# ANNUAL
# BIBLIOGRAPHY
# OF ENGLISH LANGUAGE
# AND LITERATURE
# FOR 1989

ANNUAL

# BIBLIOGRAPHY

OF

# ENGLISH LANGUAGE

# AND LITERATURE

## FOR 1989

VOLUME 64

EDITOR
ELIZABETH ERSKINE

AMERICAN EDITORS
MARY JEAN DeMARR
D. GENE ENGLAND
*Indiana State University, Terre Haute*

Modern Humanities Research Association

1993

The *Annual Bibliography*
*of English Language and Literature*
may be ordered from the Hon. Treasurer MHRA
King's College, Strand, London WC2R 2LS, England

Unsolicited offprints, photocopies or other material for reporting, and correspondence about such matters, ought to be sent direct to the Editor, *Annual Bibliography of English Language and Literature*, University Library, West Road, Cambridge CB3 9DR, England

ISBN 0 947623 53 1
ISSN 0066-3786

*Printed in Great Britain by*
W. S. MANEY & SON LIMITED
HUDSON ROAD    LEEDS LS9 7DL

Contributors — *continued*

| | |
|---|---|
| *Poland:* | IRENA DOBRZYCKA, University of Warsaw |
| | JACEK FISIAK, Adam Mickiewicz University, Poznań |
| *Romania:* | FLORENTINA VASILE ⎫ Biblioteca Nationala a Romaniei, |
| | MIRCEA STEFANCU ⎭ Bucharest |
| *Republic of South Africa:* | FRANCES STOY, South African Library, Cape Town |
| | DOROTHY DRIVER, University of Cape Town |
| *Spain:* | PABLO DOMÍNGUEZ, University of La Laguna, Tenerife |
| *Sweden:* | GÖRAN EKROTH, Royal Library, Stockholm |
| | KERSTIN ASSARSSON-RIZZI, Library of the Royal Academy of Letters, History and Antiquities, Stockholm |

*UK and Republic of Ireland:*

J. H. ALEXANDER, University of Aberdeen
JOHN R. ALLRED
CECILY CLARK
W. G. DAY, Winchester College
J. G. W. ERSKINE, Stranmillis College, Belfast
ISOBEL FOX, Library, Trinity College, Dublin
MICHAEL C. HEAD, Robert Gordon's Institute of Technology, Aberdeen
JOYCE M. HILL, University of Leeds
ROBERT INGLESFIELD, University of London
LESLEY JOHNSON, University of Leeds
VERA JOHNSTON
PETER MEREDITH, University of Leeds
JAMES OGDEN, University College of Wales, Aberystwyth
SHEILA RAINEY
PRISCILLA SCHLICKE, Robert Gordon's Institute of Technology, Aberdeen
JOHN TURNER, University College of Wales, Aberystwyth
COLIN WILCOCKSON, Pembroke College, Cambridge

*USA:*

B. J. ALEXANDER, Tarleton State University, Stephenville, TX
BRENDA AMETER, Troy State University, Dothan, AL
DAVID R. CHENEY, University of Toledo, Toledo, OH
EUGENE R. CUNNAR, New Mexico State University, Las Cruces, NM
ALICE CUSHMAN, Tarleton State University, Stephenville, TX
G. RONALD DOBLER, Morehead State University, Morehead, KY
RAYMOND F. DOLLE, Indiana State University, Terre Haute, IN
ALVIN I. DUST, University of Waterloo, Waterloo, Ont.
GORDON ERIKSEN, Kalamazoo, MI
MARC GLASSER, Morehead State University, Morehead, KY
MICHAEL HANNAFORD, Indiana State University, Terre Haute, IN
STYRON HARRIS, East Tennessee State University, Johnson City, TN
JAMES A. HOUCK, Youngstown State University, Youngstown, OH
CHARNA HOWSON, Indiana State University, Terre Haute, IN
HARRIET HUDSON, Indiana State University, Terre Haute, IN
FRED ISAAC, Berkeley, CA
RICHARD S. KEATING, United States Air Force Academy, Colorado Springs, CO
JAMES R. KELLY, George Washington University, Washington, DC

Contributors — *continued*

CHARLES J. NOLAN, JR, United States Naval Academy,
  Annapolis, MD
ROBERT PERRIN, Indiana State University, Terre Haute, IN
BETTY JO HICKS PETERS, Morehead State University, Morehead, KY
JOHN S. PHILLIPSON, University of Akron, Akron, OH
RENÉE HANNAFORD RAMSEY, Indiana State University,
  Terre Haute, IN
WILLIAM L. SIPPLE, Robert Morris College, Coraopolis, PA
PAULA M. WOODS, Baylor University, Waco, TX
*For USSR:*   PETER HELLYER, Slavonic & East European Collections, British
  Library, London

# CONTENTS

# SOURCES AND ABBREVIATIONS 1989

While the editors make every effort to maintain regular coverage of the periodicals listed below, no undertaking is given that every journal listed has been fully reported. Issues which have not been available to contributors during the report year are covered as soon as possible thereafter. Articles may also be reported from periodicals not included in this list, for example when a magazine publishes a special literary number. In such cases the place of publication is given in each entry for that periodical. The editors will be glad to hear of errors and omissions, and of new journals requiring coverage.

In many cases journals are referred to in this volume by their main titles alone (e.g. Ariel, Bibliotheck), without this title being shown separately below as an abbreviation.

*USSR serials.* Titles of serials published in the USSR are sometimes cited differently in different sources. In particular 'gosudarstvennyï', etc., 'state', is sometimes included, sometimes not. This should be allowed for by users of the *Bibliography*.

| | |
|---|---|
| AAA | Arbeiten aus Anglistik und Amerikanistik (Univ. of Graz) |
| AAAPSS | Annals of the American Academy of Political and Social Science (Philadelphia, PA) |
| AAnth | American Anthropologist (Washington, DC) |
| AArt | American Artist (New York) |
| AAS | Anglo-American Studies (Salamanca) |
| ABC | American Book Collector (Ossining, New York) |
| Abhath al-Yarmouk (Irbid, Jordan) | |
| ABN | Arnold Bennett Newsletter (Glencoe, IL) |
| ABPR | American Book Publishing Record (New York) |
| ABS | American Behavioral Scientist (Beverly Hills, CA) |
| ABV (Sofia) | |
| Academia Scientiarum Fennica, dissertationes humanarum litterarum (Helsinki) | |
| ACLSN | American Council of Learned Societies Newsletter (New York) |
| ACM | Aligarh Critical Miscellany (Aligarh Muslim Univ., India) |
| Acta Academiae Aboensis, Ser. A: Humaniora (Åbo, Finland) | |
| Acta Jutlandica (Aarhus Univ., Denmark) | |
| Acta Universitatis Tamperensis (Tampere, Finland) | |
| ActLitH | Acta Litteraria Academiae Scientiarum Hungaricae (Budapest) |
| AD | Armchair Detective (New York) |
| al-Adāb al-Ajnabīyah (Syria) | |
| Adena (Louisville, KY) | |
| AEB | Analytical and Enumerative Bibliography (Northern Illinois Univ., DeKalb) |
| AEH | Anglican and Episcopal History (Austin, TX). *Formerly* HMPEC |
| Africana Notes and News (Johannesburg) | |
| Agenda (London) | |
| Agora: a journal in the humanities and social sciences (State Univ. of New York, Potsdam) | |
| AH | American Heritage: the magazine of history (New York) |
| AHR | American Historical Review (Washington, DC) |
| AHum | American Humor: an interdisciplinary newsletter (Virginia Commonwealth Univ., Richmond) |
| AI | American Imago: a psychoanalytic journal for culture, science and the arts (Wayne State Univ., Detroit, MI) |
| AIQ | American Indian Quarterly (Univ. of California, Berkeley) |
| AJES | Aligarh Journal of English Studies (Aligarh Muslim Univ., India) |

AJH American Jewish History (Waltham, MA)
AJP American Journal of Philology (Baltimore, MD)
AJPS American Journal of Political Science (Austin, TX)
AJS American Journal of Sociology (Chicago)
Aktual'nye problemy leksikologii i slovoobrazovaniiâ (Novosibirsk Univ., USSR)
AL American Literature: a journal of literary history, criticism and bibliography (Durham, NC)
'Ālam al-Fikr (Kuwait)
AlaR Alabama Review: a journal of Alabama history (University, AL)
ALH Acta Linguistica Hafniensia: international journal of general linguistics (Copenhagen)
ALitA American Literature Abstracts (San Jose State College, CA)
ALLC Bulletin Association for Literary and Linguistic Computing Bulletin (Cambridge)
ALLC Journal Association for Literary and Linguistic Computing Journal (Cambridge)
Allegorica (Univ. of Texas at Arlington)
Allt om böcker (Lund)
ALM Archives des Lettres Modernes: études de critique et d'histoire littéraire (Paris)
ALR American Literary Realism, 1870–1910 (Univ. of Texas at Arlington)
ALS Australian Literary Studies (Univ. of Queensland, St Lucia)
AM American Mercury (Torrance, CA)
America: national Catholic weekly review (New York)
American Presbyterians (Philadelphia, PA)
AmerS American Studies International (George Washington Univ., Washington, DC)
AmeSt American Studies (Seoul National Univ., Korea)
Amfiteatru (Bucharest)
AmLH American Literary History (Oxford)
AmLib American Libraries (Chicago)
AmQ American Quarterly (Univ. of Pennsylvania, Philadelphia)
AmS American Studies (Univ. of Kansas, Lawrence)
AmSS American Studies in Scandinavia (Oslo)
Amst Amerikastudien/American Studies (Munich)
Analecta cartusiana (Univ. of Salzburg)
Andvari (Reykjavik)
ANF Arkiv för nordisk filologi/Archives for Scandinavian Philology (Lund)
Ang Anglia: Zeitschrift für englische Philologie (Tübingen)
Angles Angles in the English-speaking world (Univ. of Copenhagen)
Anglistik & Englischunterricht (Heidelberg)
Annales Academiae Scientarum Fennicae (Helsinki)
Annales Universitatis Turkuensis, Ser.B. (Turku, Finland)
AnnMed Annuale Mediaevale (Duquesne Univ., Pittsburgh, PA)
ANQ American Notes and Queries (Lexington, KY)
AnthL Anthropological Linguistics (Indiana Univ., Bloomington)
AnthQ Anthropological Quarterly (Washington, DC)
Antic (Auckland)
Antwerp Papers in Linguistics
Anuario de filología (Univ. del Zulia, Maracaibo, Venezuela)
AnUBLLS Analele Universității București. Limbi și literaturi străine. (Bucharest)
AnUCFil Analele Universității Craiova. Seria Științe filologice (Craiova, Romania)
AnUGSU Analele Universității din Galați. Fascicula I. Științe sociale și umaniste (Galați, Romania)

AnUILingv     Analele științifice ale Universității 'Al.I.Cuza' din Iași. (Serie nouă.) Secțiunea III. e. Lingvistică (Jassy, Romania)
AnUILit     Analele științifice ale Universității 'Al.I.Cuza' din Iași. (Serie nouă.) Secțiunea III. f. Literatură (Jassy, Romania)
AnUTFil     Analele Universității din Timișoara. Seria Științe filologice (Timișoara, Romania)
AP     Acta Philologica (Warsaw)
APAIS     Australian Public Affairs Information Service (Canberra)
APC     Abstracts of Popular Culture (Univ. of Maryland, College Park)
APJPH     American Presbyterians: journal of Presbyterian history (Philadelphia, PA). *Formerly* JPH
Apollo: the international magazine of art and antiques (London)
APP     American Poetry and Poetics (Madison, SD)
APQ     American Philosophical Quarterly (Bowling Green State Univ., OH)
APR     American Poetry Review (Philadelphia, PA)
APSR     American Political Science Review (Washington, DC)
AQ     Arizona Quarterly (Univ. of Arizona, Tucson)
AR     Antioch Review (Yellow Springs, OH)
Arbor: revista general de investigacion y cultura (Madrid)
arcadia: Zeitschrift für vergleichende Literaturwissenschaft (Berlin)
Archiv     Archiv für das Studium der neueren Sprachen und Literaturen (Berlin)
Archiv für Geschichte des Buchwesens (Frankfurt)
Archiv für Kulturgeschichte (Cologne)
Archives et bibliothèques de Belgique (Brussels)
ArchivR     Archiv für Reformationsgeschichte/Archive for Reformation History (Gütersloh, W. Germany)
ArchL     Archivum Linguisticum: a review of comparative philology and general linguistics (Univ. of Leeds)
Arda: årsskrift för Arda-forskningen (Uppsala)
Arena: a Marxist journal of criticism and discussion (North Carlton, Vic.)
Argumentation (Dordrecht)
ArH     Archivo Hispalense: revista histórica, literaria y artística (Seville)
Ariadne: University of Crete School of Philosophy Yearbook (Rethymnon)
Ariel: a review of international English literature (Univ. of Calgary, Alta.)
ArizW     Arizona and the West: a journal of history (Univ. of Arizona, Tucson)
ArkHQ     Arkansas Historical Quarterly (Univ. of Arkansas, Fayetteville)
Arnoldian (U.S. Naval Academy, Annapolis, MD). *See* NCP
Artes: tidskrift för litteratur, konst och musik (Stockholm)
ArtJ     Art Journal (New York)
ASch     American Scholar (Washington, DC)
ASci     American Scientist (New Haven, CT)
ASE     Anglo-Saxon England (Emmanuel College, Cambridge)
ASocR     American Sociological Review (Washington, DC)
Assays: critical approaches to medieval and Renaissance texts (Carnegie–Mellon Univ., Pittsburgh, PA)
Ateneu (Bacău, Romania)
Atlantis (Univ. of Oviedo, Spain)
AtlMon     Atlantic Monthly (Boston, MA)
ATQ     American Transcendental Quarterly: journal of New England writers (Univ. of Rhode Island, Kingston)
AUMLA     Journal of the Australasian Universities Language and Literature Association: a journal of literary criticism, philology and linguistics (Univ. of Tasmania, Hobart)
AUR     Aberdeen University Review
AusQ     Australian Quarterly (Sydney)
Australasian Drama Studies (Univ. of Queensland, St Lucia).

Australasian Journal of American Studies (La Trobe Univ., Bundoora, Vic.)
Australasian Journal of Philosophy (La Trobe Univ., Bundoora, Vic.)
Australian Academic and Research Libraries (Ultimo, N.S.W.)
Australian Author (Milsons Point, N.S.W.)
Australian Cultural History (Australian National Univ., Canberra)
Australian Historical Bibliography (Univ. of New South Wales, Kensington)
Australian Journal of Education (Hawthorn, Vic.)
Australian Journal of Linguistics (Univ. of Queensland, St Lucia)
Australian Journal of Screen Theory (Univ. of New South Wales, Kensington)
Australian Library Journal (Ultimo, N.S.W.)
Australian National Bibliography (Canberra)
Australian Review of Applied Linguistics (Brisbane)

| | |
|---|---|
| AWest | The American West (Palo Alto, CA) |
| AWR | Anglo-Welsh Review (Tenby, Dyfed) |
| BALF | Black American Literature Forum (Indiana State Univ., Terre Haute) |

Bălgarski ezik (Sofia)
Bălgarski ezik i literatura (Sofia)
Bălgarski žurnalist (Sofia)
Balkan Studies (Thessaloniki)
Balkansko ezikoznanie/Linguistique Balkanique (Sofia)
Ball State Monographs: Publications in English (Muncie, IN)

| | |
|---|---|
| BALLF | Bulletin de l'Académie de Langue et de Littérature Française (Brussels) |
| BANQ | Biblionews and Australian Notes and Queries: journal for book collectors (Cremorne, N.S.W.) |
| BAR | British Archaeological Reports (Oxford) |
| BaratR · | Barat Review: a journal of literature and the arts (Barat College, Lake Forest, IL) |
| BB · | Bulletin of Bibliography (Westport, CT) |
| BBB | Black Books Bulletin (Chicago) |
| BC · | Book Collector (London) |
| BDC | Barnhart Dictionary Companion (Cold Spring, NY) |

Belgian Journal of Linguistics (Brussels)

| | |
|---|---|
| BF | Book Forum (New York) |
| BHM | Bulletin of the History of Medicine (Baltimore, MD) |
| BHS | Bulletin of Hispanic Studies (Liverpool) |

Bibliographical Society of Australia and New Zealand Bulletin (Univ. of Adelaide)
Bibliographie de Belgique: Belgische Bibliografie (Brussels)
Bibliotekar (Sofia)
Bibliotheck: a Scottish journal of bibliography and allied topics (Mitchell Library, Glasgow)

| | |
|---|---|
| BIHS | Bulletin of the Institute for Humanistic Science (Inha Univ., Incheon, Korea) |

Bildung und Erziehung (Düsseldorf)

| | |
|---|---|
| BIS | Browning Institute Studies: an annual of Victorian literary and cultural history (Univ. of Maryland, College Park, MD) |
| BJA | British Journal of Aesthetics (Oxford) |
| BJECS | British Journal for Eighteenth Century Studies (Oxford) |
| BJRL | Bulletin of the John Rylands University Library of Manchester |
| BkIA | Books at Iowa (Univ. of Iowa, Iowa City) |
| BkW | Book World (Washington Post, Washington, DC) |

Blake: an illustrated quarterly (Univ. of New Mexico, Albuquerque)

| | |
|---|---|
| BlakeS | Blake Studies (Memphis State Univ., TN) |
| BLJ | British Library Journal (London) |

BLM: Bonniers litterära magasin (Stockholm)

| | |
|---|---|
| BLR | Bodleian Library Record (Oxford) |
| BLSMPAB | Bulletin de la Classe des Lettres et Sciences Morales et Politiques de l'Académie de Belgique (Brussels) |
| BN | Beiträge zur Namenforschung (Heidelberg) |

Bókaormurinn (Reykjavik)
Boundary 2: a journal of postmodern literature and culture (State Univ. of New York, Binghamton)
BPJ                   Beloit Poetry Journal (Ellsworth, ME)
BR                    Bilingual Review/Revista bilingue (State Univ. of New York, Binghamton)
BRH                   Bulletin of Research in the Humanities (New York)
British National Bibliography (London)
Brno Studies in English (Univ. J. E. Purkyne, Brno, Czechoslovakia)
Broadsheet (Auckland)
Brussels Preprints in Linguistics
BSch                  Black Scholar: journal of black studies and research (San Francisco, CA)
BSEAA                 XVIIe–XVIIIe: Bulletin de la Société d'Études anglo-américains des XVIIᵉ et XVIIIᵉ siècles (Paris)
BSJ                   Baker Street Journal: an irregular quarterly of Sherlockiana (New York)
BSN                   Browning Society Notes (Platt, nr Sevenoaks, Kent)
BST                   Brontë Society Transactions (Haworth)
BSUF                  Ball State University Forum (Muncie, IN)
Bulletin (Sydney)
Bulletin des Anglicistes Médiévistes (Paris)
Bulletin de la Société linguistique de Paris
BuR                   Bucknell Review: a scholarly journal of letters, arts and science (Cranbury, NJ)
Burlington Magazine (London)
BurnsC                Burns Chronicle and Club Directory (Kilmarnock)
BW                    Book World (Chicago Tribune)
CAE                   Collection of articles and essays (Hankuk Univ. of Foreign Studies, Korea)
Cahiers de l'APLIUT (Paris)
Cahiers de linguistique théorique et appliquée (Bucharest). See RRL
Cahiers Internationaux de Symbolisme (Univ. de l'État, Mons)
Caliban (Univ. of Toulouse–Le Mirail, Toulouse)
Cambridge Review: a journal of University life and thought (Cambridge)
CamQ                  Cambridge Quarterly
CanD                  Canadian Drama/Art dramatique canadien (Univ. of Waterloo, Ont.)
CanL                  Canadian Literature/Littérature canadienne: a quarterly of criticism and review (Univ. of British Columbia, Vancouver)
CanP                  Canadian Poetry (Univ. of Western Ontario, London)
CanRCL                Canadian Review of Comparative Literature/Revue canadienne de littérature comparée (Univ. of Alberta, Edmonton)
CanTR                 Canadian Theatre Review (Toronto)
CaQ                   California Quarterly: a journal of fiction and poetry (Univ. of California, Davis)
CarnM                 Carnegie Magazine (Pittsburgh, PA)
Carrell: journal of the Friends of the University of Miami Library (Coral Gables, FL)
CathHR                Catholic Historical Review (Washington, DC)
CathW                 Catholic World (New York)
Cauce (Seville)
CB                    Classical Bulletin (Asbury College, Wilmore, KY)
CC                    Crosscurrents (West Nyack, NY)
CCC                   College Composition and Communication (Urbana, IL)
CCTE                  Proceedings of Conference of College Teachers of English at Texas (Commerce, TX)
CE                    College English (Urbana, IL)
CEACrit               CEA Critic: an official journal of the College English Association (Bucknell Univ., Lewisburg, PA)

CEAF — CEA Forum: an official journal of the College English Association (Bucknell Univ., Lewisburg, PA)

CEBAL — Copenhagen School of Economics and Business Administration, Language Dept

CEl — Cahiers élisabethains: études sur la Pré-Renaissance et la Renaissance anglaises (Université Paul Valéry, Montpellier)

Cencrastus: Scottish and international literature, arts and affairs (Edinburgh)

Centrum: working papers of the Minnesota Center for Advanced Studies in Language, Style and Literary Theory (Univ. of Minnesota, Minneapolis)

CH — California History (San Francisco)

Chaucer Newsletter (New Chaucer Society, Univ. of Oklahoma, Norman)

ChauR — Chaucer Review (University Park, PA)

ChCen — Christian Century: an ecumenical weekly (Chicago)

Chelsea (New York)

ChiR — Chicago Review (Univ. of Chicago)

CHist — Church History (Wallingford, PA)

ChrisL — Christianity and Literature (Baylor Univ., Waco, TX)

ChronC — Chronicles of Culture (Rockford, IL)

Chronica (Scripps College, Claremont, CA)

ChronOkla — Chronicles of Oklahoma (Oklahoma City)

CHum — Computers and the Humanities (Osprey, FL)

CI — Critical Inquiry (Chicago)

CIF — Cuadernos de investigación filológica (Colegio Univ. de la Rioja, Logroño, Spain)

CimR — Cimarron Review (Oklahoma State Univ., Stillwater)

Cithara: essays in Judaeo-Christian tradition (St Bonaventure Univ., NY)

CJ — Classical Journal (Florida State Univ., Tallahassee)

CJa — Cizí jazyky ve škole (Prague)

CJIS — Canadian Journal of Irish Studies (Univ. of British Columbia, Vancouver)

CJL — Canadian Journal of Linguistics/Revue canadienne de linguistique (Carleton Univ., Ottawa)

CL — Comparative Literature (Univ. of Oregon, Eugene)

CLAJ — College Language Association Journal (Morehouse College, Atlanta, GA)

Classic (Johannesburg)

CLB — Charles Lamb Bulletin (Sevenoaks, Kent)

CLC — Columbia Library Columns (Columbia Univ., New York)

CLEd — Children's Literature in Education (New York)

CLIO: journal of literature, history, and the philosophy of history (Indiana Univ.–Purdue Univ., Fort Wayne, IN)

CLit — College Literature (West Chester Univ., PA)

CLQ — Colby Library Quarterly (Colby College, Waterville, ME)

CLS — Comparative Literature Studies (Univ. of Illinois, Urbana–Champaign)

Clues: a journal of detection (Bowling Green State Univ., OH)

CM — Classica et Mediaevalia (Roskilde, Denmark)

CMF — Casopis pro moderní filologii (Prague) See PP

CML — Classical and Modern Literature: a quarterly (Terre Haute, IN)

ColJR — Columbia Journalism Review (Columbia Univ., New York)

Colloquium: the Australian and New Zealand theological review (Auckland)

ColoM — Colorado Magazine (Denver)

ColoQ — Colorado Quarterly (Univ. of Colorado, Boulder)

Comitatus: a journal of medieval and Renaissance studies (Univ. of California, Los Angeles)

CommEd — Communication Education (Annandale, VA)

Commentary: journal of significant thought and opinion on contemporary issues (New York)

ComMon — Communication Monographs (Annandale, VA)

Communication & Cognition (Ghent)

CompCrit — Comparative Criticism: a yearbook (Cambridge)
CompDr — Comparative Drama (Western Michigan Univ., Kalamazoo)
ComQ — Communication Quarterly (Villanova Univ., PA)
Concerning Poetry (Western Washington State College, Bellingham)
Confrontation (Brooklyn, NY)
ConLit — Contemporary Literature (Univ. of Wisconsin–Madison)
ConnHSB — Connecticut Historical Society Bulletin (Hartford)
Connoisseur (London).
Conradiana: a journal of Joseph Conrad studies (Texas Tech Univ., Lubbock)
Contemporanul (Bucharest)
Contrast: South African literary journal (Cape Town)
ConvLit — Convorbiri literare (Bucharest)
Coranto: journal of the Friends of the Libraries, University of Southern
    California (Los Angeles)
CP — Classical Philology (Chicago)
CR — Centennial Review (Michigan State Univ., East Lansing)
CREL — Cahiers roumains d'études littéraires (Bucharest)
Cresset: a review of literature, the arts and public affairs (Valparaiso Univ., IN)
Crit — Critique: studies in modern fiction (Washington, DC)
Critical Arts: a journal for media studies (Univ. of Natal, Durban, South Africa)
Critical Review (Australian National Univ., Canberra)
Criticism: a quarterly for literature and the arts (Detroit, MI)
Critique: revue générale des publications françaises et étrangères (Paris)
CritQ — Critical Quarterly (Manchester)
CRL — College and Research Libraries (Chicago)
Cronica (Jassy, Romania)
Crosscurrent (Hamilton, NZ)
Crux: a guide to teaching English language and literature (Pretoria)
CSR — Christian Scholar's Review: a Christian quarterly of the arts
    and sciences (Union, ME)
Current Affairs Bulletin (Univ. of Sydney)
Current Writing: text and reception in Southern Africa (Univ. of Natal, Durban)
Čuždoezikovo obučenie (Sofia)
CVE — Cahiers victoriens et édouardiens (Univ. Paul Valéry,
    Montpellier)
CW — Classical World (Duquesne Univ., Pittsburgh, PA)
Cweal — Commonweal (New York)
CWH — Civil War History: a journal of the middle period
    (Kent State Univ., OH)
DA — Dissertation Abstracts International (Ann Arbor, MI)
Daedalus: journal of the American Academy of Arts and Sciences (Cambridge, MA)
DalR — Dalhousie Review: a Canadian quarterly of literature and
    opinion (Dalhousie Univ., Halifax, N.S.)
Damascus University Journal
Dansk bogfortegnelse (Copenhagen)
Danske studier (Birkerød, Denmark)
Degrés (Brussels)
DelH — Delaware History (Wilmington)
Delta: revue du Centre d'Études et de Recherche sur les Écrivains du Sud aux
    États-Unis (Univ. Paul Valéry, Montpellier)
Descant: Texas Christian University literary journal (Fort Worth)
Deutsche Bibliographie (Frankfurt)
Deutsches Archiv für Erforschung des Mittelalters (Munich)
DHLR — D. H. Lawrence Review (Univ. of Delaware, Newark)
Diacritics: a journal of contemporary criticism (Baltimore, MD)
Dialog (Warsaw)
Diavazo (Athens)
Dic — Dictionaries: journal of the Dictionary Society of North America
    (Univ. of Michigan, Ann Arbor)
Dick — Dickensian (London)

Dirasāt (Amman)
Direction      Direction Line: newsletter for bibliographers and textual critics (Univ. of Texas at Austin)
Dix-huitième siècle (Paris)
DLAJ      DeKalb Literary Arts Journal (DeKalb Community Coll., Clarkston, GA)
Dodona: University of Ioannina School of Philosophy yearbook (Ioannina, Greece)
Dolphin (Univ. of Aarhus)
DQ      Denver Quarterly (Univ. of Denver, CO)
DQR: Dutch Quarterly Review of Anglo-American Letters (Amsterdam)
DreiS      Dreiser Studies (Indiana State Univ., Terre Haute)
DS      Dickinson Studies (Brentwood, MD)
DSA      Dickens Studies Annual: essays on Victorian fiction (Southern Illinois Univ., Carbondale)
DSN      Dickens Studies Newsletter (Univ. of Louisville, KY)
DUJ      Durham University Journal
DVLG      Deutsche Vierteljahrsschrift für Literaturwissenschaft und Geistesgeschichte (Stuttgart)
DWB      Dietsche Warande en Belfort: tijdschrift voor letterkunde, kunst en geestesleven (Antwerp)
DWPELL      Dutch Working Papers in English Language and Linguistics (Univ. of Leiden)
EA      Études anglaises (Paris)
EAL      Early American Literature (Chapel Hill, NC)
EAS      Essays and Studies (London)
EC      Essays in Criticism: a quarterly journal of literary criticism (Oxford)
ECanW      Essays on Canadian Writing (Toronto)
ECent      Eighteenth Century: theory and interpretation (Texas Tech Univ., Lubbock)
ECI      Eighteenth-Century Ireland (Trinity College Dublin)
ECL      Eighteenth-Century Life (College of William and Mary, Williamsburg, VA)
ECS      Eighteenth-Century Studies (St Olaf College, Northfield, MN)
Edda: nordisk tidsskrift for litteraturforskning (Oslo)
EDH      Essays by Divers Hands (London)
Edinburgh Review (Edinburgh Univ.)
EducF      Educational Forum (Ohio State Univ., Columbia)
EHR      English Historical Review (Harlow, Essex)
Éire–Ireland: journal of Irish studies (St Paul, MN)
EJ      English Journal (Urbana, IL)
EL      Études de lettres (Univ. of Lausanne)
ELH (Baltimore, MD)
ELit      Essays in Literature (Western Illinois Univ., Macomb)
ELN      English Language Notes (Univ. of Colorado, Boulder)
ELR      English Literary Renaissance (Univ. of Massachusetts, Amherst)
ELT      English Literature in Transition (1800–1920) (Univ. of North Carolina, Greensboro')
Enc      Encounter (London)
Eng      English (Oxford)
EngA      English in Africa (Rhodes Univ., Grahamstown, South Africa)
English Academy Review (English Academy of Southern Africa, Johannesburg)
English in Aotearoa (N.Z. Assn for the teaching of English, Wellington)
English in Australia (Norwood, S. Australia)
English Usage      English Usage in Southern Africa (Univ. of South Africa, Pretoria)
EngS      English Studies: a journal of English language and literature (Lisse, The Netherlands)
EngSt      English Studies (Seoul National Univ., Korea)

EON      Eugene O'Neill Newsletter (Suffolk Univ., Boston, MA). *See* EOR

EOR      Eugene O'Neill Review (Suffolk Univ., Boston, MA). *Formerly* EON

Ephemera (Nancy, France)

Epoch: a magazine of contemporary literature (Cornell Univ., Ithaca, NY)

ERec      English Record (Buffalo, NY)

ERGS      ETC.: a review of general semantics (San Francisco)

ESA      English Studies in Africa: a journal of the humanities (Johannesburg)

ESCan      English Studies in Canada (Univ. of Alberta, Edmonton)

Esprit (Paris)

ESQ: a journal of the American renaissance (Washington State Univ., Pullman)

Esquire (New York)

ESRS      Emporia State Research Studies (Emporia State Univ., KS)

Ethics: an international journal of social, political and legal philosophy (Chicago)

Études germaniques (Paris)

Études irlandaises (Université de Lille III, Villeneuve d'Ascq, France)

Études sur le XVIIIe siècle (Université Libre de Bruxelles)

Euphorion: Zeitschrift für Literaturgeschichte (Heidelberg)

Europe: revue littéraire mensuel (Paris)

EWeltyN      Eudora Welty Newsletter (Univ. of Toledo, OH)

EWN      Evelyn Waugh Newsletter (State Univ. of New York, Garden City)

Exemplaria (State Univ. of New York, Binghamton)

Exp      Explicator (Washington, DC)

Expl      Exploration (Illinois State Univ., Normal)

Explorations (Government College, Lahore)

ExRC      Explorations in Renaissance Culture (Univ. of Southern Mississippi, Hattiesburg)

Extrapolation: journal of the scholarly study of science fiction and fantasy (Kent, OH)

Ezik i literatura (Sofia)

Factotum (ESTC, British Library)

FAJ      Feminist Art Journal (Brooklyn, NY)

Familia (Oradea, Romania)

FAR      French American Review (Texas Christian Univ., Fort Worth)

Fenix (Biblioteca Nacional, Lima)

FF      Folklore Forum (Bloomington, IN)

FHA      Fitzgerald/Hemingway Annual (Univ. of South Carolina, Columbia)

FHQ      Florida Historical Quarterly (Univ. of South Florida, Tampa)

Field: contemporary poetry and poetics (Oberlin College, OH)

Filologija (Sofia)

Fine Print (San Francisco)

FJ      Faulkner Journal (Ada, OH)

FK      Filológiai Közlöny/Philological review (Budapest)

FL      Folia linguistica: acta Societatis Linguisticae Europaeae (The Hague)

FLH      Folia Linguistica Historica (The Hague)

FM      Filosofska misăl (Sofia)

FMJ      Folk Music Journal (Sheffield)

FMod      Filología moderna (Univ. Complutense, Madrid)

FOB      Flannery O'Connor Bulletin (Georgia College, Milledgeville)

Focus      Focus on Robert Graves (Univ. of Colorado, Boulder)

Folk Life: a journal of ethnological studies (Cardiff)

Folklore (Univ. College, London)

Form (Dhaka)

Fort Hare Papers (Fort Hare Univ., Alice, South Africa)

Fortnight (Belfast)
Forum (Romania)
ForumH                Forum (Houston) (Univ. of Houston, TX)
ForumL                Forum der Letteren: Tijdschrift voor Taal- en Letterkunde
                      (Leiden)
FQ                    Four Quarters (La Salle College, Philadelphia, PA)
Frankfurter Hefte (Bonn)
Friends' Quarterly (London)
FRP                   Film Research in Progress (Univ. of North Carolina, Chapel
                      Hill)
FS                    Faulkner Studies: an annual of research, criticism, and reviews
                      (Univ. of Miami, Coral Gables, FL)
Fund og forskning i det Kongelige Biblioteks Samlinger (Copenhagen)
FurmS                 Furman Studies (Furman Univ., Greenville, SC)
GaHQ                  Georgia Historical Quarterly (Savannah, GA)
Gambit: international theatre review (London)
GaR                   Georgia Review (Univ. of Georgia, Athens)
Gaskell Society Journal (Univ. of Manchester)
Genders (Univ. of Texas, Austin)
Genre (Univ. of Oklahoma, Norman)
Germanica Olomucensia, Acta Universitatis Palackianae, Facultas Philosophica,
      Philologia (Palacký Univ., Olomouc, Czechoslovakia)
GGA                   Göttingische gelehrte Anzeigen (Göttingen)
GHJ                   George Herbert Journal (Sacred Heart Univ., Bridgeport, CT)
De Gids (Amsterdam)
GL                    General Linguistics (University Park, PA)
GLOT: Tijdschrift voor taalwetenschap (Dordrecht)
GLR                   Great Lakes Review: a journal of Midwest culture
                      (Central Michigan Univ., Mt Pleasant)
Glyph: textual studies (Minneapolis, MN)
Godišnik na VITIZ 'Krǎstju Sarafov' (Sofia)
Gothic (Baton Rouge, LA)
GPJ                   Great Plains Journal (Lawton, OK)
GPQ                   Great Plains Quarterly (Lincoln, NB)
GR                    Germanic Review (Washington, DC)
Gradiva: a journal of contemporary theory and practice (State Univ. of New York,
      Stony Brook)
Greyfriar: Siena studies in literature (Siena College, Loudonville, NY)
GRM                   Germanisch-romanische Monatsschrift (Heidelberg)
Growing Point (Northampton)
GSB                   General Semantics Bulletin (Institute of General Semantics,
                      Lakeville, CT)
GSUFNF                Godišnik na Sofijskija universitet. Fakultet po klasičeski i novi
                      filologii (Sofia)
GSUFSF                Godišnik na Sofijskija universitet. Fakultet po slavjanski filologii
                      (Sofia)
Häften för Kritiska Studier (Stockholm)
HAHR                  Hispanic American Historical Review (Durham, NC)
Harper's (New York)
HC                    Hollins Critic (Hollins College, Roanoke, VA)
Hecate: a women's interdisciplinary journal (Univ. of Queensland, St Lucia)
Helikon: vilagirodalmi figyelo (Budapest)
Helios (Texas Tech Univ., Lubbock)
Hellenika (Salonica)
Hemisphere: an Asian-Australian magazine (Canberra)
HemR                  Hemingway Review (Ohio Northern Univ., Ada)
HGP                   Heritage of the Great Plains (Emporia State Univ., KS)
Hist                  History (London)
HistJ                 Historical Journal (Cambridge)
Historian: a journal of history (Allentown, PA)

Historical News (Christchurch, N.Z.)
Historical Studies (Univ. of Melbourne)
Historiographia Linguistica (Amsterdam)
Historische Sprachforschung (Göttingen). *Formerly* ZVS

| | |
|---|---|
| HJ | Higginson Journal (Brentwood, MD) |
| HJR | Henry James Review (Louisiana State Univ., Baton Rouge) |
| HLB | Harvard Library Bulletin (Harvard Univ., Cambridge, MA) |
| HLQ | Huntington Library Quarterly: a journal for the history and interpretation of English and American civilization (San Marino, CA) |
| HMPEC | Historical Magazine of the Protestant Episcopal Church (Austin, TX). *See* AEH |

Honest Ulsterman (Belfast)

| | |
|---|---|
| HopQ | Hopkins Quarterly (Mohawk College, Hamilton, Ont.) |

Horisont: organ för Svenska Osterbottens litteraturforening (Krylbo, Sweden)
Horizon (New York)

| | |
|---|---|
| HR | Hudson Review (New York) |
| HSCL | Harvard Studies in Comparative Literature (Harvard Univ., Cambridge, MA) |
| HSE | Hungarian Studies in English (Debrecen, Hungary) |
| HSJ | Housman Society Journal (Bromsgrove, Worcestershire) |
| HT | History Today (London) |
| HTR | Harvard Theological Review (Harvard Divinity School, Cambridge, MA) |

Humanist (Amherst, NY)

| | |
|---|---|
| HUSL | Hebrew University Studies in Literature and the Arts (Jerusalem) |
| HZ | Historische Zeitschrift (Munich) |
| IAN | Izvestiía Akademii nauk S.S.S.R. Seriía literatury i íazyka (Moscow) |
| IARB | Inter-American Review of Bibliography/Revista interamericana de bibliografia (Washington, DC) |

ICAME Journal: International Computer Archive of Modern English (Norwegian Computing Centre for the Humanities, Bergen)
ICarbS: journal of the Friends of the Morris Library at Southern Illinois University (Carbondale, IL)

| | |
|---|---|
| IE | Indiana English (Indiana State Univ., Terre Haute) |
| IF | Indogermanische Forschungen: Zeitschrift für Indogermanistik und allgemeine sprachwissenschaft (Berlin) |
| IHB | Indiana History Bulletin (Indianapolis) |
| IHJ | Illinois Historical Journal (Springfield, IL) |
| IJAL | International Journal of American Linguistics (Chicago) |
| IJAS | Indian Journal of American Studies (Hyderabad) |
| IJPP | Interpretation: a journal of political philosophy (City Univ. of New York, Flushing) |
| IKS | Inmun Kwahak (The Journal of the Humanities) (Sungkyunkwan Univ., Korea) |
| IKY | Inmun Kwahak (The Journal of the Humanities) (Yonsei Univ., Korea) |

Illusions: a New Zealand magazine of film, television and theatre criticism (Wellington)

| | |
|---|---|
| IMH | Indiana Magazine of History (Indiana Univ., Bloomington) |

Independent (London)
Indiana University Publications, Humanities Series (Bloomington)

| | |
|---|---|
| IndS | Independent Shavian (New York) |

Infini (Paris)

| | |
|---|---|
| INH | Inmun Nonchong (The Journal of the Humanities) (Hanyang Univ., Korea) |
| InL | Inostrannaía literatura (Moscow) |

Innsbrucker Beiträge zur Sprachwissenschaft (Innsbruck)

Inostrannye îâzyki v shkole (Moscow)
International Folklore Review (London)
Interpretations: a journal of ideas, analysis, and criticism (Memphis State
    Univ., TN)
International Medieval Bibliography (Univ. of Leeds)

| | |
|---|---|
| IowaR | Iowa Review (Univ. of Iowa, Iowa City) |
| IPQ | International Philosophical Quarterly (Fordham Univ., Bronx, NY) |
| IR | Intercollegiate Review: a journal of scholarship and opinion (Bryn Mawr, PA) |
| IRAL | International Review of Applied Linguistics in Language Teaching (Heidelberg) |

Irish Booklore (Belfast)
Irish Folk Music Studies (Dublin)
Isis (Philadelphia, PA)

| | |
|---|---|
| ISJR | Iowa State Journal of Research (Iowa State Univ., Ames) |

Islands: a New Zealand quarterly of arts and letters (Auckland)
Issledovaniîâ po romano-germanskomu îâzykozaniîû (Volgogradskiĭ pedagogicheskiĭ
    institut, Volgograd)

| | |
|---|---|
| IT | Index to Theses accepted for higher degrees by the Universities of Great Britain and Ireland (and the Council for National Academic Awards) (ASLIB) (London) |
| ItalA | Italian Americana (State Univ. of New York, Buffalo) |

Italian Studies (Univ. of Hull)
Italica (Univ. of Wisconsin, Madison)

| | |
|---|---|
| ITL | ITL Review of Applied Linguistics (Leuven) |
| IUR | Irish University Review: a journal of Irish Studies (University College, Dublin) |

Izraz (Sarajevo, Yugoslavia)

| | |
|---|---|
| JA | Journal of Aesthetics and Art Criticism (Temple Univ., Philadelphia, PA) |
| JAC | Journal of American Culture (Bowling Green State Univ., OH) |
| JAE | Journal of Aesthetic Education (Univ. of Illinois at Urbana–Champaign) |
| JAF | Journal of American Folklore (Washington, DC) |

Jagger Journal (J.W. Jagger Library, Univ. of Cape Town)

| | |
|---|---|
| JAH | Journal of American History (Bloomington, IN) |
| JAML | Journal of Arts Management and Law (Washington, DC) |
| JAR | Journal of Anthropological Research (Univ. of New Mexico, Albuquerque) |
| JASAT | Journal of the American Studies Association of Texas (Wayland College, Plainview) |
| JAStud | Journal of American Studies (Cambridge) |
| JazA | Jazykovědné aktuality (Prague) |
| JBCD | Journal of the Book Club of Detroit |
| JBecS | Journal of Beckett Studies (Ohio State Univ., Lima) |
| JBS | Journal of British Studies (Chicago) |
| JC | Journal of Communication (Philadelphia, PA) |
| JCanStud | Journal of Canadian Studies/Revue d'études canadiennes (Trent Univ., Peterborough, Ont.) |
| JCF | Journal of Canadian Fiction (Montreal) |
| JCL | Journal of Commonwealth Literature (Oxford) |
| JCSJ | John Clare Society Journal (Peterborough) |
| JCT | Joseph Conrad Today (State Univ. College of New York, Oswego) |
| JDJ | John Donne Journal: studies in the age of Donne (North Carolina State Univ., Raleigh) |
| JEGP | Journal of English and Germanic Philology (Univ. of Illinois at Urbana–Champaign) |

| | |
|---|---|
| JEL | Journal of English Linguistics (Univ. of Wisconsin, Whitewater) |
| JELL | Journal of the English Language and Literature (Seoul) |
| JELLC | Journal of the English Language and Literature, Chungchong (Daejeon, Korea) |
| JEPNS | Journal of the English Place-Name Society (Univ. of Nottingham) |
| JES | Journal of Ethnic Studies (Western Washington Univ., Bellingham, WA) |
| JEurS | Journal of European Studies (Univ. of Exeter) |
| Jewish Affairs (Johannesburg) | |
| JFR | Journal of Folklore Research (Bloomington, IN) |
| JGE | Journal of General Education (University Park, PA) |
| JH | Journal of the Humanities (Seoul National Univ., Korea) |
| JHI | Journal of the History of Ideas (Temple Univ., Philadelphia, PA) |
| JHM | Journal of the History of Medicine and Allied Sciences (New Haven, CT) |
| JHP | Journal of the History of Philosophy (Emory Univ., Atlanta, GA) |
| JHY | Journal of the Humanities (Yeungnam Univ., Gyongsan, Korea) |
| JIES | Journal of Indo-European Studies (Butte, MT) |
| JISHS | Journal of the Illinois State Historical Society (Springfield) |
| JIWE | Journal of Indian Writing in English (Gulbarga, India) |
| JJJ | James Joyce Journal (Seoul) |
| JJQ | James Joyce Quarterly (Univ. of Tulsa, OK) |
| JLN | Jack London Newsletter (Southern Illinois Univ., Carbondale) |
| JLS | Journal of Literary Studies/Tydskrif vir Literatuurwetenskap (SAVAL, Pretoria) |
| JMH | Journal of Modern History (Chicago) |
| JMissH | Journal of Mississippi History (Jackson) |
| JML | Journal of Modern Literature (Temple Univ., Philadelphia, PA) |
| JMMLA | Journal of the Midwest Modern Language Association (Univ. of Iowa, Iowa City) |
| JMRS | Journal of Medieval and Renaissance Studies (Durham, NC) |
| JNL | Johnsonian News Letter (Columbia Univ., New York) |
| JNPH | Journal of Newspaper and Periodical History (London) |
| JNT | Journal of Narrative Technique (Eastern Michigan Univ., Ypsilanti) |
| JNZL | Journal of New Zealand Literature (Wellington) |
| Journal of the English Literary Club (Peshawar, Pakistan) | |
| Journal of Librarianship (London) | |
| Journal of Pacific History (Australian National Univ., Canberra) | |
| Journal of Pragmatics: an interdisciplinary bi-monthly of language studies (Amsterdam) | |
| Journal of Semantics (Dordrecht) | |
| Journal of Social Sciences and Humanities (Karachi) | |
| Journal of the Southwest (Univ. of Arizona, Tucson) | |
| JP | Journal of Philosophy (Columbia Univ., New York) |
| JPC | Journal of Popular Culture (Bowling Green State Univ., OH) |
| JPH | Journal of Presbyterian History (Philadelphia, PA). See APJPH |
| JPhon | Journal of Phonetics (Colchester) |
| JPHS | Journal of the Printing Historical Society (London) |
| JPol | Journal of Politics (Univ. of Florida, Gainesville) |
| JPR | Journal of Psycholinguistic Research (New York) |
| JPRAS | Journal of Pre-Raphaelite and Aesthetic Studies (Peterborough, NH) |
| JPRS | Journal of Pre-Raphaelite Studies (Peterborough, NH) |

| | |
|---|---|
| JQ | Journalism Quarterly (Univ. of South Carolina, Columbia) |
| JR | Journal of Religion (Chicago) |
| JRead | Journal of Reading (Newark, DE) |
| JRMMRA | Journal of the Rocky Mountain Medieval and Renaissance Association (Northern Arizona Univ., Flagstaff) |
| JRS | Journal of Ritual Studies (Pittsburgh Univ., PA) |
| JRUL | Journal of the Rutgers University Libraries (New Brunswick, NJ) |
| JSAA | Journal of Southern African Affairs (Univ. of Maryland, College Park) |
| JSAL | Journal of South Asian Literature (Michigan State Univ., East Lansing) |
| JSH | Journal of Southern History (Rice Univ., Houston, TX) |
| JSHR | Journal of Speech and Hearing Research (Rockville, MD) |
| JSSE | Journal of the Short Story in English (Angers, France) |

Judaism: a quarterly journal of Jewish life and thought (New York)
Junior Bookshelf (Huddersfield)

| | |
|---|---|
| JWCI | Journal of the Warburg and Courtauld Institutes (Univ. of London) |
| JWest | Journal of the West (Manhattan, KS) |
| JWMS | Journal of the William Morris Society (Kew, Surrey) |

Kalki: studies in James Branch Cabell (Oradell, NJ)
Karamu (Eastern Illinois Univ., Charleston)

| | |
|---|---|
| KF . | Keystone Folklore (Univ. of Pennsylvania, Philadelphia) |
| KFR | Kentucky Folklore Record: a regional journal of folklore and life (Western Kentucky Univ., Bowling Green). *See* SF |
| KH | Kansas History: a journal of the Central Plains (Topeka, KS) |

Kirke og kultur (Oslo)

| | |
|---|---|
| KJ | Kipling Journal (London) |

Klagenfurter Beiträge zur Sprachwissenschaft (Klagenfurt, Austria)

| | |
|---|---|
| KN | Kwartalnik Neofilologiczny (Warsaw) |

Knizhnaîa letopis' (Moscow)
Književna smotra (Zagreb)

| | |
|---|---|
| Kp | Kunapipi (Univ. of Aarhus) |
| KQ | Kansas Quarterly (Kansas State Univ., Manhattan) |
| KR | Kenyon Review (Kenyon College, Gambier, OH) |

Kritik: tidsskrift for litteratur, forskning, undervisning (Copenhagen)

| | |
|---|---|
| KSJ | Keats–Shelley Journal: Keats, Shelley, Byron, Hunt, and their circles (Univ. of Pennsylvania, Philadelphia) |
| KSR | Keats–Shelley Review (Univ. of York) |
| LaH | Louisiana History (Univ. of Southwestern Louisiana, Lafayette) |

Landfall: a New Zealand literary magazine (Christchurch)

| | |
|---|---|
| Lang | Language (Washington, DC) |

Langage et l'Homme (Brussels)
Langages: sémiotiques textuelles (Paris)

| | |
|---|---|
| LangMono | Language Monographs (Arlington, VA) |
| LangS | Language and Style: an international journal (City Univ. of New York, Flushing) |
| LankaG | Lanka Guardian (Colombo) |

Lantern: journal for art, knowledge and culture (Pretoria)

| | |
|---|---|
| LAR | Library Association Record (London) |

La Trobe Library Journal (Bundoora, Vic.)
Laurels: a magazine devoted to French-American friendship (New York)

| | |
|---|---|
| LC | Library Chronicle (Univ. of Pennsylvania, Philadelphia) |
| LCUT | Library Chronicle (Univ. of Texas at Austin) |
| LDeus | Letras de Deusto (Univ. of Deusto, Bilbao, Spain) |

Leabharlann/Irish Library (Armagh)

Leeds Medieval Studies (Univ. of Leeds)
Leeds Studies in English (Univ. of Leeds)
Leeds Texts and Monographs (Univ. of Leeds)
Legacy: a journal of nineteenth-century American women writers (Univ. of
    Massachusetts, Amherst)
Letopis' zhurnal'nykh stateĭ (Moscow)
LeuB               Leuvense Bijdragen: tijdschrift voor Germaanse filologie
                       (Katholieke Univ. van Leuven)
Lexi (Athens)
LF                 Literaturen front (Sofia)
LGJ               Lost Generation Journal (Salem, MO)
LH                Lincoln Herald: magazine of Lincoln and the Civil War
                       (Harrogate, TN)
LI                 Linguistic Inquiry (Cambridge, MA)
Library (Oxford)
Library History (London)
Library Review: a quarterly devoted to information transfer, conservation and
    exploitation (Glasgow)
Libros (Madrid)
Linen Hall Review (Linen Hall Library, Belfast)
LingR            Linguistic Reporter (Arlington, VA)
Lingua: international review of general linguistics (Amsterdam)
Linguistic Review (Dordrecht)
Linguistica (Prague)
Linguistics and Philosophy: an international journal (Dordrecht)
Linguistics in the Netherlands (Dordrecht)
Linq: literature in North Queensland (James Cook Univ., Townsville, Qld.)
Listener (London)
LitM             Literární měsíčník (Prague)
Literator: bulletin van die letterkundige dept., Universiteit van Potchefstroom/
    Literator: bulletin of the literature dept., University of Potchefstroom (South
    Africa)
Literaturna misăl (Sofia)
LitEW          Literature East and West (Austin, TX)
LitFQ          Literature/Film Quarterly (Salisbury State College, MD)
LitR            Literary Review: international journal of contemporary writing
                     (Fairleigh Dickinson Univ., Madison, NJ)
Littératures (Univ. of Toulouse)
Livres de l'année (Paris)
Livres du mois (Paris)
Livres-Hebdo (Paris)
LJ                 Library Journal (New York)
LJGG          Literaturwissenschaftliches Jahrbuch im Auftrage der Görres-
                     Gesellschaft (Berlin)
LL                 Language Learning: a journal of applied linguistics
                     (Univ. of Michigan, Ann Arbor)
LM                Lesbók Morgunblaðsins (Reykjavik)
LMR           Literary Magazine Review (Kansas State Univ., Manhattan)
Long-Islander (Huntington, NY)
Long Room (Friends of Trinity Coll. Library, Dublin)
Lore and Language (Univ. of Sheffield)
LQ                Library Quarterly: a journal of investigation and discussion in
                     the field of library science (Chicago)
LRB            London Review of Books
LRN           Literary Research Newsletter (Manhattan College,
                     Bronx, NY)
LU                Lion and the Unicorn: a critical journal of children's literature
                     (Brooklyn College, NY)
Luceafărul (Bucharest)

LWU                Literatur in Wissenschaft und Unterricht (Univ. of Kiel)
Lyrikvännen (Stockholm)
MA                 Moyen Âge: revue historique (Brussels)
Maal og minne (Oslo)
MÆ                 Medium Ævum (Magdalen College, Oxford)
MalaR              Malahat Review (Victoria, BC)
Mankind (Univ. of Sydney)
Manuscripta: a journal devoted to manuscript studies (Saint Louis Univ., MO)
Manuscriptum: revista trimestriala editata de muzeul literaturii Romanae
    (Bucharest)
al-Ma'rifah (Syria)
MarkR              Markham Review (Wagner College, Staten Island, NY)
Mark Twain Circular (Charleston, SC)
MassR              Massachusetts Review: a quarterly of literature, arts and public
                   affairs (Univ. of Massachusetts, Amherst)
MBL                Modern British Literature (Butler, PA)
MCMT               Main Currents in Modern Thought (New Rochelle, NY)
Meanjin: a magazine of literature, art and discussion (Univ. of Melbourne)
MEB                Missouri English Bulletin (Lincoln Univ., Jefferson City, MO)
Med                Mediævistik: Internationale Zeitschrift für interdisziplinäre
                   Mittelalterforschung (Frankfurt)
MedArch            Medieval Archaeology (London)
MedHum             Medievalia et Humanistica: studies in medieval and
                   Renaissance culture (North Texas State Univ., Denton)
Medieval Prosopography (Kalamazoo, MI)
MedRen             Medieval & Renaissance Drama in England (New York)
MedStud            Mediaeval Studies (Toronto)
MELUS: the journal of the Society for the Study of the Multi-Ethnic Literature of the
    United States (State Univ. of New York, Albany)
Menckeniana (Baltimore, MD)
Mentalities (Hamilton, N.Z.)
Meridian (La Trobe Univ., Bundooora, Vic.)
MESN               Medieval English Studies Newsletter (Tokyo)
METh               Medieval English Theatre (Univ. of Lancaster)
MF                 Mystery Fancier (Memphis, TN)
MFR                Mississippi Folklore Register (East Central Junior College,
                   Decatur, MS)
MFS                Modern Fiction Studies (Purdue Univ., West Lafayette, IN)
MHM                Maryland Historical Magazine (Baltimore)
MHR                Missouri Historical Review (Columbia, MO)
MichA              Michigan Academician (Ann Arbor)
MichH              Michigan History (Lansing)
MichQR             Michigan Quarterly Review (Univ. of Michigan, Ann Arbor)
MidA               Mid-America: a historical review (Loyola Univ., Chicago)
Midamerica: the yearbook of the Society for the Study of Midwestern Literature
    (Michigan State Univ., East Lansing)
Mid-America Folklore (Batesville, AR)
Midland History (Chichester, Sussex)
MidQ               Midwest Quarterly: a journal of contemporary thought
                   (Pittsburg State Univ., KS)
Midwestern Folklore: Journal of the Hoosier Folklore Society (Indiana State Univ.,
    Terre Haute). Formerly MJLF
Midwestern Miscellany (Michigan State Univ., East Lansing)
Miesięcznik Literacki (Warsaw)
MillNL             Mill News Letter (Univ. of Toronto)
MinnH              Minnesota History (St Paul)
MinnR              Minnesota Review: a journal of committed writing (State Univ.
                   of New York, Stony Brook)
Misc               Miscelánea (Univ. of Zaragoza)
MissQ              Mississippi Quarterly: the journal of Southern culture
                   (Mississippi State Univ.)

| | |
|---|---|
| MJLF | Midwestern Journal of Language and Folklore (Indiana State Univ., Terre Haute). *See* Midwestern Folklore |
| MLJ | Modern Language Journal (Madison, WI) |

MLN: Modern Language Notes (Baltimore, MD)

| | |
|---|---|
| MLQ | Modern Language Quarterly (Univ. of Washington, Seattle) |
| MLR | Modern Language Review (London) |
| MLS | Modern Language Studies (Brown Univ., Providence, RI) |
| MMN | Marianne Moore Newletter (Philadelphia, PA) |
| MN | Mystery Nook (Wheaton, MD) |
| ModAge | Modern Age (Bryn Mawr, PA) |
| ModDr | Modern Drama (Univ. of Toronto) |

Monist: an international quarterly of general philosophical inquiry (La Salle, IL)
Montana: the magazine of Western history (Helena, MT)
Moreana: time trieth truth (Angers, France)
Mosaic: journal for the interdisciplinary study of literature (Univ. of Manitoba, Winnipeg)
Most (Mostar, Yugoslavia)

| | |
|---|---|
| MP | Modern Philology (Chicago) |
| MPS | Modern Poetry Studies (Buffalo, NY) |
| MQ | Milton Quarterly (Ohio Univ., Athens) |
| MS | Moderna språk (Linkoping, Sweden) |
| MSE | Massachusetts Studies in English (Univ. of Massachusetts, Amherst) |
| MsM | MS: the new magazine for women (New York) |
| MSNH | Mémoires de la Société Néophilologique de Helsinki |
| MSS | Manuscripts (Burbank, CA) |
| MSSN | Medieval Sermon Studies Newsletter (Univ. of Warwick) |
| MStud | Milton Studies (Univ. of Pittsburgh, PA) |
| MTJ | Mark Twain Journal (College of Charleston, SC) |
| MULRN | McMaster University Library Research News (Hamilton, Ont.) |

Münchener Studien zur Sprachwissenschaft (Munich)

| | |
|---|---|
| MundusA | Mundus Artium: a journal of international literature and the arts (Univ. of Texas at Dallas, Richardson) |
| MusQ | Musical Quarterly (New York) |
| MV | Minority Voices: an interdisciplinary journal of literature and the arts (University Park, PA) |

Mythlore: a journal of J. R. R. Tolkien, C. S. Lewis, Charles Williams, general fantasy and mythic studies (Los Angeles, CA)
Nabokovian (Univ. of Kansas, Lawrence)
Nachrichten der Akademie der Wissenschaften in Göttingen
Nagyvilág (Budapest)

| | |
|---|---|
| NAmerR | North American Review (Univ. of Northern Iowa, Cedar Falls) |

Names (New York)

| | |
|---|---|
| Nat | Nation (New York) |

Natalia (Pietermaritzburg, South Africa)
National Times: Australia's national weekly newspaper of business and affairs (Sydney)

| | |
|---|---|
| NatR | National Review: a journal of fact and opinion (New York) |

Natural Language and Linguistic Theory (Dordrecht)
Nauchnye trudy Kubanskogo universiteta (Krasnodar, USSR)
Nauchnye trudy Kuĭbyshevskogo universiteta (Kuĭbyshev, USSR)
Naučni trudove. Filologija Plovidvski Universitet 'Paisij Hilendarski' (Plovdiv, Bulgaria)

| | |
|---|---|
| NC | New Comparison (Univ. of Warwick) |
| NCarF | North Carolina Folklore Journal (Appalachian State Univ., Boone) |
| NCathW | New Catholic World (Mahwah, NJ) |
| NCC | Nineteenth-Century Contexts (Northeastern Univ., Boston, MA). *Formerly* RPP |
| NCF | Nineteenth-Century Fiction (Berkeley, CA) |

NCHR          North Carolina Historical Review (Raleigh)
NCL           Notes on Contemporary Literature (West Georgia College,
              Carrollton)
NCP           Nineteenth-Century Prose (U.S. Naval Academy, Annapolis,
              MD). *Formerly* Arnoldian
NCrit         New Criterion (New York)
NDEJ          Notre Dame English Journal (Univ. of Notre Dame, IN)
NDFN          Nauchnye doklady vyssheĭ shkoly. Filologicheskie nauki
              (Moscow)
NDH           North Dakota History: journal of the Northern Plains
              (Bismarck, ND)
NDQ           North Dakota Quarterly (Univ. of N. Dakota, Grand Forks)
Nea Poreia (Thessalonika)
NebH          Nebraska History (Lincoln, NE)
NELM News (National English Literary Museum, Grahamstown, South Africa)
Neohelicon: acta comparationis litterarum universarum (Akademiai Kiadó,
    Budapest)
Neophilologus (Groningen)
NEQ           New England Quarterly: an historical review of New England
              life and letters (Boston, MA)
NER           New England Review (Hanover, NH)
Neue Sammlung: Vierteljahres-Zeitschrift für Erziehung und Gesellschaft (Stuttgart)
New Coin Poetry (Rhodes Univ., Grahamstown, South Africa)
NewL          New Leader: a bi-weekly of news and opinion (New York)
New Letters: a magazine of fine writing (Univ. of Missouri, Kansas City)
New Literature Review (Univ. of New England, Armidale, N.S.W.)
New Perspectives: Technikon Natal journal for research and education (Durban)
NewSt         New Statesman: an independent political and literary review
              (London)
New Zealand Journal of French Studies (Palmerston North)
New Zealand Monthly Review (Christchurch)
New Zealand National Bibliography (Wellington)
New Zealand Slavonic Journal (Victoria Univ., Wellington)
New Zealand Speech–Language Therapists' Journal (Christchurch)
New Zealand Women's Studies Journal (Auckland). *See* Women's Studies Journal
NGM           National Geographic (Washington, DC)
NHJ           Nathaniel Hawthorne Journal (Englewood, CO)
NHR           Nathaniel Hawthorne Review (Bowdoin College, Brunswick,
              ME)
Nieman Reports (Harvard Univ., Cambridge, MA)
NIF           Newsletter on Intellectual Freedom (Chicago)
Nimrod (Univ. of Tulsa, OK)
NJH           New Jersey History (Newark, NJ)
NJL           Nordic Journal of Linguistics (Oslo)
NK            Narodna kultura (Sofia)
NLB           Newberry Library Bulletin (Chicago)
NLH           New Literary History: a journal of theory and interpretation
              (Baltimore, MD)
NM            Neuphilologische Mitteilungen (Helsinki)
NMAL          Notes on Modern American Literature (St John's Univ.,
              Jamaica, NY)
NMS           Nottingham Medieval Studies (Univ. of Nottingham)
NMW           Notes on Mississippi Writers (Univ. of Southern Mississippi,
              Hattiesburg)
NoB           Namn och bygd: tidskrift för nordisk ortsnamnforskning/
              Journal for Nordic place-name research (Uppsala)
Nomina: journal of name studies relating to Great Britain and Ireland (Univ. of Hull)
NOR           New Orleans Review (Loyola Univ., New Orleans, LA)
Nordlyd: Tromsö University Working Papers on Language and Linguistics (Tromsö,
    Norway)

Norsk bokfortegnelse (Oslo)
Novel: a forum on fiction (Brown Univ., Providence, RI)

| | |
|---|---|
| NovM | Novyĭ Mir (Moscow) |
| NOWELE | North-Western European Language Evolution: NOWELE (Odense Univ., Denmark) |
| NQ | Notes and Queries (Oxford) |
| NR | New Republic: a journal of opinion (Washington, DC) |
| NRam | New Rambler: the journal of the Johnson Society of London (Farningham, Kent) |
| NRF | Nouvelle revue française (Paris) |
| NSch | New Scholasticism (Catholic Univ. of America, Washington, DC) |
| NSG | Newsletter of Study Group on Eighteenth-Century Russia (Univ. of East Anglia, Norwich) |
| NwMSUS | Northwest Missouri State University Studies: bulletin of Northwest Missouri State University (Maryville) |
| NwOQ | Northwest Ohio Quarterly (Bowling Green State Univ., OH) |
| NWT | Nieuw Wereld Tijdschrift (Liezele-Purs, Belgium) |
| NY | New Yorker |
| NYF | New York Folklore (State Univ. of New York, Buffalo) |
| NYH | New York History (Cooperstown, NY) |
| NYHSQ | New York Historical Society Quarterly (New York) |
| NYRB | New York Review of Books |
| NYTB | New York Times Book Review |
| NYTM | New York Times Magazine |
| NZEN | New Zealand English Newsletter |
| NZJH | New Zealand Journal of History (Univ. of Auckland) |
| NZLib | New Zealand Libraries (Wellington) |
| NZList | New Zealand Listener (Wellington) |
| NZZ | Neue Zürcher Zeitung (Zürich) |
| Ob | Obsidian: black literature in review (Detroit, MI) |

Occasional Papers in Language and Linguistics (Univ. of Canterbury, Christchurch, NZ)
Odyssey: a journal of the humanities (Oakland Univ., Rochester, MI)

| | |
|---|---|
| OE | Ons Erfdeel: algemeen nederlands tweemaandelijks kultureel tijdschrift (Rekkem, Belgium) |
| OEN | Old English Newsletter (State Univ. of New York, Binghamton) |
| OhioanaQ | Ohioana Quarterly (Columbus, OH) |
| OhioH | Ohio History (Columbus) |
| OhioR | Ohio Review (Ohio Univ., Athens) |
| OL | Orbis litterarum: international review of literary studies (Copenhagen) |
| OldN | Old Northwest (Miami Univ., Oxford, OH) |

OLSON: journal of the Charles Olson Archives (Univ. of Connecticut, Storrs)

| | |
|---|---|
| OnS | On-Stage Studies (Univ. of Colorado, Boulder) |

Opera News (New York)

| | |
|---|---|
| OpL | Open Letter (Toronto) |

Oral English (Le Moyne Coll., Syracuse, NY)
Oral History (Univ. of Essex)
Orana: journal for school and children's librarians (Ultimo, N.S.W.)
Orbis: bulletin international de documentation linguistique (Univ. Catholique de Louvain)
Ord och bild: nordisk kulturtidskrift (Stockholm)

| | |
|---|---|
| OreHQ | Oregon Historical Quarterly (Portland) |

Orizont (Timişoara, Romania)
Ortnamnssällskapets i Uppsala årsskrift (Uppsala)
Overland (Mt Eliza, Vic.)

| | |
|---|---|
| PAAS | Proceedings of the American Antiquarian Society (Worcester, MA) |
| PacH | Pacific Historian (Univ. of the Pacific, Stockton, CA) |

PacHR                    Pacific Historical Review (Berkeley, CA)
Pacific Philosophical Quarterly (Univ. of Southern California, Los Angeles)
PacNQ                    Pacific Northwest Quarterly (Univ. of Washington, Seattle)
PADS                     Publications of the American Dialect Society (Univ. of Kansas,
                         Lawrence)
Paideuma (Univ. of Maine, Orono)
Paintbrush: a journal of poetry, translations and letters (Georgia Southwestern
    College, Americus)
El país: panorama semanal (Madrid)
Palimpsest (Iowa City)
Pamiętnik Teatralny (Warsaw)
Panorama (Sofia)
PAPS                     Proceedings of the American Philosophical Society (University
                         Park, PA)
Parergon: bulletin of the Australian and New Zealand Association for Medieval and
    Renaissance Studies (Univ. of Sydney)
ParisR                   Paris Review (Flushing, NY)
Parousia (Univ. of Athens)
Past and Present: a journal of historical studies (Corpus Christi College, Oxford)
Paunch (Buffalo, NY)
PBSA                     Papers of the Bibliographical Society of America
                         (Williamsburg, MA)
PBSC                     Papers of the Bibliographical Society of Canada (Toronto)
PCL                      Perspectives on Contemporary Literature (Univ. of Louisville,
                         KY)
PCP                      Pacific Coast Philology (San Diego State Univ., CA)
Pegasus (Soungjeon Univ., Korea)
PEW                      Philosophy East and West: a quarterly journal of Asian and
                         comparative thought (Univ. of Hawaii, Honolulu)
PH                       Przegląd Humanistyczny (Warsaw)
PhilL                    Philosophy and Literature (Baltimore, MD)
Philosophy (Cambridge)                                    .
PhilP                    Philological Papers (West Virginia Univ., Morgantown)
PhilR                    Philosophy and Rhetoric (University Park, PA)
PhilS                    Philosophical Studies: an international journal for philosophy in
                         the analytic tradition (Dordrecht)
PhilT                    Philosophy Today (Celina, OH)
Phylon: Atlanta University review of race and culture (Atlanta, GA)
PJAS                     Pakistan Journal of American Studies (Islamabad)
PL                       Papers in Linguistics: international journal of human
                         communication (Edmonton, Alta.) See RLSI
Pl                       Ploughshares: a journal of new writing (Cambridge, MA)
Plamăk (Sofia)
Planet (Aberystwyth)
Playboy (Chicago)
Plays and Players (Croydon, Surrey)
PLL                      Papers on Language and Literature (Southern Illinois Univ.,
                         Edwardsville)
PMHB                     Pennsylvania Magazine of History and Biography
                         (Philadelphia)
PMHS                     Proceedings of the Massachusetts Historical Society (Boston)
PMLA: Publications of the Modern Language Association of America (New York)
PMMLA                    Papers of the Midwest MLA (New York)
PN Review (Manchester)
PoeM                     Poe Messenger (Richmond, VA)
PoeS                     Poe Studies (Pullman, WA)
PoeSAN                   Poe Studies Association Newsletter (Pennsylvania State Univ.,
                         DuBois)
PoetA                    Poetica: Zeitschrift für Sprach- und Literaturwissenschaft
                         (Bochum)

PoetC　　　　　　　　Poet and Critic (Iowa State Univ., Ames)
Poetics: international review for the theory of literature (Amsterdam)
Poétique: revue de théorie et d'analyse littéraires (Paris)
Poetry (Chicago)
PoetT　　　　　　　　Poetica: an international journal of linguistic-literary studies
　　　　　　　　　　　　(Tokyo)
Polycom (Carlton, Vic.)
PP　　　　　　　　　　Philologica Pragensia: journal of modern philology (Prague)
　　　　　　　　　　　　*Includes, as supplement,* CMF
PPQ　　　　　　　　　Pacific Philosophical Quarterly (Univ. of Southern California,
　　　　　　　　　　　　Los Angeles)
PPR　　　　　　　　　Philosophy and Phenomenological Research (Buffalo, NY)
PQ　　　　　　　　　　Philological Quarterly (Univ. of Iowa, Iowa City)
PR　　　　　　　　　　Partisan Review (Boston Univ., MA)
Prague Studies in English
Praxis: a journal of cultural criticism (Univ. of California, Los Angeles)
Private Library (Pinner, Middlesex)
Problemi na izkustvoto (Sofia)
Prose Studies (London)
Prospects: an annual journal of American cultural studies (Columbia Univ., New
　　York)
PrS　　　　　　　　　Prairie Schooner (Univ. of Nebraska, Lincoln)
PRv　　　　　　　　　Philosophical Review (Cornell Univ., Ithaca, NY)
Przewodnik bibliograficzny (Warsaw)
PSiCL　　　　　　　　Papers and Studies in Contrastive Linguistics (Poznań)
PSQ　　　　　　　　　Political Science Quarterly (New York)
PT　　　　　　　　　　Poetics Today (Jerusalem)
PTFS　　　　　　　　Publications of the Texas Folklore Society (Nacogdoches, TX)
PubH　　　　　　　　Publishing History (Cambridge)
Publications of the Department of English, University of Turku (Finland)
PULC　　　　　　　　Princeton University Library Chronicle (Princeton, NJ)
Puls (Sofia)
Push from the Bush (Clayton, Vic.)
PW　　　　　　　　　Poetry Wales: Cylchgrawn Cenedlaethol o Farddoniaeth
　　　　　　　　　　　　Newydd (Bridgend)
QH　　　　　　　　　Quaker History (Haverford, PA)
QJLC　　　　　　　　Quarterly Journal of the U.S. Library of Congress
　　　　　　　　　　　　(Washington, DC)
QJS　　　　　　　　　Quarterly Journal of Speech (Annandale, VA)
QNL　　　　　　　　　Quarterly Newsletter (Book Club of California, San Francisco)
QQ　　　　　　　　　Queen's Quarterly: a Canadian review (Queen's Univ.,
　　　　　　　　　　　　Kingston, Ont.)
Quadrant (Sydney)
Quaerendo: a quarterly journal from the Low Countries devoted to manuscripts and
　　printed books (Leiden)
Quarterly Bulletin of the South African Library (Cape Town)
Queen City Heritage: the journal of the Cincinnati Historical Society (Cincinnati,
　　OH)
Quest: a feminist quarterly (Washington, DC)
RAEI　　　　　　　　Revista alicantina de estudios ingleses (Alicante)
RALS　　　　　　　　Resources for American Literary Study (Longwood College,
　　　　　　　　　　　　Farmville, VA.)
Ramuri (Craiova, Romania)
RANAM　　　　　　　Recherches anglaises et américaines: a quarterly review (Univ.
　　　　　　　　　　　　des Sciences Humaines, Strasbourg)
Rapports d'activités de l'Institut de Phonétique (Brussels)
Raritan: a quarterly review (Rutgers Univ., New Brunswick, NJ)
Ravi (Lahore)
RBPH　　　　　　　　Revue belge de philologie et d'histoire (Brussels)
RCEI　　　　　　　　Revista canaria de estudios ingleses (Univ. of La Laguna,
　　　　　　　　　　　　Tenerife)

Reading Time (Curtin, A.C.T.)
REAL            Re: Artes Liberales (Stephen F. Austin State Univ.,
                Nacogdoches, TX)
RECTR           Restoration and Eighteenth-Century Theatre Research (Loyola
                Univ. of Chicago)
REEDNewsletter  Records of Early English Drama Newsletter (Univ. of Toronto)
Ren             Renascence: essays on values in literature (Milwaukee, WI)
RenD            Renaissance Drama (Univ. of New Orleans, LA)
Rendezvous: Idaho State University journal of arts and letters (Pocatello, ID)
RenP            Renaissance Papers (Duke Univ., Durham, NC)
RenR            Renaissance and Reformation/Renaissance et réforme (Univ. of
                Toronto)
Repérages (Nantes)
Representations (Berkeley, CA)
Republika (Zagreb)
RES             Review of English Studies: a quarterly journal of English
                literature and the English language (Oxford)
Restoration: studies in English literary culture, 1660–1700 (Univ. of Tennessee,
   Knoxville)
Review (Charlottesville, VA)
Revista interamericana de bibliografía. See IARB
RevL            Revue de Louisiane/Louisiana Review (Lafayette)
Revue des lettres modernes: histoire des idées des littératures (Paris)
Revue du cinéma/Image et son: revue culturelle de cinéma (Paris)
Revue internationale de philosophie (Wetteren, Belgium)
Revue romane (Copenhagen)
RFil            Revista de filología (Univ. of La Laguna, Tenerife)
RG              Revue générale (Brussels)
RHT             Revue d'histoire du théâtre (Paris)
RiceUS          Rice University Studies (Houston, TX)
RITL            Revista de istorie şi teorie literară (Bucharest)
RL              Religion and Literature (Univ. of Notre Dame, IN)
RLC             Revue de littérature comparée (Paris)
RLSI            Research in Language and Social Interaction (Edmonton,
                Alta.)
RMP             Rheinisches Museum für Philologie (Frankfurt)
RMRLL           Rocky Mountain Review of Language and Literature (Boise
                State Univ., ID)
RMS             Renaissance and Modern Studies (Univ. of Nottingham)
RN              Revue nouvelle (Brussels)
RNL             Review of National Literatures (Whitestone, NY)
RodR            Rodna reč (Sofia)
Romanskoe i germanskoe fâzykoznanie (Minskiĭ pedagogicheskiĭ institut, Minsk,
   USSR)
RomLit          România literară (Bucharest)
RomN            Romance Notes (Univ. of North Carolina, Chapel Hill)
RORD            Research Opportunities in Renaissance Drama (Univ. of
                Kansas, Lawrence)
RPA             Revue de Phonétique appliquée (Paris)
RPh             Romance Philology (Berkeley, CA)
RPP             Romanticism Past and Present (Northeastern Univ., Boston,
                MA (See NCC)
RQ              Renaissance Quarterly (New York)
RR              Romantic Review (Columbia Univ., New York)
RRCNU           Research Review of Chungbuk National University (Chongju,
                Korea)
RRL             Revue roumaine de linguistique (Bucharest) Includes, as
                supplement, Cahiers de linguistique théorique et appliquée
RSWSU           Research Studies of Washington State University (Pullman)
RUC             Revista de la Universidad Complutense de Madrid

| | |
|---|---|
| RULB | Revue de l'Université Libre de Bruxelles |
| RusL | Russkaiâ literatura (Leningrad) |
| RussR | Russian Review: an American quarterly devoted to Russia past and present (Cambridge, MA) |
| SAC | Studies in the Age of Chaucer: the yearbook of the New Chaucer Society (Univ. of Tennessee, Norman) |
| SAF | Studies in American Fiction (Northeastern Univ., Boston, MA) |
| SAH | Studies in American Humor (Southwest Texas State Univ., San Marcos) |
| SAJournal of Linguistics/SA Tydskrif vir Taalkunde (Lynn East) | |
| SAL | Southwestern American Literature (Denton, TX) |
| Samlaren: tidskrift för svensk litteraturvetenskaplig forskning (Uppsala) | |
| Samtiden (Oslo) | |
| SAP | Studia Anglica Posnaniensia (Poznań) |
| SAQ | South Atlantic Quarterly (Durham, NC) |
| SaS | Slovo a slovesnot/Word and writing (Prague) |
| SATJ | South African Theatre Journal (Sunnyside) |
| SAtlR | South Atlantic Review (Univ. of North Carolina, Chapel Hill) |
| SatR | Saturday Review: a review of literature and the creative arts (Washington, DC) |
| Săvremennik (Sofia) | |
| SB | Studies in Bibliography: papers of the Bibliographical Society of the University of Virginia (Univ of Virginia, Charlottesville) |
| SBrown | Studies in Browning and his Circle: a journal of criticism, history and bibliography (Baylor Univ., Waco, TX) |
| ScanR | Scandinavian Review (New York) |
| SCHM | South Carolina Historical Magazine (Charleston) |
| SchP | Scholarly Publishing (Toronto) |
| Science Fiction: a review of speculative literature (Univ. of Western Australia, Nedlands) | |
| SCL | Studii şi cercetări lingvistice (Bucharest) |
| SCN | Seventeenth-Century News (Pennsylvania State Univ., University Park) |
| ScottN | Scott Newsletter (Univ. of Aberdeen) |
| SCR | South Central Review (Texas A & M Univ., College Station) |
| Scriblerian and Kit-Cats: a newsjournal devoted to Pope, Swift, and their circle, the Kit-Cats and Dryden (Temple Univ., Philadelphia, PA) | |
| Scriptorium: international review of manuscript studies (Brussels) | |
| SDR | South Dakota Review (Univ. of South Dakota, Vermillion) |
| SE | Southern Exposure (Durham, NC) |
| Secolul 20: revista de literatura universala (Bucharest) | |
| SEEJ | Slavic and East European Journal (Univ. of Arizona, Tucson) |
| SEL | Studies in English Literature/Eibungaku Kenkyu (Tokyo) |
| SELit | Studies in English Literature 1500–1900 (Rice Univ., Houston, TX) |
| Septemvri (Sofia) | |
| SEVEN: an Anglo-American literary review (Wheaton Coll., IL) | |
| Seventeenth Century (Univ. of Durham) | |
| SewR | Sewanee Review (Unit. of the South, Sewanee, TN) |
| SEz | Săpostavitelno ezikoznaie (Sofia) |
| SF | Southern Folklore (Western Kentucky Univ., Bowling Green). *Merger* of KFR and SFQ |
| SFN | Shakespeare on Film Newsletter (Univ. of Vermont, Burlington) |
| SFQ | Southern Folklore Quarterly (Univ. of Florida, Gainesville). *See* SF |
| SFS | Science-Fiction Studies (McGill Univ., Montreal) |
| SGM | Scottish Geographical Magazine (Edinburgh) |
| Shakespeare in Southern Africa (Rhodes Univ., Grahamstown) | |
| Shakespeare Society of Southern Africa Newsletter (Rhodes Univ., Grahamstown) | |

Shakespeare Society of Southern Africa Occasional Papers (Rhodes Univ., Grahamstown)
Shaw: the annual of Bernard Shaw studies (University Park, PA)
Shen                Shenandoah (Washington and Lee Univ., Lexington, VA)
SHQ                 Southwestern Historical Quarterly (Austin, TX)
ShR                 Shakespeare Review (Seoul)
ShS                 Shakespeare Survey: an annual survey of Shakespearean study
                    and production (Oxford)
SHum                Studies in the Humanities (Indiana Univ. of Pennsylvania,
                    Indiana)
SIcon               Studies in Iconography (Arizona State Univ., Tempe)
Sigma (Univ. Paul Valéry, Montpellier)
Signs: journal of women in culture and society (Chicago)
Sinsear (Dublin)
Sistemnoe opisanie leksiki germanskikh îâzykov (Leningrad State Univ.)
Sites: a journal for radical perspectives (Palmerston North, N.Z.)
SixCT               Sixteenth Century Journal: an interdisciplinary journal for
                    Renaissance and Reformation students and scholars
                    (Northeast Missouri State Univ., Kirksville)
SJO                 Jahrbuch der deutschen Shakespeare-Gesellschaft Ost
                    (Weimar)
SJP                 Southern Journal of Philosophy (Memphis State Univ., TN)
SJS                 San Jose Studies (San Jose State Univ., CA)
SJW                 Jahrbuch der deutschen Shakespeare-Gesellschaft West (Univ.
                    of Würzburg)
Skírnir (Reykjavik)
SL                  Studies in Language (Amsterdam)
SLang               Scottish Language: an annual review (Univ. of Aberdeen)
SlavR               Slavic Review: American quarterly of Soviet and East European
                    studies (Stanford Univ., CA)
SLI                 Studies in the Literary Imagination (Georgia State Univ.,
                    Atlanta)
SLJ                 Scottish Literary Journal (Univ. of Aberdeen)
SLN                 Sinclair Lewis Newsletter (St Cloud State College, MN)
Slovoobrazovanie i ego mesto v kurse obucheniîâ inostrannomu îâzyku (Leningrad
State Univ.)
SLRC                Studii de literatură română şi comparată Universitatea din
                    Timişoara (Romania)
Smithsonian (Washington, DC)
SN                  Studia Neophilogica: a journal of Germanic and Romance
                    philology (Stockholm)
SNH                 Studies in Nathaniel Hawthorne (Nathaniel Hawthorne Soc. of
                    Korea, Seoul)
SNL                 Shakespeare Newsletter (Evanston, IL)
SNTM                Sbornik nauchnykh trudov Moskovskogo pedagogicheskogo
                    instituta inostrannykh îâzykov (Moscow)
SNTT                Sbornik nauchnykh trudov Tashkentskogo universiteta
                    (Tashkent)
Social Dynamics (Cape Town)
Societas Scientiarum Fennica: commentationes humanarum litterarum (Helsinki)
SoCR                South Carolina Review (Clemson Univ., SC)
SocSJ               Social Science Journal (Colorado State Univ., Fort Collins)
SoHR                Southern Humanities Review (Auburn Univ., AL)
SoLJ                Southern Literary Journal (Univ. of North Carolina, Chapel
                    Hill)
SoQ                 Southern Quarterly: a journal of the arts in the South (Univ. of
                    Southern Mississippi, Hattiesburg)
SoR                 Southern Review: a literary and critical quarterly magazine
                    (Louisiana State Univ., Baton Rouge)

SoRA Southern Review: literary and interdisciplinary essays (Univ. of Adelaide)
SoS Southern Studies: an interdisciplinary journal of the South (Northwestern State Univ. of Louisiana, Natchitoches)
Soundings: an interdisciplinary journal (Vanderbilt Univ., Nashville, TN)
South African Journal of Linguistics (Lynn East). *See* SA Journal of Linguistics
South-Central Names Institute Publications (East Texas State Univ., Commerce)
Southerly: a review of Australian literature (Univ. of Sydney)
SP Studies in Philology (Univ. of North Carolina, Chapel Hill)
Span (Christchurch, N.Z.)
Spec Speculum: a journal of medieval studies (Cambridge, MA)
Spect Spectator (London)
SpenN Spenser Newsletter (State Univ. of New York, Albany)
Spenser Studies: a Renaissance poetry annual (Princeton Univ., NJ)
Spin (Palmerston North, NZ)
Spirit: a magazine of poetry (Seton Hall Univ., South Orange, NJ)
Splash (Auckland)
SPR Southern Poetry Review (Univ. of North Carolina, Charlotte)
Die Sprache: Zeitschrift für Sprachwissenschaft (Wiesbaden)
Spr Sprachkunst: Beiträge zur Literaturwissenschaft (Vienna)
SQ Shakespeare Quarterly (Washington, DC)
SR Studies in Romanticism (Boston Univ., MA)
SRev Southwest Review (Southern Methodist Univ., Dallas, TX)
SRO Shakespearean Research and Opportunities: the report of the MLA Conference (City Univ. of New York)
SS Scandinavian Studies (Urbana, IL)
SSF Studies in Short Fiction (Newberry College, SC)
SShA: ėkonomika, politika, ideologiiā (Moscow)
SSJ Southern Speech Communication Journal (Appalachian State Univ., Boone, NC)
SSL Studies in Scottish Literature (Univ. of South Carolina, Columbia)
SSMLN Society for the Study of Midwestern Literature Newsletter (Michigan State Univ., East Lansing)
SSQ Social Science Quarterly (Austin, TX)
SStud Shakespeare Studies (Univ. of New Mexico, Albuquerque)
SStudT Shakespeare Studies (Tokyo)
Staffrider (Braamfontein, South Africa)
Standpunte (Auckland Park, South Africa)
Steaua (Cluj-Napoca, Romania)
SteiQ Steinbeck Quarterly (Ball State Univ., Muncie, IN)
Streven (Antwerp)
StUCNPhil Studia Universitatis Babes-Bolyai, Cluj-Napoca. Series Philologia (Cluj-Napoca, Romania)
StudAJL Studies in American Jewish Literature (University Park, PA)
StudCanL Studies in Canadian Literature (Univ. of New Brunswick, Fredericton)
StudECC Studies in Eighteenth-Century Culture (Arizona State Univ., Tempe)
Studier fra sprog- og oldtidsforskning (Copenhagen)
Studier i modern språkvetenskap/Stockholm Studies in Modern Philology (Univ. of Stockholm)
Studies: an Irish quarterly review (Dublin)
Studies in Language (Faculty of Arts, Univ. of Joensun, Finland) ·
StudL Studia Linguistica: revue de linguistique générale et comparée (Malmo, Sweden)
StudME Studies in Medieval English Language and Literature (Japan Society for Medieval English Studies, Tokyo)
StudN Studies in the Novel (North Texas State Univ., Denton)
Style (Northern Illinois Univ., DeKalb)

Svensk bokförteckning/Swedish National Bibliography (Stockholm)
Svensk litteraturidskrift (Stockholm)
Svenska tidskriftsartiklar (Lund)
SvL            Světová literatura (Prague)
SW             South and West: an international literary quarterly (Fort Smith,
               AR)
Swift Studies (Munster: Ehrenpreis Centre for Swift Studies)
SwS            Southwestern Studies (Univ. of Texas at El Paso)
Sydney Morning Herald (Broadway, N.S.W.)
Sydney Studies in Society and Culture
Sydsvenska ortnamnssällskapets årsskrift: annual journal of the South Swedish
   Place-Name Society (Lund)
Symposium: a quarterly journal in modern foreign literatures (Washington, DC)
Synthesis: bulletin du Comité National de Littérature Comparée de la République
   Socialiste de Roumanie (Bucharest)
SZ             Stimmen der Zeit: Monatsschrift für das Geistesleben der
               Gegenwart (Freiburg im Breisgau)
T              Teatår (Sofia)
TamkR          Tamkang Review: a journal mainly devoted to comparative
               studies between Chinese and foreign literatures (Taipei,
               Taiwan)
TAPS           Transactions of the American Philosophical Society
               (Philadelphia, PA)
TBR            Texas Books in Review (Univ. of North Texas, Denton)
TCBS           Transactions of the Cambridge Bibliographical Society
               (Cambridge)
TCL            Twentieth-century Literature: a scholarly and critical journal
               (Hofstra Univ., Hempstead, NY)
TDR            Drama Review: international journal documenting historical
               and contemporary trends in the performing arts (Cambridge,
               MA)
Te             Teatr (Moscow)
Te Reo: journal of the Linguistic Society of New Zealand (Univ. of Auckland)
Text & Context: a journal of interdisciplinary studies (North Staffs Poly., Stoke-on-
   Trent)
Textures (Univ. of the Orange Free State, Bloemfontein)
TfL            Tidskrift för litteraturvetenskap (Umeå, Sweden)
TFSB           Tennessee Folklore Society Bulletin (Middle Tennessee State
               Univ., Murfreesboro)
THA            Thomas Hardy Annual (London)
TheatreS       Theatre Survey (State Univ. of New York, Albany)
Themes in Drama (Cambridge)
Theologie und Philosophie (Freiburg im Breisgau)
Theologische Zeitschrift (Basel Univ.)
Theoria: a journal of studies in the arts, humanities and social sciences (Univ. of
   Natal, Pietermaritzburg, South Africa)
THES           Times Higher Education Supplement (London)
This Australia (Collingwood, Vic.)
THJ            Thomas Hardy Journal (Canterbury)
ThN            Thackeray Newsletter (Mississippi State Univ., Starkville)
Thomist: a speculative quarterly review of theology and philosophy (Washington,
   DC)
Thoreau Society Booklet (State Univ. College, Geneseo, NY)
Thoth (Syracuse Univ., NY)
Thought: a review of culture and ideas (Fordham Univ., Bronx, NY)
THQ            Tennessee Historical Quarterly (Nashville)
Threshold (Belfast)
Tijdschrift voor de Studie van de Verlichting en van het vrije Denken (Centrum voor
   de Studie van de Verlichting en van Let Vrije Denken, Vrije Universiteit, Brussels)
Time (New York)

| | |
|---|---|
| TJ | Theatre Journal (Baltimore, MD) |
| TJQ | Thoreau Quarterly: a journal of literary and philosophical studies (Univ. of Minnesota, Minneapolis) |
| TLR | Turnbull Library Record (Wellington, N.Z.) |

TLS: Times Literary Supplement (London)

| | |
|---|---|
| TM | Temps modernes (Paris) |
| TMM | Tímarit Máls og menningar (Reykjavik) |
| TN | Theatre Notebook: journal of the history and technique of British theatre (London) |

Tocher (Univ. of Edinburgh)
Topic: a journal of the liberal arts (Washington and Jefferson College, Washington, PA)

| | |
|---|---|
| TPB | Tennessee Philological Bulletin: proceedings of the annual meeting of the Tennessee Philological Association (Memphis, TN) |
| TQ | Texas Quarterly (Univ. of Texas at Austin) |

Traditio: studies in ancient and medieval history, thought, and religion (Bronx, NY)

| | |
|---|---|
| Trans | Translation (Columbia Univ., New York) |

Transilvania (Sibiu, Romania)

| | |
|---|---|
| TRB | Tennyson Research Bulletin (Lincoln) |
| TRI | Theatre Research International (Oxford) |

Tribuna (Cluj–Napoca, Romania)
TriQuarterly (Northwestern Univ., Evanston, IL)
Trudove na Velikotărnovskija universitet 'Kiril i Metodij' (Tărnovo, Bulgaria)
Trudy Samarkandskogo universiteta (Samarkand)

| | |
|---|---|
| TS | Theatre Studies: the journal of the Ohio State University Theatre Research Institute (Columbus, OH) |
| TSB | Thoreau Society Bulletin: devoted to the life and writings of Henry David Thoreau (State Univ. College, Geneseo, NY) |
| TSE | Tulane Studies in English (Tulane Univ., New Orleans, LA) |
| TSL | Tennessee Studies in Literature (Univ. of Tennessee, Knoxville) |
| TSLL | Texas Studies in Literature and Language: a journal of the humanities (Univ. of Texas at Austin) |
| TSWL | Tulsa Studies in Women's Literature (Univ. of Tulsa, OK) |
| TTJE | Texas Tech Journal of Education (Texas Tech Univ., Lubbock) |

Twainian (Perry, MO)
Twórczość (Warsaw)

| | |
|---|---|
| TWR | Thomas Wolfe Review (Univ. of Akron, OH) |

Tygodnik Powszechny (Cracow, Poland)

| | |
|---|---|
| UASPY | University of Athens School of Philosophy Yearbook |

Uchenye zapiski Tartuskogo universiteta. Trudi po romano-germanskoĭ filologii (Tartu, USSR)

| | |
|---|---|
| UCTSE | University of Cape Town Studies in English (Univ. of Cape Town) |
| UDR | University of Dayton Review (Dayton, OH) |
| UES | Unisa English Studies: journal of the Department of English (Univ. of South Africa, Pretoria) |
| UHQ | Utah Historical Quarterly (Salt Lake City) |
| UHSL | University of Hartford Studies in Literature: a journal of interdisciplinary criticism (West Hartford, CT) |
| UJH | University Journal: Humanities (Busan National Univ., Korea) |

Ulster Folklife (Cultra, Co. Down)

| | |
|---|---|
| UMPWS | University of Michigan Papers in Women's Studies (Ann Arbor) |
| UMSE | University of Mississippi Studies in English (University, MS) |

Unicorn: a miscellaneous journal (Brooklyn, NY)

| | |
|---|---|
| Univ | Universitas: Zeitschrift für Wissenschaft, Kunst und Literatur (Stuttgart) |

University of Colorado Studies, Series in Bibliography (Boulder)

University of Colorado Studies, Series in Language and Literature (Boulder)
University of Tulsa Monograph Series (Tulsa, OK)
Untold (Christchurch, N.Z.)

| | |
|---|---|
| UPQ | University: a Princeton quarterly (Princeton, NJ) |
| Upstream (Cape Town) | |
| UPub | University Publishing: an international quarterly review of books published by university presses (Berkeley, CA) |
| URLB | University of Rochester Library Bulletin (Rochester, NY) |
| USFLQ | University of South Florida Language Quarterly (Univ. of South Florida, Tampa) |
| USLL | Utah Studies in Literature and Linguistics (Univ. of Utah, Salt Lake City) |
| USP | Under the Sign of Pisces: Anaïs Nin and her circle (Ohio State Univ., Columbus) |
| UTQ | University of Toronto Quarterly: a Canadian journal of the humanities (Toronto) |
| UTSPY | University of Thessaloniki School of Philosophy Yearbook |
| UWR | University of Windsor Review (Univ. of Windsor, Ont.) |
| Vatra (Tîrgu-Mureş, Romania) | |
| VC | Virginia Cavalcade (Richmond, VA) |
| Vestnik Khar'kovskogo universiteta. Inostrannye îâzyki (Khar'kov, USSR) | |
| VH | Vermont History (Montpelier, VT) |
| VIA | Voprosy îâzykoznaniîâ (Moscow) |
| Viator: medieval and Renaissance studies (Univ. of California, Los Angeles) | |
| Views on Language and Language Teaching (Athens) | |
| VIJ | Victorians Institute Journal (East Carolinia Univ., Greenville, NC) |
| Vinduet: Gyldendals tidsskrift för litteratur (Oslo) | |
| VisCom | Visionary Company: a magazine of the Twenties (Mercy Coll., Dobbs Ferry, NY) |
| VKU | Vestnik Kievskogo universiteta. Romano-germanskaîâ filologiîâ (Kiev) |
| VLit | Voprosy literatury (Moscow) |
| VLU | Vestnik Leningradskogo universiteta. Istoriîâ, îâzyk, literatura (Leningrad) |
| VMHB | Virginia Magazine of History and Biography (Richmond VA) |
| VMKANTL | Verslagen en mededelingen van de Koninklijke Academie voor Nederlandse Taal- en Letterkunde (Antwerp) |
| VMU | Vestnik Moskovskogo universiteta. Ser. 9: filologiîâ (Moscow) |
| VN | Victorian Newsletter (Western Kentucky Univ., Bowling Green) |
| VNRN | Vladimir Nabokov Research Newsletter. See Nabokovian |
| VP | Victorian Poetry (West Virginia Univ., Morgantown) |
| VPR | Victorian Periodicals Review (Southern Illinois Univ., Edwardsville) |
| VQR | Virginia Quarterly Review: a national journal of literature and discussion (Univ. of Virginia, Charlottesville) |
| VR | Viaţa românească (Bucharest) |
| VS | Victorian Studies: a journal of the humanities, arts and sciences (Indiana Univ., Bloomington) |
| VWM | Virginia Woolf Miscellany (Rohnert Park, CA) |
| VWQ | Virginia Woolf Quarterly (Cherry Hill, NJ) |
| WAL | Western American Literature (Utah State Univ., Logan) |
| WBEP | Wiener Beiträge zur englischen Philologie (Vienna) |
| WCR | West Coast Review: a quarterly magazine of the arts (Simon Fraser Univ., Burnaby, BC) |
| WCWR | William Carlos Williams Review (Swarthmore College, PA) |
| WD | Writer's Digest (Cincinnati, OH) |
| WE | Winesburg Eagle: the official publication of the Sherwood Anderson Society (Univ. of Richmond, VA) |

Westerly: a quarterly review (Univ. of Western Australia, Nedlands)
WF                    Western Folklore (Glendale, CA)
Whimsy; proceedings of the Whim Conference (Tempe, AZ)
WHR                   Western Humanities Review (Univ. of Utah, Salt Lake City)
WIRS                  Western Illinois Regional Studies (Western Illinois Univ.,
                      Macomb)
WJSC                  Western Journal of Speech Communication (California State
                      Univ., Los Angeles)
WLB                   Wilson Library Bulletin (Bronx, NY)
WLT                   World Literature Today: a literary quarterly of the University
                      of Oklahoma (Norman)
WLWE                  World Literature Written in English (Univ. of Guelph, Ont.)
WMH                   Wisconsin Magazine of History (Madison, WI)
WMQ                   William and Mary Quarterly: a magazine of early American
                      history and culture (Williamsburg, VA)
Women and Literature: a journal of women writers and the literary treatment of
      women up to 1900 (Rutgers Univ., New Brunswick, NJ)
Women's Studies: an interdisciplinary journal (City Univ. of New York, Flushing)
Women's Studies Journal (Auckland). *Formerly* New Zealand Women's Studies
      Journal
Word & Image (London)
WordsC                Wordsworth Circle (Temple Univ., Philadelphia, PA)
Working Papers (Speech and Language Research Centre, Macquarie University,
      North Ryde, N.S.W.)
WPQ                   Western Political Quarterly (Salt Lake City, UT)
Writer (Boston MA)
WSJ                   Wallace Stevens Journal (Clarkson College, Potsdam, NY)
WT                    Water Table (Seattle, WA)
WVH                   West Virginia History (Charleston, WV)
WWQR                  Walt Whitman Quarterly Review (Univ. of Iowa, Iowa City)
Yankee (Dublin, NH)
YCC                   Yearbook of Comparative Criticism (University Park, PA)
YCGL                  Yearbook of Comparative and General Literature (Indiana
                      Univ., Bloomington)
YER                   Yeats Eliot Review: a journal of criticism and scholarship
                      (Univ. of Alberta, Edmonton)
YES                   Yearbook of English Studies (Univ. of Warwick)
YFS                   Yale French Studies (New Haven, CT)
YLG                   Yale University Library Gazette (New Haven, CT)
YLS                   Yearbook of Langland Studies (Michigan State Univ., East
                      Lansing)
YR                    Yale Review (New Haven, CT)
YREAL                 REAL: Yearbook of Research in English and American
                      Literature (Berlin)
YSE                   Yale Studies in English (New Haven, CT)
YYY                   Youngeo Youngmunhak (English Language and Literature)
                      (Yeungnam Univ., Korea)
ZAA                   Zeitschrift für Anglistik und Amerikanistik (Leipzig)
ZDL                   Zeitschrift für Dialektologie und Linguistik (Stuttgart)
Život (Sarajevo, Yugoslavia)
ZP                    Zeitschrift für Phonetik, Sprachwissenschaft und
                      Kommunikationsforschung (Berlin, E. Germany)
ZRG                   Zeitschrift für Religions- und Geistesgeschichte (Cologne)
ZRL                   Zagadnienia Rodzajów Literackich (Łódź, Poland)
ZVS                   Zeitschrift für Vergleichende Sprachforschung/Journal of
                      Comparative Linguistic Research into Indo-European
                      Philology (Göttingen). *See* Historische Sprachforschung
Życie Literackie (Cracow)

# ANNUAL BIBLIOGRAPHY OF ENGLISH LANGUAGE AND LITERATURE
## 1989

# FESTSCHRIFTEN AND OTHER COLLECTIONS

### American Literary Landscapes:
### the Fiction and the Fact

**1.** BELL, IAN F. A.; ADAMS, D. K. (eds). American literary landscapes: the fiction and the fact. London: Vision Press; New York: St Martin's Press, 1988. pp. 176. Rev. by Bryan Wollf in TLS, 16 June, 672.

CLARKE, GRAHAM. 'To emanate a look': Whitman, photography and the spectacle of self. 78–101

HABEGGER, ALFRED. Henry James's *Bostonians* and the fiction of democratic vulgarity. 102–21

HARDING, BRIAN. The myth of the myth of the garden. 44–60

KRUPNICK, MARK. Lionel Trilling and the politics of style. 152–70

MICHAELS, WALTER BENN. Frank Norris, Josiah Royce and the ontology of corporations. 122–51

MOTTRAM, ERIC. 'Thought is always prior to fact': an introduction. 9–28

MULVEY, CHRISTOPHER. Anglo-American fictions: national characteristics in nineteenth-century travel literature. 61–77

MURRAY, DAVID. From speech to text: the making of American Indian autobiographies. 29–43

### American Literature in Belgium

**2.** DEBUSSCHER, GILBERT; MAUFORT, MARC (eds). American literature in Belgium. Amsterdam: Rodopi, 1988. pp. 265. (Costerus, 66.)

CALLENS, JOHAN. Initiation in Jack Richardson's *In the Final Year of Grace*. 163–74

CLAYTON, JOHN J. Saul Bellow's *Seize the Day*: a study in midlife transition. 135–47

CUNLIFFE, MARCUS. America's imaginary wars. 251–60

DEBUSSCHER, GILBERT. Tennessee Williams's Black Nativity: an unpublished libretto. 127–33

DUYTSCHAEVER, JORIS. Faulkner's *Light in August* and the vicissitudes of narcissism: the case of Gail Hightower. 99–115

## Anglica Wratislaviensia, 14

MacQueen, Angus. Form and the search for meaning in William Langland's *Piers Plowman*. 81–93

Trebisz, Małgorzata. The necklace motif in *La Parure, Paste* and *A String of Beads*. 95–104

## Anglistentag 1987 Tübingen

**4.** Ludwig, Hans-Werner (ed.). Anglistentag 1987 Tübingen. Tübingen; Giessen: Hoffmann, 1988. pp. 435. (Tagungsberichte des Anglistentags: Verbands deutscher Anglisten, 9.)

Ahrends, Günter. Literarischer Text und szenische Realisation: Einführende Bemerkungen zum Verhältnis zweier Zeichensysteme. 14–24

Ahrends, Günter. Vom Text des Autors zum Text der Aufführung: Andrea Breths Interpretation von Edward Bonds *Summer*. 124–39

Bassnett, Susan. Poetry, translation and the process of discovery. 145–53

Beilharz, Manfred. Textüberlegungen zur Inszenierung von Shakespeares *Ein Sommernachtstraum*. 38–44

Bergner, Heinz; Stein, Dieter. Introduction. 285–7 (To part 2.)

Boas, Hans Ulrich. Parametrization in generative grammar. 406–9

Edmondson, Willis J. Speaker and hearer as discourse roles. 397–405

Enkemann, Jürgen. Nichtliterarische Theaterformen: zu ihrem Vordringen in Großbritannien seit den 60er Jahren. 57–71

Erdmann, Peter. *Habeas corpus* – über die Nützlichkeit von Sprachdaten bei der Beschreibung des Englischen. 319–29

Fischer, Andreas. Concordances, computer corpora and diachronic lexicology. 348–9 (Abstract.)

Fischer-Seidel, Therese. Die unausweichliche Modalität des Sichtbaren: Wahrnehmung und Kategorien des Dramas im Theater Becketts. 106–23

Frank, Armin Paul. Literary translation and alterity: some distinctions. 271–82

Görlach, Manfred. Corpus problems of text collections: linguistic aspects of the canon. 365–81

Hickey, Raymond. Proposals for a corpus database system for linguistics. 288–99

Hüllen, Werner. On the translation of English compound verbs into German: an investigation based on Alex Haley's *Roots/Wurzeln*. 238–57

Kuck, Gerd Leo. Arie Zingers Stuttgarter *Macbeth*: Bearbeitung und Tendenzen. 45–6

LEITNER, GERHARD.   Wie anders ist das Englische in Indien? 385–96

MARTENS, KLAUS.   It was the mockingbird not the nightingale: how an American bird homes in on the German tradition. 198–208

MENGEL, EWALD.   Strategies of dealing with 'alterity' in John Mortimer's *The Captain of Köpernick*. 222–37

MINDT, DIETER.   EDV-gestützte Forschungen zur Semantik. 330–44

PLATZ, NORBERT H.   Die Orchestrierung des menschlichen Stimmpotentials: zur Klangästhetik des modernen englischen und amerikanischen Dramas. 72–90

RIEDEL, WOLFGANG.   National metaphor in Anglo-Irish literature. 434–5 (Abstract.)

RIEHLE, WOLFGANG.   Zur Relevanz von Shakespeares Plautusrezeption in der *Comedy of Errors*. 91–105

SCHNEIDER, EDGAR W.   Advantages and limitations of text corpora in the study of lexis. 300–18

SCHWANITZ, DIETRICH.   Drama and interaction. 47–56

SNELL-HORNBY, MARY.   The unfamiliar image: metaphor as a problem in translation. 258–70

STANZEL, PETER.   Englische und Deutsche Kriegsdichtung 1914–18: eine komparatistische Versuch. 410–11 (Abstract.)

VIERECK, WOLFGANG.   A corpus of dialectal English computerised. 345–7 (Abstract.)

VON KOPPENFELS, WERNER.   'When thou hast done thou hast not Don(n)e': Entfremdung und Verfremdung eines metaphysical poet. 154–74

WENZEL, PETER.   Uneinheitliche Einheitlichkeit: eine Auseinandersetzung mit dem Konzept der 'unity' in der anglo-amerikanischen Literaturkritik. 412–33

WOLPERS, THEODOR.   Dickens' Stadtebilder – Englisch und Deutsche: zum 'Realismus' als Übersetzungsproblem. 175–97

## Anglistentag 1988 Göttingen

5.  MÜLLENBROCK, HEINZ-JOACHIM; NOLL-WIEMANN, RENATE (eds). Anglistentag 1988 Göttingen. Tübingen: Niemeyer. pp. xi, 368. (Tagungsberichte des Anglistentags: Verbands deutscher Anglisten, 10.)

ARENS, WERNER.   Destruction and regeneration as Blakean contraries in Patrick White's *Riders in the Chariot*. 126–45

BARNES, JOHN.   Home thoughts from abroad: the sense of place in Australian writing. 52–65

BODE, CHRISTOPH.   Literary value and evaluation: the case for relational concepts. 309–24

BUBLITZ, WOLFRAM.   Repetition in spoken discourse, 352–68

CERNY, LOTHAR.   Blake's Satan and the idea of limit. 325–37

DELBRIDGE, ARTHUR.   The *Macquarie*, an international national dictionary. 66–79

GOETSCH, PAUL.   Fictive oral storytelling in *Lord Jim*. 179–95

HALFORD, BRIGITTE K.   Non-syntactic discourse units – the liberties of spoken English. 234–43

KASTOVSKY, DIETER.   Typological changes in the history of English word-formation. 281–93

KÖNIG, EKKEHARD.   A new bilingual dictionary for function words. 294–306

LIPKA, LEONHARD.   The state of the art in lexicology. 250–63

NEUHAUS, H. JOACHIM.   Shakespeare's wordforms, a database view. 264–80

PLATZ, NORBERT H.   Influence or choice? Henry Handel Richardson's *Maurice Guest* and its relation to German culture. 115–25

PRIESSNITZ, HORST.   The 'vossification' of Ludwig Leichhardt: Leichhardt's career in 19th and 20th century Australian poems. 102–14

SCHAEFER, URSULA.   'A song of myself': propositions on the vocality of Old English poetry. 196–208

STEIN, THOMAS MICHAEL.   'You have work to do, my reader': David Ireland's *A Woman of the Future* as modernist fictional autobiography. 146–55

STILZ, GERHARD.   'Offensively Australian': the international character of Australian literary nationalism in the 1880s and 1890s. 87–101

TRISTRAM, HILDEGARDE L. C.   Why James Joyce also lost his 'brain of forgetting': patterns of memory and media in Irish writing. 220–33

UNGERER, FRIEDRICH.   Scope as syntactic principle. 338–51

VOLK-BIRKE, SABINE.   Literacy and orality in late 14th century vernacular sermons and in Chaucer. 209–19

WINKGENS, MEINHARD.   Die kulturelle Symbolik von Mündlichkeit und Schriftlichkeit in George Eliots Roman *Daniel Deronda*. 163–78

WOLPERS, THEODOR.   Göttingen als Vermittlungszentrum englischer Literatur im 18. Jahrhundert. 31–51

## 2. Anglisticko-amerikanistická konference/ Second Conference on English and American Studies

6.   HLADKÝ, JOSEF (ed.).   2. Anglisticko-amerikanistická konference/ Second conference on English and American studies. Brno: Brno UP. pp. 47. (Abstracts.)

ARBEIT, MARCEL.   Allen Tate – prozaik. (Allen Tate the prose writer.) 16

BAŠTÍN, ŠTEFAN.   Ideové a estetické paralely medzi satirou a čiernym humorom. (Aesthetic boundaries between satire and black humour.) 16–17

CHAMONIKOLASOVÁ, JANÁ.   Zájmena ve FVP. (Pronouns in functional sentence perspective.) 20

DUŠKOVÁ, LIBUŠE.   K úloze prostředků textové koheze jako indikátorů funkčních stylů. (On the role of the devices of text cohesion as indicators of functional styles.) 18

FIRBAS, JAN.   Dva přístupy k analýze mluvené věty. (Two approaches to the analysis of a spoken sentence.) 18

GILBERTOVÁ, IVA.   Wole Soyinka: dvě rané hry. (Wole Soyinka: two early plays.) 18–19

GOLKOVÁ, EVA.   Větné začátky v angličtine a češtině. (Sentence starters in English and Czech.) 19–20

GRMELOVÁ, ANNA.   Tématické a strukturální diversifikace povídek D. H. Lawrence pod vlivem 1. světové války. (Thematic and structural diversification of D. H. Lawrence's stories as influenced by World War I.) 20

HILSKÝ, MARTIN.   Hříšné hříčky: jazyk rané shakespearovské komedie z hlediska překladatelského. (Sinful puns: the language of early Shakespearean comedy from a translator's viewpoint.) 45

HORNÁT, JAROSLAV.   Pan Pickwick a Sam Weller. (Mr Pickwick and Sam Weller.) 21

JAŘAB, JOSEF.   Allen Ginsberg po letech. (Allen Ginsberg several years later.) 22–3

KLÉGR, ALEŠ.   Zkušenosti z práce kolokačním slovníku. (Experience in working out a dictionary of word combinations.) 24

KNITTLOVÁ, DAGMAR.   Stylistická ekvivalence v překladech prózy. (Stylistic equivalence in prose translations.) 24

KOLÁŘ, PAVEL.   Přítomnost v orientaci časového systému. (Present time within the tense system.) 25

KOUŘILOVÁ, MAGDA.   Štruktúra a funkcia v anglijskom odbornom prehovore. (Structure and function in English technical utterances.) 25–6

KŘEHLÍKOVÁ, EVA.   Interpretace povídek Marka Twaina v českych překladech 19. století. (Mark Twain's short stories as interpreted in Czech translations of the nineteenth century.) 26

KUDRNÁČOVÁ, NADĚŽDA.   K problematice jednoho užití pojmu záměr. (Problems of using the term 'intention'.) 27

NOSEK, JIŘÍ.   Jazyková typologie a kategorie určenosti. (Linguistic typology and the category of determination.) 31

PALENSKÁ, VĚRA.   Karibská poválečná románova tvorba. (Postwar fiction in the Caribbean.) 31

PANTUCKOVÁ, LIDMILLA.   Anglická a ameriká literatura v Nerudově časopisu *Obrazy života*. (English and American literature as reflected in the Czech literary journal *Images of Life*.) 32

PEPRNÍK, JAROSLAV.   Češi v současné britské a americké literatuře. (The Czechs in contemporary British and American literature.) 33

POLÁČKOVÁ, MILENA.   Slovní hříčky a problémy překladu z angličtiny do češtiny. (Puns and the problem of translating them from English into Czech.) 33–4

POSPÍŠIL, TOMÁŠ.   Čtyři romány E. L. Doctorowa ve světle jeho autorských zájmů. (Four novels of E. L. Doctorow in the light of his interests.) 35–6

PUCI, JÁN.   Poznámky k niektorým štýlotvorným činitelom anglického publicistického štylu. (On some stylistic features of English journalese.) 36–7

RŮŽIČKA, MILAN.   Elipsa a aktuální členění vétné. (Ellipsis and functional sentence perspective.) 39–40

RUŽIČKOVÁ, EVA.   Analýza l'udských potrieb. (An analysis of human necessities.) 40

RYBÁROVÁ, VIERA.   Rozprávacská situácia v románě Virginie Woolfovej *K majáku*. (The narrator's position in Virginia Woolf's novel *To the Lighthouse*.) 40–1

SPARLING, DON.   Timothy Findley's fictions. 41

SŘÍBRNÝ, ZDENĚK.   Zpráva o chystaném slovníku spisovatelů píšících anglicky. (A report on a dictionary of authors writing in English.) 42

SVOBODA, ALEŠ.   Funkční perspektiva nadvětná. (A hyper-syntactic functional perspective.) 42–3

SÝKOROVÁ, LIBUŠE.   K problematice anglických kokolací. (Problems of English word combinations.) 43

TAHAL, KAREL.   Některé sémantické rysy *ing*-ových slovesných tvarů. (Some semantic features of verbal *ing*-forms.) 43–4

TARNYIKOVÁ, JARMILA.   Text a textura. (Textlinguistics and texture.) 44

URBANOVÁ, LUDMILLA.   Linguistics and didactic specifications of the English language of conversation. 44–5

## Approaching Postmodernism

**7.**  FOKKEMA, DOUWE; BERTENS, HANS (eds).   Approaching Postmodernism: papers presented at a workshop on Postmodernism, 21–23 September 1984, University of Utrecht. Amsterdam; Philadelphia, PA: Benjamins, 1986. pp. x, 300. (Utrecht publications in general and comparative literature, 21.) Rev. by Steven Connor in MLR (84:3) 701.

BERTENS, HANS. The Postmodern *Weltanschauung* and its relation with Modernism: an introductory survey. 9–51

CALINESCU, MATEI. Postmodernism and some paradoxes of periodization. 239–54

D'HAEN, THEO. Postmodernism in American fiction and art. 211–31

FOKKEMA, DOUWE. Preliminary remarks. 1–8

FOKKEMA, DOUWE. The semantic and syntactic organization of Postmodernist texts. 81–98

HOFFMANN, GERHARD. The absurd and its forms of reduction in Postmodern American fiction. 185–210

LETHEN, HELMUT. Modernisism cut in half: the exclusion of the avant-garde and the debate on Postmodernism. 233–8

McHALE, BRIAN. Change of dominant from Modernist to Postmodernist writing. 53–79

SULEIMAN, SUSAN RUBIN. Naming and difference: reflections on 'Modernism *versus* Postmodernism' in literature. 255–70 (Revised version of conference paper, New York, 1983.)

TODD, RICHARD. The presence of Postmodernism in British fiction: aspects of style and selfhood. 99–117

## The Arthurian Tradition: Essays in Convergence

**8.** BRASWELL, MARY FLOWERS; BUGGE, JOHN (eds). The Arthurian tradition: essays in convergence. Tuscaloosa; London: Alabama UP, 1988. pp. xi, 258.

ASHE, GEOFFREY. The convergence of Arthurian studies. 10–28

ATKINSON, STEPHEN C. B. 'Now I se and undirstonde': the Grail Quest and the education of Malory's reader. 90–108

BLACKER-KNIGHT, JEAN. Transformations of a theme: the depoliticization of the Arthurian world in the *Roman de Brut*. 54–74

BOYD, DAVID L. Tennyson's Camelot revisited: an Augustinian approach to the *Idylls*. 163–74

BUGGE, JOHN. Arthurian myth devalued in Walker Percy's *Lancelot*. 175–87

ECKHARDT, CAROLINE D. Prophecy and nostalgia: Arthurian symbolism at the close of the English Middle Ages. 109–26

FRIES, MAUREEN. Boethian themes and tragic structure in Geoffrey of Monmouth's *Historia regum britanniae*. 29–42

MANCOFF, DEBRA N. 'An ancient idea of chivalric greatness': the Arthurian revival and Victorian history painting. 127–43

MOORMAN, CHARLES. 'Yet some men say . . . that Kynge Arthure ys nat ded.' 188–99

NELSON, JAN A. A Jungian interpretation of sexually ambiguous imagery in Chrétien's *Erec et Enide*. 75–89

PARINS, MARYLYN JACKSON. Malory's expurgators. 144–62

THOMPSON, MARY L. H. A possible source of Geoffrey's Roman war? 43–53

## Australian English:
## the Language of a New Society

**9.** COLLINS, PETER; BLAIR, DAVID (eds). Australian English: the language of a new society. St Lucia: Queensland UP. pp. xiv, 358.

BALL, PETER; GALLOIS, CYNTHIA; CALLAN, VICTOR J. Language attitudes: a perspective from social psychology. 89–102, 331–5

BERNARD, J. R. Quantitative aspects of the sounds of Australian English. 187–204, 342–3

BERNARD, J. R. Regional variation in Australian English: a survey. 255–9, 347–8

BLAIR, DAVID. The development and current state of Australian English: a survey. 171–5, 340–1

BRADLEY, DAVID. Regional dialects in Australian English phonology. 260–70, 348–9

BRYANT, PAULINE. Regional variation in the Australian English lexicon. 301–14, 321, 350

CLARK, J. E. Some proposals for a revised phonetic transcription of Australian English. 205–13, 343–4

COCHRANE, G. R. Origins and development of the Australian accent. 176–86, 318, 341–2

COLLINS, PETER. Divided and debatable usage in Australian English. 138–49, 339–40

COLLINS, PETER. Sociolinguistics in Australia: a survey. 3–20, 332–5

EAGLESON, ROBERT. Popular and professional attitudes to prestige dialects. 150–7, 317, 340

GUNN, JOHN S. The shearing shed society. 77–88, 316, 331 (Language of woolgrowing in Australia.)

HIROAKI, OASA. Phonology of current Adelaide English. 271–87, 349

POYNTON, CATE. Terms of address in Australian English. 59–69, 316, 329

REEVE, JAN. Community attitudes to Australian English. 111–26, 337

SUSSEX, ROLAND. The Americanisation of Australian English. 158–68, 317

TAYLOR, BRIAN. American, British and other foreign influences on Australian English since World War II. 225–54, 318–21, 345–7

TURNER, G. W.    Some problems in Australian etymology. 214–24, 344–5

## La beauté

**10.**  ANON. (ed.).    La beauté. Pau: Univ. de Pau et des Pays de l'Adour. pp. 207. (Centre de Recherche Médiatisation et Systèmes de Représentation.) (Convergences, 5.)

BULCKAEN-MESSINA, DENISE.    Smollett et Hogarth: rencontre autour d'une ligne de beauté. 9–26

BUTLER, LANCE.    Éthique/esthétique dans *Characteristicks* de Shaftesbury. 27–36

CHEVALIER, JEAN-LOUIS.    Sur la beauté: étude d'un sonnet de St Vincent Millay. 37–50

GAUTHIER, DOMINIQUE.    Fragments de beauté chez deux poètes d'Irlande du Nord: Derek Mahon et Michael Longley. 109–24

LAVABRE, SIMONE.    Swinburne et la beauté. 125–30

PARSONS, MICHAEL.    Beauté et laideur dans *Paradise Lost* de John Milton. 131–48

SUBERCHICOT, ALAIN.    La beauté dans l'œuvre de Rodney Pybus, 169–84

## 'Bright Shootes of Everlastingnesse': the Seventeenth-Century Religious Lyric

**11.**  SUMMERS, CLAUDE J.; PEBWORTH, TED-LARRY (eds).    'Bright shootes of everlastingnesse': the seventeenth-century religious lyric. Columbia: Missouri UP, 1987. pp. xv, 222. (Essays in seventeenth-century literature, 2.) Rev. by Jonathan F. S. Post in RQ (42:1) 151–2; by Phillip Rogers in QQ (95:2) 1988, 464–6; by John R. Mulder in GHJ (11:2) 1988, 63–9; by William C. Johnson in Six CT (19:1) 1988, 122–3; by E. Beatrice Batson in ChrisL (37:3) 1988, 55–7; by N. H. Keeble in NQ (36:3) 391–2.

CLARK, JAMES ANDREW.    *The Coronet*: Marvell's 'curious frame' of allusion. 145–61

HESTER, M. THOMAS.    Re-signing the text of the self: Donne's *As Due by Many Titles*. 59–71

PINKA, PATRICIA G.    Timely timelessness in two Nativity poems. 162–72

RADZINOWICZ, MARY ANN.    *Anima mea* psalms and John Donne's religious poetry. 40–58

REVARD, STELLA P.    The seventeenth-century religious ode and its classical models. 173–91

ROBERTS, LORRAINE.    Crashaw's Epiphany Hymn: faith out of darkness. 134–44

SCHOENFELDT, MICHAEL C.   Standing on ceremony: the comedy of manners in Herbert's *Love (III)*. 116–33

SESSIONS, WILLIAM A.   Abandonment and the English religious lyric in the seventeenth century. 1–19

SHULLENBERGER, WILLIAM.   *Ars praedicandi* in George Herbert's poetry. 96–115

SUMMERS, CLAUDE J.   The Bride of the Apocalypse and the quest for true religion: Donne, Herbert, and Spenser. 72–95

WITTREICH, JOSEPH.   'In copious legend, or sweet lyric song': typology and the perils of the religious lyric. 192–215

YOUNG, R. V.   Donne's Holy Sonnets and the theology of grace. 20–39

## The Bumper Book

**12.**   METCALF, JOHN (ed.).   The bumper book. Toronto: ECW Press, 1986. pp. 238. Rev. by I. S. Maclaren in CanL (120) 198–200; by Stephen Scobie in QQ (95:1) 1988, 190.

FAWCETT, BRIAN.   Some proposals for the reification of poetry in Canada. 92–103

GAREBIAN, KEITH.   Seasons of discontent. 140–53

GIBSON, DOUGLAS.   'Edited any good books lately?' 108–15

KEITH, W. J.   The quest for the (instant) Canadian classic. 155–65

MACKLEM, MICHAEL.   Seed money. 119–27

MACLEOD, JACK.   The importance of not being earnest: some mutterings on Canadian humour. 79–88

MATHEWS, LAWRENCE.   Hacking at the parsnips: *The Mountain and the Valley* and the critics. 188–201

MILLS, JOHN.   Notes of a natural son. 28–38

ROSS, MORTON L.   The canonization of *As for Me and My House*: a case study. 170–85

SNIDER, NORMAN.   Robertson Davies: the view from High Table. 69–77

SOLECKI, SAM.   Some kicks against the prick: John Metcalf in his essays. 207–23

SUTHERLAND, FRASER.   Frisking Laura Secord. 14–25

SUTHERLAND, FRASER.   In defence of Laura Secord. 6–13

WEISS, ALLAN.   Professing support: in defence of academia's role in Canadian literature. 130–9

## A Centre of Excellence

**13.**   DRUCE, ROBERT (ed.).   A centre of excellence: essays presented to Seymour Betsky. Amsterdam: Rodopi, 1987. pp. vi (unnumbered), 216. (Costerus, 58.) Rev. by Sylvère Monod in EA (41:2) 1988, 193–4.

BARFOOT, C. C.   Reading the word in Geoffrey Hill. 65–88

BEAVER, HAROLD.   Doodling America: Poe's *MS. Found in a Bottle*. 15–27

BETSKY-ZWEIG, SARAH.   Lawrence and Cézanne. 103–26

DRUCE, ROBERT.   Man, the machine, and a radiant fool. 127–44

FIEDLER, LESLIE A.   *Martin Chuzzlewit* – a great bad book. 43–8

FORD, BORIS.   *Wuthering Heights*. 29–42

FRY, AUGUST J.   The return of Joseph Jefferson Jackson, a study in American myth. 89–102

HARDY, BARBARA.   The figure of narration in *Hamlet*. 1–14

HOLBROOK, DAVID.   Truth, campaigns and freedom. 197–216

HUMPHREYS, ARTHUR.   The livingness of literature. 173–7

INGLIS, FRED.   Popular culture and the meaning of feeling. 145–60

KNIGHTS, L. C.   Cambridge criticism: what was it? 161–71

KNIGHTS, L. C.   Postscript. 193–5

MARTIN, GRAHAM.   Cambridge criticism & 'history'. 179–82

ROBSON, W. W.   Values and knowledge. 185–8

SALINGAR, LEO.   Life and thought. 189–91

WESTENDORP, TJEBBE A.   'He backed me into a corner and blockaded me with a chair': strategies of Mark Twain's literary campaigns. 49–63

## Children and their Books

**14.**   AVERY, GILLIAN; BRIGGS, JULIA (eds).   Children and their books: a celebration of the work of Iona and Peter Opie. Oxford: Clarendon Press. pp. xvi, 424.

ALDERSON, BRIAN.   Collecting children's books: self-indulgence and scholarship. 7–17

AVERY, GILLIAN.   The Puritans and their heirs. 95–118

BATCHELOR, JOHN.   Dodgson, Carroll, and the emancipation of Alice. 181–99

BAYLEY, JOHN.   The child in Walter de la Mare. 337–49

BELL, OLIVIA; BELL, ALAN.   Children's manuscript magazines in the Bodleian Library. 399–412

BRIGGS, JULIA.   Women writers and writing for children: from Sarah Fielding to E. Nesbit. 221–50

BROGAN, HUGH.   Tolkien's Great War. 351–67

CARPENTER, HUMPHREY.   Excessively impertinent bunnies: the subversive element in Beatrix Potter. 271–98

COCKSHUT, A. O. J.   Children's diaries. 381–98

EVERETT, BARBARA.   Henry James's children. 317–35

FLINT, KATE.   Arthur Hughes as illustrator for children. 201–20

HURST, CLIVE.   Selections from the accession diaries of Peter Opie. 19–44

LURIE, ALISON.   William Mayne. 369–79

PHILIP, NEIL.   *The Wind in the Willows*: the vitality of a classic. 299–316

ROBSON, W. W.   E. Nesbit and *The Book of Dragons*. 251–70

ST CLAIR, WILLIAM.   William Godwin as children's bookseller. 165–79

SMITH, NIGEL.   A child prophet: Martha Hatfield as *The Wise Virgin*. 79–93

THOMAS, KEITH.   Children in early modern England. 45–77

ZIPES, JACK.   The origins of the fairy tale for children or, How script was used to tame the beast in us. 119–34

### Confluences II: centre(s) de pouvoirs(s) et d'influence(s)

**15.**   HIMY, ARMAND; ROBIN, MAURICE (eds).   Confluences II: centre(s) de pouvoir(s) et d'influence(s). Nanterre: Université Paris X, Centre de Recherches sur les Origines de la Modernité et les Pays Anglophones. pp. 176.

ARNAUD, PIERRE.   La lutte pour le pouvoir au sein de la famille dans *The Vicar of Wakefield*. 139–50

DHUICQ, BERNARD.   'Landed gentry' et 'merchants' dans le théâtre d'Aphra Benn. 71–85

DOMMERGUES, ANDRÉ.   Aldous Huxley: pouvoir et société. 123–35

HIMY, ARMAND.   *Measure for Measure*, ou le puritanisme comme centre du pouvoir. 21–40

LERAY, JOSETTE.   Lieux et langages du pouvoir dans les romans d'Ivy Compton-Burnett. 163–76

### Convention and Innovation in Literature

**16.**   D'HAEN, THEO; GRÜBEL, RAINER; LETHEN, HELMUT (eds).   Convention and innovation in literature. Amsterdam; Philadelphia, PA: Benjamins. pp. xxii, 434. (Utrecht publications in general and comparative literature, 24.)

BERTENS, HANS.   The convention of the new beginning in Theroux's *The Mosquito Coast*. 389–403

BUSBY, KEITH.   *Cristal et Clarie*: a novel romance? 77–103

DE VOOGD, P. J.   Literature of displacement: René Harding rejects George Eliot. 349–59

D'HAEN, THEO.   Genre convention in postmodern fiction. 405–20

D'HAEN, THEO; GRÜBEL, RAINER; LETHEN, HELMUT. Introduction: the decline and rise of convention. vii–xxii

FOKKEMA, DOUWE. The concept of convention in literary theory and empirical research. 1–16

FRY, AUGUST J. A note on *convention* and *innovation*: the *Odes* of John Keats. 225–34

GEYER-RYAN, HELGA; LETHEN, HELMUT. The rhetoric of forgetting: Brecht and the historical avant-garde. 305–48

LEFEVERE, ANDRÉ. The dynamics of the system: convention and innovation in literary history. 37–55

OVERSTEEGEN, J. J. Genre: a modest proposal. 17–35

TODD, RICHARD. Convention and innovation in British fiction 1981–1984: the contemporaneity of magic realism. 361–88

VAN DEN BROECK, RAYMOND. Literary conventions and translated literature. 57–75

WESTERWEEL, BART. The well-tempered lady and the unruly horse: convention and submerged metaphor in Renaissance literature and art. 105–22

## Critical Approaches to Anglo-Irish Literature

**17.** ALLEN, MICHAEL; WILCOX, ANGELA (eds). Critical approaches to Anglo-Irish literature. Gerrards Cross: Smythe. pp. ix, 193. (Irish literary studies, 29.)

BELSEY, CATHERINE. Mobilizing Byzantium. 1–16

COUGHLAN, PATRICIA. Doubles, shadows, sedan-chairs and the past: the 'ghost stories' of J. S. Le Fanu. 17–39

DEANE, SEAMUS. National character and national audience: races, crowds and readers. 40–52

FITZGIBBON, GERALD. Garnering the facts: unreliable narrators in some plays of Brian Friel. 53–62

FLEISCHMANN, RUTH. Fathers vanquished and victorious: a historical reading of Synge's *Playboy*. 63–74

FOGARTY, MARGARET E. 'It is myself that I remake': the shaping of self of W. B. Yeats's *Autobiographies*. 75–85

FOSTER, JOHN WILSON. The critical condition of Ulster. 86–102

HUGHES, EAMONN. The political unconscious in the autobiographical writings of Patrick Kavanagh. 103–10

KENNEALLY, MICHAEL. The autobiographical imagination and Irish literary autobiographies. 111–31

PAULIN, TOM. English political writers on Ireland: Robert Southey to Douglas Hurd. 132–45

Rix, Walter.   James Joyce's *The Dead*: the symbolist inspiration and its narrative reflection. 146–65

Roe, Nicholas.   *Wordsworth at the Flax-Dam*: an early poem by Seamus Heaney. 166–70

## The Critical Spirit and the Will to Believe:
## Essays in Nineteenth-Century Literature and Religion

**18.**   Jasper, David; Wright, T. R. (eds).   The critical spirit and the will to believe: essays in nineteenth-century literature and religion. Basingstoke: Macmillan. pp. xii, 239.

Ashton, Rosemary.   Doubting clerics: from James Anthony Froude to *Robert Elsmere* via George Eliot. 69–87

Barcus, James E.   The successful failure of ordering structures in Tennyson's *Idylls of the King*. 131–44

Fraser, Hilary.   Truth to nature: science, religion and the Pre-Raphaelites. 53–68

Jay, Elisabeth.   Doubt and the Victorian woman. 88–103

Kent, John.   A renovation of images: nineteenth-century Protestant *Lives of Jesus* and the Roman Catholic alleged appearances of the Blessed Virgin Mary. 37–52

Milbank, Alison.   Doubting Castle: the gothic mode of questioning. 104–19

Prickett, Stephen.   Poetics and narrative: biblical criticism and the nineteenth-century novel. 1–22

Ryan, Robert M.   The genealogy of honest doubt: F. D. Maurice and *In Memoriam*. 120–30

Wheeler, Michael.   'Can these dry bones live?': questions of belief in a future life. 23–36

## Discharging the Canon:
## Cross-Cultural Readings in Literature

**19.**   Hyland, Peter (ed.).   Discharging the canon: cross-cultural readings in literature. Singapore: Singapore UP, 1986. pp. xi, 190. Rev. by Ian Reid in AUMLA (72) 361–5.

Birch, David.   Cunning beneath the verbs: demythologising Singapore English poetry. 147–90

Chew, Shirley.   Wordsworth's *Prelude*: a prospect in the mind. 133–46

Chua Chen Lok.   The European participant and the third-world revolution: André Malraux's *Les Conquérants* and D. H. Lawrence's *The Plumed Serpent*. 101–11

Hyland, Peter.   Introduction: discharging the canon. 1–9

Koh Tai Ann.   The Empire's orphans: stayers and quitters in *A Bend in the River* and *Scorpion Orchid*. 38–53

KWAN-TERRY, JOHN.   Of pines, beards and several Chinamen: one way of looking at Wallace Stevens. 54–72

LE BLOND, MAX.   Drama in Singapore: towards an English language theatre. 112–25

LIM, SHIRLEY.   The dispossessing eye: reading Wordsworth on the equatorial line. 126–32

YONG, MARGARET.   Explorations in the heart of darkness: turning landscape into art in *Slipstream* and *The Year of Living Dangerously*. 10–37

### Diversity Itself:
### Essays in Australian Arts and Culture

**20.**   QUARTERMAINE, PETER (ed.).   Diversity itself: essays in Australian arts and culture. Exeter: Univ. of Exeter for AmCAS, 1986. pp. x, 179. (Exeter studies in American and Commonwealth arts, 1.)

BIRD, DELYS.   Writing women/reading women: the double-voiced discourse of Australian women's fiction. 91–107

CRAVEN, IAN.   'Achieving' culture in the Australian cinema. 121–41

GRANT, DON.   Australian studies and Australian identity. 77–90

GUNEW, SNEJA.   Constructing Australian subjects: critics, writers, multicultural writers. 51–62

ROSS, BRUCE CLUNIES.   Les Murray's vernacular republic. 21–37

SENN, WERNER.   Setting up an Australian literature course: some conceptual and practical reflections. 63–75

TURNER, GRAEME.   Film and fiction: dealing with Australian narrative. 109–20

### The English Emblem and the Continental Tradition

**21.**   DALY, PETER M. (ed.).   The English emblem and the continental tradition. New York: AMS Press, 1988. pp. xiii, 263. (AMS studies in the emblem, 1.) (In honour of Karl Josef Höltgen.) Rev. by Jean Michel Massing in TLS, 21 July, 806.

BATH, MICHAEL.   Collared stags and bridled lions: Queen Elizabeth's household accounts. 225–57

DALY, PETER M.   England and the emblem: the cultural context of English emblem books. 1–60

DIMLER, G. RICHARD.   Edmund Arwaker's translation of the *Pia Desideria*: the reception of a continental Jesuit emblem book in seventeenth-century England. 203–24

MANNING, JOHN.   Unpublished and unedited emblems by Geffrey Witney: further evidence of the English adaptation of continental traditions. 83–107

TUNG, MASON.   From personifications to emblems: a study of Peacham's use of Ripa's *Iconologia* in *Minerva Britanna*. 109–50

YOUNG, ALAN R.   The English tournament imprese. 61–81

YOUNG, ALAN R.   Wenceslaus Hollar, the London book trade, and two unidentified English emblem books. 151–202

## Essais sur le dialogue: contrastivités

**22.**   LAVÉDRINE, JEAN (ed.).   Essais sur le dialogue: contrastivités. Grenoble: Univ. des Langues et Lettres, 1987. pp. 195. (Publications du Centre de Recherches Thématiques et Formelles, 3.) Rev. by Georges Bourcier in EA (42:4) 459–60.

ABITEBOUL, MAURICE.   L'art de la contrastivité dans *Hamlet*. 143–61

BOURQUIN, GUY.   La traduction automatique comme instrument d'investigation en analyse contrastive. 7–16

CHEVILLET, FRANÇOIS.   Les pronoms allocutoires en français et en anglais: éléments pour une réflexion socio-historique contrastive. 17–36

CHEVILLET, FRANÇOIS.   Un exemple de contrastivité lexicale: les lexèmes français *plancher*, anglais 'floor'. 87–110

JAUDEL, PHILIPPE.   Traduire Conrad. 37–49

MARIGNY, JEAN.   Difficultés de traduction dans les littératures de l'irréel. 51–65

MORÈRE, PIERRE.   Un problème de traduction philosophique: 'fancy'/'imagination' dans le Livre I du *Traité de la Nature Humaine* de David Hume. 111–22

## Essays on English and American Literature and a Sheaf of Poems

**23.**   BAKKER, J.; VERLEUN, J. A.; VAN DER VRIESENAERDE, J. (eds). Essays on English and American literature and a sheaf of poems: offered to David Wilkinson on the occasion of his retirement from the Chair of English Literature at the University of Groningen. Amsterdam: Rodopi, 1987. pp. 241. (Costerus, 63.)

apROBERTS, ROBERT P.   A contribution to the thirteenth labour: purging the *Troilus* of incest. 11–25

BAKKER, J.   Saul Bellow: a writer's despair. 177–90

BARFOOT, C. C.   Life divided, death undivided in *The Mill on the Floss*. 81–99

BIRRELL, T. A.   The printed books of Dame Margaret Nicollson: a pre-Reformation collection. 27–33

DALESKI, H. M.   Joyce's 'Circe': a tale of dragons. 151–63

DE VOOGD, PETER JAN.   'The great object of remark': Samuel Johnson and Laurence Sterne. 65–74

FRY, AUGUST J.   The clouding of the wine: reading Thomas Pynchon's *The Crying of Lot 49*. 143–9

GRAHAM, KENNETH.   The tangible dream. 33–53

KROOK, DOROTHEA.   *The Aspern Papers*: a counter-introduction. 223–34

MACKINNON, A. H.   The Augustan intellectual and the ignoble savage: Houyhnhym versus Hottentot. 55–63

RIEWALD, J. G.   Sir Max Beerbohm: a bibliographical checklist 1950–1985. 192–222

RULAND, RICHARD.   Kate Chopin and *The Awakening*. 119–30

VAN CASPEL, PAUL P. J.   Blake and Joyce: strange syzygy. 101–17

VERLEUN, JAN.   Conrad's modernity and humanity. 131–40

WALTHEER, ELIZABETH.   Geoffrey Hill's critical nostalgia. 165–71

WESTENDORP, TJEBBE.   How pleasant to meet Mr Eliot! An account of a forgotten interview. 173–6

## Essays on English Language in Honour of Bertil Sundby

**24.**   BREIVIK, LEIV EGIL; HILLE, ARNOLDUS; JOHANSSON, STIG (eds). Essays on English language in honour of Bertil Sundby. Oslo: Novus. pp. xxii, 396. (Studia anglistica norvegica, 4.)

ANDRÉSEN, BJØRN STÅLHANE.   The London School of Phonology: essence and roots. 1–11

BENSKIN, MICHAEL.   Some aspects of Cumbrian English, mainly mediaeval. 13–46

BJØRGE, ANNE KARI.   'I poor man is singing': subject–verb concord in eighteenth-century English grammar. 47–65

BREIVIK, LEIV EGIL.   On the diachrony of the English particle comparative. 67–83

DAHL, TRINE.   Compound adjectives in English general and special language. 85–94

ELSNESS, JOHAN.   The English present perfect: has it seen its best days? 95–106

FIRBAS, JAN.   Interpreting Psalm 91 from the point of view of functional sentence perspective. 107–16

HAUGLAND, KARI E.   Some practical aspects of trade names and trademarks in terminology and translation: a brief report from the translation of an ESP text. 117–29

HILLE, ARNOLDUS.   Old English *līcþrōwere* 'a leper' and Old Norse *líkþrá* 'leprosy'. 131–44

JACOBSON, SVEN.   Some grammatical trends in American newspaper language. 145–54

KRISTENSSON, GILLIS.   Place-names and linguistic geography. 155–64

LEWIS, ROBERT E.   The phonic status of Middle English initial <sch>. 165–77

### Les États-Unis: images du travail et des loisirs

## L'étranger dans la littérature et la pensée anglaises

**26.** RIGAUD, N. J. (ed.).   L'étranger dans la littérature et la pensée anglaises. Actes du Colloque, Aix-en-Provence, 11–12 mars 1988. Aix-en-Provence: Univ. of Provence for Centre Aixois de Recherches Anglaises. pp. xiii, 308. (CARA, 9.)

BUTLER, LANCE ST JOHN.   Qui est étranger dans les romans de Thomas Hardy? 189–204

CHEYRE-BERNARD, CATHERINE.   Abigail et Jessica: extranéité ou aliénation? 13–28

CODACCIONI, MARIE-JOSÉ.   L'étrangère dans le temps. 237–45

COSTA DE BEAUREGARD, RAPHAËLLE.   D'étranges manières: remarques à propos de l'étrangeté de l'étranger dans *Othello*. 29–51

DORANGEON, SIMONE.   *A Theatre for Wordlings*, ou l'influence des 'étrangers' de Londres sur la formation de Spenser. 1–12

DUPERRAY, MAX.   L'étranger dans le contexte post-moderniste: *The Comfort of Strangers* d'Ian McEwan. 291–306

GOSCILO, MARGARET.   The dual outsider in Henry James's *The Princess Casamassima*. 205–18

HÉROU, JOSETTE.   Macaronis et kickshaw-mongers: representation des italiens et des français sur la scène comique en Angleterre, au 18e siècle. 129–47

HUGHES, DEREK.   The Dryden–Davenant *Tempest* and some seventeenth-century images of the stranger. 83–108

LÉVY, MAURICE.   Étranges étrangers: ou, le fantastique selon Lovecraft. 219–36

LURBE, PIERRE.   Statut des étrangers et statut de l'étranger chez John Toland. 109–27

MATHIS, GILLES.   En tête à texte avec l'étrange: la métamorphose de Jack dans *Lord of the Flies*. 247–78

PAKNADEL, FÉLIX.   Trois anglaises en France pendant la Révolution. 149–63

PARIS, MICHÈLE.   A propos des frasques de la princesse Caroline: le regard sur l'étranger au début du 19e siècle. 165–88

RIGAUD, N. J.   La problématique de l'étranger dans *The Custom of the Country* de J. Fletcher. 53–72

SALEM, DANIEL.   L'étranger dans *A Slight Ache* de Pinter. 279–90

SCHRICKE, GILBERT.   Monsieur de Paris, mauvais anglais et faux étranger: *The Gentleman Dancing Master* de Wycherley. 73–82

## The European Tragedy of Troilus

**27.** BOITANI, PIERO (ed.).   The European tragedy of Troilus. Oxford: Clarendon Press; New York: OUP. pp. xiii, 361.

ANDREW, MALCOLM.   The fall of Troy in *Sir Gawain and the Green Knight* and *Troilus and Criseyde*. 75–93

ANTONELLI, ROBERTO.   The birth of Criseyde – an exemplary triangle: 'classical' Troilus and the question of love at the Anglo-Norman court. 21–48

BENSON, C. DAVID.   True Troilus and false Cresseid: the descent from tragedy. 153–70

BOITANI, PIERO.   Antiquity and beyond: the death of Troilus. 1–19

BOITANI, PIERO.   Eros and thanatos: Cressida, Troilus, and the modern age. 281–305

BREWER, DEREK.   Comedy and tragedy in *Troilus and Criseyde*. 95–109

LOMBARDO, AGOSTINO.   Fragments and scraps: Shakespeare's *Troilus and Cressida*. 199–217

MANN, JILL.   Shakespeare and Chaucer: 'What is Criseyde worth?' 219–42

NATALI, GIULIA.   A lyrical version: Boccaccio's *Filostrato*. 49–73

REICHL, KARL.   Chaucer's *Troilus*: philosophy and language. 133–52

RUFINI, SERGIO.   'To make that maxim good': Dryden's Shakespeare. 243–80

TORTI, ANNA.   From 'history' to 'tragedy': the story of Troilus and Criseyde in Lydgate's *Troy Book* and Henryson's *Testament of Cresseid*. 171–97

WINDEATT, BARRY.   Classical and medieval elements in Chaucer's *Troilus*. 111–31

## Explorations in the Field of Nonsense

**28.**   TIGGES, WIM (ed.).   Explorations in the field of nonsense. Amsterdam: Rodopi, 1987. pp. 255. (DQR studies in literature, 3.)

BOELENS, TYSGER.   The bad manners of nonsense: an inquiry into the nonsensical orthodoxy of Stefan Themerson's *The Adventures of Peddy Bottom*. 229–44

BURGESS, ANTHONY.   Nonsense. 17–21

EDE, LISA S.   Edward Lear's limericks and their illustrations. 103–16

EDE, LISA S.   An introduction to the nonsense literature of Edward Lear and Lewis Carroll. 47–60

ELDERHORST, CONSTANCE.   John Donne's *First Anniversary* as an anatomical anamorphosis. 97–102

GALESTIN, PAUL.   The Marx Brothers: verbal and visual nonsense in their films. 149–60

LANTERS, JOSÉ.   'Still life' versus real life: the English writings of Brian O'Nolan. 161–81

PEZE, ESTHER.   Situational nonsense in postmodern American fiction. 215–27

SEWELL, ELIZABETH.   Is Flannery O'Connor a nonsense writer? 183–213

SEWELL, ELIZABETH.   Nonsense verse and the child. 135–48

THEMERSON, STEFAN.   On nonsense and on logic-fiction. 3–16

TIGGES, WIM.   An anatomy of nonsense. 23–46

TIGGES, WIM.   The limerick: the sonnet of nonsense? 117–33

TIGGES, WIM (comp.).   A select annotated bibliography on literary nonsense. 245–55

VAN LEEUWEN, HENDRIK.   The liaison of visual and written nonsense. 61–95

## Feminism and Psychoanalysis

**29.**   FELDSTEIN, RICHARD; ROOF, JUDITH (eds).   Feminism and psychoanalysis. Ithaca, NY; London: Cornell UP. pp. ix, 359.

FELDSTEIN, RICHARD.   Reader, text, and ambiguous referentiality in *The Yellow Wallpaper*. 269–79

JOHNSON, BARBARA.   Is female to male as ground is to figure? 255–68

KAHANE, CLAIRE.   Hysteria, feminism, and the case of *The Bostonians*. 280–97

NEELY, CAROL THOMAS.   Constructing female sexuality in the Renaissance: Stratford, London, Windsor, Vienna. 209–29

POOVEY, MARY.   The anathematized race: the governess and *Jane Eyre*. 230–54

SPRENGNETHER, MADELON.   (M)other Eve: some revisions of the Fall in fiction by contemporary women writers. 298–322

## An Historic Tongue

**30.**   NIXON, GRAHAM; HONEY, JOHN (eds).   An historic tongue: studies in English linguistics in memory of Barbara Strang. London; New York: Routledge, 1988. pp. xiv, 247.

BAGHDIKIAN, SONIA.   Ambiguous negations in Chaucer and Queen Elizabeth. 41–8

BEAL, JOAN.   Goodbye to all 'that'? The history and present behaviour of optional *that*. 49–66

BLAKE, N. F.   Negation in Shakespeare. 89–111

FISCHER, OLGA.   The rise of the *for NP to V* construction: an explanation. 67–88 (Revised version of conference paper, Sheffield, 1983.)

FRANKIS, JOHN.   The great vowel-shift and other vowel-shifts. 133–7

GÖRLACH, MANFRED.   *Varietas delectat*: forms and functions of English around the world. 167–208 (Revised version of Studium Linguistik (15) 1984, 10–35.)

HOEY, MICHAEL.   The discourse properties of the criminal statute. 145–66 (Conference paper, Univ. of Houston, 1985.)

HOGG, RICHARD M.   Snuck: the development of irregular preterite forms. 31–40

HONEY, JOHN.   'Talking proper': schooling and the establishment of English 'Received Pronunciation'. 209–27

LASS, ROGER.   Cyn(e)wulf revisited: the problem of the runic signatures. 17–30

NIXON, GRAHAM.   The methods of urban linguistic surveys. 228–41

OSSELTON, NOEL E.   Thematic genitives. 138–44

REED, JOHN O.   Englishmen and their moods: Renaissance grammar and the English verb. 112–30

STANLEY, E. G.   The difficulty of establishing borrowings between Old English and the continental West Germanic languages. 3–16

## The Historical Renaissance:
### New Essays on Tudor and Stuart Literature and Culture

**31.** DUBROW, HEATHER; STRIER, RICHARD (eds).   The historical Renaissance: new essays on Tudor and Stuart literature and culture. Chicago; London: Chicago UP, 1988. pp. ix, 377. Rev. by Lauro Martines in RQ (42:3) 572–4; by Christopher Hill in GHJ (12:2) 43–54; by Miranda Johnson Haddad in SQ (40:4) 514–17.

DUBROW, HEATHER.   'The sun in water': Donne's Somerset epithalamium and the poetics of patronage. 197–219

DUBROW, HEATHER; STRIER, RICHARD.   Introduction: the historical Renaissance. 1–12

GARBER, MARJORIE.   Descanting on deformity: Richard III and the shape of history. 79–103

HELGERSON, RICHARD.   Barbarous tongues: the ideology of poetic form in Renaissance England. 273–92 (Revised version of conference paper, Western Michigan Univ., 1984.)

HULSE, CLARK.   Spenser, Bacon, and the myth of power. 315–46

KELLEY, DONALD R.   Ideas of resistance before Elizabeth. 48–76

KINNEY, ARTHUR F.   Sir Philip Sidney and the uses of history. 293–314

MANLEY, LAWRENCE.   From matron to monster: Tudor–Stuart London and the languages of urban description. 347–74

MARCUS, LEAH S.   *Cymbeline* and the unease of topicality. 134–68

MUELLER, JANEL.  A Tudor Queen finds voice: Katherine Parr's *Lamentation of a Sinner*. 15–47 (Revised version of conference paper, Purdue Univ., 1987.)

QUILLIGAN, MAUREEN.   Sidney and his Queen. 171–96

SCHOENFELDT, MICHAEL C.   'Subject to ev'ry mounters bended knee': Herbert and authority. 242–69

STRIER, RICHARD.   Faithful servants: Shakespeare's praise of disobedience. 104–33

### History and Violence in Anglo-Irish Literature

**32.** DUYTSCHAEVER, JORIS; LERNOUT, GEERT (eds).   History and violence in Anglo-Irish literature. (Papers from the first Easter Conference on Anglo-Irish Literature, Antwerp, 9 April 1986.) Amsterdam: Rodopi, 1988. pp. 135. (Costerus, 71.)

D'HAEN, THEO.   Desmond Hogan and Ireland's postmodern past. 79–84

DIELTJENS, LOUIS.   The Abbey Theatre as a cultural formation. 47–65

DUYTSCHAEVER, JORIS.   History in the poetry of Derek Mahon. 97–110

KENNELLY, BRENDAN.   Poetry and violence. 5–28

LEERSSEN, JOEP.   Táin after táin: the mythical past and the Anglo-Irish. 29–46

LERNOUT, GEERT.   Banville and being: *The Newton Letter* and history. 67–77

McCORMACK, W. J.   *Finnegans Wake* in Irish literary history. 111–35

VERSTRAETE, GINETTE.   Brian Friel's drama and the limits of language. 85–96

### The Idea of the Novel in the Eighteenth Century

**33.** UPHAUS, ROBERT W. (ed.).   The idea of the novel in the eighteenth century. East Lansing, MI: Colleagues Press; Woodbridge: Boydell & Brewer, 1988. pp. x, 143. (Studies in literature, 1500–1800, 3.)

BEASLEY, JERRY C.   Life's episodes: story and its form in the eighteenth century. 21–45

DUSSINGER, JOHN A.   'The language of real feeling': internal speech in the Jane Austen novel. 97–115

MYERS, MITZI.   The dilemmas of gender as double-voiced narrative: or, Maria Edgeworth mothers the Bildungsroman. 67–96

RICHETTI, JOHN.   The novel and society: the case of Daniel Defoe. 47–66

RICHTER, DAVID H.   The reception of the gothic novel in the 1790s. 117–37

WEINSHEIMER, JOEL.   Fiction and the force of example. 1–19

## Instead of Flowers: Papers in Honour of Mats Rydén on the Occasion of his Sixtieth Birthday, August 27, 1989

**34.** ODENSTEDT, BENGT; PERSSON, GUNNAR (eds). Instead of flowers: papers in honour of Mats Rydén on the occasion of his sixtieth birthday, August 27, 1989. Umeå: Acta Universitatis Umensis; Stockholm: Almqvist & Wiksell. pp. v, 136. (Umeå studies in the humanities, 90.)

ANDERSON, JOHN. Periphrases and paradigms. 1–10

BÄCKLUND, INGEGERD. Cues to the audience: on some structural markers in English monologue. 29–39

BAER, KERSTIN. Friendship in Otwavian fashion. 11–14

BRORSTRÖM, SVERKER. Periphrastic *do* v. the *do*-less form in the letters of Lady Brilliana Harley (b. 1600? – d. 1643). 15–28

COLMAN, FRAN. The crunch is the key: on computer research on Old English personal names. 41–55

ELERT, CLAES-CHRISTIAN; ELERT, KERSTIN. Daisy and Lily . . . : women's first names derived from plant names. 57–68

GRANQVIST, RAOUL. Us and them: distancing practices of the colonial travelogue. 69–86

HOVDE, CARL F. *The Maine Woods, Cape Cod* and the shape of Thoreau's career. 87–98

JACOBSON, SVEN. Some observations on article variation in English. 98–108

JOHANNESSON, NILS-LENNART. Subject topicalization in Ælfric's homilies. 109–21

KRISTENSSON, GILLIS. The linguistic status of East Anglia in late Middle English. 123–30 (Review-article.)

MAGNUSSON, ULF. The verb *do* in the LOB Corpus. 131–45

MELCHERS, GUNNEL. Twartree ösfil Shetlan flooers. (Two or three useful Shetland flowers.) 147–53

ODENSTEDT, BENGT. The Frisian inscription from Britsum: a re-appraisal. 155–61

OMBERG, MARGARET. Gustav Vasa's adventures in 18th-century English drama. 163–73

ORESTRÖM, BENGT. A love affair. 175–7

PERSSON, GUNNAR. On the semantics of collective nouns in English. 179–88

RYNELL, ALARIK. English nicknames for Napoleon in contemporary caricatures. 197–204

SHRIMPTON, NEVILLE; NJIE, SULAYMAN. Editing Krio texts. 205–22 (Afro-English creole of Sierra Leone.)

SVARTVIK, JAN. Instead of native speakers. 259–67

Tottie, Gunnel. What does *uh-(h)uh* mean? American English vocalizations and the Swedish learner. 269–81

Zettersten, Arne. The pristine place-names of the Tristan da Cunha group. 297–310

### Les lieux de passage

**35.** Anon. (ed.). Les lieux de passage. Pau: Univ. de Pau et des Pays de l'Adour. pp. 162. (Centre de Recherche Médiatisation et Systèmes de Représentation.) (Convergences, 6.)

Chevalier, Jean-Louis. *The Door* et quelques autres portes: à propos d'un poème de Charles Tomlinson. 119–28

Floc'h, Sylvain. Arches et arcanes: la mystique de l'échange chez D. H. Lawrence. 129–34

Gauthier, Dominique. Du labyrinthe au temple: le pont comme seuil mythique dans *The Bridge* de Hart Crane. 135–44

Jacquin, Bernard. Enfermement et rites de passage dans la fiction de William Golding. 93–100

Pilet, Françoise. Une lecture de *Through the Tunnel* de Doris Lessing. 101–8

### Literatura angielska i amerykanska: problemy recepcji

**36.** Zagórska, Anna; Bystydzieńska, Grażyna (eds). Literatura angielska i amerykańska: problemy recepcji. (English and American literature: problems of reception.) Lublin: Uniwersytet Marii Curie-Skłodowsklej. pp. 243.

Bielecka, Daniela. Dickens in Poland. 119–35

Bystydzieńska, Grażyna. Laurence Sterne'a gra z czytelnikiem (*Podróz sentymentalna*). (Laurence Sterne – playing games with the reader (*Sentimental Journey*).) 94–107

Chrzanowska-Karpińska, Ewa. John Barth's *Lost in the Fun-House* as a comic metafiction. 209–27

Eland-Jankowska, Ewa. On the reception of Shakespeare in early American theatre. 57–73

Jedrzejkiewicz, Maria. Problemy recepcji powieści Iris Murdoch (na przykładzie lektury *The Sea, the Sea*). (The problem of the reception of Iris Murdoch's novels (exemplified by *The Sea, the Sea*).) 153–77

Kowalik, Barbara. Poetry and testimony: a relationship between some late-medieval poems and their readers. 46–56

Kurowska, Elżbieta. The modern English novel in Polish and English literary criticism in the 1930s. 136–52

Kutnik, Jerzy. The reader's plight in Raymond Federman's fiction. 223–34

LUBICZ-PYRZOWSKA, BARBARA. Perspektywy semiotyzacji opowiadań E. M. Forstera w świetle kategorii gatunkowych i ponadga-
tunkowych. (Applying semiotics to E. M. Forster's short stories:
figurative and non-figurative criteria.) 178–93

LYRA, FRANCISZEK. Toward a history of American literature in
Poland. 194–208

MOLLOY, SHAUN. Guilty pleasures of the text and unauthorized
versions. 40–5

NOWICKI, WOJCIECH. Uwagi o adresacie przedmow osiemnastowiecznej powiesci angielskiej. (Notes on the fictive reader in English
eighteenth-century novels.) 85–93

OSTROWSKI, WITOLD. Social aspects of literary evaluation in
England and in Poland. 7–26

STAMIROWSKA, KRYSTYNA. The reading of fiction. 27–39

WĄCIOR, SŁAWOMIR. Adresat w poezji Thomasa Traherne'a: szkic
problematyki. (The fictive reader in Thomas Traherne's poetry: an
outline of the problem.) 74–84

ZGORZELSKI, ANDRZEJ. Lektura jako kontakt osobowy. (Reading as a
personal contact.) 235–43

## Literature and the Art of Creation

**37.** WELCH, ROBERT; BUSHRUI, SUHEIL BADI (eds). Literature and the
art of creation: essays and poems in honour of A. Norman Jeffares.
Gerrards Cross: Smythe; Totowa, NJ: Barnes & Noble, 1988. pp. ix,
323.

BROWN, TERENCE. Canon Sheehan and the Catholic intellectual.
7–17

DAICHES, DAVID. W. B. Yeats: tones of voice. 18–25

DUNN, T. A. The imperial bawd. 26–32

HARMON, MAURICE. Pangur Ban and the scholar critic. 33–42

HAYLEY, BARBARA. Lafcadio Hearn, W. B. Yeats and Japan. 43–60

HORDEN, JOHN. Renaissance emblem books: a comment on terminology. 61–70

KNIGHT, G. WILSON. My life's work, with a discussion of Francis
Berry's poetry. 71–80

KOSOK, HEINZ. Dion Boucicault's 'American' plays: considerations
on defining national literatures in English. 81–97

MARTIN, AUGUSTINE. Julia Cahill, Father McTurnan, and the
geography of nowhere. 98–111

MORPURGO, J. E. The poet and Barabbas: Keats, his publishers and
editors. 112–23

RAVENSCROFT, ARTHUR. South African novelists as prophets. 124–39

RUTHERFORD, ANNA.   Stone people in a stone country: Alan Paton's *Too Late the Phalarope*. 140–52

SADDLEMYER, ANN.   The theatrical voice: *The Words upon the Window-Pane*. 153–73

SUTHERLAND, JAMES.   Who was Peter Grimes? 179–85

THOMSON, ALASTAIR W.   Method and decorum in *Don Juan*. 186–203

WELCH, ROBERT.   Seneca and the English Renaissance: the old world and the new. 204–18

ZACH, WOLFGANG.   Fascination and scandal: on John Gay's *Beggar's Opera* and the doctrine of poetic justice. 219–37

## The Living Middle Ages:
## Studies in Mediaeval Literature and its Tradition

**38.**  BÖKER, UWE; MARKUS, MANFRED; SCHÖWERLING, RAINER (eds). The living Middle Ages: studies in mediaeval literature and its tradition: a festschrift for Karl Heinz Göller. Stuttgart: Belser. pp. 383.

ARENS, WERNER.   Late Middle English political poetry as 'public poetry'. 167–81

BOITANI, PIERO.   Some dead master: Brunetto, Dante and Eliot. 277–93

BÖKER, UWE.   The epistle mendicant in mediaeval and Renaissance literature: the sociology and poetics of a genre. 137–65

BREUER, ROLF.   Christian tragedy/tragedy of Christianity. 183–95

BREWER, DEREK.   Chaucer's anti-Ricardian poetry. 115–28

DUBRUCK, EDELGARD E.   Inviting tacit agreement: the Pardoner's Tale and its modern reception. 103–13

ERZGRÄBER, WILLI.   The beginnings of a written literature in Old English times. 25–43

FICHTE, J. O.   *The Awntyrs off Arthure*: an unconscious change of the paradigm of adventure. 129–36

GLEISSNER, REINHARD.   Some observations on Old English *cyswucu* in the A-version of the Old English *West-Saxon Gospels*. 45–68

GRIEM, EBERHARD.   Medieval elements and their functions in some contemporary English novels. 305–18

HAAS, RENATE.   The social functions of F. J. Furnivall's medievalism. 319–32

HIETSCH, OTTO.   Enshrined in speech: medieval life and modern leavings. 333–71

KAYLOR, NOEL HAROLD, JR.   The Nun's Priest's Tale as Chaucer's anti-tragedy. 87–102

KOHL, STEPHAN.   The Renaissance lover, the medieval sinner, and timelessness: Alexander Theroux's *Darconville's Cat*. 295–304

MARKUS, MANFRED.   The spelling peculiarities in the *Ormulum* from an interdisciplinary point of view: a reappraisal. 69–86

MITCHELL, JEROME.   Scott and Malory. 211–26

MÜLLENBROCK, HEINZ-JOACHIM.   The Middle Ages in eighteenth-century England: a guide to periodization? 197–209

SCHÖWERLING, RAINER.   Sir Walter Scott and the tradition of the historical novel before 1814 – with a checklist. 227–62

## Making a Spectacle: Feminist Essays on Contemporary Women's Theatre

**39.**   HART, LYNDA (ed.).   Making a spectacle: feminist essays on contemporary women's theatre. Ann Arbor: Michigan UP. pp. viii (unnumbered), 347. (Women and culture.) Rev. by Kate Davy in TJ (41:3) 429–31.

ARNOLD, STEPHANIE.   Dissolving the half shadows: Japanese American women playwrights. 181–94

AUSTIN, GAYLE.   The madwoman in the spotlight: plays of Maria Irene Fornes. 76–85

BACKES, NANCY.   Body art: hunger and satiation in the plays of Tina Howe. 41–60

BRESLAUER, JAN; KEYSSAR, HELENE.   Making magic public: Megan Terry's traveling family circus. 169–80

CARLSON, SUSAN.   Revisionary endings: Pam Gems's *Aunt Mary* and *Camille.* 103–17

CASE, SUE-ELLEN.   Toward a butch-femme aesthetic. 282–99

CURB, ROSEMARY.   Mirrors moving beyond frames: Sandra Shotlander's *Framework* and *Blind Salome.* 300–17

DESHAZER, MARY K.   Rejecting necrophilia: Ntozake Shange and the warrior re-visioned. 86–100

DIAMOND, ELIN.   (In)visible bodies in Churchill's theater. 259–81

DOLAN, JILL.   Bending gender to fit the canon: the politics of production. 318–44

GONZÁLEZ, YOLANDA BROYLES.   Toward a re-vision of Chicano theatre history: the women of El Teatro Campesino. 209–38

GUERRA, JONNIE.   Beth Henley: female quest and the family-play tradition. 118–30

HART, LYNDA.   'They don't even look like maids any more': Wendy Kesselman's *My Sister in This House.* 131–46

HART, LYNDA.   Introduction: performing feminism. 1–21

HELLE, ANITA PLATH.   Re-presenting women writers onstage: a retrospective to the present. 195–208

PATRAKA, VIVIAN M.    Mass culture and metaphors of menace in Joan Schenkar's plays. 25–40

REINELT, JANELLE.    Michelene Wandor: artist and ideologue. 239–55

SPENCER, JENNY S.    Marsha Norman's 'she-tragedies'. 147–65

WILKERSON, MARGARET B.    Music as metaphor: new plays of Black women. 61–75

## A Mazing Space: Writing Canadian Women Writing

**40.**  NEUMAN, SHIRLEY; KAMBOURELI, SMARO (eds).    A mazing space: writing Canadian women writing. Edmonton, Alta: Longspoon Press; NeWest Press 1986. pp. xi, 427. Rev. by Coral Ann Howells in CanL (120) 177–9; by Marilyn Randell in QQ (95:2) 1988, 447–9.

BARBOUR, DOUGLAS.    Day thoughts on Anne Wilkinson's poetry. 179–90

BENNETT, DONNA.    Naming the way home. 228–45

BESSAI, DIANE.    Sharon Pollock's women: a study in dramatic process. 126–36

BUSS, HELEN M.    Canadian women's autobiography: some critical directions. 154–64

BUTLING, PAULINE.    Paradox and play in the poetry of Phyllis Webb. 191–204

FRIEWALD, BINA.    'Femininely speaking': Anna Jameson's *Winter Studies and Summer Rambles in Canada*. 61–73

GODARD, BARBARA.    Voicing difference: the literary production of native women. 87–107

GUNNARS, KRISTJANA.    Laura Goodman Salverson's confessions of a divided self. 148–53

HARASYM, SARAH.    Ringing rounds on the proper name. 324–33

HARRIS, CLAIR.    Poets in limbo. 115–25

HUTCHEON, LINDA.    'Shape shifters': Canadian women novelists and the challenge to tradition. 219–27

IRVINE, LORNA.    Starting from the beginning every time. 246–55

KAMBOURELI, SMARO.    The body as audience and performance in the writing of Alice Munro. 31–8

McMULLEN, LORRAINE.    Lily Dougall's vision of Canada. 137–47

MURRAY, HEATHER.    Women in the wilderness. 74–83

NEUMAN, SHIRLEY.    Importing difference. 392–405

PERREAULT, JEANNE.    Narrative strategies and feminist fundamentals in *The True Story of Ida Johnson*. 270–5

RICOU, LAURIE.    Phyllis Webb, Daphne Marlatt and simultitude. 205–15

ROOKE, CONSTANCE.   Fear of the open heart. 256–69

STANLEY, MARNI L.   Travelers' tales: showing and telling, slamming and questing. 51–60

THESEN, SHARON.   Poetry and the dilemma of expression. 380–4

TOSTEVIN, LOLA LEMIRE.   Breaking the hold on the story: the feminine economy of language. 385–91

VAN HERK, ARITHA.   Double crossings: booking the lover. 276–86

WAH, FRED.   Which at first seems to be a going back for origins: notes on a reading of some American women writers. 374–9

WILLIAMSON, JANICE.   Framed by history: Marjorie Pickthall's devices and desire. 167–78

## Medieval English Studies Presented to George Kane

**41.** KENNEDY, EDWARD DONALD; WALDRON, RONALD; WITTIG, JOSEPH S. (eds).   Medieval English studies presented to George Kane. Woodbridge; Wolfeboro, NH: Boydell & Brewer, 1988. pp. xviii, 327. Rev. by Thomas Garbáty in YLS (3) 159–63.

ADAMS, ROBERT.   Mede and mercede: the evolution of the economics of grace in the *Piers Plowman* B and C versions. 217–32

ALFORD, JOHN A.   The idea of reason in *Piers Plowman*. 199–215

ALLEN, ROSAMUND.   The date and provenance of *King Horn*: some interim reassessments. 99–125

BATELY, JANET.   On some aspects of the vocabulary of the West Midlands in the early Middle Ages: the language of the Katherine Group. 55–77

BLOOMFIELD, MORTON W.   History *and* literature in the vernacular in the Middle Ages? 309–15

BREWER, DEREK.   The other, the self: speculations concerning an aspect of Western culture and medieval literature. 317–27

COWEN, J. M.   The Miller's Tale, line 3325: 'merry maid and gallant groom'? 147–52

DAHOOD, ROGER.   The use of coloured initials and other division markers in early versions of the *Ancrene Riwle*. 79–97

DAVENPORT, W. A.   Patterns in Middle English dialogues. 127–45

FISHER, JOHN H.   *Piers Plowman* and the Chancery tradition. 267–78

HUSSEY, S. S.   Chaucer's Host. 153–61

JACOBS, NICOLAS.   Some creative misreadings in *Le Bone Florence of Rome*: an experiment in textual criticism. 279–84

KASKE, R. E.   The character Hunger in *Piers Plowman*. 187–97 (Conference paper, Cornell Univ., 1986.)

LADD, C. A.   'Look out for the little words.' 163–5

LUMIANSKY, R. M.    Concerning three names in *Le Morte Darthur* – 'Roone', 'The Welshe Kyng' and 'Chastelayne' – and Malory's possible revision of his book. 301–8

MIDDLETON, ANNE.    Making a good end: John But as a reader of *Piers Plowman*. 243–66

PEARSALL, DEREK.    Poverty and poor people in *Piers Plowman*. 167–85

ROBERTS, JANE.    *Guthlac A*: sources and source hunting. 1–18

RUSSELL, G. H.    The imperative of revision in the C version of *Piers Plowman*. 233–42

STANLEY, E. G.    Rhymes in English medieval verse: from Old English to Middle English. 19–54

WALDRON, RONALD.    Trevisa's original prefaces on translation: a critical edition. 285–99

## Multiple Worlds, Multiple Words

**42.**    MAES-JELINEK, HENA; MICHEL, PIERRE; MICHEL-MICHOT, PAUL-ETTE (eds).    Multiple worlds, multiple words: essays in honour of Irène Simon. Liège: English Dept, Univ. of Liège, 1988. pp. xv, 322.

BRADBURY, MALCOM.    Persons of letters. 5–14

CORIN, FERNAND.    Rites of passage in Iris Murdoch's *The Good Apprentice*. 15–25

DANCHIN, PIERRE.    Coventry Patmore and Francis Thompson: the story of a brief friendship (1894–1896). 27–37

DELBAERE-GARANT, JEANNE.    The artist as clown of God: Golding's *The Paper Man*. 39–49

DEROLEZ, RENÉ.    Hrothgar King of Denmark. 51–8

DIERICKX, JEAN.    Equivalent messages: headlines in *Le Monde* and their translation into English. 59–68

DOR, JULIETTE.    Reversals in the Nun's Priest's Tale. 69–77

DRAPER, RONALD P.    Hardy's love poetry. 79–96

ELLRODT, ROBERT.    Time and the body in the works of Sir Thomas Browne. 97–101

ERZGRÄBER, WILLI.    European literature in the late Middle Ages in its political and social contexts. 103–21

GENET, JACQUELINE.    Yeats's *Deirdre* as a chess-game and a poet's game. 123–38

GRABES, HERBERT.    Deliberate intertextuality: the function of quotation and allusion in the early poetry of T. S. Eliot. 139–52

LAPREVOTTE, GUY.    Note on Arbuthnot's use of official documents in *The History of John Bull*. 153–9

MAES-JELINEK, HENA.    A web of horizons: 'Otherland' in Christopher Koch's *The Doubleman*. 161–73

MERTENS-FONCK, PAULE. Tradition and feminism in Middle English literature: source-hunting in the Wife of Bath's portrait and in *The Owl and the Nightingale*. 175–92

MICHEL, PIERRE. Quentin Compson and the narrative perspective in Faulkner's *Absalom, Absalom!*. 193–202

MICHEL-MICHOT, PAULETTE. Fowles's 'Poor Koko': a metaphor of the quest. 203–11

NOËL, JACQUES, *et al.* Computational lexicography and multi-lingualism. 213–27

PAGNOULLE, CHRISTINE. Dramatic irony in David Jones's poem *The Tribune's Visitation*. 229–37

RUTHERFORD, ANNA. Miles Franklin: the outside track. 239–56

SCHRICKX, WILLEM. *All's Well That Ends Well* and its historical relevance. 257–74

SERVOTTE, HERMAN. Auden and Kierkegaard. 275–82

SMIDT, KRISTIAN. Levels and discontinuities in *Titus Andronicus*. 283–93

SUTHERLAND, JAMES. A note on the foreseen and the fortuitous in poetry. 295–301

ZANDVOORT, R. W. Mr Fezziwig's Ball. 303–9

### 'News that Stays News': the Enactment of Present and Future in American Literature

**43.** PORTER, GERALD (ed.). 'News that stays news': the enactment of present and future in American literature. Vaasa, Finland: Univ. of Vaasa. pp. 75. (Proceedings of the Univ. of Vaasa, 137.)

AALTONEN, SIRKKU. 'De meuleh de world': patterns of dominance in Zora Neale Hurston's *Their Eyes Were Watching God*. 22–30

KANKAANRANTA, ANNE. A different quest of roots as shown in Toni Morrison's novel *Song of Solomon*. 31–41

PORTER, GERALD. Adding a murder ballad to the American sonbag: technical and cultural factors in *The Lexington Miller*. 65–72

PORTER, GERALD. The art of the impossible: two early American utopias. 42–54

### Nineteenth-Century Lives

**44.** LOCKRIDGE, LAURENCE; MAYNARD, JOHN; STONE, DONALD D. (eds). Nineteenth-century lives: essays presented to Jerome Hamilton Buckley. Bibliography by DAVID M. STAINES. Cambridge; New York: CUP. pp. xix, 216.

ALTICK, RICHARD D. Writing the life of J. J. Ridley. 26–58

ATWOOD, MARGARET. Biographobia: some personal reflections on the act of biography. 1–8

Cohen, Morton N.   Lewis Carroll: 'dishcoveries' – and more. 112–24

Kelvin, Norman.   Patterns in time: the decorative and the narrative in the work of William Morris. 140–68

Kiely, Robert.   Charles Dickens: the lives of some important nobodies. 59–81

Miller, J. Hillis.   Prosopopoeia and *Praeterita*. 125–39

Rose, Phyllis.   Fact and fiction in biography. 188–202

Rosenberg, John D.   Mr Darwin collects himself. 82–111

Stetz, Margaret Diane.   Life's 'half-profits': writers and their readers in fiction of the 1890s. 169–87

Woodring, Carl.   Shaping life in *The Prelude*. 9–25

## Omnium Gatherum: Essays for Richard Ellmann

**45.**   Dick, Susan, *et al.* (eds).   Omnium gatherum: essays for Richard Ellmann. Gerrards Cross: Smythe. pp. xix, 499. Rev. by Patricia Craig in TLS, 27 Oct., 1192.

Albright, Daniel.   Beckett's recent activities: the liveliness of dead imagination. 374–83

Armstrong, Alison.   Transition years: James Joyce and Modernist art. 351–9

Butler, Christopher.   The concept of Modernism. 49–59

Cantrell, Carol H.   'Sufficient ground to stand on': Pound, Williams, and American history. 153–60

Culler, Jonathan.   Wilde's criticism: theory and practice. 402–6

Cullingford, Elizabeth Butler.   Labour and memory in the love poetry of W. B. Yeats. 204–19

Desai, R. W.   In search of Horatio's identity (via Yeats). 191–203

Dick, Susan.   'The writing "I" has vanished': Virginia Woolf's last short fictions. 134–45

Dick, Susan, *et al.*   Richard Ellmann: the critic as artist. xiii–xviii

Diggory, Terence.   Yeats's stream of consciousness. 253–66

Donoghue, Denis.   Notes on a late poem by Stevens. 167–74

Eagleton, Terry.   Joyce and mythology. 310–19

Ellmann, Richard.   Joyce as letter writer. 304–9 (Text of radio broadcast, 28 April 1984.)

Feidelson, Charles.   Henry James, history, and 'story'. 104–21

Flannery, James.   Yeats: the masker and the masks. 267–79

Huttar, Charles A.   Poe's angels. 82–4

Johnson, Bruce.   A Modernist noesis. 60–70

KERMODE, FRANK.    Northrop Frye and the Bible. 71–81

KIBERD, DECLAN.    Isabel Archer: the New Woman as American. 85–103

KUCH, PETER.    'What can I but enumerate old themes?' 234–52

LAUGHLIN, JAMES.    Richard Ellmann's Michaux: a publisher's recollections. 23–8

LITZ, A. WALTON.    Strange meetings: Eliot, Pound, and Laforgue. 146–52

McDONALD, CHRISTIE.    'Oranges – apples – sugarsticks . . .' Joycean associations: an interview with Richard Ellmann. 37–41

McMILLAN, DOUGALD.    The fatal circle: composition and direction of *Come and Go*. 384–93

MANGANIELLO, DOMINIC.    The consolation of art: Oscar Wilde and Dante. 394–401

MASON, ELLSWORTH.    Ellmann's road to Xanadu. 4–12

MERCIER, VIVIAN.    *All That Fall*: Samuel Beckett and the Bible. 360–73

REYNOLDS, MARY T.    Mr Leopold Bloom and the lost Vermeer. 320–32

ROBERTSON, WILLIAM K.    A portrait of James Joyce's biographer. 42–8 (Interview with Richard Ellmann.)

RONSLEY, JOSEPH.    The difficult debut of Denis Johnston's *Old Lady*. 175–90

ROSENBAUM, S. P.    Lytton Strachey and the prose of Empire. 122–33

SADDLEMYER, ANN.    'Yours affly, Dobbs': George Yeats to her husband, winter 1931–32. 280–303

SCHENDLER, SYLVAN.    'Heroic work, heroic being': avoid the valedictory. 1–3

SCHNEIDER, DANIEL J.    D. H. Lawrence's physical religion: the debt to Tylor, Frobenius, and Nuttall. 161–6

SENN, FRITZ.    'There's a medium in all things': Joycean readings. 333–50

STALLWORTHY, JON.    W. B. Yeats and that high horse. 220–33

WHITAKER, THOMAS R.    Playing in earnest. 407–23

## On Modern Poetry

**46.**  BELL, VEREEN; LERNER, LAURENCE (eds).    On modern poetry: essays presented to Donald Davie. Nashville, TN: Vanderbilt UP, 1988. pp. x, 256.

BELL, VEREEN.    Grace dissolved in place: a reading of *Ash Wednesday*. 1–14

BERGONZI, BERNARD.   Poetry of the Desert War: British poets in Egypt 1940–45. 15–35

GUNN, THOM.   Three hard women: HD, Marianne Moore, Mina Loy. 37–52

HARPER, GEORGE MILLS.   'Necessary murder': the Auden circle and the Spanish Civil War. 67–80

HEANEY, SEAMUS.   Or, Solitude: a reading. 81–7

JARMAN, MARK.   A shared humanity: In the Stopping Train and The Whitsun Weddings, 89–101

KILROY, JAMES.   Four late poems of Lorine Niedecker. 119–32

LERNER, LAURENCE.   On ambiguity, Modernism, and sacred texts. 133–44

MacINTYRE, ALASDAIR.   Poetry as political philosophy: notes on Burke and Yeats. 145–57

PRATT, WILLIAM.   Pound and Yeats: the poetics of friendship. 159–80

RAWSON, CLAUDE.   Bards, boardrooms, and blackboards: John Ashbery, Wallace Stevens, and the academicization of poetry. 181–91

STEAD, C. K.   Stendhal's mirror and Yeats's looking-glass: a reconsideration of The Tower. 193–211

TOMLINSON, CHARLES.   Some presences on the scene: a vista of postwar poetry. 215–32

VENDLER, HELEN.   Donald Davie: self-portraits in verse. 233–53

VON HALLBERG, ROBERT.   Ezra Pound in Paris. 53–65

## One Hundred Years of English Studies in Dutch Universities

**47.**  BUNT, G. H. V., et al. (eds).   One hundred years of English studies in Dutch universities: seventeen papers read at the Centenary Conference, Groningen, 15–16 January 1986. Amsterdam: Rodopi, 1987. pp. vii, 274. (Costerus, 64.) Rev. by Georges Bourcier in EA (42:4) 444.

AARTS, F. G. A. M.   Dutch progress in English syntax: Zandvoort's Handbook of English Grammar and after. 67–79

AERTSEN, H.   The use of dialect words in Middle English alliterative poetry. 173–85

BAKKER, J.   Emily Dickinson's secret. 239–48

BERTENS, HANS.   The attack on epistemology in recent American fiction. 249–59

BEUKEMA, FRITS; VERHEIJEN, RON.   Particle constructions in English. 109–25

BLOM, J. M.   George Gissing. 225–37

DENISON, DAVID.   On word order in Old English. 139–55

DRAGSTRA, H. H.   The modernity of modern Chaucer criticism. 187–97

EWBANK, INGA-STINA.   Victorian novels and feminist criticism. 47–66

GRAY, DOUGLAS.   Chaucer and *gentilesse*. 1–27

HANNAY, MIKE.   English comma placement: a functional view. 81–92

NASH, WALTER.   Usage, users, and the used: some reflections on contemporary English. 29–46

PEEREBOOM, J. J.   Hervey and the facts as he saw them. 211–24

POSTHUMUS, J.   Short forms of English loans in Dutch. 93–107

STUURMAN, FRITS.   Approaching *ought (to)*. 127–38

TIEKEN-BOON VAN OSTADE, INGRID.   Negative *do* in eighteenth-century English: the power of prestige. 157–71

WESTERWEEL, BART.   Macbeth, time and prudence. 199–210

### Papers from the First Nordic Conference on Text Comprehension in Man and Machine

**48.**   DAHL, ÖSTEN; FRAURUD, KARI (eds).   Papers from the first Nordic Conference on Text Comprehension in Man and Machine. Stockholm: Inst. of Linguistics, Stockholm Univ. pp. vi, 208.

EJERHED, EVA.   Denotational semantics of natural language. 63–74

FRAURUD, KARI.   Towards a non-uniform treatment of definite NP's in discourse. 75–87

HELLMAN, CHRISTINA.   Integrative processes in disfavouring conditions: a self-paced reading study. 113–24

JANSSON, CARL GUSTAF.   A top down, abductive and schema-based approach to text comprehension: an artificial intelligence perspective from Yale. 125–38

KÄLLGREN, GUNNEL.   Automatic indexing and generating of content graphs from unrestricted text. 147–60

PREBENSEN, HENRIK.   Experiments in noun phrase comprehension on the computer. 161–72

ROMMETVEIT, RAGNAR.   On perspectives and fixation of perspectives in texts. 173–84

SEM, HELLA FRISAK.   Discourse in situation schema theory. 99–111

THRANE, TORBEN.   PAKA: a program for automated knowledge acquisition. 195–208

### The Philosopher as Writer: the Eighteenth Century

**49.**   GINSBERG, ROBERT (ed.).   The philosopher as writer: the eighteenth century. Selingrove, PA: Susquehanna UP; London; Toronto: Assoc. UPs, 1987. pp. 245. Rev. by Ken Edward Smith in BJECS (12) 223.

FINKE, LAURIE A.   'A philosophic wanton': language and authority in Wollstonecraft's *Vindication of the Rights of Women*. 155–76

GINSBERG, ROBERT.  Introduction to eighteenth-century philosophic writing. 7–11

GINSBERG, ROBERT.  The literary structure and strategy of Hume's essay on the standard of taste. 199–237

MARKLEY, ROBERT.  Style as philosophical structure: the contexts of Shaftesbury's *Characteristicks*. 140–54

SIEBERT, DONALD T.  'Ardor of youth': the manner of Hume's *Treatise*. 177–98

SOLOMON, HARRY M.  Reading philosophical poetry: a hermeneutics of metaphor for Pope's *Essay on Man*. 122–39

## The Play out of Context: Transferring Plays from Culture to Culture

**50.**  SCOLNICOV, HANNA; HOLLAND, PETER (eds).  The play out of context: transferring plays from culture to culture. Cambridge; New York; Melbourne: CUP. pp. viii, 227.

GLAAP, ALBERT-REINER.  *Whose Life is it Anyway?* in London and on Broadway: a contrastive analysis of the British and American versions of Brian Clark's play. 214–23

HABICHT, WERNER.  Shakespeare and theatre politics in the Third Reich. 110–20

HOLLAND, PETER.  Space: the final frontier. 45–62

PAVIS, PATRICE.  Problems of translation for the stage: interculturism and post-modern theatre. Trans. by LOREN KRUGER. 25–44

REDMOND, JAMES.  'If the salt have lost his savour': some 'useful' plays in and out of context on the London stage. 63–88

SCOLNICOV, HANNA.  Mimesis, mirror, double. 89–98

SHAKED, GERSHON.  The play: gateway to cultural dialogue. Trans. by JEFFREY GREEN. 7–24

VON LEDEBUR, RUTH.  The adaptation and reception in Germany of Edward Bond's *Saved*. 199–213

## The Private Self: Theory and Practice of Women's Autobiographical Writings

**51.**  BENSTOCK, SHARI (ed.).  The private self: theory and practice of women's autobiographical writings. London: Routledge; Chapel Hill: North Carolina UP, 1988. pp. vii, 319. Rev. by Laura Marcus in TLS, 14 July, 768.

BENSTOCK, SHARI.  Authorizing the autobiographical. 10–33

FOX-GENOVESE, ELIZABETH.  My statue, my self: autobiographical writings of Afro-American women. 63–89

FRIEDMAN, SUSAN STANFORD.  Women's autobiographical selves: theory and practice. 34–62

KAPLAN, DEBORAH. Representing two cultures: Jane Austen's letters. 211–29

MARCUS, JANE. Invincible mediocrity: the private selves of public women. 114–46

MCGAVRAN, JAMES HOLT, JR. Dorothy Wordsworth's journals: putting herself down. 230–53

MYERS, MITZI. Pedagogy as self-expression in Mary Wollstonecraft: exorcising the past, finding a voice. 192–210

NUSSBAUM, FELICITY A. Eighteenth-century women's autobiographical commonplaces. 147–71

SPACKS, PATRICIA MEYER. Female rhetorics. 177–91

WALKER, NANCY. 'Wider than the sky': public presence and private self in Dickinson, James, and Woolf. 272–303

### Reflections on Chomsky

**52.** GEORGE, ALEXANDER (ed.). Reflections on Chomsky. Oxford; New York: Blackwell. pp. xii, 271. Rev. by Gilbert Harman in TLS, 18 Aug., 898.

BROMBERGER, SYLVAIN. Types and tokens in linguistics. 58–89

BURGE, TYLER. Wherein is language social? 175–91

DAVIES, MARTIN. Tacit knowledge and subdoxastic states. 131–52

DUMMETT, MICHAEL. Language and communication. 192–212

GEORGE, ALEXANDER. How not to become confused about linguistics. 90–110

HIGGINBOTHAM, JAMES. Knowledge of reference. 153–74

HINTIKKA, JAAKKO. Logical form and linguistic theory. 41–57

HORNSTEIN, NORBERT. Meaning and the mental: the problem of semantics after Chomsky. 23–40

PEACOCKE, CHRISTOPHER. When is a grammar psychologically real? 111–30

PUTNAM, HILARY. Model theory and the 'factuality' of semantics. 213–32

WRIGHT, CRISPIN. Wittgenstein's rule-following considerations and the central project of theoretical linguistics. 233–64

### Rethinking Historicism: Critical Readings in Romantic History

**53.** LEVINSON, MARJORIE (ed.). Rethinking historicism: critical readings in Romantic history. Oxford; New York: Blackwell. pp. 149. Rev. by Frank Kermode in LRB (11:20) 21–3.

BUTLER, MARILYN. Repossessing the past: the case for an open literary history. 64–84

HAMILTON, PAUL.   Keats and critique. 108–42

LEVINSON, MARJORIE.   Introduction. 1–17

LEVINSON, MARJORIE.   The new historicism: back to the future. 18–63

McGANN, JEROME.   The third world of criticism. 85–107

## Rewriting the Renaissance: the Discourses of Sexual Difference in Early Modern Europe

**54.** FERGUSON, MARGARET W.; QUILLIGAN, MAUREEN; VICKERS, NANCY J. (eds).   Rewriting the Renaissance: the discourses of sexual difference in early modern Europe. Chicago; London: Chicago UP, 1986. pp. xxxi, 426. (Women in culture and society.) Rev. by James Fitzmaurice in SixCT (18:3) 1987, 427; by Retha Warnicke in JRMMRA (8) 1987, 209–10; by Derek Attridge in RQ (40:4) 1988, 810–14; by Elizabeth H. Hageman in SQ (39:2) 1988, 247–51.

GOLDBERG, JONATHAN.   Fatherly authority: the politics of Stuart family images. 3–32

GUILLORY, JOHN.   Dalila's house: *Samson Agonistes* and the sexual division of labor. 106–22

HALPERN, RICHARD.   Puritanism and Maenadism in *A Mask*. 88–105

HULSE, CLARK.   Stella's wit: Penelope Rich as reader of Sidney's sonnets. 272–86

JORDAN, CONSTANCE.   Feminism and the humanists: the case of Sir Thomas Elyot's *Defence of Good Women*. 242–58

KAHN, COPPÉLIA.   The absent mother in *King Lear*. 33–49

MONTROSE, LOUIS ADRIAN.   *A Midsummer Night's Dream* and the shaping fantasies of Elizabethan culture: gender, power, form. 65–87

ORGEL, STEPHEN.   Prospero's wife. 50–64

SILBERMAN, LAUREN.   Singing unsung heroines: androgynous discourse in Book 3 of *The Faerie Queene*. 259–71

STALLYBRASS, PETER.   Patriarchal territories: the body enclosed. 123–42

WALLER, MARGUERITE.   Usurpation, seduction, and the problematics of the proper: a 'deconstructive', 'feminist' rereading of the seductions of Richard and Anne in Shakespeare's *Richard III*. 159–74

## Shakespeare and the Sense of Performance

**55.** THOMPSON, MARVIN; THOMPSON, RUTH (eds).   Shakespeare and the sense of performance: essays in the tradition of performance criticism in honor of Bernard Beckerman. Newark: Delaware UP; London; Toronto: Assoc. UPs. pp. 259. Rev. by Robert Hapgood in TLS, 25 Aug., 927.

BERRY, RALPH.   Hamlet and the audience: the dynamics of a relationship. 24–8

BRAUNMULLER, A. R.   Editing the staging/staging the editing. 139–49

BROWN, JOHN RUSSELL.   The nature of speech in Shakespeare's plays. 48–59

CHARNEY, MAURICE.   Asides, soliloquies, and offstage speech in *Hamlet*: implications for staging. 116–31 (Revised version of conference paper, W. Berlin, 1986, pub. in Shakespeare Bulletin (4) 1986, 5–8.)

CLAYTON, THOMAS.   'Balancing at work': (r)evoking the script in performance and criticism. 228–49

DESSEN, ALAN C.   Much virtue in *as*: Elizabethan stage locales and modern interpretation. 132–8

EWBANK, INGA-STINA.   From narrative to dramatic language: *The Winter's Tale* and its source. 29–47

FOAKES, R. A.   Stage images in *Troilus and Cressida*. 150–61

GOLDMAN, MICHAEL.   Performer and role in Marlowe and Shakespeare. 91–102

GURR, ANDREW.   The 'state' of Shakespeare's audiences. 162–79

McGUIRE, PHILIP C.   Egeus and the implications of silence. 103–15

PEAT, DEREK.   Looking back to front: the view from the Lords' room. 180–94

RICHMOND, HUGH M.   Peter Quince directs *Romeo and Juliet*. 219–27

ROSENBERG, MARVIN.   Subtext in Shakespeare. 79–90

STYAN, J. L.   Stage space and the Shakespeare experience. 195–209

SWANDER, HOMER.   Shakespeare and Beckett: what the words know. 60–78

THOMPSON, MARVIN; THOMPSON, RUTH.   Performance criticism: from Granville-Barker to Bernard Beckerman and beyond. 13–23

WICKHAM, GLYNNE.   Reflections arising from recent productions of *Love's Labour's Lost* and *As You Like It*. 210–18

## Studies in Earlier Old English Prose

**56.**   SZARMACH, PAUL E. (ed.).   Studies in earlier Old English prose: sixteen original contributions. Albany: New York State UP, 1986. pp. vi, 420. Rev. by E. G. Stanley in MLR (84:4) 911–12.

BERKHOUT, CARL T.   Appendix: research on early Old English literary prose, 1973–82. 401–9

BOLTON, W. F.   How Boethian is Alfred's *Boethius*? 153–68

CLEMENT, RICHARD W.   The production of the *Pastoral Care*: King Alfred and his helpers. 129–52

CROSS, J. E.   The Latinity of the ninth-century Old English martyrologist. 275–99

FRY, DONALD K.   Bede fortunate in his translator: the Barking nuns. 345–62

GATCH, MILTON McC.   King Alfred's version of Augustine's *Soliloquia*: some suggestions on its rationale and unity. 17–45

HORGAN, DOROTHY M.   The Old English *Pastoral Care*: the scribal contribution. 108–27

KOTZOR, GÜNTER.   The Latin tradition of martyrologies and the *Old English Martyrology*. 301–33

LIGGINS, ELIZABETH M.   Syntax and style in the Old English *Orosius*. 245–73

MEANEY, AUDREY L.   St Neots, Æthelweard and the compilation of the *Anglo-Saxon Chronicle*: a survey. 193–243

MORRISH, JENNIFER.   King Alfred's letter as a source on learning in England in the ninth century. 87–107

RICHARDS, MARY P.   The manuscript contexts of the Old English laws: tradition and innovation. 171–92

ROBERTS, JANE.   The Old English prose translation of Felix's *Vita sancti Guthlaci*. 363–79

SZARMACH, PAUL E.   The earlier homily: *De parasceve*. 381–99

WATERHOUSE, RUTH.   Tone in Alfred's version of Augustine's *Soliloquies*. 47–85

YERKES, DAVID.   The translation of Gregory's *Dialogues* and its revision: textual history, provenance, authorship. 335–43

## Studies in Fantastic Fiction

**57.** ZGORZELSKI, ANDRZEJ (ed.).   Studies in fantastic fiction. Gdansk: Uniwersytet Gdánski, 1988. pp. 112. (Zeszyty naukowe wyzdialu humanistycznego filologia angielska, 8.)

CZEŻYK, MARIOLA.   Extratextual perspectives of two trilogies. 75–89

LUBICH-PYRZOWSKA, BARBARA.   Perspectives of semiotization in E. M. Forster's short stories in the light of genological and suprageno-logical categories. 7–18

MALCOLM, DAVID.   Two *Theys*: a comparison of the fantastic in two texts. 19–30

SZCZERBICKA, ANNA.   The child motif in the short stories of R. Bradbury. 31–74

WĄGROCKA, JADWIGA.   *The Whole Man*: autothematic use of fairy tale. 91–100

## Studies in Medieval English Romances: Some New Approaches

**58.** BREWER, DEREK (ed.).   Studies in medieval English romances: some new approaches. Cambridge: Brewer; Wolfeboro, NH: Boydell & Brewer, 1988. pp. v (unnumbered), 197. Rev. by Marcella McCarthy in NQ (36:4) 491–2.

BREWER, DEREK.  Escape from the mimetic fallacy. 1–10

BURTON, JULIE.  Folktale, romance and Shakespeare. 176–97

LUTTRELL, CLAUDE.  The folk-tale element in *Sir Gawain and the Green Knight*. 92–112

McCARTHY, TERENCE.  *Le Morte Darthur* and romance. 148–75

PEARSALL, DEREK.  The development of Middle English romance. 11–35

SCOTT, ANNE.  Plans, predictions, and promises: traditional story techniques and the configuration of word and deed in *King Horn*. 37–68

SHIPPEY, T. A.  Breton *lais* and modern fantasies. 69–91

WINDEATT, BARRY.  *Troilus* and the disenchantment of romance. 129–47

WRIGLEY, CHRISTOPHER.  *Sir Gawain and the Green Knight*: the underlying myth. 113–28

### The Sun is God: Painting, Literature and Mythology in the Nineteenth Century

**59.**  BULLEN, J. B. (ed.).  The sun is god: painting, literature and mythology in the nineteenth century. Oxford: Clarendon Press; New York: OUP. pp. viii, 230.

ANON.  Introduction. 1–11

ARMSTRONG, ISOBEL.  Tennyson's *The Lady of Shalott*: Victorian mythography and the politics of narcissism. 49–107

BEER, GILLIAN.  'The death of the sun': Victorian solar physics and solar myth. 159–80

BIRCH, DINAH.  'The sun is god': Ruskin's solar mythology. 109–23

BULLEN, J. B.  The gods in Wessex exile: Thomas Hardy and mythology. 181–98

BUTLER, MARILYN.  Romantic manichaeism: Shelley's *On the Devil, and Devils* and Byron's mythological dramas. 13–37

CONNOR, STEVEN.  Conclusion: myth and meta-myth in Max Müller and Walter Pater. 199–222

GAGE, JOHN.  J. M. W. Turner and solar myth. 39–48

MORGAN, THAÏS E.  The sun of faith, the shadow of doubt: language and knowledge in Swinburne's myth of Apollo. 125–58

### La violence dans la littérature et la pensée anglaises

**60.**  RIGAUD, NADIA (ed.).  La violence dans la littérature et la pensée anglaises. Aix-en-Provence: Univ. of Provence for Centre Aixois de Recherches Anglaises. pp. 176. (CARA, 10.)

ABITEBOUL, MAURICE.  Ferdinand dans *The Duchess of Malfi* de John Webster ou la violence en procès. 19–30

BUTLER, LANCE ST JOHN.   Failed violence in Victorian fiction. 97–110

DARRAGI, RAFIK.   Le spectacle: réflexions sur la violence et le théâtre jacobéen. 1–18

DENIZOT, PAUL.   Violence d'un idéal ou idéal, de la violence? Réflexions sur le *London Chronicle* de 1789. 47–64

DUPERRAY, MAX.   Enchaînements et dechaînements: la violence et la répétition dans *The White Hotel* (1981) de D. M. Thomas. 159–74

GARCES, JEAN-PIERRE.   Stryver, ou une autre expression de la violence dans *A Tale of Two Cities*. 85–96

LURBE, PIERRE.   Violence et sacrifice dans *Peter Grimes* de Benjamin Britten. 121–38

SOUPEL, SERGE.   Modalités de la violence dans *The Life and Strange Adventures of Robinson Crusoe of York, Mariner* (1719). 31–46

TOBOUL, DENISE.   Violence et irrationalité dans l'œuvre romanesque d'Angus Wilson. 139–58

### Writing the Female Voice: Essays on Epistolary Literature

**61.**   GOLDSMITH, ELIZABETH C. (ed.).   Writing the female voice: essays on epistolary literature. Boston, MA: Northeastern UP. pp. xiii, 296.

ANON.   Introduction. vii–xiii

BORINSKY, ALICIA.   No body there: on the politics of interlocution. 245–56

CARSON, JAMES.   Narrative cross-dressing and the critique of authorship in the novels of Richardson. 95–113

EPSTEIN, JULIA.   Fanny's fanny: epistolarity, eroticism, and the transsexual text. 135–53

KAUFFMAN, LINDA.   Special delivery: twenty-first-century epistolarity in *The Handmaid's Tale*. 221–44

SPACKS, PATRICIA MEYER.   Female resources: epistles, plot, and power. 63–76

WILLIAMS, CAROLYN.   'Trying to do without God': the revision of epistolary address in *The Color Purple*. 273–85

### Zborník filozofickej fakulty

**62.**   BÁZLIK, MIROSLAV (ed.).   Zborník filozofickej fakulty. (Papers of the Faculty of Philosophy.) Bratislava: Slovenské pedagogické nakladatel'stvo. pp. 148. (Universitas Comenia, philologica.)

BAŠTÍN, ŠTEFAN.   The comic vision of life in the fiction of Joseph Heller. 89–103

BÁZLIK, MIROSLAV.   A contrastive analysis of the Slovak prepositional constructions with the accusative and their English equivalents. 9–29

BÖHMEROVÁ, ADELA.   Contrastive analysis of some aspects of grammatical negation in English and in Slovak. 31–48

HUTTOVÁ, MÁRIA.   Hardy's Wessex tragedy or melodrama. 105–13

KUBIŠOVÁ, ALŽBETA.   Expressing time relations in English as a problem of Slovak learners. 49–59

OLEXA, JOSEF.   Romantic and realistic features in the composition of *Wuthering Heights.* 115–23

RUŽIČKOVA, EVA.   On verbs referring to a state of mind and feeling. 61–7

STANÍK, IVAN.   Norman Mailer as a radical and observer. 125–37

VACHEK, JOSEF.   Some remarks on English and Slovak vocalic systems: a chapter from comparative phonology of English and Slovak. 69–76

VILIKOVSKÝ, JÁN.   The context of literary translation. 139–47

# BIBLIOGRAPHY

## GENERAL

**63.** DRAUDT, MANFRED. The rationale of current bibliographical methods: printing house studies, computer-aided compositor studies, and the use of statistical methods. ShS (40) 1988, 145–53.

**64.** FRANK, FREDERICK S. Montague Summers: a bibliographical portrait. Metuchen, NJ; London: Scarecrow Press, 1988. pp. xviii, 277. (Great bibliographers, 7.)

**65.** FREDEMAN, WILLIAM E. Two uncollected bibliographers: Simon Harcourt Nowell-Smith and Michael Trevanion of Erewhon. BC (38:4) 465–82. ('Michael Trevanion' pseudonym of Nowell-Smith.)

**66.** McCANN, WESLEY. Bibliographical studies in Ulster: an historical survey. Linen Hall Review (6:1) 16–17.

**67.** McKENZIE, D. F. Bibliography and the sociology of texts. London: British Library, 1986. pp. x, 70. (Panizzi Lectures, 1985.) Rev. by Jerome McGann in LRB (10:4) 1988, 20–1; by Hugh Amory in BC (36:3) 1987, 411–18; by Clive Hurst in NQ (35:4) 1988, 505–6.

**68.** MYERS, ROBIN; HARRIS, MICHAEL (eds). Pioneers in bibliography. Winchester: St Paul's Bibliographies, 1988. pp. 117. Rev. by John Hewish in Library (11:3) 272–3.

**69.** STOKES, ROY. A bibliographical companion. Metuchen, NJ: Scarecrow Press. pp. x, 298. (Dictionary of bibliographical terms.)

## BINDING

**70.** AYTON, ANDREW. Domesday Book re-bound, c. 1346. NQ (36:3) 298–9.

**71.** BENNETT, BRUCE. Of books and covers: Peter Cowan. Overland (114) 58–62. (Sign systems in the cover designs on Peter Cowan's books.)

**72.** CARTER, JOHN. *Binding Variants* with *More Binding Variants in English Publishing 1820–1900.* Newcastle, DE: Oak Knoll Books. pp. 258, (plates) 14. Rev. by Frank Broomhead in Private Library (2:3) 186–8.

**73.** COLLINS, JOHN. A binding by John Partridge? in the Royal Hospital, Chelsea, 1687–88. BC (38:2) 229–31. (English and foreign bookbindings, 48.)

**74.** FOOT, MIRJAM M. An Irish binding by William McKenzie, 1784. BC (38:1) 66–7. (English and foreign bookbindings, 47.)

**75.** McDONNELL, JOSEPH; HEALY, PATRICK. Gold-tooled bookbindings commissioned by Trinity College Dublin in the eighteenth century. (Bibl. 1988, 40.) Rev. by David McKitterick in BC (38:1) 118–19; by Mirjam M. Foot in Library (11:3) 280–2.

**76.** MORRIS, JOHN. An Egyptian binding by Robert Hamilton, Edinburgh, 1820. BC (38:4) 514–15. (English and foreign bookbindings, 50.)

## BOOK ILLUSTRATION

For work on the illustrations, etc., of William Blake, see under
'Eighteenth Century Authors: William Blake'.

**77.** ALDERSON, BRIAN. Sing a song of sixpence: the English picture
book tradition and Randolph Caldecott. Cambridge; New York: CUP
in assn with British Library, 1986. pp. 112. (Catalogue of exhibition at
British Library, October 1986–January 1987.) Rev. by Charles Lillard
in CanL (118) 1988, 155.

**78.** BATH, MICHAEL. Collared stags and bridled lions: Queen
Elizabeth's household accounts. *In* (pp. 225–57) **21.**

**79.** BROSCH, RENATE. Vision und Illusion. Coleridges *The Rime of the
Ancient Mariner* von Doré illustriert. GRM (39) 41–57.

**80.** DALY, PETER M. England and the emblem: the cultural context of
English emblem books. *In* (pp. 1–60) **21.**

**81.** —— (ed.). The English emblem and the continental tradition.
*See* **21.**

**82.** —— DUER, LESLIE T.; RASPA, ANTHONY (eds). The English
emblem tradition: vol. 1, Jan van der Noot, *A Theatre for Worldlings*;
Paolo Giovio, *The Worthy Tract of Paulus Jovius*; Lodovico Domenici,
*Certain Noble Devises both Militarie and Amorous*; Geffrey Whitney, *A Choice
of Emblemes*. Toronto; London: Toronto UP, 1988. pp. xvi, 483. (Index
emblematicus.) Rev. by Jean Michel Massing in TLS, 21 July, 806.

**83.** DIEHL, HUSTON. An index of icons in English emblem books
1500–1700. Norman; London: Oklahoma UP, 1986. pp. xiv, 258. Rev.
by Karl Josef Höltgen in RES (39:153) 1988, 149–50, by Patricia
Demers in JRMMRA (8) 1987, 210–12; by William E. Engel in SQ
(39:2) 1988, 263–5.

**84.** DIMLER, G. RICHARD. Edmund Arwaker's translation of the *Pia
Desideria*: the reception of a continental Jesuit emblem book in
seventeenth-century England. *In* (pp. 203–24) **21.**

**85.** EDE, LISA S. Edward Lear's limericks and their illustrations. *In*
(pp. 103–16) **28.**

**86.** FLINT, KATE. Arthur Hughes as illustrator for children. *In*
(pp. 201–20) **14.**

**87.** FOX, CELINA. Graphic journalism in England during the 1830s
and 1840s. New York; London: Garland, 1988. pp. 343, (plates) 199.
(Outstanding theses in the fine arts from British universities.) (Cf. bibl.
1975, 1049.) Rev. by David McKitterick in BC (38:2) 264.

**88.** HAYMAN, DAVID. *Ulysses* and Motherwell: illustrating an affinity.
JJQ (26:4) 583–605.

**89.** HENRY, AVRIL (ed.). Biblia pauperum. Aldershot: Scolar Press;
Ithaca, NY: Cornell UP, 1987. pp. x, 178. (Facsim. of first ed., 1460?)
Rev. in BC (37:3) 1988, 326–7.

**90.** HODNETT, EDWARD. Five centuries of English book illustration.
(Bibl. 1988, 49.) Rev. by David McKitterick in BC (38:2) 262–4.

**91.** HORDEN, JOHN. Renaissance emblem books: a comment on
terminology. *In* (pp. 61–70) **37.**

**92.** LEATHLEAN, HOWARD.   Henry Noel Humphreys and the getting-up of books in the mid-nineteenth century. BC (38:2) 192–209.

**93.** LUBORSKY, RUTH SAMSON.   The illustrations to *The Shepheardes Calender*: II. Spenser Studies (9) 1988, 249–53.

**94.** MACCARTHY, FIONA.   Eric Gill. London: Faber & Faber. pp. xiii, 338. Rev. by Malcolm Yorke in Listener (121) 9 Feb., 25.

**95.** MANNING, JOHN.   Unpublished and unedited emblems by Geffrey Whitney: further evidence of the English adaptation of continental traditions. *In* (pp. 83–107) **21.**

**96.** MATHEWSON, STEPHEN.   Thomas Hart Benton's centennial, with attention to the Missouri regionalist's illustrations of Mark Twain's books. KQ (20:4) 1988, 23–48.

**97.** TIGGES, WIM (ed.).   Explorations in the field of nonsense. *See* **28.**

**98.** TUNG, MASON.   From personifications to emblems: a study of Peacham's use of Ripa's *Iconologia* in *Minerva Britanna*. *In* (pp. 109–50) **21.**

**99.** VAN LEEUWEN, HENDRIK.   The liaison of visual and written nonsense. *In* (pp. 61–95) **28.**

**100.** VINK, JAMES.   A concealed figure in the woodcut to the *Januarye Eclogue*. Spenser Studies (7) 1987, 297–8.

**101.** WARD, GERALD W. (ed.).   The American illustrated book in the nineteenth century. Charlottesville: Virginia UP for Henry Francis du Pont Winterthur Museum, 1987. pp. 273. (Proceedings of the four-teenth Annual North American Print Conference at Winterthur Museum, Winterthur, DE, 1982.) Rev. by David McKitterick in BC (38:2) 262–5.

**102.** WOOD, M.   Popular satire in early nineteenth-century radicalism, with special reference to Hone and Cruikshank. Unpub. doct. diss., Univ. of Oxford. [Abstr. in IT (39:3) 1114.]

**103.** WRIGHT, S. A.   The big Bible, Royal I.E. ix in the British Library and manuscript illumination in London in the early fifteenth century. Unpub. doct. diss., Univ. of London, 1986. [Abstr. in IT (36:1) 12.]

**104.** YOUNG, ALAN R.   The English tournament imprese. *In* (pp. 61–81) **21.**

**105.** —— Wenceslaus Hollar, the London book trade, and two un-identified English emblem books. *In* (pp. 151–202) **21.**

## BOOK PRODUCTION, PRINTING, AND TYPOGRAPHY

**106.** BARLOW, WILLIAM P., JR.   A Baskerville collection. BC (38:2) 171–91. (Contemporary collectors, 53.)

**107.** BOWMAN, J. H.   Robert Proctor's 'Otter' Greek type. TCBS (9:4) 381–98.

**108.** CLOONAN, MICHÈLE VALERIE.   Paper-covered books, from their first known use in 1482 to the introduction of cloth, *ca* 1825. Unpub. doct. diss., Univ. of Illinois at Urbana-Champaign, 1988. [Abstr. in DA (49) 2435A.]

**109.**  COLERIDGE, K. A.; CAVE, RODERICK.    Early printing in New Zealand: two papers. Wellington: Dept of Librarianship, Victoria Univ. of Wellington. pp. 33. (Occasional papers in bibliography and librarianship, 6.)

**110.**  FELTES, N. N.    Modes of production of Victorian novels. (Bibl. 1988, 65.) Rev. by John Sutherland in RES (39:154) 1988, 311–12.

**111.**  HUGHES, PETER.    'Sneers, jeers ... and red rantings': Bob Lowry's early printing at Auckland University College. TLR (22:1) 5–31.

**112.**  KELVIN, NORMAN.    Patterns in time: the decorative and the narrative in the work of William Morris. *In* (pp. 140–68) **44.**

**113.**  McATEER, E.    Typeface effects in written language: functions of typeface change for signalling meaning within a text. Unpub. doct. diss., Univ. of Glasgow. [Abstr. in IT (39:2) 481.]

**114.**  MOORE, J. K.    Copy and print in English books of the sixteenth and seventeenth centuries. Unpub. doct. diss., Univ. of Oxford. [Abstr. in IT (39:3) 1104.]

**115.**  MOSLEY, JAMES.    British type specimens before 1831: a hand-list. (Bibl. 1987, 123.) Rev. by Paul S. Koda in AEB (ns 1:4) 1987, 249–50.

**116.**  MYERS, ROBIN; HARRIS, MICHAEL (eds).    Aspects of printing from 1600. Oxford: Oxford Polytechnic Press, 1987. pp. xii, 174. (Publishing pathways.)

**117.**  SLIGHTS, WILLIAM W. E.    The edifying margins of Renaissance English books. RQ (42:4) 682–716.

**118.**  TRIBBLE, EVELYN BYRD.    Margins and marginality: some uses of printed page in early modern England. Unpub. doct. diss., Univ. of California, Berkeley, 1988. [Abstr. in DA (50) 1316A.]

**119.**  WOOLLEY, BENJAMIN.    Printed matters. Listener (122) 20 July, 13. (Desktop publishing.)

# MANUSCRIPTS

**120.**  ALLEN, ROSAMUND.    The date and provenance of *King Horn*: some interim reassessments. *In* (pp. 99–125) **41.**

**121.**  ANON.    Katherine Mansfield manuscripts in the Alexander Turnbull Library. Wellington: Alexander Turnbull Library, 1988. pp. xii, 136.

**122.**  —— (ed.).    British literary manuscripts from the Bodleian Library, Oxford: series 1, The English Renaissance, *c.* 1500–*c.* 1700: an inventory to part 1 of the Harvester microform collection. Brighton: Harvester Microform, 1988. pp. x, 34. (Britain's literary heritage.)

**123.**  —— (ed.).    Catalogue of manuscripts in the Houghton Library, Harvard University. Alexandria, VA: Chadwyck-Healey, 1986/87. 8 vols, 359 microfiche: vol. 1, pp. viii, 464; vols 2–7 pp. vi, 464, vol. 8, pp. vi, 454. Rev. by J. P. Hudson in Library (11:2) 166–9.

**124.**  BOFFEY, JULIA.    Manuscripts of English courtly love lyrics in the later Middle Ages. (Bibl. 1988, 86.) Rev. by A. S. G. Edwards in Spec

(64:1) 125-7; by Carol J. Harvey in JRMMRA (10) 99-100; by O. S. Pickering in Archiv (226:1) 99-106.

**125.** BROWN, MICHELLE B.    A new fragment of a ninth-century English Bible. ASE (18) 33-43.

**126.** CHAUDHURI, SUKANTA.    Marlowe, madrigals, and a new Elizabethan poet. RES (39:154) 1988, 199-216.

**127.** CHOPRA, VISHNU R.    From manuscript to print: Stephen Leacock's *The Transit of Venus*. CanL (121) 42-53.

**128.** CLARK, JOHN P. H.; TAYLOR, CHERYL (eds).    Walter Hilton's Latin writings. Salzburg: Institut für Anglistik und Amerikanistik, Salzburg Univ., 1987. 2 vols. pp. vi, 479. (Analecta cartusiana, 124.) Rev. by Siegfried Wenzel in Spec (64:4) 969-71.

**129.** CRICK, J. C.    The reception of Geoffrey of Monmouth's *Historia regum britannie*: the evidence of manuscripts and textual history. Unpub. doct. diss., Univ. of Cambridge. [Abstr. in IT (39:2) 499.]

**130.** CRICK, JULIA C.    The *Historia regum britannie* of Geoffrey of Monmouth: 3, A summary catalogue of the manuscripts. Woodbridge; Wolfeboro, NH: Boydell & Brewer. pp. xxii, 378.

**131.** CROSS, J. E.    The Latinity of the ninth-century Old English martyrologist. *In* (pp. 275-99) **56.**

**132.** DAHOOD, ROGER.    The use of coloured initials and other division markers in early versions of the *Ancrene Riwle*. *In* (pp. 79-97) **41.**

**133.** DEBUSSCHER, GILBERT.    Tennessee Williams's Black Nativity: an unpublished libretto. *In* (pp. 127-33) **2.**

**134.** DOYLE, A. I. (introd.).    The Vernon Manuscript: a facsimile of Bodleian Library, Oxford, MS Eng. Poet.a.1. (Bibl. 1988, 96.) Rev. by Manfred Görlach in Ang (107:3/4) 520-3; by Richard Beadle in TLS, 13 Jan., 46.

**135.** ECKHARDT, CAROLINE D.    Geoffrey of Monmouth's *Prophetia Merlini* and the construction of Liège University MS 369c. Manuscripta (32:3) 1988, 76-84.

**136.** FEIN, SUSANNA GREER.    *Haue Mercy of Me* (Psalm 51): an unedited alliterative poem from the London Thornton manuscript. MP (86:3) 223-41.

**137.** FISHER, JOHN H.    *Piers Plowman* and the Chancery tradition. *In* (pp. 267-78) **41.**

**138.** GLASSCOE, MARION.    Visions and revisions: a further look at the manuscripts of Julian of Norwich. SB (42) 103-20.

**139.** GREEN, RICHARD FIRTH.    The lost exemplar of the Z-text of *Piers Plowman* and its 20-line pages. MÆ (56:2) 1987, 307-10.

**140.** HANNA, RALPH, III.    The scribe of Huntington HM 114. SB (42) 120-33.

**141.** HARTZELL, K. D.    An eleventh-century English missal fragment in the British Library. ASE (18) 45-97.

**142.** HOAD, LINDA (ed.).    Literary manuscripts at the National Library of Canada. Ottawa: National Library of Canada, 1984. pp. 35. Rev. by Helen Hoy in CanL (116) 1988, 204-5.

**143.** HORGAN, DOROTHY M. The Old English *Pastoral Care*: the scribal contribution. *In* (pp. 108–27) **56.**

**144.** HOWARD-HILL, T. H. Buc and the censorship of *Sir John Van Olden Barnavelt* in 1619. RES (39:153) 1988, 39–63.

**145.** HUNT, TONY. The trilingual glossary in MS London, BL Sloane 146 ff.69$^v$–72$^r$. EngS (70:4) 289–310.

**146.** JACOBS, NICOLAS. Some creative misreadings in *Le Bone Florence of Rome*: an experiment in textual criticism. *In* (pp. 279–84) **41.**

**147.** JONES, CLYVE. The Harley family and the Harley papers. BLJ (15:2) 123–33.

**148.** JUMP, HARRIET. Two new Akenside manuscripts. RES (39:154) 1988, 217–30.

**149.** KANE, GEORGE (ed.). *Piers Plowman*: the A version, Will's visions of Piers Plowman and Do-Well: an edition in the form of Trinity College Cambridge MS R.3.14, corrected from other manuscripts, with variant readings. (Bibl. 1964, 2288.) London: Athlone Press; Berkeley: California UP, 1988. pp. ix, 461. (Revised ed.: first ed. 1960.) Rev. by E. G. Stanley in NQ (36:3) 363–6.

**150.** —— DONALDSON, E. TALBOT (eds). *Piers Plowman*: the B version, Will's visions of Piers Plowman, Do-Well, Do-Better, and Do-Best: an edition in the form of Trinity College Cambridge MS B.15.17, corrected and restored from the known evidence, with variant readings. (Bibl. 1979, 3755.) London: Athlone Press; Berkeley, California UP, 1988. pp. vii, 681. (Revised ed.: first ed. 1975.) Rev. by E. G. Stanley in NQ (36:3) 363–6.

**151.** KINNEY, DANIEL. Rewriting Thomas More: a devotional anthology. Manuscripta (33:1) 29–35. (Cambridge University Library MS Dd. xii. 41.)

**152.** LISZKA, THOMAS R. MS Laud misc. 108 and the early history of the *South English Legendary*. Manuscripta (33:2) 75–91.

**153.** LOVE, HAROLD. Scribal texts and literary communities: the Rochester circle and Osborn b.105. SB (42) 219–35. (*Poems on Several Occasions*.)

**154.** McGOLDRICH, L. The literary manuscripts and literary patronage of the Beauchamp and Neville families in the late Middle Ages, *c.* 1390–1500. Unpub. doct. diss., CNAA, 1985. [Abstr. in IT (36:2) 483.]

**155.** MARX, C. WILLIAM; DRENNAN, JEANNE F. (eds). The Middle English prose *Complaint of Our Lady* and *Gospel of Nicodemus*, ed. from Cambridge, Magdalene College, MS Pepys 2498. Heidelberg: Winter, 1987. pp. 232. (Middle English texts, 19.) Rev. by Klaus Bitterling in Ang (107:3/4) 526–8.

**156.** MEANEY, AUDREY L. St Neots, Æthelweard and the compilation of the *Anglo-Saxon Chronicle*: a survey. *In* (pp. 193–243) **56.**

**157.** MINNIS, A. J. (ed.). Latin and vernacular: studies in late-medieval texts and manuscripts. Cambridge: Brewer; Wolfeboro, NH: Boydell & Brewer. pp. vii, 155. (York manuscripts conferences: proceedings, 1.)

**157a.** MODERT, JO.  Here for the first time, a Jane Austen letter, Persuasions (6) 1984, 18–20.

**158.** MOFFAT, DOUGLAS (ed.).  *The Soul's Address to the Body* (the Worcester fragments). East Lansing, MI: Colleagues Press, 1987. pp. viii, 136. Rev. by E. G. Stanley in YLS (1) 1987, 150–2.

**159.** OGILVIE-THOMSON, S. J. (eds).  Richard Rolle: prose and verse, ed. from MS Longleat 29 and related manuscripts. Oxford: OUP, 1988. pp. xcvi, 273. (EETS, 293.)

**160.** PÄCHT, OTTO.  Book illumination in the Middle Ages: an introduction. (Bibl. 1988, 124.) Rev. by Walter Cahn in Spec (64:3) 750–1.

**161.** PICKERING, O. S.  The present popularity of Middle English manuscript studies: some recent work reviewed. Archiv (226:1) 99–106.

**162.** RICHARDS, MARY P.  The manuscript contexts of the Old English laws: tradition and innovation. *In* (pp. 171–92) **56.**

**163.** RICKS, CHRISTOPHER; DAY, AIDAN (eds).  Tennyson: the manuscripts and proofs at the Tennyson Research Centre: Lincoln M1–M37, N12, P7–P38. New York; London: Garland. pp. xi, 302. (Tennyson archive, 16.)

**164.** ―――― Tennyson: the manuscripts and proofs at the Tennyson Research Centre: Lincoln P85++–P109. New York; London: Garland. pp. xi, 306. (Tennyson archive, 17.)

**165.** ―――― Tennyson: the manuscripts and proofs at the Tennyson Research Centre: Lincoln P109–P179. New York; London: Garland. pp. xi, 318. (Tennyson archive, 18.)

**166.** ―――― Tennyson: the manuscripts and proofs at the Tennyson Research Centre: Lincoln P179–P194. New York; London: Garland. pp. xi, 311. (Tennyson archive, 19.)

**167.** ―――― Tennyson: the manuscripts and proofs at the Tennyson Research Centre: Lincoln P194–P205. New York; London: Garland. pp. xi, 294. (Tennyson archive, 20.)

**168.** ―――― Tennyson: the manuscripts and proofs at the Tennyson Research Centre: Lincoln P205–P210++. New York; London: Garland. pp. xi, 303. (Tennyson archive, 21.)

**169.** ―――― Tennyson: the manuscripts and proofs at the Tennyson Research Centre: Lincoln P213–P216. New York; London: Garland. pp. xi, 324. (Tennyson archive, 22.)

**170.** ―――― Tennyson: the manuscripts and proofs at the Tennyson Research Centre: Lincoln P217 and miscellaneous poems. New York; London: Garland. pp. xi, 289. (Tennyson archive, 23.)

**171.** ―――― Tennyson: the manuscripts at Trinity College, Cambridge: loose papers, *In Memoriam* (notebook 13) and notebooks 14–17. New York; London: Garland, 1988. pp. xiv, 304. (Tennyson archive, 11.)

**172.** ―――― Tennyson: the manuscripts at Trinity College Cambridge: notebooks 18–25. New York; London: Garland, 1988. pp. xi, 348. (Tennyson archive, 12.)

**173.** —————— Tennyson: the manuscripts at Trinity College Cambridge: notebooks 26–29. New York; London: Garland, 1988. pp. xi, 321. (Tennyson archive, 13.)

**174.** ————— ————— Tennyson: the manuscripts at Trinity College Cambridge: notebooks 30–36. New York; London: Garland, 1988. pp. ix, 411. (Tennyson archive, 14.)

**175.** —————— Tennyson: the manuscripts at Trinity College Cambridge: notebooks 37–40 and loose papers O.15.42, O.15.42(A), Add. MS a.187(16) and R.7.50. New York; London: Garland, 1988. pp. xi, 344. (Tennyson archive, 15.)

**176.** SCATTERGOOD, JOHN.   Two unrecorded poems from Trinity College Dublin MS 490. RES (38:149) 1987, 46–9.

**177.** SCHERF, KATHLEEN.   Three new poems by Malcolm Lowry. CanL (121) 55–8.

**178.** SMITH, MARGARET M.; BOUMELHA, PENNY.   Index of English literary manuscripts: vol. 3, 1700–1800, part I, Addison–Fielding. (Bibl. 1987, 196.) Rev. by Ian Jack in RES (39:153) 1988, 151–2.

**179.** STREITBERGER, W. R.   Edmond Tyllney, Master of the Revels and censor of plays: a descriptive index to his diplomatic manual on Europe. New York: AMS Press, 1986. pp. xiv, 146. (AMS studies in the Renaissance, 15.) Rev. by N. W. Bawcutt in RES (39:154) 1988, 288–9; by E. A. J. Honigmann in YES (19) 313–14.

**180.** TAYLOR, GARY.   William Shakespeare, Richard James and the House of Cobham. RES (38:151) 1987, 334–54.

**181.** THOMPSON, JOHN J.   Robert Thornton and the London Thornton manuscript: British Library MS Additional 31042. Cambridge: Brewer; Wolfeboro, NH: Boydell & Brewer. pp. xiii, 84, (plates) 56. (Manuscript studies, 2.) Rev. by Richard Beadle in TLS, 13 Jan., 46.

**182.** THORP, NIGEL.   The glory of the page: medieval and Renaissance illuminated manuscripts from Glasgow University Library. London: Harvey Miller for Glasgow Univ. Library and the Art Gallery of Ontario, 1987. pp. 228. Rev. in BC (37:3) 1988, 325–6.

**183.** TOKOO, TATSUO (ed.).   Percy Bysshe Shelley: vol. 8, Bodleian MS Shelley d.3: a facsimile edition with full transcription and textual notes. New York; London: Garland, 1988. pp. xxx, 203. (Bodleian Shelley manuscripts.)

**184.** VOSS, MANFRED.   Quinns Edition der kleineren Cleopatraglossare: Corrigenda und Addenda. AAA (14:2) 127–40. (British Library MS Cotton Cleopatra A.III.)

**185.** WALDRON, RONALD.   Trevisa's original prefaces on translation: a critical edition. *In* (pp. 285–99) **41.**

**186.** WEBBER, M. T. J.   A study of the books of Salisbury Cathedral and of the scribal activities, studies and interests of the canons in the late eleventh and early twelfth centuries. Unpub. doct. diss., Univ. of Oxford, 1988. [Abstr. in IT (39:2) 500.]

**187.** WILSON, EDWARD.   The debate of the carpenter's tools. RES (38:152) 1987, 445–70. (Bodleian Library MS Ashmole 61.)

**188.** WRIGHT, S. A.   The big Bible, Royal I.E. ix in the British Library and manuscript illumination in London in the early fifteenth century. *See* **103.**

**189.** WRIGHT, STEPHEN K.   The manuscript of *Sanctus Tewdricus*: rediscovery of a 'lost miracle play' from St Omers. SB (42) 236–45.

**190.** YERKES, DAVID.   The translation of Gregory's *Dialogues* and its revision: textual history, provenance, authorship. *In* (pp. 335–43) **56.**

# COLLECTING AND THE LIBRARY

**191.** AHEARN, ALLEN.   Book collecting: a comprehensive guide. New York: Putnam. pp. 20. Rev. by Michael M. Thomas in BkW 12 Nov., 6.

**192.** ALDERSON, BRIAN.   Collecting children's books: self-indulgence and scholarship. *In* (pp. 7–17) **14.**

**193.** ANON. (comp.).   Chuo daigaku toshokan Hardu collection kaidai mokuroku. (A descriptive catalogue of the Hardy collection in Chuo University Library.) Tokyo: Chuo Univ. Library, 1988. pp. viii, 288,

**194.** —— Katherine Mansfield manuscripts in the Alexander Turnbull Library. *See* **121.**

**195.** —— (ed.).   Catalogue of manuscripts in the Houghton Library, Harvard University. *See* **123.**

**196.** BANDRY, ANNE.   First reactions to *Tristram Shandy* in the Oates Collection. Shandean (1) 27–52. (Cambridge University Library.)

**197.** BARKER, NICOLAS.   The library catalogue of Laurence Sterne. Shandean (1) 9–24.

**198.** BARLOW, WILLIAM P., JR.   A Baskerville collection. *See* **106.**

**199.** BELL, ALAN.   The Edinburgh tercentennial: founded 1689, still going strong . . . . BC (38:4) 445–63. (Advocates' Library, Edinburgh.)

**200.** BELL, OLIVIA; BELL, ALAN.   Children's manuscript magazines in the Bodleian Library. *In* (pp. 399–412) **14.**

**201.** BIRRELL, T. A.   English monarchs and their books: from Henry VII to Charles II. London: British Library, 1987. pp. x, 65. (Panizzi lectures, 1986.) Rev. by Julian Roberts in Library History (8:2) 1988, 47–8.

**202.** —— The printed books of Dame Margaret Nicollson: a pre-Reformation collection. *In* (pp. 27–33) **23.**

**203.** BLEIER, CAROL.   The Pierpont Morgan Library: changing of the guard. WLB (62:8) 1988, 41–4.

**204.** BRODSKY, LOUIS DANIEL; HAMBLIN, ROBERT W. (eds).   Faulkner: a comprehensive guide to the Brodsky Collection: vol. 2, The letters. (Bibl. 1985, 170.) Rev. by Calvin S. Brown in SewR (94:1) 1986, 167–80.

**205.** —————— Faulkner: a comprehensive guide to the Brodsky Collection: vol. 3, *The De Gaulle Story*. (Bibl. 1987, 215.) Rev. by Calvin S. Brown in SewR (94:1) 1986, 167–80.

**206.** BURDETTE, LIVIA.   The Hillier Shakespeare Collection: origin, scope and prospects. Shakespeare in Southern Africa (1) 1987, 62–4. (The Hillier Collection in Durban Municipal Library.)

**207.** BUSH, SARGENT, JR; RASMUSSEN, CARL J. The library of Emmanuel College, Cambridge, 1584–1637. (Bibl. 1988, 139.) Rev. by Francis J. Bremer in EAL (24:1) 77–9.

**208.** CAIRNS, EDITH M. Catalogue of the collection of children's books, 1617–1939, in the library of the University of Reading. Reading: Univ. Library, 1988. pp. xii, 265. (Reading Univ. Library pubs, 5.) Rev. by Clive Hurst in BC (38:2) 261–2.

**209.** CAMPBELL, LOUISE; STEER, FRANCIS. A catalogue of manuscripts in the College of Arms' collections: vol. I. Introd. by SIR ANTHONY WAGNER. London: College of Arms, 1988. pp. xxvii, 614. Rev. by Ann Payne in TLS, 14 Apr., 400.

**210.** CARLEY, JAMES P. John Leland and the contents of the English pre-Dissolution libraries. TCBS (9:4) 330–57.

**211.** CLEMENT, RICHARD W. Short-title catalogue of the Clubb Anglo-Saxon Collection. OEN (21:2) 1988 (Appendix B) B1–B24.

**212.** CONNOLLY, JOSEPH. Children's modern first editions: their value to collectors. London: MacDonald Orbis, 1988. pp. 336. Rev. by Patricia Craig in LRB (11:11) 26–7.

**213.** COOMBS, DOUGLAS. Spreading the word: the library work of the British Council. London; New York: Mansell, 1988. pp. xi, 298. (Information adviser.) Rev. by D. J. Foskett in Journal of Librarianship (21:1) 1988, 70–6.

**214.** DAY, J. C. Library provision in nineteenth century Northumberland. Unpub. M.Phil. diss., Univ. of Strathclyde, 1987. [Abstr. in IT (38:4) 1432.]

**215.** DAY, W. G. The Oates Collection, Cambridge University Library. Shandean (1) 25–6. (Of Sterne.)

**216.** DUTSCHKE, C. W., *et al.* Guide to medieval and Renaissance manuscripts in the Huntington Library. San Marino, CA: Huntington Library. 2 vols. pp. 886. Rev. by Andrew G. Watson in TLS, 24 Nov., 1307.

**217.** —— ROUSE, R. H.; FERRARI, M. Medieval and Renaissance manuscripts in the Claremont libraries. (Bibl. 1987, 227.) Rev. by Georges Dogaer in Quaerendo (18:1) 1988, 76–7.

**218.** EDEL, LEON; TINTNER, ADELINE R. (eds). The library of Henry James. Ann Arbor, MI: UMI Research Press, 1987. pp. 106. (Studies in modern literature, 90.) Rev. by P. N. Furbank in TLS, 25 Mar. 1988, 335–6.

**219.** ELLIS, A. C. O. School libraries and the Cross Commission. LAR (90:1) 1988, 33–5.

**220.** FARNIE, D. A. Enriqueta Augustina Rylands (1843–1908), founder of the John Rylands Library. BJRL (71:2) 3–38.

**221.** FIELD, CLIVE D. Sources for the study of Protestant nonconformity in the John Rylands University Library of Manchester. BJRL (71:2) 103–39.

**222.** FINCH, JEREMIAH J. A catalogue of the libraries of Sir Thomas Browne and Dr Edward Browne, his son. Leiden: Brill; Leiden UP,

1986. pp. xiv, 177. (Pubs of the Sir Thomas Browne Institute, ns 7.) Rev. by Giles Mandelbrote in BC (37:2) 1988, 279–81.

**223.** FREEMAN, ARTHUR.   William Street, 1746, revisited: thirty-two new books from the library of Jonathan Swift. BC (38:1) 68–78.

**224.** FUGGLES, J. F.   The Librarians of the National Trust. Library Review (37:1) 1988, 35–9.

**225.** GILLESPIE, MICHAEL PATRICK; STOCKER, ERIK BRADFORD. James Joyce's Trieste library: a catalogue of materials at the Harry Ransom Humanities Research Center, the University of Texas at Austin. (Bibl. 1987, 234.) Rev. by J. C. C. Mays in RES (39:156) 1988, 589.

**226.** GLENN, JOHN; WALSH, DAVID.   Catalogue of the Francis Trigge chained library, St Wulfram's Church, Grantham. Wolfeboro, NH: Woodbridge: Boydell & Brewer, 1988. pp. vii, 82. Rev. by John Goldfinch in Library (11:4) 367–9; by David McKitterick in BC (38:3) 309–10.

**227.** GRAY, JOHN.   Independent libraries: survivors look to the future. Linen Hall Review (6:2) 12–13.

**228.** GRENVILLE, KATE.   From *The Getting of Wisdom* to *Illywhacker*: the library and our literary heritage. Australian Library Journal (13:8) 55–69.

**229.** HAMMERMAN, HARLEY J.   On collecting O'Neill. EOR (13:1) 47–54.

**230.** HERGENHAN, LAURIE.   The C. Hartley Grattan manuscript collection: a critical introduction. LCUT (42/43) 1988, 51–75. (Collection at Univ. of Texas at Austin.)

**231.** HIBBERD, DOMINIC.   A donation to the Wilfred Owen collection at Oxford. NQ (36:2) 197–8.

**232.** HOAD, LINDA (ed.).   Literary manuscripts at the National Library of Canada. *See* **142.**

**233.** HODGSON, JOHN.   A Gaskell collection at Canterbury. Gaskell Society Journal (3) 42–5.

**234.** HUMPHREYS, K. W.   A national library in theory and in practice. London: British Library, 1988. pp. x, 86. (Panizzi Lectures, 1987.) Rev. by B. J. Enright in Library (11:4) 375–8.

**235.** HURST, CLIVE.   Selections from the accession diaries of Peter Opie. *In* (pp. 19–44) **14.**

**236.** JAMKHANDI, SUDHAKAR R.   Australian literary publications in the C. Hartley Grattan collection. LCUT (42/43) 1988, 39–49. (Collection at Univ. of Texas at Austin.)

**237.** JONES, CLYVE.   The Harley family and the Harley papers. *See* **147.**

**238.** KANEVSKII, B. P.   Britanskaya biblioteka. (The British Library.) Moscow: All-Union Bibliophiles' Soc., 1987. pp. 47.

**239.** KEELING, DENIS F. (ed.).   British library history: bibliography, 1981–1984. London: Library Assn, 1987. pp. 190. Rev. by Donald G. Davis, Jr, in Library History (8:1) 1988, 17–19.

**240.** KELLEY, PHILIP; COLEY, BETTY A. The Browning collections: a reconstruction with other memorabilia. (Bibl. 1987, 245.) Rev. by John Maynard in AEB (ns 1:4) 1987, 259–64.

**241.** KER, N. R. Books, collectors and libraries: studies in the medieval heritage. Ed. by ANDREW G. WATSON. (Bibl. 1987, 246.) Rev. by S. J. Ogilvie-Thomson in RES (38:150) 1987, 235–6.

**242.** KIESSLING, NICOLAS K. The library of Robert Burton. (Bibl. 1988, 156, where scholar's forename misspelt.) Rev. by David McKitterick in BC (38:3) 307–8; by Robin Robbins in BC (38:4) 550–1; by James McConica in LRB (11:5) 14–15.

**243.** LEFANU, WILLIAM. A catalogue of books belonging to Dr Jonathan Swift: a facsimile of Swift's autograph with introduction and alphabetic catalogue. Cambridge: Cambridge Univ. Library, 1988. pp. vii, 70. (Cambridge Bibliographical Soc. monographs, 10.) Rev. by M. J. Jannetta in Library (11:3) 279–80.

**244.** LISTER, ANTHONY. The Althorp library of second Earl Spencer, now in the John Rylands Library of Manchester: its formation and growth. BJRL (71:2) 67–86.

**245.** LOUGHNEY, KATHARINE. Shakespeare on film at the Library of Congress. SFN (14:1) 4, 6.

**246.** McDONNELL, J. M. William Pickering (1796–1854): antiquarian bookseller, publisher and book designer: a study in the early nineteenth-century book trade. Unpub. doct. diss., CNAA, 1985. [Abstr. in IT (36:2) 451.]

**247.** McKITTERICK, DAVID. Balancing the record. BC (38:3) 301–20 (review-article). (Catalogues of small libraries.)

**248.** —— Cambridge University Library: a history: vol. 2, The eighteenth and nineteenth centuries. Cambridge: CUP, 1986. pp. xviii, 812. Rev. in BC (36:1) 1987, 9–20; by P. A. Hoare in Library History (7:5) 1987, 163–7; by Kenneth Humphreys in Library (9:4) 1987, 402–5; by David Vaisey in TLS, 26 Feb. 1988, 228.

**249.** McLAREN, JOHN. Iris Milutinovic – between two worlds. LCUT (42/43) 1988, 143–59.

**250.** MARRS, SUZANNE. The Welty collection: a guide to the Eudora Welty manuscripts and documents at the Mississippi Department of Archives and History. Jackson; London: Mississippi UP, 1988. pp. viii, 245.

**251.** MEREDITH, MICHAEL (ed.). Meeting the Brownings. New York: Armstrong Browning Library of Baylor Univ., 1986. pp. 128. (Catalogue of exhibition in Winfield, KS, 1986.) Rev. by Margaret Smith in RES (39:154) 1988, 315.

**252.** MOORE, J.; TENER, J.; STEELE, A. (eds). The Alice Munro papers: first accession. Calgary, Alta: Calgary UP, 1986. pp. xxxv, 211. (Canadian archival inventory: Literary papers, 7.) Rev. by Helen Hoy in CanL (116) 1988, 203–4.

**253.** MORGAN, PAUL. Frances Wolfreston and 'hor bouks': a seventeenth-century woman book-collector. Library (11:3) 197–219.

**254.** MOSS, WILLIAM. Confederate broadside poems: an annotated descriptive bibliography based on the collection of the Z. Smith Reynolds Library of Wake Forest University. Westport, CT; London: Meckler, 1988. pp. xii, 173. (Literary bibliographies from Meckler Corporation.)

**255.** PARKS, STEPHEN. The Elizabethan Club of Yale University and its library. Introd. by ALAN BELL. New Haven, CT; London: Yale UP, 1986. pp. 280. (Elizabethan Club, 8.) Rev. by T. A. Birrell in EngS (70:2) 170–2.

**256.** POWELL, DAVID. The John Clare collection in Northampton Public Library. JCSJ (8) 37–43.

**257.** POYAS, FRANK B. C. Hartley Grattan: the man and the collection. LCUT (42/43) 1988, 11–37. (Collection at Univ. of Texas at Austin.)

**258.** RASTELLI, LUCY GORDON. People don't come here to read best-sellers: the Vatican Library. WLB (63:6) 47–50.

**259.** REIZBAUM, MARILYN. Zurich James Joyce Foundation. JJQ (26:2) 284–6.

**260.** RILEY, DAVID W. English books of the seventeenth to nineteenth centuries in the John Rylands University Library of Manchester, with particular reference to history and literature. BJRL (71:2) 87–102.

**261.** RITCHIE, NEIL. Collecting Sitwelliana. Private Library (2:3) 178–85.

**262.** ST CLAIR, GUY. Their hidden glories: England's cathedral libraries. WLB (63:5) 65–71.

**263.** SCHILLER, JUSTIN G. One collector's progress. BkW, 14 May, 1, 22. (Collecting children's literature.)

**264.** SHERBO, ARTHUR. Dean Thomas Gaisford's copy of Robert Dodsley's *Collection of Poems* (1758). MP (86:1) 1988, 53–5.

**265.** SHERCLIFF, W. H. Morality to adventure: Manchester Polytechnic's collection of children's books 1840–1939. Manchester: Manchester Polytechnic Library in assn with Bracken Books and Studio Editions, 1988. pp. viii, 203, (plates) 7. Rev. by Clive Hurst in BC (38:2) 261–2, by Patricia Craig in LRB (11:11) 26–7; by John Barr in Library (11:3) 286–7.

**266.** SIMSOVA, SILVA. Librarians as readers: bibliopsychological studies 1966–1984. London: Data Help, 1987. pp. 100 + 1 fiche + disk. Rev. by David P. Fisher in Journal of Librarianship (20:4) 1988, 304–7.

**267.** SULLIVAN, ERNEST W., II; MURRAH, DAVID J. (eds). The Donne Dalhousie discovery: proceedings of a symposium on the acquisition and study of the John Donne and Joseph Conrad collections at Texas Tech University. Lubbock, TX: Friends of the Univ. Library/ Southwest collection, 1987. pp. vii, 72. Rev. by Paul Parrish in SCN (47:1/2) 9.

**268.** TAYLOR, FRANK. The John Rylands Library, 1936–72. BJRL (71:2) 39–66.

**269.** TAYLOR, ROBERT N., *et al.* Lewis Carroll at Texas: the Warren Weaver Collection and related Dodgson materials at the Harry Ransom

Humanities Research Center. (Bibl. 1985, 251.) Rev. by Margaret Watson in NQ (35:1) 1988, 113–14.

**270.** TENER, J., *et al.* (eds). The Robert Kroetsch papers: first accession. Calgary, Alta: Calgary UP, 1986. pp. xlvii, 371. (Canadian archival inventory: literary papers, 3.) Rev. by Helen Hoy in CanL (116) 1988, 204–5.

**271.** THORP, NIGEL. The glory of the page: medieval and Renaissance illuminated manuscripts from Glasgow University Library. *See* **182.**

**272.** TUCK, JOHN P. Some sources for the history of popular culture in the John Rylands University Library of Manchester. BJRL (71:2) 159–80.

**273.** WARRINGTON, BERNARD. William Pickering, bookseller and book collector. BJRL (71:1) 121–38.

**274.** WEBBER, M. T. J. A study of the books of Salisbury Cathedral and of the scribal activities, studies and interests of the canons in the late eleventh and early twelfth centuries. *See* **186.**

**275.** WEBER, WILLIAM. Thomas Tudway and the Harleian collection of 'ancient' church music. BLJ (15:2) 187–205.

**276.** WICKHAM, D. E. The A. Edward Newton catalogues. Private Library (2:2) 82–92.

**277.** WOUDHUYSEN, H. R. Sir John Harington's printed books. TLS, 10 Nov., 1249.

**278.** ZELLER, ROBERT. 'I hope here be truths': R. G. Howarth as editor of Joseph Furphy. LCUT (42/43) 1988, 103–19. (Howarth Collection at HRHC.)

# TEXTUAL STUDIES

**279.** ADAMSON, C. A. Materials towards an edition of MS Shelley Adds.e.8. Unpub. doct. diss., Univ. of Oxford. [Abstr. in IT (39:3) 1109.]

**280.** ALLEN, ROSAMUND. The date and provenance of *King Horn*: some interim reassessments. *In* (pp. 99–125) **41.**

**281.** ARNGART, O. A commentary on *The Hunting of the Cheviot* text. EngS (70:6) 484–9. (Bodleian MS Ashmole 48.)

**282.** BARNETT, GERALD BRUCE. The representation of medieval English texts. Unpub. doct. diss., Univ. of Washington, 1988. [Abstr. in DA (50) 135A.]

**283.** BARR, H. A study of *Mum and the Sothsegger* in its political and literary contexts. Unpub. doct. diss., Univ. of Oxford. [Abstr. in IT (39:3) 1104.]

**284.** BAWCUTT, PRISCILLA. 'The copill': a crux in *The Kingis Quair*. RES (38:150) 1987, 211–14.

**285.** BOWERS, FREDSON. Regularization and normalization in modern critical texts. SB (42) 79–102.

**286.** BREWER, CHARLOTTE. The textual principles of Kane's A text. YLS (3) 67–90.

**287.** BROWN, D. E. The Scottish origin-legend before Fordun. Unpub. doct. diss., Univ. of Edinburgh. [Abstr. in IT (39:4) 1650.]

**288.** CABLE, THOMAS. Middle English meter and its theoretical implications. YLS (2) 1988, 47–69.

**289.** CHAUDHURI, SUKANTA. Marlowe, madrigals, and a new Elizabethan poet. *See* **126.**

**290.** CHOPRA, VISHNU R. From manuscript to print: Stephen Leacock's *The Transit of Venus. See* **127.**

**291.** CLARK, JOHN P. H.; TAYLOR, CHERYL (eds). Walter Hilton's Latin writings. *See* **128.**

**292.** CLAYTON, MARY. The Assumption homily in CCCC 41. NQ (36:3) 293–5.

**293.** CLEMENT, RICHARD W. The production of the *Pastoral Care*: King Alfred and his helpers. *In* (pp. 129–52) **56.**

**294.** COOPER, R. A.; PEARSALL, D. A. The *Gawain* poems: a statistical approach to the question of common authorship. RES (39:155) 1988, 365–85.

**295.** CRICK, J. C. The reception of Geoffrey of Monmouth's *Historia regum britannie*: the evidence of manuscripts and textual history. *See* **129.**

**296.** CROSS, J. E. The Latinity of the ninth-century Old English martyrologist. *In* (pp. 275–99) **56.**

**297.** CURETON, KEVIN K. Chaucer's revision of *Troilus and Criseyde*. SB (42) 153–84.

**298.** DAHOOD, ROGER. The use of coloured initials and other division markers in early versions of the *Ancrene Riwle*. *In* (pp. 79–97) **41.**

**299.** DALZIEL, P. A critical edition of Thomas Hardy's uncollected stories. Unpub. doct. diss., Univ. of Oxford. [Abstr. in IT (39:3) 1110–11.]

**300.** DEBUSSCHER, GILBERT. Tennessee Williams's Black Nativity: an unpublished libretto. *In* (pp. 127–33) **2.**

**301.** DE GRUSON, GENE (ed.). The lost first edition of Upton Sinclair's *The Jungle*. Atlanta, GA: St Luke's Press, 1988. pp. xxxi, 349. Rev. by David Roediger in MidQ (31:1) 138–9.

**302.** DIXON, PETER; BANCROFT, VICKY. Sheridan's second prologue to *The Rivals*: a case for emendation. NQ (36:4) 479–80.

**303.** DONNO, ELIZABETH STORY. Abraham Fleming: a learned corrector in 1586–87. SB (42) 200–11.

**304.** DUGGAN, HOYT N. Notes toward a theory of Langland's meter. YLS (1) 1987, 41–70.

**305.** DUNCAN, THOMAS G. The text and verse-form of 'Adam lay i-bowndyn'. RES (38:150) 1987, 215–21.

**306.** DU SAUTOY, PETER. Editing *Ulysses*: a personal account. JJQ (27:1) 69–76.

**307.** EDWARDS, A. S. G. Pynson's and Thynne's editions of Chaucer's *House of Fame*. SB (42) 185–6.

**308.** —— The text of Chaucer's *House of Fame*: editing and authority. PoetT (29/30) 80–92.

**309.** FEIN, SUSANNA GREER. *Haue Mercy of Me* (Psalm 51): an unedited alliterative poem from the London Thornton manuscript. *See* **136.**

**310.** FIELD, LESLIE. Thomas Wolfe and his editors: establishing a true text for the posthumous publications. (Bibl. 1988, 187.) Rev. by Frank W. Shelton in AL (61:1) 122–4; by Carol Johnston in SoCR (21:2) 85–6.

**311.** FINLKAYSON, JOHN. *The Simonie*: two authors? Archiv (226:1) 39–51.

**312.** —— Textual variants in Chaucer's *House of Fame*: Thynne as editor. EngS (70:5) 385–94.

**313.** FISHER, JOHN H. *Piers Plowman* and the Chancery tradition. *In* (pp. 267–78) **41.**

**314.** FLEISSNER, ROBERT F. Robert Frost stonewalls it again: the newly discovered variant lines. ELN (27:2) 57–61. ('Some May Know What They Seek in School and Church.')

**315.** GERRITSEN, JOHAN. Correction and erasure in the Vespasian Psalter Gloss. EngS (70:6) 477–83.

**316.** —— Emending *Beowulf* 2253 – some matters of principle. Neophilologus (73:3) 448–53.

**317.** GLASSCOE, MARION. Visions and revisions: a further look at the manuscripts of Julian of Norwich. *See* **138.**

**318.** GOTTFRIED, RUDOLF BRAND. *A View of the Present State of Ireland* by Edmund Spenser: the text of Bodleian MS Rawlinson B 478, edited with an introduction and notes. Unpub. doct. diss., Yale Univ., 1935. [Abstr. in DA (49) 1809A.]

**319.** GREETHAM, D. C. Textual and literary theory: redrawing the matrix. SB (42) 1–24.

**320.** HAYES, KEVIN J. Textual anomalies in the 1900 Doubleday, Page *Sister Carrie*. ALR (22:1) 53–68.

**321.** HENDRICK, GEORGE. Neopragmatism and convention in textual editing. AEB (ns 1:4) 1987, 225–6.

**322.** HIGDON, DAVID LEON. Conrad, *Under Western Eyes*, and the mysteries of revision. RES (39:154) 1988, 231–44.

**323.** HINDEN, MICHAEL. Missing lines in *Long Day's Journey into Night*. ModDr (32:2) 178–82.

**324.** HOLLAND, S. E. An edition of the *Admonitio ad claustrales* from Worcester Cathedral MS Q.51. Unpub. doct. diss., Univ. of Durham, 1988. [Abstr. in IT (38:4) 1438.]

**325.** HORDEN, JOHN: VANDER MOTTEN, J. P. *Five New Plays*: Sir William Killigrew's two annotated copies. Library (11:3) 253–71.

**326.** HORGAN, DOROTHY M. The Old English *Pastoral Care*: the scribal contribution. *In* (pp. 108–27) **56.**

**327.** HOUSUM, MARY ELIZABETH. A critical edition of Middle English *Sir Cleges*. Unpub. doct. diss., Catholic Univ. of America, 1988. [Abstr. in DA (49) 1797A.]

**328.** HOWARD-HILL, T. H. Buc and the censorship of *Sir John Van Olden Barnavelt* in 1619. *See* **144.**

**329.** —— Modern textual theories and the editing of plays. Library (11:2) 89–115.

**330.** Hoy, Helen. 'Rose and Janet': Alice Munro's metafiction. CanL (121) 59–83. (Versions of *Who Do You Think You Are?*.)

**331.** Hunt, Tony. The trilingual glossary in MS London, BL Sloane 146 ff. 69ᵛ–72ʳ. *See* **145.**

**332.** Jacobs, Nicolas. Some creative misreadings in *Le Bone Florence of Rome*: an experiment in textual criticism. *In* (pp. 279–84) **41.**

**333.** Johnston, A. F. (ed.). Editing early English drama: special problems and new directions. Papers given at the nineteenth Annual Conference on Editorial Problems, University of Toronto, 4–5 November 1983. New York: AMS Press, 1987. pp. 143. Rev. by Mary Erler in Library (11:2) 158–60.

**334.** Joyce, Steven James. Transformations and text: the rehearsal copies of George Bernard Shaw's *Buoyant Billions* in critical perspective. Unpub. doct. diss., Univ. of North Carolina at Chapel Hill, 1988. [Abstr. in DA (49) 2649A.]

**335.** Jump, Harriet. Two new Akenside manuscripts. *See* **148.**

**336.** Kain, Richard M. The case of the lost cyclist; or, What happened to Harry Thrift (*U*10.1259). JJQ (26:4) 607.

**337.** Kane, George (ed.). *Piers Plowman*: the A version, Will's visions of Piers Plowman and Do-Well: an edition in the form of Trinity College Cambridge MS R.3.14, corrected from other manuscripts, with variant readings. *See* **149.**

**338.** —— Donaldson, E. Talbot (eds). *Piers Plowman*: the B version, Will's visions of Piers Plowman, Do-Well, Do-Better, and Do-Best: an edition in the form of Trinity College Cambridge MS B.15.17, corrected and restored from the known evidence, with variant readings. *See* **150.**

**339.** King, Kathryn Rose. Studies toward a critical edition of Thomas Hardy's *Wessex Tales*. Unpub. doct. diss., Emory Univ., 1988. [Abstr. in DA (50) 147A.]

**340.** Kotzer, Günter. The Latin tradition of martyrologies and the *Old English Martyrology*. *In* (pp. 301–33) **56.**

**341.** Lass, Roger. Cyn(e)wulf revisited: the problem of the runic signatures. *In* (pp. 17–30) **30.**

**342.** Liszka, Thomas R. MS Laud misc. 108 and the early history of the *South English Legendary*. *See* **152.**

**343.** Love, Harold. Scribal texts and literary communities: the Rochester circle and Osborn b. 105. *See* **153.**

**344.** McGoldrich, L. The literary manuscripts and literary patronage of the Beauchamp and Neville families in the late Middle Ages, *c.* 1390–1500. *See* **154.**

**345.** McKenzie, D. F. Bibliography and the sociology of texts. *See* **67.**

**346.** McMillan, Dougald. The fatal circle: composition and direction of *Come and Go*. *In* (pp. 384–93) **45.**

**347.** Marcus, Leah S. Textual indeterminacy and ideological difference: the case of *Doctor Faustus*. RenD (20) 1–29.

**348.** MARX, C. WILLIAM; DRENNAN, JEANNE F. (eds). The Middle English prose *Complaint of Our Lady* and *Gospel of Nicodemus*, ed. from Cambridge, Magdalene College, MS Pepys 2498. *See* **155.**

**349.** MATHESON, LISTER M. *Piers Plowman* B.13.331 (330): some 'shrewed' observations. YLS (1) 1987, 108–16.

**350.** MEANEY, AUDREY L. St Neots, Æthelweard and the compilation of the *Anglo-Saxon Chronicle*: a survey. *In* (pp. 193–243) **56.**

**351.** MEKEMSON, MARY J. A critical, modern-spelling edition of James Shirley's *The Opportunity*. Unpub. doct. diss., Univ. of Wisconsin–Madison, 1988. [Abstr. in DA (49) 2232A.]

**352.** MIDDLETON, ANNE. Making a good end: John But as a reader of *Piers Plowman*. *In* (pp. 243–66) **41.**

**353.** MINNIS, A. J. (ed.). Latin and vernacular: studies in late-medieval texts and manuscripts. *See* **157.**

**354.** MITCHELL, BARBARA. The long and short of it: two versions of *Who Has Seen the Wind*. CanL (119) 1988, 8–22.

**355.** MOFFAT, DOUGLAS (ed.). *The Soul's Address to the Body* (the Worcester fragments). *See* **158.**

**356.** NAGAWARA, MAKOTO. *A True Story* and its manuscript: Mark Twain's image of the American Black. PoetT (29/30) 143–56.

**357.** NELLES, WILLIAM. From 'Tourist Town' to *Let Noon Be Fair*: the posthumous revision of Motley's last novel. AEB (ns 2:2) 1988, 61–7.

**358.** NEMESVARI, RICHARD. Choice of copy-text and treatment of accidentals in Thomas Hardy's *The Trumpet-Major*. Library (11:4) 357–62.

**359.** NEMESVARI, RICHARD ANDREW. Towards a critical edition of Thomas Hardy's *The Trumpet-Major*. Unpub. doct. diss., Queen's Univ. at Kingston (Ont.), 1988. [Abstr. in DA (49) 3371–2A.]

**360.** NEUFELDT, LEONARD N. Neopragmatism and convention in textual editing, with examples from the editing of Thoreau's autograph journal. AEB (ns 1:4) 1987, 227–36.

**361.** OGILVIE-THOMSON, S. J. (ed.). Richard Rolle: prose and verse, ed. from MS Longleat 29 and related manuscripts. *See* **159.**

**362.** O'KEEFFE, P. Wyndham Lewis's *Tarr*: an edition of the novel, based on the 1918 American version. Unpub. doct. diss., Univ. of Liverpool. [Abstr. in IT (39:3) 1117–18.]

**363.** O'MARA, V. M. A study of unedited late Middle English sermons that occur singly or in small groups. Unpub. doct. diss., Univ. of Leeds, 1987. [Abstr. in IT (38:4) 1455.]

**364.** OSTOVICH, HELEN. 'Manfrede'? Reconstruction of a misprint in Jonson's *Every Man Out of his Humour* (1600). NQ (36:3) 320–1.

**365.** OSTOVICH, HELEN MYRA. A modern critical edition of Ben Jonson's *Every Man Out of His Humour*. Unpub. doct. diss., Univ. of Toronto, 1988. [Abstr. in DA (49) 2672A.]

**366.** PARINS, MARYLYN JACKSON. Malory's expurgators. *In* (pp. 144–62) **8.**

**367.** PESCH, JOSEF W. Dot dropping(s) . . . a 'pre-text'? JJQ (27:1) 136–7.

**368.** RAMSEY, ROY VANCE.    F. N. Robinson's editing of the *Canterbury Tales*. SB (42) 134–52.

**369.** RAYLOR, TIMOTHY.    Samuel Hartlib's copy of *Upon Sir John Suckling's Hundred Horse*. NQ (36:4) 445–7.

**370.** REYNOLDS, M. L.    *Aurora Leigh* by Elizabeth Barrett Browning: an edition with textual variants, explanatory annotation and critical introduction. Unpub. doct. diss., Univ. of London, 1986. [Abstr. in IT (39:1) 33.]

**371.** RICHARDS, MARY P.    The manuscript contexts of the Old English laws: tradition and innovation. *In* (pp. 171–92) **56.**

**372.** RICKS, CHRISTOPHER; DAY, AIDAN (eds).    Tennyson: the manuscripts and proofs at the Tennyson Research Centre: Lincoln M1–M37, N12, P38. *See* **163.**

**373.** —————— Tennyson: the manuscripts and proofs at the Tennyson Research Centre: Lincoln P85++–P109. *See* **164.**

**374.** —————— Tennyson: the manuscripts and proofs at the Tennyson Research Centre: Lincoln P109–P179. *See* **165.**

**375.** —————— Tennyson: the manuscripts and proofs at the Tennyson Research Centre: Lincoln P179–P194. *See* **166.**

**376.** —————— Tennyson: the manuscripts and proofs at the Tennyson Research Centre: Lincoln P194–P205. *See* **167.**

**377.** —————— Tennyson: the manuscripts and proofs at the Tennyson Research Centre: Lincoln P205–P210++. *See* **168.**

**378.** —————— Tennyson: the manuscripts and proofs at the Tennyson Research Centre: Lincoln P213–P216. *See* **169.**

**379.** —————— Tennyson: the manuscripts and proofs at the Tennyson Research Centre: Lincoln P217 and miscellaneous poems. *See* **170.**

**380.** —————— Tennyson: the manuscripts at Trinity College Cambridge: loose papers, *In Memoriam* (notebook 13) and notebooks 14–17. *See* **171.**

**381.** —————— Tennyson: the manuscripts at Trinity College Cambridge: notebooks 18–25. *See* **172.**

**382.** —————— Tennyson: the manuscripts at Trinity College Cambridge: notebooks 26–29. *See* **173.**

**383.** —————— Tennyson: the manuscripts at Trinity College Cambridge: notebooks 30–36. *See* **174.**

**384.** —————— Tennyson: the manuscripts at Trinity College Cambridge: notebooks 37–40 and loose papers O.15.42, O.15.42(A), Add. MS a.187(16) and R.7.50. *See* **175.**

**385.** ROBERTS, JANE.    The Old English prose translation of Felix's *Vita Sancti Guthlaci*. *In* (pp. 363–79) **56.**

**386.** ROSSER, MARION DORTCH.    A critical edition of the Middle English *Horn Childe and Maiden Rimnild*. Unpub. doct. diss., Univ. of Southwestern Louisiana. [Abstr. in DA (50) 1668–9A.]

**387.** RUSSELL, G. H.    The imperative of revision in the C version of *Piers Plowman*. *In* (pp. 233–42) **41.**

**388.** SANDBERG, ROBERT A.    'The adjustment of screens': putative narrators, authors, and editors in Melville's unfinished 'Burgundy Club' book. TSLL (31:3) 426–50.

**389.** SANDBERG, ROBERT ALLEN. Melville's unfinished 'Burgundy Club' book: a reading edition edited from the manuscripts with introduction and notes. Unpub. doct. diss., Northwestern Univ. [Abstr. in DA (50) 948A.]

**390.** SCATTERGOOD, JOHN. Two unrecorded poems from Trinity College Dublin MS 490. *See* **176.**

**391.** SCHERF, KATHLEEN. Three new poems by Malcolm Lowry. *See* **177.**

**392.** SCHERF, KATHLEEN DOROTHY. The collected poetry of Malcolm Lowry: a critical edition with a commentary. Unpub. doct. diss., Univ. of British Columbia, 1988. [Abstr. in DA (49) 3721A.]

**393.** SHEPHERD, S. H. A. Four Middle English Charlemagne romances: a revaluation of the non-cyclic verse texts and the holograph *Sir Ferumbras*. Unpub. doct. diss., Univ. of Oxford, 1988. [Abstr. in IT (39:2) 484.]

**394.** SHILLINGSBURG, PETER L. An inquiry into the social status of texts and modes of textual criticism. SB (42) 55–79.

**395.** SPROUSE, JAMES R. The textual relationships of the unexpanded Middle English *Northern Homily Cycle*. Manuscripta (33:2) 92–108.

**395a.** SPROUSE, JAMES RICHARDSON. An edition of the sermon for the Second Sunday of Advent from the manuscripts of the unexpanded Middle English Northern Homily Cycle: textual and dialectical introductions, text, table of variant readings, and glossary. Unpub. doct. diss., Univ. of Tennessee. [Abstr. in DA (50) 1669A.]

**396.** STEVICK, ROBERT D. Two notes on *Christ II*. Leeds Studies in English (20) 293–309.

**397.** STREATFIELD, K. M. A critical edition of six occasional sermons by Jeremy Taylor (1613–1667). Unpub. doct. diss., Univ. of Edinburgh. [Abstr. in IT (39:4) 1603.]

**398.** STREITBERGER, W. R. Edmond Tyllney, Master of the Revels and censor of plays: a descriptive index to his diplomatic manual on Europe. *See* **179.**

**399.** SZARMACH, PAUL E. The earlier homily: *De parasceve*. *In* (pp. 381–99) **56.**

**400.** TAYLOR, GARY. William Shakespeare, Richard James and the House of Cobham. *See* **180.**

**401.** THOMPSON, JOHN J. Robert Thornton and the London Thornton manuscript: British Library MS Additional 31042. *See* **181.**

**402.** TOKOO, TATSUO (ed.). Percy Bysshe Shelley: vol. 8, Bodleian MS Shelley d.3: a facsimile edition with full transcription and textual notes. *See* **183.**

**403.** VAN HEERTUM, FRANCISCA WILHELMINA. A critical edition of Joseph Swetnam's *The Araignment of Lewd, Idle, Froward and Unconstant Women* (1615). Nijmegen, The Netherlands: Cicero Press. pp. xiii, 369.

**404.** VON ALBRECHT, MICHAEL. Fate or hate? A textual problem in Shaw's *Major Barbara*. NQ (36:2) 196–7.

**405.** Voss, Manfred. Quinns Edition der kleineren Cleopatra-glossare: Corrigenda und Addenda. *See* **184.**

**406.** Waldron, Ronald. Trevisa's original prefaces on translation: a critical edition. *In* (pp. 285–99) **41.**

**407.** Werstine, Paul. Provenance and printing history in two Revels editions: review article. MedRen (1) 1984, 243–62.

**408.** Wilson, Edward. The debate of the carpenter's tools. *See* **187.**

**409.** Wilson, John. *Havelok the Dane*, line 1349: 'til'. NQ (36:2) 150–1.

**410.** Witek, Therese Damm. The *Life Studies* manuscripts: Robert Lowell and the revisable self. Unpub. doct. diss., Vanderbilt Univ., 1988. [Abstr. in DA (50) 688A.]

**411.** Yerkes, David. The translation of Gregory's *Dialogues* and its revision: textual history, provenance, authorship. *In* (pp. 335–43) **56.**

# HISTORY OF PUBLISHING AND BOOKSELLING

**412.** Alblas, J. B. H. Johannes Boekholt (1656–1693), the first Dutch publisher of John Bunyan and other English authors, with a descriptive bibliography of his publications. (Bibl. 1988, 226, where title incorrect.) Rev. by Susan Roach in Library (11:2) 165–6.

**413.** Barlow, William P., Jr. A Baskerville collection. *See* **106.**

**414.** Bell, Maureen. Hannah Allen and the development of a Puritan publishing business, 1646–51. PubH (26) 5–66.

**415.** Black, Jeremy. The English press in the eighteenth century. Philadelphia: Pennsylvania UP, 1987. (Bibl. 1988, 232.) Rev. by Robert R. Rea in AHR (94:2) 432–8.

**416.** —— In search of a scandalous pamphlet: Sir Robert Walpole and the attempt to suppress the publication of opposition literature in the United Provinces. PubH (25) 5–11.

**417.** Borchardt, D. H.; Kirsop, W. (eds). The book in Australia: essays towards a cultural and social history. Melbourne: Australian Reference Pubs in assn with the Centre for Bibliographical and Textual Studies, Monash Univ., 1988. pp. vii, 214.

**418.** Bots, H.; Evers, M. Book news in Locke's correspondence (1683–1692). DQR (19:3) 230–42.

**419.** Bradlow, Frank R. Africana in the Tauchnitz edition. Quarterly Bulletin of the South African Library (44:2) 68–77.

**420.** Butt, A. R. The nineteenth-century book trade in Sind. Unpub. doct. diss., Univ. of Wales, 1988. [Abstr. in IT (39:3) 1139–40.]

**421.** Cave, Roderick. The Grey Walls Press Crown Classics. Private Library (2:3) 100–17.

**422.** Christianson, C. Paul. A community of book artisans in Chaucer's London. Viator (20) 207–18.

**423.** —— Memorials of the book trade in medieval London: the archives of Old London Bridge. Cambridge: Brewer, 1987. pp. ix, 66. (Manuscript studies, 3.) Rev. in BC (37:3) 1988, 328; by A. I. Doyle in Library (11:2) 155–6.

**424.** —— Paternoster Row and the Tudor book-trade community. Library (11:4) 352–6.

**425.** COLE, RICHARD CARGILL.   Irish booksellers and English writers 1740–1800. (Bibl. 1987, 372.) Rev. by J. D. Fleeman in RES (38:152) 1987, 568–9.

**426.** DUFFY, MAUREEN.   A thousand capricious chances: a history of the Methuen list 1889–1989. London: Methuen. pp. 162.

**427.** EDWARDS, RUSSELL; HALL, DAVID J.   'So much admired': die Insel-Bücherei and the King Penguin series. Edinburgh: Salvia, 1988. pp. vi, 108.

**428.** EILENBERG, SUSAN.   Mortal pages: Wordsworth and the reform of copyright. ELH (56:2) 351–74.

**429.** ELIOT, SIMON.   Unequal partnerships: Besant, Rice and Chatto 1876–82. PubH (26) 73–109.

**430.** FEATHER, JOHN.   Publishers and politicians: the remaking of the law of copyright in Britain, 1775–1842: 1, Legal deposit and the battle of library tax; 2, The right of authors. PubH (24) 1988, 49–76; (25) 45–72.

**431.** FERDINAND, C. Y.   Benjamin Collins, the *Salisbury Journal*, and the provincial book trade. Library (11:2) 116–38.

**432.** —— Richard Baldwin, Junior, bookseller. SB (42) 254–64.

**433.** GASKELL, PHILIP.   A bibliography of the Foulis Press. Charlottesville: Virginia UP, 1986. (Bibl. 1987, 379.) Rev. by Brian Gerrard in AEB (ns 2:4) 1988, 175–81.

**434.** GERRARD, BRIAN.   Bibliography of the Foulis Press. AEB (ns 2:4) 1988, 175–81 (review-article).

**435.** HARTLEY, JEAN.   Philip Larkin, the Marvell Press and me. Manchester: Carcanet Press. pp. 208. Rev. by Blake Morrison in TLS, 7 July, 740, by Patrick Taylor-Martin in Listener (121) 1 June, 28.

**436.** HORDEN, JOHN.   'In the Savoy': John Nutt and his family. PubH (24) 1988, 2–26.

**437.** HUFFMAN, CLIFFORD CHALMERS.   Elizabethan impressions: John Wolfe and his press. New York: AMS Press, 1988. pp. xii, 203. (AMS studies in the Renaissance, 21.) Rev. by Paul Morgan in Library (11:4) 366–7.

**438.** JOHNSON, GERALD D.   William Barley, 'publisher and seller of bookes', 1591–1614. Library (11:1) 10–46.

**439.** KERNAN, ALVIN.   Printing technology, letters and Samuel Johnson. (Bibl. 1987, 392.) Rev. by C. John Sommerville in AHR (94:1) 133–4; by David Womersley in RES (39:156) 1988, 559–60; by Paul Alkon in ELN (26:1) 1988, 73–5.

**440.** KINANE, VINCENT.   Some aspects of the Cuala Press. Private Library (2:3) 118–29.

**441.** LAUE, JUDY MYERS.   Rufus Wilmot Griswold's *The Female Poets of America*: the politics of anthologizing. Unpub. doct. diss., Univ. of Southern California, 1988. [Abstr. in DA (49) 1803A.]

**442.** LEATHLEAN, HOWARD.   Henry Noel Humphreys and the getting-up of books in the mid-nineteenth century. *See* **92**.

**443.** LISTER, ANTHONY.   William Ford (1771–1832), 'the universal bookseller'. BC (38:3) 343–71.

**444.** LONG, MOIRA.   The Foulis Press. TLR (22:2) 113–18.

**445.** LORD, C. P.   Image and reality: the chapbook perspective on women in early modern Britain. Unpub. M.Phil. diss., Univ. of St Andrews. [Abstr. in IT (39:1) 46.]

**446.** MCCANN, WESLEY.   An unrecorded Belfast edition of John Taylor's *Verbum Sempiternum*. Linen Hall Review (6:2) 14–15.

**447.** MCDONNELL, J. M.   William Pickering (1796–1854): antiquarian bookseller, publisher and book designer: a study in the early nineteenth-century book trade. *See* **246.**

**448.** MCELRATH, JOSEPH R., JR; CRISLER, JESSE S.   The bowdlerization of *McTeague*. AL (61:1) 97–101.

**449.** MOON, MARJORIE.   John Harris's books for youth 1801–1843. (Bibl. 1988, 257.) Rev. by John Barr in Library (11:3) 286.

**450.** MOORE, J. K.   Copy and print in English books of the sixteenth and seventeenth centuries. *See* **114.**

**451.** MORPURGO, J. E.   The poet and Barabbas: Keats, his publishers and editors. *In* (pp. 112–23) **37.**

**452.** MYERS, ROBIN; HARRIS, MICHAEL (eds).   Aspects of printing from 1600. *See* **116.**

**453.** —————— Bibliophily. (Bibl. 1986, 412.) Rev. by David Pearson in BJECS (11) 1988, 212–13.

**454.** —————— Economics of the British book trade, 1605–1939. (Bibl. 1986, 413.) Rev. by David Pearson in BJECS (11) 1988, 212–13.

**455.** PERKIN, M. R. (ed.).   The book trade in Liverpool 1806–50: a directory. Liverpool: Liverpool Bibliographical Soc., 1987. pp. xxiv, 403 + 6 fiches. (Book trade in the North West project occasional pubs, 2.) Rev. by Peter B. Freshwater in Library History (8:1) 1988, 20–2.

**456.** PETRIK, PAULA.   Desk-top publishing. HT (39) Oct., 12–19.

**457.** PIPER, ALAN J.; FOSTER, MERYL R.   Evidence of the Oxford booktrade, about 1300. Viator (20) 155–9.

**458.** RAINEY, LAWRENCE S.   The price of Modernism: reconsidering the publication of *The Waste Land*. YR (78:2) 279–300.

**459.** RIVERS, ISABEL (ed.).   Books and their readers in eighteenth-century England. (Bibl. 1986, 428.) Rev. by Cecil Price in RES (38:149) 1987, 79–80.

**460.** ROY, G. ROSS.   The Brash and Reid editions of *Tam o'Shanter*. BurnsC (98) 38–44.

**461.** RUSSELL, GILLIAN.   Lamb's *Specimens of English Dramatic Poets*: the publishing context and the principles of selection. CLB (65) 1–8.

**462.** ST CLAIR, WILLIAM.   William Godwin as children's bookseller. *In* (pp. 165–79) **14.**

**463.** STERN, MADELEINE B.   Nicholas Gouin Dufief of Philadelphia: Franco-American bookseller, 1778–1834. Philadelphia, PA: Philobiblon Club, 1988. pp. 84. (Studies in Philadelphia booklore, 1.) (Limited edition of 300 copies.)

**464.** TIERNEY, JAMES E. (ed.). The correspondence of Robert Dodsley, 1733–1764. Cambridge: CUP, 1988. pp. xxxviii, 599. (Cambridge studies in publishing and printing history.) Rev. by Pat Rogers in TLS, 14 July, 770.

**465.** TODD, WILLIAM B.; BOWDEN, ANN. Tauchnitz international editions in English, 1841–1955. New York: Bibliographical Soc. of America, 1988. pp. xxiv, 1078. Rev. by David McKitterick in BC (38:4) 555–7; by John Stephens in Library (11:3) 290–4.

**466.** WARRINGTON, BERNARD. William Pickering, bookseller and book collector. See **273**.

**467.** WEST, JAMES L. W., III. American authors and the literary marketplace since 1900. Philadelphia: Pennsylvania UP, 1988. pp. 172. Rev. by Michael T. Gilmore in NEQ (62:4) 612–17.

**468.** WHITEMAN, BRUCE; STEWART, CHARLOTTE; FUNNELL, CATHERINE. A bibliography of Macmillan of Canada imprints, 1906–1980. (Bibl. 1986, 445.) Rev. by George L. Parker in CanL (116) 1988, 115–16.

**469.** WOLF, EDWIN, II. The book culture of a colonial American city: Philadelphia books, bookmen and booksellers. Oxford: Clarendon Press, 1988. pp. viii, 227. (Lyell Lectures in Bibliography, 1985/86.) Rev. by James Raven in TLS, 17 June 1988, 686; by Nicolas Barker in BC (38:4) 557–9; by Wayne Wiegand in JAH (76:1) 241–2; by Trevor Colburn in PMHB (113:4) 644–6.

**470.** WOODRUFF, JAMES F. The background and significance of the *Rambler*'s format. PubH (4) 1978, 113–33.

**471.** WOOLMER, J. HOWARD. The Poetry Bookshop, 1912–1935: a bibliography. Introd. by PENELOPE FITZGERALD. Revere, PA: Woolmer/ Brotherton; Winchester: St Paul's Bibliographies, 1988. pp. xxxii, 186. Rev. by Richard Fifoot in Library (11:3) 288–9; by John Byrne in TLS, 10 Mar., 247; by Colin Franklin in BC (38:2) 259–60.

**472.** YOUNG, ALAN R. Wenceslaus Hollar, the London book trade, and two unidentified English emblem books. *In* (pp. 151–202) **21**.

**473.** ZBORAY, RONALD J. The book peddler and literary dissemination: the case of Parson Weems. PubH (25) 27–44.

**474.** ZIONKOWSKI, LINDA JOAN. The value of words: writing and the eighteenth-century commerce in letters. Unpub. doct. diss., Northwestern Univ., 1988. [Abstr. in DA (49) 3373A.]

## CONTEMPORARY PUBLISHING AND BOOKSELLING

**475.** CLAY, STEVEN; ABEL, DAVID. Recent examples of bookmaking in the United States. BkIA (51) 6–31.

**476.** COATES, JOSEPH. A book lover's Christmas. BW, 3 Dec., 1, 12.

**477.** GIBSON, DOUGLAS. 'Edited any good books lately?' *In* (pp. 108–15) **12**.

**478.** GREENFIELD, GEORGE. Scribblers for bread: aspects of the

English novel since 1945. London: Hodder & Stoughton. pp. 320. Rev. by Philip Oakes in Listener (121) 27 Apr., 27.

**479.** HASTED, ANNE; MEAD, ROGER; WHEELER, SHARON.   PLR loans: a statistical exploration. Stockton-on-Tees: Registrar of Public Lending Right, 1988. pp. 269. Rev. by Douglas Betts in Journal of Librarianship (21:1) 62–9.

**480.** JONES, ROBERT M.   Glad Hand Press. Private Library (2:2) 52–81.

**481.** KNIFFEL, LEONARD.   Books made to order: libraries as publishers. AmLib (20:8) 735–9.

**482.** McCORMACK, THOMAS.   The fiction editor, the novel, and the novelist. New York: St Martin's Press, 1988; London: Sidgwick & Jackson. pp. 202.

**483.** MACKLEM, MICHAEL.   Seed money. In (pp. 119–27) **12.**

**484.** O'BRIEN, GEORGE.   Dubliners and other poets. BkW, 5 Mar., 15. (Publishing in the Republic of Ireland.)

**485.** SMITH, CHARLOTTE M.   The Tamazunchale Press: a bibliographic checklist. BkIA (50) 28–34.

**486.** STREITFELD, DAVID.   A gentlemanly business. BkW, 21 May, 15.

**487.** —— Gloom on publishers' row. BkW, 31 Dec., 15.

**488.** —— Rhyme and reason. BkW, 26 Mar., 14. (Publishing poetry.)

**489.** SUMSION, JOHN.   PLR in practice: a report to the Advisory Committee. Stockton-on-Tees: Registrar of Public Lending Right, 1988. pp. 151. Rev. by Douglas Betts in Journal of Librarianship (21:1) 62–9.

**490.** SUTHERLAND, JOHN.   New ground for the book trade. LRB (11:18) 16.

# SCHOLARLY METHOD

**491.** BAKER, NANCY L.   A research guide for undergraduate students: English and American literature. (Bibl. 1984, 507.) New York: Modern Language Assn. pp. 61. (Third ed.: first ed. 1982.)

**492.** DRAUDT, MANFRED.   The rationale of current bibliographical methods: printing house studies, computer-aided compositor studies, and the use of statistical methods. *See* **63**.

**493.** FRANKING, HOLLY.   Stylometry: a statistical method for determining authorship, textual integrity, and chronology. Unpub. doct. diss., Univ. of Kansas, 1988. [Abstr. in DA (50) 449A.]

**494.** GIBSON, DOUGLAS.   'Edited any good books lately?' *In* (pp. 108–15) **12**.

**495.** HERGENHAN, LAURIE.   Editing *The Penguin New Literary History of Australia*. *In* (pp. 86–91) GEORGE SHAW (ed.), 1988 and all that: new views of Australia's past. Brisbane: Queensland UP, 1988. pp. 140.

**496.** HOWARD-HILL, T. H.   Modern textual theories and the editing of plays. *See* **329**.

**497.** JOHNSTON, A. F. (ed.).   Editing early English drama: special problems and new directions. Papers given at the nineteenth Annual Conference on Editorial Problems, University of Toronto, 4–5 November 1983. *See* **333**.

**498.** KÄLLGREN, GUNNEL.   Automatic indexing and generating of content graphs from unrestricted text. *In* (pp. 147–60) **48**.

**499.** KANE, THOMAS S.   The new Oxford guide to writing. New York; Oxford: OUP, 1988. pp. viii, 327.

**500.** LINDEMANN, ERIKA.   Longman bibliography of composition and rhetoric 1984–1985. New York; London: Longman, 1987. pp. xv, 318. (Longman series in college composition and communication.)

**501.** NIXON, GRAHAM.   The methods of urban linguistic surveys. *In* (pp. 228–41) **30**.

**502.** SHAND, G. B.; SHADY, RAYMOND C. (eds).   Play-texts in old spelling: papers from the Glendon conference. (Bibl. 1986, 44.) Rev. by Philip R. Rider in MedRen (4) 297–303.

**503.** SHILLINGSBURG, PETER L.   Scholarly editing in the computer age: theory and practice. (Bibl. 1987, 469.) Rev. by Tim William Machan in SAC (11) 286–8.

**504.** SMITH, ADRIAN.   The dangers of citation counting. LAR (90:4) 1988, 220.

**505.** SVARTVIK, JAN.   Instead of native speakers. *In* (pp. 259–67) **34**.

# LANGUAGE, LITERATURE, AND THE COMPUTER

**506.** AARTS, JAN; MEIJS, WILLEM (eds). Corpus linguistics: recent developments in the use of computer corpora in English language research. (Bibl. 1987, 476.) Rev. by Guy Bourquin in EA (42:2) 205–7.

**507.** ABERCROMBIE, JOHN R. Computer programs for literary analysis. Philadelphia: Pennsylvania UP, 1984. pp. 203. Rev. by David M. Axler in JAF (99:393) 1986, 360–1.

**508.** AKKERMAN, ERIK; MASEREEUW, PIETER; MEIJS, WILLEM. Designing a computerized lexicon for linguistic purposes: ASCOT report, no. 1. Amsterdam: Rodopi, 1985. pp. 80. (Costerus, 51.) Rev. by Guy Bourquin in EA (42:2) 205–7.

**509.** —— VOOGD-VAN ZUTPHEN, HETTY; MEIJS, WILLEM. A computerized lexicon for word-level tagging. (Bibl. 1988, 299.) Rev. by Guy Bourquin in EA (42:2) 205–7.

**510.** BERGNER, HEINZ; STEIN, DIETER. Introduction. *In* (pp. 285–7) **4.** (To part 2.)

**511.** BLANK, JAN. AUSTLIT (Australian Literary Database): it's no Furphy. Australian Academic and Research Libraries (20:2) 71–8.

**512.** BOGURAEV, BRAN; BRISCOE, TED (eds). Computational lexicography for natural language processing. London: Longman. pp. xiv, 310.

**513.** BOURQUIN, GUY. La traduction automatique comme instrument d'investigation en analyse contrastive. *In* (pp. 7–16) **22.**

**514.** BURROWS, J. F. Computation into criticism: a study of Jane Austen's novels and an experiment in method. (Bibl. 1988, 301.) Rev. by Helmut Bonheim in YES (19) 332–3; by Park Honan in BJECS (11) 1988, 100–1.

**515.** COLMAN, FRAN. The crunch is the key: on computer research on Old English personal names. *In* (pp. 41–55) **34.**

**516.** CONTI, DIANE COASSIN. Word processing and the composing process. Unpub. doct. diss., Columbia Univ. Teachers College, 1987. [Abstr. in DA (50) 126–7A.]

**517.** COTTRELL, GARRISON W. A connectionist approach to word sense disambiguation. London: Pitman. pp. xi, 220. (Research notes in artificial intelligence.)

**518.** DAHL, ÖSTEN; FRAURUD, KARI (eds). Papers from the first Nordic Conference on Text Comprehension in Man and Machine. *See* **48.**

**519.** DE HAAN, PIETER. Postmodifying clauses in the English noun phrase: a corpus based study. Amsterdam: Rodopi. pp. 252. (Language and computers, 3.)

**520.** DRAUDT, MANFRED. The rationale of current bibliographical methods: printing house studies, computer-aided compositor studies, and the use of statistical methods. *See* **63**.

**521.** FISCHER, ANDREAS. Concordances, computer corpora and diachronic lexicology. *In* (pp. 348–9) **4.** (Abstract.)

**522.** GRAY, PAUL. A scholarly Everest gets bigger: the *Oxford English Dictionary* updates and goes electronic. Time, 27 Mar., 95, 98.

**523.** HAUGLAND, KARI E. Some practical aspects of trade names and trademarks in terminology and translation: a brief report from the translation of an ESP text. *In* (pp. 117–29) **24.**

**524.** HELLMAN, CHRISTINA. Integrative processes in disfavouring conditions: a self-paced reading study. *In* (pp. 113–24) **48.**

**525.** HICKEY, RAYMOND. Proposals for a corpus database system for linguistics. *In* (pp. 288–99) **4.**

**526.** JANOUŠEK, MIROSLAV. If Cal = Calit then LL = LL + x, or, notes on computer assisted literature learning. Germanica Olomucensia (7) 103–12.

**527.** JANSSON, CARL GUSTAF. A top down, abductive and schema-based approach to text comprehension: an artificial intelligence perspective from Yale. *In* (pp. 125–38) **48.**

**527a.** JOHANSSON, STIG; HOFLAND, KNUT. Frequency analysis of English vocabulary and grammar: based on the LOB Corpus: vol. 1, Tag frequencies and word frequencies; vol. 2, Tag combinations and word combinations. Oxford: Clarendon Press; New York: OUP. pp. 400; 380.

**528.** JONES, CARLA FAUST. The Literary Detective computer analysis of stylistic differences between *The Dark Tower* and C. S. Lewis' Deep Space trilogy. Mythlore (15:3) 11–15.

**529.** KÄLLGREN, GUNNEL. Automatic indexing and generating of content graphs from unrestricted text. *In* (pp. 147–60) **48.**

**530.** KIPFER-WESTERLUND, B. A. Towards the onomasiological dictionary: the use of the computer in providing diversified access. Unpub. doct. diss., Univ. of Exeter. [Abstr. in IT (38:4) 1453.]

**531.** KORN, ERIC. Miracles of miniaturization. TLS, 15 Jan., 34. (The OED on CD-ROM.)

**532.** KYTÖ, MERJA. Progress report on the diachronic part of the Helsinki Corpus. ICAME Journal (13) 12–15.

**533.** LUDWIG, HANS-WERNER (ed.). Anglistentag 1987 Tübingen. *See* **4.**

**534.** MAGNUSSON, ULF. The verb *do* in the LOB Corpus. *In* (pp. 131–45) **34.**

**535.** MARDER, LOUIS. Testing computerized authorship programs. SNL (39:3/4) 30–1.

**536.** MEIJER, HANS. Programmar: a translation generator. Nijmegen: Bloembergen Santee, 1986. pp. 256.

**537.** NAGAO, MAKOTO. Machine translation: how far can it go? Trans. by NORMAN D. COOK. Oxford: OUP. pp. xii, 150.

**538.** NEUHAUS, H. JOACHIM. The Shakespeare dictionary database. ICAME Journal (13) 3–11.

**539.** —— Shakespeare's wordforms, a database view. *In* (pp. 264–80) **5.**

**540.** NOËL, JACQUES, *et al.* Computational lexicography and multi-lingualism. *In* (pp. 213–27) **42.**

**541.** PRADEILLES, ANNE. Une analyse titrologique des 'Memoir(s)' publiés en Grande-Bretagne (1780–1790). BSEAA (28) 39–70.

**542.** PREBENSEN, HENRIK. Experiments in noun phrase comprehension on the computer. *In* (pp. 161–72) **48.**

**543.** QI-BO, ZHU. A quantitative look at the Guangzhou Petroleum English Corpus. ICAME Journal (13) 28–38.

**544.** RAUFF, JAMES VERNON. Machine translation with two-level grammars. Unpub. doct. diss., Northwestern Univ., 1988. [Abstr. in DA (49) 2203A.]

**545.** RISSANEN, MATTI. Three problems connected with the use of diachronic corpora. ICAME Journal (13) 16–19.

**546.** ROKOŠNÁ, DANIELA. Oxfordský slovník anglického jazyka na kompaktnom disku. (The *Oxford English Dictionary* on compact disc.) CJa (33) 129–30.

**547.** SCHNEIDER, EDGAR W. Advantages and limitations of text corpora in the study of lexis. *In* (pp. 300–18) **4.**

**548.** SOUTER, CLIVE. The COMMUNAL project: extracting a grammar from the Polytechnic of Wales Corpus. ICAME Journal (13) 20–7.

**549.** SVARTVIK, JAN. Instead of native speakers. *In* (pp. 259–67) **34.**

**550.** THRANE, TORBEN. PAKA: a program for automated knowledge acquisition. *In* (pp. 195–208) **48.**

**551.** VIERECK, WOLFGANG. A corpus of dialectal English computerised. *In* (pp. 345–7) **4.** (Abstract.)

**552.** WOOLLEY, BENJAMIN. Fog factors. Listener (121) 22 June, 19. (Readability of text.)

# NEWSPAPERS AND OTHER PERIODICALS

**553.** ARMSTRONG, ALISON.   Transition years: James Joyce and Modernist art. *In* (pp. 351–9) **45.**

**554.** BASKER, JAMES G.   Tobias Smollett: critic and journalist. Newark: Delaware UP; London: Assoc. UPs, 1988. pp. 358. (Cf. bibl. 1987, 523.)

**555.** BLACK, JEREMY.   Meddling in French domestic politics: a project for a British-funded newspaper in 1732. PubH (26) 67–71.

**556.** BOND, DONALD F. (ed.).   The Tatler. (Bibl. 1988, 329.) Rev. by Gwin J. Kolb in MP (87:2) 184–6; by Pat Rogers in LRB (11:5) 16–17; by Simon Varey in BJECS (12) 234–5.

**557.** CENTING, RICHARD R.   Ohio magazines. OhioanaQ (32:4) 206. (*Don De Quille Journal.*)

**558.** —— Ohio magazines. OhioanaQ (32:3) 133. (*Mark; Bylines.*)

**559.** —— Ohio magazines. OhioanaQ (32:1) 6. (*Newsletter of the Margaret Atwood Society.*)

**560.** COOK, MICHAEL L.; MILLER, STEPHEN T.   Mystery, detective and espionage fiction: a checklist of fiction in U.S. pulp magazines, 1915–1974. New York; London: Garland, 1988. 2 vols., pp. xvi, 1183. (Fiction in the pulp magazines, 1.) (Garland reference library of the humanities, 838.)

**561.** COWELL, PATTIE.   Colonial poets and the magazine trade, 1741–1775. EAL (24:2) 112–19.

**562.** DENIZOT, PAUL.   Publicité et liberté dans la presse britannique à la fin du XVIIIe siècle. BSEAA (29) 159–77.

**563.** —— Violence d'un idéal ou idéal de la violence? Réflexions sur le *London Chronicle* de 1789. *In* (pp. 47–64) **60.**

**564.** DLUGOS, JAMES STEVEN, JR.   Seeing the past: conceptions of American literature in early national periodicals. Unpub. doct. diss., Univ. of Virginia. [Abstr. in DA (50) 1656A.]

**565.** DROTNER, KIRSTEN.   English children and their magazines, 1751–1945. New Haven, CT; London: Yale UP, 1988. pp. x, 272. Rev. by Patricia Craig in LRB (11:11) 26–7.

**566.** ELIOT, SIMON.   Unequal partnerships: Besant, Rice and Chatto 1876–82. *See* **429.**

**567.** ELLIS, FRANK H. (ed.).   Swift *vs* Mainwaring: *The Examiner* and *The Medley.* (Bibl. 1988, 340.) Rev. by Michael Treadwell in RES (38:149) 1987, 77–9; by David Nokes in BJECS (10) 1987, 98–9.

**568.** FERDINAND, C. Y.   Benjamin Collins, the *Salisbury Journal,* and the provincial book trade. *See* **431.**

**569.** FITZPATRICK, BARBARA LANING.   The text of Tobias Smollett's *Life and Adventures of Sir Launcelot Greaves,* the first serialized novel. Unpub. doct. diss., Duke Univ., 1987. [Abstr. in DA (49) 2228A.]

**570.** Fox, Celina.   Graphic journalism in England during the 1830s and 1840s. *See* **87.**

**571.** Griffiths, D. M.   The social and economic history of *The Standard* and Fleet Street: 1653–1900. Unpub. doct. diss., City Univ. [Abstr. in IT (39:1) 21.]

**572.** Groves, David.   Thomas De Quincey and a review of *Blackwood's Magazine*. Library (11:2) 147–9.

**573.** Hill, Anthony Duane.   J. A. Jackson's page in *Billboard*: a voice for Black performance during the Harlem renaissance between 1920–25. Unpub. doct. diss., New York Univ., 1988. [Abstr. in DA (49) 2454A.]

**574.** Houghton, Walter E., *et al.* (eds).   The Wellesley Index to Victorian periodicals, 1824–1900: vol. 4, Tables of contents and identification of contributors with bibliographies of their articles and stories and an index of initials and pseudonyms. (Bibl. 1988, 353.) Rev. by Richard D. Altick in MP (87:1) 101–4; by P. L. Shillingsburg in AEB (2:3) 1988, 126–8.

**575.** James, Caryn.   Big little magazines: a reader's guide. NYTB, 30 Apr., 32.

**576.** Ketcham, Michael G.   Transparent designs: reading, performance and form in the *Spectator* papers. (Bibl. 1988, 356.) Rev. by Richard W. F. Kroll in BJECS (11) 1988, 226.

**577.** Lyons, Mary E.   The last Transcendentalist. CathW (232) 60–4. (Isaac Hecker.)

**578.** McBride, J. P.   The *Dublin University Magazine*: cultural nationality and Tory ideology in an Irish literary and political journal 1833–1852. Unpub. doct. diss., Trinity Coll. Dublin, 1987. [Abstr. in IT (39:4) 1630.]

**579.** Maughan-Brown, David.   The anthology as reliquary? *Ten Years of 'Staffrider'* and *The 'Drum' Decade*. Current Writing (1) 3–21.

**580.** Meyer, Bruce Miller.   Sergeant of *Outposts*: one editor's role in post-war British poetry, 1944–1987. Unpub. doct. diss., McMaster Univ., 1988. [Abstr. in DA (49) 3371A.]

**581.** Milne, J. M.   The politics of *Blackwood's*, 1817–1846: a study in the political, economic and social articles in *Blackwood's Edinburgh Magazine*, 1817–1846 and of selected contributors. Unpub. doct. diss., Univ. of Newcastle-upon-Tyne, 1984. [Abstr. in IT (36:4) 1394.

**582.** Mofokeng, Boitumelo.   Where are the women? *Ten Years of 'Staffrider'*. Current Writing (1) 41–2.

**583.** Ndebele, Njabulo S.   The ethics of intellectual combat. Current Writing (1) 23–35. (*Refers to* **579.**)

**584.** Nelson, Carolyn; Seccombe, M.   Periodical publications, 1641–1700: a survey with illustrations. (Bibl. 1986, 658.) Rev. by Heather Creaton in JNPH (3:3) 1987, 25–6.

**585.** —— Seccombe, Matthew.   British newspapers and periodicals 1641–1700: a short-title catalogue of serials printed in England, Scotland, Ireland and British America. (Bibl. 1988, 370.) Rev. by

Michael Harris in Library (11:4) 378–83; by John Feather in NQ (36:3) 396–8.

**586.** OLIPHANT, A. W.; VLADISLAVIC, I. (eds). Ten years of *Staffrider* magazine, 1978–1988. Johannesburg: Ravan, 1988. Rev. by Francis Faller in Upstream (7:3) 72–3.

**587.** SHELDEN, MICHAEL. Friends of promise: Cyril Connolly and the world of *Horizon*. London: Hamilton. pp. xii, 254. Rev. by Frances Spalding in Listener (121) 16 Feb., 25; by John Bayley in LRB (11:5) 3, 5.

**588.** SHERBO, ARTHUR. Further additions to the Nichols file of the *Gentleman's Magazine*. SB (42) 249–54.

**589.** ——Matters English in *The Critic* (1881–1906). RES (39:154) 1988, 245–57.

**590.** —— *Nil nisi bonum*: Samuel Johnson in *The Gentleman's Magazine*, 1785–1800. CLit (16:2) 168–81.

**591.** SHEVELOW, KATHRYN. Women and print culture: the construction of feminity in the early periodical. London: Routledge. pp. 235.

**592.** SUPER, R. H. Matthew Arnold's *Literature and Dogma*, the *Cornhill Magazine*, and censorship. NQ (36:2) 187–8.

**593.** SUTHERLAND, JAMES. The Restoration newspaper and its development. (Bibl. 1987, 614.) Rev. by John Morrill in RES (39:153) 1988, 111–13.

**594.** SWIFT, PATRICK; WRIGHT, DAVID (eds). An anthology from *X*: a quarterly review of literature and the arts, 1959–1962. Oxford; New York: OUP, 1988. pp. xix, 270.

**595.** TAYLOR, RICHARD C. A source for Goldsmith's Tony Lumpkin in *The Connoisseur*. ELN (26:3) 30–6.

**596.** THOMAS, SUE. Indexes to fiction in *Chambers's Journal of Popular Literature, Science and Art*, later *Chambers's Journal*, 3rd to 6th series of *Chambers's Edinburgh Journal*, 1854–1910. St Lucia: Dept of English, Univ. of Queensland. pp. v, 103. (Victorian fiction research guides, 17.)

**597.** VANN, J. DON. Victorian novels in serial. (Bibl. 1987, 618.) Rev. by Nicola Bradbury in RES (38:149) 1987, 98–9.

**598.** VON RICHTHOFEN, P. M. The *Booster/Delta* nexus: Henry Miller and his friends in the literary world of Paris and London on the eve of the Second World War. Unpub. doct. diss., Univ. of Durham, 1987. [Abstr. in IT (38:4) 1463.]

**599.** WHITE, BRUCE ALLEN. Elbert Hubbard's *The Philistine, a Periodical of Protest* (1895–1915): a major American 'little magazine'. Unpub. doct. diss., Univ. of Maryland College Park, 1988. [Abstr. in DA (49) 2223A.]

**600.** WILLIAMS, JANE (ed.). Tambimuttu: bridge between two worlds. London: Owen. pp. xviii, 290. (Limited edition of 1,000 copies.) Rev. by Ian Hamilton in TLS, 1 Dec., 1335.

**601.** WILLIS, PATRICIA C. American modern: Scofield Thayer, Marianne Moore, and *The Dial*. YR (78:2) 301–17.

**602.** WOODRUFF, JAMES F. The background and significance of the *Rambler's* format. *See* **470**.

# THE ENGLISH LANGUAGE

## GENERAL STUDIES

### LANGUAGE AND LINGUISTICS

**603.** AITCHISON, JEAN. Words in the mind: an introduction to the mental lexicon. pp. x, 229. (Bibl. 1987, 630, where pagination incorrect.) Rev. by Hartmut Günther in Yearbook of Morphology (1) 1988, 296–9.

**604.** AVRAMIDES, ANITA. Meaning and mind: an examination of a Gricean account of language. Cambridge, MA; London: MIT Press. pp. xi, 202. Rev. by Simon Blackburn in TLS, 17 Nov., 1265–6.

**605.** BARTSCH, RENATE. Norms of language: theoretical and practical aspects. London: Longman, 1987. pp. xv, 348. (Longman linguistics library.) (Trans. of **606**.)

**606.** —— Sprachnormen: Theorie und Praxis. Tübingen: Niemeyer, 1985. pp. ix, 341.

**607.** BEDNARCZYK, MAREK ANTONI. Categories of asynchronous systems. Unpub. doct. diss., Univ. of Sussex, 1987. [Abstr. in DA (49) 2197A.]

**608.** BREIVIK, LEIV EGIL; HILLE, ARNOLDUS; JOHANSSON, STIG (eds). Essays on English language in honour of Bertil Sundby. See **24**.

**609.** BUTLER, M. L. Logical syntax and the limits of sense in the philosophy of Frege and Wittgenstein. Unpub. doct. diss., Univ. of Sheffield, 1988. [Abstr. in IT (39:2) 463–4.]

**610.** CHAFE, WALLACE; NICHOLS, JOHANNA (eds). Evidentiality: the linguistic coding of epistemology. (Bibl. 1987, 640.) Rev. by Ellen Basso in AAnth (90:1) 1988, 216–17.

**611.** COMRIE, BERNARD (ed.). The world's major languages. London; Sydney: Croom Helm, 1987. pp. xiii, 1025. Rev. by Walter Nash in LRB (10:1) 1988, 22–3.

**612.** CRANMER, ROBIN. Fundamental aspects of Wittgenstein's later conception of language. Unpub. doct. diss., Univ. of Oxford, 1987. [Abstr. in DA (49) 2198A.]

**613.** CRYSTAL, DAVID. The Cambridge encyclopedia of language. (Bibl. 1988, 400.) Rev. by Hans Andersson in MS (83:1) 12–15.

**614.** DAVIES, MARTIN. Tacit knowledge and subdoxastic states. In (pp. 131–52) **52**.

**615.** FILL, ALWIN. Wörter zu Pflugscharen. Versuch einer Ökologie der Sprache. Vienna: Böhlau, 1987. pp. 178.

**616.** FIRBAS, JAN. Interpreting Psalm 91 from the point of view of functional sentence perspective. In (pp. 107–16) **24**.

**617.** GEORGE, ALEXANDER (ed.). Reflections on Chomsky. See **52**.

**618.** GRACE, GEORGE W. The linguistic construction of reality. London; New York; Sydney: Croom Helm, 1987. pp. 152. Rev. by Jarmila Tárnyiková in PP (32) 212–14.

**619.** GRANDY, RICHARD E.    On Grice on language. JP (86:10) 514–25.
**620.** HARRIS, ROY.    The language machine. London: Duckworth, 1987. pp. 182.
**621.** HASAN, RUQAIYA.    Linguistics, language, and verbal art. Oxford: OUP. pp. xiv, 124. (Second ed.: first ed. 1985.)
**622.** HLADKÝ, JOSEF (ed.).    2. Anglisticko-amerikanistická konference/ Second conference on English and American studies. See **6.**
**623.** HOCKETT, C. F.    Refurbishing our foundations: elementary linguistics from an advanced point of view. Amsterdam; Philadelphia, PA: Benjamins, 1987. pp. x, 181. (Amsterdam studies in the theory and history of linguistic science, 4: Current issues in linguistic theory, 56.) Rev. by François Chevillet in EA (42:4) 452–3.
**624.** HÖHLEIN, HELGA; MARSDEN, PETER H.; POLLNER, CLAUSDIRK. Auswahlbibliographie zum Studium der anglistischen Sprachwissenschaft. Mit Kommentaren. (Bibl. 1987, 662.) Rev. by Georges Bourcier in EA (42:4) 458.
**625.** ILLICH, IVAN; SANDERS, BARRY.    ABC: the alphabetization of the popular mind. London; New York: Boyars, 1988; Harmondsworth: Penguin. pp. xi, 166.
**626.** LEŠKA, O.; NEKVAPIL, J.; ŠOLTYS, O.    The dynamics of linguistic description and linguistic systems. PP (32:1) 18–32.
**627.** LUDWIG, HANS-WERNER (ed.).    Anglistentag 1987 Tübingen. See **4.**
**628.** MAES-JELINEK, HENA; MICHEL, PIERRE; MICHEL-MICHOT, PAULETTE (eds).    Multiple worlds, multiple words: essays in honour of Irène Simon. See **42.**
**629.** MÜLLENBROCK, HEINZ-JOACHIM; NOLL-WIEMANN, RENATE (eds). Anglistentag 1988 Göttingen. See **5.**
**630.** ODENSTEDT, BENGT; PERSSON, GUNNAR (eds).    Instead of flowers: papers in honour of Mats Rydén on the occasion of his sixtieth birthday, August 27, 1989. See **34.**
**631.** PROGOVAC, LJILJANA.    A binding approach to polarity sensitivity. Unpub. doct. diss., Univ. of Southern California, 1988. [Abstr. in DA (49) 2642A.]
**632.** PYLKKÖ, PAULI OLAVI.    Logic, formal languages, and formal language identification: some logical properties of the languages in the Chomsky hierarchy, and an interrogative model of formal language identification. Unpub. doct. diss., Florida State Univ., 1988. [Abstr. in DA (49) 1789A.]
**633.** RAMAT, PAOLO.    Linguistic typology. Berlin; New York; Amsterdam: Mouton de Gruyter, 1987. pp. xii, 244. Rev. by François Chevillet in EA (42:2) 198–9.
**634.** ROBERTS, P. M.    Action, intention and language: a Davidsonian study. Unpub. doct. diss., Univ. of Edinburgh. [Abstr. in IT (39:4) 1607.]
**635.** SAVITCH, WALTER J., et al. (eds).    The formal complexity of natural language. Dordrecht; Lancaster; Boston, MA: Reidel, 1987. pp. xv, 451. (Studies in linguistics and philosophy, 33.)

**636.** SMITH, N. V.    The twitter machine: reflections on language. Oxford: Blackwell. pp. viii, 275. Rev. by Terence Moore in TLS, 17 Nov., 1266.

**637.** STEELE, ROSS; THREADGOLD, TERRY (eds).    Language topics: essays in honour of Michael Halliday: vols 1 and 2. (Bibl. 1987, 34–5.) Rev. by François Chevillet in EA (42:3) 333–5.

**638.** STEINER, GEORGE.    Real presences: is there anything *in* what we say? London: Faber & Faber. pp. 236. (Cf. bibl. 1986, 787.) Rev. by Roger Scruton in TLS, 19 May, 533–4.

**639.** STUBBS, MICHAEL.    Educational linguistics. (Bibl. 1986, 853.) Rev. by Friedrich Wilhelm Gester in Ang (107:1/2) 119–23.

**640.** SVARTVIK, JAN.    Instead of native speakers. *In* (pp. 259–67) **34**.

**641.** TRNKA, BOHUMIL.    Kapitoly z funkční jazykovědy. (Studies in functional linguistics.) Ed. by JIŘÍ NOSEK. Prague: Charles UP, 1988. pp. 212. (Acta Universitatis Carolinae, Philologica, 103.)

**642.** VACHEK, JOSEF.    Written language revisited. Ed. by PHILIP A. LUELSDORFF. Amsterdam: Benjamins. pp. xiv, 210.

**643.** VAN VOORST, J.    Event structure. Amsterdam; Philadelphia, PA: Benjamins, 1988. pp. x, 181. (Amsterdam studies in the theory and history of linguistic science, 4: Current issues in linguistic theory, 59.) Rev. by R. Declerck in LeuB (78:3) 275–304.

**644.** VARANTOLA, KRISTA.    Natural language *vs* purpose-built languages: the human factor. NM (90:2) 173–83.

**645.** WRIGHT, CRISPIN.    Wittgenstein's rule-following considerations and the central project of theoretical linguistics. *In* (pp. 233–64) **52**.

**646.** WYBURGH, M.    Language, spaces and self: a question of a-prioris. Unpub. doct. diss., Univ. of Essex, 1987. [Abstr. in IT (36:4) 1385.]

## THE ENGLISH LANGUAGE

**647.** BURCHFIELD, R. W.    Unlocking the English language. London: Faber & Faber. pp. xii, 202. (T. S. Eliot Memorial Lectures.) Rev. by Martin Fagg in Listener (122) 5 Oct., 34.

**648.** CROWLEY, TONY.    The politics of discourse: the standard language question in British cultural debates. Basingstoke: Macmillan. pp. vi, 302.

**649.** GREENBAUM, SIDNEY; WHITCUT, JANET.    Longman guide to English usage. (Bibl. 1988, 422.) Rev. by Walter Nash in LRB (11:2) 16–17.

**650.** LASS, ROGER.    The shape of English: structure and history. (Bibl. 1988, 423.) Rev. by Jean Pauchard in EA (42:2) 194–5.

**651.** MALLESS, STAN; McQUAIN, JEFF.    The elements of English: a glossary of basic terms for literature, composition, and grammar. Lanham, MD; London: Madison, 1988. pp. xiv, 73. (Second revised ed.: first pub. 1986 as *A Handlist to English*.)

**652.** NASH, WALTER.    English usage: a guide to first principles. (Bibl. 1987, 708.) Rev. by Rodney Sampson in EngS (70:5) 460–1.

**653.** ——Usage, users, and the used: some reflections on contemporary English. *In* (pp. 29–46) **47.**

**654.** SHIBATANI, KATAYOSHI; OOTSU, YUKIO; TSUDA, AOI. Eigogaku taikei dai 6-kan: eigogaku no kanren bunya. (English philology and linguistics, 6: related studies.) Tokyo: Taishukan. pp. xxiv, 574.

**655.** SUNG, CHAN-KYUNG. Hanguk youngeo youngmunhak yeongusa, 1945–1965. (A history of the study of English language and literature in Korea, 1945–1965.) IKS (19) 67–161.

**656.** SUTHERLAND, JOHN. Nice words and bad language. TLS, 1 Dec., 1332.

**657.** TOTTIE, GUNNEL; BÄCKLUND, INGEGERD (eds). English in speech and writing: a symposium. (Bibl. 1986, 16.) Rev. by Klaus-Dieter Barnickel in Ang (107:3/4) 469–73.

**658.** TYNAN, JOHN. Presuppositional phenomena in English. Atlantis (11:1/2) 9–19.

## HISTORY OF LANGUAGE

**659.** ADAMSKA-SAŁACIAK, ARLETA. On explaining language change teleologically. SAP (22) 53–74.

**660.** ANTTILA, RAIMO (ed.). Historical and comparative linguistics. Amsterdam: Benjamins. pp. xv, 462. (Amsterdam studies in the theory and history of linguistic science, 4: Current issues in linguistic theory, 6.) (Second revised ed.: first ed. 1972.)

**661.** BENJAMIN, ANDREW E.; CANTOR, GEOFFREY N.; CHRISTIE, JOHN R. R. (eds). The figural and the literal: problems of language in the history of science and philosophy, 1630–1800. (Bibl. 1987, 714.) Rev. by Alain Morvan in EA (42:3) 341–2.

**662.** CROWLEY, TERRY. An introduction to historical linguistics. Port Moresby: Papua New Guinea UP; Suva: Inst. of Pacific Studies, Univ. of the South Pacific, 1987. pp. vi, 306. Rev. by Scott Allen in Te Reo (32) 95–9.

**663.** HOCK, HANS HEINRICH. Principles of historical linguistics. Berlin; New York; Amsterdam: Mouton de Gruyter, 1986. pp. xiii, 722. (Trends in linguistics: studies and monographs, 34.) Rev. by W. van der Wurff in EngS (70:5) 441–9.

**664.** KYTÖ, MERJA. Progress report on the diachronic part of the Helsinki Corpus. *See* **532.**

**665.** PADLEY, G. A. Grammatical theory in western Europe, 1500–1700: trends in vernacular grammar, II. Cambridge: CUP, 1988. pp. x, 534.

**666.** RISSANEN, MATTI. Three problems connected with the use of diachronic corpora. *See* **545.**

**667.** VAN DER WURFF, W. One thousand and one principles of historical linguistics. EngS (70:5) 441–9 (review-article).

**668.** WASWO, RICHARD. Language and meaning in the Renaissance. (Bibl. 1988, 431.) Rev. by David Quint in RQ (42:3) 534–7; by Edward Benson in SixCT (20:2) 348–9.

**669.** WATKINS, CALVERT. New parameters in historical linguistics, philology, and culture history. Lang (65:4) 783–99.

## HISTORY AND DEVELOPMENT OF ENGLISH

**670.** AZAD, Y.   The government of tongues: common usage and the 'prescriptive' tradition 1650 to 1800. Unpub. doct. diss., Univ. of Oxford. [Abstr. in IT (39:3) 1108.]

**671.** BATES, C.   Courtship and courtliness: studies in Elizabethan courtly language and literature. Unpub. doct. diss., Univ. of Oxford, 1988. [Abstr. in IT (39:3) 1105.]

**672.** BENSKIN, MICHAEL.   Some aspects of Cumbrian English, mainly mediaeval. *In* (pp. 13–46) **24.**

**673.** BREMMER, ROLF H.   Late medieval and early modern opinions on the affinity between English and Frisian: the growth of a commonplace. FLH (9:1) 1988, 167–91.

**674.** COLMAN, FRAN.   Neutralization: on characterizing distinctions between Old English proper names and common nouns. Leeds Studies in English (20) 249–70.

**675.** EATON, ROGER, *et al.* (eds).   Papers from the 4th International Conference on English Historical Linguistics. (Bibl. 1988, 436.) Rev. by Suzanne Romaine in RES (38:152) 1987, 533–4.

**676.** EVANS, G. R.   'Thus it is Englished': the use of English in scholastic disputation in the mid-sixteenth century. RES (39:156) 1988, 519–22.

**677.** FISIAK, JAČEK (ed.).   A bibliography of writings for the history of the English language. (Bibl. 1983, 189.) Berlin; New York: Mouton de Gruyter, 1987. pp. xi, 216. (Second ed.: first ed. 1983.) Rev. by J. R. J. North in SL (13:2) 518–21; by Xavier Dekeyser in LeuB (78:2) 232–4.

**678.** GRANT, RAYMOND J. S.   The B text of the Old English Bede: a linguistic commentary. Amsterdam; Atlanta, GA: Rodopi. pp. iii, 497. (Costerus, 73.)

**679.** HIETSCH, OTTO.   Enshrined in speech: medieval life and modern leavings. *In* (pp. 333–71) **38.**

**680.** HOFSTETTER, WALTER.   Winchester und der spätaltenglische Sprachgebrauch: Untersuchungen zur geographischen und zeitlichen Verbreitung altenglischer Synonyme. Munich: Fink, 1987. pp. xxxii, 611. (Münchener Universitäts-Schriften. Philosophische Fakultat: Texte und Untersuchungen zur englischen Philologie, 14.) Rev. by E. G. Stanley in NQ (36:2) 216.

**681.** IGLESIAS RÁBADE, LUIS.   The language of pleading in the manorial courts of late 13th-century England, with examples drawn from the court of the manor of Hales Owen. RECI (18) 231–42.

**682.** KELLY, ANN CLINE.   Swift and the English language. Philadelphia: Pennsylvania UP, 1988. pp. xiii, 169. Rev. by Serge Soupel in EA (42:1) 101–2.

**683.** KRISTENSSON, GILLIS.   The linguistic status of East Anglia in late Middle English. *In* (pp. 123–30) **34.**

**684.** —— A survey of Middle English dialects 1290–1350: the West Midland counties. (Bibl. 1987, 747.) Rev. by Lister M. Matheson in Spec (64:2) 459–60; by E. G. Stanley in NQ (36:3) 363.

**685.** McIntosh, Angus; Samuels, M. L.; Benskin, Michael.   Guide to *A Linguistic Atlas of Late Medieval English*. Aberdeen: Aberdeen UP, 1987. pp. 23. Rev. by Angelika Lutz in Ang (107:3/4) 495–502.

**686.** —————— A linguistic atlas of late medieval English. (Bibl. 1987, 751.) Rev. by Angelika Lutz in Ang (107:3/4) 495–502; by Edward Wilson in RES (39:153) 1988, 94–6.

**687.** Millward, C. M.   A biography of the English language. New York; London: Holt, Rinehart & Winston. pp. xx, 386.

**688.** Mitchell, Bruce.   On Old English: selected papers. (Bibl. 1988, 444.) Rev. by T. A. Shippey in NQ (36:4) 488–9.

**689.** Nixon, Graham; Honey, John (eds).   An historic tongue: studies in English linguistics in memory of Barbara Strang. *See* **30.**

**690.** Ooizumi, Akio; Iwasaki, Haruo (eds).   Chaucer no eigo: kenkyu no kadaito houhou. (Studies in Chaucer's English: some problems and methods.) Tokyo: Eichousha. pp. 240.

**691.** Salmon, Vivian; Burness, Edwina (eds).   A reader in the language of Shakespeare's drama. (Bibl. 1987, 755.) Rev. by Henri Suhamy in EA (42:4) 469; by D. Delabastita in LeuB (78:2) 227–9; by Alan Ward in NQ (36:2) 234–5; by Russ McDonald in SQ (40:3) 360–3.

**692.** Seebold, Elmar.   Winchester und Canterbury: zum spätaltenglischen Sprachgebrauch. Ang (107:1/2) 52–60.

**693.** Sluder, Brenda.   Differences between Chancery English and the English of John of Trevisa. ELN (27:2) 13–18.

**694.** Stones, Lionel; Phillips, Seymour.   English in the Public Records: three late thirteenth-century examples. NMS (32) 1988, 196–205.

**695.** Sundby, Bertil.   DENG: a dictionary of English normative grammar, 1700–1800: ambiguity. Bergen: Dept of English, Univ. of Bergen, 1987. pp. 17. (Linguistic project reports, 16.)

**696.** —— DENG: a dictionary of English normative grammar 1700–1800: collocations, idioms, tautologies. Bergen: Dept of English, Univ. of Bergen, 1987. pp. 55. (Linguistic project reports, 14.)

**697.** —— DENG: a dictionary of English normative grammar 1700–1800: prescriptive labelling: problems and principles, with a prescriptive index. Bergen: Dept of English, Univ. of Bergen, 1987. pp. 32. (Linguistic project reports, 17.)

**698.** Tajima, Matsuji.   Old and Middle English language studies: a classified bibliography, 1923–1985. (Bibl. 1988, 452.) Rev. by J. R. J. North in SL (13:2) 518–21.

**699.** Wakelin, Martyn F.   The archaeology of English. London: Batsford, 1988. pp. 191.

## HISTORY OF LINGUISTICS

**700.** Andrésen, Bjørn Stålhane.   The London School of Phonology: essence and roots. *In* (pp. 1–11) **24.**

**701.** Brown, Keith.   Linguistics today. (Bibl. 1984, 683.) Rev. by N. F. Blake in Lore and Language (8:2) 106–7.

**702.** DE RIJK, L. M.    Through language to reality: studies on medieval semantics and metaphysics. Ed. by E. P. Bos. London: Variorium Reprints. pp. 322. (Collected studies, 302.)

**703.** GORDON, W. TERRENCE.    Language, philosophy and linguistics in *inter-bellum* Britain. Historiographia Linguistica (16:3) 263–77 (review-article).

**704.** HARRIS, ROY.    The ideological implications of onomatopoeia in the eighteenth century. StudECC (17:1) 1987, 209–16.

**705.** —— (ed.).    Linguistic thought in Britain, 1914–1945. London: Duckworth, 1988. pp. xi, 201. Rev. by W. Terrence Gordon in Historiographia Linguistica (16:3) 361–77.

**706.** —— TAYLOR, TALBOT J.    Landmarks in linguistic thought: the Western tradition from Socrates to Saussure. London: Routledge. pp. xviii, 199. (Routledge history of linguistic thought.)

**707.** HÜLLEN, WERNER.    'Their manner of discourse'. Nachdenken über Sprache im Umkreis der Royal Society. Tübingen: Narr. pp. 292.

**708.** KOERNER, KONRAD.    Practicing linguistic historiography: selected essays. Amsterdam: Benjamins. pp. ix, 454. (Amsterdam studies in the theory and history of linguistic science, 4: Current issues in linguistic theory, 50.)

**709.** MCKUSICK, JAMES C.    Coleridge's philosophy of language. (Bibl. 1986, 825.) Rev. by L. A. Rabinowitz in UES (27:2) 28–9.

**710.** PRICKETT, STEPHEN.    Radicalism and linguistic theory: Horne Tooke on Samuel Pegge. YES (19) 1–17.

**711.** REED, JOHN O.    Englishmen and their moods: Renaissance grammar and the English verb. *In* (pp. 112–30) **30.**

# PHONETICS AND PHONOLOGY

## GENERAL STUDIES

**712.** AKAMATSU, TSUTOMU. The theory of neutralization and the archiphoneme in functional phonology. Amsterdam; Philadelphia, PA: Benjamins, 1988. pp. xxi, 533. (Amsterdam studies in the theory and history of linguistic science, 4: Current issues in linguistic theory, 43.) (Cf. bibl. 1986, 1404.)

**713.** AWANESS, LAZIM MIHRAN. Some resonatory facts about the function of the supraglottal organs in speech sounds [sic] production. Journal of Education and Science (Univ. of Mosul, Iraq) (1) 1979, 53–63.

**714.** BAGEMIHL, BRUCE. Alternate phonologies and morphologies. Unpub. doct. diss., Univ. of British Columbia, 1988. [Abstr. in DA (49) 3700A.]

**715.** CHARETTE, MONIK. Some constraints on governing relations in phonology. Unpub. doct. diss., McGill Univ. [Abstr. in DA (50) 936A.]

**716.** COCHRANE, G. R. Origins and development of the Australian accent. In (pp. 176–86, 318, 341–2) **9.**

**717.** KELLY, JOHN; LOCAL, JOHN. Doing phonology: observing, recording, interpreting. Manchester: Manchester UP. pp. vii, 286.

**718.** SCHLINDWEIN, DEBORAH. The phonological geometry of morpheme concatenation. Unpub. doct. diss., Univ. of Southern California, 1988. [Abstr. in DA (49) 2204A.]

**719.** VANDEPITTE, SONIA. A pragmatic function of intonation: tone and cognitive environment. Lingua (79:4) 265–97.

## HISTORICAL PHONETICS AND PHONOLOGY OF ENGLISH

**720.** BARRACK, CHARLES M. Keyser, Kiparsky and Postal versus Sievers. Lingua (77:3/4) 223–96.

**721.** DIETZ, KLAUS. Die historische Schichtung phonologischer Isoglossen in den englischen Dialekten: altenglische Isoglossen. Ang (107:3/4) 295–329.

**722.** FRANKIS, JOHN. The great vowel-shift and other vowel-shifts. In (pp. 133–7) **30.**

**723.** GREEN, THOMAS A. Linguistic manipulation in the Punch and Judy script. Lore and Language (8:2) 33–41.

**724.** HICKEY, R. The realization of dental obstruents adjacent to /r/ in the history of English. NM (90:2) 167–72.

**725.** HONEY, JOHN. 'Talking proper': schooling and the establishment of English 'Received Pronunciation'. In (pp. 209–27) **30.**

**726.** IKEGAMI, MASA T. Rhyme and pronunciation: some studies of English rhymes from *Kyng Alisaunder* to Skelton. (Bibl. 1986, 1441.) Rev. by Alan Ward in MÆ (56:1) 1987, 116–17.

**727.** JUUL, ARNE; NIELSEN, HANS FREDE (eds). *Our Changing Speech*: two BBC talks by Daniel Jones; with a supplement: *Daniel Jones*

*(1881–1967)* by BEVERLEY COLLINS. Copenhagen: National Institute for Educational Media, 1985. pp. xvii, 62.

**728.** KAMINASHI, KEIKO.   Old English stress, high vowel deletion and gemination: two prosodic plane theory. StudL (43:2) 77–118.

**729.** LEWIS, ROBERT E.   The phonic status of Middle English initial <sch>. *In* pp. 165–77) **24.**

**730.** McCULLY, C. B.   The phonology of English rhythm and metre, with special reference to Old English. Unpub. doct. diss., Univ. of Manchester, 1988. [Abstr. in IT (39:2) 481.]

**731.** MARKUS, MANFRED.   The spelling peculiarities in the *Ormulum* from an interdisciplinary point of view: a reappraisal. *In* (pp. 69–86) **38.**

**732.** MELCHERS, GUNNEL.   *Hween, kenee, tlock*: on the realization of initial *k*-clusters in some varieties of English. *In* (pp. 237–44) **24.**

**733.** MUGGLESTONE, L. C.   A.J. Ellis, 'Standard English' and the prescriptive tradition. RES (39:153) 1988, 87–92.

**734.** —— Samuel Johnson and the use of /h/. NQ (36:4) 431–3.

**735.** —— Studies in the pronunciation of standard English in the late eighteenth and nineteenth centuries according to the evidence of contemporary writers on the language. Unpub. doct. diss., Univ. of Oxford, 1988. [Abstr. in IT (39:1) 27.]

**736.** RITT, NIKOLAUS.   The processes amounting to MEOSL and its exceptions. *In* (pp. 153–66) MANFRED MARKUS (ed.), Historical English: on the occasion of Karl Brunner's 100th birthday. Innsbruck: Institut für Anglistik, 1988. pp. ix, 244. (Innsbrucker Beiträge zur Kulturwissenschaft: Anglistische Reihe, 1.)

**737.** RUSSOM, GEOFFREY.   Old English metre and linguistic theory. (Bibl. 1988, 491, where scholar's name incomplete.) Rev. by Wolfgang Obst in Ang (107:3/4) 506–10.

## PHONETICS AND PHONOLOGY OF CONTEMPORARY ENGLISH

**738.** BERNARD, J. R.   Quantitative aspects of the sounds of Australian English. *In* (pp. 187–204, 342–3) **9.**

**739.** BOROWSKY, TONI.   Structure preservation and the syllable coda in English. Natural Language and Linguistic Theory (7:2) 145–66.

**740.** BRADLEY, DAVID.   Regional dialects in Australian English phonology. *In* (pp. 260–70, 348–9) **9.**

**741.** CAISSE, MICHELLE.   Modeling English vowel durations. Unpub. doct. diss., Univ. of California, Berkeley, 1988. [Abstr. in DA (50) 936A.]

**742.** CLARK, J. E.   Some proposals for a revised phonetic transcription of Australian English. *In* (pp. 205–13, 343–4) **9.**

**743.** DOCHERTY, G. J.   An experimental phonetic study of the timing of voicing in English obstruents. Unpub. doct. diss., Univ. of Edinburgh. [Abstr. in IT (39:4) 1617.]

**744.** ESSER, JÜRGEN; POLOMSKI, ANDRZEJ.   Comparing reading and speaking intonation. Amsterdam: Rodopi, 1988. pp. 252.

**745.** FABER, DAVID.　Some problems of English nucleus placement. Unpub. doct. diss., Univ. of Manchester, 1987. [Abstr. in DA (49) 3349A; in IT (39:3) 1098.]

**746.** FORDYCE, JAMES FORREST.　Studies in sound symbolism with special reference to English. Unpub. doct. diss., Univ. of California, Los Angeles, 1988. [Abstr. in DA (49) 2639–40A.]

**747.** GHALIB, GHALIB B. M.; FALIH, HALEEM H.　A contrastive–phonetic explanation of the occurrence versus non-occurrence of errors in the production of some English consonants. Journal of Education and Science (Univ. of Mosul, Iraq) (7) (Humanities and Education) 61–79.

**748.** GOMAA, M. A. M.　The nature of word-accent in English with special reference to duration and perception. Unpub. doct. diss., Univ. of Glasgow, 1988. [Abstr. in IT (39:1) 25.] (Restricted access.)

**749.** GORDON, ELIZABETH.　That colonial twang: New Zealand speech and New Zealand identity. In (pp. 77–90) DAVID NOVITZ and BILL WILLMOTT (eds), Culture and identity in New Zealand. Wellington: GP Books. pp. ix, 302.

**750.** GUIERRE, LIONEL (ed.).　Règles et exercices de prononciation anglaise. Paris: Colin; London: Longman, 1987. pp. 128. Rev. by Georges Bourcier in EA (42:4) 455–6.

**751.** HIROAKI, OASA.　Phonology of current Adelaide English. In (pp. 271–87, 349) **9**.

**752.** HONEY, JOHN.　Does accent matter? The Pygmalion factor. London: Faber & Faber. pp. xii, 208.

**753.** HORNE, MERLE.　Towards a discourse-based model of English sentence intonation. Lund: Dept of Linguistics and Phonetics, Lund Univ., 1987. 2 vols. pp. 41; 122.) (Doct. diss., Lund Univ.)

**754.** HUGHES, ARTHUR; TRUDGILL, PETER.　English accents and dialects: an introduction to social and regional varieties of British English. (Bibl. 1987, 863.) Rev. by François Chevillet in EA (42:2) 207–8.

**755.** INKELAS, SHARON.　Prosodic constituency in the lexicon. Unpub. doct. diss., Stanford Univ. [Abstr. in DA (50) 1648A.]

**756.** KAGER, R. W. J.　A metrical theory of stress and destressing in English and Dutch. Dordrecht: ICG. pp. xvii, 244.

**757.** KIM, CHONG-HOON.　Youngeo eui eumjeol gwa geu gujo. (The English syllable and its structure.) Unpub. doct. diss., Korea Univ., Seoul. pp. 217.

**758.** KNOWLES, GERALD.　Patterns of spoken English: an introduction to English phonetics. (Bibl. 1988, 507.) Rev. by François Chevillet in EA (42:2) 197–8.

**759.** KREIDLER, CHARLES W.　The pronunciation of English: a course book in phonology. Oxford: Blackwell. pp. xiii, 335.

**760.** LIMBRICK, V. R.　Palatalization and affriction in South African English – a sample study. English Usage (20:2) 20–38.

**761.** McALLISTER, J. M.　Lexical stress and lexical access: effects in read and spontaneous speech. Unpub. doct. diss., Univ. of Edinburgh. [Abstr. in IT (39:4) 1621.]

**762.** McKenna, G. E.   Vowel duration in the standard English of Scotland. Unpub. M.Litt. diss., Univ. of Edinburgh. [Abstr. in IT (39:4) 1621.]

**763.** Milliken, Margaret E.   Phonological divergence and intelligibility: a case study of English and Scots. Unpub. doct. diss., Cornell Univ., 1988. [Abstr. in DA (49) 3015A.]

**764.** Moftah, A. A.   A comparative study of some prosodic features of British English and Cairene Arabic. Unpub. doct. diss., Univ. of Leeds, 1988.[Abstr. in IT (39:3) 1099.]

**765.** Nixon, Graham.   The methods of urban linguistic surveys. *In* (pp. 228–41) **30.**

**766.** Ono, Koji.   Eigo no gairaigo kyousei taikei nitsuite. (On the stress system of English loan vocabulary.) SEL (66:1) 97–109.

**767.** Park, Joo-Hyun.   Youngeo eui rhythm gwa wunyul iron. (Rhythm and prosodic theory in English.) Unpub. doct. diss., Seoul National Univ.

**768.** Peet, Margot Tamara.   Postlexical palatalization in English: an acoustic–phonetic study. Unpub. doct. diss., Univ. of California, Berkeley, 1988. [Abstr. in DA (50) 939–40A.]

**769.** Prunet, Jean-François.   Spreading and locality domains in phonology. Unpub. doct. diss., McGill Univ., 1987. [Abstr. in DA (49) 3707A.]

**770.** Stevens, Kenneth N.; Keyser, Samuel Jay.   Primary features and their enhancement in consonants. Lang (65:1) 81–106.

**771.** Szpyra, Jolanta.   The phonology–morphology interface: cycles, levels and words. London: Routledge. pp. xiii, 270. (Croom Helm linguistics.)

**772.** Tench, P. W.   The roles of intonation in English discourse. Unpub. doct. diss., Univ. of Wales, 1988. [Abstr. in IT (39:3) 1099–100.]

**773.** Vachek, Josef.   Some remarks on English and Slovak vocalic systems: a chapter from comparative phonology of English and Slovak. *In* (pp. 69–76) **62.**

**774.** Yousif, M. N.   Experiments in the application of the stress rule presented in the SPE on selected cases in single words. Journal of Education and Science (Univ. of Mosul, Iraq) (7) (Humanities and Education) 81–8.

**775.** Zec, Draga.   Sonority constraints on prosodic structure. Unpub. doct. diss., Stanford Univ. [Abstr. in DA (50) 678A.]

## SPELLING, PUNCTUATION, HANDWRITING

**776.** Coulmas, Florian.   The writing systems of the world. Oxford: Blackwell. pp. ix, 302. (Language library.)

**777.** Ellis, Michael Edmond.   Patterns of spelling variation in the *Anglo-Saxon Chronicle* manuscripts. Unpub. doct. diss., Univ. of Kentucky, 1988. [Abstr. in DA (49) 1808A.]

**778.** Hannay, Mike.   English comma placement: a functional view. *In* (pp. 81–92) **47.**

**779.** LEULSDORFF, PHILIP. Constraints on error variables in grammar: bilingual misspelling orthographies. Amsterdam; Philadelphia, PA: Benjamins, 1986. pp. xix, 505.

**780.** LEWIS, ROBERT E. The phonic status of Middle English initial <sch>. *In* (pp. 165–77) **24.**

**781.** MARKUS, MANFRED. The spelling peculiarities in the *Ormulum* from an interdisciplinary point of view: a reappraisal. *In* (pp. 69–86) **38.**

**782.** SALMON, VIVIAN. John Rastell and the normalization of early sixteenth-century orthography. *In* (pp. 289–301) **24.**

# GRAMMAR
## GENERAL STUDIES

**783.** ABRAHAM, WERNER. Language universals: the Chomskyan approach *vs* Greenberg's typological approach. Belgian Journal of Linguistics (4) 9–25.

**784.** BARLOW, MICHAEL. A situated theory of agreement. Unpub. doct. diss., Stanford Univ., 1988. [Abstr. in DA (49) 3700A.]

**785.** BENNIS, HANS; HOEKSTRA, TEUN. PRO and the binding theory. Linguistics in the Netherlands 1989 (6) 11–20.

**786.** BOAS, HANS ULRICH. Parametrization in generative grammar. *In* (pp. 406–9) **4.**

**787.** CARPENTER, B. Phrase meaning and categorial grammar. Unpub. doct. diss., Univ. of Edinburgh. [Abstr. in IT (39:4) 1616.]

**788.** CHUNG, EUN-KU. GB iron gwa anaphora eui euimi haesuk. (The interpretation of anaphora in GB theory.) JELLC (30) 239–53.

**789.** COMRIE, BERNARD. Language universals and linguistic typology: syntax and morphology. (Bibl. 1982, 2050.) Oxford: Blackwell. pp. xii, 264. (Second ed.: first ed. 1981.)

**790.** CORVER, NORBERT. Left branch extractions and DP. Linguistics in the Netherlands 1989 (6) 31–40.

**791.** DE VRIES, GERTRUD. (Un)specified NPs and scope. Linguistics in the Netherlands 1989 (6) 163–72.

**792.** FUKUMIRA, TORAJI. Eigo to eigogaku: dentoushugi to henkei seisei bunpou. (English and English linguistics: traditionalism and transformational generative grammar.) Tokyo: Taishukan. pp. vi, 208.

**793.** GEORGE, ALEXANDER. How not to become confused about linguistics. *In* (pp. 90–110) **52.**

**794.** HALLIDAY, M. A. K. An introduction to functional grammar. (Bibl. 1985, 1529.) Rev. by M. Toolan in EngS (70:3) 280–2; by Hilton Hubbard in English Usage (20:2) 69–73.

**795.** HAMITOUCHE, FATIHA. Studies in word order: a functional pragmatic approach. Unpub. doct. diss., Univ. of Essex, 1988. [Abstr. in DA (49) 3703A.]

**796.** HENDRIKSE, A. P. Syntactic structures as pragmatic options. SL (13:2) 333–79.

**797.** HONG, YOUNG-YEAH. The empty category principle: antecedent-government. Unpub. doct. diss., Ewha Woman's Univ., Seoul.

**798.** JO, IN-HEE. A unitary analysis of emphatic self-forms as intensifying adverbs. JELLC (30) 255–90.

**799.** KANG, BEOMMO. Functional inheritance, anaphora, and semantic interpretation in a generalized categorial grammar. Unpub. doct. diss., Brown Univ., 1988. [Abstr. in DA (49) 2202A.]

**800.** KEENAN, EDWARD L. Universal grammar: 15 essays. (Bibl. 1987, 954.) Rev. by François Chevillet in EA (42:2) 202–3.

**801.** KEMMER, SUZANNE E. The middle voice: a typological and diachronic study. Unpub. doct. diss., Stanford Univ., 1988. [Abstr. in DA (49) 3704A.]

**802.** KIM, YANG SOON.　Licensing principles and phrase structure. Unpub. doct. diss., Univ. of Wisconsin–Madison, 1988. [Abstr. in DA (49) 3350A.]

**803.** KO, TAE-HONG.　Youngeo myungryeongbeob yeongu: hyeondae youngeo jungsim euro. (A study of the English imperative: centred in modern English.) JUJH (22)1986, 141–65.

**804.** KOKTOVÁ, EVA.　Sentence adverbials in a functional description. (Bibl. 1988, 550.) Rev. by Frederica Venier in Journal of Pragmatics (13:2) 292–6.

**805.** KUBOTA, MASAHITO.　Why 'to VP' ha younin kanoude aru. (Why 'to VP' is acceptable.) SEL (66:1) 51–64.

**806.** LASNIK, HOWARD.　Essays on anaphora. Dordrecht: Kluwer. pp. ix, 179. (Studies in natural language and linguistic theory, 16.)

**807.** ——URIAGEREKA, JUAN.　A course in GB syntax: lectures on binding and empty categories. (Bibl. 1988, 554.) Rev. by Juhani Rudanko in SN (61:2) 233–7.

**808.** LEE, DAE SOK.　The nature of intransitivity reflected in passives. Unpub. doct. diss., Univ. of Washington, 1988. [Abstr. in DA (49) 2202A.]

**809.** LEFFEL, KATHERINE ALLYSON GILMORE.　Free X-bar theory and barriers to movement and government. Unpub. doct. diss., Univ. of Florida, 1988. [Abstr. in DA (49) 3705A.]

**810.** LYS, FRANZISKA.　An analysis of aspectual compositionality in English and German. Unpub. doct. diss., Northwestern Univ., 1988. [Abstr. in DA (49) 3351A.]

**811.** McDANIEL, DANA.　Partial and multiple wh-movement. Natural Language and Linguistic Theory (7:4) 565–604.

**812.** MEL'ČUK, IGOR' ALEKSANDROVIČ; PERTSOV, NIKOLAJ V.; KITTREDGE, RICHARD.　Surface syntax of English: a formal model within the meaning–text framework. (Bibl. 1987, 970.) Rev. by Georges Bourcier in EA (42:2) 196–7.

**813.** MORRILL, G. V.　Extraction and coordination in phrase structure grammar and categorial grammar. Unpub. doct. diss., Univ. of Edinburgh. [Abstr. in IT (39:4) 1621.]

**814.** NAPOLI, DONNA JO.　Predication theory: a case study for indexing theory. Cambridge: CUP. pp. ix, 369. (Cambridge studies in linguistics, 50.)

**815.** NUYTS, JAN.　Negatives are not fond of travelling: a cognitive–pragmatic reconsideration of negative raising. Amsterdam: Univ. of Amsterdam, Inst. for General Linguistics, 1987. pp. 55. (Working papers in functional grammar, 21.)

**816.** PARK, S. H.　A parody on government and governments. YYY (5) 145–58.

**817.** PEACOCKE, CHRISTOPHER.　When is a grammar psychologically real? *In* (pp. 111–30) **52**.

**818.** POPOWICH, F. P.    Reflexives and tree unification grammar. Unpub. doct. diss., Univ. of Edinburgh. [Abstr. in IT (39:4) 1622.]

**819.** RADFORD, ANDREW.    Transformational grammar: a first course. Cambridge: CUP, 1988. pp. xii, 625. (Cambridge textbooks in linguistics.) Rev. by Bas Aarts in EngS (70:5) 456–8.

**820.** RICE, SALLY ANN.    Towards a cognitive model of transitivity. Unpub. doct. diss., Univ. of California, San Diego, 1987. [Abstr. in DA (49) 1789A].

**821.** SCALISE, SERGIO.    The notion of 'head' in morphology. Yearbook of Morphology (1) 1988, 229–45.

**822.** SCHOLTEN, CHRISTINA GEERTRUIDA MARIA.    Principles of universal grammar and the auxiliary verb phenomenon. Unpub. doct. diss., Univ. of Maryland College Park, 1988. [Abstr. in DA (49) 2642–3A.]

**823.** SEELY, THOMAS DANIEL.    Anaphoric relations, chains, and paths. Unpub. doct. diss., Univ. of Massachusetts, 1988. [Abstr. in DA (49) 3709A.]

**824.** SEKI, SHIGEKI.    Chikaku to teiji. (Perception and presentation.) SEL (66:1) 81–96.

**825.** SEO, SANG-OK.    Sortal incorrectness eui euimironjeok bunsuk. (Semantic analysis of sortal incorrectness.) JELLC (29) 1987, 197–242. (Mis-categorization.)

**826.** SOAMES, SCOTT.    Subject–auxiliary inversion and gaps in generalized phrase structure grammar. Linguistics and Philosophy (12:3) 373–82.

**827.** SUH, SOO-HYEON.    Jaegwisa eui nonri hyungtae. (The logical form of an anaphor.) EngSt (13) 93–105.

**828.** URIAGEREKA, JUAN.    On government. Unpub. doct. diss., Univ. of Connecticut, 1988. [Abstr. in DA (49) 3710A.]

**829.** VEIKHMAN, G. A.    The text and its constituents: the syntactical aspect. PP (32:4) 175–84.

**830.** WESTERGAARD, MARIT R.    Definite NP anaphora: a pragmatic approach. (Bibl. 1988, 574.) Rev. by Ekkehard König in Ang (107:1/2) 116–19.

**831.** WIERZBICKA, ANNA.    The semantics of grammar. Amsterdam: Benjamins, 1988. pp. x, 617. (Studies in language companion series, 18.)

## GRAMMAR OF CONTEMPORARY ENGLISH

**832.** ATTAL, JEAN-PIERRE.    Grammaire et usage de l'anglais. (Bibl. 1987, 1017.) Rev. by John D. Gallagher in EA (42:4) 456–7.

**833.** BOOHER, DIANNA.    Good grief, good grammar. New York: Fawcett/Crest. pp. 304. Rev. in BW, 9 July, 9.

**834.** BURLAKOVA, V. V. (ed.).    Spornyje voprosy anglijskoj grammatiki. (Moot points of English grammar.) Leningrad: Leningrad UP, 1988.

**835.** CHERCHI, LUCIEN.    La grammaire anglaise au fil des textes.

Dijon: Aleï, 1986. pp. 288. Rev. by Jean Lavédrine in EA (42:2) 199–201.
836. COTTLE, BASIL. The language of literature: English grammar in action. (Bibl. 1986, 1933.) Rev. by Alan Ward in RES (38:150) 1987, 234–5; by E. G. Stanley in NQ (36:1) 84–7; by J. M. Kirk in Lore and Language (8:2) 108–9.
837. DUŠKOVÁ, LIBUŠE, et al. Mluvnice současné angličtiny na pozadí češtiny. (A grammar of present-day English against the background of Czech.) Prague: Academia, 1988. pp. 673.
838. EDMISTON, CYNTHIA DENISE. English grammar as a stratified system of signs. Unpub. doct. diss., Rice Univ., 1988. [Abstr. in DA (49) 3013A.]
839. GLÄSER, ROSEMARIE. Phraseologie der englischen Sprache. Tübingen: Niemeyer, 1986. pp. 201. Rev. by Friedrich Ungerer in Ang (107:3/4) 473–7; by Eckhart Weiher in Archiv (226:2) 416–21.
840. GREENBAUM, SIDNEY. Good English and the grammarian. London; New York: Longman, 1988. pp. xi, 152. (English language, 17.) Rev. by Walter Nash in LRB (11:2) 16–17.
841. HATFULL, DEREK. The grammar's inside English. Westerham: Hatfull. pp. 112.
842. LAMPRECHT, ADOLF. Grammatik der englischen Sprache. Neufassung. Berlin: Cornelsen- Velhagen & Klasing; Volk und Wissen, 1986. pp. 420. Rev. by Wolfgang Zydatiss in Ang (107:1/2) 106–10.
843. LEECH, GEOFFREY; CRUICKSHANK, BENITA; IVANIČ, ROZ. An A–Z of English grammar and usage. London: Arnold. pp. xv, 575.
844. LEGENHAUSEN, LIENHARD. Grammatical fuzziness im Englischen. AAA (14:1) 73–88.
845. LEITNER, GERHARD (ed.). The English reference grammar: language and linguistics, writers and readers. Tübingen: Niemeyer, 1986. pp. 450. (Linguistische Arbeiten, 172.) Rev. by Friedrich Wilhelm Gester in Ang (107:1/2) 100–5.
846. OKUNO, TADATOKU. Henkei bunpou niyoru eigo no bunseki. (The analysis of English through transformational grammar.) Tokyo: Kaitaku. pp. x, 366.
847. SCHENDL, HERBERT. Semantic verb classes and the use of diagnostics in Old English. In (pp. 124–39) MANFRED MARKUS (ed.), Historical English: on the occasion of Karl Brunner's 100th birthday. Innsbruck: Institut für Anglistik, 1988. pp. ix, 244. (Innsbrucker Beiträge zur Kulturwissenschaft: Anglistische Reihe, 1.)

## MORPHOLOGY OF CONTEMPORARY ENGLISH

848. BAGEMIHL, BRUCE. Alternate phonologies and morphologies. See 714.
849. BATES, DAWN E. Prominence relations and structure in English compound morphology. Unpub. doct. diss., Univ. of Washington, 1988. [Abstr. in DA (50) 675A.]
850. BAUER, LAURIE. Irregularity in past non-finite verb-forms. NZEN (3) 13–15.

**851.** DAHL, TRINE. Compound adjectives in English general and special language. *In* (pp. 85–94) **24.**

**852.** INKELAS, SHARON. Prosodic constituency in the lexicon. *See* **755.**

**853.** KASTOVSKY, DIETER. Wortbildung und Semantik. Düsseldorf: Schwann-Bagel; Berne: Francke, 1982. pp. 334. (Studienreihe Englisch, 14.) Rev. by Rudolf Emons in Ang (104:1/2) 1986, 136–44.

**854.** KNUTOVÁ, GABRIELA; KUSTROVÁ, MARCELA. Konverzia ako jeden z najproduktívnejších slovotvorných tvoreniu slovies v angličtine. (Conversion as one of the most productive verb-forming types of word formation in English). CJa (33) 12–15.

**855.** PILCH, HERBERT. Syntax des englischen tatpuruṣa. *In* (pp. 259–75) **24.**

**856.** SCHLINDWEIN, DEBORAH. The phonological geometry of morpheme concatenation. *See* **718.**

**857.** SUH, JUNG-IL. Subjunctive debate. JHY (8:2) 1987, 1–27. (In Korean.)

**858.** SZPYRA, JOLANTA. The phonology–morphology interface: cycles, levels and words. *See* **771.**

## HISTORICAL MORPHOLOGY OF ENGLISH

**859.** CHEVILLET, FRANÇOIS. Les pronoms allocutoires en français et en anglais: éléments pour une réflexion socio-historique contrastive. *In* (pp. 17–36) **22.**

**860.** KASTOVSKY, DIETER. Typological changes in the history of English word-formation. *In* (pp. 281–93) **5.**

**861.** MCINTOSH, ANGUS. English compounds containing OE *-lāc, -læcan*, ON *-leik* and some related matters. *In* (pp. 221–36) **24.**

**862.** MAUSCH, HANNA. Personal pronouns and markedness: an interpretation of grammatically conditioned changes. SAP (22) 81–90.

**863.** OGURA, MICHIKO. Simple reflexives, compound reflexives, and compound forms of 'refl/non-refl pron + self' in Old and Middle English. StudME (4) 49–72.

**864.** PADDOCK, HAROLD. On explaining macrovariation in the sibilant and nasal suffixes of English. FLH (9:1) 1988, 235–69.

**865.** SHEEN, DING-TAOU. The historical development of reciprocal pronouns in Middle English with selected early modern English comparisons. Unpub. doct. diss., Ball State Univ., 1988. [Abstr. in DA (50) 1295A.]

**866.** TERASAWA, JUN. Metrical constraints on Old English compounds. PoetT (31) 1–16.

**867.** VIERECK, WOLFGANG. Diachronic English morphology and the notion of frequency. *In* (pp. 367–73) **24.**

**868.** ZBIERSKA-SAWALA, ANNA. On the status of French derivational suffixes in Early Middle English. SAP (22) 91–9.

## SINGLE MORPHEMES

**869.** *-ing*] SØRENSEN, KNUD. On adjectives in *-ing and -y*. *In* (pp. 355–66) **24.**

**870.**   *-ious/-uous*] KJELLMER, GÖRAN.   '*-uous*' and '*-ious*': on instability of the English suffix system. NM (90:3/4) 321–6.

**871.**   *-y*] SØRENSEN, KNUD.   On adjectives in *-ing* and *-y*. *In* (pp. 355–66) **24.**

## SYNTAX OF CONTEMPORARY ENGLISH

**872.**   AARTS, F. G. A. M.   Dutch progress in English syntax: Zandvoort's *Handbook of English Grammar* and after. *In* (pp. 67–79) **47.**

**873.**   ABBAS, HASSOONEI HASHIM.   Some remarks on the prepositions 'in', 'on' and 'to' in English and standard Arabic. Al-Mustansiriya Literary Review (Al-Mustansiriya Univ., Baghdad) (11) 1985, 41–50.

**874.**   ABDEL-LATIF, N. M.   A contrastive analysis of interrogative structures in English and Arabic. Unpub. doct. diss., Univ. of Wales, 1986. [Abstr. in IT (39:1) 23.]

**875.**   ABDELMOUMENE, N.   Sentential complementation in French, English and Arabic. Unpub. doct. diss., Univ. of Essex. [Abstr. in IT (38:4) 1451.]

**876.**   AKIMOTO, YOSHIHARU.   A study of verbo-nominal structures in English. Tokyo: Shinozaki. pp. vi, 410.

**877.**   ANDERSON, JOHN.   Periphrases and paradigms. *In* (pp. 1–10) **34.**

**878.**   ARIMOTO, MASATAKE.   Jougoyouso no bunseki to hobun kouzou. (The distribution of pleonastic elements and the complement structure of English.) SEL (66:1) 65–80.

**879.**   BAKER, C. L.   English syntax. Cambridge, MA; London: MIT Press. pp. xv, 504.

**880.**   BAUER, LAURIE.   Marginal modals in New Zealand English. Te Reo (32) 3–16.

**881.**   BÁZLIK, MIROSLAV.   A contrastive analysis of the Slovak prepositional constructions with the accusative and their English equivalents. *In* (pp. 9–29) **62.**

**882.**   —— Z konfrontácie subjektu v angličtine a v slovenčine. (Confronting the subject in English and Slovak.) CJa (33) 108–11.

**883.**   —— (ed.).   Zbornik filozofickej fakulty. *See* **62.**

**884.**   BEUKEMA, FRITS; VERHEIJEN, RON.   Particle constructions in English. *In* (pp. 109–25) **47.**

**885.**   BISCHOFF, GUNTHER.   Better times: Programm zum Gebrauch der englischen Zeiten. (Bibl. 1987, 1094.) Rev. by Thomas K. Koller in AAA (14:2) 187–8.

**886.**   BÖHMEROVÁ, ADELA.   Contrastive analysis of some aspects of grammatical negation in English and in Slovak. *In* (pp. 31–48) **62.**

**887.**   BREWER, N. M.   Modality and factivity: one perspective on the meaning of the English modal auxiliaries. Unpub. doct. diss., Univ. of Leeds, 1988. [Abstr. in IT (38:4) 1452; in DA (49) 1786A.]

**888.**   CHEN, PI-FEN LIU.   A study of the article system in English. Unpub. doct. diss., Michigan State Univ., 1988. [Abstr. in DA (49) 3012–13A.]

**889.**   CHESTERMAN, ANDREW.   Definiteness in English and Finnish. Unpub. doct. diss., Univ. of Reading, 1988. [Abstr. in DA (49) 3349A.]

**890.** CHUNG, EUN-KU.   Youngeo eui choeung hyunsang: kineungjeok bunsuk. (Anaphora in English: a functional analysis.) Unpub. doct. diss., Sungkyunkwan Univ., Seoul.

**891.** CORNISH, FRANCIS.   Anaphoric relations in English and French: a discourse perspective. Dover, NH: Croom Helm, 1986. (Bibl. 1988, 633.) Rev. by Marie-Paule Woodley in MLR (84:3) 682–3.

**892.** COTTE, PIERRE.   La négation: domaine anglais. St Étienne: Université de St Étienne, 1988. pp. 171.

**893.** DE HAAN, PIETER.   Postmodifying clauses in the English noun phrase: a corpus based study. See **519**.

**894.** DUŠKOVÁ, LIBUŠE.   On the function of the English possessive case. PP (32:1) 6–13.

**895.** ELSNESS, JOHAN.   The English present perfect: has it seen its best days? In (pp. 95–106) **24**.

**896.** FOX, BARBARA A.   Discourse structure and anaphora: written and conversational English. (Bibl. 1987, 1116.) Rev. by François Chevillet in EA (42:3) 335–6; by Francis Cornish in Lingua (79:2/3) 229–43.

**897.** FRAURUD, KARI.   Towards a non-uniform treatment of definite NP's in discourse. In (pp. 75–87) **48**.

**898.** Entry cancelled.

**899.** GOLKOVÁ, EVA.   Větné začátky v angličtině a češtině. (Sentence starters in English and Czech.) In (pp. 19–20) **6**.

**900.** HAJIČOVÁ, EVA.   Negation scope: ambiguity or vagueness? PP (32:1) 13–18.

**901.** HANNAY, MICHAEL.   English existentials in functional grammar. Dordrecht: Foris, 1985. pp. xiv, 230. (Functional grammar, 3.)

**902.** HASSAN, ABDUL, SH. QASSIM.   The object in English and Arabic: a contrastive study. Al-Mustansiriya Literary Review (Al-Mustansiriya Univ., Baghdad) (12) 1985, 69–91.

**903.** EL-HASSAN, SHAHIR.   Stativity and variation in English adjectives and nouns. SAP (22) 101–17.

**904.** HEGGIE, LORIE A.   The syntax of copular structures. Unpub. doct. diss., Univ. of Southern California, 1988. [Abstr. in DA (49) 3703A.]

**905.** HINTIKKA, JAAKKO.   Logical form and linguistic theory. In (pp. 41–57) **52**.

**906.** HOEKSTRA, ERIC.   Binding, objects and the structure of the English VP. Linguistics in the Netherlands 1989 (6) 71–80.

**907.** HÖSSELBARTH, LUTZ.   Zu einigen theoretischen Aspekten der Beschreibung englischer Kausalkonjunktionen. PP (32:1) 32–43.

**908.** HU, JIAZHEN.   Temporal interpretation in English. Unpub. doct. diss., Univ. of Arizona, 1988. [Abstr. in DA (50) 127A.]

**909.** HUDSON, RICHARD.   English passives, grammatical relations and default inheritance. Lingua (79:1) 17–48.

**910.** HUETTNER, ALISON K.   Adjunct infinitives in English. Unpub. doct. diss., Univ. of Massachusetts. [Abstr. in DA (50) 1293A.]

**911.** INADA, TOSHIAKI. Hobun no kouzou. (The structure of comple-mentation.) Tokyo: Taishukan. pp. viii, 240.

**912.** JACOBSON, SVEN. Some observations on article variation in English. *In* (pp. 99–108) **34.**

**913.** JØRGENSEN, ERIK. It + COPULA + PREDICATIVE + for + (PRO)NOUN + to-INFINITIVE. EngS (70:2) 167–8.

**914.** KIM, HYANG-RYUN. Iconicity in syntactic coding of topic continuity based on English narrative. JELL (35) 785–810.

**915.** KIM, JONG-DO. Youngeo eui sang yeongu. (A study of aspect in English.) Unpub. doct. diss., Yonsei Univ., Seoul.

**916.** KOLÁŘ, PAVEL. Přítomnost v orientaci časového systému. (Present time within the tense system.) *In* (p. 25) **6.**

**917.** KUBIŠOVÁ, ALŽBETA. Expressing time relations in English as a problem of Slovak learners. *In* (pp. 49–59) **62.**

**918.** KWON, CHUNG-JA. A study on pronominal variable binding in English. Unpub. doct. diss., Sogang Univ., Seoul.

**919.** LEE, KEUM-HEE. Youngeo eui tonghap gyeok iron. (A unified theory of case in English.) EngSt (13) 106–27.

**920.** LEITZKE, EVA. (De)nominale Adjektive im heutigen Englisch: Untersuchungen zur Morphologie, Syntax, Semantik und Pragmatik von Adjectiv-Nomen-Kombinationen der Typen 'atomic energy' und 'criminal lawyer'. Tübingen: Niemeyer, pp. x, 200. (Linguistische Arbeiten, 221.)

**921.** LYSVÅG, PER. Adverbials from left to right. *In* (pp. 195–208) **24.**

**922.** MCCAWLEY, JAMES D. The syntactic phenomena of English. Chicago; London: Chicago UP, 1988. 2 vols. pp. xviii, 768.

**923.** MACKENZIE, J. LACHLAN. Aspects of nominalization in English and Dutch. Amsterdam: Univ. of Amsterdam, Inst. for General Linguistics, 1986. pp. 32. (Working papers in functional grammar, 15.)

**924.** —— The representation of nominal predicates in the fund: a new proposal. Amsterdam: Univ. of Amsterdam, Inst. for General Linguistics, 1987. pp. 18. (Working papers in functional grammar, 25.)

**925.** MCNULTY, ELAINE MARIE. The syntax of adjunct predicates. Unpub. doct. diss., Univ. of Connecticut, 1988. [Abstr. in DA (49) 3706A.]

**926.** MEYER, CHARLES F. Restrictive apposition: an indeterminate category. EngS (70:2) 147–66.

**927.** MIN, JAE-KHI. A syntactic review of English nominalization. JELL (35) 149–69.

**928.** NOSEK, JIŘÍ. Jazyková typologie a kategorie určenosti. (Linguistic typology and the category of determination.) *In* (p. 31) **6.**

**929.** OGIHARA, TOSHIYUKI. Temporal reference in English and Japanese. Unpub. doct. diss., Univ. of Texas at Austin. [Abstr. in DA (50) 1648–9A.]

**930.** OHKADO, MASAYUKI. INFL and negating particles. Lingua (77:1) 1–12.

**931.** OSSELTON, NOEL E. Thematic genitives. *In* (pp. 138–44) **30.**

**932.** POLÁČKOVÁ, MILENA. Analytické verbonominální konstrukce v překladu mezi češtinou a angličtinou. (Analytical verb-noun constructions in English-Czech and Czech-English translations). ČMF (71) 19–25.

**933.** PREBENSEN, HENRIK.    Experiments in noun phrase comprehension on the computer. *In* (pp. 161–72) **48.**

**934.** RIGTER, BOB; BEUKEMA, FRITS.    First explorations in English syntax: part 2, A government and binding approach to English sentence structures. (Bibl. 1985, 1647.) Rev. by Bas Aarts in EngS (69:3) 1988, 286–7.

**935.** RUŽIČKOVÁ, EVA.    On verbs referring to a state of mind and feeling. *In* (pp. 61–7) **62.**

**936.** SCHOPF, ALFRED.    Das Verzeitungssystem des Englischen und seine Textfunktion. Tübingen: Niemeyer, 1984. pp. xvi, 418. (Linguistische Arbeiten, 140.) Rev. by Wolfram Bublitz in Ang (105:3/4) 1987, 429–32.

**937.** SCHWARTZ, LEE ANN.    Coordination: an ATN perspective. Unpub. doct. diss., Georgetown Univ., 1987. [Abstr. in DA (49) 3708–9A.]

**938.** SIGURD, BENGT.    A supplementary relativization hierarchy based on the complexity of the relative phrase. StudL (43:1) 33–46.

**939.** SUZUKI, TATSUYA.    The structure of English gerunds. Unpub. doct. diss., Univ. of Washington, 1988. [Abstr. in DA (49) 2204A.]

**940.** SWAN, TORIL.    A note on initial adverbials and word order in English and Norwegian. *In* (pp. 331–44) **24.**

**941.** TSUZUKI, MASAKO.    Eigo ni okeru nijiteki jutsugo no kousatsu: kekkano jutsugo to byoushano jutsugo. (Secondary predicate constructions in English: resultative predicates and depictive predicates.) SEL (66:1) 33–50.

**942.** UNGERER, FRIEDRICH.    Scope as syntactic principle. *In* (pp. 338–51) **5.**

**943.** —— Syntax der englischen Adverbialen. Tübingen: Niemeyer, 1988. pp. xi, 415. (Linguistische Arbeiten, 215.) Rev. by J. Buysschaert in LeuB (78:2) 230–1.

**944.** VAN OIRSOUW, ROBERT R.    The syntax of coordination. London: Croom Helm, 1987. pp. 295. (Croom Helm linguistics.) Rev. by Anneke Neijt in Lingua (78:4) 343–56.

**945.** VON RANDOW, ELISE.    Valente Substantive des Englischen. Tübingen: Narr, 1986. pp. 307. (Tübinger Beiträge zur Linguistik, 294.) Rev. by Thomas Herbst in Ang (107:3/4) 455–63.

**946.** WARREN, BEATRICE.    Pseudo-problematic pseudo-adjectives. EngS (70:4) 248–56.

**947.** WEBER, ELIZABETH GEAN.    Varieties of questions in English conversation: a study of the role of morphosyntax in declarative and nonclausal forms. Unpub. doct. diss., Univ. of California, Los Angeles. [Abstr. in DA (50) 941A.]

**948.** YANG, HEI-SOON.    On definite reference in English. JELL (35) 811–28.

**949.** ZAGONA, KAREN.   Verb phrase syntax: a parametric study of English and Spanish. Dordrecht; Boston, MA; London: Kluwer, 1988. pp. xiii, 213. (Studies in natural language and linguistic theory, 13.)

**950.** ZRIBI-HERTZ, ANNE.   Anaphor building and narrative point of view: English reflexive pronouns in sentence and discourse. Lang (65:4) 695–727.

## HISTORICAL SYNTAX OF ENGLISH

**951.** BAGHDIKIAN, SONIA.   Ambiguous negations in Chaucer and Queen Elizabeth. *In* (pp. 41–8) **30.**

**952.** BJØRGE, ANNE KARI.   'I poor man is singing': subject–verb concord in eighteenth-century English grammar. *In* (pp. 47–65) **24.**

**953.** BLAKE, N. F.   Negation in Shakespeare. *In* (pp. 89–111) **30.**

**954.** BLOCKLEY, MARY.   Old English coordination, apposition, and the syntax of English poetry. MP (87:2) 115–31.

**955.** BREIVIK, LEIV EGIL.   On the diachrony of the English particle comparative. *In* (pp. 67–83) **24.**

**956.** BRINTON, LAUREL J.   The development of English aspectual systems: aspectualizers and post-verbal particles. Cambridge: CUP, 1988. pp. xii, 307. (Cambridge studies in linguistics, 49.)

**957.** DENISON, DAVID.   Auxiliary + impersonal in Old English. FLH (9:1) 1988, 139–66.

**958.** ——On word order in Old English. *In* (pp. 139–55) **47.**

**959.** FILL, ALWIN.   Purism and word formation: word substitution in 16th and 19th century English. *In* (pp. 231–44) MANFRED MARKUS (ed.), Historical English: on the occasion of Karl Brunner's 100th birthday. Innsbruck: Institut für Anglistik, 1988. pp. ix, 244. (Innsbrucker Beiträge zur Kulturwissenschaft: Anglistische Reihe, 1.)

**960.** FISCHER, OLGA.   The rise of the *for NP to V* construction: an explanation. *In* (pp. 67–88) **30.**

**961.** GOOSSENS, LOUIS.   The auxiliarization of English modals. Amsterdam: Univ. of Amsterdam, Inst. for General Linguistics, 1986, pp. 45. (Working papers in functional grammar, 7.)

**962.** HOUSTON, JOHN PORTER.   Shakespearean sentences: a study in style and syntax. (Bibl. 1988, 676.) Rev. by Russ McDonald in RQ (42:4) 881–3; by Anthony Graham-White in TJ (41:4) 572.

**963.** JACK, GEORGE.   Evidence of a jussive infinitive in Middle English. NM (90:3/4) 255–71.

**964.** JOHANNESSON, NILS-LENNART.   Subject topicalization in Ælfric's homilies. *In* (pp. 109–21) **34.**

**965.** KETTEMANN, BERNHARD.   The transition from the impersonal to the personal use of the verb *like* in late Middle English and early Modern English — some previously neglected determinants of variation. *In* (pp. 210–18) MANFRED MARKUS (ed.), Historical English: on the occasion of Karl Brunner's 100th birthday. Innsbruck: Institut für Anglistik, 1988. pp. ix, 244. (Innsbrucker Beiträge zur Kulturwissenschaft: Anglistische Reihe, 1.)

**966.** KOOPMAN, WILLEM F.    Old English constructions with three verbs. FLH (9:1) 1988, 271–300.

**967.** LIGGINS, ELIZABETH M.    Syntax and style in the Old English *Orosius*. In (pp. 245–73) **56.**

**968.** MANABE, KAZUMI.    The syntactic and stylistic development of the infinitive in Middle English. Fukuoka: Kyushu UP. pp. 206.

**969.** MITCHELL, BRUCE.    *Beowulf*: six notes, mostly syntactical. Leeds Studies in English (20) 311–18.

**970.** MUKHIN, ANATOLIJ M.; SHAMANAYEVA, ALLA N.    Groups of transitive verbs with dative in Old English. FLH (9:1) 1988, 193–212.

**971.** OGURA, MICHIKO.    Verbs with the reflexive pronoun and constructions with *self* in Old and early Middle English. Cambridge: Brewer. pp. xiv, 113.

**972.** RAINER, MARIA EVA.    Das Perfekt im Spätmittel- und Frühneuenglischen: eine Frequenz- und Funktionsanalyse anhand von Brieftexten. Innsbruck: Institut für Anglistik und Amerikanistik. pp. 216. (Innsbrucker Beiträge zur Kulturwissenschaft: Anglistische Reihe, 2.) Rev. by Thomas K. Koller in AAA (14:2) 185–7.

**973.** TIEKEN-BOON VAN OSTADE, INGRID.    Negative *do* in eighteenth-century English: the power of prestige. In (pp. 157–71) **47.**

**974.** TOYAMA, KIKUO.    On the agreement of the subject and predicative adjective/past participle in Old English prose. StudME (4) 31–47.

**975.** VAN GELDEREN, ELLY.    The historical rationale behind split infinitives and kindred constructions. Archiv (226:1) 1–18.

**976.** VON SEEFRANZ-MONTAG, ARIANE.    Syntaktische Funktionen und Wortstellungsveränderung: Die Entwicklung 'subjektiver' Konstruktionen in einigen Sprachen. (Bibl. 1987, 1226.) Rev. by Angelika Lutz in Ang (106:3/4) 1988, 466–73.

## SINGLE SYNTACTICAL ITEMS

**977.** *be*] STYAN, EVELYN MARIE MATHESON.    Elementary sentences containing 'be': a semantic analysis of subject–predicate relations. Unpub. doct. diss., McGill Univ., 1988. [Abstr. in DA (50) 128A.]

**978.** *be/have*] RYDÉN, MATS; BRORSTRÖM, SVERKER.    The 'be/have' variation with intransitives in English: with special reference to the late modern period. (Bibl. 1987, 1238.) Rev. by Georges Bourcier in EA (42:4) 458–9; by Rodney Sampson in EngS (70:5) 458–9.

**979.** *but*] BLAKEMORE, DIANE.    Denial and contrast: a relevance theoretic analysis of *but*. Linguistics and Philosophy (12:1) 15–37.

**980.** *direct/directly*] OPDAHL, LISE.    'Did they purchase it direct – or directly?': on *direct* and *directly* as verb modifiers in present-day British and American English. In (pp. 245–57) **24.**

**981.** *do*] BRORSTRÖM, SVERKER.    Periphrastic *do* v. the *do*-less form in the letters of Lady Brilliana Harley (b. 1600? – d. 1643). In (pp. 15–28) **34.**

**982.** *do*] MAGNUSSON, ULF.    The verb *do* in the LOB Corpus. In (pp. 131–45) **34.**

**983.** *do*] TIEKEN-BOON VAN OSTADE, INGRID. Negative *do* in eighteenth-century English: the power of prestige. *In* (pp. 157–71) **47.**

**984.** *each other/one another*] STUURMAN, FRITS. 'Each other' – 'one another': to reciprocate. EngS (70:4) 356–9.

**985.** *even if/even though*] KJELLMER, GÖRAN. 'Even if' and 'even though'*. EngS (70:3) 256–69.

**986.** *from ... to ...*] GERSON, STANLEY. 'From ... to ...' as an intensifying collocation. EngS (70:4) 360–71.

**987.** *have*] BRUGMAN, CLAUDIA MARLEA. The syntax and semantics of 'have' and its complements. Unpub. doct. diss., Univ. of California, Berkeley, 1988. [Abstr. in DA (50) 935A.]

**988.** *help/help to*] BURCHFIELD, ROBERT. 'Help' or 'help to'? MS (83:2) 119–21. (Also in Sunday Times, London, 26 June 1988.)

**989.** *intention*] KUDRNÁČOVÁ, NADĚŽDA. K problematice jednoho užití pojmu zámĕr. (Problems of using the term 'intention'.) *In* (p. 27) **6.**

**990.** *ought (to)*] STUURMAN, FRITS. Approaching *ought (to)*. *In* (pp. 127–38) **47.**

**991.** *that*] BEAL, JOAN. Goodbye to all 'that'? The history and present behaviour of optional *that*. *In* (pp. 49–66) **30.**

**992.** *that*] SEPPÄNEN, AIMO. *That*-clauses as complements of prepositions. *In* (pp. 315–30) **24.**

**993.** *well*] FINELL, ANNE. 'Well' now and then. Journal of Pragmatics (13:4) 653–6.

# VOCABULARY

## GENERAL STUDIES

**994.** BERG, THOMAS.   On the internal structure of polysyllabic monomorphemic words: the case for superrimes. StudL (43:1) 5–32.

**995.** BOCHNER, HARRY.   The forms of words: a theory of lexical relationships. Unpub. doct. diss., Harvard Univ., 1988. [Abstr. in DA (49) 3012A.]

**996.** HOWARD, PHILIP.   Winged words. London: Hamilton, 1988. pp. xv, 292. Rev. by Martin Fagg in Listener (120) 7 July, 28.

**997.** RUŽIČKOVA, EVA.   On verbs referring to a state of mind and feeling. In (pp. 61–7) **62.**

**998.** SCHNEIDER, EDGAR W.   Advantages and limitations of text corpora in the study of lexis. In (pp. 300–18) **4.**

## VOCABULARY OF CONTEMPORARY ENGLISH

**999.** BENNETT, T. J. A.   Aspects of English colour collocations and idioms. Heidelberg: Winter, 1988. pp. 301. (Anglistische Forschungen, 197.) Rev. by Alwin Fill in AAA (14:1) 119–20.

**1000.** HILSKÝ, MARTIN.   Hříšné hříčky: jazyk rané shakespearovské komedie z hlediska překladatelského. (Sinful puns: the language of early Shakespearean comedy from a translator's viewpoint). In (p. 45) **6.**

**1001.** JOHANSSON, STIG; HOFLAND, KNUT.   Frequency analysis of English vocabulary and grammar: based on the LOB Corpus: vol. 1, Tag frequencies and word frequencies; vol. 2, Tag combinations and word combinations. See **527a.**

**1002.** KRÁMSKÝ, JIŘÍ.   Synonyma v angličtině. (Synonyms in English.) Part 39. CJa (32) 219–23, 260–3, 307–11, 349–53; (33) 11–15, 66–70.

**1003.** KRATZ, HENRY.   Raunch. SN (61:2) 175–82. (Vulgarisms in the vocabulary of *Little Red Rooster* by Greg Matthews.)

**1004.** LEITCH, ROGER (ed.).   The book of Sandy Stewart. Edinburgh: Scottish Academic Press, 1988. pp. 129. Rev. by J. C. Massey in Lore and Language (8:2) 119–20.

**1005.** MORT, SIMON (ed.).   Longman Guardian new words. (Bibl. 1986, 1781.) Rev. by Václav Řeřicha in CJa (32) 425–6.

**1006.** OČENÁŠ, BENJAMÍN.   Eufemismy, džentilizmy a sobrikety v angličtine. (Euphemisms, genteelisms and sobriquets in English.) CJa (32) 404–7.

**1007.** PEPRNÍK, JAROSLAV.   Pojmenování barev v angličtině a češtině. (Colour terms in English and Czech.) In (pp. 439–52) MILAN HRALA (ed.), Translatologica Pragensia (2:1). Prague: Charles UP, 1986. pp. 624. (Acta Universitatis Carolinae; Philologica 1–3.)

**1008.** PERSSON, GUNNAR.   On the semantics of collective nouns in English. In (pp. 179–88) **34.**

**1009.** POLÁČKOVÁ, MILENA.   Slovní hříčky a problémy překladu z angličtiny do češtiny. (Puns and the problem of translating them from English into Czech.) In (pp. 33–4) **6.**

**1010.** SALE, JONATHAN.	Street whys. Listener (122) 31 Aug., 7. (Children's secret language and backslang.)

**1011.** SEIDL, JENNIFER.	English idioms: exercises on idioms. Oxford: OUP. pp. 94. (Second ed.: orig. pub. 1982 as *Idioms in Practice*.)

**1012.** SÝKOROVÁ, LIBUŠE.	K problematice anglických kolokací. (Problems of English word combinations.) *In* (p. 43) **6.**

**1013.** TILLER, DALE KEATING.	Structure in the affective lexicon. Unpub. doct. diss., Univ. of Oxford, 1988. [Abstr. in DA (50) 1295A.]

**1014.** TOMAKHIN, G. D.	Amerika čerez amerikanizmy. (America through americanisms.) (Bibl. 1987, 1321.) Rev. by Jaroslav Peprník in CJa (31:4) 1988, 285–8.

**1015.** WALLACE, BILL.	A glossary of New Zealand blade–shearing terms. NZEN (3) 21–9.

## HISTORICAL VOCABULARY OF ENGLISH

**1016.** BATELY, JANET.	On some aspects of the vocabulary of the West Midlands in the early Middle Ages: the language of the Katherine Group. *In* (pp. 55–77) **41.**

**1017.** CLAIBORNE, ROBERT.	The roots of English: a reader's handbook of words' origins. New York: Times Books. pp. 335. Rev. in BkW, 17 Sept., 13.

**1018.** COATES, RICHARD.	Old English words not hitherto noted in place-names: some instances from Hampshire. JEPNS (21) 1988/89, 5–14.

**1019.** DANNER, HORACE G.	An introduction to an academic vocabulary: words clusters from Latin, Greek and German: a vade mecum for the serious student. Lanham, MD; London: UP of America, 1985. pp. xix, 217.

**1020.** FISCHER, ANDREAS.	Concordances, computer corpora and diachronic lexicology. *In* (pp. 348–9) **4.** (Abstract.)

**1020a.** HILL, BETTY.	Seven Old English glosses to the Lindisfarne Gospels. NQ (36:2) 148–50.

**1021.** HUGHES, GEOFFREY.	Words in time: a social history of the English vocabulary. (Bibl. 1988, 742.) Rev. by Walter Nash in LRB (11:2) 16–17.

**1022.** KING-HELE, D. G.	Antedatings of *OED* from Erasmus Darwin's *Botanic Garden*. NQ (36:3) 355–8.

**1023.** MANNING, JOHN.	Antedating, postdatings, and additions to *OED* from Thomas Palmer's *Two Hundred Poosees*. NQ (36:4) 429–31.

**1024.** —— Thomas Palmer and proverbs: antedatings and additions to Tilley from *Two Hundred Poosees.* NQ (36:4) 427–9.

**1025.** NICHOLS, ANN ELJENHOLM.	Lollard language in the Croxton *Play of the Sacrament.* NQ (36:1) 23–5.

**1026.** O'NEILL, PATRICK P.	Further Old English glosses on Sedulius in BN Lat. 8092. Ang (107:3/4) 415.

**1027.** RUSSELL, THOMAS W., III.	Shakespearean coinages: fewer than supposed? ELN (26:3) 8–18.

**1028.** STANLEY, E. G.   The difficulty of establishing borrowings between Old English and the continental West Germanic languages. *In* (pp. 3–16) **30.**

**1029.** STEVENS, MARK KEMBLE.   The significance of John Skelton's contribution to English vocabulary. Unpub. doct. diss., Florida State Univ., 1988. [Abstr. in DA (50) 693–4A.]

**1030.** SVEC, PATRICIA WARD.   Water words in *Beowulf*: principles of selection. BSUF (30:1) 5–13.

**1031.** VIATOR, TIMOTHY J.   Corrections to *OED* from Colley Cibber's *Woman's Wit*. NQ (36:3) 355.

**1032.** WATANABE, SHOUICHI.   Eigo gogen no sobyou. (A brief survey of English etymology.) Tokyo: Taishukan, pp. x, 244.

**1033.** WEST, GILIAN.   A glossary to the language of debt at the climax of *1 Henry IV*. NQ (36:3) 323–4.

**1034.** WRIGHT, L. C.   Technical vocabulary to do with life on the River Thames in London, *c*. A.D. 1270–1500. Unpub. doct. diss., Univ. of Oxford, 1988. [Abstr. in IT (39:2) 485.]

## SINGLE WORDS AND PHRASES

**1035.** *æl*] SCHENDL, HERBERT.   OE *æl* ('fire') – a ghost-word? NM (90:2) 143–5.

**1036.** *amir*] COATES, RICHARD.   Two measure-terms in Gaelic and early Modern Scots. NQ (36:1) 27–8.

**1037.** *amphibologies*] CIGMAN, GLORIA.   Amphibologies and heresy: *Troilus and Criseyde*. EA (42:4) 385–400.

**1038.** *avaunced*] REVARD, CARTER.   *Title* and *auaunced* in *Piers Plowman* B.11.290. YLS (1) 1987, 116–21.

**1039.** *catalempsi*] NORRI, JUHANI.   A note on the entries 'catalempsi' and 'goute festre' in the *Middle English Dictionary*. NQ (36:1) 25–7.

**1040.** *copill*] BAWCUTT, PRISCILLA.   'The copill': a crux in *The Kingis Quair*. See **284.**

**1041.** *country dance*] ZANDVOORT, R. W.   Mr Fezziwig's Ball. *In* (pp. 303–9) **42.**

**1042.** *cræft*] STEVENS GIRSCH, ELIZABETH BALDWIN.   A semantic analysis of Old English *cræft* and related words. Unpub. doct. diss., Univ. of Toronto. [Abstr. in DA (50) 1653–4A.]

**1043.** *cyswucu*] GLEISSNER, REINHARD.   Some observations on Old English *cyswucu* in the A-version of the Old English *West-Saxon Gospels*. *In* (pp. 45–68) **38.**

**1044.** *eisegan stefne*] HASENFRATZ, ROBERT.   *Eisegan stefne* (*Christ and Satan* 36a), the *Visio Pauli*, and '*ferrea vox*' (*Aeneid* 6, 626). MP (86:4) 398–403.

**1045.** *falding*] SHARPE, RICHARD.   ME *falding*, MIr. *fallaing*: Irish mantles in medieval England. Ang (107:3/4) 416–29.

**1046.** *fancy*] MORÈRE, PIERRE.   Un problème de traduction philosophique: 'fancy'/'imagination' dans de Livre 1 du *Traité de la Nature Humaine* de David Hume. *In* (pp. 11–22) **22.**

**1047.** *feminal*] McCARREN, V. P.   Middle English *feminal* – a ghost word. MÆ (58:1) 113–17.

**1048.** *flagrant/fragrant*] NICHOL, DONALD W.   'Flagrant' versus 'fragrant' in Beaumont, Pope, Pound, and Burgess. MP (87:1) 76–82.

**1049.** *floor*] CHEVILLET, FRANÇOIS.   Un exemple de contrastivité lexicale: les lexèmes français *plancher*, anglais 'floor'. *In* (pp. 87–110) **22.**

**1050.** *gengþ*] BURROW, J. A.   A note on *The Owl and the Nightingale*, line 376. NQ (36:4) 427.

**1051.** *gentilesse*] GRAY, DOUGLAS.   Chaucer and *gentilesse*. *In* (pp. 1–27) **47.**

**1052.** *goute festre*] NORRI, JUHANI.   A note on the entries 'catalempsi' and 'goute festre' in the *Middle English Dictionary*. See **1039.**

**1053.** *hor-docks*] POUSSA, PATRICIA.   Hordocks in Lear's crown. Lore and Language (8:2) 69–71.

**1054.** *imagination*] MORÈRE, PIERRE.   Un problème de traduction philosophique: 'fancy'/'imagination' dans le Livre I du *Traité de la Nature Humaine* de David Hume. *In* (pp. 11–22) **22.**

**1055.** *līcþrōwere*] HILLE, ARNOLDUS.   Old English *līcþrōwere* 'a leper' and Old Norse *líkþrá* 'leprosy'. *In* (pp. 131–44) **24.**

**1056.** *like*] KETTEMANN, BERNHARD.   The transition from the impersonal to the personal use of the verb *like* in late Middle English and early Modern English – some previously neglected determinants of variation. See **965.**

**1057.** *lof*] GREEN, BRIAN .   'Lof': interlocking denotations in *Beowulf*. UES (27:2) 21–5.

**1058.** *love*] ORESTRÖM, BENGT.   A love affair. *In* (pp. 175–7) **34.**

**1059.** *love*] ÖSTMAN, JAN-OLA.   English 'love': temporary or permanent. Journal of Pragmatics (13:6) 1019–22.

**1060.** *maile*] COATES, RICHARD.   Two measure-terms in Gaelic and early Modern Scots. See **1036.**

**1061.** *male chauvinism*] PÜTZ, MANFRED.   Male chauvinism. NQ (36:3) 360–1.

**1062.** *mede/mercede*] ADAMS, ROBERT.   Mede and mercede: the evolution of the economics of grace in the *Piers Plowman* B and C versions. *In* (pp. 217–32) **41.**

**1063.** *mede/mercede*] TSUJI, YASUAKI.   'Mede' and 'mercede': theological aspects of the metaphor of Latin grammar in *Piers Plowman* C-text. StudME (4) 73–89.

**1064.** *milde*] TYSON, D. B.; ROBERTS, JANE.   More about 'milde' as a royal honorific. NQ (36:3) 299 300

**1065.** *on the weekend*] BAUER, LAURIE.   A note on the New Zealand weekend. NZEN (3) 15–16.

**1066.** *platonic love*] GOOCH, PAUL W.   Platonic love: lexicographical curiosities. NQ (36:3) 358–60.

**1067.** *saebeorg*] HALL, J. R.   Old English 'saebeorg': *Exodus* 442a, *Andreas* 308a. PLL (25:2) 127–34.

**1068.** *same*] LOSADA DURÁN, JOSÉ RAMÓN.   Same/mismo y otros identificadores. RAEI (2) 101–17.

**1069.**   *searolice*] STEVICK, ROBERT D.   Two notes on *Christ II*. *See* **396.**

**1070.**   *sepe*] DEKEYSER, XAVIER.   Adjacent and distant antecedents and the compound relative 'sepe' in Old English prose. LeuB (78:4) 385–99.

**1071.**   *snuck*] HOGG, RICHARD M.   Snuck: the development of irregular preterite forms. *In* (pp. 31–40) **30.**

**1072.**   *swete*] McCARTHY, TERENCE.   Malory's 'swete madame'. MÆ (56:1) 1987, 89–94.

**1073.**   *þegu*] KRISTENSSON, GILLIS.   OE *þegu 'received land'. NQ (36:4) 426–7.

**1074.**   *time or setdown*] HIGGINS, MICHAEL.   A note on 'time or setdown' in *Ulysses*. NQ (36:2) 200–1.

**1075.**   *title*] REVARD, CARTER.   *Title* and *auaunced* in *Piers Plowman* B.11.290. *See* **1038.**

**1076.**   *tom-cod*] BENTLEY, D. M. R.   An addition to *OED* from Thomas Cary's *Abram's Plains*. NQ (36:2) 165–6.

**1077.**   *ymaginatif*] ELDREDGE, L. M.   Some medical evidence on Langland's imaginatif. YLS (3) 131–6.

**1078.**   *yon*] ENGLER, BALZ.   'Yon' and the pragmatics of poetry. EngS (70:6) 560–5.

# LEXICOGRAPHY
## GENERAL STUDIES
**1079.** AKKERMAN, ERIK; MASEREEUW, PIETER; MEIJS, WILLEM. Designing a computerized lexicon for linguistic purposes: ASCOT report, no. 1. *See* **508.**

**1080.** BAILEY, RICHARD W. (ed.). Dictionaries of English: prospects for the record of our language. Ann Arbor: Michigan UP, 1987; Cambridge: CUP. pp. viii, 161.

**1081.** BAMMESBERGER, ALFRED (ed.). Problems of Old English lexicography: studies in memory of Angus Cameron. (Bibl. 1988, 805.) Rev. by Myra Stokes in RES (38:149) 1987, 64–5; by Klaus Dietz in Archiv (226:2) 421–5.

**1082.** BOGURAEV, BRAN; BRISCOE, TED (eds). Computational lexicography for natural language processing. *See* **512.**

**1083.** BORNEMANN, EVA. Translation and lexicography: a practical view. Paintbrush (16) 99–104.

**1084.** BURCHFIELD, ROBERT (ed.). Studies in lexicography. (Bibl. 1988, 810.) Rev. by A. R. Tellier in EA (42:2) 201–2.

**1085.** DELBRIDGE, ARTHUR. The *Macquarie*, an international national dictionary. *In* (pp. 66–79) **5.**

**1086.** DI VIRGILIO, PAUL. The dictionary's role as semantic universe in the genesis and translation of the literary work. Paintbrush (16) 69–78.

**1087.** GRAY, PAUL. A scholarly Everest gets bigger: the *Oxford English Dictionary* updates and goes electronic. *See* **522.**

**1088.** HARTMANN, REINHARD. Lexicography, translation and the so-called language barrier. Paintbrush (16) 9–20.

**1089.** HEDRICK, ELIZABETH. Fixing the language: Johnson, Chesterfield, and *The Plan of a Dictionary*. ELH (55:2) 1988, 421–42.

**1090.** KIPFER-WESTERLUND, B. A. Towards the onomasiological dictionary: the use of the computer in providing diversified access. *See* **530.**

**1091.** KISTER, KEN. The big dictionaries: hordes and hordes of words. WLB (62:6) 1988, 38–43.

**1092.** KLÉGR, ALEŠ. Zkušenosti z práce na kolokačním slovníku. (Experience in working out a dictionary of word combinations.) *In* (p. 24) **6.**

**1093.** KÖNIG, EKKEHARD. A new bilingual dictionary for function words. *In* (pp. 294–306) **5.**

**1094.** KORN, ERIC. Miracles of miniaturization. *See* **531.**

**1095.** KROMANN, HANS-PEDER. Neue Orientierung der zweisprachigen Wörterbücher. Zur funktionalen zweisprachigen Lexikographie. Paintbrush (16) 55–65.

**1096.** KUSSMAUL, PAUL. Kontext und einsprachiges Wörterbuch in der Übersetzerausbildung. Paintbrush (16) 107–19.

**1097.** LIPKA, LEONHARD. The state of the art in lexicology. *In* (pp. 250–63) **5.**

**1098.** NEUHAUS, H. JOACHIM.    Shakespeare's wordforms, a database view. *In* (pp. 264–80) **5.**

**1099.** NOËL, JACQUES, *et al.*    Computational lexicography and multilingualism. *In* (pp. 213–27) **42.**

**1100.** PETTI, VINCENT.    Notes on dictionary making. MS (83:3) 201–7.

**1101.** REGAN, VINCENT DAVID.    A conception of language embodied in the dictionary. Unpub. doct. diss., Indiana Univ., 1988. [Abstr. in DA (49) 2642A.]

**1102.** ROKOŠNÁ, DANIELA.    Oxfordský slovník anglického jazyka na kompaktnom disku. *See* **546.**

**1103.** ROSSENBECK, KLAUS.    Lexikologische und lexikographische Probleme fachsprachlicher Phraseologie aus Kontrastiver Sicht. Paintbrush (16) 197–210.

**1104.** RYAN, J. S.    Clerks to the language – the twentieth-century New Zealand lexicographers of English. SAP (22) 3–29.

**1105.** SAMOL, EMIL.    Noah Webster a lexikografia. (Noah Webster and lexicography.) CJa (32) 411–13.

**1106.** ŠARČEVIĆ, SUSAN.    Lexicography and translation across cultures. Paintbrush (16) 211–21.

**1107.** SCHMID, ANNEMARIE.    Wörterbücher als Hilfe zur Übersetzung von Phraseologismen. Paintbrush (16) 121–7.

**1108.** SENN, FRITZ.    Beyond the lexicographer's reach: literary overdetermination. Paintbrush (16) 79–87.

**1109.** SHENKER, ISRAEL.    Annals of lexicography: the dictionary factor. NY, 3 Apr., 86–100.

**1110.** SNELL-HORNBY, MARY; PÖHL, ESTHER (eds).    Symposium: translation and the lexicographer: papers read at the Euralex Colloquium held at Innsbruck 2–5 July 1987: a special monograph. Paintbrush (16) 225–33.

**1111.** STEIN, GABRIELE.    The emerging role of English in the dictionaries of Renaissance Europe. FLH (9:1) 1988, 29–138.

**1112.** —— The English dictionary before Cawdrey. Tübingen: Niemeyer, 1985. pp. vii, 444. (Lexicographica: ser. maior, 9.) Rev. by Helmut Gneuss in Ang (107:3/4) 478–82.

**1113.** TOURY, GIDEON.    The meaning of translation-specific lexical items and its representation in the dictionary. Paintbrush (16) 45–53.

**1114.** WEIJERS, OLGA.    Lexicography in the Middle Ages. Viator (20) 139–53.

**1115.** WOOD, NIGEL.    Johnson's revisions to his Dictionary, 1755–1773. NRam 1987/88, 23–8.

## DICTIONARIES OF ENGLISH

**1116.** AMOS, ASHLEY CRANDELL, *et al.* (eds).    Dictionary of Old English: vol. 1, Preface and lists of texts and index of editions; vol. 2, Fascicle D. Material assembled by ANGUS CAMERON. (Bibl. 1987, 1481.) Rev. by Michael Korhammer in Ang (107:1/2) 127–30; by Daniel

Donoghue in Spec (64:1) 155–7; by Hans Sauer in Archiv (225:2) 1988, 370–5; by Janet Bately in NQ (35:2) 1988, 198.

**1117.** ANON.   Collins pocket reference English dictionary. London: Collins, 1988. pp. x, 566.

**1118.** —— Collins pocket reference thesaurus. London : Collins, 1988. pp. ix, 564.

**1119.** —— (ed.).   The New Hamlyn encyclopedic world dictionary. London: Hamlyn, 1988. pp. xl, 1973. (Second ed.: previously pub. as *Encyclopedic World Dictionary*, 1971.)

**1120.** AYTO, JOHN.   The Longman register of new words. Harlow: Longman. pp. 425.

**1121.** BAILIE, JOHN; KITCHIN, MOYNA.   The essential guide to English usage. (Bibl. 1979, 1716.) London: Chancellor Press, 1983. pp. 319. (Previously pub. as *The Hamlyn Guide to English Usage*, 1979.)

**1122.** BAKER, SIDNEY JOHN.   A dictionary of Australian slang. Melbourne: Viking O'Neil, 1988. pp. 88.

**1123.** BEALE, PAUL (ed.).   A concise dictionary of slang and unconventional English: from *A Dictionary of Slang and Unconventional English* by ERIC PARTRIDGE. (Bibl. 1984, 1423.) London: Routledge. pp. xxvi, 534. Rev. by Peter Reading in TLS, 17 Nov., 1267.

**1124.** BEECHING, CYRIL LESLIE.   A dictionary of eponyms. (Bibl. 1983, 1635.) London: Library Assn. pp. ix, 218. (Third ed.: first ed. 1979.)

**1125.** BENSON, MORTON; BENSON, EVELYN; ILSON, ROBERT.   The BBI combinatory dictionary of English: a guide to word combinations. (Bibl. 1988, 830.) Rev. by Alan S. Kaye and Ken McDaniel in Lingua (77:3/4) 375–83.

**1126.** BURCHFIELD, R. W. (ed.).   The compact edition of the *Oxford English Dictionary*: vol. 3. Oxford: OUP, 1987. pp. xvii, 1412. (Supplement to *Oxford English Dictionary*, vols. 1–4.) Rev. by Knud Sørensen in EngS (69:6) 1988, 573.

**1127.** —— A supplement to the *Oxford English Dictionary*: vol. 4, Se–Z. (Bibl. 1988, 831.) Rev. by Basil Cottle in RES (38:151) 1987; by Gabriele Stein in Ang (107:3/4) 482–91; by Jaroslav Peprník in CJa (33) 85–9.

**1128.** CLARK, JOHN O. E.   Word for word: a dictionary of synonyms. London: Harrap, 1988. pp. 668. (Harrap's reference.)

**1129.** FLEXNER, STUART BERG.   The Random House dictionary of the English language. (Bibl. 1988, 834.) Rev. by Lachlan Mackinnon in TLS, 21 Apr., 431; by Hans Andersson in MS (83:2) 159–63.

**1130.** GREEN, JONATHON.   Newspeak: a dictionary of jargon. London: Routledge & Kegan Paul, 1985. pp. 263. Rev. by W. Bennett in Lore and Language (8:2) 114–15.

**1131.** HARP, RICHARD L. (ed.).   Dr Johnson's critical vocabulary: a selection from his *Dictionary*. Lanham, MD; London: UP of America, 1987. pp. xlv, 268. Rev. by Isobel Grundy in YES (18) 1988, 324–6.

**1132.** HORNBY, A. S.; COWIE, A. P. (eds).   Oxford advanced learner's dictionary of current English. (Bibl. 1978, 1653.) Oxford: OUP. pp. xix, 1579. (Fourth ed.: first ed. 1948.)

**1133.**  HUNT, TONY.   The trilingual glossary in MS London, BL Sloane 146 ff. 69ᵛ–72ʳ. *See* **145.**

**1134.**  McGILL, DAVID.   The dinkum Kiwi dictionary. Lower Hutt, NZ: Mills. pp. 118.

**1135.**  MACLEOD, ISEABAIL; MARTIN, RUTH; CAIRNS, PAULINE (eds). The pocket Scots dictionary. (Bibl. 1988, 842, where scholars' forenames abbreviated.) Rev. by John M. Kirk in SLang (8) 65–82.

**1136.**  MANSER, MARTIN H. (ed.).   Chambers dictionary of synonyms and antonyms. Edinburgh: Chambers; Cambridge: CUP. pp. vii, 405.

**1137.**  MORTON, JAMES.   Lowspeak: a dictionary of criminal and sexual slang. London: Angus & Robertson. pp. 154. Rev. by Peter Reading in TLS, 17 Nov., 1267.

**1138.**  MYERS, JACK; SIMMS, MICHAEL.   Longman dictionary and handbook of poetry. New York; London: Longman, 1987. pp. xv, 366. (Longman English and humanities.) Rev. by E. G. Stanley in NQ (36:2) 213–14.

**1139.**  NEUHAUS, H. JOACHIM.   The Shakespeare dictionary database. *See* **538.**

**1140.**  PAROS, LAWRENCE.   The erotic tongue: a sexual lexicon. Seattle, WA: Madrona, 1984; London: Arlington, 1988. pp. xii, 241.

**1141.**  PHYTHIAN, B. A.   A concise dictionary of confusables. Sevenoaks: Headway; Hodder & Stoughton. pp. v, 198.

**1142.**  PRATT, T. K. (ed.).   Dictionary of Prince Edward Island English. Toronto; London; Toronto UP, 1988. pp. xxvii, 192.

**1143.**  PRINCE, GERALD.   A dictionary of narratology. Lincoln: Nebraska UP, 1987; Aldershot: Scolar Press, 1988. pp. ix, 188. Rev. by Colin Crowder in NC (7) 183–5, by Leigh Hafrey in TLS, 13 Jan., 41.

**1144.**  ROOM, ADRIAN.   Dictionary of changes in meaning. (Bibl. 1987, 1342.) Rev. by H. C. Walkiden in Lore and Language (8:1) 136–7.

**1145.**  —— Dictionary of true etymologies. pp. 193. (Bibl. 1986, 1788, where pagination incorrect.) Rev. by H. C. Walkiden in Lore and Language (8:1) 136–7.

**1146.**  SIMPSON, J. A.; WEINER, E. S. C. (eds).   The Oxford English dictionary. Oxford: Clarendon Press; New York: OUP. 20 vols. pp. 21, 728. (Second ed.) Rev. by Hugh Kenner in NYTB, 14 Apr., 3; by Geoffrey Hill in TLS, 21 Apr., 411–14.

**1147.**  SINCLAIR, JOHN, *et al.* (eds).   Collins COBUILD English language dictionary. (Bibl. 1988, 854.) Rev. by F. G. A. M. Aarts in EngS (70:3) 282–5.

**1148.**  SIXSMITH, ANGUS.   The glossamery of roistering slang. London: Bagwash, 1987. pp. viii, 47.

**1149.**  STEVENSON, JAMES A. C.; MACLEOD, ISEABAIL.   Scoor-oot: a dictionary of Scots words and phrases in current use. London: Athlone Press. pp. 256. Rev. by John M. Kirk in SLang (8) 65–82.

**1150.**  SUMMERS, DELLA (ed.), *et al.*   Longman dictionary of contemporary English. Munich: Langenscheidt, 1987. (Bibl. 1987, 1512.) Rev. by

Ewald Standop in Ang (107:1/2) 130–4; by Aleš Klégr in PP (31:4) 1988, 217–19; by Arne Olofsson in MS (82:4) 1988, 296–303.

**1151.** TRAPIDO, JOEL (gen. ed.). An international dictionary of theatre language. Westport, CT; London: Greenwood Press, 1985. pp. xxxvi, 1032. Rev. by Alan Woods in TJ (38:3) 1986, 382–3.

**1152.** URDANG, LAURENCE (ed.). Longman synonym dictionary. (Bibl. 1986, 1796.) Rev. by Basil Cottle in RES (38:152) 1987, 532.

**1153.** WALES, KATIE. A dictionary of stylistics. Harlow: Longman. pp. xii, 504. (Studies in language and linguistics.) Rev. by Louis Milic in TLS, 17 Nov., 1266.

**1154.** WIERZBICKA, ANNA. English speech act verbs: a semantic dictionary. Sydney: Academic Press, 1987. pp. viii, 397.

**1155.** WILKES, G. A. A dictionary of Australian colloquialisms. (Bibl. 1985, 1435.) Rev. by Peter Craven in TLS, 17 Nov., 1267.

# NAMES

## GENERAL STUDIES

**1156.** CALLARY, EDWARD; SEITS, LAURENCE E. (eds). The how, why, and whence of names: vol. 4. DeKalb: Illinois Name Soc., 1984. pp. 134.

**1157.** CAMERON, KENNETH. Bynames of location in Lincolnshire Subsidiary Rolls. NMS (32) 1988, 156–64.

**1158.** CARLSSON, STIG. Studies on Middle English local bynames in East Anglia. Lund: Lund UP; Bromley: Chartwell-Bratt. pp. 193. (Lund studies in English, 79.) (Doct. diss., Lund Univ.) Rev. by O. Arngart in EngS (70:6) 587–8.

**1159.** COATES, RICHARD. Old English words not hitherto noted in place-names: some instances from Hampshire. See **1018.**

**1160.** COLMAN, FRAN. The crunch is the key: on computer research on Old English personal names. In (pp. 41–55) **34.**

**1161.** CONSTANTINESCU, ILINCA. Asimilarea numelor proprii engelezesti în limba rômană. (The assimilation of English proper names into Romanian.) SCL (40:3) 219–25.

**1162.** DRUMMOND, PETER. Placenames of the Monklands. Coatbridge: Monklands Library Services Dept, 1987. pp. 38.

**1163.** DUNKLING, LESLIE; WRIGHT, GORDON. A dictionary of pub names. London: Routledge & Kegan Paul, 1987. pp. xiv, 305.

**1164.** ELERT, CLAES-CHRISTIAN; ELERT, KERSTIN. Daisy and Lily . . . : women's first names derived from plant names. In (pp. 57–68) **34.**

**1165.** FELLOWS-JENSEN, GILLIAN. Scandinavian settlement names in the North-West. (Bibl. 1987, 1542, where scholar's name incorrect.) Rev. by Svante Strandberg in NoB (77) 138–40.

**1166.** GUILFOYLE, CHERRELL. Othello, Otuel, and the English Charlemagne romances. RES (38:149) 1987, 50–5.

**1167.** HANKS, PATRICK; HODGES, FLAVIA. A dictionary of surnames. Oxford: OUP, 1988. pp. liv, 826. Rev. by E. G. Stanley in NQ (36:3) 373–4.

**1168.** HAUGLAND, KARI E. Some practical aspects of trade names and trademarks in terminology and translation: a brief report from the translation of an ESP text. In (pp. 117–29) **24.**

**1169.** KRISTENSSON, GILLIS. The linguistic status of East Anglia in late Middle English. In (pp. 123–30) **34.**

**1170.** —— Place-names and linguistic geography. In (pp. 155–64) **24.**

**1171.** NICOLAISEN, W. F. H. Place-name maps: how reliable are they? In (pp. 261–8) LENA PETERSON et al. (eds), Studia onomastica: festskrift till Thorsten Andersson den 23 februari 1989. Stockholm: Almqvist & Wiksell. pp. xxiv, 454.

**1172.** OČENÁŠ, BENJAMÍN. Eufemizmy, džentilizmy a sobrikety v angličtine. See **1006.**

**1173.** POYNTON, CATE. Terms of address in Australian English. In (pp. 59–69, 316, 329) **9.**

**1174.** ROBSON, JOHN M. Surnames and status in Victorian England. QQ (95:3) 1988, 642–61.

**1175.** SANDRED, KARL-INGE.   The Scandinavians in Norfolk: observations on some river-side place-names in Norwich. *In* (pp. 337–47)
LENA PETERSON *et al.* (eds), Studia onomastica: festskrift till Thorsten
Andersson den 23 februari 1989. Stockholm: Almqvist & Wiksell.
pp. xxiv, 454.

**1176.** SVENSSON, ÖRJAN.   Saxon place-names in East Cornwall. (Bibl.
1988, 882.) Rev. by Georges Bourcier in EA (42:2) 195–6; by Gillian
Fellows-Jensen in NoB (77) 163–8.

**1177.** ZETTERSTEN, ARNE.   The pristine place-names of St Helena.
*In* (pp. 389–96) **24.**

**1178.** —— The pristine place-names of the Tristan da Cunha group. *In*
(pp. 297–310) **34.**

## SINGLE NAMES

**1179.** *Amounderness*] FELLOWS-JENSEN, GILLIAN.   'Amounderness' and
'Holderness'. *In* (pp. 87–94) LENA PETERSON *et al.* (eds), Studia
onomastica: festskrift till Thorsten Andersson den 23 februari 1989.
Stockholm: Almqvist & Wiksell. pp. xxiv, 454.

**1180.** *Bonaparte*] RYNELL, ALARIK.   English nicknames for Napoleon
in contemporary caricatures. *In* (pp. 197–204) **34.**

**1181.** *Brampton/Frampton*] ARNGART, O.   The place-names 'Bramp-
ton', 'Frampton': final comments. SN (61:2) 167–8.

**1182.** *Chastelayne*] LUMIANSKY, R. M.   Concerning three names in *Le
Morte Darthur* – 'Roone', 'The Welshe Kyng' and 'Chastelayne' – and
Malory's possible revision of his book. *In* (pp. 301–8) **41.**

**1183.** *finna land*] OSBORN, MARIJANE.   Beowulf's landfall in 'finna
land'. NM (90:2) 137–42.

**1184.** *fornetes folm*] RYDÉN, MATS.   Two Old English names for
orchids. *In* (pp. 277–88) **24.**

**1185.** *hām/hamm*] KOLB, EDUARD.   *Hamm*: a long-suffering place-name
word. Ang (107:1/2) 49–51.

**1186.** *Hobbit*] O'BRIEN, DONALD.   On the origin of the name 'Hobbit'.
Mythlore (16:2) 32–8.

**1187.** *Holderness*] FELLOWS-JENSEN, GILLIAN.   'Amounderness' and
'Holderness'. *See* **1179.**

**1188.** *Hollin*] ATKIN, M. A.   'Hollin' names in north-west England.
Nomina (12) 1988/89, 77–88.

**1189.** *hræfres leac*] RYDÉN, MATS.   Two Old English names for orchids.
*In* (pp. 277–88) **24.**

**1190.** *Napoleon*] RYNELL, ALARIK.   English nicknames for Napoleon in
contemporary caricatures. *In* (pp. 197–204) **34.**

**1191.** *Nigel of Canterbury*] RIGG, A. G.   Nigel of Canterbury: what was
his name? MÆ (56:2) 1987, 304–7.

**1192.** *Hōra*] COLE, ANN.   The meaning of the OE place-name element
*ōra*. JEPNS (21) 1988/89, 15–22.

**1193.** *Pakistan*] STUBBINGS, FRANK H.   *Now or Never* – an elusive
pamphlet important for the history of the name *Pakistan*. NQ (36:4)
433–4.

**1194.**  *Roone*] LUMIANSKY, R. M.   Concerning three names in *Le Morte Darthur* – 'Roone', 'The Welshe Kyng' and 'Chastelayne' – and Malory's possible revision of his book. *In* (pp. 301–8) **41.**

**1195.**  *Shaw/Shay*] GELLING, MARGARET.   'Shaw'/'shay': the phonological problem. Nomina (12) 1988/89, 103–4.

**1196.**  *Shay*] HIGHAM, MARY C.   'Shay' names – a need for reappraisal? Nomina (12) 1988/89, 89–102.

**1197.**  *Theydon*] KRISTENSSON, GILLIS.   The place-name Theydon (Essex). NQ (36:1) 7–8.

**1198.**  *The Welshe Kyng*] LUMIANSKY, R. M.   Concerning three names in *Le Morte Darthur* – 'Roone', 'The Welshe Kyng' and 'Chastelayne' – and Malory's possible revision of his book. *In* (pp. 301–8) **41.**

# MEANING
## SEMANTICS
**1199.** ABBOTT, BARBARA. Nondescriptionality and natural kind terms. Linguistics and Philosophy (12:3) 269–91.

**1200.** BADR, BASIM M. Semantic change in English. Al-Mustansiriya Literary Review (Al-Mustansiriya Univ., Baghdad) (12) 1985, 5–27.

**1201.** BERG, THOMAS. On the internal structure of polysyllabic monomorphemic words: the case for superrimes. *See* **994.**

**1202.** BROMBERGER, SYLVAIN. Types and tokens in linguistics. *In* (pp. 58–89) **52.**

**1203.** CIENKI, ALAN JOSEPH. Spatial cognition and the semantics of prepositions in English, Polish, and Russian. Unpub. doct. diss., Brown Univ., 1988. [Abstr. in DA (49) 2198A.]

**1204.** COLLINS, PETER. Divided and debatable usage in Australian English. *In* (pp. 138–49, 339–40) **9.**

**1205.** COTTRELL, GARRISON W. A connectionist approach to word sense disambiguation. *See* **517.**

**1206.** DAHL, ÖSTEN; FRAURUD, KARI (eds). Papers from the first Nordic Conference on Text Comprehension in Man and Machine. *See* **48.**

**1207.** DAVIES, MARTIN. 'Two examiners marked six scripts': interpretations of numerically qualified sentences. Linguistics and Philosophy (12:3) 293–323.

**1208.** DUMMETT, MICHAEL. Language and communication. *In* (pp. 192–212) **52.**

**1209.** EJERHED, EVA. Denotational semantics of natural language. *In* (pp. 63–74) **48.**

**1210.** FALTZ, LEONARD. A role for influence in meaning change. SL (13:2) 317–31.

**1211.** FISHER, ALEC. Suppositions in argumentation. Argumentation (3:4) 401–13.

**1212.** FREEDMAN, D. The intentionality, causality and metaphysics of naming. Unpub. doct. diss., Univ. of Oxford, 1988. [Abstr. in IT (39:2) 464.]

**1213.** GORDON, W. TERRENCE. Semantics: a bibliography, 1965–1978. Metuchen, NJ; London: Scarecrow Press, 1980. pp. xiv, 307.

**1214.** —— Semantics: a bibliography, 1979–1985. Metuchen, NJ; London: Scarecrow Press, 1987. pp. xii, 292.

**1215.** GRICE, PAUL. Studies in the way of words. Cambridge, MA; London: Harvard UP. pp. viii, 394. Rev. by Simon Blackburn in TLS, 17 Nov., 1265–6.

**1216.** HAND, MICHAEL. Who plays semantical games? PhilS (56:3) 251–72.

**1217.** HELLMAN, CHRISTINA. Integrative processes in disfavouring conditions: a self-paced reading study. *In* (pp. 113–24) **48.**

**1218.** HIGGINBOTHAM, JAMES. Elucidations of meaning. Linguistics and Philosophy (12:4) 465–517.

**1219.** —— Knowledge of reference. *In* (pp. 153–74) **52.**
**1220.** HINTIKKA, JAAKKO. Logical form and linguistic theory. *In* (pp. 41–57) **52.**
**1221.** HORGAN, T. Attitudinatives. Linguistics and Philosophy (12:2) 133–65.
**1222.** HORNSTEIN, NORBERT. Meaning and the mental: the problem of semantics after Chomsky. *In* (pp. 23–40) **52.**
**1223.** HUNTLEY, RUTH ANN. The influence of verb semantics in sentence processing. Unpub. doct. diss., Univ. of Florida, 1987. [Abstr. in DA (49) 2201A.]
**1224.** INNIS, ROBERT E. (ed.). Semiotics: an introductory anthology. (Bibl. 1986, 2207.) Rev. by Christopher Hutton in RES (38:151) 1987, 425–6.
**1225.** KAMAREDDINE, F. D. Semantics in a Frege structure. Unpub. doct. diss., Univ. of Edinburgh. [Abstr. in IT (39:4) 1619.]
**1226.** KASTOVSKY, DIETER. Wortbildung und Semantik. *See* **853.**
**1227.** KIM, HYUNG-KOOK. Semantic transfer. IKS (19) 53–65.
**1228.** KNITTLOVÁ, DAGMAR. The intensifying connotation component and its translation counterparts. Germanica Olomucensia (7) 121–8.
**1229.** KÜPER, CHRISTOPH. Sprache und Metrum. Semiotik und Linguistik des Verses. (Bibl. 1988, 923.) Rev. by Ewald Standop in Ang (107:3/4) 503–6; by Walter Bernhart in AAA (14:2) 179–82.
**1230.** LAKOFF, ROBIN. The way we were, or, the real actual truth about generative semantics. Journal of Pragmatics (13:6) 939–88.
**1231.** LASERSOHN, PETER NATHAN. A semantics for groups and events. Unpub. doct. diss., Ohio State Univ., 1988. [Abstr. in DA (49) 2641A.]
**1232.** LAWLER, JOHN M. Lexical semantics in the commercial transaction frame: 'value', 'worth', 'cost' and 'price'. SL (13:2) 381–404.
**1233.** LUDLOW, PETER. Implicit comparison classes. Linguistics and Philosophy (12:4) 519–33.
**1234.** MAY, ROBERT. Interpreting logical form. Linguistics and Philosophy (12:4) 387–435.
**1235.** MILLER, A. Semantic theory and sentential understanding: a discussion of tacit knowledge and compositionality. Unpub. M.Litt. diss., Univ. of St Andrews. [Abstr. in IT (39:1) 26.]
**1236.** MINDT, DIETER. EDV-gestützte Forschungen zur Semantik. *In* (pp. 330–44) **4.**
**1237.** PHARIES, DAVID A. Charles S. Peirce and the linguistic sign. (Bibl. 1986, 1388, where misplaced and title misspelt.) Rev. by David Justice in RPh (42:1) 1988, 77–9.
**1238.** POWELL, JOHN WELDON. Language as signs. Unpub. doct. diss., Univ. of Oregon, 1988. [Abstr. in DA (50) 705A.]
**1239.** PUTNAM, HILARY. Model theory and the 'factuality' of semantics. *In* (pp. 213–32) **52.**
**1240.** ROMMETVEIT, RAGNAR. On perspectives and fixation of perspectives in texts. *In* (pp. 173–84) **48.**

**1241.** Rosenberg, Marvin. Sign theory and Shakespeare. ShS (40) 1988, 33–40.

**1242.** Ružičková, Eva. Analýza l'udských potrieb. (An analysis of human necessities.) *In* (p. 40) **6.**

**1243.** Schendl, Herbert. Semantic verb classes and the use of diagnostics in Old English. *See* **847.**

**1244.** Segal, Gabriel. A preference for sense and reference. JP (86:2) 73–89.

**1245.** Sem, Helle Frisak. Discourse in situation schema theory. *In* (pp. 99–111) **48.**

**1246.** Seuren, Pieter A. M. Discourse semantics. Appendix by A. Weijters. (Bibl. 1987, 1713.) Rev. by Paul Werth in Lingua (78:4) 321–42.

**1247.** Shalinsky, Allison. A cognitive semantics for first-person statements. Unpub. doct. diss., Univ. of California, San Diego, 1988. [Abstr. in DA (49) 2688–9A.]

**1248.** Sheriff, John K. The fate of meaning: Charles Peirce, structuralism and literature. Princeton, NJ; Guildford: Princeton UP. pp. xviii, 149.

**1249.** Silverman, Kaja. The subject of semiotics. (Bibl. 1984, 1810.) Rev. by Christopher Hutton in RES (38:149) 1987, 121–2.

**1250.** Styan, Evelyn Marie Matheson. Elementary sentences containing 'be': a semantic analysis of subject–predicate relations. *See* **977.**

**1251.** Tahal, Karel. Některé sémantické rysy *ing*-ových slovesných tvarů. (Some semantic features of verbal *ing*-forms.) *In* (pp. 43–4) **6.**

**1252.** Themerson, Stefan. On nonsense and on logic-fiction. *In* (pp. 3–16) **28.**

**1253.** Traugott, Elizabeth Closs. On the rise of epistemic meanings in English: an example of subjectification in semantic change. Lang (65:1) 31–55.

**1254.** Weijters, A. J. M. M. Denotation in discourse: analysis and algorithm. Nijmegen: Weijters. pp. 249.

**1255.** Werth, Paul. The rise and rise of generative semantics. Lingua (78:4) 321–42 (review-article).

**1256.** Wierzbicka, Anna. The semantics of grammar. *See* **831.**

**1257.** Wilensky, Robert. Primal content and actual content: an antidote to literal meaning. Journal of Pragmatics (13:2) 163–86.

## PRAGMATICS

**1258.** Benoit, Pamela J. Relationship arguments: an interactionist elaboration of speech acts. Argumentation (3:4) 423–37.

**1259.** Bublitz, Wolfram. Ausdrücke des Kenntnisnehmens (Hörer-signale) oder des Stellungsnehmens (Redebeiträge): 'yes' und verwandte Formen. FL (23:1/2) 67–104.

**1260.** Carls, Uwe. Der Topikalisierungsprozeß im Englischen und im Deutschen. AAA (14:1) 89–100.

**1261.** CHAMONIKOLASOVÁ, JANÁ.    Zájmena ve FVP. (Pronouns in functional sentence perspective.) *In* (p. 20) **6.**

**1262.** EDMONDSON, WILLIS J.    Speaker and hearer as discourse roles. *In* (pp. 397–405) **4.**

**1263.** ESSER, JÜRGEN.    Untersuchungen zum gesprochenen Englisch: ein Beitrag zur strukturellen Pragmatik. (Bibl. 1986, 750.) Rev. by Milena Turbová in PP (32) 218–20.

**1264.** FILL, ALWIN.    Purism and word formation: word substitution in 16th and 19th century English. *See* **959.**

**1265.** —— Sprache und Streit: pragmalinguistische Perspektiven. Linguistische Berichte (Brunswick) (121) 206–14.

**1266.** FOSTER, DANIEL GEORGE.    The effects of linguistic and non-linguistic context on the deictic interpretation of noun phrases. Unpub. doct. diss., Louisiana State Univ. and Agricultural and Mechanical College, 1988. [Abstr. in DA (49) 2200A.]

**1267.** FRASER, BRUCE; ROSS, HÁJ; ULICHNY, POLLY.    Repeat performances. Journal of Pragmatics (13:4) 651–3.

**1268.** FRIGGIERI, JOE.    Austin on actions and speech actions. Unpub. doct. diss., Univ. of Oxford, 1987. [Abstr. in DA (49) 2666A.]

**1269.** HAFT-VAN REES, M. AGNES.    Conversation, relevance, and argumentation. Argumentation (3:4) 385–93.

**1270.** HUSPEK, MICHAEL.    Linguistic variability and power: an analysis of 'you know/I think' variation in working class speech. Journal of Pragmatics (13:5) 661–83.

**1271.** JACOBS, SCOTT.    Speech acts and arguments. Argumentation (3:4) 345–65.

**1272.** JAYEZ, JACQUES.    Problems of context and knowledge. Argumentation (3:3) 303–19.

**1273.** KURZON, DENNIS.    It is hereby performed . . . : explorations in legal speech acts. Amsterdam: Benjamins, 1987. pp. vii, 81. (Pragmatics and beyond, 7, 6.) Rev. by P. M. Tiersma in SL (13:1) 245–7.

**1274.** LAUERBACH, GERDA E.    'We don't want war, but . . . ': speech act schemata and inter-schema inference transfer. Journal of Pragmatics (13:1) 25–51.

**1275.** LJUNG, MAGNUS.    English emotives. *In* (pp. 185–94) **24.**

**1276.** MEILAND, JACK W.    Argument as inquiry and argument as persuasion. Argumentation (3:3) 185–96.

**1277.** NICOLOFF, FRANCK.    Threats and illocutions. Journal of Pragmatics (13:4) 501–22.

**1278.** OLESKY, WIESLAW.    Contrastive pragmatics. Amsterdam: Benjamins. pp. xii, 282. (Pragmatics and beyond, 3.)

**1279.** OSTMAN, JAN-OLA.    Testing iconicity: sentence structure and politeness. Belgian Journal of Linguistics (4) 145–63.

**1280.** PRIMATAROVA-MILTSCHEVA, ANTOINETTE.    Indirect directives in monological argumentation. Argumentation (3:4) 415–22.

**1281.** QUIRK, RANDOLPH.    Words at work: lectures on textual structure. (Bibl. 1986, 1828.) Rev. by Ronald Landheer in Journal of Pragmatics (13:2) 297–301.

**1282.** REBOUL, ANNE. Relevance and argumentation: how bald can you get? Argumentation (3:3) 285–302.

**1283.** RŮŽIČKA, MILAN. Elipsa a aktuální členěni větné. (Ellipsis and functional sentence perspective.) *In* (pp. 39–40) **6.**

**1284.** SEARLE, JOHN R. How performatives work. Linguistics and Philosophy (12:5) 535–58.

**1285.** SPERBER, DAN; WILSON, DEIRDRE. Relevance: communication and cognition. (Bibl. 1988, 965.) Rev. by Paul Meara in MLR (84:4) 894–5; by Alastair Fowler in LRB (11:7) 16–17.

**1286.** SVOBODA, ALEŠ. Funkční perspektiva nadvětná. (A hypersyntactic functional perspective). *In* (pp. 42–3) **6.**

**1287.** TABE, SHIGERU. A pragmatic analysis of English sentences: the CBS theory. Tokyo: Liber, 1988. pp. xiv, 206.

**1288.** TÁRNYIKOVÁ, JARMILA. Ke komunikativní funkci anglického vokativu. (On the communicative function of the English vocative). CJa (32) 264–8.

**1289.** ——Komunikativní funkce anglických vět typu 'Life is life'. (The communicative function of English sentences of the type 'Life is life'.) CJa (32) 115–18.

**1290.** ——Language manifestation of communicative strategies. Germanica Olomucensia (7) 113–20.

**1291.** ——Text a textura. (Textlinguistics and texture.) *In* (p. 44) **6.**

**1292.** THOMAS, J. A. The dynamics of discourse: a pragmatic analysis of confrontational interaction. Unpub. doct. diss., Univ. of Lancaster, 1986. [Abstr. in IT (36:3) 908.]

**1293.** THOMAS, STEPHEN. Using translation to overcome cross-cultural pragmatic failure. NC (8) 75–84.

**1294.** VANDEPITTE, SONIA. A pragmatic function of intonation: tone and cognitive environment. *See* **719.**

**1295.** VAN EEMEREN, FRANS H.; GROOTENDORST, ROB. Speech act conditions as tools for reconstructing argumentative discourse. Argumentation (3:4) 367–83.

**1296.** VERBIEST, AGNES. Confrontation in conversations: the adjacency pair as a tool of the descriptive component of a pragma-dialectical analysis. Argumentation (3:4) 395–400.

**1297.** WALTON, DOUGLAS N. Dialogue theory for critical thinking. Argumentation (3:2) 169–84.

**1298.** WARDHAUGH, RONALD. How conversation works. New York: Blackwell, 1985. (Bibl. 1985, 893.) Rev. by Karen Ann Hunold in Journal of Pragmatics (13:4) 625–30.

**1299.** WIERZBICKA, ANNA. English speech act verbs: a semantic dictionary. *See* **1154.**

**1300.** WIKBERG, KAY. On the role of the lexical verb in discourse. *In* (pp. 375–88) **24.**

**1301.** YAMAGUCHI, HARUHIKO. On 'unspeakable sentences': a pragmatic review. Journal of Pragmatics (13:4) 577–96 (review-article).

## RHETORIC AND FIGURES OF SPEECH

**1302.** BAUMLIN, JAMES S.; BAUMLIN, TITA FRENCH.   Psyche/logos: mapping the terrains of mind and rhetoric. CE (51:3) 245–61.

**1303.** CALENDRILLO, LINDA THERESA.   The art of memory and rhetoric. Unpub. doct. diss., Purdue Univ., 1988. [Abstr. in DA (49) 3011A.]

**1304.** CONDON, DENIS.   The foundations of the Cornell School of Rhetoric. Unpub. doct. diss., Univ. of Pittsburgh, 1988. [Abstr. in DA (50) 1482A.]

**1305.** ESPY, WILLARD R.   The garden of eloquence: a rhetorical bestiary. Includes portions of the first *Garden of Eloquence* published in 1577 by Henry Peacham. New York; London: Harper & Row, 1983. pp. 221.

**1306.** FONG, HEATHERBELL NANCY.   The stony idiom of the brain: a study in the semantics and syntax of metaphors. Unpub. doct. diss., Univ. of California, San Diego, 1988. [Abstr. in DA (50) 937A.]

**1307.** HAUSMAN, CARL R.   Metaphor and art: interactionism and reference in the verbal and nonverbal arts. Cambridge: CUP. pp. xi, 238.

**1308.** HERMAN, WILLIAM.   The basic writer's rhetoric. New York; London: Holt, Rinehart, & Winston, 1988. pp. xiii, 247.

**1309.** HORNER, WINIFRED BRYAN.   The present state of scholarship in historical and contemporary rhetoric. Columbia; London: Missouri UP, 1983. pp. vi, 230. Rev. by Brian Vickers in MLR (84:2) 455–7.

**1310.** IMPSON, MARIBETH.   The concept of ethos in classical and modern rhetoric. Unpub. doct. diss., Univ. of Kansas, 1988. [Abstr. in DA (50) 1297A.]

**1311.** KENT, THOMAS.   Beyond system: the rhetoric of paralogy. CE (51:5) 492–507.

**1312.** KLUMPP, JAMES F.; HOLLIHAN, THOMAS A.   Rhetorical criticism as moral action. QJS (75:1) 84–96.

**1313.** KÖVECSES, ZOLTÁN.   Metaphors of anger, pride and love: a lexical approach to the structure of concepts. Amsterdam: Benjamins, 1986. pp. vi, 147. (Pragmatics and beyond, 7, 8.) Rev. by Cliff Goddard in Lingua (77:1) 90–8.

**1314.** KRAJEWSKI, BRUCE JAMES.   Traveling with Hermes: hermeneutics and rhetoric. Unpub. doct. diss., Univ. of Iowa, 1988. [Abstr. in DA (49) 2205–6A.]

**1315.** LOGUE, CALVIN M.; DORGAN, HOWARD (eds).   A new diversity in contemporary Southern rhetoric. Baton Rouge; London: Louisiana State UP, 1987. pp. viii, 268.

**1316.** MACKIN, JAMES ANDREW, JR.   Toward an ethics of rhetoric: an ecological model for assessing public moral argument. Unpub. doct. diss., Univ. of Texas at Austin. [Abstr. in DA (50) 1482–3A.]

**1317.** MILLER, JOYCE RAUSCH.   Language during the late Renaissance years: an historical survey of issues and circumstances responsible for changes in attitudes toward rhetoric during the seventeenth century. Unpub. doct. diss., Michigan State Univ. [Abstr. in DA (50) 692A.]

**1318.** NASH, WALTER.   Rhetoric: the wit of persuasion. Oxford: Blackwell. pp. xii, 241. (Language library.)

**1319.** ROSTECK, THOMAS.   Irony, argument, and reportage in television documentary: *See It Now* versus Senator McCarthy. QJS (75:3) 277–98.

**1320.** SEBBERSON, DAVID.   Investigations for a critical theory of rhetoric: issues in practical reasoning and rhetorical proof. Unpub. doct. diss., Univ. of Maryland College Park, 1988. [Abstr. in DA (49) 2637A.]

**1321.** SHUGER, DEBORA K.   Sacred rhetoric: the Christian grand style in the English Renaissance. Princeton, NJ: Princeton UP, 1988. pp. x, 290. Rev. by Craig Kallendorf in SCN (47:1/2) 3–4; by Richard A. Muller in SixCT (20:4) 687–8; by Anthony Low in ChrisL (38:3) 79–81.

**1322.** SLOANE, THOMAS O.   Reinventing *inventio*. CE (51:5) 461–73.

**1323.** SWANSON, JON CHARLES.   The rhetoric of evangelization: a study of pragmatic constraints on organizational systems of rhetoric. Unpub. doct. diss., Univ. of Texas at Austin. [Abstr. in DA (50) 1484–5A.]

**1324.** VICKERS, BRIAN.   In defence of rhetoric. (Bibl. 1988, 1009.) Rev. by Don Bialostosky in CE (51:3) 325–9; by Miriam Dow in CE (51:8) 875–8.

**1325.** WEBER, DONALD.   Rhetoric and history in Revolutionary New England. New York; Oxford: OUP, 1988. pp. xiv, 207. Rev. by Michael P. Kramer in AL (61:4) 688–9; by Melvin Yazawa in JAH (75:4) 1304–5; by Harry S. Stout in EAL (24:2) 152–5.

**1326.** WOODS, MARJORIE CURRY.   An unfashionable rhetoric in the fifteenth century. QJS (75:3) 312–20.

**1327.** YOUNGKIN, BETTY ROGERS.   The contributions of Walter J. Ong to the study of rhetoric: history and metaphor. Unpub. doct. diss., Texas A&M Univ. [Abstr. in DA (50) 1485A.]

# MEDIUM AND REGISTER

## SPOKEN DISCOURSE

**1328.** ACKERMAN, BRUCE.   Why dialogue? JP (86:1) 5–12.

**1329.** AIJMER, KARIN.   Themes and tails: the discourse functions of dislocated elements. NJL (12:2) 137–54.

**1330.** AL-AZZAWI, MOHAMMED-BASIL; HASSAN, JASSIM MOHAMED. Notes on sentence patterns in conversational English. Al-Mustansiriya Literary Review (Al-Mustansiriya Univ., Baghdad) (12) 1985, 29–41.

**1331.** BÄCKLUND, INGEGERD.   Cues to the audience: on some structural markers in English monologue. *In* (pp. 29–39) **34.**

**1332.** BIBER, DOUGLAS.   Variation across speech and writing. Cambridge: CUP, 1988. pp. xiii, 299. Rev. by Bengt Altenberg in StudL (43:2) 167–74.

**1333.** BOSCH, PETER.   Agreement and anaphora: a study in the role of pronouns in syntax and discourse. (Bibl. 1986, 1086, where scholar's name misspelt.) Rev. by Hannes Rieser in Journal of Pragmatics (13:3) 486–96.

**1334.** BUBLITZ, WOLFRAM.   Ausdrücke des Kenntnisnehmens (Hörersignale) oder des Stellungsnehmens (Redebeiträge): 'yes' und verwandte Formen. *See* **1259.**

**1335.** —— Repetition in spoken discourse. *In* (pp. 352–68) **5.**

**1336.** —— Supportive fellow-speakers and cooperative conversations. Amsterdam: Benjamins, 1988. pp. 308. Rev. by Anna-Brita Stenström in SN (43:1) 63–6.

**1337.** —— Topical coherence in spoken discourse. SAP (22) 31–51.

**1338.** COHEN, LEONARD G.   Syntactic blends in English parole. Frankfurt; Berne; New York; Paris: Lang, 1987. pp. 178. (Forum Anglicum, 15.) Rev. by Christian Mair in AAA (14:2) 190–1.

**1339.** CORNISH, FRANCIS.   Discourse structure and anaphora: written and conversational English. Lingua (79:2/3) 229–43 (review-article).

**1340.** ERDMANN, PETER.   *Habeas corpus* – über die Nützlichkeit von Sprachdaten bei der Beschreibung des Englischen. *In* (pp. 319–29) **4.**

**1341.** FARAG, S. M.   A linguistic analysis of spoken and written narrative discourse. Unpub. doct. diss., Univ. of Aston, 1986. [Abstr. in IT (36:2) 466.]

**1342.** FIRBAS, JAN.   Dva přístupy k analýze mluvené věty. (Two approaches to the analysis of a spoken sentence.) *In* (p. 18) **6.**

**1343.** FORD, CECILIA E.   Grammar in ordinary interaction: the pragmatics of adverbial clauses in conversational English. Unpub. doct. diss., Univ. of California, Los Angeles, 1988. [Abstr. in DA (49) 3702A.]

**1344.** FRASER, JOHN.   Playing for real: discourse and authority. UTQ (56:3) 1987, 416–34.

**1345.** FRAURUD, KARI.   Towards a non-uniform treatment of definite NP's in discourse. *In* (pp. 75-87) **48.**

**1346.** FROW, JOHN.   Formal method in discourse analysis. Journal of Pragmatics (13:3) 333–41.

1347.   GOODY, JACK.   The interface between the written and the oral. (Bibl. 1987, 1829.) Rev. by A. Ebeogu in Lore and Language (8:1) 112–15.

1348.   HALFORD, BRIGITTE K.   Non-syntactic discourse units – the liberties of spoken English. *In* (pp. 234–43) **5**.

1349.   HORNE, MERLE.   Towards a discourse-based model of English sentence intonation. *See* **753**.

1350.   HUSPEK, MICHAEL.   Linguistic variability and power: an analysis of 'you know/I think' variation in working class speech. *See* **1270**.

1351.   KIM, HYANG-YEON.   Topic continuity in English discourse. Unpub. doct. diss., Sungkyunkwan Univ., Seoul.

1352.   KIM, IL-UNG.   Damwha eui jjaim gwa geu jeongae. (The organization of discourse and its progression.) UJH (34) 23–59.

1353.   KLEIN-ANDREU, FLORA (ed.).   Discourse perspectives on syntax. New York; London: Academic Press, 1983. pp. xvii, 266. Rev. by Jarmila Tárnyiková in PP (32:1) 49–52.

1354.   LEE, CHINGKWEI ADRIENNE.   Information structure in planned, written, and unplanned, spoken discourse. Unpub. doct. diss., Univ. of South Carolina, 1988. [Abstr. in DA (49) 3014A.]

1355.   LESSL, THOMAS M.   The priestly voice. QJS (75:2) 183–97.

1356.   LIFSON, MARTHA RONK.   Learning by talking: conversation in *As You Like It.* ShS (40) 1988, 91–105.

1357.   LJUNG, MAGNUS.   English emotives. *In* (pp. 185–94) **24**.

1358.   MATSON, DONALD BRUCE.   Theme, focus, action and the forms of discourse. Unpub. doct. diss., Univ. of California, San Diego, 1988. [Abstr. in DA (50) 944A.]

1359.   NOBLE, BART EDWARD.   A comparison of objective and subjective measurement procedures in assessing the intelligibility of connected discourse. Unpub. doct. diss., Univ. of Texas at Austin. [Abstr. in DA (50) 1483A.]

1360.   PIAZZA, ROBERTA.   A conversational analysis of theatrical discourse: repair procedures as the expression of dramatic interaction. Unpub. doct. diss., Columbia Univ. Teachers College, 1987. [Abstr. in DA (49) 3352A.]

1361.   RICHARDS, BERNARD.   Chambers of horrors. Listener (121) 23 Feb., 9–11. (Clichés and mixed metaphors on radio).

1362.   SCHIFFRIN, DEBORAH.   Discourse markers. Cambridge: CUP, 1987. pp. x, 364. (Studies in interactional sociolinguistics, 5.) Rev. by Kathryn Woolard in AAnth (93:3) 1988, 739.

1363.   SEM, HELLA FRISAK.   Discourse in situation schema theory. *In* (pp. 99–111) **48**.

1364.   SKREBNEV, J. M.   Vvedenie v kollokvialistiku. (Introduction to colloquial language.) Saratov: Saratov UP, 1985. pp. 209.

1365.   SPARKS, F. M.   Deixis and conversation analysis. Unpub. M.Phil. diss., Univ. of Sussex, 1988. [Abstr. in IT (38:4) 1454.]

1366.   STIRLING, L. F.   Switch-reference and logophoricity in discourse representation theory. Unpub. doct. diss., Univ. of Edinburgh. [Abstr. in IT (39:4) 1623.]

**1367.** TANNEN, DEBORAH.   Talking voices: repetition, dialogue, and imagery in conversational discourse. Cambridge: CUP. pp. 240. (Studies in interactional sociolinguistics, 6.)

**1368.** TAYLOR, TALBOT J.; CAMERON, DEBORAH.   Analysing conversation: rules and units in the structure of talk. (Bibl. 1987, 1858.) Rev. by Michael Toolan in Journal of Pragmatics (13:2) 251–74.

**1369.** TENCH, P. W.   The roles of intonation in English discourse. *See* **772.**

**1370.** TOOLAN, MICHAEL.   Ruling out rules in the analysis of conversation. Journal of Pragmatics (13:2) 251–74 (review-article).

**1371.** TOTTIE, GUNNEL.   What does *uh-(h)uh* mean? American English vocalizations and the Swedish learner. *In* (pp. 269–81) **34.**

**1372.** TRIKI, M.   Linguistic and perceptual subjectivity: towards a typology of narrative voice. Unpub. doct. diss., Univ. of Essex. [Abstr. in IT (39:3) 1100.]

**1373.** URBANOVÁ, LUDMILLA.   Linguistics and didactic specifications of the English language of conversation. *In* (pp. 44–5) **6.**

**1374.** VERSTER, LEONORE; WEIDEMAN, ALBERT.   'Two roads diverged ...': an analysis of the achievement of partings. SA Journal of Linguistics (6:4) 1988, 55–68.

**1375.** WATTS, RICHARD J.   Taking the pitcher to the 'well': native speakers' perception of their use of discourse markers in conversation. Journal of Pragmatics (13:2) 203–37.

**1376.** WEBER, ELIZABETH GEAN.   Varieties of questions in English conversation: a study of the role of morphosyntax in declarative and nonclausal forms. *See* **947.**

**1377.** WEIJTERS, A. J. M. M.   Denotation in discourse: analysis and algorithm. *See* **1254.**

**1378.** WELLS, W. H. G.   Focus in spoken English. Unpub. doct. diss., Univ. of York. [Abstr. in IT (38:4) 1454.]

**1379.** WIKBERG, KAY.   On the role of the lexical verb in discourse. *In* (pp. 375–88) **24.**

## STYLISTICS OF LITERARY TEXTS

**1380.** ASHCROFT, W. D.   Language issues facing Commonwealth writers: a reply to D'Costa. JCL (22:1) 1987, 99–118. (*Refers to* bibl. 1984, 1063.)

**1381.** BANFIELD, ANN.   Unspeakable sentences: narration and representation in the language of fiction. (Bibl. 1987, 1872.) Rev. by Haruhiko Yamaguchi in Journal of Pragmatics (13:4) 577–96.

**1382.** BIBER, DOUGLAS.   Variations across speech and writing. *See* **1332.**

**1383.** —— FINEGAN, EDWARD.   Drift and the evolution of English style: a history of three genres. Lang (65:3) 487–517. (Fiction, essays and letters.)

**1384.** BIRCH, DAVID.   Cunning beneath the verbs: demythologising Singapore English poetry. *In* (pp. 147–90) **19.** (Revised version of conference paper, Melbourne, February 1985.)

**1385.** BLAKE, N. F.   The language of Shakespeare. Basingstoke: Macmillan. pp. x, 154. (Language of literature.) (Repr. of bibl. 1985, 966; orig. pub. as *Shakespeare's Language: an Introduction.*)

**1386.** BOASE-BEIER, JEAN.   Poetic compounds: the principles of poetic language in modern English poetry. Tübingen: Niemeyer, 1987. pp. vii, 202. (Linguistische Arbeiten, 179.) Rev. by Geert Booij in Yearbook of Morphology 1988 (1) 285–91.

**1387.** BURNLEY, DAVID.   The language of Chaucer. Basingstoke: Macmillan. pp. xvi, 264. (Language of literature.) (Repr. of bibl. 1987, 3500; orig. pub. as *A Guide to Chaucer's Language.*)

**1388.** CALDER, A. C.   The dramatic language of Shakespeare's *Henry VI*: a stylistic and theatrical study. Unpub. doct. diss., Univ. of Aberdeen. [Abstr. in IT (39:3) 1106.]

**1389.** CARTER, RONALD; SIMPSON, PAUL (eds).   Language, discourse and literature: an introductory reader in discourse stylistics. London: Unwin Hyman. pp. xii, 298.

**1390.** COOPMANS, PETER.   Where stylistic and syntactic processes meet: locative inversion in English. Lang (65:4) 728–51.

**1391.** Entry cancelled.

**1392.** COWAN, LAURA JEAN.   'An altering speech': syntax in the early poetry of W. H. Auden. Unpub. doct. diss., Princeton Univ., 1988. [Abstr. in DA (49) 3367A.]

**1393.** CROMBIE, WINIFRED.   Free verse and prose style: an operational definition and description. (Bibl. 1988, 1050.) Rev. by Kenneth Millard in NQ (36:2) 283–4.

**1394.** DAKHNO, M. P.   Rol' stilisticheskikh priemov v formirovanii kontseptual'noĭ informatsii dramaturgicheskogo teksta: na materiale p'es Dzh. B. Pristli. (The role of stylistic devices in the formation of the conceptual information of the dramatic text: based on material from J. B. Priestley's plays.) SNTM (334) 74–81.

**1395.** DOTY, KATHLEEN.   Dialogue, deixis and narration in a dramatic adaptation. PoetT (31) 42–59. (Albee's adaptation of *The Ballad of the Sad Café.*)

**1396.** DUSSINGER, JOHN A.   'The language of real feeling': internal speech in the Jane Austen novel. *In* (pp. 97–115) **33.**

**1397.** FABB, NIGEL, *et al.* (eds).   The linguistics of writing: arguments between language and literature. (Bibl. 1988, 1056.) Rev. by Josiane Paccaud in EA (42:4) 453–4; by Roger Fowler in MLR (84:4) 897–8.

**1398.** FARAG, S. M.   A linguistic analysis of spoken and written narrative discourse. *See* **1341.**

**1399.** FIRBAS, JAN.   Interpreting Psalm 91 from the point of view of functional sentence perspective. *In* (pp. 107–16) **24.**

**1400.** FOKKEMA, DOUWE.   The semantic and syntactic organization of Postmodernist texts. *In* (pp. 81–98) **7.**

**1401.** FOWLER, ROGER. Linguistic criticism. (Bibl. 1987, 1888.) Rev. by Hildegard Tristram in Ang (107:1/2) 95–9.

**1402.** GANTS, N. V.; KUZNETŜOVA, L. B. Funkt̂sional'nostilisti-cheskie kharakteristiki minimal'nykh dvusostavnykh predlozheniĭ s podlezhashchim 'it' v dialogakh p'es Shekspira. (Functional-stylistic characteristics of minimal binominal sentences with the subject 'it' in the dialogues of Shakespeare's plays.) Analiz stileĭ zarubezhnoĭ khudo-zhestvennoĭ i nauchnoĭ literatury (Leningrad) (6) 110–14.

**1403.** GÖRLACH, MANFRED. Corpus problems of text collections: linguistic aspects of the canon. *In* (pp. 365–81) **4.**

**1404.** GREENWAY, WILLIAM. The urn and the rock: poets teaching poetry. CEAF (20:1/2) 2–4.

**1405.** HALÁSZ, LÁSZLÓ (ed.). Literary discourse: aspects of cognitive and social psychological approaches. Berlin: de Gruyter, 1987. pp. 242. Rev. by A. Ebeogu in Lore and Language (8:2) 115.

**1406.** HAMEED, SALIH MAHDI. Some stylistic features in *To Autumn*. Journal of Education and Science (Univ. of Mosul, Iraq) (3) 1981, 17–36.

**1407.** HOLTON, SYLVIA WALLACE. Down home and uptown: the representation of Black speech in American fiction. Madison, NJ: Fairleigh Dickinson UP; London; Toronto: Assoc. UPs, 1984. pp. 226. Rev. by Walter Edwards in BALF (23:3) 615–20.

**1408.** HOPKINS, MARY FRANCES. The rhetoric of heteroglossia in Flannery O'Connor's *Wise Blood*. QJS (75:2) 198–211.

**1409.** KOBERNICK, MARK. Semiotics of the drama and the style of Eugene O'Neill. Amsterdam: Benjamins. pp. xiv, 159. (Foundations of semiotics, 19.)

**1410.** LIGGINS, ELIZABETH M. Syntax and style in the Old English *Orosius*. *In* (pp. 245–73) **56.**

**1411.** LUBICZ-PYRZOWSKA, BARBARA. Perspektywy semiotyzacji opowiadań E. M. Forstera w świetle kategorii gatunkowych i ponadga-tunkowych. (Applying semiotics to E. M. Forster's short stories: figurative and non-figurative criteria.) *In* (pp. 178–93) **36.**

**1412.** MATHIS, GILLES. Analyse stylistique du *Paradis perdu* de John Milton: l'univers poétique: échos et correspondances. Aix-en-Provence: Université de Provence, 1987. 4 vols. pp. 1490. Rev. by Thomas Healy in MLR (84:3) 718; by Mary Ann Radzinowicz in RQ (42:1) 146–9.

**1413.** MORTON, A. Q. Authorship: the nature of the habit. TLS, 17 Feb., 164. (Stylometry.)

**1414.** NAJA, LAYAL WAJIH. A stylistic analysis of a passage from *Wuthering Heights*. Al-Mustansiriya Literary Review (Al-Mustansiriya Univ., Baghdad) (11) 1985, 59–67.

**1415.** POMORSKA, KRYSTYNA; RUDY, STEPHEN (eds). Language in literature. By ROMAN JAKOBSON. Cambridge, MA; London: Harvard UP, 1987. pp. 548. Rev. by David Shepherd in MLR (84:4) 1049–50; by F. W. Galan in TLS, 13 Jan., 41.

**1416.** PROTŜENKO, I. B. Kompozit̂sionno-stilisticheskie osobennosti p'esy Dzhozefa Khellera *N'iu Kheĭven my bombili.* (The compositional-stylistic peculiarities of Joseph Heller's play *We Bombed New Haven.*) Analiz stileĭ zarubezhnoĭ-khudozhestvennoĭ i nauchnoĭ literatury (Leningrad) (6) 84–93.

**1417.** REYES, MARIE. A semantics for literary texts. Unpub. doct. diss., Concordia Univ., 1988. [Abstr. in DA (50) 1295A.]

**1418.** SABIN, MARGERY. The dialect of the tribe: speech and community in modern fiction. Oxford; New York: OUP, 1987. pp. x, 310. Rev. by Deirdre Byrne in UES (27:2) 39–40.

**1419.** SEWELL, DAVID R. Mark Twain's languages: discourse, dialogue and linguistic variety. (Bibl. 1987, 1903.) Rev. by John S. Whitley in JAStud (23:3) 496–7.

**1420.** SHOR, IU. V. Stilisticheskie osobennosti angliĭskogo goticheskogo romana: na materiale romana A. Radklif *Udol'fskie taĭny.* (The stylistic peculiarities of the English gothic novel: based on material from Ann Radcliffe's *The Mysteries of Udolpho.*) Analiz stileĭ zarubezhnoĭ khudozhestvennoĭ i nauchnoĭ literatury (Leningrad) (6) 57–65.

**1421.** SÖDERLIND, JOHANNES. Immediate phrase repetition in language and in music. *In* (pp. 345–54) **24.**

**1422.** STANDOP, EWALD. Abriß der englischen Metrik: mit einer Enführung in die Prosodie der Prosa (Satzintonation) und einen Aufsatz uber Rhythmus von JOST TRIER. Tübingen: Francke. pp. viii, 163.

**1423.** STANLEY, E. G. King Alfred's prefaces. RES (39:155) 1988, 349–64.

**1424.** SURETTE, LEON. Metaphor and metonymy: Jakobson reconsidered. UTQ (56:4) 1987, 557–74.

**1425.** TAN, P. K. W. A stylistics of drama, with particular reference to Stoppard's *Travesties* and parody. Unpub. doct. diss., Univ. of Edinburgh. [Abstr. in IT (39:4) 1635.]

**1426.** TODD, LORETO. The language of Irish literature. Basingstoke: Macmillan. pp. xii, 193. (Language of literature.)

**1427.** UNAL-HODSON, H. C. A stylistic evaluation of point of view in James Joyce's *The Boarding House.* Unpub. M.Litt. diss., Univ. of Edinburgh. [Abstr. in IT (39:4) 1635.]

**1428.** WALES, KATIE. A dictionary of stylistics. *See* **1153.**

## STYLISTICS OF NON-LITERARY TEXTS

**1429.** CORNISH, FRANCIS. Discourse structure and anaphora: written and conversational English. *See* **1339.**

**1430.** DUŠKOVÁ, LIBUŠE. K úloze prostředků textové koheze jako indikátorů funkčních stylů. (On the role of the devices of text cohesion as indicators of functional styles.) *In* (p. 18) **6.**

**1431.** DUVAL, GILLES. Divination, morals and courtesy: some aspects of English chap-literature of the eighteenth century. Lore and Language (8:1) 31–43.

**1432.** ELSHERSHABI, MUHAMMAD ATTIA HASAN. Substitution and lexical cohesion in the editorial argumentative discourse of Arabic and

American English. Unpub. doct. diss., Univ. of South Carolina, 1988. [Abstr. in DA (49) 1786A.]

**1433.** EWALD, HELEN ROTHSCHILD. Schematic and text-based arrangement options, the reading process, and rhetorical competence. CEAF (20:1/2) 5–11.

**1434.** FAREH, SHEHDEH ISMAIL. Paragraph structure in Arabic and English expository discourse. Unpub. doct. diss., Univ. of Kansas, 1988. [Abstr. in DA (50) 1292A.]

**1435.** GREEN, DAVID. Shaping political consciousness: the language of politics in America from McKinley to Reagan. Ithaca, NY; London: Cornell UP, 1987. pp. xiii, 277. Rev. by Marcus Cunliffe in JAH (75:4) 1345–6.

**1436.** GREEN, THOMAS A. Linguistic manipulation in the Punch and Judy script. *See* **723.**

**1437.** HOEY, MICHAEL. The discourse properties of the criminal statute. *In* (pp. 145–66) **30.**

**1438.** JACOBSON, SVEN. Some grammatical trends in American newspaper language. *In* (pp. 145–54) **24.**

**1439.** KAPLAN, ROBERT B. English as language of science. Vox (Canberra) (2) 49–53.

**1440.** KIM, HYANG-RYUN. Iconicity in syntactic coding of topic continuity based on English narrative. *See* **914.**

**1441.** KOUŘILOVÁ, MAGDA. Štruktúra a funkcia v anglijskom odbornom prehovore. (Structure and function in English technical utterances.) *In* (pp. 25–6) **6.**

**1442.** LEE, CHINGKWEI ADRIENNE. Information structure in planned, written, and unplanned, spoken discourse. *See* **1354.**

**1443.** McATEER, E. Typeface effects in written language: functions of typeface change for signalling meaning within a text. *See* **113.**

**1444.** MOORE, T. C. A study of the development of the liturgy in the Anglican tradition to 1556. Unpub. M.Litt. diss., Univ. of Stirling, 1988. [Abstr. in IT (39:1) 5–6.]

**1445.** NASH, WALTER. The language of humour. (Bibl. 1987, 1937.) Rev. by Philip Drew in RES (38:149) 1987, 63–4; by J. M. Kirk in Lore and Language (8:2) 121.

**1446.** PUCI, JÁN. Poznámky k niektorým štýlotvorným činitelom anglického publicistického štýlu. (On some stylistic factors of English journalese.) *In* (pp. 36–7) **6.**

**1447.** QI-BO, ZHU. A quantitative look at the Guangzhou Petroleum English Corpus. *See* **543.**

**1448.** REID, CHRISTOPHER. Edmund Burke and the practice of political writing. (Bibl. 1986, 1196.) Rev. by John Cannon in BJECS (10) 1987, 228–9.

**1449.** STONES, LIONEL; PHILLIPS, SEYMOUR. English in the Public Records: three late thirteenth-century examples. *See* **694.**

**1450.** WARD, R. J. A stylistic analysis of administrative English through a qualitative and quantitative investigation of government leaflets. Unpub. doct. diss., Univ. of Wales. [Abstr. in IT (39:3) 1100.]

**1451.** WILLIAMS, M. P.    A comparison of the textual structures of Arabic and English written texts. Unpub. doct. diss., Univ. of Leeds. [Abstr. in IT (39:3) 1100.]

**1452.** WOOLLEY, BENJAMIN.    Fog factors. *See* **552.**

## DIALECTS
### GENERAL STUDIES
**1453.** JOSEPH, JOHN EARL.   Eloquence and power: the rise of language standards and standard languages. London: Pinter, 1987. pp. xi, 199. (Open linguistics.)

**1454.** KASTOVSKY, DIETER; SZWEDEK, ALEKSANDER (eds); PŁOCIŃSKA, BARBARA (asst ed.).   Linguistics across historical and geographical boundaries: in honour of Jacek Fisiak on the occasion of his fiftieth birthday: vol. 1, Linguistic theory and historical linguistics; vol. 2, Descriptive, contrastive and applied linguistics. (Bibl. 1987, 1955.) Rev. by Wilhelm Elmer in Ang (106:1/2) 1988, 145–6.

**1455.** TRUDGILL, PETER.   Dialects in contact. pp. viii, 174. (Bibl. 1986, 859, where pagination incorrect.) Rev. by Beat Glauser in Ang (107:3/4) 492–5.

### DIALECTS OF THE BRITISH ISLES
**1456.** ADAMS, J. R. R.   A preliminary checklist of works containing Ulster dialect, 1700–1900. Linen Hall Review (6:3) 10–12.

**1457.** AERTSEN, H.   The use of dialect words in Middle English alliterative poetry. In (pp. 173–85) **47.**

**1458.** BENSKIN, MICHAEL.   Some aspects of Cumbrian English, mainly mediaeval. In (pp. 13–46) **24.**

**1459.** COATES, RICHARD.   Two measure-terms in Gaelic and early Modern Scots. See **1036.**

**1460.** DIETZ, KLAUS.   Die historische Schichtung phonologischer Isoglossen in den englischen Dialekten: altenglische Isoglossen. See **721.**

**1461.** DOLAN, TERENCE (introd.).   English as we speak it in Ireland. By P. W. JOYCE. Dublin: Wolfhound Press, 1988. pp. xxiv, 356. (Repr. of second ed.: 1910.)

**1462.** FENTON, ALEXANDER.   Wirds an' wark 'e seasons roon: on an Aberdeenshire farm. Aberdeen: Aberdeen UP, 1987. pp. x, 84. Rev. by Leslie W. Wheeler in SLang (6) 1987, 57–9.

**1463.** GRAHAM, WILLIAM.   The handy guide to Scots. Edinburgh: Ramsay Head Press, 1986. pp. 78.

**1464.** HERBISON, IVAN.   Language, literature and cultural identity: an Ulster-Scots perspective. Ballymena: Dunclug Press. pp. 9. (Contribution to series *The Cultural Identity of Ulster* read at Conway Mill, Belfast, 23 Apr. 1989.)

**1465.** KRISTENSSON, GILLIS.   The linguistic status of East Anglia in late Middle English. In (pp. 123–30) **34.**

**1466.** —— Place-names and linguistic geography. In (pp. 155–64) **24.**

**1467.** —— A survey of Middle English dialects 1290–1350: the West Midland counties. (Bibl. 1987, 747.) Rev. by John McNeal Dodgson in Nomina (12) 1988/89, 188–90.

**1468.** LEITCH, ROGER (ed.).   The book of Sandy Stewart. See **1004.**

**1469.** LETLEY, EMMA.   From Galt to Douglas Brown: nineteenth-century fiction and Scots language. (Bibl. 1988, 1158.) Rev. in

Edinburgh Review (83) 141–2; by Graham Tulloch in SLJ (supp. 31)
20–3; by Joachim Schwend in Cencrastus (33) 44–5.
**1470.** LOVELACE, MARTIN J.   *The Language of Old Burton, Burton
Bradstock, Dorset.* By DOUGLAS NORTHOVER. With notes of parallels to
Newfoundland usage. Lore and Language (8:2) 3–31. (Glossary.)
**1471.** MACAFEE, C. I.   Some studies in the Glasgow vernacular.
Unpub. doct. diss., Univ. of Glasgow, 1988. [Abstr. in IT (39:1) 26.]
**1472.** MACAFEE, CAROLINE; MACLEOD, ISEABAIL (eds).   The 'nuttis
schell': essays on the Scots language presented to A.J. Aitken. (Bibl.
1988, 1159.) Rev. by Thomas Crawford in AUR (52) 336–7.
**1473.** McKENNA, G. E.   Vowel duration in the standard English of
Scotland. *See* **762.**
**1474.** MANNING, SUSAN.   Scotland and America: national literatures?
National languages? Cencrastus (32) 41–6.
**1475.** MELCHERS, GUNNEL.   *Hween, kenee, tlock*: on the realization of
initial *k*-clusters in some varieties of English. *In* (pp. 237–44) **24.**
**1476.** —— Twartree ösfil Shetlan flooers. (Two or three useful Shetland flowers.) *In* (pp. 147–53) **34.**
**1477.** MILLIKEN, MARGARET E.   Phonological divergence and
intelligibility: a case study of English and Scots. *See* **763.**
**1478.** MUNRO, MICHAEL.   The patter: another blast. Edinburgh:
Canongate, 1988. pp. ix, 99. (Glasgow dialect.)
**1479.** NICKEL, GERHARD; STALKER, JAMES C. (eds).   Problems of
standardization and linguistic variation in present-day English. (Bibl.
1986, 847, where title incorrect.) Rev. by Friedrich Wilhelm Gester in
Archiv (226:2) 404–9.
**1480.** PADDOCK, HAROLD.   On explaining macrovariation in the
sibilant and nasal suffixes of English. *See* **864.**
**1481.** PEPPER, JOHN.   John Pepper's Ulster handbook. Belfast:
Appletree, 1987. pp. 72.
**1482.** RIACH, W. A. D.   A Galloway glossary. Aberdeen: Assn for
Scottish Literary Studies, 1988. pp. xii, 49. (Occasional papers, 7.)
**1483.** SMITH, J. B.   'The old eel that come up through Breydon
Water': Arthur Ransome's work as a key to folklife and folk speech. Lore
and Language (8:2) 51–62.
**1484.** STEVENSON, JAMES A. C.; MACLEOD, ISEABAIL.   Scoor-oot: a
dictionary of Scots words and phrases in current use. *See* **1149.**
**1485.** UPTON, CLIVE; SANDERSON, STEWART; WIDDOWSON, JOHN.
Word maps: a dialect atlas of England. (Bibl. 1987, 2041.) Rev. by Aleš
Klégr in CJa (32) 1988, 190–2; by François Chevillet in EA (42:2)
208–9.
**1486.** VIERECK, WOLFGANG.   A corpus of dialectal English computerised. *In* (pp. 345–7) **4.** (Abstract.)

## DIALECTS OF NORTH AMERICA

**1487.** ALVAREZ, LOUIS; KOLKER, ANDREW.   American tongues. New
York: Center for New American Media, 1986. Rev. by Elizabeth S.
Girsch in IE (12:2), 1988, 31–2.

**1488.** BERGIN, KENDALL RUSSELL. The development of rating scales for Black English grammar, pronunciation, rhythm/intonation, and overall Black English usage. Unpub. doct. diss., Univ. of Tennessee, 1988. [Abstr. in DA (50) 429A.]

**1489.** DE WOLF, GAELAN THORNLEY DODDS. A study of selected social and regional factors in Canadian English: a comparison of phonological variables and grammatical items in Ottawa and Vancouver. Unpub. doct. diss., Univ. of Victoria, B.C., 1988. [Abstr. in DA (49) 2639A.]

**1490.** HISCOCK, PHILIP. Newfoundland folklore and language: a bibliography. St John's: Memorial Univ. of Newfoundland. pp. 56. (Regional language studies Newfoundland, 12.)

**1491.** HLAVSOVÁ, JELENA. On some newly-coined words in American English. CJa (33) 71–3.

**1492.** LAAGER, DOROTHY MARY. English, made in U.S.A. Unpub. doct. diss., State Univ. of New York at Stony Brook, 1988. [Abstr. in DA (50) 1294A.]

**1493.** LOGUE, CALVIN M.; DORGAN, HOWARD (eds). A new diversity in contemporary Southern rhetoric. *See* **1315.**

**1494.** MANNING, SUSAN. Scotland and America: national literatures? National languages? *See* **1474.**

**1495.** PENFIELD, JOYCE; ORNSTEIN-GALICIA, JACOB L. Chicano English: an ethnic contact dialect. (Bibl. 1986, 875.) Rev. by Christian Mair in AAA (14:2) 191–2.

**1496.** PIERCE, JAMES ALFRED. Sociolinguistic relationships in attitudes toward Anglo and Mexican American varieties of English in Corpus Christi, Texas. Unpub. doct. diss., Univ. of Texas at Austin. [Abstr. in DA (50) 1649A.]

**1497.** PRATT, T. K. (ed.). Dictionary of Prince Edward Island English. *See* **1142.**

**1498.** RICHARDS, DONNA JEAN. Prestige and standard in Canadian English: evidence from the survey of Vancouver English. Unpub. doct. diss., Univ. of British Columbia, 1988. [Abstr. in DA (49) 3708A.]

**1499.** ROSTEN, LEO. The joys of Yinglish. New York: McGraw-Hill. Rev. by Richard Shepard in NYTB, 8 Oct., 11.

**1500.** SCHNEIDER, EDGAR W. American earlier Black English: morphological and syntactic variables. Tuscaloosa; London: Alabama UP. pp. xiv, 314. (Trans. of bibl. 1985, 875.)

**1501.** SIMPSON, DAVID. The politics of American English, 1776–1850. (Bibl. 1988, 1188.) Rev. by Basil Cottle in RES (39:153) 1988, 93–4.

**1502.** WADE-LEWIS, MARGARET. The African substratum in American English. Unpub. doct. diss., New York Univ., 1988. [Abstr. in DA (49) 3016A.]

## DIALECTS OF THE REST OF THE WORLD

**1503.** ALI, AHMED. English in South Asia – a historical perspective. Third World International (Karachi) (13:5) 82–6.

**1504.** ARMUDA, A. A. Yoruba/English code-switching in Nigeria:

aspects of its functions and form. Unpub. doct. diss., Univ. of Reading, 1986. [Abstr. in IT (36:3) 902.]

**1505.** Attah, M. O.    Acceptability and intelligibility of selected accents of English in Benue State. Unpub. doct. diss., Univ. of Wales, 1985. [Abstr. in IT (36:2) 465.]

**1506.** Baker, Sidney John.    A dictionary of Australian slang. *See* **1122.**

**1507.** Bauer, Laurie.    Irregularity in past non-finite verb-forms. *See* **849.**

**1508.** —— Marginal modals in New Zealand English. *See* **880.**

**1509.** —— A note on the New Zealand weekend. *See* **1065.**

**1510.** Baumgardner, Robert J.    The Pakistanization of English. The Nation (Lahore) 7 Nov., 3.

**1511.** Bayard, Donn.    'Me say that? No way!': the social correlates of American lexical diffusion in New Zealand English. Te Reo (32) 17–60.

**1512.** Bernard, J. R.    Quantitative aspects of the sounds of Australian English. *In* (pp. 187–204, 342–3) **9.**

**1513.** —— Regional variation in Australian English: a survey. *In* (pp. 255–9, 347–8) **9.**

**1514.** Blair, David.    The development and current state of Australian English: a survey. *In* (pp. 171–5, 340–1) **9.**

**1515.** Bradley, David.    Regional dialects in Australian English phonology. *In* (pp. 260–70, 348–9) **9.**

**1516.** Bryant, Pauline.    Regional variation in the Australian English lexicon. *In* (pp. 301–14, 321, 350) **9.**

**1517.** Clark, J. E.    Some proposals for a revised phonetic transcription of Australian English. *In* (pp. 205–13, 343–4) **9.**

**1518.** Cochrane, G. R.    Origins and development of the Australian accent. *In* (pp. 176–86, 318, 341–2) **9.**

**1519.** Collins, Peter.    Divided and debatable usage in Australian English. *In* (pp. 138–49, 339–40) **9.**

**1520.** —— Blair, David (eds).    Australian English: the language of a new society. *See* **9.**

**1521.** Cooper, P. A.    An evaluation of attitudes towards conservative and extreme South African dialects. English Usage (20:2) 39–53.

**1522.** Delbridge, Arthur.    The *Macquarie*, an international national dictionary. *In* (pp. 66–79) **5.**

**1523.** Donaldson, Bruce Christopher.    The influence of English on Afrikaans: a case study of linguistic change in a language contact situation. Pretoria: Serva, 1988. pp. vi, 312. (Cf. bibl. 1987, 1953.)

**1524.** Gordon, Elizabeth.    That colonial twang: New Zealand speech and New Zealand identity. *See* **749.**

**1525.** —— Deverson, Tony.    Finding a New Zealand voice: attitudes towards English used in New Zealand. Auckland: New House. pp. 96.

**1526.** Gordon, Ian A.    British regional survivals in New Zealand English. NZEN (3) 5–8.

**1527.** Görlach, Manfred. *Varietas delectat*: forms and functions of English around the world. *In* (pp. 167–208) **30.**

**1528.** Hauptfleisch, Temple. Citytalk, theatretalk: dialect, dialogue and multilingual theatre in South Africa. EngA (16:1) 71–91.

**1529.** Hirsh, Walter (ed.). New Zealand English – alive and very well. Auckland: Office of the Race Relations Conciliator. pp. 28.

**1530.** Hornadge, Bill. The Australian slanguage: a look at what we say and how we say it. Melbourne: Mandarin, pp. 306.

**1531.** Khan, F. Linguistic variation in Indian English: a sociolinguistic study. Unpub. doct. diss., Univ. of Reading. [Abstr. in IT (39:2) 480.]

**1532.** Kohli, Devindra. Indian English: a *khichri* of words. TLS, 1 Dec., 1332, 1340.

**1533.** Leitner, Gerhard. Wie anders ist das Englische in Indien? *In* (pp. 385–96) **4.**

**1534.** Limbrick, V. R. Palatalization and affriction in South African English – a sample study. *See* **760.**

**1535.** Mabbett, I. W. 'Gender/inclusive language', literature and freedom. Quadrant (34:5) 36–40.

**1536.** McGill, David. The dinkum Kiwi dictionary. *See* **1134.**

**1537.** O'Grady, John. Aussie English: an explanation of the Australian idiom. Sydney: Weldon. pp. 104.

**1538.** Patterson, John. Maori concepts in Pakeha English. English in Aotearoa (8) 19–24.

**1539.** Picard, J. H. English . . . where do we go from here? English Usage (20:1) 23–31.

**1540.** Sanyal, S. C. English language in India and Indo-Anglian prose style. Ilfracombe: Stockwell, 1987. pp. 91.

**1541.** Sharp, Iain. New Zildish. Pacific Way (Auckland), Jan., 8–9.

**1542.** Sussex, Roland. The Americanisation of Australian English. *In* (pp. 158–68, 317) **9.**

**1543.** Taylor, Brian. American, British and other foreign influences on Australian English since World War II. *In* (pp. 225–54, 318–21, 345–7) **9.**

**1544.** Turner, G. W. Some problems in Australian etymology. *In* (pp. 214–24, 344–5) **9.**

**1545.** Wallace, Bill. A glossary of New Zealand blade-shearing terms. *See* **1015.**

## ENGLISH AS A WORLD LANGUAGE

**1546.** Smith, M. Van Wyk. Some thoughts on English as a lingua franca. Theoria (73) 31–8.

## PIDGINS AND CREOLES

**1547.** Ashcroft, W. D. Language issues facing Commonwealth writers: a reply to D'Costa. *See* **1380.**

**1548.** Dabydeen, David. On not being Milton: nigger talk in England today. Landfall (43:2) 180–91.

**1549.** GILBERT, G. G. (ed.). Pidgin and creole languages: essays in memory of John E. Reinecke. Honolulu: Hawaii UP, 1987. pp. 502. Rev. by Matthias Perl in ZP (41:3) 1988, 397–9.

**1550.** HOLM, JOHN A. Pidgins and creoles: vol. 2, Reference survey. Cambridge: CUP. pp. xxi, 704.

**1551.** MAIR, CHRISTIAN. Naipaul's *Miguel Street* and Selvon's *Lonely Londoners* – two approaches to the use of Caribbean creole in fiction. JCL (24:1) 138–54.

**1552.** ROMAINE, SUZANNE. Pidgin and creole languages. (Bibl. 1988, 1231.) Rev. by Bo Seltén in StudL (43:1) 59–63.

**1553.** SHRIMPTON, NEVILLE; NJIE, SULAYMAN. Editing Krio texts. *In* (pp. 205–22) **34.** (Afro-English creole of Sierra Leone.)

**1554.** ZIMA, PETR. Are there empirically-based universal features of language creolizations? PP (32:3) 152–61.

## SOCIOLINGUISTICS

**1555.** AHN, JUNG-HUN. Euisa sotong gwa ingan gwangae. (Communication and human relations.) UJH (34) 163–88.

**1556.** ARMUDA, A. A. Yoruba/English code-switching in Nigeria: aspects of its functions and form. *See* **1504.**

**1557.** BALL, PETER; GALLOIS, CYNTHIA; CALLAN, VICTOR J. Language attitudes: a perspective from social psychology. *In* (pp. 89–102, 331–5) **9.**

**1558.** BLEICH, DAVID. The double perspective: language, literacy, and social relations. New York; Oxford: OUP, 1988. pp. xiv, 347.

**1559.** BURGE, TYLER. Wherein is language social? *In* (pp. 175–91) **52.**

**1560.** BYUN, MYUNG-SUO. Language maintenance and shift: a domain analysis. JELL (35) 829–43.

**1561.** CHAIKA, ELAINE. Language: the social mirror. (Bibl. 1985, 824.) Cambridge, MA; London: Newbury House. pp. xx, 374. (Second ed.: first ed. 1982.)

**1562.** COCHRAN, EFFIE PAPATZIKOU. Generic masculine pronominal usage and sex-linked occupational stereotypes among high school students. Unpub. doct. diss., Columbia Univ. Teachers College, 1988. [Abstr. in DA (50) 126A.]

**1563.** COLLINS, PETER. Sociolinguistics in Australia: a survey. *In* (pp. 3–20, 332–5) **9.**

**1564.** —— BLAIR, DAVID (eds). Australian English: the language of a new society. *See* **9.**

**1565.** EAGLESON, ROBERT. Popular and professional attitudes to prestige dialects. *In* (pp. 150–7, 317, 340) **9.**

**1566.** FISHMAN, JOSHUA A. Language and ethnicity in minority sociolinguistic perspective. Clevedon: Multilingual Matters. pp. ix, 717. (Multilingual matters, 45.)

**1567.** GORDON, ELIZABETH; DEVERSON, TONY. Finding a New Zealand voice: attitudes towards English used in New Zealand. *See* **1525.**

**1568.** GUNN, JOHN S. The shearing shed society. *In* (pp. 78–88, 316, 331) **9.** (Language of woolgrowing in Australia.)

**1569.** HABERLAND, HARTMUT. Whose English, nobody's business. Journal of Pragmatics (13:6) 927–38.

**1570.** HAMERS, JOSIANE F.; BLANC, MICHEL H. A. Bilinguality and bilingualism. Cambridge: CUP. pp. xii, 324. Rev. by Kenji Hakuta in TLS, 17 Nov., 1263.

**1571.** HONEY, JOHN. 'Talking proper': schooling and the establishment of English 'Received Pronunciation'. *In* (pp. 209–27) **30.**

**1572.** HORN, PETER. Men talk women talk. Pretexts (1:1) 64–72.

**1573.** JAYASURIYA, LAKSIR. Language and culture in Australian public policy. Vox (Canberra) (2) 42–8.

**1574.** KHAN, F. Linguistic variation in Indian English: a sociolinguistic study. *See* **1531.**

**1575.** KRESS, GUNTHER. History and language: towards a social account of linguistic change. Journal of Pragmatics (13:3) 445–66.

**1576.** LANCE, MARK NORRIS. Normative inferential vocabulary: the explicitation of social linguistic practice. Unpub. doct. diss., Univ. of Pittsburgh, 1988. [Abstr. in DA (50) 461A.]

**1577.** MABBETT, I. W. 'Gender/inclusive language', literature and freedom. *See* **1535.**

**1578.** MONTGOMERY, MARTIN. An introduction to language and society. (Bibl. 1986, 1013.) Rev. by Miroslav Bázlik in Jazykovedný časopis (Bratislava) 1989, 96–8.

**1579.** PIERCE, JAMES ALFRED. Sociolinguistic relationships in attitudes toward Anglo and Mexican American varieties of English in Corpus Christi, Texas. *See* **1496.**

**1580.** PREISLER, BENT. Linguistic sex roles in conversation: social variation in the expression of tentativeness in English. New York; Berlin: Mouton de Gruyter, 1986. pp. xviii, 347. (Contributions to the sociology of language, 45.)

**1581.** REEVE, JAN. Community attitudes to Australian English. *In* (pp. 111–26, 337) **9.**

**1582.** ROMAINE, SUZANNE. Bilingualism. Oxford; New York: Blackwell. pp. 337. (Language in society, 13.) Rev. by Kenji Hakuta in TLS, 17 Nov., 1263.

**1583.** ŠIMEČEK, VÁCLAV. Vztah jazyka a společnosti jako předmět sociolingvistiky. (Language and society as the object of sociolinguistics.) CJa (32) 302–7, 337–42.

**1584.** STRNADOVÁ, ZDENKA. English as a sexist language. PP (32:1) 44–9.

**1585.** ŠVEJCER, A. D. Contemporary sociolinguistics: theory, problems, methods. Amsterdam: Benjamins, 1986. pp. vii, 193. (Linguistic and literary studies in Eastern Europe, 15.) Rev. by John Harris in MLR (84:3) 681–2.

**1586.** —— NIKOL'SKIJ, L. B. Introduction to sociolinguistics. Amsterdam: Benjamins, 1986. pp. xii, 181. (Linguistic and literary studies in Eastern Europe, 14.) Rev. by John Harris in MLR (84:3) 681–2.

**1587.** WOLFSON, NESSA; MANES, JOAN (eds).   Language of inequality.
Berlin; New York; Amsterdam: Mouton de Gruyter, 1985. pp. xvi, 412.
(Contributions to the sociology of language, 36.) Rev. by Alberto M.
Mioni in Journal of Pragmatics (13:3) 467–72.

# TRANSLATION AND COMPARATIVE LINGUISTICS

**1588.** ABBAS, HASSOONEI HASHIM. Some remarks on the prepositions 'in', 'on' and 'to' in English and standard Arabic. *See* **873.**

**1589.** ABDEL-LATIF, N. M. A contrastive analysis of interrogative structures in English and Arabic. *See* **874.**

**1590.** ABDELMOUMENE, N. Sentential complementation in French, English and Arabic. *See* **875.**

**1591.** AZIZ, YOWELL Y. Style shift in English–Arabic translation. Journal of Education and Science (Univ. of Mosul, Iraq) (4) 1981, 5–36.

**1592.** BÁZLIK, MIROSLAV. Z konfrontácie subjektu v angličtine a v slovenčine. *See* **882.**

**1593.** BIRKENHAUER, KLAUS; BIRKENHAUER, RENATE. Shaping tools for the literary translator's trade. Paintbrush (16) 89–98.

**1594.** BORNEMANN, EVA. Translation and lexicography: a practical view. *See* **1083.**

**1595.** BOURQUIN, GUY. La traduction automatique comme instrument d'investigation en analyse contrastive. *In* (pp. 7–16) **22.**

**1596.** CARLS, UWE. Der Topikalisierungsprozeß im Englischen und Deutschen. *See* **1260.**

**1597.** CARPENTER, RAYMOND L. Translation among English, French, German, Russian, and Japanese. SocSJ (26:2) 199–204.

**1598.** CHESTERMAN, ANDREW. Definiteness in English and Finnish. *See* **889.**

**1599.** CHEVILLET, FRANÇOIS. Les pronoms allocutoires en français et en anglais: éléments pour une réflexion socio-historique contrastive. *In* (pp. 17–36) **22.**

**1600.** CHOE, YONG-JAE. Daejo bunsuk eui jaepyeongga. (Contrastive analysis: a reappraisal.) ET (34) 1987, 23–39. (Comparison of two or more languages or subsystems of languages.)

**1601.** CIENKI, ALAN JOSEPH. Spatial cognition and the semantics of prepositions in English, Polish, and Russian. *See* **1203.**

**1602.** COMRIE, BERNARD. Translatability and language universals. Belgian Journal of Linguistics (4) 53–67.

**1603.** DIERICKX, JEAN. Equivalent messages: headlines in *Le Monde* and their translation into English. *In* (pp. 59–68) **42.**

**1604.** DI VIRGILIO, PAUL. The dictionary's role as semantic universe in the genesis and translation of the literary work. *See* **1086.**

**1605.** ELSHERSHABI, MUHAMMAD ATTIA HASAN. Substitution and lexical cohesion in the editorial argumentative discourse of Arabic and American English. *See* **1432.**

**1606.** FAREH, SHEHDEH ISMAIL. Paragraph structure in Arabic and English expository discourse. *See* **1434.**

**1607.** GERZYMISCH-ARBOGAST, HEIDRUN. The role of sense relations in translating vague business and economic texts. Paintbrush (16) 187 95.

**1608.** HARTMANN, REINHARD. Lexicography, translation and the so-called language barrier. *See* **1088.**

**1609.** HASSAN, ABDUL, SH. QASSIM. The object in English and Arabic: a contrastive study. *See* **902.**

**1610.** HAUGLAND, KARI E. Some practical aspects of trade names and trademarks in terminology and translation: a brief report from the translation of an ESP text. *In* (pp. 117–29) **24.**

**1611.** HAWKINS, JOHN A. A comparative typology of English and German: unifying the contrasts. (Bibl. 1988, 1292.) Rev. by Manfred Markus in Ang (107:1/2) 110–15.

**1612.** HÜLLEN, WERNER. On the translation of English compound verbs into German: an investigation based on Alex Haley's *Roots/ Wurzeln. In* (pp. 238–57) **4.**

**1613.** JAUDEL, PHILIPPE. Traduire Conrad. *In* (pp. 37–49) **22.**

**1614.** KAGER, R. W. J. A metrical theory of stress and destressing in English and Dutch. *See* **756.**

**1615.** KLEIN-LATAUD, CHRISTINE. Les transports de la métaphore. CanL (117) 1988, 81–91.

**1616.** KNITTLOVÁ, DAGMAR. Stylistická ekvivalence v překladech prózy. (Stylistic equivalence in prose translations.) *In* (p. 24) **6.**

**1617.** KODŽAHINKOV, IVAN. Săpostavitelen analiz na zoomorfni harakteristiki v bălgarskija i anglijskija ezik. (Comparative analysis of zoomorphous characteristics in English and Bulgarian.) SEz (14:3) 13–19.

**1618.** KÖNIG, EKKEHARD. A new bilingual dictionary for function words. *In* (pp. 294–306) **5.**

**1619.** KROMANN, HANS-PEDER. Neue Orientierung der zwei-sprachigen Wörterbücher. Zur funktionalen zweisprachigen Lexiko-graphie. *See* **1095.**

**1620.** KUSSMAUL, PAUL. Kontext und einsprachiges Wörterbuch in der Übersetzerausbildung. *See* **1096.**

**1621.** LAVÉDRINE, JEAN. Essais sur le dialogue: contrastivités. *See* **22.**

**1622.** LYS, FRANZISKA. An analysis of aspectual compositionality in English and German. *See* **810.**

**1623.** MACKENZIE, J. LACHLAN. Aspects of nominalization in English and Dutch. *See* **923.**

**1624.** MARIGNY, JEAN. Difficultés de traduction dans les littératures de l'irréel. *In* (pp. 56–65) **22.**

**1625.** MEIJER, HANS. Programmar: a translation generator. *See* **536.**

**1626.** MORÈRE, PIERRE. Un problème de traduction philosophique: 'fancy'/'imagination' dans le Livre I du *Traité de la Nature Humaine* de David Hume.

**1627.** NAGAO, MAKOTO. Machine translation: how far can it go? Trans. by NORMAN D. COOK. *See* **537.**

**1628.** NIRANJANA, TEJASWINI. Bringing the text to legibility:

translation, poet-structuralism, and the colonial context. Unpub. doct. diss., Univ. of California, Los Angeles, 1988. [Abstr. in DA (49) 2671A.]

**1629.** OGIHARA, TOSHIYUKI. Temporal reference in English and Japanese. *See* **929.**

**1630.** PEPRNÍK, JAROSLAV. Pojmenování barev v angličtině a češtině. *See* **1007.**

**1631.** PICKEN, CATRIONA (ed.). The translator's handbook. (Bibl. 1984, 37.) London: Aslib. pp. vi, 382. (Revised ed.: first ed. 1983.)

**1632.** POLÁČKOVÁ, MILENA. Analytické verbonominální konstrukce v překladu mezi češtinou a angličtinou. *See* **932.**

**1633.** POSTHUMUS, J. Short forms of English loans in Dutch. *In* (pp. 93–107) **47.**

**1634.** PROCHÁZKA, MARTIN. Cultural invention and cultural awareness: translational activities and author's subjectivity in the culture of the Czech national revival. NC (8) 57–65.

**1635.** RAUFF, JAMES VERNON. Machine translation with two-level grammars. *See* **544.**

**1636.** ROSSENBECK, KLAUS. Lexikologische und lexikographische Probleme fachsprachlicher Phraseologie aus kontrastiver Sicht. *See* **1103.**

**1637.** SANDVED, ARTHUR O. From *Piers Plowman* to *Peter Plogmann*: on translating Langland's poem into Norwegian. *In* (pp. 303–13) **24.**

**1638.** ŠARČEVIĆ, SUSAN. Lexicography and translation across cultures. *See* **1106.**

**1639.** SCHMID, ANNEMARIE. Wörterbücher als Hilfe zur Übersetzung von Phraseologismen. *See* **1107.**

**1640.** SENN, FRITZ. Beyond the lexicographer's reach: literary over-determination. *See* **1108.**

**1641.** SNELL-HORNBY, MARY. The unfamiliar image: metaphor as a problem in translation. *In* (pp. 258–70) **4.**

**1642.** ——— PÖHL, ESTHER (eds). Symposium: translation and the lexicographer: papers read at the Euralex Colloquium held at Innsbruck 2–5 July 1987: a special monograph. *See* **1110.**

**1643.** STANZEL, PETER. Englische und Deutsche Kriegsdichtung 1914–18: eine komparatistische Versuch. *In* (pp. 410–11) **4.** (Abstract.)

**1644.** SWAN, TORIL. A note on initial adverbials and word order in English and Norwegian. *In* (pp. 331–44) **24.**

**1645.** TEJADA, PALOMA. Traducción y caracterización lingüística: la prosa anglosajona. RCEI (18) 243–9.

**1646.** THOMAS, STEPHEN. Using translation to overcome cross-cultural pragmatic failure. *See* **1293.**

**1647.** TOURY, GIDEON. The meaning of translation-specific lexical items and its representation in the dictionary. *See* **1113.**

**1648.** WILLIAMS, M. P. A comparison of the textual structures of Arabic and English written texts. *See* **1451.**

**1649.** ZAGONA, KAREN. Verb phrase syntax: a parametric study of English and Spanish. *See* **949.**

# TRADITIONAL CULTURE, FOLKLORE AND FOLKLIFE

## GENERAL

**1650.** AXLER, DAVID M. Some potential approaches to the folkloristic study of science fiction. KF (4:1) 7–18.

**1651.** BREIDENSTEIN, PATRICIA ANN. On the creation of organizational folk theories: an analysis of storytelling and language behavior. Unpub. doct. diss., Purdue Univ., 1988. [Abstr. in DA (50) 571A.]

**1652.** DAVIDSON, H. R. ELLIS. Katharine Briggs: story-teller. Cambridge: Lutterworth Press, 1986. pp. xiii, 209.

**1653.** DOTY, WILLIAM G. Mythography: the study of myths and rituals. Tuscaloosa: Alabama UP, 1986. pp. xix, 326. Rev. by Robert A. Segal in JAF (102:403) 110–12.

**1654.** EVANS, GEORGE EWART. Spoken history. London: Faber & Faber, 1987. pp. 255. Rev. by D. Hey in Lore and Language (8:1) 109–11.

**1655.** GAMMERDINGER, HARRY ALBERT, JR. The use of film and videotape to document and present folklore. Unpub. doct. diss., Indiana Univ., 1988. [Abstr. in DA (49) 3122A.]

**1656.** KIGHTLY, CHARLES. The perpetual almanack of folklore. London: Thames & Hudson, 1987. pp. 208.

**1657.** SEXTON, R. D. Travelling people in the United Kingdom. Unpub. doct. diss., Univ. of Southampton. [Abstr. in IT (38:4) 1476.]

**1658.** STERN, STEPHEN. Dorson's use and adaptation of prevailing historical models of American folklore. JFR (26:1) 43–50.

**1659.** THOMAS, H. NIGEL. From folklore to fiction: a study of folk heroes and rituals in the Black American novel. New York; London: Greenwood Press, 1988. pp. xii, 200. (Contributions in Afro-American and African studies, 118.)

## AREA STUDIES AND COLLECTIONS (MISCELLANEOUS)

**1660.** DODD, GERALD. Ghosts and legends of Brontëland. Haworth: Bobtail, 1986. pp. 41.

**1661.** FENTON, ALEXANDER. Wirds an' wark 'e seasons roon: on an Aberdeenshire farm. *See* **1462.**

**1662.** FIFE, AUSTIN; FIFE, ALTA. Exploring western Americana. Ann Arbor, MI; London: UMI Research Press, 1988. pp. xviii, 279. (American material culture and folklife.)

**1663.** FOWKE, EDITH. Canadian folklore. Toronto; Oxford: OUP, 1988. pp. vii, 149. (Perspectives on Canadian culture.)

**1664.** GAVINS, RAYMOND. North Carolina Black folklore and song in the age of segregation: toward another meaning of survival. NCHR (66:4) 412–42.

**1665.** HISCOCK, PHILIP. Newfoundland folklore and language: a bibliography. *See* **1490.**

**1666.** LaBORWIT, MELANIE. Folklore and native American traditions. NDH (56:4) 10–15.

**1667.** LISTER, MARTIN. Cornish times past: a cornucopia of Cornish fact and fantasy. Saltash: Tamara, 1987. pp. 56.

**1668.** MERRILL, JOHN N. Derbyshire folklore. Matlock: JNM Pubs. 1988. pp. v, 124.

**1669.** MOONSAMMY, RITA ZORN; COHEN, DAVID STEVEN; WILLIAMS, LORRAINE E. Pineland folklife. New Brunswick, NJ: Rutgers UP, 1987. pp. 234. Rev. by W. Bennett in Lore and Language (8:2) 120–1.

**1670.** SAMUELSEN, SUE; KEPNER, RAY. Bocce Ball meets Hacky-Sack: a western Pennsylvania Independence Day gathering. KF (3:2) 1984, 26–35.

**1671.** SEAL, GRAHAM. The hidden culture: folklore in Australian society. Melbourne; Oxford: OUP. pp. 180.

**1672.** WELSCH, ROGER. Reflections on Plains folklore. NDH (56:4) 5–9.

**1673.** WOLFORD, JOHN B. Shaker studies and folklore: an overview. FF (22:1/2) 78–107.

## PROVERBS, PROVERBIAL EXPRESSIONS, RIDDLES, RHYMES AND DITES

**1674.** MAC CON IOMAIRE, LIAM (comp.). Ireland of the proverb. Dublin: Town House, 1988. pp. xii, 232.

**1675.** MacNEIL, JOE NEIL. Tales until dawn/Sgeul gu latha: the world of a Cape Breton Gaelic story-teller. Trans. and ed. by JOHN SHAW. Edinburgh: Edinburgh UP, 1987. pp. 484. Rev. by J. C. Massey in Lore and Language (8:1) 124–5. (Parallel Gaelic and English text.)

**1676.** MIEDER, WOLFGANG. Tradition and innovation in folk literature. London; Hanover, NH: New England UP in assn with Univ. of Vermont, 1987. pp. xx, 293. Rev. by Juliette Wood in MLR (84:4) 909–11.

## WRITTEN AND PRINTED MATERIALS, INSCRIPTIONS, EPITAPHS, GRAFFITI

**1677.** BARRICK, MAC E. The role of print in superstition maintenance. KF (3:2) 1984, 1–19.

**1678.** DUNDES, ALAN; PAGTER, CARL R. When you're up to your ass in alligators: more urban folklore from the paperwork empire. Detroit, MI: Wayne State UP, 1987. pp. 271. Rev. by W. Bennett in Lore and Language (8:2) 109–10.

**1679.** EXELL, A. W.   The history of the ladybird: with some diversions on this and that. Shipston-on-Stour: Drinkwater. pp. iv, 43.
**1679a.** HOLLOWAY, JOHN (sel.).   The Oxford book of local verses. Oxford; New York: OUP, 1987. pp. xxii, 350. Rev. by Patricia Beer in TLS, 17 July 1987, 764.
**1680.** HOLTZBERG, MAGGIE.   Some like it hot: printing and the rhetoric of tradition. KF (3:2) 1984, 36–55.

# SPOKEN NARRATIVE

**1681.** BAKER, RONALD.   Xenophobia in 'beauty and the beast' and other animal/monster–groom tales. Midwestern Folklore (15:2) 71–8.
**1682.** BAKER, RONALD L.   Hoosier folk legends. Bloomington: Indiana UP, 1982, pp. xix, 264. Rev. by Bill Ellis in Lore and Language (8:2) 82–3.
**1683.** BALLINGER, FRANCHOT.   Living sideways: social themes and social relationships in native American trickster tales. AIQ (13:1) 15–30.
**1684.** BAUMAN, RICHARD.   Story, performance and event: contextual studies of oral narrative. (Bibl. 1986, 2432, where title misspelt.) Rev. by Patricia Waterman in AAnth (90:1) 1988, 220–1.
**1685.** BELLAMY, JOHN.   Robin Hood: an historical enquiry. (Bibl. 1986, 2433.) Rev. by John Scattergood in YES (19) 301–4.
**1686.** BOSKIN, JOSEPH.   Sambo: the rise and demise of an American jester. (Bibl. 1988, 1349, where subtitle incorrect.) Rev. by Daniel Royot in EA (42:4) 495.
**1687.** BOTTIGHEIMER, RUTH B.   'Beauty and the beast': marriage and money – motif and motivation. Midwestern Folklore (15:2) 79–88.
**1688.** BROWN, CAROLYN S.   The tall tale in American folklore and literature. (Bibl. 1988, 1353.) Rev. by James C. Austin in AmerS (29:1) 1988, 91.
**1689.** BROWN, D. E.   The Scottish origin-legend before Fordun. *See* **287.**
**1690.** BRUNVAND, JAN HAROLD.   The vanishing hitchhiker: American urban legends and their meaning. (Bibl. 1981, 2293.) Rev. by Bill Ellis in Lore and Language (8:2) 77–9.
**1691.** BURTON, JULIE.   Folktale, romance and Shakespeare. *In* (pp. 176–97) **58.**
**1692.** COTTERELL, ARTHUR.   The illustrated encyclopedia of myths and legends. London: Cassell. pp. 260.
**1693.** DELANEY, FRANK.   Legends of the Celts. Sevenoaks: Hodder & Stoughton. pp. xxxi, 237.
**1694.** DELANEY, JAMES G.   David Thomson. Lore and Language (8:2) 63–7.
**1695.** DREVER, HELEN.   Tales of the Scottish clans. Edinburgh: Chambers. pp. 85. (Chambers mini guides.)
**1696.** DUNDES, ALAN.   Cracking jokes: studies of sick humor cycles

and stereotypes. Berkeley, CA: Ten Speed Press, 1987. pp. 198. Rev. by
N. F. Blake in Lore and Language (8:2) 109.

**1697.** —— (ed.).    *Little Red Riding Hood*: a casebook. Madison;
London: Wisconsin UP. pp. 251. Rev. by Marina Warner in TLS,
24 Nov., 1309.

**1698.** —— Sacred narrative: readings in the theory of myth. Berkeley,
CA; Los Angeles, CA; London: California UP, 1984. pp. ix, 352. Rev. by
Marta Weigle in JAF (99:391) 1986, 91–2.

**1699.** ELLIS, BILL.    The vanishing American legend: oral narrative
and textmaking in the 1980s. Lore and Language (8:2) 75–102
(review-article).

**1700.** EVANS, GWLADYS.    Hampshire haunts and legends. Winchester: Fox, 1988. pp. 48.

**1701.** FINE, GARY ALAN.    Magic settings: the reflection of middle-
class life in 'beauty and the beast'. Midwestern Folklore (15:2) 89–100.

**1702.** FOLEY, JOHN MILES.    The theory of oral composition: history
and methodology. Bloomington: Indiana UP, 1988. pp. xv, 170. Rev. by
Jeff Opland in JAF (102:406) 489–91.

**1703.** —— (ed.).    Oral tradition in literature: interpretation in context. Columbia: Missouri UP, 1986. pp. xviii, 190. Rev. by Michael
Harney in RPh (43:2) 359–64.

**1704.** FREEMAN-WITTHOF, BONITA.    Thematic problems in North
American Indian narrative. KF (3:2) 1984, 20–5.

**1705.** GOSE, ELLIOTT B., JR.    The world of the Irish wonder tale: an
introduction to the study of fairy tales. (Bibl. 1986, 2449.) Rev. by
Gerald Thomas in CanL (115) 1987, 242–4.

**1706.** GOSS, MICHAEL.    The evidence for phantom hitch-hikers. (Bibl.
1985, 2030.) Rev. by Bill Ellis in Lore and Language (8:2) 97–9.

**1707.** GRAY, AFFLECK.    Legends of the Cairngorms. Edinburgh:
Mainstream, 1987. pp. 265.

**1708.** GULOTTA, DONNA SHEINBERG.    Fairy tales and Arthurian
legends in the novels of Henry James: the emergence of self. Unpub.
doct. diss., State Univ. of New York at Buffalo, 1988. [Abstr. in DA (50)
449A.]

**1709.** HEARNE, BETSY.    *Beauty and the Beast*: visions and revisions of an
old tale. Chicago; London: Chicago UP. pp. 284. Rev. by Marina
Warner in TLS, 24 Nov., 1309.

**1710.** JAMES, BERYL.    Tales of the Tinners' Way. Redruth: Dyllansow
Truran, 1988. pp. 83.

**1710a.** JENKINS, E. R.    The presentation of African folk tales in some
South African English children's versions. *In* EDGARD SIENAERT and
NIGEL BELL (eds), Catching winged words; oral tradition and education. Durban: Natal Univ. Oral Documentation and Research Centre,
1988. pp. vii, 282.

**1711.** KIGHTLY, CHARLES.    Country voices: life and lore in farm and
village. London: Thames & Hudson, 1984. pp. 240.

**1712.** KILGANNON, EILY (comp.).    Folktales of the Yeats country.
Cork: Mercier. pp. 96.

**1713.** LEERSSEN, JOEP.    Táin after táin: the mythical past and the Anglo-Irish. *In* (pp. 29–46) **32.**

**1714.** LENIHAN, EDMUND.    In search of Biddy Early. Cork: Mercier, 1987. pp. 113.

**1715.** LUTTRELL, CLAUDE.    The folk-tale element in *Sir Gawain and the Green Knight. In* (pp. 92–112) **58.** (Repr. from SP (77:2) 1981, 105–27.)

**1716.** McCARTHY, CHRISTINE M.    Some ghostly tales of Shropshire. Shrewsbury: Shropshire Libraries, 1988. pp. ix, 98.

**1717.** MacNEIL, JOE NEIL.    Tales until dawn/Sgeul gu latha: the world of a Cape Breton Gaelic story-teller. *See* **1675.**

**1718.** MALOTKI, EKKEHART.    Gullible Coyote Una'ihu: a bilingual collection of Hopi Coyote stories. Tucson: Arizona UP, 1985. pp. xii, 180. Rev. by A. Ebeogu in Lore and Language (8:1) 125.

**1719.** MATTHEWS, CAITLIN; MATTHEWS, JOHN.    The Aquarian guide to British and Irish mythology. Wellingborough: Aquarian, 1988. pp. 176.

**1720.** MATTHEWS, JOHN (ed.).    An Arthurian reader: selections from Arthurian legend, scholarship and story. Wellingborough: Aquarian, 1988. pp. 351.

**1721.** ——STEWART, BOB.    Warriors of Arthur. London: Blandford Press, 1987. pp. 192.

**1722.** MERCATANTE, ANTHONY S.    The Facts on File encyclopedia of mythology and legend. New York; Oxford: Facts on File, 1988. pp. xviii, 807.

**1723.** MEYER, RUDOLF.    The wisdom of fairy tales. Edinburgh: Floris, 1988. pp. 267.

**1724.** MIEDER, WOLFGANG.    Tradition and innovation in folk literature. *See* **1676.**

**1725.** PEPPER, DENNIS.    A book of tall stories. Oxford: OUP, 1987. pp. 160.

**1726.** PHILIP, NEIL (ed.).    The Cinderella story. Harmondsworth: Penguin. pp. ix, 177. (Penguin folklore library.) Rev. by Marina Warner in TLS, 24 Nov., 1309.

**1727.** RADNER, JOAN N.    'The woman who went to hell': coded values in Irish folk narrative. Midwestern Folklore (15:2) 109–18.

**1728.** RAINE, KATHLEEN (introd.).    Fairy and folk tales of Ireland. Ed. by W. B. YEATS. Gerrards Cross: Smythe, 1988. pp. xxvi, 441. (Third ed.: first ed. 1892.)

**1729.** REAVER, J. RUSSELL (ed.).    Florida folktales. Gainesville: Florida UP, 1987. pp. xvi, 179. Rev. by Peggy A. Bulger in JAF (102:404) 228–9.

**1730.** RELPH, J. T. (ed.).    A bit o' Cumbrian crack: tales and poems in the dialects of Cumberland, Westmorland and Lancashire north of the Sands. Penrith: Lakeland Dialect Soc. pp. 157.

**1731.** SPIVEY, TED R.    Beyond modernism: toward a new myth criticism. (Bibl. 1988, 1386.) Rev. by Sue Wienhorst in ChrisL (38:2) 90–1.

**1732.** Sullivan, C. W.   Welsh Celtic myth in modern fantasy. Westport, CT; London: Greenwood Press. pp. xvi, 181. (Contributions to the study of science fiction and fantasy, 35.)

**1733.** Tedlock, Dennis.   The spoken word and the work of interpretation. (Bibl. 1988, 1331.) Rev. by Bill Ellis in Lore and Language (8:2) 87–9.

**1734.** Thomas, Joyce.   Inside the wolf's belly: aspects of the fairy tale. Sheffield: Sheffield Academic Press. pp. 308.

**1735.** Ward, Donald.   'Beauty and the beast': fact and fancy, past and present. Midwestern Folklore (15:2) 119–25.

**1736.** Wolitarsky, Margaret Gaffney.   Portrait of a lady: a study of the ugly woman tradition in literature from fairytales and folk tales to seventeenth-century drama. Unpub. doct. diss., Lehigh Univ., 1988. [Abstr. in DA (49) 1813A.]

**1737.** Wonham, Henry.   Character development of the ring-tailed roarer in American literature. SF (46:3) 265–79.

**1738.** Wonham, Henry B.   In the name of wonder: the emergence of tall narrative in American writing. AmQ (41:2) 284–307.

**1739.** Wrigley, Christopher.   *Sir Gawain and the Green Knight*: the underlying myth. *In* (pp. 113–28) **58.**

**1739a.** Zipes, Jack.   The origins of the fairytale for children or, How script was used to tame the beast in us. *In* (pp. 119–34) **14.**

# SONG AND MUSIC

**1740.** Arngart, O.   A commentary on *The Hunting of the Cheviot* text. *See* **281.**

**1741.** Carlin, Richard.   English and American folk music. New York; Oxford: Facts on File, 1987. pp. x, 118.

**1742.** Cooke, Peter.   The fiddle tradition of the Shetland Isles. (Bibl. 1986, 2510.) Rev. by J. C. Massey in Lore and Language (8:2) 107.

**1743.** Donaldson, William.   The Jacobite song: political myth and national identity. Aberdeen: Aberdeen UP, 1988. pp. x, 166. Rev. by Murray G. H. Pittock in SLJ (supp. 30) 5–6.

**1744.** Edwards, Carol L.; Manley, Kathleen E. B. (eds).   Narrative folksong: new directions: essays in appreciation of W. Edson Richmond. Greeley: Dept of English, Univ. of Northern Colorado, 1985. pp. 482. Rev. by C. W. Neilands in Lore and Language (8:2) 110–11.

**1745.** Fish, Lydia M.   General Edward G. Lansdale and the folksongs of Americans in the Vietnam War. JAF (102:406) 390–411.

**1746.** Gibbons, Roy W.   The CCFCS collection of musical instruments: 3, Chordophones. Ottawa: National Museums of Canada, 1984. pp. 267. (Canadian Centre for Folk Culture Studies.)

**1747.** Göller, Karl Heinz.   *Child Roland and the King of Elfland* as the source for Shakespeare's *King Lear* III.iv.186–188. LJGG (27) 1986, 308–9.

**1748.** Hill, Errol G.   Calypso and war. BALF (23:1) 61–88.

**1749.** MAIK, LINDA L.   Mothers in ballads: Freud's maternal paradigm. SF (46:2) 117–32.

**1750.** MARQUIS, GREG.   Country music: the folk music of Canada. QQ (95:2) 1988, 291–309.

**1751.** NELSON, ESTHER L.   Holiday singing & dancing games. New York: Sterling, 1980. pp. 72.

**1752.** PETERS, ERSKINE.   The poetics of the Afro-American spiritual. BALF (23:3) 559–78.

**1753.** PICKERING, MICHAEL; GREEN, TONY (eds).   Everyday culture: popular song and the vernacular milieu. Milton Keynes: Open UP, 1987. pp. x, 194. Rev. by A. Ebeogu in Lore and Language (8:1) 133–5.

**1754.** PORTER, GERALD.   Adding a murder ballad to the American songbag: technical and cultural factors in *The Lexington Miller. In* (pp. 65–72) **43.**

**1755.** RICE, H. WILLIAM.   Two work songs in *Cane.* BALF (23:3) 593–9.

**1756.** ROSENBERG, NEIL V.   Bluegrass: a history. Urbana: Illinois UP, 1985. pp. 447. Rev. by A. Ward in Lore and Language (8:1) 137–40. (Bluegrass Ramblers.)

**1757.** SCHAEFFER, DEBORAH L.   Irish folk music: a selected discography. New York; London: Greenwood Press. pp. x, 180. (Discographies.)

**1758.** SHULDHAM-SHAW, PATRICK; LYLE, EMILY B.; HALL, PETER A. (eds).   The Greig–Duncan folk song collection: vol. 3. (Bibl. 1988, 1422.) Rev. by David Buchan in SLJ (supp. 30) 19–21.

**1759.** STEINER, MARGARET LYNN.   Aesthetic and social dynamics in the folksong tradition of a Northern Irish community. Unpub. doct. diss., Indiana Univ., 1988. [Abstr. in DA (49) 3466A.]

**1760.** TURNBULL, MALCOLM T. R. B.   Joseph Hislop and the songs of Burns. BurnsC (98) 59–62.

**1761.** WORK, FREDERICK, J.   A search for a song (1902). SoLJ (22:1) 14–19.

## DANCE AND DRAMA

**1762.** DAVIS, SUSAN GRAY.   Parades and power: street theatre in nineteenth-century Philadelphia. Philadelphia, PA: Temple UP, 1986; Berkeley; London: California UP, 1988. pp. xi, 235. Rev. by Rachelle H. Saltzman in JAF (102:405) 365–7; by Regina Bendix in FF (19:2) 1986, 206–9.

**1763.** DRAKE, JON.   The fool and the hobby horse: their role in ritual dramas of Britain. Oxford: Drake, 1988. pp. 49.

**1764.** FEES, C.   Christmas mumming in a north Cotswold town, with special reference to tourism, urbanisation, and immigration-related social change. Unpub. doct. diss., Univ. of Leeds, 1988. [Abstr. in IT (38:4) 1450.] (Chipping Campden.)

**1765.** GREEN, THOMAS A.   Linguistic manipulation in the Punch and Judy script. *See* **723.**

**1766.** JACOBS, LAURA.   Folk movements. NewL (72:16) 22–3.

**1767.** Jones, Dave.   The Welsh Border Morris dances of Herefordshire, Worcestershire and Shropshire. n.p. (Great Britain): Jones, 1988. pp. 52.

**1768.** Nelson, Esther L.    Holiday singing & dancing games. *See* **1751.**

**1769.** Stokes, James D.    Robin Hood and the churchwardens in Yeovil. MedRen (3) 1986, 1–25.

**1770.** Taft, Michael.    Folk drama on the Great Plains: the mock wedding in Canada and the United States. NDH (56:4) 16–23.

## CUSTOM AND BELIEF

**1771.** Barber, Paul.    Vampires, burial, and death: folklore and reality. New Haven, CT; London: Yale UP, 1988. pp. viii, 236. Rev. by Felix J. Oinas in JFR (26:2) 179–80.

**1772.** Doyle, Mary Agnes.    Games of lamentation: the Irish wake performance tradition. Unpub. doct. diss., Northwestern Univ., 1988. [Abstr. in DA (49) 2346–7A.]

**1773.** Gray, Affleck.    The big grey man of Ben MacDhui: myth or monster? Introd. by Sydney Scroggie. Moffat: Lochar. pp. xiii, 146. (Second ed.: first ed. 1970.)

**1774.** Green, Miranda.    Gods of the Celts. Gloucester: Sutton, 1986. pp. 257.

**1775.** Holtzberg, Maggie.    Some like it hot: printing and the rhetoric of tradition. *See* **1680.**

**1776.** Hufford, David J.    The terror that comes in the night: an experience-centred study of supernatural assault traditions. Philadelphia: Pennsylvania UP, 1982. pp. xxiv, 278. (Pubs. of the American Folklore Soc., 7.) Rev. by Peter M. Rojcewicz in KF (3:2) 55–9.

**1777.** Isern, Thomas D.    The folklore of farming on the North American Plains. NDH (56:4) 30–6.

**1778.** Kightly, Charles.    The customs and ceremonies of Britain: an encyclopaedia of living traditions. London: Thames & Hudson, 1986. pp. 248.

**1779.** —— The perpetual almanack of folklore. *See* **1656.**

**1780.** Leitch, Roger (ed.).    The book of Sandy Stewart. *See* **1004.**

**1781.** Otten, Charlotte F. (ed.).    A lycanthropy reader: werewolves in western culture. (Bibl. 1988, 1437.) Rev. by Juliette Wood in MLR (84:3) 693–4.

**1782.** Payne, David.    *The Wizard of Oz*: therapeutic rhetoric in a contemporary media ritual. QJS (75:1) 25–39.

**1783.** Ross, Anne.    The pagan Celts. London: Batsford, 1986. pp. 160. (Second ed.: first ed. 1980.) Rev. by D. E. Bland in Lore and Language (8:2) 127–8.

## MATERIAL CULTURE, TECHNIQUES, AND OCCUPATIONS, FOLK ARTS AND CRAFTS

**1784.** Humphrey, Theodore C.; Humphrey, Lin T. (eds).    'We gather together': food and festival in American life. Ann Arbor, MI;

London: UMI Research Press, 1988. pp. xii, 289. (American material culture and folklife.)

**1785.** KIGHTLY, CHARLES. Country voices: life and lore in farm and village. *See* **1711.**

**1786.** MARTIN, ANGUS. Kintyre country life. Edinburgh: Donald, 1987. pp. 126.

**1787.** POUNDS, NORMAN J. G. Hearth and home: a history of material culture. Bloomington: Indiana UP. pp. x, 437. Rev. by Robert E. Walls in JFR (26:2) 176.

# CHILDREN'S TRADITIONS

**1788.** ECKLEY, GRACE. Children's lore in *Finnegans Wake*. Syracuse, NY: Syracuse UP, 1985. pp. xxi, 250. (Irish studies.) Rev. by John Kidd in TLS, 5 Sept. 1987, 980; by Henry F. Beechold in Eire–Ireland (22:1) 1987, 159–60.

**1789.** JENKINS, E. R. The presentation of African folktales in some South African English children's versions. *See* **1710a.**

**1790.** KOSKE, MARY SUSAN. Finnish and American adolescent fantasy and humor: an analysis of personal and social folklore in educational contexts. Unpub. doct. diss., Indiana Univ., 1988. [Abstr. in DA (49) 2769–70A.]

**1791.** OPIE, IONA (comp.). Tail feathers from Mother Goose: the Opie rhyme book. London: Walker, 1988. pp. 124.

**1792.** TRUSSELL-CULLEN, ALAN. A pocket full of posies: a history of nursery rhymes. Auckland; Melbourne: Shortland & Rigby. pp. 32.

# ENGLISH LITERATURE

## GENERAL

### GENERAL LITERARY STUDIES

**1793.** ADAMS, ROGER (comp.). Famous writers on cricket. London: Partridge, 1988. pp. 107.

**1794.** ALDRIDGE, A. OWEN. Literature and the study of man. JELL (35) 57–82.

**1795.** ALLEN, JANE, *et al*. Out on the shelves: a bibliography of lesbian literature. Newcastle-under-Lyme: Assn of Assistant Librarians. pp. 81.

**1796.** ALLEN, M.; WILCOX, A. (eds). Critical approaches to Anglo-Irish literature. *See* **17.**

**1797.** ANON. (ed.). La beauté. *See* **10.**

**1798.** —— IASAIL: Bibliography bulletin for 1988. IUR (19:2) 314–67.

**1799.** BACH, RAYMOND E. The sacrificial child: a phenomenological study of a literary theme. Unpub. doct. diss., Stanford Univ., 1988. [Abstr. in DA (49) 3714–15A.]

**1800.** BAKER-SMITH, DOMINIC; BARFOOT, C. C. (eds). Between dream and nature: essays on utopia and dystopia. (Bibl. 1987, 11.) Rev. by Gilbert Bonifas in EA (42:4) 445.

**1801.** BAKKER, J.; VERLEUN, J. A.; VAN DER VRIESENAERDE, J. (eds). Essays on English and American literature and a sheaf of poems: offered to David Wilkinson on the occasion of his retirement from the Chair of English Literature at the University of Groningen. *See* **23.**

**1802.** BARRICELLI, JEAN-PIERRE. Melopoiesis: approaches to the study of literature and music. New York; London: New York UP, 1988. pp. xvi, 342.

**1803.** BAYM, NINA, *et al*. (eds). The Norton anthology of American literature: vol. 1. (Bibl. 1986, 2591.) New York; London: Norton. pp. xxx, 2459. (Third ed.: first ed. 1979.)

**1804.** BÁZLIK, MIROSLAV (ed.). Zborník filozofickej fakulty. *See* **62.**

**1805.** BELL, IAN F. A.; ADAMS, D. K. (eds). American literary landscapes: the fiction and the fact. *See* **1.**

**1806.** BLAND, CHRISTOPHER; KELLY, LINDA (eds). Feasts. London: Constable, 1987. pp. 266.

**1807.** BLOCH, ERNST. The utopian function of art and literature: selected essays. (Bibl. 1988, 1461.) Rev. by Ernest Goodheart in PR (56:3) 661–5.

**1808.** BOITANI, PIERO. Eros and thanatos: Cressida, Troilus, and the modern age. *In* (pp. 281–305) **27.**

**1809.** BOLD, ALAN. Scotland: a literary guide. London: Routledge. pp. ix, 327. Rev. in Edinburgh Review (83) 154–5.

**1810.** BOYLE, NICHOLAS; SWALES, MARTIN (eds). Realism in European literature: essays in honour of J. P. Stern. (Bibl. 1987, 2422.) Rev. by Terence Wright in MLR (84:2) 426–8.

**1811.** BRADY, LAURA ANN. Collaborative literary writing: issues of authorship and authority. Unpub. doct. diss., Univ. of Minnesota, 1988. [Abstr. in DA (49) 3016A.]

**1812.** BREUER, HORST. Historische Literaturpsychologie: von Shakespeare bis Beckett. Tübingen: Francke. pp. 227.

**1813.** BREWER, DEREK. The other, the self: speculations concerning an aspect of Western culture and medieval literature. *In* (pp. 317–27) **41.**

**1814.** BROWN, TERENCE. Ireland's literature: selected essays. Mullingar: Lilliput Press; Totowa, NJ: Barnes & Noble, 1988. pp. ix, 262. Rev. by Patricia Craig in TLS, 26 May, 577.

**1815.** BUNT, G. H. V., *et al.* (eds). One hundred years of English studies in Dutch universities: seventeen papers read at the Centenary Conference, Groningen, 15–16 January 1986. *See* **47.**

**1816.** BURGESS, ANTHONY. Nonsense. *In* (pp. 17–21) **28.**

**1817.** CARRERA SUÁREZ, ISABEL. Scottish studies in Spanish universities. SLJ (16:1) 59–64.

**1818.** CARTER, MARGARET L. (ed.). The vampire in literature: a critical bibliography. Ann Arbor, MI: UMI Research Press. pp. viii, 136. Rev. by Joe R. Christopher in Mythlore (16:2) 55–7.

**1819.** CAVE, TERENCE. Recognitions: a study in poetics. (Bibl. 1988, 1467.) Rev. by Colin Burrow in Eng (38) 162–8.

**1820.** CIXOUS, HÉLÈNE; CLÉMENT, CATHÉRINE. The newly born woman. Trans. by BETSY WING. Manchester: Manchester UP, 1986. pp. xviii, 169. (Theory and history of literature, 24.) Rev. by Elizabeth Wright and Dianne Chisholm in MLR (84:2) 418–19.

**1821.** COETZEE, J. M. White writing: on the culture of letters in South Africa. Sandton, South Africa: Radix; New Haven, CT; London: Yale UP, 1988. pp. 193. Rev. by George Packer in Nat (247:20) 1988, 724–8; by Mike Marais in Upstream (6:4) 1988, 59–60; by Martin Trump in UES (27:1) 62–3.

**1822.** CONRAD, PETER. The Everyman history of English literature. (Bibl. 1986, 2611.) Rev. by Basil Cottle in RES (38:149) 1987, 111–12.

**1823.** COOTE, JOHN (ed.). The Faber book of the sea: an anthology. London: Faber & Faber. pp. x, 406.

**1824.** DABYDEEN, DAVID (ed.). The Black presence in English literature. (Bibl. 1986, 2615.) Rev. by Zohreh T. Sullivan in YES (19) 361–2.

**1825.** DANE, JOSEPH A. Parody: critical concepts versus literary practices, Aristophanes to Sterne. Norman; London: Oklahoma UP, 1988. pp. vii, 261. Rev. by Christopher Robinson in NQ (36:4) 516–17.

**1826.** DAVIS, BONNIE SCHNURBUSCH. A rationale for the reconstruction of the American literary canon. Unpub. doct. diss., Saint Louis Univ., 1988. [Abstr. in DA (50) 639A.]

**1827.**  DEANE, SEAMUS.   A short history of Irish literature. (Bibl. 1987, 2443.) Rev. by R. A. Cave in RES (39:154) 1988, 323–4.

**1828.**  D'HAEN, THEO; GRÜBEL, RAINER; LETHEN, HELMUT.   Introduction: the decline and rise of convention. *In* (pp. vii–xxii) **16.**

**1829.**  ——————— (eds).   Convention and innovation in literature. *See* **16.**

**1830.**  DICKINS, GORDON.   An illustrated literary guide to Shropshire. Shrewsbury: Shropshire Libraries, 1987. pp. viii, 128. (Second ed.: first pub. as *A Literary Guide to Shropshire*, 1980.)

**1831.**  DONOGHUE, DENIS.   Reading America: essays on American literature. (Bibl. 1987, 2447.) Rev. by Michael Allen in Studies (78:4) 434–5; by Sven Birkets in PR (56:3) 495–9.

**1832.**  DRUCE, ROBERT.   Man, the machine, and a radiant fool. *In* (pp. 127–44) **13.**

**1833.**  —— (ed.).   A centre of excellence: essays presented to Seymour Betsky. *See* **13.**

**1834.**  DU PRIEST, TRAVIS.   'Read, mark, learn and inwardly digest': metaphors for reading. Cresset (53:1) 16–19.

**1835.**  DUYTSCHAEVER, JORIS; LERNOUT, GEERT (eds).   History and violence in Anglo-Irish literature. *See* **32.**

**1836.**  ELLIOTT, EMORY (gen. ed.); BANTA, MARTHA, *et al.* (assoc. eds). Columbia literary history of the United States. (Bibl. 1988, 1476.) Rev. by John W. Rathbun in ALR (22:1) 87–8; by Cathy N. Davidson in CR (33:1) 89–90; by Andrew Hook in NQ (36:2) 268–70.

**1837.**  ELLRODT, ROBERT; BRUGIÈRE, BERNARD (eds).   Âge d'Or et apocalypse. (Bibl. 1986, 2.) Rev. by Maurice Lévy in EA (42:4) 447–9.

**1838.**  ENRIGHT, D. J.   The alluring problem: an essay on irony. (Bibl. 1988, 1479.) Rev. by David Dowling in CanL (119) 1988, 118.

**1839.**  —— (ed.).   The Faber book of fevers and frets. London: Faber & Faber. pp. xiii, 364. Rev. by Roy Porter in TLS, 8 Dec., 1367.

**1840.**  FELDSTEIN, RICHARD; ROOF, JUDITH (eds).   Feminism and psychoanalysis. *See* **29.**

**1841.**  FORD, BORIS (ed.).   American literature. (Bibl. 1988, 1487.) Rev. by Stuart Hutchinson in NQ (36:3) 412–13.

**1842.**  FOWLER, ALASTAIR.   A history of English literature: forms and kinds from the Middle Ages to the present. Cambridge, MA: Harvard UP, 1987. (Bibl. 1988, 1488.) Rev. by Miranda Johnson Haddad in SCN (47:1/2) 5–6; by John Pafford in NQ (36:3) 374–6.

**1843.**  FRÜHWALD, WOLFGANG.   Symposium: Apokalypse und Antichrist in der europäischen Literatur. Einleitung. LJGG (29) 1988, 219–23.

**1844.**  GAIR, REAVLEY (gen. ed.).   A literary and linguistic history of New Brunswick. Fredericton, N.B.: Fiddlehead; Goose Lane, 1985. pp. 286. Rev. by Thomas B. Vincent in CanL (116) 1988, 131–2.

**1845.**  GOLDSTEIN, LAURENCE.   The flying machine and modern literature. Bloomington: Indiana UP, 1986. (Bibl. 1986, 2647.) Rev. by Stuart James in SewR (96:3) 1988, lxvi–lxvii.

**1846.** GORDIMER, NADINE. Censorship and the artist. Staffrider (7:2) 1988, 11–16.

**1847.** GRATZER, WALTER (ed.). The Longman literary companion to science. Harlow: Longman. pp. xx, 517.

**1848.** GREEN, SUSAN GALE. The narrative construction of women in literary texts. Unpub. doct. diss., Univ. of Washington, 1988. [Abstr. in DA (50) 146A.]

**1849.** GUILHAMET, LEON. Satire and the transformation of genre. (Bibl. 1988, 1495.) Rev. in QQ (95:4) 1988, 968–9; by Frans De Bruyn in BJECS (12) 228–9; by Ronald Rompkey in DalR (67:2/3) 1987, 370–1; by Raman Selden in DUJ (81:2) 319–20; by J. V. Guerinot in SCN (47:1/2) 4.

**1850.** HAAPALA, A. K. What is a work of literature? Unpub. doct. diss., Univ. of London, 1988. [Abstr. in IT (39:1) 28–9.]

**1851.** HAMBER, J. P. Word, words, words. Shakespeare Society of Southern Africa Occasional Papers and Reviews (4:2) 1–6.

**1852.** HARMON, MAURICE. Pangur Ban and the scholar critic. In (pp. 33–42) **37**.

**1853.** HARVEY, A. D. Literature into history. Basingstoke: Macmillan, 1988. pp. vii, 207.

**1854.** HILL, GEOFFREY. The lords of limit: essays on literature and ideas. New York: OUP, 1984. pp. ix, 203. (Bibl. 1984, 2132, where pagination incorrect.) Rev. by Eleanor McNees in ELN (23:3) 1986, 75–6; by David Gervais in CamQ (15:3) 1986, 243–5; by William Logan in EC (37:4) 1987, 329–35.

**1855.** HIMY, ARMAND; ROBIN, MAURICE (eds). Confluences II: centre(s) de pouvoirs(s) et d'influence(s). See **15**.

**1856.** HLADKÝ, JOSEF (ed.). 2. Anglisticko-amerikanistická konference/Second conference on English and American studies. See **6**.

**1857.** HOCHMAN, BARUCH. Character in literature. (Bibl. 1986, 2659.) Rev. by Thomas Docherty in RES (38:151) 1987, 423–5.

**1858.** HYLAND, PETER. Introduction: discharging the canon. In (pp. 1–9) **19**.

**1859.** INGRAMS, RICHARD. England: an anthology. London: Collins. pp. 239.

**1860.** IVASHEVA, V. V. Sud'by angliĭskikh pisateleĭ: dialogi vchera i segodnĭa. (The fate of English writers: dialogues of yesterday and today.) Moscow: Sovestkiĭ pisatel'. pp. 443.

**1861.** JASPER, DAVID. The study of literature and religion: an introduction. Basingstoke: Macmillan. pp. xii, 158. (Studies in literature and religion.)

**1862.** JONES, D. L. An anatomy of allegory: a study of the genre, its rhetorical traditions and its American renaissance. Unpub. doct. diss., Univ. of Sussex. [Abstr. in IT (38:4) 1455.]

**1863.** JOSIPOVICI, GABRIEL. Writing, reading, and the study of literature. NLH (21:1) 75–96. (Inaugural lecture, Univ. of Sussex, 1986.)

**1864.** KIM, WOO-CHANG.   Miguk si e isseoseo eui jayeon. (Nature in American literature.) AmeSt (10) 1987. 19–53.

**1865.** KISTNER, ULRIKE.   Literature and the national question. JLS (5:3/4) 302–14.

**1866.** KOESTENBAUM, WAYNE.   Double talk: the erotics of male literary collaboration. New York; London: Routledge. pp. x, 214.

**1867.** LACY, NORRIS J. (ed.); ASHE, GEOFFREY, et al. (assoc. eds).   The Arthurian encyclopedia. (Bibl. 1988, 1923.) Rev. by Muriel Whitaker in CanL (118) 1988, 180–2.

**1868.** LANE, MAGGIE.   Literary daughters. London: Hale. pp. 222.

**1869.** LASS, ABRAHAM H.; KIREMIDJIAN, DAVID; GOLDSTEIN, RUTH M.   The Facts on File dictionary of classical, biblical, and literary allusions. New York; Oxford: Facts on File, 1987. pp. viii, 240.

**1870.** LEAL, D. C.   The concept of parable. Unpub. doct. diss., Univ. of Leeds, 1988. [Abstr. in IT (38:4) 1444.]

**1871.** LEERSSEN, JOSEPH TH.   Mere Irish and fíor-Ghael: studies in the idea of Irish nationality, its development and literary expression prior to the nineteenth century. (Bibl. 1988, 1511.) Rev. by George O'Brien in YES (19) 348–9.

**1872.** LEFEVERE, ANDRÉ.   The dynamics of the system: convention and innovation in literary history. In (pp. 37–55) **16.**

**1873.** LERNER, LAURENCE.   The frontiers of literature. Oxford: Blackwell, 1988. pp. viii, 291.

**1874.** LEVIN, IŪ.   Angliiâ–Rossiiâ: literaturnye sviazi. (England–Russia: literary connections.) VLit (1989:2) 167–77.

**1875.** LUDWIG, HANS-WERNER (ed.).   Anglistentag 1987 Tübingen. See **4.**

**1876.** LYRA, FRANCISZEK.   Toward a history of American literature in Poland. In (pp. 194–208) **36.**

**1877.** MACCORNACK, KATHARINE GRISWOLD.   The mental spaces of allegory. Unpub. doct. diss., Brown Univ., 1988. [Abstr. in DA (49) 2134A.]

**1878.** McGANN, JEROME J.   Social values and poetic acts: the historical judgment of literary work. (Bibl. 1988, 1519.) Rev. by Claude Rawson in LRB (11:6) 17–19.

**1879.** MAES-JELINEK, HENA; MICHEL, PIERRE; MICHEL-MICHOT, PAULETTE (eds).   Multiple worlds, multiple words: essays in honour of Irène Simon. See **42.**

**1880.** MANNING, SUSAN.   Scotland and America: national literatures? National languages? See **1474.**

**1881.** MESEROLE, HARRISON T.   A selected, annotated list of current articles on American literature. AL (61:1) 167–74; (61:2) 337–44; (61:3) 536–45; (61:4) 742–9.

**1882.** MEYER, WILLIAM E. H., JR.   The hypervisual meaning of the American West. PhilT (33:1) 28–41.

**1883.** MILLER, KARL.   Authors. Oxford: Clarendon Press; New York: OUP. pp. xiii, 218. Rev. by Liz Heron in Listener (122) 12 Oct., 31–2.

**1884.** MOONEY, BEL (ed.). From this day forward: an anthology of marriage. London: Murray. pp. 373.

**1885.** MOORMAN, CHARLES. 'Yet some men say ... that Kynge Arthure ys nat ded.' *In* (pp. 188–99) **8**.

**1886.** MORETTI, FRANCO. Signs taken for wonders: essays in the sociology of literary forms. Trans. by SUSAN FISCHER, DAVID FORGACS, and DAVID MILLER. (Bibl. 1983, 2630.) London: Verso, 1988. pp. vi, 314. (Revised ed.: first ed. 1983.)

**1887.** MOTTRAM, ERIC. 'Thought is always prior to fact': an introduction. *In* (pp. 9–28) **1**.

**1888.** MÜLLENBROCK, HEINZ-JOACHIM; NOLL-WIEMANN, RENATE (eds). Anglistentag 1988 Göttingen. *See* **5**.

**1889.** NEW, W. H. A history of Canadian literature. Basingstoke: Macmillan. pp. x, 380. (Macmillan history of literature.)

**1890.** NEWMAN, JENNY (ed.). The Faber book of seductions. London; Boston, MA: Faber & Faber, 1988. pp. xxix, 366.

**1891.** NEWTON, K. M. In defence of literary interpretation: theory and practice. (Bibl. 1986, 2710.) Rev. by Francis Berry in RES (39:153) 1988, 155–6.

**1892.** NOVITZ, DAVID. Knowledge, fiction and imagination. Philadelphia, PA: Temple UP, 1987. pp. vii, 262. Rev. by Peter Lamarque in PhilL (13:2) 365–74.

**1893.** NUTTALL, A. D. The stoic in love: selected essays on literature and ideas. New York; London: Harvester Wheatsheaf. pp. xii, 209. Rev. by Frank Kermode in LRB (11:20) 21–3.

**1894.** OLIVER, DOUGLAS. Poetry and narrative in performance. Basingstoke: Macmillan. pp. xix, 189. (Language, discourse, society.)

**1895.** O'NEILL, PATRICK. Ireland and Germany: a study in literary relations. Berne; Frankfurt; New York: Lang, 1985. pp. 358. (Canadian studies in German language and literature, 33.) Rev. by Heinz Kosok in Ang (107:3/4) 540–4.

**1896.** ONG, WALTER J. Orality and literacy: the technologizing of the world. (Bibl. 1984, 33.) Rev. by Meinhard Winkgens in LJGG (26) 1985, 442–5.

**1897.** ONOGE, OMAFUME F. Literature, culture and national development. Classic (4:1) 18–23, 27.

**1898.** OUSBY, IAN (ed.). The Cambridge guide to literature in English. (Bibl. 1988, 1529.) Rev. by Claude Rawson in TLS, 21 Apr., 429–30.

**1899.** OVERSTEEGEN, J. J. Genre: a modest proposal. *In* (pp. 17–35) **16**.

**1900.** PANDIT, LALITA. Waiting: narratives of deferral from Shakespeare to Henry James. Unpub. doct. diss., State Univ. of New York at Buffalo, 1988. [Abstr. in DA (49) 3734A.]

**1901.** PATTERSON, DAVID. The affirming flame: religion, language, literature. Norman; London: Oklahoma UP, 1988. pp. x, 175. Rev. by Norman R. Cary in ChrisL (38:3) 64–5.

**1902.** PAULSON, WILLIAM R.   The noise of culture: literary texts in a world of information. (Bibl. 1988, 1532.) Rev. by Walter J. Ong in MP (87:2) 215–18.

**1903.** POIRIER, RICHARD.   The renewal of literature: Emersonian reflections. (Bibl. 1988, 1535.) Rev. by Douglas Crase in Nat (244:22) 1987, 766–70; by Nina Baym in NYTB, 22 Mar. 1987, 37.

**1904.** POSNER, RICHARD A.   Law and literature: a misunderstood relation. (Bibl. 1988, 1537.) Rev. by James D. Freedman in BkW, 22 Jan.; by Peter Shaw in Commentary (87:5) 68–70.

**1905.** PUNTER, DAVID.   The hidden script: writing and the unconscious. (Bibl. 1988, 2531.) Rev. by Thomas Docherty in RES (38:150) 1987, 287–9.

**1906.** RIGAUD, NADIA (ed.).   La violence dans la littérature et la pensée anglaises. *See* **60**.

**1907.** RILEY, DAVID W.   English books of the seventeenth to nineteenth centuries in the John Rylands University Library of Manchester, with particular reference to history and literature. *See* **260**.

**1908.** ROGERS, PAT (ed.).   The Oxford illustrated history of English literature. (Bibl. 1988, 1541, where '(ed.)' omitted.) Rev. by John Pafford in NQ (36:3) 374–6.

**1909.** ROSS, MALCOLM.   The impossible sum of our traditions: reflections on Canadian literature. Introd. by DAVID STAINES. (Bibl. 1986, 2732, where introducer's name omitted.) Rev. by D. M. R. Bentley in DalR (66:4) 1986, 532–9.

**1910.** ROSS, TREVOR THORNTON.   'Albion's Parnassus': the making of the English literary canon. Unpub. doct. diss., Univ. of Toronto, 1988. [Abstr. in DA (50) 149–50A.]

**1911.** SALZMAN, JACK (ed.).   The Cambridge handbook of American literature. (Bibl. 1986, 2736.) Rev. by Richard King in RES (39:153) 1988, 157–8.

**1912.** SCHIRMER, WALTER F.   Geschichte der englischen und amerikanischen Literatur: von den Anfängen bis zur Gegenwart. (Bibl. 1987, 2550.) Rev. by Adolf Barth in LJGG (26) 1985, 428–31.

**1913.** SEEBER, HANS ULRICH.   Auf dem Weg zum Vortex: Zentralbewegung, Ästhetik des Sublimen und das Wasser der Moderne in englischen London-Texten des 19. Jahrhunderts. PoetA (21:3/4) 302–28.

**1914.** SEKINE, MASARU (ed.).   Irish writers and society at large. (Bibl. 1985, 2253.) Rev. by Hilary Pyle in RES (38:150) 1987, 286–7.

**1915.** SHAPIRO, SUSAN C.   'Yon plumed dandebrat': male 'effeminacy' in English satire and criticism. RES (39:155) 1988, 400–12.

**1916.** SHEIDLOWER, DAVID.   Some prose about prose about prose. RCEI (18) 71–4.

**1917.** SIWANI, JOYCE.   Women writers in Africa ... conspicuous by their absence. Classic (4:1) 2–3.

**1918.** SKINNER, DOUGLAS REID.   What English means to me. Crux (23:2) 3–8.

**1919.** SMITH, GODFREY (ed.). The English reader: an anthology. London: Pavilion, 1988. pp. 300.

**1920.** SPENDER, DALE; TODD, JANET (eds). Anthology of British women writers. London: Unwin Hyman. pp. xvii, 925. Rev. by Angela Leighton in TLS, 22 Sept., 1024.

**1921.** SPENGEMANN, WILLIAM C. A mirror for Americanists: reflections on the idea of American literature. Hanover, NH: New England UP for Dartmouth College. pp. vii, 183.

**1922.** SPIVAK, GAYATRI CHAKRAVORTY. In other worlds: essays in cultural politics. Introd. by COLIN MACCABE. (Bibl. 1988, 1551.) Rev. by Roger Fowler in MLR (84:4) 898–9.

**1923.** STALLYBRASS, PETER; WHITE, ALLON. The politics and poetics of transgression. Ithaca, NY: Cornell UP, 1986. (Bibl. 1988, 1552.) Rev. by Clair Wills in QQ (95:1) 1988, 201–3.

**1924.** STEINER, WENDY. Pictures of romance: form against context in painting and literature. (Bibl. 1988, 1554.) Rev. by Eugene E. Cunnar in RMRLL (43:4) 263–5.

**1925.** STEPHENS, MEIC (comp.). A dictionary of literary quotations. London: Routledge. pp. x, 193.

**1926.** —— (ed.). The Oxford companion to the literature of Wales. (Bibl. 1988, 1556.) Rev. by Nicolas Jacobs in RES (38:151) 1987, 415–16.

**1927.** STÜRZL, ERWIN A. Gaben der Zeit/Fruits of time. Salzburg: Institut für Anglistik und Amerikanistik, Salzburg Univ. 2 vols. pp. xiv, 425; 316. (Salzburg studies in English literature: Poetic drama & poetic theory, 27:7.)

**1928.** SUNG, CHAN-KYUNG. Hanguk youngeo youngmunhak yeongusa, 1945–1965. *See* **655.**

**1929.** TIGERMAN, KATHLEEN. Spirituality and language: our shamanic heritage. Unpub. doct. diss., Univ. of Wisconsin–Milwaukee, 1988. [Abstr. in DA (49) 2645A.]

**1930.** TIGGES, WIM. An anatomy of nonsense. *In* (pp. 23–46) **28.**

**1931.** —— (comp.). A selected annotated bibliography on literary nonsense. *In* (pp. 245–55) **28.**

**1932.** —— (ed.). Explorations in the field of nonsense. *See* **28.**

**1933.** TODD, LORETO. The language of Irish literature. *See* **1426.**

**1934.** TUCK, JOHN P. Some sources for the history of popular culture in the John Rylands University Library of Manchester. *See* **272.**

**1935.** WALKER, NANCY; DRESNER, ZITA (eds). Redressing the balance: American women's literary humor from colonial times to the 1980s. Jackson; London: Mississippi UP, 1988. pp. xxxiv, 454.

**1936.** WARD, DAVID. Chronicles of darkness. London: Routledge. pp. xxi, 191.

**1937.** WELCH, ROBERT; BUSHRUI, SUHEIL BADI (eds). Literature and the art of creation: essays and poems in honour of A. Norman Jeffares. *See* **37.**

**1938.** WEXELBLATT, ROBERT. *Ex nihilo*; or, For openers. MidQ (30:2) 137–50. (Opening lines of books.)

**1939.** WILLIAMS, RAYMOND.    What I came to say. Introd. by FRANCIS MULHERN. London: Century Hutchinson. pp. vii, 280. Rev. by Chris Baldick in TLS, 3 Nov., 1205.

**1940.** WISEMAN, ADELE.    *Memoirs of a Book Molesting Childhood* and other essays. Oxford; Toronto: OUP, 1987. pp. 200. Rev. by Glenn Deer in CanL (120) 152–3.

**1941.** WITKIN, MILDRED STARR.    The Jewess in English literature: a mediating presence. Unpub. doct. diss., City Univ. of New York, 1988. [Abstr. in DA (49) 2236A.]

**1942.** WOLITARSKY, MARGARET GAFFNEY.    Portrait of a lady: a study of the ugly woman tradition in literature from fairytales and folk tales to seventeenth-century drama. *See* **1736.**

**1943.** WRIGHT, T. R.    Theology and literature. Oxford: Blackwell, 1988. pp. viii, 243. (Signposts in theology.) Rev. by André Bordeaux in EA (42:4) 441–2; by Lewis F. Archer in ChrisL (38:4) 79–80.

**1944.** WYCHE-SMITH, SUSAN LEE.    The magic circle: writers and ritual. Unpub. doct. diss., Univ. of Washington, 1988. [Abstr. in DA (49) 2645A.]

**1945.** WYNNE-DAVIES, MARION (ed.).    Bloomsbury guide to English literature. London: Bloomsbury. pp. x, 1066. Rev. by Christopher Potter in Listener (122) 19 Oct., 30–1.

**1946.** YAE, YOUNG-SOO.    Miguk munhak gwa jayeonjueui. (Naturalism in American literature.) JELL (35) 511–35.

**1947.** YAEGER, PATRICIA.    Honey-mad women: emancipatory strategies in women's writing. New York: Columbia UP, 1988. pp. x, 317. (Gender and culture.) Rev. by Gail L. Mortimer in RMRLL (43:4) 271–2.

**1948.** ZAGÓRSKA, ANNA; BYSTYDZIEŃSKA, GRAŻYNA (eds).    Literatura angielska i amerykańska: problemy recepcji. *See* **36.**

**1949.** ZINMAN, JANE ANN.    Readers, writers, and the grounds for a textual divorce. Unpub. doct. diss., Ohio State Univ., 1988. [Abstr. in DA (49) 2206A.]

## DRAMA AND THE THEATRE

**1950.** AGOSTINI, RENÉ.    Théâtre et narratologie: perspectives d'une esthétique du récit dramatique. CVE (29) 83–97.

**1951.** AHRENDS, GÜNTER.    Literarischer Text und szenische Realisation: Einführende Bemerkungen zum Verhältnis zweier Zeichensysteme. *In* (pp. 14–24) **4.**

**1952.** ANDERSON, DAVID JAMES.    Theatre criticism: a minor art with a major problem. Unpub. doct. diss., Ohio State Univ., 1988. [Abstr. in DA (49) 2453–4A.]

**1953.** BERGAN, RONALD.    The great theatres of London: an illustrated companion. Introd. by ANTHONY HOPKINS. London: Admiral, 1987. pp. 200.

**1954.** BRUSTEIN, ROBERT.    Who needs theatre? Dramatic opinions. New York: Atlantic Monthly Press, 1987; London: Faber & Faber. pp. xv, 234. Rev. by Jane Ellert Tammany in TJ (41:3) 434–6.

**1955.** CASE, SUE-ELLEN.   Feminism and theatre. Basingstoke; New York: Macmillan, 1988. pp. 149. (New directions in theatre.) Rev. by Lynda Hart in TJ (41:2) 261; by Rosette C. Lamont in ModDr (32:1) 159–61.

**1956.** DEVLIN, DIANA.   Mask and scene: an introduction to a world view of theatre. Basingstoke: Macmillan, 1988. pp. v, 221.

**1957.** EDDERSHAW, MARGARET.   Grand fashionable nights: Kendal Theatre 1575–1985. Lancaster: Centre for North West Regional Studies, Univ. of Lancaster, 1988. pp. vii, 57. (Occasional papers, 17.)

**1958.** ESSLIN, MARTIN.   The field of drama: how the signs of drama create meaning on stage and screen. (Bibl. 1988, 1580.) Rev. by Burnet M. Hobgood in JAE (23:4) 116–18; by Peter Larlham in JRS (3:2) 327–9.

**1959.** FLETCHER, STEVE; JOPLING, NORMAN (eds).   Harrap's book of 1000 plays. London: Harrap. pp. 352.

**1960.** HAY, PETER (comp.).   Theatrical anecdotes. New York; Oxford: OUP, 1987. pp. xiii, 392.

**1961.** HOWARD-HILL, T. H.   Modern textual theories and the editing of plays. *See* **329.**

**1962.** HUNT, BARBARA JOAN.   The paradox of Christian tragedy. Troy, NY: Whitston, 1985. pp. 147. Rev. by Darryl Tippens in SCR (4:4) 1987, 108–10; by June Schlueter in ChrisL (37:1) 1987, 75–7.

**1963.** KASE-POLISINI, JUDITH (ed.).   Drama as a meaning maker. Lanham, MD; London: UP of America. pp. xiv, 247.

**1964.** KELSALL, MALCOLM.   Studying drama: an introduction. (Bibl. 1987, 2600.) Rev. by Georges Bas in EA (42:2) 192.

**1965.** KIM, JIN-NA.   An extended notion of recognition in drama. JELL (35) 775–84.

**1966.** KUBIAK, ANTHONY JAMES.   *Phobos* and performance: the stages of terror. Unpub. doct. diss., Univ. of Wisconsin–Milwaukee, 1988. [Abstr. in DA (49) 2026A.]

**1967.** LEONARD, WILLIAM TORBERT.   Masquerade in black. Metuchen, NJ; London: Scarecrow Press, 1986. pp. xii, 431. (The history of 'blackface' in the theatre.)

**1968.** LEVIN, HARRY.   Playboys and killjoys: an essay on the theory and practice of comedy. (Bibl. 1988, 1583.) Rev. by Neil Rhodes in NQ (36:3) 376–7.

**1969.** MASON, H. A.   The tragic plane. (Bibl. 1988, 1584.) Rev. by Harriett Hawkins in RES (38:150) 1987, 227–8.

**1970.** OLIVA, JUDY LEE.   Theatricalizing politics: David Hare and a tradition of British political drama. Unpub. doct. diss., Northwestern Univ., 1988. [Abstr. in DA (49) 2027A.]

**1971.** PAVIS, PATRICE.   Problems of translation for the stage: inter-culturism and post-modern theatre. Trans. by LOREN KRUGER. *In* (pp. 25–44) **50.**

**1972.** PFISTER, MANFRED.   The theory and analysis of drama. Trans. by JOHN HALLIDAY. Cambridge: CUP, 1988. pp. xix, 339. (European studies in English literature.) (First pub. as *Das Drama*, Munich, 1987.) Rev. by Jonathan Hope in NC (8) 182–3.

**1973.** REDMOND, JAMES (ed.).    Drama, sex and politics. Cambridge: CUP, 1985. pp. xiii, 251. (Themes in drama, 7.) Rev. by Georges Bas in EA (42:2) 192–4.

**1974.** ——(ed.).    The theatrical space. Cambridge: CUP, 1987. pp. xii, 276. (Themes in drama, 9.) Rev. by Georges Bas in EA (42:2) 192–4.

**1975.** RIGAUD, N. J. (ed.).    L'étranger dans la littérature et la pensée anglaises. See **26.**

**1976.** SALEM, JAMES M. (ed.).    Drury's guide to best plays. By FRANCIS K. W. DRURY. (Bibl. 1953/54, 86.) Metuchen, NJ; London: Scarecrow Press, 1987. pp. 480. (Fourth ed.: first ed. 1953.)

**1977.** SCHECHNER, RICHARD.    Performance theory. London: Routledge, 1988. pp. xv, 304. (Revised ed.: orig. pub. as *Essays on Performance Theory*, 1977.)

**1978.** SCHWANITZ, DIETRICH.    Drama and interaction. *In* (pp. 47–56) **4.**

**1979.** SCOLNICOV, HANNA.    Mimesis, mirror, double. *In* (pp. 89–98) **50.**

**1980.** ——HOLLAND, PETER (eds).    The play out of context: transferring plays from culture to culture. See **50.**

**1981.** SHAKED, GERSHON.    The play: gateway to cultural dialogue. Trans. by JEFFREY GREEN. *In* (pp. 7–24) **50.**

**1982.** SILK, MICHAEL.    The autonomy of comedy. CompCrit (10) 1988, 3–37.

**1983.** SIMON, BENNETT.    Tragic drama and the family: psychoanalytic studies from Aeschylus to Beckett. New Haven, CT; London: Yale UP, 1988. pp. xiii, 274.

**1984.** SWIFT, CAROLYN.    Stage by stage. Dublin: Poolbeg, 1985. pp. 312.

**1985.** TAN, P. K. W.    A stylistics of drama, with particular reference to Stoppard's *Travesties* and parody. See **1425.**

**1986.** TETZELI VON ROSADOR, KURT.    Formen der Historizität im englischen Geschichtsdrama. LJGG (28) 1987, 243–61.

**1987.** THOMSON, PETER; SALGĀDO, GĀMINI.    The Everyman companion to the theatre. (Bibl. 1985, 2324.) Rev. by J. W. Saunders in RES (38:149) 1987, 112–14.

**1988.** TRAPIDO, JOEL (gen. ed.).    An international dictionary of theatre language. See **1151.**

**1989.** TURNER, VICTOR.    Are there universals of performance? CompCrit (9) 1987, 47–58.

**1990.** WIKANDER, MATTHEW H.    The play of truth and state: historical drama from Shakespeare to Brecht. (Bibl. 1988, 1589.) Rev. by Ann Thompson in MLR (84:3) 714–15.

## FICTION

**1991.** ABBOTT, H. PORTER.    Diary fiction: writing as action. (Bibl. 1988, 1591.) Rev. by Alan Kennedy in UTQ (56:3) 1987, 449–51.

**1992.** ALKON, PAUL K.   Origins of futuristic fiction. Athens: Georgia UP, 1987. pp. xii, 341. Rev. by John Huntington in MP (87:2) 1814; by Arthur B. Evans in SFS (16:1) 94–102.
**1993.** ANON. (ed.).   Introduction. *In* (pp. vii–xiii) **61.**
**1994.** AXLER, DAVID M.   Some potential approaches to the folkloristic study of science fiction. *See* **1650.**
**1995.** AYMAR, BRANDT (ed.).   Men at sea: the best sea stories of all time from Homer to William F. Buckley, Jr. New York: Crown, 1988; London: Barrie & Jenkins. pp. xiii, 640.
**1996.** BACON-SMITH, CAMILLE.   Introduction to special issue: science fiction. KF (4:1) 1–6.
**1997.** BOONE, JOSEPH ALLEN.   Tradition counter tradition: love and the form of fiction. (Bibl. 1988, 1596.) Rev. by Élisabeth Béranger in EA (42:4) 451–2.
**1998.** BOOTH, WAYNE C.   The company we keep: an ethics of fiction. (Bibl. 1988, 1597.) Rev. by Eugene Goodheart in LRB (11:6) 23–4.
**1999.** BORUAH, BIJOY H.   Fiction and emotion: a study in aesthetics and the philosophy of mind. Oxford: Clarendon Press, 1988. pp. viii, 133.
**2000.** BORUCHOFF, DAVID ALAN.   In his own words: monologue and monologism in the picaresque confession. Unpub. doct. diss., Harvard Univ., 1988. [Abstr. in DA (49) 3019–20A.]
**2001.** BUSSING, SABINE.   Aliens in the home: the child in horror fiction. New York; London: Greenwood Press, 1987. pp. xxi, 203. (Contributions to the study of childhood and youth, 4.)
**2002.** CHAMBERLAIN, DANIEL FRANK.   Figures and facets of narrative perspective in fiction. Unpub. doct. diss., Univ. of Toronto, 1988. [Abstr. in DA (49) 2643–4A.] (*Jacob's Room.*)
**2003.** COHAN, STEVEN.   Violation and repair in the English novel: the paradigm of experience from Richardson to Woolf. (Bibl. 1988, 1600.) Rev. by Grant Campbell in QQ (95:3) 1988, 735–7.
**2004.** COLLINS, JERRE CHURCHILL.   Narratives and time. Unpub. doct. diss., Univ. of Wisconsin–Milwaukee, 1988. [Abstr. in DA (50) 942A.]
**2005.** DALESKI, H. M.   Unities: studies in the English novel. (Bibl. 1987, 2626.) Rev. by Thomas Docherty in RES (38:151) 1987, 422–3.
**2006.** DÄLLENBACH, LUCIEN.   The mirror in the text. Trans. by JEREMY WHITELEY and EMMA HUGHES. Cambridge: Polity Press; Oxford: Blackwell. pp. 262.
**2007.** DAVIS, LENNARD J.   Resisting novels: ideology and fiction. New York; Toronto: Methuen, 1987. (Bibl. 1987, 2627.) Rev. by Terrence Craig in CanL (121) 154–7; by Thomas Docherty in RES (39:156) 1988, 602–3; by David Bunn in JLS (5:3/4) 343–60.
**2008.** DERWIN, SUSAN.   The renunciation of mimesis: theory and practice of the novel. Unpub. doct. diss., Johns Hopkins Univ., 1988. [Abstr. in DA (50) 132A.] (*The Second Coming.*)
**2009.** EVANS, ARTHUR B.   Futures of the past. SFS (16:1) 94–102 (review-article).

**2010.** FAIRBANKS, CAROL.   Prairie women: images in American and Canadian fiction. (Bibl. 1988, 1603.) Rev. by Karen S. Langlois in HLQ (52:3) 433–7; by Barbara W. Rippey in JWest (28:1) 124; by Ann Leger Anderson in CanL (115) 1987, 249–51.

**2011.** FIELD, TREVOR.   Form and function in the diary novel. Basingstoke: Macmillan. pp. xii, 198.

**2012.** FÖLDÉNYI, LÁSZLO F.   Novel and individuality. Neophilologus (73:1) 1–13.

**2013.** FOLEY, BARBARA.   Telling the truth: the theory and practice of documentary fiction. (Bibl. 1986, 2920, where entry misplaced.) Rev. by Peter J. Rabinowitz in MP (86:4) 450–2; by Shari Zeck in JMMLA (20:1) 1986, 111–17; by Carl Plantinga in JA (45:3) 316–18; by A. S. Byatt in TLS, 1987, 16 Jan., 65.

**2014.** GELLEY, ALEXANDER.   Narrative crossings: theory and pragmatics of prose fiction. (Bibl. 1987, 2632.) Rev. by Mark G. Sokolyansky in MLR (84:3) 686–7; by Leigh Hafrey in TLS, 13 Jan., 41.

**2015.** GOLDSMITH, ELIZABETH C. (ed.).   Writing the female voice: essays on epistolary literature. *See* **61.**

**2016.** GRAHAM, JAY.   Beyond fragmentation: toward a theory of imagination and the tradition of greatness in fiction. BSUF (26:3) 1985, 45–52.

**2017.** GUNN, JAMES (ed.).   The new encyclopedia of science fiction. London; New York: Viking Press, 1988. pp. xix, 524. Rev. by Gary K. Wolfe in SFS (16:3) 379–83; by John Clute in TLS, 21 Apr., 430.

**2018.** HAIN, BONNIE ANN.   Virtue, vartue: rewriting theories of the novel. Unpub. doct. diss., State Univ. of New York at Stony Brook, 1988. [Abstr. in DA (50) 952A.]

**2019.** HANTZIS, DARLENE MARIE.   'You are about to begin reading': the nature and function of second person point of view in narrative. Unpub. doct. diss., Louisiana State Univ. and Agricultural and Mechanical College, 1988. [Abstr. in DA (49) 3550A.]

**2020.** HARTMAN, DONALD K.; DROST, JEROME.   Themes and settings in fiction: a bibliography of bibliographies. Introd. by ARTHUR EFRON. New York; London: Greenwood Press, 1988. pp. xv, 223. (Bibliographies and indexes in world literature, 14.)

**2021.** HOOPER, BRAD.   Short story writers and their work: a guide to the best. Chicago; London: American Library Assn, 1988. pp. 60.

**2022.** KEEFER, JANICE KULYK.   Under eastern eyes: a critical reading of Maritime fiction. (Bibl. 1987, 2640.) Rev. by Laurie Ricou in CanL (121) 140–1.

**2023.** KNOX-SHAW, PETER.   The explorer in English fiction. (Bibl. 1987, 2643.) Rev. by Douglas Hewitt in RES (39:156) 1988, 601–2.

**2024.** KUNDERA, MILAN.   The art of the novel. Trans. by LINDA ASHER. London: Faber & Faber, 1988. pp. 165. Rev. by Stuart Gillespie in CamQ (18:2) 232–7; by Stephen Wall in LRB (11:6) 24–6.

**2025.** LEIBY, DAVID ALLEN.   The tooth that gnaws: a poetics of time travel narratives. Unpub. doct. diss., Univ. of California, Los Angeles, 1987. [Abstr. in DA (48) 1988, 3111A.]

**2026.** LLOYD-SMITH, ALLAN GARDNER.   Uncanny American fiction: Medusa's face. Basingstoke: Macmillan. pp. xii, 186.

**2027.** McDERMOTT, HUBERT.   Novel and romance: the *Odyssey* to *Tom Jones*. Basingstoke: Macmillan. pp. xi, 257.

**2028.** McLEISH, KENNETH.   Bloomsbury good reading guide. London: Bloomsbury, 1988. pp. x, 310.

**2029.** MARTENS, LORNA.   The diary novel. (Bibl. 1988, 1618.) Rev. by Miriam Allott in RES (38:149) 1987, 118.

**2030.** MOSES, MICHAEL VALDEZ.   The tragic novel: heroism and the politics of modernity. Unpub. doct. diss., Univ. of Virginia, 1987. [Abstr. in DA (49) 3360–1A.]

**2031.** NEW, W. H.   Dreams of speech and violence: the art of the short story in Canada and New Zealand. (Bibl. 1987, 2656.) Rev. in QQ (95:4) 1988, 968–9; by Gary Boire in Landfall (43:1) 119–24; by Reginald Berry in NZList, 26 Aug., 71–72; by Helen Tiffin in CanL (121) 131–3.

**2032.** PAVEL, THOMAS G.   Fictional worlds. (Bibl. 1988, 1622.) Rev. by David Dowling in CanL (119) 1988, 118–19.

**2033.** PEPPER, DENNIS (comp.).   An Oxford book of Christmas stories. Oxford: OUP, 1988. pp. 223.

**2034.** PIERCE, JOHN J.   Foundations of science fiction: a study in imagination and evolution. (Bibl. 1987, 2662.) Rev. by Patrick Parrinder in SFS (16:2) 231–2.

**2035.** PRADO, C. G.   Making believe: philosophical reflections on fiction. Westport, CT; London: Greenwood Press, 1984. pp. viii, 169. (Contributions in philosophy, 25.) Rev. by Carolyn Korsmeyer in JA (46:1) 1987, 90–1.

**2036.** RIDGWAY, JIM; BENJAMIN, MICHELE.   PsiFi: psychological theories and science fictions. Leicester: British Psychological Soc., 1987. pp. ix, 229.

**2037.** RIGAUD, N. J. (ed.).   L'étranger dans la littérature et la pensée anglaises. *See* **26.**

**2038.** ROBBINS, BRUCE.   The servant's hand: English fiction from below. (Bibl. 1988, 1624.) Rev. by Gerald C. Sorenson in StudN (20:2) 1988, 114–16.

**2039.** RUPPERT, PETER.   Reader in a strange land: the activity of reading literary utopias. Athens; London: Georgia UP, 1986. pp. xiv, 193. Rev. by Kenneth M. Roemer in SFS (15:1) 1988, 88–93.

**2040.** SEIDEL, KATHRYN LEE.   The Southern belle in the American novel. (Bibl. 1988, 1626.) Rev. by Carol Mitchell in SF (46:2) 194–6.

**2041.** SEIDEL, MICHAEL.   Exile and the narrative imagination. (Bibl. 1988, 1627.) Rev. by Richard C. Wood in SewR (96:3) 1988, lix–lxi; by John Richetti in MP (86:3) 335–8.

**2042.** SEJOURNÉ, PHILIPPE.   Technique and artifice in the short story. JSSE (12) 11–20.

**2043.** SPEHNER, NORBERT.   Écrits sur la science-fiction: bibliographie analytique des études et essais sur la science-fiction publiés entre 1900 et

1987. Longueil, Qué.: Éditions du Préambule, 1988. pp. 535. Rev. by Arthur B. Evans in SFS (16:2) 240–2.

**2044.** SPENDER, DALE. Mothers of the novel: 100 good women writers before Jane Austen. (Bibl. 1987, 2671.) Rev. by Helen Wilcox in BJECS (11) 1988, 101–2; by Ann Messenger in CanL (115) 1987, 234–5.

**2045.** STAMIROWSKA, KRYSTYNA. The reading of fiction. *In* (pp. 27–39) **36.**

**2046.** STURGESS, PHILIP. Narrativity and its definition. YREAL (6) 17–38.

**2047.** TRACY, LAURA. Catching the drift: authority, gender and narrative strategy in fiction. New Brunswick, NJ; London: Rutgers UP, 1988. pp. ix, 229.

**2048.** TRISTRAM, PHILIPPA. Living space in fact and fiction. London: Routledge. pp. xiv, 306.

**2049.** VEEDER, WILLIAM; GRIFFIN, SUSAN M. (eds). The art of criticism: Henry James on the theory and the practice of fiction. (Bibl. 1987, 2675.) Rev. by Ronald Mason in NQ (36:4) 535–6.

## LITERATURE FOR CHILDREN

**2050.** ALDERSON, BRIAN. Collecting children's books: self-indulgence and scholarship. *In* (pp. 7–17) **14.**

**2051.** —— Sing a song of sixpence: the English picture book tradition and Randolph Caldecott. *See* **77.**

**2052.** ATKINSON, DOROTHY (ed.). The children's bookroom: reading and the use of books. Stoke on Trent: Trentham. pp. 141.

**2053.** AVERY, GILLIAN; BRIGGS, JULIA (eds). Children and their books: a celebration of the work of Iona and Peter Opie. Introd. by IONA OPIE. *See* **14.**

**2054.** BELL, OLIVIA; BELL, ALAN. Children's manuscript magazines in the Bodleian Library. *In* (pp. 399–412) **14.**

**2055.** CAIRNS, EDITH M. (comp.). Catalogue of the collection of children's books, 1617–1939, in the library of the University of Reading. *See* **208.**

**2056.** HOWARD, ELIZABETH F. America as story: historical fiction for secondary schools. Chicago; London: American Library Assn, 1988. pp. xviii, 137.

**2057.** HURST, CLIVE. Selections from the accession diaries of Peter Opie. *In* (pp. 19–44) **14.**

**2058.** MARSHALL, MARGARET R. An introduction to the world of children's books. (Bibl. 1983, 3099.) Aldershot: Gower, 1988. pp. 327. (Second ed.: first ed. 1982.) Rev. by BC in Junior Bookshelf (52:5) 1988, 225.

**2059.** NIKOLAJEVA, MARIA. The magic code: the use of magical patterns in fantasy for children. (Bibl. 1988, 1639.) Rev. by Pat Reynolds in Mythlore (16:1) 45–6; by Lena Kåreland in Samlaren (110) 136–9.

**2060.** SCHILLER, JUSTIN G. One collector's progress. *See* **263.**

**2061.** SHIELDS, NANCY E.   Index to literary criticism for young adults. Metuchen, NJ; London: Scarecrow Press, 1988. pp. ix, 408.

**2062.** STOKES, KATHY JO.   Children's journey stories as an epic subgenre. Unpub. doct. diss., Univ. of Nebraska–Lincoln, 1988. [Abstr. in DA (50) 131A.]

**2063.** STONE, MICHAEL.   Interview with Barbara Giles. Span (29) 1–11.

**2064.** SULLIVAN, DALE LEE.   A rhetoric of children's literature as epideictic discourse. Unpub. doct. diss., Rensselaer Polytechnic Institute, 1988. [Abstr. in DA (49) 3204A.]

## POETRY

**2065.** AMIS, KINGSLEY (ed.).   The Amis anthology. London: Hutchinson, 1988. pp. xvi, 360. Rev. by John Bayley in LRB (11:2) 13–14.

**2066.** BARRELL, JOHN.   Poetry, language and politics. (Bibl. 1988, 1646.) Rev. by John Higgins in Upstream (7:1) 71–3.

**2067.** BLASING, MUTLU KONUK.   American poetry: the rhetoric of its forms. (Bibl. 1988, 1647.) Rev. by Peter Stitt in ELN (26:3) 90–2; by Mathew Fisher in SoHR (23:1) 87–8; by Julian D. Gill in JAStud (23:1) 121–2; by David Shevin in OhioanaQ (32:1) 9–11.

**2068.** BLOOM, HAROLD.   Ruin the sacred truths: poetry and belief from the Bible to the present. Cambridge, MA; London: Harvard UP. pp. 11, 204. (Charles Eliot Norton lectures, 1987/88.) Rev. by Harold Beaver in TLS, 18 Aug., 900.

**2069.** BROGAN, TERRY V. F.   Verseform: a comparative bibliography. Baltimore, MD; London: Johns Hopkins UP. pp. xv, 122.

**2070.** CURTIS, TONY (ed.).   The poetry of Pembrokeshire. Bridgend: Seren. pp. 134.

**2071.** EASTHOPE, ANTONY.   Poetry and phantasy. Cambridge: CUP. pp. 227.

**2072.** EDWARDS, MICHAEL.   Poetry and possibility. Totowa, NJ: Barnes & Noble, 1988. (Bibl. 1988, 1651.) Rev. by Marcia Leveson in UES (27:1) 68; by Larry Allums in ChrisL (39:1) 91–2.

**2073.** —— The project of a Christian poetics. ChrisL (39:1) 63–76.

**2074.** ENGLER, BALZ.   'Yon' and the pragmatics of poetry. *See* **1078.**

**2075.** EVERETT, BARBARA.   Poets in their time: essays on English poetry from Donne to Larkin. (Bibl. 1987, 2715.) Rev. by Paul Hammond in RES (39:154) 1988, 330–1; by Michael Williams in UES (27:1) 66–8.

**2076.** FARRINGDON, JILL.   The language of gender. PW (24:3) 23–5.

**2077.** FITTER, C.   Landscape in poetry: descriptive approaches and cultural contexts in Christian and antecedent traditions to the period of Milton. Unpub. doct. diss., Univ. of Oxford. [Abstr. in IT (39:3) 1101.]

**2078.** FITZGERALD, WILLIAM.   Agonistic poetry: the Pindaric mode in Pindar, Horace, Hölderlin and the English ode. Berkeley; London: California UP, 1987. pp. xiv, 242. Rev. by Edgar C. Reinke and Jacob Fuchs in CML (9:2) 164–70.

**2079.** GRAY, STEPHEN (ed.).   The Penguin book of verse. Harmondsworth: Penguin. pp. xxv, 402.

**2080.** HARRIS, CANDICE RAE.   The decline of the country-house poem in England: a study in the history of ideas. Unpub. doct. diss., Univ. of North Texas, 1988. [Abstr. in DA (49) 3033A.]

**2081.** HARRISON, MICHAEL; STUART-CLARK, CHRISTOPHER (sels). Peace and war: a collection of poems. Oxford: OUP. pp. 208.

**2082.** HAUGHTON, HUGH (ed.).   The Chatto book of nonsense poetry. pp. 530. (Bibl. 1988, 1656, where pagination incorrect.) Rev. by John Bayley in LRB (11:2) 13–14.

**2083.** HOLLANDER, JOHN.   Melodious guile: fictive pattern in poetic language. New Haven, CT; London: Yale UP. pp. x, 262. Rev. by Lachlan Mackinnon in TLS, 11 Aug., 880; by Alastair Fowler in LRB (11:21) 24–5.

**2084.** HOŠEK, CHAVIVA; PARKER, PATRICIA (eds).   Lyric poetry: beyond New Criticism. (Bibl. 1986, 2927.) Rev. by Gabriella Bedetti in Genre (20:1) 1987, 91–5.

**2085.** JACOBS, ALAN.   'The natural sin of language': poetic authority and the Christian lyric. Unpub. doct. diss., Univ. of Virginia, 1987. [Abstr. in DA (49) 3369A.]

**2086.** KELLY, A. A. (ed.).   Pillars of the house: an anthology of verse by Irish women from 1690 to the present. Dublin: Wolfhound Press, 1987. pp. 174.

**2087.** KINSELLA, THOMAS (ed.).   The new Oxford book of Irish verse. (Bibl. 1987, 2725.) Rev. by Hilary Pyle in RES (38:152) 1987, 592–3.

**2088.** LASKI, MARGHANITA (sel.).   Common ground: an anthology. Manchester: Carcanet Press. pp. 295.

**2089.** LERNER, LAURENCE.   On ambiguity, Modernism, and sacred texts. *In* (pp. 133–44) **46.**

**2090.** LILLEY, K.   To dy in writinge: figure and narrative in masculine elegy. Unpub. doct. diss., Univ. of London, 1988. [Abstr. in IT (39:1) 29.]

**2091.** LINDE, PETER.   Droger och diktare. (Drugs and poets.) Stockholm: Carlsson. pp. 221.

**2092.** LINZEY, ANDREW; REGAN, TOM (eds).   Song of creation: an anthology of poems in praise of animals. Basingstoke: Abbey, 1988. pp. xx, 155.

**2093.** MCALLASTER, ELVA.   As apostles for poetry. ChrisL (38:4) 65–75.

**2094.** MCMAHON, SEAN (ed.).   My native land: a celebration of Britain. Dublin: Poolbeg, 1987. pp. 360.

**2095.** MANN, CHRIS ZITHULELE.   A poem called *Farmyard in the City* with a few observations on prosody and quantum mechanics. Upstream (7:4) 46–53.

**2096.** MELLER, HORST.   Zum Verstehen englischer Gedichte. (Bibl. 1985, 2468.) Rev. by Willi Erzgräber in LJGG (28) 1987, 395–7.

**2097.** MURRAY, LES.   Poems and the mystery of embodiment. Meanjin (47:3) 1988, 519–33.

**2098.** MYERS, JACK; SIMMS, MICHAEL.   Longman dictionary and handbook of poetry. *See* **1138.**

**2099.** NEMIROFF, GRETA HOFMANN (ed.).   Celebrating Canadian women: prose and poetry by and about women. Markham, Ont.: Fitzhenry & Whiteside. pp. xvii, 406.

**2100.** PETTINGELL, PHOEBE.   Tales of Eros in verse. NewL (72:5) 15–16.

**2101.** ROBERTS, MARIE.   British poets and secret societies: Free-masons and clandestine brotherhoods. (Bibl. 1988, 1675.) Rev. by Ken E. Smith in BJECS (10) 1987, 109–10.

**2102.** ROSE-INNES, HENRIETTA.   Cross-cultural interchange of under-standing through poetry. Crux (23:4) 37–9.

**2103.** ROSENTHAL, M. L. (gen. ed.).   Poetry in English: an anthology. New York; Oxford: OUP, 1987. pp. xxxviii, 1196.

**2104.** SACKS, PETER M.   The English elegy: studies in the genre from Spenser to Yeats. (Bibl. 1987, 2746.) Rev. by Andrew V. Ettin in ELN (27:1) 69–71.

**2105.** SEWELL, ELIZABETH.   Nonsense verse and the child. *In* (pp. 135–48) **28.** (Repr. from Lion and Unicorn (40) 1980/81, 30–48.)

**2106.** STREITFELD, DAVID.   Rhyme and reason. *See* **488.**

**2107.** SUHAMY, HENRI.   La poétique. Paris: Presses Universitaires de France, 1986. pp. 128. (Que sais-je?, 2311.)

**2108.** SUTHERLAND, JAMES.   A note on the foreseen and the fortuitous in poetry. *In* (pp. 295–301) **42.**

**2109.** SWANGER, DAVID.   The heart's education: why we need poetry. JAE (23:2) 45–54.

**2110.** TILLOTSON, KATHLEEN.   Palgrave's *Golden Treasury* and Tenny-son: another source. TRB (5:2) 1988, 49–54.

**2111.** WILLIAMS, MILLER.   Patterns of poetry: an encyclopedia of forms. Baton Rouge: Louisiana State UP, 1986. pp. 204. Rev. by Stephan Cushman in SewR (96:1) 1988, ii, iv, vi.

## PROSE

**2112.** CAMPBELL, MARY BAINE.   The rhetoric of exotic travel litera-ture, 400–1600. Unpub. doct. diss., Boston Univ., 1985. [Abstr. in DA (50) 1652A.]

**2113.** GORDON, ELEANOR RISTEEN.   The authority of the essay: philosophical, rhetorical, and cognitive considerations of person. Unpub. doct. diss., Univ. of Illinois at Chicago, 1988. [Abstr. in DA (50) 449A.]

**2114.** PRYOR, FELIX (ed.).   The Faber book of letters: letters written in the English language 1578–1939. (Bibl. 1988, 1687.) Rev. in BkW, 16 Apr., 13; by Bennett Schiff in Smithsonian (20:3) 168.

**2115.** RAYMENT, N.   Empiricism and the nature tradition. Unpub. doct. diss., Univ. of Loughborough, 1988. [Abstr. in IT (39:1) 29.]

## BIOGRAPHY AND AUTOBIOGRAPHY

**2116.** ABBS, PETER. The development of autobiography in Western culture: from Augustine to Rousseau. Unpub. doct. diss., Univ. of Sussex, 1986. [Abstr. in DA (49) 1790A.]

**2117.** ÁLVAREZ, MARÍA ANTONIA. Importancia y evolución de la autobiografía en Norteamérica. Atlantis (11:1/2) 113–23.

**2118.** ATWOOD, MARGARET. Biographobia: some personal reflections on the act of biography. *In* (pp. 1–8) **44.**

**2119.** BATTS, JOHN STUART. Private chronicles in public places. CanL (121) 12–25.

**2120.** BENSTOCK, SHARI (ed.). The private self: theory and practice of women's autobiographical writings. *See* **51.**

**2121.** BRUMBLE, H. DAVID, III. American Indian autobiography. Berkeley; London: California UP, 1988. pp. xi, 278. Rev. by Hertha D. Wong in AL (61:4) 686–8.

**2122.** BUSCH, FREDERICK. Public or purloined? Novelists' letters, biographers' rights. Harper's (279) Aug., 58–61.

**2123.** CLINE, CHERYL. Women's diaries, journals, and letters: an annotated bibliography. New York; London: Garland. pp. xxxviii, 716. (Garland reference library of the humanities, 780.)

**2124.** COCKSHUT, A. O. J. Children's diaries. *In* (pp. 381–98) **14.**

**2125.** DAVIS, GWENN; JOYCE, BEVERLY A. Personal writings by women to 1900: a bibliography of American and British writers. London: Mansell. pp. xx, 294. (Bibliographies of writings by American and British women to 1900, 1.) Rev. in OhioanaQ (32:3) 137.

**2126.** ELBAZ, ROBERT. The changing nature of the self: a critical study of the autobiographic discourse. (Bibl. 1988, 1692.) Rev. by A. O. J. Cockshut in NQ (36:2) 284.

**2127.** EPSTEIN, WILLIAM H. Recognizing biography. Philadelphia: Pennsylvania UP, 1987. pp. x, 231. Rev. by Albert Pailler in EA (42:4) 443.

**2128.** GILMORE, LEIGH. Autobiographics: women's autobiography and the poetics of identity. Unpub. doct. diss., Univ. of Washington, 1988. [Abstr. in DA (49) 1791A.]

**2129.** HASSAM, ANDREW. Reading other people's diaries. UTQ (56:3) 1987, 435–42.

**2130.** HEIDT, EDWARD R. Narrative voice in autobiographical writing. Unpub. doct. diss., Univ. of Southern California. [Abstr. in DA (50) 147A.]

**2131.** HINZ, EVELYN J. A speculative introduction: life-writing as drama. Mosaic (20:4) 1987, v–xii.

**2132.** KIRSHENBLATT-GIMBLETT, BARBARA. Authoring lives. JFR (26:2) 123–49.

**2133.** KRUPAT, ARNOLD. For those who come after: a study of native American autobiography. (Bibl. 1987, 2773.) Rev. by Bernard A. Hirsch in AmerS (29:2) 1988, 94–5.

**2134.** MJÖBERG, JÖRAN.   Nyare anglosaxiska författarbiografier: personkarakteristik och metodik. (Recent Anglo-Saxon author biographies: method and the way of characterizing personality.) TfL (18:2/3) 82–99.

**2135.** RAMPERSAD, ARNOLD.   Psychology and Afro-American biography. YR (78:1) 1988, 1–18.

**2136.** WHITTEMORE, REED.   Pure lives: the early biographers. (Bibl. 1988, 1697.) Rev. by Calhoun Winton in ModAge (32:2) 1988, 142–4; by Dante Cantrill in RMRLL (43:4) 269–71; by James M. Morris in CRL (50:3) 363–4, 367.

## RELATED STUDIES

**2137.** ANYIDOHO, KOFI.   To be heard and to be seen: translating oral poetry. Crosscurrent (2:3/4) 55–67.

**2138.** BOITANI, PIERO.   Antiquity and beyond: the death of Troilus. In (pp. 1–19) **27.**

**2139.** BUTLER, THOMAS (ed.).   Memory: history, culture and the mind. Oxford: Blackwell. pp. ix, 189. (Wolfson College lectures.)

**2140.** CHEVREL, YVES.   La littérature comparée. Paris: Presses Universitaires de France. pp. 127. (Que sais-je?, 127.)

**2141.** EDELSTEIN, ALEX S.; ITO, YOUICHI; KEPPLINGER, HANS MATHIAS.   Communication and culture: a comparative approach. Introd. by MAXWELL McCOMBS. New York; London: Longman. pp. xxvi, 342. (Communications.)

**2142.** FORSYTH, NEIL.   The old enemy: Satan and the combat myth. (Bibl. 1988, 1702.) Rev. by Peter Brown in Spec (64:3) 699–701.

**2143.** FRANCE, PETER: GLEN, DUNCAN (eds).   European poetry in Scotland: an anthology of translations. Edinburgh: Edinburgh UP. pp. xviii, 224.

**2144.** FRANK, ARMIN PAUL.   Literary translation and alterity: some distinctions. In (pp. 271–82) **4.**

**2145.** FRYKMAN, ERIK.   Skottland: då och nu: härs och tvärs. (Scotland: past and present: back and forth.) Stockholm: Norstedt. pp. 271, (plates) 8. Rev. by Hans Andersson in MS (83:4) 356–8.

**2146.** HAWKES, J. G. (ed.).   The history and social influence of the potato. By REDCLIFFE N. SALAMAN. With a chapter on industrial uses by W. G. BURTON. (Bibl. 1949, 875.) Cambridge; New York: CUP, 1985. pp. xliv, 685. (Second ed.: first ed., 1949.) Rev. by D. Hey in Lore and Language (5:1) 1986, 127–8.

**2147.** HERMANS, THEO (ed.).   The manipulation of literature: studies in literary translation. (Bibl. 1987, 2794.) Rev. by Jo Labanyi in MLR (84:2) 420–1.

**2148.** HONIG, EDWIN.   The poet's other voice: conversations on literary translation. (Bibl. 1988, 1704.) Rev. by Jo Labanyi in MLR (84:2) 421–2.

**2149.** HUNTER, IAN.   Culture and government: the emergence of literary education. Basingstoke: Macmillan, 1988. pp. xi, 317. (Language, discourse, society.)

**2150.** KERBER, LINDA K.   Diversity and the transformation of American studies. AmQ (41:3) 415–31.

**2151.** KITTEL, HARALD (ed.).   Die literarische Übersetzung: Stand und Perspektiven ihrer Erforschung. Berlin: Schmidt, 1988. pp. xiii, 238.

**2152.** LONGMAN, TREMPER, III.   Literary approaches to biblical interpretation. Grand Rapids, MI: Academie; Leicester: Apollos, 1987. pp. xi, 164. (Foundations of contemporary interpretation, 3.)

**2153.** MARTIN, STODDARD.   Orthodox heresy: the rise of 'magic' as religion and its relation to literature. Basingstoke: Macmillan. pp. viii, 322.

**2154.** MILLER, SEUMAS.   Ideology, language and thought. Theoria (74) 97–105.

**2155.** MORRISON, KARL F.   'I am you': the hermeneutics of empathy in Western literature, theology and art. Princeton NJ: Princeton UP. pp. 366. Rev. by Brian Stock in TLS, 21 Apr., 434.

**2156.** NOONAN, JOHN T., JR.   Bribes. New York: Macmillan; London: Collier Macmillan, 1984. pp. xxiii, 839. Rev. by John A. Yunck in YLS (1) 1987, 153–5.

**2157.** NOVITZ, DAVID.   Art, narrative, and human nature. PhilL (13:1) 57–74.

**2158.** OSTROWSKI, WITOLD.   Social aspects of literary evaluation in England and in Poland. *In* (pp. 7–26) **36.**

**2159.** PATTERSON, ANNABEL.   Pastoral and ideology: Virgil to Valéry. Berkeley: California UP; Oxford: Clarendon Press, 1987. pp. xiv, 344. Rev. by Anthony Low in RQ (42:2) 332–4; by William W. Batstone in MP (87:2) 170–3; by Stuart Gillespie in CamQ (18:3) 322–5.

**2160.** PETILLON, PIERRE-YVES.   *1630 & All That*: de l'Amérique puritaine. EA (42:1) 68–84.

**2161.** SMITH, JESSIE CARNEY (ed.).   Images of Blacks in American culture: a reference guide to information sources. Introd. by NIKKI GIOVANNI. Westport, CT; London: Greenwood Press, 1988. pp. 390. Rev. in OhioanaQ (32:3) 137.

**2162.** THOMPSON, KENNETH (ed.).   Discourse and the two cultures: science, religion and the humanities. Lanham, MD; London: UP of America, 1988. pp. xviii, 288. (Exxon Education Foundation series on rhetoric and political discourse, 19.)

**2163.** VAN DEN BROECK, RAYMOND.   Literary conventions and translated literature. *In* (pp. 57–75) **16.**

**2164.** —— (introd.).   Translated! Papers on literary translation and translation studies. By JAMES S. HOLMES. Amsterdam: Rodopi, 1988. pp. 117. (Approaches to translation studies, 7.) Rev. by Theo Hermans in NC (8) 196–7.

**2165.** VILIKOVSKÝ, JÁN.   The context of literary translation. *In* (pp. 139–47) **62.**

**2166.** WILLIAMS, DAVID R.   Wilderness lost: the religious origins of the American mind. Selinsgrove, PA; London: Susquehanna UP, 1987. pp. 292. Rev. by Mary Kateri Fitzgerald in ChrisL (38:4) 83–5.

**2167.** WOODCOCK, GEORGE.  More than an echo: notes on the craft of translation. CanL (117) 1988, 72–9.
**2168.** ZGORZELSKI, ANDRZEJ.  Lektura jako kontakt osobowy. (Reading as personal contact.) *In* (pp. 235–43) **36.**

## LITERARY THEORY

This section is intended to cover general writings **about** literary history, criticism and critical theory. For general works **of** literary history and criticism, see under 'General Literary Studies'.

**2169.** AGOSTINI, RENÉ.  Théâtre et narratologie: perspectives d'une esthétique du récit dramatique. *See* **1950.**
**2170.** ANDERSON, DAVID JAMES.  Theatre criticism: a minor art with a major problem. *See* **1952.**
**2171.** BIRCH, DAVID.  Language, literature and critical practice: ways of analysing text. New York; London: Routledge. pp. xiv, 214. (Interface.)
**2172.** CRISP, PETER.  Essence, realism and literature. Eng (38) 55–68.
**2173.** DAVIS, ROBERT CON; FINKE, LAURIE (eds).  Literary criticism and theory: the Greeks to the present. New York; London: Longman. pp. xxi, 952. (Longman English and humanities.)
**2174.** DYSERINCK, HUGO: FISCHER, MANFRED S. (eds).  Internationale Bibliographie zur Geschichte und Theorie der Komparatistik. (Bibl. 1986, 3023.) Rev. by Adrian Marino in Archiv (224:1) 1987, 124–8.
**2175.** EARTHMAN, ELISE ANN.  The lonely, quiet concert: readers creating meaning from literary texts. Unpub. doct. diss., Stanford Univ. [Abstr. in DA (50) 1583–4A.]
**2176.** FANTO, JAMES ANTHONY.  The making of a literary critic: professionalism and the strategies of authority. Unpub. doct. diss., Univ. of Michigan, 1988. [Abstr. in DA (49) 2210A.]
**2177.** GIVENS, TERRYL L.  Mimesis and the limits of semblance. Unpub. doct. diss., Univ. of North Carolina at Chapel Hill, 1988. [Abstr. in DA (49) 2648–9A.]
**2178.** GREETHAM, D. C.  Textual and literary theory: redrawing the matrix. *See* **319.**
**2179.** HARPHAM, GEOFFREY GALT.  Ethics and the double standard of criticism. SoHR (23:4) 343–55.
**2180.** HAWTHORN, JEREMY.  Unlocking the text: fundamental issues in literary theory. London: Arnold, 1987. pp. vi, 138. Rev. by Douglas Hewitt in NQ (36:1) 137.
**2181.** HEBEL, UDO J.  Intertextuality, allusion, and quotation: an international bibliography of critical studies. New York; London: Greenwood Press. pp. xii, 175. (Bibliographies and indexes in world literature, 18.)
**2182.** KELLY, NANCY WEBB.  *Homo ludens, homo aestheticus*: the transformation of 'free play' in the rise of literary criticism. Unpub. doct. diss., Stanford Univ., 1988. [Abstr. in DA (49) 2644A.]

**2183.** KIRWAN, J.    Literary theory and literary aesthetics. Unpub. doct. diss., Univ. of Edinburgh, 1988. [Abstr. in IT (39:4) 1625; in DA (50) 1650A.]

**2184.** KRAEMER, DONALD JAMES, JR.    Creating and controlling plurality: a critique of some attempts to unify the profession of literary studies. Unpub. doct. diss., Univ. of Oregon, 1988. [Abstr. in DA (49) 3712A.]

**2185.** KRAJEWSKI, BRUCE JAMES.    Traveling with Hermes: hermeneutics and rhetoric. *See* **1314.**

**2186.** LEVINSON, MARJORIE (ed.).    Rethinking historicism: critical readings in Romantic history. *See* **53.**

**2187.** McGANN, JEROME J.    The beauty of inflections: literary investigations in historical method and theory. (Bibl. 1986, 3032.) Rev. by Thérèse Tessier in EA (42:2) 191.

**2188.** MANLOVE, COLIN.    Critical thinking: a guide to interpreting literary texts. London: Macmillan. pp. 188.

**2189.** MEROD, JIM.    The political responsibility of the critic. (Bibl. 1987, 2820.) Rev. by John Clifford in CE (51:5) 520–3.

**2190.** MOLLOY, SHAUN.    Guilty pleasures of the text and unauthorized versions. *In* (pp. 40–5) **36.**

**2191.** MOODY, H. L. B.    Literary appreciation: a practical guide to the interpretation and appreciation of literature, especially unseen passages of poetry and prose. (Bibl. 1968, 2185.) Harlow: Longman, 1987. pp. x, 211. (New ed.: first ed. 1968.)

**2192.** NOAKES, SUSAN.    Timely reading: between exegesis and interpretation. Ithaca, NY; London: Cornell UP, 1988. pp. xv, 249.

**2193.** RAJAN, BALACHANDRA.    The form of the unfinished: English poetics from Spenser to Pound. (Bibl. 1986, 3042.) Rev. by Francis Berry in RES (38:149) 1987, 119–20.

**2194.** ROSSLYN, FELICITY.    Spiders, bees and silkworms: the case against literary theory. CamQ (17:1) 1988, 3–16.

**2195.** SEAMON, ROGER.    The story of the moral: the function of thematizing in literary criticism. JA (47:3) 229–36.

**2196.** Entry cancelled.

**2197.** SELDEN, RAMAN (ed.).    The theory of criticism: from Plato to the present: a reader. (Bibl. 1988, 1726.) Rev. by M. A. Williams in UES (27:1) 64–5; by Maud Ellmann in TLS, 17 Feb., 172.

**2198.** SNYDER, JOHN.    Tragedy, satire, the essay and a dialectical theory of genre. YREAL (6) 1–15.

**2199.** SUSSMAN, HENRY.    High resolution: critical theory and the problem of literacy. New York; Oxford: OUP. pp. xiv, 256.

**2200.** WENZEL, PETER.    Uneinheitliche Einheitlichkeit: eine Auseinandersetzung mit dem Konzept der 'unity' in der anglo-amerikanischen Literaturkritik. *In* (pp. 412–33) **4.**

# OLD ENGLISH

## GENERAL AND ANONYMOUS

### General Literary Studies; Editions and Studies of Anonymous Writings (except *Beowulf*)

**2201.** ANDERSON, EARL R.   Liturgical influence in *The Dream of the Rood*. Neophilologus (73:2) 293–304.

**2202.** ANDERSON, JAMES E.   Two literary riddles in the Exeter Book: Riddle 1 and the Easter Riddle. (Bibl. 1988, 1729.) Rev. by Hans Sauer in Ang (107:3/4) 517–20.

**2203.** ASTELL, ANN W.   Holofernes's head: 'tacen' and teaching in the Old English *Judith*. ASE (18) 117–33.

**2204.** BALL, CHRISTOPHER.   Byrhtnoth's weapons. NQ (36:1) 8–9. (*Battle of Maldon*.)

**2205.** BELANOFF, PAT.   The fall(?) of the Old English female poetic image. PMLA (104:5) 822–31.

**2206.** BERKHOUT, CARL T.   Appendix: research on early Old English literary prose, 1973–82. *In* (pp. 401–9) **56.**

**2207.** —— Old English bibliography 1987. OEN (21:2) 1988, 43–70.

**2208.** —— *et al.* Bibliography for 1988. ASE (18) 245–92.

**2209.** BHATTACHARYA, P.   Aspects of prose style in Old and early Middle English. Unpub. M.Litt. diss., Univ. of Oxford, 1988. [Abstr. in IT (39:2) 484.]

**2210.** BIGGS, FREDERICK M.   The eschatological conclusion of the Old English *Physiologus*. MÆ (58:2) 286–97.

**2211.** BJORK, ROBERT E.   The Old English verse saints' lives: a study in direct discourse and iconography of style. Buffalo, NY; Toronto UP, 1985. (Bibl. 1986, 3074.) Rev. by N. F. Blake in MLR (84:2) 431–2; by Jocelyn Price in Ang (107:1/2) 161–7.

**2212.** —— 'Sundor æt rune': the voluntary exile of *The Wanderer*. Neophilologus (73:1) 119–29.

**2213.** BLOCKLEY, MARY.   Old English coordination, apposition, and the syntax of English poetry. *See* **954.**

**2214.** BODDEN, MARY-CATHERINE (ed. and trans.).   The Old English *Finding of the True Cross*. Cambridge: Brewer, 1987. pp. xii, 132. Rev. by A. S. G. Edwards in MLR (84:2) 430–1; by Rosemarie Potz McGierr in EngS (70:2) 173–4.

**2215.** BRAGG, LOIS.   *Wulf and Eadwacer, The Wife's Lament*, and women's love lyrics of the Middle Ages. GRM (39) 257–67.

**2216.** BROWN, JOHN HENNING.   Spatial form in Maxims i, a seventh-century 'Waste Land' poem. Unpub. doct. diss., Univ. of South Florida. [Abstr. in DA (50) 1309A.]

**2217.** BROWN, PHYLLIS RUGG; CRAMPTON, GEORGIA RONAN; ROBINSON, FRED C. (eds).   Modes of interpretation in Old English literature: essays in honour of Stanley B. Greenfield. (Bibl. 1988, 1738.) Rev. by

D. G. Scragg in RES (39:154) 1988, 277–8; by N. F. Blake in MLR (84:4) 912–13.

**2218.** BROWN, RAY. The begging scop and the generous king in *Widsith*. Neophilologus (73:2) 281–92.

**2219.** BUSSE, WILHELM. Altenglische Literatur und ihre Geschichte: zur Kritik des gegenwärtigen Deutungssystems. Dusseldorf: Droste, 1987. pp. 314. (Studia humaniora, 7.) Rev. by Ursula Schaefer in Ang (107:1/2) 152–5; by Andreas Fischer in Archiv (226:1) 139–41; by John C. Pope in Spec (64:1) 135–43; by E. G. Stanley in NQ (36:2) 216–18.

**2220.** CHANCE, JANE. Woman as hero in Old English literature. (Bibl. 1988, 1742.) Rev. by Charlotte Brewer in RES (39:154) 1988, 280–1; by Jonathan W. Nicholls in MLR (84:1) 115.

**2221.** CLEMENT, RICHARD W. Short-title catalogue of the Clubb Anglo-Saxon Collection. See **211.**

**2222.** COLMAN, FRAN. The crunch is the key: on computer research on Old English personal names. *In* (pp. 41–55) **34.**

**2223.** DEKEYSER, XAVIER. Adjacent and distant antecedents and the compound relative 'seþe' in Old English prose. See **1070.**

**2224.** DONOGHUE, DANIEL. Style in Old English poetry: the test of the auxiliary. (Bibl. 1987, 2852.) Rev. by A. A. MacDonald in SL (13:2) 525–7; by Bruce Mitchell in Spec (64:2) 407–9.

**2225.** EDDEN, VALERIE (ed.). Medieval sermon studies newsletter: 21 and 22. Coventry: English Dept, Univ. of Warwick, 1988. pp. xxiv; xvii.

**2226.** ERZGRÄBER, WILLI. The beginnings of a written literature in Old English times. *In* (pp. 25–43) **38.** (Conference paper, February 1988.)

**2227.** Entry cancelled.

**2228.** FULK, R. D. West Germanic parasiting, Sievers' law, and the dating of Old English verse. SP (86:2) 117–38.

**2229.** GARDINER-STALLAERT, NICOLE. From the sword to the pen: an analysis of the concept of loyalty in Old English secular heroic poetry. New York; Berne; Frankfurt; Paris: Lang. pp. xiv, 370. (American univ. studies, 4: English language and literature, 65.)

**2230.** GATCH, MILTON McC. The unknowable audience of the Blickling homilies. ASE (18) 99–115.

**2231.** GERRITSEN, JOHAN. Correction and erasure in the Vespasian Psalter Gloss. See **315.**

**2232.** GIOVINE, MARIA T. Aspects of romance in Old English literature. Unpub. doct. diss., New York Univ., 1988. [Abstr. in DA (49) 3032–3A.]

**2233.** HALL, J. R. Old English 'sæbeorg': *Exodus* 442a, *Andreas* 308a. See **1067.**

**2234.** HALL, THOMAS N. The twelvefold division of the Red Sea in two Old English prose texts. MÆ (58:2) 298–304.

**2235.** HASENFRATZ, ROBERT. *Eisegen stefne* (*Christ and Satan* 36a), the *Visio Pauli*, and '*ferrea vox*' (*Aeneid* 6, 626). See **1044.**

**2236.** HEFFERNAN, CAROL FALVO. The phoenix at the fountain:

images of woman and eternity in Lactantius's *Carmen de Ave Phoenice* and the Old English *Phoenix*. Newark: Delaware UP; London: Assoc. UPs, 1988. pp. 175. Rev. by E. G. Stanley in NQ (36:2) 218–20.

**2237.** HILL, BETTY. Seven Old English glosses to the Lindisfarne Gospels. *See* **1020a.**

**2238.** HILL, MARGARETT HUTTON. Studies in theme and structure: *Piers Plowman A, Amelia,* and *Andreas.* Unpub. doct. diss., State Univ. of New York at Stony Brook, 1988. [Abstr. in DA (50) 1653A.]

**2239.** HILL, THOMAS D. Saturn's time riddle: an insular Latin analogue for *Solomon and Saturn* II lines 282–291. RES (39:154) 1988, 273–6.

**2240.** HORGAN, A. D. *The Wanderer* – Boethian poem? RES (38:149) 1987, 40–6.

**2241.** JACOBS, NICOLAS. Syntactical connection and logical disconnections: the case of *The Seafarer.* MÆ (58:1) 105–13.

**2242.** JONES, JOHN MARK. The metaphor that will not perish: *The Dream of the Rood* and the new hermeneutic. ChrisL (38:2) 63–72.

**2243.** KENNEDY, EDWARD DONALD; WALDRON, RONALD; WITTIG, JOSEPH S. (eds). Medieval English studies presented to George Kane. *See* **41.**

**2244.** KOTZOR, GÜNTER. The Latin tradition of martyrologies and the *Old English Martyrology. In* (pp. 301–33) **56.**

**2245.** LAPIDGE, MICHAEL; GNEUSS, HELMUT (eds). Learning and literature in Anglo-Saxon England: studies presented to Peter Clemoes on the occasion of his sixty-fifth birthday. (Bibl. 1988, 1768.) Rev. by Roberta Frank in UTQ (56:3) 1987, 461–3.

**2246.** LERER, SETH. The riddle and the book: Exeter Book Riddle 42 in its context. PLL (25:1) 3–18.

**2247.** LESLIE, R. F. (ed.). Three old English elegies: *The Wife's Lament; The Husband's Message; The Ruin.* (Bibl. 1966, 2108.) Exeter: Univ. of Exeter, 1988. pp. xii, 86. (Exeter medieval English texts and studies.) (Revised ed.: first ed. 1961.)

**2248.** LIGGINS, ELIZABETH M. Syntax and style in the Old English *Orosius. In* (pp. 245–73) **56.**

**2249.** LOCHERBIE-CAMERON, M. A. L. Byrhtnoth, his noble companion and his sister's son. MÆ (57:2) 1988, 159–71.

**2250.** LOGSDON, GAY MARIE. *Maldon, Brunanburh, Finnsburh Fragment,* and *Finnsburh Episode*: an inquiry into tradition and alternative styles in Old English poetry. Unpub. doct. diss., Univ. of Texas at Austin. [Abstr. in DA (50) 1666–7A.]

**2251.** LUCAS, PETER J. A new reading of *Christ III,* 1476b. MÆ (58:1) 103–5.

**2252.** LUTZ, ANGELIKA (ed.). Die Version G der Angelsächischen Chronik: Rekonstruktion und Edition. (Bibl. 1988, 2876, where subtitle omitted.) Rev. by E. G. Stanley in RES (39:154) 1988, 281–2.

**2253.** MEANEY, AUDREY L. St Neots, Æthelweard and the compilation of the *Anglo-Saxon Chronicle*: a survey. *In* (pp. 193–243) **56.**

**2254.** MJÖBERG, JÖRAN. Nyare anglosaxiska författarbiografier: personkarakteristik och metodik. *See* **2134.**

**2255.** MOMMA, HARUKO. The 'gnomic formula' and some additions to Bliss's Old English metrical system. NQ (36:4) 423–6.

**2256.** MONTEVERDE, MARGARET PYNE. The patterning of history in Old English literature. Unpub. doct. diss., Ohio State Univ., 1988. [Abstr. in DA (49) 2232–3A.]

**2257.** NELSON, MARIE. Structures of opposition in Old English poems. Amsterdam: Rodopi. pp. 195. (Costerus, 74.)

**2258.** NELSON, NANCY SUSAN. Heroism and failure in Anglo-Saxon poetry: the ideal and the real within the comitatus. Unpub. doct. diss., Univ. of North Texas. [Abstr. in DA (50) 1668A.]

**2259.** PINSKER, HANS; ZIEGLER, WALTRAUD (eds). Die altenglischen Rätsel des Exeterbuchs. (Bibl. 1988, 1780.) Rev. by Reinhard Gleissner in Ang (107:1/2) 140–5.

**2260.** REICHL, KARL. Formulaic diction in Old English poetry. *In* (pp. 42–70) A. T. HATTO (gen. ed.), Traditions of heroic and epic poetry: vol. 2, Characteristics and techniques. Ed. by J. B. HAINSWORTH. London: Modern Humanities Research Assn. pp. vii, 319. (Pubs of the MHRA, 13.)

**2261.** RENOIR, ALAIN. The hero on the beach: Germanic theme and Indo-European origin. NM (90:1) 111–16.

**2262.** RICHARDS, MARY P. The manuscript contexts of the Old English laws: tradition and innovation. *In* (pp. 171–92) **56.**

**2263.** RICHARDSON, JOHN. Two notes on the time frame of *The Wanderer* (lines 22 and 73–87). Neophilologus (73:1) 158–9.

**2264.** ROBERTS, JANE. *Guthlac A*: sources and source hunting. *In* (pp. 1–18) **41.**

**2265.** —— The Old English prose translation of Felix's *Vita sancti Guthlaci*. *In* (pp. 363–79) **56.**

**2266.** ROWE, ELIZABETH ASHMAN. Irony in the Old English and Old Norse interrogative situation. Neophilologus (73:3) 477–9.

**2267.** SAUER, HANS. Die 72 Völker und Sprachen der Welt: einige Ergänzungen. Ang (107:1/2) 61–4. (*Refers to* bibl. 1983, 3238.)

**2268.** SCHAEFER, URSULA. 'A song of myself': propositions on the vocality of Old English poetry. *In* (pp. 196–208) **5.**

**2269.** STANLEY, E. G. Rhymes in English medieval verse: from Old English to Middle English. *In* (pp. 19–54) **41.**

**2270.** SWANTON, MICHAEL. English literature before Chaucer. (Bibl. 1987, 2901.) Rev. by Peter J. Lucas in NQ (36:1) 78; by Karl Reichl in Archiv (226:1) 144–7; by Daniel G. Calder in Spec (64:3) 769–71.

**2271.** SZARMACH, PAUL E. The earlier homily: *De parasceve*. *In* (pp. 381–99) **56.**

**2272.** —— (ed.). Studies in earlier Old English prose: sixteen original contributions. *See* **56.**

**2273.** TAKAHASHI, HIROSHI. Koeishi no shisou to gengo. (The language and ideas of Old English poetry.) Tokyo: Kaibunsha. pp. 236.

**2274.** TEJADA, PALOMA. Traducción y caracterización lingüística: la prosa anglosajona. *See* **1645.**

**2275.** TERASAWA, JUN. Metrical constraints on Old English compounds. *See* **866.**

**2276.** TOYAMA, KIKUO. On the agreement of the subject and predicative adjective/past participle in Old English prose. *See* **974.**

**2277.** TRAHERN, JOSEPH B., JR (ed.). Year's work in Old English studies 1987. OEN (22:1) 1988, 33–178.

**2278.** VICKREY, JOHN F. *Exodus* and the robe of Joseph. SP (86:1) 1–17.

**2279.** —— *Genesis* 598: 'þe for þam larum com'. Neophilologus (73:3) 454–60.

**2280.** —— On *Genesis* 623–5. EngS (70:2) 97–106.

**2281.** —— *The Seafarer* 12–17, 25–30, 55–57: 'Dives' and the fictive speaker. SN (61:2) 145–56.

**2282.** VOSS, MANFRED. Quinns Edition der kleineren Cleopatraglossare: Corrigenda und Addenda. *See* **184.**

**2283.** WERT, ELLEN L. The poems of the Anglo-Saxon Chronicles: poetry of convergence. Unpub. doct. diss., Temple Univ. [Abstr. in DA (50) 1654A.]

**2284.** WHITE, STEPHEN D. Kinship and lordship in early medieval England: the story of Sigeberht, Cynewulf, and Cyneheard. Viator (20) 1–18.

**2285.** WILLIAMS, DOUGLAS. *The Seafarer* as an evangelical poem. Lore and Language (8:1) 19–30. (In memory of Stanley B. Greenfield.)

**2286.** YERKES, DAVID. The translation of Gregory's *Dialogues* and its revision: textual history, provenance, authorship. *In* (pp. 335–43) **56.**

**2287.** —— (ed.). The Old English *Life of Machutus*. (Bibl. 1986, 3182.) Rev. by Jane Roberts in UTQ (56:4) 1987, 588–90.

### Related Studies

**2288.** BERSCHIN, WALTER. Biographie und Epochenstil im lateinischen Mittelalter: vol. 1, Von der Passio Perpetuae zu den Dialogi Gregors des Grossen; vol. 2, Merowingische Biographie: Italien, Spanien und die Inseln im frühen Mittelalter. Stuttgart: Hiersemann, 1986; 1988. pp. xii, 358; xii, 337. (Quellen und Untersuchungen zur lateinischen Philologie des Mittelalters, 8–9.)

**2289.** BURNS, J. H. (ed.). The Cambridge history of medieval political thought *c.* 350–*c.* 1450. Cambridge; New York: CUP, 1988. pp. viii, 808. Rev. by David Wallace in SAC (11) 194–202.

**2290.** CLAYTON, MARY. The Assumption homily in CCCC 41. *See* **292.**

**2291.** DAVIS, PATRICIA; SCHLUETER, MARY. The Latin Riddle of the Exeter Book. Archiv (226:1) 92–9.

**2292.** DUMVILLE, DAVID; KEYNES, SIMON (gen. eds). The Anglo-Saxon Chronicle: a collaborative edition: vol. 3, MS A: a semi-diplomatic edition with introduction and notes. Ed. by JANET M. BATELY. (Bibl. 1987, 2922.) Rev. by Lucia Kornexl in Archiv (226:1)

142–4; by D. G. Scragg in Ang (107:1/2) 146–9; by N. F. Blake in YES (19) 298–9; by E. G. Stanley in RES (39:153) 1988, 96–7.

**2293.** ELLIOTT, RALPH W. V.   Runes: an introduction. (Bibl. 1963, 1360.) Manchester: Manchester UP. pp. xiv, 151. (Second ed.: first ed. 1959.) Rev. by J. T. Hooker in TLS, 17 Nov., 1264.

**2294.** ELLIS, MICHAEL EDMOND.   Patterns of spelling variation in the *Anglo-Saxon Chronicle* manuscripts. *See* **777.**

**2295.** FRY, DONALD K.   Bede fortunate in his translator: the Barking nuns. *In* (pp. 345–62) **56.**

**2296.** GLEISSNER, REINHARD.   Some observations on Old English *cyswucu* in the A-version of the Old English *West-Saxon Gospels. In* (pp. 45–68) **38.**

**2297.** GRANT, RAYMOND J. S.   The B text of the Old English Bede: a linguistic commentary. *See* **678.**

**2298.** HOLLANDER, LEE (ed. and trans.).   The Poetic Edda. Austin: Texas UP, 1986. pp. xxix, 343. (Second ed.: first ed. 1964.) Rev. by Stephen A. Mitchell in Spec (63:1) 1988, 170.

**2299.** HOOKE, DELLA (ed.).   Anglo-Saxon settlements. Oxford: Blackwell. pp. 319. Rev. by H. R. Loyn in TLS, 5 May, 492.

**2300.** KIRBY, IAN J.   A runic fragment from Eshaness, Shetland. Nytt om Runer (Oslo) (4) 16–17.

**2301.** LE GOFF, JACQUES.   The birth of purgatory. Trans. by ARTHUR GOLDHAMMER. London: Scolar Press, 1984. pp. ix, 430. Rev. by Alexander Murray in MÆ (56:1) 1987, 115–16.

**2302.** LINDSTRÖM, BENGT.   Corrigendum to SN (60:1) 23–35, 'The Old English Translation of Alcuin's *Liber de virtutibus et vitiis*'. SN (61:1) 128. (*Refers to* bibl. 1988, 1770.)

**2303.** McKINNELL, JOHN (ed. and trans.).   *Viga-Glums Saga*, with the tales of Ögmund Bash and Thorvald Chatterbox. Edinburgh: Canongate; UNESCO, 1987. pp. 160. (New saga library; UNESCO collection of representative works, Icelandic ser.) Rev. by H. Twycross-Martin in DUJ (81:1) 1988, 155–7.

**2304.** MARENBON, JOHN.   Early medieval philosophy (480–1150): an introduction. (Bibl. 1983, 3294.) London: Routledge, 1988. pp. xv, 197. (Revised ed.: first ed. 1983.)

**2305.** ODENSTEDT, BENGT.   The Frisian inscription from Britsum: a reappraisal. *In* (pp. 155–61) **34.**

**2306.** OHLGREN, THOMAS H.   The joys of Valhalla: a cross fragment from Jurby, Isle of Man. OEN (21:2) 1988, 40–1.

**2307.** OLSAN, LEA.   The *Arcus* charms and Christian magic. Neophilologus (73:3) 438–47.

**2308.** ORTENBERG, V. N.   Aspects of monastic devotions to the saints in England, *ca* 950 to *ca* 1100: the liturgical and iconographical evidence. Unpub. doct. diss., Univ. of Cambridge, 1987. [Abstr. in IT (36:4) 1367.]

**2309.** REYNOLDS, SUSAN.   Kingdoms and communities in Western Europe, 900–1300. Oxford: Clarendon Press, 1984. pp. viii, 387. Rev. by P. Wormald in MÆ (56:1) 1987, 112–13.

**2310.** STEIN, WALTER JOHANNES. The ninth century and the Holy Grail. London: Temple Lodge, 1988. pp. xiii, 267.

**2311.** STONEHAM, WILLIAM P. Another Old English note signed 'Coleman'. MÆ (56:1) 1987, 78–82.

**2312.** WALLACE-HADRILL, J. M. Bede's *Ecclesiastical History of the English People*: a historical commentary. Oxford: Clarendon Press. pp. 299. (Oxford medieval texts.) Rev. by H. R. Loyn in TLS, 5 May, 492.

**2313.** WINTERBOTTOM, M. Notes on the Life of Edward the Confessor. MÆ (56:1) 1987, 82–4.

**2314.** WISSOLIK, RICHARD DAVID. The Bayeux Tapestry: its English connection and its peripheral narrative. Unpub. doct. diss., Duquesne Univ., 1988. [Abstr. in DA (50) 451–2A.]

## AUTHORS
### Ælfric

**2315.** DEROLEZ, RENÉ. 'Those things are difficult to express in English. . . .' EngS (70:6) 469–76.

**2316.** FAUSBØLL, ELSE (ed.). Fifty-six Ælfric fragments: the newly-found Copenhagen fragments of Ælfric's *Catholic Homilies*, with facsimiles. (Bibl. 1988, 1808.) Rev. by N. F. Blake in MLR (84:2) 431; by A. Meaney in EngS (70:1) 78–80; by David N. Dumville in Archiv (226:1) 132–4; by M. R. Godden in RES (39:156) 1988, 529–31.

**2317.** JOHANNESSON, NILS-LENNART. Subject topicalization in Ælfric's homilies. *In* (pp. 109–21) **34.**

**2318.** REINSMA, LUKE M. Æelfric: an annotated bibliography. New York; London: Garland, 1987. pp. x, 306. (Garland reference library of the humanities, 617.) Rev. by Helmut Gneuss in Ang (107:1/2) 159–61; by Theodore H. Leinbaugh in Spec (64:3) 760–2.

**2319.** SZARMACH, PAUL E. The earlier homily: *De parasceve*. *In* (pp. 381–99) **56.**

### Aldhelm

**2320.** GWARA, SCOTT JAMES. Aldhelm's 'p's and 'q's in the *Epistola ad Ehfridum*. NQ (36:3) 290–3.

### Alfred

**2321.** BOLTON, W. F. How Boethian is Alfred's *Boethius*? *In* (pp. 153–68) **56.**

**2322.** CLEMENT, RICHARD W. The production of the *Pastoral Care*: King Alfred and his helpers. *In* (pp. 129–52) **56.**

**2323.** FRANTZEN, ALLEN J. King Alfred. (Bibl. 1988, 1815.) Rev. by Daniel Donoghue in Spec (64:2) 425–7.

**2324.** GATCH, MILTON McC. King Alfred's version of Augustine's *Soliloquia*: some suggestions on its rationale and unity. *In* (pp. 17–45) **56.**

**2325.** HORGAN, DOROTHY M. The Old English *Pastoral Care*: the scribal contribution. *In* (pp. 108–27) **56.**

**2326.** MORRISH, JENNIFER. King Alfred's letter as a source on learning in England in the ninth century. *In* (pp. 87–107) **56.**

**2327.** STANLEY, E. G. King Alfred's prefaces. *See* **1423.**

**2328.** STANLEY, ERIC.   Notes on Old English poetry. Leeds Studies in English (20) 319–44.

**2329.** WATERHOUSE, RUTH.   Tone in Alfred's version of Augustine's *Soliloquies. In* (pp. 47–85) **56.**

### Byrhtferth

**2330.** DEROLEZ, RENÉ.   'Those things are difficult to express in English. . . .' *See* **2315.**

### Cædmon

**2331.** OSBORN, MARIJANE.   Translation, translocation, and the native context of *Cædmon's Hymn.* NC (8) 13–23.

**2332.** STANLEY, ERIC.   Notes on Old English poetry. *See* **2328.**

### Cynewulf

**2333.** LASS, ROGER.   Cyn(e)wulf revisited: the problem of the runic signatures. *In* (pp. 17–30) **30.**

**2334.** STEVICK, ROBERT D.   Two notes on *Christ II. See* **396.**

### Wulfstan

**2335.** CROSS, J. E.   Wulfstan's *Incipit de baptismo* (Bethurum VIII A): a revision of sources. NM (90:3/4) 237–42.

**2336.** —— BROWN, ALAN.   Literary impetus for Wulfstan's *Sermo Lupi.* Leeds Studies in English (20) 271–91.

### *BEOWULF*

**2337.** ARCANA, JUDITH.   *Beowulf:* the defeat of the old religion. BSUF (29:3) 1988, 21–36.

**2338.** BALCOM, CYNTHIA ANN.   Ideal structures in Hrothgar's *Ræd.* Unpub. doct. diss., Univ. of Massachusetts. [Abstr. in DA (50) 1308A.]

**2339.** CHRISTENSEN, BONNIEJEAN.   Tolkien's creative technique: *Beowulf* and *The Hobbit.* Mythlore (15:3) 4–10.

**2340.** DENTON, ROBERT F.   *Beowulf,* the Thorkelin transcripts, and the resistance to reading. AEB (ns 2:3) 1988, 101–6.

**2341.** DEROLEZ, RENÉ.   Hrothgar King of Denmark. *In* (pp. 51–8) **42.**

**2342.** FAJARDO-ACOSTA, FIDEL.   The serpent in the mirror: heroism and tragedy in *Beowulf.* Unpub. doct. diss., Univ. of Iowa, 1988. [Abstr. in DA (49) 2210A.]

**2343.** GERRITSEN, JOHAN.   Emending *Beowulf* 2253 – some matters of principle. *See* **316.**

**2344.** GREEN, BRIAN.   'Lof': interlocking denotations in *Beowulf. See* **1057.**

**2345.** HILL, JOHN M.   Revenge and superego mastery in *Beowulf.* Assays (5) 3–36.

**2346.** HUGHES, ERIL BARNETT.   Time in *Beowulf*: an application of narratology. Unpub. doct. diss., Univ. of Arkansas, 1988. [Abstr. in DA (49) 1797A.]

**2347.** HUISMAN, ROSEMARY.   The three tellings of Beowulf's fight with Grendel's mother. Leeds Studies in English (20) 217–48.

**2348.** KIERNAN, KEVIN S.   The Thorkelin transcripts of *Beowulf.* (Bibl. 1987, 163.) Rev. by Rolf H. Bremmer, Jr, in EngS (70:2) 172–3; by T. A. Shippey in Spec (64:3) 727–9.

**2349.** LOGSDON, GAY MARIE.   *Maldon, Brunanburh, Finnsburh Fragment,* and *Finnsburh Episode*: an inquiry into tradition and alternative styles in Old English poetry. *See* **2250.**

**2350.** MEANEY, AUDREY L.   'Scyld Scefing' and the dating of *Beowulf* – again. BJRL (71:1) 7–40. (T. Northcote Toller Memorial Lecture, 1988.)

**2351.** MITCHELL, BRUCE.   *Beowulf*: six notes, mostly syntactical. *See* **969.**

**2352.** MIZUNO, TOMOAKI.   Beowulf as a terrible stranger. JIES (17:1/2) 1–46.

**2353.** MÜLLER, WOLFGANG G.   Syntaktisch-semasiologische Analyse des Grendel-Kampfes im *Beowulf*. LJGG (29) 1988, 9–22.

**2354.** NEAR, MICHAEL RAYMOND.   The formal attire of being: self-consciousness and the representation of identity in Augustine's *Confessions*, the Old English *Beowulf*, and Chaucer's *Troilus*. Unpub. doct. diss., Univ. of California, Berkeley, 1988. [Abstr. in DA (49) 3359A.]

**2355.** OSBORN, MARIJANE.   Beowulf's landfall in 'finna land'. *See* **1183.**

**2356.** OVERING, GILLIAN R.   Reinventing Beowulf's voyage to Denmark. OEN (21:2) 1988, 30–9.

**2357.** SMITS, KATHRYN.   Die 'Stimmen' des schweigenden Königs. Ein Erzählmotiv im *Beowulf*, im *Nibelungenlied* und im *Parzival*. LJGG (27) 1986, 23–45.

**2358.** STANLEY, E. G.   A *Beowulf* allusion, 1790. NQ (36:2) 148.

**2359.** STANLEY, ERIC.   Notes on Old English poetry. *See* **2328.**

**2360.** SVEC, PATRICIA WARD.   Water words in *Beowulf*: principles of selection. *See* **1030.**

**2361.** TRIPP, RAYMOND P., JR.   Did Beowulf have an 'inglorious youth'? SN (61:2) 129–43.

# MIDDLE ENGLISH
# AND FIFTEENTH CENTURY
## GENERAL AND ANONYMOUS

**General Literary Studies;**
**Editions and Studies of Anonymous Writings**
**(except Drama and the Writings of the Gawain Poet)**

**2362.** ACKERMAN, ROBERT W.; DAHOOD, ROGER (eds). *Ancrene Riwle*: introduction and part I. (Bibl. 1988, 1844.) Rev. by Bella Millett in MÆ (56:1) 1987, 117–18.

**2363.** ADAMS, ALISON, *et al.* (eds). The changing face of Arthurian romance: essays on Arthurian prose romances in memory of Cedric E. Pickford. (Bibl. 1988, 1845.) Rev. by Mark Lambert in MLR (84:3) 704.

**2364.** ADAMS, ROBERT. Annual bibliography: 1985. YLS (1) 1987, 161–73.

**2365.** AERS, DAVID (ed.). Medieval literature: criticism, ideology and history. (Bibl. 1986, 33.) Rev. by Pamela Gradon in RES (38:152) 1987, 535–7; by Anne Samson in MLR (84:4) 917–18.

**2366.** AERTSEN, H. The use of dialect words in Middle English alliterative poetry. *In* (pp. 173–85) **47.**

**2367.** AILES, M. J. A comparative study of the medieval French and Middle English verse texts of the *Fierabras* legend. Unpub. doct. diss., Univ. of Reading. [Abstr. in IT (39:2) 482.]

**2368.** ALLEN, ROSAMUND. The date and provenance of *King Horn*: some interim reassessments. *In* (pp. 99–125) **41.**

**2369.** ARENS, WERNER. Late Middle English political poetry as 'public poetry'. *In* (pp. 167–81) **38.**

**2370.** ARMOUR-HILEMAN, VICTORIA LEE. Otherworld motifs and paradigms: a study of Celtic influence on early English literature. Unpub. doct. diss., Univ. of Iowa, 1988. [Abstr. in DA (50) 950A.]

**2371.** ARNGART, O. A commentary on *The Hunting of the Cheviot* text. *See* **281.**

**2372.** BARNETT, GERALD BRUCE. The representation of medieval English texts. *See* **282.**

**2373.** BARR, H. A study of *Mum and the Sothsegger* in its political and literary contexts. *See* **283.**

**2374.** BARRATT, ALEXANDRA. The Five Wits and their structural significance in part II of *Ancrene Wisse*. MÆ (56:1) 1987, 12–24.

**2375.** —— Flying in the face of tradition: a new view of *The Owl and the Nightingale*. UTQ (56:4) 1987, 471–85.

**2376.** BARRON, W. R. J. English medieval romance. (Bibl. 1988, 1853.) Rev. by Claude Gauvin in EA (42:4) 463; by Rosalind Field in Eng (38) 251–5.

**2377.** BATELY, JANET. On some aspects of the vocabulary of the West Midlands in the early Middle Ages: the language of the Katherine Group. *In* (pp. 55–77) **41.**

**2378.** BAWCUTT, PRISCILLA. 'The copill': a crux in *The Kingis Quair*. *See* **284.**

**2379.** —— RIDDY, FELICITY (eds). Longer Scottish poems: vol. 1, 1375–1650. (Bibl. 1988, 1856.) Rev. by A. A. MacDonald in EngS (70:2) 175–7; by Dieter Mehl in Archiv (226:2) 425–8.

**2380.** BENNETT, J. A. W. Middle English literature. Ed. and completed by DOUGLAS GRAY. (Bibl. 1988, 1858.) Rev. by A. C. Spearing in YLS (2) 1988, 155–9; by Götz Schmitz in Archiv (226:1) 147–51; by Dieter Mehl in Ang (107:1/2) 175–80; by Albert E. Hartung in Spec (64:4) 922–5; by John M. Hill in SAC (11) 180–2; by Derek Pearsall in RES (13:153) 1988, 97–9.

**2381.** BENSON, C. DAVID. True Troilus and false Cresseid: the descent from tragedy. *In* (pp. 153–70) **27.**

**2382.** BHATTACHARYA, P. Aspects of prose style in Old and early Middle English. *See* **2209.**

**2383.** BLOOMFIELD, MORTON W. History *and* literature in the vernacular in the Middle Ages? *In* (pp. 309–15) **41.**

**2384.** —— DUNN, CHARLES W. The role of the poet in early societies. Cambridge: Brewer. pp. x, 166.

**2385.** BÖKER, UWE. The epistle mendicant in mediaeval and Renaissance literature: the sociology and poetics of a genre. *In* (pp. 137–65) **38.**

**2386.** —— MARKUS, MANFRED; SCHÖWERLING, RAINER (eds). The living Middle Ages: studies in mediaeval literature and its tradition: a festschrift for Karl Heinz Göller. *See* **38.**

**2387.** BOSSY, MICHEL-ANDRÉ (ed. and trans.). Medieval debate poetry: vernacular works. New York; London: Garland, 1987, pp. xxxi, 191. (Garland library of medieval literature, 52, ser. A.) Rev. by Jan M. Ziolkowski in Spec (64:4) 925.

**2388.** BRAGG, LOIS. *Wulf and Eadwacer*, *The Wife's Lament*, and women's love lyrics of the Middle Ages. *See* **2215.**

**2389.** BRASWELL, LAUREL (ed.). The Index of Middle English prose: handlist 4, A handlist of Douce manuscripts containing Middle English prose in the Bodleian Library, Oxford. (Bibl. 1987, 3029.) Rev. by Jeremy Griffiths in SAC (11) 191–4; by N. F. Blake in EngS (70:5) 453–4.

**2390.** BRASWELL, MARY FLOWERS; BUGGE, JOHN (eds). The Arthurian tradition: essays in convergence. *See* **8.**

**2391.** BREMMER, ROLF HENDRICK, JR (ed.). *The Fyve Wyttes*: a late Middle English devotional treatise: edited from BL MS Harley 2398. (Bibl. 1987, 3030.) Rev. by Jerzy Welna in LeuB (78:2) 225–6; by Alexandra Barratt in EngS (70:5) 452–3; by Veronica M. O'Mara in Archiv (226:1) 171–2; by André Crépin in EA (42:3) 338.

**2392.** BREUER, ROLF. Christian tragedy/tragedy of Christianity. *In* (pp. 183–95) **38.**

**2393.** BREWER, DEREK. Escape from the mimetic fallacy. *In* (pp. 1–10) **58.**

**2394.** —— (ed.). Studies in medieval English romances: some new approaches. *See* **58.**

**2395.** Bunt, Gerrit Hendrik Volken (ed.). William of Palerne, an alliterative romance: re-edited from MS King's College Cambridge 13. (Bibl. 1987, 3032.) Rev. by Marjorie Rigby in RES (39:149) 1987, 67–8; by E. G. Stanley in NQ (36:2) 220–1; by Joanne A. Charbonneau in YLS (1) 1987, 140–3; by Thorlac Turville-Petre in MÆ (56:1) 1987, 125.

**2396.** Burrow, J. A. The ages of man: a study in medieval writing and thought. (Bibl. 1988, 1862.) Rev. by Derek Pearsall in MLR (84:1) 111–12; by John B. Friedman in YLS (3) 142–5; by Hildegard Tristram in Ang (107:1/2) 183–8; by Alison Lee in Eng (36) 1987, 267–71; by Christina von Nolcken in RES (38:152) 1987, 534–5.

**2397.** —— A note on *The Owl and the Nightingale*, line 376. See **1050.**

**2398.** Burton, Julie. Folktale, romance and Shakespeare. *In* (pp. 176–97) **58.**

**2399.** Cable, Thomas. Middle English meter and its theoretical implications. *See* **288.**

**2400.** Cherniss, Michael D. Boethian apocalypse: studies in Middle English vision poetry. (Bibl. 1987, 3040.) Rev. by Esther C. Quinn in Spec (64:3) 688–90.

**2401.** Copeland, Rita. Literary theory in the later Middle Ages. RPh (41:1) 1987, 58–71 (review-article).

**2402.** Craig, Cairns (gen. ed.). The history of Scottish literature: vol. 1, Origins to 1660. Ed. by R. D. S. Jack. (Bibl. 1988, 1870.) Rev. by Elizabeth Archibald in SLJ (supp. 31) 1–3.

**2403.** Crane, Susan Dannenbaum. Insular romance: politics, faith, and culture in Anglo-Norman and Middle English literature. (Bibl. 1988, 1871.) Rev. by Tony Hunt in RES (39:154) 1988, 283–4; by Joseph A. Dane in RPh (42:3) 381–4.

**2404.** Cubitt, Catherine. International medieval bibliography: publications of January–June 1987. Leeds: Univ. of Leeds, 1988. pp. lvi, 256.

**2405.** Dahood, Roger. Design in part I of *Ancrene Riwle*. MÆ (56:1) 1987, 1–11.

**2406.** —— The use of coloured initials and other division markers in early versions of the *Ancrene Riwle*. *In* (pp. 79–97) **41.**

**2407.** Davenport, W. A. Patterns in Middle English dialogues. *In* (pp. 127–45) **41.**

**2408.** Dean, Christopher. Arthur of England: English attitudes to King Arthur and the Knights of the Round Table in the Middle Ages and the Renaissance. Toronto; London: Toronto UP, 1987. pp. xii, 229. Rev. by Phillip Rogers in QQ (94:4) 1988, 920–1; by Helen Cooper in NQ (36:1) 89–90.

**2409.** DiMarco, Vincent. Annual bibliography: 1986; 1987; 1988. YLS (1) 1987, 174–89; (2) 1988, 179–203; (3) 181–213.

**2410.** Dove, Mary. The perfect age of man's life. (Bibl. 1986, 3326.) Rev. by John B. Friedman in YLS (3) 145–52; by Alison Lee in Eng (36) 1987, 267–71; by Götz Schmitz in Archiv (225:2) 1988, 375–9; by Jane

Chance in SAC (11) 208–12; by Thorlac Turville-Petre in RES (39:155) 1988, 424–5.

**2411.** DUBROW, HEATHER; STRIER, RICHARD. Introduction: the historical Renaissance. *In* (pp. 1–12) **31.**

**2412.** DUNCAN, BONNIE ISRAEL. Middle English poems in Harley MS 2253: semiosis and reading scribes. Unpub. doct. diss., Univ. of Iowa, 1988. [Abstr. in DA (50) 1310A.]

**2413.** DUNCAN, THOMAS G. The text and verse-form of 'Adam lay i-bowndyn'. *See* **305.**

**2414.** EBIN, LOIS A. Illuminator, makar, *vates*: visions of poetry in the fifteenth century. Lincoln; London: Nebraska UP, 1988. pp. xiv, 253. Rev. by David J. Parkinson in SLJ (supp. 31) 4–5.

**2415.** ECKHARDT, CAROLINE D. Prophecy and nostalgia: Arthurian symbolism at the close of the English Middle Ages. *In* (pp. 109–26) **8.**

**2416.** EDDEN, VALERIE (ed.). Medieval sermon studies newsletter: 21 and 22. *See* **2225.**

**2417.** EDWARDS, A. S. G.; PEARSALL, DEREK (eds). Middle English prose: essays on bibliographical problems. (Bibl. 1983, 97.) Rev. by G. A. Lester in Lore and Language (8:1) 109.

**2418.** EHRHART, MARGARET J. The judgment of the Trojan prince Paris in medieval literature. Philadelphia: Pennsylvania UP, 1987. pp. xv, 290. (Middle Ages.) Rev. by Noel Harold Kaylor, Jr, in SAC (11) 212–15; by Renate Blumenfeld Kosinski in Spec (64:2) 409–12.

**2419.** ELLIOTT, R. W. V. Landscape and language in Middle English alliterative poetry. PoetT (29/30) 1–16.

**2420.** EVANS, D. SIMON. Medieval religious literature. (Bibl. 1987, 3060.) Rev. by John Scattergood in YES (19) 301–4; by David N. Klausner in Spec (64:2) 412–14.

**2421.** FACINELLI, DIANE A. Treasonous criticisms of Henry IV: the loyal poet of *Richard the Redeless* and *Mum and the Sothsegger*. JRMMRA (10) 51–62.

**2422.** FEIN, SUSANNA. The poetic art of *Death and Life*. YLS (2) 1988, 103–23.

**2423.** FEIN, SUSANNA GREER. *Haue Mercy of Me* (Psalm 51): an unedited alliterative poem from the London Thornton manuscript. *See* **136.**

**2424.** FERGUSON, ARTHUR B. The chivalric tradition in Renaissance England. (Bibl. 1987, 3064.) Rev. by Carol M. Meale in Spec (64:4) 942–5.

**2425.** FEWSTER, CAROL. Traditionality and genre in Middle English romance. (Bibl. 1987, 3065.) Rev. by Rosalind Field in Eng (38) 251–5

**2426.** FICHTE, J. O. *The Awntyrs off Arthure*: an unconscious change of the paradigm of adventure. *In* (pp. 129–36) **38.**

**2427.** FLEMING, C. E. M. E. Ideas of the self in medieval English literature. Unpub. doct. diss., Univ. of Liverpool, 1988. [Abstr. in IT (39:3) 1104.]

**2428.** FORDE, SIMON; CUBITT, CATHERINE. International medieval bibliography: publications of July–December 1987. Leeds: Univ. of Leeds, 1988. pp. lv, 262.

**2429.** FRIEDMAN, JOHN B.    The ages of man. YLS (3) 137–52 (review-article).

**2430.** FURROW, MELISSA.    Middle English fabliaux and modern myth. ELH (56:1) 1–18.

**2431.** FURROW, MELISSA M. (ed.).    Ten fifteenth-century comic poems. (Bibl. 1987, 3067.) Rev. by Andrew Wawn in MLR (84:2) 435–6.

**2432.** GALVÁN, FERNANDO.    Medieval English studies in Spain: a first bibliography. Atlantis (11:1/2) 191–207.

**2433.** GELLRICH, JESSE M.    The idea of the book in the Middle Ages: language theory, mythology and fiction. (Bibl. 1988, 1892, where punctuation of title incorrect.) Rev. by Joseph A. Dane in UTQ (56:2) 1986/87, 365–7; by Rita Copeland in RPh (42:3) 366–70.

**2434.** GOWANS, LINDA.    Cei and the Arthurian legend. (Bibl. 1988, 1895.) Rev. by Marcella McCarthy in NQ (36:4) 497–8.

**2435.** GRAY, DOUGLAS (ed.).    The collected papers of Nevill Coghill, Shakespearian and medievalist. (Bibl. 1988, 2063.) Rev. by Paul R. Thomas in JRMMRA (10) 111–12; by Helen Cooper in NQ (36:2) 226.

**2436.** —— The Oxford book of late medieval verse and prose. (Bibl. 1988, 1897.) Rev. by John Frankis in RES (38:152) 1987, 591–2; by Stephan Kohl in Ang (107:1/2) 199–203.

**2437.** GREEN, RICHARD FIRTH.    Legal satire in *The Tale of Beryn*. SAC (11) 43–62.

**2438.** GUILFOYLE, CHERRELL.    Othello, Otuel, and the English Charlemagne romances. *See* **1166.**

**2439.** HARRIS, SALLY SPONSEL.    An edition of selections from the *Northern Homily Collection*. Unpub. doct. diss., Univ. of Minnesota, 1988. [Abstr. in DA (49) 2229A.]

**2440.** HARTUNG, ALBERT E. (gen. ed.).    A manual of the writings in Middle English 1050–1500: vol. 7. Fasc. 17, John Gower, ed. by JOHN H. FISHER *et al.*; Fasc. 18, Piers Plowman, ed. by ANNE MIDDLETON; Fasc. 19, Travel and geographical writings, ed. by CHRISTIAN K. ZACHER; Fasc. 20, Works of religious and philosophical instruction, ed. by ROBERT R. RAYMO. New Haven: Connecticut Academy of Arts and Sciences, 1986. pp. viii, 403 (2193–595 in the continuous pagination). Rev. by Derek Pearsall in YLS (1) 1987, 148–50.

**2441.** HARVEY, E. RUTH (ed.).    The court of Sapience. (Bibl. 1988, 1904.) Rev. by John Scattergood in MÆ (56:1) 1987, 134–6.

**2442.** HASENFRATZ, ROBERT JOSEPH.    'To ears of flesh and blood': some uses of the sensational in medieval English literature. Unpub. doct. diss., Pennsylvania State Univ., 1988. [Abstr. in DA (50) 439–40A.]

**2443.** HATHAWAY, NEIL.    *Compilatio*: from plagiarism to compiling. Viator (20) 19–44.

**2444.** HEFFERNAN, THOMAS J. (ed.).    The popular literature of medieval England. (Bibl. 1988, 1906.) Rev. by Stephen Knight in YLS (2) 1988, 159–63; by Marjory Rigby in RES (38:151) 1987, 380–1.

**2445.** HEINRICHS, KATHERINE.   Love and Hell: the denizens of Hades in the love poems of the Middle Ages. Neophilologus (73:4) 593–604.

**2446.** HENRY, AVRIL (ed.).   The mirour of mans saluacione: a Middle English translation of *Speculum humanae salvationis*: a critical edition of the fifteenth-century manuscript illustrated from *Der Spiegel der menschen Behältnis*, Speyer, Drach, *c.* 1475. (Bibl. 1988, 1908.) Rev . by Richard Firth Green in SAC (11) 228–31; by S. J. Ogilvie-Thomson in RES (39:156) 1988, 537–8.

**2447.** —— The pilgrimage of the lyfe of the manhode. Translated anonymously into prose from the first recension of Guillaume Deguileville's poem *Le Pèlerinage de la vie humaine*: vol. 1, Introduction and text (Bibl. 1987, 3091.) Rev. by N. F. Blake in MLR (83:3) 1988, 659–60; by Rosemarie Potz McGurr in EngS (69:1) 1988, 85–6.

**2448.** HIRSH, JOHN C. (ed.).   *Barlam and Iosaphat*: a Middle English Life of Buddha. (Bibl. 1988, 1909, where title misspelt.) Rev. by Marjory Rigby in RES (39:156) 1988, 533–4.

**2449.** HOLLADAY, D.   A study of the tradition of the concepts of measure and discretion and its interpretation in some Middle English texts. Unpub. M.Phil. diss., Univ. of Exeter. [Abstr. in IT (39:4) 1628.]

**2450.** HORNER, PATRICK J.   The Index of Middle English prose: handlist 3, A handlist of manuscripts containing Middle English prose in the Digby Collection, Bodleian Library, Oxford. (Bibl. 1987, 3097.) Rev. by S. J. Ogilvie-Thomson in RES (39:154) 1988, 284–5; by H. L. Spencer in SAC (11) 238–41.

**2451.** HOUSUM, MARY ELIZABETH.   A critical edition of Middle English *Sir Cleges. See* **327.**

**2452.** HUDSON, ANNE.   Lollards and their books. (Bibl. 1987, 3098.) Rev. by John Frankis in RES (39:153) 1988, 100–1; by Margaret Aston in MÆ (56:2) 1987, 326–8.

**2453.** JACKSON, W. A.; FERGUSON, F. S.; PANTZER, KATHARINE F. (eds).   A short-title catalogue of books printed in England, Scotland, and Ireland and of English books printed abroad 1475–1640: vol. 1, A–H. By A. W. POLLARD and G. R. REDGRAVE. (Bibl. 1987, 3103.) Rev. by Gordon Williams in RES (39:153) 1988, 148–9; by David Pearson in MLR (84:4) 919–21; by Richard C. Clement in SixCT (19:3) 1988, 520–1.

**2454.** JACOBS, NICOLAS.   Some creative misreadings in *Le Bone Florence of Rome*: an experiment in textual criticism. *In* (pp. 279–84) **41.**

**2455.** KASKE, R. E.; GROOS, ARTHUR; TWOMEY, MICHAEL W. Medieval Christian literary imagery: a guide to interpretation. Toronto; London: Toronto UP, 1988. pp. xxiii, 247. (Toronto medieval bibliographies, 11.)

**2456.** KENDALL, RITCHIE D.   The drama of dissent: the radical poetics of nonconformity, 1380–1590. (Bibl. 1988, 1920.) Rev. by Arthur F. Kinney in MedRen (4) 258–63; by O. B. Hardison, Jr, in Spec (64:2) 456–7.

**2457.** KENNEDY, EDWARD DONALD; WALDRON, RONALD; WITTIG, JOSEPH S. (eds). Medieval English studies presented to George Kane. *See* **41**.

**2458.** KING, JOHN N. English Reformation literature: the Tudor origins of the Protestant tradition. (Bibl. 1985, 2836.) Rev. by Douglas H. Parker in RenR (12:4) 1988, 328–30.

**2459.** KOWALIK, BARBARA. Poetry and testimony: a relationship between some late-medieval poems and their readers. *In* (pp. 46–56) **36**.

**2460.** KRATZMANN, GREGORY; SIMPSON, JAMES (eds). Medieval English religious and ethical literatures: essays in honour of G. H. Russell. (Bibl. 1988, 1920.) Rev. by A. J. Minnis in YLS (3) 163–8; by Anne Hudson in MLR (84:2) 432–3.

**2461.** KRUGER, STEVEN F. Dreams in search of knowledge: the middle vision of Chaucer and his contemporaries. Unpub. doct. diss., Stanford Univ., 1988. [Abstr. in DA (49) 2651A.]

**2462.** LACY, NORRIS J.; ASHE, GEOFFREY. The Arthurian encyclopedia. (Bibl. 1988, 1922.) Rev . by A. H. Diverres in RPh (42:3) 358–61.

**2463.** LAWTON, DAVID A. The diversity of Middle English alliterative poetry. Leeds Studies in English (20) 143–72.

**2464.** LESTER, GEOFFREY (ed.). The earliest English translation of Vegetius' *De re militari*; ed. from Oxford MS Bodl. Douce 291. Heidelberg: Winter, 1988. pp. 229. (Middle English texts, 21.)

**2465.** LINDBERG, CONRAD (ed.). The Middle English Bible: vol. 2, The Book of Baruch. (Bibl. 1988, 2846.) Rev. by Henry Hargreaves in RES (38:150) 1987, 236–7.

**2466.** LISZKA, THOMAS R. MS Laud misc. 108 and the early history of the *South English Legendary. See* **152**.

**2467.** LYNCH, KATHRYN L. The high medieval dream vision: poetry, philosophy, and literary form. Stanford, CA: Stanford UP, 1988. pp. xiv, 263. Rev. by Lois Roney in JRMMRA (10) 97–9; by Anne Eggebroten in ChrisL (38:3) 66–7; by William F. Pollard in SAC (11) 263–5.

**2468.** MCGERR, ROSEMARIE P. Medieval concepts of literary closure: theory and practice. Exemplaria (1:1) 149–79.

**2469.** MCGOLDRICH, L. The literary manuscripts and literary patronage of the Beauchamp and Neville families in the late Middle Ages, *c.* 1390–1500. *See* **154**.

**2470.** MCSPARRAN, FRANCES (ed.). Octovian. Ed. from Lincoln, Dean and Chapter Library, MS 91, and Cambridge, University Library MS Ff.2.38. (Bibl. 1988, 1928, where title incorrect.) Rev. by Ann Squires in DUJ (81:1) 1988, 158.

**2471.** MARX, C. WILLIAM; DRENNAN, JEANNE F. (eds). The Middle English prose *Complaint of Our Lady* and *Gospel of Nicodemus*, ed. from Cambridge, Magdalene College, MS Pepys 2498. *See* **155**.

**2472.** MATSUDA, TAKAMI. Death and transience in the Vernon refrain series. EngS (70:3) 193–205.

**2473.** MATTHEWS, JOHN (ed.). An Arthurian reader; selections from Arthurian legend, scholarship and story. *See* **1720**.

**2474.** MEARNS, RODNEY (ed.).    *The Vision of Tundale*, edited from BL Cotton Caligula A II. (Bibl. 1988, 1930.) Rev. by Kathryn Kerby-Fulton in YES (19) 299–300.

**2475.** MERTENS-FONCK, PAULE.    Tradition and feminism in Middle English literature: source-hunting in the Wife of Bath's portrait and in *The Owl and the Nightingale*. *In* (pp. 175–92) **42.**

**2476.** MILLER, JACQUELINE T.    Poetic license: authority and authorship in medieval and Renaissance contexts. (Bibl. 1988, 1931.) Rev. by A. C. Spearing in Spec (64:1) 189–91.

**2477.** MINNIS, A. J.    Medieval theory of authorship: scholastic literary attitudes in the later Middle Ages. (Bibl. 1988, 1933.) Rev. by Rita Copeland in RPh (41:1) 1987, 58–71.

**2478.** —— (ed.).    Latin and vernacular: studies in late-medieval texts and manuscripts. *See* **157.**

**2479.** —— SCOTT, A. B. (eds); WALLACE, DAVID (asst ed.).    Medieval literary theory and criticism, *c.* 1100–*c.* 1375: the commentary-tradition. Oxford: Clarendon Press; New York: OUP, 1988. pp. xvi, 538.

**2480.** MOFFAT, DOUGLAS (ed.).    *The Soul's Address to the Body*: the Worcester fragments. East Lansing, MI: Colleagues Press, 1987. pp. viii, 133. (Medieval texts and studies, 1.) Rev. by Erik Kooper in EngS (70:3) 270–1; by Christine Franzen in NQ (36:1) 79; by O. S. Pickering in Archiv (226:1) 155–7; by A. S. G. Edwards in MLR (84:2) 429–30.

**2481.** MORGAN, GWENDOLYN ANNE.    Medieval balladry and the courtly tradition. Unpub. doct. diss., Univ. of South Florida. [Abstr. in DA (50) 1301A.]

**2482.** MOUS, PETER H. J. (ed.).    The southern version of *Cursor Mundi*: vol. 4, lines 17289–21346. (Bibl. 1988, 1936.) Rev. by James R. Sprouse in SAC (11) 265–7.

**2483.** MUELLER, JANEL M.    The native tongue and the word: developments in English prose style 1380–1580. (Bibl. 1988, 1937.) Rev. by B. D. H. Miller in RES (38:151) 1987, 378–9; by Anne Hudson in MÆ (56:1) 1987, 130–2.

**2484.** MÜLLENBROCK, HEINZ-JOACHIM. The Middle Ages in eighteenth-century England: a guide to periodization? *In* (pp. 197–209) **38.**

**2485.** NEVANLINNA, SAARA (ed.).    The Northern Homily Cycle: the expanded version in MSS Harley 4196 and Cotton Tiberius E vii, parts 1–3: vol. 38, From Advent to Septuagesima. (Bibl. 1977, 3051.) Rev. by Karla Taylor in MLR (84:3) 707–8.

**2486.** —— The Northern Homily Cycle: the expanded version in MSS Harley 4196 and Cotton Tiberius E vii, parts 1–3: vol. 41, From Septuagesima to the Fifth Sunday after Trinity. (Bibl. 1973, 3322.) Rev. by Karla Taylor in MLR (84:3) 707–8.

**2487.** —— The Northern Homily Cycle: the expanded version in MSS Harley 4196 and Cotton Tiberius E vii, parts 1–3: vol. 43, From the Fifth to the Twenty-Fifth Sunday after Trinity. (Bibl. 1988, 1938.) Rev. by Karla Taylor in MLR (85:3) 707–8.

**2488.** NEWMAN, FRANCIS X.    Social unrest in the Middle Ages: papers of the fifteenth Annual Conference of the Center for Medieval and Early Renaissance Studies. (Bibl. 1987, 63.) Rev. by Judith M. Bennett in YLS (2) 1988, 163–6; by F. C. de Vries in RES (39:155) 1988, 425–6; by John Scattergood in YES (19) 301–4.

**2489.** O'MARA, VERONICA M. An unknown Middle English translation of a Brigittine work. NQ (36:2) 162–4. (*Revelations.*)

**2490.** PAGE, STEPHEN FREDERICK. Literature and culture in late medieval East Anglia. Unpub. doct. diss., Ohio State Univ., 1988. [Abstr. in DA (49) 2233A.]

**2491.** PATTERSON, LEE. Negotiating the past: the historical understanding of medieval literature. (Bibl. 1988, 1942.) Rev. by John M. Ganim in SAC (11) 267–70; by Derek Brewer in Spec (64:3) 751–3.

**2492.** PEARCY, ROY J. '*La Prière du plus grand péril*' in medieval English literature. Leeds Studies in English (20) 119–41.

**2493.** PEARSALL, DEREK. The development of Middle English romance. *In* (pp. 11–35) **58.** (Repr. from MedStud (27) 1965, 91–116.)

**2494.** —— (ed.). Manuscripts and texts: editorial problems in later Middle English literature: essays from the 1985 conference at the University of York. (Bibl. 1988, 1943.) Rev. by Charles A. Owen in SAC (11) 270–3; by N. F. Blake in MLR (84:4) 914–16.

**2495.** PHILLIPS, HELEN. The ghost's baptism in *The Awntyrs off Arthure*. MÆ (58:1) 49–58.

**2496.** PICKERING, O. S. A Middle English prose miracle of the Virgin, with hidden verses. MÆ (57:2) 1988, 219–39.

**2497.** —— The present popularity of Middle English manuscript studies: some recent work reviewed. *See* **161.**

**2498.** —— (ed.). The South English ministry and passion, ed. from St John's College, Cambridge, MS B.6. (Bibl. 1987, 3151.) Rev. by A. S. G. Edwards in YES (19) 300–1; by R. Hamer in MÆ (56:1) 1987, 118–19; by Thomas J. Heffernan in Spec (64:3) 755–6.

**2499.** —— POWELL, SUSAN. The Index of Middle English prose: handlist 6, A handlist of manuscripts containing Middle English prose in Yorkshire libraries and archives. Cambridge: Brewer; Wolfeboro, NH: Boydell & Brewer. pp. xviii, 81.

**2500.** PSAKI, FRANCIES REGINA. The medieval lyric-narrative hybrid: formal play and narratorial subjectivity. Unpub. doct. diss., Cornell Univ. [Abstr. in DA (50) 682A.]

**2501.** RANSOM, DANIEL. Poets at play: irony and parody in the Harley Lyrics. (Bibl. 1986, 3413.) Rev. by Ian Bishop in YES (19) 304–5; by Michael J. Franklin in MÆ (56:1) 1987, 128–30.

**2502.** REGNIER-BÖHLER, DANIELLE (ed.). La légende arthurienne: le Graal et la table ronde. Paris: Laffont. pp. 1206. (Bouquins.)

**2503.** REMLEY, PAUL G. *Muscipula diaboli* and medieval English antifeminism. EngS (70:1) 1–14.

**2504.** RICHARDSON, MALCOLM. Medieval English vernacular correspondence: notes toward an alternative rhetoric. Allegorica (10) 95–118.

**2505.** RIDER, JEFF.   Other voices: historicism and the interpretation of medieval texts. Exemplaria (1:2) 293–312.

**2506.** RIMMER, E. M.   The role of the hero in the romances of Britain. Unpub. M.Litt. diss., Univ. of Stirling, 1988. [Abstr. in IT (39:1) 30.]

**2507.** RINGLER, WILLIAM A., JR.   Bibliography and index of English verse printed 1476–1558. London: Mansell, 1988. pp. viii, 440. Rev. by David McKitterick in TLS, 9 June, 645.

**2508.** ROSE, MARY BETH (ed.).   Women in the Middle Ages and the Renaissance: literary and historical perspectives. (Bibl. 1988, 1952.) Rev. by Jonathan W. Nicholls in MLR (84:1) 114–15.

**2509.** ROSSER, MARION DORTCH.   A critical edition of the Middle English *Horn Childe and Maiden Rimnild*. See **386.**

**2510.** ROSTON, MURRAY.   Renaissance perspectives in literature and the visual arts. (Bibl. 1988, 1953.) Rev. by Constance Jordan in ELN (27:2) 67–71; by Ernest B. Gilman in RQ (42:4) 871–4.

**2511.** SARGENT, MICHAEL G.   James Grenehalgh as textual critic. Salzburg: Institut für Anglistik und Amerikanistik, Salzburg Univ., 1984. 2 vols. pp. 589. (Analecta cartusiana, 85.) Rev. by Bella Millett in MÆ (56:1) 1987, 136–7.

**2512.** SCATTERGOOD, JOHN.   Two unrecorded poems from Trinity College Dublin MS 490. See **176.**

**2513.** ——— (ed.).   Literature and learning in medieval and Renaissance England: essays presented to Fitzroy Pyle. (Bibl. 1987, 40.) Rev. by Anne Samson in YES (19) 307.

**2514.** SCHEPS, WALTER; LOONEY, J. ANNA.   Middle Scots poets: a reference guide to James I of Scotland, Robert Henryson, William Dunbar, and Gavin Douglas. (Bibl. 1988, 3169.) Rev. by Sally Mapstone in RES (38:151) 1987, 383–4.

**2515.** SCOTT, ANNE.   Plans, predictions, and promises: traditional story techniques and the configuration of word and deed in *King Horn*. In (pp. 37–68) **58.**

**2516.** SCOTT, ANNE MARIE.   'Do nu ase þu sedes': word and deed in *King Horn, Havelok the Dane*, and the Franklin's Tale. Unpub. doct. diss., Brown Univ., 1988. [Abstr. in DA (49) 2214A.]

**2517.** SEARS, ELIZABETH.   The ages of man: medieval interpretations of the life cycle. (Bibl. 1987, 3356.) Rev. by John B. Friedman in YLS (3) 137–42.

**2518.** SHEPHERD, S. H. A.   Four Middle English Charlemagne romances: a revaluation of the non-cyclic verse texts and the holograph *Sir Ferumbras*. See **393.**

**2519.** SKEY, MIRIAM.   The death of Herod in the *Cursor Mundi*. MÆ (57:1) 1988, 74–80.

**2520.** SMALLWOOD, T. M.   'God was born in Bethlehem ...': the tradition of a Middle English charm. MÆ (58:2) 206–23.

**2521.** SMITHERS, G. V.   The style of *Hauelok*. MÆ (57:2) 1988, 190–218.

**2522.** SPEARING, A. C.   Medieval to Renaissance in English poetry.

(Bibl. 1988, 1960.) Rev. by Michael G. Brennan in RES (38:149) 68–9; by David Lawton in YLS (1) 1987, 155–9.

**2523.** —— Readings in medieval poetry. (Bibl. 1988, 1961.) Rev. by Joerg O. Fichte in SAC (11) 290–3; by George Jack in EngS (70:1) 83–4.

**2524.** SPROUSE, JAMES R.    The textual relationships of the un-expanded Middle English *Northern Homily Cycle*. *See* **395.**

**2525.** SPROUSE, JAMES RICHARDSON.    An edition of the sermon for the Second Sunday of Advent from the manuscripts of the unexpanded Middle English Northern Homily Cycle: textual and dialectical intro-ductions, text, table of variant readings, and glossary. *See* **395a.**

**2526.** STANLEY, E. G.    Rhymes in English medieval verse: from Old English to Middle English. *In* (pp. 19–54) **41.**

**2527.** STAUFFENBERG, HENRY J. (ed.).    The southern version of *Cursor Mundi*: vol. 3, lines 12713–17082. (Bibl. 1988, 1963.) Rev. by Derek Pearsall in RES (39:153) 1988, 99–100.

**2528.** STEPHEN, RUSSELL J.    The English dream vision: anatomy of a form. Columbus: Ohio State UP, 1988. pp. ix, 244. Rev. by Rosemarie Potz McGerr in CR (33:2) 188–9.

**2529.** STEVENS, JOHN.    Words and music in the Middle Ages: song, narrative, dance and drama, 1050–1350. Cambridge: CUP, 1986, pp. xviii, 554. (Cambridge studies in music.) Rev. by Jeremy Yudkin in Spec (64:3) 765–9.

**2530.** STIEVE, EDWIN M.    Medical and moral interpretations of plague and pestilence in late Middle English texts. Unpub. doct. diss., Michigan State Univ., 1988. [Abstr. in DA (49) 3037A.]

**2531.** SUZUKI, EIICHI (ed.).    Chueigo touinshi no gengo to buntai. (The language and style of Middle English alliterative poetry.) Tokyo: Gaku. pp. vi, 136.

**2532.** SZITTYA, PENN R.    The antifraternal tradition in medieval literature. (Bibl. 1988, 1965.) Rev. by Christina von Nolcken in MP (86:3) 292–4; by John Scattergood in YES (19) 301–4; by Katherine Walsh in YLS (2) 1988, 174–6; by S. Ogilvie-Thomson in RES (39:153) 1988, 159.

**2533.** THOMPSON, JOHN J.    Literary associations of an anonymous Middle English paraphrase of Vulgate Psalm L. MÆ (57:1) 1988, 38–55.

**2534.** —— Robert Thornton and the London Thornton manuscript: British Library MS Additional 31042. *See* **181.**

**2535.** TRIGG, STEPHANIE.    The rhetoric of excess in *Winner and Waster*. YLS (3) 91–108.

**2536.** TURVILLE-PETRE, THORLAC.    Alliterative poetry of the later Middle Ages: an anthology. London: Routledge. pp. xiii, 261. (Rout-ledge medieval English texts.)

**2537.** —— The author of *The Destruction of Troy*. MÆ (57:2) 1988, 264–9.

**2538.** URQUHART, E. A.    Fifteenth-century literary culture with particular reference to the patterns of patronage, focussing on the

Stafford family during the fifteenth century. Unpub. doct. diss., Univ. of Sheffield, 1988. [Abstr. in IT (39:2) 484.]

**2539.** VALDMAN, BERTRAND ANDRÉ. The metaphor of commerce and the quest of the self in Arthurian romance literature. Unpub. doct. diss., Stanford Univ., 1987. [Abstr. in DA (48) 1988, 2870A.]

**2540.** VANCE, EUGENE. From topic to tale: logic and narrativity in the Middle Ages. Introd. by WLAD GODZICH. Minneapolis: Minnesota UP, 1987. pp. xxxiii, 131. (Theory and history of literature, 47.) Rev. by Donald Maddox in Spec (64:1) 231–5.

**2541.** WALLNER, BJÖRN (ed.). The Middle English translation of Guy de Chauliac's treatise on 'Apostemes': Book II of *The Great Surgery*. Ed. from MS New York Academy of Medicine 12 and related MSS: part 1, Text; part 2, Introduction, notes, glossary, marginalia and Latin appendix. Lund: Lund UP; Bromley: Chartwell-Bratt, 1988; 1989. 2 vols. pp. 190; 185. (Skrifter utgivna av Vetenskapssocieteten i Lund, 80, 82.)

**2542.** WALSH, C. R. *Sir Perceval of Galles*: a critical study. Unpub. M.Phil. diss., Univ. of Exeter. [Abstr. in IT (39:4) 1628.]

**2543.** WENZEL, SIEGFRIED. Preachers, poets, and the early English lyric. (Bibl. 1988, 1972.) Rev. by S. J. Ogilvie-Thomson in RES (39:155) 1988, 423–4; by Thomas G. Duncan in MLR (84:2) 432–4.

**2544.** WHITMAN, JON. Allegory: the dynamics of an ancient and medieval technique. (Bibl. 1988, 1974.) Rev. by John Bowers in YLS (3) 174–8; by Gordon Teskey in MP (86:4) 418–21.

**2545.** WILSON, EDWARD. The debate of the carpenter's tools. See **187.**

**2546.** WILSON, JOHN. *Havelok the Dane*, line 1349: 'til'. See **409.**

**2547.** WOODS, MARJORIE CURRY. An unfashionable rhetoric in the fifteenth century. See **1326.**

## Drama

**2548.** ANON. *Homo, memento, finis*: the iconography of just judgment in medieval art and drama. Kalamazoo: Medieval Inst., Western Michigan Univ., 1985. pp. xi, 219, (plates) 27. (Early drama, art and music monographs, 6.) Rev. by Peter W. Travis in MedRen (4) 256–8.

**2549.** BALKIN, MARTHA MUNSELL. The Renaissance tool villain and his medieval heritage. Unpub. doct. diss., Univ. of Notre Dame, 1988. [Abstr. in DA (49) 1795–6A.]

**2550.** BUCHANAN-OLIVER, MARGO. *Media vitae in morte sumus*: patterns of life and death in the English mediaeval morality drama, with special reference to the play *Mankind*. Unpub. doct. diss., Univ. of Auckland.

**2551.** CLOPPER, LAWRENCE M. The Chester Cycle: review article. MedRen (2) 1985, 283–91.

**2552.** DAVIDSON, CLIFFORD. From creation to doom: the York Cycle of Mystery plays. (Bibl. 1986, 3460.) Rev. by Alexandra F. Johnston in MedRen (3) 1986, 305–7.

**2553.** DOUGLAS, AUDREY; GREENFIELD, PETER (eds). Records of early English drama: Cumberland, Westmorland, Gloucestershire. (Bibl. 1988, 2285.) Rev. by Clifford Davidson in MedRen (4) 237–40.

**2554.** EL ITREBY, ELIZABETH J.    The N-Town play of *The Woman Taken in Adultery* central to a recapitulative 'redemption trilogy'. BSUF (26:3) 1985, 3–13.

**2555.** EPP, GARRETT PETER JANTZ.    The imitation of the word: the York Cycle and the poetics of realism. Unpub. doct. diss., Univ. of Toronto, 1988. [Abstr. in DA (49) 2666A.]

**2556.** FIONDELLA, MARIS G.    Framing and ideology in the Towneley *Creation* play. Exemplaria (1:2) 401–27.

**2557.** HAPPÉ, PETER.    Acting the York Mystery plays: a consideration of modes. METh (10:2) 1988, 112–16.

**2558.** HARRIS, MAX.    Flesh and spirits: the battle between virtues and vices in medieval drama re-assessed. MÆ (57:1) 1988, 56–64.

**2559.** HILLIARD, MARGARET WILSON.    To sacrifice a child: the development of a theme in medieval and Renaissance drama. Unpub. doct. diss., Univ. of Tennessee. [Abstr. in DA (50) 1664–5A.]

**2560.** JOHNSTON, A. F. (ed.).    Editing early English drama: special problems and new directions. Papers given at the nineteenth Annual Conference on Editorial Problems, University of Toronto, 4–5 November 1983. *See* **333.**

**2561.** KROLL, NORMA.    Cosmic characters and human form: dramatic interaction and conflict in the Chester Cycle *Fall of Lucifer*. MedRen (2) 1985, 33–50.

**2562.** LANCASHIRE, IAN.    Dramatic texts and records of Britain: a chronological topography to 1558. (Bibl. 1986, 3472.) Rev. by Thomas Pettitt in RenR (12:4) 1988, 318–24.

**2563.** LUMIANSKY, R. M.; MILLS, DAVID (eds).    The Chester Mystery Cycle: essays and documents. (Bibl. 1986, 3475.) Rev. by Lawrence M. Clopper in MedRen (2) 1985, 283–91.

**2564.** —————— The Chester Mystery Cycle: vol. 2, Commentary and glossary. (Bibl. 1988, 1983.) Rev. by Sarah Carpenter in RES (39:154) 1988, 285–7; by Alexandra F. Johnston in NQ (36:3) 371–2.

**2565.** MEREDITH, PETER (ed.).    The Mary play from the N-Town manuscript. London; New York: Longman, 1987. pp. vii, 185. Rev. by Claude Gauvin in EA (42:4) 461–3.

**2566.** —————— TAILBY, JOHN E. (eds).    The staging of religious drama in Europe in the later Middle Ages: texts and documents in English translation. (Bibl. 1986, 3479, where title incomplete.) Rev. by Steven Urkowitz in MedRen (3) 1986, 335–7.

**2567.** MILLS, DAVID.    Netta Syrett and *The Old Miracle Plays of England*. METh (10:2) 1988, 117–28.

**2568.** NEUSS, PAULA (ed.).    Aspects of early English drama. (Bibl. 1985, 2931.) Rev. by John Wasson in MedRen (3) 1986, 337–8.

**2569.** NICHOLS, ANN ELJENHOLM.    Lollard language in the Croxton *Play of the Sacrament*. *See* **1025.**

**2570.** RIGGIO, MILLA COZART.    The staging of medieval drama: pictures and icons. CEACrit (51:4) 31–9.

**2571.** SOMERSET, J. A. B.    Local drama and playing places at

Shrewsbury: new findings from the Borough Records. MedRen (2) 1985, 1–31.

**2572.** SPINRAD, PHOEBE S.    The summons of death on the medieval and Renaissance English stage. Columbus: Ohio State UP, 1987. pp. xii, 334. Rev. by James M. Gibson in ChrisL (38:3) 69–70.

**2573.** STEVENS, MARTIN.    Four Middle English Mystery Cycles: textual, contextual and critical interpretations. (Bibl. 1987, 3237.) Rev. by Alan H. Nelson in ELN (27:2) 62–5; by Daniel F. Pigg in SAC (11) 293–6.

**2574.** SUEMATSU, YOSHIMICHI.    The Towneley *Mactacio Abel* seen through the Fall of Man and Christ's Passion. StudME (4) 91–109.

**2575.** TRAVIS, PETER W.    Dramatic design in the Chester Cycle. (Bibl. 1985, 2938.) Rev. by J. A. B. Somerset in MedRen (4) 310–13.

**2576.** TRINGHAM, NIGEL K.    The Whitsuntide commemoration of St William of York: a note. REEDNewsletter (14:2) 10–12.

**2577.** TYDEMAN, WILLIAM.    English medieval theatre, 1400–1500. (Bibl. 1987, 3243.) Rev. by David Mills in RES (38:150) 1987, 239–40; by Peter Meredith in MLR (84:4) 923–4; by Alexandra F. Johnston in NQ (36:3) 372–3.

**2578.** WASSON, JOHN.    Professional actors in the Middle Ages and early Renaissance. MedRen (1) 1984, 1–11.

**2579.** WASSON, JOHN M. (ed.).    Records of early English drama: Devon. Toronto; London; Buffalo, NY: Toronto UP, 1986. pp. lxxvi, 623. Rev. by William Tydeman in MedRen (4) 314–18.

**2580.** WENZEL, SIEGFRIED.    'Somer game' and sermon references to a Corpus Christi play. MP (86:3) 274–83.

**2581.** WICKHAM, GLYNNE.    The medieval theatre. (Bibl. 1976, 3673.) Cambridge: CUP, 1987. pp. xiv, 260. (Third ed.: first ed. 1974.)

**2582.** WRIGHT, STEPHEN K.    The manuscript of *Sanctus Tewdricus*: rediscovery of a 'lost miracle play' from St Omers. *See* **189.**

## Related Studies

**2583.** ALLEN, PETER L.    *Ars amandi, ars legendi*: love poetry and literary theory in Ovid, Andrea Capellanus, and Jean de Meun. Exemplaria (1:1) 181–205.

**2584.** ANTONELLI, ROBERTO.    The birth of Criseyde – an exemplary triangle: 'classical' Troilus and the question of love at the Anglo-Norman court. *In* (pp. 21–48) **27.**

**2585.** ASHBY-BEACH, GENETTE.    *The Song of Roland*: a generative study of the formulaic language in the single combat. Amsterdam: Rodopi, 1985. pp. 190. (Faux titre, 20.) Rev. by Roger Pensom in MÆ (56:2) 1987, 329–30.

**2586.** ASHE, GEOFFREY.    The convergence of Arthurian studies. *In* (pp. 10–28) **8.**

**2587.** BAKER, J. H.    A French vocabulary and conversation-guide in a fifteenth-century legal notebook. MÆ (58:1) 80–102.

**2588.** BARBER, RICHARD; BARKER, JULIET.    Tournaments, jousts, chivalry and pageants in the Middle Ages. Woodbridge: Boydell. pp. 225.

**2589.** BENNETT, JUDITH M.   Women in the medieval English countryside: gender and household in Brigstock before the Plague. Oxford; New York: OUP, 1987. pp. xv, 322. Rev. by Priscilla Martin in YLS (3) 153–6.

**2590.** BERSCHIN, WALTER.   Biographie und Epochenstil im lateinischen Mittelalter: vols 1 and 2. *See* **2288.**

**2591.** BLACKER-KNIGHT, JEAN.   Transformations of a theme: the depoliticization of the Arthurian world in the *Roman de Brut. In* (pp. 54–74) **8.**

**2592.** BROOK, LESLIE C.   Guigemar and the white hind. MÆ (56:1) 1987, 94–101.

**2593.** BURNS, J. H. (ed.).   The Cambridge history of medieval political thought *c.* 350–*c.* 1450. *See* **2289.**

**2594.** BUSBY, KEITH.   *Cristal et Clarie*: a novel romance? *In* (pp. 77–103) **16.**

**2595.** CAMPBELL, THOMAS P.; DAVIDSON, CLIFFORD (eds).   The Fleury playbook. (Bibl. 1987, 3268.) Rev. by John Stevens in NQ (36:1) 90–1.

**2596.** CAVANAUGH, SUSAN H.   The identification of a lost English analogue of the 'Death of Begon' episode from the Old French epic *Garin de Loherain.* MÆ (57:1) 1988, 64–7.

**2597.** CHAMBERS, FRANK M.   An introduction to Old Provençal versification. Philadelphia: American Philosophical Soc., 1985. pp. viii, 299. Rev. by J. H. Marshall in MÆ (56:2) 1987, 341–2.

**2598.** CLASSEN, ALBRECHT.   Emergence from the dark: female epistolary literature in the Middle Ages. JRMMRA (10) 1–15.

**2599.** —— Emperor Sigismund's visit to England in 1416: its observation and reflection in late medieval chronicles. Archiv (226:2) 276–90.

**2600.** COBBAN, ALAN B.   The medieval English universities: Oxford and Cambridge to *c.* 1500. Berkeley: California UP; Aldershot: Scolar Press, 1988. pp. xvii, 465. Rev. by Damian Leader in RQ (42:4) 826–8.

**2601.** —— The role of colleges in the medieval universities of northern Europe, with special reference to England and France. BJRL (71:1) 49–70.

**2602.** COOK, ROBERT FRANCIS.   The sense of the song in *The Song of Roland.* Ithaca, NY; London: Cornell UP, 1987. pp. xix, 266. Rev. by Ross G. Arthur in SAC (11) 202–4.

**2603.** COURTENAY, WILLIAM J.   Schools and scholars in fourteenth-century England. Princeton, NJ: Princeton UP, 1987. pp. xix, 435. Rev. by Denis N. Baker in YLS (3) 156–9.

**2604.** CRICK, J. C.   The reception of Geoffrey of Monmouth's *Historia regum britannie*: the evidence of manuscripts and textual history. *See* **129.**

**2605.** CRICK, JULIA C.   The *Historia regum britannie* of Geoffrey of Monmouth: 3, A summary catalogue of the manuscripts. *See* **130.**

**2606.** CUMMINS, JOHN.   The hound and the hawk: the art of medieval hunting. London: Weidenfeld & Nicholson, 1988. pp. x, 306.

**2607.** CURTIS, RENÉE L. (ed.).   Le Roman de Tristan en prose: vol. 3.

Cambridge: Brewer, 1985. pp. lxi, 294. (Arthurian studies, 14.) Rev. by Keith Busby in MÆ (56:2) 1987, 335–6.

**2608.** DE RIJK, L. M.   Through language to reality: studies on medieval semantics and metaphysics. Ed. by E. P. Bos. *See* **702.**

**2609.** DRONKE, PETER.   Dante and medieval Latin traditions. (Bibl. 1988, 2010.) Rev. by Cecil Grayson in RES (38:151) 1987, 379–80.

**2610.** DUGGAN, LAWRENCE G.   Was art really the 'book' of the illiterate? Word & Image (5:3) 227–51.

**2611.** DUMONT, STEPHEN.   Theology as a science and Duns Scotus's distinction between intuitive and abstractive cognition. Spec (64:3) 579–99.

**2612.** ECO, UMBERTO.   Art and beauty in the Middle Ages. Trans. by HUGH BREDIN. New Haven, CT; London: Yale UP, 1986. pp. x, 131. Rev. by Martine Rey in JRMMRA (9) 1988, 172–3.

**2613.** ELLIS, ROGER.   'Viderunt eam filie Syon': the spirituality of the English house of a medieval contemplative order from its beginnings to the present day. Salzburg: Institut für Anglistik und Amerikanistik, Salzburg Univ., 1984. pp. 190. (Analecta cartusiana, 68; The contemplative life in Great Britain: Carthusians, Benedictines, Bridgettines, 2.) Rev. by Bella Millett in MÆ (56:1) 1987, 137–8.

**2614.** ERLER, MARY; KOWALESKI, MARYANNE (eds).   Women and power in the Middle Ages. Athens; London: Georgia UP, 1988. pp. 277. Rev. by Charlotte C. Morse in SAC (11) 215–18; by Joan M. West in JRMMRA (10) 101–2.

**2615.** ERZGRÄBER, WILLI.   European literature in the late Middle Ages in its political and social contexts. *In* (pp. 103–21) **42.**

**2616.** FLECKENSTEIN, JOSEF (ed.).   Das ritterliche Turnier im Mittelalter. Beiträge zu einer vergleichenden Formen- und Verhaltensgeschichte des Rittertums. Göttingen: Vandenhoeck & Ruprecht, 1986. pp. 669, (plates) 23. Rev. by D. H. Green in MLR (84:4) 901–2.

**2617.** FRIES, MAUREEN.   Boethian themes and tragic structure in Geoffrey of Monmouth's *Historia regum britannie. In* (pp. 29–42) **8.**

**2618.** GIES, FRANCES; GIES, JOSEPH.   Marriage and the family in the Middle Ages. New York; London: Harper & Row, 1987. pp. viii, 369. (Perennial library.) Rev. by Judith M. Bennett in Spec (64:2) 432–3.

**2619.** GRASSI, CAROLUS A. (ed.).   Tractatus de quantitate; et Tractatus de corpore Christi. St Bonaventure, NY: St Bonaventure UP, 1986. pp. 253. (Opera philosophica et theologica: opera theologica, 10.) Rev. by Thomas Michael Tomasic in Spec (64:3) 711–13.

**2620.** GREEN, JUDITH A.   The government of England under Henry I. Cambridge: CUP, 1986, pp. xii, 303. (Cambridge studies in medieval life and thought, 4:3.) Rev. by T. N. Bisson in Spec (64:2) 436–8.

**2621.** GRILLO, P. R.   Was Marie de France the daughter of Waleran II, Count of Meulan? MÆ (57:2) 1988, 269–74.

**2622.** HAHN, CYNTHIA.   Purification, sacred action, and the vision of God: viewing medieval narratives. Word & Image (5:1) 71–84.

**2623.** HAMBURGER, JEFFREY.   The visual and the visionary: the image in late medieval monastic devotions. Viator (20) 161–82.

**2624.** HANNA, RALPH, III.     Sir Thomas Berkeley and his patronage. Spec (64:4) 878–916.

**2625.** HAROIAN, GILLISANN.     The Cornish mermaid: the fine thread of androgyny in the *Ordinalia*. MedRen (4) 1–11.

**2626.** HENRY, AVRIL (ed.).     Biblia pauperum. *See* **89.**

**2627.** HINDMAN, SANDRA L.     Christine de Pizan's *Epistre Othea*: painting and politics at the court of Charles VI. Toronto: Pontifical Inst. of Mediaeval Studies, 1986. pp. xxii, 229. (Studies and texts, 77.)

**2628.** HUGHES, JONATHAN.     Pastors and visionaries: religion and secular life in late medieval London. Woodbridge; Wolfeboro, NH: Boydell & Brewer, 1988. pp. 419.

**2629.** HULT, DAVID F.     Steps forward and steps backward: more on Chrétien's *Lancelot*. Spec (64:2) 307–16.

**2630.** HUNT, TONY.     *Deliciae clericorum*: intellectual and scientific pursuits in two Dorset monasteries. MÆ (56:2) 1987, 159–82.

**2631.** IGLESIAS RÁBADE, LUIS.     The language of pleading in the manorial courts of late 13th-century England, with examples drawn from the court of the manor of Hales Owen. *See* **681.**

**2632.** ILLINGWORTH, R. N.     The structure of the *Passion* of Clermont-Ferrand. MÆ (57:2) 1988, 274–84.

**2633.** JAGER, ERIC.     Reading the *Roman* inside out: the dream of Croesus as a *caveat lector*. MÆ (57:1) 1988, 67–74.

**2634.** JEFFERSON, LISA.     The keys to the enchantments of Dolorous Gard. MÆ (58:1) 59–79.

**2635.** JEFFREY, DAVID LYLE (ed.).     The law of love: English spirituality in the age of Wyclif. Grand Rapids, MI: Eerdmans, 1988. pp. x, 404. Rev. by William Reynolds in ChrisL (38:4) 87–9.

**2636.** KELLER, HANS-ERICH, *et al.* (eds).     Studia occitanica in memoriam Paul Remy: vol. 2, The Narrative–Philology. Kalamazoo: Medieval Inst., Western Michigan Univ., 1986. pp. 441. Rev. by M. B. Booth in MLR (84:1) 154–5; by William D. Paden in Spec (64:3) 725–7.

**2637.** KEMP, B. R. (ed.).     Reading Abbey cartularies: BL MSS, Egerton 3031, Harley 1708, and Cotton Vespasian E xxv: 1, General documents and those relating to English counties other than Berkshire. London: Royal Historical Soc., 1986. pp. xvi, 486. (Camden fourth ser., 31.) Rev. by William T. Reedy in Spec (64:2) 454–6.

**2638.** KENNEDY, ANGUS J. (ed.).     Christine de Pizan's *Epistre de la prison de vie humaine*. Glasgow: Glasgow UP, 1984. pp. 83. Rev. by Kenneth Varty in MÆ (56:1) 1987, 145–6.

**2639.** KESSLER, HERBERT L.     Reading ancient and medieval art. Word & Image (5:1) 1–18.

**2640.** KRISTELLER, PAUL OSKAR.     The active and the contemplative life in Renaissance Humanism. *In* (pp. 133–52) BRIAN VICKERS (ed.), Arbeit, Musse, Meditation: Betrachtungen zur *Vita activa* und *Vita contemplativa*. Zurich: Centre for Renaissance Studies, 1985. pp. xvi, 311. Rev. by F. C. De Vries in RES (39:154) 1988, 325–7.

**2641.** LEGGE, M. D.     Bishop Odo in the Bayeux tapestry. MÆ (56:1) 1987, 84–5.

**2642.** LE GOFF, JACQUES.    The birth of purgatory. *See* **2301.**

**2643.** LEWRY, P. OSMUND (ed.).    On time and imagination: *De tempore, De spiritu fantastico.* Oxford: OUP for the British Academy, 1987. pp. xxxviii, 186. (Auctores britannici medii aevi, 9.) Rev. by George Marcil in Spec (64:4) 982–4.

**2644.** McGUIRE, BRIAN PATRICK.    Purgatory, the communion of saints, and medieval change. Viator (20) 61–84.

**2644a.** McLOUGHLIN, J. P.    John of Salisbury (*c.* 1120–1180): the career and attitudes of a schoolman in church politics. Unpub. doct. diss., Trinity Coll. Dublin, 1988. [Abstr. in IT (39:4) 1645–6.]

**2645.** MARENBON, JOHN.    Early medieval philosophy (480–1150): an introduction. *See* **2304.**

**2646.** MARKUS, MANFRED.    The spelling peculiarities in the *Ormulum* from an interdisciplinary point of view: a reappraisal. *In* (pp. 69–86) **38.**

**2647.** MILLER, D. A.    The twinning of Arthur and Cei: an Arthurian tessera. JIES (17:1/2) 47–76.

**2648.** MORIARTY, CATHERINE (ed.).    The voice of the Middle Ages in personal letters, 1100–1500. Oxford: Lennard. pp. 332. Rev. by Tom Shippey in TLS, 20 Oct., 1162.

**2649.** MURDOCH, BRIAN.    The holy hostage: *De filio mulieris* in the Middle Cornish play *Beunans Meriasek*. MÆ (58:2) 258–73.

**2650.** MYERS, A. R.    London in the age of Chaucer. Norman; London: Oklahoma UP, 1988. pp. xi, 236. (Centers of civilization, 31.) Rev. by Richard H. Jones in Spec (64:4) 1013–16.

**2651.** NATALI, GIULIA.    A lyrical version: Boccaccio's *Filostrato. In* (pp. 49–73) **27.**

**2651a.** NEDERMAN, CARY J.    The changing face of tyranny: the reign of King Stephen in John of Salisbury's political thought. NMS (33) 1–20.

**2652.** NELSON, JAN A.    A Jungian interpretation of sexually ambiguous imagery in Chrétien's *Erec et Enide. In* (pp. 75–89) **8.**

**2653.** O'MARA, V. M.    A study of unedited late Middle English sermons that occur singly or in small groups. *See* **363.**

**2654.** ORMROD, W. M.    The personal religion of Edward III. Spec (64:4) 849–77.

**2655.** ORTENBERG, V. N.    Aspects of monastic devotions to the saints in England, *ca* 950 to *ca* 1100: the liturgical and iconographical evidence. *See* **2308.**

**2656.** PADEN, WILLIAM D.    Tenebrism in the *Song of Roland*. MP (86:4) 339–56.

**2657.** PENSOM, ROGER.    Thibaut de Champagne and the art of the trouvère. MÆ (57:1) 1988, 1–26.

**2658.** PIPER, ALAN J.; FOSTER, MERYL R.    Evidence of the Oxford booktrade, about 1300. *See* **457.**

**2659.** PRICE, JOCELYN.    *La vie de Sainte Modwenne*: a neglected Anglo-Norman hagiographic text, and some implications for English secular literature. MÆ (57:2) 1988, 172–89.

**2660.** REYNOLDS, SUSAN.   Kingdoms and communities in Western Europe, 900–1300. *See* **2309.**

**2661.** ROWE, J. G. (ed.).   Aspects of late medieval government and society: essays presented to J. R. Lander. Toronto; Buffalo, NY; London: Toronto UP, 1986. pp. xix, 226. Rev. by Claude Gauvin in EA (42:4) 464–5.

**2662.** SHIPPEY, T. A.   Breton *lais* and modern fantasies. *In* (pp. 69–91) **58.**

**2663.** SHORT, IAN.   The patronage of Beneit's *Vie de Thomas Becket*. MÆ (56:2) 1987, 239–56.

**2664.** SINCLAIR, K. V. (ed.).   The Hospitallers' 'Riwle' (Miracula et Regula Hospitalis Sancti Johannis Jerosolimitani.) London: ANTS, 1984. pp. xlix, 96. (Anglo-Norman texts, 42.) Rev. by Dafydd Evans in MÆ (56:1) 1987, 145.

**2665.** SMITH, FORREST S.   Secular and sacred visionaries in the late Middle Ages. New York: Garland, 1986. pp. xi, 334. (Garland pubs in comparative literature.) Rev. by Avril Henry in YLS (3) 169–71.

**2666.** SOLTERER, HELEN.   Letter writing and picture reading: medieval textuality and the *Bestiaire d'amour*. Word & Image (5:1) 131–47.

**2667.** STEWART, R. J. (ed.).   Merlin and woman: the second Merlin Conference, London, June 1987. London; New York: Blandford Press, 1988. pp. 190.

**2668.** STOCK, BRIAN.   Activity, contemplation, work and leisure between the eleventh and the thirteenth centuries. *In* (pp. 87–108) BRIAN VICKERS (ed.), Arbeit, Musse, Meditation: Betrachtungen zur *Vita activa* und *Vita contemplativa*. Zurich: Centre for Renaissance Studies, 1985. pp. xvi, 311. Rev. by F. C. De Vries in RES (39:154) 1988, 325–7.

**2669.** STUARD, SUSAN MOSHER.   Women in medieval history and historiography. Philadelphia: Pennsylvania UP, 1987. pp. xvi, 205. (Middle Ages.) Rev. Judith M. Bennett in Spec (64:1) 221–2.

**2670.** SULLIVAN, RICHARD E.   The Carolingian age: reflections on its place in the Middle Ages. Spec (64:2) 267–306.

**2671.** TATTERSALL, JILL.   Anthropophagi and eaters of raw flesh in French literature of the Crusade period: myth, tradition and reality. MÆ (57:2) 1988, 240–53.

**2672.** TAYLOR, JOHN.   English historical literature in the fourteenth century. Oxford: Clarendon Press; New York; Toronto: OUP, 1987. pp. xii, 349. Rev. by Antonia Gransden in NMS (33) 137–8.

**2673.** THOMPSON, MARY L. H.   A possible source of Geoffrey's Roman war? *In* (pp. 43–53) **8.**

**2674.** TROTTER, D. A.   The influence of Bible commentaries on Old French Bible translations. MÆ (56:2) 1987, 257–75.

**2675.** USHER, JONATHAN.   Frame and novella gardens in the *Decameron*. MÆ (58:2) 274–85.

**2676.** WARREN, W. L.   The governance of Norman and Angevin England, 1086–1272. Stanford, CA: Stanford UP; London: Arnold, 1987. pp. xvi, 237. (The governance of England, 2.) Rev. by Stephanie Evans Christelow in Spec (64:4) 1049–51.

**2677.** WEIJERS, OLGA.   Lexicography in the Middle Ages. *See* **1114.**
**2678.** WHITE, GRAHAM.   Pelagianisms. Viator (20) 233–54.
**2679.** WISSOLIK, RICHARD DAVID.   The Bayeux Tapestry: its English connection and its peripheral narrative. *See* **2314.**
**2680.** WRIGHT, S. A.   The big Bible, Royal I.E.ix in the British Library and manuscript illumination in London in the early fifteenth century. *See* **103.**
**2681.** ZIOLKOWSKI, JAN (ed.).   Miracles of the Virgin Mary, in verse/Miracula sancte dei genitricis virginis Marie, versifice. Ed. from British Library MS Cotton Vespasian D.xix. Toronto: Pontifical Inst. of Mediaeval Studies, 1986. pp. 101. (Toronto mediaeval Latin texts, 17.) Rev. by David Carlson in Spec (64:2) 475–7.

## AUTHORS
### (except Chaucer and the Gawain Poet)
### William Caxton
**2682.** FUSTER, MIGUEL.   La veracidad del prólogo y los epílogos de *Recuyell*: claves para una interpretación biográfica de W. Caxton. RAEI (2) 53–64.
### Charles of Orleans
**2683.** CROPP, GLYNNIS M.   Fortune and the poet in ballades of Eustache Deschamps, Charles d'Orleans and François Villon. MÆ (58:1) 125–32.
### Gavin Douglas
**2684.** CANITZ, AUGUSTE ELFRIEDE CHRISTA.   Gavin Douglas's prologues to his *Eneados*: the narrator in quest of a new homeland. Unpub. doct. diss., Univ. of British Columbia, 1988. [Abstr. in DA (49) 3729A.]
### William Dunbar
**2685.** EVANS, DEANNA DELMAR.   Dunbar's *Tretis*: the seven deadly sins of carnivalesque disguise. Neophilologus (73:1) 130–41.
**2686.** SWENSON, KAREN.   Mary as 'wall' in Dunbar's *Ane Ballat of Our Lady*. ELN (27:1) 1–6.
**2687.** TING, J. A.   A critical and contextual study of the poetry of William Dunbar. Unpub. doct. diss., Univ. of Oxford, 1988. [Abstr. in IT (39:2) 490.]
### John Gower
**2688.** GITTES, KATHARINE S.   Gower's Helen of Troy and the contemplative way of life. ELN (27:1) 19–24.
**2689.** HARTUNG, ALBERT E. (gen. ed.).   A manual of the writings in Middle English 1050–1500: vol. 7, Fasc. 17, John Gower. *See* **2440.**
**2690.** PICKLES, J. D.; DAWSON, J. L. (eds).   A concordance to John Gower's *Confessio Amantis*. (Bibl. 1988, 2050.) Rev. by Claude Gauvin in EA (42:4) 465–6; by R. F. Yeager in SAC (11) 276–9; by Katharine S. Gittes in JRMMRA (10) 94–5.
**2691.** SHAW, JUDITH.   The role of the shared bed in John Gower's tales of incest. ELN (26:3) 4–7.
**2692.** WHITE, HUGH.   The naturalness of Amans' love in *Confessio Amantis*. MÆ (56:2) 1987, 316–22.

### Robert Henryson

**2693.** TORTI, ANNA. From 'history' to 'tragedy': the story of Troilus and Criseyde in Lydgate's *Troy Book* and Henryson's *Testament of Cresseid. In* (pp. 171–97) **27.**

### William Herebert

**2694.** REIMER, STEPHEN R. (ed.). The works of William Herebert, OFM. Toronto: Pontifical Inst. of Mediaeval Studies, 1987. pp. ix, 173. (Studies and texts, 81.) (Cf. bibl. 1985, 3091.) Rev. by Siegfried Wenzel in SAC (11) 279–83.

### Walter Hilton

**2695.** CLARK, JOHN P. H.; TAYLOR, CHERYL (eds). Walter Hilton's Latin writings. *See* **128.**

**2696.** CLEVE, GUNNEL. Mystic themes in Walter Hilton's *Scale of Perfection*, Book I. Salzburg: Institut für Anglistik und Amerikanistik, Salzburg Univ. pp. vii, 110. (Salzburg studies in English literature: Elizabethan and Renaissance studies, 92:19.)

### Thomas Hoccleve

**2697.** GREETHAM, D. C. Self-referential artifacts: Hoccleve's persona as a literary device. MP (86:3) 242–51.

**2698.** STANLEY, E. G. Chaucer's metre after Chaucer: I, Chaucer to Hoccleve. NQ (36:1) 11–23.

### Julian of Norwich

**2699.** GLASSCOE, MARION. Visions and revisions: a further look at the manuscripts of Julian of Norwich. *See* **138.**

**2700–1.** Entries cancelled.

**2702.** JANTZEN, GRACE M. Julian of Norwich: mystic and theologian. London: SPCK, 1987; New York: Paulist Press, 1988. pp. x, 230. Rev. by John-Julian Swanson in SAC (11) 247–9.

**2703.** MILLER, GAYLE HOUSTON. Imagery and design in Julian of Norwich's *Revelations of Divine Love*. Unpub. doct. diss., Univ. of Georgia, 1988. [Abstr. in DA (49) 3359A.]

### Margery Kempe

**2704.** FIENBERG, NONA. Thematics of value in *The Book of Margery Kempe*. MP (87:2) 132–41.

### William Langland

**2705.** ADAMS, ROBERT. 'Mede' and 'mercede': the evolution of the economics of grace in the *Piers Plowman* B and C versions. *In* (pp. 217–32) **41.**

**2706.** ALFORD, JOHN A. The idea of reason in *Piers Plowman. In* (pp. 199–215) **41.**

**2707.** ——*Piers Plowman*: a glossary of legal diction. Cambridge: Brewer; Wolfeboro, NH: Boydell & Brewer, 1988. pp. xxxi, 170. (Piers Plowman studies, 5.)

**2708.** —— (ed.). A companion to Piers Plowman. (Bibl. 1988, 2059.) Rev. by S. S. Hussey in NQ (36:4) 492–3.

**2709.** ALLEN, DAVID G. The Dismas *distinctio* and the forms of *Piers Plowman* B.10–13. YLS (3) 31–48.

**2710.** BLAND, CYNTHIA RENÉE. Langland's use of the term *ex vi transicionis*. YLS (2) 1988, 125–35.

**2711.** BOWERS, JOHN M. The crisis of will in *Piers Plowman*. (Bibl. 1988, 2060.) Rev. by Robert Adams in YLS (1) 1987, 135–40; by Anne Middleton in Spec (64:1) 130–4.

**2712.** BREWER, CHARLOTTE. The textual principles of Kane's A text. *See* **286.**

**2713.** CABLE, THOMAS. Middle English meter and its theoretical implications. *See* **288.**

**2714.** CLOPPER, LAWRENCE M. The life of the dreamer, the dreams of the wanderer in *Piers Plowman*. SP (86:3) 261–85.

**2715.** COOPER, HELEN. Langland's and Chaucer's Prologues. YLS (1) 1987, 71–81.

**2716.** DAVLIN, MARY CLEMENTE. A game of heuene: word play and the meaning of *Piers Plowman* B. Cambridge: Brewer; Wolfeboro, NH: Boydell & Brewer. pp. 147. (Piers Plowman studies, 7.)

**2717.** —— *Piers Plowman* and the books of wisdom. YLS (2) 1988, 23–33.

**2718.** DOLAN, T. P. Langland and FitzRalph: two solutions to the mendicant problem. YLS (2) 1988, 35–45.

**2719.** DONALDSON, E. TALBOT; ECONOMOU, GEORGE; BARNES, RICHARD. On translating *Piers Plowman*. YLS (3) 1–29.

**2720.** DUGGAN, HOYT N. The authenticity of the Z-text of *Piers Plowman*: further notes on metrical evidence. MÆ (56:1) 1987, 25–45.

**2721.** —— Notes toward a theory of Langland's meter. *See* **304.**

**2722.** ELDREDGE, L. M. Some medical evidence on Langland's imaginatif. *See* **1077.**

**2723.** ERZGRÄBER, WILLI. Apokalypse und Antichrist in der englischen Literatur des 14. Jahrhunderts: William Langlands *Piers Plowman*, Joachim von Fiore und der Chiliasmus des Mittelalters. LJGG (29) 1988, 233–51.

**2724.** FINLAYSON, JOHN. *The Simonie*: two authors? *See* **311.**

**2725.** FISHER, JOHN H. *Piers Plowman* and the Chancery tradition. *In* (pp. 267–78) **41.**

**2726.** GOLDSMITH, MARGARET E. The figure of Piers Plowman: the image on the coin. (Bibl. 1987, 3432.) Rev. by Guy Bourquin in EA (42:2) 211–12.

**2727.** GREEN, RICHARD FIRTH. The lost exemplar of the Z-text of *Piers Plowman* and its 20-line pages. *See* **139.**

**2728.** GRIFFITHS, LAVINIA. Personification in *Piers Plowman*. (Bibl. 1988, 2064.) Rev. by Richard Kenneth Emmerson in YLS (1) 1987, 144–5; by Guy Bourquin in EA (42:2) 210–11.

**2729.** HARTUNG, ALBERT E. (gen. ed.). A manual of the writings in Middle English 1050–1500: vol. 7, Fasc. 18, Piers Plowman. *See* **2440.**

**2730.** HICKSON, ROBERT DAVID, JR. The virtue of hope and the humility of God: Piers Plowman's vision of 'Goddes Body' and the desolation of ingratitude. Unpub. doct. diss., Univ. of North Carolina at Chapel Hill, 1988. [Abstr. in DA (50) 682A.]

**2731.** HILL, MARGARETT HUTTON.   Studies in theme and structure: *Piers Plowman A, Amelia*, and *Andreas*. See **2238.**

**2732.** HILL, THOMAS D.   Seth the 'seeder' in *Piers Plowman* C.10.249. YLS (1) 1987, 105–8.

**2733.** HOBAN, S.   *Piers Plowman* considered in the terms of the mediaeval dream-vision form. Unpub. M.Phil. diss., Univ. of York. [Abstr. in IT (38:4) 1455.]

**2734.** HOLLOWAY, JULIA BOLTON.   The pilgrim and the book: a study of Dante, Langland, and Chaucer. New York; Berne; Frankfurt: Lang, 1987. pp. xxiii, 321. (American univ. studies, 4; English language and literature, 42.) Rev. by Howard H. Schless in Spec (64:4) 973–6; by Christian K. Zacher in SAC (11) 234–8.

**2735.** KANE, GEORGE.   Chaucer and Langland: historical and textual approaches. London: Athlone Press; Berkeley: California UP. pp. x, 302. Rev. by Marie Zaerr in RMRLL (43:4) 249–50.

**2736.** —— (ed.).   *Piers Plowman*: the A version, Will's visions of Piers Plowman and Do-Well: an edition in the form of Trinity College Cambridge MS R.3.14, corrected from other manuscripts, with variant readings. See **149.**

**2737.** —— DONALDSON, E. TALBOT (eds).   *Piers Plowman*: the B version, Will's visions of Piers Plowman, Do-Well, Do-Better, and Do-Best: an edition in the form of Trinity College Cambridge MS B.15.17, corrected and restored from the known evidence, with variant readings. See **150.**

**2738.** KASKE, R. E.   The character Hunger in *Piers Plowman*. *In* (pp. 187–97) **41.**

**2739.** KIRK, ELIZABETH D.   Langland's plowman and the recreation of fourteenth-century religious metaphor. YLS (2) 1988, 1–21.

**2740.** LAWTON, DAVID.   The subject of *Piers Plowman*. YLS (1) 1987, 1–30.

**2741.** MacQUEEN, ANGUS.   Form and the search for meaning in William Langland's *Piers Plowman*. *In* (pp. 81–93) **3.**

**2742.** MATHESON, LISTER M.   *Piers Plowman* B.13.331 (330): some 'shrewed' observations. See **349.**

**2743.** MIDDLETON, ANNE.   Making a good end: John But as a reader of *Piers Plowman*. *In* (pp. 243–66) **41.**

**2744.** —— The passion of Seint Averoys [B.13.91]: 'deuynyng' and divinity in the banquet scene. YLS (1) 1987, 31–40.

**2745.** PEARSALL, DEREK.   Poverty and poor people in *Piers Plowman*. *In* (pp. 167–85) **41.**

**2746.** PEVERETT, M. D. G.   Medieval conceptions of reason and the modes of thought in *Piers Plowman*. Unpub. doct. diss., Univ. of Durham, 1988. [Abstr. in IT (39:3) 1105.]

**2747.** REVARD, CARTER.   *Title* and *auaunced* in *Piers Plowman* B.11.290. See **1038.**

**2748.** RUSSELL, G. H.   The imperative of revision in the C version of *Piers Plowman*. *In* (pp. 233–42) **41.**

**2749.** RUSSELL, GEORGE.   'As they read it': some notes on early responses to the C-version of *Piers Plowman*. Leeds Studies in English (20) 173–89.

**2750.** SANDVED, ARTHUR O.   From *Piers Plowman* to *Peter Plogmann*: on translating Langland's poem into Norwegian. *In* (pp. 303–13) **24**.

**2751.** SCHMIDT, A. V. C.   The clerkly maker: Langland's poetic art. (Bibl. 1988, 2072.) Rev. by Hoyt N. Duggan in YLS (2) 1988, 167–74; by Derek Pearsall in SAC (11) 288–90.

**2752.** SHERBO, ARTHUR.   Samuel Pegge, Thomas Holt White, and *Piers Plowman*. YLS (1) 1987, 122–8.

**2753.** SHOAF, R. A.   'Speche þat spire is of grace': a note on *Piers Plowman* B.9.104. YLS (1) 1987, 128–33.

**2754.** SIMPSON, JAMES.   Spirituality and economics in Passus 1–7 of the B text. YLS (1) 1987, 83–103.

**2755.** SMITH, B. ALLISON.   The dreamer's questions: keys to the structure of meaning in *Piers Plowman* B. Unpub. doct. diss., Catholic Univ. of America. [Abstr. in DA (50) 1301–2A.]

**2756.** TARVERS, JOSEPHINE KOSTER.   The Abbess's ABC. YLS (2) 1988, 137–41. (Conference paper, Kalamazoo, 1987.)

**2757.** TAVORMINA, M. TERESA.   'Gendre of generacion': *Piers Plowman* B.16.222. ELN (27:2) 1–9.

**2758.** —— 'Maledictus qui non reliquit semen': the curse on infertility in *Piers Plowman* B.XVI and C.XVIII. MÆ (58:1) 117–25.

**2759.** TSUJI, YASUAKI.   'Mede' and 'mercede': theological aspects of the metaphor of Latin grammar in *Piers Plowman* C-text. *See* **1063**.

**2760.** VON NOLCKEN, CHRISTINA.   *Piers Plowman*, the Wycliffites, and *Pierce the Plowman's Creed*. YLS (2) 1988, 71–102.

**2761.** WELDON, JAMES F. G.   Gesture of perception: the pattern of kneeling in *Piers Plowman* B.18–19. YLS (3) 49–66.

**2762.** WHITE, HUGH.   Nature and salvation in *Piers Plowman*. Cambridge: Brewer; Wolfeboro, NH: Boydell & Brewer, 1988. pp. viii, 128. (Piers Plowman studies, 6.) Rev. by Wendy Scase in NQ (36:3) 366–7; by Eugenie R. Freed in UES (27:1) 35–7; by A. V. C. Schmidt in YLS (3) 171–4.

## Laȝamon

**2763.** HALL, AUDLEY S.   The fiction of history: a structural analysis of Laȝamon's *Brut*. Unpub. doct. diss., Univ. of Arkansas, 1987. [Abstr. in DA (49) 1796A.]

**2764.** LE SAUX, FRANÇOISE H. M.   Laȝamon's *Brut*: the poem and its sources. Cambridge: Brewer. pp. viii, 244. (Arthurian studies, 19.)

**2765.** RIDER, JEFF.   The fictional margin: the Merlin of the *Brut*. MP (87:1) 1–12.

## John Lydgate

**2766.** EDWARDS, A. S. G.   An unidentified extract from Lydgate's *Troy Book*. NQ (36:3) 307–8.

**2767.** MOONEY, LINNE R.   Lydgate's *Kings of England* and another verse chronicle of the kings. Viator (20) 255–89.

**2767a.** STANLEY, E. G.    Chaucer's metre after Chaucer: II, Lydgate and Barclay. NQ (36:2) 151–62.
**2768.** TORTI, ANNA.    From 'history' to 'tragedy': the story of Troilus and Criseyde in Lydgate's *Troy Book* and Henryson's *Testament of Cresseid*. *In* (pp. 171–97) **27.**

### Sir Thomas Malory

**2769.** ATKINSON, STEPHEN C. B.    'Now I se and undirstonde': the Grail Quest and the education of Malory's reader. *In* (pp. 90–108) **8.**
**2770.** KENNEDY, BEVERLY.    Knighthood in the *Morte Darthur*. Woodbridge: Boydell & Brewer, 1985. (Bibl. 1987, 3465.) Rev. by James W. Spisak in Spec (64:2) 457–9; by Flora Alexander in RES (38:152) 1987, 543–4.
**2771.** LA FARGE, CATHERINE.    Conversation in Malory's *Morte Darthur*. MÆ (56:2) 1987, 225–38.
**2772.** LEE, A.    Thomas Malory and fifteenth-century chivalric literature. Unpub. doct. diss., Univ. of Oxford. [Abstr. in IT (39:3) 1104–5.]
**2773.** LUMIANSKY, R. M.    Concerning three names in *Le Morte Darthur* – 'Roone', 'The Welshe Kyng' and 'Chastelayne' – and Malory's possible revision of his book. *In* (pp. 301–8) **41.**
**2774.** MCCARTHY, TERENCE.    Malory's 'swete madame'. *See* **1072.**
**2775.** —— *Le Morte Darthur* and romance. *In* (pp. 148–75) **58.**
**2776.** —— Reading the *Morte Darthur*. Cambridge: Brewer, 1988. pp. xv, 187. (Arthurian studies, 20.)
**2777.** MAHONEY, DHIRA B.    Malory's great guns. Viator (20) 291–310.
**2778.** MITCHELL, JEROME.    Scott and Malory. *In* (pp. 211–26) **38.**
**2779.** PARINS, MARYLYN JACKSON.    Malory's expurgators. *In* (pp. 144–62) **8.**
**2780.** —— (ed.).    Malory: the critical heritage. (Bibl. 1988, 2082 where scholar's name incomplete.) Rev. by P. J. C. Field in NQ (36:4) 496–7.
**2781.** RIDDY, FELICITY.    Sir Thomas Malory. (Bibl. 1987, 3471.) Rev. by J. A. Burrow in NQ (36:1) 82–3.
**2782.** SPISAK, JAMES W. (ed.).    Studies in Malory. (Bibl. 1987, 3472.) Rev. by O. D. Macrae-Gibson in RES (38:150) 1987, 240–1.

### Sir John Mandeville

**2783.** HIGGINS, IAIN MACLEOD.    The world of a book of the world: *Mandeville's Travels* in Middle English (British Library MS Cotton Titus C.xvi.) Unpub. doct. diss., Harvard Univ., 1988. [Abstr. in DA (50) 440A.]

### Robert Mannyng

**2784.** TURVILLE-PETRE, THORLAC.    Politics and poetry in the early fourteenth century: the case of Robert Manning's *Chronicle*. RES (39:153) 1988, 1–28.

### John Mirk

**2785.** FLETCHER, ALAN J.    John Mirk and the Lollards. MÆ (56:2) 1987, 217–24.

### Richard Rolle

**2786.** ALLEN, ROSAMUND S. (ed. and trans.).    Richard Rolle: the

English writings. London: SPCK. pp. 232. (Paulist Press, classics of Western spirituality.)

**2787.** MOYES, MALCOLM ROBERT (ed.).    Richard Rolle's *Expositio super novem lectiones mortuorum*: an introduction and contribution towards a critical edition. (Bibl. 1988, 2087.) Rev. by A. S. G. Edwards in Spec (64:4) 1033–4.

**2788.** OGILVIE-THOMSON, S. J. (ed.).    Richard Rolle: prose and verse, ed. from MS Longleat 29 and related manuscripts. *See* **159.**

**2789.** SARGENT, MICHAEL G.    Richard Rolle, Sorbonnard? MÆ (57:2) 1988, 284–90.

### Thomas of Hales

**2790.** HORRALL, SARAH M. (ed.).    *The Lyf of Oure Lady*: the ME translation of Thomas of Hales' *Vita Sancte Marie*, ed. from MS St George's Chapel, Windsor Castle, E.I.I. (Bibl. 1987, 3482.) Rev. by A. S. G. Edwards in YES (19) 300–1.

### John Trevisa

**2791.** HANNA, RALPH, III.    Sir Thomas Berkely and his patronage. *See* **2624.**

**2791a.** SLUDER, BRENDA.    Differences between Chancery English and the English of John of Trevisa. *See* **693.**

**2792.** WALDRON, RONALD.    Trevisa's 'Celtic complex' revisited. NQ (36:3) 303–7. (*Refers to* bibl. 1947, 1422.)

**2793.** —— Trevisa's original prefaces on translation: a critical edition. *In* (pp. 285–99) **41.**

### John Wyclif

**2794.** GRADON, PAMELA (ed.).    English Wycliffite sermons: vol. II. Oxford: Clarendon Press, 1988. pp. xcv, 378. (Oxford English texts.) Rev. by Siegfried Wenzel in NQ (36:3) 370–1.

**2795.** HUDSON, ANNE.    The premature Reformation: Wycliffite texts and Lollard history. Oxford: Clarendon Press; New York: OUP, 1988. pp. xii, 556. Rev. by Donald Dean Smeeton in SixCT (20:3) 507; by Priscilla H. Barnum in Spec (64:4) 976–9; by Tom Shippey in LRB (11:3) 8–9.

**2796.** KENNY, ANTHONY (ed.).    Wyclif in his times. (Bibl. 1988, 2092.) Rev. by Christina von Nolcken in YLS (2) 1988, 145–9; by John Scattergood in YES (19) 301–4.

**2797.** LINDBERG, CONRAD.    Towards an English Wyclif canon. *In* (pp. 179–84) **24.**

**2798.** LUPTON, LEWIS.    Wyclif's wicket: sign of a credible faith. London: Olive Tree, 1984. pp. 179. (History of the Geneva Bible, 16.) Rev. by Christina von Nolcken in YLS (2) 1988, 150–3.

**2799.** SPADE, PAUL VINCENT; WILSON, GORDON ANTHONY (eds). Summa insolubilium. (Bibl. 1988, 2095.) Rev. by Anne Hudson in RES (39:153) 1988, 160.

**2800.** VON NOLCKEN, CHRISTINA.    *Piers Plowman*, the Wycliffites, and *Pierce the Plowman's Creed*. *See* **2760.**

**2801.** —— Wyclif in our times: the Wyclif sexcentenary, 1984. YLS (2) 1988, 143–54 (review-article).

## GEOFFREY CHAUCER
### General Studies,
### and Works other than *The Canterbury Tales* and
### *Troilus and Criseyde*

**2802.** AERS, DAVID.   Chaucer. (Bibl. 1988, 2098.) Rev. by J. D. Burnley in RES (38:152) 1987, 539–40; by Derek Pearsall in MLR (84:1) 112–13.

**2803.** ALLEN, MARK; FISHER, JOHN H.   The essential Chaucer: an annotated bibliography of major modern studies. (Bibl. 1987, 3491.) Rev. by C. C. Morse in NQ (36:4) 489–90; by Russell A. Peck in Spec (64:2) 381.

**2804.** ARRATHOON, LEIGH A. (ed.).   Chaucer and the craft of fiction. Rochester, MI: Solaris Press, 1986. pp. xxv, 430. Rev. by Peter Brown in SAC (10) 1988, 119–22.

**2805.** BAGHDIKIAN, SONIA.   Ambiguous negations in Chaucer and Queen Elizabeth. *In* (pp. 41–8) **30.**

**2806.** BAIRD-LANGE, LORRAYNE Y.; BOWERS, BEGE K.   An annotated Chaucer bibliography, 1987. SAC (11) 303–77.

**2807.** Entry cancelled.

**2808.** BENSON, LARRY D. (gen. ed.).   The Riverside Chaucer. (Bibl. 1988, 2103.) Rev. by Betsy Bowden in EC (38:1) 1988, 75–9.

**2809.** BIRNEY, EARLE.   Essays on Chaucerian irony. Ed., with an essay on irony, by BERYL ROWLAND. (Bibl. 1988, 2104.) Rev. by J. A. Burrow in RES (38:151) 1987, 48–9.

**2810.** BLAKE, N. F.   The Chaucer canon: methodological assumptions. NM (90:3/4) 295–310.

**2811.** BOITANI, PIERO.   Chaucer and the imaginary world of fame. (Bibl. 1988, 2105.) Rev. by John C. Hirsh in MÆ (56:1) 1987, 123–4.

**2812.** —— MANN, JILL (eds).   The Cambridge Chaucer companion. (Bibl. 1988, 2106.) Rev. by Phillipa Hardman in RES (39:156) 1988, 534–5; by Paul G. Ruggiers in Spec (64:2) 391–2; by J. Norton-Smith in NQ (36:1) 80–1.

**2813.** BOFFEY, JULIA.   Richard Pynson's *Book of Fame* and the *Letter of Dido*. Viator (19) 1988, 339–53.

**2814.** BOWDEN, BETSY.   Chaucer aloud: the varieties of textual interpretation. (Bibl. 1988, 2107.) Rev. by Richard Osburg in SAC (11) 186–8; by Alan T. Gaylord in Spec (64:3) 670–4; by Charlotte C. Morse in NQ (36:1) 81–2.

**2815.** BOWERS, BEGE K.   Chaucer research in progress, 1988–1989. NM (90:3/4) 273–94.

**2816.** BREWER, DEREK.   Chaucer's anti-Ricardian poetry. *In* (pp. 115–28) **38.**

**2817.** BURNLEY, DAVID.   The language of Chaucer. See **1387.**

**2818.** CHRISTIANSON, C. PAUL.   A community of book artisans in Chaucer's London. See **422.**

**2819.** COLLETTE, CAROLYN P.   Chaucer and Victorian medievalism: culture and society. PoetT (29/30) 115–25.

**2820.** DAVENPORT, W. A. Chaucer: complaint and narrative. Cambridge: Brewer; Wolfeboro, NH: Boydell & Brewer, 1988. pp. 232. (Chaucer studies, 14.) Rev. by Catherine Batt in Eng (38) 69–76.

**2821.** DE WEEVER, JACQUELINE. Chaucer name dictionary: a guide to astrological, biblical, historical, literary, and mythological names in the works of Geoffrey Chaucer. (Bibl. 1987, 3507.) Rev. by Emerson Brown, Jr, in SAC (11) 204–8.

**2822.** DONALDSON, E. TALBOT. The swan at the well: Shakespeare reading Chaucer. (Bibl. 1987, 3508.) Rev. by Peter Bement in RES (38:152) 1987, 559–60.

**2823.** DRAGSTRA, H. H. The modernity of modern Chaucer criticism. *In* (pp. 187–97) **47.**

**2824.** EDWARDS, A. S. G. Pynson's and Thynne's editions of Chaucer's *House of Fame*. See **307.**

**2825.** —— The text of Chaucer's *House of Fame*: editing and authority. *See* **308.**

**2826.** EDWARDS, ROBERT R. The dream of Chaucer: representation and reflection in the early narratives. Durham, NC; London: Duke UP. pp. xvi, 189.

**2827.** ELLIOTT, RALPH W. V. Literary dialect in Chaucer, Hardy, and Alan Garner. SEL (English number) 37–56.

**2828.** FICHTE, JOERG O. (ed.). Chaucer's frame tales: the physical and metaphysical. (Bibl. 1987, 3515.) Rev. by Sigmund Eisner in JRMMRA (10) 96–7; by John Bugge in SAC (11) 218–21.

**2829.** FICHTE, JÖRG O. Chaucer's work in German literary scholarship to 1914. PoetT (29/30) 93–101.

**2830.** FINLAYSON, JOHN. Textual variants in Chaucer's *House of Fame*: Thynne as editor. *See* **312.**

**2831.** FISHER, JOHN H. (ed.). The complete poetry and prose of Geoffrey Chaucer. (Bibl. 1981, 3796.) New York; London: Holt, Rinehart & Winston. pp. xiii, 1040. (Second ed.: first ed. 1977.)

**2832.** HAAS, RENATE. From the *Vormärz* to the Empire: the sociopolitical context of the golden age of German Chaucer scholarship. PoetT (29/30) 102–14.

**2833.** Entry cancelled.

**2834.** HEWITT, KATHLEEN. Loss and restitution in the *Book of the Duchess*. PLL (25:1) 19–35.

**2835.** HORNSBY, JOSEPH ALLEN. Chaucer and the law. Norman, OK: Pilgrim, 1988. pp. ix, 180. Rev. by George D. Gopen in SAC (11) 241–7.

**2836.** JEFFREY, DAVID LYLE (ed.). Chaucer and scriptural tradition. (Bibl. 1986, 3702.) Rev. by Helen Cooper in MÆ (56:1) 1987, 119.

**2837.** JORDAN, ROBERT M. Chaucer's poetics and the modern reader. (Bibl. 1988, 2132.) Rev. by John P. Hermann in SAC (11) 250–3.

**2838.** KANE, GEORGE. Chaucer and Langland: historical and textual approaches. *See* **2735.**

**2839.** Entry cancelled.

**2840.** KELLY, H. A. Chaucer and Shakespeare on tragedy. Leeds Studies in English (20) 191–206.

**2841.** KELLY, HENRY ANSGAR.    Chaucer and the cult of Saint Valentine. (Bibl. 1988, 2135.) Rev. by John P. McCall in Spec (64:2) 453–4.

**2842.** KNIGHT, STEPHEN. Chaucer's British rival. Leeds Studies in English (20) 87–98. (Dafydd ap Gwilym.)

**2843.** —— Geoffrey Chaucer. (Bibl. 1988, 2137.) Rev. by J. D. Burnley in RES (38:152) 1987, 540; by Alison Lee in Eng (36) 1987, 52–5.

**2844.** KOFF, LEONARD MICHAEL.    Chaucer and the art of storytelling. Berkeley; London: California UP, 1988. pp. ix, 298.

**2845.** KOOPER, ERIK SIMON.    Love, marriage and salvation in Chaucer's *Book of the Duchess* and *Parlement of Foules*. Unpub. doct. diss., Rijksuniversiteit te Utrecht, 1985. [Abstr. in DA (49) 2651A.]

**2846.** KRUGER, STEVEN F.    Dreams in search of knowledge: the middle vision of Chaucer and his contemporaries. See **2461.**

**2847.** LADD, C. A.    'Look out for the little words.' *In* (pp. 163–5) **41.**

**2848.** LAWTON, DAVID.    Chaucer's narrators. (Bibl. 1988, 2139.) Rev. by Helen Cooper in RES (38:151) 1987, 382–3; by C. David Benson in Spec (64:1) 182–3.

**2849.** LEYERLE, JOHN; QUICK, ANNE.    Chaucer: a bibliographical introduction. (Bibl. 1988, 2140.) Rev. by Helen Cooper in RES (38:152) 1987, 541; by J. Norton-Smith in NQ (36:1) 79–81.

**2850.** LYNCH, KATHRYN L.    The *Book of the Duchess* as a philosophical vision: the argument of form. Genre (21:3) 1988, 279–305.

**2851.** MACHAN, TIM WILLIAM.    Techniques of translation: Chaucer's *Boece*. (Bibl. 1987, 3524.) Rev. by Derek Pearsall in MLR (84:1) 113–14; by Roger Ellis in MÆ (56:2) 1987, 324–5.

**2852.** McKENNA, STEVEN R.    Orality, literacy, and Chaucer: a study of performance, textual authority, and proverbs in the major poetry. Unpub. doct. diss., Univ. of Rhode Island, 1988. [Abstr. in DA (49) 3370A.]

**2853.** MASUI, MICHIO.    Studies in Chaucer's language of feeling. (Bibl. 1988, 2146.) Rev. by E. G. Stanley in NQ (36:3) 369.

**2854.** MEHL, DIETER.    Geoffrey Chaucer: an introduction to his narrative poetry. (Bibl. 1988, 2147.) Rev. by Phillipa Hardman in RES (39:156) 1988, 535.

**2855.** MITCHELL, JEROME.    Scott, Chaucer, and medieval romance: a study in Sir Walter Scott's indebtedness to the literature of the Middle Ages. Lexington: Kentucky UP, 1987. pp. xi, 268. Rev. by N. F. Blake in Lore and Language (8:1) 128–9; by Ruth Beckett in SLJ (supp. 30) 7–9.

**2856–7.**    Entries cancelled.

**2858.** NEWMAN, JOHN KEVIN.    The English tradition: Chaucer and Milton. *In* (pp. 339–98) JOHN KEVIN NEWMAN, The classical epic tradition. Madison; London: Wisconsin UP, 1986. pp. 566. (Wisconsin studies in classics.)

**2859.** NIEKER, MARK.    Apprehensive moments: Conrad, Chaucer, and the *Sefer Yetsira*. Cithara (29:1) 48–71. (*Parliament of Fowls, Heart of Darkness.*)

**2860.** OLSON, GLENDING.   Juan Garcia de Castrojeriz and John of Wales: a note on Chaucer's reading. Spec (64:1) 106–10.

**2861.** OLSSON, KURT.   Poetic invention and Chaucer's *Parlement of Foules*. MP (87:1) 13–35.

**2862.** OOIZUMI, AKIO; IWASAKI, HARUO (eds).   Chaucer no eigo: kenkyu no kadaito houhou. *See* **690**.

**2863.** PECK, RUSSELL A.   Chaucer's *Romaunt of the Rose* and *Boece*, *Treatise on the Astrolabe*, *Equatorie of the Planetis*, lost works, and Chaucerian apocrypha: an annotated bibliography, 1900–1985. Toronto; London: Toronto UP in assn with Univ. of Rochester, 1988. pp. xx, 402. (Chaucer bibliographies.) Rev. by Warren Ginsberg in SAC (11) 273–6.

**2864.** PIZZORNO, PATRIZIA GRIMALDI.   *The Book of the Duchess*: a re-vision in a dream. Unpub. doct. diss., Harvard Univ., 1988. [Abstr. in DA (49) 2212A.]

**2865.** PURDON, L. O.   Chaucer's use of 'woad' in *The Former Age*. PLL (25:2) 216–19.

**2866.** ROONEY, ANNE.   *The Book of the Duchess*: hunting and the '*ubi sunt*' tradition. RES (38:151) 1987, 299–314.

**2867.** ROWE, DONALD W.   Through nature to eternity: Chaucer's *Legend of Good Women*. Lincoln; London: Nebraska UP, 1988. pp. x, 218. Rev. by Janet M. Cowen in SAC (11) 283–6; by Dieter Mehl in NQ (36:3) 367–8.

**2868.** SCHABER, BENNET JAY.   The lettered body: Chaucer in the place of analysis. Unpub. doct. diss., Brown Univ., 1988. [Abstr. in DA (49) 3359A.]

**2869.** SCHLESS, HOWARD H.   Chaucer and Dante: a revaluation. (Bibl. 1988, 2153.) Rev. by James Simpson in MÆ (56:1) 1987, 120–1.

**2870.** SCOTT-MACNAB, DAVID.   A re-examination of Octovyen's hunt in *The Book of the Duchess*. MÆ (56:2) 1987, 183–99.

**2871.** STANLEY, E. G.   Chaucer's metre after Chaucer: I, Chaucer to Hoccleve. *See* **2698**.

**2872.** —— Chaucer's metre after Chaucer: II, Lydgate and Barclay. *See* **2767a**.

**2873.** TAKADA, YASUNARI.   'The brooch of Thebes' and 'the girdle of Venus': courtly love in an oppositional perspective. PoetT (29/30) 17–38.

**2874.** TAYLOR, ANTHONY BRIAN.   Chaucer's non-involvement in *Pyramus and Thisbe*. NQ (36:3) 317–20.

**2875.** WALLACE, DAVID.   Chaucer and the early writings of Boccaccio. (Bibl. 1988, 2160.) Rev. by James Simpson in MÆ (56:2) 1987, 323–4.

## The Canterbury Tales

**2876.** ALEXANDER, MICHAEL.   *The Miller's Tale* by Geoffrey Chaucer. pp. viii, 72. (Bibl. 1986, 3732, where pagination incorrect.) Rev. by Derek Pearsall in MLR (84:1) 113.

**2877.** ANDERSON, DAVID.   Before the Knight's Tale: imitation of classical epic in Boccaccio's *Teseida*. Philadelphia, PA: Philadelphia UP, 1988. pp. xiii, 269. (Middle Ages.) Rev. by N. R. Havely in SAC (11) 177–80.

**2877a.** BAUMLIN, TITA FRENCH.   Theology and discourse in the Pardoner's Tale, the Parson's Tale, and the Retraction. Ren (41:3) 127–42.

**2878.** BENSON, C. DAVID.   Chaucer's drama of style: poetic variety and contrast in *The Canterbury Tales*. (Bibl. 1988, 2167.) Rev. by Helen Cooper in RES (38:152) 1987, 540–1; by Richard Firth Green in Spec (64:3) 658–60.

**2879.** BESTUL, THOMAS H.   Chaucer's Parson's Tale and the late medieval tradition of religious meditation. Spec (64:3) 600–19.

**2880.** BISHOP, IAN.   The narrative art of *The Canterbury Tales*: a critical study of the major poems. (Bibl. 1987, 3552.) Rev. by Catherine Batt in Eng (38) 69–76; by Helen Cooper in NQ (36:3) 370.

**2881.** BLAKE, N. F.   The textual tradition of *The Canterbury Tales*. (Bibl. 1988, 2169.) Rev. by Helen Cooper in RES (38:150) 1987, 237–8.

**2882.** BLAMIRES, ALCUIN.   The Wife of Bath and Lollardy. MÆ (58:2) 224–42.

**2883.** BLOCH, R. HOWARD.   Chaucer's maiden's head: the Physician's Tale and the poetics of virginity. Representations (28) 113–34.

**2884.** COOPER, HELEN.   Langland's and Chaucer's Prologues. *See* **2715.**

**2885.** COWEN, J. M.   The Miller's Tale, line 3325: 'merry maid and gallant groom'? *In* (pp. 147–52) **41.**

**2886.** DINSHAW, CAROLYN.   The law of man and its 'abhomynacions'. Exemplaria (1:1) 117–48.

**2887.** DOR, JULIETTE.   Reversals in the Nun's Priest's Tale. *In* (pp. 69–77) **42.**

**2888.** DORRELL, L.   Chaucer, Shakespeare and the Constance–Griselda legend: a study of the Clerk's Tale, the Man of Law's Tale and Shakespeare's last plays. Unpub. M.Litt. diss., Univ. of Oxford, 1988. [Abstr. in IT (39:3) 1103–4.]

**2889.** DuBRUCK, EDELGARD E.   Inviting tacit agreement: the Pardoner's Tale and its modern reception. *In* (pp. 103–13) **38.**

**2890.** ELLIOTT, RALPH.   Chaucer's garrulous heroine: Alice of Bath. StudME (4) 1–30.

**2891.** ELLIS, ROGER.   Patterns of religious narrative in *The Canterbury Tales*. (Bibl. 1988, 2176.) Rev. by Traugott Lawler in MLR (84:3) 708–10; by Alison Lee in Eng (36) 1987, 52–5; by Helen Cooper in RES (39:153) 1988, 102–3.

**2892.** ENGLE, LARS.   Chaucer, Bakhtin, and Griselda. Exemplaria (1:2) 429–59.

**2893.** —— Bakhtin, Chaucer, and anti-essentialist humanism. Exemplaria (1:2) 489–97.

**2894.** FARRELL, THOMAS J.   Privacy and the boundaries of fabliau in the Miller's Tale. ELH (56:4) 773–95.

**2895.** —— The style of the Clerk's Tale and the functions of its glosses. SP (86:3) 286–309.

**2896.** FLETCHER, ALAN J.   The preaching of the Pardoner. SAC (11) 15–35.

**2897.** FRADENBURG, LOUISE O.   Criticism and anti-semitism, and the Prioress's Tale. Exemplaria (1:1) 69–115.

**2898.** FRANK, ROBERT WORTH, JR.   Inept Chaucer. SAC (11) 5–14. (Presidential address to the New Chaucer Society.)

**2899.** GILLMEISTER, HEINER.   Chaucer's Pardoner's Tale as a poetic sermon. PoetT (29/30) 58–79.

**2900.** GOURLAY, ALEXANDER S.   What was Blake's Chaucer? SB (42) 272–83.

**2901.** GRAY, DOUGLAS.   Chaucer and *gentilesse*. In (pp. 1–27) **47.**

**2902.** GRIFFITHS, GWEN.   Receding images of initiators and recipients – yet another reflection on the Merchant's Tale. PLL (25:3) 242–63.

**2903.** GRUDIN, MICHAELA PAASCHE.   Chaucer's Clerk's Tale as political paradox. SAC (11) 63–92.

**2904.** GUNNELL, DONNA DENISE PRESCOTT.   *Des Contes à rire*: Chaucer's and Boccaccio's adaptations of certain Old French fabliaux. Unpub. doct. diss., Southern Illinois Univ. at Carbondale, 1988. [Abstr. in DA (50) 439A.]

**2905.** HALE, DAVID G.   Another Latin source for the Nun's Priest on dreams. NQ (36:1) 10–11.

**2905a.** HARLEY, MARTA POWELL.   The Reeve's 'Four gleedes' and St Fursey's vision of the four fires of the afterlife. MÆ (56:1) 1987, 85–9.

**2906.** HARWOOD, BRITTON J.   The 'fraternitee' of Chaucer's guildsmen. RES (39:155) 1988, 413–17.

**2907.** HILBERRY, JANE ELIZABETH.   The silent woman: speech, gender, and authority in Chaucer and Shakespeare. Unpub. doct. diss., Indiana Univ., 1988. [Abstr. in DA (50) 953A.]

**2908.** HITCHCOX, KATHRYN LANGFORD.   Alchemical discourse in the *Canterbury Tales*: signs of gnosis and transmutation. Unpub. doct. diss., Rice Univ., 1988. [Abstr. in DA (49) 3033A.]

**2909.** HOLLOWAY, JULIA BOLTON.   The pilgrim and the book: a study of Dante, Langland, and Chaucer. See **2734.**

**2910.** HUSSEY, S. S.   Chaucer's Host. In (pp. 153–61) **41.**

**2910a.** KAYLOR, NOEL HAROLD, JR.   The Nun's Priest's Tale as Chaucer's anti-tragedy. In (pp. 87–102) **38.**

**2911.** KEMPTON, DANIEL.   Chaucer's *Tale of Melibee*: 'A litel thyng in prose'. Genre (21:3) 1988, 263–78.

**2912.** KENDRICK, LAURA.   Chaucerian play: comedy and control in the *Canterbury Tales*. (Bibl. 1988, 2184.) Rev. by Mary Flowers Braswell in SAC (11) 253–6.

**2913.** KIM, JONG-HWAN.   Dramatic irony in Chaucer's The Franklin's Tale. JELL (35) 3–12.

**2914.** KOLVE, V. A.   Chaucer and the imagery of narrative: the first five Canterbury Tales. (Bibl. 1988, 2186.) Rev. by J. D. Burnley in Lore and Language (8:1) 118–19.

**2915.** LESTER, G. A.    Chaucer's unkempt knight. ELN (27:1) 25–9.

**2916.** McCLELLAN, WILLIAM.    Bakhtin's theory of dialogic discourse, medieval rhetorical theory, and the multi-voiced structure of the Clerk's Tale. Exemplaria (1:2) 461–88.

**2917.** —— Lars Engle – 'Chaucer, Bakhtin, and Griselda': a response. Exemplaria (1:2) 499–506.

**2917a.** MASUI, MICHIO (ed.).    A new rime index to *The Canterbury Tales* based on Manly and Rickert's text of *The Canterbury Tales*. (Bibl. 1988, 2190.) Rev. by E. G. Stanley in NQ (36:3) 369–70.

**2917b.** MERTENS-FONCK, PAULE.    Tradition and feminism in Middle English literature: source-hunting in the Wife of Bath's portrait and in *The Owl and the Nightingale. In* (pp. 175–92) **42.**

**2918.** MOORE, BRUCE.    The Reeve's 'rusty blade'. MÆ (58:2) 304–12.

**2919.** OKUDA, HIROKO.    'Thynk wel that love is free': Chaucer no kishino hanashino higekiteki ai. ('Thynk wel that love is free': tragic love in the Knight's Tale.) SEL (66:1) 3–15.

**2920.** PATTERSON, LEE.    'What man artow?': authorial self-definition in *The Tale of Sir Thopas* and *The Tale of Melibee*. SAC (11) 117–75.

**2921.** PEARCY, ROY J.    '*La Prière du plus grand péril*' in medieval English literature. *See* **2492.**

**2922.** PEARSALL, DEREK.    *The Canterbury Tales*. (Bibl. 1987, 3591.) Rev. by John B. Friedman in YES (19) 305–6; by Sally Mapstone in NQ (36:2) 222–3; by Vincent DiMarco in Ang (107:1/2) 192–7; by Helen Cooper in MÆ (56:2) 1987, 325–6; by Phillipa Hardman in RES (38:152) 1987, 542–3.

**2923.** RAMSEY, ROY VANCE.    F. N. Robinson's editing of the *Canterbury Tales. See* **368.**

**2924.** RICHMAN, GERALD.    Rape and desire in the Wife of Bath's Tale. SN (61:2) 161–5.

**2925.** ROBINSON, MICHÈLE.    Figuring out women: Chaucer's reading of the antifeminist tradition. Unpub. doct. diss., Johns Hopkins Univ., 1988. [Abstr. in DA (49) 1797A.]

**2926.** ROGERS, WILLIAM E.    Upon the ways: the structure of *The Canterbury Tales*. (Bibl. 1988, 2197.) Rev. by Helen Cooper in RES (39:154) 1988, 337.

**2927.** RUGGIERS, PAUL G.; BAKER, DONALD C. (gen. eds).    A variorum edition of the works of Geoffrey Chaucer: vol. 2, part 17, The Physician's Tale, ed. by HELEN STORM CORSA. (Bibl. 1988, 2199.) Rev. by N. F. Blake in EngS (69:5) 571–2; by Lorrayne Y. Baird-Lange in Spec (64:4) 931–3.

**2928.** —— —— A variorum edition of the works of Geoffrey Chaucer: vol. 2, part 20, The Prioress's Tale, ed. by BEVERLY BOYD. (Bibl. 1988, 2199.) Rev. by A. S. G. Edwards in SAC (11) 189–91; by N. F. Blake in EngS (70:3) 271–2; by Florence H. Ridley in Spec (64:3) 682–4.

**2929.** RUUD, JAY.    'In meetre in many a sondry wyse': fortune's wheel and the Monk's Tale. ELN (26:4) 6–11.

**2930.** SCANLON, LARRY.    The authority of fable: allegory and irony in the Nun's Priest's Tale. Exemplaria (1:1) 43–68.

**2931.** SEYMOUR, M. C.   Some satiric pointers in the Squire's Tale. EngS (70:4) 311–14.

**2932.** SIMMONS-O'NEILL, ELIZABETH.   'Sires, by youre leve, that am nat I': romance and pilgrimage in Chaucer and the *Gawain/Morgne*-poet. Unpub. doct. diss., Univ. of Washington, 1988. [Abstr. in DA (50) 135A.]

**2933.** STEPHENS, JOHN; RYAN, MARCELLA.   Metafictional strategies and the theme of sexual power in the Wife of Bath's and Franklin's Tales. NMS (33) 56–75.

**2934.** VOLK-BIRKE, SABINE.   Literacy and orality in late 14th century vernacular sermons and in Chaucer. *In* (pp. 209–19) **5.**

**2935.** WENZEL, SIEGFRIED.   Chaucer's Pardoner and his relics. SAC (11) 37–41.

**2936.** WILCOCKSON, COLIN.   Geoffrey Chaucer, The Clerk's Tale: notes. Harlow: Longman, 1987. pp. 64. (York notes.)

**2937.** WILLIAMS, DAVID.   *The Canterbury Tales*: a literary pilgrimage. (Bibl. 1988, 2208.) Rev. by N. F. Blake in EngS (70:1) 81–2; by Monica E. McAlpine in Spec (64:1) 237–8.

**2938.** ZHANG, JOHN Z.   Writing in lines 1303–27 of the Knight's Tale. ELN (26:4) 1–5.

### Troilus and Criseyde

**2939.** ANDREW, MALCOLM.   The fall of Troy in *Sir Gawain and the Green Knight* and *Troilus and Criseyde*. *In* (pp. 75–93) **27.**

**2940.** apROBERTS, ROBERT P.   A contribution to the thirteenth labour: purging the *Troilus* of incest. *In* (pp. 11–25) **23.**

**2941.** BOITANI, PIERO (ed.).   The European tragedy of Troilus. *See* **27.**

**2942.** BREWER, DEREK.   Comedy and tragedy in *Troilus and Criseyde*. *In* (pp. 95–109) **27.**

**2943.** CIGMAN, GLORIA.   Amphibologies and heresy: *Troilus and Criseyde*. *See* **1037.**

**2944.** CURETON, KEVIN K.   Chaucer's revision of *Troilus and Criseyde*. *See* **297.**

**2945.** FRANK, ROBERT WORTH, JR.   Inept Chaucer. *See* **2898.**

**2946.** HANLY, MICHAEL GERARD.   The relation of Chaucer's *Troilus and Criseyde* to the *Roman de Troyle* of Beauvau, Seneschal of Anjou. Unpub. doct. diss., Univ. of California, Irvine, 1988. [Abstr. in DA (49) 2213A.]

**2947.** HEINRICHS, KATHERINE.   'Lovers' consolations of philosophy' in Boccaccio, Machaut, and Chaucer. SAC (11) 93–115.

**2948.** KOKONIS, MICHAEL.   Rhetoric and sophistry in Chaucer's *Troilus and Criseyde*. Aristotle Univ. of Thessaloniki Yearbook of English Studies (1) 367–99.

**2949.** MACHAN, TIM WILLIAM.   *Troilus and Criseyde* IV. 897–903. ELN (27:2) 10–12.

**2950.** MANN, JILL.   Shakespeare and Chaucer: 'What is Criseyde worth?' CamQ (18:2) 109–28.

**2951.** —— Shakespeare and Chaucer: 'What is Criseyde worth?' *In* (pp. 219–42) **27.** (Repr. of **2950.**)

**2952.** NEAR, MICHAEL RAYMOND. The formal attire of being: self-consciousness and the representation of identity in Augustine's *Confessions*, the Old English *Beowulf*, and Chaucer's *Troilus*. See **2354.**

**2953.** REICHL, KARL. Chaucer's *Troilus*: philosophy and language. *In* (pp. 133–52) **27.**

**2954.** SHAFIK-GHALY, SALWA WILLIAM. Towards a medieval narratology: discourse and narration in Chrétien's *Yvain* and Chaucer's *Troilus*. Unpub. doct. diss., Univ. of Alberta, 1988. [Abstr. in DA (49) 3716–17A.]

**2955.** SHIGEO, HISASHI. *Troilus and Criseyde* as a play of love: a defense of Criseyde. PoetT (29/30) 39–57.

**2956.** SHOAF, R. A. (ed.). *Troilus and Criseyde*. Text established by A. C. BAUGH. East Lansing, MI: Colleagues Press; Woodbridge: Boydell & Brewer. pp. xxxii, 312.

**2957.** WINDEATT, BARRY. Classical and medieval elements in Chaucer's *Troilus*. *In* (pp. 111–31) **27.**

**2958.** —— *Troilus* and the disenchantment of romance. *In* (pp. 129–47) **58.**

## THE GAWAIN POET

**2959.** ANDREW, MALCOLM. The fall of Troy in *Sir Gawain and the Green Knight* and *Troilus and Criseyde*. *In* (pp. 75–93) **27.**

**2960.** ARTHUR, ROSS G. Medieval sign theory and *Sir Gawain and the Green Knight*. (Bibl. 1987, 3620.) Rev. by Russell A. Peck in Spec (64:3) 647–50; by S. H. A. Shepherd in NQ (36:4) 494–6.

**2961.** BURROW, J. A. Two notes on the Middle English *Patience*, lines 56 and 329. NQ (36:3) 300–3.

**2962.** CLEIN, WENDY. Concepts of chivalry in *Sir Gawain and the Green Knight*. (Bibl. 1988, 2220.) Rev. by Ian Bishop in NQ (36:4) 493–4.

**2963.** COOKE, W. G. *Sir Gawain and the Green Knight*: a restored dating. MÆ (58:1) 34–48.

**2964.** COOPER, R. A.; PEARSALL, D. A. The *Gawain* poems: a statistical approach to the question of common authorship. See **294.**

**2965.** FINLAYSON, JOHN. Sir Gawain, knight of the queen, in *Sir Gawain and the Green Knight*. ELN (27:1) 7–13.

**2966.** FLINT, MICHAEL. *Sir Gawain and the Green Knight*: modality in description. SN (61:2) 157–60.

**2967.** FREEMAN, ADAM; THORMANN, JANET. *Sir Gawain and the Green Knight*: an anatomy of chastity. AI (45:4) 1988, 389–410.

**2968.** GILLIGAN, JANET. Numerical composition in the Middle English *Patience*. SN (61:1) 7–11.

**2969.** GINSBERG, WARREN. Place and dialectic in *Pearl* and Dante's *Paradiso*. ELH (55:4) 1988, 731–53.

**2970.** GOEDHALS, JAMES BARRIE. Perspectives on the Gawain poet: an examination of the texts, and of modern criticism from 1945 to the present. Unpub. doct. diss., Univ. of South Africa.

**2971.** GREEN, RICHARD FIRTH.   Gawain's five fingers. ELN (27:1) 14–18.

**2972.** HORGAN, A. D.   Gawain's 'pure pentaungel' and the virtue of faith. MÆ (56:2) 1987, 310–16.

**2973.** JOHNSON, LYNN STALEY.   The voice of the Gawain-poet. (Bibl. 1988, 2224.) Rev. by A. V. C. Schmidt in MÆ (56:1) 1987, 126–8.

**2974.** KAMPS, IVO.   Magic, women, and incest: the real challenges in *Sir Gawain and the Green Knight*. Exemplaria (1:2) 313–36.

**2975.** LUTTRELL, CLAUDE.   The folk-tale element in *Sir Gawain and the Green Knight. In* (pp. 92–112) **58.**

**2976.** MORGAN, GERALD.   The action of the hunting and bedroom scenes in *Sir Gawain and the Green Knight*. MÆ (56:2) 1987, 200–16.

**2977.** NICHOLLS, JONATHAN.   The matter of courtesy: medieval courtesy books and the Gawain-poet. (Bibl. 1988, 2227.) Rev. by P. J. Mroczkowski in RES (38:152) 1987, 537–9.

**2978.** RASTETTER, S. J.   The liturgical background to the Middle English *Pearl*. Unpub. doct. diss., Univ. of Manchester. [Abstr. in IT (39:4) 1628.]

**2979.** SCHMIDT, A. V. C.   'Latent content' and 'the testimony in the text': symbolic meaning in *Sir Gawain and the Green Knight*. RES (38:150) 1987, 145–68.

**2980.** SHARON-ZISSER, SHIRLEY.   The endless knot; aspects of self-reflexivity in *Sir Gawain and the Green Knight*. YREAL (6) 67–99.

**2981.** SILVERSTEIN, THEODORE (ed.).   Sir Gawain and the Green Knight: a new critical edition. (Bibl. 1986, 3827.) Rev. by Gerald Morgan in MÆ (56:1) 1987, 125–6.

**2982.** SIMMONS-O'NEILL, ELIZABETH.   'Sires, by youre leve, that am nat I': romance and pilgrimage in Chaucer and the Gawain/Morgne-poet. *See* **2932.**

**2983.** SÖDERLIND, JOHANNES.   Immediate phrase repetition in language and in music. *In* (pp. 345–54) **24.**

**2984.** TOLIMIERI, JANE.   Medieval concepts of time and their influence on structure and meaning in the works of the Gawain-poet. Unpub. doct. diss., Univ. of Connecticut, 1988. [Abstr. in DA (49) 3718–19A.]

**2985.** WHITE, HUGH.   Blood in *Pearl*. RES (38:149) 1987, 1–13.

**2986.** WRIGLEY, CHRISTOPHER.   *Sir Gawain and the Green Knight*: the underlying myth. *In* (pp. 113–28) **58.**

# SIXTEENTH CENTURY
## GENERAL
### General Literary Studies

**2987.** ANDERSON, JUDITH H.    Biographical truth: the representation of historical persons in Tudor–Stuart writing. (Bibl. 1988, 2237.) Rev. by Scott Colley in MedRen (3) 1986, 289–93; by Karen Batley in UES (27:2) 26.

**2988.** ANON. (ed.).    British literary manuscripts from the Bodleian Library, Oxford: series 1, The English Renaissance, c. 1500–c. 1700: an inventory to part 1 of the Harvester microform collection. *See* **122.**

**2989.** ARMOUR-HILEMAN, VICTORIA LEE.    Otherworld motifs and paradigms: a study of Celtic influence on early English literature. *See* **2370.**

**2990.** AUSTERN, LINDA PHYLLIS.    'Sing againe syren': the female musician and sexual enchantment in Elizabethan life and literature. RQ (42:3) 420–48.

**2991.** BATES, C.    Courtship and courtliness: studies in Elizabethan courtly language and literature. *See* **671.**

**2992.** BERGER, HARRY, JR.    Second world and green world: studies in Renaissance fiction-making. Introd. by JOHN PATRICK LYNCH. Berkeley; London: California UP, 1988. pp. xxiii, 519. Rev. by Alastair Fowler in LRB (11:21) 24–5.

**2993.** BÖKER, UWE.    The epistle mendicant in mediaeval and Renaissance literature: the sociology and poetics of a genre. *In* (pp. 137–65) **38.**

**2994.** BRENNAN, MICHAEL.    Literary patronage in the English Renaissance: the Pembroke family. (Bibl. 1988, 2240.) Rev. by John Gouws in NQ (36:4) 499–500; by V. Houliston in CamQ (18:3) 327–35.

**2995.** CHENEY, DONALD.    Recent studies in the English Renaissance. SELit (28:1) 1988, 149–96.

**2996.** COBB, H. A.    Representations of Elizabeth I: three sites of ambiguity and contradiction. Unpub. doct. diss., Univ. of Oxford. [Abstr. in IT (39:3) 1106.]

**2997.** DALY, PETER M.    England and the emblem: the cultural context of English emblem books. *In* (pp. 1–60) **21.**

**2998.** —— (ed.).    The English emblem and the continental tradition. *See* **21.**

**2999.** —— DUER, LESLIE T.; RASPA, ANTHONY (eds).    The English emblem tradition: vol. 1, Jan van der Noot, *A Theatre for Worldlings*; Paolo Giovio, *The Worthy Tract of Paulus Jovius*; Lodovico Domenici, *Certain Noble Devises both Militarie and Amorous*; Geffrey Whitney, *A Choice of Emblemes*. *See* **82.**

**3000.** DEAN, CHRISTOPHER.    Arthur of England: English attitudes to King Arthur and the Knights of the Round Table in the Middle Ages and the Renaissance. *See* **2408.**

**3001.** DIEHL, HUSTON.   An index of icons in English emblem books 1500–1700. *See* **83**.

**3002.** DUBROW, HEATHER; STRIER, RICHARD.   Introduction: the historical Renaissance. *In* (pp. 1–12) **31**.

**3003.** ————— (eds).   The historical Renaissance: new essays on Tudor and Stuart literature and culture. *See* **31**.

**3004.** FERGUSON, MARGARET W.; QUILLIGAN, MAUREEN; VICKERS, NANCY J. (eds).   Rewriting the Renaissance: the discourses of sexual difference in early modern Europe. *See* **54**.

**3005.** GOLDBERG, JONATHAN.   Voice terminal echo: postmodernism and English Renaissance texts. (Bibl. 1988, 2246.) Rev. by Margarita Stocker in MLR (84:1) 126; by Richard Strier in RQ (42:2) 347–51; by Elaine Eldridge in SCN (47:1/2) 1.

**3006.** GREENBLATT, STEPHEN.   Renaissance self-fashioning: from More to Shakespeare. (Bibl. 1985, 3368.) Rev. by Alan Sinfield in MedRen (2) 1985, 324–8.

**3007.** HANNAY, MARGARET PATTERSON (ed.).   Silent but for the word: Tudor women as patrons, translators, and writers of religious works. (Bibl. 1987, 3654.) Rev. by Josephine A. Roberts in RES (38:152) 1987, 544–5.

**3008.** HOLSTUN, JAMES.   Ranting at the new historicism. ELR (19:2) 189–225.

**3009.** HORDEN, JOHN.   Renaissance emblem books: a comment on terminology. *In* (pp. 61–70) **37**.

**3010.** JUNGMAN, ROBERT E.   *Western Wind* and Tibullus I, 45–48. ELN (27:2) 19–26.

**3011.** KINNEY, ARTHUR F.   Humanist poetics: thought, rhetoric, and fiction in sixteenth-century England. (Bibl. 1988, 2251.) Rev. by Charles Ross in MP (86:4) 421–3; by Philip Rollinson in MedRen (4) 263–4; by Michael G. Brennan in RES (39:156) 1988, 541–2.

**3012.** LINDENBAUM, PETER.   Changing landscapes: anti-pastoral sentiment in the English Renaissance. (Bibl. 1988, 2254.) Rev. by Theodore B. Leinwand in MedRen (4) 273–5; by Michael G. Brennan in RES (39:156) 1988, 541–2.

**3013.** LLOYD, PETER.   Perspectives and identities: the Elizabethan writer's search to know his world. London: Rubicon. pp. 234.

**3014.** MILWARD, PETER; TATSUMI, TOYOHIKO (comps).   Renaissance to shin sekai. (The Renaissance and the New World.) Tokyo: Aratake Press. pp. viii, 128. (Renaissance sousho, 19.)

**3015.** MORSE, DAVID.   England's time of crisis: from Shakespeare to Milton: a cultural history. Basingstoke: Macmillan. pp. viii, 391.

**3016.** PARKER, PATRICIA; QUINT, DAVID (eds).   Literary theory/ Renaissance texts. (Bibl. 1988, 2258.) Rev. by Peter Erickson in MedRcn (4) 282–9.

**3017.** PATTERSON, ANNABEL.   Censorship and interpretation: the conditions of writing and reading in early modern England. (Bibl. 1987, 3670.) Rev. by Germaine Warkentin in UTQ (56:3) 1987, 456–60; by Achsah Guibbory in JDJ (6:2) 1987, 295–8.

**3018.** RICHMOND, HUGH M.   Puritans and libertines: Anglo–French literary relations in the Reformation. (Bibl. 1986, 3860.) Rev. by William Edinger in MedRen (2) 1985, 337–43.

**3019.** SCHENDL, HERBERT.   Elizabethan concordances: some considerations. MESN (21) 24–7.

**3020.** SCHOENBAUM, S.   Shakespeare and others. (Bibl. 1986, 3861.) Rev. by Peter Bement in RES (38:152) 1987, 556–7.

**3021.** SLIGHTS, WILLIAM W. E.   The edifying margins of Renaissance English books. *See* **117.**

**3022.** STEIN, ARNOLD.   The house of death: messages from the English Renaissance. (Bibl. 1988, 2263.) Rev. by Kevin Dunn in SQ (40:2) 245–8; by G. R. Evans in RES (39:155) 1988, 467.

**3023.** TITLESTAD, P. J. H.   Religion, politics and literature: the Elizabethan background new modelled. Shakespeare in Southern Africa (2) 1988, 42–50.

**3024.** TRIBBLE, EVELYN BYRD.   Margins and marginality: some uses of printed page in early modern England. *See* **118.**

**3025.** VAN DORSTEN, J. A.   The Anglo-Dutch Renaissance: seven essays. Ed. by J. VAN DEN BERG and ALASTAIR HAMILTON. With contributions by A. G. H. BACHRACH and ROY STRONG. Leiden; New York: Brill, 1988. pp. iii (unnumbered), 90. (Publications of the Sir Thomas Browne Inst., 10.) (Tribute to van Dorsten.)

**3026.** VON KOPPENFELS, WERNER.   Lust in action: Über einige Metamorphosen Ovids in der elisabethanischen Literatur. SJW 242–65.

**3027.** WOODBRIDGE, LINDA.   Women and the English Renaissance: literature and the nature of womankind, 1540–1620. (Bibl. 1987, 3689.) Rev. by Elizabeth H. Hageman in MedRen (4) 318–22.

**3028.** YOUNG, ALAN R.   Wenceslaus Hollar, the London book trade, and two unidentified English emblem books. *In* (pp. 151–202) **21.**

## Drama and the Theatre

**3029.** AGNEW, JEAN-CHRISTOPHE.   Worlds apart: the market and the theater in Anglo-American thought, 1550–1750. (Bibl. 1988, 2267.) Rev. by Lars Engle in SQ (40:3) 372–4; by Robert D. Hume in MLR (84:4) 921–2.

**3030.** ANDERSON, L. M.   Jefferson Hope as tragic revenger. BSJ (39:3) 135–43. (Sir Arthur Conan Doyle's *A Study in Scarlet* as revenge tragedy.)

**3031.** ANON. (ed.).   Igirisu Renaissance no shosou: engeki, bunka, shisou no tenkai. (Aspects of the English Renaissance: evolution in drama, culture and thought.) Tokyo: Chuo UP. pp. xx, 492. (Chuo Univ. Inst. for Humanities Research.)

**3032.** ASTINGTON, JOHN H.   Descent machinery in the playhouses. MedRen (2) 1985, 119–33.

**3033.** BALKIN, MARTHA MUNSELL.   The Renaissance tool villain and his medieval heritage. *See* **2549.**

**3034.** BARBER, CHARLES.   The theme of honour's tongue: a study of social attitudes in the English drama from Shakespeare to Dryden. (Bibl. 1985, 3396.) Rev. by Éliane Cuvelier in EA (42:2) 212–13.

**3035.** BARKER, S. A.   An examination of the relationship between English drama 1550–1642 and contemporary military science. Unpub. doct. diss., Univ. of Wales, 1988. [Abstr. in IT (39:3) 1105.]

**3036.** BELSEY, CATHERINE.   The subject of tragedy: identity and difference in Renaissance drama. (Bibl. 1988, 2271.) Rev. by Harriett Hawkins in RES (38:150) 1987, 278–9; by Paul Gaudet in MedRen (4) 217–23.

**3037.** BERGERON, DAVID M. (ed.).   Pageantry in the Shakespearean theater. (Bibl. 1988, 2273.) Rev. by Anne Lancashire in UTQ (56:3) 1987, 463–4.

**3038.** BERRY, HERBERT.   The first public playhouses, especially the Red Lion. SQ (40:2) 133–48.

**3039.** —— Shakespeare's playhouses. (Bibl. 1988, 2274.) Rev. by S. P. Cerasano in SQ (40:3) 366–9.

**3040.** BEVINGTON, DAVID.   Editing Renaissance drama in paperback. RenD (19) 1988, 127–47.

**3041.** BOSWELL, JACKSON CAMPBELL.   Seven actors in search of a biographer. MedRen (2) 1985, 51–6. (Thomas Moyle, Simon Fish, John Roo, Richard Spenser, — Ramsey, Andrew Hewit, Myles Somelymes.)

**3042.** BRADEN, GORDON.   Renaissance tragedy and the Senecan tradition: anger's privilege. (Bibl. 1988, 2275.) Rev. by Harriett Hawkins in RES (38:150) 1987, 279–80; by Marion Trousdale in MedRen (4) 223–7.

**3043.** BRAUNMULLER, A. R.; BULMAN, J. C. (eds).   Comedy from Shakespeare to Sheridan: change and continuity in the English and European dramatic tradition: essays in honour of Eugene M. Waith. (Bibl. 1987, 15.) Rev. by Arthur F. Kinney in HLQ (52:4) 509–16.

**3044.** BRISTOL, MICHAEL D.   Carnival and theater: plebeian culture and the structure of authority in Renaissance England. (Bibl. 1988, 2276.) Rev. by Thomas Cartelli in MedRen (4) 228–31; by Frank E. Manning in TDR (33:1) 20–2.

**3045.** BUELER, LOIS E.   The structural uses of incest in English Renaissance drama. RenD (15) 1984, 115–45.

**3046.** CARPENTER, SARAH.   Drama and politics: Scotland in the 1530s. METh (10:2) 1988, 81–90.

**3047.** CERASANO, S. P.   The 'business' of shareholding, the Fortune playhouses, and Francis Grace's will. MedRen (2) 1985, 231–51.

**3048.** —— Raising a playhouse from the dust. SQ (40:4) 483–90. (The Rose Theatre.)

**3049.** —— Shakespeare's elusive Globe: review article. MedRen (3) 1986, 265–75.

**3050.** CLARE, JANET.   'Greater themes for insurrection's arguing': political censorship of the Elizabethan and Jacobean stage. RES (38:150) 1987, 169–83.

**3051.** COHEN, WALTER.   Drama of a nation: public theater in Renaissance England and Spain. (Bibl. 1987, 3706.) Rev. by Jonathan

Dollimore in MedRen (4) 231–7; by David Mills in RES (38:149) 1987, 70–2.

**3052.** —— Intrigue tragedy in Renaissance England and Spain. RenD (15) 1984, 175–200.

**3053.** COMAN, ALAN C.   The Congleton accounts: further evidence of Elizabethan and Jacobean drama in Cheshire. REEDNewsletter (14:1) 3–18.

**3054.** COOK, ANN JENNALIE.   The privileged playgoers of Shakespeare's London, 1576–1642. (Bibl. 1986, 3886.) Rev. by Stephen Booth in MedRen (2) 1985, 306–11.

**3055.** COOKE, W. G.   Queen Elizabeth never slept here: Cassandra, Duchess of Chandos, as an authority for royal progresses. REEDNewsletter (14:1) 18–20.

**3056.** DAVIDSON, CLIFFORD; GIANAKARIS, C. J.; STROUPE, JOHN H. (eds).   Drama in the Renaissance: comparative and critical essays. (Bibl. 1987, 19.) Rev. by Lawrence Manley in YES (19) 318–9.

**3057.** DESSEN, ALAN C.   Elizabethan stage conventions and modern interpreters. (Bibl. 1987, 3710.) Rev. by D. F. Rowan in MedRen (3) 1986, 307–10.

**3058.** —— Modern productions and the Elizabethan scholar. RenD (18) 1987, 205–23.

**3059.** —— Much virtue in *as*: Elizabethan stage locales and modern interpretation. *In* (pp. 132–8) **55.**

**3060.** DUTTON, RICHARD.   *Hamlet, An Apology for Actors*, and the sign of the Globe. ShS (41) 35–43.

**3061.** FEINBERG, ANAT.   'Like demie Gods the Apes began to move': the ape in the English theatrical tradition, 1580–1660. CEl (35) 1–13.

**3062.** FORKER, CHARLES R.   'A little more than kin, and less than kind': incest, intimacy, narcissism, and identity in Elizabethan and Stuart drama. MedRen (4) 13–51.

**3063.** GAIR, W. REAVLEY.   The Children of Paul's: the story of a theatre company, 1553–1608. (Bibl. 1987, 3715.) Rev. by William B. Long in MedRen (3) 1986, 320–4.

**3064.** GARNER, SHIRLEY NELSON.   'Let her paint an inch thick': painted ladies in Renaissance drama and society. RenD (20) 123–39.

**3065.** GREGORY, DAMIEN.   Coming up roses? HT (39) July, 3–4. (Excavation of the Rose Theatre.)

**3066.** GURR, ANDREW.   The Shakespearian stages, forty years on. ShS (41) 1–12.

**3067.** —— ORRELL, JOHN.   Rebuilding Shakespeare's Globe. London: Weidenfeld & Nicolson. pp. 197. Rev. by Keith Brown in TLS, 8 Sept., 966.

**3068.** HADORN, PETER THOMAS.   Power, propaganda and subversion: chivalry on the English Renaissance stage. Unpub. doct. diss., Univ. of Illinois at Urbana-Champaign. [Abstr. in DA (50) 1311A.]

**3069.** HALLETT, CHARLES A.; HALLETT, ELAINE S.   The revenger's madness: a study of revenge tragedy motifs. (Bibl. 1985, 3873.) Rev. by Harry Keyishian in MedRen (1) 1984, 271–4.

**3070.** HASSEL, R. CHRIS, JR. Renaissance drama and the English church year. (Bibl. 1982, 4179.) Rev. by Alice-Lyle Scoufos in MedRen (2) 1985, 328–30.

**3071.** HATTAWAY, MICHAEL. Elizabethan popular theatre: plays in performance. (Bibl. 1988, 2293.) Rev. by William B. Long in MedRen (4) 247–52.

**3072.** HILLIARD, MARGARET WILSON. To sacrifice a child: the development of a theme in medieval and Renaissance drama. See **2559.**

**3073.** HOWARD, JEAN E. Scripts and/versus playhouses: ideological production and the Renaissance public stage. RenD (20) 31–49.

**3074.** HUNTER, G. K. The beginnings of Elizabethan drama: revolution and continuity. RenD (17) 1986, 29–52.

**3075.** HYDE, THOMAS. Identity and acting in Elizabethan tragedy. RenD (15) 1984, 93–114.

**3076.** KAWACHI, YOSHIKO. Calendar of English Renaissance drama, 1558–1642. New York; London: Garland, 1986. pp. xvii, 351. (Garland reference library of the humanities, 661.) Rev. by Kristian Smidt in EngS (70:1) 86–8.

**3077.** KNUTSON, ROSLYN L. Evidence for the assignment of plays to the repertory of Shakespeare's Company. MedRen (4) 63–89.

**3078.** KOHLER, RICHARD C. Excavating Henslowe's Rose. SQ (40:4) 475–82.

**3079.** KURTZ, MARTHA ANNE. 'Present laughter': comedy in the Elizabethan history play. Unpub. doct. diss., Univ. of Toronto. [Abstr. in DA (50) 1666A.]

**3080.** LANCASHIRE, IAN. History of a transition: review article. MedRen (3) 1986, 277–88.

**3081.** —— (ed.). Two Tudor interludes: *The Interlude of Youth* and *Hick Scorner*. Baltimore, MD: Johns Hopkins UP, 1980. (Bibl. 1983, 4027.) Rev. by Paul Werstine in MedRen (1) 1984, 255–62.

**3082.** LEGGATT, ALEXANDER. English drama: Shakespeare to the Restoration, 1590–1660. Rev. by S. McCafferty in NQ (36:3) 378–9.

**3083.** LEVENSON, JILL L. Recent studies in Elizabethan and Jacobean drama. SELit (28:2) 1988, 331–89.

**3084.** LEVIN, RICHARD. Women in the Renaissance theatre audience. SQ (40:2) 165–74.

**3085.** LEWIS, CYNTHIA. 'Wise men, folly-fall'n': characters named Antonio in English Renaissance drama. RenD (20) 197–236.

**3086.** LIMON, JERZY. Gentlemen of a company: English players in central and eastern Europe, 1590–1660. (Bibl. 1988, 2300.) Rev. by Peter Hollindale in RES (38:150) 1987, 247–8; by Ann Thompson in MLR (84:3) 714.

**3087.** LINDLEY, DAVID (ed.). The court masque. (Bibl. 1987, 3734.) Rev. by Catherine M. Shaw in MedRen (4) 275–8; by Brian Gibbons in RES (38:149) 1987, 116–17.

**3088.** LONG, WILLIAM B. 'A bed/for woodstock': a warning for the unwary. MedRen (2) 1985, 91–118. (*Thomas of Woodstock.*)

**3089.** McALINDON, T. English Renaissance tragedy. (Bibl. 1988,

2302.) Rev. by Roma Gill in RES (39:156) 1988, 543–4; by Richard Dutton in MLR (84:3) 712–13.

**3090.** McKinnell, John. Drama and ceremony in the last years of Durham Cathedral Priory. METh (10:2) 1988, 91–111.

**3091.** MacLean, Sally-Beth. Leicester and the Evelyns: new evidence for the Continental tour of Leicester's men. RES (39:156) 1988, 487–93.

**3092.** McMillin, Scott. Building stories: Greg, Fleay, and the plot of *2 Seven Deadly Sins*. MedRen (4) 53–62.

**3093.** McPherson, David. Three charges against sixteenth- and seventeenth-century playwrights: libel, bawdy, and blasphemy. MedRen (2) 1985, 269–82.

**3094.** Maguire, Nancy Klein (ed.). Renaissance tragicomedy: explorations in genre and politics. New York: AMS Press, 1987. pp. 244. (AMS studies in the Renaissance, 20.). Rev. by Eugene M. Waith in RQ (42:3) 576–9.

**3095.** Mansfield, R. G. The protean player: the concept and practice of doubling in the plays of Shakespeare and his contemporaries, *c.* 1576–1631. Unpub. doct. diss., Univ. of East Anglia. [Abstr. in IT (39:3) 1096.]

**3096.** Marder, Louis. Foundation of the Rose Theatre discovered. SNL (39:1/2) 19–20.

**3097.** —— Remains of the Globe discovered. SNL (39:3/4) 25–6.

**3098.** Mills, David. William Aldersey's *History of the Mayors of Chester*. REEDNewsletter (14:2) 2–10.

**3099.** Mullaney, Steven. The place of the stage: license, play, and power in Renaissance England. (Bibl. 1988, 2310.) Rev. by Elaine Eldridge in SCN (47:1/2) 17; by Mary Janell Metzger in SixCT (20:3) 524; by John Drakakis in RQ (42:3) 580–2.

**3100.** Orgel, Stephen. Nobody's perfect; or, Why did the English stage take boys for women? SAQ (88:1) 7–29.

**3101.** Orlin, Lena Cowen. Man's house as his castle in *Arden of Feversham*. MedRen (2) 1985, 57–89.

**3102.** Orrell, John. The human stage: English theatre design, 1567–1640. Cambridge: CUP, 1988. pp. xix, 292. Rev. by R. A. Foakes in RQ (42:4) 879–81; by Andrew Gurr in SQ (40:2) 248–50; by Duncan Smith in TJ (41:4) 573–5; by Keith Brown in TLS, 8 Sept., 966.

**3103.** Paster, Gail Kern. Leaky vessels: the incontinent women of city comedy. RenD (18) 1987, 43–65.

**3104.** Pavel, Thomas G. The poetics of plot: the case of English Renaissance drama. (Bibl. 1988, 2313.) Rev. by James Hansford in RES (39:149) 1987, 69–70.

**3105.** Peat, Derek. Looking back to front: the view from the Lords' room. *In* (pp. 180–94) **55**.

**3106.** Pilkington, Mark C. Playing in the Guildhall, Bristol. REEDNewsletter (14:2) 15–19.

**3107.** Pinciss, G. M. Literary creations: conventional characters in the drama of Shakespeare and his contemporaries. (Bibl. 1988, 2315.) Rev. by Joel G. Fink in TJ (41:3) 417–18.

**3108.** POPHAM, SHELBY ANNE. 'Tis a tale told: narrative in Renaissance pastoral drama in Italy, France, and England. Unpub. doct. diss., Univ. of California, Los Angeles, 1988. [Abstr. in DA (49) 1793–4A.]

**3109.** POTTER, LOIS (gen. ed.). The 'Revels' history of drama in English: vol. 2, 1500–1576. By NORMAN SANDERS *et al.* London; New York: Methuen, 1980. pp. xxxvii, 290. Rev. by Ian Lancashire in MedRen (3) 1986, 277–88.

**3110.** ROBINSON, J. W. The art and meaning of *Gammer Gurton's Needle.* RenD (14) 1983, 45–77.

**3111.** ROSE, MARY BETH. The expense of spirit: love and sexuality in English Renaissance drama. Ithaca, NY; London: Cornell UP, 1988. pp. xi, 239. Rev. by Lorraine Helms in TJ (41:3) 416–17.

**3112.** —— Moral conceptions of sexual love in Elizabethan comedy. RenD (15) 1984, 1–29.

**3113.** ROZETT, MARTHA TUCK. The doctrine of election and the emergence of Elizabethan tragedy. (Bibl. 1988, 2319.) Rev. by Lois Potter in MedRen (4) 294–6.

**3114.** SANDONA, MARK. Patience and the agents of Renaissance drama. Unpub. doct. diss., Harvard Univ. [Abstr. in DA (50) 945A.]

**3115.** SCOTT, MARGARET. Machiavelli and the Machiavel. RenD (15) 1984, 147–74.

**3116.** SOMERSET, J. A. B. Local drama and playing places at Shrewsbury: new findings from the Borough Records. *See* **2571.**

**3117.** SPINRAD, PHOEBE S. The summons of death on the medieval and Renaissance English stage. *See* **2572.**

**3118.** STREITBERGER, W. R. Edmond Tyllney, Master of the Revels and censor of plays: a descriptive index to his diplomatic manual on Europe. *See* **179.**

**3119.** —— Henry VIII's entertainment for the Queen of Scots, 1516: a new Revels account and Cornish's play. MedRen (1) 1984, 29–35.

**3120.** TWAIJ, MOHAMMED BAQIR. The common themes [*sic*] *The True Tragedy of Richard the Third* and Shakespeare's *Richard III.* Al-Mustansiriya Literary Review (Al-Mustansiriya Univ., Baghdad) (8) 1984, 79–105.

**3121.** TYLUS, JANE. Veiling the stage: the politics of innocence in Renaissance drama. TJ (41:1) 16–29.

**3122.** VINCE, RONALD. Renaissance theatre: a historiographical handbook. Westport, CT: Greenwood Press, 1984. pp. xi, 204. Rev. by Stuart M. Kurland in MedRen (3) 1986, 349–51.

**3123.** WAITH, EUGENE M. Patterns and perspectives in English Renaissance drama. Newark: Delaware UP; London: Assoc. UPs, 1988. pp 312. Rev. by Arthur F. Kinney in HLQ (52:4) 509–16.

**3124.** WASSON, JOHN. Professional actors in the Middle Ages and early Renaissance. *See* **2578.**

**3125.** WASSON, JOHN M. (ed.). Records of early English drama: Devon. *See* **2579.**

**3126.** WEIMANN, ROBERT.   Shakespeare und die Macht der Mimesis: Autorität und Repräsentation im elisabethanischen Theater. Berlin; Weimar: Aufbau, 1988. pp. 370. (Dokumentation, Essayistik, Literaturwissenschaft.)

**3127.** WELCH, ROBERT.   Seneca and the English Renaissance: the old world and the new. *In* (pp. 204–18) **37.**

**3128.** WERSTINE, PAUL.   Provenance and printing history in two Revels editions: review article. *See* **407.**

**3129.** WHITE, PAUL WHITFIELD.   Predestinarian theology in the mid-Tudor play *Jacob and Esau.* RenR (12:4) 1988, 291–302.

**3130.** WIGGINS, M. J.   The assassin in English Renaissance drama, 1558–1642. Unpub. doct. diss., Univ. of Oxford. [Abstr. in IT (39:3) 1107.]

**3131.** WRIGHT, STEPHEN K.   *The Historie of King Edward the Fourth*: a chronicle play on the Coventry Pageant wagons. MedRen (3) 1986, 69–81.

### Fiction

**3132.** CREIGH, GEOFFREY; BELFIELD, JANE (eds).   *The Cobler of Caunterburie* and *Tarltons Newes out of Purgatorie.* (Bibl. 1987, 3759.) Rev. by Neil Rhodes in NQ (36:1) 93–4.

**3133.** DI BIASE, CARMINE GIUSEPPE.   Elizabethan framed tales and the Italian *novella.* Unpub. doct. diss., Ohio State Univ., 1988. [Abstr. in DA (49) 2226A.]

**3134.** LUCAS, C.   Writing for women: a study of woman as reader in Elizabethan romance. Unpub. doct. diss., Univ. of Exeter. [Abstr. in IT (39:2) 485.]

**3135.** SAVORY, S. J.   Artificial realism: form and content in Elizabethan fiction. Unpub. doct. diss., Univ. of Bradford, 1988. [Abstr. in IT (39:4) 1629.]

### Literature for Children

**3136.** WOODEN, WARREN W.   Children's literature of the English Renaissance. Ed. by JEANIE WATSON. (Bibl. 1988, 2335.) Rev. by Mary Burgan in AHR (94:4) 1092; by Peter Hollindale in RES (39:155) 1988, 428–9.

### Poetry

**3137.** BENSON, C. DAVID.   True Troilus and false Cresseid: the descent from tragedy. *In* (pp. 153–70) **27.**

**3138.** BURROW, C. J.   The English Humanist epic 1580–1614. Unpub. doct. diss., Univ. of Oxford, 1988. [Abstr. in IT (39:3) 1105.]

**3139.** BUTLER, GEORGE FRANK.   The spiritual odyssey and the Renaissance epic. Unpub. doct. diss., Univ. of Connecticut, 1988. Abstr. in DA (49) 2209A.

**3140.** CHAUDHURI, SUKANTA.   Renaissance pastoral: and its English developments. Oxford: Clarendon Press. pp. ix, 487. (Cf. bibl. 1986, 3836.)

**3141.** Cook, Elizabeth.   Seeing through words: the scope of late Renaissance poetry. (Bibl. 1988, 2339.) Rev. by Michael G. Brennan in RES (38:152) 1987, 560–1; by Dick Higgins in SCN (47:1/2) 11–12.

**3142.** David, Gail Pliam.   Diverse (in)versions: female heroics in the Renaissance pastoral romance and in women's pastoral fiction from Fanny Burney to George Eliot. Unpub. doct. diss., Univ. of California, Davis, 1988. [Abstr. in DA (50) 448–9A.]

**3143.** Doughtie, Edward (ed.).   *Liber Lilliati*: Elizabethan verse and song (Bodleian MS Rawlinson poetry, 148). (Bibl. 1987, 3769.) Rev. by Patricia Thomson in YES (19) 311–13.

**3144.** Ferry, Anne.   The art of naming. Chicago; London: Chicago UP, 1988. pp. xix, 203. Rev. by Jonathan Goldberg in SQ (40:3) 374–6; by Eugene D. Hill in SixCT (20:3) 489–90.

**3145.** Grossman, Marshall.   Literary forms and historical consciousness in Renaissance poetry. Exemplaria (1:2) 247–64.

**3146.** Hardison, O. B.   Prosody and purpose in the English Renaissance. Baltimore, MD; London: Johns Hopkins UP. pp. xvi, 342.

**3147.** Helgerson, Richard.   Barbarous tongues: the ideology of poetic form in Renaissance England. *In* (pp. 273–92) **31.**

**3148.** Knapp, Jeffrey Dana.   An empire nowhere: England and America, from *Utopia* to *The Tempest*. Unpub. doct. diss., Univ. of California, Berkeley, 1988. [Abstr. in DA (49) 3370A.]

**3149.** Low, Anthony.   The georgic revolution. (Bibl. 1988, 2348.) Rev. by Rivkah Zim in RES (38:149) 1987, 114–15; by Stanley Stewart in JDJ (6:2) 1987, 299–303.

**3150.** Maynard, Winifred.   Elizabethan lyric poetry and its music. (Bibl. 1988, 2350.) Rev. by Patricia Thomson in MLR (84:1) 117–19; by Linda Phyllis Austern in MP (86:3) 294–6.

**3151.** Moody, Ellen.   Six elegiac poems, possibly by Anne Cecil de Vere, Countess of Oxford. ELR (19:2) 152–70.

**3152.** Pigman, G. W., III.   Grief and English Renaissance elegy. (Bibl. 1987, 3786.) Rev. by Anthony Low in JDJ (6:2) 1987, 285–8; by James Egan in SCN (47:1/2) 13–14.

**3153.** Ringler, William A., Jr.   Bibliography and index of English verse printed 1476–1558. *See* **2507.**

**3154.** Smith, A. J.   The metaphysics of love: studies in Renaissance love poetry from Dante to Milton. (Bibl. 1987, 3788.) Rev. by Cedric C. Brown in RES (38:149) 1987, 65–6.

**3155.** Smith, Debra Morris.   The business of the poet: poetic self-awareness from Sidney to Johnson. Unpub. doct. diss., Michigan State Univ., 1988. [Abstr. in DA (50) 693A.]

**3156.** Smith, Kathy Overhulse.   Making much of time: rhetorical strategies of Renaissance *carpe diem* poetry. Unpub. doct. diss., Univ. of Missouri–Columbia, 1988. [Abstr. in DA (49) 3372A.]

**3157.** Westerweel, Bart.   The well-tempered lady and the unruly horse: convention and submerged metaphor in Renaissance literature and art. *In* (pp. 105–22) **16.**

**3158.** Zim, Rivkah.   English metrical psalms: poetry as praise and prayer, 1535–1601. (Bibl. 1988, 2363.) Rev. by Gijsbert J. Siertsemea in HLQ (52:4) 517–18; by Michael G. Brennan in NQ (36:3) 377–8; by Noel J. Kinnamon in ChrisL (38:2) 81–2.

## Prose

**3159.** HILL, GEOFFREY.    Of diligence and jeopardy. TLS, 17 Nov., 1273–6 (review-article).
**3160.** MERCER, JOHN M.    Adaptation of conventions in the Elizabethan prose dedication. ExRC (15) 49–58.
**3161.** RASHKOW, ILONA NEMESNYIK.    Upon the dark places: English Renaissance biblical translation. Unpub. doct. diss., Univ. of Maryland College Park, 1988. [Abstr. in DA (49) 2234A.]
**3162.** SHUGER, DEBORA K.    Sacred rhetoric: the Christian grand style in the English Renaissance. See **1321.**

## Related Studies

**3163.** AMUSSEN, SUSAN DWYER.    An ordered society: gender and class in early modern England. Oxford: Blackwell, 1988. pp. xi, 203. Rev. by Merry E. Wiesner in SixCT (20:4) 706–7.
**3164.** ASTON, MARGARET.    England's iconoclasts: 1, Laws against images. Oxford: Clarendon Press. pp. xiv, 548. Rev. by Diarmaid MacCulloch in SixCT (20:3) 491.
**3165.** BATH, MICHAEL.    Collared stags and bridled lions: Queen Elizabeth's household accounts. In (pp. 225–57) **21.**
**3166.** BAUMANN, UWE.    Seneca-Rezeption im neulateinischen Drama der englischen Renaissance. LJGG (30) 55–77.
**3167.** BOZEMAN, THEODORE DWIGHT.    To live ancient lives: the primitivist dimension in Puritanism. Chapel Hill: North Carolina UP, 1988. pp. x, 413. (Institute of early American history and culture.) Rev. by John Gatta in SCN (47:1/2) 14–15; by John S. Erwin in JAH (76:3) 909–10.
**3168.** BRAND, PETER.    Disguise in Renaissance comedy. CompCrit (10) 1988, 69–92.
**3169.** CAHN, SUSAN.    Industry of devotion: the transformation of women's work in England, 1500–1660. New York: Columbia UP, 1987. pp. 252. Rev. by Merry E. Wiesner in SixCT (20:1) 144.
**3170.** COLLINS, STEPHEN L.    From divine cosmos to sovereign state: an intellectual history of consciousness and the idea of order in Renaissance England. Oxford; New York: OUP. pp. ix, 235. Rev. by Alan Rudrum in TLS, 22 Sept., 1036.
**3171.** COLLINSON, PATRICK.    The birthpangs of Protestant England: religious and cultural change in the sixteenth and seventeenth centuries. New York: St Martin's Press; Basingstoke: Macmillan, 1988. pp. xiii, 188. (Anstey Memorial Lectures, 3.) Rev. by Peter F. Macluso in SixCT (20:4) 723–4.
**3172.** COULIANO, IOAN P.    Eros and magic in the Renaissance. Trans. by MARGARET COOK. Introd. by MIRCEA ELIADE. Chicago; London: Chicago UP, 1987. pp. xxi, 264. (Orig. pub. as *Eros et Magie à la*

*Renaissance, 1485.* Paris: Flammarion, 1984.) Rev. by Robert Boenig in SCN (47:3/4) 53–4; by Mary Winkler in SixCT (20:2) 300–1; by Lorraine Helms in TJ (41:3) 416.

**3173.** DAVIES, HORTON. Like angels from a cloud: the English metaphysical preachers, 1588–1645. (Bibl. 1988, 2376.) Rev. by G. R. Evans in RES (39:153) 1988, 160–1.

**3174.** DEMOLEN, RICHARD L. The spirituality of Erasmus of Rotterdam. (Bibl. 1988, 2377.) Rev. by Anne M. O'Donnell in RQ (42:2) 308–10.

**3175.** GILLESPIE, GERALD. Garden and labyrinth of time: studies in Renaissance and Baroque literature. New York; Berne; Frankfurt; Paris: Lang, 1988. pp. 335. (Germanic studies in America, 56.) Rev. by Alan Menhennet in NC (7) 187–90.

**3176.** GODMAN, PETER. Johannes Secundus and Renaissance Latin poetry. RES (39:154) 1988, 258–72.

**3177.** HOFFMANN, MANFRED. Faith and piety in Erasmus's thought. SixCT (20:2) 241–58.

**3178.** HOUSTON, R. A. Literacy in early modern Europe: culture and education 1500–1800. London: Longman, 1988. pp. ix, 266.

**3179.** INGRAM, MARTIN. Church courts, sex and marriage in England, 1570–1640. Cambridge: CUP, 1987. pp. xiii, 412. Rev. by J. Sears McGee in RQ (42:4) 857–9; by Sherrin Marshall in SixCT (20:2) 354–5; by Wm Kent Hackmann in JRMMRA (10) 113–14.

**3180.** JAMES, MERVYN. Society, politics and culture: studies in early modern England. (Bibl. 1986, 4017.) Rev. by C. W. Brooks in DUJ (81:1) 1988, 150–1; by John Scattergood in YES (19) 301–4.

**3181.** JOHNSTON, ALEXANDRA F. English guilds and municipal authority. RenR (13:1) 69–88.

**3182.** KELLEY, DONALD R. Ideas of resistance before Elizabeth. *In* (pp. 48–76) **31.**

**3183.** KINNEY, ARTHUR F. Continental humanistic poetics: studies in Erasmus, Castiglione, Marguerite de Navarre, Rabelais, and Cervantes. Amherst; London: Massachusetts UP. pp. xviii, 367.

**3184.** LAKE, PETER. Anglicans and Puritans? Presbyterianism and English Conformist thought from Whitgift to Hooker. London: Unwin Hyman, 1988. pp. 262. Rev. by W. Speed Hill in SCN (47:3/4) 39–40; by James B. McSwain in SixCT (20:3) 485–6.

**3185.** MANLEY, LAWRENCE. From matron to monster: Tudor–Stuart London and the languages of urban description. *In* (pp. 347–74) **31.**

**3186.** MERKEL, INGRID; DEBUS, ALLEN G. (eds). Hermeticism and the Renaissance: intellectual history and the occult in early modern Europe. Washington, DC: Folger Library, 1988. pp. 438. Rev. by Charles G. Nauert in RQ (42:3) 550–2.

**3187.** MULRYNE, J. R.; SHEWRING, MARGARET (eds). War, literature and the arts in sixteenth-century Europe. Basingstoke: Macmillan. pp. xii, 210. (Warwick studies in the European humanities.)

**3188.** PARRY, G. J. R. A Protestant vision: William Harrison and the reformation of Elizabethan England. Cambridge: CUP, 1987. pp. ix,

348. (Cambridge studies in the history and theory of politics.) Rev. by Arthur J. Slavin in RQ (41:4) 1988, 727–31; by Ronald H. Fritze in SixCT (19:2) 1988, 277–8.

**3189.** QUESTIER, M. C.  Some aspects of English recusant polemical literature. Unpub. M.Phil. diss., Univ. of Sussex, 1988. [Abstr. in IT (38:4) 1473.]

**3190.** SEYMOUR, IAN.  The political magic of John Dee. HT (39) Jan., 29–35.

**3191.** SLAVIN, ARTHUR J.  Defining the divorce. SixCT (20:1) 105–11 (review-article).

**3192.** SPEVACK, MARVIN; BINNS, J. W.; WECKERMANN, HANS-JÜRGEN (gen. eds).  *Cancer* [Anon.]; *Fraus honesta*, by Edmund Stubbe. Ed. by THOMAS W. BEST. Hildesheim; Zurich; New York: Olms, 1987. pp. iv, 23, (facsims) 510. (Renaissance Latin drama in England, 2:2.)

**3193.** ———————— *Iephte*, by John Christopherson; *Herodes*, by William Goldingham. Ed. by CHRISTOPHER UPTON. Hildesheim; Zurich; New York: Olms, 1988. pp. iv, 18, (facsims) 80. (Renaissance Latin drama in England, 2:7.)

**3194.** ———————— *Leander*; *Labyrinthus*, by Walter Hawkesworth. Ed. by SUSAN BROCK. Hildesheim; Zurich; New York: Olms, 1987. pp. ii, 16, (facsims) 181. Renaissance Latin drama in England, 2:3.)

**3195.** ———————— *Risus anglicanus* [Anon.]; *Loiola*, by John Hacket. Ed. by MALCOLM M. BRENNAN. Hildesheim; Zurich; New York: Olms, 1988. pp. iv, 15, (facsims) 180. (Renaissance drama in England, 2:6.)

**3196.** SURTZ, EDWARD; MURPHY, VIRGINIA (eds).  The divorce tracts of Henry VIII. Introd. by JOHN GUY. Angers: Moreana, 1988. pp. xliv, 487. Rev. by David Loades in RQ (42:3) 566–8; by Arthur J. Slavin in SixCT (20:1) 105–11.

**3197.** THOMAS, KEITH.  Children in early modern England. *In* (pp. 45–77) **14.**

**3198.** VREDVELD, HARRY.  'That familiar proverb': folly as the elixir of youth in Erasmus's *Moriae encomium*. RQ (42:1) 78–91.

**3199.** WUNDERLI, RICHARD; BROCE, GERALD.  The final moment before death in early modern England. SixCT (20:2) 259–75.

**3200.** YOUNG, ALAN.  Tudor and Jacobean tournaments. (Bibl. 1988, 2418.) Rev. by David M. Bergeron in RQ (42:2) 322–4; by David Loades in DUJ (81:1) 1988, 147–8.

**3201.** YOUNG, ALAN R.  The English tournament imprese. *In* (pp. 61–81) **21.**

**3202.** ——— Tudor Arthurianism and the Earl of Cumberland's tournament pageants. DalR (67:2/3) 1987, 176–89.

## Literary Theory

This section is intended to contain studies **about** the literary theory, literary historiography, literary criticism, etc., produced *in* the sixteenth century. For modern works **of** literary history and criticism dealing generally with this period, see under 'Sixteenth Century: General Literary Studies'.

**3203.** BERGVALL, Åke.  The 'enabling of judgement': Sir Philip

Sidney and the education of the reader. Uppsala: Acta Universitatis
Upsaliensis; Stockholm: Almqvist & Wiksell. pp. 137. (Studia anglistica upsaliensia, 70.) (Doct. diss., Uppsala Univ.)
**3204.** CREWE, JONATHAN. Hidden designs: the critical profession and
Renaissance literature. (Bibl. 1988, 2419.) Rev. by Michael G. Brennan
in RES (39:154) 1988, 287–8; by Peter Stallybrass in RQ (42:1) 130–3.
**3205.** GONZÁLEZ, JOSÉ MANUEL. Two critical aspects of *An Apologie
for Poetry*. Atlantis (11:1/2) 39–51.
**3206.** GRANT, PATRICK. Literature and the discovery of method in the
English Renaissance. (Bibl. 1987, 3844.) Rev. by Suzanne Gossett in
MedRen (4) 243–7.
**3207.** MIRBACH, LUCIA. Form und Gehalt der Substantivischen
Reihungen in George Puttenhams *The Arte of English Poesie* (1589).
Tübingen: Niemeyer. pp. viii, 179 + 3 fiches. (Linguistische Arbeiten,
219.)

## AUTHORS
### William Alabaster
**3208.** SPEVACK, MARVIN; BINNS, J. W.; WECKERMANN, HANS-JÜRGEN
(gen. eds). *Antigone*, by Thomas Watson; *Roxana*, by William Alabaster; *Adrastus parentans sive vindicta*, by Peter Mease. Ed. by JOHN
COLDEWEY and BRIAN F. COPENHAVER. Hildesheim; Zurich; New York:
Olms, 1987. pp. iv, 22, (facsims) 137. (Renaissance Latin drama in
England, 2:4.)

### Roger Ascham
**3209.** DELLANEVA, JOANN. Reflecting lesser lights: the imitation of
minor writers in the Renaissance. RQ (42:3) 449–79.
**3210.** NOYES, GERTRUDE ELIZABETH. A study of Roger Ascham's
literary citations with particular reference to his knowledge of the
Classics. Unpub. doct. diss., Yale Univ., 1937. [Abstr. in DA (50)
1314A.]

### William Baldwin
**3211.** RINGLER, WILLIAM A., JR; FLACHMANN, MICHAEL (eds). *Beware
the Cat*: the first English novel. San Marino, CA: Huntington Library,
1988. pp. xxx, 126. Rev. by Katherine Duncan-Jones in TLS, 7 Apr.,
369.

### Alexander Barclay
**3212.** STANLEY, E. G. Chaucer's metre after Chaucer: II, Lydgate and
Barclay. *See* **2767a.**

### Barnabe Barnes
**3213.** LATHAM, JACQUELINE F. M. Machiavelli, policy, and *The
Devil's Charter*. MedRen (1) 1984, 97–108.

### Henry Chettle
**3214.** COMENSOLI, VIVIANA. Refashioning the marriage code: the
*Patient Grissil* of Dekker, Chettle and Haughton. RenR (13:2) 199–214.

### John Colet
**3215.** LOCHMAN, DANIEL T. Colet and Erasmus: the *Disputatiuncula*
and the controversy of letter and spirit. SixCT (20:1) 77–87.

## William Cornish the Younger

**3216.** STREITBERGER, W. R.    Henry VIII's entertainment for the Queen of Scots, 1516: a new Revels account and Cornish's play. *See* **3119.**

## Thomas Cranmer

**3217.** EVANS, G. R.    'Thus it is Englished': the use of English in scholastic disputation in the mid-sixteenth century. *See* **676.**

**3218.** MOORE, T. C.    A study of the development of the liturgy in the Anglican tradition to 1556. *See* **1444.**

## Samuel Daniel

**3219.** DALY, PETER M.; DUER, LESLIE T.; RASPA, ANTHONY (eds). The English emblem tradition: vol. 1, Jan van der Noot, *A Theatre for Worldlings*; Paolo Giovio, *The Worthy Tract of Paulus Jovius*; Lodovico Domenici, *Certain Noble Devises both Militarie and Amorous*; Geffrey Whitney, *A Choice of Emblemes*. *See* **82.**

## Queen Elizabeth I

**3220.** BAGHDIKIAN, SONIA.    Ambiguous negations in Chaucer and Queen Elizabeth. *In* (pp. 41–8) **30.**

**3221.** CRANE, MARY THOMAS.    '*Video et taceo*': Elizabeth I and the rhetoric of counsel. SELit (28:1) 1988, 1–15.

## Sir Thomas Elyot

**3222.** JORDAN, CONSTANCE.    Feminism and the humanists: the case of Sir Thomas Elyot's *Defence of Good Women*. *In* (pp. 242–58) **54.**

## John Foxe

**3223.** SPEVAK, MARVIN; BINNS, J. W.; WECKERMANN, HANS-JÜRGEN (gen. eds).    *Absalom*, by Thomas Watson; *Christus triumphans*, by John Foxe. Ed. by JOHN HAZEL SMITH. Hildesheim; Zurich; New York; Olms, 1988. pp. iv, 38, (facsims) 167. (Renaissance Latin drama in England, 2:5.)

## Thomas Garter

**3224.** KERR, HEATHER.    Thomas Garter's *Susanna*: 'pollicie' and 'true report'. AUMLA (72) 183–202.

## George Gascoigne

**3225.** ERIKSEN, ROY T.    George Gascoigne's and Mary Sidney's versions of Psalm 130. CEl (36) 1–9.

## Arthur Golding

**3226.** TAYLOR, ANTHONY BRIAN.    Shakespeare, Studley, and Golding. RES (39:155) 1988, 522–7.

## Barnabe Googe

**3227.** KENNEDY, JUDITH M. (ed.).    Eclogues, epitaphs, and sonnets. Toronto; Buffalo, NY; London: Toronto UP. pp. vii, 223.

## John Gough

**3228.** DUNNAN, D. S.    A note on John Gough's *The Dore of Holy Scripture*. NQ (36:3) 309–10. (Prologue to the 1540 Wycliffite Bible.)

## Robert Greene

**3229.** BARBOUR, A. REID.    Deciphering Renaissance prose narrative: plenism and the fictions of control. Unpub. doct. diss., Univ. of Rochester, 1988. [Abstr. in DA (49) 1806A.]

**3230.** CRUPI, CHARLES W. Robert Greene. Boston, MA: G. K. Hall, 1985. pp. xvi, 182. (Twayne's English authors, 416.) Rev. by Elizabeth Heale in YES (19) 309–11.

**3231.** EWBANK, INGA-STINA. From narrative to dramatic language: *The Winter's Tale* and its source. *In* (pp. 29–47) **55.**

**3232.** HIEATT, CHARLES W. Multiple plotting in *Friar Bacon and Friar Bungay.* RenD (16) 1985, 17–34.

**3233.** LEKHAL, CATHERINE. The historical background of Robert Greene's *The Scottish History of James IV* or 'Cross the foe before he have betrayed you' (III. 3. 29). CEl (35) 27–45.

### Everard Guilpin

**3234.** KERINS, FRANK. The crafty enchaunter: ironic satires and Jonson's *Every Man Out of His Humour.* RenD (14) 1983, 125–50.

### Sir John Harington (1561–1612)

**3235.** WOUDHUYSEN, H. R. Sir John Harington's printed books. *See* **277.**

### Gabriel Harvey

**3236.** DIESEL, JOHN. Thomas Nashe and Gabriel Harvey: the controversy. CAE (22) 409–17.

### William Haughton

**3237.** COMENSOLI, VIVIANA. Refashioning the marriage code: the *Patient Grissil* of Dekker, Chettle and Haughton. *See* **3214.**

### Raphael Holinshed

**3238.** DONNO, ELIZABETH STORY. Abraham Fleming: a learned corrector in 1586–87. *See* **303.**

### Thomas Kyd

**3239.** ARDOLINO, FRANK R. *Corrida* of blood in *The Spanish Tragedy*: Kyd's use of revenge as national destiny. MedRen (1) 1984, 37–49.

**3240.** GONZÁLEZ, JOSÉ MANUEL. Lo español en *The Spanish Tragedy.* RAEI (2) 91–100.

**3241.** GRIFFITHS, Y. J. Motivation in Kyd's *Spanish Tragedy* with a consideration of *The Oresteia* of Aeschylus. Unpub. doct. diss., Univ. of Liverpool. [Abstr. in IT (39:3) 1106.

**3242.** HAMMERSMITH, JAMES P. The death of Castile in *The Spanish Tragedy.* RenD (16) 1985, 1–16.

**3243.** KOHLER, RICHARD C. Kyd's ordered spectacle: 'Behold . . ./What 'tis to be subject to destiny.' MedRen (3) 1986, 27–49.

### John Leland

**3244.** CARLEY, JAMES P. John Leland and the contents of the English pre-Dissolution libraries: Lincolnshire. *See* **210.**

### Sir David Lindsay

**3245.** RIACH, D. W. A reconstruction of the 1552 performance at Cupar of Sir David Lindsay's *Ane Satyre of the Thrie Estaitis.* Unpub. M.Litt. thesis, Univ. of Edinburgh, 1986. [Abstr. in IT (36:4) 1379.]

**3246.** WALKER, GREG. Sir David Lindsay's *Ane Satire of the Thrie Estaitis* and the politics of reformation. SLJ (16:2) 5–17.

**Thomas Lupton**

**3247.** CONCOLATO, MARIA GRAZIA PALERMO (ed.). All for money. (Bibl. 1985, 3592.) Rev. by Katherine Duncan-Jones in NQ (36:1) 92–3.

**John Lyly**

**3248.** BARBOUR, A. REID. Deciphering Renaissance prose narrative: plenism and the fictions of control. *See* **3229.**

**Christopher Marlowe**

**3249.** BELT, DEBRA ANNE. The poetics of hostile response: writers and critical readers in sixteenth-century England. Unpub. doct. diss., Johns Hopkins Univ., 1988. [Abstr. in DA (49) 2225A.]

**3250.** BIRRINGER, JOHANNES H. Marlowe's *Dr Faustus* and *Tamburlaine*: theological and theatrical perspectives. (Bibl. 1985, 3595.) Rev. by David Kaula in MedRen (3) 1986, 293–7.

**3251.** BREUER, ROLF. Christian tragedy/tragedy of Christianity. *In* (pp. 183–95) **38.**

**3252.** BURNETT, MARK THORNTON. Marlovian echoes in Ford's *Perkin Warbeck*. NQ (36:3) 347–9.

**3253.** CHAUDHURI, SUKANTA. Marlowe, madrigals, and a new Elizabethan poet. *See* **126.**

**3254.** DABBS, THOMAS WINN. The making of Marlowe: a genealogy of a nineteenth-century author. Unpub. doct. diss., Univ. of South Carolina. [Abstr. in DA (50) 1662A.]

**3255.** DUANE, CAROL LEVENTEN. Marlowe's mixed messages: a model for Shakespeare? MedRen (3) 1986, 51–67.

**3256.** EMPSON, WILLIAM. Faustus and the censor: the English Faustbook and Marlowe's *Doctor Faustus*. Ed. by JOHN HENRY JONES. (Bibl. 1988, 2458.) Rev. by John Jowett in NQ (36:1) 94–5.

**3257.** ERIKSEN, ROY T. 'What resting place is this?': aspects of time and place in *Doctor Faustus* (1616). RenD (16) 1985, 49–74.

**3258.** GECKLE, GEORGE L. *Tamburlaine* and *Edward II*. Basingstoke: Macmillan, 1988. pp. 107. (Text and performance.)

**3259.** GILL, ROMA (ed.). The complete works of Christopher Marlowe: vol. 1, *All Ovids Elegies*; *Lucans First Booke*; *Dido Queene of Carthage*; *Hero and Leander*. (Bibl. 1987, 3901.) Rev. by Richard Dutton in MLR (84:4) 923; by Katherine Duncan-Jones in RES (39:155) 1988, 430–1.

**3260.** GOLDMAN, MICHAEL. Performer and role in Marlowe and Shakespeare. *In* (pp. 91–102) **55.**

**3261.** HARDIN, RICHARD F. Irony and privilege in Marlowe. CR (33:3) 207–27.

**3262.** JONES, ROBERT C. Engagement with knavery: point of view in *Richard III*, *The Jew of Malta*, *Volpone*, and *The Revenger's Tragedy*. (Bibl. 1987, 4714, where entry misplaced and subtitle omitted.) Rev. by Lois Potter in NQ (35:1) 1988, 85–6; by Richard Dutton in MLR (83:4) 1988, 949; by Marc Maufort in RBPH (3) 607–13.

**3263.** KEEFER, MICHAEL H. History and the canon: the case of *Dr Faustus*. UTQ (56:4) 1987, 498–522.

**3264.** LEECH, CLIFFORD. Christopher Marlowe: poet for the stage. Ed. by ANNE LANCASHIRE. New York: AMS Press, 1986. pp. x, 250.

(AMS studies in the Renaissance, 11.) Rev. by Roma Gill in RES (38:152) 1987, 552–3; by Richard Dutton in MLR (84:4) 922–3; by R. A. Foakes in MedRen (4) 266–8.

**3265.** LEVIN, RICHARD. The contemporary perception of Marlowe's Tamburlaine. MedRen (1) 1984, 51–70.

**3266.** LINDLEY, ARTHUR. The unbeing of the overreacher: Proteanism and the Marlovian hero. MLR (84:1) 1–17.

**3267.** McCLOSKEY, SUSAN. The worlds of *Edward II*. RenD (16) 1985, 35–48.

**3268.** MARCUS, LEAH S. Textual indeterminacy and ideological difference: the case of *Doctor Faustus. See* **347.**

**3269.** MILLER, DAVID LEE. The death of the modern: gender and desire in Marlowe's *Hero and Leander*. SAQ (88:4) 757–87.

**3270.** PORTER, JOSEPH A. Marlowe, Shakespeare, and the canonization of heterosexuality. SAQ (88:1) 127–47.

**3271.** SHAPIRO, JAMES. 'Steale from the deade?': the presence of Marlowe in Jonson's early plays. RenD (18) 1987, 67–99.

**3272.** SHEPHERD, SIMON. Marlowe and the politics of Elizabethan theatre. (Bibl. 1988, 2470.) Rev. by Harry Keyishian in MedRen (4) 303–10.

**3273.** TAYLOR, ANTHONY BRIAN. Tamburlaine's doctrine of strife and John Calvin. ELN (27:1) 30–1.

**3274.** THURN, DAVID H. Sights of power in *Tamburlaine*. ELR (19:1) 3–21.

**3275.** TRUSSLER, SIMON (ed.). *Dr Faustus*: a programme/text. London: Methuen. pp. xviii, 33.

**3276.** TYDEMAN, WILLIAM (ed.). Dr Faustus. (Bibl. 1987, 3911.) Rev. by Richard Dutton in MLR (84:4) 923–4.

### Alexander Montgomerie

**3277.** JACK, R. D. S. Alexander Montgomerie. (Bibl. 1988, 2475.) Rev. by Sally Mapstone in RES (38:152) 1987, 548.

### Sir Thomas More

**3278.** BAUMANN, UWE; HEINRICH, HANS PETER. Thomas Morus: humanistische schriften. Introd. by HUBERTUS SCHULTE HERBRUGGEN. Darmstadt: Wissenschaftliche, 1986. pp. viii, 226. (Erträge der Forschung, 243.) Rev. by R. J. Schoeck in RQ (42:4) 854–5.

**3279.** FREDRICKS, DANIEL DAVID. Drama in the life and works of Thomas More. Unpub. doct. diss., Univ. of North Carolina at Greensboro, 1988. [Abstr. in DA (49) 2228–9A.]

**3280.** HOUSE, SEYMOUR BAKER. Sir Thomas More and Holy Orders: More's view of the English clergy, both secular and regular. Unpub. doct. diss., Univ. of St Andrews, 1987. [Abstr. in IT (36:4) 1367; in DA (49) 274–5A.]

**3281.** JURT, JOSEPH. Das Bild der Stadt in den utopischen Entwürfen von Filarete bis L.-S. Mercier. LJGG (27) 1986, 233–52.

**3282.** KINNEY, DANIEL. Rewriting Thomas More: a devotional anthology. *See* **151.**

**3283.** MARC'HADOUR, GERMAIN; GALIBOIS, ROLAND (eds and trans). Érasme de Rotterdam et Thomas More: correspondance. Sherbrooke, Que.: Sherbrooke UP, 1985. pp. l, 286. Rev. by Margaret Mann Phillips in Moreana (23:89) 1986, 57–8; by Maurice Lebel in Moreana (23:90) 1986, 73–6.

**3284.** MARIUS, RICHARD. Thomas More: a biography. (Bibl. 1987, 3924.) Rev. by James Patrick in ModAge (32:2) 1988, 144–7.

**3285.** PIEPER, ANNEMARIE. Der philosophische Begriff der Utopie und die klassischen Utopisten. LJGG (27) 1986, 219–31.

**3286.** SILVANI, GIOVANNA. Woman in Utopia from More to Huxley. *In* (pp. 135–52) CARMELINA IMBROSCIO (ed.), Requiem pour l'utopie? Tendances autodestructives du paradigme utopique. Introd. by RAYMOND TROUSSON. Pisa: Goliardica, 1986. pp. 222. (Histoire et critiques des idées, 6.) Rev. by Abigail E. Lee in MLR (84:4) 902–4.

### Thomas Nashe

**3287.** BARBOUR, A. REID. Deciphering Renaissance prose narrative: plenism and the fictions of control. *See* **3229.**

**3288.** DE, ESHA NIYOGI. 'The purpose of playing': theater and ritual in the Revesby Folk Play, *Summer's Last Will and Testament*, and *Hamlet*. Unpub. doct. diss., Purdue Univ., 1988. [Abstr. in DA (49) 2665–6A.]

**3289.** DIESEL, JOHN. Thomas Nashe and Gabriel Harvey: the controversy. *See* **3236.**

**3290.** HOGG, JAMES (ed.). Essais sur Thomas Nashe. By ANTOINE DEMADRE. Salzburg: Institut für Anglistik und Amerikanistik, Salzburg Univ., 1987. 2 vols. pp. ii, 507. (Salzburg studies in English literature: Elizabethan and Renaissance studies, 90.) Rev. by Éliane Cuvelier in EA (42:4) 466–7.

**3291.** HUTSON , LORNA. Thomas Nashe in context. Oxford: Clarendon Press. pp. xiii, 294. (Oxford English monographs.)

**3292.** SIMONS, LOUISE. Rerouting *The Unfortunate Traveller*: strategies for coherence and direction. SELit (28:1) 1988, 17–38.

### Anne Cecil de Vere, Countess of Oxford

**3293.** MOODY, ELLEN. Six elegiac poems, possibly by Anne Cecil de Vere, Countess of Oxford. *See* **3151.**

### Queen Katherine Parr

**3294.** MUELLER, JANEL. A Tudor Queen finds voice: Katherine Parr's *Lamentation of a Sinner*. *In* (pp. 15–47) **31.**

### Henry Peacham the Elder

**3295.** ESPY, WILLARD R. The garden of eloquence: a rhetorical bestiary. *See* **1305.**

### George Peele

**3296.** BINNIE, PATRICIA (ed.). The old wives tale. (Bibl. 1985, 3656.) Rev. by Paul Werstine in MedRen (1) 1984, 243–55.

**3296a.** WERSTINE, PAUL. Provenance and printing history in two Revels editions: review article. *See* **407.**

### Mary Herbert, Countess of Pembroke

**3297.** BRENNAN, MICHAEL G. Nicholas Breton's *The Passions of the Spirit* and the Countess of Pembroke. RES (38:150) 1987, 221–5.

**3298.** ERIKSEN, ROY T.    George Gascoigne's and Mary Sidney's versions of Psalm 130. *See* **3225.**

**3299.** HANNAY, MARGARET P.    'Princes you as men must dy': Genevan advice to monarchs in the *Psalmes* of Mary Sidney. ELR (19:1) 22–41.

**3300.** —— Unpublished letters by Mary Sidney, Countess of Pembroke. Spenser Studies (6) 1985, 165–90.

### George Puttenham

**3301.** MIRBACH, LUCIA.    Form und Gehalt der Substantivischen Reihungen in George Puttenhams *The Arte of English Poesie* (1589). *See* **3207.**

### Margaret Roper

**3302.** KAUFMAN, PETER IVER.    Absolute Margaret: Margaret More Roper and 'well learned' men. SixCT (20:3) 443–56.

### George Ruggle

**3303.** SPEVACK, MARVIN; BINNS, J. W.; WECKERMANN, HANS-JÜRGEN (gen. eds).    *Ignoramus.* Ed. by E. F. J. TUCKER. Hildesheim; Zurich; New York: Olms, 1987. pp. iv, 19, (facsims) 202. (Renaissance Latin drama in England, 2:1.)

### Thomas Sackville

**3304.** HULTIN, NEIL C.; OBER, WARREN U.    John Payne Collier, Thomas Crofton Croker and the Hoby epitaph. Neophilologus (73:1) 142–9.

### Thomas Salter

**3305.** HOLMES, JANIS BUTLER (ed.).    A critical edition of Thomas Salter's *The Mirrhor of Modestie.* New York: Garland, 1987. pp. 207. (Renaissance imagination, 32.) Rev. by Mary Jane Metzger in SixCT (20:1) 143.

### Sir Philip Sidney

**3306.** BACHINGER, KATRINA.    Gender positions: the intertextuality of gender difference in Margaret Atwood, Katherine Mansfield, Joyce Carol Oates, Edgar Allan Poe, Sir Philip Sidney and others. Unpub. Habilitationsschrift, Univ. of Salzburg.

**3307.** BERGVALL, ÅKE.    The 'enabling of judgement': Sir Philip Sidney and the education of the reader. *See* **3203.**

**3308.** BERRY, EDWARD.    Sidney's May game for the Queen. MP (86:3) 252–64.

**3309.** CERNY, LOTHAR.    'Beautie and the use thereof': eine Interpretation von Sir Philip Sidneys *Arcadia.* (Bibl. 1985, 3663.) Rev. by Götz Schmitz in Archiv (225:1) 1988, 155–9.

**3310.** DUNDAS, JUDITH.    'The heaven's ornament': Spenser's tribute to Sidney. EA (42:2) 129–39.

**3311.** FONSECA, TEREZINHA A.    The 'Correlitiue knowledge of thinges': relations and intertextuality in *Astrophil and Stella* and *A Defence of Poetry.* Unpub. doct. diss., New York Univ., 1988. [Abstr. in DA (49) 3032A.]

**3312.** GONZÁLEZ, JOSÉ MANUEL.    Two critical aspects of *An Apologie for Poetry. See* **3205.**

**3313.** HABER, JUDITH DEBORAH.    Pastoral and the poetics of self-contradiction. Unpub. doct. diss., Univ. of California, Berkeley, 1988. [Abstr. in DA (50) 952A.]

**3314.** HANNAY, MARGARET P.    'My sheep are thoughts': self-reflexive pastoral in *The Faerie Queene*, Book VI, and the *New Arcadia*. Spenser Studies (9) 1988, 137–59.

**3315.** HENINGER, S. K., JR.    Spenser and Sidney at Leicester House. Spenser Studies (8) 1987, 239–49.

**3316.** HULSE, CLARK.    Stella's wit: Penelope Rich as reader of Sidney's sonnets. *In* (pp. 272–86) **54.**

**3317.** KAY, DENNIS (ed.).    Sir Philip Sidney: an anthology of modern criticism. Oxford: Clarendon Press, 1987. pp. xiv, 327.

**3318.** KINNEY, ARTHUR F.    Sir Philip Sidney and the uses of history. *In* (pp. 293–314) **31.**

**3319.** KUIN, ROGER.    The gaps and the whites: indeterminacy and undecideability in the sonnet sequences of Sidney, Spenser, and Shakespeare. Spenser Studies (8) 1987, 251–85.

**3320.** LEVAO, RONALD.    Renaissance minds and their fictions: Cusanus, Sidney, Shakespeare. (Bibl. 1988, 2513.) Rev. by Katherine Duncan-Jones in RES (38:151) 1987, 384–5.

**3321.** MANGANARO, ELISE SALEM.    Songs and sonnets in *Astrophil and Stella*: a reading of Sidney's poetics. ExRC (15) 121–35.

**3322.** MARTIN, CHRISTOPHER.    Sidney and the limits of eros. Spenser Studies (7) 1986, 239–59.

**3323.** PIGEON, RENÉE MARIE.    Prose fiction adaptations of Sidney's *Arcadia*. Unpub. doct. diss., Univ. of California, Los Angeles, 1988. [Abstr. in DA (49) 2233A.]

**3324.** PRESCOTT, ANNE LAKE.    King David as a 'right poet': Sidney and the Psalmist. ELR (19:2) 131–61.

**3325.** PRESTON, C. E.    Emblematic pictorialism and narrative structures in *New Arcadia* and *Pericles*. Unpub. doct. diss., Univ. of Oxford, 1988. [Abstr. in IT (39:1) 30.]

**3326.** QUILLIGAN, MAUREEN.    Sidney and his Queen. *In* (pp. 171–96) **31.**

**3327.** SCHLEINER, LOUISE.    Spenser and Sidney on the *vaticinium*. Spenser Studies (6) 1985, 129–45.

**3328.** SKRETKOWICZ, VICTOR (ed.).    The Countess of Pembroke's Arcadia (the *New Arcadia*). (Bibl. 1988, 2521.) Rev. by Christopher Martin in SixCT (20:4) 717–18; by Michael McCanles in RQ (42:1) 133–5.

**3329.** STILLMAN, ROBERT E.    Sidney's poetic justice: the *Old Arcadia*, its eclogues, and Renaissance pastoral traditions. (Bibl. 1988, 2522.) Rev. by Judith Dundas in MLR (84:1) 120–1.

**3330.** VAN DORSTEN, J. A.    The Anglo-Dutch Renaissance: seven essays. Ed. by J. VAN DEN BERG and ALASTAIR HAMILTON. With contributions by A. G. H. BACHRACH and ROY STRONG. *See* **3025.**

**3331.** WEBSTER, JOHN (ed.).    William Temple's *Analysis* of Sir Philip

Sidney's *Apology for Poetry*. (Bibl. 1987, 3974.) Rev. by Lothar Cerny in
Ang (107:1/2) 216–20.

## John Skelton

**3332.** EADE, J. C.    The Saturnian date in Skelton's *Speculum Principis*.
NQ (36:2) 165.

**3333.** KINNEY, ARTHUR F.    John Skelton: priest as poet: seasons of
discovery. (Bibl. 1988, 2529.) Rev. by Andrew D. Weiner in RQ (42:1)
127–30.

**3334.** STEVENS, MARK KEMBLE.    The significance of John Skelton's
contribution to English vocabulary. *See* **1029.**

**3335.** WILSON, JANET.    Skelton's *Ware the Hauke* and the 'circumstances' of sin. MÆ (58:2) 243–57.

## Edmund Spenser

**3336.** ALPERS, PAUL.    Spenser's late pastorals. ELH (56:4) 797–817.

**3337.** BAKER, DAVID J.    'Some quirk, some subtle evasion': legal
subversion in Spenser's *A View of the Present State of Ireland*. Spenser
Studies (6) 1985, 147–63.

**3338.** BARKAN, LEONARD.    The gods made flesh: metamorphosis and
the pursuit of paganism. New Haven, CT; London: Yale UP, 1986.
pp. xvi, 398. Rev. by J. B. Trapp in MLR (84:3) 691–3; by Jonathan
Bate in THES (746) 1987, 19; by Elizabeth D. Harvey in RenR (13:2)
233–6; by Janet L. Smarr in JEGP (87:2) 1988, 252–4; by William C.
Carroll in RQ (41:1) 1988, 155–8; by Steven Max Miller in JRMMRA
(9) 1988, 157–8; by Clark Hulse in SQ (39:3) 1988, 363–4; by David
Hopkins in Eng (37) 1988, 49–54.

**3339.** BATES, CATHERINE.    Images of government in *The Faerie Queene*,
Book II. NQ (36:3) 314–15.

**3340.** BEDNARZ, JAMES P.    Imitations of Spenser in *A Midsummer
Night's Dream*. RenD (14) 1983, 79–102.

**3341.** BELLAMY, ELIZABETH J.    Reading desire backwards: belated-
ness in Spenser's Arthur. SAQ (88:4) 789–809.

**3342.** BELT, DEBRA.    Hostile audiences and the courteous reader in
*The Faerie Queene*, Book VI. Spenser Studies (9) 1988, 107–35.

**3343.** BELT, DEBRA ANNE.    The poetics of hostile response: writers
and critical readers in sixteenth-century England. *See* **3249.**

**3344.** BENSON, PAMELA J.    Florimell at sea: the action of grace in *Faerie
Queene*, Book III. Spenser Studies (6) 1985, 83–94.

**3345.** BERGER, HARRY, JR.    Revisionary play: studies in Spenserian
dynamics. Introd. by LOUIS MONTROSE. Berkeley; London: California UP, 1988. pp. xi, 482.

**3346.** BERNARD, JOHN D    Ceremonies of innocence: pastoralism in
the poetry of Edmund Spenser. Cambridge: CUP. pp. ix, 242.

**3347.** BIEMAN, ELIZABETH.    Plato baptized: towards the interpretation of Spenser's mimetic fictions. Toronto; London: Toronto UP,
1988. pp. x, 325. Rev. by Eugene D. Hill in SixCT (20:3) 492–3.

**3348.** BORRIS, KENNETH.    'Diuelish ceremonies': allegorical satire of
Protestant extremism in *The Faerie Queene* VI. viii. 31–51. Spenser Studies
(8) 1987, 175–209.

**3349.** —— Fortune, occasion, and the allegory of the quest in Book Six of *The Faerie Queene*. Spenser Studies (7) 1986, 123–45.

**3350.** BOUCHARD, GARY MICHAEL. From campus to *campus*: the relationship of the university world to the literary pastoral worlds of Edmund Spenser, Phineas Fletcher, and John Milton. Unpub. doct. diss., Loyola Univ. of Chicago, 1988. [Abstr. in DA (49) 1806–7A.]

**3351.** CARTER, F. M. M. The protean image: a study of dance as an image in English Renaissance literature with special reference to Spenser and Milton. Unpub. doct. diss., Univ. of Oxford. [Abstr. in IT (39:3) 1106.]

**3352.** CARTMELL, DEBORAH. 'Beside the shore of siluer streaming *Thamesis*': Spenser's *Ruines of Time*. Spenser Studies (6) 1985, 77–82.

**3353.** CAVANAGH, SHEILA T. 'That fairest vertue': discourses of chastity in Spenser and Shakespeare. Unpub. doct. diss., Brown Univ., 1988. [Abstr. in DA (49) 2226A.]

**3354.** CHANG, HERAN. The two feminine archetypes – elementary and transformative – found in Edmund Spenser's *The Faerie Queene*. ShR (15) 149–64.

**3355.** CHENEY, PATRICK. 'And doubted her to deeme an earthly wight': male neoplatonic 'magic' and the problem of female identity in Spenser's allegory of the two Florimells. SP (86:3) 310–40.

**3356.** —— The old poet presents himself: *Prothalamion* as a defense of Spenser's career. Spenser Studies (8) 1987, 211–38.

**3357.** CHRISTIAN, MARGARET. 'The ground of storie': genealogy in *The Faerie Queene*. Spenser Studies (9) 1988, 61–79.

**3358.** CUMMINGS, ROBERT. Spenser's 'twelve private morall virtues'. Spenser Studies (8) 1987, 35–59.

**3359.** DORANGEON, SIMONE. *A Theatre for Worldlings*, ou l'influence des 'étrangers' de Londres sur la formation de Spenser. *In* (pp. 1–12) **26.**

**3360.** DUNDAS, JUDITH. 'The heaven's ornament': Spenser's tribute to Sidney. *See* **3310.**

**3361.** ESOLEN, ANTHONY M. Irony and the pseudo-physical in *The Faerie Queene*. Spenser Studies (8) 1987, 61–78.

**3362.** ESOLEN, ANTHONY MICHAEL. A rhetoric of Spenserian irony. Unpub. doct. diss., Univ. of North Carolina at Chapel Hill, 1987. [Abstr. in DA (49) 2227A.]

**3363.** FIKE, MATTHEW ALLEN. The descent into hell in *The Faerie Queene*. Unpub. doct. diss., Univ. of Michigan, 1988. [Abstr. in DA (49) 3731–2A.]

**3364.** FRANTZ, DAVID O. The union of Florimell and Marinell: the triumph of hearing. Spenser Studies (6) 1985, 115–27.

**3365.** FRUEN, JEFFREY P. 'True glorious type': the place of Gloriana in *The Faerie Queene*. Spenser Studies (7) 1986, 147–73.

**3366.** FRUSHELL, RICHARD C. Spenser and the eighteenth-century schools. Spenser Studies (7) 1986, 175–98.

**3367.** FUKUDA, SHOHACHI. The numerological patterning of *Amoretti* and *Epithalamion*. Spenser Studies (9) 1988, 33–48.

**3368.** García Landa, José Ángel.   'Another game in view': the representation of the poet in *The Faerie Queene*. RAEI (2) 65–81.

**3369.** Gleckner, Robert F.   Blake and Spenser. (Bibl. 1986, 4253.) Rev. by J. M. Q. Davies in RES (39:153) 1988, 118–20.

**3370.** Goldberg, Jonathan.   Colin to Hobbinol: Spenser's familiar letters. SAQ (88:1) 107–26.

**3371.** Gottfried, Rudolf Brand.   *A View of the Present State of Ireland* by Edmund Spenser: the text of Bodleian MS Rawlinson B 478, edited with an introduction and notes. *See* **318.**

**3372.** Graves, Roy Neil.   Two newfound poems by Edmund Spenser: the buried short-line runes in *Epithalamion* and *Prothalamion*. Spenser Studies (7) 1986, 199–238.

**3373.** Greene, Roland.   *The Shepheardes Calender*, dialogue, and periphrasis. Spenser Studies (8) 1987, 1–33.

**3374.** Gross, Kenneth.   Spenserian poetics: idolatry, iconoclasm, and magic. (Bibl. 1988, 2542.) Rev. by Patricia Thomson in RES (38:152) 1987, 545–7.

**3375.** Hannay, Margaret P.   'My sheep are thoughts': self-reflexive pastoral in *The Faerie Queene*, Book VI, and the *New Arcadia*. *See* **3313.**

**3376.** Heale, Elizabeth.   *The Faerie Queene*: a reader's guide. (Bibl. 1987, 4007.) Rev. by Charles Larson in SixCT (20:1) 154.

**3377.** Heberle, Mark.   The limitations of friendship. Spenser Studies (8) 1987, 101–18.

**3378.** Heninger, S. K., Jr.   Spenser and Sidney at Leicester House. *See* **3314.**

**3379.** Hieatt, A. Kent.   Arthur's deliverance of Rome? (Yet again.) Spenser Studies (9) 1988, 243–8.

**3380.** —— The projected continuation of *The Faerie Queene*: 'Rome Delivered'? Spenser Studies (8) 1987, 335–42.

**3381.** Hulse, Clark.   Spenser, Bacon, and the myth of power. *In* (pp. 315–46) **31.**

**3382.** Kane, Sean.   Spenser's moral allegory. Toronto; London: Toronto UP. pp. xiii, 237. Rev. by John A. Thomas in RMRLL (43:4) 250–2.

**3383.** Kaske, Carol V.   Rethinking Loewenstein's 'viper thoughts'. Spenser Studies (8) 1987, 325–9.

**3384.** King, John N.   Was Spenser a Puritan? Spenser Studies (6) 1985, 1–31.

**3385.** Krier, T. M.   The mysteries of the Muses: Spenser's *Faerie Queene*, II.3, and the epic tradition of the goddess observed. Spenser Studies (7) 1986, 59–91.

**3386.** Kucich, Greg.   The duality of Romantic Spenserianism. Spenser Studies (8) 1987, 287–307.

**3387.** —— The Spenserian psychodrama of *Prometheus Unbound*. NCC (12:1) 1988, 61–84.

**3388.** Kuin, Roger.   The gaps and the whites: indeterminacy and undecideability in the sonnet sequences of Sidney, Spenser, and Shakespeare. *See* **3319.**

**3389.** LOEWENSTEIN, JOSEPH. A note on the structure of Spenser's *Amoretti*: viper thoughts. Spenser Studies (8) 1987, 311–23.

**3390.** LUBORSKY, RUTH SAMSON. The illustrations to *The Shepheardes Calender*: II. *See* **93.**

**3391.** LUPTON, JULIA REINHARD. Home-making in Ireland: Virgil's *Eclogue* I and Book VI of *The Faerie Queene*. Spenser Studies (8) 1987, 119–45.

**3392.** McCABE, RICHARD A. The pillars of eternity: time and providence in *The Faerie Queene*. Blackrock, Co. Dublin: Irish Academic Press. pp. 256. (Dublin studies in medieval and Renaissance literature.)

**3393.** MALEY, WILLIAM. Spenser and Ireland: a select bibliography. Spenser Studies (9) 1988, 227–42.

**3394.** MALLETTE, RICHARD. The Protestant art of preaching in Book One of *The Faerie Queene*. Spenser Studies (7) 1986, 3–25.

**3395.** —— The Protestant ethics of love in Book II of *The Faerie Queene*. ChrisL (38:4) 45–64.

**3396.** MILLER, DAVID LEE. The poem's two bodies: the poetics of the 1590 *Faerie Queene*. Princeton, NJ: Princeton UP, 1988. pp. xiii, 297. Rev. by Bruce Thomas Boehrer in SixCT (20:3) 523.

**3397.** MOREY, JAMES H. Spenser's mythic adaptations in *Muiopotmos*. Spenser Studies (9) 1988, 49–59.

**3398.** NEUSE, RICHARD T. Planting works in the soul: Spenser's Socratic garden of Adonis. Spenser Studies (8) 1987, 79–100.

**3399.** PRESCOTT, ANNE LAKE. Response to Deborah Cartmell. Spenser Studies (7) 1987, 289–94.

**3400.** —— The thirsty deer and the lord of life: some contexts for *Amoretti* 67–70. Spenser Studies (6) 1985, 33–76.

**3401.** ROCHE, THOMAS P., JR. A response to A. Kent Hieatt. Spenser Studies (8) 1987, 343–7.

**3402.** ROLLINSON, PHILIP. Arthur, Maleger, and the interpretation of *The Faerie Queene*. Spenser Studies (7) 1986, 103–21.

**3403.** ROOKS, JOHN. Art, audience and performance in the Bowre of Bliss. MLS (18:2) 1988, 23–36.

**3404.** SCHARNHORST, GARY. Hawthorne and *The Poetical Works of Edmund Spenser*: a lost review. AL (61:4) 668–73.

**3405.** SCHLEINER, LOUISE. Spenser and Sidney on the *vaticinium*. *See* **3327.**

**3406.** SCOTT, SHIRLEY CLAY. From Polydorus to Fradubio: the history of a *topos*. Spenser Studies (7) 1986, 27–57.

**3407.** SHAVER, ANNE. Rereading Mirabella. Spenser Studies (9) 1988, 211–26.

**3408.** SHEPHERD, SIMON. Spenser. New York; London: Harvester Wheatsheaf. pp. ix, 135. (Harvester new readings.)

**3409.** SHIMAMURA, NOBUO. Eikoku jojoushi no shikisai to hyougen: *Yousei Jouou* to *Rakuen Soushitu*. (The expression of colour in the English epic: *The Faerie Queene* and *Paradise Lost*.) Tokyo: Yachiyo. pp. viii, 206.

**3410.** SHORE, DAVID R. Spenser and the poetics of pastoral: a study of the world of Colin Clout. (Bibl. 1988, 2560.) Rev. by Judith Dundas in MLR (84:1) 119–20.

**3411.** SILBERMAN, LAUREN.   Singing unsung heroines: androgynous discourse in Book 3 of *The Faerie Queene*. *In* (pp. 259–71) **54.**

**3412.** STALLYBRASS, PETER.   Patriarchal territories: the body enclosed. *In* (pp. 123–42) **54.**

**3413.** STEWART, STANLEY.   Spenser and the Judgement of Paris. Spenser Studies (9) 1988, 161–209.

**3414.** STUMP, DONALD V.   The two deaths of Mary Stuart: historical allegory in Spenser's Book of Justice. Spenser Studies (9) 1988, 81–105.

**3415.** SUMMERS, CLAUDE J.   The Bride of the Apocalypse and the quest for true religion: Donne, Herbert, and Spenser. *In* (pp. 72–95) **11.**

**3416.** THORNTON, BRUCE.   Rural dialectic: pastoral, georgic, and *The Shepheardes Calender*. Spenser Studies (9) 1988, 1–20.

**3417.** TONKIN, HUMPHREY.   *The Faerie Queene*. London: Unwin Hyman. pp. xii, 282. (Unwin critical library.)

**3418.** TRATNER, MICHAEL.   'The thing S. Paule ment by ... the courteousness that he spake of': religious sources for Book VI of *The Faerie Queene*. Spenser Studies (8) 1987, 147–74.

**3419.** VARDANIS, ALEX A.   The temptations of despaire: Jeffers and *The Faerie Queene*. Spenser Studies (9) 1988, 255–7.

**3420.** VINK, JAMES.   A concealed figure in the woodcut to the *Januarye Ecologue. See* **100.**

**3421.** WALDMAN, LOUIS.   Spenser's pseudonym 'E.K.' and humanist self-naming. Spenser Studies (9) 1988, 21–31.

**3422.** WALL, JOHN N.   Transformations of the word: Spenser, Herbert, Vaughan. Athens; London: Georgia UP, 1988. pp. xv, 428. Rev. by Daniel W. Doerksen in GHJ (12:2) 55–9.

**3423.** WALL, JOHN N., JR.   Orion once more: revisiting the sky over Faerieland. Spenser Studies (8) 1987, 331–4.

**3424.** —— Orion's flaming head: Spenser's *Faerie Queene*, II.ii.46 and the feast of the twelve days of Christmas. Spenser Studies (7) 1986, 93–101.

**3425.** WEATHERBY, HAROLD L.   *Axiochus* and the Bower of Bliss: some fresh light on sources and authorship. Spenser Studies (6) 1985, 95–113.

**3426.** WELCH, ROBERT.   Seneca and the English Renaissance: the old world and the new. *In* (pp. 204–18) **37.**

**3427.** WELLS, ROBIN HEADLAM.   Spenser and the politics of music. HLQ (52:4) 447–68.

**3428.** YOON, HERAN C.   Colin Clout in love again: a study of Edmund Spenser's pastoralism in *Amoretti* and *Epithalamion*. Unpub. doct. diss., George Washington Univ., 1988. [Abstr. in DA (50) 151A.]

**3429.** YOON, JUNG-MOOK.   The significance of Guyon's faint in Book 2 of *The Faerie Queene*. JELL (35) 13–27.

### John Studley

**3430.** TAYLOR, ANTHONY BRIAN.   Shakespeare, Studley, and Golding. *See* **3226.**

## William Tyndale

**3431.**  DANIELL, DAVID (ed.).  Tyndale's *New Testament*; translated from the Greek by William Tyndale in 1534; in a modern spelling edition. New Haven, CT; London: Yale UP. pp. xxxvi, 429. Rev. by Geoffrey Hill in TLS, 17 Nov., 1273–6; by Ann Loades in Listener (122) 28 Sept., 35.

**3432.**  HILL, GEOFFREY.  Of diligence and jeopardy. *See* **3159.**

## Thomas Watson

**3433.**  SPEVACK, MARVIN; BINNS, J. W.; WECKERMANN, HANS-JÜRGEN (gen. eds).  *Absalom*, by Thomas Watson: *Christus triumphans*, by John Foxe. Ed. by JOHN HAZEL SMITH. *See* **3223.**

**3434.**  —————— *Antigone*, by Thomas Watson; *Roxana*, by William Alabaster; *Adrastus parentans sive vindicta*, by Peter Mease. Ed. by JOHN COLDEWEY and BRIAN F. COPENHAVER. *See* **3208.**

## Geffrey Whitney

**3435.**  MANNING, JOHN.  Unpublished and unedited emblems by Geffrey Whitney: further evidence of the English adaptation of continental traditions. *In* (pp. 83–107) **21.**

## Thomas Wilson

**3436.**  MEDINE, PETER E.  Thomas Wilson. (Bibl. 1987, 4048.) Rev. by Elizabeth Heale in YES (19) 309–11.

## Sir Thomas Wyatt

**3437.**  ADAMS, MICHAEL.  Sir Thomas Wyatt and the progress of Mannerism in Renaissance English lyric. Unpub. doct. diss., Univ. of Michigan, 1988. [Abstr. in DA (49) 3728A.]

**3438.**  CALDWELL, ELLEN C. (comp.).  Recent studies in Sir Thomas Wyatt (1970–1987). ELR (19:2) 226–46.

**3439.**  MASON, H. A. (ed.).  Sir Thomas Wyatt: a literary portrait: selected poems. (Bibl. 1988, 2582, where title incomplete.) Rev. by Patricia Thomson in RES (39:153) 1988, 103–4.

# WILLIAM SHAKESPEARE
## Editions and Textual Criticism

**3440.**  ADEY, LOUISE.  Reading between the lines: Tieck's prolegomena to the Schlegel–Tieck edition of Shakespeare. BJRL (71:3) 89–103.

**3441.**  BERGER, THOMAS L.  The second quarto of *Othello* and the question of textual 'authority'. AEB (ns 2:4) 1988, 141–59.

**3442.**  BEVINGTON, DAVID.  Bantam Shakespeare: the complete works. New York: Bantam Books, 1988. Rev. by Jeanne Addison Roberts in SQ (40:2) 239–40.

**3443.**  —— (ed.).  Henry IV, part I. (Bibl. 1988, 2586.) Rev. by Joan Rees in RES (39:155) 1988, 431–2.

**3444.**  BRAUNMULLER, A. R.  Editing the staging/staging the editing. *In* (pp. 139–49) **55.**

**3445.**  —— (ed.).  The life and death of King John. Oxford: Clarendon Press. pp. ix, 303. (Oxford Shakespeare.)

**3446.**  DORSCH, T. S. (ed.).  The comedy of errors. Cambridge: CUP.

pp. xiv, 115. (New Cambridge Shakespeare.) Rev. by T. W. Craik in DUJ (81:1) 1988, 158–60.

**3447.** EVANS, MAURICE (ed.).    The narrative poems. London: Penguin. pp. 263. (New Penguin Shakespeare.)

**3448.** EVERETT, BARBARA.    New readings in *Hamlet* (and some principles of emendation). RES (39:154) 1988, 177–98.

**3449.** FERGUSON, W. CRAIG.    Compositor identification in *Romeo* Q1 and *Troilus.* SB (42) 211–18.

**3450.** GABLER, HANS WALTER.    Assumption fruitfully disturbed. SJW 344–50 (review-article).

**3451.** HIBBARD, G. R. (ed.).    Hamlet. (Bibl. 1988, 2596.) Rev. by T. H. Howard-Hill in RES (39:155) 1988, 432–4.

**3452.** HOWARD, JEAN E.; O'CONNOR, MARION F.    Shakespeare reproduced: the text in history and ideology. New York: Methuen, 1987. (Bibl. 1987, 4070.) Rev. by John Drakakis in SQ (40:3) 342–5; by Richard G. Barlow in TJ (41:4) 575–7.

**3453.** JACKSON, MACDONALD P.    The year's contributions to Shakespearian study: 3, Editions and textual studies. ShS (40) 1988, 224–36; (41) 228–45.

**3454.** JOWETT, JOHN.    Cuts and casting: author and book-keeper in the Folio text of *2 Henry IV.* AUMLA (72) 275–95.

**3455.** —— The thieves in *1 Henry IV.* RES (38:151) 1987, 325–33.

**3456.** KING, NEIL (ed.).    Macbeth. Cheltenham: Thornes. pp. 95.

**3457.** MAHOOD, M. M. (ed.).    The merchant of Venice. (Bibl. 1987, 4081.) Rev. by Lawrence Danson in SQ (40:2) 240–3; by Katherine Duncan-Jones in NQ (36:1) 98–9.

**3458.** MONTGOMERY, WILLIAM.    The original staging of *The First Part of the Contention* (1594). ShS (41) 13–22.

**3459.** NICHOLLS, GRAHAM.    Measure for measure. (Bibl. 1986, 4889.) Rev. by Martin Wiggins in NQ (36:3) 386–7.

**3460.** OOBA, KENJI (ed.).    Julius Caesar. Tokyo: Taishukan. pp. xx, 288.

**3461.** OZ, AVRAHAM (ed. and trans.).    Ha-sokher mi-Veneziyah. (The Merchant of Venice.) Tel Aviv(?): Massadah. pp. 171. (Second ed.: first ed. 1975.) (National Council of Culture and the Arts, translations from world literature.)

**3462.** PATTERSON, ANNABEL.    Back by popular demand: the two versions of *Henry V.* RenD (19) 1988, 29–62.

**3463.** SASAYAMA, TAKASHI (ed.).    Othello. Tokyo: Taishukan. pp. xviii, 312. (In Japanese.)

**3464.** SEMPLE, HILARY (gen. ed.).    Macbeth: complete and unabridged. Ed. by ELISABETH LICKINDORF. London: Hodder & Stoughton, 1988. pp. xv, 96. (Bankside edition.)

**3465.** SPEVACK, MARVIN (ed.).    Julius Caesar. Cambridge: CUP, 1988. pp. xv, 184. (New Cambridge Shakespeare.)

**3466.** SPRINKLE-JACKSON, KATHRYN.    *King Lear* IV.iv.4: a proposal for emendation. ELN (26:4) 15–23.

**3467.** TAYLOR, ANTHONY BRIAN. The case for Pistol's 'base tike'. NQ (36:3) 324–5.

**3468.** THOMSON, LESLIE. Broken brackets and 'mended texts: stage directions in the Oxford Shakespeare. RenD (19) 1988, 175–93.

**3469.** WAITH, EUGENE M. (ed.). The two noble kinsmen. Oxford: Clarendon Press. pp. ix, 233. (Oxford Shakespeare.)

**3470.** WATT, R. J. C. Three cruces in *Measure for Measure*. RES (38:150) 1987, 227–33.

**3471.** WELLS, STANLEY; TAYLOR, GARY. William Shakespeare: a textual companion. (Bibl. 1988, 2610.) Rev. by Hans Walter Gabler in SJW 347–50; by George Walton Williams in CEl (35) 103–17; by E. A. J. Honigmann in NQ (36:1) 95–8.

**3472.** ———— (eds). The complete works. (Bibl. 1988, 2611.) Rev. by R. A. Foakes in MLR (84:2) 436–7; by Hans Walter Gabler in SJW 344–7; by George Walton Williams in CEl (35) 103–17.

**3473.** ———— The complete works, original-spelling edition. (Bibl. 1988, 2612.) Rev. by R. A. Foakes in MLR (84:2) 438–9; by Hans Walter Gabler in SJW 344–7; by Brian Gibbons in RES (39:156) 1988, 544–6; by George Walton Williams in CEl (35) 103–17.

**3474.** WERSTINE, PAUL. McKerrow's *Suggestion* and twentieth-century Shakespeare textual criticism. RenD (19) 1988, 149–73. (*Refers to* bibl. 1935, 2032.)

## General Scholarship and Criticism

**3475.** ADAMS, ROBERT M. Shakespeare: the four romances. New York; London: Norton. pp. xiii, 178. Rev. in BkW, 19 Nov., 13.

**3476.** ANDERSON, LINDA. A kind of wild justice: revenge in Shakespeare's comedies. (Bibl. 1988, 2615.) Rev. by Eugene D. Hill in SixCT (20:1) 118.

**3477.** ANDREWS, JOHN F. (ed.). William Shakespeare: his world, his work, and his influence. (Bibl. 1988, 2616.) Rev. by Arthur F. Kinney in HLQ (52:2) 310–13.

**3478.** ANNZAI, TETSUO (ed.). Nihon no Shakespeare 100 nen. (A hundred years of Shakespeare studies in Japan.) Tokyo: Aratake. pp. xviii, 190.

**3479.** ANON. A Shakespeare bibliography of periodical publications in South Africa in 1985 and 1986. Shakespeare in Southern Africa (1) 1987, 85–7. (Rhodes Univ., Dept of Librarianship.)

**3480.** ——— (ed.). Shakespeare no higeki. (Shakespeare's tragedies.) Tokyo: Kenkyusha, 1988. pp. viii, 280. (Japan Shakespeare Society.)

**3481.** BANESHIK, PERCY. Shakespeare in Johannesburg. Shakespeare Society of Southern Africa Occasional Papers and Reviews (4:1) 6–12.

**3482.** BARBER, C. L.; WHEELER, RICHARD P. The whole journey: Shakespeare's power of development. (Bibl. 1988, 2618.) Rev. by Kenneth Muir in MLR (84:4) 924–5; by Carol Thomas Neely in RQ (42:2) 351–4.

**3483.** BARKAN, LEONARD. The gods made flesh: metamorphosis and the pursuit of paganism. *See* **3338.**

**3484.**  BATE, JONATHAN.  Shakespeare and the English Romantic imagination. (Bibl. 1988, 2621.) Rev. by Esther H. Schor in SQ (40:1) 121–3.

**3485.**  BEINER, G.  *Agon* in Shakespearian comedy. YREAL (6) 149–85.

**3486.**  BERGERON, DAVID M.; DESOUSA, GERALDO U.  Shakespeare: a study and research guide. (Bibl. 1976, 4448.) Lawrence: Kansas UP, 1987. pp. viii, 202. (Second ed.: first ed. 1975.) Rev. by James J. Yoch, Jr, in SQ (40:1) 113–16.

**3487.**  BLAKE, N. F.  The language of Shakespeare. *See* **1385.**

**3488.**  —— Negation in Shakespeare. *In* (pp. 89–111) **30.**

**3489.**  BLISS, LEE.  Three plays in one: Shakespeare and *Philaster.* MedRen (2) 1985, 153–70.

**3490.**  BRADBROOK, M. C.  Shakespeare in his context: the constellated Globe. Introd. by ANDREW GURR. Hemel Hempstead: Harvester Wheatsheaf. pp. xii, 207. (Collected papers of Muriel Bradbrook, 4.)

**3491.**  BRADSHAW, GRAHAM.  Shakespeare's scepticism. (Bibl. 1988, 2627.) Rev. by Balz Engler in EngS (70:5) 455–6; by Tom Mason in CanQ (18:4) 428–45; by Alastair Fowler in LRB (11:5) 15–16; by Lawrence Normand in NQ (36:3) 381.

**3492.**  BRENNAN, ANTHONY.  Onstage and offstage worlds in Shakespeare's plays. London: Routledge. pp. ix, 321.

**3493.**  —— Shakespeare's dramatic structures. (Bibl. 1987, 4115.) Rev. by Andrew Gurr in RES (38:151) 1987, 388–9; by Stephen J. Phillips in NQ (36:2) 233–4.

**3494.**  BRONSON , BERTRAND H.; O'MEARA, JEAN M. (eds).  Selections from Johnson on Shakespeare. (Bibl. 1988, 2628.) Rev. by Murray G. H. Pittock in BJECS (12) 111–12.

**3495.**  BROWNLOW, F. W.  John Shakespeare's recusancy: new light on an old document. SQ (40:2) 186–91.

**3496.**  BURDETTE, LIVIA.  The Hillier Shakespeare Collection: origin, scope and prospects. *See* **206.**

**3497.**  CALDERWOOD, JAMES L.  Shakespeare and the denial of death. Amherst: Massachusetts UP, 1987. pp. xi, 233. Rev. by Arthur Kirsch in SQ (40:3) 348–9; by Park Honan in NQ (36:3) 382.

**3498.**  CARTELLI, THOMAS.  *Bartholomew Fair* as urban Arcadia: Jonson responds to Shakespeare. RenD (14) 1983, 151–72.

**3499.**  CAVANAGH, SHEILA T.  'That fairest vertue': discourses of chastity in Spenser and Shakespeare. *See* **3353.**

**3500.**  CAVELL, STANLEY.  Disowning knowledge in six plays of Shakespeare. (Bibl. 1988, 2635.) Rev. by Gilles Montsarrat in EA (42:4) 467–8; by Park Honan in NQ (36:1) 101–2.

**3501.**  CHARNEY, MAURICE (ed.).  'Bad' Shakespeare: revaluations of the Shakespeare canon. Rutherford, NJ; Fairleigh Dickinson UP; London; Toronto: Assoc. UPs, 1988. pp. 213. Rev. by Alexander Leggatt in SQ (40:3) 352–4.

**3502.**  CHEADLE, BRIAN.  The 'new historicism': approaching Shakespeare's practice. Shakespeare in Southern Africa (2) 1988, 31–41.

**3503.** CLEMEN, WOLFGANG.    Shakespeare's sololoquies. Trans. by CHARITY SCOTT STOKES. (Bibl. 1987, 4130.) Rev. by Joan Rees in NQ (36:1) 99; by Ulrich Suerbaum in SJW 374-6; by Kristian Smidt in EngS (70:2) 179–80.

**3504.** COHEN, DEREK.    Shakespearean motives. New York: St Martin's Press, 1988. (Bibl. 1988, 2638.) Rev. by Alexander Leggatt in SQ (40:1) 102–4; by Peggy Muñoz Simonds in JRMMRA (10) 112–13.

**3505.** CONWAY, DANIEL J.    Erotic arguments: rhetoric and sexuality in seventeenth-century English stage adaptations of Plutarch. Unpub. doct. diss., Univ. of Minnesota. [Abstr. in DA (50) 1139A.]

**3506.** COX, C. B.; PALMER, D. J. (eds).    Shakespeare's wide and universal stage. (Bibl. 1986, 4417.) Rev. by J. A. J. van Zyl in Shakespeare in Southern Africa (1) 1987, 82–4.

**3507.** COX, JOHN D.    Shakespeare and the dramaturgy of power. Princeton, NJ; Guildford: Princeton UP. pp. xviii, 282. Rev. by Peter Erickson in RQ (42:4) 883–5.

**3508.** CUYLER, GRENVILLE.    Shakespeare and Jung. Unpub. doct. diss., Univ. of Birmingham, 1985. [Abstr. in DA (49) 3731A.]

**3509.** DAMANT, D. G.    Some reflections on Shakespeare's 'anticlericalism'. Shakespeare in Southern Africa (1) 1987, 39–45.

**3510.** D'AMICO, JACK.    The politics of madness: Junius Brutus in Machiavelli and Shakespeare. MidQ (30:4) 405–22.

**3511.** DASH, IRENE G.    Wooing, wedding, and power: women in Shakespeare's plays. (Bibl. 1986, 4425.) Rev. by Elaine Upton Pugh in MedRen (2) 1985, 311–13.

**3512.** DEAN, PAUL.    Shakespeare's causes. CEl (36) 25–35.

**3513.** DESSEN, ALAN C.    Shakespeare and the late moral plays. (Bibl. 1988, 2646.) Rev. by R. W. F. Martin in RES (39:153) 1988, 104–5.

**3514.** DOBSON, M.    Authorizing Shakespeare: adaptation and canonization, 1660–1769. Unpub. doct. diss., Univ. of Oxford. [Abstr. in IT (39:3) 1103.]

**3515.** DOLLIMORE, JONATHAN.    Radical tragedy: religion, ideology, and power in the drama of Shakespeare and his contemporaries. (Bibl. 1988, 2647.) Rev. by Harry Keyishian in MedRen (2) 1985, 314–20.

**3516.** —— SINFIELD, ALAN (eds).    Political Shakespeare: new essays in cultural materialism. (Bibl. 1987, 4140.) Rev. by David Ellis in CamQ (18:1) 94–5; by A. W. Stadler in Shakespeare in Southern Africa (1) 75–7; by Charles R. Forker in MedRen (3) 1986, 310–15.

**3517.** DOMINIK, MARK.    Shakespeare and *The Birth of Merlin*. New York: Philosophical Library, 1985. pp. 214. Rev. by Peter Bement in RES (38:152) 1987, 560.

**3518.** DORRELL, L.    Chaucer, Shakespeare and the Constance–Griselda legend: a study of the Clerk's Tale, the Man of Law's Tale and Shakespeare's last plays. See **2888.**

**3519.** DRAKAKIS, JOHN (ed.).    Alternative Shakespeares. (Bibl. 1987, 4143.) Rev. by David Ellis in CamQ (18:1) 92–3.

**3520.** DREHER, DIANE ELIZABETH.    Domination and defiance: fathers and daughters in Shakespeare. (Bibl. 1988, 2649.) Rev. by Ann Thompson in YES (19) 316–17.

**3521.** DUANE, CAROL LEVENTEN. Marlowe's mixed messages: a model for Shakespeare? *See* **3255.**

**3522.** DUTTON, RICHARD. William Shakespeare: a literary life. Basingstoke: Macmillan. pp. xii, 180. (Macmillan literary lives.)

**3523.** —— The year's contributions to Shakespearian study: 2, Shakespeare's life, times, and stage. ShS (40) 1988, 211–24; (41) 214–228.

**3524.** EAGLESON, ROBERT D. (ed.). A Shakespeare glossary. By C. T. ONIONS. (Bibl. 1988, 2651.) Rev. by Basil Cottle in RES (39:154) 1988, 291–2.

**3525.** EAGLETON, TERRY. William Shakespeare. (Bibl. 1988, 2652.) Rev. by Ann Thompson in MLR (84:3) 716.

**3526.** ECKER, GISELA. Der weibliche Körper bei Shakespeare im Spiel von An- und Abwesenheit. SJW 223–41.

**3527.** EDWARDS, PHILIP. Shakespeare: a writer's progress. (Bibl. 1988, 2653.) Rev. by Joan Rees in RES (38:150) 1987, 243–4; by J. A. Bryant, Jr, in SQ (40:1) 116–17; by G. K. Hunter in MLR (84:1) 121–2.

**3528.** ELAM, KEIR. Shakespeare's universe of discourse: language-games in the comedies. (Bibl. 1988, 2654.) Rev. by B. D. H. Miller in RES (38:150) 1987, 245–6.

**3529.** ELLIS, DAVID. The Groucho tendency in recent criticism of Shakespeare. CamQ (18:1) 86–97 (review-article).

**3530.** EMPSON, WILLIAM. Essays on Shakespeare. Ed. by DAVID B. PIRIE. (Bibl. 1988, 2655.) Rev. by Philip V. McGuire in TJ (41:1) 114–15.

**3531.** ERICKSON, PETER. Patriarchal structures in Shakespeare's drama. (Bibl. 1988, 2656.) Rev. by Peter Bement in RES (38:152) 1987, 557–8.

**3532.** EVANS, MALCOLM. Signifying nothing: truth's true contents in Shakespeare's text. (Bibl. 1988, 2657.) New York; London: Harvester Wheatsheaf. pp. xii, 317. (Second ed.: first ed. 1986.) Rev. by Charles H. Frey in MedRen (4) 240–3.

**3533.** FAAS, EKBERT. Shakespeare's poetics. (Bibl. 1988, 2660.) Rev. by T. H. Howard-Hill in RES (38:151) 1987, 386–7.

**3534.** FARRELL, KIRBY. Play, death and heroism in Shakespeare. Chapel Hill; London: North Carolina UP. pp. xi, 235.

**3535.** FINEMAN, JOEL. Shakespeare's ear. Representations (28) 6–13.

**3536.** FISCHER, SANDRA K. 'He means to pay': value and metaphor in the Lancastrian tetralogy. SQ (40:2) 149–64.

**3537.** FOAKES, R. A. (ed.). Coleridge's criticism of Shakespeare: a selection. London: Athlone Press. pp. xii, 195.

**3538.** FRASER, RUSSELL. Young Shakespeare. (Bibl. 1988, 2664.) Rev. by Robert Y. Turner in RQ (42:2) 354–6; by S. Schoenbaum in TLS, 20 Jan., 63.

**3539.** FREY, CHARLES H. Experiencing Shakespeare: essays on text, classroom, and performance. Columbia: Missouri UP, 1988. pp. xv, 207. Rev. by Robert Hapgood in SQ (40:2) 228–30.

**3540.** FRYE, NORTHROP.    Northrop Frye on Shakespeare. Ed. by
ROBERT SANDLER. (Bibl. 1988, 2665.) Rev. by E. A. J. Honigmann in
YES (19) 314–16; by A. W. Lyle in RES (39:155) 1988, 434–5.

**3541.** GANTS, N. V.; KUZNETSOVA, L. B.    Funktsional'no-
stilisticheskie kharakteristiki minimal'nykh dvusostavnykh predlozheniĭ s podlezhashchim 'it' v dialogakh p'es Shekspira. *See* **1402.**

**3542.** GANZEL, DEWEY.    Fortune and men's eyes: the career of John
Payne Collier. (Bibl. 1987, 4066.) Rev. by G. P. Jones in MedRen (3)
1986, 255–63.

**3543.** GARBER, MARJORIE.    Shakespeare's ghost writers: literature as
uncanny causality. (Bibl. 1988, 2667.) Rev. by Margreta DeGrazia in
SQ (40:3) 345–8; by Derick R. C. Marsh in NQ (36:2) 235–6.

**3544.** GIBBONS, BRIAN.    The human body in *Titus Andronicus* and other
early Shakespeare plays. SJW 209–22.

**3545.** GLINOGA, CELSO ALAN.    Shakespeare in einer neokolonialen
Gesellschaft: das Beispiel Philippinen. SJO (125) 29–34.

**3546.** GOLDBERG, JONATHAN.    Rebel letters: postal effects from
*Richard II* to *Henry IV*. RenD (19) 1988, 3–28.

**3547.** GOLDMAN, MICHAEL.    Acting and action in Shakespearean
tragedy. (Bibl. 1988, 2669.) Rev. by Peter Bement in RES (38:152)
1987, 558–9.

**3548.** GOOCH, BRYAN N. S.    Music for Shakespeare: coming to terms
with a neglected heritage. Archiv (226:2) 360–5.

**3549.** GRADY, HUGH H.    Instituting Shakespeare: hegemony and
Tillyard's historical criticism. Assays (5) 37–61.

**3550.** GRAY, J. C. (ed.).    Mirror up to Shakespeare: essays in honour
of G. R. Hibbard. (Bibl. 1986, 4461, where dedicatee's second initial
incorrect.) Rev. by Jeanne Addison Roberts in MedRen (3) 1986,
328–9.

**3551.** GREENBLATT, STEPHEN.    Shakespearean negotiations: the circulation of social energy in Renaissance England. Berkeley: California UP, 1988. (Bibl. 1988,2673.) Rev. by Jane Donawerth in SixCT
(20:3) 501–2; by John Drakakis in NQ (36:4) 503–5; by Peter Burke in
LRB (11:1) 18–19; by Steven Mullaney in SQ (40:4) 495–500.

**3552.** GREENWOOD, JOHN.    Shifting perspectives and the stylish style:
mannerism in Shakespeare and his Jacobean contemporaries. Toronto;
Buffalo, NY; London: Toronto UP, 1988. pp. viii, 227. Rev. by Lucy
Gent in RQ (42:2) 361–3; by Gunther Klotz in SJO (125) 189–91.

**3553.** GUILFOYLE, CHERRELL.    Othello, Otuel, and the English
Charlemagne romances. *See* **1166.**

**3554.** HARRISON, ROBERT LEE, JR.    The recurring author: William
Shakespeare, a case study through content analysis. Unpub. doct. diss.,
American Univ., 1988. [Abstr. in DA (49) 3645A.]

**3555.** HASSAN, DINESH SHANKAR.    Shakespeare's early comedies: a
study of their plots. Unpub. doct. diss., Univ. of Cincinnati, 1988.
[Abstr. in DA (49) 3368A.]

**3556.** HAWKES, TERENCE.    That Shakespeherian rag: essays on a
critical process. (Bibl. 1988, 2678.) Rev. by Ann Thompson in MLR

(84:3) 716; by Ian Steadman in Shakespeare in Southern Africa (1) 1987, 81–2.

**3557.** HELMS, LORRAINE. Playing the woman's part: feminist criticism and Shakespearean performance. TJ (41:2) 190–200.

**3558.** HENRY, KAREN SCHWAB. The shattering of resemblance: the mirror in Shakespeare. Unpub. doct. diss., Tufts Univ. [Abstr. in DA (50) 1664A.]

**3559.** HERRMAN, ANNE. Travesty and transgression: transvestism in Shakepeare, Brecht and Churchill. TJ (41:2) 133–54.

**3560.** HILBERRY, JANE ELIZABETH. The silent woman: speech, gender, and authority in Chaucer and Shakespeare. See **2907.**

**3561.** HILSKÝ, MARTIN. Hříšné hříčky: jazyk rané shakespearovské komedie z hlediska překladatelského. In (pp. 45) **6.**

**3562.** HILTSCHER, MICHAEL. Aus der Geschichte der deutschen Shakespeare-Forschung: Nicolaus Delius 1813–1888. SJW 387–97.

**3563.** HOLDERNESS, GRAHAM (ed.). The Shakespeare myth. (Bibl. 1988, 2682.) Rev. by Howard Mills in Eng (38) 77–83; by Robert Hapgood in TLS, 25 Aug., 927.

**3564.** —— POTTER, NICK; TURNER, JOHN. Shakespeare: the play of history. Iowa City: Iowa UP, 1987. (Bibl. 1987, 4176.) Rev. by Eric S. Mallin in RQ (42:2) 359–61; by Paul N. Siegel in ELN (27:2) 65–7; by Phyllis Lewsen in Shakespeare in Southern Africa (2) 1988, 112–14.

**3565.** HOMAN, SIDNEY. Shakespeare's theater of presence: language, spectacle and the audience. (Bibl. 1988, 2684.) Rev. in QQ (95:1) 1988, 208–9.

**3566.** HORWICH, RICHARD. 'I sing but after you': Shakespeare's internal parody. SELit (28:2) 1988, 219–40.

**3567.** —— Shakespeare's dilemmas. New York; Berne; Frankfurt: Lang, 1988. pp. x, 221. (American univ. studies, 4: English language and literature, 61.) Rev. by J. A. Bryant, Jr, in SQ (40:3) 355–7.

**3568.** HORWITZ, EVE. Freedom of speech and Shakespeare's women characters. Shakespeare in Southern Africa (2) 1988, 51–9.

**3569.** HUNT, MAURICE. Homeopathy in Shakespearean comedy and romance. BSUF (29:3) 1988, 45–57.

**3570.** ISER, WOLFGANG. Shakespeares Historien: Genesis und Geltung. Konstanz: Konstanz UP, 1988. pp. 239.

**3571.** ISHIKAWA, MINORU. Shakespeare yondai higeki. (Four great Shakespearean tragedies.) Tokyo: Keio Tsushin. pp. vi, 218.

**3572.** JONES-DAVIES, MARIE-THÉRÈSE. Shakespeare: le théâtre du monde. (Bibl. 1988, 2689.) Rev. by Kenneth Muir in EA (42:1) 100–1.

**3573.** KALLFELZ COX, M. L. 'Unsex me here': the political roles of women: Shakespeare and the modern world. Unpub. doct. diss., Univ. of Essex, 1988. [Abstr. in IT (39:3) 1106.]

**3574.** KATRITZKY, LINDE. Shakespeare in den *Nachtwachen* von Bonaventura. SJO (125) 103–15.

**3575.** KAWAI, SHOICHIRO. The four basic dramatic functions of characters in Shakespeare's comedies. SStudT (25) 1987, 41–67.

**3576.** KAWAJI, YOSHIKO. Shakespeare worldwide: translation and adaptation, 12. Tokyo: Yushoudo. pp. x, 218.

**3577.** KELLY, H. A. Chaucer and Shakespeare on tragedy. *See* **2840.**

**3578.** KHAN, MAQBOOL H. Tolstoy's critique of Shakespeare. ACM (2:1) 60–73.

**3579.** KIM, HAN. Shakespeare eui malgigeuk eul tonghae bon Shakespeare eui guwonkwan. (A study of Shakespeare's view of time and human salvation.) JELL (35) 537–57.

**3580.** KOMAROVA, V. P. Metafory i allegorii v proizvedeniĭakh Shekspira. (Metaphors and allegories in the works of Shakespeare.) Leningrad: Leningrad UP. pp. 199.

**3581.** LEE, HYUNG-SHIK. Two worlds in Shakespeare's comedies. JELL (35) 735–45.

**3582.** LEFRANC, ABEL. Under the mask of William Shakespeare. Trans. by CECIL CRAGG. Braunton, Devonshire: Merlin, 1988. pp. 538.

**3583.** LEIBBRANDT, SHIRLEY A. A Shakespeare bibliography of periodical publications in South Africa in 1987. Shakespeare in Southern Africa (2) 1988, 131–4.

**3584.** LEMMER, ANDRÉ. 'The play's the thing': some thoughts on the teaching of Shakespeare at school. Shakespeare Society of Southern Africa Occasional Papers and Reviews (1:1) 1986, 2–7.

**3585.** LEVI, PETER. The life and times of William Shakespeare. New York: Holt, Rinehart & Winston. (Bibl. 1988, 2708.) Rev. in BkW, 12 Nov., 17; by S. Schoenbaum in TLS, 20 Jan., 63.

**3586.** LOMAX, MARION. Stage images and traditions: Shakespeare to Ford. (Bibl. 1988, 2713.) Rev. by Victor Bourgy in EA (42:4) 470–1; by David Stevens in TJ (41:1) 115–16; by Maurice Charney in RQ (42:1) 140–2.

**3587.** LUKACHER, NED. Anamorphic stuff: Shakespeare, catharsis, and Lacan. SAQ (88:4) 863–98.

**3588.** McDONALD, RUSS. Shakespeare and Jonson/Jonson and Shakespeare. Brighton: Harvester; Lincoln: Nebraska UP, 1988. pp. x, 239.

**3589.** MACKINNON, LACHLAN. Shakespeare the aesthete: an exploration of literary theory. (Bibl. 1988, 2717.) Rev. by Howard Mills in Eng (38) 77–83.

**3590.** MAGISTER, KARL-HEINZ. Shakespeare Bibliographie für 1987, mit Nachträgen aus früheren Jahren. SJO (125) 225–302.

**3591.** MAHON, JOHN W.; PENDLETON, THOMAS A. (eds). 'Fanned and winnowed opinions': Shakespearean essays presented to Harold Jenkins. (Bibl. 1987, 23.) Rev. by Juliet McLauchlan in NQ (36:3) 385–6; by A. E. Voss in Shakespeare in Southern Africa (2) 1988, 114–15.

**3592.** MAHOOD, M. M. Shakespeare in states unknown. Shakespeare in Southern Africa (1) 1987, 1–9.

**3593.** MANSFIELD, R. G. The protean player: the concept and practice of doubling in the plays of Shakespeare and his contemporaries, *c.* 1576–1631. *See* **3095.**

**3594.** MARCUS, LEAH S. Puzzling Shakespeare: local reading and its discontents. Berkeley; London: California UP, 1988. pp. xiii, 267. (New historicism: studies in cultural poetics, 6.) Rev. by Robert Hapgood in TLS, 25 Aug., 927.

**3595.** MARDER, LOUIS.   Remains of the Globe discovered. *See* **3097.**

**3596.** —— Testing computerized authorship programs. *See* **535.**

**3597.** MAROWITZ, CHARLES.   Reconstructing Shakespeare or harlotry in bardolatry. ShS (40) 1988, 1–10.

**3598.** MARVEL, LAURA MELISSA.   Tragedies of identity in the works of Shakespeare and Beckett. Unpub. doct. diss., Univ. of Notre Dame. [Abstr. in DA (49) 3034–5A.]

**3599.** MEHL, DIETER.   Shakespeare's tragedies: an introduction. (Bibl. 1988, 2722.) Rev. by Richard Dutton in MLR (84:3) 711–12; by F. David Hoeniger in SQ (40:1) 112–13; by Claire Saunders in RES (39:156) 1988, 546.

**3600.** MERRIAM, T.   Taylor's statistics in *A Textual Companion*. NQ (36:3) 341–2.

**3601.** MILWARD, PETER.   Biblical influences in Shakespeare's great tragedies. (Bibl. 1988, 2724.) Rev. by Coburn Freer in SQ (40:1) 106–8.

**3602.** —— Shakespeare's other dimensions. Tokyo: Renaissance Kenkyusho. pp. 146.

**3603.** MORRIS, HARRY.   Last things in Shakespeare. (Bibl. 1987, 4221.) Rev. by Joan Rees in RES (38:150) 1987, 243; by Kenneth Muir in MLR (84:4) 924.

**3604.** MUIR, KENNETH.   Shakespeare: contrasts and controversies. (Bibl. 1986, 4540.) Rev. by Peter Bement in RES (38:152) 1987, 555–6.

**3605.** —— (sel.).   Interpretations of Shakespeare: British Academy Shakespeare lectures. (Bibl. 1986, 4541.) Rev. by E. A. J. Honigmann in YES (19) 314–16.

**3606.** NAGARAJAN, S.; VISWANATHAN, S. (eds).   Shakespeare in India. (Bibl. 1987, 4226.) Rev. by Jyotsna Singh in TJ (41:1) 113–14.

**3607.** NETHERSOLE, REINGARD.   'Shakespeare without end': Shakespeare and European literature. Shakespeare in Southern Africa (1) 1987, 52–61.

**3608.** NEUHAUS, H. JOACHIM.   The Shakespeare dictionary database. *See* **538.**

**3609.** —— Shakespeare's wordforms, a database view. *In* (pp. 264–80) **5.**

**3610.** NEVO, RUTH.   Shakespeare's other language. New York: Methuen, 1987. (Bibl. 1987, 4230.) Rev. by John Drakakis in NQ (36:2) 231–3.

**3611.** NOVY, MARIANNE.   *Daniel Deronda* and George Eliot's female (re)vision of Shakespeare. SELit (28:4) 1988, 671–92.

**3612.** NUTTALL, A. D.   A new mimesis: Shakespeare and the representation of reality. (Bibl. 1986, 4547.) Rev. by Lubomír Doležel in CompCrit (11) 253–7.

**3613.** O'DAIR, SHARON KAY.   The social self of the hero in Shakespearean tragedy. Unpub. doct. diss., Univ. of California, Berkeley, 1988. [Abstr. in DA (50) 956A.]

**3614.** ORKIN, MARTIN.    Shakespeare against apartheid. (Bibl. 1988, 2735.) Rev. by Laurence Wright in Shakespeare in Southern Africa (1) 1987, 72–4.

**3615.** ORNSTEIN, ROBERT.    Shakespeare's comedies: from Roman farce to romantic mystery. (Bibl. 1988, 2736.) Rev. by Frank Ardolino in SixCT (20:4) 704–5.

**3616.** ORRELL, JOHN.    The quest for Shakespeare's Globe. (Bibl. 1986, 4548.) Rev. by S. P. Cerasano in MedRen (3) 1986, 265–75.

**3617.** OZU, JIRO.    Ishowo kaku Shakespeare. (Shakespeare writing his will.) Tokyo: Iwanami. pp. vi, 314.

**3618.** —— Shakespeare toujou. (Enter Shakespeare.) Tokyo: Kinokuniya. pp. vi, 222.

**3619.** PARK, SUN-BOO.    Shakespeare munhak gwa modernism (1). (Shakespearean literature and modernism (1).) ShR (15) 23–54.

**3620.** PARKER, BARBARA L.    A precious seeing: love and reason in Shakespeare's plays. (Bibl. 1987, 4242.) Rev. by Park Honan in NQ (36:1) 101–2.

**3621.** PARKER, G. F.    Johnson's Shakespeare. Oxford: Clarendon Press; New York: OUP. pp. xx, 204. Rev. by Robert Hapgood in TLS, 25 Aug., 927.

**3622.** PARKER, PATRICIA; HARTMAN, GEOFFREY (eds).    Shakespeare and the question of theory. (Bibl. 1988, 2738.) Rev. by Thomas Docherty in RES (38:152) 1987, 553–5; by David Ellis in CamQ (18:1) 96–7.

**3623.** PASTER, GAIL KERN.    The idea of the city in the age of Shakespeare. (Bibl. 1988, 2739.) Rev. by Nancy Elizabeth Hodge in MedRen (4) 289–94.

**3624.** PFISTER, MANFRED.    Zur Theoretisierung des Körpers. SJW 174–7.

**3625.** POOLE, ADRIAN.    Tragedy: Shakespeare and the Greek example. (Bibl. 1988, 2742.) Rev. by A. D. Nuttall in RES (39:154) 1988, 329–30; by Felicity Rosslyn in CamQ (18:2) 208–15.

**3626.** PORTER, JOSEPH A.    Marlowe, Shakespeare, and the canonization of heterosexuality. *See* **3270.**

**3627.** POWERS, KATHLEEN EMILY.    Shakespeare's use of lies and deceptions in the comedies. Unpub. doct. diss., Brown Univ., 1988. [Abstr. in DA (49) 2233A.]

**3628.** RABKIN, GERALD.    Shakespeare our ideologist. MLS (18:2) 1988, 3–22.

**3629.** RACKIN, PHYLLIS.    Temporality, anachronism, and presence in Shakespeare's English histories. RenD (17) 1986, 101–23.

**3630.** RANALD, MARGARET LOFTUS.    Shakespeare and his social context: essays in osmotic knowledge and literary interpretation. (Bibl. 1988, 2745.) Rev. by Carolyn Ruth Swift in SQ (40:3) 357–8.

**3631.** RASMUSSEN, ERIC.    Shakespeare's hand in *The Second Maiden's Tragedy.* SQ (40:1) 1–26.

**3632.** RICHER, JEAN.    Lecture astrologique des pièces romaines de Shakespeare: *Titus Andronicus, Jules César, Antoine et Cléopâtre, Coriolan.*

Paris: Trédaniel, 1988. pp. 94. Rev. by François Laroque in CEl (35) 121.

**3633.** ROHMER, ROLF. Sprachen des Welttheaters – Kontroverse und Dialog mit Shakespeare. SJO (125) 7–19.

**3634.** ROSENBERG, MARVIN. Sign theory and Shakespeare. *See* **1241.**

**3635.** ROVINE, HARVEY. Silence in Shakespeare: drama, power, and gender. Ann Arbor, MI; London: UMI Research Press, 1987. pp. 114. (Theater and dramatic studies, 45.) (Cf. bibl. 1986, 4565.) Rev. by Jay L. Halio in SQ (40:3) 354–5; by J. Pat Rice in TJ (41:3) 418–20.

**3636.** ROWSE, A. L. Discovering Shakespeare: a chapter in literary history. London: Weidenfeld & Nicolson. pp. xiii, 177. Rev. by S. Schoenbaum in TLS, 6 Oct., 1091.

**3637.** —— HEDGECOE, JOHN. In Shakespeare's land: a journey through the landscape of Elizabethan England. London: Weidenfeld & Nicolson, 1986. pp. 200.

**3638.** RUNIA, ANTHONY P. The codas to Shakespeare's tragedies. YREAL (6) 101–47.

**3639.** RUSSELL, THOMAS W., III. Shakespearean coinages: fewer than supposed? *See* **1027.**

**3640.** RYAN, KIERNAN. Shakespeare. New York; London: Harvester Wheatsheaf. pp. xi, 130. (Harvester new readings.)

**3641.** SALINGAR, LEO. Dramatic form in Shakespeare and the Jacobeans. (Bibl. 1988, 2751.) Rev. by R. W. F. Martin in RES (39:154) 1988, 289–90; by E. A. J. Honigmann in YES (19) 314–16.

**3642.** SCHOENBAUM, MARILYN (ed.). A Shakespeare merriment: an anthology of Shakespearean humor. New York; London: Garland, 1988. pp. xxii, 266. (Garland reference library of the humanities, 836.) Rev. in BkW, 19 Feb., 13.

**3643.** SCHUMAN, SAMUEL. Nabokov and Shakespeare's trees. NCL (18:3) 1988, 8–10.

**3644.** SCOTT, MICHAEL. Shakespeare and the modern dramatist. Basingstoke: Macmillan, 1988. pp. viii, 164. (Contemporary interpretations of Shakespeare.)

**3645.** SCRAGG, LEAH. Discovering Shakespeare's meaning. (Bibl. 1988, 2752.) Rev. by Howard Mills in Eng (38) 77–83; by Martin Coyle in NQ (36:3) 384.

**3646.** SEEHASE, GEORG. Ein Plädoyer für Shakespeare aus Südafrika. SJO (125) 35–9.

**3647.** SHAHEEN, NASEEB. Biblical references in Shakespeare's tragedies. Newark, NJ: Delaware UP; London; Toronto: Assoc. UPs, 1987. pp. 245. Rev. by Cynthia Lewis in SQ (40:1) 108–12.

**3648.** SHERBO, ARTHUR. Lord Hailes, Shakespeare critic. SQ (40:2) 175–85.

**3649.** al-SHETAWI, MAHMOUD F. Shakespeare in Arabic: an overview. NC (8) 114–26.

**3650.** SHIN, KYUM-SOO. Shakespeare heuigeuk eseoeui useum eui yeongu: romantic comedies reul jungsim euro. (A study of laughter in

Shakespeare's comedy based on his romantic comedies.) Unpub. doct. diss., Sungkyunkwan Univ., Seoul.

**3651.** SMIDT, KRISTIAN.   Unconformities in Shakespeare's early comedies. New York: St Martin's Press, 1986. (Bibl. 1986, 4593.) Rev. by Sidney Thomas in SQ (40:2) 230–2.

**3652.** SMITH, M. W. A.; CALVERT, HUGH.   Word-links as a general indicator of chronology of composition. NQ (36:3) 338–41.

**3653.** SPEVACK, MARVIN.   The art of dying in Shakespeare. SJW 169–73.

**3654.** STEVENS, PAUL.   Imagination and the presence of Shakespeare in *Paradise Lost*. (Bibl. 1988, 2764.) Rev. by Nigel Smith in RES (38:150) 1987, 249–50.

**3655.** STOCKHOLDER, KAY.   Dream works: lovers and families in Shakespeare's plays. (Bibl. 1988, 2765.) Rev. by Valerie Traub in SQ (40:1) 100–2.

**3656.** TARLINSKAJA, MARINA.   Shakespeare's verse: iambic pentameter and the poet's idiosyncrasies. (Bibl. 1987, 4269.) Rev. by Anthony Graham-White in TJ (41:4) 572–3; by Russ McDonald in SQ (40:3) 360–3.

**3657.** TAYLOR, ANTHONY BRIAN.   Shakespeare, Studley, and Golding. See **3226.**

**3658.** —— Two notes on Shakespeare and the translators. RES (38:152) 1987, 523–6.

**3659.** TAYLOR, GARY.   Reinventing Shakespeare: a cultural history from the Restoration to the present. New York: Weidenfeld & Nicolson; London: Hogarth Press. pp. 461. Rev. by Michael Dirda in BkW, 27 Aug., 1,4; by Gary Schmidgall in NYTB, 17 Sept., 28.

**3660.** —— William Shakespeare, Richard James and the House of Cobham. See **180.**

**3661.** TENNENHOUSE, LEONARD.   Power on display: the politics of Shakespeare's genres. (Bibl. 1988, 2768.) Rev. by Ann Thompson in MLR (84:3) 715; by M.S. in TJ (41:2) 254–5; by Peggy Muñoz Simonds in JRMMRA (10) 109–10; by Thomas Docherty in RES (39:155) 1988, 435–6.

**3662.** THOMAS, SHIRLEY FORBES.   'One that's dead is quick': a study of counterfeit death and resurrection in relation to plot, character, and theme in the plays of William Shakespeare. Unpub. doct. diss., Univ. of Arkansas, 1988. [Abstr. in DA (49) 1812A.]

**3663.** THOMAS, VIVIAN.   The moral universe of Shakespeare's problem plays. (Bibl. 1988, 2770.) Rev. by Annette L. Combrink in Shakespeare in Southern Africa (2) 1988, 118–20; by J. G. Saunders in RES (39:156) 1988, 547–8; by Peter Happé in NQ (36:1) 100–1.

**3664.** THOMPSON, MARVIN; THOMPSON, RUTH.   Performance criticism: from Granville-Barker to Bernard Beckerman and beyond. *In* (pp. 13–23) **55.**

**3665.** TIFFANY, GRACE CLEVELAND.   Power plays: the construction of kingship in Shakespeare's Henriad. Unpub. doct. diss., Univ. of Notre Dame. [Abstr. in DA (50) 957A.]

**3666.** TRUSSLER, SIMON.    Shakespearean concepts: a dictionary of terms and conventions, influences and institutions, themes, ideas and genres in the Elizabethan and Jacobean drama. London: Methuen. pp. 185.

**3667.** UMEDA, BAIO.    Shakespeare no kotoba asobi. (Word-play in Shakespeare.) Tokyo: Eihosha. pp. 390.

**3668.** URKOWITZ, STEVEN.    Memorial reconstruction: decline of a theory. SNL (39:1/2) 10.

**3669.** VAN DEN BERG, KENT T.    Playhouse and cosmos: Shakespearean theater as metaphor. (Bibl. 1987, 4277, where scholar's name misspelt.) Rev. by R. S. White in RES (38:150) 1987, 244–5.

**3670.** VEST, JAMES M.    Reflections of Ophelia (and of Hamlet) in Alfred Hitchcock's *Vertigo*. JMMLA (22:1) 1–9.

**3671.** VOSEVICH, KATHI ANN.    The rhetoric of Shakespeare's women: figures, sense, and structure. Unpub. doct. diss., Univ. of Denver, 1988. [Abstr. in DA (49) 1812A.]

**3672.** WARREN, CHARLES.    T. S. Eliot on Shakespeare. (Bibl. 1988, 2778.) Rev. by William Harmon in SewR (96:1) 1988, 111–12.

**3673.** WEIMANN, ROBERT.    Shakespeare und die Macht der Mimesis: Autorität und Repräsentation im elisabethanischen Theater. *See* **3126.**

**3674.** WELLS, ROBIN HEADLAM.    Shakespeare, politics, and the state. (Bibl. 1988, 2784.) Rev. by Paul Yachnin in RenR (12:4) 1988, 324–5; by Ann Thompson in MLR (84:3) 714; by Janet Clare in RES (39:155) 1988, 436–8.

**3675.** WELLS, STANLEY.    Enjoying Shakespeare. Shakespeare in Southern Africa (2) 1988, 1–14.

**3676.** ⸺ Shakespeare: a bibliography. London: British Council. pp. 54.

**3677.** ⸺ (ed.).    The Cambridge companion to Shakespeare studies. New York: CUP, 1986. (Bibl. 1986, 4619.) Rev. by Lois Potter in MLR (84:3) 710–11; by Marion Jones in RES (39:155) 1988, 438–9.

**3678.** WHITE, R. S.    The year's contributions to Shakespearian study: 1, Critical studies. ShS (40) 1988, 185–211; (41) 193–214.

**3679.** WILDERS, JOHN.    New prefaces to Shakespeare. Oxford: Blackwell, 1988. pp. ix, 284. Rev. by Tony Davies in Shakespeare in Southern Africa (2) 1988, 116–17; by Joan Rees in NQ (36:3) 379–80.

**3680.** WILES, DAVID.    Shakespeare's clown: actor and text in the Elizabethan playhouse. (Bibl. 1988, 2789.) Rev. by Kristian Smidt in EngS (70:2) 180–2; by David Ellis in CamQ (18:1) 86–91.

**3681.** WILLIAMSON, MARILYN L.    The patriarchy of Shakespeare's comedies. (Bibl. 1988, 2791.) Rev. by Ann Thompson in YES (19) 316–17.

**3682.** WILSON, ROBERT R.    Shakespeare's narrative: the craft of bemazing ears. SJO (125) 85–102.

**3683.** WRIGHT, GEORGE T.    Shakespeare's metrical art. Berkeley; London: California UP, 1988. pp. xiv, 349. Rev. by Peter Levi in NQ (36:3) 387–9; by Anthony Graham-White in TJ (41:4) 573.

**3684.** WRIGHT, LAURENCE.   Shakespeare and the bomber pilot – a reply to Colin Gardner. Shakespeare in Southern Africa (2) 1988, 83–9.
**3685.** ZBIERSKI, HENRYK.   William Shakespeare. Warsaw: Wiedza Powszechna, 1988. pp. 1300.
**3686.** ZIEGLER, GEORGIANNA (ed.).   Shakespeare study today: the Horace Howard Furness Memorial Lectures. (Bibl. 1987, 4292, where scholar's forename misspelt and title incomplete.) Rev. by Joan Rees in RES (38:150) 1987, 241–2; by Lois Potter in MLR (84:3) 711.

## Productions

**3687.** ALSENAD, ABEDALMUTALAB ABOOD.   Professional production of Shakespeare in Iraq: an exploration of cultural adaptation. Unpub. doct. diss., Univ. of Colorado at Boulder, 1988. [Abstr. in DA (49) 2023A.]
**3688.** AMATO, ROB.   The Baxter Theatre and Handspring Puppet Company's production of *A Midsummer Night's Dream* at the Monument Theatre, Grahamstown, July 1988. Shakespeare in Southern Africa (2) 1988, 102–5.
**3689.** ASHCROFT, PEGGY; EWBANK, INGA-STINA.   Playing Shakespeare. ShS (40) 1988, 11–19. (Interview.)
**3690.** ASTINGTON, JOHN H.   Malvolio and the dark house. ShS (41) 55–62.
**3691.** BEILHARZ, MANFRED.   Textüberlegungen zur Inszenierung von Shakespeares *Ein Sommernachtstraum*. In (pp. 38–44) **4.**
**3692.** BERKOFF, STEVEN.   I am Hamlet. London: Faber & Faber. pp. x, 209. Rev. by David Nokes in TLS, 20 Oct., 1151.
**3693.** BERRY, RALPH.   Hamlet and the audience: the dynamics of a relationship. In (pp. 24–8) **55.**
**3694.** BOLTZ, INGEBORG; JAUSLIN, CHRISTIAN.   Verzeichnis der Shakespeare-Inszenierungen und Bibliographie der Kritiken: Spielzeit 1987/88. SJW 311–31.
**3695.** BRAUNMULLER, A. R.   Editing the staging/staging the editing. In (pp. 139–49) **55.**
**3696.** BROWN, JOHN RUSSELL.   The nature of speech in Shakespeare's plays. In (pp. 48–59) **55.**
**3697.** BULMAN, J. C.; COURSEN, H. R. (eds).   Shakespeare on television: an anthology of essays and reviews. Hanover, NH; London: New England UP, 1988. pp. xi, 324. Rev. by Thomas L. Berger in SQ (40:2) 237–9; by Peter Hyland in NQ (36:4) 505–6.
**3698.** CAMERON-WEBB, GAVIN.   *End of the World* and *Hamlet*. OnS (12) 11–31.
**3699.** CHARNEY, MAURICE.   Asides, soliloquies, and offstage speech in *Hamlet*: implications for staging. In (pp. 116–31) **55.**
**3700.** CLAYTON, THOMAS.   'Balancing at work': (r)evoking the script in performance and criticism. In (pp. 228–49) **55.**
**3701.** COLLICK, JOHN.   Shakespeare, cinema and society. Manchester: Manchester UP. pp. 208. (Cultural politics.)
**3702.** CORLISS, RICHARD.   King Ken comes to conquer: a brash

British star turns *Henry V* into an antiwar movie. Time, 13 Nov., 119–20. (Kenneth Branagh's film version of *Henry V.*)

**3703.** COURSEN, H. R.   Recently viewed on TV and tape: *Midsummer Night's Dream*; *Macbeth*. SFN (14:1) 7,12.

**3704.** —— The Renaissance Theatre's television *Twelfth Night*. SFN (13:2) 3.

**3705.** CROWL, SAMUEL.   'Hid indeed within the centre': The Hall/ Finney *Hamlet*. ShS (41) 45–53.

**3706.** DAVIES, ANTHONY.   Filming Shakespeare's plays: the adaptations of Laurence Olivier, Orson Welles, Peter Brook and Akira Kurosawa. (Bibl. 1988, 2802.) Rev. by Sidney Gottlieb in SQ (40:4) 523–24; by Colin Gardner in Shakespeare in Southern Africa (2) 1988, 109–12.

**3707.** DAVIES, E. A.   'Alfa-Romeo and Juliet' in Stratford. Shakespeare Society of Southern Africa Occasional Papers and Reviews (1:1) 1986, 8–11. (*Romeo and Juliet* at Stratford-upon-Avon, 1986.)

**3708.** DESSEN, ALAN C.   Much virtue in *as*: Elizabethan stage locales and modern interpretation. *In* (pp. 132–8) **55.**

**3709.** DÖRNEMANN, KURT.   Shakespeare an der Ruhr. SJW 42–58.

**3710.** DUTTON, RICHARD.   The year's contributions to Shakespearian study: 2, Shakespeare's life, times, and stage. *See* **3523.**

**3711.** EDGECOMBE, RODNEY.   A view of Shakespeare and ballet. Shakespeare in Southern Africa (1) 1987, 46–51.

**3712.** ELAND-JANKOWSKA, EWA.   On the reception of Shakespeare in early American theatre. *In* (pp. 57–73) **36.**

**3713.** EWBANK, INGA-STINA.   From narrative to dramatic language: *The Winter's Tale* and its source. *In* (pp. 29–47) **55.**

**3714.** FOAKES, R. A.   Stage images in *Troilus and Cressida*. *In* (pp. 150–61) **55.**

**3715.** FOULKES, RICHARD.   Charles Calvert's *Henry V.* ShS (41) 23–34. (Manchester, 1872.)

**3716.** —— Shakespeare and the Victorian stage. (Bibl. 1987, 4314.) Rev. by Jan McDonald in SQ (40:2) 235–7; by John Stokes in YES (19) 342–3.

**3717.** GAINES, ROBERT A.   John Neville takes command: the story of the Stratford Shakespearean Festival in production. Stratford, Ont.: Street Press, 1987. pp. 339. Rev. by Keith Garebian in QQ (95:4) 1988, 966–7.

**3718.** GOLDMAN, MICHAEL.   Performer and role in Marlowe and Shakespeare. *In* (pp. 91–102) **55.**

**3719.** GRANQVIST, RAOUL.   Some traits of cultural nationalism in the reception of Shakespeare in 19th-century USA. OL (43:1) 1988, 32–57.

**3720.** GURR, ANDREW.   The Shakespearian stages, forty years on. *See* **3066.**

**3721.** —— The 'state' of Shakespeare's audiences. *In* (pp. 162–79) **55.**

**3722.** —— *The Tempest*'s tempest at Blackfriars. ShS (41) 91–102.

**3723.** GUSHURST, BRUNA.   Polanski's determining of power in *Macbeth*. SFN (13:2) 7.

**3724.** HABICHT, WERNER. Shakespeare and theatre politics in the Third Reich. *In* (pp. 110–20) **50.**

**3725.** HAMBURGER, MAIK. New concepts of staging *A Midsummer Night's Dream.* ShS (40) 1988, 51–61.

**3726.** —— Shakespeare auf den Bühnen der DDR in der Spielzeit 1987/88. SJO (125) 155–71.

**3727.** HOLDERNESS, GRAHAM. The taming of the shrew. Manchester: Manchester UP. pp. viii, 133. (Shakespeare in performance.)

**3728.** HORTMANN, WILHELM. Spielorte und Bühnenräume. Zur Szenographie von Shakespeare-Inszenierungen der jünsten Vergangenheit. SJW 13–41.

**3729.** JANSEN, HANS. Als Ophelia die Unschuld verlor: Erinnerung an Peter Zadeks 'wilde' Shakespeare-Inszenierungen. SJW 59–67.

**3730.** JAUSLIN, CHRISTIAN. Bühnenbericht 1987/88. SJW 297–310.

**3731.** KAWAJI, YOSHIKO. Shakespeare worldwide: translation and adaptation, 12. *See* **3576.**

**3732.** KERBER, JAN. Die Erfahrung Welt – die Begegnung Theater: Berichte am runden Tisch. SJO (125) 55–62.

**3733.** KING, CHRISTINE E.; COVEN, BRENDA. Joseph Papp and the New York Shakespeare festival: an annotated bibliography. New York; London: Garland, 1988. pp. xxxii, 369. (Garland reference library of the humanities, 793.)

**3734.** KLIMAN, BERNICE W. Branagh's *Henry V*: allusion and illusion. SFN (14:1) 1, 9–10.

**3735.** KNIGHT, DUDLEY. Acting is re-acting. OnS (12) 33–52.

**3736.** KNIGHT, G. WILSON. My life's work, with a discussion of Francis Berry's poetry. *In* (pp. 71–80) **37.**

**3737.** KNOX-SHAW, PETER. Under a waning moon: *Twelfth Night* at Maynardville. Shakespeare in Southern Africa (2) 1988, 96–9.

**3738.** KUCK, GERD LEO. Arie Zingers Stuttgarter *Macbeth*: Bearbeitung und Tendenzen. *In* (pp. 45–6) **4.**

**3739.** LEVENSON, JILL L. Romeo and Juliet. (Bibl. 1987, 4330.) Rev. by Martin Wiggins in NQ (36:3) 387.

**3740.** LOUGHNEY, KATHARINE. Shakespeare on film at the Library of Congress. *See* **245.**

**3741.** LYONS, BRIDGET GELLERT (ed.). Chimes at midnight. New Brunswick, NJ; London: Rutgers UP, 1988. pp. x, 340. (Rutgers films in print.)

**3742.** McGUIRE, PHILIP C. Egeus and the implications of silence. *In* (pp. 103–15) **55.**

**3743.** MERCER, PETER. *Hamlet* and the acting of revenge. Iowa City: Iowa UP, 1987. (Bibl. 1987, 4333.) Rev. by Jerzy Limon in SQ (40:3) 365–6.

**3744.** MONTGOMERY, WILLIAM. The original staging of *The First Part of the Contention* (1594). *See* **3458.**

**3745.** NAGRAJAN, S. Some stage versions of *Measure for Measure.* ACM (2:1) 26–59.

**3746.** NEIGHBARGER, RANDY LYN. Music for London Shakespeare productions, 1660–1830. Unpub. doct. diss., Univ. of Michigan, 1988. [Abstr. in DA (49) 3546A.]

**3747.**   NOURYEH, ANDREA.   Understanding Xanadu: an alternative way of viewing Orson Welles's Shakespearean films. SFN (14:1) 3.

**3748.**   OTTEN, ELIZABETH.   Jane Howell's *Winter's Tale*: the message, not the medium. SFN (14:1) 5.

**3749.**   PEAT, DEREK.   Looking back to front: the view from the Lords' room. *In* (pp. 180–94) **55.**

**3750.**   PHILLIPS, STEPHEN J.   History in men's lives: a study of two cycles of Shakespeare's histories produced at Stratford in the nineteen-sixties and nineteen-seventies. Unpub. doct. diss., Univ. of Exeter, 1988. [Abstr. in DA (49) 1464A.]

**3751.**   RATHBONE, N. (comp.).   Professional Shakespeare productions in the British Isles, January–December 1986. ShS (41) 183–91.

**3752.**   RICCI, DIGBY.   *Twelfth Night*: Joseph Ribeiro's production for the Wits School of Dramatic Art. Shakespeare in Southern Africa (2) 1988, 105–8.

**3753.**   RICHMOND, HUGH M.   King Richard III. Manchester; New York: Manchester UP, 1989. pp. viii, 158. (Shakespeare in performance.)

**3754.**   —— Peter Quince directs *Romeo and Juliet*. *In* (pp. 219–27) **55.**

**3755.**   ROSENBERG, MARVIN.   Subtext in Shakespeare. *In* (pp. 79–90) **55.**

**3756.**   RUTTER, CAROL.   Clamorous voices: Shakespeare's women today. Ed. by FAITH EVANS. London: Women's Press, 1988. pp. xxvii, 131. (Interviews with RSC actresses.)

**3757.**   SCHRADER, WILLI.   Shakespeare-Rezeption in der DDR im Lichte der Shakespeare-Tage in Weimar. SJW 68–87.

**3758.**   SEMPLE, HILARY; LICKINDORF, ELISABETH; PINTER, KAROLY. *Othello* at Johannesburg's Market Theatre: three views on the recent production. Shakespeare in Southern Africa (1) 1987, 67–71. (Janet Suzman's production.)

**3759.**   AL-SHETAWI, MAHMOUD F.   Shakespeare in Arabic: an overview. *See* **3649.**

**3760.**   SHRIMPTON, NICHOLAS.   Shakespeare performances in London, Manchester and Stratford-upon-Avon 1985–6. ShS (40) 1988, 169–83.

**3761.**   SINGH, JYOTSNA.   Different Shakespeares: the Bard in colonial/postcolonial India. TJ (41:4) 445–58.

**3762.**   STYAN, J. L.   Stage space and the Shakespeare experience. *In* (pp. 195–209) **55.**

**3763.**   —— Understanding Shakespeare in performance. Shakespeare in Southern Africa (1) 1987, 19–29.

**3764.**   SUZMAN, JANET.   *Othello* – a belated reply. Shakespeare in Southern Africa (2) 1988, 90–6.

**3765.**   SWANDER, HOMER.   Shakespeare and Beckett: what the words know. *In* (pp. 60–78) **55.**

**3766.**   TATSPAUGH, PATRICIA E.   Notes from London: *Hamlet*. SFN (14:1) 7.

**3767.** TERRIS, OLWEN (ed.).    Shakespeare: a list of audio-visual materials available in the UK. London: British Universities Film & Video Council, 1987. pp. vi, 41. (Second ed.: first ed. 1986.)

**3768.** THOMPSON, MARVIN; THOMPSON, RUTH (eds).    Shakespeare and the sense of performance: essays in the tradition of performance criticism in honor of Bernard Beckerman. *See* **55.**

**3769.** TIWARI, ATUL.    Die Integration Shakespeares in das indische Nationaltheater. Ein sozio-historischer Überblick. SJO (125) 40–54.

**3770.** TYLEE, CLAIRE M.    The text of Cressida and every ticklish reader: *Troilus and Cressida*, the Greek camp scene. ShS (41) 63–76.

**3771.** VAN ZYL, JOHN.    A thrice-told tale: the television production of *The Winter's Tale*. Shakespeare in Southern Africa (2) 1988, 100–2.

**3772.** WARREN, ROGER.    Cymbeline. Manchester: Manchester UP. pp. vii, 132. (Shakespeare in performance.)

**3773.** —— Shakespeare's late plays at Stratford, Ontario. ShS (40) 1988, 155–68. (1986 productions.)

**3774.** WELLS, STANLEY.    Shakespeare performances in London and Stratford-upon-Avon, 1986–7. ShS (41) 159–81.

**3775.** WICKHAM, GLYNNE.    Reflections arising from recent productions of *Love's Labour's Lost* and *As You Like It. In* (pp. 210–18) **55.**

**3776.** WILLEMS, MICHÈLE (ed.).    Shakespeare à la télévision. Rouen: Publications de l'Université de Rouen, 1987. pp. 195.

**3777.** WORTHEN, W. B.    Deeper meanings and theatrical technique: the rhetoric of performance criticism. SQ (40:4) 441–55.

**3778.** ZANDER, HORST.    Shakespeare 'bearbeitet': eine Untersuchung am Beispiel der Historien-Inszenierungen 1945–1975 in der Bundesrepublik Deutschland. (Bibl. 1985, 4094.) Rev. by Ruth Freifrau von Ledebur in Archiv (225:1) 1988, 176–81.

**3779.** ZBIERSKI, HENRYK; CZUBAK, MARZENA.    Das Schicksal des Fortinbras: Theater kontra Text. SJO (125) 79–84.

## Separate Works

See also under 'Editions' and 'Productions', above.

*All's Well That Ends Well*

**3780.** KEITH, RHONDA.    Jane Austen and Shakespeare. Persuasions (6) 1984, 30.

**3781.** PALMER, DAVID J.    Comedy and the Protestant spirit in Shakespeare's *All's Well That Ends Well*. BJRL (71:1) 95–107.

**3782.** ROARK, CHRISTOPHER.    Lavatch and service in *All's Well That Ends Well*. SELit (28:2) 1988, 241–58.

**3783.** SCHRICKX, WILLEM.    *All's Well That Ends Well* and its historical relevance. *In* (pp. 257–74) **42.**

**3784.** SIMONDS, PEGGY MUÑOZ.    Sacred and sexual motifs in *All's Well That Ends Well*. RQ (42:1) 33–59.

**3785.** SUMMERS, ELLEN LOUISE.    The ends of *All's Well That Ends Well*. Unpub. doct. diss., Univ. of North Carolina at Chapel Hill, 1988. [Abstr. in DA (49) 2672–3A.]

**3786.** WEISS, WOLFGANG. 'There is language in her eye, her cheek, her lip': Körper und Körpersprache in *Troilus and Cressida, All's Well That Ends Well* und *Measure for Measure.* SJW 196–208.

**3787.** WILKES, G. A. *All's Well That Ends Well* and 'the common stock of narrative tradition'. Leeds Studies in English (20) 207–16.

*Antony and Cleopatra*

**3788.** DUNN, T. A. The imperial bawd. *In* (pp. 26–32) **37.**

**3789.** JANKOWSKI, THEODORA A. 'As I am Egypt's queen': Cleopatra, Elizabeth I, and the female body politic. Assays (5) 91–110.

**3790.** MILES, GARY B. How Roman are Shakespeare's 'Romans'? SQ (40:3) 257–83.

**3791.** MITCHELL, ROBIN NORMAN. Tragic identity: studies in Euripides and Shakespeare. Unpub. doct. diss., Brown Univ., 1988. [Abstr. in DA (49) 2211A.]

**3792.** SINGH, JYOTSNA. Renaissance antitheatricality, antifeminism, and Shakespeare's *Antony and Cleopatra.* RenD (20) 99–121.

**3793.** THOMSON, LESLIE. *Antony and Cleopatra*, Act 4 Scene 16: 'a heavy sight'. ShS (41) 77–90.

**3794.** WINE, MARTIN. *Antony and Cleopatra* by William Shakespeare. Introd. by HAROLD BROOKS. Basingstoke: Macmillan, 1987. pp. xii, 92. (Macmillan master guides.)

*As You Like It*

**3795.** LIFSON, MARTHA RONK. Learning by talking: conversation in *As You Like It. See* **1356.**

**3796.** ORKIN, MARTIN. Touchstone's swiftness and sententiousness. ELN (27:1) 42–7.

**3797.** ORMEROD, DAVID. Orlando, Jaques, and Maurice Scève. NQ (36:3) 325–7.

**3798.** PRIEST, DALE G. *Oratio* and *negotium*: manipulative modes in *As You Like It.* SELit (28:2) 1988, 273–86.

**3799.** SMIDT, KRISTIAN. All even in Arden? Notes on the composition of *As You Like It.* EngS (70:6) 490–503.

**3800.** WICKHAM, GLYNNE. Reflections arising from recent productions of *Love's Labour's Lost* and *As You Like It. In* (pp. 210–18) **55.**

**3801.** WILLIS, PAUL J. 'Tongues in trees': the book of nature in *As You Like It.* MLS (18:3) 1988, 65–74.

*The Comedy of Errors*

**3802.** MCMANUS, EVA BEASLEY. The growth toward mature love in four of Shakespeare's romances and comedies. Unpub. doct. diss., Univ. of Tennessee, 1988. [Abstr. in DA (49) 2670A.]

**3803.** RIEHLE, WOLFGANG. Zur Relevanz von Shakespeares Plautus-rezeption in der *Comedy of Errors. In* (pp. 91–105) **4.**

**3804.** TAYLOR, ANTHONY BRIAN. Men as 'masters to their females': Shakespeare and Calvin. NQ (36:3) 321–2.

**3805.** TAYLOR, GARY. Textual and sexual criticism: a crux in *The Comedy of Errors.* RenD (19) 1988, 195–225.

*Coriolanus*

**3806.** BERRY, RALPH.   Shakespeare and social class. Atlantic Highlands, NJ: Humanities Press, 1988. pp. xxii, 198. Rev. by S. Gorley Putt in SQ (40:3) 359–60.

**3807.** MILES, GARY B.   How Roman are Shakespeare's 'Romans'? *See* **3790.**

*Cymbeline*

**3808.** FLACHMANN, MICHAEL.   All corners of the world: spatial and moral geography in *Cymbeline*. OnS (12) 73–6.

**3809.** McMANUS, EVE BEASLEY.   The growth toward mature love in four of Shakespeare's romances and comedies. *See* **3802.**

**3810.** MARCUS, LEAH S.   *Cymbeline* and the unease of topicality. *In* (pp. 134–68) **31.**

**3811.** SIMONDS, PEGGY MUÑOZ.   The iconography of primitivism in *Cymbeline*. RenD (16) 1985, 95–120.

**3812.** —— The marriage topos in Cymbeline: Shakespeare's variations on a classical theme. ELR (19:1) 94–117.

*Hamlet*

**3813.** ABITEBOUL, MAURICE.   L'art de la contrastivité dans *Hamlet*. *In* (pp. 143–61) **22.**

**3814.** BALDO, JONATHAN.   'His form and cause conjoin'd': reflections on 'cause' in *Hamlet*. RenD (16) 1985, 75–94.

**3815.** BERLIN, NORMAND.   O'Neill's Shakespeare. EOR (13:1) 5–13.

**3816.** BERRY, RALPH.   Hamlet and the audience: the dynamics of a relationship. *In* (pp. 24–8) **55.**

**3817.** BONNEFOY, YVES.   Readiness, ripeness: *Hamlet, Lear*. Trans. by MARTIN SORRELL. CompCrit (10) 1988, 191–206.

**3818.** BYLES, JOAN MONTGOMERY.   The problem of the self and the other in the language of Ophelia, Desdemona and Cordelia. AI (46:1) 37–59.

**3819.** CANTOR, PAUL.   Shakespeare: *Hamlet*. Cambridge; New York; Melbourne: CUP. pp. xvi, 106. (Landmarks of world literature.)

**3820.** CHARNEY, MAURICE.   Asides, soliloquies, and offstage speech in *Hamlet*: implications for staging. *In* (pp. 116–31) **55.**

**3821.** —— Hamlet's fictions. New York; London: Routledge, 1988. pp. x, 168. Rev. by Alexander Leggatt in RQ (42:4) 886–8; by Park Honan in NQ (36:3) 382–3.

**3822.** CODDON, KARIN S.   'Suche strange desygns': madness, subjectivity, and treason in *Hamlet* and Elizabethan culture. RenD (20) 51–75.

**3823.** COHEN, MICHAEL.   *Hamlet* in my mind's eye. Athens; London: Georgia UP. pp. ix, 173.

**3824.** COOKSON, LINDA; LOUGHREY, BRYAN (eds).   Critical essays on *Hamlet*: William Shakespeare. Harlow: Longman, 1988. pp. 128. (Longman literature guides.)

**3825.** DE, ESHA NIYOGI.   'The purpose of playing': theater and ritual in the Revesby Folk Play, *Summer's Last Will and Testament*, and *Hamlet*. See **3288**.

**3826.** DESAI, R. W.    In search of Horatio's identity (via Yeats). *In* (pp. 191–203) **45**.

**3827.** DUTTON, RICHARD.    *Hamlet, An Apology for Actors*, and the sign of the Globe. See **3060**.

**3828.** FRYE, ROLAND MUSHAT.    The Renaissance *Hamlet*: issues and responses in 1600. (Bibl. 1988, 2861.) Rev. by Sheldon Zitner in UTQ (56:2) 1986/87, 367–71.

**3829.** GREINER, BERNHARD.    Explosion einer Erinnerung in einer abgestorbenen dramatischen Struktur: Heiner Müllers *Shakespeare Factory*. SJW 88–112.

**3830.** HARDY, BARBARA.    The figure of narration in *Hamlet*. *In* (pp. 1–14) **13**.

**3831.** HARESNAPE, GEOFFREY.    *Hamlet* and bereavement: loss of fathers. English Academy Review (6) 61–70.

**3832.** HOLLERAN, JAMES V.    Maimed funeral rites in *Hamlet*. ELR (19:1) 65–93.

**3833.** HUGHES, PETER.    Playing with grief: *Hamlet* and the act of mourning. CompCrit (9) 1987, 111–33.

**3834.**    Entry cancelled.

**3835.** KIM, JIN-A.    An extended notion of recognition: a study of *Hamlet*, *The Three Sisters*, and *Footfalls*. Unpub. doct. diss., Univ. of Michigan, 1988. [Abstr. in DA (49) 3716A.]

**3836.** LOEWENSTEIN, JOSEPH.    Plays agonistic and competitive: the textual approach to Elsinore. RenD (19) 1988, 63–96.

**3837.** McGEE, ARTHUR.    The Elizabethan *Hamlet*. (Bibl. 1988, 2869.) Rev. by Willem Schrickx in EngS (70:1) 88–9; by Eric Sams in NQ (36:1) 99–100; by Margaret Loftus Ranald in RQ (42:2) 357–8; by Alastair Fowler in LRB (11:5) 15–16.

**3838.** MacLEAN, PATRICK.    About *Hamlet*: the enigma of King Claudius. OnS (12) 84–8.

**3839.** MOWAT, BARBARA.    The form of *Hamlet's* fortunes. RenD (19) 1988, 97–126.

**3840.** MUTTALEB, F. A.    Shakespeare, Chekhov and the problem of the Russian *Hamlet*. Unpub. doct. diss., Univ. of Essex. [Abstr. in IT (39:3) 1101.]

**3841.** NOLLET, THOMAS.    'Nothing either good or bad': sophistry and self-delusion in *Hamlet*. ACM (2:1) 1–25.

**3842.** O'MEARA, JOHN.    *Hamlet* and the fortunes of sorrowful imagination: a re-examination of the genesis and fate of the Ghost. CEl (35) 15–25.

**3843.** OMESCO, ION.    *Hamlet, ou la tentation du possible*. Paris: Presses Universitaires de France, 1987. pp. x, 278. Rev. by J.-M. Maguin in CEl (35) 120–1; by Heinz Hohenwald in SJO (125) 196–8.

**3844.** REINHARD, KENNETH; LUPTON, JULIA.    Shapes of grief: Freud, *Hamlet*, and mourning. Genders (4) 50–67.

**3845.** SCHULTZ, BRIGITTE.   'The time is out of joint': the reception of Shakespeare's *Hamlet* in Polish plays. NC (8) 99–113.

**3846.** TAWFEEK, S. B.   Chance, divinity and human endeavour in *Hamlet*. Journal of Education and Science (Univ. of Mosul, Iraq) (1) 1979, 31–6.

**3847.** TRUSS, LYNNE.   The player prince. Listener (121) 30 Mar., 15.

**3848.** VAUGHAN-LEE, L. C.   Imaginal response: an adaptation of Jung's 'active imagination' into a mode of responding to archetypal images in Shakespeare's *Hamlet*. Unpub. doct. diss., CNAA. [Abstr. in IT (39:4) 1625.]

**3849.** WADDINGTON, RAYMOND B.   Lutheran Hamlet. ELN (27:2) 27–42.

**3850.** YOUNG, CHARLES E., JR.   Words, words, words. CLit (16:3) 240–54.

*Henry IV*

**3851.** BERGER, HARRY, JR.   What did the king know and when did he know it? SAQ (88:4) 811–62.

**3852.** PFEIFFER, K. LUDWIG.   Körper, Handeln, System: *Henry IV* und andere Beispiele. SJW 178–95.

**3853.** REES, JOAN.   Falstaff, St Paul, and the hangman. RES (38:149) 1987, 14–22.

**3854.** SHIN, WOONG-JAE.   Prince Hal's escape from the taint of bastardy: Shakespeare's blood-conscious modifications of his sources. ShR (15) 55–71.

**3855.** TRAUB, VALERIE.   Prince Hal's Falstaff: positioning psychoanalysis and the female reproductive body. SQ (40:4) 456–74.

**3856.** VILLQUIN, JEAN-PIERRE.   *1 Henry IV*, de l'épopée à la parodie. Repérages (12) 37–58.

**3857.** WEST, GILIAN.   A glossary to the language of debt at the climax of *1 Henry IV*. See **1033**.

*Henry V*

**3858.** GURR, ANDREW.   Why Captain Jamy in *Henry V*? Archiv (226:2) 365–73.

**3858a.** TRAUB, VALERIE.   Prince Hal's Falstaff: positioning psychoanalysis and the female reproductive body. See **3855**.

**3859.** WALCH, GÜNTER.   *Henry V* as working-house of ideology. ShS (40) 1988, 63–8.

*Henry VI*

**3860.** BERNTHAL, CRAIG ALLEN.   'In danger for the breach of law': trial scenes in Shakespeare's *2 Henry VI*, *The Merchant of Venice* and *Measure for Measure*. Unpub. doct. diss., Michigan State Univ., 1988. [Abstr. in DA (49) 3030A.]

**3861.** CALDER, A. C.   The dramatic language of Shakespeare's *Henry VI*: a stylistic and theatrical study. See **1388**.

**3862.** DOMBROWA, REGINA. Strukturen in Shakespeares *King Henry the Sixth*. (Bibl. 1985, 4170.) Rev. by Hugo Keiper in GRM (38:1/2) 1988, 229–31.

**3863.** GARBER, MARJORIE. Descanting on deformity: Richard III and the shape of history. *In* (pp. 79–103) **31.**

*Julius Caesar*

**3864.** MILES, GARY B. How Roman are Shakespeare's 'Romans'? *See* **3790.**

**3864a.** MIOLA, ROBERT S. Shakespeare and his sources: observations on the critical history of *Julius Caesar*. ShS (40) 1988, 69–76.

**3865.** PASTER, GAIL KERN. 'In the spirit of men there is no blood': blood as trope of gender in *Julius Caesar*. SQ (40:3) 284–98.

**3866.** SCOTT, WILLIAM O. The speculative eye: problematic self-knowledge in *Julius Caesar*. ShS (40) 1988, 77–89.

*King Lear*

**3867.** ADDYMAN, M. E. The character of hysteria in Shakespeare's England: an introduction. Unpub. doct. diss., Univ. of York. [Abstr. in IT (38:4) 1456.]

**3868.** BATE, JONATHAN. Ovid and the mature tragedies: metamorphosis in *Othello* and *King Lear*. ShS (41) 133–44.

**3869.** BONNEFOY, YVES. Readiness, ripeness: *Hamlet, Lear*. *See* **3817.**

**3870.** BUTLER, F. G. Lear's crown of weeds. EngS (70:5) 395–406.

**3871.** BUTLER, GUY. Jacobean psychiatry: Edgar's curative stratagems. Shakespeare in Southern Africa (2) 1988, 15–30.

**3872.** BYLES, JOAN MONTGOMERY. The problem of the self and the other in the language of Ophelia, Desdemona and Cordelia. *See* **3818.**

**3873.** CALLAGHAN, DYMPNA. Women and gender in Renaissance tragedy: a study of *King Lear, Othello, The Duchess of Malfi* and *The White Devil*. New York; London: Harvester Wheatsheaf. pp. viii, 187. (Cf. bibl. 1987, 4455.)

**3874.** COOKSON, LINDA; LOUGHREY, BRYAN (eds). Critical essays on *King Lear*: William Shakespeare. Harlow: Longman, 1988. pp. 150. (Longman literature guides.)

**3875.** CZUBAK, MARZENA. Life and sterility in *King Lear*. SAP (22) 163–74.

**3876.** DOLOFF, STEVEN. 'Cry you mercy, I took you for a joint-stool': a note on King Lear's trial of the chairs (III.vi.20–83). NQ (36:3) 331–2.

**3877.** GÖLLER, KARL HEINZ. *Child Roland and the King of Elfland* as the source for Shakespeare's *King Lear* III.iv. 186–188. *See* **1747.**

**3878.** HAWKES, TERENCE. Lear's maps: a general survey. SJW 134–47.

**3879.** KAHN, COPPÉLIA. The absent mother in *King Lear*. *In* (pp. 33–49) **54.**

**3879a.** KERNAN, ALVIN. Meaning and emptiness in *King Lear* and *The Tempest*. RenD (18) 1987, 225–58.

**3880.** KIM, MIJA.   King Lear's sanity: the fool and Cordelia. CAE (22) 43–53.

**3881.** KIRBY, IAN J.   The passing of King Lear. ShS (41) 145–57.

**3882.** ORKIN, MARTIN.   Cruelty, *King Lear* and the South African Land Act 1913. ShS (40) 1988, 135–43.

**3883.** POUSSA, PATRICIA.   Hordocks in Lear's crown. *See* **1053.**

**3884.** RAY, ROBERT H. (ed.).   Approaches to teaching Shakespeare's *King Lear*. (Bibl. 1988, 2927.) Rev. by Ralph Alan Cohen in SQ (40:4) 502–5.

**3885.** ROSEN, ALAN CHARLES.   Versions of catastrophe: Shakespeare, Defoe, Scholem. Unpub. doct. diss., Boston Univ., 1988. [Abstr. in DA (49) 1794A.]

**3886.** STRIER, RICHARD.   Faithful servants: Shakespeare's praise of disobedience. *In* (pp. 104–33) **31.**

**3887.** TAYLOR, GARY; WARREN, MICHAEL (eds).   The division of the kingdoms: Shakespeare's two versions of *King Lear*. (Bibl. 1987, 4474.) Rev. by George Walton Williams in MedRen (2) 1985, 343–50.

**3888.** THOMPSON, ANN.   King Lear. Atlantic Highlands, NJ: Humanities Press, 1988. (Bibl. 1988, 2931.) Rev. by Ralph Alan Cohen in SQ (40:4) 502–5; by Martin Elliott in NQ (36:4) 501–2.

**3889.** WHITTIER, GAYLE.   Cordelia as prince: gender and language in *King Lear*. Exemplaria (1:2) 367–99.

*A Lover's Complaint*

**3890.** KERRIGAN, JOHN.   Keats and *Lucrece*. ShS (41) 103–18. (Keats's marginalia to his copy of Shakespeare's *Poetical Works*.)

*Love's Labour's Lost*

**3891.** BERRY, RALPH.   Shakespeare and social class. *See* **3806.**

**3892.** WICKHAM, GLYNNE.   Reflections arising from recent productions of *Love's Labour's Lost* and *As You Like It*. *In* (pp. 210–18) **55.**

*Macbeth*

**3893.** CALDERWOOD, JAMES L.   If it were done: Macbeth and tragic action. (Bibl. 1988, 2937.) Rev. by R. A. Foakes in RES (39:154) 1988, 292–3; by James L. Sanderson in RQ (42:1) 138–40; by Jyotsna Singh in SQ (40:2) 232–5.

**3894.** CODDON, KARIN S.   'Unreal mockery': unreason and the problem of spectacle in *Macbeth*. ELH (56:3) 485–501.

**3895.** COOKSON, LINDA; LOUGHREY, BRYAN (eds).   Critical essays on *Macbeth*: William Shakespeare. Harlow: Longman, 1988. pp. 141. (Longman literature guides.)

**3896.** GREINER, BERNHARD.   Explosion einer Erinnerung in einer abgestorbenen dramatischen Struktur: Heiner Müllers *Shakespeare Factory*. *See* **3829.**

**3897.** HAMMOND, PAUL.   Macbeth and the ages of man. NQ (36:3) 332–3.

**3898.** HARDY, BARBARA. The narrators in *Macbeth*. London: Univ. of London, 1987. pp. 29. (Hilda Hulme Lecture, 1986.)

**3899.** JANTON, PIERRE. Sonship and fatherhood in Macbeth. CEl (35) 47–58.

**3900.** KESTNER, JOSEPH. Dynamic encounter. Opera News (52:9) 1988, 32–5, 43. (*Macbeth* as inspiration for Verdi.)

**3901.** LAROQUE, FRANÇOIS. Magic in *Macbeth*. CEl (35) 59–84.

**3902.** LISTON, WILLIAM T. 'Male and female created he them': sex and gender in *Macbeth*. CLit (16:3) 232–9.

**3903.** LOVE, H. W. Seeing the difference: good and evil in the world of *Macbeth*. AUMLA (72) 203–28.

**3904.** LYNCH, KATHRYN L. 'What hands are here?': the hand as generative symbol in *Macbeth*. RES (39:153) 1988, 29–38.

**3905.** McGRAIL, MARY ANN. Shakespeare's dramas of tyranny: *Macbeth, Richard III, The Winter's Tale*, and *The Tempest*. Unpub. doct. diss., Harvard Univ., 1988. [Abstr. in DA (50) 450A.]

**3906.** TAWFEEK, S. B. Time in *Macbeth*. Journal of Education and Science (Univ. of Mosul, Iraq) (2) 1980, 5–15.

**3907.** WESTERWEEL, BART. Macbeth, time and prudence. *In* (pp. 199–210) **47.**

*Measure for Measure*

**3908.** BERNTHAL, CRAIG ALLEN. 'In danger for the breach of law': trial scenes in Shakespeare's *2 Henry VI*, *The Merchant of Venice* and *Measure for Measure. See* **3860.**

**3909.** HAWKES, TERENCE. Take me to your Leda. ShS (40) 1988, 21–32.

**3910.** HIMY, ARMAND. *Measure for Measure*, ou le puritanisme comme centre de pouvoir. *In* (pp. 21–40) **15.**

**3911.** JEON, KEUN-SOON. *Measure for Measure* e natanan ingan eui oemyeon gwa naemyeonjeok moseup. (The appearance and reality of human nature in *Measure for Measure*.) ShR (15) 165–80.

**3912.** LEZRA, JACQUES. Pirating reading: the appearance of history in *Measure for Measure*. ELH (56:2) 255–92.

**3913.** NEELY, CAROL THOMAS. Constructing female sexuality in the Renaissance: Stratford, London, Windsor, Vienna. *In* (pp. 209–29) **29.**

**3914.** NEVO, RUTH. *Measure for Measure*: mirror for mirror. ShS (40) 1988, 107–22.

**3915.** SHELL, MARC. The end of kinship: *Measure for Measure*, incest, and the ideal of universal siblinghood. (Bibl. 1988, 2963.) Rev. by Mark Rose in SQ (40:1) 97–100; by Mary Ann Bushman in RMRLL (43:4) 256–8.

**3916.** SMITH, NIGEL. The two economies of *Measure for Measure*. Eng (36) 1987, 197–232.

**3917.** WATTS, CEDRIC. William Shakespeare, *Measure for Measure*. Harmondsworth: Penguin, 1986. pp. 149. (Penguin critical studies.)

**3918.** WEISS, WOLFGANG. 'There is language in her eye, her cheek, her lip': Körper und Körpersprache in *Troilus and Cressida, All's Well That Ends Well* und *Measure for Measure*. See **3786**.

**3919.** WIDMAYER, MARTHA ELLEN. The great 'fever on goodness': *Measure for Measure* and the war over reform. Unpub. doct. diss., Univ. of Miami, 1988. [Abstr. in DA (50) 694A.]

*The Merchant of Venice*

**3920.** BERNTHAL, CRAIG ALLEN. 'In danger for the breach of law': trial scenes in Shakespeare's *2 Henry VI, The Merchant of Venice* and *Measure for Measure*. See **3860**.

**3921.** CHEYRE-BERNARD, CATHERINE. Abigail et Jessica: extranéité ou aliénation? *In* (pp. 13–28) **26**.

**3922.** ENGEHAUSEN, FRANK. Shylock, Antonio und die zietgenössische Diskussion um die Rechtmäßigkeit des Geldverleihs für Zinsen. SJW 148–68.

**3923.** FINN, STEPHEN M. Antonio: the other Jew in *The Merchant of Venice*. Literator (10:1) 16–25.

**3924.** HAMEED, SALIH MAHDI. The Prince of Morocco in *The Merchant of Venice*. Journal of Education and Science (Univ. of Mosul, Iraq) (7) (Humanities and Education) 5–24.

**3925.** HANSEN, NIELS BUGGE. The metamorphosis of Shylock. SJO (125) 72–8.

**3926.** HOMAN, SIDNEY. Shakespeare and the triple play: from study to stage to classroom. Lewisburg, PA: Bucknell UP; London; Toronto: Assoc. UPs, 1988. pp. 239. Rev. by Carol J. Carlisle in SQ (40:4) 505–8.

**3927.** KUHNS, RICHARD; TOVEY, BARBARA. Portia's suitors. PhilL (13:2) 325–31.

**3928.** SEMPLE, HILARY. Shakespeare and race. Shakespeare in Southern Africa (1) 1987, 30–8.

**3929.** WHEELER, THOMAS. *The Merchant of Venice*: an annotated bibliography. (Bibl. 1986, 4905.) Rev. by Lars Engle in SQ (40:2) 244–5.

*The Merry Wives of Windsor*

**3930.** BERRY, RALPH. Shakespeare and social class. See **3806**.

**3931.** FOLEY, STEPHEN. Falstaff in love and other stories. Exemplaria (1:2) 227–46.

**3932.** LEHNERT, MARTIN. *The Merry Wives of Windsor*, IV, i. Ein sprachlich-literarisches Kabinettstück, oder Shakespeare und Latein. SJO (125) 63–71.

**3933.** MCMANUS, EVA BEASLEY. The growth toward mature love in four of Shakespeare's romances and comedies. See **3802**.

**3934.** NEELY, CAROL THOMAS. Constructing female sexuality in the Renaissance: Stratford, London, Windsor, Vienna. *In* (pp. 209–29) **29**.

*A Midsummer Night's Dream*

**3935.** BEDNARZ, JAMES P. Imitations of Spenser in *A Midsummer Night's Dream*. See **3340**.

**3936.** COHEN, ROBERT.    Quince's moon-disfiguring reality in *A Midsummer Night's Dream*. OnS (12) 53–60.
**3937.** DOLAN, MAUREEN.    *A Midsummer Night's Dream*: sources and origins. OnS (12) 79–85.
**3938.** GRAHAM, KENNETH.    The tangible dream. *In* (pp. 33–53) **23.**
**3939.** McGUIRE, PHILIP C.    Egeus and the implications of silence. *In* (pp. 103–15) **55.**
**3940.** MONTROSE, LOUIS ADRIAN.    *A Midsummer Night's Dream* and the shaping fantasies of Elizabethan culture: gender, power, form. *In* (pp. 65–87) **54.**
**3941.** SLIGHTS, WILLIAM W. E.    The changeling in *A Dream*. SELit (28:2) 1988, 259–72.
**3942.** TAYLOR, ANTHONY BRIAN.    Chaucer's non-involvement in *Pyramus and Thisbe*. *See* **2874.**

*Much Ado About Nothing*

**3943.** COOKSON, LINDA; LOUGHREY, BRYAN (eds).    Critical essays on *Much Ado About Nothing*: William Shakespeare. Harlow: Longman. pp. 138. (Longman literature guides.)
**3944.** IBRAHIM, ABDULLA MAHMOOD.    Villainy in *Much Ado About Nothing*. Journal of Education and Science (Univ. of Mosul, Iraq) (1) 1979, 5–16.
**3945.** TAYLOR, MARK.    Presence and absence in *Much Ado About Nothing*. CR (33:1) 1–12.

*Othello*

**3946.** BATE, JONATHAN.    Ovid and the mature tragedies: metamorphosis in *Othello* and *King Lear*. *See* **3868.**
**3947.** BYLES, JOAN MONTGOMERY.    The problem of the self and the other in the language of Ophelia, Desdemona and Cordelia. *See* **3818.**
**3948.** CALLAGHAN, DYMPNA.    Women and gender in Renaissance tragedy: a study of *King Lear, Othello, The Duchess of Malfi* and *The White Devil*. *See* **3873.**
**3949.** CASOLE, STEPHEN.    A question of fidelity. Opera News (52:12) 1988, 16–18. (*Othello* into *Otello*.)
**3950.** COSTA DE BEAUREGARD, RAPHAËLLE.    D'étranges manières: remarques à propos de l'étrangeté de l'étranger dans *Othello*. *In* (pp. 29–51) **26.**
**3951.** DAUBER, ANTOINETTE B.    Allegory and irony in *Othello*. ShS (40) 1988, 123–33.
**3952.** FAWCETT, MARY LAUGHLIN.    'Such noise as I can make': chastity and speech in *Othello* and *Comus*. RenD (16) 1985, 159–80.
**3953.** GROSS, KENNETH.    Slander and skepticism in *Othello*. ELH (56:4) 819–52.
**3954.** HOLLAND, PETER.    The resources of characterization in *Othello*. ShS (41) 119–32.
**3955.** LAROQUE, FRANÇOIS.    An additional note to '*Othello* and popular traditions'. CEl (33) 1988, 57–8. (*Refers to* bibl. 1987, 4541.)

**3956.** McNEELY, TREVOR.   Supersubtle Shakespeare: *Othello* as a rhetorical allegory. DQR (19:4) 243–63.

**3957.** MARSH, DERICK.   *Othello* re-read. Sydney Studies in English (14) 1988/89, 3–12.

**3958.** MÜLLER-SCHWEFE, GERHARD.   Shakespeare-Parodien im deutschsprachigen Raum: Karl Meisls *Othellerl, Der Mohr von Wien*. SJW 266–90.

**3959.** NEILL, MICHAEL.   Unproper beds: race, adultery, and the hideous in *Othello*. SQ (40:4) 383–412.

**3960.** RIAZ, SAHIBZADA M.   The two images of Desdemona. ARIEL (Jamshoro, Pakistan) (13) 1987/88, 73–83.

**3961.** RICKS, DAVID.   *Digenes Akrites* not a source for *Othello*. NQ (36:3) 328–9.

**3962.** ROSSLYN, FELICITY.   Nature erring from itself: *Othello* again. CamQ (18:3) 289–302.

**3963.** RUDNYTSKY, PETER L.   *A Woman Killed with Kindness* as subtext of *Othello*. RenD (14) 1983, 103–24.

**3964.** RYDING, S.   Scanning this thing further: Iago's ambiguous advice. SQ (40:2) 195–6.

**3965.** SEMPLE, HILARY.   Shakespeare and race. *See* **3928.**

**3966.** STALLYBRASS, PETER.   Patriarchal territories: the body enclosed. *In* (pp. 123–42) **54.**

**3967.** VILLQUIN, JEAN-PIERRE.   Dramaturgie des images poétiques dans *Othello*. Repérages (11) 47–72.

**3968.** YOON, CHUNG-EUN.   *Othello* e natanan sarang. (Love in *Othello*.) ShR (15) 73–105.

*Pericles*

**3969.** MICHAEL, NANCY C.   *Pericles*: an annotated bibliography. (Bibl. 1987, 4552.) Rev. by Richard Hillman in SQ (40:1) 117–21.

**3970.** PRESTON, C. E.   Emblematic pictorialism and narrative structures in *New Arcadia* and *Pericles*. *See* **3325.**

**3971.** SMITH, M. W. A.   Function words and the authorship of *Pericles*. NQ (36:3) 333–6.

*The Phoenix and the Turtle*

**3972.** CONSTABLE, JOHN.   *The Phoenix and the Turtle*: 'Either was the other's mine': a new reading. NQ (36:3) 327.

**3973.** MARDER, LOUIS.   *The Phoenix and the Turtle*: another unsolved mystery. SNL (39:3/4) 40–2.

*The Rape of Lucrece*

**3974.** KERRIGAN, JOHN.   Keats and *Lucrece*. *See* **3890.**

**3975.** WILSON, R. RAWDON.   Shakespearean narrative: *The Rape of Lucrece* reconsidered. SELit (28:1) 1988, 39–59.

*Richard II*

**3976.** BERGER, HARRY, JR.    *Richard II*, III.ii: an exercise in imaginary audition. ELH (55:4) 1988, 755–96.

**3977.** COOKSON, LINDA; LOUGHREY, BRYAN (eds).    Critical essays on *Richard II*: William Shakespeare. Harlow: Longman. pp. 142. (Longman literature guides.)

**3978.** GURR, ANDREW.    The 'state' of Shakespeare's audiences. *In* (pp. 162–79) **55.**

**3979.** HOMAN, SIDNEY.    Shakespeare and the triple play: from study to stage to classroom. *See* **3926.**

**3980.** KIM, YUN-CHEOL.    Shakespeare's unhistorical inventions and deviations from Holinshed, and their dramatic functions in *Richard II*. JELL (35) 747–58.

**3981.** LEE, DAE-SUK.    The cyclical pattern of *Richard II*: the ironic and ambivalent rise and fall of history. ShR (15) 107–27.

**3982.** NOON, G.    Richard versus Bullingbrook: Heaven versus Machiavelli? ESA (32:1) 41–52.

**3983.** ROBINSON, IAN.    *Richard II* and Woodstock. Doncaster: Brynmill, 1988. pp. 51.

*Richard III*

**3984.** GARBER, MARJORIE.    Descanting on deformity: Richard III and the shape of history. *In* (pp. 79–103) **31.**

**3985.** HAMEL, GUY.    Time in *Richard III*. ShS (40) 1988, 41–9.

**3986.** HAMMERSMITH, JAMES P.    The melodrama of *Richard III*. EngS (70:1) 28–36.

**3987.** JONES, ROBERT C.    Engagement with knavery: point of view in *Richard III, The Jew of Malta, Volpone*, and *The Revenger's Tragedy*. *See* **3262.**

**3988.** KONG, SUNG-UK.    Metadrama roseoeui *Richard III*. (Metadramatic aspects of *Richard III*.) ShR (15) 1–12.

**3989.** McGRAIL, MARY ANN.    Shakespeare's dramas of tyranny: *Macbeth, Richard III, The Winter's Tale*, and *The Tempest*. *See* **3905.**

**3990.** MATUS, IRVIN LEIGH.    An early reference to the Coventry Mystery plays in Shakespeare? SQ (40:2) 196–7.

**3991.** TWAIJ, MOHAMMED BAQIR.    The common themes [*sic*] *The True Tragedy of Richard the Third* and Shakespeare's *Richard III*. *See* **3120.**

**3992.** WALLER, MARGUERITE.    Usurpation, seduction, and the problematics of the proper: a 'deconstructive', 'feminist' rereading of the seductions of Richard and Anne in Shakespeare's *Richard III*. *In* (pp. 159–74) **54.**

*Romeo and Juliet*

**3993.** ANDREWS, MICHAEL CAMERON.    Music's 'silver sound': a note on *Romeo and Juliet*. NQ (36:3) 322–3.

**3994.** MONGA, LUIGI.    *Romeo and Juliet* revisited: more *novelle* from the Italian Renaissance. Manuscripta (33:1) 47–53.

**3995.** PORTER, JOSEPH A.   Shakespeare's Mercutio: his history and drama. Chapel Hill; London: North Carolina UP, 1988. pp. 281.

**3996.** PRIOR, ROGER.   'Runnawayes eyes': a genuine crux. SQ (40:2) 191–5.

**3997.** REED, MELISSA ANN.   Recurring images of symbolic action in Shakespeare's *Tragedy of Romeo and Juliet*: initiating the bard. Unpub. doct. diss., Univ. of Minnesota, 1988. 2 vols. [Abstr. in DA (49) 2028A.]

**3998.** RICHMOND, HUGH M.   Peter Quince directs *Romeo and Juliet*. *In* (pp. 219–27) **55.**

**3999.** SHIKODA, MITSUO.   Juliet, the nursling of the nurse. SStudT (25) 1987, 25–39.

**4000.** TRUSSLER, SIMON (ed.).   *Romeo and Juliet*, by William Shakespeare: a programme/text. London: Methuen. pp. xxii, 50.

**4001.** WHITTIER, GAYLE.   The sonnet's body and the body sonnetized in *Romeo and Juliet*. SQ (40:1) 27–41.

*The Sonnets*

**4002.** BERMANN, SANDRA L.   The sonnet over time: a study in the sonnets of Petrarch, Shakespeare and Baudelaire. Chapel Hill; London: North Carolina UP, 1988. pp. ix, 174. (Univ. of North Carolina studies in comparative literature, 63.)

**4003.** ENGLE, LARS.   Afloat in thick deeps: Shakespeare's sonnets on certainty. PMLA (104:5) 832–43.

**4004.** KENNEDY, WILLIAM J.   Commentary into narrative: Shakespeare's *Sonnets* and Vellutello's commentary on Petrarch. Allegorica (10) 119–33.

**4005.** KUIN, ROGER.   The gaps and the whites: indeterminacy and undecideability in the sonnet sequences of Sidney, Spenser, and Shakespeare. *See* **3319.**

**4006.** SIMONDS, PEGGY MUÑOZ.   Eros and Anteros in Shakespeare's Sonnets 153 and 154: an iconographical study. Spenser Studies (7) 1986, 261–86.

**4007.** WEISER, DAVID K.   Mind in character: Shakespeare's speaker in the *Sonnets*. (Bibl. 1988, 3030.) Rev. by Peter Happé in NQ (36:4) 502–3.

*The Taming of the Shrew*

**4008.** HENKEL, NIKOLAUS.   Beobachtungen zu Shakespeare, *The Taming of the Shrew*, Act III, lines 26–44. *In* (pp. 121–2) NIKOLAUS HENKEL, Deutsche Übersetzungen lateinischer Schultexte: ihre Verbreitung und Funktion im Mittelalter und in der frühen Neuzeit. Munich; Zurich: Artemis, 1988. pp. xi, 358. (Münchener Texte und Untersuchungen zur deutschen Literatur des Mittelalters, 90.)

**4009.** MIKESELL, MARGARET LAEL.   'Love wrought these miracles': marriage and genre in *The Taming of the Shrew*. RenD (20) 141–67.

*The Tempest*

**4010.** COLE, DAVID L.   Drake's brave new world and *The Tempest*. CEACrit (51:4) 40–52.

**4011.** COOKSON, LINDA; LOUGHREY, BRYAN (eds). Critical essays on *The Tempest*: William Shakespeare. Harlow: Longman, 1988. pp. 146. (Longman literature guides.)

**4012.** HOMAN, SIDNEY. Shakespeare and the triple play: from study to stage to classroom. *See* **3926.**

**4013.** HULME, PETER. Colonial encounters: Europe and the native Caribbean, 1492–1797. (Bibl. 1988, 3035.) Rev. by Karina Williamson in RES (39:153) 1988, 153–5.

**4014.** KERNAN, ALVIN. Meaning and emptiness in *King Lear* and *The Tempest*. *See* **3879a.**

**4015.** MCGRAIL, MARY ANN. Shakespeare's dramas of tyranny: *Macbeth, Richard III, The Winter's Tale,* and *The Tempest*. *See* **3905.**

**4016.** ORGEL, STEPHEN. Prospero's wife. *In* (pp. 50–64) **54.**

**4017.** ROE, RICHARD PAUL. The perils of the *Tempest*. SNL (39:3/4) 36–7.

**4018.** SKURA, MEREDITH ANNE. Discourse and the individual: the case of colonialism in *The Tempest*. SQ (40:1) 42–69.

**4019.** SLIGHTS, WILLIAM W. E. 'His art doth give the fashion': generic fashions and fashioning in *The Tempest*. BSUF (30:1) 20–32.

**4020.** SOROKA, O. Prospero – pobedivshiĭ Hamlet. (Prospero – a vanquished Hamlet.) Te (1989:8) 166–71.

**4021.** WARD, DAVID. 'Now I will believe that there are unicorns': *The Tempest* and its theatre. Eng (36) 1987, 95–110.

*Timon of Athens*

**4022.** NUTTALL, A. D. Timon of Athens. New York; London: Harvester Wheatsheaf. pp. xxii, 164. (Harvester new critical introductions to Shakespeare.) Rev. by Frank Kermode in LRB (11:18) 20.

*Titus Andronicus*

**4023.** BLOCK, JUDITH. *Titus Andronicus*: 'a wildness of tigers'. OnS (12) 88–93.

**4024.** FINK, JOEL. The conceptualization and realization of violence in *Titus Andronicus*. OnS (12) 1–10.

**4025.** GIBBONS, BRIAN. The human body in *Titus Andronicus* and other early Shakespeare plays. *See* **3544.**

**4026.** GREEN, DOUGLAS E. Interpreting 'her martyr'd signs': gender and tragedy in *Titus Andronicus*. SQ (40:3) 317–26.

**4027.** HUNT, MAURICE. Compelling art in *Titus Andronicus*. SELit (28:2) 1988, 197–218.

**4028.** JACKSON, MACD. P. *Titus Andronicus*: play, ballad, and prose history. NQ (36:3) 315–17. (*Refers to* bibl. 1988, 3046.)

**4029.** KENDALL, GILLIAN MURRAY. 'Lend me thy hand': metaphor and mayhem in *Titus Andronicus*. SQ (40:3) 299–316.

**4030.** PARKER, DOUGLAS H. Shakespeare's use of comic conventions in *Titus Andronicus*. UTQ (56:4) 1987, 486–97.

**4031.** SMIDT, KRISTIAN. Levels and discontinuities in *Titus Andronicus*. *In* (pp. 283–93) **42.**

**4032.** WEIMANN, GUNDULA.   Zur Funktion des Antihelden im Text *Anatomie Titus Fall of Rome. Ein Shakespearekommentar* von Heiner Müller: Aarons Welttheater im Kunstwerk der tatsächlichen Schlacht ein lebendiges Erbe. SJO (125) 116–20.

### Troilus and Cressida

**4033.** ADAMSON, JANE.   *Troilus and Cressida.* (Bibl. 1987, 4603.) Rev. by Lawrence Normand in NQ (36:3) 380–1.

**4034.** BOITANI, PIERO (ed.).   The European tragedy of Troilus. *See* **27.**

**4035.** CHARNES, LINDA.   'So unsecret to ourselves': notorious identity and the material subject in Shakespeare's *Troilus and Cressida.* SQ (40:4) 413–40.

**4036.** FOAKES, R. A.   Stage images in *Troilus and Cressida. In* (pp. 150–61) **55.**

**4037.** HOOKER, DEBORAH A.   Coming to Cressida through Irigaray. SAQ (88:4) 899–932.

**4038.** HYLAND, PETER.   William Shakespeare: *Troilus and Cressida.* London: Penguin. pp. 96. (Penguin critical studies.)

**4039.** LOMBARDO, AGOSTINO.   Fragments and scraps: Shakespeare's *Troilus and Cressida. In* (pp. 199–217) **27.**

**4040.** MANN, JILL.   Shakespeare and Chaucer: 'What is Criseyde worth?' *See* **2950.**

**4041.** RUFINI, SERGIO.   'To make that maxim good': Dryden's Shakespeare. *In* (pp. 243–80) **27.**

**4042.** WEISS, WOLFGANG.   'There is language in her eye, her cheek, her lip': Körper und Körpersprache in *Troilus and Cressida, All's Well That Ends Well* und *Measure for Measure. See* **3786.**

### Twelfth Night

**4043.** BELT, DEBRA ANNE.   The poetics of hostile response: writers and critical readers in sixteenth-century England. *See* **3249.**

**4044.** GRAS, HENK.   *Twelfth Night, Every Man out of his Humour,* and the Middle Temple Revels of 1597–98. MLR (84:3) 545–64.

**4045.** HUNT, MAURICE.   *Twelfth Night* and the Annunciation. PLL (25:3) 264–71.

**4046.** OSBORNE, LAURIE.   Letters, lovers, Lacan; or, Malvolio's not-so-purloined letter. Assays (5) 63–89.

### The Two Gentlemen of Verona

**4047.** GIRARD, RENÉ.   Love delights in praises: a reading of *The Two Gentlemen of Verona.* PhilL (13:2) 231–47.

**4048.** PERRY, THOMAS AMHERST.   *The Two Gentlemen of Verona* and the Spanish *Diana.* MP (87:1) 73–6.

**4049.** SCHLÜTER, KURT.   Zu Shakespeares früher Komödie: *The Two Gentlemen of Verona.* LJGG (30) 45–53.

**4050.** SHIN, WOONG-JAE.   *Two Gentlemen of Verona* and *Diana Enamorada*: Shakespeare's class-orientated modifications of his sources. JELL (35) 717–33.

*The Two Noble Kinsmen*

**4051.** HICKMAN, ANDREW.   *Bonduca*'s two ignoble armies and *The Two Noble Kinsmen*. MedRen (4) 143–71.

*Venus and Adonis*

**4052.** HART, JONATHAN.   'Till forging nature be condemned of treason': representational strife in *Venus and Adonis*. CEl (36) 37–47.

*The Winter's Tale*

**4053.** ADDYMAN, M. E.   The character of hysteria in Shakespeare's England: an introduction. *See* **3867.**

**4054.** BURTON, JULIE.   Folktale, romance and Shakespeare. *In* (pp. 176–97) **58.**

**4055.** DYMOND, G. B.   Rhetoric and character in *The Winter's Tale*. Unpub. M.Litt. diss., Univ. of Oxford, 1988. [Abstr. in IT (39:1) 30.]

**4056.** EWBANK, INGA-STINA.   From narrative to dramatic language: *The Winter's Tale* and its source. *In* (pp. 29–47) **55.**

**4057.** FLEISSNER, ROBERT F.   What *The Winter's Tale* unveils: who is 'the best'? NQ (36:3) 336–8.

**4058.** HILTON, JULIAN.   The Galatea principle: learning machines. CompCrit (11) 111–35.

**4059.** McGRAIL, MARY ANN.   Shakespeare's dramas of tyranny: *Macbeth, Richard III, The Winter's Tale*, and *The Tempest*. *See* **3905.**

**4060.** McMANUS, EVA BEASLEY.   The growth toward mature love in four of Shakespeare's romances and comedies. *See* **3802.**

**4061.** SANDERS, WILBUR.   *The Winter's Tale*. (Bibl. 1987, 4620.) Rev. by Michèle Willems in EA (42:4) 470.

**4062.** WRIGHT, LAURENCE.   When does the tragi-comic disruption start? *The Winter's Tale* and Leontes' 'affection'. EngS (70:3) 225–32.

# SEVENTEENTH CENTURY

## GENERAL

### General Literary Studies

**4063.** Anon (ed.). British literary manuscripts from the Bodleian Library, Oxford: series 1, The English Renaissance, *c.* 1500–*c.* 1700: an inventory to part 1 of the Harvester microform collection. *See* **122.**

**4064.** Archer, Stanley (ed.). Abstracts of recent articles. SCN (47:1/2) 25–6; (47:3/4) 58–63.

**4065.** Atkins, John. Sex in literature: vol. 4, High noon: the seventeenth and eighteenth centuries. (Bibl. 1983, 4857.) Rev. by Carol Houlihan Flynn in MLR (82:4) 1987, 921.

**4066.** Austern, Linda Phyllis. 'Sing againe syren': the female musician and sexual enchantment in Elizabethan life and literature. *See* **2990.**

**4067.** Barash, Carol Lynn. Augustan women's mythmaking: English women writers and the body of monarchy, 1660–1720. Unpub. doct. diss., Princeton Univ. [Abstr. in DA (50) 1308A.]

**4068.** Battigelli, Anna F., *et al.* Some current publications. Restoration (13:2) 95–114.

**4069.** Berger, Harry, Jr. Second world and green world: studies in Renaissance fiction-making. Introd. by John Patrick Lynch. *See* **2992.**

**4070.** Böker, Uwe. The epistle mendicant in mediaeval and Renaissance literature: the sociology and poetics of a genre. *In* (pp. 137–65) **38.**

**4071.** Breinig, Helmbrecht; Halfmann, Ulrich (eds). Die amerikanische Literatur bis zum Ende des 19. Jahrhunderts. Tübingen: Francke, 1985. pp. 358. Rev. by Klaus Lubbers in LJGG (28) 1987, 385–8.

**4072.** Camé, Jean-François. Myth and poetry in XVIIth century England. Montpellier: Centre d'Études et de Recherches Élisabéthaines, Université Paul Valéry. pp. 226. (Astraea, 2.)

**4073.** Cheney, Donald. Recent studies in the English Renaissance. *See* **2995.**

**4074.** Corns, Thomas N. (ed.). The literature of controversy: polemical strategy from Milton to Junius. (Bibl. 1987, 42.) Rev. by David Womersley in NQ (36:1) 107–8.

**4075.** Daly, Peter M. England and the emblem: the cultural context of English emblem books. *In* (pp. 1–60) **21.**

**4076.** —— (ed.). The English emblem and the continental tradition. *See* **21.**

**4077.** Dean, Christopher. Arthur of England: English attitudes to King Arthur and the Knights of the Round Table in the Middle Ages and the Renaissance. *See* **2408.**

**4078.** De Prospo, R. C. The latest early American literature. EAL (24:3) 248–56.

**4079.** DIEHL, HUSTON. An index of icons in English emblem books 1500–1700. *See* **83.**

**4080.** DIETZ, BERND (ed.). Estudios literarios ingleses: la restauración. Madrid: Cátedra. pp. 300.

**4081.** DOLLE, RAYMOND F. (ed.). Americana abstracts. SCN (47:1/2) 26–9; (47:3/4) 63–4.

**4082.** DRAKE, VALERIE CHRISTINE. 'I matter not how I appear to man': a view of women's lives concentrating on the writings of non-elite women, 1640–1663. Unpub. doct. diss., CNNA, 1988. [Abstr. in DA (49) 1133–4A; in IT (39:2) 501.]

**4083.** DUBROW, HEATHER; STRIER, RICHARD (eds). The historical Renaissance: new essays on Tudor and Stuart literature and culture. *See* **31.**

**4084.** FERGUSON, MARGARET W.; QUILLIGAN, MAUREEN; VICKERS, NANCY J. (eds). Rewriting the Renaissance: the discourses of sexual difference in early modern Europe. *See* **54.**

**4085.** GOLDBERG, JONATHAN. James I and the politics of literature: Jonson, Shakespeare, Donne, and their contemporaries. (Bibl. 1987, 4639.) Rev. by Alexander Leggatt in MedRen (3) 1986, 324–7.

**4086.** GUIBBORY, ACHSAH. The map of time: seventeenth-century English literature and ideas of pattern in history. (Bibl. 1988, 3080.) Rev. by Paul Hammond in RES (39:153) 1988, 105–6; by John M. Steadman in MP (86:3) 304–6.

**4087.** HAGSTRUM, JEAN H. Eros and vision: the Restoration to Romanticism. Evanston, IL: Northwestern UP. pp. xx, 290. Rev. by David Nokes in TLS, 11 Aug., 880.

**4088.** HOLSTUN, JAMES. Ranting at the new historicism. *See* **3008.**

**4089.** HÖLTGEN, KARL JOSEF. Aspects of the emblem: studies in the English emblem tradition and the European context. (Bibl. 1988, 3086.) Rev. by John Manning in RES (39:154) 1988, 327–8; by Lothar Hönnighausen in LJGG (29) 1988, 362–4.

**4090.** HORDEN, JOHN. Renaissance emblem books: a comment on terminology. *In* (pp. 61–70) **37.**

**4091.** HUME, ROBERT D. Recent studies in the Restoration and eighteenth century. SELit (28:3) 1988, 514–57.

**4092.** HUNTER J. PAUL. Canon of generations, generation of canons. MLS (18:1) 1988, 38–46.

**4093.** KEEBLE, N. H. The literary culture of nonconformity in later seventeenth-century England. Athens: Georgia UP, 1987. (Bibl. 1988, 3087.) Rev. by Thomas H. Luxon in RQ (42:4) 893–7; by Leo F. Solt in AHR (94:1) 132–3.

**4094.** KIBBEY, ANN. The interpretation of material shapes in Puritanism: a study of rhetoric, prejudice, and violence. (Bibl. 1988, 3089.) Rev. by Nigel Smith in RES (39:153) 1988, 107–8; by Paul Lindholt in SewR (96:3) 1988, 466–8.

**4095.** KROOK, ANNE KARIN. The genesis of authority: scripture, satire, and interpretation in English literature, 1660–1760. Unpub. doct. diss., Cornell Univ. [Abstr. in DA (50) 691A.]

**4096.** Kupersmith, William. Roman satirists in seventeenth-century England. (Bibl. 1987, 4657.) Rev. by Katharine Eisaman Maus in MedRen (4) 264–6.

**4097.** Lawson, Bruce Jonathan. 'A king he seems, and something more': providentialism and Machiavellianism in the poetry, prose and pulpit oratory about Oliver Cromwell. Unpub. doct. diss., Univ. of Southern California, 1988. [Abstr. in DA (49) 1810A.]

**4098.** Leerssen, J. Th. Skeletons in the cupboard: the 'Glorious' Revolution and Ireland. DQR (19:3) 214–29.

**4099.** Lewis, Jayne Elizabeth. The voluble body: re-inventing the neoclassical fable. Unpub. doct. diss., Princeton Univ., 1988. [Abstr. in DA (50) 148A.]

**4100.** Lord, C. P. Image and reality: the chapbook perspective on women in early modern Britain. See **445.**

**4101.** McCarthy, Finbarr. A rage for order: the ideological implications of form in early Southern writing. Unpub. doct. diss., Tulane Univ., 1988. [Abstr. in DA (49) 3725A.]

**4102.** McGowan, Ian (ed.). The Restoration and eighteenth century. Basingstoke: Macmillan. pp. xxviii, 584. (Macmillan anthologies of English literature, 3.)

**4103.** Marcus, Leah S. The politics of mirth: Jonson, Herrick, Milton, Marvell and the defense of old holiday pastimes. (Bibl. 1988, 3094.) Rev. by John D. Cox in MP (86:3) 298–300; by Achsah Guibbory in QQ (95:2) 1988, 469–71.

**4104.** Marshall, Ian Stuart. Mountains to match the man: national identity and the mountain in American literature, beginnings to 1860. Unpub. doct. diss., Univ. of Delaware, 1988. [Abstr. in DA (49) 2660A.]

**4105.** Messenger, Ann. His and hers: essays in Restoration and eighteenth-century literature. (Bibl. 1987, 4662.) Rev. by Janice Farrar Thaddeus in JEGP (87:3) 1988, 444–6; by Kendall in TJ (40:1) 1988, 126–7.

**4106.** Morrison, John J., et al. (eds). Short-title catalogue of books printed in England, Scotland, Ireland, Wales, and British America and of English books printed in other countries 1641–1700: vol. 3, P1–Z28. By Donald Wing. (Bibl. 1988, 3095.) Rev. by Theodore Hofmann in Library (11:4) 383–8.

**4107.** Morse, David. England's time of crisis: from Shakespeare to Milton: a cultural history. See **3015.**

**4108.** Myers, William (ed.). Restoration and revolution. (Bibl. 1987, 4664.) Rev. by Nora Crow Jaffe in YES (19) 325–7.

**4109.** Popkin, Susan M. Some current publications. Restoration (13:1) 49–58.

**4110.** Radcliffe, David Hill. Meditations and literary history, 1600–1750: generic mixture and generic change. Unpub. doct. diss., Univ. of Virginia, 1987. [Abstr. in DA (50) 149A.]

**4111.** Ross, Harry J. Trapped by society, imprisoned in the wilderness: captivity in American literature, 1680–1860. Unpub. doct. diss., Northwestern Univ. [Abstr. in DA (50) 948A.]

**4112.** ROUSSEL, ROY. The conversation of the sexes: seduction and equality in selected seventeenth- and eighteenth-century texts. (Bibl. 1988, 3099.) Rev. by Antonia Forster in SCN (47:1/2) 19–20.

**4113.** SHARPE, KEVIN. Criticism and compliment: the politics of literature in the England of Charles I. (Bibl. 1988, 3103.) Rev. by Hervé Abalain in EA (42:4) 473–4.

**4114.** —— ZWICKER, STEVEN N. (eds). Politics of discourse: the literature and history of seventeenth-century England. (Bibl. 1988, 3104.) Rev. by Robert C. Evans in SixCT (20:1) 151–2; by Esther S. Cope in JMH (61:4) 764–5.

**4115.** SLIGHTS, WILLIAM W. E. The edifying margins of Renaissance English books. See **117**.

**4116.** SMITH, NIGEL. Perfection proclaimed: language and literature in English radical religion, 1640–1660. Oxford: Clarendon Press. pp. vii, 396.

**4117.** TRIBBLE, EVELYN BYRD. Margins and marginality: some uses of printed page in early modern England. See **118**.

**4118.** VON FRANK, ALBERT J. The sacred game: provincialism and frontier consciousness in American literature, 1630–1860. (Bibl. 1988, 3108.) Rev. by A. Robert Lee in RES (38:152) 1987, 582–3.

**4119.** WALLACE, JOHN M. (ed.). The golden and the brazen world: papers in literature and history, 1650–1800. (Bibl. 1986, 5092.) Rev. by David Nokes in BJECS (10) 1987, 222–3.

**4120.** WEISS, KLAUS. Grunlegung einer puritanischen Mimesislehre: eine literatur- und geistesgeschichtliche Studie der Schriften Edward Taylors und anderer puritanischer Autoren. Munich; Vienna; Zürich: Schöningh, 1984. (Bibl. 1985, 4412.) Rev. by Alfred Schopf in LJGG (28) 1987, 360–5.

**4121.** WILDING, MICHAEL. Dragons teeth: literature in the English Revolution. (Bibl. 1988, 3111.) Rev. by Roger Lejosne in EA (42:3) 339–40; by David Womersley in NQ (36:1) 107–8; by James Holstun in SCN (47:1/2) 1–3; by Mary Ann Radzinowicz in MP (87:2) 174–6; by James G. Turner in RQ (42:3) 593–7.

**4122.** WILSON, KATHARINA M.; WARNKE, FRANK J. (eds). Women writers of the seventeenth century. Athens; London: Georgia UP. pp. 545. Rev. by Sharon Valiant in RMRLL (43:4) 236–8.

**4123.** YOUNG, ALAN R. Wenceslaus Hollar, the London book trade, and two unidentified English emblem books. In (pp. 151–202) **21**.

### Drama and the Theatre

**4124.** ARULANANDAM, SANTHA DEVI. The London Prodigal: a critical edition in modern spelling. Unpub. doct. diss., Univ. of Auckland.

**4125.** ASTINGTON, JOHN H. Descent machinery in the playhouses. See **3032**.

**4126.** BALKIN, MARTHA MUNSELL. The Renaissance tool villain and his medieval heritage. See **2549**.

**4127.** BARKER, S. A.    An examination of the relationship between English drama 1550–1642 and contemporary military science. *See* **3035.**

**4128.** BERGERON, DAVID M.    Art within *The Second Maiden's Tragedy.* MedRen (1) 1984, 173–86.

**4129.** BEVINGTON, DAVID.    Editing Renaissance drama in paperback. *See* **3040.**

**4130.** BEVIS, RICHARD W.    English drama: Restoration and eighteenth century, 1660–1789. (Bibl. 1988, 3116, where scholar's initial omitted.) Rev. by David Wykes in NQ (36:4) 508–9; by Robert Folkenflik in TLS, 10 Mar., 253.

**4131.** BILBY, MONIKA.    'Heroick vertue': changing ideas of feminine greatness in the heroic drama of the late seventeenth century. Unpub. doct. diss., Univ. of Maryland College Park, 1988. [Abstr. in DA (50) 951A.]

**4132.** BORCHARDT, CORDELIA.    Der Akademiker als satirischer Sprecher in Dramen um 1600. Archiv (226:2) 291–309.

**4133.** BOWERS, FREDSON (ed.).    Jacobean and Caroline dramatists. Detroit, MI: Gale Research, 1987. pp. xxii, 370. (Dictionary of literary biography, 58.) Rev. by William Proctor Williams in NQ (36:2) 236.

**4134.** BOWERS, RICK.    Players, Puritans, and 'theatrical propaganda', 1642–1660. DalR (67:4) 1987, 463–79.

**4135.** BUELER, LOIS E.    The structural uses of incest in English Renaissance drama. *See* **3045.**

**4136.** BURNS, EDWARD.    Restoration comedy: crises of desire and identity. (Bibl. 1987, 4692.) Rev. by James Ogden in BJECS (12) 230–1.

**4137.** BUTLER, MARTIN.    A provincial masque of *Comus*, 1636. RenD (17) 1986, 149–74.

**4138.** ——— Theatre and crisis, 1632–1642. (Bibl. 1986, 5104.) Rev. by Douglas Howard in MedRen (3) 1986, 292–301.

**4139.** CARSON, NEIL A.    A companion to Henslowe's Diary. Cambridge: CUP, 1988. pp. xii, 151. Rev. by William Proctor Williams in NQ (36:2) 231.

**4140.** CAUDILL, HELEN SUE.    Plague as a force in Jacobean tragedy. Unpub. doct. diss., Univ. of Pittsburgh, 1988. [Abstr. in DA (49) 1807A.]

**4141.** CERASANO, S. P.    The 'business' of shareholding, the Fortune playhouses, and Francis Grace's Will. *See* **3047.**

**4142.** ——— Competition for the King's Men? Alleyn's Blackfriars venture. MedRen (4) 173–86.

**4143.** ——— Shakespeare's elusive Globe: review article. *See* **3049.**

**4144.** CLARE, JANET.    'Greater themes for insurrection's arguing': political censorship of the Elizabethan and Jacobean stage. *See* **3050.**

**4145.** COHEN, WALTER.    Intrigue tragedy in Renaissance England and Spain. *See* **3052.**

**4146.** COMAN, ALAN C.    The Congleton accounts: further evidence of Elizabethan and Jacobean drama in Cheshire. *See* **3053.**

**4147.** CORBIN, PETER; SEDGE, DOUGLAS.    An annotated critical bibliography of Jacobean and Caroline comedy (excluding Shakespeare).

New York; London: Harvester Wheatsheaf, 1988. pp. xii, 235. (Harvester Wheatsheaf annotated critical bibliographies.)

**4148.** DANCHIN, PIERRE (ed.). The prologues and epilogues of the Restoration, 1660–1700: part II, 1677–1690. (Bibl. 1986, 5108.) Rev. by Harold Love in MLR (83:1) 1988, 151–2.

**4149.** DARRAGI, RAFIK. Le spectacle: réflexions sur la violence et le théâtre jacobéen. *In* (pp. 1–18) **60.**

**4150.** DESSEN, ALAN C. Modern productions and the Elizabethan scholar. *See* **3058.**

**4151.** DOBSON, M. Authorizing Shakespeare: adaptation and canonization, 1660–1769. *See* **3514.**

**4152.** DOLLIMORE, JONATHAN. Subjectivity, sexuality, and transgression: the Jacobean connection. RenD (17) 1986, 53–81.

**4153.** DUTTON, RICHARD. *Hamlet, An Apology for Actors*, and the sign of the Globe. *See* **3060.**

**4154.** FEINBERG, ANAT. 'Like demie Gods the Apes began to move': the ape in the English theatrical tradition, 1580–1660. *See* **3061.**

**4155.** FLORES, STEPHAN PAUL. Recognition and repression: ideology and dramatic success on the London stage, 1660–1680. Unpub. doct. diss., Univ. of Michigan, 1988. [Abstr. in DA (49) 2228A.]

**4156.** FORKER, CHARLES R. 'A little more than kin, and less than kind': incest, intimacy, narcissism, and identity in Elizabethan and Stuart drama. *See* **3062.**

**4157.** FREER, COBURN. The poetics of Jacobean drama. (Bibl. 1986, 5113.) Rev. by Paul Bertram in MedRen (2) 1985, 321–3.

**4158.** GARNER, SHIRLEY NELSON. 'Let her paint an inch thick': painted ladies in Renaissance drama and society. *See* **3064.**

**4159.** GEWIRTZ, ARTHUR. Restoration adaptations of early seventeenth-century comedies. Lanham, MD: UP of America, 1982. pp. xxiv, 190. Rev. by Eric Pump in TS (31/32) 1984/85–1985/86, 123–4; by Derek Hughes in YES (17) 1987, 290–1.

**4160.** GREENWOOD, JOHN. Shifting perspectives and the stylish style: mannerism in Shakespeare and his Jacobean contemporaries. *See* **3552.**

**4161.** GURR, ANDREW. The Shakespearian stages, forty years on. *See* **3066.**

**4162.** HADORN, PETER THOMAS. Power, propaganda and subversion: chivalry on the English Renaissance stage. *See* **3068.**

**4163.** HOWARD, JEAN E. Scripts and/versus playhouses: ideological production and the Renaissance public stage. *See* **3073.**

**4164.** HYDE, THOMAS. Identity and acting in Elizabethan tragedy. *See* **3075.**

**4165.** INGRAM, WILLIAM. The playhouse as an investment, 1607–1614: Thomas Woodford and Whitefriars. MedRen (2) 1985, 209–30.

**4166.** JORDAN, CONSTANCE. Gender and justice in *Swetnam the Woman-Hater*. RenD (18) 1987, 149–69.

**4167.** KAWACHI, YOSHIKO. Calendar of English Renaissance drama, 1558–1642. *See* **3076.**

**4168.** KNUTSON, HAROLD C. The triumph of wit: Molière and

Restoration comedy. Columbus: Ohio State UP, 1988. pp. xi, 192. Rev. by David Whitton in TJ (41:4) 563–4.

**4169.** KNUTSON, ROSLYN L.    Evidence for the assignment of plays to the repertory of Shakespeare's Company. *See* **3077.**

**4170.** KURTZ, MARTHA ANNE.    'Present laughter': comedy in the Elizabethan history play. *See* **3079.**

**4171.** LEHMANN, ELMAR.    Ordnung und Chaos: das englische Restaurationsdrama 1660–1685. Amsterdam: Grüner, 1988. pp. 194. (Beihefte zu Poetica, 19.)

**4172.** LEINWAND, THEODORE B.    The city staged: Jacobean comedy, 1603–1613. (Bibl. 1988, 3135.) Rev. by Carol Leventen in MedRen (4) 268–72; by Ann Jennalie Cook in MP (86:4) 423–5; by Lawrence Manley in YES (19) 318–19; by Martin Garrett in RES (39:155) 1988, 429–30.

**4173.** LETUNOVSKAÎÂ, I. V.    Angliiskaîâ tragediîâ pervoĭ treti XVII veka. (English tragedy of the first third of the seventeenth century.) VKU (23) 119–21.

**4174.** LEVENSON, JILL L.    Recent studies in Elizabethan and Jacobean drama. *See* **3083.**

**4175.** LEWIS, CYNTHIA.    'Wise men, folly-fall'n': characters named Antonio in English Renaissance drama. *See* **3085.**

**4176.** LIMON, JERZY.    Dangerous matter: English drama and politics, 1623/24. (Bibl. 1988, 3137.) Rev. by Martin Garrett in RES (39:155) 1988, 429–30.

**4177.** McGEE, C. E.; MEAGHER, JOHN C.    Preliminary checklist of Tudor and Stuart entertainments: 1614–1625. RORD (30) 1988, 17–128.

**4178.** McPHERSON, DAVID.    Three charges against sixteenth- and seventeenth-century playwrights: libel, bawdy, and blasphemy. *See* **3093.**

**4179.** MAGUIRE, NANCY KLEIN (ed.).    Renaissance tragicomedy: explorations in genre and politics. *See* **3094.**

**4180.** MANSFIELD, R. G.    The protean player: the concept and practice of doubling in the plays of Shakespeare and his contemporaries, *c.* 1576–1631. *See* **3095.**

**4181.** MURRAY, TIMOTHY.    Theatrical legitimation: allegories of genius in seventeenth-century England and France. (Bibl. 1988, 3143.) Rev. by Michael G. Brennan in NQ (36:2) 239–40; by Peter Hyland in SCN (47:3/4) 45–6; by Jonathan Crewe in RQ (42:4) 888–91; by H. Waverly Deutsch in TJ (41:2) 253–4.

**4182.** ORRELL, JOHN.    The human stage: English theatre design, 1567–1640. *See* **3102.**

**4183.** PASTER, GAIL KERN.    Leaky vessels: the incontinent women of city comedy. *See* **3103.**

**4184.** PEARSON, JACQUELINE.    The prostituted muse: images of women and women dramatists, 1642–1737. New York; London: Harvester Wheatsheaf, 1988. pp. xii, 308.

**4185.** PEAT, DEREK.    Looking back to front: the view from the Lords' room. *In* (pp. 180–94) **55.**

**4186.** POPHAM, SHELBY ANNE. 'Tis a tale told: narrative in Renaissance pastoral drama in Italy, France, and England. *See* **3108.**

**4187.** RIGAUD, N. J. La veuve dans la comédie anglaise au temps du Shakespeare, 1600–1625: femme mystifiée, femme de raison. Aix-en-Provence: Univ. of Provence, 1986. pp. 280.

**4188.** ROBERTS, DAVID. The ladies: female patronage of Restoration drama, 1660–1700. Oxford: Clarendon Press; New York: OUP. pp. 188. (Cf. bibl. 1988, 3146.) Rev. by David Nokes in LRB (11:11) 20–2.

**4189.** ROSE, MARY BETH. The expense of spirit: love and sexuality in English Renaissance drama. *See* **3111.**

**4190.** —— Moral conceptions of sexual love in Elizabethan comedy. *See* **3112.**

**4191.** SANDONA, MARK. Patience and the agents of Renaissance drama. *See* **3114.**

**4192.** SCOTT, MARGARET. Machiavelli and the Machiavel. *See* **3115.**

**4193.** SEVILLE, D. Political criticism and caricature in selected Jacobean plays. Unpub. M.Phil. diss., Univ. of Sheffield, 1988. [Abstr. in IT (38:4) 1457.] (*A Game at Chess, Eastward Ho!, The Isle of Gulls, Sejanus, Philotas.*)

**4194.** SHAPIRO, MICHAEL. Lady Mary Wroth describes a 'boy actress'. MedRen (4) 187–94.

**4195.** SPINRAD, PHOEBE S. The summons of death on the medieval and Renaissance English stage. *See* **2572.**

**4196.** SPIVACK, CHARLOTTE. Alienation and illusion: the play-within-the-play on the Caroline stage. MedRen (4) 195–210.

**4197.** STALLYBRASS, PETER. Reading the body: *The Revenger's Tragedy* and the Jacobean theater of consumption. RenD (18) 1987, 121–48.

**4198.** STOKES, JAMES. More on *The Rival Friends* and the death of Dr Butts. REEDNewsletter (14:2) 13–15.

**4199.** STREITBERGER, W. R. (ed.). Jacobean and Caroline Revels accounts, 1603–1642. London: Malone Soc., 1986. pp. xxxv, 182. (Malone Soc. collections, 13.) Rev. by Gordon McMullan in NQ (36:2) 236–7.

**4200.** STURGESS, KEITH. Jacobean private theatre. New York: Routledge & Kegan Paul, 1987. (Bibl. 1988, 3149.) Rev. by Georges Bas in EA (42:4) 471–3; by Marc Maufort in RBPH (3) 607–13; by Michelle Marrapodi in SCN (47:3/4) 46–7.

**4201.** STYAN, J. L. Restoration comedy in performance. (Bibl. 1988, 3150.) Rev. by Harold Love in MLR (84:4) 930–1; by James Ogden in BJECS (12) 230–1; by John Conaghan in RES (39:155) 1988, 442–3.

**4202.** TRICOMI, ALBERT H. Anti-court drama in England, 1603–1642. Charlottesville; London: Virginia UP. pp. 235. Rev. by Alexander Leggatt in RQ (42:3) 582–5.

**4203.** TYLUS, JANE. Veiling the stage: the politics of innocence in Renaissance drama. *See* **3121.**

**4204.** VINCE, RONALD. Renaissance theatre: a historiographical handbook. *See* **3122.**

**4205.** WAITH, EUGENE M.    Patterns and perspectives in English Renaissance drama. *See* **3123.**

**4206.** WARD, T. E.    Compound magic: virtuosity, theatricality and the experience of theatre in the early Jacobean period. Unpub. doct. diss., Univ. of East Anglia, 1988. [Abstr. in IT (39:3) 1107.]

**4207.** WEBER, HAROLD.    The Restoration rake-hero: transformations in sexual understanding in seventeenth-century England. (Bibl. 1988, 3152a.) Rev. by Susan Staves in MP (86:3) 306–9; by Ellen Pollak in AHR (94:3) 760–1; by John Conaghan in RES (39:155) 1988, 442–3.

**4208.** WELCH, ROBERT.    Seneca and the English Renaissance: the old world and the new. *In* (pp. 204–18) **37.**

**4209.** WIGGINS, M. J.    The assassin in English Renaissance drama, 1558–1642. *See* **3130.**

**4210.** WYMER, ROWLAND.    Suicide and despair in the Jacobean drama. (Bibl. 1988, 3158.) Rev. by M. Garrett in RES (38:152) 1987, 549.

**4211.** ZIMBARDO, ROSE A.    A mirror to nature: transformations in drama and aesthetics, 1660–1732. (Bibl. 1987, 4745.) Rev. by Harold Love in MLR (84:2) 439–40.

**4212.** ZONINA, N. V.    Angliĭskaĭa drama pervoĭ poloviny XVII v.: k probleme vzaimovliĭaniĭ narodnogo i pridvornogo iskusstva. (English drama of the first half of the seventeenth century: the problem of mutual influences between popular and courtly art.) VLU (1989:2) 38–46. (Summary in English.)

## Fiction

**4213.** AERCKE, KRISTIAAN PAUL GUIDO.    Theatrical technique in seventeenth-century prose fiction. Unpub. doct. diss., Univ. of Georgia, 1988. [Abstr. in DA (49) 2647A.]

**4214.** CLARK, JUDITH PETTERSON.    *The Life and Death of Mrs Mary Frith, Commonly Called Mal Cutpurse* (1662): an annotated facsimile reprint. Unpub. doct. diss., Miami Univ. [Abstr. in DA (50) 1661A.]

**4215.** MCKEON, MICHAEL.    The origins of the English novel, 1600–1740. (Bibl. 1988, 3156.) Rev. by Maximillian E. Novak in MLR (84:2) 440–2; by Stephen Kohl in PoetA (21:2) 431–8; by John Richetti in StudN (20:3) 1988, 351–4; by Arthur B. Ferguson in AHR (94:1) 131–2; by Homer Obed Brown in ELH (55:4) 1988, 917–54; by Jane Tylus in RQ (42:1) 156–9.

**4216.** PIGEON, RENÉE MARIE.    Prose fiction adaptations of Sidney's *Arcadia. See* **3323.**

**4217.** SCHOFIELD, MARY ANNE; MACHESKI, CECILIA (eds).    Fetter'd or free? British women novelists, 1670–1815. (Bibl. 1987, 25.) Rev. by Kate Flint in RES (38:152) 1987, 585–6; by Edna L. Steeves in MLS (18:1) 1988, 199–201.

**4218.** SPENCER, JANE.    The rise of the woman novelist: from Aphra Behn to Jane Austen. (Bibl. 1988, 3157.) Rev. by Helen Wilcox in BJECS (11) 1988, 101–2; by Mona Scheuermann in StudN (20:2) 1988, 234–6.

**4219.** TODD, JANET.   The sign of Angellica: women, writing and fiction, 1660–1800. London: Virago Press. pp. vii, 328. Rev. by Terry Castle in TLS, 2 June, 607–8.

## Literature for Children

**4220.** AVERY, GILLIAN.   The Puritans and their heirs. *In* (pp. 95–118) **14.**

## Poetry

**4221.** ABBOUD, JA'FAR.   Unnatural naturalism: the *carpe diem* motif in seventeenth-century poetry. Journal of Education and Science (Univ. of Mosul, Iraq) (8) (Humanities and Education) 19–39.

**4222.** BEECH, MARTIN.   Meteor imagery in English poetry, *c.* 1600 to *c.* 1900. NC (7) 99–112.

**4223.** BONIN, MICHAEL RICHARD.   The epigram in the early seventeenth century. Unpub. doct. diss., Univ. of California, Los Angeles. [Abstr. in DA (50) 447–8A.]

**4224.** BURROW, C. J.   The English Humanist epic 1580–1614. *See* **3138.**

**4225.** BUTLER, GEORGE FRANK.   The spiritual odyssey and the Renaissance epic. *See* **3139.**

**4226.** CHAUDHURI, SUKANTA.   Renaissance pastoral: and its English developments. *See* **3140.**

**4227.** CRAWFORD, THOMAS; HEWITT, DAVID; LAW, ALEXANDER (eds). Longer Scottish poems: vol. 2, 1650–1830. (Bibl. 1988, 3160.) Rev. by A. A. MacDonald in EngS (70:2) 175–7.

**4228.** DOODY, MARGARET ANNE.   The daring muse: Augustan poetry reconsidered. (Bibl. 1987, 4758.) Rev. by Cecil Price in RES (38:151) 1987, 392–3.

**4229.** FERRY, ANNE.   The art of naming. *See* **3144.**

**4230.** GREER, GERMAINE, *et al.* (eds).   Kissing the rod: an anthology of seventeenth-century women's verse. New York: Farrar, Straus, & Giroux, 1988. (Bibl. 1988, 3163.) Rev. by Sharon Valiant in RMRLL (43:4) 236–8.

**4231.** GROSSMAN, MARSHALL.   Literary forms and historical consciousness in Renaissance poetry. *See* **3145.**

**4232.** HELGERSON, RICHARD.   Barbarous tongues: the ideology of poetic form in Renaissance England. *In* (pp. 273–92) **31.**

**4233.** JORGENS, ELISE BICKFORD.   Politics and women in Cavalier song: a report from a collection of secular song manuscripts. ExRC (15) 25–48.

**4234.** KNAPP, JEFFREY DANA.   An empire nowhere: England and America, from *Utopia* to *The Tempest*. *See* **3148.**

**4235.** LORD, GEORGE DEFOREST.   Classical presences in seventeenth-century English poetry. (Bibl. 1988, 3169.) Rev. by J. V. Guerinot in SCN (47:1/2) 4–5.

**4236.** MUELLER, JANEL.   Women among the metaphysicals: a case, mostly, of being Donne for. MP (87:2) 142–58.

**4237.** PHILLIPS, PATRICIA. The adventurous muse: theories of originality in English poetics 1650–1760. (Bibl. 1988, 3174.) Rev. by Mark Thackeray in RES (38:149) 1987, 120–1.

**4238.** SESSIONS, WILLIAM A. Abandonment and the English religious lyric in the seventeenth century. *In* (pp. 1–19) **11.**

**4239.** SMITH, DEBRA MORRIS. The business of the poet: poetic self-awareness from Sidney to Johnson. *See* **3155.**

**4240.** SMITH, KATHY OVERHULSE. Making much of time: rhetorical strategies of Renaissance *carpe diem* poetry. *See* **3156.**

**4241.** SUMMERS, CLAUDE J.; PEBWORTH, TED-LARRY (eds). 'Bright shootes of everlastingnesse': the seventeenth-century religious lyric. *See* **11.**

**4242.** TERRY, R. G. Studies in English burlesque poetry, 1663–1785. Unpub. doct. diss., Univ. of Cambridge. [Abstr. in IT (39:2) 486.]

**4243.** THOMSON, E. Poetry and the court in the reign of Charles I. Unpub. doct. diss., Univ. of Oxford. [Abstr. in IT (39:3) 1107–8.]

**4244.** TOLIVER, HAROLD. Lyric provinces in the English Renaissance. (Bibl. 1988, 3178.) Rev. by Patricia Thomson in YES (19) 311–13.

**4245.** WADA, TETSUZO. Keiji joushiron sokou. (An essay on the Metaphysical poets.) Tokyo: Chusekisha. pp. 228.

**4246.** WESTERWEEL, BART. The well-tempered lady and the unruly horse: convention and submerged metaphor in Renaissance literature and art. *In* (pp. 105–22) **16.**

**4247.** WITTREICH, JOSEPH. 'In copious legend, or sweet lyric song': typology and the perils of the religious lyric. *In* (pp. 192–215) **11.**

### Prose

**4248.** ERNST, CHARLES ALBERT SCHEURINGER. Contextualizing the character: generic studies of text and canon, rhetoric, style, and quantitative analysis in the seventeenth-century English prose character. Unpub. doct. diss., Univ. of Pennsylvania, 1988. [Abstr. in DA (49) 3367A.]

**4249.** GREY, ROBIN SANDRA. The complicity of imagination: seventeenth-century English prose and the ideology of assimilation in Emerson, Thoreau, and Melville. Unpub. doct. diss., Univ. of California, Los Angeles, 1988. [Abstr. in DA (49) 3362–3A.]

**4250.** MERCER, JOHN M. Adaptation of conventions in the Elizabethan prose dedication. *See* **3160.**

**4251.** RASHKOW, ILONA NEMESNYIK. Upon the dark places: English Renaissance biblical translation. *See* **3161.**

**4252.** SHUGER, DEBORA K. Sacred rhetoric: the Christian grand style in the English Renaissance. *See* **1321.**

### Biography and Autobiography

**4253.** FALLER, LINCOLN B. Turned to account: the forms and functions of criminal biography in late seventeenth- and early

eighteenth-century England. Cambridge: CUP, 1987. pp. xiv, 347. Rev.
by Kevin L. Cope in StudN (20:4) 1988, 428–9.

**4254.** GRAHAM, ELSPETH, *et al.* (eds). Her own life: autobiographical
writings by seventeenth-century Englishwomen. London; New York:
Routledge. pp. v, 250.

**4255.** MASCUCH, M. Social mobility in English autobiography
1600–1750. Unpub. doct. diss., Univ. of Cambridge. [Abstr. in IT
(39:2) 501.]

## Related Studies

**4256.** ASHLEY, MAURICE. Charles I and Oliver Cromwell: a study in
contrasts and comparisons. London: Methuen, 1987. pp. 244. Rev. by
William Proctor Williams in SCN (47:1/2) 20–1; by William T. Walker
in SixCT (20:2) 308.

**4257.** BARBOUR, JAMES; QUIRK, THOMAS (eds). Essays on Puritans
and Puritanism. Albuquerque: New Mexico UP, 1986. pp. xii, 221. Rev.
by Frank Shuffelton in EAL (24:1) 75–7.

**4258.** BAUMANN, UWE. Seneca-Rezeption im neulateinischen Drama
der englischen Renaissance. *See* **3166.**

**4259.** BOZEMAN, THEODORE DWIGHT. To live ancient lives: the
primitivist dimension in Puritanism. *See* **3167.**

**4260.** BRAND, PETER. Disguise in Renaissance comedy. *See* **3168.**

**4261.** BYRNE, MURIEL ST CLARE (ed.). The Lisle letters. (Bibl. 1984,
4517.) Rev. by William B. Long in MedRen (1) 1984, 263–7.

**4262.** CAHN, SUSAN. Industry of devotion: the transformation of
women's work in England, 1500–1660. *See* **3169.**

**4263.** CHAN, S. K. H. The Puritan meditative tradition, 1599–1691: a
study of ascetical piety. Unpub. doct. diss., Univ. of Cambridge, 1984.
[Abstr. in IT (36:1) 3.]

**4264.** COLLINS, STEPHEN L. From divine cosmos to sovereign state:
an intellectual history of consciousness and the idea of order in
Renaissance England. *See* **3170.**

**4265.** COLLINSON, PATRICK. The birthpangs of Protestant England:
religious and cultural change in the sixteenth and seventeenth centuries.
*See* **3171.**

**4266.** DRAKE, VALERIE CHRISTINE. 'I matter not how I appear to
man': a view of women's lives concentrating on the writings of non-elite
women, 1640–1663. *See* **4082.**

**4267.** FLEMING, JULIET. *The French Garden*: an introduction to
women's French. ELH (56:1) 19–51.

**4268.** FREUDENTHAL, GIDEON. Atom and individual in the age of
Newton: on the genesis of the mechanistic world view. Trans. by PETER
MCLAUGHLIN. Dordrecht; Boston, MA: Reidel, 1986. pp. xv, 276.
(Boston studies in the philosophy of science, 88.) Rev. by David Kubrin
in JHP (27:1) 154–6.

**4269.** GEORGE, MARGARET. Women in the first capitalist society:
experiences in seventeenth-century England. Urbana: Illinois UP;

Brighton: Harvester Press, 1988. pp. 260. Rev. by Merry E. Wiesner in
RQ (42:3) 574–5.

**4270.** GILLESPIE, GERALD.   Garden and labyrinth of time: studies in
Renaissance and Baroque literature. *See* **3175.**

**4271.** GOLDBERG, JONATHAN.   Fatherly authority: the politics of
Stuart family images. *In* (pp. 3–32) **54.**

**4272.** HOBBS, CLAIRE.   Cutting off the king's head: discourse and
subjection. Unpub. doct. diss., Univ. of Essex, 1988. [Abstr. in DA (49)
3360A.]

**4273.** HOFFER, PETER CHARLES (ed.).   An American Enlightenment:
selected articles on colonial intellectual history. New York; London:
Garland, 1988. pp. ix, 339. (Early American history.)

**4274.** HOLSTUN, JAMES.   A rational millennium: Puritan utopias of
seventeenth-century England and America. (Bibl. 1988, 3201.) Rev. by
Christopher Hill in RQ (42:3) 600–2.

**4275.** HORNER, BRUCE MERLE.   The rhetorics of seventeenth-century
English songs. Unpub. doct. diss., Univ. of Pittsburgh, 1988. [Abstr. in
DA (49) 1809A.]

**4276.** HOUSTON, R. A.   Literacy in early modern Europe: culture and
education 1500–1800. *See* **3178.**

**4277.** HÜLLEN, WERNER.   'Their manner of discourse.' Nachdenken
über Sprache im Umkreis der Royal Society. *See* **707.**

**4278.** INGRAM, MARTIN.   Church courts, sex and marriage in
England, 1570–1640. *See* **3179.**

**4279.** KERBER, LINDA K.   Women and individualism in American
history. MassR (30:4) 589–609.

**4280.** KNIGHT, JANICE LYNN.   A garden enclosed: the tradition of
heart-piety in Puritan New England. Unpub. doct. diss., Harvard
Univ., 1988. [Abstr. in DA (50) 443A.]

**4281.** KORSTEN, FRANS.   The eve of the Glorious Revolution: the
Catholic threat. DQR (19:3) 189–201.

**4282.** MANLEY, LAWRENCE.   From matron to monster: Tudor–Stuart
London and the languages of urban description. *In* (pp. 347–74) **31.**

**4283.** MARKLEY, ROBERT.   Isaac Newton's theological writings:
problems and prospects. Restoration (13:1) 35–48.

**4284.** MARTIN, JEAN-PIERRE.   Le puritanisme américain en Nouvelle-
Angleterre (1620–1693). Bordeaux: Presses Universitaires de Bordeaux. pp. 260.

**4285.** PEÑALBA GARCÍA, MERCEDES.   Visiones eutópicas de América
en la identidad coloquial puritana. RAEI (2) 127–42.

**4286.** POPKIN, RICHARD H. (ed.).   Millenarianism and Messianism in
English literature and thought 1650–1800: Clark Library lectures,
1981–1982. Leiden; New York: Brill, 1988. pp. 210. (Pubs from the
Clark Library Professorship, UCLA, 10.) Rev. by Geoffrey F. Nuttall in
TLS, 11 Aug., 880.

**4287.** PORTER, ROY.   Mind-forg'd manacles: a history of madness in
England from the Restoration to the Regency. London: Athlone Press,
1987. pp. xii, 412. Rev. by John Wiltshire in CamQ (18:2) 198–207.

**4288.** QUESTIER, M. C.　Some aspects of English recusant polemical literature. *See* **3189.**

**4289.** ROBBINS, STEPHEN LEE.　Manifold afflictions: the life and writings of William Aspinwall, 1605–1662. Unpub. doct. diss., Oklahoma State Univ., 1988. [Abstr. in DA (49) 3028A.]

**4290.** SCHWOERER, LOIS G.　Images of Queen Mary II, 1689–95. RQ (42:4) 717–48.

**4291.** SEPPER, DENNIS L.　Descartes and the eclipse of imagination, 1618–1630. JHP (27:3) 379–403.

**4292.** SHAPIN, STEVEN; SCHAFFER, SIMON.　*Leviathan* and the air-pump: Hobbes, Boyle, and the experimental life: including a translation of *Dialogus physicus de natura aeris*. Princeton, NJ: Princeton UP, 1985. pp. xiv, 440. Rev. by A. P. Martinich in JHP (27:2) 308–9.

**4293.** SMITH, NIGEL.　A child prophet: Martha Hatfield as *The Wise Virgin*. *In* (pp. 79–93) **14.**

**4294.** THOMAS, KEITH.　Children in early modern England. *In* (pp. 45–77) **14.**

**4295.** TREVOR-ROPER, HUGH.　Catholics, Anglicans and Puritans: seventeenth-century essays. Chicago: Chicago UP; London: Secker & Warburg, 1987, pp. xiii, 317. Rev. by James M. Rosenheim in MP (87:2) 176–8; by James H. Sims in SCN (47:3/4) 33–4.

**4296.** YOCH, JAMES J.　A very wild regularity: the character of landscape in the work of Inigo Jones. RORD (30) 1988, 7–15.

**4297.** YOUNG, ALAN R.　The English tournament imprese. *In* (pp. 61–81) **21.**

## Literary Theory

This section is intended to contain studies **about** the literary theory, literary historiography, literary criticism, etc., produced *in* the seventeenth century. For modern works **of** literary history and criticism dealing generally with this period, see under 'Seventeenth Century: General Literary Studies'.

**4298.** ENGELL, JAMES.　Forming the critical mind: Dryden to Coleridge. Cambridge, MA; London: Harvard UP. pp. x, 322.

## AUTHORS
### Edmund Arwaker

**4299.** DIMLER, G. RICHARD.　Edmund Arwaker's translation of the *Pia Desideria*: the reception of a continental Jesuit emblem book in seventeenth-century England. *In* (pp. 203–24) **21.**

### Francis Bacon

**4300.** ANDERSON, JUDITH H.　'But we shall teach the lad another language': history and rhetoric in Bacon, Ford, and Donne. RenD (20) 169–96.

**4301.** FLANNERY, KATHRYN.　Models of reading: seventeenth-century productions of Bacon's texts. Assays (5) 111–33.

**4302.** HULSE, CLARK.　Spenser, Bacon, and the myth of power. *In* (pp. 315–46) **31.**

**4303.** KIERNAN, MICHAEL (ed.).    The Essayes or Counsels, Civill and Morall. (Bibl. 1987, 4838.) Rev. by David Norbrook in RES (38:152) 1987, 551–2; by Brian Vickers in MLR (83:2) 1988, 403–5.
**4304.** PIEPER, ANNEMARIE.    Der philosophische Begriff der Utopie und die klassischen Utopisten. *See* **3285.**
**4305.** WEISER, DAVID K.    Bacon's borrowed imagery. RES (38:151) 1987, 315–24.
**4306.** WHITNEY, CHARLES.    Francis Bacon and modernity. (Bibl. 1986, 5277.) Rev. by David Norbrook in RES (38:152) 1987, 551; by Robin Attfield in JHP (26:4) 1988, 665–7; by Achsah Guibbory in JEGP (87:4) 1988, 579–82.

### Beaumont and Fletcher

**4307.** BLISS, LEE.    Three plays in one: Shakespeare and *Philaster*. *See* **3489.**
**4308.** BOWERS, FREDSON (gen. ed.).    The dramatic works in the Beaumont and Fletcher canon; vol. 5, *The Mad Lover, The Loyal Subject, The Humorous Lieutenant, Women Pleased, The Island Princess.* (Bibl. 1983, 5038.) Rev. by William Proctor Williams in MedRen (2) 1985, 299–306.
**4309.** CRAIK, T. W. (ed.).    The maid's tragedy. (Bibl. 1988, 3232.) Rev. by Gordon McMullan in NQ (36:3) 389–91.
**4310.** RADEL, NICHOLAS F.    'Then thus I turne my language to you': the transformation of theatrical language in *Philaster.* MedRen (3) 1986, 129–47.
**4311.** TURNER, ROBERT Y.    Heroic passion in the early tragicomedies of Beaumont and Fletcher. MedRen (1) 1984, 109–30.
**4312.** ZITNER, SHELDON P. (ed.).    The Knight of the Burning Pestle. (Bibl. 1987, 485.) Rev. by Anne Lancashire in RES (38:151) 1987, 389–90; by Michael Hattaway in MedRen (4) 322–4.

### Francis Beaumont

**4313.** BLISS, LEE.    Francis Beaumont. (Bibl. 1988, 3236.) Rev. by Emily C. Bartels in RQ (42:1) 142–4; by Richard G. Barlow in SCN (47:1/2) 17–18.
**4314.** NICHOL, DONALD W.    'Flagrant' versus 'fragrant' in Beaumont, Pope, Pound, and Burgess. *See* **1048.**

### Aphra Behn

**4315.** BALLASTER, R. M.    Seductive forms: women's amatory fiction from 1684 to 1740 with particular reference to Aphra Behn, Delarivier Manley and Eliza Haywood. Unpub. doct. diss., Univ. of Oxford. [Abstr. in IT (39:3) 1108.]
**4316.** DHUICQ, BERNARD.    'Landed gentry' et 'merchants' dans le théâtre d'Aphra Behn. *In* (pp. 71–85) **14.**
**4317.** MENDELSON, SARA HELLER.    The mental world of Stuart women: three studies. (Bibl. 1988, 3240, where title incorrect.) Rev. by Retha M. Warnicke in RQ (42:1) 152–4.
**4318.** O'DONNELL, MARY ANN.    Aphra Behn: an annotated bibliography of primary and secondary sources. (Bibl. 1986, 5290.) Rev. by Sharon Valiant in RMRLL (43:4) 235–6.
**4319.** RUSSELL, B. W.    A critical introduction to Aphra Behn's *The*

*Emperor of the Moon.* Unpub. M.Litt. diss., Univ. of Lancaster, 1988.
[Abstr. in IT (39:2) 484.]

## Edward Benlowes

**4320.** KENNEDY, RICHARD F.   Allusions to Herbert in John Spencer
and Edward Benlowes. GHJ (12:1) 1988, 45–7.

## Anne Bradstreet

**4321.** MARAGOU, HELENA.   The portrait of Alexander the Great in
Anne Bradstreet's *The Third Monarchy.* EAL (23:1) 1988, 70–81.

## Nicholas Breton

**4322.** BRENNAN, MICHAEL G.   Nicholas Breton's *The Passions of the
Spirit* and the Countess of Pembroke. *See* **3297.**

## Richard Brome

**4323.** BERRY, HERBERT.   The Globe bewitched and *El hombre fiel.*
MedRen (1) 1984, 211–30.

**4324.** EVANS, ROBERT C.   Richard Brome's death. NQ (36:3) 351.

**4325.** STEEN, SARA JAYNE (ed.).   The English Moore; or, The mock-
marriage. Columbia: Missouri UP, 1983. pp. x, 164. Rev. by Henry D.
Janzen in MedRen (3) 1986, 344–7; by William Proctor Williams in NQ
(33:2) 1986, 235–6.

## Sir Thomas Browne

**4326.** ELLRODT, ROBERT.   Time and the body in the works of Sir
Thomas Browne. *In* (pp. 97–101) **42.**

**4327.** FAVRE, ALBERT.   Sir Thomas Browne: *Pseudodoxia Epidemica*:
révélation d'une personnalité? Le Livre 5. EA (42:2) 140–50.

**4328.** FINCH, JEREMIAH J.   A catalogue of the libraries of Sir Thomas
Browne and Dr Edward Browne, his son. *See* **222.**

**4329.** GALEF, DAVID.   Mrs Woolf and Mr Browne. NQ (36:2) 202–3.

**4330.** SUNUNU, ANDREA.   Recent studies in Sir Thomas Browne
(1970–1986). ELR (19:1) 118–29.

## George Villiers, Second Duke of Buckingham

**4331.** YARDLEY, B. C.   The political career of George Villiers, 2nd
Duke of Buckingham (1628–87). Unpub. doct. diss., Univ. of Oxford.
[Abstr. in IT (39:3) 1130.]

## John Bunyan

**4332.** BATSON, BEATRICE.   John Bunyan's *Grace Abounding* and *The
Pilgrim's Progress*: an overview of literary studies, 1960–1987. New York;
London: Garland, 1988. pp. xx, 245. (Garland reference library of the
humanities, 773.) Rev. by Sara van den Berg in ChrisL (38:2) 86–7.

**4333.** FORREST, JAMES F.; SHARROCK, ROGER (eds).   The life and
death of Mr Badman: presented to the world in a familiar dialogue
between Mr Wiseman and Mr Attentive. Oxford: Clarendon Press;
New York; OUP, 1988. pp. xlii, 188. (Oxford English texts.) Rev. by
John Drury in TLS, 4 Nov., 1233.

**4334.** HILL, CHRISTOPHER.   A turbulent, seditious, and factious
people: John Bunyan and his church 1628–1688. (Bibl. 1988, 3258.)
Rev. by Tom Shippey in LRB (11:3) 8–9; by Roger Sharrock in DUJ
(81:2) 318–19.

**4335.** KEEBLE, N. H. (ed.).   John Bunyan: conventicle and Parnassus: tercentenary essays. (Bibl. 1988, 3259.) Rev. by Graham Midgley in NQ (36:3) 395–6.

**4336.** KIM, SUNG-KYOON.   Bunyan eui *Mr Badman* yeongu: an embryo novel. (A study of Bunyan's *Mr Badman*: an embryo novel.) JELL (35) 407–27.

**4337.** SHARROCK, ROGER (gen. ed.).   The barren fig-tree; The strait gate; The heavenly foot-man. Ed. by GRAHAM MIDGLEY. (Bibl. 1988, 3263.) Rev. by Malcolm Hardman in YES (19) 323–4; by Nigel Smith in RES (39:156) 1988, 553–5.

**4338.** —— Christian behaviour; The holy city; The resurrection of the dead. Ed. by J. SEARS MCGEE. (Bibl. 1988, 3264.) Rev. by N. H. Keeble in NQ (35:3) 1988, 374–5; by Nigel Smith in RES (39:156) 1988, 553–5.

**4339.** —— Good news for the vilest of men; The advocateship of Jesus Christ. Ed. by RICHARD L. GREAVES. (Bibl. 1988, 3265.) Rev. by Nigel Smith in RES (38:149) 1987, 74–5.

**4340.** THOMAS, RONALD R.   The novel and the afterlife: the end of the line in Bunyan and Beckett. MP (86:4) 385–97.

### Robert Burton

**4341.** CONN, JOEY.   Robert Burton and the *Anatomy of Melancholy*: an annotated bibliography of primary and secondary sources. New York; London: Greenwood Press, 1988. pp. xii, 105. (Bibliographies and indexes in world literature, 15.)

**4342.** FAULKNER, THOMAS C.; KIESSLING, NICOLAS K.; BLAIR, RHONDA L. (eds).   The anatomy of melancholy: vol. 1, Text. Oxford: Clarendon Press; New York: OUP. pp. lxxi, 675. Rev. by A. D. Nuttall in LRB (11:22) 18–19.

**4343.** GIBSON, JOSEPH RICHARD.   Babylon anatomized: Burton's use of Augustine. Unpub. doct. diss., McMaster Univ. [Abstr. in DA (50) 1311A.]

**4344.** JACKSON, STANLEY W.   Robert Burton and psychological healing. JHM (44:2) 160–78.

**4345.** O'CONNELL, MICHAEL.   Robert Burton. (Bibl. 1988, 3275.) Rev. by Elizabeth Heale in YES (19) 309–11.

**4346.** SCHMELZER, MARY MURPHY.   "Tis all one': *The Anatomy of Melancholy* as belated copious discourse. Unpub. doct. diss., Temple Univ., 1988. [Abstr. in DA (49) 3735–6A.]

**4347.** STEED, PATRICIA L.   The dialectical 'I': invention and self in Robert Burton's *Anatomy of Melancholy*. Unpub. doct. diss., Texas Woman's Univ., 1988. [Abstr. in DA (49) 3037A.]

### Thomas Campion

**4348.** LINDLEY, DAVID (ed.); SOWERBY, ROBIN (addl notes and trans.). De puluerea coniuratione. (On the Gunpowder Plot.) Sidney Sussex MS 59. (Bibl. 1987, 4894.) Rev. by JWB in CEl (35) 120.

### Thomas Carew

**4349.** HANNAFORD, RENÉE.   'My unwashed muse': sexual play and sociability in Carew's *A Rapture*. ELN (27:1) 32–9.

## George Chapman

**4350.** BEACH, VINCENT WOODROW, JR.   George Chapman's *Bussy D'Ambois* (*c.* 1604) and Jacobean social attitudes. Unpub. doct. diss., City Univ. of New York, 1988. [Abstr. in DA (49) 2225A.]

**4351.** DUNDAS, JUDITH.   'Arachnean eyes': a mythological emblem in the poetry of George Chapman. JDJ (6:2) 1987, 275–83.

**4352.** HOLADAY, ALLAN (gen. ed.); EVANS, G. BLAKEMORE; BERGER, THOMAS L. (asst eds).   The plays of George Chapman, a critical edition: the tragedies with *Sir Gyles Goosecappe*. (Bibl. 1988, 3288.) Rev. by John Jowett in NQ (36:1) 102–4.

**4353.** IDE, RICHARD S.   Exploiting the tradition: the Elizabethan revenger as Chapman's 'complete man'. MedRen (1) 1984, 159–72.

**4354.** KRASNER, JAMES N.   *The Tragedy of Bussy D'Ambois* and the creation of heroism. MedRen (4) 107–21.

**4355.** MONTUORI, DEBORAH.   The confusion of self and role in Chapman's *Bussy D'Ambois*. SELit (28:2) 1988, 287–99.

**4356.** RASMUSSEN, ERIC.   Shakespeare's hand in *The Second Maiden's Tragedy. See* **3631.**

**4357.** SNARE, GERALD.   The mystification of George Chapman. Durham, NC; London: Duke UP. pp. x, 186.

**4358.** SOELLNER, ROLF.   Chapman's *Caesar and Pompey* and the fortunes of Prince Henry. MedRen (2) 1985, 135–51.

## Walter Charleton

**4359.** LINDEN, STANTON J.   Walter Charleton and Henry Vaughan's *Cock-Crowing.* NQ (36:1) 38–9.

## Edward Hyde, Earl of Clarendon

**4360.** DZELZAINIS, MARTIN.   Edward Hyde and Thomas Hobbes's *Elements of Law, Natural and Politic.* HistJ (32:2) 303–17.

## William Congreve

**4361.** KRAFT, ELIZABETH.   Why didn't Mirabell marry the Widow Languish? Restoration (13:1) 26–34.

**4362.** Entry cancelled.

**4363.** SNIDER, ALVIN.   Professing a libertine in *The Way of the World.* PLL (25:4) 376–97.

## Thomas Coryate

**4364.** JONES, ANN ROSALIND.   Italians and others: Venice and the Irish in *Coryat's Crudities* and *The White Devil*. RenD (18) 1987, 101–19.

## Charles Cotton

**4365.** HARTLE, P. N.   'Mr Cotton, of merry memory': Charles Cotton (1630–1687), poet. Neophilologus (73:4) 605–19.

## John Cotton

**4366.** BUSH, SARGENT, JR.   John Cotton's correspondence: a census. EAL (24:2) 91–111.

**4367.** SHAW, NANCY JOY.   Speaking for the spirit: Cotton, Shepard, Edwards, Emerson. Unpub. doct. diss., Cornell Univ., 1988. [Abstr. in DA (49) 3065–6A.]

## Abraham Cowley

**4368.** COLTRANE, ROBERT.   Cowley's revisions in *Cutter of Coleman Street.* Restoration (13:2) 68–75.

**4369.** FRONTAIN, RAYMOND-JEAN. 'Ruddy and goodly to look at withal': Drayton, Cowley, and the Biblical model for Renaissance hom[m]osexuality. CEl (36) 11–24.

**4370.** NEW, MELVYN. Cowley and Sterne. NQ (36:4) 447.

**4371.** RADCLIFFE, DAVID HILL. Sylvan states: social and literary formations in *sylvae* by Jonson and Cowley. ELH (55:4) 1988, 797–809.

**4372.** REVARD, STELLA P. The seventeenth-century religious ode and its classical models. *In* (pp. 173–91) **11.**

### Ralph Crane

**4373.** HAAS, VIRGINIA L. Ralph Crane: a status report. AEB (ns 3:1) 3–10.

### Richard Crashaw

**4374.** HAMMILL, GRAHAM. Stepping to the temple. SAQ (88:4) 933–59.

**4375.** HEALY, THOMAS F. Richard Crashaw. (Bibl. 1987, 4921.) Rev. by Michael G. Brennan in NQ (36:1) 106–7.

**4376.** REVARD, STELLA P. The seventeenth-century religious ode and its classical models. *In* (pp. 173–91) **11.**

**4377.** ROBERTS, JOHN R. Richard Crashaw: an annotated bibliography of criticism, 1632–1980. (Bibl. 1987, 4922.) Rev. by Robert Ellrodt in EA (42:2) 214; by Alan Rudrum in RES (38:150) 1987, 250–1.

**4378.** ROBERTS, LORRAINE. Crashaw's Epiphany Hymn: faith out of darkness. *In* (pp. 134–44) **11.**

### Sir William Davenant

**4379.** EDMOND, MARY. Rare Sir William Davenant: poet laureate, playwright, Civil War general, Restoration theatre manager. (Bibl. 1988, 3297.) Rev. by J. P. Vander Motten in EngS (70:3) 274–6.

**4380.** HUGHES, DEREK. The Dryden–Davenant *Tempest* and some seventeenth-century images of the stranger. *In* (pp. 83–108) **26.**

### Thomas Dekker

**4381.** ADLER, DORIS. Dekker observed: review article. MedRen (1) 1984, 231–42.

**4382.** BARBOUR, A. REID. Deciphering Renaissance prose narrative: plenism and the fictions of control. *See* **3229.**

**4383.** CHAMPION, LARRY S. 'Disaster with my so many joys': structure and perspective in Massinger and Dekker's *The Virgin Martyr*. MedRen (1) 1984, 199–209.

**4384.** —— Thomas Dekker and the traditions of English drama. (Bibl. 1985, 4630.) Rev. by Harry Keyishian in MedRen (3) 1986, 301–5.

**4385.** COMENSOLI, VIVIANA. Refashioning the marriage code: the *Patient Grissil* of Dekker, Chettle and Haughton. *See* **3214.**

**4386.** DAWSON, ANTHONY B. Witchcraft/bigamy: cultural conflict in *The Witch of Edmonton*. RenD (20) 77–98.

**4387.** MUIR, NORMAN R. Middle-class heroism and the cardinal virtue fortitude in Thomas Dekker's *Honest Whore* plays. ExRC (15) 83–96.

**4388.** MULHOLLAND, PAUL A. (ed.). The roaring girl. (Bibl. 1987, 4931.) Rev. by Lorna Hutson in NQ (36:2) 237–8.

## John Donne
**4389.** ANDERSON, JUDITH H. 'But we shall teach the lad another language': history and rhetoric in Bacon, Ford, and Donne. *See* **4300.**

**4390.** BEAL, PETER. More Donne manuscripts. JDJ (6:2) 1987, 213–18.

**4391.** BEIER, NAHIA MARY. A unity of truth: the metaphysical poetics of John Donne. Unpub. doct. diss., Univ. of Virginia, 1987. [Abstr. in DA (49) 3729A.]

**4392.** CHAMBERS, A. B. *Goodfriday, 1613. Riding Westward*: looking back. JDJ (6:2) 1987, 185–201.

**4393.** CLEBSCH, WILLIAM A. (ed.). Biathanatos. Chico, CA: Scholars Press, 1983. pp. 114. Rev. by W. Speed Hill in JDJ (6:1) 1987, 109–33.

**4394.** CORTHELL, RONALD J. Donne's 'disparitie': inversion, gender, and the subject of love in some *Songs and Sonets*. Exemplaria (1:1) 17–42.

**4395.** CRAIK, T. W.; CRAIK, R. J. (eds). Selected poetry and prose. (Bibl. 1988, 3308.) Rev. by Marie L. K. Lally in SCN (47:1/2) 13.

**4396.** DEMOOR, MARYSA. The whisper of John Donne in Dante Gabriel Rossetti's *The Stream's Secret*. NQ (36:2) 190–1.

**4397.** DOCHERTY, THOMAS. John Donne, undone. (Bibl. 1988, 3309.) Rev. by Neil Rhodes in RES (39:155) 1988, 439–40.

**4398.** DUBROW, HEATHER. 'The sun in water': Donne's Somerset epithalamium and the poetics of patronage. *In* (pp. 197–219) **31.**

**4399.** DUYCK, RUDY. V. S. Naipaul and John Donne: the morning after. JCL (24:1) 155–62.

**4400.** ELDERHORST, CONSTANCE. John Donne's *First Anniversary* as an anatomical anamorphosis. *In* (pp. 97–102) **28.**

**4401.** FLYNN, DENNIS. Donne's *Ignatius His Conclave* and other libels on Robert Cecil. JDJ (6:2) 1987, 163–83.

**4402.** GRANQVIST, RAOUL. Lustan och döden: teman i John Donnes poesi. (Lust and death: themes in the poetry of John Donne.) Horisont (36:2) 6–14.

**4403.** HASKIN, DAYTON. New historical contexts for appraising the Donne revival from A. B. Grosart to Charles Eliot Norton. ELH (56:4) 869–95.

**4404.** HESTER, M. THOMAS. Re-signing the text of the self: Donne's *As Due by Many Titles*. *In* (pp. 59–71) **11.**

**4405.** JOHNSON, JEFFREY STEPHENS. The centrique part: John Donne's *Elegies*. Unpub. doct. diss., Univ. of Missouri–Columbia, 1987. [Abstr. in DA (49) 2668A.]

**4406.** KIM, YOUNG-NAM. John Donne gwa 'tonghapdoen gamsusung' e daehan sogo. (John Donne and the problem of 'unified sensibility'.) JELLC (30) 1–20.

**4407.** LOW, ANTHONY. Donne and the new historicism. JDJ (7:1) 1988, 125–31 (review-article).

**4408.** —— Love and science: cultural change in Donne's *Songs and Sonnets*. SLI (22:1) 5–16.

**4409.** MAKURENKOVA, S. A. Byl li Dzhon Donn Dzhonom Donnom? (Was John Donne John Donne?) NDFN (1989:2) 74–7.

**4410.** MAROTTI, ARTHUR F. John Donne, coterie poet. (Bibl. 1988,

3315.) Rev. by Cedric C. Brown in RES (38:152) 1987, 560–1; by Gerald Hammond in MLR (84:1) 124–5.

**4411.** MARSHALL, ANN HERNDON. Godly decorum: Anglican approaches to history, imitation, and the arts in the sermons of John Donne and selected works of George Herbert. Unpub. doct. diss., Univ. of Virginia, 1987. [Abstr. in DA (50) 148–9A.]

**4412.** MENAGHAN, JOHN MICHAEL. Text as stage: Donne, Browning, Eliot and the idea of the 'dramatic'. Unpub. doct. diss., Univ. of California, Berkeley, 1988. [Abstr. in DA (50) 955A.]

**4413.** MUELLER, JANEL. Women among the metaphysicals: a case, mostly, of being Donne for. *See* **4236.**

**4414.** MÜLLER, WOLFGANG G. Liturgie und Lyrik: John Donnes *The Litanie.* LJGG (27) 1986, 65–80.

**4415.** PRIOR, R. J. John Donne: text and context. Unpub. doct. diss., Univ. of Nottingham, 1987. [Abstr. in IT (38:4) 1456–7.]

**4416.** RADZINOWICZ, MARY ANN. *Anima mea* psalms and John Donne's religious poetry. *In* (pp. 40–58) **11.**

**4417.** RICHARDS, BERNARD. The 'bed's feet' in Donne's *A Nocturnal upon St Lucy's Day.* NQ (36:1) 28–9.

**4418.** SELLIN, PAUL R.; VEENENDAAL, AUGUSTUS J., JR. A 'pub crawl' through old The Hague: shady light on life and art among English friends of John Donne in the Netherlands, 1627–1635. JDJ (6:2) 1987, 235–60.

**4419.** SHAWCROSS, JOHN T. The concept of *sermo* in Donne and Herbert. JDJ (6:2) 1987, 203–12.

**4420.** SLOANE, THOMAS O. Donne, Milton, and the end of Humanist rhetoric. (Bibl. 1988, 3322.) Rev. by Cedric C. Brown in RES (38:150) 1987, 248–9.

**4421.** STANWOOD, P. G.; ASALS, HEATHER ROSS (eds). John Donne and the theology of language. Columbia: Missouri UP, 1986. pp. viii, 376. (Selections from Donne's sermons.) Rev. by Winfried Schleiner in MP (86:3) 296–7.

**4422.** STRIER, RICHARD. John Donne awry and squint: the *Holy Sonnets,* 1608–1610. MP (86:4) 357–84.

**4423.** SULLIVAN, ERNEST W., II. Updating the John Donne listings in Peter Beal's *Index of English Literary Manuscripts.* JDJ (6:2) 1987, 219–34.

**4424.** —— MURRAH, DAVID J. (eds). The Donne Dalhousie discovery: proceedings of a symposium on the acquisition and study of the John Donne and Joseph Conrad collections at Texas Tech University. *See* **267.**

**4425.** SUMMERS, CLAUDE; PEBWORTH, TED-LARRY (eds). The eagle and the dove: reassessing John Donne. (Bibl. 1988, 3324.) Rev. by Gerald Hammond in MLR (84:1) 125.

**4426.** SUMMERS, CLAUDE J. The Bride of the Apocalypse and the quest for true religion: Donne, Herbert, and Spenser. *In* (pp. 72–95) **11.**

**4427.** VON KOPPENFELS, WERNER. 'When thou hast done thou hast not Don(n)e': Entfremdung und Verfremdung eines metaphysical poet. *In* (pp. 154–74) **4.**

**4428.** WALKER, JULIA M. Left/write: of lock-jaw and literary criticism. JDJ (7:1) 1988, 133–9 (review-article).

**4429.** WARNKE, FRANK J. John Donne. Boston, MA: G. K. Hall, 1987. pp. 143. (Twayne's English authors, 444.) Rev. by Ann Baynes Coiro in RQ (42:3) 585–7.

**4430.** WHITE, WILLIAM ROBERT. A performer's analysis of Benjamin Britten's 'The *Holy Sonnets* of John Donne'. Unpub. doct. diss., Univ. of Texas at Austin, 1988. [Abstr. in DA (50) 300A.]

**4431.** WRIGHT, NANCY E. The *figura* of the martyr in John Donne's sermons. ELH (56:2) 293–309.

**4432.** YOUNG, R. V. Donne's Holy Sonnets and the theology of grace. *In* (pp. 20–39) **11.**

### Michael Drayton

**4433.** FRONTAIN, RAYMOND-JEAN. 'Ruddy and goodly to look at withal': Drayton, Cowley, and the Biblical model for Renaissance hom[m]osexuality. *See* **4369.**

### John Dryden

**4434.** ALLOTT, TERENCE. 'Brutes turn'd politicians': the seventeenth-century fable. NC (7) 20–32.

**4435.** ANNZAI, TETSUO (ed.). Nihon no Shakespeare 100 nen. *See* **3478.**

**4436.** BENTLEY, CHRISTOPHER. Dryden's Presbyterian wolf. NQ (36:4) 450–1. (*The Hind and the Panther.*)

**4437.** BRENNAN, MICHAEL G. Sir William Trumbull and Dryden's *An Essay of Dramatick Poesie*. NQ (36:1) 41–6.

**4438.** BROWN, STEPHEN WILLIAM. Changing concepts of character and plot from Dryden to Sterne. Unpub. doct. diss., Queen's Univ. at Kingston (Ont.), 1988. [Abstr. in DA (49) 3366A.]

**4439.** CLAYTON, RONALD. Dryden's advice to Danby. NQ (36:4) 447–50.

**4440.** CLINGHAM, G. J. Pope's Bolingbroke and Dryden's 'happy man'. NQ (36:1) 56–8.

**4441.** CLINGHAM, GREGORY J. Johnson's criticism of Dryden's odes in praise of St Cecilia. MLS (18:1) 1988, 165–80.

**4442.** COMBE, KIRK. Clandestine protest against William III in Dryden's translations of Juvenal and Persius. MP (87:1) 36–50.

**4443.** CONWAY, DANIEL J. Erotic arguments: rhetoric and sexuality in seventeenth-century English stage adaptations of Plutarch. *See* **3505.**

**4444.** CORSE, TAYLOR. *Festina lente*: Dryden and Oldham. Restoration (13:1) 17–25.

**4445.** DAVIES, H. NEVILLE. *All for Love*: text and contexts. CEl (36) 49–71.

**4446.** DURANT, JACK D. Freedom and bondage in *All for Love*. CEACrit (51:2/3) 20–30.

**4447.** FROST, WILLIAM. John Dryden: dramatist, satirist, translator. New York: AMS Press, 1988. pp. xv, 258. (AMS studies in the seventeenth century, 3.) Rev. by Kirk Combe in NQ (36:4) 514.

**4448.** GARDINER, ANNE BARBEAU. Divine and royal art: history as hand-formed artwork in Dryden's *Threnodia Augustalis* (1685). PLL (25:4) 398–424.

**4449.** HAMMOND, PAUL. An echo of Dryden in Oldham's *The Thirteenth Satyr of Juvenal, Imitated.* NQ (36:4) 451.

**4450.** —— A precedent for the buzzard in *The Hind and the Panther.* NQ (36:4) 450.

**4451.** HOPKINS, DAVID. Dryden and the Garth–Tonson *Metamorphoses.* RES (39:153) 1988, 64–74.

**4452.** —— John Dryden. (Bibl. 1988, 3344.) Rev. by BH in BJECS (10) 1987, 109.

**4453.** HUGHES, DEREK. The Dryden–Davenant *Tempest* and some seventeenth-century images of the stranger. *In* (pp. 83–108) **26.**

**4454.** KEENER, FREDERICK M. Pope, Dryden, Milton, and the poets' secret. ELH (56:1) 81–96.

**4455.** OGDEN, JAMES. Horace and Milton in *Mac Flecknoe.* NQ (36:1) 50.

**4456.** POYET, ALBERT. John Dryden, poète satirique. Unpub. doct. diss., Univ. de la Sorbonne Nouvelle, Paris III, 1988. [Abstr. in EA (42:1) 117–18.]

**4457.** ROPER, ALAN (gen. ed.). The works of John Dryden: vol. 5, Poems; The works of Virgil in English. Ed. by WILLIAM FROST and VINTON A. DEARING. (Bibl. 1988, 3352.) Rev. by William Malin Porter in MP (87:2) 179–81; by Stanley Archer in SCN (47:3/4) 42.

**4458.** —— The works of John Dryden: vol. 13, Plays: *All for Love, Oedipus, Troilus and Cressida.* Ed. by MAXIMILLIAN E. NOVAK and GEORGE R. GUFFEY. (Bibl. 1986, 5425, where misplaced.) Rev. by Paul Hammond in RES (38:150) 1987, 251–2; by Derek Hughes in YES (19) 322–3.

**4459.** RUFINI, SERGIO. 'To make that maxim good': Dryden's Shakespeare. *In* (pp. 243–80) **27.**

**4460.** SATO, ISAO. Dryden to shuuhen shijin no honyaku riron. (Dryden's theory of translation.) Tokyo: New Current International. pp. 92.

**4461.** SLOMAN, JUDITH. Dryden: the poetics of translation. Ed. by ANNE MCWHIR. (Bibl. 1987, 5027.) Rev. by Paul Hammond in RES (38:149) 1987, 75–7.

**4462.** WALKER, KEITH (ed.). John Dryden. (Bibl. 1988, 3354.) Rev. by Tom Mason in RES (39:155) 1988, 443–4.

**4463.** WINN, JAMES ANDERSON. John Dryden and his world. (Bibl. 1988,3356.) Rev. by Albert Poyet in EA (42:3) 340–1; by Phillip Harth in MP (86:4) 425–7; by Brean S. Hammond in BJECS (12) 232–3; by William Roosen in AHR (94:5) 1371; by Anne Barbeau Gardiner in JMH (61:4) 765–8; by David Wykes in NQ (36:2) 242–3.

**4464.** YAMAMURA, TAKEO. Dryden kara Hopkins e: 17 seiki to 20 seiki no soukan kankei. (From Dryden to Hopkins: the relationship between the 17th century and the 20th century.) Tokyo: Apollon. pp. 380, viii.

## Sir George Etherege

**4465.** OGÉE, FRÉDÉRIC. 'All the world will be seen in the park tonight': seeing and being seen in Etherege's *The Man of Mode*. Restoration (13:2) 86–94.

### John Evelyn

**4466.** MacLean, Sally-Beth. Leicester and the Evelyns: new evidence for the Continental tour of Leicester's men. *See* **3091.**

**4467.** Vickers, Brian. Public and private life in seventeenth-century England: the Mackenzie–Evelyn debate. *In* (pp. 257–78) Brian Vickers (ed.), Arbeit, Musse, Meditation: Betrachtungen zur *Vita activa* und *Vita contemplativa*. Zurich: Centre for Renaissance Studies, 1985. pp. xvi, 311. Rev. by F. C. De Vries in RES (39:154) 1988, 325–7.

### George Farquhar

**4468.** Stafford-Clark, Max. Letters to George: the account of a rehearsal. London: Hern. pp. xvi, 189. (Letters written during rehearsals of *The Recruiting Officer*.) Rev. by Ed Thomason in Listener (122) 17 Aug., 25–6.

### Owen Felltham

**4469.** Stewart, Stanley. Authorial representation and Owen Felltham's *Resolves*. Cithara (28:2) 7–33.

### Nathan Field

**4470.** Woolford, John; Karlin, Daniel. A new source for the form of *Pippa Passes*. NQ (36:2) 184–5. (Fletcher and Field's *Four Plays, or, Moral Representations in One*.)

### John Fletcher

**4471.** Gurr, Andrew. *The Tempest*'s tempest at Blackfriars. *See* **3722.**

**4472.** Hickman, Andrew. *Bonduca*'s two ignoble armies and *The Two Noble Kinsmen*. *See* **4051.**

**4473.** Howard-Hill, T. H. Buc and the censorship of *Sir John Van Olden Barnavelt* in 1619. *See* **144.**

**4474.** Prager, Carolyn. The problem of slavery in *The Custom of the Country*. SELit (28:2) 1988, 301–17.

**4475.** Rigaud, N. J. La problématique de l'étranger dans *The Custom of the Country* de J. Fletcher. *In* (pp. 53–72) **26.**

**4476.** Squier, Charles L. John Fletcher. Boston, MA: G. K. Hall, 1986. pp. 167. (Twayne's English authors, 433.) Rev. by Emily C. Bartels in RQ (42:1) 142–4.

**4477.** Turner, Robert Y. Responses to tyranny in John Fletcher's plays. MedRen (4) 123–41.

**4478.** Waith, Eugene M. (ed.). The two noble kinsmen. *See* **3469.**

**4479.** Woolford, John; Karlin, Daniel. A new source for the form of *Pippa Passes*. *See* **4470.**

### Phineas Fletcher

**4480.** Bouchard, Gary Michael. From campus to *campus*: the relationship of the university world to the literary pastoral worlds of Edmund Spenser, Phineas Fletcher, and John Milton. *See* **3350.**

### John Ford

**4481.** Anderson, Donald K., Jr. 'Concord in discord': the plays of John Ford, 1586–1986. New York: AMS Press, 1986. pp. xiv, 298. (AMS studies in the Renaissance, 17.) Rev. by Marie L. Kessel in SCN (47:1/2) 19.

**4482.** ANDERSON, JUDITH H. 'But we shall teach the lad another language': history and rhetoric in Bacon, Ford, and Donne. *See* **4300.**

**4483.** BARBOUR, REID. John Ford and resolve. SP (86:3) 341–66.

**4484.** BURNETT, MARK THORNTON. Marlovian echoes in Ford's *Perkin Warbeck. See* **3252.**

**4485.** DAWSON, ANTHONY B. Witchcraft/bigamy: cultural conflict in *The Witch of Edmonton. See* **4386.**

**4486.** FOSTER, VERNA ANN. Perkin without the Pretender: re-examining the dramatic center of Ford's play. RenD (16) 1985, 141–58.

**4487.** GOMEZ, CHRISTINE. Profaning the sacred: the juxtaposition of incest and marriage in Ford, Ibsen and Osborne. ACM (2:1) 74–84.

**4488.** KESSEL, MARIE L. *The Broken Heart*: an allegorical reading. MedRen (3) 1986, 217–30.

**4489.** NEILL, MICHAEL (ed.). John Ford: critical re-visions. Cambridge: CUP, 1988. pp. xi, 278.

### Fulke Greville, Lord Brooke

**4490.** GOUWS, JOHN (ed.). The prose works of Fulke Greville, Lord Brooke. (Bibl. 1988, 3373.) Rev. by Michael G. Brennan in RES (38:151) 1987, 385–6; by Katherine Duncan-Jones in MLR (84:1) 122–4.

**4491.** QUILLIGAN, MAUREEN. Sidney and his Queen. *In* (pp. 171–96) **31.**

### Sir Robert Harley (1579–1656)

**4492.** EALES, JAQUELINE. Sir Robert Harley, K. B., (1579–1656) and the 'Character' of a Puritan. BLJ (15:2) 134–57.

### George Herbert

**4493.** ANDERSON, JAN. Further biblical allusions in Herbert's *Love* poems. GHJ (12:1) 1988, 41–4.

**4494.** BIENZ, JOHN. Herbert's 'daily labour': an eschatological pattern in *The Church*. GHJ (12:1) 1988, 1–15.

**4495.** BLOCH, CHANA. Spelling the word: George Herbert and the Bible. (Bibl. 1987, 5070.) Rev. by Michael Piret in RES (38:149) 1987, 73–4.

**4496.** COSTELLO, JOAN KUZMA. True child, servant, and guest of his master: images of household rules in George Herbert's *The Temple*. BSUF (30:1) 39–51.

**4497.** DAVIDSON, CLIFFORD. George Herbert and stained glass windows. GHJ (12:1) 1988, 29–39.

**4498.** DICKSON, DONALD R. The fountain of living waters: the typology of the waters of life in Herbert, Vaughan, and Traherne. (Bibl. 1987, 5075.) Rev. by Ernest B. Gilman in RQ (42:3) 587–9; by Elizabeth Mackenzie in NQ (36:3) 392–4; by Gary A. Stringer in SCN (47:1/2) 12; by Cristina Malcolmson in GHJ (12:1) 1988, 48–52; by Edward E. Ericson in ChrisL (38:2) 76–8.

**4499.** ETCHELLS, RUTH (sel. and introd.). A selection of poems by

Herbert, the lenten poet, exploring his pilgrimage of faith. Tring: Lion, 1988. pp. 48. (Poets and prophets.)

**4500.** GODDARD, KEVIN. Reading George Herbert. UES (27:2) 12–19.

**4501.** —— 'That which while I use I am with thee': St Augustine's influence on George Herbert's mimetic art. ESA (32:2) 63–78.

**4502.** GOTTLIEB, SIDNEY. Herbert's political allegory of *Humilitie*. HLQ (52:4) 469–80.

**4503.** KENNEDY, RICHARD F. Allusions to Herbert in John Spencer and Edward Benlowes. *See* **4320.**

**4504.** KRONENFELD, JUDY. Post-Saussurean semantics, Reformation religious controversy, and contemporary critical disagreement. Assays (5) 135–65.

**4505.** LYNCH, DENISE. Herbert's *Love (III)* and Augustine on wisdom. ELN (27:1) 40–1.

**4506.** MARSHALL, ANN HERNDON. Godly decorum: Anglican approaches to history, imitation, and the arts in the sermons of John Donne and selected works of George Herbert. *See* **4411.**

**4507.** MARTIN, LOUIS FERDINAND. Numerical structures in *The Temple*: Augustinian aesthetics and George Herbert. Unpub. doct. diss., Univ. of North Carolina at Chapel Hill, 1988. [Abstr. in DA (49) 2670A.]

**4508.** OLSON, JOHN. Biblical narratives and Herbert's dialogue poems. GHJ (12:1) 1988, 17–28.

**4509.** PAHLKA, WILLIAM H. Saint Augustine's meter and George Herbert's will. (Bibl. 1987, 5096.) Rev. by Mark Taylor in GHJ (12:1) 1988, 59–62.

**4510.** PINKA, PATRICIA G. Timely timelessness in two Nativity poems. *In* (pp. 162–72) **11.**

**4511.** PRUSS, INGRID. George Herbert's *Prayer (1)*: from metaphor to mystery. GHJ (12:2) 17–26.

**4512.** PRUSS, INGRID R. George Herbert: the anxiety of receiving and the rewriting of the self. Unpub. doct. diss., Vanderbilt Univ., 1988. [Abstr. in DA (50) 693A.]

**4513.** RAY, JOAN KLINGEL. Myth, microcosm, and method in George Herbert's *Prayer (1)*. GHJ (12:2) 37–42.

**4514.** ROBERTS, JOHN R. George Herbert: an annotated bibliography of modern criticism, revised edition, 1905–1984. (Bibl. 1980, 5841.) Columbia: Missouri UP, 1988. pp. xix, 433. (Second ed.: first ed. 1978.) Rev. by Jeffrey Johnson in ChrisL (38:4) 85–6.

**4515.** SCHOENFELDT, MICHAEL C. Standing on ceremony: the comedy of manners in Herbert's *Love (III)*. *In* (pp. 116–33) **11.**

**4516.** —— 'Subject to ev'ry mounters bended knee': Herbert and authority. *In* (pp. 242–69) **31.**

**4517.** SHAWCROSS, JOHN T. The concept of *sermo* in Donne and Herbert. *See* **4419.**

**4518.** SHULLENBERGER, WILLIAM. *Ars praedicandi* in George Herbert's poetry. *In* (pp. 96–115) **11.**

**4519.** SINGLETON, MARION WHITE.   God's courtier: configuring a different grace in George Herbert's *Temple*. (Bibl. 1988, 3392.) Rev. by N. H. Keeble in NQ (36:3) 392; by Donald R. Dickson in SCN (47:1/2) 9–11; by Anthony Low in GHJ (12:1) 1988, 53–8.

**4520.** STEWART, STANLEY.   George Herbert. (Bibl. 1987, 5102.) Rev. by C. F. Main in RQ (42:1) 144–6; by Claude Summers in GHJ (12:2) 60–6.

**4521.** SUMMERS, CLAUDE J.   The Bride of the Apocalypse and the quest for true religion: Donne, Herbert, and Spenser. *In* (pp. 72–95) **11.**

**4522.** WALL, JOHN N.   Transformations of the word: Spenser, Herbert, Vaughan. *See* **3422.**

**4523.** WESTERWEEL, BART.   Patterns and patterning: a study of four poems by George Herbert. (Bibl. 1986, 5507.) Rev. by Dick Higgins in SCN (47:1/2) 11–12.

**4524.** YOUNG, DIANE.   The orator's church and the poet's temple. GHJ (12:2) 1–15.

### Edward, Lord Herbert of Cherbury

**4525.** HILL, EUGENE D.   Edward, Lord Herbert of Cherbury. (Bibl. 1988, 3377.) Rev. by Stanley Archer in SCN (47:3/4) 53.

### Robert Herrick

**4526.** COIRO, ANN BAYNES.   Robert Herrick's *Hesperides* and the epigram book tradition. Baltimore, MD; London: Johns Hopkins UP, 1988. pp. viii, 272. Rev. by Mary Thomas Crane in RQ (42:2) 363–5; by Michael G. Brennan in NQ (36:4) 507–8.

**4527.** LANDRUM, DAVID WAYNE.   Laudian themes in the poetry of Robert Herrick. Unpub. doct. diss., Purdue Univ., 1988. [Abstr. in DA (50) 691A.]

### Thomas Heywood

**4528.** ATKINSON, DAVID.   An approach to the main plot of Thomas Heywood's *A Woman Killed with Kindness*. EngS (70:1) 15–27.

**4529.** BERRY, HERBERT.   The Globe bewitched and *El hombre fiel*. *See* **4323.**

**4530.** DUTTON, RICHARD.   *Hamlet, An Apology for Actors*, and the sign of the Globe. *See* **3060.**

**4531.** GURR, ANDREW.   *The Tempest*'s tempest at Blackfriars. *See* **3722.**

**4532.** GUTIERREZ, NANCY A.   The irresolution of melodrama: the meaning of adultery in *A Woman Killed with Kindness*. Exemplaria (1:2) 265–91.

**4533.** KIEFER, FREDERICK.   Heywood as moralist in *A Woman Killed with Kindness*. MedRen (3) 1986, 83–98.

**4534.** RUDNYTSKY, PETER L.   *A Woman Killed with Kindness* as subtext of *Othello*. *See* **3963.**

**4535.** WRIGHT, STEPHEN K.   *The Historie of King Edward the Fourth*: a chronicle play on the Coventry Pageant wagons. *See* **3131.**

**4536.** YOUNG, ALAN R.   Thomas Heywood's pageants: new forms of evidence. RORD (30) 1988, 129–51.

## Edmund Hickeringill

**4537.** HAMMOND, PAUL. A precedent for the buzzard in *The Hind and the Panther*. See **4450**.

## Thomas Hobbes

**4538.** DZELZAINIS, MARTIN. Edward Hyde and Thomas Hobbes's *Elements of Law, Natural and Politic*. See **4360**.

**4539.** JOHNSTON, DAVID. The rhetoric of *Leviathan*: Thomas Hobbes and the politics of cultural transformation. Princeton, NJ: Princeton UP, 1986. pp. xx, 243. (Studies in moral, political and legal philosophy.) Rev. by Sheldon Wein in DalR (67:1) 1987, 145–6; by A. Jane Arscott in QQ (95:1) 1988, 213–14; by A. P. Martinich in JHP (27:3) 474–6.

**4540.** MARA, GERALD. Hobbes's counsel to sovereigns. JPol (50:2) 1988, 390–411.

**4541.** SHAVER, ROBERT WILLIAM. Hobbes, Rousseau, and *amour propre*. Unpub. doct. diss., Univ. of Pittsburgh. [Abstr. in DA (50) 1684A.]

**4542.** SORELL, TOM. Hobbes. (Bibl. 1988, 3410.) Rev. by A. P. Martinich in JHP (27:1) 152–4.

**4543.** TUCK, RICHARD. Hobbes. Oxford: OUP. pp. viii, 127. (Past masters.)

## Anne Hutchinson

**4544.** LANG, AMY SCHRAGER. Prophetic woman: Anne Hutchinson and the problem of dissent in the literature of New England. (Bibl. 1987, 4811, where entry misplaced.) Rev. by Susan L. Mizruchi in NEQ (62:1) 105–15; by Eileen Dreyer in CamQ (18:3) 334–8.

## Lucy Hutchinson

**4545.** NARVESON, KATHERINE. The source for Lucy Hutchinson's *On Theology*. NQ (36:1) 40–1.

## James I and VI, King of England and Scotland

**4546.** AKRIGG, G. P. V. (ed.). Letters of King James VI and I. (Bibl. 1986, 5532.) Rev. by Susan Zimmerman in MedRen (3) 1986, 231–43.

**4547.** MANNING, GILLIAN. An echo of King James in Jonson's *Bartholomew Fair*. NQ (36:3) 342–4.

**4548.** MARCUS, LEAH S. *Cymbeline* and the unease of topicality. *In* (pp. 134–68) **31**.

**4549.** ZIMMERMAN, SUSAN. Popular *vs* scholarly editions of Renaissance letters: review article. MedRen (3) 1986, 231–43.

## Edward Johnson

**4550.** MARTIN-DIAZ, JAMES ROBERT. Edward Johnson: the herald of New England. Unpub. doct. diss., State Univ. of New York at Buffalo, 1988. [Abstr. in DA (49) 2660A.]

## Ben Jonson

**4551.** ADACHI, MAMI. Song as device: Ben Jonson's use of seduction songs in *Volpone* and *The Devil is an Ass*. SStudT (25) 1987, 1–23.

**4552.** BARTON, ANNE. Ben Jonson, dramatist. (Bibl. 1988, 3412.) Rev. by Michael Warren in MedRen (4) 213–17.

**4553.** BEMENT, PETER (ed.). The alchemist. New York: Methuen, 1988. (Bibl. 1987, 5131.) Rev. by Miranda Johnson in SCN (47:3/4) 49.

**4554.** BENET, DIANA. 'The master-wit is the master-fool': Jonson, *Epicoene*, and the moralists. RenD (16) 1985, 121–39.

**4555.** BERGERON, DAVID M. 'Lend me your dwarf': romance in *Volpone*. MedRen (3) 1986, 99–113.

**4556.** BUTLER, MARTIN (ed.). The selected plays of Ben Jonson: vol. 2, *The Alchemist, Bartholomew Fair, The New Inn, A Tale of a Tub*. Cambridge: CUP. pp. xx, 534. (Plays by Renaissance and Restoration dramatists.)

**4557.** CARTELLI, THOMAS. *Bartholomew Fair* as urban Arcadia: Jonson responds to Shakespeare. *See* **3498.**

**4558.** CHENEY, PATRICK. Jonson's *The New Inn* and Plato's myth of the hermaphrodite. RenD (14) 1983, 173–94.

**4559.** DAVIDSON, CLIFFORD. Judgment, iconoclasm, and anti-theatricalism in Jonson's *Bartholomew Fair*. PLL (25:4) 349–63.

**4560.** DUNCAN, DOUGLAS. Ben Jonson and the Lucianic tradition. (Bibl. 1982, 5434.) Rev. by Rolf Soellner in MedRen (1) 1984, 267–70.

**4561.** DUTTON, RICHARD. Ben Jonson: to the first folio. (Bibl. 1988, 3418.) Rev. by Douglas M. Lanier in MedRen (3) 1986, 316–19.

**4562.** FLACHMANN, MICHAEL. *Epicoene*: a comic hell for a comic sinner. MedRen (1) 1984, 131–42.

**4563.** GRAS, HENK. *Twelfth Night, Every Man out of his Humour*, and the Middle Temple Revels of 1597–98. *See* **4044.**

**4564.** HATTAWAY, MICHAEL (ed.). The new inn. (Bibl. 1985, 4815.) Rev. by Anne Lancashire in RES (38:151) 1987, 390–1; by Ejner J. Jensen in MedRen (4) 252–5.

**4565.** HAYNES, JONATHAN. Representing the underworld: *The Alchemist*. SP (86:1) 18–41.

**4566.** JONES, ROBERT C. Engagement with knavery: point of view in *Richard III, The Jew of Malta, Volpone*, and *The Revenger's Tragedy*. *See* **3262.**

**4567.** KERINS, FRANK. The crafty enchaunter: ironic satires and Jonson's *Every Man Out of His Humour. See* **3234.**

**4568.** LANIER, DOUGLAS M. The prison-house of the canon: allegorical form and posterity in Ben Jonson's *The Staple of Newes*. MedRen (2) 1985, 253–67.

**4569.** LANIER, DOUGLAS MERCER. 'Better markes': towards a rhetoric of Jonsonian authority. Unpub. doct. diss., Duke Univ., 1988. [Abstr. in DA (49) 2669A.]

**4570.** LEGGATT, ALEXANDER. Ben Jonson: his vision and his art. (Bibl. 1986, 5568.) Rev. by Scott Colley in MedRen (2) 1985, 331–3.

**4571.** McDONALD, RUSS. Shakespeare and Jonson/Jonson and Shakespeare. *See* **3588.**

**4572.** MANNING, GILLIAN. An echo of King James in Jonson's *Bartholomew Fair. See* **4547.**

**4573.** MAUS, KATHARINE EISAMAN. Ben Jonson and the Roman frame of mind. (Bibl. 1987, 5156.) Rev. by William Blissett in MedRen (3) 1986; 333–5.

**4574.** —— Satiric and ideal economies in the Jonsonian imagination. ELR (19:1) 42–64.

**4575.** MILES, ROSALIND. Ben Jonson: his life and work. (Bibl. 1988, 3427.) Rev. by John Ferns in RES (39:155) 1988, 440–2.

**4576.** MILLARD, BARBARA C. 'An acceptable violence': sexual contest in Jonson's *Epicoene*. MedRen (1) 1984, 143–58.

**4577.** MILLER, ANTHONY. 'These forc'd joyes': imitation, celebration, and exhortation in Ben Jonson's *Ode to Sir William Sidney*. SP (86:1) 42–68.

**4578.** MILLER, CLARENCE H. The meaning of the concluding lines of Ben Jonson's *Epitaph on Elizabeth, L. H.* PLL (25:1) 36–43.

**4579.** MÜLLER, KURT. Satire und Metadrama: Das Theatermotiv in Ben Jonson's *Volpone*. LJGG (30) 79–91.

**4580.** NEWMAN, KAREN. City talk: women and commodification in Jonson's *Epicoene*. ELH (56:3) 503–18.

**4581.** OSTOVICH, HELEN. 'Jeered by confederacy': group aggression in Jonson's comedies. MedRen (3) 1986, 115–28.

**4582.** —— 'Manfrede'? Reconstruction of a misprint in Jonson's *Every Man Out of his Humour* (1600). *See* **364.**

**4583.** OSTOVICH, HELEN MYRA. A modern critical edition of Ben Jonson's *Every Man Out of His Humour*. *See* **365.**

**4584.** PARKER, R. B. (ed.). Volpone; or, The fox. (Bibl. 1987, 5159.) Rev. by Thomas L. Berger in MedRen (3) 1986, 338–43.

**4585.** PROCTER, JOHANNA (ed.). The selected plays of Ben Jonson: vol. 1, *Sejanus, Volpone, Epicoene; or, The Silent Woman*. Introd. by MARTIN BUTLER. Cambridge: CUP. pp. xix, 444. (Plays by Renaissance and Restoration dramatists.)

**4586.** QUIGLEY, DANIEL JAMES. Ben Jonson's conceptual unity. Unpub. doct. diss., Univ. of Notre Dame, 1988. [Abstr. in DA (49) 2233A.]

**4587.** RADCLIFFE, DAVID HILL. Sylvan states: social and literary formations in *sylvae* by Jonson and Cowley. *See* **4371.**

**4588.** RIGGS, DAVID. Ben Jonson: a life. Cambridge, MA; London: Harvard UP. pp. viii, 399. Rev. by Guy Davenport in BW, 1 Jan., 5; by David Bevington in NYTB, 19 Mar., 20; by Charles Nicholl in LRB (11:16) 18–19.

**4589.** RONAN, CLIFFORD J. Snakes in *Catiline*. MedRen (3) 1986, 149–63.

**4590.** ROWE, GEORGE E. Distinguishing Jonson: imitation, rivalry, and the direction of a dramatic career. Lincoln; London: Nebraska UP, 1988. pp. xii, 220. Rev. by Peter Hyland in NQ (36:4) 506–7.

**4591.** SCHULER, ROBERT M. Jonson's alchemists, epicures, and Puritans. MedRen (2) 1985, 171–208.

**4592.** SCODEL, JOSHUA. Genre and occasion in Jonson's *On My First Sonne*. SP (86:2) 235–59.

**4593.** SHAPIRO, JAMES. 'Steale from the deade?': the presence of Marlowe in Jonson's early plays. *See* **3271.**

**4594.** SILVER, J. M. Language, power and identity in the drama of

Ben Jonson. Unpub. doct. diss., Univ. of London, 1986. [Abstr. in IT (39:1) 31.]

**4595.** SLIGHTS, WILLIAM W. E.    Unfashioning the man of mode: a comic countergenre in Marston, Jonson, and Middleton. RenD (15) 1984, 69–91.

**4596.** SWEENEY, JOHN GORDON, III.    Jonson and the psychology of public theater: 'To coin the spirit, spend the soul'. (Bibl. 1988, 3432.) Rev. by Russ McDonald in MedRen (3) 1986, 347–9.

**4597.** WOMACK, PETER.    Ben Jonson. (Bibl. 1988, 3434.) Rev. by John Ferns in RES (39:155) 1988, 440–2.

### Sir William Killigrew

**4598.** HORDEN, JOHN; VANDER MOTTEN, J. P.    *Five New Playes*: Sir William Killigrew's two annotated copies. *See* **325.**

### R. Kirkham

**4599.** TRICOMI, ALBERT H.    R. Kirkham's *Alfred; or, Right Re-enthroned.* OEN (22:1) 1988, 30–1.

### Nathaniel Lee

**4600.** VERDURMEN, J. PETER.    *Lucius Junius Brutus* and Restoration tragedy: the politics of trauma. JEurS (19:2) 81–98.

### John Locke

**4601.** ASHCRAFT, RICHARD.    Locke's *Two Treatises of Government.* Boston, MA: Allen & Unwin, 1987. (Bibl. 1987, 5174.) Rev. by Andrew Reeve in MLR (84:4) 928–30.

**4602.** —— Revolutionary politics and Locke's *Two Treatises of Government.* (Bibl. 1988, 3439.) Rev. by J. Douglas Rabb in QQ (95:2) 1988, 487–9.

**4603.** BOTS, H.; EVERS, M.    Book news in Locke's correspondence (1683–1692). *See* **418.**

**4604.** CARUTH, CATHY LYNNE.    Empirical truths and critical fictions: Locke, Wordsworth, Kant, Freud. Unpub. doct. diss., Yale Univ., 1988. [Abstr. in DA (50) 1299A.]

**4605.** FOX, CHRISTOPHER.    Locke and the Scriblerians: identity and consciousness in early eighteenth-century Britain. Berkeley: California UP, 1988. pp. x, 174. Rev. by John Mullan in TLS, 4 Aug., 853.

**4606.** GRANT, RUTH W.    Locke's political anthropology and Lockean individualism. JPol (50:1) 1988, 42–63.

**4607.** HARRISON, BERNARD.    The defence of Wit: Sterne, Locke and the particular. CompCrit (10) 1988, 93–120.

**4608.** MILLER, JOYCE RAUSCH.    Language during the late Renaissance years: an historical survey of issues and circumstances responsible for changes in attitudes toward rhetoric during the seventeenth century. *See* **1317.**

**4609.** NEILL, ALEX.    Locke on habituation, autonomy, and education. JHP (27:2) 225–45.

**4610.** PETERS, JOHN DURHAM.    John Locke, the individual, and the origin of communication. QJS (75:4) 387–99.

**4611.** SHIN, KYUNG-WON. Search for personal identity in Locke and Wordsworth. JELL (35) 627–50.

### Richard Lovelace

**4612.** ANSELMENT, RAYMOND A. 'Clouded majesty': Richard Lovelace, Sir Peter Lely, and the Royalist spirit. SP (86:3) 367–87.

**4613.** HAMMOND, GERALD. Selected poems. (Bibl. 1987, 5189.) Rev. by Michael G. Brennan in NQ (36:1) 105–6.

**4614.** RANDALL, DALE B. J. Reading the light in Lovelace's *The Grasshopper*. CLit (16:2) 182–9.

### Sir George Mackenzie

**4615.** VICKERS, BRIAN. Public and private life in seventeenth-century England: the Mackenzie–Evelyn debate. *See* **4467.**

### Gervase Markham

**4616.** MOFFAT, S. A study of Gervase Markham's *English Arcadia*. Unpub. M.Phil. diss., Univ. of Dundee. [Abstr. in IT (38:4) 1456.]

### John Marston

**4617.** BENNETT, ROBERT BEALE. The royal ruse: malcontentedness in John Marston's *The Malcontent*. MedRen (1) 1984, 71–84.

**4618.** BLAKE, ANN. 'The humour of children': John Marston's plays in the private theatres. RES (38:152) 1987, 471–82.

**4619.** BURNETT, MARK THORNTON. 'I will not swell like a tragedian': Marston's *Antonio's Revenge* in performance. NM (90:3/4) 311–20.

**4620.** COLLEY, SCOTT. Marston, Calvinism, and satire. MedRen (1) 1984, 85–96.

**4621.** GECKLE, GEORGE L. John Marston's drama: themes, images, sources. (Bibl. 1983, 5338, where scholar's initial omitted.) Rev. by Dietrich Rolle in Ang (107:1/2) 228–31.

**4622.** JACKSON, MACDONALD P.; NEILL, MICHAEL (eds). The selected plays of John Marston. (Bibl. 1988, 3450.) Rev. by Martin Garrett in RES (39:154) 1988, 293–4.

**4623.** KERINS, FRANK. The crafty enchaunter: ironic satires and Jonson's *Every Man Out of His Humour*. *See* **3234.**

**4624.** ROBERTSON, KAREN. *Antonio's Revenge*: the tyrant, the Stoic, and the passionate man. MedRen (4) 91–106.

**4625.** SHELBURNE, STEVEN R. Principled satire: decorum in John Marston's *The Metamorphosis of Pigmalions Image and Certaine Satyres*. SP (86:2) 198–218.

**4626.** SLIGHTS, WILLIAM W. E. Unfashioning the man of mode: a comic countergenre in Marston, Jonson, and Middleton. *See* **4595.**

### Andrew Marvell

**4627.** BRODY, JULES. The resurrection of the body: a new reading of Marvell's *To His Coy Mistress*. ELH (56:1) 53–79.

**4628.** BRUNNER, LARRY. 'Love at lower rate': a Christian reading of *To His Coy Mistress*. ChrisL (38:4) 25–44.

**4629.** CLARK, JAMES ANDREW. *The Coronet*: Marvell's 'curious frame' of allusion. *In* (pp. 145–61) **11.**

**4630.** DUYFHUIZEN, BERNARD. Textual harassment of Marvell's Coy

Mistress: the institutionalization of masculine criticism. CE (50:4) 1988, 411–23.

**4631.** GRIFFIN, PATSY. "'Twas no *religious house* till now': Marvell's *Upon Appleton House*. SELit (28:1) 1988, 61–76.

**4632.** HABER, JUDITH DEBORAH.    Pastoral and the poetics of self-contradiction. *See* **3313.**

**4633.** JAECKLE, DANIEL P.    Marvell's dialogics of history: *Upon Appleton House*, XI–XXXV. JDJ (6:2) 1987, 261–73.

**4634.** SIMONS, JOHN.    Marvell's tulips. NQ (36:4) 434. (*Upon Appleton House*.)

**4635.** STEWART, JAMES C. Q.    Two images in Marvell. ELN (26:4) 12–14.

**4636.** STOCKER, MARGARITA.    Apocalyptic Marvell: the Second Coming in seventeenth-century poetry. (Bibl. 1986, 5638.) Rev. by Gordon Campbell in YES (19) 320–1; by Jonathan F. S. Post in RQ (42:1) 149–51.

**4637.** VICKERS, BRIAN.    Machiavelli and Marvell's *Horatian Ode*. NQ (36:1) 32–8.

**4638.** WILCHER, ROBERT (ed.).    Andrew Marvell: selected poetry and prose. (Bibl. 1988, 5642.) Rev. by Marie L. K. Lally in SCN (47:1/2) 13.

### Philip Massinger

**4639.** CHAMPION, LARRY S.    'Disaster with my so many joys': structure and perspective in Massinger and Dekker's *The Virgin Martyr*. *See* **4383.**

**4640.** HOWARD, DOUGLAS (ed.).    Philip Massinger: a critical reassessment. (Bibl. 1985, 4871.) Rev. by Martin Garrett in RES (38:149) 1987, 72–3.

**4641.** HOWARD-HILL, T. H.    Buc and the censorship of *Sir John Van Olden Barnavelt* in 1619. *See* **144.**

**4642.** PRAGER, CAROLYN.    The problem of slavery in *The Custom of the Country*. *See* **4474.**

**4643.** TRICOMI, ALBERT H.    *A New Way to Pay Old Debts* and the country-house poetic tradition. MedRen (3) 1986, 177–87.

### Cotton Mather

**4644.** CANUP, JOHN.    Cotton Mather and 'Criolian degeneracy'. EAL (24:1) 20–34.

### Increase Mather

**4645.** HALL, MICHAEL G.    The last American Puritan: the life of Increase Mather, 1639–1723. Middletown, CT: Wesleyan UP, 1988. pp. xv, 438. Rev. by Ross Miller in NEQ (62:1) 116–24; by Ronald S. Bosco in EAL (24:3) 257–9.

### Middleton and Rowley

**4646.** HOLDSWORTH, R. V.    Notes on *The Changeling*. NQ (36:3) 344–6.

**4647.** RANDALL, DALE B. J.    Some new perspectives on the Spanish setting of *The Changeling* and its source. MedRen (3) 1986, 189–216.

### Thomas Middleton

**4648.** BERGERON, DAVID M.    Art within *The Second Maiden's Tragedy*. *See* **4128.**

**4648a.** HOWARD-HILL, T. H. More on 'William Prynne and the Allegory of Middleton's *Game at Chess*'. NQ (36:3) 349–51. (*Refers to* bibl. 1983, 5371.)

**4649.** LOUGHREY, BRYAN; TAYLOR, NEIL (eds). Five plays. Harmondsworth: Penguin, 1988 pp. xxxiv, 421. (Penguin classics.) (*A Trick to Catch The Old One*; *The Revenger's Tragedy*; *A Chaste Maid in Cheapside*; *Women Beware Women*; *The Changeling* (with William Rowley).) Rev. by T. W. Craik in DUJ (81:1) 1988, 158–60.

**4650.** McKINLEY, M. The morality of games in some works by Thomas Middleton. Unpub. M.Litt. diss., Univ. of Oxford, 1988. [Abstr. in IT (39:2) 485.]

**4651.** MUIR, NORMAN R. Middle-class heroism and the cardinal virtue fortitude in Thomas Dekker's *Honest Whore* plays. See **4387.**

**4652.** RASMUSSEN, ERIC. Shakespeare's hand in *The Second Maiden's Tragedy*. See **3631.**

**4653.** SLIGHTS, WILLIAM W. E. Unfashioning the man of mode: a comic countergenre in Marston, Jonson, and Middleton. See **4595.**

**4654.** THOMSON, LESLIE. 'On y$^e$ walls': the staging of *Hengist, King of Kent*, v.ii. MedRen (3) 1986, 165–76.

**4655.** VAN DEN BROEK, A. G. Take the number seven in Cheapside. SELit (28:2) 1988, 319–30.

**4656.** WHITSON, CAROLINE BAGBY. Social contract theory in the plays of Thomas Middleton. Unpub. doct. diss., Univ. of Arkansas, 1987. [Abstr. in DA (49) 1812–13A.]

## John Milton

**4657.** BAUMAN, MICHAEL. Milton's Arianism. Frankfurt; Berne; New York: Lang, 1987. pp. xvi, 378. (Sprache und Literatur: Regensburger Arbeiten zur Anglistik und Amerikanistik, 26.) Rev. by Thomas N. Corns in NQ (36:2) 240–1.

**4658.** BENNETT, JOAN S. Reviving liberty: radical Christian humanism in Milton's great poems. Cambridge, MA; London: Harvard UP. pp. xiv, 233. Rev. by James H. Sims in SCN (47:3/4) 33–4; by Neil Forsyth in TLS, 22 Sept., 1036.

**4659.** BERKELEY, DAVID SHELLEY. Michael's new commandment 'with promise': *Paradise Lost* XI. 530–46. PLL (24:2) 1988, 134–41.

**4660.** BLESSINGTON, FRANCIS C. *Paradise Lost*: ideal and tragic epic. Boston, MA: G. K. Hall, 1988. pp. xiv, 144. (Twayne's master studies, 12.) Rev. by Michael A. Mikolajczak in SCN (47:1/2) 7–8.

**4661.** BOOCKER, JOSEPH DAVID. *Paradise Lost* as Reformation history. Unpub. doct. diss., Univ. of Nebraska–Lincoln, 1988. [Abstr. in DA (50) 144A.]

**4662.** BOUCHARD, GARY MICHAEL. From campus to *campus*: the relationship of the university world to the literary pastoral worlds of Edmund Spenser, Phineas Fletcher, and John Milton. See **3350.**

**4663.** BRADLEY, J. G. R. Critical and creative responses to Milton's *Lycidas*, 1740–1860. Unpub. doct. diss., Univ. of Manchester. [Abstr. in IT (39:4) 1627.]

**4664.** BROWN, CEDRIC C. John Milton's aristocratic entertainments.

(Bibl. 1988, 3487.) Rev. by J. Martin Evans in RES (38:152) 1987, 562–3.

**4665.** —— The *komos* in Milton. JDJ (5:1/2) 1986, 235–66.

**4666.** BUTLER, MARTIN.    A provincial masque of *Comus*, 1636. *See* **4137.**

**4667.** CAMÉ, JEAN-FRANÇOIS.    *Lycidas*: étude mythique. BSEAA (29) 57–69.

**4668.** —— Myth and poetry in XVIIth century England. *See* **4072.**

**4669.** CARTER, F. M. M.    The protean image: a study of dance as an image in English Renaissance literature with special reference to Spenser and Milton. *See* **3351.**

**4670.** CERNY, LOTHAR.    Blake's Satan and the idea of limit. *In* (pp. 325–37) **5.**

**4671.** CHOI, JUNG-WOON.    Milton eui gangyeolhan seosasi e natanan Satan gwa Jesus eui image. (The images of Satan and Jesus in Milton's brief epic.) INH (14) 1987, 197–220. (*Paradise Regained.*)

**4672.** COIRO, ANN BAYNES.    'To repair the ruins of our first parents': *Of Education* and fallen Adam. SELit (28:1) 1988, 133–47.

**4673.** CONNORS, S. G.    Living within the light of high endeavours: Wordsworth's poetry of 1800–1805 and the influence of John Milton. Unpub. doct. diss., Univ. of Wales, 1986. [Abstr. in IT (39:1) 32.]

**4674.** CRUMP, GALBRAITH M. (ed.).    Approaches to teaching Milton's *Paradise Lost*. New York: Modern Language Assn of America, 1986. pp. x, 201. (Approaches to teaching masterpieces of world literature.) Rev. by Lois Potter in MLR (84:1) 128.

**4675.** CUNNINGHAM, MERRILEE.    The epic narrator in Milton's *Paradise Regained*. RenR (13:2) 215–32.

**4676.** DANIEL, CLAY LEE.    Some aspects of death in Milton's poetry. Unpub. doct. diss., Texas A&M Univ., 1988. [Abstr. in DA (49) 3367A.]

**4677.** DAVIES, J. M. Q.    'Attempting to be no more than man we become less': Blake's *Comus* designs and the two faces of Milton's Puritanism. DUJ (81:2) 197–219.

**4678.** DAVIES, STEVIE; HUNTER, WILLIAM B.    Milton's Urania: 'the meaning, not the name I call'. SELit (28:1) 1988, 95–111.

**4679.** DE VINCK, JOSÉ JOHN.    Occidentalism: the classic and the values of culture. Unpub. doct. diss., State Univ. of New York at Binghamton. [Abstr. in DA (49) 3020A.]

**4680.** DIBENEDETTO, VINCENT PAUL.    Education, poetic restoration, and the narrator of *Paradise Lost*. Unpub. doct. diss., Univ. of Toronto, 1988. [Abstr. in DA (49) 2666A.]

**4681.** DILLON, STEVEN C.    Tragic idyll: studies in the poetics of Virgil, Milton, and Tennyson. Unpub. doct. diss., Yale Univ., 1988. [Abstr. in DA (50) 1309–10A.]

**4682.** DOUKE, KOUICHIRO.    Milton to kindai. (Milton and the modern.) Tokyo: Kenkyusha. pp. 442, x.

**4683.** E JEON, JO-YOUNG.    John Steinbeck eui *In Dubious Battle* gwa John Milton eui *Paradise Lost* eui sinwha wa yeongwanhayeo. (The relationship between John Steinbeck's *In Dubious Battle* and John Milton's mythology in *Paradise Lost.*) JELLC (30) 129–51.

**4684.** ENTZMINGER, ROBERT L.   Divine word: Milton and the redemption of language. (Bibl. 1987, 5267.) Rev. by G. R. Evans in RES (38:150) 1987, 292.

**4685.** ETCHELLS, RUTH (sel. and introd.).   A selection of poems by John Milton, 1608–1674, exploring his pilgrimage of faith. Tring: Lion, 1988. pp. 48. (Poets and prophets.)

**4686.** FAWCETT, MARY LAUGHLIN.   'Such noise as I can make': chastity and speech in *Othello* and *Comus. See* **3952.**

**4687.** FEATHERINGILL, RON CHARLES.   The tension between divine will and human free will in Milton and the classical epic tradition. Unpub. doct. diss., Univ. of California, Riverside, 1988. [Abstr. in DA (49) 1793A.]

**4688.** FERRY, ANNE.   Milton's creation of Eve.   SELit (28:1) 1988, 113–32.

**4689.** FISH, STANLEY.   Spectacle and evidence in *Samson Agonistes.* CI (15:3) 556–86.

**4690.** FRANSON, J. KARL.   The Diodatis in Chester. NQ (36:4) 435.

**4691.** GRAY, DAVID.   John 10:18 and the typology of *Samson Agonistes.* ELN (27:2) 49–52.

**4692.** GREGORY, E. R.   Milton's use of *'musae mansuetiores'* in his first prolusion. MQ (22:2) 1988, 66–8.

**4693.** GROSE, CHRISTOPHER.   Milton and the sense of tradition. New Haven, CT: Yale UP, 1988. pp. 240. Rev. by Robert L. Entzminger in RQ (42:4) 891–3; by Keith W. F. Stavely in SCN (47:3/4) 36–7; by Neil Forsyth in TLS, 22 Sept., 1036.

**4694.** GROSSMAN, MARSHALL.   'Authors to themselves': Milton and the revelation of history. Cambridge: CUP, 1987. pp. xii, 243. Rev. by Thomas N. Corns in NQ (36:3) 395.

**4695.** GUILLORY, JOHN.   Dalila's house: *Samson Agonistes* and the sexual division of labor. *In* (pp. 106–22) **54.**

**4696.** HALPERN, RICHARD.   Puritanism and Maenadism in *A Mask.* *In* (pp. 88–105) **54.**

**4697.** HASAN, NAWAL M.   'Daughter of God and man': a reconsideration of Milton's Eve in *Paradise Lost.* Al-Mustansiriya Literary Review (Al-Mustansiriya Univ., Baghdad) (8) 1984, 123–44.

**4698.** HONEYGOSKY, STEPHEN RAYMOND.   Milton's house of God: church, scripture, sacrament. Unpub. doct. diss., Univ. of Wisconsin–Madison, 1988. [Abstr. in DA (49) 2667A.]

**4699.** HOWISON, PATRICIA M.   Memory and will: selective amnesia in *Paradise Lost.* UTQ (56:4) 1987, 523–39.

**4700.** HUNTER, WILLIAM B., JR.   Milton's *Comus*: family piece. (Bibl. 1986, 5731.) Rev. by Philip B. Rollinson in MedRen (2) 1985, 330–1.

**4701.** KEENER, FREDERICK M.   Pope, Dryden, Milton, and the poets' secret. *See* **4454.**

**4702.** KELLEY, MAURICE.   On the state of Milton's *De Doctrina Christiana.* ELN (27:2) 43–8.

**4703.** KENDRICK, CHRISTOPHER.   Milton: a study in ideology and form. (Bibl. 1988, 3505.) Rev. by Douglas Chambers in RES (39:153) 1988, 108–9; by Gordon Campbell in MLR (84:1) 127.

**4704.** KNOESPEL, KENNETH J.   Milton and the hermeneutics of time: seventeenth-century chronologies and the science of history. SLI (22:1) 17–35.

**4705.** LARGENT, REGINA M.   A multilevel celebration: Milton's Morning Hymn. MQ (22:2) 1988, 63–6. (*Paradise Lost*, Book 5.)

**4706.** LEVINE, JOSEPH M.   Bentley's Milton: philology and criticism in eighteenth-century England. JHI (50:4) 549–68.

**4707.** LIEB, MICHAEL.   The sinews of Ulysses: form and convention in Milton's works. Pittsburgh, PA: Duquesne UP. pp. 174. (Duquesne studies: Language and literature, 9.) Rev. by John Mulryan in Cithara (29:1) 74–5.

**4708.** LINDEN, STANTON J.   The 'Seminarie of all sects and their dissentions': Thomas Vaughan and Milton's Limbo of Vanity. PLL (25:4) 364–75.

**4709.** LOEWENSTEIN, DAVID A.   *Areopagitica* and the dynamics of history. SELit (28:1) 1988, 77–93.

**4710.** MACCALLUM, HUGH.   Milton and the sons of God: the divine image in Milton's epic poetry. (Bibl. 1988, 3513.) Rev. by G. R. Evans in RES (39:154) 1988, 294–5.

**4711.** MCCARTY, WILLARD.   The catabatic structure of Satan's quest. UTQ (56:2) 1986/87, 283–307.

**4712.** MARTIN, R. W. F.   Milton's hell-hounds. NQ (36:1) 31–2.

**4713.** MARTINDALE, CHARLES.   John Milton and the transformation of ancient epic. (Bibl. 1988, 3517.) Rev. by George deForest Lord in MLR (84:4) 927–8; by J. Martin Evans in RES (39:156) 1988, 552–3.

**4714.** MATHIS, GILLES.   Analyse stylistique du *Paradis perdu* de John Milton: l'univers poétique: echos et correspondances. *See* **1412.**

**4715.** —— Architectures sonores et continuité mélodique dans *L'Allegro*, *Il Penseroso*, *Comus* et *Lycidas*. BSEAA (29) 95–132.

**4716.** MILLER, LEO.   A German critique of Milton's *Areopagitica* in 1647. NQ (36:1) 29–30.

**4717.** —— John Milton and the Oldenburg Safeguard: new light on Milton and his friends in the Commonwealth from the diaries and letters of Hermann Mylius, agonist in the early history of modern diplomacy. (Bibl. 1988, 3522.) Rev. by Amos C. Miller in AHR (94:2) 437; by J. Max Patrick in SCN (47:1/2) 6; by John Morrill in RES (38:151) 1987, 391–2.

**4718.** —— The Milton/Cromwell letter to Transylvania. NQ (36:4) 435–42.

**4719.** MILLER, TIMOTHY C.   Milton's religion of the spirit and 'the state of the Church' in Book XII of *Paradise Lost*. Restoration (13:1) 7–16.

**4720.** MUSTAZZA, LEONARD.   'Such prompt eloquence': language as agency and character in Milton's epics. Lewisburg, PA: Bucknell UP; London; Toronto: Assoc. UPs, 1988. pp. 173. Rev. by Rachel Trubowitz in SCN (47:3/4) 35–6.

**4721.** MYERS, WILLIAM. Milton and free will: an essay in criticism and philosophy. (Bibl. 1988, 3525.) Rev. by G. R. Evans in RES (39:156) 1988, 604–5; by Thomas Healy in MLR (84:3) 717.

**4722.** NEWMAN, JOHN KEVIN. The English tradition: Chaucer and Milton. *See* **2858.**

**4723.** NIELSEN, ROSEMARY M.; SOLOMON, ROBERT H. The faith of lover and reader in *Odes* 1.5: Horace and Milton. RBPH (67:1) 75–92.

**4724.** NYQUIST, MARY; FERGUSON, MARGARET W. (eds). Remembering Milton: essays on the texts and traditions. (Bibl. 1987, 5321.) Rev. by Thomas N. Corns in NQ (36:3) 394–5.

**4725.** OGDEN, JAMES. Horace and Milton in *Mac Flecknoe*. *See* **4455.**

**4726.** OLEĬNIK, V. T. Lermontov i Mil'ton: *Demon* i *Poteri︠a︡nnyĭ raĭ.* (Lermontov and Milton: *The Demon* and *Paradise Lost.*) IAN (T.48:4) 299–315.

**4727.** PARKER, CATHERINE A. INNES. The location of the Pinnacle of the Temple: a note on *Paradise Regained.* NQ (36:4) 442–5.

**4728.** PARSONS, MICHAEL. Beauté et laideur dans *Paradise Lost* de John Milton. *In* (pp. 131–48) **10.**

**4729.** PATRIDES, C. A. An annotated critical bibliography of John Milton. (Bibl. 1987, 5323.) Rev. by Thomas Healy in MLR (84:3) 717–18; by Michael Fixler in RES (39:156) 1988, 604.

**4730.** PEDLEY, PHILIP EDWARD. Hierarchy in Milton: a biography of an idea. Unpub. doct. diss., Univ. of Pennsylvania, 1988. [Abstr. in DA (49) 2672A.]

**4731.** PING, TANG SOO. *Frankenstein, Paradise Lost,* and 'the majesty of goodness'. CLit (16:3) 255–60.

**4732.** PINKA, PATRICIA G. Timely timelessness in two Nativity poems. *In* (pp. 162–72) **11.**

**4733.** PIRONON, JEAN. Retour à *Lycidas.* BSEAA (29) 71–94.

**4734.** REVARD, STELLA P. The seventeenth-century religious ode and its classical models. *In* (pp. 173–91) **11.**

**4735.** ROE, NICHOLAS. Wordsworth, Milton, and the politics of poetic influence. YES (19) 112–26.

**4736.** ROSEN, ALAN. The monomachia sequence in *Paradise Lost.* SEL (65:2) 159–74.

**4737.** RUMRICH, JOHN PETER. Metamorphosis in *Paradise Lost.* Viator (20) 311–25.

**4738.** SCHAAR, C. Satan as deconstructor. EngS (70:6) 504–6.

**4739.** SCHWARTZ, REGINA M. Remembering and repeating: Biblical Creation in *Paradise Lost.* Cambridge: CUP. pp. ix, 144. Rev. by Neil Forsyth in TLS, 22 Sept., 1036.

**4740.** SELLARS, R. Bloom, Freud, and Milton: misprision, psychoanalysis, and the question of the text. Unpub. doct. diss., Univ. of Oxford. [Abstr. in IT (39:3) 1101.]

**4741.** SHERBO, ARTHUR. Two notes on Gray's poems. NQ (36:1) 62.

**4742.** SHIMAMURA, NOBUO. Eikoku jojoushi no shikisai to hyougen: *Yousei Jouou* to *Rakuen Soushitu. See* **3409.**

**4743.** STAVELY, KEITH W. F. Puritan legacies: *Paradise Lost* and

the New England tradition, 1630–1890. (Bibl. 1988, 3540.) Rev. by
James G. Turner in RQ (42:3) 593–7; by Mason I. Lowance, Jr, in AHR
(94:3) 840–1.

**4744.** STERNE, LAURENCE; KOLLMEIER, HAROLD H. (eds). A concordance to the English prose of John Milton. Binghamton, NY: Center for
Medieval and Renaissance Studies, 1985. pp. xxii, 1492. (Medieval &
Renaissance texts & studies, 35.) Rev. by Michael Fixler in RES
(38:152) 1987, 594.

**4745.** SWAIM, KATHLEEN M. Before and after the Fall: contrasting
modes in *Paradise Lost*. (Bibl. 1987, 5354.) Rev. by Jacqueline T. Miller
in RQ (42:2) 365–7; by Frederick M. Keener in YES (19) 321–2; by
Irène Simon in RES (39:154) 1988, 295–7.

**4746.** TRAVERS, MICHAEL ERNEST. The devotional experience in the
poetry of John Milton. Lewiston, NY: Mellen, 1988. pp. 163. (Studies in
art and religious interpretation, 10.) (Cf. bibl. 1986, 5812.) Rev. by
Rachel Trubowitz in SCN (47:1/2) 7; by George Musacchio in ChrisL
(38:4) 86–7.

**4747.** WALKER, JULIA M. (ed.). Milton and the idea of woman.
Urbana: Illinois UP, 1988. pp. ix, 262. Rev. by Raymond-Jean Frontain
in ChrisL (39:1) 96–8.

**4748.** WATT, R. J. C. The lacuna in Milton's *On the Death of a Fair
Infant*. NQ (36:1) 30–1.

**4749.** WITTREICH, JOSEPH. Feminist Milton. (Bibl. 1988, 3556.) Rev.
by Diane McColley in RQ (42:3) 589–93.

**4750.** —— Interpreting *Samson Agonistes*. (Bibl. 1988, 3557.) Rev. by
J. Martin Evans in RES (39:153) 1988, 109–11; by Janel Mueller in MP
(86:3) 300–4; by Thomas Healy in MLR (84:1) 128–9.

## John Oldham

**4751.** BROOKS, HAROLD F. (ed.); SELDEN, RAMAN (asst ed.). The
poems of John Oldham. (Bibl. 1987, 5371.) Rev. by Charles Gullans in
SCN (47:3/4) 42–4; by Claude Rawson in LRB (11:1) 19–21; by Ian
Jack in NQ (36:1) 110; by D. L. Farley-Hills in RES (39:155) 1988,
445–6.

**4752.** CORSE, TAYLOR. *Festina lente*: Dryden and Oldham. *See* **4444.**

**4753.** HAMMOND, PAUL. An echo of Dryden in Oldham's *The
Thirteenth Satyr of Juvenal, Imitated. See* **4449.**

**4754.** —— John Oldham and the renewal of classical culture. (Bibl.
1988, 3564.) Rev. by Margarita Stocker in BJECS (11) 1988, 91.

## 'Orinda' (Katherine Philips)

**4755.** THOMAS, PATRICK. Katherine Philips ('Orinda'). Cardiff:
Wales UP for the Welsh Arts Council, 1988. pp. 73. (Writers of Wales.)

## Thomas Otway

**4756.** ATKINS, JANET E. (introd.). The dramatic censor: remarks
upon the tragedy of *Venice Preserv'd*. Los Angeles, CA: Clark Memorial
Library, 1985. pp. xii, 84. (Augustan Reprint Soc. pubs, 233–4.) Rev. by
G. J. Clingham in BJECS (10) 1987, 235–6.

**4757.** BAER, KERSTIN. Friendship in Otawian fashion. *In* (pp.
11–14) **34.**

**4758.** CONWAY, DANIEL J.   Erotic arguments: rhetoric and sexuality in seventeenth-century English stage adaptations of Plutarch. *See* **3505.**

**4759.** MURRAY, BARBARA A.   The butt of Otway's political moral in *The History and Fall of Caius Marius* (1680). NQ (36:1) 48–50.

### Thomas Palmer

**4760.** MANNING, JOHN.   Antedatings, postdatings, and additions to *OED* from Thomas Palmer's *Two Hundred Poosees*. *See* **1023.**

**4761.** Entry cancelled.

**4762.** MANNING, JOHN.   Thomas Palmer and proverbs: antedatings and additions to Tilley from *Two Hundred Poosees*. *See* **1024.**

### Henry Peacham the Younger

**4763.** TUNG, MASON.   From personifications to emblems: a study of Peacham's use of Ripa's *Iconologia* in *Minerva Britanna*. *In* (pp. 109–50) **21.**

### William Penn

**4764.** DUNN, MARY MAPLES, *et al.* (eds).   The papers of William Penn: vol. 3, 1685–1700; vol. 4, 1702–1718. Philadelphia: Pennsylvania UP, 1986; 1987. pp. xix, 794; xvii, 823. Rev. by R. Melvin Keiser in QH (78:1) 50–2.

### Samuel Pepys

**4765.** HOEFNAGEL, DICK.   Charles Dickens's annotated copy of Pepys's *Memoirs*. Dick (85:3) 163–6.

**4766.** PODGORKSIĬ, A. V.   Sĭumĭuel Pepis i ego *Dnevnik*. (Samuel Pepys and his *Diary*.) NDFN (1989:3) 73–7.

### William Prynne

**4767.** HOWARD-HILL, T. H.   More on 'William Prynne and the Allegory of Middleton's *Game at Chess*'. *See* **4648.**

### Francis Quarles

**4768.** HORDEN, JOHN.   *The Christian Pilgrim*, 1652, and Francis Quarles's *Emblemes and Hieroglyphikes*, 1643. Emblematica (New York) (4:1) 63–90.

### John Wilmot, Earl of Rochester

**4769.** LOVE, HAROLD.   Scribal texts and literary communities: the Rochester circle and Osborn b.105. *See* **153.**

**4770.** ROGAL, SAMUEL J.   The control of honest expression: offensive language in Rochester's poetry. BSUF (30:1) 33–8.

**4771.** VIETH, DAVID M. (ed.).   John Wilmot, Earl of Rochester: critical essays. (Bibl. 1988, 3587.) Rev. by J. V. Guerinot in SCN (47:3/4) 44.

### Mary Rowlandson

**4772.** DEROUNIAN, KATHRYN ZABELLE.   A note on Mary (White) Rowlandson's English origins. EAL (24:1) 70–2.

### William Rowley

**4773.** DAWSON, ANTHONY B.   Witchcraft/bigamy: cultural conflict in *The Witch of Edmonton*. *See* **4386.**

**4773a.** DOMINIK, MARK.   Shakespeare and *The Birth of Merlin*. *See* **3517.**

**4774.** LOUGHREY, BRYAN; TAYLOR, NEIL (eds).   Five plays. *See* **4649.**

### Thomas Shadwell

**4775.** MULCAHY, ELIZABETH.   God's plenty: the drama of Thomas

Shadwell. Unpub. doct. diss., Univ. of Miami, 1988. [Abstr. in DA (50) 692A.]

**4776.** SLAGLE, JUDITH B. 'A great rabble of people': the ribbon-weavers in Thomas Shadwell's *The Virtuoso*. NQ (36:3) 351–4.

**4776a.** TASCH, PETER A. *The Beggar's Opera* and *The Libertine*. NQ (36:1) 52.

## Thomas Shepard

**4777.** CAPPELLO, MARY. The authority of self-definition in Thomas Shepard's *Autobiography* and *Journal*. EAL (24:1) 35–51.

**4778.** SHAW, NANCY JOY. Speaking for the spirit: Cotton, Shepard, Edwards, Emerson. *See* **4367.**

**4779.** WERGE, THOMAS. Thomas Shepard. Boston, MA: G. K. Hall, 1987. pp. 129. (Twayne's US authors, 519.) Rev. by Michael McGiffert in EAL (23:2) 1988, 227–9.

## James Shirley

**4780.** BURNER, SANDRA A. James Shirley: a study of literary coteries and patronage in seventeenth-century England. Lanham, MD: London: UP of America, 1988. pp. xiv, 234.

**4781.** HUEBERT, RONALD (ed.). The lady of pleasure. Wolfeboro, NH: Manchester UP, 1986. (Bibl. 1988, 3596.) Rev. by Harold Love in MLR (84:4) 925–6; by William Zunder in EngS (70:1) 89–91; by Brian Gibbons in RES (39:156) 1988, 550–2.

**4782.** MEKEMSON, MARY J. A critical, modern-spelling edition of James Shirley's *The Opportunity*. *See* **351.**

**4783.** YEARLING, E. M. (ed.). The cardinal. Wolfeboro, NH: Manchester UP, 1986. (Bibl. 1988, 3599.) Rev. by Harold Love in MLR (84:4) 926; by William Zunder in EngS (70:1) 89–91; by Brian Gibbons in RES (39:156) 1988, 550–2.

## Captain John Smith

**4784.** KUPPERMAN, KAREN ORDAHL. (ed.). Captain John Smith: a select edition of his writings. (Bibl. 1988, 3600a, where scholar's second forename omitted.) Rev. by Carla Mulford in SoQ (27:4) 5–15.

## Thomas Southerne

**4785.** JORDAN, ROBERT; LOVE, HAROLD (eds). The works of Thomas Southerne. (Bibl. 1988, 3602.) Rev. by David Womersley in NQ (36:4) 511–13.

## John Spencer

**4786.** KENNEDY, RICHARD F. Allusions to Herbert in John Spencer and Edward Benlowes. *See* **4320.**

## Sir John Suckling

**4787.** RAYLOR, TIMOTHY. Samuel Hartlib's copy of *Upon Sir John Suckling's Hundred Horse*. *See* **369.**

## Joseph Swetnam

**4788.** VAN HEERTUM, FRANCISCA WILHELMINA. A critical edition of Joseph Swetnam's *The Araignment of Lewd, Idle, Froward and Unconstant Women* (1615). *See* **403.**

## Edward Taylor

**4789.** GRABO, NORMAN S. Edward Taylor. (Bibl. 1963, 2820.)

Boston, MA: G. K. Hall, 1988. pp. 176. (Revised ed.: first ed. 1961.) Rev. by J. Daniel Patterson in EAL (24:3) 264–6.

**4790.** ROWE, KAREN E. Saint and singer: Edward Taylor's typology and the poetics of meditation. (Bibl. 1988, 3604.) Rev. by Michael Schuldiner in HLQ (52:2) 295–303.

**4791.** WOOLSEY, STEPHEN ALFRED. 'My handy works, are Words, and Wordiness': Edward Taylor and the life of language. Unpub. doct. diss., Drew Univ., 1988. [Abstr. in DA (49) 1805A.]

### Jeremy Taylor

**4792.** McFADDEN, ROBERTA SUZANNE LePAGE. 'Exquisite equilibrium': an analysis of the prose style of Jeremy Taylor. Unpub. doct. diss., Fordham Univ., 1988. [Abstr. in DA (49) 1810A.]

**4793.** STREATFIELD, K. M. A critical edition of six occasional sermons by Jeremy Taylor (1613–1667). See **397**.

### John Taylor

**4794.** McCANN, WESLEY. An unrecorded Belfast edition of John Taylor's *Verbum Sempiternum*. See **446**.

### Sir William Temple

**4795.** DOWNIE, J. A. (introd.). Swift, Temple and the Du Cros affair: part 2, *A Letter from Monsieur de Cros* (1693) and *Reflections upon Two Pamphlets* (1693). (Bibl. 1987, 5416.) Rev. by Alain Morvan in EA (42:1) 102–3.

### Cyril Tourneur

**4796.** JONES, ROBERT C. Engagement with knavery: point of view in *Richard III, The Jew of Malta, Volpone*, and *The Revenger's Tragedy*. See **3262**.

**4796a.** LOUGHREY, BRYAN; TAYLOR, NEIL (eds). Five plays. See **4649**.

**4797.** STALLYBRASS, PETER. Reading the body: *The Revenger's Tragedy* and the Jacobean theater of consumption. See **4197**.

**4798.** TRUSSLER, SIMON (ed.). *The Revenger's Tragedy*: a programme/text. (Bibl. 1987, 5419.) Rev. by Richard G. Barlow in SCN (47:3/4) 48–9.

### Thomas Traherne

**4799.** BALAKIER, JAMES J. Thomas Traherne's Dobell series and the Baconian model of experience. EngS (70:3) 233–47.

**4800.** CHAMBERS, D. D. C. (ed.). Thomas Traherne: *Commentaries of Heaven*: the poems. Salzburg: Institut für Anglistik und Amerikanistik, Salzburg Univ. pp. xvii, 173. (Salzburg studies in English language and literature: Elizabethan and Renaissance studies, 92:22.)

**4801.** WĄCIOR, SŁAWOMIR. Adresat w poezji Thomasa Traherne'a: Szkic problematyki. (The fictive reader in Thomas Traherne's poetry: an outline of the problems.) *In* (pp. 74–84) **36**.

### Sir John Vanbrugh

**4802.** CORDNER, MICHAEL (ed.). Four comedies. Harmondsworth: Penguin. pp. 419. (Penguin classics.) (*The Relapse, The Provok'd Wife, The Confederacy, A Journey to London*.)

**4802a.**  JONES, CLYVE.  'To dispose in earnest, of a place I got in jest': eight new letters of Sir John Vanbrugh, 1722–1726. NQ (36:4) 461–9.

### Henry Vaughan

**4803.**  HILL, GEOFFREY.  A Pharisee to Pharisees: reflections on Vaughan's *The Night*. Eng (38) 97–113.

**4804.**  LINDEN, STANTON J.  Walter Charleton and Henry Vaughan's *Cock-Crowing*. See **4359**.

**4805.**  WALL, JOHN N.  Transformations of the word: Spenser, Herbert, Vaughan. See **3422**.

### Thomas Vaughan

**4806.**  LINDEN, STANTON J.  The 'Seminarie of all sects and their dissentions': Thomas Vaughan and Milton's Limbo of Vanity. See **4708**.

### John Webster

**4807.**  ABITEBOUL, MAURICE.  Ferdinand dans *The Duchess of Malfi* de John Webster ou la violence en procès. *In* (pp. 19–30) **60**.

**4808.**  BLISS, LEE.  The world's perspective: John Webster and the Jacobean drama. (Bibl. 1987, 5446.) Rev. by Charles R. Forker in MedRen (2) 1985, 296–9.

**4809.**  CALLAGHAN, DYMPNA.  Women and gender in Renaissance tragedy: a study of *King Lear, Othello, The Duchess of Malfi* and *The White Devil*. See **3873**.

**4810.**  CARNEGIE, DAVID.  Webster's *The Duchess of Malfi* on TV. SFN (12:1) 1987, 1–2.

**4811.**  CAVE, RICHARD A.  *The White Devil* and *The Duchess of Malfi*. Basingstoke: Macmillan, 1988. pp. 74. (Text and performance.) Rev. by Martin Wiggins in NQ (36:3) 386.

**4812.**  DESAI, RUPIN W.  'Spectacles fashioned with such perspective art': a phenomenological reading of Webster's *The White Devil*. MedRen (1) 1984, 187–98.

**4813.**  GRUNDY, JOAN.  *Two on a Tower* and *The Duchess of Malfi*. THJ (5:2) 55–60.

**4814.**  JONES, ANN ROSALIND.  Italians and others: Venice and the Irish in *Coryat's Crudities* and *The White Devil*. See **4364**.

**4815.**  KISTNER, A. L.; KISTNER, M. K.  *The White Devil* and John Webster. SN (61:1) 13–21.

**4816.**  PEARSON, JACQUELINE.  Tragedy and tragicomedy in the plays of John Webster. (Bibl. 1985, 5103.) Rev. by Charles R. Forker in MedRen (1) 1984, 275–8.

**4817.**  RANDALL, DALE B. J.  The rank and earthy background of certain physical symbols in *The Duchess of Malfi*. RenD (18) 1987, 171–203.

### John Weever

**4818.**  HONIGMANN, E. A. J.  John Weever: a biography of a literary associate of Shakespeare and Jonson, together with a photographic facsimile of Weever's *Epigrammes* (1599). (Bibl. 1988, 3629.) Rev. by H. R. Woudhuysen in Library (11:2) 160–3.

### Michael Wigglesworth

**4819.**  CHERNIAVSKY, EVA.  Night pollution and the floods of confession in Michael Wigglesworth's *Diary*. AQ (45:2) 15–33.

### John Wilkins
**4820.**  ALSOP, J. D.   John Wilkins and Winstanley. NQ (36:1) 46–8.

### Roger Williams
**4821.**  LaFANTASIE, GLENN W. (ed.); COCROFT, ROBERT S., *et al.* (asst eds).   The correspondence of Roger Williams: vol. 1, 1629–1653; vol. 2, 1654–1682. From an unpublished manuscript by BRADFORD F. SWAN. Hanover, NH; London: New England UP for the Rhode Island Historical Soc., 1988. pp. xciv, 867.

### Gerrard Winstanley
**4822.**  BRADSTOCK, A. W.   A Christian contribution to revolutionary praxis? An examination of the significance of religious belief for the political philosophies of Gerrard Winstanley and Camilo Torres. Unpub. doct. diss., Univ. of Kent. [Abstr. in IT (39:2) 461.]

### Lady Mary Wroth
**4823.**  SHAPIRO, MICHAEL.   Lady Mary Wroth describes a 'boy actress'. *See* **4194.**

**4824.**  SWIFT, CAROLYN RUTH.   Feminine self-definition in Lady Mary Wroth's *Love's Victorie* (*c.* 1621). ELR (19:2) 171–88.

### William Wycherley
**4825.**  SCHRICKE, GILBERT.   Monsieur de Paris, mauvais anglais et faux étranger: *The Gentleman Dancing-Master* de Wycherley. *In* (pp. 73–82) **26.**

# EIGHTEENTH CENTURY

## GENERAL

### General Literary Studies

**4826.** ADAMS, J. R. R.   A preliminary checklist of works containing Ulster dialect, 1700–1900. *See* **1456.**

**4827.** BARASH, CAROL LYNN.   Augustan women's myth-making: English women writers and the body of monarchy, 1660–1720. *See* **4067.**

**4828.** BERNINGHAUSEN, THOMAS FREDERICK.   American claimants: England in the American literary imagination from Benjamin Franklin to Henry James. Unpub. doct. diss., State Univ. of New York at Buffalo, 1988. [Abstr. in DA (49) 3722A.]

**4829.** BERTELSEN, LANCE.   The Nonsense Club: literature and popular culture, 1749–1764. (Bibl. 1988, 3638.) Rev. by Brean S. Hammond in RES (39:153) 1988, 116–17; by Francis Doherty in BJECS (11) 1988, 95–6; by Ann Jessie Van Sant in MLR (84:4) 931–2.

**4830.** BOUCÉ, PAUL-GABRIEL; HALIMI, SUZY (eds).   Le corps et l'âme en Grande-Bretagne au XVIIIe siècle. Colloques 1983–85 du Centre d'Études Anglaises du XVIIIe siècle. (Bibl. 1986, 14.) Rev. by Marialuisa Bignami in YES (19) 327.

**4831.** BRADLEY, J. G. R.   Critical and creative responses to Milton's *Lycidas*, 1740–1860. *See* **4663.**

**4832.** BREINIG, HELMBRECHT; HALFMANN, ULRICH (eds).   Die amerikanische Literatur bis zum Ende des 19. Jahrhunderts. *See* **4071.**

**4833.** BROMWICH, DAVID.   A choice of inheritance: self and community from Edmund Burke to Robert Frost. Cambridge, MA; London: Harvard UP. pp. xi, 317. Rev. in BkW, 6 Aug., 13.

**4834.** CANFIELD, J. DOUGLAS.   Female rebels and patriarchal paradigms in some neoclassical works. StudECC (18) 153–66.

**4835.** CARETTA, VINCENT.   The snarling muse: verbal and visual political satire from Pope to Churchill. (Bibl. 1988, 3647.) Rev. by Jenny Mezciems in RES (39:154) 1988, 300–1.

**4836.** CARTER, JENNIFER J.; PITTOCK, JOAN H. (eds).   Aberdeen and the Enlightenment: proceedings of a conference held at the University of Aberdeen. (Bibl. 1987, 1.) Rev. by F. W. Freeman in SLJ (supp. 30) 1–2.

**4837.** CHADEN, CARYN.   'To advantage dress'd': clothing and public identity from *A Tale of a Tub* to *Sartor Resartus*. Unpub. doct. diss., Univ. of Virginia. [Abstr. in DA (50) 1309A.]

**4838.** CHRISTIANSEN, RUPERT.   Romantic affinities: portraits from an age 1780–1830. (Bibl. 1988, 3649.) Rev. by Angela Leighton in TLS, 12 Feb. 1988, 168.

**4839.** COPLEY, STEPHEN (ed.).   Literature and the social order in eighteenth-century England. (Bibl. 1986, 5947.) Rev. by Nora Crow Jaffe in YES (19) 325–7.

**4840.** DAHL, ANTHONY GEORGE.   Literature of the Bahamas: the march towards national identity. Unpub. doct. diss., Univ. of Minnesota, 1988. [Abstr. in DA (49) 3016–17A.]

**4841.** DEANE, SEAMUS. The French Revolution and Enlightenment in England, 1789–1832. Cambridge, MA; London: Harvard UP, 1988. pp. xii, 212.

**4842.** DE PROSPO, R. C. The latest early American literature. *See* **4078.**

**4843.** DERINGER, LUDWIG. The Pacific Northwest in American and Canadian literature since 1776: the present state of scholarship. OreHQ (90:3) 305–27.

**4844.** DE VOOGD, PETER J. Aeneas to Camilla: or, a critical bibliography of recent eighteenth-century studies. DQR (19:1) 37–50.

**4845.** DIEDRICH, MARIA. Ausbach aus der Knechtschaft. Das amerikanische 'slave narrative' zwischen Unabhängigkeitserklärung und Bürgerkrieg. (Bibl. 1987, 5483.) Rev. by Friederike Hajek in AAA (14:1) 121–2.

**4846.** DLUGOS, JAMES STEVEN, JR. Seeing the past: conceptions of American literature in early national periodicals. *See* **564.**

**4847.** DWYER, JOHN. Virtuous discourse: sensibility and community in late eighteenth-century Scotland. (Bibl. 1988, 3654.) Rev. by Lars Hartveit in EngS (70:3) 276–7; by George Davie in AUR (53) 45–6.

**4848.** EDWARDS, MARY JANE. Early Canadian literature in English: a survey and a challenge. CE (51:5) 508–16.

**4849.** ENSSLEN, KLAUS. Einführung in die schwarzamerikanische Literatur. Stuttgart: Kohlhammer, 1982. pp. 256. (Sprache und Literatur, 117.) Rev. by Rolf Franzbecker in LJGG (26) 1985, 437–40.

**4850.** GINSBERG, ROBERT. Introduction to eighteenth-century philosophic writing. *In* (pp. 7–11) **49.**

**4851.** —— (ed.). The philosopher as writer: the eighteenth century. *See* **49.**

**4852.** HAGSTRUM, JEAN H. Eros and vision: the Restoration to Romanticism. *See* **4087.**

**4853.** HETHERINGTON, CAROL; PETERSSON, IRMTRAUD. Annual bibliography of studies in Australian literature: 1988. ALS (14:1) 78–103.

**4854.** HUME, ROBERT D. Recent studies in the Restoration and eighteenth century. *See* **4091.**

**4855.** HUNTER, J. PAUL. Canon of generations, generation of canons. *See* **4092.**

**4856.** JAMESON, FREDRIC. Nationalism, colonialism and literature: modernism and imperialism. Derry: Field Day, 1988. pp. 24. (Field Day pamphlets, 14.)

**4857.** JAMKHANDI, SUDHAKAR R. Australian literary publications in the C. Hartley Grattan Collection. *See* **236.**

**4858.** JORDANOVA, L. J. (ed.). Languages of nature: critical essays on science and literature. (Bibl. 1986, 5965.) Rev. by D. G. Charlton in BJECS (11) 1988, 107.

**4859.** KANIO, MITSUO. Yami, hishou, soshite seishin no naraku: igirisu koten shugi kara roman shugi e. (Darkness, flight and the pit of the soul: from English Classicism to Romanticism.) Tokyo: Eihousha. pp. vi, 438.

**4860.** KLANCHER, JON P.    The making of English reading audiences, 1790–1832. (Bibl. 1987, 5495.) Rev. by Janet Todd in BJECS (12) 224–5; by Paul Hamilton in NQ (36:3) 403–4; by Patricia Meyer Spacks in YES (19) 335–7.

**4861.** KNIGHT, CHARLES A.    The images of nations in eighteenth-century satire. ECS (22:4) 489–511.

**4862.** KROOK, ANNE KARIN.    The genesis of authority: scripture, satire, and interpretation in English literature, 1660–1760. See **4095.**

**4863.** LAWSON-PEEBLES, ROBERT.    Landscape and written expression in Revolutionary America: the world turned upside down. Cambridge; New York: CUP, 1988. pp. xii, 384. (Cambridge studies in American literature and culture.) Rev. by Donald A. Ringe in AL (61:2) 280–1; by Stephen Fender in LRB (11:2) 22–3; by Philip F. Gura in JAH (76:3) 919; by Cheryl Z. Oreovicz in SAF (17:2) 247–8.

**4864.** LEWIS, JAYNE ELIZABETH.    The voluble body: re-inventing the neoclassical fable. See **4099.**

**4865.** LORD, C. P.    Image and reality: the chapbook perspective on women in early modern Britain. See **445.**

**4866.** LUND, ROGER D.    Martinus Scriblerus and the search for the soul. PLL (25:2) 135–50.

**4867.** McCARTHY, FINBARR.    A rage for order: the ideological implications of form in early Southern writing. See **4101.**

**4868.** McGOWAN, IAN (ed.).    The Restoration and eighteenth century. See **4102.**

**4869.** MACKINNON, A. H.    The Augustan intellectual and the ignoble savage: Houyhnhym versus Hottentot. In (pp. 55–63) **23.**

**4870.** MARSHALL, IAN STUART.    Mountains to match the man: national identity and the mountain in American literature, beginnings to 1860. See **4104.**

**4871.** MEEHAN, MICHAEL.    Liberty and poetics in eighteenth-century England. (Bibl. 1987, 5500.) Rev. by Francis Doherty in RES (38:151) 1987, 393–4; by Nora Crow Jaffe in YES (19) 325–7.

**4872.** MULLAN, JOHN.    Sentiment and sociability: the language of feeling in the eighteenth century. (Bibl. 1988, 3672.) Rev. by Andrew Varney in NQ (36:4) 517–18.

**4873.** MÜLLENBROCK, HEINZ-JOACHIM.    The Middle Ages in eighteenth-century England: a guide to periodization? In (pp. 197–209) **38.**

**4874.** NOKES, DAVID.    Raillery and rage: a study of eighteenth-century satire. (Bibl. 1987, 5502.) Rev. by Frans De Bruyn in BJECS (12) 228–9.

**4875.** NUSSBAUM, FELICITY; BROWN, LAURA (eds).    The new eighteenth century: theory, politics, English literature. (Bibl. 1988, 3675.) Rev. by Serge Soupel in EA (42:3) 345–6.

**4876.** OKAJI, REI.    Igirisu roman shugi to keimou shisou. (English Romanticism and the Enlightenment.) Tokyo: Chuo UP. pp. xii, 314.

**4877.** PATEY, DOUGLAS LANE; KEEGAN, TIMOTHY (eds). Augustan studies: essays in honor of Irvin Ehrenpreis. (Bibl. 1987,8.) Rev. by Simon Varey in BJECS (11) 1988, 224–6.

**4878.** PAUL, RONALD. Romantics and reactionaries: some English responses to the French Revolution. MS (83:2) 114–18.

**4879.** PRICKETT, STEPHEN. England and the French Revolution. Basingstoke: Macmillan. pp. xi, 183. (Context and commentary.) Rev. by Michael Rossington in Eng (38) 261–7.

**4880.** RADCLIFFE, DAVID HILL. Meditations and literary history, 1600–1750: generic mixture and generic change. See **4110**.

**4881.** RAWSON, CLAUDE. Order from confusion sprung: studies in eighteenth-century literature from Swift to Cowper. (Bibl. 1988, 3683.) Rev. by Maximillian E. Novak in BJECS (12) 112–13; by Joan H. Pittock in Eng (36:155) 1987, 163–8.

**4882.** ROGERS, PAT. Eighteenth-century encounters: studies in literature and society in the age of Walpole. (Bibl. 1988, 3684.) Rev. by Howard Erskine-Hill in BJECS (10) 1987, 224–6; by Joan H. Pittock in Eng (36:155) 1987, 163–8.

**4883.** —— Literature and popular culture in eighteenth-century England. (Bibl. 1988, 3685.) Rev. by Howard Erskine-Hill in BJECS (10) 1987, 224–5; by Joan H. Pittock in Eng (36:155) 1987, 163–8.

**4884.** ROSS, HARRY J. Trapped by society, imprisoned in the wilderness: captivity in American literature, 1680–1860. See **4111**.

**4885.** ROUSSEAU, G. S.; PORTER, ROY (eds). Sexual underworlds of the Enlightenment. Manchester: Manchester UP, 1987. pp. x, 294. Rev. by Serge Soupel in EA (42:3) 346–7.

**4886.** SALE, ROGER. Closer to home: writers and places in England, 1780–1830. (Bibl. 1988, 3688.) Rev. by R. K. R. Thornton in BJECS (12) 223–4.

**4887.** SAMBROOK, JAMES. The eighteenth century: the intellectual and cultural context of English literature, 1700–1789. (Bibl. 1988, 3689.) Rev. by Thomas Woodman in BJECS (11) 1988, 91–2.

**4888.** SCANLAN, JOHN. A scholar's work: Edmond Malone and eighteenth-century literature. Unpub. doct. diss., Univ. of Michigan, 1988. [Abstr. in DA (49) 3735A.]

**4889.** SIDORENKO, L. V. Literaturno–ėsteticheskie spory ob ostroumii v Anglii pervoĭ chetverti XVIII veka. (Literary–aesthetic debates on wit in England in the first quarter of the eighteenth century.) VLU (1989:3) 33–42.

**4890.** SIMON, RICHARD KELLER. The labyrinth of the comic: theory and practice from Fielding to Freud. (Bibl. 1988, 3691.) Rev. by Mark Sokolyansky in MLR (84:3) 687–8; by Peter M. Briggs in StudN (20:1) 1988, 116–19.

**4891.** SIMPSON, KENNETH. The protean Scot: the crisis of identity in eighteenth-century Scottish literature. (Bibl. 1988, 3693.) Rev. in Edinburgh Review (83) 136–7; by J. Derrick McClure in TLS, 26 May, 579; by Susan Manning in Cencrastus (35) 41–2; by Robert Crawford in SLJ (supp. 31) 8–9.

**4892.** SISKIN, CLIFFORD.  The historicity of Romantic discourse. New York; Oxford: OUP, 1988. pp. viii, 225.

**4893.** STAFFORD, BARBARA MARIA.  Voyage into substance: art, science, nature and the illustrated travel account, 1760–1840. (Bibl. 1985, 5157.) Rev. by G. S. Rousseau in JMH (61:1) 128–30; by Sylvana Tomaselli in BJECS (10) 1987, 105–6.

**4894.** TIEKEN-BOON VAN OSTADE, INGRID.  Negative *do* in eighteenth-century English: the power of prestige. *In* (pp. 157–71) **47.**

**4895.** TODD, JANET.  Sensibility: an introduction. New York: Methuen, 1986. (Bibl. 1988, 3696.) Rev. by Coral Ann Howells in BJECS (11) 1988, 93; by Rebecca Ferguson in BJECS (12) 108–9.

**4896.** WARD, WILLIAM S.  A literary history of Kentucky. Knoxville: Tennessee UP, 1988. pp. xviii, 484. Rev. by William J. Sowder in AL (61:4) 728–9.

**4897.** WEISSINGER, THOMAS.  Current bibliography. BALF (23:2) 401–10; (23:4) 815–23.

**4898.** WELSH, KEITH EDWARD.  Edmund Burke, Friedrich Engels, and ideas of community in eighteenth- and nineteenth-century British fiction and poetry. Unpub. doct. diss., Indiana Univ., 1988. [Abstr. in DA (50) 957A.]

**4899.** WILDE, WILLIAM H.; HOOTON, JOY; ANDREWS, BARRY (eds). The Oxford companion to Australian literature. (Bibl. 1988, 3700.) Rev. by Basil Cottle in RES (39:154) 1988, 334–5.

**4900.** WILLIAMS, CAROLYN.  The changing face of change: fe/male in/constancy. BJECS (12) 13–28.

**4901.** ZIONKOWSKI, LINDA JOAN.  The value of words: writing and the eighteenth-century commerce in letters. *See* **474.**

## Drama and the Theatre

**4902.** BANK, ROSEMARIE.  Frontier melodrama. DQR (19:2) 136–45.

**4903.** BARNETT, DENE; MASSY-WESTROPP, JEANETTE.  The art of gesture: the practices of 18th-century acting. Heidelberg: Winter, 1987. pp. 503. (Reihe Siegen, 64.) Rev. by Volker Kapp in LJGG (31) 415–17.

**4904.** BILBY, MONIKA.  'Heroick vertue': changing ideas of feminine greatness in the heroic drama of the late seventeenth century. *See* **4131.**

**4905.** DE, ESHA NIYOGI.  'The purpose of playing': theater and ritual in the Revesby Folk Play, *Summer's Last Will and Testament*, and *Hamlet*. *See* **3288.**

**4906.** DERITTER, WILLIAM JONES, JR.  Authors and audiences: the development of eighteenth-century literary forms. Unpub. doct. diss., Univ. of Virginia, 1988. [Abstr. in DA (49) 3731A.]

**4907.** DOBSON, M.  Authorizing Shakespeare: adaptation and canonization, 1660–1769. *See* **3514.**

**4908.** HÉROU, JOSETTE.  Macaronis et kickshaw-mongers: représentation des italiens et des français sur la scène comique en Angleterre au 18e siècle. *In* (pp. 129–47) **26.**

**4909.** HUME, ROBERT D.  Henry Fielding and the London theatre,

1728–1737. (Bibl. 1988, 3704.) Rev. by Robert Folkenflik in TLS, 10 Mar., 253.

**4910.** PEARSON, JACQUELINE.   The prostituted muse: images of women and women dramatists, 1642–1737. *See* **4184.**

**4911.** WOODS, LEIGH.   Garrick claims the stage: acting as a social emblem in eighteenth-century England. (Bibl. 1985, 5193.) Rev. by Pat Rogers in BJECS (11) 1988, 96.

### Fiction

**4912.** BARKER, GERARD A.   Grandison's heirs: the paragon's progress in the late eighteenth-century English novel. (Bibl. 1986, 6039, where title incomplete.) Rev. by Terence Wright in BJECS (10) 1987, 106–7.

**4913.** BEASLEY, JERRY C.   Life's episodes: story and its form in the eighteenth century. *In* (pp. 21–45) **33.**

**4914.** —— Novels of the 1740s. (Bibl. 1986, 6041.) Rev. by Jenny Mezciems in RES (38:150) 1987, 254–5.

**4915.** BENDER, JOHN.   Imagining the penitentiary: fiction and the architecture of mind in eighteenth-century England. (Bibl. 1988, 3714.) Rev. by Timothy Erwin in JA (47:4) 385–7; by Lincoln B. Faller in MP (86:4) 430–3; by Alistair M. Duckworth in ELN (26:4) 80–5; by Alain Morvan in EA (42:3) 344–5.

**4916.** BERRY, JOHN CHARLES.   British serial production: author, audience, text. Unpub. doct. diss., Univ. of Rochester. [Abstr. in DA (50) 1660–1A.]

**4917.** CAHALAN, JAMES M.   The Irish novel: a critical history. (Bibl. 1988, 3716.) Rev. by Joseph McMinn in Fortnight (273) 23; by Patricia Craig in TLS, 26 May, 577.

**4918.** CASTLE, TERRY.   Masquerade and civilization: the.carnival-esque in eighteenth-century English culture and fiction. (Bibl. 1987, 5540.) Rev. by Robin Howells in BJECS (11) 1988, 93–4; by Sylvia Kasey Marks in StudN (20:1) 1988, 102–4.

**4919.** CLAYTON, JAY.   Romantic vision and the novel. (Bibl. 1988, 3717.) Rev. by Garrett Stewart in ELN (26:4) 85–8.

**4920.** CLOUGH, MONICA (ed.).   Hartly House, Calcutta: a novel of the days of Warren Hastings. London: Pluto. pp. xxiii, 302. (Writers abroad.)

**4921.** CZON, SEUNG-GUL.   Choki miguk heukin soseol yeongu. (A study of the early Afro-American novel.) AmeSt (12) 1–20.

**4922.** DAVID, GAIL PLIAM.   Diverse (in)versions: female heroics in the Renaissance pastoral romance and in women's pastoral fiction from Fanny Burney to George Eliot. *See* **3142.**

**4923.** DAVIDSON, CATHY N.   Revolution and the word: the rise of the novel in America. (Bibl. 1988, 3720.) Rev. by Cynthia S. Jordan in EAL (24:1) 73–5; by Bernard Rosenthal in StudN (20:4) 1988, 426–7.

**4924.** DAY, GEOFFREY.   From fiction to the novel. (Bibl. 1987, 5543.) Rev. by Margaret Kirkham in BJECS (12) 226–7.

**4925.** DAY, WILLIAM PATRICK.   In the circles of fear and desire: a study of gothic fantasy. (Bibl. 1987, 5544.) Rev. by Patricia Thomson in RES (38:150) 1987, 282–3.

**4926.** DeRitter, William Jones, Jr.    Authors and audiences: the development of eighteenth-century literary forms. *See* **4906.**

**4927.** Derry, S. G.    Tradition, imitation, and innovation: Jane Austen and the development of the novel, 1740–1818. Unpub. doct. diss., Univ. of Durham. [Abstr. in IT (39:3) 1111.]

**4928.** Fisher, Benjamin Franklin, iv.    The gothic's gothic: study aids to the tradition of the tale of terror. New York; London: Garland, 1988. pp. xix, 485. (Garland reference library of the humanities, 567.)

**4929.** Flint, Christopher.    Disrupted legacies: family structure and narrative form in the eighteenth-century novel. Unpub. doct. diss., Univ. of Pennsylvania, 1988. [Abstr. in DA (50) 145–6a.]

**4930.** Fraiman, Susan Diana.    Deforming novels: women writers and the Bildungsroman. Unpub. doct. diss., Columbia Univ., 1988. [Abstr. in DA (49) 3732a.] (Jane Austen, Fanny Burney, Charlotte Brontë, George Eliot.)

**4931.** Guthrie, D. F. N.    'A thousand wrecks!': rake's progresses in some eighteenth-century English novels. Unpub. doct. diss., Univ. of Oxford. [Abstr. in IT (39:3) 1108.]

**4932.** Hahn, H. George; Behm, Carl, iii.    The eighteenth-century British novel and its background: an annotated bibliography and guide to topics. (Bibl. 1986, 6054.) Rev. by Michael Irwin in RES (38:152) 1987, 566–7.

**4933.** Hedrick, Elizabeth Ann.    Authority divided: benevolence and form in the English sentimental novel. Unpub. doct. diss., Columbia Univ., 1986. [Abstr. in DA (49) 3732a.]

**4934.** Hill, Mary K.    Bath and the eighteenth-century novel. Bath: Bath UP. pp. 76.

**4935.** Jordan, Cynthia S.    Second stories: the politics of language, form, and gender in early American fictions. Chapel Hill; London: North Carolina UP. pp. xv, 242. (Gender and American culture.)

**4936.** Kelly, Gary.    English fiction of the Romantic period 1789–1830. London: Longman. pp. xii, 330. (Longman literature in English.)

**4937.** Konigsberg, Ira.    Narrative technique in the English novel: Defoe to Austen. (Bibl. 1987, 5554.) Rev. by Park Honan in BJECS (11) 1988, 100–1.

**4938.** Lemmens, Cheryl Ann.    Dark recesses of the soul: victimization in selected British fiction from *Clarissa* to *The Collector*. Unpub. doct. diss., Univ. of Toronto. [Abstr. in DA (50) 1666a.]

**4939.** Lovell, Terry.    Consuming fiction. (Bibl. 1987, 5557.) Rev. by Johan Svedjedal in Samlaren (110) 165–7.

**4940.** Lubot, Donna L.    Domestic relations: patterns of empowerment in women's fiction, 1720–1820. Unpub. doct. diss., Univ. of Delaware, 1988. [Abstr. in DA (49) 2231a.]

**4941.** McCormick, Marjorie Jean.    Mothers in the English novel: from stereotype to archetype. Unpub. doct. diss., Vanderbilt Univ. [Abstr. in DA (50) 1667a.]

**4942.** MISHRA, V. C.    The gothic sublime: theory, practice and interpretation. Unpub. doct. diss., Univ. of Oxford. [Abstr. in IT (39:3) 1112.]

**4943.** MOLYNEAUX, MARIBEL WALDO.    Women and work: on the margins of the marketplace. Unpub. doct. diss., Univ. of Pennsylvania, 1988. [Abstr. in DA (49) 2670–1A.]

**4944.** NAPIER, ELIZABETH R.    The failure of gothic: problems of disjunction in an eighteenth-century literary form. (Bibl. 1988, 3731.) Rev. by David Worrall in BJECS (12) 107–8; by Judith Wilt in MLR (84:3) 720–1.

**4945.** NOWICKI, WOJCIECH.    Uwagi o adresacie przedmów osiemnastowiecznej powieści angielskiej. (Notes on the fictive reader of prefaces in English eighteenth-century novels.) In (pp. 85–93) **36.**

**4946.** PIGEON, RENÉE MARIE.    Prose fiction adaptations of Sidney's *Arcadia. See* **3323.**

**4947.** PROBYN, CLIVE T.    English fiction of the eighteenth century, 1700–1789. (Bibl. 1987, 5570.) Rev. by Alain Morvan in EA (42:3) 343; by James McLaverty in NQ (36:1) 111.

**4948.** RABB, MELINDA ALLIKER.    Making and rethinking the canon: general introduction and the case of *Millenium Hall.* MLS (18:1) 1988, 3–16.

**4949.** RICHTER, DAVID H.    The reception of the gothic novel in the 1790s. In (pp. 117–37) **33.**

**4950.** SCHEUERMANN, MONA.    Social protest in the eighteenth-century English novel. (Bibl. 1986, 6069.) Rev. by Robert W. Uphaus in StudN (20:3) 1988, 356–9.

**4951.** SCHÖWERLING, RAINER.    Sir Walter Scott and the tradition of the historical novel before 1814 – with a checklist. In (pp. 227–62) **38.**

**4952.** SHROFF, HOMAI J.    The eighteenth-century novel: the idea of the gentleman. (Bibl. 1986, 6070.) Rev. by Claire Lamont in BJECS (11) 1988, 99.

**4953.** SMITH, SANDRA JO.    Father–daughter relationships in fiction and society (1790–1890). Unpub. doct. diss., Vanderbilt Univ. [Abstr. in DA (50) 1669A.]

**4954.** SOVOV'EVA, N. A.    Frantsuzskaia revoliutsiia i angliiskii iakobinskii roman. (The French Revolution and the English Jacobin novel.) VMU (1989:5) 42–51.

**4955.** SPACKS, PATRICIA MEYER.    Female resources: epistles, plot, and power. Persuasions (9) 1987, 88–98.

**4956.** TAVOR, EVE.    Scepticism, society and the eighteenth-century novel. (Bibl. 1988, 3737.) Rev. by Ken Edward Smith in BJECS (11) 1988, 99–100.

**4957.** TODD, JANET.    The sign of Angellica: women, writing and fiction, 1660–1800. *See* **4219.**

**4958.** TOMPKINS, JANE.    Sensational designs: the cultural work of American fiction, 1790–1860. (Bibl. 1988, 3741.) Rev. by Allan Lloyd Smith in JAStud (23:1) 95–9.

**4959.** Ty, Eleanor Rose. Romantic revolutionaries: women novelists of the 1790s. Unpub. doct. diss., McMaster Univ., 1987. [Abstr. in DA (49) 2235A.] (Mary Wollstonecraft, Mary Hays, Helen Maria Williams, Elizabeth Inchbald, Charlotte Smith.)

**4960.** Uphaus, Robert W. (ed.). The idea of the novel in the eighteenth century. *See* **33**.

**4961.** Varnado, S. L. Haunted presence: the numinous in gothic fiction. Tuscaloosa; London: Alabama UP, 1987. pp. 160. Rev. by David Ketterer in SFS (16:3) 397–9; by Paul W. Nisley in ChrisL (38:3) 84–5.

**4962.** Weinsheimer, Joel. Fiction and the force of example. *In* (pp. 1–19) **33**.

**4963.** Wolf, Werner. Schauerroman und Empfindsamkeit: zur Beziehung zwischen 'gothic novel' und empfindsamen Roman in England. Ang (107:1/2) 1–33.

### Literature for Children

**4964.** Avery, Gillian. The Puritans and their heirs. *In* (pp. 95–118) **14**.

**4965.** Briggs, Julia. Women writers and writing for children: from Sarah Fielding to E. Nesbit. *In* (pp. 221–50) **14**.

**4966.** Drotner, Kirsten. English children and their magazines, 1751–1945. *See* **565**.

**4967.** Summerfield, Geoffrey. Fantasy and reason: children's literature in the eighteenth century. (Bibl. 1988, 3749.) Rev. by Wendy R. Katz in DalR (67:1) 1987, 146–8; by Terry Jones in CLEd (20:2) 129–30.

### Poetry

**4968.** Barry, Kevin. Language, music, and the sign: a study in aesthetics, poetics and poetic practice from Collins to Coleridge. (Bibl. 1987, 5585.) Rev. by Nicholas Roe in NQ (36:1) 115–16.

**4969.** Beech, Martin. Meteor imagery in English poetry, *c.* 1600 to *c.* 1900. *See* **4222**.

**4970.** Cowell, Pattie. Colonial poets and the magazine trade, 1741–1775. *See* **561**.

**4971.** Duval, Gilles. Divination, morals and courtesy: some aspects of English chap-literature of the eighteenth century. *See* **1431**.

**4972.** Engler, Bernd. Die amerikanische Ode: Gattungsgeschichtliche Untersuchungen. Paderborn; Munich; Vienna; Zurich: Schöningh, 1985. pp. 235. (Beiträge zur englischen und amerikanischen Literatur, 4.) Rev. by Werner Oberholzner in LJGG (27) 1986, 370–3.

**4973.** Frushell, Richard C. Spenser and the eighteenth-century schools. *See* **3366**.

**4974.** Herbison, Ivan. Language, literature and cultural identity: and Ulster-Scots perspective. *See* **1464**.

**4975.** Jarvis, Frederick. Clouds of glory: poets of the Romantic movement. Braunton, Devonshire: Merlin, 1988. pp. 189.

**4976.** LAMB, B. J. K. 'What opening worlds': a study of cosmic themes and imagery in eighteenth-century verse. Unpub. doct. diss., Univ. of Manchester. [Abstr. in IT (39:2) 485–6.]

**4977.** LONSDALE, ROGER (ed.). Eighteenth-century women poets: an Oxford anthology. Oxford; New York: OUP. pp. xlvii, 555. Rev. by Terry Castle in TLS, 10 Nov., 1227–8; by Margaret Anne Doody in LRB (11:24) 3–5; by Naomi Lewis in Listener (122) 30 Nov., 30–1.

**4978.** —— The new Oxford book of eighteenth-century verse. (Bibl. 1986, 6102.) Rev. by Joan H. Pittock in BJECS (11) 1988, 102–4.

**4979.** MERRETT, ROBERT JAMES. England's Orpheus: praise of Handel in eighteenth-century poetry. Mosaic (20:2) 1987, 97–110.

**4980.** NAKAGAWA, TADASHI. Shishin tono tawamure: 18 seiki eishi koudoku. (Wandering with the muse: a reading of eighteenth-century English poetry.) Tokyo: Apollon. pp. 214.

**4981.** SCHULZ, MAX F. Paradise preserved: recreations of Eden in eighteenth- and nineteenth-century England. (Bibl. 1988, 3752.) Rev. by Chris Brooks in RES (38:150) 1987, 280–1.

**4982.** SHERBO, ARTHUR. Dean Thomas Gaisford's copy of Robert Dodsley's *Collection of Poems* (1758). See **264.**

**4983.** SMITH, DEBRA MORRIS. The business of the poet: poetic self-awareness from Sidney to Johnson. See **3155.**

**4984.** TERRY, R. G. Studies in English burlesque poetry, 1663–1785. See **4242.**

**4985.** TINKLER-VILLANI, V. Visions of Dante in English poetry: translations of the *Commedia* from Jonathan Richardson to William Blake. Amsterdam: Rodopi. pp. viii, 358. (Costerus, 72.) Rev. by Robert Wells in TLS, 1 Dec., 1339.

**4986.** WELCH, ROBERT. A history of verse translation from the Irish, 1789–1897. Gerrards Cross: Smythe, 1988. pp. xii, 200. Rev. by Peter Denman in IUR (19:2) 393–7.

### Prose

**4987.** ALTMAN, JANET GURKIN. Political ideology in the letter manual (France, England, New England). StudECC (18) 1988, 105–22.

**4988.** DUVAL, GILLES. Divination, morals and courtesy: some aspects of English chap-literature of the eighteenth century. See **1431.**

**4989.** FAVRET, MARY A. The idea of correspondence in British Romantic literature. Unpub. doct. diss., Stanford Univ., 1988. [Abstr. in DA (49) 3731A.]

**4990.** REDFORD, BRUCE. The converse of the pen: acts of intimacy in the eighteenth-century familiar letter. (Bibl. 1988, 3765.) Rev. by Bernard Beatty in BJECS (12) 236–7; by Peter Sabor in QQ (95:4) 1988, 925–7.

### Biography and Autobiography

**4991.** ANDREWS, WILLIAM L. To tell a free story: the first century of Afro-American autobiography, 1760–1865. (Bibl. 1988, 3768.) Rev. by John C. Shields in BALF (23:1) 159–67.

**4992.** Entry cancelled.

**4993.** DOLLE, RAYMOND.    Freeing the first person. BALF (23:4) 785–91 (review-article).

**4994.** EDWARDS, PAUL.    Pioneering amongst the Black British Georgians. BALF (23:4) 792–8 (review-article).

**4995.** FALLER, LINCOLN B.    Turned to account: the forms and functions of criminal biography in late seventeenth- and early eighteenth-century. *See* **4253.**

**4996.** MASCUCH, M.    Social mobility in English autobiography 1600–1750. *See* **4255.**

**4997.** NUSSBAUM, FELICITY A.    Eighteenth-century women's autobiographical commonplaces. *In* (pp. 147–71) **51.**

**4998.** PRADEILLES, ANNE.    Une analyse titrologique des 'Memoir(s)' publiés en Grande-Bretagne (1780–1790). *See* **541.**

**4999.** SANDIFORD, KEITH A.    Measuring the moment: strategies of protest in eighteenth-century Afro-English writing. London; Toronto: Assoc. UPs; Selinsgrove, PA: Susquehanna UP, 1988. pp. 191. Rev. by Paul Edwards in BALF (23:4) 792–8; by Larry E. Hudson in NC (7) 180–2.

**5000.** STEPANOWSKY, PAULA; HARPER, CONRAD K.    Views from both directions: courtship and marriage in letters and diaries from the age of Jane Austen. Persuasions (10) 1988, 117–26.

**5001.** WHEELER, DAVID (ed.).    Domestick privacies: Samuel Johnson and the art of biography. Lexington: Kentucky UP, 1987. pp. vii, 190. Rev. by David R. Anderson in SCN (47:3/4) 38–9.

## Related Studies

**5002.** ADAMS, J. R. R.    The printed word and the common man: popular culture in Ulster, 1700–1900. Belfast: Inst. of Irish Studies, Queen's Univ. of Belfast, 1987. pp. 218.

**5003.** BARBOUR, JAMES; QUIRK, THOMAS (eds).    Essays on Puritans and Puritanism. *See* **4257.**

**5004.** BARNOUW, JEFFREY.    Feeling in Enlightenment aesthetics. StudECC (18) 323–42.

**5005.** BARRELL, JOHN.    The political theory of painting from Reynolds to Hazlitt: 'the body of the public'. (Bibl. 1987, 5612.) Rev. by Stephen Bann in CompCrit (10) 1988, 255–66.

**5006.** BURLEY, PETER.    Witness to the Revolution: American and British commentators in France, 1788–94. London: Weidenfeld & Nicolson. pp. xxi, 238.

**5007.** CAPELLE, ALEX.    L'éphémère présence culturelle française en Virginie à la fin du XVIIIe siècle. BSEAA (28) 71–86.

**5008.** DUFAU, MICHELLE-MARIE.    Le jardin des patriotes à Stowe (Buckinghamshire). BSEAA (28) 91–131.

**5009.** FISKE, ROGER.    English theatre music in the eighteenth century. (Bibl. 1975, 6136.) Oxford: OUP, 1986. pp. xvi, 684. (Second ed.: first ed. 1973.)

**5010.** HARDING, BRIAN. The myth of the myth of the garden. *In* (pp. 44–60) **1.**

**5011.** HARRIS, ROY. The ideological implications of onomatopoeia in the eighteenth century. *See* **704.**

**5012.** HOFFER, PETER CHARLES (ed.). An American Enlightenment: selected articles on colonial intellectual history. *See* **4273.**

**5013.** HOUSTON, R. A. Literacy in early modern Europe: culture and education 1500–1800. *See* **3178.**

**5014.** JEHLEN, MYRA. American incarnation: the individual, the nation and the continent. (Bibl. 1987, 5629.) Rev. by Sam B. Girgus in ALR (21:3) 72–4.

**5015.** KERBER, LINDA K. Women and individualism in American history. *See* **4279.**

**5016.** KNIGHT, JANICE LYNN. A garden enclosed: the tradition of heart-piety in Puritan New England. *See* **4280.**

**5017.** MALMGREEN, GAIL (ed.). Religion in the lives of English women, 1760–1930. London; Sydney: Croom Helm; Bloomington: Indiana UP, 1986. pp. x, 295. Rev. by Isobel Grundy in MLR (84:3) 718–19.

**5018.** MINKEMA, KENNETH PIETER. The Edwardses: a ministerial family in eighteenth-century New England. Unpub. doct. diss., Univ. of Connecticut, 1988. [Abstr. in DA (49) 3484A.]

**5019.** NEUBAUER, JOHN. The emancipation of music from language: departure from mimesis in eighteenth-century aesthetics. (Bibl. 1987, 5638.) Rev. by James A. Winn in MP (86:4) 433–5.

**5020.** PARK, WILLIAM. Rococo and neo-Palladian. EA (42:2) 151–67.

**5021.** POPKIN, RICHARD H. (ed.). Millenarianism and Messianism in English literature and thought 1650–1800: Clark Library lectures, 1981–1982. *See* **4286.**

**5022.** PORTER, ROY. Mind-forg'd manacles: a history of madness in England from the Restoration to the Regency. *See* **4287.**

**5023.** RAZZAK, FAKHIR ABDUL. *The Arabian Nights* in England. Al-Mustansiriya Literary Review (Al-Mustansiriya Univ., Baghdad) (8) 1984, 15–52.

**5024.** SCHWARTZ, RICHARD B. Daily life in Johnson's London. (Bibl. 1985, 5277.) Rev. by Nora Crow Jaffe in YES (19) 325–7.

**5025.** STOUT, HARRY S. The New England soul: preaching and religious culture in Colonial New England. (Bibl. 1988, 3219.) Rev. by Donald Weber in MP (86:4) 443–5.

**5026.** THALE, MARY. London debating societies in the 1790s. HistJ (32:1) 57–86.

**5027.** THOMAS, KEITH. Children in early modern England. *In* (pp. 45–77) **14.**

**5028.** WASZEK, NORBERT. The Scottish Enlightenment and Hegel's account of 'civil society'. Dordrecht; London: Kluwer Academic, 1988. pp. xvii, 286. (International archives of the history of ideas, 120.)

**5029.** WEBER, DONALD. Rhetoric and history in Revolutionary New England. *See* **1325.**

**5030.** WITHINGTON, ANN FAIRFAX.    Republican bees: the political economy of the beehive in eighteenth-century America. StudECC (18) 39–77.

**5031.** WOLPERS, THEODOR.    Göttingen als Vermittlungszentrum englischer Literatur im 18. Jahrhundert. *In* (pp. 31–51) **5.**

**5032.** ZACHS, W. J.    The life and writings of Gilbert Stuart 1743–86: a social and literary study. Unpub. doct. diss., Univ. of Edinburgh. [Abstr. in IT (39:4) 1630.]

### Literary Theory

This section is intended to contain studies **about** the literary theory, literary historiography, literary criticism, etc., produced *in* the eighteenth century. For modern works **of** literary history and criticism dealing generally with this period, see under 'Eighteenth Century: General Literary Studies'.

**5033.** ENGELL, JAMES.    Forming the critical mind: Dryden to Coleridge. *See* **4298.**

**5034.** LEVINE, JOSEPH M.    Bentley's Milton: philology and criticism in eighteenth-century England. *See* **4706.**

**5035.** PATEY, DOUGLAS LANE.    The eighteenth century invents the canon. MLS (18:1) 1988, 17–37.

**5036.** RICHTER, DAVID H.    The reception of the gothic novel in the 1790s. *In* (pp. 117–37) **33.**

### AUTHORS

#### Abigail Adams

**5037.** CAPPON, LESTER J. (ed.).    The Adams–Jefferson letters: the complete correspondence between Thomas Jefferson and Abigail and John Adams. Chapel Hill; London: North Carolina UP for the Inst. of Early American History and Culture, 1988. pp. xix, 638.

#### John Adams

**5038.** CAPPON, LESTER J. (ed.).    The Adams–Jefferson letters: the complete correspondence between Thomas Jefferson and Abigail and John Adams. *See* **5037.**

**5039.** FARRELL, JAMES M.    John Adams's *Autobiography*: the Ciceronian paradigm and the quest for fame. NEQ (62:4) 505–28.

#### Joseph Addison

**5040.** MCCREA, BRIAN.    The canon and the eighteenth century: a modest proposal and a tale of two tubs. MLS (18:1) 1988, 58–73.

#### Mark Akenside

**5041.** JUMP, H.    Mark Akenside and the poetry of current events: 1738–1770. Unpub. doct. diss., Univ. of Oxford. [Abstr. in IT (39:3) 1108.]

**5042.** JUMP, HARRIET.    Two new Akenside manuscripts. *See* **148.**

#### John Arbuthnot

**5043.** FOX, CHRISTOPHER.    Locke and the Scriblerians: identity and consciousness in early eighteenth-century Britain. *See* **4605.**

**5044.** LAPREVOTTE, GUY. Note on Arbuthnot's use of official documents in *The History of John Bull*. *In* (pp. 153–9) **42.**

### Mary Astell

**5045.** PERRY, RUTH. The celebrated Mary Astell: an early English feminist. (Bibl. 1987, 5656.) Rev. by Mary Beth Rose in JMH (61:4) 769–71.

### Joel Barlow

**5046.** VAN DOVER, J. K. The design of anarchy: *The Anarchiad*, 1786–1787. EAL (24:3) 237–47.

### James Beattie

**5047.** KING, EVERARD H. Robert Burns and James Beattie, minstrels 'of the north countrie'. DalR (67:1) 1987, 45–53.

### William Beckford

**5048.** COPE, KEVIN L. Moral travel and the pursuit of nothing: *Vathek* and *Siris* as philosophical monologue. StudECC (18) 167–86.

**5049.** RABAIOTTI, RENATO. Beckford's *A Dialogue in the Shades* and Dibdin's *The Lincolne Nosegay*. BC (38:2) 210–28.

### George Berkeley

**5050.** BOX, M. A. How much of Berkeley did Hume read? NQ (36:1) 65–6.

**5051.** COPE, KEVIN L. Moral travel and the pursuit of nothing: *Vathek* and *Siris* as philosophical monologue. *See* **5048.**

### William Blake

**5052.** ANON. William Blake and his contemporaries: a loan exhibition in aid of the Friends of the Fitzwilliam Museum. Cambridge: Fitzwilliam Museum, 1986. pp. 112. Rev. by David McKitterick in BC (36:3) 1987, 305–6.

**5053.** ANSARI, A. A. Blake's *Mental Traveller*. ACM (2:2) 218–30.

**5054.** BAINE, RODNEY M.; BAINE, MARY R. The scattered portions: William Blake's biological symbolism. (Bibl. 1987, 5677, where second scholar's name omitted.) Rev. by Andrew Lincoln in RES (39:153) 1988, 117–18; by Margaret Storch in MLR (84:4) 936–7; by David Fuller in BJECS (12) 109–10.

**5055.** BENTLEY, G. E., JR. *Blake Records* supplement: being new materials relating to the life of William Blake discovered since the publication of *Blake Records* (1969). Oxford: Clarendon Press; New York: OUP, 1988. pp. xlviii, 152. Rev. by L. M. Findlay in NQ (36:4) 520–1.

**5056.** BETHEA, DEAN WENTWORTH. Visionary warfare: Blake, Hamann, and Boehme against ideology. Unpub. doct. diss., Univ. of Tennessee. [Abstr. in DA (50) 1651A.]

**5057.** BIDNEY, MARTIN. Blake and Goethe: psychology, ontology, imagination. Columbia: Missouri UP, 1988. pp. xvi, 184. Rev. by John Mee in NQ (36:4) 521.

**5058.** BRACHER, MARK. 'Being form'd': thinking through Blake's *Milton*. (Bibl. 1987, 5686.) Rev. by Andrew Lincoln in RES (38:149) 1987, 86–7.

**5059.** BROGAN, HOWARD O.    William Blake and the literary canon. CEAF (20:3/4) 10–12.

**5060.** BROOKS, HAROLD F.    Blake and Jung: 2, The fall into disintegration. ACM (2:2) 158–74.

**5061.** BUSH, GLEN.    Revolutionary visions: Blake, Ginsberg and Ferlinghetti. ACM (2:2) 175–85.

**5062.** BUTTER, P. H.    Blake's *The French Revolution*. YES (19) 18–27.

**5063.** CERNY, LOTHAR.    Blake's Satan and the idea of limit. *In* (pp. 325–37) **5.**

**5064.** CHILDERS, JOSEPH.    Opposing the paradigm: the example of Blake. DalR (66:3) 1986, 301–10.

**5065.** CLARK, JOHN M.    Writing *Jerusalem* backwards: William Blake in *Exiles*. JJQ (26:2) 183–97.

**5066.** CONNOLLY, THOMAS E.    *Little Girl Lost, Little Girl Found*: Blake's reversal of the innocence–experience pattern. CLit (16:2) 148–66.

**5067.** COX, P. T.    Unnatural refuge: aspects of pastoral in William Blake's epic poetry. Unpub. doct. diss., Univ. of York. [Abstr. in IT (38:4) 1457.]

**5068.** CREHAN, STEWART.    Blake in context. (Bibl. 1985, 5313.) Rev. by Ken E. Smith in BJECS (10) 1987, 110.

**5069.** DAVIES, J. M. Q.    'Attempting to be no more than man we become less': Blake's *Comus* designs and the two faces of Milton's Puritanism. *See* **4677.**

**5070.** ESSICK, ROBERT N.    William Blake and the language of Adam. Oxford: Clarendon Press. pp. x, 272.

**5071.** FERBER, MICHAEL.    The social vision of William Blake. (Bibl. 1988, 3814.) Rev. by Andrew Lincoln in RES (38:149) 1987, 85–6; by Nelson Hilton in MLS (18:1) 1988, 195–7; by David Worrall in BJECS (10) 1987, 110–12.

**5072.** FLETCHER, JOHN.    Poetry, gender and primal fantasy. *In* (pp. 109–41) VICTOR BURGIN, JAMES DONALD, and CORA KAPLAN (eds), Formations of fantasy. London; New York: Methuen, 1986. pp. x, 221. Rev. by Maria Del Sapio in YES (19) 362–3.

**5073.** FULLER, DAVID.    Blake's heroic argument. (Bibl. 1988, 3815.) Rev. by Ken Edward Smith in BJECS (12) 231–2; by Raman Selden in DUJ (81:1) 1988, 160–2; by Jon Mee in NQ (36:2) 244–5.

**5074.** GARDNER, STANLEY.    Blake's *Innocence and Experience* retraced. (Bibl. 1986, 6233.) Rev. by David Fuller in BJECS (12) 109–10.

**5075.** GOURLAY, ALEXANDER S.    What was Blake's Chaucer? *See* **2900.**

**5076.** GUTH, DEBORAH.    Innocence re-called: the implied reader in Blake's *Songs of Innocence*. CLQ (25:1) 4–11.

**5077.** HAGSTRUM, JEAN H.    The Romantic body: love and sexuality in Keats, Wordsworth, and Blake. (Bibl. 1988, 3817.) Rev. by V. A. De Luca in UTQ (56:4) 1987, 586–7; by François Piquet in EA (42:2) 215–16.

**5078.** HAMPSEY, JOHN C.    Blake's bound children. BSUF (27:3) 1986, 20–37.

**5079.** HILTON, NELSON.   Blake and the apocalypse of the canon. MLS (18:1) 1988, 134–49.

**5080.** —— (ed.).   Essential articles for the study of William Blake. Hamden, CT: Archon, 1986. pp. 333. Rev. by Ken Edward Smith in BJECS (11) 1988, 97–8.

**5081.** —— VOGLER, THOMAS A. (eds).   Unnam'd forms: Blake and textuality. Berkeley: California UP, 1986. pp. xiii, 267.

**5082.** HIRST, DESIRÉE.   The problems posed by William Blake's religious position. ACM (2:2) 186–202.

**5083.** LANSVERK, MARVIN DUANE LANDERHOLM.   The wisdom of many, the vision of one: the proverbs of William Blake. Unpub. doct. diss., Univ. of Washington, 1988. [Abstr. in DA (50) 147–8A.]

**5084.** LARRISSY, EDWARD.   William Blake. (Bibl. 1988, 3823.) Rev. by Michael Ackland in AUMLA (72) 352–5.

**5085.** LINDSAY, DAVID W.   Blake: *Songs of Innocence and Experience.* Basingstoke: Macmillan. pp. 91. (Critics debate.)

**5086.** LUNDEEN, KATHLEEN.   Urizen's quaking word. CLQ (25:1) 12–27.

**5087.** MCARTHUR, MURRAY.   Stolen writings: Blake's *Milton,* Joyce's *Ulysses,* and the nature of influence. Ann Arbor, MI; London: UMI Research Press, 1988. pp. 180. (Studies in modern literature, 87.) Rev. by Robert Spoo in JJQ (26:2) 291–5.

**5088.** MCGANN, JEROME.   The third world of criticism. *In* (pp. 85–107) **53.**

**5089.** MCKEEVER, KERRY ELLEN.   Disseminating Cain: sublime sacrifices in Byron, Blake and Coleridge. Unpub. doct. diss., Univ. of California, Irvine, 1988. [Abstr. in DA (50) 149A.]

**5090.** MASON, MICHAEL (ed.).   William Blake.   Oxford: OUP, 1988. pp. xxvi, 601. (Oxford authors.) Rev. by David Fuller in DUJ (81:2) 321–2; by L. M. Findlay in NQ (36:4) 519–20.

**5091.** MEE, J. A.   The political rhetoric of William Blake's early prophecies. Unpub. doct. diss., Univ. of Cambridge. [Abstr. in IT (38:3) 1011.]

**5092.** MILLER, DAN; BRACHER, MARK; AULT, DONALD (eds).   Critical paths: Blake and the argument of method. Durham, NC: Duke UP, 1987. pp. 380. Rev. by Ken Edward Smith in BJECS (12) 231–2.

**5093.** NANAVUTTY, PILOO.   Blake and the *Ramayana.* ACM (2:2) 211–17.

**5094.** OH, MOON-KIL.   Nangmanjeok sangsangryeok yeongu: Blake wa Wordsworth bikyo. (A comparative study of the Romantic imagination: William Blake and William Wordsworth.) Unpub. doct. diss., Chung Ang Univ., Seoul.

**5095.** PALEY, MORTON D.   The art of 'the Ancients'. HLQ (52:1) 97–124.

**5096.** PETERFREUND, STUART.   Blake on charters, weights and measures as forms of social control. SLI (22:1) 37–59.

**5097.** PHILLIPS, MICHAEL (ed.).   An Island in the Moon. Introd. by HAVEN O'MORE. Cambridge: CUP in assn with the Inst. of Traditional

Science, 1987. pp. viii, 110 (facsims). Rev. by David McKitterick in BC (37:3) 1988, 423–4.

**5098.** PIQUET, FRANÇOIS.    Shadows of prophecy: Blake and the Millenarian ideology. YES (19) 28–35.

**5099.** RAINE, KATHLEEN.    The apocalypse – Blake and Michelangelo. ACM (2:2) 139–57.

**5100.** RAMSEY, M. K.    The Established Church in the work of William Blake, 1757–1827. Unpub. M.Phil. diss., Univ. of St Andrews. [Abstr. in IT (39:1) 31.]

**5101.** RICHARDSON, ALAN.    The politics of childhood: Wordsworth, Blake, and catechistic method. ELH (56:4) 853–68.

**5102.** SORENSEN, PETER JULIAN.    Gnostic myth and ritual in the poetry of William Blake. Unpub. doct. diss., Washington State Univ., 1988. [Abstr. in DA (49) 3737A.]

**5103.** STEVENSON, W. H. (ed.).    William Blake: selected poetry. London: Penguin, 1988. pp. 300. (Penguin poetry library.)

**5104.** VAN CASPEL, PAUL P. J.    Blake and Joyce: strange syzygy. *In* (pp. 101–17) **23.**

**5105.** VINE, S. P.    The spectre in Blake's poetry. Unpub. doct. diss., Univ. of Southampton. [Abstr. in IT (39:1) 31–2.]

**5106.** WERNER, BETTE CHARLENE.    Blake's vision of the poetry of Milton: illustrations to six poems. Lewisburg, PA: Bucknell UP; London; Toronto: Assoc. UPs, 1986. pp. 319. Rev. by Gordon Campbell in BJECS (12) 225.

**5107.** YOUNGQUIST, PAUL BRUCE.    Madness and Blake's myth. Unpub. doct. diss., Univ. of Virginia, 1988. [Abstr. in DA (49) 3738A.]

**5108.** ZGORZELSKI, ANDRZEJ.    Strategia wizji unaoczniających w wierzu W. Blake'a *The Tyger.* (The strategy of visions forming mental images in Blake's poem *The Tyger.*) KN (36:2) 115–32.

## James Boswell

**5109.** DANZIGER, MARLIES K.; BRADY, FRANK (eds).    Boswell: the great biographer, 1789–1795. New York: McGraw-Hill; London: Heinemann. pp. xxvii, 371. Rev. by Donald Greene in BkW, 27 Aug., 1, 10.

**5110.** DURING, SIMON.    Waiting for the post: some relations between modernity, colonization and writing. JLS (5:3/4) 279–301.

**5111.** KULLMAN, COLBY H.    Boswell interviews Rousseau: a theatrical production. SoCR (21:2) 30–45.

**5111a.** LUSTIG, IRMA S.; POTTLE, FREDERICK A. (eds).    Boswell: the English experiment: 1785–1789. (Bibl. 1988, 3842.) Rev. by A. F. T. Lurcock in RES (39:156) 1988, 562–3; by Paul Clayton in NQ (36:1) 115.

**5112.** VANCE, JOHN A. ed.).    Boswell's *Life of Johnson*: new questions, new answers. (Bibl. 1987, 5746.) Rev. by G. J. Clingham in Eng (36:155) 1987, 168–78.

## .Hugh Henry Brackenridge

**5113.** LOOBY, CHRISTOPHER JAMES.    The utterance of America. Unpub. doct. diss., Columbia Univ. [Abstr. in DA (50) 1305A.]

**5114.** SMITH, HERB. Hugh Henry Brackenridge's debt to the stage-Irish convention. BSUF (30:1) 14–19.

### Anne Bradstreet

**5115.** DORIANI, BETH M. 'Then have I . . . said with David': Anne Bradstreet's Andover manuscript poems and the influence of the psalm tradition. EAL (24:1) 52–69.

### Frances Brooke

**5116.** BERLAND, K. J. H. The true pleasurable philosopher: some influences on Frances Brooke's *History of Emily Montague*. DalR (66:3) 1986, 286–300.

### Henry Brooke

**5117.** OMBERG, MARGARET. Gustav Vasa's adventures in 18th-century English drama. *In* (pp. 163–73) **34.**

### Edmund Burke

**5118.** FURNISS, T. E. Edmund Burke's revolution: the discourse of aesthetics, gender, and political economy in Burke's *Philosophical Enquiry* and *Reflections on the Revolution in France*. Unpub. doct. diss., Univ. of Edinburgh. [Abstr. in IT (38:3) 990.]

**5119.** FURNISS, TOM. Burke, Paine, and the language of *assignats*. YES (19) 54–70.

**5120.** GARNETT, MARK A. Hazlitt against Burke: radical versus conservative? DUJ (81:2) 229–39.

**5121.** HALIMI, SUZY. La notion de progrès dans *Reflections on the Revolution in France* d'Edmund Burke. EA (42:1) 55–67.

**5122.** HAMPSHER-MONK, IAIN. The political philosophy of Edmund Burke. London; New York: Longman, 1987. pp. 284. (Documents in political ideas.) Rev. by Marie-Cécile Revauger in EA (42:4) 478–9.

**5123.** LOCK, F. P. Burke's *Reflections on the Revolution in France*. (Bibl. 1988, 3850.) Rev. by L. G. Mitchell in RES (38:150) 1987, 293.

**5124.** MACINTYRE, ALASDAIR. Poetry as political philosophy: notes on Burke and Yeats. *In* (pp. 145–57) **46.**

**5125.** TURNER, JOHN. Burke, Paine, and the nature of language. YES (19) 36–53.

### Fanny Burney (Mme D'Arblay)

**5126.** DEVLIN, D. D. Emily Brontë and Fanny Burney. NQ (36:2) 183.

**5127.** —— The novels and journals of Fanny Burney. (Bibl. 1987, 5763.) Rev. by R. L. Brett in RES (39:154) 1988, 338.

**5128.** DOODY, MARGARET ANNE. Frances Burney: the life in the works. (Bibl. 1988, 3854.) Rev. by Alethea Hayter in LRB (11:17) 22–3; by Nigel Andrew in Listener (121) 18 May, 33; by David Nokes in TLS, 25 Aug., 911–12.

**5129.** HEMLOW, JOYCE (ed.). Fanny Burney: selected letters and journals. (Bibl. 1988, 3855.) Rev. by Helen Wilcox in BJECS (11) 1988, 227–8.

**5130.** SIMONS, JUDY. Fanny Burney. (Bibl. 1988, 3860.) Rev. by Coral Ann Howells in BJECS (11) 1988, 97.

**5131.** —— (introd.). Cecilia, or, Memoirs of an heiress. (Bibl. 1986,

6322.) Rev. by Peter Sabor in MLR (84:4) 933–4; by Helen Wilcox in BJECS (11) 1988, 227–8.

**5132.** STRAUB, KRISTINA. Divided fictions: Fanny Burney and feminine strategy. Lexington: Kentucky UP, 1987. pp. viii, 237. Rev. by Paula R. Backscheider in MP (87:1) 93–5.

### Robert Burns

**5133.** BENTMAN, RAYMOND. Robert Burns. Boston, MA: G. K. Hall, 1987. pp. 155. (Twayne's English authors, 452.)

**5134.** BOYLE, ANDREW M. The Ayrshire book of Burns-lore. Ayr: Alloway, 1985. pp. 143.

**5135.** DAICHES, DAVID. Burns and Pope. SLJ (16:1) 5–20.

**5136.** HEMPSTEAD, JAMES L. William Corbet, the 'steady friend' of Robert Burns. BurnsC (98) 49–56.

**5137.** KING, EVERARD H. Robert Burns and James Beattie, minstrels 'of the north countrie'. *See* **5047.**

**5138.** LINDSAY, MAURICE. The Burns encyclopedia. (Bibl. 1980, 6613.) Rev. in BurnsC (98) 10–12.

**5139.** MACKAY, JAMES A. A recollection of Burns from 1836. BurnsC (98) 83–5.

**5140.** —— *The Selkirk Grace*: fact and fable. BurnsC (98) 24–30.

**5141.** —— The world-wide memorials to Robert Burns. BurnsC (98) 77–82.

**5142.** —— (ed.). The complete letters of Robert Burns. Ayr: Alloway, 1987. pp. 862.

**5143.** PEEL, R. Those jolly beggars. BurnsC (98) 73–6.

**5144.** PITTOCK, JOAN H. Burns: *Tam o'Shanter* and *Cutty Sark*. DUJ (81:2) 191–6.

**5145.** ROY, G. ROSS. The Brash and Reid editions of *Tam o'Shanter*. *See* **460.**

**5146.** —— (ed.). The letters of Robert Burns: vol. 1, 1780–1789; vol. 2, 1790–1796. Ed. by J. DE LANCEY FERGUSON. (Bibl. 1986, 6345.) Rev. by Thomas Crawford in RES (38:150) 1987, 256–8; by Douglas S. Mack in NQ (34:4) 1987, 556.

**5147.** SEMPLE, HILARY. 'Brother-mortals': Robert Burns and Es'kia Mphahlele. Contrast (17:4) 25–41.

**5148.** STRAWHORN, JOHN. Robert Burns and Professor Stewart. BurnsC (98) 63–72.

**5149.** SUTHERLAND, BILL (comp.). History of the Burns Howff Club of Dumfries. Dumfries: Burns Howff Club, 1988. pp. 55.

**5150.** TURNBULL, MALCOLM T. R. B. Joseph Hislop and the songs of Burns. *See* **1760.**

**5151.** VEITCH, JAMES. The life of Robert Burns. Ayr: Alloway; Burns Federation, 1985. pp. 24.

### William Byrd

**5152.** LOCKRIDGE, KENNETH A. The diary and life of William Byrd II of Virginia, 1674–1744. Chapel Hill; London: North Carolina UP for the Inst. of Early American History and Culture, 1987. pp. x, 201. Rev. by J. A. Leo Lemay in SoQ (27:2) 107–9.

### Elizabeth Carter

**5153.** SPACKS, PATRICIA MEYER. Female rhetorics. *In* (pp. 177–91) **51.**

### Thomas Cary

**5154.** BENTLEY, D. M. R. An addition to *OED* from Thomas Cary's *Abram's Plains. See* **1076.**

**5155.** —— (ed.). Abram's plains: a poem. London, Ont.: Canadian Poetry Press, 1986. pp. xlviii, 43. Rev. by David Latham in CanL (122/23) 141–3.

### Thomas Chatterton

**5156.** BRIGGS, J. A. The real life of Thomas Chatterton: a world discovered and devised. Unpub. doct. diss., Univ. of Durham. [Abstr. in IT (39:3) 1108.]

**5157.** FREEMAN, ARTHUR; HOFMANN, THEODORE. The ghost of Coleridge's first effort: *A Monody on the Death of Chatterton.* Library (11:4) 328–35.

### Philip Dormer Stanhope, Earl of Chesterfield

**5158.** HEDRICK, ELIZABETH. Fixing the language: Johnson, Chesterfield, and *The Plan of a Dictionary. See* **1089.**

### Colley Cibber

**5159.** DERITTER, JONES. 'How came this muff here?': a note on *Tom Jones.* ELN (26:4) 41–6.

**5160.** VIATOR, TIMOTHY J. Corrections to *OED* from Colley Cibber's *Woman's Wit. See* **1031.**

**5161.** —— A missing scene change in Cibber's *Perolla and Izadora.* NQ (36:3) 354–5.

### John Cleland

**5162.** EPSTEIN, JULIA. Fanny's fanny: epistolarity, eroticism, and the transsexual text. *In* (pp. 135–53) **61.**

**5163.** ROUSSEAU, G. S.; PORTER, ROY (eds). Sexual underworlds of the Enlightenment. *See* **4885.**

### Catharine Cockburn (Catharine Trotter)

**5164.** OMBERG, MARGARET. Gustav Vasa's adventures in 18th-century English drama. *In* (pp. 163–73) **34.**

### Charles Coffey

**5165.** CHESLEY, BRENT. Probable sources for Garrick's pantomime. NQ (36:1) 61–2.

### William Collins

**5166.** STEWART, MARY MARGARET. William Collins, Samuel Johnson, and the use of biographical details. SELit (28:3) 1988, 471–82.

### George Colman the Elder

**5167.** TAYLOR, RICHARD C. A source for Goldsmith's Tony Lumpkin in *The Connoisseur. See* **595.**

### William Cowper

**5168.** HUTCHINGS, W. B. William Cowper and 1789. YES (19) 71–93.

**5169.** KING, JAMES. William Cowper: a biography. (Bibl. 1988, 3883.) Rev. by Karina Williamson in RES (38:152) 1987, 567–8; by Robert James Merrett in DalR (66:4) 1986, 564–7; by Vincent Newey in BJECS (12) 105–7.

**5170.** —— RYSKAMP, CHARLES (eds). The letters and prose writings of William Cowper: vol. 5, Prose 1756–*c.* 1799 and cumulative index. (Bibl. 1986, 6369.) Rev. by Karina Williamson in RES (39:154) 1988, 301–3.

**5171.** SPACKS, PATRICIA MEYER. Forgotten genres. MLS (18:1) 1988, 47–57.

### George Crabbe

**5172.** DALRYMPLE-CHAMPNEYS, NORMA; POLLARD, ARTHUR (eds). The complete poetical works. (Bibl. 1988, 3885.) Rev. by Jerome McGann in LRB (11:6) 16–17.

**5173.** FAULKNER, THOMAS C. (ed.); BLAIR, RHONDA L. (asst ed.). Selected letters and journals of George Crabbe. (Bibl. 1988, 3886.) Rev. by R. L. Brett in RES (38:149) 1987, 84–5.

**5174.** LURBE, PIERRE. Violence et sacrifice dans *Peter Grimes* de Benjamin Britten. *In* (pp. 121–38) **60.**

**5175.** SUTHERLAND, JAMES. Who was Peter Grimes? *In* (pp. 179–85) **37.**

### 'J. Hector St John de Crèvecœur'
### (Michel-Guillaume Jean de Crèvecœur)

**5176.** ALLEN, GAY WILSON; ASSELINEAU, ROGER. St John de Crèvecœur: the life of an American farmer. (Bibl. 1988, 3888.) Rev. by Bernard Chevignard in EA (42:2) 229–30.

### Erasmus Darwin

**5177.** KING-HELE, D. G. Antedatings of *OED* from Erasmus Darwin's *Botanic Garden. See* **1022.**

**5178.** KING-HELE, DESMOND. Erasmus Darwin and the Romantic poets. (Bibl. 1986, 6381.) Rev. by J. C. C. Mays in RES (38:151) 1987, 396–7.

### Daniel Defoe

**5179.** ASAMOAH, LORD EMMANUEL. The moral Defoe: the moral writings, *Moll Flanders*, and *Roxana*. Unpub. doct. diss., Ohio Univ., 1988. [Abstr. in DA (50) 447A.]

**5180.** BACKSCHEIDER, PAULA R. Daniel Defoe: ambition and innovation. (Bibl. 1987, 5808.) Rev. by J. A. Downie in RES (39:156) 1988, 557–8.

**5181.** —— Daniel Defoe: his life. Baltimore, MD; London: Johns Hopkins UP. pp. xv, 671. Rev. by John Kenyon in BkW, 10 Dec., 15.

**5182.** BELL, IAN A. Defoe's fiction. (Bibl. 1988, 3894.) Rev. by Paula R. Backscheider in MLS (18:1) 1988, 201–2; by J. A. Downie in BJECS (10) 1987, 97–8.

**5183.** BLEWETT, DAVID. Moll Flanders in Chichester. NQ (36:1) 51–2.

**5184.** BROWN, STEPHEN. Making history novel: Defoe's *Due Preparations* and *A Journal of the Plague Year*. DalR (67:2/3) 1987, 190–201.

**5185.** COLVIN, ANNE HUTTA. The celluloid Crusoe: a study of cinematic Robinsonades. Unpub. doct. diss., Temple Univ. [Abstr. in DA (50) 1464–5A.]

**5186.** CURTIS, LAURA A. The attribution of *A Vindication of the Press* to Daniel Defoe. StudECC (18) 1988, 433–44.

**5187.** DANON, RUTH. Work in the English novel: the myth of vocation. (Bibl. 1988, 3898.) Rev. by Sheila M. Smith in RES (38:150) 1987, 284–5.

**5188.** DIJKSTRA, BRAM. Defoe and economics: the fortunes of *Roxana* in the history of interpretation. New York: St Martin's Press, 1987. (Bibl. 1987, 5816.) Rev. by Maximillian E. Novak in MP (87:1) 89–92; by Robert W. Uphaus in StudN (20:3) 1988, 356–9.

**5189.** FRICK, WERNER. Providenz, Rationalität, Gesellschaft: Funktionen der Vorsehung im europäischen Sozialroman des frühen 18. Jahrhunderts. *In* (pp. 101–53) WERNER FRICK, Providenz und Kontingenz: Untersuchungen zur Schicksalssemantik im deutschen und europäischen Roman des 17. und 18. Jahrhunderts: vol. 1. Tübingen: Niemeyer, 1988. 2 vols. pp. xv, 559. (Hermaea germanistische Forschungen, ns 55: 1/2.)

**5190.** FURBANK, P. N.; OWENS, W. R. The canonisation of Daniel Defoe. (Bibl. 1988, 3902.) Rev. by Hugh Amory in BC (38:3) 410–14; by Pat Rogers in LRB (11:5) 16–17; by Andrew Varney in NQ (36:4) 514–15.

**5191.** GLENN-LAUGA, CATHERINE. The 'hearerly' text: seashells on the seashore. JLS (5:2) 194–214.

**5192.** HENTZI, GARY PAUL. Parables of restlessness: narrative contradiction and the problem of the subject in five novels by Daniel Defoe. Unpub. doct. diss., Columbia Univ., 1988. [Abstr. in DA (50) 1311–12A.] (*Colonel Jack, Robinson Crusoe, A Journal of the Plague Year, Moll Flanders, Roxana.*)

**5193.** HUDSON, NICHOLAS. 'Why God no kill the Devil?': the diabolical disruption of order in *Robinson Crusoe*. RES (39:156) 1988, 494–501.

**5194.** KALB, GERTRUD. Daniel Defoe. Heidelberg: Winter, 1985. pp. 144.

**5195.** KAY, CAROL. Political constructions: Defoe, Richardson, and Sterne in relation to Hobbes, Hume, and Burke. Ithaca, NY; London: Cornell UP, 1988. pp. xi, 286.

**5196.** KREBS, JEAN-DANIEL. La pícara, l'aventurière, la pionnière: fonctions de l'héroïne picaresque à travers les figures de Justina, Courage et Moll. arcadia (24) 239–52.

**5197.** LADEN, MARIE-PAULE. Self-imitation in the eighteenth-century novel. (Bibl. 1988, 3904.) Rev. by Simon Davies in BJECS (12) 235–6.

**5198.** MEIER, THOMAS KEITH. Defoe and the defense of commerce. Victoria, B.C.: Victoria UP, 1987. pp. 117. (English literary studies monographs, 38.)

**5199.** RICHETTI, JOHN. The novel and society: the case of Daniel Defoe. *In* (pp. 47–66) **33.**

**5200.** RICHETTI, JOHN J. Daniel Defoe. (Bibl. 1988, 3908.) Rev. by Michael M. Boardman in MP (87:2) 187–8.

**5201.** Roosen, William.    Daniel Defoe and diplomacy. Selinsgrove, PA: Susquehanna UP, 1986. pp. 144.

**5202.** Rosen, Alan Charles.    Versions of catastrophe: Shakespeare, Defoe, Scholem. *See* **3885.**

**5203.** Shaw, Narelle L.    Ancients and moderns in Defoe's *Consolidator*. SELit (28:3) 1988, 391–400.

**5204.** Sim, Stuart.    Interrogating an ideology: Defoe's *Robinson Crusoe*. BJECS (10) 1987, 163–73.

**5205.** Soulier-Detis, Elisabeth.    Colliers, gants et manchon: les pulsions dévoilées. BSEAA (28) 145–62. (*Roxana, A Sentimental Journey, Tom Jones.*)

**5206.** Soupel, Serge.    Modalités de la violence dans *The Life and Strange Adventures of Robinson Crusoe of York, Mariner* (1719). *In* (pp. 31–46) **60.**

**5207.** Stojčeva, Tatjana.    Poznazijat i nepoznatijat Robinzon Kruzo. (The known and the unknown Robinson Crusoe.) Ezik i literatura (44:4) 72–81.

**5208.** Trotter, David.    Circulation: Defoe, Dickens and the economies of the novel. London: Macmillan, 1988. pp. vii, 148. (Language, discourse, society.) Rev. by John Sutherland in LRB (10:20) 1988, 22–3.

### Mary Delany

**5209.** Spacks, Patricia Meyer.    Female rhetorics. *In* (pp. 177–91) **51.**

### Samuel Derrick

**5210.** Atkins, Janet E. (introd.).    The dramatic censor: remarks upon the tragedy of *Venice Preserv'd*. *See* **4756.**

### Robert Dodsley

**5210a.** Tierney, James E. (ed.).    The correspondence of Robert Dodsley, 1733–1764. *See* **464.**

### Stephen Duck

**5211.** Goodridge, John A.    Some predecessors of Clare: 'honest Duck'. JCSJ (8) 5–10.

### Jonathan Edwards

**5212.** Burman, Ronald Sidney.    A study of the dynamics of conversion and identity in the life and works of Jonathan Edwards. Unpub. doct. diss., Univ. of Minnesota, 1988. [Abstr. in DA (50) 442A.]

**5213.** Hatch, Nathan O.; Stout, Harry S. (eds).    Jonathan Edwards and the American experience. (Bibl. 1988, 3919.) Rev. by Suzanne B. Geissler in JAH (75:4) 1303.

**5214.** Holbrook, Clyde A.    Jonathan Edwards, the valley and nature: an interpretive essay. (Bibl. 1988, 3920.) Rev. by Stephen J. Stein in EAL (23:3) 1988/89; by John Stilgoe in AmerS (92:2) 1988, 98.

**5215.** Lee, Sang-Hyun.    The philosophical theology of Jonathan Edwards. Princeton, NJ; Guildford: Princeton UP, 1988. pp. xiii, 248. Rev. by Amy Plantinga Pauw in JAH (76:3) 913–14.

**5216.** Shaw, Nancy Joy.    Speaking for the spirit: Cotton, Shepard, Edwards, Emerson. *See* **4367.**

**5217.** WESTRA, HELEN PETTER. 'Above all others': Jonathan Edwards and the gospel ministry. APJPH (67:3) 209–20.

**5218.** WILLIAMS, DAVID R. Experience and appearance in America's moral wilderness: Edwards' humiliation, Franklin's rationalization, and Huck Finn's damnation. Cresset (52:4) 5–11.

### Olaudah Equiano

**5219.** ACHOLONU, CATHERINE OBIANJU. The home of Olaudah Equiano – a linguistic and anthropological search. JCL (22:1) 1987, 5–16.

**5220.** COSTANZO, ANGELO. Surprizing narrative: Olaudah Equiano and the beginnings of Black autobiography. (Bibl. 1987, 5848.) Rev. by Raymond Dolle in BALF (23:4) 785–91; by William L. Andrews in JSH (55:3) 468–9.

**5221.** DOLLE, RAYMOND. Freeing the first person. *See* **4993.**

**5222.** WATERS, CARVER WENDELL. Voice in the slave narratives of Olaudah Equiano, Frederick Douglass, and Solomon Northrup. Unpub. doct. diss., Univ. of Southwestern Louisiana, 1988. [Abstr. in DA (49) 1805A.]

### George Farquhar

**5223.** DIXON, PETER (ed.). The recruiting officer. Dover, NH: Manchester UP, 1986. (Bibl. 1986, 6435.) Rev. by Jessica Munns in MLR (84:1) 130–1.

**5224.** KENNY, SHIRLEY STRUM (ed.). The works of George Farquhar. (Bibl. 1988, 3924.) Rev. by Christopher Murray in IUR (19:2) 405–6; by D. J. Womersley in NQ (36:4) 510–11.

### Henry Fielding

**5225.** BATTESTIN, MARTIN C. Dating Fielding's letters to Lady Mary Wortley Montagu. SB (42) 246–8.

**5226.** —— BATTESTIN, RUTHE R. Henry Fielding: a life. London: Routledge. pp. xvii, 738. Rev. by W. B. Carnochan in TLS, 20 Oct., 1145–6; by William Scammell in Listener (122) 21 Dec., 64–5.

**5227.** BAUER, DANIEL JOSEPH. Creative ambiguity: satirical portraiture in the *Ju-lin wai-shih* and *Tom Jones*. Unpub. doct. diss., Univ. of Wisconsin–Madison, 1988. [Abstr. in DA (49) 3715A.]

**5228.** BROWN, STEPHEN WILLIAM. Changing concepts of character and plot from Dryden to Sterne. *See* **4438.**

**5229.** BURLING, WILLIAM J. 'Merit infinitely short of service': Fielding's pleas in the *Journal of a Voyage to Lisbon*. EngS (70:1) 53–62.

**5230.** CAMPBELL, JILL CATHERINE. 'Natural masques': gender and identity in Fielding's early works. Unpub. doct. diss., Yale Univ., 1988. [Abstr. in DA (50) 1309A.]

**5231.** CHOE, OK-YOUNG. *Tom Jones*: Tom as a romance hero. CAE (22) 343–61.

**5232.** CLEARY, THOMAS R. Henry Fielding: political writer. (Bibl. 1988, 3929.) Rev. by Christine Gerrard in BJECS (10) 1987, 95–6.

**5233.** DERITTER, JONES. 'How came this muff here?': a note on *Tom Jones*. *See* **5159.**

**5234.** EMERY, TED A. *Tom Jones* on the Italian stage: the *Orfano* trilogy of Pietro Chiari. StudECC (18) 311–22.

**5235.** GOLDEN, MORRIS. Public context and imagining self in *Amelia*. UTQ (56:3) 1987, 377–91.

**5236.** GOLDGAR, BERTRAND A. (ed.). *The Covent-Garden Journal*; and, *A Plan of the Universal Register Office*. Oxford: Clarendon Press; New York: OUP, 1988. pp. lxiv, 517. (Wesleyan edition of the works of Henry Fielding.) Rev. by Jeremy Black in NQ (36:3) 399–400.

**5237.** HILL, MARGARETT HUTTON. Studies in theme and structure: *Piers Plowman A*, *Amelia*, and *Andreas*. *See* **2238.**

**5238.** LEWIS, PETER. Fielding's burlesque drama: its place in the tradition. Edinburgh: Edinburgh UP for Univ. of Durham, 1987. pp. viii, 220. (Univ. of Durham series, 2.) Rev. by Robert Folkenflik in TLS, 10 Mar., 253.

**5239.** LYNCH, JAMES J. Henry Fielding and the Heliodoran novel: romance, epic, and Fielding's new province of writing. Rutherford, NJ: Fairleigh Dickinson UP; London; Toronto: Assoc. UPs, 1986. pp. 128. Rev. by David Nokes in BJECS (11) 1988, 229–30.

**5240.** MILHOUS, JUDITH; HUME, ROBERT D. Edward Phillips and the authorship of *Marforio* (1736). ELN (26:1) 1988, 22–5.

**5241.** NOKES, DAVID (ed.). Henry Fielding, *Joseph Andrews*. Harmondsworth: Penguin, 1987. pp. 104. (Penguin masterstudies.)

**5242.** SABOR, PETER (introd.). Remarks on *Clarissa*. (Bibl. 1987, 5877.) Rev. by G. J. Clingham in BJECS (10) 1987, 235–6.

**5243.** SELLERS, MURRAY McCOWEN. Energy – framed and potent: narration in Fielding's *Tom Jones*. Unpub. doct. diss., Univ. of Florida, 1988. [Abstr. in DA (50) 693A.]

**5244.** SIMPSON, K. G. (ed.). Henry Fielding: justice observed. (Bibl. 1988, 3942.) Rev. by Michael Irwin in RES (38:152) 1987, 565–6; by Murray G. H. Pittock in BJECS (10) 1987, 234–5.

**5245.** SMALLWOOD, ANGELA J. Fielding and the woman question: the novels of Henry Fielding and feminist debate 1700–1750. Hemel Hempstead: Harvester Wheatsheaf. pp. x, 230.

**5246.** SOULIER-DETIS, ELISABETH. Colliers, gants et manchon: les pulsions dévoilées. *See* **5205.**

**5247.** VAREY, SIMON. Henry Fielding. (Bibl. 1988, 3946.) Rev. by David Nokes in BJECS (11) 1988, 229–30.

**5248.** WILNER, ARLENE FISH. Henry Fielding and the knowledge of character. MLS (18:1) 1988, 181–94.

### Hannah Webster Foster

**5249.** DAVIDSON, CATHY N. (ed.). The coquette. (Bibl. 1987, 5887.) Rev. by David Seed in BJECS (12) 110–11.

### Benjamin Franklin

**5250.** BUXMAN, MELVIN H. (ed.). Critical essays on Benjamin Franklin. Boston, MA: G. K. Hall, 1987. pp. viii, 214. Rev. by Christopher Looby in EAL (24:1) 79–80.

**5251.** LOOBY, CHRISTOPHER JAMES. The utterance of America. *See* **5113.**

**5252.** WILLCOX, WILLIAM B. (ed.); ARNOLD, DOUGLAS M., *et al.* (assoc. eds). The papers of Benjamin Franklin: vol. 25, October 1, 1777 through February 28, 1788. (Bibl. 1986, 6478.) Rev. by James H. Hutson in PMHB (111:4) 1987, 555–60.

**5253.** WILLIAMS, DAVID R. Experience and appearance in America's moral wilderness: Edwards' humiliation, Franklin's rationalization, and Huck Finn's damnation. *See* **5218.**

### David Garrick

**5254.** CHESLEY, BRENT. Probable sources for Garrick's pantomime. *See* **5165.**

### Sir Samuel Garth

**5255.** HOPKINS, DAVID. Dryden and the Garth–Tonson *Metamorphoses*. *See* **4451.**

**5256.** SENA, JOHN F. The best-natured man: Sir Samuel Garth, physician and poet. New York: AMS Press, 1986. pp. xii, 216. (AMS studies in the eighteenth century, 9.) Rev. by Malcolm Kelsall in RES (39:155) 1988, 446–7.

### John Gay

**5257.** BOSKER, MARGO. Polly Peachum as interpreted by John Gay and Peter Hacks. MichA (20:2) 1988, 133–8.

**5258.** DU SORBIER, FRANÇOISE. Marge et pouvoir dans *The Beggar's Opera*. BSEAA (29) 133–45.

**5259.** FULLER, JOHN (ed.). Dramatic works. (Bibl. 1986, 6486.) Rev. by Cecil Price in RES (39:156) 1988, 558–9.

**5260.** RICHARDSON, P. Virgilian forms and the ideal of civilization in English poetry 1700–1720. Unpub. doct. diss., Univ. of Manchester. [Abstr. in IT (39:4) 1629–30.)

**5261.** TASCH, PETER A. *The Beggar's Opera* and *The Libertine*. *See* **4776a.**

**5262.** ZACH, WOLFGANG. Fascination and scandal: on John Gay's *Beggar's Opera* and the doctrine of poetic justice. *In* (pp. 219–37) **37.**

### Edward Gibbon

**5263.** CRADDOCK, PATRICIA. Gibbon's choice of Lausanne, 1783–94. StudECC (18) 359–73.

**5264.** CRADDOCK, PATRICIA B. Edward Gibbon, luminous historian, 1772–1794. Baltimore, MD; London: Johns Hopkins UP. pp. xv, 432. Rev. by Linda Colley in LRB (11:9) 20–2.

**5265.** —— Edward Gibbon: a reference guide. Boston, MA: G. K. Hall, 1987. pp. xlix, 476. (Reference guides to literature.) Rev. by Michel Baridon in EA (42:1) 103–4.

**5266.** GARDNER, JOSEPH H. 'To cease upon the midnight': Keats and Gibbon. ELN (26:4) 47–9.

**5267.** PORTER, ROY. Edward Gibbon: making history. London: Weidenfeld & Nicolson, 1988. pp. x, 187. (Historians on historians.) Rev. by Linda Colley in LRB (11:9) 20–2.

**5268.** WOMERSLEY, D. J. Gibbon's apostasy. BJECS (11) 1988, 51–70.

**5269.** WOMERSLEY, DAVID.    A complex allusion in Gibbon's letters. BJECS (10) 1987, 55–7.

**5270.** —— A complex allusion in Gibbon's *Memoirs*. NQ (36:1) 68–70.

### William Godwin (1756–1836) ('Edward Baldwin')

**5271.** CLEMIT, P.    The intellectual novel in the Romantic period: William Godwin and his school. Unpub. doct. diss., Univ. of Oxford, 1988. [Abstr. in IT (39:1) 32.]

**5272.** HALE, DOROTHY J.    Profits of altruism: Caleb Williams and Arthur Mervyn. ECS (22:1) 1988, 47–69.

**5273.** HINDLE, M.    William Godwin's *Caleb Williams*: a critical edition. Unpub. doct. diss., Univ. of Essex. [Abstr. in IT (39:4) 1630.]

**5274.** MARSHALL, PETER (ed.).    The anarchist writings of William Godwin. London: Freedom Press, 1986. pp. 182. Rev. by Martin Fitzpatrick in BJECS (12) 217–18.

**5275.** —— Damon and Delia. Croesor, Gwynedd: Zena; Cardiff: Wales UP. pp. 182. (Facsim. reprint.) Rev. by Richard Lansdown in TLS, 25 Aug., 912.

**5276.** MARSHALL, PETER H.    William Godwin. (Bibl. 1987, 5910.) Rev. by Robert Lance Snyder in ChrisL (38:2) 84–6.

**5277.** PHILP, MARK.    Godwin's *Political Justice*. Ithaca, NY: Cornell UP, 1986. (Bibl. 1986, 6503.) Rev. by John P. Clark in AHR (94:2) 438–9; by Peter Marshall in YES (19) 328–30.

**5278.** ST CLAIR, WILLIAM.    The Godwins and the Shelleys: the biography of a family. London: Faber & Faber. pp. xiv, 572. Rev. by Richard Lansdown in TLS, 25 Aug., 912; by Paul Foot in LRB (11:18) 21–2; by Martin Fagg in Listener (121) 29 June, 25; by Brian Aldiss in BkW, 24 Dec., 9, 13; by Leslie A. Marchand in NYTB, 5 Nov., 38.

**5279.** —— William Godwin as children's bookseller. *In* (pp. 165–79) **14.**

**5280.** WARREN, LELAND E.    Caleb Williams and the 'fall' into writing. Mosaic (20:1) 1987, 57–69.

**5281.** WEHRS, DONALD R.    Rhetoric, history, rebellion: *Caleb Williams* and the subversion of eighteenth-century fiction. SELit (28:3) 1988, 497–511.

### Oliver Goldsmith

**5282.** ARNAUD, PIERRE.    La lutte pour le pouvoir au sein de la famille dans *The Vicar of Wakefield*. *In* (pp. 139–50) **14.**

**5283.** BROOKS, CHRISTOPHER.    The political sub-text of Goldsmith's *The Good Natur'd Man*. ELN (26:3) 25–9.

**5284.** CHILTON, LESLIE ANNE.    Catching Pegasus by the tail: Oliver Goldsmith's *The Citizen of the World* as commercial literature. Unpub. doct. diss., Arizona State Univ., 1988. [Abstr. in DA (50) 144–5A.]

**5285.** KENNELLY, LAURA B.    A gloss on Jehu's judgement of Hume. NQ (36:4) 477.

**5286.** —— Hawthorne and Goldsmith: British history in *Young Goodman Brown* and *Biographical Stories*. JAStud (23:2) 295–7.

**5287.** KENNELLY, LAURA BALLARD.    Goldsmith's *History* in *The Antique Ring*. NHR (15:1) 24–5.

**5288.** LUCAS, JOHN (ed.). Selected writings. Manchester: Fyfield Press, 1988. pp. 180.

**5289.** TAYLOR, RICHARD C. A source for Goldsmith's Tony Lumpkin in *The Connoisseur*. See **595**.

**5290.** TAYLOR, RICHARD CAMERON. Goldsmith as journalist. Unpub. doct. diss., Pennsylvania State Univ., 1988. [Abstr. in DA (50) 451A.]

### Thomas Gray

**5291.** CAMAIORA, LUISA CONTI. Gray – Keats – Hopkins: poetry and the poetic presence. Lecce: Milella, 1985. pp. 169. Rev. by Marialuisa Bignami in MLR (84:2) 444-5.

**5291a.** SHERBO, ARTHUR. Two notes on Gray's poems. See **4741**.

### Elizabeth Griffith

**5292.** MASSEFSKI, HEIDI MINTZ. From London to Philadelphia: the misattribution of Elizabeth Griffith's *Essays, Addressed to Young Married Women (1782)*. NQ (36:4) 480-2.

### Eliza Haywood

**5293.** BALLASTER, R. M. Seductive forms: women's amatory fiction from 1684 to 1740 with particular reference to Aphra Behn, Delarivier Manley and Eliza Haywood. See **4315**.

**5294.** LOCKWOOD, THOMAS. Eliza Haywood in 1749: *Dalinda, and Her Pamphlet on the Pretender*. NQ (36:4) 475-7.

### Lord Hervey

**5295.** PEEREBOOM, J. J. Hervey and the facts as he saw them. *In* (pp. 211-24) **47**.

### Lemuel Hopkins

**5296.** VAN DOVER, J. K. The design of anarchy: *The Anarchiad*, 1786-1787. See **5046**.

### David Hume

**5297.** BAKER, RICHARD LEE, JR. By the eyes of faith alone: faith, reason, and design in David Hume's *Dialogues Concerning Natural Religion*. Unpub. doct. diss., Univ. of Texas at Austin, 1988. [Abstr. in DA (50) 459A.]

**5298.** BECKWITH, FRANCIS JOSEPH. David Hume's argument against miracles: contemporary attempts to rehabilitate it and a response. Unpub. doct. diss., Fordham Univ. [Abstr. in DA (49) 3749A.]

**5299.** BOX, M. A. How much of Berkeley did Hume read? See **5050**.

**5300.** CASTIGLIONE, DARIO. A mitigated skepticism: a study of David Hume's philosophical and political thought in its intellectual context. Unpub. doct. diss., Univ. of Sussex, 1986. [Abstr. in DA (49) 3750A.]

**5301.** CHRISTENSEN, JEROME. Practicing Enlightenment: Hume and the formation of a literary career. (Bibl. 1987, 5938.) Rev. by W. B. Carnochan in MLR (84:2) 442-4; by David Womersley in RES (39:155) 1988, 449-50; by Alain Morvan in EA (42:1) 104-5.

**5302.** GINSBERG, ROBERT. The literary structure and strategy of Hume's essay on the standard of taste. *In* (pp. 199-237) **49**.

**5303.** KENNELLY, LAURA B. A gloss on Jehu's judgement of Hume. See **5285**.

**5304.** McIntyre, Jane L.   Personal identity and the passions. JHP (27:4) 545–57.

**5305.** Morère, Pierre.   Un problème de traduction philosophique: 'fancy'/'imagination' dans le Livre I du *Traité de la Nature Humaine* de David Hume. *In* (pp. 111–22) **22.**

**5306.** Pakaluk, Michael.   Quine's 1946 lectures on Hume. JHP (27:3) 445–59.

**5307.** Siebert, Donald T.   'Ardor of youth': the manner of Hume's *Treatise. In* (pp. 177–98) **49.**

**5308.** —— Hume as philosophical traveler: from 'wild agreeable prospects' to a 'very pretty machine'. StudECC (18) 187–98.

**5309.** Tilley, John Joseph.   'Humean' rationality, morality, and reasons for action. Unpub. doct. diss., Univ. of Wisconsin–Madison, 1988. [Abstr. in DA (49) 3755A.]

**5310.** Tweyman, Stanley.   Scepticism and belief in Hume's *Dialogues Concerning Natural Religion.* (Bibl. 1986, 6542.) Rev. by M. A. Stewart in JHP (27:3) 481–5.

**5311.** Wilson, Fred.   Is Hume a sceptic with regard to the senses? JHP (27:1) 49–73.

### David Humphreys

**5312.** Van Dover, J. K.   The design of anarchy: *The Anarchiad,* 1786–1787. *See* **5046.**

### Francis Hutcheson

**5313.** Darling, John.   The moral teaching of Francis Hutcheson. BJECS (12) 165–74.

### Elizabeth Inchbald

**5314.** Manvell, Roger.   Elizabeth Inchbald: England's principal woman dramatist and independent woman of letters in 18th century London: a biographical study. (Bibl. 1988, 3990.) Rev. by Ellen Donkin in TJ (41:3) 423.

**5315.** —— (introd. and notes).   Selected comedies. (Bibl. 1987, 5948.) Rev. by Ellen Donkin in TJ (41:3) 423–5.

### Thomas Jefferson

**5316.** Cappon, Lester J. (ed.).   The Adams–Jefferson letters: the complete correspondence between Thomas Jefferson and Abigail and John Adams. *See* **5037.**

**5317.** Cunningham, Noble E., Jr.   In pursuit of reason: the life of Thomas Jefferson. Baton Rouge: Louisiana State UP, 1987. pp. xvi, 414. Rev. by Frank Shuffelton in EAL (23:2) 1988, 217–19.

**5318.** Tauber, Gisela.   Thomas Jefferson: relationships with women. AI (45:4) 1988, 431–47.

### Soame Jenyns

**5319.** Rompkey, Ronald.   Soame Jenyns. (Bibl. 1986, 6549.) Rev. by Elaine Hepple in BJECS (12) 229–30.

**5320.** Winnett, A. R.   The problem of evil in the 18th century: Dr Johnson and Soame Jenyns. NRam (27) 1987/88, 46–7.

### Dr Samuel Johnson

**5321.** Abbott, John L.   Defining the Johnsonian canon: authority, intuition, and the uses of evidence. MLS (18:1) 1988, 89–98.

**5322.** ALKON, PAUL.   Johnson and time criticism. MP (85:4) 1988, 543–57.

**5323.** —— FOLKENFLIK, ROBERT.   Samuel Johnson: pictures and words. Papers presented at a Clark Library seminar, 23 October, 1982. (Bibl. 1986, 6552.) Rev. by Isobel Grundy in BJECS (10) 1987, 103–5.

**5324.** BRACK, O. M., JR.   Johnson's *Life of Admiral Blake* and the development of a biographical technique. MP (85:4) 1988, 523–31.

**5325.** BROWNELL, MORRIS R.   Samuel Johnson's attitude to the arts. Oxford: Clarendon Press. pp. xvii, 195.

**5326.** CLINGHAM, GREGORY J.   Johnson's criticism of Dryden's odes in praise of St Cecilia. *See* **4441.**

**5327.** CURLEY, THOMAS M.   Johnson's tour of Scotland and the idea of Great Britain. BJECS (12) 135–44.

**5328.** DeMARIA, ROBERT, JR.   Johnson's *Dictionary* and the language of learning. (Bibl. 1988, 3997.) Rev. by David Womersley in RES (39:153) 1988, 113–14; by Allen Reddick in MP (86:3) 312–16; by Murray G. H. Pittock in BJECS (12) 111–12.

**5329.** —— The politics of Johnson's *Dictionary*. PMLA (104:1) 64–74.

**5330.** DE VOOGD, PETER JAN.   'The great object of remark': Samuel Johnson and Laurence Sterne. *In* (pp. 65–74) **23.**

**5331.** DITCHFIELD, G. M.   Dr Johnson at Oxford, 1759. NQ (36:1) 66–8.

**5332.** DURING, SIMON.   Waiting for the post: some relations between modernity, colonization and writing. *See* **5110.**

**5333.** ENGELL, JAMES.   Johnson and his age. (Bibl. 1987, 5965.) Rev. by Isobel Grundy in BJECS (10) 1987, 103–5.

**5334.** FINCH, G. J.   Reason, imagination and will in *Rasselas* and *The Vanity of Human Wishes*. Eng (38) 195–209.

**5335.** FLEEMAN, J. D. (ed.).   A journey to the Western Islands of Scotland. (Bibl. 1987, 5968.) Rev. by David Womersley in RES (38:149) 1987, 82–3; by Isobel Grundy in BJECS (10) 1987, 103–5.

**5336.** GILMORE, THOMAS B.   Implicit criticism of Thomson's *Seasons* in Johnson's *Dictionary*. MP (86:3) 265–73.

**5337.** GOLD, JOEL J. (ed.).   Samuel Johnson: *A Voyage to Abyssinia*. (Bibl. 1987, 5970, where scholar's forename abbreviated.) Rev. by Isobel Grundy in BJECS (10) 1987, 103–5; by Claire Lamont in RES (38:149) 1987, 81–2.

**5338.** GRAY, JAMES.   'The Athenian blockheads': new light on Johnson's Oxford. NRam (27) 1987/88, 30–45.

**5339.** GREENE, DONALD (ed.).   Samuel Johnson.   (Bibl. 1988, 4001.) Rev. by Jenny Mezciems in RES (39:154) 1988, 298–9.

**5340.** GROSS, GLORIA.   Mentoring Jane Austen: reflections on 'my dear Dr Johnson'. Persuasions (11) 53–60.

**5341.** GRUNDY, ISOBEL.   Samuel Johnson and the scale of greatness. (Bibl. 1988, 4002.) Rev. by G. J. Clingham in RES (38:151) 1987, 394–6.

**5342.** HARP, RICHARD L. (ed.).   Dr Johnson's critical vocabulary: a selection from his *Dictionary*. *See* **1131.**

**5343.** HEBERDEN, ERNEST.   Dr Heberden and Dr Johnson. NRam (27) 1987/88, 9–21.

**5344.** HEDRICK, ELIZABETH.   Fixing the language: Johnson, Chesterfield, and *The Plan of a Dictionary. See* **1089.**

**5345.** HUDSON, N. J.   Samuel Johnson and the literature of common life. BJECS (11) 1988, 39–50.

**5346.** HUTCHINGS, W. B.   Johnson and Juvenal. NRam (1987/88) 21–2.

**5347.** JEMIELITY, THOMAS.   Prophetic voices and satiric echoes. Cithara (29:1) 30–47.

**5348.** KAMINSKI, THOMAS.   The early career of Samuel Johnson. (Bibl. 1987, 5975.) Rev. by A. F. T. Lurcock in NQ (36:1) 113–14.

**5349.** KORSHIN, PAUL J. (ed.).   Johnson after two hundred years. (Bibl. 1987, 5979.) Rev. by Thomas F. Bonnell in MP (86:4) 427–30; by Murray G. H. Pittock in BJECS (12) 111–12.

**5350.** LAMONT, CLAIRE.   Dr Johnson, the Scottish Highlander, and the Scottish Enlightenment. BJECS (12) 47–55.

**5351.** MANER, MARTIN.   The philosophical biographer: doubt and dialectic in Johnson's *Lives of the Poets.* Athens; London: Georgia UP, 1988. pp. xi, 187.

**5352.** MUGGLESTONE, L. C.   Samuel Johnson and the use of /h/. *See* **734.**

**5353.** NASSIR, GHAZI Q.   A history and criticism of Samuel Johnson's oriental tales. Unpub. doct. diss., Florida State Univ. [Abstr. in DA (50) 692A.]

**5354.** PAGE, NORMAN (ed.).   Dr Johnson: interviews and recollections. (Bibl. 1987, 5983.) Rev. by A. F. T. Lurcock in NQ (36:1) 114; by J. D. Fleeman in NRam (27) 1987/88, 48–50.

**5355.** PARKER, G. F.   Johnson's Shakespeare. *See* **3621.**

**5356.** RAWLINSON, DAVID H.   Presenting its evils to our minds: imagination in Johnson's pamphlets. EngS (70:4) 315–27.

**5357.** REINERT, THOMAS.   Johnson and conjecture. SELit (28:3) 1988, 483–96.

**5358.** SHERBO, ARTHUR.   *Nil nisi bonum*: Samuel Johnson in *The Gentleman's Magazine,* 1785–1800. *See* **590.**

**5359.** SOLIMAN, SOLIMAN Y.   *Rasselas*: certain aspects of technique. Journal of Education and Science (Univ. of Mosul, Iraq) (3) 1981, 5–15.

**5360.** STAFFORD, FIONA.   Dr Johnson and the ruffian: new evidence in the dispute between Samuel Johnson and James Macpherson. NQ (36:1) 70–7.

**5361.** STEWART, MARY MARGARET.   William Collins, Samuel Johnson, and the use of biographical details. *See* **5166.**

**5362.** WALSH, MARCUS.   Samuel Johnson on poetic lice and fleas. NQ (36:4) 470.

**5363.** WEINSHEIMER, JOEL.   Fiction and the force of example. *In* (pp. 1–19) **33.**

**5364.** WHEELER, DAVID (ed.).   Domestick privacies: Samuel Johnson and the art of biography. *See* **5001.**

**5365.** WINNETT, A. R. The problem of evil in the 18th century: Dr Johnson and Soame Jenyns. *See* **5320.**

**5366.** WOOD, NIGEL. Johnson's revisions to his *Dictionary*, 1755–1773. *See* **1115.**

**5367.** WOODRUFF, JAMES F. The background and significance of the *Rambler*'s format. *See* **470.**

### Richard Payne Knight

**5368.** ROUSSEAU, G. S.; PORTER, ROY (eds). Sexual underworlds of the Enlightenment. *See* **4885.**

### Charlotte Lennox

**5369.** DALZIEL, MARGARET (ed.). The female Quixote; or, The adventures of Arabella. Introd. by MARGARET ANNE DOODY. Oxford: OUP. pp. xxxvii, 428. (World's classics.)

### M. G. Lewis

**5370.** KAUHL, GUDRUN. On the release from monkish fetters: Matthew Lewis reconsidered. DQR (19:4) 264–80.

### George Lillo

**5371.** REDMOND, JAMES. 'If the salt have lost his savour': some 'useful' plays in and out of context on the London stage. *In* (pp. 63–88) **50.**

### William Livingston

**5372.** WILSON, ROB. William Livingston's *Philosophic Solitude* and the ideology of the natural sublime. EAL (24:3) 217–36.

### James Macpherson

**5373.** O'HALLORAN, CLARE. Irish re-creation of the Gaelic past: the challenge of Macpherson's Ossian. Past & Present (124) 69–95.

**5374.** PROCHÁZKA, MARTIN. Cultural invention and cultural awareness: translational activities and author's subjectivity in the culture of the Czech national revival. *See* **1634.**

**5375.** STAFFORD, FIONA. Dr Johnson and the ruffian: new evidence in the dispute between Samuel Johnson and James Macpherson. *See* **5360.**

**5376.** —— The sublime savage: a study of James Macpherson and the poems of Ossian. (Bibl. 1988, 4042.) Rev. in Edinburgh Review (83) 147–8; by Joan H. Pittock in SLJ (supp. 31) 9–12; by Neil Rennie in LRB (11:3) 20–2.

### Bernard Mandeville

**5377.** DAVIDSON, I. S. The literary and philosophical context of the debate about Mandeville's *Fable of the Bees*. Unpub. doct. diss., Univ. of Wales, 1987. [Abstr. in IT (39:1) 31.]

**5378.** MCKEE, FRANCIS. Two brief notes on Bernard Mandeville. NQ (36:1) 52–3.

### Mary de la Rivière Manley

**5379.** BALLASTER, R. M. Seductive forms: women's amatory fiction from 1684 to 1740 with particular reference to Aphra Behn, Delarivier Manley and Eliza Haywood. *See* **4315.**

### Lady Mary Wortley Montagu

**5380.** BATTESTIN, MARTIN C. Dating Fielding's letters to Lady Mary Wortley Montagu. *See* **5225.**

**5381.** RICHARDSON, P.    Virgilian forms and the ideal of civilization in English poetry 1700–1720. *See* **5260.**

**5382.** SPACKS, PATRICIA MEYER. Female rhetorics. *In* (pp. 177–91) **51.**

### John Newton

**5383.** SPACKS, PATRICIA MEYER.    Forgotten genres. *See* **5171.**

### Jonathan Odell

**5384.** EDELBERG, CYNTHIA DUBIN.    Jonathan Odell: loyalist poet of the American Revolution. Durham, NC: Duke UP, 1987. pp. xv, 205. Rev. by Robert D. Arner in AL (60:2) 1988, 293–4; by Charles E. Modlin in EAL (23:2) 1988, 229–30; by Carla Mulford in NJH (106:1/2) 1988, 86–99.

### Thomas Paine

**5385.** AYER, A. J.    Thomas Paine. New York: Atheneum; London: Secker & Warburg, 1988. pp. xi, 195. Rev. by William Randel in AL (61:3) 473–4.

**5386.** FURNISS, TOM.    Burke, Paine, and the language of *assignats*. *See* **5119.**

**5387.** NORMAN, CHARLES J.    *The American Crisis* by Thomas Paine: a rhetorical analysis. Unpub. doct. diss., Lehigh Univ., 1988. [Abstr. in DA (49) 1803A.]

**5388.** POWELL, DAVID.    Tom Paine: the greatest exile. (Bibl. 1986, 6692.) Rev. by Martin Fitzpatrick in BJECS (11) 1988, 73.

**5389.** TURNER, JOHN.    Burke, Paine, and the nature of language. *See* **5125.**

### Thomas Parnell

**5390.** RAWSON, CLAUDE; LOCK, F. P. (eds).    Collected poems of Thomas Parnell. Newark, NJ: Delaware UP; London: Assoc. UPs. pp. 717. Rev. by Donald Davie in TLS, 8 Dec., 1365.

**5391.** WOODMAN, THOMAS M.    Thomas Parnell. Boston, MA: G. K. Hall, 1985. pp. x, 137. (Twayne's English authors, 397.) Rev. by Yvonne Noble in BJECS (10) 1987, 229–30.

### Samuel Pegge the Younger

**5392.** PRICKETT, STEPHEN.    Radicalism and linguistic theory: Horne Tooke on Samuel Pegge. *See* **710.**

**5393.** SHERBO, ARTHUR.    Samuel Pegge, Thoms Holt White, and *Piers Plowman See* **2752.**

### Thomas Percy

**5394.** DAVIS, BERTRAM H.    Thomas Percy: a scholar-cleric in the age of Johnson. Philadelphia: Pennsylvania UP. pp. xi, 361. Rev. by Roy Foster in TLS, 14 July, 770.

### Edward Phillips

**5395.** MILHOUS, JUDITH; HUME, ROBERT D.    Edward Phillips and the authorship of *Marforio* (1736). *See* **5240.**

### John Pinkerton

**5396.** STANLEY, E. G.    A *Beowulf* allusion, 1790. *See* **2358.**

### Hester Lynch Piozzi (Mrs Thrale)

**5397.** McCARTHY, WILLIAM.    The repression of Hester Lynch Piozzi: or how we forgot a revolution in authorship. MLS (18:1) 1988, 99–111.

**5398.** NUSSBAUM, FELICITY A.     Eighteenth-century women's auto-biographical commonplaces. *In* (pp. 147–71) **51.**

### Alexander Pope

**5399.** AMIN, JA'FAR ABBOUD M.     Pride or love in *The Rape of the Lock?* Journal of education and Science (Univ. of Mosul, Iraq) (6) (Humanities and education) 1987, 49–71.

**5400.** ATKINS, G. DOUGLAS.     Quests of difference: reading Pope's poems. (Bibl. 1988, 4043.) Rev. by J. Douglas Canfield in MP (86:3) 309–12.

**5401.** BERRY, REGINALD.     A Pope chronology. (Bibl. 1988, 4045.) Rev. by Kirk Combe in NQ (36:4) 513–14; by Michael Williams in UES (27:2) 27–8.

**5402.** BROWN, LAURA.     Alexander Pope. (Bibl. 1988, 4048.) Rev. by Michael Ackland in AUMLA (72) 350–2.

**5403.** BROWN, STEPHEN WILLIAM.     Changing concepts of character and plot from Dryden to Sterne. *See* **4438.**

**5404.** CLINGHAM, G. J.     Pope's Bolingbroke and Dryden's 'happy man'. *See* **4440.**

**5405.** COOKE, MICHAEL G.     Byron, Pope, and the Grand Tour. YR (78:3) 352–69.

**5406.** DAICHES, DAVID.     Burns and Pope. *See* **5135.**

**5407.** DAMROSCH, LEOPOLD, JR.     The imaginative world of Alexander Pope. (Bibl. 1987, 6043.) Rev. by Pat Rogers in ELN (26:3) 88–90; by Douglas H. White in MP (87:2) 188–91; by Karina Williamson in EC (38:3) 1988, 254–8; by Brean S. Hammond in BJECS (12) 237.

**5408.** FAIRER, DAVID.     The poetry of Alexander Pope. Harmondsworth: Penguin. pp. xii, 160. (Penguin critical studies.)

**5409.** FERGUSON, REBECCA.     The unbalanced mind: Pope and the rule of passion. (Bibl. 1988, 4064.) Rev. by David Fairer in BJECS (11) 1988, 105–6.

**5410.** FOX, CHRISTOPHER.     Locke and the Scriblerians: identity and consciousness in early eighteenth-century Britain. *See* **4605.**

**5411.** GRIFFIN, ROBERT J.     Wordsworth's Pope: the language of his former heart. ELH (54:3) 1987, 695–715.

**5412.** HAMMOND, BREAN S.     Pope. (Bibl. 1988, 4067.) Rev. by Pat Rogers in RES (38:152) 1987, 563–4.

**5413.** INGRAM, ALLAN.     Intricate laughter in the satire of Swift and Pope. (Bibl. 1987, 6049.) Rev. by Brean S. Hammond in BJECS (10) 1987, 233–4.

**5414.** JEMIELITY, THOMAS.     Prophetic voices and satiric echoes. *See* **5347.**

**5414a.** KEENER, FREDERICK M.     Pope, Dryden, Milton, and the poets' secret. *See* **4454.**

**5415.** MARTIN, PETER.     Pursuing innocent pleasures: the gardening world of Alexander Pope. (Bibl. 1988, 4079.) Rev. by Graham Midgley in RES (39:154) 1988, 299–300.

**5416.** NICHOL, DONALD W.     'Flagrant' versus 'fragrant' in Beaumont, Pope, Pound, and Burgess. *See* **1048.**

**5417.** —— Pope, Warburton, Knapton, and Cole: a longstanding connection. NQ (36:1) 54–6.

**5418.** NUTTALL, A. D. Pope's *Essay on Man*. (Bibl. 1985, 5661.) Rev. by Murray G. H. Pittock in BJECS (11) 1988, 223–4.

**5419.** O'GRADY, DEIRDRE. The influence of the translations of the works of Alexander Pope on eighteenth-century Italian literature. NC (8) 24–35.

**5420.** POLLAK, ELLEN. The poetics of sexual myth: gender and ideology in the verse of Swift and Pope. (Bibl. 1988, 4085.) Rev. by Janet Todd in BJECS (10) 1987, 231–3.

**5421.** QUINTERO, RUBEN DAVID. Literate culture: the rhetoric of Pope's poetry, 1711–1729. Unpub. doct. diss., Harvard Univ., 1988. [Abstr. in DA (49) 3035A.]

**5422.** RICHARDSON, P. Virgilian forms and the ideal of civilization in English poetry 1700–1720. *See* **5260.**

**5423.** ROSSLYN, FELICITY (ed.). Pope's Iliad: a selection with commentary. Bristol: Bristol Classical Press, 1985. pp. xxvii, 228. Rev. by BH in BJECS (10) 1987, 96–7.

**5424.** ROUSSEAU, G. S.; ROGERS, PAT (eds). The enduring legacy: Alexander Pope tercentenary essays. Cambridge; New York: CUP, 1988. pp. xiii, 286.

**5425.** SOLOMON, HARRY M. Reading philosophical poetry: a hermeneutics of metaphor for Pope's *Essay on Man*. *In* (pp. 122–39) **49.**

**5426.** SPACKS, PATRICIA MEYER. Forgotten genres. *See* **5171.**

**5427.** STRINER, RICHARD. The inverted world: cosmic visions in the poetry of Pope. CEACrit (51:4) 11–30.

**5428.** TODD, DENNIS. 'One vast egg': Leibniz, the new embryology and Pope's *Dunciad*. ELN (26:4) 24–40.

**5429.** WILLIAMS, ROBERT W. Pope and the 'microscopic eye'. Sydney Studies in English (14) 1988/89, 21–37.

## Matthew Prior

**5430.** DE VOOGD, PETER J. William III, the Siege of Namur, Prior and Sterne. DQR (19:3) 202–13.

**5431.** NELSON, NICHOLAS H. Dramatic textures and philosophical debate in Prior's *Dialogues of the Dead*. SELit (28:3) 1988, 427–41.

## Ann Radcliffe

**5432.** COTTOM, DANIEL. The civilized imagination: a study of Ann Radcliffe, Jane Austen, and Sir Walter Scott. (Bibl. 1988, 4097.) Rev. by Peter Faulkner in BJECS (10) 1987, 101.

**5433.** EDE, W. R. The gentlewoman as creative artist in the life and romances of Ann Radcliffe: 1764–1823. Unpub. doct. diss., Univ. of Wales, 1986. [Abstr. in IT (39:1) 31.]

**5434.** MACDONALD, D. L. Bathos and repetition: the uncanny in Radcliffe. JNT (19:2) 197–204.

**5435.** SHOR, ÎU. V. Stilisticheskie osobennosti angliĭskogo goticheskogo romana: na materiale romana A. Radklif *Udol'fskie taĭny*. *See* **1420.**

## Allan Ramsay (1713–1784)

**5436.** LAW, ALEXANDER. Allan Ramsay and the Easy Club. SLJ (16:2) 18–40.

## Samuel Richardson

**5437.** BRODER, JANICE SUSAN. Re: Readings of *Clarissa*: toward a theory of reader's competence. Unpub. doct. diss., Brandeis Univ., 1988. [Abstr. in DA (49) 1807A.]

**5438.** BROPHY, ELIZABETH BERGEN. Samuel Richardson. Boston, MA: G. K. Hall, 1987. pp. xii, 134. (Twayne's English authors, 454.)

**5439.** BROWN, STEPHEN WILLIAM. Changing concepts of character and plot from Dryden to Sterne. *See* **4438.**

**5440.** CARSON, JAMES. Narrative cross-dressing and the critique of authorship in the novels of Richardson. *In* (pp. 95–113) **61.**

**5441.** CHABER, LOIS A. From moral man to godly man: 'Mr Locke' and Mr B in part 2 of *Pamela*. StudECC (18) 1988, 213–61.

**5442.** DOODY, MARGARET ANNE; STUBER, FLORIAN. *Clarissa* censored. MLS (18:1) 1988, 74–88.

**5443.** —— SABOR, PETER (eds). Samuel Richardson: tercentenary essays. Cambridge: CUP. pp. xvii, 306. Rev. by Rosemary Ashton in LRB (11:22) 22.

**5444.** FAWCETT, NANCY RUTH. A safe place: Jane Austen and the Richardsonian inheritance. Unpub. doct. diss., McMaster Univ., 1988. [Abstr. in DA (49) 3367–8A.]

**5445.** HARRIS, JOCELYN. Samuel Richardson. (Bibl. 1988, 4105.) Rev. by Sylvia Kasey Marks in StudN (20:4) 1988, 432–3.

**5446.** HYNES, PETER. Curses, oaths, and narrative in Richardson's *Clarissa*. ELH (56:2) 311–26.

**5447.** KAY, CAROL. Political constructions: Defoe, Richardson, and Sterne in relation to Hobbes, Hume, and Burke. *See* **5195.**

**5448.** LAMB, JONATHAN. The fragmentation of originals and *Clarissa*. SELit (28:3) 1988, 443–59.

**5449.** MARKS, SYLVIA KASEY. *Sir Charles Grandison*: the compleat conduct book. Lewisburg, PA: Bucknell UP; London; Toronto: Assoc. UPs, 1986. pp. 173. Rev. by Lila V. Graves in StudN (20:1) 1988, 109–11.

**5450.** MYER, VALERIE GROSVENOR (ed.). Samuel Richardson: passion and prudence. (Bibl. 1988, 4113.) Rev. by Loraine Fletcher in StudN (20:1) 1988, 111–14.

**5451.** STRAUB, KRISTINA. Reconstructing the gaze: voyeurism in Richardson's *Pamela*. StudECC (18) 1988, 419–31.

**5452.** YODER, R. PAUL. Clarissa regained: Richardson's redemption of Eve. ECL (13:2) 87–99.

## Col. Robert Rogers

**5453.** TANNER, LAURA E.; KRASNER, JAMES N. Exposing the 'sacred juggle': revolutionary rhetoric in Robert Rogers' *Ponteach*. EAL (24:1) 4–19.

## Elizabeth Singer Rowe

**5454.** MADIGAN, MARY KATHLEEN. Forever yours: the subgenre of the letter from the dead to the living with thematic analyses of the works of Elizabeth Singer Rowe and Meta Klopstock. Unpub. doct. diss., Univ. of North Carolina at Chapel Hill, 1988. [Abstr. in DA (50) 681A.]

### Susanna Rowson
**5455.** DAVIDSON, CATHY N. (ed.).   Charlotte Temple. (Bibl. 1987, 6117.) Rev. by David Seed in BJECS (12) 110–11.
**5456.** PARKER, PATRICIA L.   Susanna Rowson.   Boston, MA: G. K. Hall, 1986. pp. 146. (Twayne's US authors, 498.) Rev. by Ivy Schweitzer in EAL (23:2) 1988, 221–5.

### Robert Samber
**5457.** BLOM, J. M.   The life and works of Robert Samber (1682–±1745). EngS (70:6) 507–50.

### Mary Scott
**5458.** HOLLADAY, GAE (introd.).   The female advocate; a poem occasioned by reading Mr Duncombe's *Feminead*. Los Angeles, CA: William Andrews Clark Memorial Library, 1984. pp. xiv, viii, 41. (Augustan Reprint Soc., 224.) (Facsim. of text first pub. 1774). Rev. by James Egan in SCN (47:1/2) 12–13.

### Sarah Scott
**5459.** RABB, MELINDA ALLIKER.   Making and rethinking the canon: general introduction and the case of *Millenium Hall*. *See* **4948**.
**5460.** Entry cancelled

### Anthony Ashley Cooper, Third Earl of Shaftesbury
**5461.** BUTLER, LANCE.   Éthique/esthétique dans *Characteristicks* de Shaftesbury. *In* (pp. 27–36) **10**.
**5462.** LOTTES, WOLFGANG.   *The Judgment of Hercules*: Shaftesbury und die 'ut pictura poesis'-Tradition. Ang (107:3/4) 330–43.
**5463.** MARKLEY, ROBERT.   Style as philosophical structure: the contexts of Shaftesbury's *Characteristicks*. *In* (pp. 140–54) **49**.
**5464.** PORTIER, FRANÇOIS.   Un Mécène anglais et des artistes italiens au début du XVIIIe siècle: Lord Shaftesbury, Antonio Verrio et Paolo de Matteis. EA (42:4) 401–10.
**5465.** PROSTKO, JACK.   'Natural conversation set in view': Shaftesbury and moral speech. ECS (23:1) 42–61.

### Richard Brinsley Sheridan
**5466.** DIXON, PETER; BANCROFT, VICKY.   Sheridan's second prologue to *The Rivals*: a case for emendation. *See* **302**.
**5467.** MORWOOD, JAMES.   The life and works of Richard Brinsley Sheridan. (Bibl. 1988, 4123.) Rev. by Brean S. Hammond in RES (38:149) 1987, 83–4.
**5468.** MURRAY, GERALDINE.   A Sheridan emendation. NQ (36:4) 482–3.
**5469.** PARKER, ANNE.   'Absolute sense' in Sheridan's *The Rivals*. BSUF (27:3) 1986, 10–19.
**5470.** RANGER, PAUL.   *The School for Scandal* by Richard Sheridan. Basingstoke: Macmillan, 1986. pp. x, 83. (Macmillan master guides.) Rev. by Cecil Price in MLR (84:4) 933.
**5471.** ROWE, JEREMY.   *The Rivals* by Richard Sheridan. (Bibl. 1986, 6806.) (Macmillan master guides.) Rev. by Cecil Price in MLR (84:4) 932–3.

### Christopher Smart
**5472.** WALSH, MARCUS (ed.).   The poetical works of Christopher

Smart: vol. 3, A translation of the Psalms of David. (Bibl. 1988, 4127.) Rev. by J. P. Vander Motten in EngS (70:2) 183–4.

**5473.** ——; WILLIAMSON, KARINA (eds). The poetical works of Christopher Smart: vol. 2, Religious poetry 1763–1771. (Bibl. 1986, 6814.) Rev. by Cecil Price in RES (38:150) 1987, 255–6.

**5474.** WILLIAMSON, KARINA (ed.). The poetical works of Christopher Smart: vol. 4, Miscellaneous poems, English and Latin. (Bibl. 1987, 6137.) Rev. by J. P. Vander Motten in EngS (70:2) 183–4.

### Charlotte Smith

**5475.** EHRENPREIS, ANNE HENRY (ed.). The old manor house. Introd. by JUDITH PHILLIPS STANTON. Oxford: OUP. pp. xxix, 546. (World's classics.)

### Tobias Smollett

**5476.** BASKER, JAMES G. Tobias Smollett: critic and journalist. See **554.**

**5477.** BULCKAEN-MESSINA, DENISE. Smollett et Hogarth: rencontre autour d'une ligne de beauté. In (pp. 9–26) **10.**

**5478.** CHESLEY, BRENT. Probable sources for Garrick's pantomime. See **5165.**

**5479.** FITZPATRICK, BARBARA LANING. The text of Tobias Smollett's *Life and Adventures of Sir Launcelot Greaves*, the first serialized novel. See **569.**

**5480.** GUTHRIE, NEIL. A possible source for Smollett's *Peregrine Pickle*. NQ (36:1) 58.

**5481.** KELLY, LIONEL (ed.). Tobias Smollett: the critical heritage. (Bibl. 1987, 6153.) Rev. by John Valdimir Price in NQ (36:1) 112–13.

**5482.** LEWIS, JOANNE. Death and the comic marriage: Lismahago in *Harlequin Skeleton*. StudECC (18) 1988, 405–17.

**5483.** SPECTOR, ROBERT D. Tobias Smollett: an eighteenth-century man of letters. PLL (25:2) 225–31.

### Sir Richard Steele

**5484.** DAMMERS, RICHARD H. Familial relationships in Steele's plays. BSUF (26:3) 1985, 14–20.

**5485.** McCREA, BRIAN. The canon and the eighteenth century: a modest proposal and a tale of two tubs. See **5040.**

### Laurence Sterne

**5486.** BANDRY, ANNE. First reactions to *Tristram Shandy* in the Oates Collection. See **196.**

**5487.** BARKER, NICOLAS. The library catalogue of Laurence Sterne. See **197.**

**5488.** BROWN, STEPHEN WILLIAM. Changing concepts of character and plot from Dryden to Sterne. See **4438.**

**5489.** BYRD, MAX. Tristram Shandy. (Bibl. 1988, 4144.) Rev. by W. G. Day in BJECS (10) 1987, 92.

**5490.** BYSTYDZIEŃSKA, GRAŻYNA. Laurence Sterne'a gra z czytelnikiem (*Podróz sentymentalna*). (Laurence Sterne – playing games with the reader (*Sentimental Journey*).) In (pp. 94–107) **36.**

**5491.** CASH, ARTHUR H. Laurence Sterne: the later years. (Bibl. 1988, 4145.) Rev. by Oliver W. Ferguson in SewR (96:3) 1988, lxiv–lxvi; by Jeffrey Smitten in RES (39:153) 1988, 114–15.

**5492.** DAVIDSON, ELIZABETH LIVINGSTON. The man of opinion and the man of sentiment: the relationship between *Tristram Shandy* and *A Sentimental Journey*. Unpub. doct. diss., State Univ. of New York at Stony Brook, 1987. [Abstr. in DA (50) 1662A.]

**5493.** DAY, W. G. The Oates Collection, Cambridge University Library. *See* **215.**

**5494.** DE VOOGD, PETER J. A portrait and a flourish. Shandean (1) 129–32. (Previously unknown picture of Sterne and possible source for woodcut of flourish in vol. 9 of *Tristram Shandy*.)

**5495.** —— Stephen Croft's chimney-piece: or, was this the fireplace? Shandean (1) 109–15.

**5496.** —— William III, the Siege of Namur, Prior and Sterne. *See* **5430.**

**5497.** DE VOOGD, PETER JAN. 'The great object of remark': Samuel Johnson and Laurence Sterne. *In* (pp. 65–74) **23.**

**5498.** GÖBEL, WALTER; UHLIG, CLAUS. Zur Kritik erkenntnis-theoretischer Systeme in Laurence Sternes *Tristram Shandy*. LJGG (26) 1985, 101–20.

**5499.** HARRISON, BERNARD. The defence of Wit: Sterne, Locke and the particular. *See* **4607.**

**5500.** HAWLEY, JUDITH. Two textbooks on *Tristram Shandy*. Shandean (1) 137–48 (review-article).

**5501.** ISER, WOLFGANG. Laurence Sternes *Tristram Shandy*: ins-zenierte Subjektivität. (Bibl. 1988, 4149.) Rev. by Peter Wagner in EA (42:4) 476–7.

**5502.** —— Laurence Sterne, *Tristram Shandy*. (Bibl. 1988, 4150.) Rev. by Judith Hawley in Shandean (1) 137–48.

**5503.** KAY, CAROL. Political constructions: Defoe, Richardson, and Sterne in relation to Hobbes, Hume, and Burke. *See* **5195.**

**5504.** KIM, CHUNG-SOOK. *Tristram Shandy* wa metafiction. (*Tristram Shandy* and metafiction.) JELL (35) 429–44.

**5505.** LEE, ABIGAIL E. Sterne's legacy to Juan Goytisolo: a Shan-dyian reading of *Juan sin tierra*. MLR (84:2) 351–7.

**5506.** LENARD, GEORGEANN T. An adaptation of Max Weber's theory of *Herrschaft* to Laurence Sterne's *Tristram Shandy*. Unpub. doct. diss., Temple Univ. [Abstr. in DA (50) 954A.]

**5507.** MACEY, SAMUEL L. The linear and circular time schemes in Sterne's *Tristram Shandy*. NQ (36:4) 477–9.

**5508.** MONKMAN, KENNETH. More of Sterne's *Politicks* 1741–42. Shandean (1) 53–108.

**5509.** —— Two Sterne letters, and some fragments. Shandean (1) 116–23.

**5510.** MONTANDON, ALAIN. La réception de Laurence Sterne en Allemagne. Clermont-Ferrand: Faculté des lettres et sciences humaines de l'université de Clermont-Ferrand, 1986. pp. iv, 393. Rev. by Ian

Campbell Ross in BJECS (11) 1988, 231–2; by Nicholas Cronk in RES (38:150) 1987, 292–3.

**5511.** MOORE, PAUL. Sterne, Tristram, Yorick, birds and beasts. BJECS (10) 1987, 43–54.

**5512.** NEW, MELVYN. Approaches to teaching Sterne's *Tristram Shandy*. New York: Modern Language Assn of America. pp. x, 174. (Approaches to teaching world literature, 20.) Rev. by W. G. Day in Shandean (1) 149–52.

**5513.** —— Cowley and Sterne. *See* **4370.**

**5514.** —— (gen. ed.). The life and opinions of Tristram Shandy, gentleman. (Bibl. 1986, 6855.) Rev. by Ian Campbell Ross in Review (9) 1987, 329–51.

**5515.** REISSIG, ERICH. Sterne televised. Shandean (1) 133–4. (On Bayerische Rundfunk.)

**5516.** RIELY, JOHN. Sterne in Paris, an unpublished letter. Shandean (1) 125–8.

**5517.** ROSS, IAN CAMPBELL; NASSAR, NOHA SAAD. Trim(-tram), like master, like man: servant and sexton in Sterne's *Tristram Shandy* and *A Political Romance*. NQ (36:1) 62–5.

**5518.** SMYTH, JOHN VIGNAUX. A question of eros: irony in Sterne, Kierkegaard, and Barthes. (Bibl. 1988, 4153.) Rev. by Serge Soupel in EA (42:2) 214–15.

**5519.** SOULIER-DETIS, ELISABETH. Colliers, gants et manchon: les pulsions dévoilées. *See* **5205.**

**5520.** WHITE, BARBARA ANNE. Undercurrent strategies: the encyclopedic narratives of Sterne, Melville, Poe and Rainer. Unpub. doct. diss., State Univ. of New York at Buffalo, 1988. [Abstr. in DA (49) 2651A.]

**5521.** WHITTAKER, RUTH. Tristram Shandy. Milton Keynes; Philadelphia, PA: Open UP, 1988. pp. xii, 100. (Open guides to literature.) Rev. by Judith Hawley in Shandean (1) 137–9.

### Jonathan Swift

**5522.** ANON. *Gulliver's Travels* (abridged and adapted). Tirana: Shtëpia botuese e librit shkollor. pp. 99. (Biblioteka e nxënësit.)

**5523.** BYRN, RICHARD F. MACD. Jonathan Swift's locket for Stella Swift: a sacramental marriage 'certificate'? Swift Studies (3) 1988, 2–8.

**5524.** DIXSAUT, JEAN. Du modèle à la norme dans *Gulliver's Travels*. BSEAA (28) 87–9.

**5525.** FITZGERALD, ROBERT P. The allegory of *Gulliver's Travels*. YREAL (6) 187–215.

**5526.** FOX, CHRISTOPHER. Locke and the Scriblerians: identity and consciousness in early eighteenth-century Britain. *See* **4605.**

**5527.** FREEMAN, ARTHUR. William Street, 1746, revisited: thirty-two new books from the library of Jonathan Swift. *See* **223.**

**5528.** GRIGSBY, JOHN L. Jerzy Kosinski's *Cockpit*: a twentieth-century *Gulliver's Travels*? NCL (19:2) 8–10.

**5529.** HARVEY, DAVID. Jonathan Swift on Herodotus. NQ (36:1) 50–1.

**5530.** HINNANT, CHARLES H.    Purity and defilement in *Gulliver's Travels*. New York: St Martin's Press, 1987. (Bibl. 1987, 6212.) Rev. by Brean S. Hammond in BJECS (12) 233–4.

**5531.** HOPKINS, P. A.    Swift and Anne Long: friendship, scandal, and a missing cache of poems and letters. NQ (36:4) 452–60.

**5532.** JAGTENBERG, F. J. A.    Jonathan Swift in Nederland (1700–1800). (Jonathan Swift in the Netherlands (1700–1800).) Deventer, The Netherlands: Sub Rosa. pp. 344. (Deventer Studien, 10.)

**5533.** JEMIELITY, THOMAS.    Prophetic voices and satiric echoes. *See* **5347.**

**5534.** KELLY, ANN CLINE.    Conversation: the tie that binds. CEACrit (51:2/3) 31–41.

**5535.** —— Swift and the English language. *See* **682.**

**5536.** KENNELLY, LAURA B.    Swift's Yahoo and King Jehu: genesis of an allusion. ELN (26:3) 37–45.

**5537.** LAPRAZ-SEVERINO, FRANÇOISE.    Relativité et communication dans les *Voyages de Gulliver* de Jonathan Swift. Paris: Didier; Atelier national de reproduction des thèses, 1988. pp. 677.

**5538.** LEFANU, WILLIAM.    A catalogue of books belonging to Dr Jonathan Swift: a facsimile of Swift's autograph with an introduction and alphabetic catalogue. *See* **243.**

**5539.** McCRAE, BRIAN.    The canon and the eighteenth century: a modest proposal and a tale of two tubs. *See* **5040.**

**5540.** McNEIL, DAVID.    Swift, Bakhtin and war. DalR (67:2/3) 1987, 314–27.

**5541.** NOKES, DAVID.    Jonathan Swift, a hypocrite reversed: a critical biography. (Bibl. 1988, 4178.) Rev. by Jenny Mezciems in RES (39:155) 1988, 447–9.

**5542.** PARK, JONG-TAE.    *Gulliver's Travels* eui utopia. (Utopias in *Gulliver's Travels*.) Unpub. doct. diss., Keimyung Univ., Taegu (Korea).

**5543.** PASSMANN, DIRK F.    Mud and slime: some implications of the Yahoos' genealogy and the history of an idea. BJECS (11)1988, 1–17.

**5544.** PASSMANN, DIRK FRIEDRICH.    'Full of improbable lies': *Gulliver's Travels* und die Reiseliteratur vor 1726. (Bibl. 1987, 6227.) Rev. by Serge Soupel in EA (42:1) 101.

**5545.** PROBYN, CLIVE T.    Jonathan Swift, *Gulliver's Travels*. London: Penguin. pp. 114. (Penguin critical studies.)

**5546.** RAFROIDI, PATRICK.    Swift et le dilemme anglo-irlandais. EA (42:1) 3–12.

**5547.** REAL, HERMANN J.; VIENKEN, HEINZ J. (eds).    Proceedings of the first Münster symposium on Jonathan Swift. (Bibl. 1986, 6912.) Rev. by Peter Wagner in BJECS (10) 1987, 230–1.

**5548.** REILLY, PATRICK.    Jonathan Swift: the brave desponder. (Bibl. 1987, 6231.) Rev. by Jenny Mezciems in RES (38:150) 1987, 252–4.

**5549.** RICHARDSON, J. A.    Swift's *Argument*: laughing us into religion. ECL (13:2) 35–45.

**5550.** RICHARDSON, P. Virgilian forms and the ideal of civilization in English poetry 1700–1720. *See* **5260.**

**5551.** ROSS, ANGUS; WOOLLEY, DAVID (eds). Jonathan Swift. (Bibl. 1988, 4187.) Rev. by Jenny Mezciems in RES (39:154) 1988, 297–8.

**5552.** SPACKS, PATRICIA MEYER. Forgotten genres. *See* **5171.**

**5553.** TIPPETT, BRIAN. Gulliver's travels. Basingstoke: Macmillan. pp. 99. (Critics debate.)

**5554.** WASHINGTON, GENE. Natural horses → the noble horse → Houyhynhnms. Swift Studies (3) 1988, 91–5.

**5555.** WOOD, NIGEL. Swift. (Bibl. 1987, 6239.) Rev. by Carole Fabricant in BJECS (11) 1988, 228–9.

**5556.** ZIMMERMAN, EVERETT. Swift's narrative satires: author and authority. (Bibl. 1988, 4202.) Rev. by Pat Rogers in BJECS (10) 1987, 230.

### James Thomson

**5557.** GILMORE, THOMAS B. Implicit criticism of Thomson's *Seasons* in Johnson's *Dictionary*. *See* **5336.**

**5558.** INGLESFIELD, ROBERT. Thomson's *Winter* and *The Day Chang'd*. NQ (36:4) 469–70.

**5559.** SAMBROOK, JAMES (ed.). *Liberty, The Castle of Indolence*, and other poems. (Bibl. 1987, 6244.) Rev. by Thomas Woodman in BJECS (11) 1988, 91–2; by Donald A. Low in NQ (36:4) 515–16; by Margarette Smith in RES (38:152) 1987, 564–5.

### Bonnell Thornton

**5560.** TAYLOR, RICHARD C. A source for Goldsmith's Tony Lumpkin in *The Connoisseur*. *See* **595.**

### John Toland

**5561.** LURBE, PIERRE. Un philosémite au siècle des Lumières: John Toland. BSEAA (28) 21–37.

**5562.** —— Statut des étrangers et statut de l'étranger chez John Toland. *In* (pp. 109–27) **26.**

### John Horne Tooke

**5563.** PRICKETT, STEPHEN. Radicalism and linguistic theory: Horne Tooke on Samuel Pegge. *See* **710.**

### John Trumbull

**5564.** VAN DOVER, J. K. The design of anarchy: *The Anarchiad*, 1786–1787. *See* **5046.**

### Royall Tyler

**5565.** ENGELL, JOHN. Narrative irony and national character in Royall Tyler's *The Algerine Captive*. SAF (17:1) 19–32.

### Horace Walpole

**5566.** SABOR, PETER. Horace Walpole: a reference guide. (Bibl. 1986, 6941.) Rev. by Pat Rogers in BJECS (11) 1988, 91.

**5567.** —— (ed.). Horace Walpole: the critical heritage. (Bibl. 1988, 4208.) Rev. by Pat Rogers in BJECS (12) 212–13.

### William Warburton

**5568.** NICHOL, D. W. A Warburton–Hill letter: a supplement to Rousseau. EA (42:2) 185–7.

**5569.** NICHOL, DONALD W.    Pope, Warburton, Knapton, and Cole: a longstanding connection. *See* **5417.**

### Mercy Otis Warren

**5570.** DONNELLY, MARGUERITE ANNE.    Mercy Otis Warren (1728–1814): satirist of the American Revolution. Unpub. doct. diss., New York Univ., 1988. [Abstr. in DA (49) 2219A.]

### The Wesleys

**5571.** CAPON, JOHN.    John and Charles Wesley. London: Hodder & Stoughton, 1988. pp. 158.

### John Wesley

**5572.** BAKER, FRANK.    John Wesley, biblical commentator. BJRL (71:1) 109–20.

**5573.** JAY, ELISABETH (ed.).    The journal of John Wesley: a selection. Oxford: OUP, 1987. pp. xxix, 290. Rev. by W. R. Ward in BJECS (11) 1988, 244.

### Phillis Wheatley

**5574.** DOLLE, RAYMOND F.    Freeing the Sable Muse. BALF (23:3) 601–7 (review-article).

**5575.** SHIELDS, JOHN C. (ed.).    The collected works of Phillis Wheatley. (Bibl. 1988, 4219.) Rev. by Pattie Cowell in EAL (24:2) 157–60; by Raymond F. Dolle in BALF (23:3) 601–7.

**5576.** SMITH, CYNTHIA J.    *To Maecenas*: Phillis Wheatley's invocation of an idealized reader. BALF (23:3) 579–92.

### Gilbert White

**5577.** CHATFIELD, JUNE.    *The Natural History and Antiquities of Selborne*: two hundred years on. Selborne Association Newsletter (31) 17–22.

**5578.** JACOBSSON, ROGER.    Selborne i litteraturen: om naturskildringen. (Selborne in literature: on the description of nature.) Horisont (38:6) 2–4.

### Anne Finch, Countess of Winchilsea

**5579.** THOMPSON, DENYS (ed.).    Selected poems. (Bibl. 1988, 4222.) Rev. by David Crane in BJECS (11) 1988, 227.

### Sarah Wister

**5580.** DEROUNIAN, KATHRYN ZABELLE (ed.).    The journal and occasional writings of Sarah Wister. Rutherford, NJ: Fairleigh Dickinson UP, 1987. pp. 149. Rev. by Lee Chambers-Schiller in EAL (24:2) 160–3.

### Mary Wollstonecraft

**5581.** ALEXANDER, MEENA.    Women in Romanticism: Mary Wollstonecraft, Dorothy Wordsworth and Mary Shelley. Basingstoke: Macmillan. pp. xii, 215. (Women writers.)

**5582.** BARKER-BENFIELD, G. J.    Mary Wollstonecraft: eighteenth-century Commonwealthwoman. JHI (50:1) 95–115.

**5583.** FINKE, LAURIE A.    'A philosophic wanton': language and authority in Wollstonecraft's *Vindication of the Rights of Women. In* (pp. 155–76) **49.**

**5584.** GRUNDY, ISOBEL.    Mary Wollstonecraft and Mr Cresswick. NQ (36:2) 166. (*Refers to* bibl. 1987, 6265.)

**5585.** KLEIN, ROXANNE VERONICA. Reading and writing the place of difference: Mary Wollstonecraft, Mary Shelley and women's discourse in late eighteenth- and early nineteenth-century Britain. Unpub. doct. diss., Univ. of California, San Diego, 1988. [Abstr. in DA (49) 3733A.]

**5586.** MYERS, MITZI. Pedagogy as self-expression in Mary Wollstonecraft: exorcising the past, finding a voice. *In* (pp. 192–210) **51.**

**5587.** PAKNADEL, FÉLIX. Trois anglaises en France pendant la Révolution. *In* (pp. 149–63) **26.**

**5588.** ST CLAIR, WILLIAM. The Godwins and the Shelleys: the biography of a family. *See* **5278.**

**5589.** TODD, JANET; BUTLER, MARILYN (eds); REES-MOGG, EMMA (asst ed.). The works of Mary Wollstonecraft. London: Pickering & Chatto. 7 vols. pp. 2530. Rev. by Claire Tomalin in LRB (11:18) 23–4.

**5590.** TROUILLE, MARY SEIDMAN. Eighteenth-century women writers respond to Rousseau: sexual politics and the cult of sensibility. Unpub. doct. diss., Northwestern Univ., 1988. 2 vols. [Abstr. in DA (49) 2212A.]

**5591.** WILSON, ANNA. Mary Wollstonecraft and the search for the radical woman. Genders (6) 88–101.

### John Woolman

**5592.** HELLER, MICHAEL ALAN. Soft pursuasion: a rhetorical analysis of John Woolman's essays and *Journal*. Unpub. doct. diss., Arizona State Univ. [Abstr. in DA (50) 1657A.]

### Edward Young

**5593.** GARRETT, JAMES ROBERT, JR. Satire and the sublime: a study of Edward Young's 'graver composition', *Night Thoughts*. Unpub. doct. diss., Auburn Univ., 1988. [Abstr. in DA (50) 1310–11A.]

# NINETEENTH CENTURY

## GENERAL

### General Literary Studies

**5594.** ADAMS, J. R. R.   A preliminary checklist of works containing Ulster dialect, 1700–1900. *See* **1456.**

**5595.** ADELAIDE, DEBRA.   Australian women writers: a bibliographic guide. London: Pandora, 1988. pp. xiv, 208.

**5596.** ALEXANDER, MEENA.   Outcaste power: ritual displacement and virile maternity in Indian women writers. JCL (24:1) 12–29.

**5597.** ALLEN, MICHAEL; WILCOX, ANGELA (eds).   Critical approaches to Anglo-Irish literature. *See* **17.**

**5598.** ALTER, ROBERT.   The pleasures of reading in an ideological age. New York: Simon & Schuster. pp. 250. Rev. by Hugo Meynell in JAE (23:4) 109–10; by John B. Breslin in BkW, 13 Aug., 9.

**5599.** ALTICK, RICHARD D.   Writers, readers, and occasions: selected essays on Victorian literature and life. Columbus: Ohio State UP. pp. xii, 358. Rev. in BkW, 16 July, 13; by David Grylls in TLS, 29 Sept., 1066.

**5600.** ANON.   Introduction. *In* (pp. 1–11) **59.**

**5601.** ANTELYES, PETER ALAN.   Tales of adventurous enterprise: the American narrative of Western economic expansion in the age of Irving. Unpub. doct. diss., Columbia Univ., 1986. [Abstr. in DA (50) 137–8A.]

**5602.** APARICIO, GEORGE BERNABE.   Transcendental experience in nature and in the city: a study of Anglo-American Romanticism's anti-urban attitude. Unpub. doct. diss., Florida State Univ., 1988. [Abstr. in DA (49) 3711–12A.]

**5603.** ARKIN, MARIAN; SHOLLAR, BARBARA (eds).   Longman anthology of world literature by women, 1875–1975. Harlow; New York: Longman. pp. xlvii, 1274. Rev. by Angela Leighton in TLS, 22 Sept., 1024.

**5604.** ARONOWICZ, ANNETTE.   Freedom from ideology: secrecy in modern expression. New York; London: Garland, 1987. pp. vi, 278. (Modern European history.)

**5605.** BALDICK, CHRIS.   In Frankenstein's shadow: myth, monstrosity and nineteenth-century writing. (Bibl. 1988, 4233.) Rev. by Pierre Arnaud in EA (42:4) 479–81; by Anne K. Mellor in MP (87:2) 193–5.

**5606.** BALLARD, ELIZABETH LYONS.   Red-tinted landscape: the poetics of Indian Removal in major American texts of the nineteenth century. Unpub. doct. diss., Univ. of Oklahoma. [Abstr. in DA (50) 1655A.]

**5607.** BANTA, MARTHA.   Imaging American women: idea and ideals in cultural history. New York: Columbia UP, 1987. pp. xliii, 844. Rev. by Millicent Bell in AL (61:3) 470–3; by Susan Albertine in MP (86:4) 448–50; by David Wotton in Word & Image (5:2) 221–2; by Susan L. Mizruchi in NEQ (62:1) 105–15.

**5608.**  BARNES, JOHN.   Home thoughts from abroad: the sense of place in Australian writing. *In* (pp. 52–65) **5.**

**5609.**  BERCOVITCH, SACVAN (ed.).   Reconstructing American literary history. (Bibl. 1988, 4236.) Rev. by J. A. Leo Lemay in MLR (84:4) 960–1.

**5610.**  BERNINGHAUSEN, THOMAS FREDERICK.   American claimants: England in the literary imagination from Benjamin Franklin to Henry James. *See* **4828.**

**5611.**  BLAIR, REBECCA.   The other woman: women authors and cultural stereotypes in American literature. Unpub. doct. diss., Indiana Univ., 1988. [Abstr. in DA (49) 3024A.]

**5612.**  BLEICH, DAVID.   Sexism and the discourse of perfection. ATQ (3:1) 11–25.

**5613.**  BONGIE, CHRISTOPHER LAURENCE.   Rewriting colonialism: allegories of the 'New Imperialism', 1876–1914. Unpub. doct. diss., Stanford Univ., 1988. [Abstr. in DA (49) 2647–8A.]

**5614.**  BRADLEY, J. G. R.   Critical and creative responses to Milton's *Lycidas*, 1740–1860. *See* **4663.**

**5615.**  BREINIG, HELMBRECHT; HALFMANN, ULRICH (eds).   Die amerikanische Literatur bis zum Ende des 19. Jahrhunderts. *See* **4071.**

**5616.**  BRODHEAD, RICHARD H.   The school of Hawthorne. (Bibl. 1988, 4244.) Rev. by Beverly Voloshin in ELN (25:1) 1987, 85–9; by Michael Davitt Bell in NEQ (60:3) 1987, 500–5; by Rita K. Gollin in SAF (15:2) 1987, 251–3; by Walter Herbert, Jr, in NHR (13:2) 1987, 21–2; by Alice Hall Petry in SoHR (23:1) 88–90; by John C. Hirsh in JAStud (23:1) 183; by Allan Lloyd Smith in JAStud (23:1) 95–9; by Nicola Bradbury in RES (39:156) 1988, 567–8.

**5617.**  BROMWICH, DAVID.   A choice of inheritance: self and community from Edmund Burke to Robert Frost. *See* **4833.**

**5618.**  BULLEN, J. B. (ed.).   The sun is god: painting, literature and mythology in the nineteenth century. *See* **59.**

**5619.**  CANTOR, PAUL A.   Stoning the romance: the ideological critique of nineteenth-century literature, an afterword. SAQ (88:3) 705–20.

**5620.**  CAPPELLO, MARY CATHERINE.   Writing the spirit/reading the mind: representations of illness and health in nineteenth-century American literature. Unpub. doct. diss., State Univ. of New York at Buffalo, 1988. [Abstr. in DA (49) 3722A.]

**5621.**  CHADEN, CARYN.   'To advantage dress'd': clothing and public identity from *A Tale of a Tub* to *Sartor Resartus*. *See* **4837.**

**5622.**  CHAPMAN, RAYMOND.   The sense of the past in Victorian literature. (Bibl. 1986, 6994.) Rev. by Bernard Richards in RES (38:152) 1987, 573–5; by Malcolm Hardman in MLR (84:4) 946–7.

**5623.**  CHAPPLE, J. A. V.   Science and literature in the nineteenth century. (Bibl. 1986, 6995.) Rev. by Norman Vance in MLR (84:3) 724.

**5624.**  Entry cancelled.

**5625.**  CLAUSEN, CHRISTOPHER.   Victorian literature: can these bones live? SewR (96:2) 1988, 220–35.

**5626.**  CLEMENTS, PATRICIA.   Baudelaire and the English tradition.

(Bibl. 1988, 4253.) Rev. by Anne Varty in RES (38:151) 1987, 421–2; by Clive Scott in CompCrit (10) 1988, 267–85.

**5627.** COBB, JAMES C. The South's South: the enigma of creativity in the Mississippi delta. SoR (25:1) 72–85.

**5628.** COLLETTE, CAROLYN P. Chaucer and Victorian medievalism: culture and society. *See* **2819.**

**5629.** CRAIG, CAIRNS (gen. ed.). The history of Scottish literature: vol. 3, Nineteenth century. Ed. by DOUGLAS GIFFORD. Aberdeen: Aberdeen UP, 1988. pp. x, 472. Rev. by Murray G. H. Pittock in SLJ (supp. 31) 13–17.

**5630.** CROSS, NIGEL. The common writer: life in nineteenth-century Grub Street. (Bibl. 1987, 6299.) Rev. by Uwe Böker in LJGG (28) 1987, 376–9.

**5631.** CULLER, A. DWIGHT. The Victorian mirror of history. (Bibl. 1988, 4262.) Rev. by Marjorie Stone in DalR (66:3) 1986, 354–62; by Kathryn Sutherland in RES (39:155) 1988, 455–6.

**5632.** DAHL, ANTHONY GEORGE. Literature of the Bahamas: the march towards national identity. *See* **4840.**

**5633.** DALSIMER, KATHERINE. Female adolescence: psychoanalytic reflections on works of literature. (Bibl. 1986, 7009.) Rev. by Marjorie Stone in DalR (66:4) 1986, 561–4.

**5634.** DEANE, SEAMUS. The French Revolution and Enlightenment in England, 1789–1832. *See* **4841.**

**5635.** DEBUSSCHER, GILBERT; MAUFORT, MARC (eds). American literature in Belgium. *See* **2.**

**5636.** DERINGER, LUDWIG. The Pacific Northwest in American and Canadian literature since 1776: the present state of scholarship. *See* **4843.**

**5637.** DICK, SUSAN, *et al.* (eds). Omnium gatherum: essays for Richard Ellmann. *See* **45.**

**5638.** DLUGOS, JAMES STEVEN, JR. Seeing the past: conceptions of American literature in early national periodicals. *See* **564.**

**5639.** DOWLING, LINDA. Language and decadence in the Victorian *fin de siècle*. (Bibl. 1988, 4266.) Rev. by John Stokes in MLR (84:4) 949–50.

**5640.** EAVES, MORRIS; FISCHER, MICHAEL (eds). Romanticism and contemporary criticism. (Bibl. 1987, 6307.) Rev. by V. A. De Luca in UTQ (56:4) 1987, 576–8.

**5641.** EBY, CECIL D. The road to Armageddon: the martial spirit in English popular literature 1870–1914. (Bibl. 1987, 6308.) Rev. by John Sutherland in TLS, 6 Jan., 15.

**5642.** EDWARDS, MARY JANE. Early Canadian literature in English: a survey and a challenge. *See* **4848.**

**5643.** EDWARDS, P. D. Idyllic realism from Mary Russell Mitford to Hardy. Basingstoke: Macmillan, 1988. pp. 178.

**5644.** ELLMANN, RICHARD. A long the riverrun: selected essays. New York: Knopf; London: Hamilton, 1988. pp. viii, 277. Rev. by Angeline Goreau in NYTB, 19 Mar., 2; by Anthony Hecht in BkW, 26 Mar., 10.

**5645.** ENSSLEN, KLAUS. Einführung in die schwarzamerikanische Literatur. *See* **4849.**

**5646.** EPSTEIN, JOSEPH. Partial payments: essays on writers and their lives. New York; London: Norton. pp. 429. Rev. by T. J. Binyon in TLS, 13 Oct., 1134.

**5647.** FLETCHER, IAN (ed.). British poetry and prose, 1870–1905. (Bibl. 1987, 6313.) Rev. by R. K. R. Thornton in DUJ (81:1) 1988, 166–7; by P. M. S. Dawson in RES (39:155) 1988, 458.

**5648.** FRASER, HILARY. Beauty and belief: aesthetics and religion in Victorian literature. (Bibl. 1988, 4273.) Rev. by Chris Brooks in RES (38:152) 1987, 572–3.

**5649.** GOLDEN, TAYLOR J., *et al.* (eds). A literary history of the American West. Fort Worth: Texas Christian Press, 1986. Rev. by Christopher Merrill in NER (12:2) 208–10.

**5650.** GORDON, JAN B. *Fin-de-siècle* idols and idylls: the totalization of the marginal. PoetT (31) 30–41.

**5651.** GRAY, RICHARD. Writing the South: ideas of an American region. (Bibl. 1988, 4282.) Rev. by Pamela Rhodes in DUJ (81:1) 1988, 170–1.

**5652.** HAGSTRUM, JEAN H. Eros and vision: the Restoration to Romanticism. *See* **4087.**

**5653.** HARPER, MARCIA MITCHELL. The literary influence of Sir Edmund Gosse upon the Victorian age. Unpub. doct. diss., Northern Illinois Univ., 1988. [Abstr. in DA (49) 2229A.]

**5654.** HETHERINGTON, CAROL; PETERSSON, IRMTRAUD. Annual bibliography of studies in Australian literature: 1988. *See* **4853.**

**5655.** HOMANS, MARGARET. Bearing the word: language and female experience in nineteenth-century women's writing. (Bibl. 1988, 4291.) Rev. by Moira Ferguson in StudN (20:3) 1988, 349–51.

**5656.** HÖNNIGHAUSEN, LOTHAR. The Symbolist tradition in English literature: a study of Pre-Raphaelitism and *fin de siècle*. Trans. by GISELA HÖNNIGHAUSEN. Cambridge; New York: CUP, 1988. pp. x, 349. (European studies in English literature.)

**5657.** JAMESON, FREDRIC. Nationalism, colonialism and literature: modernism and imperialism. *See* **4856.**

**5658.** JAMKHANDI, SUDHAKAR R. Australian literary publications in the C. Hartley Grattan Collection. *See* **236.**

**5659.** JASPER, DAVID; WRIGHT, T. R. (eds). The critical spirit and the will to believe: essays in nineteenth-century literature and religion. *See* **18.**

**5660.** JONES, LAWRENCE. Versions of the dream: literature and the search for identity. *In* (pp. 187–211) DAVID NOVITZ and BILL WILLMOTT (eds), Culture and identity in New Zealand. Wellington: GP Books. pp. ix, 302.

**5661.** KANIO, MITSUO. Yami, hishou, soshite seishin no naraku: igirisu koten shugi kara roman shugi e. *See* **4859.**

**5662.** KAPLAN, AMY. The burden of history. NEQ (62:4) 586–93.

**5663.** KAPLAN, FRED. Sacred tears: sentimentality in Victorian literature. (Bibl. 1987, 6333.) Rev. by Robert Beum in SewR (96:2) 1988, xxiv–xxvi; by Valerie Purton in Dick (85:1) 51–5.

**5664.** KLAUS, H. GUSTAV. The literature of labour: two hundred years of working-class writing. (Bibl. 1987, 6339.) Rev. by John Goode in YES (19) 328.

**5665.** KLEITZ, DORSEY RODNEY. Orientalism and the American Romantic imagination: the Middle East in the works of Irving, Poe, Emerson, and Melville. Unpub. doct. diss., Univ. of New Hampshire, 1988. [Abstr. in DA (50) 685A.]

**5666.** KORPERSHOEK, A. M. A critical bibliography of nineteenth-century English literature. DQR (19:4) 307–14.

**5667.** KUCICH, GREG. The duality of Romantic Spenserianism. See **3386.**

**5668.** LAWSON-PEEBLES, ROBERT. Landscape and written expression in Revolutionary America: the world turned upside down. See **4863.**

**5669.** LEAVIS, LAWRENCE ROBIN. Creative values and contemporary literature. Nijmegen: Leavis. pp. 275.

**5670.** LEVERENZ, DAVID. Manhood and the American renaissance. Ithaca, NY; London: Cornell UP. pp. x, 372. Rev. by Richard Poirier in LRB (11:19) 18–22.

**5671.** LEVINSON, MARJORIE. Introduction. In (pp. 1–17) **53.**

**5672.** —— The new historicism: back to the future. In (pp. 18–63) **53.**

**5673.** LEVY, ANITA. Blood, kinship, and gender. Genders (5) 70–85.

**5674.** LOTTES, WOLFGANG. 'Wie ein goldener Traum': die Rezeption des Mittelalters in der Kunst der Präraffaeliten. (Bibl. 1985, 5898.) Rev. by C. J. Wells in RES (38:150) 1987, 267–9.

**5675.** PIZER, DONALD. Realism and naturalism in nineteenth-century American literature. (Bibl. 1986, 7093.) Rev. by Harold Beaver in MLR (83:2) 1988, 423–4.

**5676.** McCALL, LAURA. Symmetrical minds: literary men and women in antebellum America. Unpub. doct. diss., Univ. of Michigan, 1988. [Abstr. in DA (49) 2367A.]

**5677.** McCARTHY, FINBARR. A rage for order: the ideological impli-cations of form in early Southern writing. See **4101.**

**5678.** McCASKILL, BARBARA ANN. To rise above race: Black women writers and their readers, 1859–1939. Unpub. doct. diss., Emory Univ., 1988. [Abstr. in DA (50) 140A.]

**5679.** McDOWELL, DEBORAH E.; RAMPERSAD, ARNOLD (eds). Slavery and the literary imagination. Baltimore, MD; London: John Hopkins UP. pp. xiii, 172. (Selected papers from the English Inst, ns 13.)

**5680.** McGOWAN, JOHN P. Representation and revelation: Victorian realism from Carlyle to Yeats. (Bibl. 1988, 4303.) Rev. by Chris Brooks in RES (39:153) 1988, 131–2; by Clyde de L. Ryals in MLR (84:1) 135–6.

**5681.** MAERTZ, GREGORY GEORGE. England's *Goethezeit*: Romantic and early Victorian. Unpub. doct. diss., Harvard Univ., 1988. [Abstr. in DA (49) 3034A.]

**5682.** MAPLES, DONNA ELAINE. Building a literary heritage: a study of three generations of pioneer women, 1880–1930. Unpub. doct. diss., Univ. of Missouri–Columbia, 1988. [Abstr. in DA (50) 947A.]

**5683.** MARR, DAVID. American worlds since Emerson. (Bibl. 1988, 4306.) Rev. by Russell B. Goodman in AL (61:1) 111–12; by David Grimsted in AHR (94:4) 1162–3; by Lawrence Buell in JAH (75:4) 1331; by Neal B. Houston in RMRLL (43:1/2) 106–7.

**5684.** MARSHALL, IAN STUART. Mountains to match the man: national identity and the mountain in American literature, beginnings to 1860. See **4104.**

**5685.** MARTIN, BRIAN (ed.). The nineteenth century (1798–1900). Basingstoke: Macmillan. pp. xxvi, 640. (Macmillan anthologies of English literature, 4.)

**5686.** MAYERS, OZZIE J. The power of the pin: sewing as an act of rootedness in American literature. CE (50:6) 1988, 664–80.

**5687.** MEISEL, PERRY. The myth of the modern: a study in British literature and criticism after 1850. (Bibl. 1987, 6350.) Rev. by Rikky Rooksby in NQ (36:4) 558–9; by Eugene Goodheart in ELN (27:1) 72–4; by Jean-Michel Rabaté in EA (42:3) 352–3.

**5688.** MELDRUM, BARBARA HOWARD. Under the sun: myth and realism in Western American literature. Troy, NY: Whitston, 1985. pp. 230. Rev. by D. P. Rask in ALR (21:3) 75–7.

**5689.** MELLOR, ANNE K. (ed.). Romanticism and feminism. (Bibl. 1988, 4308.) Rev. by Catherine Burroughs in TJ (41:2) 252–3.

**5690.** MENDILOW, JONATHAN. The Romantic tradition in British political thought. (Bibl. 1986, 7077.) Rev. by Nicholas Roe in RES (38:150) 1987, 258–9; by Peter Marshall in MLR (84:4) 940–1.

**5691.** MORSE, DAVID. American Romanticism: vol. 1, From Cooper to Hawthorne: excessive America; vol. 2, From Melville to James: the enduring excessive. (Bibl. 1988, 4313, 4314.) Rev. by Christine Gerrard in RES (39:156) 1988, 595–6; by Keith Carabine in NQ (36:1) 132–3.

**5692.** MORTON, PETER. The vital science: biology and the literary imagination, 1860–1900. (Bibl. 1987, 6357, where title incomplete.) Rev. by John Batchelor in RES (38:149) 1987, 99–100.

**5693.** NEUMAN, SHIRLEY; KAMBOURELI, SMARO (eds). A mazing space: writing Canadian women writing. See **40.**

**5694.** OKAJI, REI. Igirisu roman shugi to keimou shisou. See **4876.**

**5695.** OLIVER, LAWRENCE J. Theodore Roosevelt, Brander Matthews, and the campaign for literary Americanism. AmQ (41:1) 93–111.

**5696.** PANTUCKOVÁ, LIDMILLA. Anglická a americká literatura v Nerudově časopisu Obrazy života. (English and American literature as reflected in the Czech literary journal Images of Life.) In (p. 32) **6.**

**5697.** PAUL, RONALD. Romantics and reactionaries: some English responses to the French Revolution. See **4878.**

**5698.** PFAELZER, JEAN. Nineteenth-century American utopianism: texts and contexts. ATQ (3:1) 5–10.

**5699.** PFAU, THOMAS. Rhetoric and subjectivity: the theoretical and literary figuration of Romantic self-consciousness. Unpub. doct. diss., State Univ. of New York at Buffalo. [Abstr. in DA (50) 944–5A.]

**5700.** PYLE, FOREST BARNETT, III. The ideology of imagination: subject and society in the discourse of Romanticism. Unpub. doct. diss., Univ. of Texas at Austin, 1988. [Abstr. in DA (50) 22A.]

**5701.** RAYAN, KRISHNA. Text and sub-text: suggestion in literature. (Bibl. 1987, 6371.) Rev. by Peter Kitson in NQ (36:1) 135–6.

**5702.** REED, ARDEN (ed.). Romanticism and language. (Bibl. 1987, 6372.) Rev. by V. A. De Luca in UTQ (56:4) 1987, 578–9.

**5703.** REIMAN, DONALD H. Romantic texts and contexts. (Bibl. 1988, 4325.) Rev. by Nicola Trott in CLB (65) 29–31.

**5704.** REYNOLDS, DAVID S. Beneath the American renaissance: the subversive imagination in the age of Emerson and Melville. (Bibl. 1988, 4327.) Rev. by Malini Schueller in AL (61:1) 104–6; by Philip F. Gura in PMHB (113:3) 473–4; by Elizabeth McKinsey in JAH (76:2) 597–8; by Donald R. Hettinga in ChrisL (38:3) 73–4; by Albert E. Stone in AmerS (29:2) 1988, 91–3; by James McIntosh in SAF (17:2) 243–4.

**5705.** REYNOLDS, LARRY J. European revolutions and the American literary renaissance. New Haven, CT; London: Yale UP, 1988. pp. xv, 207. Rev. by David S. Reynolds in JAH (76:3) 934–5; by Elizabeth A. Schultz in AmerS (29:2) 1988, 95.

**5706.** RICARD, SERGE (ed.). Les États-Unis: images du travail et des loisirs. See **25.**

**5707.** RIEDEL, WOLFGANG. National metaphor in Anglo-Irish literature. In (pp. 434–5) **4.** (Abstract.)

**5708.** ROSS, HARRY J. Trapped by society, imprisoned in the wilderness: captivity in American literature, 1680–1860. See **4111.**

**5709.** ROWE, ANNE E. The idea of Florida in the American literary imagination. (Bibl. 1987, 6382.) Rev. by Diane Roberts in SoQ (27:2) 97–9.

**5710.** ROWLAND, WILLIAM GORDON, JR. Writers against readers: English and American Romantic writers and the nineteenth-century reading public. Unpub. doct. diss., Univ. of Virginia, 1988. [Abstr. in DA (50) 1315A.]

**5711.** SARGENT, LYMAN TOWER. Utopian literature and communitarian experiments before Bellamy. ATQ (3:1) 135–46.

**5712.** SCHULTZ, JANE ELLEN. Women at the front: gender and genre in literature of the American Civil War. Unpub. doct. diss., Univ. of Michigan, 1988. [Abstr. in DA (49) 2282–3A.]

**5713.** SCOTT, CLIVE. Baudelaire among the English. CompCrit (10) 1988, 267–85 (review-article).

**5714.** SEEBER, HANS ULRICH. Auf dem Weg zum Vortex: Zentralbewegung, Ästhetik des Sublimen und das Wasser der Moderne in englischen London-Texten des 19. Jahrhunderts. See **1913.**

**5715.** SHERBO, ARTHUR. Matters English in The Critic (1881–1906). See **589.**

**5716.** SHLOSS, CAROL. In visible light: photography and the American writer 1840–1940. New York; Oxford: OUP, 1987. pp. viii, 308.

**5717.** SIMPSON, LEWIS P.    Slavery and the cultural imperialism of New England. SoR (25:1) 1–29.

**5718.** SISKIN, CLIFFORD.    The historicity of Romantic discourse. *See* **4892.**

**5719.** SLATOFF, WALTER J.    The look of distance: reflections on suffering and sympathy in modern literature – Auden to Agee, Whitman to Woolf. (Bibl. 1988, 4336.) Rev. by Thomas Docherty in RES (39:153) 1988, 146–7.

**5720.** SPENDER, LYNNE (ed.).    Her selection: writings by nineteenth-century Australian women. Melbourne: Penguin, 1988. pp. 272. Rev. by Hilaire Lindsay in Span (29) 110–12.

**5721.** STEIN, RICHARD L.    Victoria's year: English literature and culture, 1837–1838. New York; Oxford: OUP, 1987. pp. xiii, 314. Rev. by Lawrence Poston in MP (87:1) 98–101; by John Sutherland in TLS, 13 Jan., 43; by Lars Hartveit in EngS (70:6) 588–90.

**5722.** STOKES, JOHN.    In the nineties. Hemel Hempstead: Harvester Wheatsheaf. pp. xxii, 199. Rev. by Timothy d'Arch Smith in TLS, 8 Dec., 1367.

**5723.** STONE, MARJORIE.    Mirrors and metaphors: visions of Victorian history. DalR (66:3) 1986, 354–62 (review-article).

**5724.** TANNER, TONY.    Scenes of nature, signs of men. (Bibl. 1988, 4344, where title incorrect.) Rev. by Sam B. Girgus in ALR (22:1) 92–3.

**5725.** TAYLOR, BEVERLY; BREWER, ELISABETH.    The return of King Arthur: British and American Arthurian literature since 1800. (Bibl. 1987, 6399.) Rev. by Ulrich Müller in LJGG (26) 1985, 400–6.

**5726.** TURNER, PAUL.    English literature 1832–1890, excluding the novel. Oxford: Clarendon Press; New York: OUP. pp. x, 522. (Oxford history of English literature, 1:1.) Rev. by Richard Altick in TLS, 14 Apr., 390.

**5727.** VANCE, NORMAN.    The sinews of the spirit: the ideal of Christian manliness in Victorian literature and religious thought. (Bibl. 1988, 4346.) Rev. by Chris Brooks in RES (38:149) 1987, 95–7.

**5728.** VANDERBILT, KERMIT.    American literature and the academy: the roots, growth, and maturity of a profession. (Bibl. 1988, 4347.) Rev. by Alan Golding in MP (86:4) 411–16; by John W. Rathbun in JAStud (23:1) 104–5.

**5729.** WALKER, NANCY A.    A very serious thing: women's humor and American culture. Minneapolis: Minnesota UP, 1988. pp. xiii, 229. (American culture.) Rev. by Linda Wagner-Martin in AL (61:2) 279–80; by Elizabeth A. Schultz in AmerS (29:2) 1988, 96.

**5730.** WALTERS, JONATHAN.    The drowned woman in Victorian art and literature. Unpub. doct. diss., Univ. of Miami, 1988. [Abstr. in DA (50) 694A.]

**5731.** WARD, GERALD W.    The American illustrated book in the nineteenth century. *See* **101.**

**5732.** WARD, WILLIAM S.    A literary history of Kentucky. *See* **4896.**

**5733.** WASHINGTON, MARY HELEN.    Invented lives: narratives of

Black women, 1860–1960. New York: Anchor Press, 1988. pp. 447. Rev.
by Jewelle Gomez in Nat (246:17) 1988, 615–18.

**5734.** WATERS, MICHAEL.    The garden in Victorian literature.
Aldershot: Scolar Press, 1988. pp. 371. (Cf. bibl. 1986, 7510.) Rev. by
Arthur Pollard in TRB (5:3) 144–5.

**5735.** WEISBUCH, ROBERT.    Atlantic double-cross: American litera-
ture and British influence in the age of Emerson. (Bibl. 1988, 4351.)
Rev. by E. F. Shields in QQ (95:1) 1988, 203–5; by Christine Gerrard in
RES (39:156) 1988, 594–5.

**5736.** WEISSINGER, THOMAS.    Current bibliography. *See* **4897.** (Afro-
American writers.)

**5737.** WELSH, KEITH EDWARD.    Edmund Burke, Friedrich Engels,
and ideas of community in eighteenth- and nineteenth-century British
fiction and poetry. *See* **4898.**

**5738.** WHEELER, KATHLEEN M.    Kant and Romanticism. PhilL
(13:1) 42–56.

**5739.** WHEELER, MICHAEL.    'Can these dry bones live?': questions of
belief in a future life. *In* (pp. 23–36) **18.**

**5740.** WINCHELL, JAMES ARTHUR.    Murdered sleep: crime and aesthetics in France and England, 1850–1910. Unpub. doct. diss., Univ. of
Washington, 1988. [Abstr. in DA (49) 2212A.]

**5741.** WONHAM, HENRY.    Character development of the ring-tailed
roarer in American literature. *See* **1737.**

**5742.** WOODRING, CARL.    Nature into art: cultural transformations in
nineteenth-century Britain. Cambridge, MA: Harvard UP. pp. xii, 326.
Rev. in BkW, 24 Dec., 13.

**5743.** WORKMAN, NANCY VICTORIA.    A Victorian *Arabian Nights*
adventure: a study in intertextuality. Unpub. doct. diss., Loyola Univ.
of Chicago. [Abstr. in DA (50) 958A.]

**5744.** WYATT, DAVID.    The fall into Eden: landscape and imagination
in California. (Bibl. 1988, 4357.) Rev. by Robert F. Gleckner in AL
(61:3) 508–10; by David Miller in SewR (96:3) 1988, xlviii, l, lii; by
James Hurt in MLR (84:4) 963–4.

## Drama and the Theatre

**5745.** ALLINGHAM, PHILIP VICTOR.    Dramatic adaptations of the
Christmas books of Charles Dickens, 1844–8: texts and contexts.
Unpub. doct. diss., Univ. of British Columbia, 1988. [Abstr. in DA (49)
3728–9A.]

**5746.** BANK, ROSEMARIE.    Frontier melodrama. *See* **4902.**

**5747.** BARNES, JOHN.    Pioneers of British film: the beginnings of the
cinema in England 1894–1901: vol. 3, 1898: the rise of the photoplay.
London: Bishopsgate, 1983. pp. 255.

**5748.** CHINOY, HELEN KRICH; JENKINS, LINDA WALSH (eds).    Women
in American theatre. (Bibl. 1982, 9371.) New York: Theatre Communications Group, 1987. pp. 445. (Second ed.: first ed. 1981.) Rev. by
Karen Laughlin in ModDr (32:1) 163–7.

**5749.** DAVIS, SUSAN GRAY.    Parades and power: street theatre in nineteenth-century Philadelphia. *See* **1762.**

**5750.** DAVIS, TRACY C.    The actress in Victorian pornography. TJ (41:3) 294–315.

**5751.** EMELJANOW, VICTOR.    Victorian popular dramatists. (Bibl. 1987, 6421.) Rev. by Michael R. Booth in YES (19) 344–5.

**5752.** FAN, ADA MEI.    In and out of bounds: marriage, adultery, and women in the plays of Henry Arthur Jones, Arthur Wing Pinero, Harley Granville-Barker, John Galsworthy, and W. Somerset Maugham. Unpub. doct. diss., Univ. of Rochester, 1988. [Abstr. in DA (49) 1808A.]

**5753.** FRANKLIN, CAROLINE.    'At once above – beneath her sex': the heroine in Regency verse drama. MLR (84:2) 273–88.

**5754.** FRIEDL, BETTINA (ed.).    On to victory: propaganda plays of the woman suffrage movement. (Bibl. 1988, 4364, where '(ed.)' omitted.) Rev. by Katharine Worth in NQ (36:3) 409–10.

**5755.** GOSHER, SYDNEY PAUL.    A historical and critical survey of the South African one-act play written in English. Unpub. doct. diss., Univ. of South Africa, 1988.

**5756.** GRANQVIST, RAOUL.    Some traits of cultural nationalism in the reception of Shakespeare in 19th-century USA. *See* **3719.**

**5757.** GREYVENSTEIN, W. R.    The history and development of children's theatre in English in South Africa. Unpub. doct. diss., Rand Afrikaans Univ., 1988.

**5758.** GREYVENSTEIN, WALTER.    Let us entertain you! Children's theatre and popular entertainment. SATJ (3:2) 51–68.

**5759.** GRIMSTED, DAVID.    Melodrama unveiled: American theater and culture, 1800–1850. Introd. by LAWRENCE W. LEVINE. (Bibl. 1970, 6010.) Berkeley; London: California UP, 1987. pp. xviii, 285. (Approaches to American culture.) (Revised ed.: first ed. 1968.)

**5760.** GUSTAFSON, ANTOINETTE MCCLOSKEY.    The image of the West in American popular performance. Unpub. doct. diss., New York Univ., 1988. [Abstr. in DA (49) 3206A.]

**5761.** HIATT, RICHARD G.    Lady troupers along the Oregon trail. DQR (19:2) 113–23.

**5762.** HUME, CHARLES V.    They came to see the elephant. DQR (19:2) 83–8. (The Eagle Theatre, Sacramento, CA.)

**5763.** LARABEE, ANN E.    First-wave feminist theatre, 1890–1930. Unpub. doct. diss., State Univ. of New York at Binghamton, 1988. [Abstr. in DA (49) 2426A.]

**5764.** LAUTERBACH, CHARLES E.    Langrishe and Glenn's Black Crook tour of California, Nevada, and Mexico, 1874–1875. DQR (19:2) 124–34.

**5765.** LEONARD, WILLIAM TORBERT. Once was enough. Metuchen, NJ; London: Scarecrow Press, 1986. pp. xvii, 282. (Plays which were performed only once.)

**5766.** MCDERMOTT, DOUGLAS.    An American theatrical everyman: the career of Lambart F. Beatty, 1853–1871. DQR (19:2) 104–12.

**5767.** MURPHY, BRENDA. American realism and American drama, 1880–1940. (Bibl. 1988, 4375.) Rev. by Terry Oggel in ALR (21:3) 89–90; by David Grimsted in AmerS (29:1) 1988, 90; by James Fisher in ModDr (32:3) 453–4.

**5768.** NELSON, WALTER. Oscar Wilde and the dramatic critics: a study in Victorian theatre. Lund: Nelson. pp. 201. (Linerovägen, 33.)

**5769.** O'CONNOR, MARION. William Poel and the Elizabethan Stage Society. Cambridge: Chadwyck-Healey in assn with the Consortium for Drama and Media in Higher Education, 1987. pp. 143. (Theatre in focus.)

**5770.** PROEHL, GEOFFREY SCOTT. Coming home again: American family drama and the figure of the prodigal. Unpub. doct. diss., Stanford Univ., 1988. [Abstr. in DA (49) 2455A.]

**5771.** REBECK, THERESA. Your cries are in vain: a theory of the melodramatic heroine. Unpub. doct. diss., Brandeis Univ. [Abstr. in DA (50) 1668A.]

**5772.** SCHAUFFER, DENNIS. The first theatre in Natal. SATJ (3:1) 18–38. (The Victoria Theatre, Pietermaritzburg.)

**5773.** SCHIRER, THOMAS E. Mark Twain's theatrical dealings with three English dramatists: Charles Reade, Tom Taylor and Henry J. Byron. MichA (20:3) 1988, 361–6.

**5774.** SEKINE, MASARU (ed.). Irish writers and the theatre. (Bibl. 1987, 6437.) Rev. by Hilary Pyle in RES (39:154) 1988, 318–19.

**5775.** SMITH, LESLIE. Modern British farce: a selective study of British farce from Pinero to the present day. Totowa, NJ: Barnes & Noble; Basingstoke: Macmillan. pp. xii, 232.

**5776.** STEPHENS, JUDITH L. Gender ideology and dramatic convention in progressive era plays, 1890–1920. TJ (41:1) 45–55.

**5777.** THOMPSON, PAULA JUNE. A history and daybook of the English language theatre in New Orleans during the Civil War. Unpub. doct. diss., Louisiana State Univ. and Agricultural and Mechanical Coll., 1988. [Abstr. in DA (50) 1141A.]

**5778.** WILMORE, D. The development of stage machinery in the nineteenth-century British theatre: a study of physical and documentary evidence. Unpub. doct. diss., Univ. of Hull. [Abstr. in IT (39:3) 1097.]

### Fiction

**5779.** AHEARN, EDWARD J. Marx and modern fiction. New Haven, CT; London: Yale UP. pp. xv, 231. Rev. by Sergio Rizzo in RMRLL (43:4) 241–3.

**5780.** ALBERS, CHRISTINA EDNA. The guardian male figure in selected novels of Hawthorne, James, Howells, Wharton, Cather, and Hemingway. Unpub. doct. diss., Univ. of North Carolina at Chapel Hill, 1987. [Abstr. in DA (49) 2216A.]

**5781.** ARBERY, GLENN CANNON. Victims of likeness: quadroons and octoroons in Southern fiction. SoR (25:1) 52–71.

**5782.** ARDIS, ANN LOUISE. 'The apple and the ego of woman': a prehistory of English modernism in the 'New Woman' novels of the 1890s. Unpub. doct. diss., Univ. of Virginia, 1988. [Abstr. in DA (50) 144A.]

**5783.** ATWOOD, MARGARET; WEAVER, ROBERT (sels). The Oxford book of Canadian short stories in English. Oxford; New York; Toronto: OUP, 1986. pp. xix, 436.

**5784.** BAUER, STEFAN. Das wahrscheinliche Unwahrscheinliche. Realitätsansprüche in der Kriminalliteratur. arcadia (24) 284–96.

**5785.** BENTLEY, NANCY ANN. Contrary dictions: narrative technique and cultural conflict in antebellum American writing. Unpub. doct. diss., Harvard Univ., 1988. [Abstr. in DA (50) 442A.]

**5786.** BERRY, JOHN CHARLES. British serial production: author, audience, text. See **4916**.

**5787.** BIRD, DELYS. Writing women/reading women: the double-voiced discourse of Australian women's fiction. In (pp. 91–107) **20**.

**5788.** BJØRHOVDE, GERD. Rebellious structures: women writers and the crisis of the novel 1880–1900. (Bibl. 1987, 6450.) Rev. by Tess Cosslett in NQ (36:4) 551–2; by Anny Sadrin in EA (42:3) 350–1.

**5789.** BLAKE, ANDREW. Reading Victorian fiction: the cultural context and ideological content of the nineteenth-century novel. Basingstoke: Macmillan. pp. 201.

**5790.** BODENHEIMER, ROSEMARIE. The politics of story in Victorian social fiction. (Bibl. 1988, 4390.) Rev. by F. S. Schwarzbach in TLS, 6 Jan., 15.

**5791.** BOLD, CHRISTINE. Selling the Wild West: popular Western fiction, 1860–1960. (Bibl. 1988, 4391.) Rev. by Kenneth J. Bindas in PacHR (58:3) 387–8; by James H. Maguire in AL (59:4) 1987, 666–7; by Mark Abley in TLS, 22 May 1987, 552.

**5792.** BOSSERT, REX THOMAS. Oneiric architecture: a study in the ideology of modern utopian fiction. Unpub. doct. diss., Stanford Univ., 1988. [Abstr. in DA (49) 2664A.]

**5793.** BOYLE, THOMAS. Black swine in the sewers of Hampstead: beneath the surface of Victorian sensationalism. New York: Viking; London: Hodder & Stoughton. pp. xii, 273. Rev. by John Espy in BW, 24 Dec., 4–5.

**5794.** BURGESS, MOIRA (ed.). The other voice: Scottish women's writing since 1808: an anthology. (Bibl. 1987, 6453.) Rev. by J. M. Wilson in Landfall (43:2) 248–9.

**5795.** BUTLER, LANCE ST JOHN. Failed violence in Victorian fiction. In (pp. 97–110) **60**.

**5796.** CAMPBELL, JANE. Mythic Black fiction: the transformation of history. (Bibl. 1987, 6454.) Rev. by Kenneth W. Warren in BALF (23:2) 397–400.

**5797.** CARMIGNANI, PAUL. Sud historique, Sud mythique, Sud diégétique. Caliban (26) 5–14.

**5798.** CAWTHRA, GILLIAN. Cultural climate and linguistic style: change in English fictional prose from the late Victorian to the early modern period. Basingstoke: Macmillan. pp. viii, 168. (Cf. bibl. 1986, 7218.)

**5799.** CHASTON, JOEL DUANE.   Reading as if for life: the quixotic reader in the nineteenth-century British novel. Unpub. doct. diss., Univ. of Utah, 1988. [Abstr. in DA (49) 3366A.]

**5800.** CLINES, RAYMOND H.   A descriptive analysis of dialogue and inner speech in selected works of fiction. Unpub. doct. diss., Univ. of Rhode Island, 1988. [Abstr. in DA (50) 126A.] (*Ulysses, The Sound and the Fury, Adventures of Huckleberry Finn, Pride and Prejudice.*)

**5801.** COLEMAN, SARAH ANN.   The late Victorian era and the flowering of four literary types: a study in the sociology of literature. Unpub. doct. diss., Syracuse Univ., 1988. [Abstr. in DA (49) 3366–7A.]

**5802.** CONDER, JOHN J.   Naturalism in American fiction: the classic phase. (Bibl. 1988, 4397.) Rev. by Robert Lawson-Peebles in RES (38:149) 1987, 109–10.

**5803.** COSSLETT, TESS.   Woman to woman: female friendship in Victorian fiction. (Bibl. 1988, 4398.) Rev. by Terry Castle in TLS, 2 June, 607–8.

**5804.** CUNLIFFE, MARCUS.   America's imaginary wars. *In* (pp. 251–60) **2.**

**5805.** CZON, SEUNG-GUL.   Choki miguk heukin soseol yeongu. *See* **4921.**

**5806.** DAVID, GAIL PLIAM.   Diverse (in)versions: female heroics in the Renaissance pastoral romance and in women's pastoral fiction from Fanny Burney to George Eliot. *See* **3142.**

**5807.** DEKKER, GEORGE.   The American historical romance. (Bibl. 1988, 4405.) Rev. by Jean-Loup Bourget in EA (42:2) 231–4.

**5808.** DENNING, MICHAEL.   Mechanic accents: dime novels and working-class culture in America. (Bibl. 1988, 4406.) Rev. by Christine Bold in JAStud (23:1) 109–11.

**5809.** DERRY, S. G.   Tradition, imitation, and innovation: Jane Austen and the development of the novel, 1740–1818. *See* **4927.**

**5810.** DOLE, CAROL M.   'Now in fire and now in blood': purification rituals in the Victorian novel. Unpub. doct. diss., Cornell Univ., 1988. [Abstr. in DA (49) 3031A.]

**5811.** DONOVAN, ELLEN RENEE.   Narrative authority in nineteenth-century American literature: a study of dialogic structures. Unpub. doct. diss., Univ. of Wisconsin–Madison, 1988. [Abstr. in DA (50) 443A.]

**5812.** DRYDEN, EDGAR A.   The form of American romance. Baltimore, MD; London: Johns Hopkins UP, 1988. pp. xvi, 249. (Scott, *Waverley*; Hawthorne, *The Marble Faun*; Melville, *Pierre*; James, *Portrait of a Lady*; Faulkner, *Absalom, Absalom!*; Barth, *Letters.*)

**5813.** DRYDEN, PHYLIS CAMPBELL.   Dismemberment motifs in American literature: the incomplete and homeless body as metaphor. Unpub. doct. diss., State Univ. of New York at Albany, 1988. [Abstr. in DA (49) 2657A.]

**5814.** DUFFY, DENNIS.   Sounding the iceberg: an essay on Canadian historical novels. Toronto: ECW Press, 1986. pp. vi, 84. Rev. by Gerald Noonan in CanL (122/23) 233–4.

**5815.** EBY, CLARE VIRGINIA. Representative men: businessmen in American fiction, 1875–1914. Unpub. doct. diss., Univ. of Michigan, 1988. [Abstr. in DA (49) 2219–20A.]

**5816.** ELAM, DIANE MICHELLE. Realizing romance: genre, reference, and the novel. Unpub. doct. diss., Brown Univ., 1988. [Abstr. in DA (49) 2226–7A.]

**5817.** ELDRED, JANET M. Gender and creativity: female artist subplots from Hawthorne to Fowles. Unpub. doct. diss., Univ. of Illinois at Urbana-Champaign, 1988. [Abstr. in DA (49) 2648A.]

**5818.** FISHER, PHILIP. Hard facts: setting and form in the American novel. (Bibl. 1988, 4412.) Rev. by Richard Gray in MLR (84:2) 451–3.

**5819.** FOSTER, JOHN WILSON. Fictions of the Irish Literary Revival: a changeling art. (Bibl. 1988, 4413.) Rev. by Patricia Craig in LRB (11:5) 23.

**5820.** FRAIMAN, SUSAN DIANA. Deforming novels: women writers and the Bildungsroman. *See* **4930.**

**5821.** FRITH, G. The intimacy which is knowledge: female friendship in the novels of women writers. Unpub. doct. diss., Univ. of Warwick, 1988. [Abstr. in IT (39:4) 1627.]

**5822.** FRYCKSTEDT, MONICA CORREA. On the brink: English novels of 1866. Uppsala: Acta Universitatis Upsaliensis; Stockholm: Almqvist & Wiksell. pp. 157. (Studia anglistica upsaliensia, 69.)

**5823.** GALLAGHER, CATHERINE. The industrial reformation of English fiction: social discourse and narrative form, 1832–1867. (Bibl. 1988, 4416.) Rev. by Stephen Gill in RES (38:151) 1987, 404.

**5824.** GILMOUR, ROBIN. The novel in the Victorian age: a modern introduction. (Bibl. 1988, 4418.) Rev. by Nicola Bradbury in RES (39:153) 1988, 133–5; by Karen Scherzinger in UES (25:1) 1987, 40–1.

**5825.** GOSHGARIAN, G. M. To kiss the chastening rod: sex in American domestic fiction of the 1850s. Unpub. doct. diss., Univ. of California, Los Angeles, 1988. [Abstr. in DA (49) 2220A.]

**5826.** GREENWALD, ELISSA. Realism and the romance: Nathaniel Hawthorne, Henry James, and American fiction. Ann Arbor, MI; London: UMI Research Press. pp. xi, 195. Rev. by Leland S. Person, Jr, in AL (61:4) 692–3.

**5827.** GRIXTI, JOSEPH. Terrors of uncertainty: the cultural contexts of horror fiction. London: Routledge. pp. xviii, 214. Rev. by Robert Irwin in Listener (122) 31 Aug., 28.

**5828.** GROSS, KONRAD. Arbeit als literarisches Problem: Studien zum Verhältnis vom Roman und Gesellschaft in der viktorianischen Zeit. (Bibl. 1986, 7252.) Rev. by Norbert H. Platz in LJGG (26) 1985, 419–22.

**5829.** GWIN, MINROSE C. Black and white women of the old South: the peculiar sisterhood in American literature. (Bibl. 1988, 4420, where title incomplete.) Rev. by Carol Mitchell in SF (46:2) 197–8.

**5830.** HARDY, BARBARA. Forms of feeling in Victorian fiction. (Bibl.

1987, 6490.) Rev. by Alan Kennedy in UTQ (56:3) 1987, 447–9; by Penny Boumela in Eng (36:154) 1987, 73–7.

**5831.** HASTINGS, ALBERT WALLER. Social myth and fictional reality: the decline of fairy-tale thinking in the Victorian novel. Unpub. doct. diss., Univ. of Wisconsin–Madison, 1988. [Abstr. in DA (49) 3368A.]

**5832.** HAWTHORN, JEREMY (ed.). The nineteenth-century British novel. (Bibl. 1987, 6491.) Rev. by Sheila M. Smith in RES (39:153) 1988, 133.

**5833.** HEFFERON, MARGUERITE LEE. The nineteenth-century female Bildungsroman and the Romantic epic tradition. Unpub. doct. diss., Ohio State Univ., 1988. [Abstr. in DA (49) 2667A.]

**5834.** HENDRICKSON, RUTH ANN. Narrative strategies of erotic fictional autobiography. Unpub. doct. diss., Ohio State Univ., 1988. [Abstr. in DA (49) 2667A.]

**5835.** HERRMANN, CAROL JANE. The art of the novella, 1800–1855. Unpub. doct. diss., Brown Univ., 1988. [Abstr. in DA (49) 2210–11A.]

**5836.** HEWITT, DOUGLAS. English fiction of the early modern period, 1890–1940. Harlow: Longman. pp. xi, 275. Rev. by David Trotter in TLS, 29 Sept., 1066.

**5837.** HIO, N. The influence of Victorian literature upon Japanese literature of the Meiji period. Unpub. doct. diss., Univ. of Exeter. [Abstr. in IT (39:2) 494.]

**5838.** HOLLINGER, VERONICA. The vampire and the alien: variations on the outsider. SFS (16:2) 145–60.

**5839.** HOLTON, SYLVIA WALLACE. Down home and uptown: the representation of Black speech in American fiction. *See* **1407.**

**5840.** HOYSER, CATHERINE ELIZABETH. Literary viragos: late Victorian and Edwardian female Bildungsromane. Unpub. doct. diss., Indiana Univ., 1988. [Abstr. in DA (49) 2667–8A.]

**5841.** HUGHES, H. M. Changes in historical romance, 1890s to the 1980s: the development of the genre from Stanley Weyman to Georgette Heyer and her successors. Unpub. doct. diss., Univ. of Bradford, 1988. [Abstr. in IT (38:4) 1462.]

**5842.** HURLEY, KELLY. The novel of the gothic body: deviance, abjection, and late-Victorian popular fiction. Unpub. doct. diss., Stanford Univ., 1988. [Abstr. in DA (49) 3732–3A.]

**5843.** JADWIN, LISA. Alphabets of obliquity: female double-discourse and the rhetoric of the mid-Victorian novel. Unpub. doct. diss., Princeton Univ. [Abstr. in DA (50) 1665A.]

**5844.** JANOUŠEK, MIROSLAV. Na okraj literárních jubileí 1989: Anglická a americká literatura. (Glosses on literary anniversaries 1989: English and American literature.) CJa (32) 263–8.

**5845.** JAY, ELISABETH. Doubt and the Victorian woman. *In* (pp. 88–103) **18.**

**5846.** JOHANYAK, DEBRA. Avatars of Beatrice: the tragic dark heroine in American Romanticism. Unpub. doct. diss., Kent State Univ., 1988. [Abstr. in DA (49) 1802A.]

**5847.** JOHNSON, D. P. 'All that sort of people': the Victorian novel and the growth of the professions. Unpub. M.Phil. diss., Univ. of Hull. [Abstr. in IT (39:3) 1111.]

**5848.** JONES, ANN H.    Ideas and innovations: best sellers of Jane Austen's age. (Bibl. 1988, 4430.) Rev. by Patricia Meyer Spacks in YES (19) 335–7; by Rex Stamper in StudN (20:2) 1988, 224–5.

**5849.** JORDAN, CYNTHIA.    Second stories: the politics of language, form, and gender in early American fictions. *See* **4935.**

**5850.** JORDAN, MARY ELLEN.    Absent fathers and the sons' search for identity in four Victorian prose texts. Unpub. doct. diss., Univ. of Minnesota, 1988. [Abstr. in DA (49) 2668A.] (*David Copperfield, The Return of the Native, Apologia Pro Sua Vita, Daniel Deronda.*)

**5851.** KAPLAN, AMY.    The social construction of American Realism. Chicago; London: Chicago UP, 1988. pp. ix, 187.

**5852.** KATRAKIS, MARIA.    Gothic patterns in American short fiction of the nineteenth century. Unpub. doct. diss., Univ. of South Africa, 1988.

**5853.** KEATING, H. R. F.    Crime and mystery: the 100 best books. London: Xanadu, 1987. pp. 219.

**5854.** KEATING, PETER.    The haunted study: a social history of the English novel, 1875–1914. London: Secker & Warburg. pp. ix, 533. Rev. by David Trotter in TLS, 29 Sept., 1066; by John Sutherland in Listener (122) 7 Sept., 27; by Philip Horne in LRB (11:17) 14–16.

**5855.** KEIL, JAMES C.    Reading, writing, and recycling: literary archaeology and the creation of American literature. Unpub. doct. diss., Brandeis Univ., 1988. [Abstr. in DA (49) 1802A.]

**5856.** KEITH, W. J.    The quest for the (instant) Canadian classic. *In* (pp. 155–65) **12.**

**5857.** —— Regions of the imagination: the development of British rural fiction. (Bibl. 1988, 4432.) Rev. by R. P. Draper in THJ (5:2) 76–9; by F. S. Schwarzbach in TLS, 6 Jan., 15.

**5858.** KELLEY, KAROL L.    Models for the multitudes: social values in the American popular novel, 1850–1920. New York: Greenwood Press, 1987. pp. xxvi, 184. (Contributions to the study of childhood and youth, 3.) Rev. by Barbara Bair in StudN (20:1) 1988, 108–9; by NW in AmerS (29:1) 1988, 91.

**5859.** KELLY, GARY.    English fiction of the Romantic period 1789–1830. *See* **4936.**

**5860.** KENNEDY, ALAN.    Thinking the thinking of criticism. UTQ (56:3) 1987, 443–51 (review-article).

**5861.** KIMBLE, MARY ELLEN.    Literary presentations of pioneer women in Kansas and neighboring states. KQ (18:3) 1986, 105–20.

**5862.** KREYLING, MICHAEL.    Figures of the hero in Southern narrative. Baton Rouge; London: Louisiana State UP, 1987. pp. 201. Rev. by Philip Castille in StudN (20:4) 1988, 433–5; by David Roger in JAStud (23:1) 140–2.

**5863.** LAWRENCE, K. E.    'Gleams from a brighter world, too soon eclipsed or forfeited': religious orthodoxy in the Victorian novel. Unpub. doct. diss., Univ. of Oxford. [Abstr. in IT (39:3) 1111–12.]

**5864.** LEE, A. ROBERT (ed.).   The nineteenth-century American short story. (Bibl. 1987, 6509.) Rev. by Louise K. Barnett in MLR (84:2) 453–4; by Robert Lawson-Peebles in RES (39:154) 1988, 332–3.

**5865.** LEE, BRIAN.   American fiction, 1865–1940. (Bibl. 1987, 6510.) Rev. by Norman Vance in JAStud (23:1) 116–17.

**5866.** LEHNERT-RODIEK, GERTRUD.   Zeitreisen: Untersuchungen zu einem Motiv der erzählenden Literatur des neunzehnten und zwanzigsten Jahrhunderts. Rheinbach-Merzbach: CMZ, 1987. pp. 231. (Bonner Untersuchungen zur vergleichenden Literaturwissenschaft, 3.) Rev. by Raimund Borgmeier in arcadia (24) 103–5.

**5867.** LEMMENS, CHERYL ANN.   Dark recesses of the soul: victimization in selected British fiction from *Clarissa* to *The Collector*. See **4938.**

**5868.** LEVINE, GEORGE.   Darwin and the novelists: patterns of science in Victorian fiction. Cambridge, MA; London: Harvard UP, 1988. pp. x, 319. Rev. by Rosemary Ashton in LRB (11:13) 17.

**5869.** LEVY, ANITA BETH.   The revolution at home: domestic fictions in the human sciences. Unpub. doct. diss., Univ. of California, San Diego, 1988. [Abstr. in DA (49) 3370A.]

**5870.** LUBOT, DONNA L.   Domestic relations: patterns of empowerment in women's fiction, 1720–1820. See **4940.**

**5871.** MCCORMICK, MARJORIE JEAN.   Mothers in the English novel: from stereotype to archetype. See **4941.**

**5872.** Entry cancelled.

**5873.** MCFARLAND, JO ANNE YOUTZ.   A dialogic analysis of American utopian novels by women, 1888–1900. Unpub. doct. diss., Univ. of Utah, 1988. [Abstr. in DA (49) 2451A.]

**5874.** MCNAUGHTON, TRUDIE (ed.).   In deadly earnest: a collection of fiction by New Zealand women 1870s–1980s. Auckland: Century Hutchinson. pp. xiv, 232. Rev. by Maud Cahill in NZList, 16 Sept., 66–8.

**5875.** MASCIAROTTE, GLORIA-JEAN.   Breaking society's looking-glass: the feminine subject/the sensation novel/the textual difference. Unpub. doct. diss., Brown Univ., 1988. [Abstr. in DA (49) 2232A.]

**5876.** MECKIER, JEROME.   Hidden rivalries in Victorian fiction: Dickens, realism, and revaluation. Lexington: Kentucky UP, 1987. pp. x, 310. Rev. by Lynn Myrick in SoHR (23:3) 278–80; by Richard J. Dunn in StudN (20:2) 1988, 225–7.

**5877.** MERCHANT, PETER.   'Fresh instruction o'er the mind': exploit and example in Victorian fiction. CLEd (20:1) 9–24.

**5878.** MISHRA, V. C.   The gothic sublime: theory, practice and interpretation. See **4942.**

**5879.** MOLYNEAUX, MARIBEL WALDO.   Women and work: on the margins of the marketplace. See **4943.**

**5880.** MOORE, PATRICIA ANN.   Female emancipation at the turn of the century. Unpub. doct. diss., Univ. of Denver. [Abstr. in DA (50) 955A.]

**5881.** MORRIS, HORACE ANTHONY.   The influence of the Mill–Carlyle 'West Indian Debate' on four Victorian novelists. Unpub. doct. diss.,

Howard Univ., 1987. [Abstr. in DA (49) 1810–11A.] (Dickens, Eliot, Brontë, Thackeray.)

**5882.** MORROW, NANCY. Dreadful games: the play of desire in the nineteenth-century novel. Kent, OH; London: Kent State UP, 1988. pp. 207.

**5883.** MOTHERSOLE, B. Female philanthropy and women novelists of 1840 to 1870. Unpub. doct. diss., Brunel Univ. [Abstr. in IT (39:3) 1112.]

**5884.** MUKHERJEE, MEENAKSHI. Realism and reality: the novel and society in India. (Bibl. 1986, 7317.) Rev. by Sara Suleri in MLR (84:3) 729.

**5885.** MÜLLENBROCK, HEINZ JOACHIM. Die Entstehung der Anti-utopie im spätviktorianischen England und ihre genetischen Voraussetzungen. LJGG (27) 1986, 269–84.

**5886.** MULVEY, CHRISTOPHER. Anglo-American fictions: national characteristics in nineteenth-century travel literature. *In* (pp. 61–77) **1.**

**5887.** MUSSELWHITE, DAVID E. Partings welded together: politics and desire in the nineteenth-century English novel. (Bibl. 1988, 4446.) Rev. by Glenda A. Hudson in StudN (20:4) 1988, 437–9.

**5888.** NABHOLTZ, JOHN R. 'My reader my fellow-labourer': a study of English Romantic prose. (Bibl. 1988, 4545.) Rev. by Peter Marshall in YES (19) 330–1.

**5889.** NEW, W. H. Canadian short fiction: from myth to modern. Scarborough, Ont.: Prentice-Hall Canada, 1986. pp. xii, 516.

**5890.** NILE, RICHARD. The rise of the Australian novel. Unpub. doct. diss., Univ. of New South Wales, 1988. [Abstr. in DA (50) 136A.]

**5891.** NYSTUL, NANCY ANN. The textual inscription of sexual difference in nineteenth-century fiction. Unpub. doct. diss., Columbia Univ., 1988. [Abstr. in DA (49) 3734A.]

**5892.** OREL, HAROLD. The Victorian short story: development and triumph of a literary genre. (Bibl. 1988, 4448.) Rev. by Sheila M. Smith in RES (39:153) 1988, 132–3; by Shelagh Hunter in YES (19) 341–2.

**5893.** O'SULLIVAN, VINCENT (ed.). The unsparing scourge: Australian satirical texts 1845–1860. Nedlands: Centre for Studies in Australian Literature, Univ. of Western Australia, 1988. pp. 132. Rev. by Rob Jackaman in Landfall (42:4) 459–61.

**5894.** PARKER, HERSHEL. Flawed texts and verbal icons: literary authority in American fiction. (Bibl. 1987, 6537.) Rev. by Robert Lawson-Peebles in RES (38:149) 1987, 109.

**5895.** PETERSON, CARLA L. The determined reader: gender and culture in the novel from Napoleon to Victoria. New Brunswick, NJ: Rutgers UP, 1986. pp. x, 264. (Douglass series on women's lives and the meaning of gender.) Rev. by Andrea Lebowitz in CanL (115) 1987, 152–3; by Kate Flint in RES (38:152) 1987, 585.

**5896.** PHILLIPS, THOMAS OWEN. Educating the protagonist: secondary characters and moral choice in the Victorian Bildungsroman. Unpub. doct. diss., Univ. of North Carolina at Chapel Hill, 1988. [Abstr. in DA (50) 692A.]

**5897.**  PORTER, GERALD (ed.).  'News that stays news': the enactment of present and future in American literature. *See* **43**.

**5898.**  POWELL, B. L.    The house beautiful and its mapping of domestic and colonial space: a study of the domestic novel at the turn of the century. Unpub. doct. diss., Univ. of Sussex, 1987. [Abstr. in IT (38:4) 1460.]

**5899.**  PRICKETT, STEPHEN.    Poetics and narrative: biblical criticism and the nineteenth-century novel. *In* (pp. 1–22) **18**.

**5900.**  REED, JOHN R.    The Victorian Renaissance self. CLIO (17:2) 1988, 187–208.

**5901.**  ROBERTS, HEATHER.    Where did she come from? New Zealand women novelists 1862–1987. Wellington: Allen & Unwin; Port Nicholson Press. pp. vi, 177. Rev. by Jocelyn Harris in NZList, 16 Sept., 66.

**5902.**  ROSS, ALEXANDER M.    The imprint of the picturesque on nineteenth-century British fiction. (Bibl. 1987, 6550.) Rev. by J. B. Bullen in RES (39:154) 1988, 303–5.

**5903.**  ROTHFIELD, LAWRENCE I., JR.    Signs and symptoms: illness as discourse in the realistic novel. Unpub. doct. diss., Columbia Univ., 1986. [Abstr. in DA (50) 438–9A.]

**5904.**  ROY, PARAMA.    Kind hearts and coronets: the great house and social protest in the nineteenth-century novel. Unpub. doct. diss., Univ. of Rochester, 1988. [Abstr. in DA (50) 150A.]

**5905.**  RUPPEL, RICHARD JEFFREY.    Kipling, Conrad, and the popular exotic short fiction of the 1890's. Unpub. doct. diss., Univ. of North Carolina at Chapel Hill, 1987. [Abstr. in DA (49) 2234–5A.]

**5906.**  RUSSELL, NORMAN.    The novelist and Mammon: literary responses to the world of commerce in the nineteenth century. (Bibl. 1988, 4461.) Rev. by Sheila M. Smith in RES (38:150) 1987, 283–4.

**5907.**  SCHÖWERLING, RAINER.    Sir Walter Scott and the tradition of the historical novel before 1814 – with a checklist. *In* (pp. 227–62) **38**.

**5908.**  SCHRIBER, MARY SUZANNE.    Gender and the writer's imagination from Cooper to Wharton. Lexington: Kentucky UP, 1987. pp. ix, 214. Rev. by Charlotte Goodman in SAF (17:1) 121–3; by Shelley Fisher Fishkin in AL (61:1) 108–9.

**5909.**  SCHWARZ, DANIEL R.    The transformation of the English novel, 1890–1930. Basingstoke: Macmillan. pp. viii, 336.

**5910.**  SCHWEITZER, THOMAS G.    Breaking form's promise: writing against the Bildungsroman in nineteenth-century British fiction. Unpub. doct. diss., Rutgers Univ., 1988. [Abstr. in DA (49) 3036A.]

**5911.**  SENN, WERNER.    Setting up an Australian literature course: some conceptual and practical reflections. *In* (pp. 63–75) **20**.

**5912.**  SHELTAG, H. A. A.    The influence of the *Arabian Nights* upon nineteenth-century English fiction. Unpub. doct. diss., Univ. of Exeter. [Abstr. in IT (39:3) 1113.]

**5913.**  SHULMAN, ROBERT.    Social criticism and nineteenth-century American fictions. (Bibl. 1988, 4469, where title incomplete.) Rev. by Albert E. Stone in AmerS (29:2) 1988, 91–3; by Robert Clark in JAStud (23:1) 154–5.

**5914.** Singh, G. (ed.).    Collected essays by Q. D. Leavis: vol. 3, The novel of religious controversy. Cambridge: CUP. pp. vii, 347. Rev. by Martin Dodsworth in TLS, 8 Sept., 963–4.

**5915.** Skilton, David.    Schoolboy Latin and the mid-Victorian novelist: a study in reader competence. BIS (16) 1988, 39–55.

**5916.** Smith, Peter.    Public and private value: studies in the nineteenth-century novel. (Bibl. 1988, 4471.) Rev. by Alan Kennedy in UTQ (56:3) 1987, 446–7.

**5917.** Smith, Sandra Jo.    Father–daughter relationships in fiction and society (1790–1890). *See* **4953.**

**5918.** Spangler, George M.    The idea of degeneration in American fiction 1880–1940. EngS (70:5) 407–35.

**5919.** Stableford, Brian.    Scientific romance in Britain, 1890–1950. (Bibl. 1988, 4472, where title incorrect.) Rev. by T. S. Shippey in RES (38:152) 1987, 580–1.

**5920.** Steig, Michael.    Stories of reading: subjectivity and literary understanding. Baltimore, MD; London: Johns Hopkins UP. pp. xvii, 261.

**5921.** Stetz, Margaret Diane.    Life's 'half-profits': writers and their readers in fiction of the 1890s. *In*°(pp. 169–87) **44.**

**5922.** Suksang, Duangrudi.    Social relationships in nineteenth-century utopias by women. Unpub. doct. diss., Univ. of Iowa, 1988. [Abstr. in DA (49) 3364A.]

**5923.** Sutherland, John.    The Longman companion to Victorian fiction. Harlow: Longman, 1988. pp. 696. Rev. by Philip Horne in LRB (11:17) 14–16; by Richard Jenkyns in TLS, 28 July, 817.

**5924.** Tarella, Janet Anne.    Narcissism in marriage in the nineteenth-century British novel. Unpub. doct. diss., State Univ. of New York at Albany, 1988. [Abstr. in DA (49) 3737A.]

**5925.** Thomas, H. Nigel.    From folklore to fiction: a study of folk heroes and rituals in the Black American novel. *See* **1659.**

**5926.** Thomas, Sue.    Indexes to fiction in *Chambers's Journal of Popular Literature, Science and Art*, later *Chambers's Journal*, 3rd to 6th series of *Chambers's Edinburgh Journal*, 1854–1910. *See* **596.**

**5927.** Trodd, Anthea.    Domestic crime in the Victorian novel. Basingstoke: Macmillan. pp. 183. (Macmillan studies in Victorian literature.)

**5928.** Tuska, Jon (ed.).    The American West in fiction. (Bibl. 1988, 4478.) Rev. by Edward Lense in OhioanaQ (32:1) 26–7.

**5929.** Vargish, Thomas.    The providential aesthetic in Victorian fiction. Charlottesville: Virginia UP, 1985. pp. xi, 250. Rev. by Roger B. Henkle in Review (9) 1987, 311–17.

**5930.** Varnado, S. L.    Haunted presence: the numinous in gothic fiction. *See* **4961.**

**5931.** Virgili, Elizabeth Say.    Narrative as expression of women's theological voice. Unpub. doct. diss., Univ. of Southern California, 1988. [Abstr. in DA (49) 2426A.]

**5932.** Vrettos, Athena.    'In sickness and in health': Victorian fictions of disease. Unpub. doct. diss., Univ. of Pennsylvania, 1988. [Abstr. in DA (50) 150–1A.]

**5933.** WALD, PRISCILLA BETH. Writing America: the rhetoric of self-authorization in early modern American literature. Unpub. doct. diss., Columbia Univ. [Abstr. in DA (50) 1307A.]

**5934.** WEISS, WOLFGANG. Der anglo-amerikanische Universitäts-roman: eine historische Skizze. Darmstadt: Wissenschaftliche Buchgesellschaft, 1988. pp. xi, 182. (Erträge der Forschung, 260.) Rev. by Raimund Borgmeier in GRM (39) 484–6.

**5935.** WHEELER, MICHAEL. English fiction of the Victorian period, 1830–1890. (Bibl. 1988, 4487.) Rev. by Nicola Bradbury in RES (38:149) 1987, 98–9.

**5936.** WIENK, MARILYN DOWD. Hawthorne's heroines and the feminine ideal: the four major romances in the context of nineteenth-century women's novels. Unpub. doct. diss., State Univ. of New York at Binghamton. [Abstr. in DA (50) 446A.]

**5937.** WILLIAMS, MERRYN. Six women novelists. Basingstoke: Macmillan, 1987. pp. xxii, 123. (Macmillan modern novelists.) (Olive Schreiner, Edith Wharton, F. M. Mayor, 'Katherine Mansfield', Dorothy L. Sayers, Antonia White.) Rev. by Tess Cosslett in NQ (36:4) 551–2.

**5938.** —— Women in the English novel, 1800–1900. (Bibl. 1985, 6162a.) Rev. by Karla K. Walters in StudN (20:2) 1988, 228–9.

**5939.** WINN, SHARON A. Friends of the people: Chartists in Victorian social protest fiction. Unpub. doct. diss., Univ. of Tulsa. [Abstr. in DA (50) 957–8A.]

**5940.** WOLF, WERNER. Schauerroman und Empfindsamkeit: zur Beziehung zwischen 'gothic novel' und empfindsamem Roman in England. *See* **4963.**

**5941.** WOLPERT, ILANA PAULA. Crossing the gender line: female novelists and their male voices. Unpub. doct. diss., Ohio State Univ., 1988. [Abstr. in DA (49) 2236A.]

**5942.** WRIGHT, ROBERT GLENN. The social Christian novel. Introd. by ROBERT H. WALKER and DEWEY D. WALLACE, JR. New York; London: Greenwood Press. pp. xviii, 188. (Contributions in American studies, 93.) Rev. by John J. Murphy in AL (61:4) 702–4.

**5943.** YOUNG, MICHAEL ANDREW. The structure and ideology of romance fiction. Unpub. doct. diss., Univ. of Minnesota, 1988. [Abstr. in DA (50) 151A.]

### Literature for Children

**5944.** BRIGGS, JULIA. Women writers and writing for children: from Sarah Fielding to E. Nesbit. *In* (pp. 221–50) **14.**

**5945.** DROTNER, KIRSTEN. English children and their magazines, 1751–1945. *See* **565.**

**5946.** FLINT, KATE. Arthur Hughes as illustrator for children. *In* (pp. 201–20) **14.**

**5946a.** GREYVENSTEIN, W. R.   The history and development of children's theatre in English in South Africa. *See* **5758.**

**5947.** HONIG, EDITH LAZAROS.   Breaking the angelic image: woman power in Victorian children's fantasy. New York; London; Greenwood Press, 1988. pp. 156. (Contributions in women's studies, 97.)

**5948.** REID, C. S.   National identity in Scottish and Swiss children's and young people's books: a comparative study. Unpub. doct. diss., Univ. of Edinburgh, 1986. [Abstr. in IT (36:3) 909.]

**5949.** SHERCLIFF, W. H.   Morality to adventure: Manchester Polytechnic's collection of children's books 1840–1939. *See* **265.**

**5950.** SMEDMAN, M. SARAH.   Not always gladly does she teach, nor gladly learn: teachers in *Kunstlerinromane* for young readers. CLEd (20:3) 131–49.

**5951.** ZIPES, JACK (ed.).   Victorian fairy tales: the revolt of the fairies and elves. (Bibl. 1987, 6597.) Rev. by Marina Warner in TLS, 24 Nov., 1309.

### Poetry

**5952.** BEECH, MARTIN.   Meteor imagery in English poetry, *c.* 1600 to *c.* 1900. *See* **4222.**

**5953.** BLACK, PAMELA ANN.   The presence of the unknowable: the question of the universal in Romantic poetics and deconstructive theory. Unpub. doct. diss., Simon Fraser Univ. [Abstr. in DA (50) 1651A.]

**5954.** BRISTOW, JOSEPH (ed.).   The Victorian poet: poetics and persona. (Bibl. 1987, 6604.) Rev. by Bernard Richards in NQ (36:2) 249–50.

**5955.** CIUK, ANDRZEJ.   King Arthur and the knights of the Round Table in Victorian poetry. Opole, Poland: Wyższa Szkoła Pedagogiczna. pp. 85. (Studia i Monografie.)

**5956.** COOPER, ANDREW M.   Doubt and identity in Romantic poetry. (Bibl. 1988, 4506.) Rev. by Greg Crossan in NQ (36:3) 401–3.

**5957.** CRONIN, RICHARD.   Colour and experience in nineteenth-century poetry. Basingstoke: Macmillan, 1988, pp. 228.

**5958.** CURRAN, STUART.   Poetic form and British Romanticism. (Bibl. 1988, 4507.) Rev. by R. L. Brett in RES (39:153) 1988, 120–1; by Kenneth R. Johnston in MP (86:3) 316–19.

**5959.** DALY, GAY.   Pre-Raphaelites in love. New York: Ticknor & Fields. pp. 468. Rev. by John Espy in BW, 24 Dec., 4–5.

**5960.** DAVIS, PHILIP.   The importance of being earnest. CamQ (18:1) 73–86 (review-article).

**5961.** DE LUCA, V. A.   That deep Romantic chasm: some recent critical currents. UTQ (56:4) 1987, 575–87 (review-article).

**5962.** EDMOND, ROD.   Affairs of the hearth: Victorian narrative poetry and the ideology of the domestic. (Bibl. 1988, 4510.) Rev. by Rikky Rooksby in Eng (38) 83–7.

**5963.** ENGLER, BERND.   Die amerikanische Ode: Gattungsgeschichtliche Untersuchungen. *See* **4972.**

**5964.** EVERETT, GLENN SAWYER.    The role of the reader in the dramatic monologue. Unpub. doct. diss., Brown Univ., 1988. [Abstr. in DA (49) 2227–8A.]

**5965.** GRAY, STEPHEN (ed.).    The Penguin book of South African verse. London: Penguin. pp. xxv, 402.

**5966.** GRIFFITHS, ERIC.    The printed voice of Victorian poetry. Oxford: Clarendon Press; New York: OUP. pp. xv, 369. Rev. by Andrew St George in TLS, 12 May, 521; by Danny Karlin in LRB (11:16) 19–21.

**5967.** HAGENBÜCHLE, ROLAND.    Sprachskepsis und Sprachkritik: zum Erkenntnismodus dichterischer Sprache. LJGG (26) 1985, 205–26.

**5968.** HAUSMAN, MARGARET JANE.    Syntactic disordering in modern poetry: index, icon, symbol. Unpub. doct. diss., Brown Univ., 1988. [Abstr. in DA (49) 2210A.]

**5969.** HEFFERON, MARGUERITE LEE.    The nineteenth-century female Bildungsroman and the Romantic epic tradition. See **5833.**

**5970.** HERBISON, IVAN.    Language, literature and cultural identity: an Ulster-Scots perspective. See **1464.**

**5971.** HÖFELE, ANDREAS.    Rollen-Ich und lyrisches Ich. Zur Poetik des 'dramatic monologue'. LJGG (26) 1985, 185–204.

**5972.** JARVIS, FREDERICK.    Clouds of glory: poets of the Romantic movement. See **4975.**

**5973.** KENNEDY, EVELYN SWANSON.    A vision destroyed: the waste-land worlds of Augustus and Victoria. Unpub. doct. diss., Univ. of Tennessee, 1988. [Abstr. in DA (49) 3369A.]

**5974.** KIPPERMAN, MARK.    Beyond enchantment: German idealism and English Romantic poetry. Philadelphia: Pennsylvania UP, 1986. pp. xii, 242. Rev. by Stephen Prickett in RES (39:153) 1988, 122–3.

**5975.** KRAMER, LAWRENCE.    Music and poetry: the nineteenth century and after. (Bibl. 1988, 4516.) Rev. by Christopher R. Wilson in RES (38:152) 1987, 586–8.

**5976.** LAUE, JUDY MYERS.    Rufus Wilmot Griswold's *The Female Poets of America*: the politics of anthologizing. See **441.**

**5977.** LEE, A. ROBERT (ed.).    Nineteenth-century American poetry. (Bibl. 1988, 4517.) Rev. by R. W. Butterfield in JAStud (23:1) 157–8.

**5978.** LUCAS, JOHN.    Modern English poetry: from Hardy to Hughes: a critical survey. (Bibl. 1988, 4519.) Rev. by Peter Levi in RES (39:153) 1988, 139–41; by A. D. Moody in MLR (84:1) 139–40.

**5979.** MAIDMENT, BRIAN (ed.).    The poorhouse fugitives: self-taught poets and poetry in Victorian Britain. (Bibl. 1987, 6624.) Rev. in Edinburgh Review (82) 148–9; by Bruce Woodcock in TRB (5:2) 1988, 73–5.

**5980.** MAXWELL, C.    Looking and perception in nineteenth-century poetry. Unpub. doct. diss., Univ. of Oxford. [Abstr. in IT (39:3) 1112.]

**5981.** METZGER, LORE.    One foot in Eden: modes of pastoral in Romantic poetry. (Bibl. 1987, 6627.) Rev. by R. L. Brett in RES (39:153) 1988, 121.

**5982.** MILLER, J. HILLIS.    The linguistic moment: from Wordsworth to Stevens. (Bibl. 1988, 4522.) Rev. by Bernard O'Donoghue in RES (38:150) 1987, 285–6.

**5983.** MORASH, CHRISTOPHER (ed.). The hungry voice: the poetry of the Irish Famine. Introd. by TERENCE BROWN. Dublin: Irish Academic Press. pp. 172. Rev. by Eve Patten in Linen Hall Review (6:3) 26.

**5984.** MOSS, WILLIAM. Confederate broadside poems: an annotated descriptive bibliography based on the collection of the Z. Smith Reynolds Library of Wake Forest University. *See* **254.**

**5985.** NICHOLS, ASHTON. The poetics of epiphany: nineteenth-century origins of the modern literary moment. Tuscaloosa; London: Alabama UP, 1987. pp. xiv, 256. (Cf. bibl. 1986, 7089.) Rev. by John McGowan in SoHR (23:3) 280–2.

**5986.** O'FLINN, PAUL. How to study Romantic poetry. Basingstoke: Macmillan, 1988. pp. 131. (How to study literature.)

**5987.** O'SULLIVAN, VINCENT (ed.). The unsparing scourge: Australian satirical texts 1845–1860. *See* **5893.**

**5988.** PARTHASARATHY, R. The exile as writer: on being an Indian writer in English. JCL (24:1) 1–11.

**5989.** PRESCOTT, ROBERT ALLEN. Reweaving the rainbow: science in Romantic poetry. Unpub. doct. diss., Univ. of Illinois at Urbana-Champaign, 1988. [Abstr. in DA (49) 2672A.]

**5990.** PRIESSNITZ, HORST. The 'vossification' of Ludwig Leichhardt: Leichhardt's career in 19th and 20th century Australian poems. *In* (pp. 102–14) **5.**

**5991.** RACE, WILLIAM H. Classical and Romantic poetic journeys. CML (10:1) 27–45.

**5992.** REED, JEREMY. Madness: the price of poetry. London: Owen. pp. 208. Rev. by William Scammell in Listener (122) 23 Nov., 27.

**5993.** RICKS, CHRISTOPHER (ed.). The new Oxford book of Victorian verse. (Bibl. 1988, 4525.) Rev. by Philip Davis in CamQ (18:1) 73–6; by Simone Lavabre in EA (42:3) 350.

**5994.** SCHECKNER, PETER (ed.). An anthology of Chartist poetry: poetry of the British working class, 1830s–1850s. Rutherford, NJ; Fairleigh Dickinson UP; London; Toronto: Assoc. UPs. pp. 353.

**5995.** SHAW, W. DAVID. The lucid veil: poetic truth in the Victorian age. (Bibl. 1988, 4528.) Rev. by Stephen Regan in DUJ (81:1) 1986, 164; by Philip Davis in CamQ (18:1) 76–86.

**5996.** SHERMAN, JOAN R. (ed.). Collected Black women's poetry. New York; Oxford: OUP, 1988. 4 vols. pp. xxxvi, various pagings (facsims). (Schomburg library of nineteenth-century Black women writers.)

**5997.** SMITH, L. The enigma of visibility: theories of visual perception in the early poetry of William Morris and in the work of Ruskin and the pre-Raphaelites. Unpub. doct. diss., Univ. of Southampton. [Abstr. in IT (39:1) 33.]

**5998.** STOREY, MARK (ed.). Poetry and Ireland since 1800: a source book. London: Routledge, 1988. pp. viii, 221. (World and word.) Rev. by P. M. Diskin in NQ (36:3) 408–9.

**5999.** TAYLOR, DENNIS.    Hardy's metres and Victorian prosody: with a metrical appendix of Hardy's stanza forms. (Bibl. 1988, 4531.) Rev. by Norman Page in LRB (11:6) 26–7.

**6000.** WALKER, JEFFREY.    Bardic ethos and the American poem: Whitman, Pound, Crane, Williams, Olson. Baton Rouge; London: Louisiana UP. pp. xvi, 261.

**6001.** WATSON, J. R. (ed.).    Everyman's book of Victorian verse. (Bibl. 1988, 4533.) Rev. by Simone Lavabre in EA (42:3) 349–50; by Philip Davis in CamQ (18:1) 73–6.

**6002.** WELCH, ROBERT.    A history of verse translation from the Irish, 1789–1897. *See* **4986.**

## Prose

**6003.** ANDREADIS, HARRIETTE.    True womanhood revisited: women's private writing in nineteenth-century Texas. Journal of the Southwest (31:2) 179–204.

**6004.** BAKER, HAROLD DEAN.    The pleasure of landscape: insistent description in nineteenth-century prose. Unpub. doct. diss., Brown Univ., 1988. [Abstr. in DA (49) 2208–9A].

**6005.** BINDER, WOLFGANG.    'O, ye daughters of Africa awake! Awake! Arise! . . .': the functions of work and leisure in female slave narratives. *In* (pp. 127–44) **25.**

**6006.** BROMWICH, DAVID (ed.).    Romantic critical essays. (Bibl. 1988, 4539.) Rev. by E. D. Mackerness in NQ (36:2) 245–6.

**6007.** DAY, LAURA ANNE.    'The history of every one of us': a gender study of America's antebellum travel writers. Unpub. doct. diss., Purdue Univ., 1988. [Abstr. in DA (50) 717A.]

**6008.** FAVRET, MARY A.    The idea of correspondence in British Romantic literature. *See* **4989.**

**6009.** HAARHOFF, DORIAN.    Literary ivory: the nineteenth-century travelogue in Namibia and Victorian priorities. English Academy Review (6) 42–61.

**6010.** JORDAN, MARY ELLEN.    Absent fathers and the sons' search for identity in four Victorian prose texts. *See* **5850.**

**6011.** McFARLAND, THOMAS.    Romantic cruxes: the English essayists and the spirit of the age. (Bibl. 1988, 4544.) Rev. by E. D. Mackerness in NQ (36:2) 246–7.

**6012.** MULVEY, CHRISTOPHER.    Anglo-American fictions: national characteristics in nineteenth-century travel literature. *In* (pp. 61–77) **1.**

**6013.** STANLEY, MARNI L.    Travelers' tales: showing and telling, slamming and questing. *In* (pp. 51–60) **40.**

## Biography and Autobiography

**6014.** ALTICK, RICHARD D.    Writing the life of J. J. Ridley. *In* (pp. 26–58) **44.**

**6015.** BODZIOCK, JOSEPH CHRISTOPHER.    What I am about: creating the self in the antebellum slave narratives. Unpub. doct. diss., Univ. of Minnesota, 1988. [Abstr. in DA (50) 442A.]

**6016.** BROUGHTON, J. L.   Conversion and beyond: the changing self in Victorian autobiography. Unpub. doct. diss., Univ. of York. [Abstr. in IT (38:4) 1458.]

**6017.** BUSS, HELEN M.   Canadian women's autobiography: some critical directions. *In* (pp. 154–64) **40.**

**6018.** Entry cancelled.

**6019.** CULJAK, TONI ANN.   Versions of a 'feminist' self: the origins and representations of personal identity in nineteenth-century American feminist autobiography. Unpub. doct. diss., Univ. of Wisconsin–Madison, 1988. [Abstr. in DA (49) 3362A.]

**6020.** DUDLEY, DAVID LEWIS.   'The trouble I've seen': visions and revisions of bondage, flight, and freedom in Black American autobiography. Unpub. doct. diss., Louisiana State Univ. and Agricultural and Mechanical College, 1988. [Abstr. in DA (49) 2219A.]

**6021.** FOX-GENOVESE, ELIZABETH.   My statue, my self: autobiographical writings of Afro-American women. *In* (pp. 63–89) **51.**

**6022.** FRIEDMAN, SUSAN STANFORD.   Women's autobiographical selves: theory and practice. *In* (pp. 34–62) **51.**

**6023.** KIMBLE, MARY ELLEN.   Literary presentations of pioneer women in Kansas and neighboring states. *See* **5861.**

**6024.** LOCKRIDGE, LAURENCE; MAYNARD, JOHN; STONE, DONALD D. (eds).   Nineteenth-century lives: essays presented to Jerome Hamilton Buckley. *See* **44.**

**6025.** MARCUS, JANE.   Invincible mediocrity: the private selves of public women. *In* (pp. 114–46) **51.**

**6026.** NOVARR, DAVID.   The lines of life: theories of biography, 1880–1970. West Lafayette, IN: Purdue UP, 1986. pp. xviii, 202. Rev. by H. Porter Abbott in MLR (84:3) 696–8.

**6027.** PETERSON, LINDA H.   Victorian autobiography: the tradition of self-interpretation. (Bibl. 1987, 6666.) Rev. by A. F. T. Lurcock in RES (38:151) 1987, 429.

**6028.** ROSE, PHYLLIS.   Fact and fiction in biography. *In* (pp. 188–202) **44.**

**6029.** STEPANOWSKY, PAULA; HARPER, CONRAD K.   Views from both directions: courtship and marriage in letters and diaries from the age of Jane Austen. *See* **5000.**

**6030.** WILSON, CHARLES EDGAR, JR.   The antebellum slave narrative and American literature. Unpub. doct. diss., Univ. of Georgia, 1988. [Abstr. in DA (49) 3365A.]

### Related Studies

**6031.** ADAMS, J. R. R.   The printed word and the common man: popular culture in Ulster, 1700–1900. *See* **5002.**

**6032.** BARRY, ELAINE M. E. (introd.).   The Highlands and Islands: a nineteenth-century tour. By J. E. BOWMAN. With a contribution by CELIA MILLER. Gloucester: Sutton; New York: Hippocrene, 1986. pp. xxiv, 210. Rev. by B. Barber in Lore and Language (8:2) 106.

**6033.** BEER, GILLIAN. 'The death of the sun': Victorian solar physics and solar myth. *In* (pp. 159–80) **59.**

**6034.** CHILDERS, JOSEPH W. Politics as interpretation: 'progress', language, and party in early Victorian England. CLIO (17:1) 1987, 65–80.

**6035.** COMANZO, CHRISTIAN. Le bonheur du couple dans l'iconographie victorienne. CVE (28) 1988, 65–75.

**6036.** DIJKSTRA, BRAM. Idols of perversity: fantasies of feminine evil in *fin-de-siècle* culture. (Bibl. 1988, 4566.) Rev. by Bernard Richards in RES (39:156) 1988, 572–4.

**6037.** FOSTER, R. F. Varieties of Irishness. Fortnight (272:supp.) i–iv.

**6038.** FRASER, HILARY. Truth to nature: science, religion and the Pre-Raphaelites. *In* (pp. 53–68) **18.**

**6039.** GAGE, JOHN. J. M. W. Turner and solar myth. *In* (pp. 39–48) **59.**

**6040.** GAY, PETER. The bourgeois experience: Victoria to Freud: vol. 1, Education of the senses. (Bibl. 1984, 6499.) Rev. by Valerie Raoul in CanL (116) 1988, 173–4.

**6041.** —— The bourgeois experience: Victoria to Freud: vol. 2, The tender passion. (Bibl. 1988, 4572.) Rev. by Michael Lynch in UTQ (56:3) 1987, 451–5.

**6042.** GEMÜNDEN, GERD. Das sprachlose Subjekt: Kritik der romantischen Hermeneutik. Unpub. doct. diss., Univ. of Oregon, 1988. [Abstr. in DA (49) 3715A.]

**6043.** GOLBY, J. M. (ed.). Culture and society in Britain 1850–1890: a source book of contemporary writings. (Bibl. 1988, 4573.) Rev. by Malcolm Woodfield in MLR (84:1) 136–7.

**6044.** HARDING, BRIAN. The myth of the myth of the garden. *In* (pp. 44–60) **1.**

**6045.** HELSINGER, ELIZABETH. Constable: the making of a national painter. CI (15:2) 253–79.

**6046.** HUFFSTETLER, EDWARD WRIGHT. The voice from the burning bush: spiritual faith and the religion of American primitivism. Unpub. doct. diss., Univ. of Iowa, 1988. [Abstr. in DA (50) 947A.]

**6047.** JARRETT, DEREK. The sleep of reason: fantasy and reality from the Victorian age to the First World War. (Bibl. 1988, 4576.) Rev. by Stefan Collini in TLS, 6 Jan., 15.

**6048.** JAY, ELISABETH. Faith and doubt in Victorian Britain. (Bibl. 1987, 6698.) Rev. by Norman Vance in MLR (84:3) 723–4; by Bernard Richards in RES (39:155) 1988, 454–5.

**6049.** KENT, JOHN. A renovation of images: nineteenth-century Protestant 'lives of Jesus' and the Roman Catholic alleged appearances of the Blessed Virgin Mary. *In* (pp. 37–52) **18.**

**6050.** KERBER, LINDA K. Women and individualism in American history. *See* **4279.**

**6051.** KROEBER, KARL. British Romantic art. Berkeley; Los Angeles;

London: California UP, 1986. pp. xii, 278. Rev. by J. R. Watson in MLR (84:3) 721–3.

**6052.** LEVINE, LAWRENCE W.   Highbrow/lowbrow: the emergence of cultural hierarchy in America. Cambridge, MA; London: Harvard UP, 1988. pp. 306. Rev. by Tony Tanner in TLS, 14 July, 767; by Carlin Romano in BkW, 8 Jan., 3.

**6053.** McKILLOP, I. D.   The British Ethical Societies. Cambridge; London; New York: CUP, 1986. pp. viii, 204. Rev. by Shelagh Hunter in MLR (84:4) 942–3.

**6054.** MALMGREEN, GAIL (ed.).   Religion in the lives of English women, 1760–1930. See **5017.**

**6055.** MANCOFF, DEBRA N.   'An ancient idea of chivalric greatness': the Arthurian revival and Victorian history painting. In (pp. 127–43) **8.**

**6056.** MITCHELL, SALLY (ed.).   Victorian Britain: an encyclopedia. New York; London: Garland. pp. xxi, 986. (Garland reference library of social science, 438.) Rev. by John Sutherland in TLS, 21 Apr., 432.

**6057.** MOORE, R. LAURENCE.   Religion, secularization, and the shaping of the culture industry in antebellum America. AmQ (41:2) 216–42.

**6058.** NEAD, LYNDA.   Myths of sexuality: representations of women in Victorian Britain. Oxford: Blackwell, 1988. pp. x, 228. Rev. by David Wotton in Word & Image (5:2) 221–2.

**6059.** PARIS, MICHÈLE.   A propos des frasques de la princesse Caroline: le regard sur l'étranger au début du 19e siècle. In (pp. 165–88) **26.**

**6060.** PFEIFFER, H.; JAUSS, H. R.; GAILLARD, F. (eds).   Art social und Art industriel. Munich: Fink, 1987. pp. 479. Rev. by Gary Handwerk in arcadia (24) 320–2.

**6061.** POOVEY, MARY.   Uneven developments: the ideological work of gender in mid-Victorian England. Chicago: Chicago UP, 1988; London: Virago Press. pp. xi, 282. Rev. by Anne Summers in TLS, 7 Apr., 357.

**6062.** PORTER, ROY.   Mind-forg'd manacles: a history of madness in England from the Restoration to the Regency. See **4287.**

**6063.** RAZZAK, FAKHIR ABDUL.   The Arabian Nights in England. See **5023.**

**6064.** REGAN, TOM.   Bloomsbury's prophet: G. E. Moore and the development of his moral philosophy. (Bibl. 1987, 9615.) Rev. by R. Bouyssou in EA (42:3) 354–5.

**6065.** SIMON, SHERRY.   The true Quebec as revealed to English Canada: translated novels, 1864–1950. CanL (117) 1988, 31–43.

**6066.** STARZYK, LAWRENCE J.   Victorian artistic recursions. Mosaic (20:2) 1987, 57–70.

**6067.** WILSON, A. N.   Eminent Victorians. London: BBC. pp. 240. Rev. by Richard Shannon in TLS, 20 Oct., 1154.

**6068.** WRIGHT, T. R.   The religion of humanity: the impact of Comtean positivism on Victorian Britain. (Bibl. 1986, 7512.) Rev. by Shelagh Hunter in MLR (84:4) 941–2.

## Literary Theory
This section is intended to contain studies **about** the literary theory, literary historiography, literary criticism, etc., produced *in* the nineteenth century. For modern works **of** literary history and criticism dealing generally with this period, see under 'Nineteenth Century: General Literary Studies'.

**6069.** ENGELL, JAMES.   Forming the critical mind: Dryden to Coleridge. *See* **4298.**

**6070.** GRAFF, GERALD.   Professing literature: an institutional history. (Bibl. 1988, 4592.) Rev. by Laura Groening in DalR (67:4) 1987, 511–13; by Robert Wess in RMRLL (43:1/2) 98–9; by Alan Golding in MP (86:4) 411–16.

**6071.** GROENING, LAURA.   Modernizing academia: an American and a Canadian vision. DalR (67:4) 1987, 511–22 (review-article).

**6072.** HANDWERK, GARY J.   Irony and ethics in narrative, from Schlegel to Lacan. (Bibl. 1988, 4593.) Rev. by Thomas Docherty in RES (39:154) 1988, 336–7.

**6073.** HARRIS, ROBIN.   English studies at Toronto: a history. Toronto: Toronto UP, 1988. pp. 310. Rev. by Laura Groening in DalR (67:4) 1987, 513–22.

**6074.** JASEN, PATRICIA.   Arnoldian Humanism, English studies, and the Canadian university. QQ (95:3) 1988, 550–66.

**6075.** SCHNEIDER, MARY W.   Poetry in the age of democracy: the literary criticism of Matthew Arnold. Lawrence; London: Kansas UP. pp. xi, 228. Rev. by V. J. Emmett, Jr, in MidQ (31:1) 141–2.

**6076.** STILZ, GERHARD.   'Offensively Australian': the international character of Australian literary nationalism in the 1880s and 1890s. *In* (pp. 87–101) **5.**

**6077.** WALLACE, JAMES MICHAEL.   Literature and the proletariat in the nineteenth century: the work of William Johnson Fox. Unpub. doct. diss., Lehigh Univ. [Abstr. in DA (50) 1670–1A.]

## AUTHORS
### Henry Adams
**6078.** BOURGET, JEAN-LOUP.   Le tombeau de Henry Adams. EA (42:1) 27–38.

**6079.** BURICH, KEITH R.   Charles Eliot Norton, Henry Adams, and the Catholic Church as a symbol of order and authority. CathHR (75:3) 423–38.

**6080.** COMLEY, NANCY R.   Henry Adams' feminine fictions: the economics of maternity. ALR (22:1) 3–16.

**6081.** LEVENSON, J. C., *et al.* (eds).   The letters of Henry Adams: vol. 1, 1858–1868; vol. 2, 1868–1885; vol. 3, 1886–1892. (Bibl. 1985, 6286.) Rev. by Pierre Lagayette in EA (42:2) 182–4.

**6082.** —— The letters of Henry Adams: vol. 4, 1892–1899; vol. 5, 1899–1905; vol. 6, 1906–1918. Cambridge, MA; London: Harvard UP, 1988. pp. xxxvii, 736; ix, 726; ix, 861. Rev. by Harold Kaplan in AL (61:3) 458–61; by Pierre Lagayette in EA (42:2) 182–4.

**6083.** SAMUELS, ERNEST.   Henry Adams. Cambridge, MA; London: Harvard UP. pp. 504. (Abridges bibls 1948, 2799; 1957–8, 6727; 1964, 5155.) Rev. in BkW, 24 Sept., 13; by Hugh Brogan in NYTB, 19 Nov., 22.

**6084.** SOMMER, ROBERT F.   *Mont-Saint-Michel and Chartres*: Henry Adams's pilgrimage into history. CR (33:1) 32–51.

## Louisa M. Alcott

**6085.** ELBERT, SARAH.   A hunger for home: Louisa May Alcott and *Little Women*. (Bibl. 1987, 6746.) Rev. by Alice Hall Petry in SoHR (23:4) 380–2.

**6086.** —— A hunger for home: Louisa May Alcott's place in American culture. New Brunswick, NJ; London: Rutgers UP, 1987. pp. xix, 346.

**6087.** LAC, CHRISTINE MARIE ANDRÉE.   Women and children first: a comparative study of Louisa May Alcott and Sophie de Ségur (Rostopchine). Unpub. doct. diss., Univ. of Nebraska–Lincoln, 1988. [Abstr. in DA (50) 437A.]

**6088.** MYERSON, JOEL; SHEALY, DANIEL (eds).   The selected letters of Louisa May Alcott. (Bibl. 1987, 6748.) Rev. by Larry A. Carlson in AL (61:4) 699–700; by Thomas Mallon in BkW, 24 Sept., 4.

**6089.** PFAELZER, JEAN.   The sentimental promise and the utopian myth: Rebecca Harding Davis's *The Harmonists* and Louisa May Alcott's *Transcendental Wild Oats*. ATQ (3:1) 85–99.

**6090.** SHOWALTER, ELAINE (ed.).   Alternative Alcott. New Brunswick, NJ; London: Rutgers UP, 1988. pp. xlviii, 462. (American women writers.)

**6091.** STERN, MADELEINE B. (ed.); MYERSON, JOEL; SHEALY, DANIEL (assoc. eds).   A double life: newly discovered thrillers of Louisa May Alcott. Boston, MA: Little, Brown, 1988; London: Macmillan. pp. 246. Rev. by Heather Neill in Listener (121) 9 Mar., 34–5.

## Horatio Alger, Jr

**6092.** BENSON, BENJAMIN BRADLEY.   A semiotic approach to the myth of success in the writings of Horatio Alger, Jr. Unpub. doct. diss., Wayne State Univ., 1988. [Abstr. in DA (50) 441–2A.]

## Matthew Arnold

**6093.** ABJADIAN, AMROLLAH.   Arnold and the epic simile. EA (42:4) 411–23.

**6094.** apROBERTS, RUTH.   Matthew Arnold and Herder's *Ideen*. NCP (16:2) 1–20.

**6095.** BHATTI, MUHAMMAD ISMAIL.   Arnold's poetics and the Romantic poets. Explorations (12:1/2) 1988/89, 39–45.

**6096.** BUGEJA, MICHAEL J.   Mesmer as catalyst in *The Scholar-Gipsy*. BSUF (27:3) 1986, 38–42.

**6097.** BURT, FORREST D.; MACHANN, CLINTON.   The literary and critical career of Matthew Arnold: thirteen new letters. MP (87:2) 159–69.

**6098.** CERVO, NATHAN A.   Arnold's *Alaric at Rome* and *The Future*: the gothic face of *Zeitgeist* and modernism. NCP (16:2) 35–48.

**6099.** COLLINI, STEFAN.   Arnold. Oxford: OUP, 1988. pp. xii, 127. Rev. by Chris Baldick in TLS, 13 Jan., 43.

**6100.** CROOK, KEITH.   Matthew Arnold and Stopford Brooke. NCP (16:2) 21–33.

**6101.** GIDDINGS, ROBERT (ed.).   Matthew Arnold: between two worlds. (Bibl. 1988, 4624.) Rev. by Malcolm Hardman in MLR (84:4) 944–5.

**6102.** HASHMI, ALAMGIR.   Counterpoint in the arts: the example of *Dover Beach*. Explorations (12:1/2) 1988/89, 65–75.

**6103.** LIVINGSTON, JAMES C.   Matthew Arnold and Christianity: his religious prose writings. (Bibl. 1987, 6762, where scholar's initial omitted.) Rev. by Malcolm Hardman in MLR (84:4) 945–6; by Rosemary Ashton in RES (39:156) 1988, 577–8.

**6104.** LONGENBACH, JAMES.   Matthew Arnold and the modern apocalypse. PMLA (104:5) 844–55.

**6105.** MACHANN, CLINTON; BURT, FORREST D. (eds).   Matthew Arnold in his time and ours: centenary essays. Charlottesville: Virginia UP, 1988. pp. xvi, 220. (Papers delivered at a symposium at Texas A&M Univ., Spring 1985.) Rev. by Chris Baldick in TLS, 13 Jan., 43.

**6106.** MILBRANDT, ROGER DOUGLAS.   Three late Victorian models of artistic production: a study of Arnold, Pater and Morris. Unpub. doct. diss., Syracuse Univ. [Abstr. in DA (50) 1667–8A.]

**6107.** PAULIN, TOM.   English political writers on Ireland: Robert Southey to Douglas Hurd. *In* (pp. 132–45) **17.**

**6108.** RAPPLE, BRENDAN A.   Matthew Arnold's views on modernity and a state system of middle-class education in England: some continental influences. JGE (39:4) 1988, 206–21.

**6109.** REEVES, MARJORIE; GOULD, WARWICK.   Joachim of Fiore and the myth of the eternal evangel in the nineteenth century. Oxford: Clarendon Press; New York: OUP, 1987. pp. 365. Rev. by Nicholas Sagovsky in CamQ (18:1) 105–7; by Augustine Martin in IUR (19:2) 401–2; by Rosemary Ashton in RES (39:156) 1988, 577–8.

**6110.** RUNCIE, CATHERINE.   Matthew Arnold's Christ and the unity of culture and religion. Sydney Studies in English (14) 1988/89, 38–51.

**6111.** SCHNEIDER, MARY W.   Poetry in the age of democracy: the literary criticism of Matthew Arnold. *See* **6075.**

**6112.** SUPER, R. H.   Matthew Arnold's *Literature and Dogma*, the *Cornhill Magazine*, and censorship. *See* **592.**

**6113.** ULLMANN, S. O. A.   Arnold on Tennyson. NCP (16:2) 55–60.

**6114.** —— (ed.).   The Yale manuscript: Matthew Arnold. Ann Arbor: Michigan UP. pp. xii, 236. (Collection of documents, written by Arnold between 1843 and 1857, held by the Beinecke Rare Book and Manuscript Library of Yale University.)

### Jane Austen

**6115.** AIKEN, JOAN.   How might Jane Austen have revised *Northanger Abbey*? Persuasions (7) 1985, 42–54.

**6116.** ALEXANDER, PETER F.   *Robin Adair* as a musical clue in Jane Austen's *Emma*. RES (39:153) 1988, 84–6.

**6117.** ANON. (ed.). Collected reports of the Jane Austen Society 1976–1985. Overton, Hants: Jane Austen Society. pp. 376.

**6118.** AUSTEN-LEIGH, JOAN. Fanny Knight. Persuasions Occasional Papers (2) 1986, 1–2.

**6119.** —— My aunt, Jane Austen. Persuasions (11) 28–36.

**6120.** —— New light thrown on JA's refusal of Harris Bigg-Wither. Persuasions (8) 1986, 34–6.

**6121.** BENSON, MARY MARGARET. 'Excellently qualified to shine at a round game'. Persuasions (8) 1986, 96–100.

**6122.** —— Mothers, substitute mothers, and daughters in the novels of Jane Austen. Persuasions (11) 117–24.

**6123.** BERTELSEN, LANCE. A portrait of Mrs Bingley. Persuasions (8) 1986, 37–8.

**6124.** BIZZARO, PATRICK. Global and contextual humor in *Northanger Abbey*. Persuasions (7) 1985, 82–8.

**6125.** BOOTH, WAYNE C. Emma, *Emma*, and the question of feminism. Persuasions (5) 1983, 29–40. (Text of speech, Philadelphia, 8 October 1983.)

**6126.** BRIGANTI, CHIARA. Female characters and the vanishing author in Jane Austen, Charlotte Brontë and Charles Dickens. Unpub. doct. diss., Pennsylvania State Univ., 1988. [Abstr. in DA (49) 2664A.]

**6127.** BROWN, CORNELIA ELIZABETH. Speaking for not spoken by: contractual representation in Balzac, Austen, and Gogol. Unpub. doct. diss., Univ. of California, Berkeley, 1988. [Abstr. in DA (50) 943A.]

**6128.** BROWN, JULIA PREWITT. Jane Austen's England. Persuasions (10) 1988, 53–8.

**6129.** BURKE, HENRY G. Seeking Jane in foreign tongues. Persuasions (7) 1985, 17–20. (Collecting translations.)

**6130.** CANTRELL, D. DEAN. Her passion for ancient edifices. Persuasions (7) 1985, 89–93.

**6131.** —— Porcine tittle-tattle. Persuasions (4) 1982, 14–15.

**6132.** CASS, JOCELYN CREIGH. An amusing study: family likenesses in *Pride and Prejudice*. Persuasions (9) 1987, 49–50.

**6133.** CITRON, JO ANN. Contested narratives, contested selves: imagination and identity in four novels by Jane Austen. Unpub. doct. diss., Boston Univ., 1986. [Abstr. in DA (49) 1807–8A.]

**6134.** COHN, MAGGIE HUNT. Suppressed desires in *Mansfield Park*. Persuasions (2) 1980, 27–8.

**6135.** COLLINS, K. K. Prejudice, *Persuasion*, and the puzzle of Mrs Smith. Persuasions (6) 1984, 40–3.

**6136.** COOKSON, LINDA; LOUGHREY, BRYAN (eds). Critical essays on *Emma*: Jane Austen. Harlow: Longman, 1988. pp. 143. (Longman literature guides.)

**6137.** DAVIES, H. NEVILLE. More light on Mr Chard. Jane Austen Society Report 12–14.

**6138.** DAVIS, PATRICIA D. Jane Austen's use of Frank Churchill's letters in *Emma*. Persuasions (10) 1988, 34–8.

**6139.** DeForest, Mary.   Jane Austen and the anti-heroic tradition. Persuasions (10) 1988, 11–21.

**6140.** —— Mrs Elton and the slave trade. Persuasions (9) 1987, 11–13.

**6141.** Denman, Helen C.   Portraits of Jane Austen. Persuasions (3) 1981, 12–13.

**6142.** Derry, S. G.   Tradition, imitation, and innovation: Jane Austen and the development of the novel, 1740–1818. *See* **4927.**

**6143.** Drabble, Margaret (introd.).   Mansfield Park. London: Virago Press. pp. xx, 355. (Virago modern classics, 345.)

**6144.** —— Persuasion. London: Virago Press. pp. xviii, 247. (Virago modern classics, 344.)

**6145.** —— Pride and prejudice. London: Virago Press. pp. xviii, 298. (Virago modern classics, 342.)

**6146.** —— Sense and sensibility. London: Virago Press. pp. xx, 278. (Virago modern classics, 343.)

**6147.** Dussinger, John A.   'The language of real feeling': internal speech in the Jane Austen novel. *In* (pp. 97–115) **33.**

**6148.** Ellis, H. F.   The Chawton letters. Persuasions (3) 1981, 29–30. (Repr. from Punch, 5 June 1963.)

**6149.** Evans, Mary.   Jane Austen and the state. (Bibl. 1988, 4649.) Rev. by Margaret Kirkham in BJECS (12) 226–7.

**6150.** Fawcett, Nancy Ruth.   A safe place: Jane Austen and the Richardsonian inheritance. *See* **5444.**

**6151.** Fisher, Judith Warner.   All the 'write' moves: or, Theatrical gesture in *Sense and Sensibility*. Persuasions (9) 1987, 17–23.

**6152.** Fitzgerald, Jennifer.   Jane Austen's *Persuasion* and the French Revolution. Persuasions (10) 1988, 39–43.

**6153.** Ford, Susan Allen.   Imperfect articulations: language and structure in Jane Austen's novels. Unpub. doct. diss., Univ. of Michigan. [Abstr. in DA (50) 1664A.]

**6154.** Fried, Cathy.   Some notes on the 'parish business' in *Emma*. Persuasions (1) 1979, 17, 24.

**6155.** Gard, Roger.   *Mansfield Park*, Fanny Price, Flaubert and the modern novel. Eng (38) 1–33.

**6156.** Garside, P. D.   Jane Austen and subscription fiction. BJECS (10) 1987, 175–88.

**6157.** Gibbs, Christine.   Absent fathers: an examination of father–daughter relationships in Jane Austen's novels. Persuasions (8) 1986, 45–50.

**6158.** Gilson, David.   A bibliography of Jane Austen. (Bibl. 1986, 7582, repr. with corrections, 1985.) Rev. by Laura Mooneyham in MP (85:2) 1987, 209–11.

**6159.** Goubert, Pierre.   L'élévation sociale dans *Mansfield Park*. BSEAA (29) 147–57.

**6160.** Greene, Donald.   The curtain lifts. Persuasions (8) 1986, 55–7. (Austen's visit to Stoneleigh.)

**6161.** —— Hamstall Ridware: a neglected Austen setting. Persuasions (7) 1985, 58–61.

**6162.** —— A partial pedigree of Jane Austen. Persuasions (6) 1984, 31–4.

**6163.** GREY, J. DAVID.  Henry Austen: Jane Austen's 'perpetual sunshine'. Persuasions Occasional Papers (1) 1984, 9–12.

**6164.** —— Our little brother. Persuasions (3) 1981, 9–11. (Charles John Austen, 1779–1852.)

**6165.** —— Sibling relationships in *Mansfield Park*. Persuasions (2) 1980, 28–9.

**6166.** GROSS, GLORIA.  Mentoring Jane Austen: reflections on 'my dear Dr Johnson'. *See* **5340.**

**6167.** GROVES, DAVID.  Jane Austen in Scotland. Persuasions (7) 1985, 66; (10) 1988, 27–30.

**6168.** —— Knowing one's species better: social satire in *Persuasion*. Persuasions (6) 1984, 13–15.

**6169.** —— The two picnics in *Emma*. Persuasions (4) 1982, 6–7.

**6170.** HALPERIN, JOHN.  Inside *Pride and Prejudice*. Persuasions (11) 37–45.

**6171.** HARDY, JOHN.  Jane Austen's heroines: intimacy in human relationships. (Bibl. 1988, 4655.) Rev. by Park Honan in BJECS (10) 1987, 100–1.

**6172.** HARRIS, JOCELYN.  Jane Austen's art of memory. Cambridge: CUP. pp. xi, 272.

**6173.** HART, JOHN.  Jane Austen's sailors: gentlemen in the military capacity. Persuasions (4) 1982, 18–21.

**6174.** HELDMAN, JAMES.  Kipling, *Jane's Marriage*, and *The Janeites*. Persuasions (10) 1988, 44–7.

**6175.** —— Where is Jane Austen in *The Watsons*? Persuasions (8) 1986, 84–91.

**6176.** HILDEBRAND, ENID G.  Jane Austen and the law. Persuasions (4) 1982, 34–41.

**6177.** HONAN, PARK.  The Austen brothers and sisters. Persuasions (10) 1988, 59–64.

**6178.** —— Jane Austen: her life. (Bibl. 1988, 4656.) Rev. by Susan Morgan in MP (87:2) 191–3.

**6179.** HORWITZ, BARBARA J.  Lady Susan: the wicked mother in Jane Austen's novels. Persuasions (9) 1987, 84–8.

**6180.** HUDSON, GLENDA A.  'Precious remains of the earliest attachment': sibling love in Jane Austen's *Pride and Prejudice*. Persuasions (11) 125–31.

**6181.** HUFSTADER, ALICE.  Family patterns in *Persuasion*. Persuasions (6) 1984, 21–3.

**6182.** IVES, SIDNEY.  The withering eye, the transmuting hand, the alchemies of *Pride and Prejudice*. Persuasions (9) 1987, 41–5.

**6183.** JARVIS, W. A. W.  Mr Jefferson's case. Jane Austen Society Report 15–18.

**6184.** JENKINS, ELIZABETH.  Jane Fairfax. Jane Austen Society Report 5–7.

**6185.** KAPLAN, DEBORAH. The 'family influence' on Jane Austen's Juvenilia. Persuasions (10) 1988, 65–9.

**6186.** —— Representing two cultures: Jane Austen's letters. *In* (pp. 211–29) **51.**

**6187.** KAPLAN, LAURIE. Jane Austen and the uncommon reader. Persuasions (9) 1987, 71–5.

**6188.** KEITH, RHONDA. Jane Austen and Shakespeare. *See* **3780.**

**6189.** KELLETT, CHRISTINE ANN. Destroying the monolith: irony and identity in nineteenth-century narrative. Unpub. doct. diss., Univ. of Washington, 1988. [Abstr. in DA (50) 690A.]

**6190.** KNUTH, DEBORAH J. Sisterhood and friendship in *Pride and Prejudice*: need happiness be 'entirely a matter of chance'? Persuasions (11) 99–109.

**6191.** —— 'We fainted alternately on a sofa': female friendship in Jane Austen's Juvenilia. Persuasions (9) 1987, 64–71.

**6192.** KOPPEL, GENE. The mystery of the self in *Persuasion*. Persuasions (6) 1984, 48–54.

**6193.** —— *Pride and Prejudice*: conservative or liberal novel – or both? (A Gadamerian approach.) Persuasions (11) 132–9.

**6194.** —— The religious dimension of Jane Austen's novels. (Bibl. 1988, 4661.) Rev. by John C. Hawley in ChrisL (38:3) 72–3.

**6195.** LANE, MAGGIE. A charming place: Bath in the life and times of Jane Austen. Bath: Millstream, 1988. pp. 104.

**6196.** —— Jane Austen's Bath. Persuasions (7) 1985, 55–7.

**6197.** LE FAYE, DEIRDRE. Anna Lefroy's original memories of Jane Austen. RES (39:155) 1988, 417–21.

**6198.** —— Fanny Knight's diaries: Jane Austen through her niece's eyes. Persuasions Occasional Papers (2) 1986, 5–26.

**6199.** —— News from Chawton: a letter from Mrs George Austen. RES (38:151) 1987, 364–8.

**6200.** —— *Sanditon*: Jane Austen's manuscript and her niece's continuation. RES (38:149) 1987, 56–61.

**6201.** —— 'To dwell together in unity'. Jane Austen Society Report, 23–35.

**6202.** LITZ, A. WALTON. Jane Austen: the 'juvenilia'. Persuasions (9) 1987, 59–63.

**6203.** —— The picturesque in *Pride and Prejudice*. Persuasions (1) 1979, 13, 15, 20–4.

**6204.** McALEER, JOHN. The comedy of social distinctions in *Pride and Prejudice*. Persuasions (11) 70–6.

**6205.** McCAWLEY, DWIGHT. Assertion and aggression in the novels of Jane Austen. Persuasions (11) 77–84.

**6206.** McKELLAR, HUGH D. Attending divine service in the Revd George Austen's day. Persuasions (6) 1984, 7–9.

**6207.** —— Muted merriment: Christmas celebrations in Jane Austen. Persuasions (8) 1986, 12–16.

**6208.** —— 'The profession of a clergyman'. Persuasions (7) 1985, 28–34.

**6209.** McMASTER, JULIET.    'The beautifull Cassandra' illustrated. Persuasions (10) 1988, 99–103.

**6210.** —— 'God gave us our relations': the Watson family. Persuasions (8) 1986, 60–72.

**6211.** —— Hospitality. Persuasions (4) 1982, 26–33. (Text of speech, Toronto, 16 October 1982.)

**6212.** MARSHALL, P. SCOTT.    Techniques of persuasion in *Persuasion* – a lawyer's viewpoint. Persuasions (6) 1984, 44–7.

**6213.** MARTIN, ELLEN E.    The madness of Jane Austen: metonymic style and literature's resistance to interpretation. Persuasions (9) 1987, 76–84.

**6214.** MILLARD, MARY.    Do you not dance, Mr Elton? Persuasions (5) 1983, 14.

**6215.** —— 1807 and all that. Persuasions (8) 1986, 50–1. (Act abolishing the slave trade.)

**6216.** —— The fortune of the Misses Elliot. Persuasions (6) 1984, 34.

**6217.** —— The outs and not outs. Persuasions (2) 1980, 24–5.

**6218.** MILLER, PAMELA COOK.    Jane Austen and the power of the spoken word. Persuasions (7) 1985, 35–8.

**6219.** MODERT, JO.    The dating of some Jane Austen letters. NQ (36:2) 171–2.

**6220.** —— Here for the first time, a Jane Austen letter. *See* **157a.**

**6221.** MORRIS, EILEEN.    Jane Austen's hidden message to a publisher. Persuasions (4) 1982, 16–17.

**6222.** MORRIS, IVOR.    Mr Collins considered: approaches to Jane Austen. (Bibl. 1988, 4667.) Rev. by Margaret Kirkham in BJECS (12) 226–7.

**6223.** MOSEL, TAD.    Jane Austen's two inches of ivory. Persuasions Occasional Papers (1) 1984, 1–8.

**6224.** NARDIN, JANE.    Propriety versus morality in Jane Austen's novels. Persuasions (10) 1988, 70–5.

**6225.** NORRIS, JOHN.    'Sam is only a surgeon, you know.' Persuasions (8) 1986, 92–5.

**6226.** PARKER, KEIKO KIMURA.    A little query on Mr and Mrs. Persuasions (5) 1983, 11–12.

**6227.** PARSONS, FARNELL.    Fact and fantasy: Jane Austen's childhood reading. Persuasions (10) 1988, 90–8.

**6228.** PEDLEY, COLIN.    'The inward dispositions of the heart': Jane Austen and Jane West. NQ (36:2) 169–71.

**6229.** POOVEY, MARY.    'The true English style'. Persuasions (5) 1983, 48–51. (Shortened version of talk given at Philadelphia, 8 October 1983.)

**6230.** REDMOND, LUANNE BETHKE.    Land, law and love. Persuasions (11) 46–52.

**6231.** RUOFF, GENE W.    The triumph of *Persuasion*: Jane Austen and the creation of woman. Persuasions (6) 1984, 54–61.

**6232.** SANDOCK, MOLLIE.    Jane Austen and the political passions. Persuasions (10) 1988, 83–9.

**6233.** ——Jane Austen's politics: the English novel and the real business of life. Cresset (52:7) 8–12.

**6234.** SCHWERIN, ERNA. *Mansfield Park*: a note on the elopement of Henry and Maria. Persuasions (2) 1980, 22–3, 25.

**6235.** SHERROD, BARBARA. *Pride and Prejudice*: a classic love story. Persuasions (11) 66–9.

**6236.** SIMPSON, JANICE C. Fanny Price as Cinderella: folk and fairy-tale in *Mansfield Park*. Persuasions (9) 1987, 25–30.

**6237.** SMITH, ELLEN. Spanish translations of *Emma*. Persuasions (7) 1985, 21–7.

**6238.** STOVEL, BRUCE. Secrets, silence, and surprise in *Pride and Prejudice*. Persuasions (11) 85–91.

**6239.** SWORDS, BARBARA W. 'Woman's place' in Jane Austen's England 1770–1820. Persuasions (10) 1988, 76–82.

**6240.** TANNER, TONY. Jane Austen. (Bibl. 1988, 4674.) Rev. by Deirdre Le Faye in RES (39:154) 1988, 308–9; by Michael William in UES (27:1) 39–40; by Frederick M. Keener in YES (19) 333–4.

**6241.** TERRY, JUDITH. 'Knit your own stuff'; or, Finishing off Jane Austen. Persuasions (8) 1986, 73–83. (Completions of *The Watsons*.)

**6242.** —— Seen but not heard: servants in Jane Austen's England. Persuasions (10) 1988, 104–16.

**6243.** WATT, IAN. Jane Austen and the traditions of comic aggression in *Sense and Sensibility*. Persuasions (3) 1981, 14–15, 24–8.

**6244.** WIESENFARTH, JOSEPH. *The Watsons* as pretext. Persuasions (8) 1986, 101–11.

**6245.** —— Violet Hunt rewrites Jane Austen: *Pride and Prejudice* (1813) and *Their Lives* (1916). Persuasions (11) 61–5.

**6246.** WILLIAMS, A. SUSAN. Jane Austen. Hove: Wayland. pp. 112. (Life and works.)

**6247.** WILT, JUDITH. The powers of the instrument: or Jane, Frank, and the pianoforte. Persuasions (5) 1983, 41–7.

**6248.** WINGARD, SARA. Reversal and revelation: the five seasons of *Pride and Prejudice*. Persuasions (11) 92–8.

**6249.** ZOOK, ALMA C. Star gazing at Mansfield Park. Persuasions (8) 1986, 29–33.

### William Barnes

**6250.** HERTZ, ALAN. Exile in Eden: William Barnes's lyrics of romantic encounter. UTQ (56:2) 1986/87, 308–18.

### Robert Barr

**6251.** BRADSHAW, JAMES STANFORD. The science fiction of Robert Barr. SFS (16:2) 201–8.

**6252.** LAMB, HUGH (sel. and introd.). Stories in the dark: tales of terror by Jerome K. Jerome, Robert Barr and Barry Pain. Wellingborough: Equation. pp. 223. (Equation chillers.)

### Thomas Lovell Beddoes

**6253.** MOYLAN, CHRISTOPHER MICHAEL. Thomas Lovell Beddoes (1803–1849): medicine, politics, and therapeutic theater. Unpub. doct. diss., Boston Univ. [Abstr. in DA (50) 1313–14A.]

**6254.** VENKATESWARAN, PRAMILA. The stone and the web: Romantic irony in the works of Thomas Lovell Beddoes. Unpub. doct. diss., George Washington Univ., 1988. [Abstr. in DA (49) 3373A.]

### Henry Ward Beecher

**6255.** LEMEUNIER, YVES. L'éthique du loisir dans *Norwood* de Henry Ward Beecher. *In* (pp. 111–26) **25.**

### Edward Bellamy

**6256.** EGE, S. E. A comparative study of the works of Edward Bellamy and H. G. Wells with special reference to their utopian fiction (1888–1945). Unpub. doct. diss., Univ. of Strathclyde, 1987. [Abstr. in IT (38:4) 1462.]

**6257.** GRIFFITH, NANCY SNELL. Edward Bellamy: a bibliography. Metuchen, NJ: Scarecrow Press, 1986. pp. xi, 185. (Scarecrow author bibliographies, 78.) Rev. by Kenneth M. Roemer in SFS (16:2) 238–40.

**6258.** MATARESE, SUSAN M. Foreign policy and the American self-image: looking back at *Looking Backward*. ATQ (3:1) 45–54.

**6259.** MICHAELS, WALTER BENN. An American tragedy, or the promise of American life. Representations (25) 71–98.

**6260.** PORTER, GERALD. The art of the impossible: two early American utopias. *In* (pp. 42–54) **43.**

**6261.** ROEMER, KENNETH M. The literary domestication of Utopia: there's no *Looking Backward* without Uncle Tom and Uncle True. ATQ (3:1) 101–22.

**6262.** SCHEICK, WILLIAM J. The letter killeth: Edward Bellamy's *To Whom This May Come*. ATQ (3:1) 55–67.

**6263.** WIDDICOMBE, RICHARD TOBY. 'Dynamite in disguise': a deconstructive reading of Bellamy's utopian novels. ATQ (3:1) 69–84.

**6264.** —— Edward Bellamy: an annotated bibliography of secondary criticism. New York; London: Garland, 1988. pp. xix, 587. (Garland reference library of the humanities, 827.) Rev. by Kenneth M. Roemer in SFS (16:2) 238–40.

### Jeremy Bentham

**6265.** DINWIDDY, JOHN. Bentham. Oxford: OUP. pp. 132. (Past masters.)

### Sir Walter Besant

**6266.** ELIOT, SIMON. Unequal partnerships: Besant, Rice and Chatto 1876–82. *See* **429.**

### Ambrose Bierce ('Dod Grile')

**6267.** ST PIERRE, BRIAN (ed.). The devil's advocate: an Ambrose Bierce reader. San Francisco, CA: Chronicle Books, 1987. pp. 327. Rev. by David George in OhioanaQ (32:2) 68–72.

**6268.** TOURNEBIZE, CASSILDE. Représentation du Sud dans *Tales of Soldiers* d'Ambrose Bierce. Caliban (26) 15–20.

### R. D. Blackmore

**6269.** GARDNER, BARRY. Who was Lorna Doone? Dulverton; Brendon Arts for the Anglo-American Lorna Doone Society. pp. 36.

### Wilfrid Scawen Blunt

**6270.** FAULKNER, PETER (ed.). Jane Morris to Wilfrid Scawen Blunt:

the letters of Jane Morris to Wilfrid Scawen Blunt together with extracts from Blunt's diaries. (Bibl. 1988, 4693.) Rev. by G. A. Cevasco in MLR (84:2) 449–50.

## Dion Boucicault

**6271.** Kosok, Heinz. Dion Boucicault's 'American' plays: considerations on defining national literatures in English. *In* (pp. 81–97) **37.**

## William Lisle Bowles

**6272.** Wu, Duncan. Wordsworth's reading of Bowles. NQ (36:2) 166–7.

## The Brontës

**6273.** Anon. (comp.). Brontë, Brontë, Brontë. Tokyo: Kaibunsha. pp. 224, xii. (In Japanese.)

**6274.** Eagleton, Terry. Myths of power: a Marxist study of the Brontës. (Bibl. 1977, 6270.) London: Macmillan. pp. 150. (Second ed.: first ed. 1975.) Rev. by Arthur Pollard in BST (19:8) 378.

**6275.** Fraser, Rebecca. The Brontës: Charlotte Brontë and her family. New York: Crown. pp. 543. Rev. by Virginia Tiger in NYTB, 5 Feb., 16; by Nancy W. Ellenberger in BkW, 19 Feb., 6.

**6276.** Klaus, Meredith; Cross, Gilbert; Golen, Richard. A Brontë reading list. BST (19:7) 335–40.

**6277.** Wilks, Brian. There is a spot mid barren hills. BST (19:7) 310–20.

## Anne Brontë

**6278.** Marsden, Hilda; Inglesfield, Robert (eds). Agnes Grey. Oxford: Clarendon Press, 1988. pp. xxvii, 224. (Clarendon edition of the novels of the Brontës.) Rev. by Mark Seaward in BST (19:7) 322–3; by Douglas Hewitt in NQ (36:4) 524–5.

**6279.** Newey, Katherine M. Economics in *The Tenant of Wildfell Hall*. BST (19:7) 293–301.

## Branwell Brontë

**6280.** Butterfield, Mary; Duckett, R. J. (eds). Brother in the shadow: stories and sketches by Branwell Brontë. Bradford: Bradford Libraries and Information Service, 1988. pp. ix, 153. Rev. by Everard Flintoff in BST (19:7) 320–1.

**6281.** Flintoff, Everard. Some unpublished poems of Branwell Brontë. DUJ (81:2) 241–52.

**6282.** Goodacre, Selwyn H. The published poems of Branwell Brontë. BST (19:8) 361–8.

## Charlotte Brontë

**6283.** Alexander, Christine (ed.). An edition of the early writings of Charlotte Brontë: vol. 1, *The Glass Town Saga: 1826–1832.* (Bibl. 1988, 4709.) Rev. by Karen McLeod Hewitt in NQ (36:2) 251–2.

**6284.** Azim, F. The novel's imperial past: subjectivity and sexuality in the fictional writings of Charlotte Brontë. Unpub. doct. diss., Univ. of Sussex. [Abstr. in IT (39:3) 1109.]

**6285.** Bemelmans, J. W. M. Charlotte Brontë and the uses of creative writing: a study in function and form. Unpub. doct. diss., Univ. of Hull, 1988. [Abstr. in IT (38:4) 1457–8.]

**6286.** BETSINGER, SUE ANN. Charlotte Brontë's archetypal heroine. BST (19:7) 301–9.

**6287.** BLONDEL, JACQUES. La poésie dans le roman victorien: la fin de *Villette*. Repérages (11) 15–20.

**6288.** BRIGANTI, CHIARA. Female characters and the vanishing author in Jane Austen, Charlotte Brontë and Charles Dickens. *See* **6126.**

**6289.** DE JONG, MARY G. Different voices: moral conflict in *Jane Eyre*, *The Mill on the Floss*, and *Romola*. CEACrit (51:2/3) 55–65.

**6290.** DELOURME, CHANTAL. La mémoire fécondée: réflexions sur l'intertextualité: *Jane Eyre*, *Wide Sargasso Sea*. EA (42:3) 257–69.

**6291.** DUNN, RICHARD J. (ed.). *Jane Eyre*: authoritative text, backgrounds, criticism. New York; London: Norton, 1987. pp. viii, 499. (Norton critical editions.) (Second ed.: first ed. 1971.) Rev. by Margaret Smith in BST (19:7) 321–2.

**6292.** DUPRAS, JOSEPH A. Charlotte Brontë's *Shirley* and interpretive engendering. PLL (24:3) 1988, 301–16.

**6293.** EWBANK, INGA-STINA. Victorian novels and feminist criticism. *In* (pp. 47–66) **47.**

**6294.** FRASER, REBECCA. Charlotte Brontë. (Bibl. 1988, 4714.) Rev. by Margaret Smith in BST (19:8) 376–7; by John Sutherland in LRB (11:3) 19–22.

**6295.** —— A strange plant: Charlotte Brontë's friendship with Mrs Gaskell. BST (19:8) 341–54.

**6296.** GLEN, HEATHER (ed.). The professor. Harmondsworth: Penguin. pp. 316. (Penguin classics.)

**6297.** GROSSMANN, MAUREEN ELLEN. Small beginnings: the recovery of childhood and the recovery from childhood in the Victorian novel. Unpub. doct. diss., Univ. of California, Berkeley, 1988. [Abstr. in DA (50) 952A.]

**6298.** JENKINS, RUTH YVONNE. Reclaiming myths of power: narrative strategies of Nightingale, Brontë, Gaskell and Eliot. Unpub. doct. diss., State Univ. of New York at Stony Brook, 1988. [Abstr. in DA (50) 1312A.]

**6299.** AL-KHAFAJI, MAHMOUD FADHIL. Gothic and modern elements in *Villette*. Al-Mustansiriya Literary Review (Al-Mustansiriya Univ., Baghdad) (12) 1985, 151–68.

**6300.** LAWSON, KATHLEEN TOSH. Charlotte Brontë and Christianity: the heresy of desire. Unpub. doct. diss., Univ. of Toronto, 1988. [Abstr. in DA (50) 148A.]

**6301.** LOE, THOMAS. Rejection and progress in *Jane Eyre*. BST (19:8) 341–54.

**6302.** LORIMER LUNDBERG, PATRICIA. Gendered reading communities: the feminization of reader response criticism and a dialogics of reading. Unpub. doct. diss., Loyola Univ. of Chicago. [Abstr. in DA (50) 954–5A.]

**6303.** MACPHERSON, PAT. Reflecting on Jane Eyre. London: Routledge. pp. xiii, 120. (Heroines.)

**6304.** MAGIE, LYNNE ADELE. The daemon Eros: gothic elements in the novels of Emily and Charlotte Brontë, Doris Lessing, and Iris Murdoch. Unpub. doct. diss., Univ. of Washington, 1988. [Abstr. in DA (49) 2669A.]

**6305.** MANN, MAUREEN RUTH FORBES. The authority of language in the novels of Charlotte Brontë. Unpub. doct. diss., Univ. of Toronto, 1988. [Abstr. in DA (49) 2670A.]

**6306.** MICHIE, HELENA. 'There is no friend like a sister: sisterhood as sexual difference. ELH (56:2) 401–21.

**6307.** MILBANK, ALISON. Doubting Castle: the gothic mode of questioning. In (pp. 104–19) **18.**

**6308.** MONAHAN, MELODIE. Heading out is not going home: Jane Eyre. SELit (28:4) 1988, 589–608.

**6309.** MYER, VALERIE GROSVENOR. Charlotte Brontë: truculent spirit. (Bibl. 1988, 4722.) Rev. by Karen McLeod Hewitt in NQ (36:2) 250–1: by Margaret Smith in BST (19:7) 324–5.

**6310.** NESTOR, PAULINE. Female friendships and communities: Charlotte Brontë, George Eliot, Elizabeth Gaskell. (Bibl. 1988, 4724.) Rev. by Judy Simons in RES (38:150) 1987, 263–4; by Karla K. Walters in StudN (20:2) 1988, 228–9.

**6311.** POOVEY, MARY. The anathematized race: the governess and Jane Eyre. In (pp. 230–54) **29.**

**6312.** ROBBINS, HELEN WALKER. Wrapped in 'dishonest doubt': Charlotte Brontë and the shroud of language. Unpub. doct. diss., Duke Univ., 1988. [Abstr. in DA (49) 3035–6A.]

**6313.** ROSENGARTEN, HERBERT; SMITH, MARGARET (eds). Villette. (Bibl. 1988, 4726.) Rev. by Mark Seaward in BST (19:7) 322–3.

**6314.** SHAW, MARGARET LYNN. Producing the (con)text of Villette: Charlotte Brontë and the politics of culture. Unpub. doct. diss., Univ. of Pittsburgh, 1988. [Abstr. in DA (49) 3736A.]

**6315.** SMITH, MARGARET. Charlotte Brontë and Charles Dickens. BST (19:8) 368–9.

**6316.** —— ROSENGARTEN, HERBERT (eds). The professor. (Bibl. 1988, 4728.) Rev. by Mark Seaward in BST (19:7) 322–3; by Alexander Welsh in MP (87:2) 198–200.

**6317.** VARGISH, THOMAS. The providential aesthetic in Victorian fiction. See **5929.**

**6318.** WILLIAMS, JUDITH. Perception and expression in the novels of Charlotte Brontë. Ann Arbor, MI; London: UMI Research Press, 1988. pp. vi, 175. (Nineteenth-century studies.)

**6319.** WINNIFRITH, TOM; CHITHAM, EDWARD. Charlotte and Emily Brontë: literary lives. Basingstoke: Macmillan. pp. vi, 144. (Macmillan literary lives.) Rev. by Brian Wilks in BST (19:8) 376–7.

### Emily Brontë

**6320.** ARONSON, MARILYN RUTH. Time in the works of Emily Brontë. Unpub. doct. diss., St John's Univ. [Abstr. in DA (50) 1308A.]

**6321.** BATES, JUDITH. L'onirisme dans *Wuthering Heights* d'Emily Brontë: narration, schèmes et symbolisme. Paris: Lettres Modernes, 1988. pp. 167. (Situation, 47.)

**6322.** COOKSON, LINDA; LOUGHREY, BRYAN (eds). Critical essays on *Wuthering Heights*: Emily Brontë. Harlow: Longman, 1988. pp. 127. (Longman literature guides.)

**6323.** DAVIES, STEVIE. Emily Brontë. New York; London: Harvester Wheatsheaf. pp. xii, 180. (Key women writers.)

**6324.** DAWSON, TERENCE. The struggle for deliverance from the father: the structural principle of *Wuthering Heights*. MLR (84:2) 289–304.

**6325.** DEVLIN, D. D. Emily Brontë and Fanny Burney. *See* **5126.**

**6326.** FARRELL, JOHN P. Reading the text of community in *Wuthering Heights*. ELH (56:1) 173–208.

**6327.** FORD, BORIS. *Wuthering Heights. In* (pp. 29–42) **13.**

**6328.** GOLDFARB, RUSSELL M. The survival of Nelly Dean in *Wuthering Heights*. CEACrit (51:4) 53–63.

**6329.** GORDON, JAN B. Parlour's *parler*: the chatter of tongues ... within *Wuthering Heights*. Mentalities (6:1) 2–23.

**6330.** GORDON, MARCIA MACKE. Absence and presence in *Wuthering Heights* and *The Story of an African Farm*: charting the feminine in language. Unpub. doct. diss., Brown Univ., 1988. [Abstr. in DA (49) 2229A.]

**6331.** HEDBERG, JOHANNES. *Wuthering Heights*: a most remarkable English novel. MS (83:4) 290–8.

**6332.** HEYWOOD, CHRISTOPHER. Yorkshire slavery in *Wuthering Heights*. RES (38:150) 1987, 184–98.

**6333.** HORATSCHEK, ANNEGRET. 'In true gossip's fashion'? Das domestizierte Bewußtsein der Nelly Dean. PoetA (21:3/4) 353–88.

**6334.** JOHNSON, EDWARD HOTSPUR. *Wuthering Heights*: Bombay style. BST (19:7) 325–7. (Film review.)

**6335.** KAWAGUCHI, KYOUICHI. Shōsetsu no senryaku geimu: *Arashi-gaoka wo yomu.* (A strategic game of fiction: reading *Wuthering Heights*.) Tokyo: Fukutake. pp. 242.

**6336.** LEVY, ANITA. Blood, kinship, and gender. *See* **5673.**

**6337.** MAGIE, LYNNE ADELE. The daemon Eros: gothic elements in the novels of Emily and Charlotte Brontë, Doris Lessing, and Iris Murdoch. *See* **6304.**

**6338.** NAJA, LAYAL WAJIH. A stylistic analysis of a passage from *Wuthering Heights. See* **1414.**

**6339.** OLEXA, JOZEF. Romantic and realistic features in the composition of *Wuthering Heights. In* (pp. 115–23) **62.**

**6340.** REBELO, ETHELWYN. Heathcliff in South Africa. Upstream (7:1) 57.

**6341.** SIMPSON-HOUSLEY, PAUL; O'REILLY, ANDREA; PARK, DEBORAH CARTER. Geographic reality: symbolic landscapes of *Wuthering Heights*. BST (19:8) 369–75.

**6342.** WINNIFRITH, TOM; CHITHAM, EDWARD.   Charlotte and Emily Brontë: literary lives. *See* **6319.**

### Charles Brockden Brown

**6343.** CLEMIT, P.   The intellectual novel in the Romantic period: William Godwin and his school. *See* **5271.**

**6344.** HALE, DOROTHY J.   Profits of altruism: Caleb Williams and Arthur Mervyn. *See* **5272.**

**6345.** LOOBY, CHRISTOPHER JAMES.   The utterance of America. *See* **5113.**

### George Douglas Brown (George Douglas, 'Kennedy King')

**6346.** McCLEERY, ALISTAIR.   'The devil damn thee black': a note on *The House with the Green Shutters.* SLJ (16:1) 43–50.

### Thomas Edward Brown

**6347.** SHIMMIN, N. L.   The making of a Manx literature: regional identity in the writings of Hall Caine and T. E. Brown. Unpub. doct. diss., Univ. of Lancaster, 1988. [Abstr. in IT (39:4) 1631.]

### The Brownings

**6348.** ANTOS, ROSE; CHAMPEAU, DONESSE; RAILEY, KEVIN.   Robert and Elizabeth Barrett Browning: an annotated bibliography for 1987. BIS (17) 129–41.

**6349.** GARRISON, VIRGINIA; RAILEY, KEVIN.   Robert and Elizabeth Barrett Browning: an annotated bibliography for 1986. BIS (16) 1988, 181–93.

**6350.** KARLIN, DANIEL (ed.).   Robert Browning and Elizabeth Barrett: the courtship correspondence 1845–1846: a selection. Oxford: Clarendon Press. pp. xviii, 363. Rev. by Alethea Hayter in LRB (11:7) 19.

**6351.** KELLEY, PHILIP; HUDSON, RONALD (eds).   The Brownings' correspondence: vol. 4, January 1838–December 1840. (Bibl. 1987, 6943.) Rev. by Margaret Smith in RES (39:154) 1988, 314–15.

**6352.** —— —— The Brownings' correspondence: vol. 7, March 1843–October 1843. Winfield, KS: Wedgestone Press. pp. xii, 429.

**6353.** MEREDITH, MICHAEL (ed.).   Meeting the Brownings. *See* **251.**

### Elizabeth Barrett Browning

**6354.** BYRD, DEBORAH.   Four recent books about Elizabeth Barrett Browning. BIS (17) 115–27 (review-article).

**6355.** COOPER, HELEN.   Elizabeth Barrett Browning, woman & artist. (Bibl. 1988, 4761.) Rev. by Deborah Byrd in BIS (17) 121–2.

**6356.** DALLY, PETER.   Elizabeth Barrett Browning: a psychological portrait. London: Macmillan. pp. 214.

**6357.** FLETCHER, JOHN.   Poetry, gender and primal fantasy. *See* **5072.**

**6358.** FORSTER, MARGARET.   Elizabeth Barrett Browning: a biography. New York: Doubleday, 1988. (Bibl. 1988, 4762.) Rev. by Deborah Byrd in BIS (17) 125–7; by Nancy W. Ellenberger in BkW, 19 Feb., 6; by Donald Thomas in NYTB, 7 May, 32.

**6359.** FREIWALD, BINA.   'The praise which men give women': Elizabeth Barrett Browning's *Aurora Leigh* and the critics. DalR (66:3) 1986, 311–36.

**6360.** LEIGHTON, ANGELA. Elizabeth Barrett Browning. Blooming-ton: Indiana UP, 1986. (Bibl. 1987, 6948.) Rev. by Deborah Byrd in BIS (17) 118–21; by Patricia Thompson in RES (38:152) 1987, 575–7.
**6361.** LOOTENS, TRICIA A. Elizabeth Barrett Browning: the poet as heroine of literary history. Unpub. doct. diss., Indiana Univ., 1988. [Abstr. in DA (50) 954A.]
**6362.** MERMIN, DOROTHY. Elizabeth Barrett Browning: the origins of a new poetry. Chicago; London: Chicago UP. pp. xv, 310. (Women in culture and society.) Rev. by Deborah Byrd in BIS (17) 123–5.
**6363.** PAUL, SARAH. Strategic self-centering and the female narrator: Elizabeth Barrett Browning's *Sonnets from the Portuguese*. BIS (17) 75–91.
**6364.** REYNOLDS, M. L. *Aurora Leigh* by Elizabeth Barrett Browning: an edition with textual variants, explanatory annotation and critical introduction. *See* **370.**

### Robert Browning

**6365.** BORNSTEIN, GEORGE. Poetic remaking: the art of Browning, Yeats, and Pound. University Park: Pennsylvania State UP, 1988. pp. xi, 164. Rev. by Danny Karlin in LRB (11:16) 19–21; by Ian F. A. Bell in NQ (36:4) 547.
**6366.** BOYD, ZELDA. *The Grammarian's Funeral* and the erotics of grammar. BIS (16) 1988, 1–14.
**6367.** CROSSAN, GREG. Irresolution and dependence: the defeat of Wordsworthian ideals in Coleridge's *The Picture* and Browning's *The Last Ride Together*. AUMLA (71) 30–44.
**6368.** CROWDER, ASHBY BLAND. Browning and how he worked in good temper: a study of the revisions of *Pacchiarotto*. BIS (17) 93–113.
**6369.** ETCHELLS, RUTH (sel. and introd.). A selection of poems by Robert Browning, exploring his pilgrimage of faith. Tring: Lion, 1988. pp. 48. (Poets and prophets.)
**6370.** FRASER, HILARY. Browning and nineteenth-century historio-graphy. AUMLA (71) 13–29.
**6371.** GAY, PENELOPE. Desire and the female voice in Browning's *Men and Women* and *Dramatis Personae*. AUMLA (71) 47–63.
**6372.** GILLEN, JAY M. Rhetorical invention in the poetry of Robert Browning. Unpub. doct. diss., Johns Hopkins Univ., 1988. [Abstr. in DA (49) 1809A.]
**6373.** GREENBERG, NATHAN A. Browning and *Alcestis*. CML (9:2) 131–52.
**6374.** HEALD, S. Browning in the 1830s. Unpub. M.Phil. diss., Univ. of St Andrews. [Abstr. in IT (39:1) 32–3.]
**6375.** HEUER, HERMANN. Formen der Nostalgie bei englischen Dichtern: Coleridge und Browning. LJGG (26) 1985, 347–57.
**6376.** HÖFELE, ANDREAS. Rollen-Ich und lyrisches Ich: Zur Poetik des 'dramatic monologue'. *See* **5971.**
**6377.** HUISMAN, ROSEMARY. Who speaks and for whom? The search for subjectivity in Browning's poetry. AUMLA (71) 64–87.
**6378.** JOYCE, JOHN J. 'These filthy rags of speech': the limits of

language and Robert Browning's use of the dramatic monologue. Cithara (28:2) 34–42.

**6379.** LAWTON, DAVID. Browning's narrators. AUMLA (71) 88–105.

**6380.** LEWIS, CATHERINE REDMOND. The vicissitudes of narcissism in Browning's dramatic monologues. Unpub. doct. diss., Univ. of Florida, 1988. [Abstr. in DA (50) 954A.]

**6381.** LOWE, CAROL ANN. Rings of language in Robert Browning's *The Ring and the Book*. Unpub. doct. diss., Baylor Univ., 1988. [Abstr. in DA (49) 2231A.]

**6382.** MALLETT, PHILLIP. Browning and Petronius. NQ (36:2) 183–4.

**6383.** MENAGHAN, JOHN MICHAEL. Text as stage: Donne, Browning, Eliot and the idea of the 'dramatic'. *See* **4412.**

**6384.** O'CONNOR, LISA. The construction of a self: Guido and metaphor in Book xi of *The Ring and the Book*. AUMLA (71) 139–58.

**6385.** PETCH, SIMON. Browning's Roman lawyers. AUMLA (71) 109–38.

**6386.** PLASA, C. A. The economy of revision: Keats, Browning and T. S. Eliot. Unpub. doct. diss., Univ. of Southampton. [Abstr. in IT (39:1) 33.]

**6387.** SCHENKER, MARK JOHN. Historical transcendentalism in the works of Carlyle, Newman, and Browning. Unpub. doct. diss., Columbia Univ., 1988. [Abstr. in DA (49) 3036A.]

**6388.** SLINN, WARWICK. From textual reference to textual strategy: critical responses to Browning's poetry. AUMLA (71) 161–81.

**6389.** WOOLFORD, JOHN. Browning the revisionary. (Bibl. 1988, 4777.) Rev. by Danny Karlin in LRB (11:16) 19–21.

**6390.** —— KARLIN, DANIEL. A new source for the form of *Pippa Passes. See* **4470.**

### Edward Bulwer-Lytton (Lord Lytton)

**6391.** CLEMIT, P. The intellectual novel in the Romantic period: William Godwin and his school. *See* **5271.**

**6392.** HAWES, DONALD. Thackeray, Tennyson, and Bulwer Lytton. NQ (36:2) 182–3.

**6393.** TYSON, NANCY JANE. Thackeray and Bulwer: between the lines in *Barry Lyndon*. ELN (27:2) 53–6.

### Sir Richard Burton

**6394.** AL-TAHA, M. The Orient and three Victorian travellers: Kinglake, Burton and Palgrave. Unpub. doct. diss., Univ. of Leicester. [Abstr. in IT (38:4) 1474.]

### Samuel Butler (1835–1902)

**6395.** SHAFFER, ELINOR. Erewhons of the eye: Samuel Butler as painter, photographer and art critic. London: Reaktion, 1988; Kingston, NY: McPherson. pp. xxii, 334. Rev. in BkW, 26 Nov., 13.

### George Gordon Noel, Lord Byron

**6396.** AVETISÎÂN, V. A. Vospriîâtie Baĭrona v evropeĭskikh literaturakh nachala XIXv. (The perception of Byron in European literatures at the beginning of the nineteenth century.) NDFN (1989:5) 38–44.

**6397.** BACHINGER, KATRINA. The multi-man genre and Poe's Byrons. Salzburg: Institut für Anglistik und Amerikanistik, Salzburg Univ., 1987. pp. vi, 140. (Studies in English language and literature: Romantic reassessment, 92:2)

**6398.** BEATTY, BERNARD. Byron's *Don Juan*. (Bibl. 1988, 4786.) Rev. by Andrew Nicholson in MLR (84:1) 131–2; by William Myers in BJECS (10) 1987, 236–7.

**6399.** —— NEWEY, VINCENT (eds). Byron and the limits of fiction. Liverpool: Liverpool UP, 1988. pp. ix, 291. (Liverpool English texts and studies, 22.) Rev. by Murray G. H. Pittock in NQ (36:4) 521–3.

**6400.** BOYES, MEGAN. Love without wings: the story of the unique relationship between Elizabeth Bridget Pigot of Southwell and the young poet, Lord Byron. Derby: Boyes, 1988. pp. 100.

**6401.** BROOKS, HAROLD. 'A song from Mr Cypress'. RES (38:151) 1987, 368–74.

**6402.** BUTLER, MARILYN. Romantic manichaeism: Shelley's *On the Devil, and Devils* and Byron's mythological dramas. In (pp. 13–37) **59.**

**6403.** CALDER, ANGUS (ed.). Byron and Scotland: radical or dandy? Edinburgh: Edinburgh UP. pp. xviii, 163.

**6404.** CHRISTENSEN, JEROME. Perversion, parody, and cultural hegemony in Lord Byron's Oriental tales. SAQ (88:3) 569–603.

**6405.** COOKE, MICHAEL G. Byron, Pope, and the Grand Tour. *See* **5405.**

**6406.** CORBETT, MARTYN. Byron and tragedy. New York: St Martin's Press, 1988. (Bibl. 1988, 4794.) Rev. by Catherine Burroughs in TJ (41:2) 251–2.

**6407.** CROMPTON, LOUIS. Byron and Greek love: homophobia in 19th-century England. (Bibl. 1987, 7000.) Rev. by V. A. De Luca in UTQ (56:4) 1987, 585–6.

**6408.** ELLEDGE, W. PAUL. Immaterialistic matters: Byron, bogles, and bluebloods. PLL (25:3) 272–81.

**6409.** HIGASHINAKA, RYOUYO. Byron: shokini fuushi. (Byron's early satire.) Tokyo: Yamaguchi. pp. 212.

**6410.** ILIEV, ILIJA. Bajron i teatărăt. (Byron and the theatre.) T (42:5) 55–8.

**6411.** KELSALL, MALCOLM. Bryon's politics. (Bibl. 1987, 7008.) Rev. by Mark Storey in RES (39:154) 1988, 311.

**6412.** McGANN, JEROME. The third world of criticism. In (pp. 85–107) **53.**

**6413.** McGANN, JEROME J. (ed.). The complete poetical works: vol. 5, *Don Juan*. (Bibl. 1988, 4810.) Rev. by Mark Storey in RES (39:154) 1988, 309–11; by Thérèse Tessier in EA (42:2) 217–18.

**6414.** McKEEVER, KERRY ELLEN. Disseminating Cain: sublime sacrifices in Byron, Blake and Coleridge. *See* **5089.**

**6415.** MUSTAFA, SHAKIR M. The lame Prometheus' pilgrimage: a study of Byron's *Childe Harold's Pilgrimage*. Journal of Education and Science (Univ. of Mosul, Iraq) (3) 1981, 37–53.

**6416.** NABLOW, RALPH A.    Byron, Voltaire, and an epigram on a French woman. NQ (36:2) 174–5.

**6417.** PAGE, NORMAN.    A Byron chronology. Basingstoke: Macmillan; Boston, MA: G. K. Hall, 1988. pp. xv, 117. (Macmillan author chronologies.) Rev. by Murray G. H. Pittock in NQ (36:4) 523.

**6418.** RAIZIS, MARIOS BYRON.    O Vyron kai he pothos yia eleftheria. (Byron and the desire for freedom.) Aiolika Grammata (Athens) (104/5) 1988, 49–60.

**6419.** RICHARD, JEAN-PIERRE; BENSIMON, PAUL (trans).    Lettres et journaux intimes. Paris: Michel, 1987. pp. 438. Rev. by Thérèse Tessier in EA (42:2) 216–17.

**6420.** SÁNCHEZ CALVO, ARSENIO.    La naturaleza en *Alastor, Childe Harold* y *Endymion*. RAEI (2) 143–55.

**6421.** SHILSTONE, FREDERICK.    Byron, Kierkegaard, and the irony of 'rotation'. CLQ (25:4) 237–44.

**6422.** SHILSTONE, FREDERICK W.    Byron and the myth of tradition. Lincoln; London: Nebraska UP, 1988. pp. xvi, 283. Rev. by Frederick L. Beaty in SoCR (22:1) 136–7.

**6423.** SIMPSON, M.    Closet reading and political writing in the dramas of Byron and Shelley. Unpub. doct. diss., Univ. of Cambridge. [Abstr. in IT (39:2) 487–8.]

**6424.** SION, GEORGES.    Byron: l'homme qui a fait rêver l'Europe. BALLF (66:3/4) 1988, 155–66.

**6425.** ȘTEFĂNESCU-DRĂGĂNEȘTI, VIRGILIU.    Byron și românii. (Byron and the Romanians.) Luceafărul, 27 May, 8.

**6426.** STOREY, MARK.    Byron and the eye of appetite. pp. x, 229. (Bibl. 1986, 7800, where pagination incorrect.) Rev. by Andrew Nicholson in MLR (84:1) 132; by W. W. Robson in RES (39:153) 1988, 128–9.

**6427.** STÜRZL, ERWIN A.    Gaben der Zeit/Fruits of time. *See* **1927.**

**6428.** SULTANA, FEHMIDA.    Romantic Orientalism and Islam: Southey, Shelley, Moore, and Byron. Unpub. doct. diss., Tufts Univ. [Abstr. in DA (50) 1670A.]

**6429.** THOMSON, ALASTAIR W.    Method and decorum in *Don Juan*. *In* (pp. 186–203) **37.**

**6430.** WEST, PAUL.    Lord Byron's doctor. New York: Doubleday. pp. 277. Rev. by Brian Aldiss in BkW, 3 Sept., 5.

**6431.** WILLIAMS, MICHAEL.    Byron and the Siege of Ismail: 'Wherefore the ravishing did not begin!' UES (27:1) 9–14. (*Don Juan*.)

### George Washington Cable

**6432.** BUDD, LOUIS J.    Who's been demeaning whom? Mark Twain Circular (1) Sept. 1987, 1–2.

**6433.** DE PLANCHARD, ÉTIENNE.    Entre fleuve et marais ou les 'bayous-conteurs' dans *The Grandissimes* de G. W. Cable. Caliban (26) 81–90.

**6434.** DE PLANCHARD DE CUSSAC, ÉTIENNE.    L'œuvre romanesque de

George Washington Cable. Unpub. doct. diss., Univ. of Lyon III, 1987. [Abstr. in EA (42:2) 243.]

**6435.** JONES, SUZANNE (introd.). The Grandissimes: a story of creole life. Athens; London: Georgia UP, 1988. pp. xv, 339. (Brown Thrasher books.)

**6436.** PETRY, ALICE HALL. A genius in his way: the art of Cable's *Old Creole Days*. Rutherford, NJ: Fairleigh Dickinson UP, 1988. pp. 158. Rev. by Ellen Brown in AL (61:3) 478–80.

### Ada Cambridge

**6437.** BRADSTOCK, MARGARET. New light on Ada Cambridge. ALS (14:1) 107–13.

**6438.** —— Unspoken thoughts: a reassessment of Ada Cambridge. ALS (14:1) 51–65.

### Sir John Logan Campbell

**6439.** FITZGERALD, JOAN. Images of the self: two early New Zealand autobiographies by John Logan Campbell and Frederick Edward Maning. JCL (23:1) 1988, 16–42.

### Thomas Campbell

**6440.** ROBINSON, ERIC. John Clare: 'Bud of the Waste' in *Child Harold*: a debt to Thomas Campbell. JCSJ (8) 53–4.

### Rosa Nouchette Carey

**6441.** CRISP, JANE. Rosa Nouchette Carey (1840–1909): a bibliography. St Lucia: Dept of English, Univ. of Queensland. pp. 49. (Victorian fiction research guides: 16.)

### Thomas Carlyle

**6442.** APROBERTS, RUTH. The ancient dialect: Thomas Carlyle and comparative religion. Berkeley: California UP, 1988. pp. vii, 126. Rev. by G. G. Harper in ChrisL (38:2) 79–81.

**6443.** Entry cancelled.

**6444.** BOULOS, JOSEPH N. Carlylean echoes in *Hard Times*. Journal of Education and Science (Univ. of Mosul, Iraq) (6) (Humanities and education) 1987, 5–23.

**6445.** CUMMING, MARK. A disimprisoned epic: form and vision in Carlyle's *French Revolution*. Philadelphia: Pennsylvania UP, 1988. pp. xvi, 188.

**6446.** GOUGEON, LEN. Emerson, Carlyle, and the Civil War. NEQ (62:3) 403–23.

**6447.** JAMES, JERRY D.; BOTTOMS, RITA B. (eds). Lectures on Carlyle & his era. By FRED KAPLAN *et al.* Santa Cruz: Univ. Library, Univ. of California, Santa Cruz, 1985. pp. xii, 102. (Norman and Charlotte Strouse lectures, 2.) Rev. by William Myers in MLR (84:1) 133–4.

**6448.** LLOYD, TOM. Society and chaos: Schiller's impact on Carlyle's ideas about revolution. CLIO (17:1) 1987, 51–64.

**6449.** MACQUEEN, JOHN. The Enlightenment and Scottish literature: vol. 2, The rise of the historical novel. Edinburgh: Scottish Academic Press. pp. vii, 292.

**6450.** RABB, J. DOUGLAS. The silence of Thomas Carlyle. ELN (26:3) 70–81.

414     ENGLISH LANGUAGE AND LITERATURE     [1989

**6451.** ROSENBERG, JOHN D.   Carlyle and the burden of history. (Bibl. 1986, 7822.) Rev. by William Myers in MLR (84:1) 134.

**6452.** SCHENKER, MARK JOHN.   Historical transcendentalism in the works of Carlyle, Newman, and Browning. *See* **6387.**

**6453.** TENNYSON, G. B. (ed.).   A Carlyle reader: selections from the writings of Thomas Carlyle. (Bibl. 1985, 6605.) Rev. by William Myers in MLR (84:1) 133–4.

**6454.** WARE, TRACY.   A note on Poe and Carlyle's *German Romance.* NQ (36:2) 181.

**6455.** WISTRÖM, OLAV.   Revolutionen som språkets frigörelse. (Revolution as the liberation of language. Allt om böcker (1989:3) 16–19.

### 'Lewis Carroll' (Charles Lutwidge Dodgson)

**6456.** BATCHELOR, JOHN.   Dodgson, Carroll, and the emancipation of Alice. *In* (pp. 181–99) **14.**

**6457.** BOKIĬ, O. V.   Transformatsiia stilisticheskikh osobennosteĭ angliĭskoĭ ballady v parodiĭakh L. Kėrrolla. (The transformation of the stylistic peculiarities of the English ballad in Lewis Carroll's parodies.) Analiz stileĭ zarubezhnoĭ khudozhestvennoĭ i nauchnoĭ literatury (Leningrad) (6) 93–102.

**6458.** COHEN, MORTON N.   Lewis Carroll: 'dishcoveries' – and more. *In* (pp. 112–24) **44.**

**6459.** —— (ed.).   Lewis Carroll: interviews and recollections. Basingstoke: Macmillan. pp. xxvi, 273.

**6460.** CRAWFORD, T. D.   Making the world go round in *Alice in Wonderland.* NQ (36:2) 191–2.

**6461.** EDE, LISA S.   An introduction to the nonsense literature of Edward Lear and Lewis Carroll. *In* (pp. 47–60) **28.** (Introd. to doct. diss., Ohio State Univ., 1975.)

**6462.** NICHOLSON, MERVYN.   Food and power: Homer, Carroll, Atwood and others. Mosaic (20:3) 1987, 37–55.

**6463.** SEWELL, ELIZABETH.   Is Flannery O'Connor a nonsense writer? *In* (pp. 183–213) **28.**

**6464.** THOIRON, PHILIPPE; PAVÉ, ALAIN.   Index et concordance pour *Alice's Adventures in Wonderland* de Lewis Carroll. Paris: Champion; Geneva: Slatkine. pp. xix, 119, + 10 fiches. (Travaux de linguistique quantitative, 16.)

**6465.** THOMAS, RONALD R.   Profitable dreams in the marketplace of desire: *Alice in Wonderland, A Christmas Carol,* and *The Interpretation of Dreams.* NCC (12:1) 1988, 35–45.

**6466.** TIGGES, WIM.   An anatomy of literary nonsense. Amsterdam: Rodopi, 1988. pp. ii, 293. (Costerus, 67.)

### William Alexander Caruthers

**6467.** SALVIATI, YVETTE.   La fascination d'un Sudiste pour la frontière: *The Knights of the Golden Horse-Shoe* (1841) de William Alexander Caruthers. Caliban (26) 47–56.

### Charles W. Chesnutt

**6468.** BRUXVOORT, HAROLD JAMES.   An analysis of the fiction of

Charles W. Chesnutt. Unpub. doct. diss., Drake Univ., 1988. [Abstr. in DA (49) 2656A.]

## Kate Chopin

**6469.** BAUER, DALE M. Feminist dialogics: a theory of failed community. Albany: New York State UP, 1988. pp. xx, 204. Rev. by Paula S. Berggren in AL (61:2) 295–7.

**6470.** PITAVY-SOUQUES, DANIÈLE. Paysage langage ou l'impossible accès à la parole: une relecture de *The Awakening* de Kate Chopin. Caliban (26) 91–104.

**6471.** RULAND, RICHARD. Kate Chopin and *The Awakening*. *In* (pp. 119–30) **23.**

**6472.** RYU, CHEUNG-EUN. Nature and sexuality in the fiction of Kate Chopin. JELL (35) 131–47.

**6473.** STANGE, MARGIT. Personal property: exchange value and the female self in *The Awakening*. Genders (5) 106–19.

**6474.** TAYLOR, HELEN. Gender, race, and region in the writings of Grace King, Ruth McEnery Stuart, and Kate Chopin. Baton Rouge: Louisiana State UP. pp. xiv, 229. Rev. by Barbara C. Ewell in AL (61:4) 700–1.

**6475.** THOMAS, HEATHER KIRK. 'A vocation and a voice': a documentary life of Kate Chopin. Unpub. doct. diss., Univ. of Missouri–Columbia, 1988. [Abstr. in DA (50) 949A.]

## John Clare

**6476.** CLARE, JOHANNE. John Clare and the bounds of circumstance. (Bibl. 1987, 7082.) Rev. by Mark Storey in JCSJ (7) 1988, 54.

**6477.** GOODRIDGE, JOHN A. Some predecessors of Clare: 'honest Duck'. *See* **5211.**

**6478.** HAND, R. J. Anthologized Clare and the problem of death date. NQ (36:2) 181–2.

**6479.** MOYSE, MARY. John Clare's family tree. JCSJ (8) 24–30.

**6480.** PEDLAR, VALERIE. John Clare's *Child Harold*. JCSJ (8) 11–16.

**6481.** POWELL, DAVID. The John Clare collection in Northampton Public Library. *See* **256.**

**6482.** ROBINSON, ERIC. John Clare: 'Bud of the Waste' in *Child Harold*: a debt to Thomas Campbell. *See* **6440.**

**6483.** —— *To an Oaken Stem*: John Clare's poem recovered and reconsidered. RES (38:152) 1987, 483–91.

**6484.** —— (gen. ed.). The early poems of John Clare, 1804–1822. Ed. by ERIC ROBINSON, DAVID POWELL, and MARGARET GRAINGER. Oxford: Clarendon Press; New York: OUP. 2 vols. pp. xxiv, 599; xiii, 835. (Oxford English texts.) Rev. by Grevel Lindop in TLS, 8 Dec., 1366.

**6485.** STOREY, MARK (ed.). John Clare: selected letters. Oxford: Clarendon Press; New York: OUP, 1988. pp. xxix, 255. Rev. by Alan G. Hill in JCSJ (8) 47–8.

**6486.** STRICKLAND, EDWARD. The shipwreck metaphor in Clare. JCSJ (8) 17–23.

**6487.** WILLIAMS, MERRYN; WILLIAMS, RAYMOND (eds). John Clare:

selected poetry and prose. (Bibl. 1988, 4848.) Rev. by Margaret Grainger in RES (39:156) 1988, 565–6.

### Charles Cowden Clarke
**6488.** REEVES, FLORENCE.    Charles Cowden Clarke. CLB (65) 26–9.

### Arthur Hugh Clough
**6489.** KALIM, M. SIDDIQ.    A critical analysis of *The Bothie of Tober-na-Vuolich*. Explorations (12:1/2) 1988/89, 1–8.

### William Cobbett
**6490.** CHANDOR, K. F.    The dramatic works of William Cobbett. Unpub. doct. diss., Univ. of Exeter. [Abstr. in IT (39:3) 1110.]

**6491.** SAMBROOK, A. J.    Cobbett and the French Revolution. YES (19) 231–42.

**6492.** SCHWEIZER, K. W.; KLEIN, R.    The progress of William Cobbett, 1800–6. DUJ (81:2) 221–7.

### Samuel Taylor Coleridge
**6493.** ALLEN, PETER.    Morrow on Coleridge's *Church and State*. JHI (50:3) 485–90.

**6494.** BARTH, J. ROBERT.    Coleridge and the power of love. Columbia: Missouri UP, 1988. pp. xiii, 127. Rev. by David Jasper in ChrisL (39:1) 99–100; by Carol Jackson in Cithara (29:1) 75–7.

**6495.** BILIK, DOROTHY.    Josephus, Mosollamus, and the Ancient Mariner. SP (86:1) 87–95.

**6496.** BROSCH, RENATE.    Vision und Illusion. Coleridges *The Rime of the Ancient Mariner* von Doré illustriert. *See* **79.**

**6496a.** BYGRAVE, STEPHEN.    Coleridge and the self: Romantic egotism. (Bibl. 1986, 7897.) Rev. by Ralph Pite in Eng (36:156) 1987, 284–6.

**6497.** CROSSAN, GREG.    Irresolution and dependence: the defeat of Wordsworthian ideals in Coleridge's *The Picture* and Browning's *The Last Ride Together*. *See* **6367.**

**6498.** FOAKES, R. A. (ed.).    Coleridge's criticism of Shakespeare: a selection. *See* **3537.**

**6499.** FREEMAN, ARTHUR; HOFMANN, THEODORE.    The ghost of Coleridge's first effort: *A Monody on the Death of Chatterton*. *See* **5157.**

**6500.** GOODSON, A. C.    Verbal imagination: Coleridge and the language of modern criticism. New York; Oxford: OUP, 1988. pp. xix, 236. Rev. by James Sey in Upstream (7:4) 74–7.

**6501.** GRAVIL, RICHARD; NEWLYN, LUCY; ROE, NICHOLAS (eds).    Coleridge's imagination: essays in memory of Pete Laver. (Bibl. 1987, 7107.) Rev. by W. J. B. Owen in RES (38:150) 1987, 259–61; by Ralph Pite in Eng (36:156) 1987, 281–4.

**6502.** GREENBERG, MARTIN.    The Hamlet vocation of Coleridge and Wordsworth. (Bibl. 1988, 4865.) Rev. by Lucy Newlyn in RES (39:155) 1988, 450–1.

**6503.** HAMEED, SALIH MAHDI.    Coleridge's conception of imagination with reference to *The Ancient Mariner*. Journal of Education and Science (Univ. of Mosul, Iraq) (5) (Humanities and education) 1987, 5–17.

**6504.** HARDING, ANTHONY JOHN.    Coleridge and the inspired word.

(Bibl. 1987, 7110.) Rev. by Stephen Prickett in RES (38:149) 1987, 90–1; by June Sturrock in MLR (84:4) 935–6.

**6505.** HARTJE, MARY ELLEN. A critical index to the letters of Samuel Taylor Coleridge from 1820 to 1834 on the subjects of 'philosophy and religion' and 'literature': a presentation of his later thought. Unpub. doct. diss., Baylor Univ., 1988. [Abstr. in DA (49) 2230A.]

**6506.** HEUER, HERMANN. Formen der Nostalgie bei englischen Dichtern: Coleridge und Browning. *See* **6375.**

**6507.** HOLMES, RICHARD. Coleridge: early visions. London: Hodder & Stoughton. pp. xvi, 409. Rev. by Stephen Gill in TLS, 3 Nov., 1203–4; by Ian Thomson in Listener (122) 9 Nov., 29–30; by John Bayley in LRB (11:23) 12–14.

**6508.** JACKSON, H. J. (ed.). Selected letters. (Bibl. 1988, 4869.) Rev. by Denise Degrois in EA (42:3) 348–9.

**6509.** JASPER, DAVID. Coleridge as poet and religious thinker: inspiration and revelation. (Bibl. 1986, 7915.) Rev. by Lucy Newlyn in RES (38:149) 1987, 91–2.

**6510.** —— Preserving freedom and her friends: a reading of Coleridge's *Watchman*. YES (19) 208–18.

**6511.** —— (ed.). The interpretation of belief: Coleridge, Schleiermacher and Romanticism. (Bibl. 1988, 4870.) Rev. by Paul Hamilton in RES (39:153) 1988, 127–8.

**6512.** KITSON, PETER. Coleridge, the French Revolution, and *The Ancient Mariner*. YES (19) 197–207.

**6513.** LEFEBURE, MOLLY. A mystic peregrination: *The Ancient Mariner*. CLB (65) 8–25.

**6514.** MCKEEVER, KERRY ELLEN. Disseminating Cain: sublime sacrifices in Byron, Blake and Coleridge. *See* **5089.**

**6515.** MATTHIAS, DAVID THOMAS. The concept of sympathy in the early poetry of Samuel Taylor Coleridge and William Wordsworth. Unpub. doct. diss., Univ. of Toronto. [Abstr. in DA (50) 1667A.]

**6516.** MURPHY, JOHN FRANCIS. 'Woven hymns' of lyric and narrative: plotting nature in Coleridge and Shelley. Unpub. doct. diss., Univ. of Washington, 1988. [Abstr. in DA (49) 2671A.]

**6517.** NEWLYN, LUCY. Coleridge, Wordsworth and the language of allusion. (Bibl. 1987, 7131.) Rev. by J. R. Watson in RES (38:152) 1987, 570–1; by June Sturrock in MLR (84:4) 934–5; by Ralph Pite in Eng (36:156) 1987, 277–81.

**6518.** PAULIN, TOM. English political writers on Ireland: Robert Southey to Douglas Hurd. *In* (pp. 132–45) **17.**

**6519.** PETERFREUND, STUART. The way to immanence, Coleridge, and the problem of evil. ELH (55:1) 1988, 125–58. (*Christabel.*)

**6520.** PITE, R. R. G. Dante's influence on Coleridge and Keats: 'the circle of our vision'. Unpub. doct. diss., Univ. of Cambridge. [Abstr. in IT (38:4) 1460.]

**6521.** ROE, NICHOLAS. Wordsworth and Coleridge: the radical years. (Bibl. 1988, 4879.) Rev. by Olivia Smith Storey in CLB (65) 31–3; by

J. D. Gutteridge in NQ (36:3) 404–5; by Stuart M. Sperry in ELN (27:2) 71–3.

**6522.** RUDDICK, BILL. Recollecting Coleridge: the internalization of radical energies in Hazlitt's political prose. YES (19) 243–55.

**6523.** RUOFF, GENE W. Wordsworth and Coleridge: the making of the major lyrics, 1802–1804. London; Sydney; Tokyo: Harvester Wheatsheaf. pp. xviii, 318.

**6524.** RZEPKA, CHARLES J. The self as mind: vision and identity in Wordsworth, Coleridge, and Keats. (Bibl. 1988, 4882.) Rev. by Lucy Newlyn in RES (39:155) 1988, 451–2.

**6525.** SONG, JAE-SAM. Coleridge si eui gujo: sasangjeok mohyoung eul jungsim euro. (A study of the structure of Coleridge's poetry.) JELL (35) 175–97.

**6526.** TAKASE, AKINORI. Coleridge no bungaku to shisou. (Coleridge's literature and thought.) Tokyo: Senjo. pp. 294.

**6527.** TAKEMORI, OSAMU. S. T. Coleridge no shi *Kubla Khan* no kaishaku: shouchousei kaimeino kokoromi. (An interpretation of S. T. Coleridge's *Kubla Khan*: a study of its symbolism.) Tokyo: Apollon. pp. iv, 310.

**6528.** TAYLOR, ANYA. Coleridge's defense of the human. (Bibl. 1988, 4886.) Rev. by Stephen Prickett in RES (39:154) 1988, 306–8.

**6529.** TAYLOR, HARRY MILTON. Coleridge's statement and defence of the evangelical faith as ultimate metaphysics. Unpub. doct. diss., Drew Univ., 1938. [No abstract.]

**6530.** TRAYIANNOUDI, LITSA. Epistemology and aesthetics: the art of Coleridge's 'conversation' poetry. Aristotle Univ. of Thessaloniki Yearbook of English Studies (1) 455–67.

**6531.** VALLINS, D. M. The role of feeling in Coleridge's philosophy. Unpub. doct. diss., Univ. of Oxford. [Abstr. in IT (39:3) 1114.]

**6532.** VOSS, A. E. Xanadu: the deserted palace. Theoria (74) 59–68.

**6533.** WALKER, ERIC C. *Biographia Literaria* and Wordsworth's revisions. SELit (28:4) 1988, 569–88.

**6534.** WHEELER, KATHLEEN M. Kant and Romanticism. *See* **5738.**

**6535.** WYLIE, IAN. Young Coleridge and the philosophers of nature. Oxford: Clarendon Press. pp. x, 176. (Oxford English monographs.)

### Sara Coleridge

**6536.** MUDGE, BRADFORD KEYES. Sara Coleridge, a Victorian daughter: her life and essays. New Haven, CT; London: Yale UP. pp. xvii, 287. (Bibl. 1987, 7151.) Rev. in BkW, 3 Sept., 13; by Suzanne Raitt in TLS, 1 Dec., 1341; by Joan Smith in Listener (122) 12 Oct., 33; by John Bayley in LRB (11:23) 12–14.

### John Payne Collier

**6537.** HULTIN, NEIL C.; OBER, WARREN U. John Payne Collier, Thomas Crofton Croker and the Hoby epitaph. *See* **3304.**

**6538.** JONES, G. P. John Payne Collier's reputation: review article. MedRen (3) 1986, 255–63.

### Wilkie Collins

**6539.** BEATON, R. P. 'The world is hard on women': women and marriage in the novels of Wilkie Collins. Unpub. doct. diss., Univ. of Wales, 1988. [Abstr. in IT (39:3) 1109.]

**6540.** HELLER, WENDY TAMAR. Wilkie Collins and the female gothic: a study in the politics of genre and literary revision. Unpub. doct. diss., Yale Univ., 1988. [Abstr. in DA (50) 1311A.]

**6541.** LAWRENCE, KEITH. The religion of Wilkie Collins: three unpublished documents. HLQ (52:3) 389–402.

**6542.** MILBANK, A. Daughters of the house: modes of the gothic in the fiction of Wilkie Collins, Charles Dickens and Sheridan Le Fanu. Unpub. doct. diss., Univ. of Lancaster, 1988. [Abstr. in IT (39:2) 487.]

**6543.** O'FALLON, KATHLEEN ADELE. No longer 'condemned to narrate': undefining Wilkie Collins' fiction. Unpub. doct. diss., Univ. of Oregon, 1988. [Abstr. in DA (49) 2671A.]

**6544.** O'NEILL, PHILIP. Wilkie Collins: women, property and propriety. (Bibl. 1988, 4891.) Rev. by Coral Ann Howells in NQ (36:4) 529–30.

**6545.** PETERS, CATHERINE. Corrigendum to *The Wellesley Index*. NQ (36:2) 182.

**6546.** TAYLOR, J. B. Wilkie Collins and nineteenth-century psychology: cultural significance and fictional form. Unpub. doct. diss., Univ. of Warwick, 1987. [Abstr. in IT (39:4) 1632.]

### J. Fenimore Cooper

**6547.** HANSEN, KLAUS PETER. Die retrospektive Mentalität: Europäische Kulturkritik und amerikanische Kultur. (Bibl. 1986, 7962.) Rev. by Hartmut Heuermann in Ang (105:3/4) 1987, 517–20.

**6548.** HOUSE, KAY SEYMOUR (ed.). The pilot: a tale of the sea. (Bibl. 1987, 7166, where scholar's forename misspelt.) Rev. by Robert Lawson-Peebles in RES (39:156) 1988, 563–4.

**6549.** MOTLEY, WARREN. The American Abraham: James Fenimore Cooper and the frontier patriarch. (Bibl. 1988, 4902.) Rev. by Jeanne-Marie Santraud in EA (42:4) 493–5.

**6550.** REDEKOP, ERNST; GERACHT, MAURICE (introds). Gleanings in Europe: the Rhine. Ed. by THOMAS PHILBRICK and MAURICE GERACHT. (Bibl. 1987, 7171.) Rev. by Robert Lawson-Peebles in RES (39:156) 1988, 563–4.

**6551.** ROMERO, LORA PATRICIA. The government of the body: health reform and the American antebellum novel. Unpub. doct. diss., Univ. of California, Berkeley, 1988. [Abstr. in DA (50) 983A.]

**6552.** THOMAS, BROOK. Cross-examinations of law and literature: Cooper, Hawthorne, Stowe, and Melville. (Bibl. 1988, 4903.) Rev. by Charles Swann in JAStud (23:1) 160–2.

**6553.** WIELAND, DENNIS PAUL. The transformation of the Cooper *mythos* in the writings of Thomas McGuane. Unpub. doct. diss., Indiana Univ. of Pennsylvania. [Abstr. in DA (50) 1307A.]

### Henry Cotes

**6554.** HARVEY, A. D. Henry Cotes: an early Wordsworthian. EA (42:3) 308–12.

### Stephen Crane

**6555.** BLAIR, JOHN. The posture of a Bohemian in the poetry of Stephen Crane. AL (61:2) 215–29.

**6556.** BROER, PAUL ALLAN. Stephen Crane: man adrift. Unpub. doct. diss., City Univ. of New York, 1988. [Abstr. in DA (49) 2217A.]

**6557.** BROWN, BILL. Interlude: the agony of play in *The Open Boat*. AQ (45:3) 23–46.

**6558.** CHURCH, JOSEPH. The Black man's part in Crane's *Monster*. AI (45:4) 1988, 375–88.

**6559.** FRIED, MICHAEL. Realism, writing, and disfiguration: on Thomas Eakins and Stephen Crane. (Bibl. 1988, 4906.) Rev. by Janet Malcolm in NY, 5 Oct. 1987, 121–6.

**6560.** LINDBERG-SEYERSTED, BRITA. Ford Madox Ford and his relationship to Stephen Crane and Henry James. Oslo: Solum; Atlantic Highlands, NJ: Humanities Press, 1987. pp. 123. Rev. by Stanley Wertheim in ALR (21:3) 85–7.

**6561.** MITCHELL, LEE CLARK (ed.). New essays on *The Red Badge of Courage*. (Bibl. 1986, 7980.) Rev. by Jean Cazemajou in EA (42:3) 361–2.

**6562.** SEYMOUR, MIRANDA. A ring of conspirators: Henry James and his literary circle 1895–1915. Boston, MA: Houghton Mifflin. (Bibl. 1988, 4911.) Rev. by Helen Bevington in NYTB, 16 July, 11; by Joseph Coates in BW, 6 Aug., 3; by Leslie Hanscom in BkW, 25 June, 3, 10.

**6563.** WERTHEIM, STANLEY; SORRENTINO, PAUL (eds). The correspondence of Stephen Crane. New York: Columbia UP, 1988. 2 vols. pp. x, 772. Rev. by Edwin H. Cady in AL (61:3) 457–8; by Harold Beaver in TLS, 20 Jan., 55–6.

### Isabella Valancy Crawford

**6564.** BENTLEY, D. M. R. (ed.). Malcolm's Katie: a love story. London, Ont.: Canadian Poetry Press, 1987. pp. lxi, 101. Rev. by John Ower in CanL (122/23) 288–94.

**6565.** OWER, JOHN. Bentley's Katie, Bachofen, & psychology. CanL (122/23) 288–94 (review-article).

### S. R. Crockett

**6566.** DONALDSON, ISLAY MURRAY. The life and work of Samuel Rutherford Crockett. Aberdeen: Aberdeen UP. pp. ix, 357.

### Thomas Crofton Croker

**6567.** HULTIN, NEIL C.; OBER, WARREN U. John Payne Collier, Thomas Crofton Croker and the Hoby epitaph. See **3304**.

### Maria Susanna Cummins

**6568.** BAYM, NINA (ed.). The lamplighter. New Brunswick, NJ; London: Rutgers UP, 1988. pp. xxxiv, 437. (American women writers.)

### Charles Darwin

**6569.** ROSENBERG, JOHN D. Mr Darwin collects himself. *In* (pp. 82–111) **44**.

### Rebecca Harding Davis

**6570.** HARRIS, SHARON M. Rebecca Harding Davis: from Romanticism to Realism. ALR (21:2) 4–20.

**6571.** HARRIS, SHARON MARIE.    Rebecca Harding Davis in the context of American literary Realism/Naturalism. Unpub. doct. diss., Univ. of Washington, 1988. [Abstr. in DA (50) 139–40A.]

**6572.** PFAELZER, JEAN.    The sentimental promise and the utopian myth: Rebecca Harding Davis's *The Harmonists* and Louisa May Alcott's *Transcendental Wild Oats*. See **6089**.

**6573.** ROSE, JANE ATTERIDGE.    The fiction of Rebecca Harding Davis: a palimpsest of domestic ideology beneath a surface of Realism. Unpub. doct. diss., Univ. of Georgia, 1988. [Abstr. in DA (49) 2661A.]

### J. W. De Forest

**6574.** HIJIYA, JAMES A.    J. W. De Forest and the rise of American gentility. Hanover, NH; London: New England UP for Brown Univ., 1988. pp. xiv, 177. Rev. by Frank Bergmann in ALR (22:1) 95–6.

### 'Dan De Quille' (William Wright)

**6575.** BERKOVE, LAWRENCE I.    Dan De Quille follows the tracks of 'the Carson fossil-footprints'. Mark Twain Circular (2) July/Aug. 1988, 1–3.

**6576.** —— Jim Gillis: 'the Thoreau of the Sierras'. Mark Twain Circular (2) Mar./Apr. 1988, 1–2.

**6577.** —— (ed.).    Dan De Quille's narrations of Ohio: four sketches. NwOQ (61:1) 3–12.

**6578.** CENTING, RICHARD R.    Ohio magazines. See **557**.

**6579.** CROW, CHARLES L.    An American divine comedy? NwOQ (61:1) 17–19.

### Thomas De Quincey

**6580.** BAXTER, EDMUND (ed.).    The stranger's grave. London: Aporia, 1988. pp. 131.

**6581.** DAVIS, MARY ANN K.    De Quincey's *Confessions*: a strategy for salvation. ChrisL (38:3) 33–44.

**6582.** FERRARIO, LARRY STEVEN.    The pariah in the marketplace: the audience-centered rhetoric of Thomas De Quincey. Unpub. doct. diss., Univ. of Southern California. [Abstr. in DA (50) 1310A.]

**6583.** GROVES, DAVID.    De Quincey and Scott. ScottN (15) 2–6.

**6584.** —— Thomas De Quincey and a review of *Blackwood's Magazine*. See **572**.

**6585.** MCDONAGH, JOSEPHINE.    Do or die: problems of agency and gender in the aesthetics of murder. Genders (5) 121–34. (*On Murder Considered as One of the Fine Arts.*)

### Thomas Frognall Dibdin

**6586.** RABAIOTTI, RENATO.    Beckford's *A Dialogue in the Shades* and Dibdin's *The Lincolne Nosegay*. See **5049**.

### Charles Dickens

**6587.** ALLINGHAM, PHILIP VICTOR.    Dramatic adaptations of the Christmas books of Charles Dickens, 1844–8: texts and contexts. See **5745**.

**6588.** ALTMAN, RICK.    Dickens, Griffith, and film theory to-day. SAQ (88:2) 321–59.

**6589.** ARMSTRONG, FRANCES ELIZABETH.    Dickens and the concept of home. Unpub. doct. diss., Univ. of Toronto, 1988. [Abstr. in DA (50) 144A.]

**6590.** BARFOOT, C. C.   Swivelling Dick: Dickens as Romantic and anti-Romantic. DQR (19:4) 281–93.

**6591.** BARRETT, ELIZABETH MARY.   Competence, control, and critical practice in three Victorian novels. Unpub. doct. diss., Univ. of Toronto. [Abstr. in DA (50) 1660A.] (*Martin Chuzzlewit, Vanity Fair, The Egoist.*)

**6592.** BEAUCHAMP, GORDON.   Mechanomorphism in *Hard Times*. SLI (22:1) 61–77.

**6593.** BENTLEY, NICOLAS; SLATER, MICHAEL; BURGIS, NINA.   The Dickens index. (Bibl. 1988, 4929.) Rev. by Alan S. Watts in Dick (85:2) 118–19; by Graham Storey in TLS , 17 Feb., 173.

**6594.** BIELECKA, DANIELA.   Dickens in Poland. *In* (pp. 119–35) **36.**

**6595.** BIXENSTINE, ANITA.   Domestic relationships and family survival: troubled families in the novels of Charles Dickens and George Eliot. Unpub. doct. diss., Kent State Univ. [Abstr. in DA (50) 1661A.]

**6596.** BOULOS, JOSEPH N.   Carlylean echoes in *Hard Times*. *See* **6444.**

**6597.** BRATTIN, JOEL J.   From drama into fiction: *The Lamplighter* and *The Lamplighter's Story*. Dick (85:3) 131–9.

**6598.** BRIGANTI, CHIARA.   Female characters and the vanishing author in Jane Austen, Charlotte Brontë and Charles Dickens. *See* **6126.**

**6599.** COHEN-STEINER, OLIVIER.   Riah: enquête sur un Juif au-dessus de tout soupçon. EA (42:2) 168–81.

**6600.** COLACO, JILL.   Charles Dickens and the discourses of early Victorian capitalism. Unpub. doct. diss., Harvard Univ. [Abstr. in DA (50) 951A.]

**6601.** COLUMBUS, CLAUDETTE KEMPER.   The (un)lettered ensemble: what Charley does not learn about writing in Bleak House. SELit (28:4) 1988, 609–23.

**6602.** CONNOR, STEVEN.   'They're all in one story': public and private narratives in *Oliver Twist*. Dick (85:1) 2–16.

**6603.** COTSELL, MICHAEL.   The companion to *Our Mutual Friend*. (Bibl. 1988, 4940.) Rev. by T. J. Cribb in RES (39:153) 1988, 136–7.

**6604.** CRAWFORD, IAIN.   Pip and the monster: the joys of bondage. SELit (28:4) 1988, 625–48.

**6605.** DALDRY, GRAHAM.   Charles Dickens and the form of the novel: fiction and narrative in Dickens' work. (Bibl. 1987, 7232.) Rev. by Sylvère Monod in MLR (84:1) 138–9.

**6606.** DESSNER, LAWRENCE JAY.   A possible source for Dickens's Lammles. Dick (85:2) 105–7.

**6607.** EAGLETON, TERRY (ed.).   Hard times. New York: Methuen, 1987. (Bibl. 1987, 7239.) Rev. by Sylvère Monod in EA (42:2) 222–3.

**6608.** EIGNER, EDWIN M.   The Dickens pantomime. Berkeley; London: California UP. pp. xii, 191. Rev. by F. S. Schwarzbach in TLS, 3 Nov., 1214.

**6609.** ENEMARK, RICHARD D.   The limits of David Copperfield's retrospective authority: the many voices of a 'monologic' fiction. Unpub. doct. diss., Columbia Univ., 1986. [Abstr. in DA (49) 1808A.]

**6610.** FIEDLER, LESLIE A. *Martin Chuzzlewit* – a great bad book. *In* (pp. 43–8) **13.**

**6611.** FIELDING, K. J. (ed.). The speeches of Charles Dickens: a complete edition. (Bibl. 1964, 5540.) New York: Simon & Schuster; Brighton: Harvester Press, 1988. pp. 456. (Second ed.: first ed. 1960.) Rev. by Graham Storey in TLS, 17 Feb., 173.

**6612.** FLINT, KATE. Dickens. (Bibl. 1986, 8037.) Rev. by Kathryn Sutherland in RES (39:155) 1988, 457.

**6613.** FLOOD, TRACY SEELEY. Gnostic romance: Dickens, Conrad and the advent of Modernism. Unpub. doct. diss., Univ. of Texas at Austin, 1988. [Abstr. in DA (49) 3368A.]

**6614.** GARCES, JEAN-PIERRE. Stryver, ou une autre expression de la violence dans *A Tale of Two Cities. In* (pp. 85–96) **60.**

**6615.** GOLLIN, RITA K. Living in a world without Dickens. HLQ (52:3) 415–19.

**6616.** GREENMAN, DAVID J. Dickens's ultimate achievements in the ghost story: *To Be Taken with a Grain of Salt* and *The Signalman.* Dick (85:1) 40–8.

**6617.** GROSSMANN, MAUREEN ELLEN. Small beginnings: the recovery of childhood and the recovery from childhood in the Victorian novel. *See* **6297.**

**6618.** HAWTHORN, JEREMY. *Bleak House.* (Bibl. 1987, 7258.) Rev. by Sylvère Monod in MLR (84:1) 137–8.

**6619.** HOEFNAGEL, DICK. Charles Dickens's annotated copy of Pepys's *Memoirs. See* **4765.**

**6620.** HOPCRAFT, ARTHUR. The spirit of revolution. Listener (121) 18 May, 10–11. (TV adaptation of *A Tale of Two Cities.*)

**6621.** HORNÁT, JAROSLAV. Pan Pickwick a Sam Weller. (Mr Pickwick and Sam Weller.) *In* (p. 21) **6.**

**6622.** HORNE, LEWIS. Covenant and power in *Nicholas Nickleby*: or, the guidance of Newman Noggs. PLL (25:2) 165–77.

**6623.** JACOBSON, WENDY S. The companion to *The Mystery of Edwin Drood.* (Bibl. 1988, 4956.) Rev. by T. J. Cribb in RES (39:153) 1988, 137–8.

**6624.** JEFFREYS, SUSAN. Body heat. Listener (121) 4 May, 13–14. (Spontaneous human combustion.)

**6625.** KAPLAN, FRED. Dickens: a biography. (Bibl. 1988, 4957.) Rev. by Pat Rogers in TLS, 7 Apr., 360; by John Sutherland in LRB (11:3) 19–22; by Bruce Allen in Smithsonian (20:8) 243–4; by Michael Slater in Dick (85:3) 181–3.

**6626.** KIELY, ROBERT. Charles Dickens: the lives of some important nobodies. *In* (pp. 59–81) **44.**

**6627.** KINSLEY, JAMES (ed.). The Pickwick papers. (Bibl. 1988, 4960.) Rev. by John Sutherland in RES (39:154) 1988, 312–13.

**6628.** KOMATSUBARA, SHIGEO. Dickens no sekai. (The world of Dickens.) Tokyo: Mikasa. pp. 222.

**6629.** LARSON, JANET L.    Dickens and the broken scripture. (Bibl. 1988, 4961.) Rev. by John Warner in ChrisL (39:1) 101–3.

**6630.** LENNON, PETER.    A tale of two dummies. Listener (121) 1 June, 38. (TV review of *A Tale of Two Cities*.)

**6631.** LINK, FRANZ.    Dickens's Moddle and Melville's Bartleby 'prefer not to'. LJGG (27) 1986, 310–11.

**6632.** LONG, WILLIAM F.    Dickens and the coming of rail to Deal: an uncollected speech and its context. Dick (85:2) 67–80.

**6633.** MACKAY, CAROL HANBERY (ed.).    Dramatic Dickens. Basingstoke: Macmillan. pp. xv, 201. Rev. by F. S. Schwarzbach in TLS, 3 Nov., 1214.

**6634.** MAGNET, MYRON.    Dickens and the social order. (Bibl. 1987, 7280.) Rev. by Stephen Gill in RES (38:151) 1987, 403–4.

**6635.** MALTZ, HAROLD P.    The concealing narrator in *Great Expectations*. UES (27:1) 15–20.

**6636.** MARTIN, FRANÇOISE.    L'image de Londres chez Dickens et Gustave Doré: *Bleak House* et *London, A Pilgrimage*. CVE (28) 1988, 25–38.

**6637.** MATSUMURA, MASAIE.    Dickens no shōsetsu to sono jidai. (Dickens and his time.) Tokyo: Kenkyusha. pp. 352. xvi.

**6638.** MECKIER, JEROME.    Hidden rivalries in Victorian fiction: Dickens, realism, and revaluation. See **5876.**

**6639.** —— 'A world without Dickens!': James T. to Annie Fields, 10 June 1870. HLQ (52:3) 409–14.

**6640.** MELLOR, THOMAS GEORGE.    Charles Dickens' self-destructive women. Unpub. doct. diss., Univ. of Rhode Island, 1988. [Abstr. in DA (49) 3370–1A.]

**6641.** MILBANK, A.    Daughters of the house: modes of the gothic in the fiction of Wilkie Collins, Charles Dickens and Sheridan Le Fanu. See **6542.**

**6642.** MILLER, MICHAEL G.    The Fellowship-Porters and the Veneerings': setting, structure and justice in *Our Mutual Friend*. Dick (85:1) 30–8.

**6643.** MISENHEIMER, CAROLYN; MISENHEIMER, JAMES B.    Structural unities: paired parallel chapters in Dickens's *Bleak House*. Dick (85:3) 140–9.

**6644.** MONCRIEFF, SCOTT EUGENE.    Dickens and the reformulated family. Unpub. doct. diss., Univ. of California, Riverside, 1988. [Abstr. in DA (49) 1810A.]

**6645.** MUIR, KENNETH.    *Bleak House* revisited. ACM (2:1) 85–100.

**6646.** NADER, JOSEPH.    Human values and money in *Our Mutual Friend*. Journal of Education and Science (Univ. of Mosul, Iraq) (2) 1980, 29–39.

**6647.** NAYDER, LILLIAN ROSE.    Fictional economies: a study of Dickens and Conrad. Unpub. doct. diss., Univ. of Virginia, 1988. [Abstr. in DA (50) 692A.]

**6648.** NEWMAN, S. J.    Decline and fall off? Towards an appreciation of *Our Mutual Friend*. Dick (85:3) 99–104.

**6649.** PAGE, NORMAN. A Dickens chronology. Basingstoke: Macmillan; Boston, MA: G. K. Hall, 1988. pp. viii, 156. (Macmillan author chronologies.) Rev. by Ronald Mason in NQ (36:4) 525–6; by Graham Storey in TLS, 17 Feb., 173.

**6650.** PARKER, DAVID. Mr Pickwick and the horses. Dick (85:2) 82–98.

**6651.** PETTERSSON, TORSTEN. The maturity of David Copperfield. EngS (70:1) 63–73.

**6652.** PHELAN, JAMES. Reading for the character and reading for the progression: John Wemmick and *Great Expectations*. JNT (19:1) 70–84.

**6653.** RADER, RALPH W. The comparative anatomy of three baggy monsters: *Bleak House, Vanity Fair, Middlemarch*. JNT (19:1) 49–69.

**6654.** RAINA, BADRI. Dickens and the dialectic of growth. (Bibl. 1988, 4974.) Rev. by Andrew Sanders in MLR (84:4) 943–4.

**6655.** ROSENBERG, BRIAN C. Character and the demands of structure: the example of Dickens. CEACrit (51:2/3) 42–54.

**6656.** SADRIN, ANNY. *Great Expectations*. (Bibl. 1988, 4977.) Rev. by Margaret Cardwell in Dick (85:1) 50–1.

**6657.** SAMUEL, RAPHAEL. Dickens on stage and screen. HT (39) Dec., 44–51.

**6658.** SANDERS, ANDREW. The companion to *A Tale of Two Cities*. London: Unwin Hyman, 1988. pp. xvi, 176. (Dickens companions, 4.) Rev. by Graham Storey in TLS, 17 Feb., 173.

**6659.** SCHLICKE, PAUL. Dickens and popular entertainment. (Bibl. 1987, 7306.) Rev. by Rachel Bennett in RES (38:150) 1987, 265–6.

**6660.** —— (ed.). Hard times. Oxford: OUP. pp. xxxii, 430. (World's classics.)

**6661.** SHATTO, SUSAN. The companion to *Bleak House*. London: Unwin Hyman, 1988. pp. xii, 339. (Dickens companions, 3.) Rev. by Thom Braun in NQ (36:3) 408.

**6662.** SINYARD, NEIL. Dickensian visions in modern British film. Dick (85:2) 108–17.

**6663.** SMALLEY, R. ANN. Crossing the gulfs: the importance of the master–servant relationship in Dickens's *Bleak House*. Dick (85:3) 151–60.

**6664.** SMITH, MARGARET. Charlotte Brontë and Charles Dickens. *See* **6315.**

**6665.** SMITH, PETER. The aestheticist argument of *Our Mutual Friend*. CamQ (18:4) 363–82.

**6666.** SØRENSEN, KNUD. Dickens on the use of English. EngS (70:6) 551–9.

**6667.** STONE, HARRY (ed.). Dickens' working notes for his novels. (Bibl. 1987, 7309.) Rev. by Lars Hartveit in EngS (70:1) 93–4; by Douglas Hewitt in NQ (36:2) 252–3; by Sylvère Monod in EA (42:2) 221–2.

**6668.** STOREY, GRAHAM. Charles Dickens, *Bleak House*. (Bibl. 1987, 7311.) Rev. by Andrew Sanders in MLR (84:2) 447–8.

**6669.** —— TILLOTSON, KATHLEEN; BURGIS, NINA (eds). The letters of Charles Dickens: vol. 6, 1850–1852. (Bibl. 1988, 4985.) Rev. by Ronald Mason in NQ (36:4) 525–7.

**6670.** STUART, BARBARA LAWLOR. A hangman, a centaur, and a madman: Dickens' grotesques and the grotesque novels. Unpub. doct. diss., Emory Univ., 1988. [Abstr. in DA (50) 150A.]

**6671.** SUNG, EUN-AE. Dickens wa yeosung munjae: *Little Dorrit* gwa yeosung munhakron. (Dickens and feminism: *Little Dorrit* and feminist criticism.) EngSt (13) 1–10.

**6672.** THOMAS, RONALD R. Profitable dreams in the marketplace of desire: *Alice in Wonderland, A Christmas Carol,* and *The Interpretation of Dreams. See* **6465.**

**6673.** TROTTER, DAVID. Circulation: Defoe, Dickens and the economies of the novel. *See* **5208.**

**6674.** VARGISH, THOMAS. The providential aesthetic in Victorian fiction. *See* **5929.**

**6675.** VÉGA-RITTER, MAX. Dickens et Thackeray, essai d'analyse psychocritique: dès *Pickwick Papers* à *David Copperfield* et de *Barry Lyndon* à *Henry Esmond.* Unpub. doct. diss., Univ. Paul Valéry Montpellier III, 1986. [Abstr. in EA (42:1) 117.]

**6676.** —— Loi, innocence et crime dans *Oliver Twist.* CVE (29) 15–40.

**6677.** WATTS, ALAN S. Dickens and emigrant ships: a matter of whitewashing? Dick (85:3) 167–75.

**6678.** WELSH, ALEXANDER. From copyright to Copperfield: the identity of Dickens. (Bibl. 1988, 4992.) Rev. by Sylvère Monod in EA (42:2) 219–20.

**6679.** WOLPERS, THEODOR. Dickens' Stadtebilder – Englisch und Deutsche: zum 'Realismus' als Übersetzungsproblem. *In* (pp. 175–97) **4.**

**6680.** ZANDVOORT, R. W. Mr Fezziwig's Ball. *In* (pp. 303–9) **42.**

### Emily Dickinson

**6681.** ANON. (ed.). After a hundred years: essays on Emily Dickinson. Kyoto: Apollon, 1988. pp. iv, 256.

**6682.** BAKKER, J. Emily Dickinson's secret. *In* (pp. 239–48) **47.**

**6683.** BAYLON, DANIEL. Emily Dickinson: le mot, la mort et l'immortalité. Repérages (11) 1–14.

**6684.** BELL, ROBYN MARGARET. Emily Dickinson's bookmaking: a companion to the manuscript volumes. Unpub. doct. diss., Univ. of California, Santa Barbara, 1988. [Abstr. in DA (49) 3721A.]

**6685.** BUDICK, E. MILLER. Emily Dickinson and the life of language: a study in symbolic poetics. (Bibl. 1987, 7331.) Rev. by Louise Y. Gossett in SewR (96:3) 1988, 474–5.

**6686.** BUELL, JANET W. 'A slow solace': Emily Dickinson and consolation. NEQ (62:3) 323–45.

**6687.** FLETCHER, JOHN. Poetry, gender and primal fantasy. *See* **5072.**

**6688.** GREGORY, TANYA E. Audience in Emily Dickinson's poetry. Unpub. doct. diss., Rutgers Univ., 1988. [Abstr. in DA (50) 947A.]

**6689.** HAGENBÜCHLE, ROLAND. Emily Dickinson: Wagnis der Selbstbegegnung. Tübingen: Narr, 1988. pp. vi, 343. Rev. by Josef Raab in AL (61:4) 697–8.

**6690.** HOCKERSMITH, THOMAS E. Into degreeless noon: time, consciousness, and oblivion in Emily Dickinson. ATQ (3:3) 277–95.

**6691.** HORAN, ELIZABETH ROSA. Gabriela Mistral and Emily Dickinson: readers, audience, community. Unpub. doct. diss., Univ. of California, Santa Cruz, 1988. [Abstr. in DA (49) 3716A.]

**6692.** JOHNSON, GREG. Emily Dickinson: perception and the poet's quest. (Bibl. 1987, 7342.) Rev. by Jane Roberts in UTQ (56:4) 1987, 590–2; by Louise Y. Gossett in SewR (96:3) 1988, 475–6.

**6693.** LEDER, SHARON; ABBOTT, ANDREA. The language of exclusion: the poetry of Emily Dickinson and Christina Rossetti. (Bibl. 1987, 7343.) Rev. by Anthony H. Harrison in AL (61:1) 112–14.

**6694.** LOVING, JEROME. Emily Dickinson: the poet on the second story. (Bibl. 1987, 7348.) Rev. by Louise Y. Gossett in SewR (96:3) 1988, 472–4; by Lionel Kelly in MLR (84:4) 967; by Christine Gerrard in RES (39:156) 1988, 596–7.

**6695.** MILLER, CRISTANNE. Emily Dickinson: a poet's grammar. (Bibl. 1988, 5004.) Rev. by Lionel Kelly in MLR (84:4) 968–9.

**6696.** MURRAY, BARBARA M. The 'scarlet experiment': Emily Dickinson's abortion experience. Unpub. doct. diss., Univ. of Tennessee, 1988. [Abstr. in DA (50) 685–6A.]

**6697.** NIIKURA, TOSHIKAZU. Emily Dickinson: fuzaino shouzou. (Emily Dickinson: a portrait of absence.) Tokyo: Taishukan. pp. iv, 264.

**6698.** O'MEARA, ANNE BROWN. Representing Emily Dickinson: a study of literary practice. Unpub. doct. diss., Univ. of Minnesota. [Abstr. in DA (50) 444–5A.]

**6699.** PEARCE, DANIEL MYERS. 'The soul's superior instants': the individual psychology of Emily Dickinson's poetry. Unpub. doct. diss., Univ. of California, Riverside, 1988. [Abstr. in DA (50) 445A.]

**6700.** PHILLIPS, ELIZABETH. Emily Dickinson: personae and performance. University Park: Pennsylvania State UP, 1988. pp. x, 250. Rev. by Vivian Pollak in AL (61:3) 447–8.

**6701.** POLLAK, VIVIAN R. Dickinson: the anxiety of gender. (Bibl. 1986, 8146.) Rev. by Louise Y. Gossett in SewR (96:3) 1988, 476–8.

**6702.** —— (ed.). A poet's parents: the courtship letters of Emily Norcross and Edward Dickinson. Chapel Hill; London: North Carolina UP, 1988. pp. xxxv, 236. Rev. by Mary Elizabeth Kromer Bernhard in NEQ (62:2) 305–8.

**6703.** ST ARMAND, BARTON LEVI. Emily Dickinson and her culture: the soul's society. (Bibl. 1988, 5014.) Rev. by Louise Y. Gossett in SewR (96:3) 1988, 479–81.

**6704.** SALSKA, AGNIESZKA. Walt Whitman and Emily Dickinson: poetry of the central consciousness. (Bibl. 1987, 7358.) Rev. by Louise Y. Gossett in SewR (96:3) 1988, 478–9.

**6705.** SHAKINOVSKY, LYNN JOY. 'The house without the door': space and silence in the poetry of Emily Dickinson. Unpub. doct. diss., Univ. of Toronto, 1988. [Abstr. in DA (50) 141A.]

**6706.** STOCKS, KENNETH.   Emily Dickinson and the modern consciousness: a poet of our time. New York: St Martin's Press; Basingstoke: Macmillan, 1988. pp. vi, 124. Rev. by Wendy Martin in ALR (22:1) 93–4; by Watson Branch in NQ (36:3) 413–14; by Dorothy Huff Oberhaus in AL (61:2) 290–301.

**6707.** TAKACS, K. LINNEA.   Amatory strains: erotic love in the poetry of Emily Dickinson and Christina Rossetti. Unpub. doct. diss., Fordham Univ., 1988. [Abstr. in DA (49) 1794–5A.]

**6708.** TRIPP, RAYMOND P., JR.   Spiritual action in *My Life Had Stood – A Loaded Gun –*. PLL (25:3) 282–303.

**6709.** WALKER, NANCY.   'Wider than the sky': public presence and private self in Dickinson, James, and Woolf. *In* (pp. 272–303) **51.**

**6710.** WIELAND, ELIZABETH ANN.   Myself the term between: Emily Dickinson and the poetry of mediation. Unpub. doct. diss., Columbia Univ., 1988. [Abstr. in DA (50) 142A.]

**6711.** WOLFF, CYNTHIA GRIFFIN.   Emily Dickinson. (Bibl. 1987, 7364.) Rev. by Louise Y. Gossett in SewR (96:3) 1988, 469–72.

**6712.** —— Emily Dickinson, Elizabeth Cady Stanton, and the task of discovering a usable past. MassR (30:4) 629–44.

### Benjamin Disraeli

**6713.** WIEBE, M. G., *et al.* (eds).   Benjamin Disraeli: letters: 1838–1841. (Bibl. 1988, 5022.) Rev. by Ann Robson in QQ (95:4) 1988, 914–16.

**6714.** —— Benjamin Disraeli: letters: vol. 4, 1842–1847. Toronto; London: Toronto UP. pp. xciv, 449. Rev. by Norman Gash in TLS, 22 Sept., 1025.

**6715.**   Entry cancelled.

### Lily Dougall

**6716.** McMULLEN, LORRAINE.   Lily Dougall's vision of Canada. *In* (pp. 137–47) **40.**

### Frederick Douglass

**6717.** ANDREWS, WILLIAM L. (ed.).   My bondage and my freedom. Champaign: Illinois UP, 1988. pp. 306.

**6718.** BLIGHT, DAVID W.   'For something beyond the battlefield': Frederick Douglass and the struggle for the memory of the Civil War. JAH (75:4) 1156–77.

**6719.** GODDU, TERESA A.; SMITH, CRAIG V.   Scenes of writing in Frederick Douglass's *Narrative*: autobiography and the creation of self. SoR (25:4) 822–40.

**6720.** MILLER, DOUGLAS T.   Frederick Douglass and the fight for freedom. New York; Oxford: Facts on File, 1988. pp. viii, 152. (Makers of America.)

**6721.** OLSON, JON.   Frederick Douglass and a process of cultural literacy empowerment. Unpub. doct. diss., Univ. of Southern California, 1988. [Abstr. in DA (50) 141A.]

**6722.** WATERS, CARVER WENDELL.   Voice in the slave narratives of Olaudah Equiano, Frederick Douglass, and Solomon Northrup. *See* **5222.**

**6723.** YOUNG, IZOLA.   The development of the narrator as cultural hero in the anti-slavery writings of Frederick Douglass. Unpub. doct. diss., Howard Univ., 1987. [Abstr. in DA (49) 2224A.]

### Sir Arthur Conan Doyle

**6724.** ANDERSON, L. M.   Jefferson Hope as tragic revenger. *See* **3030.**

**6725.** BENTON, JOHN L.   Dr Watson's automobile. BSJ (39:2) 79–80.

**6726.** BERDAN, MARSHALL S.   Watson and Shaw: subtle echoes in the canon. BSJ (39:4) 206–8.

**6727.** BURR, ROBERT C.   But what about the blood, Holmes? (*The Boscombe Valley Mystery*.) BSJ (39:2) 75, 78.

**6728.** CAPLAN, RICHARD M.   Why coal-tar derivatives at Montpellier? BSJ (39:1) 29–33.

**6729.** DALBY, RICHARD (ed.).   Dracula's brood: neglected vampire classics by Sir Arthur Conan Doyle, Algernon Blackwood, M. R. James and others. Wellingborough: Equation. pp. 348. (Equation chillers.)

**6730.** DIETZ, HENRY A.   Murillo and San Pedro: an excursion in identification. BSJ (39:3) 153–69.

**6731.** FILLINGHAM, LYDIA ALIX.   'The colorless skein of life': threats to the private sphere in Conan Doyle's *A Study in Scarlet*. ELH (56:3) 667–88.

**6732.** GORDON, STUART; BOLCHAZY, LADISLAUS J.   Detecting the real Sherlock Holmes: a stylometric comparison of Doyle and Meyer. CB (65:3/4) 105–7.

**6733.** JONES, KELVIN I.   Conan Doyle and the spirits: the spiritualist career of Sir Arthur Conan Doyle. Wellingborough: Aquarian. pp. 256.

**6734.** LAVAZZI, CHARLES M.   Sherlock Holmes, high-fidelity pioneer, or, the advent of a shure thing. BSJ (39:1) 36–8.

**6735.** LINSENMEYER, JOHN.   Sherlock Holmes's university – Oxford or Cambridge? BSJ (39:2) 71–4.

**6736.** LUDWIG, JAMES.   Who is Cadogan West and what is he to Mycroft? BSJ (39:2) 102–7.

**6737.** MCGEE, TOM.   Reflections on *The Beryl Coronet*. BSJ (39:4) 214–17.

**6738.** MCWILLIAMS, DEBRA.   The pocket Petrarch. BSJ (39:1) 7–12.

**6739.** MAGINN, DIANE.   Suicide disguised as murder: a Munchausen-related event at Thor Bridge. BSJ (39:1) 13–15.

**6740.** MINYARD, APPLEWHITE.   The religious views of Sherlock Holmes. BSJ (39:4) 198–202.

**6741.** REDMOND, CHRISTOPHER.   In bed with Sherlock Holmes: sexual elements in Arthur Conan Doyle's stories of the great detective. Toronto: Simon & Pierre, 1984. pp. 207.

**6742.** REDMOND, KATE KARLSON.   The literary and factual origins of *The Adventure of the Beryl Coronet*. BSJ (39:4) 209–13.

**6743.** TURNER, BARNARD EDWARD.   Networks of discourse, networks of power: the Foucauldian thesis of 'carceral society' and its application to selected narratives of Balzac, Doyle and Twain. Unpub. doct. diss., Univ. of Oregon, 1988. [Abstr. in DA (49) 3717A.]

**6744.** VINEY, CHARLES (comp.). Sherlock Holmes in London: a photographic record of Conan Doyle's stories. London: Equation. pp. 168.

**6745.** WARNER, RICHARD. St Patrick's lament. BSJ (39:1) 17–21.

**6746.** WEIN, RICHARD A. The real mystery of *The Copper Beeches*. BSJ (39:4) 219–22.

### George Du Maurier

**6747.** CAREY, REBECCA A. J. M. Barrie and the Du Mauriers. Mythlore (15:4) 40–2.

### Sara Jeannette Duncan

**6748.** Rewriting *The Imperialists*. CanL (121) 26–38.

### Maria Edgeworth

**6749.** GALLAGHER, CATHERINE. Fictional women and real estate in Maria Edgeworth's *Castle Rackrent*. NCC (12:1) 1988, 11–18.

**6750.** KELLY, JOAN TANTUM. Four Irish writers: 1800–1932: nationalism and gender in a changing Ireland. Unpub. doct. diss., State Univ. of New York at Stony Brook, 1988. [Abstr. in DA (50) 1312A.]

**6751.** MYERS, MITZI. The dilemmas of gender as double-voiced narrative: or, Maria Edgeworth mothers the Bildungsroman. *In* (pp. 67–96) **33.**

### 'George Eliot' (Mary Ann Evans)

**6752.** ANDRES, SOPHIA. The germ and the picture in *Middlemarch*. ELH (55:4) 1988, 853–67.

**6753.** ASHTON, ROSEMARY. Doubting clerics: from James Anthony Froude to *Robert Elsmere* via George Eliot. *In* (pp. 69–87) **18.**

**6754.** BARFOOT, C. C. Life divided, death undivided in *The Mill on the Floss*. *In* (pp. 81–99) **23.**

**6755.** BEER, GILLIAN. George Eliot. (Bibl. 1987, 7423.) Rev. by Gail Cunningham in RES (38:152) 1987, 579.

**6756.** BERGESEN, FRANCES LYNN. *The Mill on the Floss*: George Eliot's emerging vision of androgyny. Unpub. doct. diss., Temple Univ., 1988. [Abstr. in DA (49) 1806A.]

**6757.** BERNARDO, SUSAN MARIE. Disruptive force in George Eliot's novels: ostracism and the development of self. Unpub. doct. diss., Bryn Mawr College, 1988. [Abstr. in DA (49) 2364A.]

**6758.** BIXENSTINE, ANITA. Domestic relationships and family survival: troubled families in the novels of Charles Dickens and George Eliot. *See* **6595.**

**6759.** BRADY, KRISTIN. Gender and history in George Eliot's *Romola*. DalR (67:2/3) 1987, 257–74.

**6760.** CARPENTER, MARY WILSON. George Eliot and the landscape of time: narrative form and Protestant apocalyptic history. Chapel Hill; London: North Carolina UP, 1986. pp. xiv, 246. Rev. by Rosemary Ashton in RES (39:153) 1988, 139.

**6761.** CARROLL, DAVID (ed.). *Middlemarch*. (Bibl. 1988, 5044.) Rev. by Rosemary Ashton in RES (39:153) 1988, 138–9.

**6762.** DE JONG, MARY G. Different voices: moral conflict in *Jane Eyre*, *The Mill on the Floss*, and *Romola*. *See* **6289.**

**6763.** EWBANK, INGA-STINA. Victorian novels and feminist criticism. *In* (pp. 47–66) **47.**

**6764.** FREADMAN, RICHARD. Eliot, James and the fictional self: a study in character and narration. New York: St Martin's Press, 1986. pp. x, 285. (Bibl. 1986, 8217, where pagination incorrect.) Rev. by Richard Hull in StudN (20:3) 1988, 345–7.

**6765.** GATES, SUSAN FIELDING. George Eliot and D. H. Lawrence: a study in influence. Unpub. doct. diss., Drew Univ., 1988. [Abstr. in DA (49) 1808–9A.]

**6766.** GRAY, BERYL (postscr.). Brother Jacob. London: Virago Press. pp. 77. (Virago modern classics, 312.)

**6767.** GROSSMANN, MAUREEN ELLEN. Small beginnings: the recovery of childhood and the recovery from childhood in the Victorian novel. *See* **6297.**

**6768.** HAN, AE-KYEONG. A feminist approach to *Middlemarch*: on Dorothea's second marriage. EngSt (13) 20–8.

**6769.** HAN, KI-WOOK. Yeosung eui sungsook gwa doklip: Maggie Tulliver wa Gwendolen Harleth eui kyungheom bikyo. (The growth and independence of a woman: the experience of Maggie Tulliver and Gwendolen Harleth.) EngSt (13) 11–19.

**6770.** HANDS, TIMOTHY. A George Eliot chronology. Basingstoke: Macmillan. pp. xiii, 195. (Macmillan author chronologies.)

**6770a.** HARDY, BARBARA. Particularities: readings in George Eliot. (Bibl. 1984, 7224.) Rev. by John Woolley in Eng (36:154) 1987, 72–3.

**6771.** HIROSE, YOSHIJI. George Eliot: higekiteki joseizou. (George Eliot: a tragic portrait of a woman.) Tokyo: Senjo. pp. iv, 190.

**6772.** HUSE, MARY KATHRYN. We belated historians: the narrators of George Eliot's novels. Unpub. doct. diss., Boston College, 1988. [Abstr. in DA (49) 3733A.]

**6773.** HYDE, VIRGINIA. George Eliot's Arthuriad: heroes and ideology in *Middlemarch*. PLL (24:4) 1988, 404–11.

**6774.** JENKINS, RUTH YVONNE. Reclaiming myths of power: narratives strategies of Nightingale, Brontë, Gaskell and Eliot. *See* **6298.**

**6775.** KELLETT, CHRISTINE ANN. Destroying the monolith: irony and identity in nineteenth-century narrative. *See* **6189.**

**6776.** LESSENICH, ROLF. Jew, artist, providential reader: neoromantic aspects in George Eliot's *Daniel Deronda*. LJGG (30) 123–39.

**6777.** McSWEENEY, KERRY (ed.). Middlemarch. (Bibl. 1987, 7454.) Rev. by John Woolley in Eng (36:154) 1987, 64–72.

**6778.** MONK, LELAND R. Standard deviations: chance and the modern novel. Unpub. doct. diss., Univ. of California, Berkeley, 1988. [Abstr. in DA (50) 955A.]

**6779.** NICHOLS, M. DAVINCI. Myth, exorcism, and Maggie Tulliver. BIS (16) 1988, 101–22.

**6780.** NORTON, ALEXANDRA M. The seeds of fiction: George Eliot's *Scenes of Clerical Life*. JNT (19:2) 217–32.

**6781.** NOVY, MARIANNE.    *Daniel Deronda* and George Eliot's female (re)vision of Shakespeare. *See* **3611.**

**6782.** PREYER, ROBERT O.    The language of discovery: William Whewell and George Eliot. BIS (16) 1988, 123–52.

**6783.** RADER, RALPH W.    The comparative anatomy of three baggy monsters: *Bleak House*, *Vanity Fair*, *Middlemarch*. *See* **6653.**

**6784.** REEVES, MARJORIE; GOULD, WARWICK.    Joachim of Fiore and the myth of the eternal evangel in the nineteenth century. *See* **6109.**

**6785.** ROSENMAN, ELLEN B.    Women's speech and the roles of the sexes in *Daniel Deronda*. TSLL (31:2) 237–56.

**6786.** SCHAEFER, CHARLES WESLEY.    *Middlemarch sub species* Spinoza: an ethical study of Mr Casaubon. Unpub. doct. diss., State Univ. of New York at Binghamton, 1988. [Abstr. in DA (49) 2235A.]

**6787.** SEELBINDER, EMILY.    Writing like a man: gender and readers in *Adam Bede* and *The House of Mirth*. Unpub. doct. diss., Univ. of North Carolina at Chapel Hill, 1987. [Abstr. in DA (49) 2221A.]

**6788.** SNELGROVE, TERESA CLARE.    Narrative organisation in the novels of George Eliot. Unpub. doct. diss., Univ. of Toronto. [Abstr. in DA (50) 1669A.]

**6789.** SVEC, PATRICIA WARD.    Viewpoint and vision in George Eliot: the novelist and her major fiction. Unpub. doct. diss., Loyola Univ. of Chicago. [Abstr. in DA (50) 956–7A.]

**6790.** TAYLOR, INA.    George Eliot: woman of contradictions. London: Weidenfeld & Nicolson. pp. xv, 255. Rev. by Anne Summers in TLS, 29 Sept., 1050; by Peter Kemp in Listener (122) 13 July, 25.

**6791.** THOMAS, JEANIE G.    An inconvenient indefiniteness: George Eliot, *Middlemarch*, and feminism. UTQ (56:3) 1987, 392–415.

**6792.** TIDMARSH, KAREN MACAUSLAND.    The art and science of fiction: the development of theory and practice in George Eliot. Unpub. doct. diss., Univ. of Virginia, 1988. [Abstr. in DA (50) 1316A.]

**6793.** UCHIDA, NORITSUGU.    George Eliot no zenki no shōsetsu. (The early novels of George Eliot.) Tokyo: Sougensha. pp. 244.

**6794.** VARGISH, THOMAS.    The providential aesthetic in Victorian fiction. *See* **5929.**

**6795.** WARD, DEAN ALAN.    The fictive 'experiments' of George Eliot and Thomas Pynchon: science, literary models, and human experience. Unpub. doct. diss., Univ. of Virginia, 1987. [Abstr. in DA (49) 3361A.]

**6796.** WELSH, ALEXANDER.    George Eliot and blackmail. (Bibl. 1988, 5073.) Rev. by Gail Cunningham in RES (38:152) 1987, 579–80.

**6797.** WINKGENS, MEINHARD.    Die kulturelle Symbolik von Mündlichkeit und Schriftlichkeit in George Eliots Roman *Daniel Deronda*. *In* (pp. 163–78) **5.**

### Mary Belson Elliott

**6798.** MOON, MARJORIE.    The children's books of Mary (Belson) Elliott, blending sound Christian principles with cheerful cultivation: a bibliography. (Bibl. 1988, 5075.) Rev. by John Barr in Library (11:1) 75–7.

## Ralph Waldo Emerson

**6799.** BARTLETT, IRVING H. (ed.). The philosopher and the activist: new letters from Emerson to Wendell Phillips. NEQ (62:2) 280–96.

**6800.** BURKHOLDER, ROBERT E.; MYERSON, JOEL. Emerson: an annotated secondary bibliography. (Bibl. 1987, 7482.) Rev. by Kenneth Walter Cameron in AEB (ns 1:4) 1987, 268–74.

**6801.** CADAVA, EDUARDO LUJAN. Nature's politics: Emerson and the institution of American letters. Unpub. doct. diss., Univ. of California, Irvine, 1988. [Abstr. in DA (49) 2217–18A.]

**6802.** CHANDRAN, K. NARAYANA. The pining gods and sages in Emerson's *Brahma*. ELN (27:1) 55–7.

**6803.** COOPER, BETSY McCULLY. The web of relation: science, poetry, and the Emersonian imagination. Unpub. doct. diss., George Washington Univ. [Abstr. in DA (50) 946A.]

**6804.** FURBUSH, ELISABETH BLISS. The epistemic transformation: Emerson and freedom in light of *Advaita* Vedanta. Unpub. doct. diss., Syracuse Univ., 1988. [Abstr. in DA (50) 139A.]

**6805.** GOLUBOFF, BENJAMIN. Emerson's *English Traits*: 'the mechanics of conversation'. ATQ (3:2) 153–67.

**6806.** GOUGEON, LEN. Emerson, Carlyle, and the Civil War. *See* **6446.**

**6807.** GREY, ROBIN SANDRA. The complicity of imagination: seventeenth-century English prose and the ideology of assimilation in Emerson, Thoreau, and Melville. *See* **4249.**

**6808.** HALL, GARY RICHARD. Emerson and the Bible: transcendentalism as scriptural interpretation and revision. Unpub. doct. diss., Univ. of California, Los Angeles. [Abstr. in DA (50) 1657A.]

**6809.** HAMALIAN, LEO. Scanning the self: the influence of Emerson on Kenneth Rexroth. SDR (27:2) 3–14.

**6810.** HELMECI, HOLLIS ELIZABETH. I, Hawthorne's allusions and ambiguous characters in *Rappaccini's Daughter*; II, Consuming greatness: the boa and the belly in Emerson's *Representative Men*. Unpub. doct. diss., Univ. of Toledo, 1988. [Abstr. in DA (50) 443A.]

**6811.** ISLAMOVA, A. K. Lew Tolstoĭ i Ėmerson: o sviâzi ėsteticheskikh sistem. (Tolstoy and Emerson: links between their aesthetic systems.) RusL (1989:1) 44–60.

**6812.** LEONARD, GEORGE J. Emerson, Whitman, and conceptual art. PhilL (13:2) 297–306.

**6813.** LYONS, ELEANOR. Ellison and the twentieth-century American scholar. SAF (17:1) 93–106.

**6814.** MICHAEL, JOHN. Emerson and skepticism: the cipher of the world. (Bibl. 1988, 5082.) Rev. by Robert E. Burkholder in AL (61:2) 289–91.

**6815.** NAGARAJAN, S. Emerson and *Advaita*: some comparisons and contrasts. ATQ (3:4) 325–36.

**6816.** ROSENWALD, LAWRENCE. Emerson and the art of the diary. New York; Oxford: OUP, 1988. pp. xvi, 159. Rev. by Albert J. von

Frank in AL (61:2) 288–9; by Joel Myerson in NEQ (62:3) 459–61; by
Harry Marten in NYTB, 12 Feb., 22.

**6817.** SATTELMEYER, ROBERT. 'When he became my enemy': Emerson and Thoreau, 1848–49. NEQ (62:2) 187–204.

**6818.** SHAW, NANCY JOY. Speaking for the spirit: Cotton, Shepard,
Edwards, Emerson. See **4367.**

**6819.** SIMPSON, LEWIS P. Slavery and the cultural imperialism of New
England. See **5717.**

**6820.** SYLVIA, RICHARD. 'The genuine poet of our time': Emerson's
views on Tennyson. TRB (5:3) 87–100.

### William C. Falkner

**6821.** ROUBEROL, JEAN. De Falkner à Faulkner: *La rose blanche de
Memphis*. Caliban (26) 105–10.

### 'Fanny Fern' (Sara Payson (Willis) Parton)

**6822.** DESMOND, STEWART E. The widow's trials: the life of Fanny
Fern. Unpub. doct. diss., New York Univ., 1988. [Abstr. in DA (49)
3362A.]

### Susan Ferrier

**6823.** FLETCHER, LORAINE. Great expectations: wealth and inheritance in the novels of Susan Ferrier. SLJ (16:2) 60–77.

### Annie Fields

**6824.** FRYER, JUDITH. What goes on in the ladies' room? Sarah Orne
Jewett, Annie Fields, and their community of women. MassR (30:4)
610–28.

### James T. Fields

**6825.** GROVES, JEFFREY D. A letter from Frederick Goddard
Tuckerman to James T. Fields. HLQ (52:3) 403–8.

**6825a.** MECKIER, JEROME. 'A world without Dickens!': James T.
Fields to Annie Fields, 10 June 1870. See **6639.**

### Martha Finley ('Martha Farquharson')

**6826.** HARDMAN, PAM. The steward of her soul: Elsie Dinsmore and
the training of a Victorian child. AmerS (29:2) 1988, 69–90.

### Edward Fitzball

**6827.** CLIFTON, LARRY STEPHEN. The theatre on the macabre: an
analysis of the sensational triad in selected plays by Edward Fitzball.
Unpub. doct. diss., Southern Illinois Univ. at Carbondale, 1987.
[Abstr. in DA (49) 2454A.]

### Harold Frederic

**6828.** ALBERTINE, SUSAN. 'With their tongues doom men to death':
Christian Science and the case of Harold Frederic. ALR (21:3) 52–66.

**6829.** FILETTI, JEAN S. *Seth's Brother's Wife*: the triumph of the
political machine. ALR (21:3) 41–51.

**6830.** JOLLIFF, WILLIAM GERALD. Harold Frederic: his position in the
context of Modernism. Unpub. doct. diss., Ohio State Univ., 1988.
[Abstr. in DA (49) 2659A.]

**6831.** SUDERMAN, ELMER. Modernization as dramatization in *The
Damnation of Theron Ware*. BSUF (27:1) 1986, 12–19.

## Mary E. Wilkins Freeman

**6832.** JOHNSEN, NORMA. The hair wreath: Mary Wilkins Freeman's artist fiction. Unpub. doct. diss., Univ. of New Hampshire. [Abstr. in DA (50) 1658A.]

**6833.** LUSHER, ROBERT M. Seeing the forest for the trees: the 'intimate connection' of Mary Wilkins Freeman's *Six Trees*. ATQ (3:4) 363–81.

## James Anthony Froude

**6834.** ASHTON, ROSEMARY. Doubting clerics: from James Anthony Froude to *Robert Elsmere* via George Eliot. *In* (pp. 69–87) **18.**

## Margaret Fuller

**6835.** CAPPER, CHARLES HERBERT. Margaret Fuller: the early years. Unpub. doct. diss., Univ. of California, Berkeley, 1984. [Abstr. in DA (50) 1065A.]

**6836.** STEELE, JEFFREY. *A Tale of Mizraim*: a forgotten story by Margaret Fuller. NEQ (62:1) 82–104.

**6837.** WATSON, DAVID. Margaret Fuller: an American romantic. Oxford: Berg, 1988. pp. xvi, 127.

## Frederick J. Furnivall

**6838.** HAAS, RENATE. The social functions of F. J. Furnivall's medievalism. *In* (pp. 319–32) **38.**

## John Galt

**6839.** GORDON, IAN A. Galt's *The Ayrshire Legatees*: genesis and development. SLJ (16:1) 35–42.

**6840.** MacQUEEN, JOHN. The Enlightenment and Scottish literature: vol. 2, The rise of the historical novel. *See* **6449.**

## Mrs Gaskell

**6841.** CRAIK, WENDY. Lore and learning in *Cousin Phillis* (1). Gaskell Society Journal (3) 68–80.

**6842.** EASSON, ANGUS (ed.). Wives and daughters. Oxford: OUP, 1987. pp. xxxvii, 740. (World's classics.)

**6843.** FRASER, REBECCA. A strange plant: Charlotte Brontë's friendship with Mrs Gaskell. *See* **6295.**

**6844.** HEYNS, MICHIEL. The steam-hammer and the sugar-tongs: sexuality and power in Elizabeth Gaskell's *North and South*. ESA (32:2) 79–94.

**6845.** HODGSON, JOHN. A Gaskell collection at Canterbury. *See* **233.**

**6846.** JENKINS, RUTH YVONNE. Reclaiming myths of power: narrative strategies of Nightingale, Brontë, Gaskell and Eliot. *See* **6298.**

**6847.** POLLARD, ARTHUR. Faith and family: fundamental values in *Mary Barton*. Gaskell Society Journal (3) 1–5.

**6848.** SHELSTON, ALAN. Elizabeth Gaskell's Manchester (1). Gaskell Society Journal (3) 46–67.

**6849.** STEVENSON, CATHERINE B. Household *vs* industrial economics in Gaskell's *North and South*. NCC (12:1) 1988, 19–25.

**6850.** WHEELER, MICHAEL. Two tales of Manchester life. Gaskell Society Journal (3) 6–28. (*Mary Barton* and *William Langshawe, the Cotton Lord*.)

**6851.** Entry cancelled.

**6852.** WRIGHT, EDGAR. *My Lady Ludlow*: forms of social change and forms of fiction (1). Gaskell Society Journal (3) 29–41.

### W. S. Gilbert

**6853.** HOFFMAN, CHERYL CONOVER. A study of the women in W. S. Gilbert's *Patience, Iolanthe*, and *Princess Ida*; or, the folly of being feminist. Unpub. doct. diss., West Virginia Univ., 1988. [Abstr. in DA (49) 3368A.]

### George Gissing

**6854.** AMDAHL, MARK LEIGH. Gissing and telling: sex, class, and art in selected fiction of George Gissing. Unpub. doct. diss., Washington State Univ., 1988. [Abstr. in DA (49) 3729A.]

**6855.** BLOM, J. M. George Gissing. *In* (pp. 225–37) **47**.

**6856.** Entry cancelled.

**6857.** COUSTILLAS, PIERRE; BRIDGWATER, PATRICK. George Gissing at work: a study of his notebook *Extracts from my Reading*. Greensboro, NC: ELT; Gerrards Cross: Smythe, 1988. (1880–1920 British authors, 2.)

**6858.** FEDERICO, ANNETTE ROSE. Masculine identity in Hardy and Gissing. Unpub. doct. diss., Case Western Reserve Univ. [Abstr. in DA (50) 1310A.]

**6859.** Entry cancelled.

**6860.** THEMAN, D. L. George Gissing and Charles Booth: a case study. Unpub. M.Litt. thesis, Edinburgh, 1986. [Abstr. in IT (36:3) 911.]

**6861.** WOODS, E. A darkness visible: Gissing, Masterman and the metaphors of class 1880–1914. Unpub. doct. diss., Univ. of Sussex. [Abstr. in IT (39:3) 1114.]

### John Gray

**6862.** FLETCHER, IAN (ed.). The poems of John Gray. (Bibl. 1988, 5127.) Rev. by Robert Wells in TLS, 6 Jan., 16.

### William J. Grayson

**6863.** HIND, NATHALIE. *The Hireling and the Slave*: la littérature au service de l'idéologie. Caliban (26) 21–9.

### Sir Henry Rider Haggard

**6864.** KATZ, WENDY R. Rider Haggard and the fiction of empire: a critical study of British imperial fiction. (Bibl. 1987, 7568.) Rev. by Brian Gasser in NQ (36:3) 410–11; by Lars Hartveit in EngS (70:6) 590–1.

**6865.** STOTT, R. The kiss of death: a demystification of the late-nineteenth-century 'femme fatale' in the selected works of Bram Stoker, Rider Haggard, Joseph Conrad and Thomas Hardy. Unpub. doct. diss., Univ. of York. [Abstr. in IT (39:3) 1113.]

### Thomas Chandler Haliburton

**6866.** DAVIES, RICHARD A. (ed.). The letters of Thomas Chandler Haliburton. Toronto; London: Toronto UP, 1988. pp. xxi, 293.

### Arthur Sherburne Hardy

**6867.** STEWART, E. KATE. Arthur Sherburne Hardy: man of

American letters. Potomac, MD: Scripta Humanistica, 1986. pp. 128.
Rev. by Glenn O. Carey in ALR (21:3) 77–9.

## Thomas Hardy

**6868.** AHN, YOUNG-SOO. Thomas Hardy si e natanan irony. (Irony in Thomas Hardy's poetry.) JELL (35) 363–84.

**6869.** ANON. (comp.). Chuo daigaku toshokan Hardu collection kaidai mokuroku. *See* **194.**

**6870.** EL-BAAJ, H. Thomas Hardy and Theodore Dreiser: a comparative study. Unpub. doct. diss., Univ. of Glasgow. [Abstr. in IT (39:4) 1624.]

**6871.** BECKINGHAM, CUSHLA R. The importance of the family in Hardy's fictional world. THJ (5:2) 62–8.

**6872.** BJORK, LENNART A. (ed.). The literary notebooks of Thomas Hardy. (Bibl. 1988, 5133.) Rev. by Dennis Taylor in SewR (96:2) 1988, 251–4.

**6873.** BLAISDELL, ROBERT EHLER. Thomas Hardy and Tess, Bathsheba, Eustacia, and Sue: 'Whose was this mighty personality?' Unpub. doct. diss., Univ. of California, Santa Barbara, 1988. [Abstr. in DA (50) 447A.]

**6874.** BULLEN, J. B. The expressive eye: fiction and perception in the work of Thomas Hardy. (Bibl. 1988, 5135.) Rev. by Simon Gatrell in RES (38:151) 1987, 404–5; by Shelagh Hunter in MLR (84:4) 948–9; by Bernard Richards in Eng (36:155) 1987, 184–7.

**6875.** —— The gods in Wessex exile: Thomas Hardy and mythology. *In* (pp. 181–98) **59.**

**6876.** BUTLER, LANCE ST JOHN. Qui est étranger dans les romans de Thomas Hardy? *In* (pp. 189–204) **26.**

**6877.** —— (ed.). Alternative Hardy. Basingstoke: Macmillan. pp. xii, 229.

**6878.** CLARKE, JOHN STOCK. The 'rival novelist' – Hardy and Mrs Oliphant. THJ (5:3) 51–61.

**6879.** COOK, CORNELIA. Thomas Hardy. Hove: Wayland. pp. 111. (Life and works.)

**6880.** CUNNINGHAM, A. D. Three faces of 'Hodge': the agricultural labourer in Hardy's work. Unpub. doct. diss., Univ. of Exeter. [Abstr. in IT (39:3) 1110.]

**6881.** CURRY, BRYAN TIMOTHY. Philosophical pessimism and gothic convention in the fiction of Thomas Hardy. Unpub. doct. diss., Indiana Univ., 1988. [Abstr. in DA (50) 951A.]

**6882.** DALZIEL, P. A critical edition of Thomas Hardy's uncollected stories. *See* **299.**

**6883.** DAVIS, WILLIAM A., JR. 'But he can be prosecuted for this': legal and sociological backgrounds of the mock marriage in Hardy's serial *Tess.* CLQ (25:1) 28–41.

**6884.** DRAPER, R. P. (ed.). Thomas Hardy: three pastoral novels: *Under the Greenwood Tree, Far from the Madding Crowd, The Woodlanders*: a casebook. (Bibl. 1987, 7606.) Rev. by Michael Thorpe in EngS (70:3) 279–80.

**6885.** DRAPER, RONALD P.    Hardy's love poetry. *In* (pp. 79–96) **42.**

**6886.** —— RAY, MARTIN S.    An annotated critical bibliography of Thomas Hardy. New York; London: Harvester Wheatsheaf. pp. vi, 227. (Harvester Wheatsheaf annotated critical bibliographies.)

**6887.** ELIAN, ABBAS ABDELRAHMAN.    Thomas Hardy and the sub-jugated husband: a study of his major fiction in its literary and cultural context. Unpub. doct. diss., Miami Univ. [Abstr. in DA (50) 145A.]

**6888.** ELLIOTT, RALPH W. V.    Literary dialect in Chaucer, Hardy, and Alan Garner. *See* **2827.**

**6889.** FEDERICO, ANNETTE ROSE.    Masculine identity in Hardy and Gissing. *See* **6858.**

**6890.** GATRELL, SIMON.    Hardy the creator: a textual biography. (Bibl. 1988, 5141.) Rev. by Robert Schweik in THJ (5:3) 79–82.

**6891.** GOODE, JOHN.    Thomas Hardy: the offensive truth. (Bibl. 1988, 5146.) Rev. by Merryn Williams in NQ (36:4) 536–7; by Norman Page in LRB (11:6) 26–7.

**6892.** GORDON, JAN B.    Gossip and the letter: ideologies of 'restor-ation' in *Jude the Obscure*. Lore and Language (8:1) 45–80.

**6893.** GOULD-TALKOFF, NEIL EVAN.    Thomas Hardy: a psycho-biography. Unpub. doct. diss., California School of Professional Psychology at Berkeley/Alameda, 1988. [Abstr. in DA (49) 1809A.]

**6894.** GROSSMAN, JULIE.    Thomas Hardy and the role of observer. ELH (56:3) 619–38.

**6895.** GRUNDY, JOAN.    *Two on a Tower* and *The Duchess of Malfi*. *See* **4813.**

**6896.** HAINING, PETER (ed.).    The supernatural tales of Thomas Hardy. London: Foulsham, 1988. pp. 288.

**6897.** HAWKINS, DESMOND (sel.).    Hardy at home: the people and places of his Wessex. London: Barrie & Jenkins. pp. 256.

**6898.** HOPKINS, ANNIS HELEN.    Biblical plot and character in Thomas Hardy's major novels. Unpub. doct. diss., Arizona State Univ. [Abstr. in DA (50) 1665A.] (*Far from the Madding Crowd, The Return of the Native, Tess of the d'Urbervilles, Jude the Obscure.*)

**6899.** HUTTOVÁ, MÁRIA.    Hardy's Wessex tragedy or melodrama. *In* (pp. 105–13) **62.**

**6900.** JACOBSON, DAN.    Of time and poetry. Commentary (88:5) 48–53.

**6901.** KING, KATHRYN ROSE.    Studies toward a critical edition of Thomas Hardy's *Wessex Tales*. *See* **339.**

**6902.** LAWRENCE, BERTA.    Fifteen letters from Madeleine Rolland to Thomas Hardy. THJ (5:1) 72–7.

**6903.** LEE, SO-YOUNG.    An essay on Tess's androgynous vision: Hardy's yin-yang principle in *Tess of d'Urbervilles*. JELL (35) 651–69.

**6904.** LING, ZHANG.    Thomas Hardy in China. THJ (5:1) 55–9.

**6905.** LONGSHORE-COLLINS, DEBORAH.    Purblind doomsters: Thomas Hardy's polyphonic examination of God. Unpub. doct. diss., Univ. of California, Riverside, 1988. [Abstr. in DA (49) 2231A.]

**6906.** McNees, Eleanor. Reverse typology in *Jude the Obscure*. ChrisL (39:1) 35–49.

**6907.** Maekawa, Tetsuro. Essays on Hardy the poet. Tokyo: Senjo. pp. 128.

**6908.** Magoon, Joseph. Bibliography of writings about Thomas Hardy for 1970 to 1985. Bournemouth: Magoon, 1988. pp. 146 (in various pagings). (Incl. supp. *Thomas Hardy Society Publications 1970–1985*.)

**6909.** Mallett, Phillip. Sexual ideology and narrative form in *Jude the Obscure*. Eng (38) 211–24.

**6910.** Mistichelli, William. Androgyny, survival, and fulfillment in Thomas Hardy's *Far from the Madding Crowd*. MLS (18:3) 1988, 53–64.

**6911.** Morgan, Rosemarie. Women and sexuality in the novels of Thomas Hardy. (Bibl. 1988, 5161.) Rev. by Merryn Williams in NQ (36:4) 536–7.

**6912.** Morrison, Ronald D. Reading Hardy's women. Unpub. doct. diss., Univ. of Kansas, 1988. [Abstr. in DA (49) 3371A.]

**6913.** Nader, Joseph. *Jude the Obscure*: the ordeal of an age of crisis. Journal of Education and Science (Univ. of Mosul, Iraq) (4) 1981, 37–49.

**6914.** Nemesvari, Richard. Choice of copy-text and treatment of accidentals in Thomas Hardy's *The Trumpet-Major*. See **358.**

**6915.** Nemesvari, Richard Andrew. Towards a critical edition of Thomas Hardy's *The Trumpet-Major*. See **359.**

**6916.** O'Neill, Patricia. The chain of unbeing: Hardy's Darwinian poetics. THJ (5:3) 66–72.

**6917.** Pappo-Musard, Cathérine. Les châteaux en Wessex de Thomas Hardy. CVE (28) 1988, 39–51.

**6918.** Patterson, Alice Conger. Naming complemental selves in the novels of Thomas Hardy. Unpub. doct. diss., Arizona State Univ., 1988. [Abstr. in DA (50) 451A.]

**6919.** Philip, Neil (ed.). Wessex heights: an illustrated selection. (Bibl. 1988, 5168.) Rev. by Furse Swann in THJ (5:3) 83–4.

**6920.** Purdy, Richard Little; Millgate, Michael (eds). The collected letters of Thomas Hardy: vol. 6, 1920–1925. (Bibl. 1988, 5169.) Rev. by Norman Page in LRB (11:6) 26–7.

**6921.** —— The collected letters of Thomas Hardy: vol. 7, 1926–1927. With addenda, corrigenda, and general index. (Bibl. 1988, 5170.) Rev. by Norman Page in LRB (11:6) 26–7; by Merryn Williams in NQ (36:4) 537; by James Gibson in THJ (5:2) 80–2.

**6922.** Rabbetts, John. From Hardy to Faulkner: Wessex to Yoknapatawpha. Basingstoke: Macmillan. pp. xvi, 268.

**6923.** Scannell, Vernon. Some Hardy poems considered: 4, *During Wind and Rain* and *Channel Firing*. THJ (5:2) 69–75.

**6924.** Schweik, Robert C. (ed.). Far from the madding crowd. (Bibl. 1988, 5173.) Rev. by Simon Gatrell in RES (38:151) 1987, 405.

**6925.** Smajda, Robert. Schopenhauer, l'Angleterre, et Thomas

Hardy. *In* (pp. 135–47) ANNE HENRY (ed.), Schopenhauer et la création littéraire en Europe. Paris: Méridiens Klincksieck. pp. 230.

**6926.** SPECTOR, STEPHEN J.    Flight of Fancy: characterization in Hardy's *Under the Greenwood Tree*. ELH (55:2) 1988, 469–85.

**6927.** SPRECHMAN, ELLEN LEW.    Hardy's heroines: a reversal of roles. Unpub. doct. diss., Univ. of Miami, 1988. [Abstr. in DA (49) 3037A.]

**6928.** STAVE, SHIRLEY ANN.    Between two worlds: heroines in Hardy's fiction. Unpub. doct. diss., Univ. of Minnesota, 1988. [Abstr. in DA (49) 3737A.]

**6929.** STEELE, BRUCE (ed.).    'Study of Thomas Hardy' and other essays. By D. H. Lawrence. (Bibl. 1987, 7692.) Rev. by Karen McLeod Hewitt in RES (38:149) 1987, 107–8; by Michael Bell in MLR (84:1) 147–8.

**6930.** STENNING, M. P.    Thomas Hardy: the stranger in the landscape. Unpub. doct. diss., Univ. of Sussex. [Abstr. in IT (38:4) 1460.]

**6931.** STOTT, R.    The kiss of death: a demystification of the late-nineteenth-century 'femme fatale' in the selected works of Bram Stoker, Rider Haggard, Joseph Conrad and Thomas Hardy. *See* **6865.**

**6932.** SUMNER, ROSEMARY.    Indeterminacy in Hardy's novels and poetry. THJ (5:2) 33–45.

**6933.** TAYLOR, RICHARD H. (ed.).    Emma Hardy diaries. (Bibl. 1987, 7699.) Rev. by R. P. Draper in RES (38:152) 1987, 594–5.

**6934.** TREZISE, SIMON.    Thomas Hardy and the hieroglyphic Napoleon. THJ (5:1) 59–72.

**6935.** VORHEES, DUANE LEROY.    Hardy, *Tess*, and psychic scotoma. JELL (35) 671–5.

**6936.** WIDDOWSON, PETER.    Hardy in history: a study in literary sociology. London: Routledge. pp. xi, 260.

**6937.** WRIGHT, T. R.    Hardy and the erotic. Basingstoke: Macmillan. pp. x, 150. (Macmillan Hardy studies.)

**6938.** WRIGHT, TERENCE.    Tess of the d'Urbervilles. (Bibl. 1987, 7706.) Rev. by Gail Cunningham in RES (39:156) 1988, 591.

### Frances Ellen Watkins Harper

**6939.** BACON, MARGARET HOPE.    'One great bundle of humanity': Frances Ellen Watkins Harper. PMHB (113:1) 21–43.

### George Washington Harris

**6940.** ROYOT, DANIEL.    'A nat'ral born durn'd fool': l'irrésistible déchéance de Sut Lovingood. Caliban (26) 57–64.

### Joel Chandler Harris

**6941.** BICKLEY, R. BRUCE, JR.    Joel Chandler Harris. Athens: Georgia UP, 1987. pp. 178. Rev. by Eric L. Montenyohl in SF (46:2) 200–1.

### Nathaniel Hawthorne

**6942.** BARSZCZ, JAMES.    The triple drama of Hawthorne's text. Unpub. doct. diss., Rutgers Univ., 1988. [Abstr. in DA (49) 3024A.]

**6943.** BAUER, DALE M.    Feminist dialogics: a theory of failed community. *See* **6469.**

**6944.** BENSE, JAMES.    Nathaniel Hawthorne's intention in *Chiefly about War Matters*. AL (61:2) 200–14.

**6945.** BENSICK, CAROL M. Hawthorne's tragicomic mode of moral allegory. RMRLL (43:1/2) 47–59.

**6946.** BOYD, RICHARD. The politics of exclusion: Hawthorne's *Life of Franklin Pierce*. ATQ (3:4) 337–51.

**6947.** COLACURCIO, MICHAEL J. (ed.). New essays on *The Scarlet Letter*. (Bibl. 1988, 5186.) Rev. by Robert Bellflower in RES (39:154) 1988, 333–4; by James H. Justus in AL (59:1) 1987, 129–32.

**6948.** CRISMAN, WILLIAM. *The Snow-Image* as a key to Hawthorne's biotechnology tales. ATQ (3:2) 169–87.

**6949.** DESALVO, LOUISE. Nathaniel Hawthorne. (Bibl. 1988, 5189.) Rev. by Allan Lloyd Smith in JAStud (23:1) 95–9.

**6950.** EMERICK, RONALD. Hawthorne and O'Connor: a literary kinship. FOB (18) 46–54.

**6951.** GREENWALD, ELISSA. Realism and the romance: Nathaniel Hawthorne, Henry James, and American fiction. See **5826.**

**6952.** GYSIN, FRITZ. Paintings in the house of fiction: the example of Hawthorne. Word & Image (5:2) 159–72.

**6953.** HARDING, BRIAN (ed.). *Young Goodman Brown* and other tales. Oxford; New York: OUP, 1987. pp. xxxvi, 398. (World's classics.)

**6954.** HARRIS, KENNETH MARC. Hypocrisy and self-deception in Hawthorne's fiction. Charlottesville: Virginia UP, 1988. pp. xi, 192. Rev. by William B. Dillingham in SAF (17:2) 245–6; by Mary Van Tassel Murtha in AL (61:2) 294–5; by Elizabeth N. Goodenough in NHR (15:1) 32–3; by Rita K. Gollin in NEQ (62:1) 143–6.

**6955.** HELMECI, HOLLIS ELIZABETH. 1, Hawthorne's allusions and ambiguous characters in *Rappaccini's Daughter*; 11, Consuming greatness: the boa and the belly in Emerson's *Representative Men*. See **6810.**

**6956.** HOWELL, A. J. *The Scarlet Letter* and *Walden*: two strategies of liberation. YYY (5) 15–20.

**6957.** HULL, RICHARD. 'I have no heavenly father': Foucauldian epistemes in *The Scarlet Letter*. ATQ (3:4) 309–23.

**6958.** HUTNER, GORDON. Secrets and sympathy: forms of disclosure in Hawthorne's novels. (Bibl. 1988, 5203.) Rev. by Rita K. Gollin in AL (61:3) 474–6.

**6959.** JOHNSON, BARBARA. Is female to male as ground is to figure? *In* (pp. 255–68) **29.**

**6960.** JONES, BUFORD. Current Hawthorne bibliography. NHR (15:1) 32–3.

**6961.** KENNELLY, LAURA B. Hawthorne and Goldsmith: British history in *Young Goodman Brown* and *Biographical Stories*. See **5286.**

**6962.** KENNELLY, LAURA BALLARD. Goldsmith's *History* in *The Antique Ring*. See **5287.**

**6963.** KIMBALL, ARTHUR SAMUEL. Amimesis and the signature: grammatological openings in *The Scarlet Letter* and *Moby-Dick*. Unpub. doct. diss., Univ. of Florida, 1988. [Abstr. in DA (49) 3724–5A.]

**6964.** LAFFRADO, LAURA. Fear of cultural excision: narration as rhetorical strategy in *The Gorgon's Head*. NHR (15:1) 7–11.

**6965.** LANG, HANS-JOACHIM.   Hawthorne in German translations: a checklist. NHR (15:1) 19–24.

**6966.** LESSENICH, ROLF.   The concept of 'felix culpa' in the novels of Nathaniel Hawthorne. LJGG (27) 1986, 81–103.

**6967.** MCINTOSH, JAMES (ed.).   Nathaniel Hawthorne's tales: authoritative texts, backgrounds, criticism. New York; London: Norton, 1987. pp. xi, 463. (Norton critical editions.) Rev. by Christine Gerrard in RES (39:156) 1988, 597–8.

**6968.** MCWILLIAMS, JOHN.   The politics of isolation. NHR (15:1) 1, 3–7.

**6969.** MAGISTRALE, TONY.   Hawthorne's woods revisited: Stephen King's *Pet Sematary*. NHR (14:1) 1988, 9–13.

**6970.** MARTIN, TERRY JON.   Hawthorne, Poe, Melville, and the rhetoric of deception. Unpub. doct. diss., State Univ. of New York at Buffalo, 1988. [Abstr. in DA (49) 3725A.]

**6971.** MILES, ROBERT.   *The Blithedale Romance*, Rousseau, and the feminine art of dress. TSLL (31:2) 215–36.

**6972.** MILLER, JOHN N.   *The Maypole of Merry Mount*: Hawthorne's festive irony. SSF (26:2) 111–24.

**6973.** —— The pageantry of revolt in *My Kinsman, Major Molineux*. SAF (17:1) 51–64.

**6974.** MILLIMAN, CRAIG ARTHUR.   Lessons of the masters: social tension as a creative necessity in the fiction of Hawthorne, James, and Joyce. Unpub. doct. diss., Louisiana State Univ. and Agricultural and Mechanical College, 1988. [Abstr. in DA (50) 1300A.]

**6975.** MIZRUCHI, SUSAN L.   The power of historical knowledge: narrating the past in Hawthorne, James, and Dreiser. Princeton, NJ: Princeton UP, 1988. pp. xviii, 313. (Cf. bibl. 1986, 8485.) Rev. by N. E. Stafford in AL (61:2) 297–8.

**6976.** MOTT, WESLEY T.   Hawthorne reviewed in a children's temperance newspaper. NHR (15:1) 25.

**6977.** NEWBERRY, FREDERICK.   The Biblical veil: sources and typology in Hawthorne's *The Minister's Black Veil*. TSLL (31:2) 169–95.

**6978.** —— Hawthorne's divided loyalties: England and America in his works. London; Toronto: Assoc. UPs, 1987. (Bibl. 1988, 5220.) Rev. by Charles Swann in JAStud (23:1) 160–2.

**6979.** OLEKSY, ELŻBIETA.   Theistic existentialism in American letters – Hawthorne and Percy. Łódz: Wydawnictwo Uniwersytetu Łódzkiego. pp. 277. (Acta universitatis Lodziensis.)

**6980.** PEARCE, ROY HARVEY.   *Gesta humanorum*: studies in the historicist mode. (Bibl. 1988, 5222.) Rev. by Terence Martin in ELN (27:2) 75–7; by Robert Clark in JAStud (23:1) 154–5.

**6981.** PERSON, LELAND S., JR.   Aesthetic headaches: women and a masculine poetics in Poe, Melville, and Hawthorne. Athens; London: Georgia UP, 1988. pp. xi, 196. Rev. by John McWilliams in AL (61:1) 109–11; by Elizabeth A. Schultz in AmerS (29:2) 1988, 95–6; by John L. Idol, Jr, in SoCR (21:2) 81–2.

**6982.** POLLOCK, BETH RUBY. The representation of Utopia: Hawthorne and the female medium. Unpub. doct. diss., Univ. of California, Berkeley, 1988. [Abstr. in DA (50) 687A.]

**6983.** ROMERO, LORA PATRICIA. The government of the body: health reform and the American antebellum novel. See **6551.**

**6984.** ROSE, MARILYN RUSSELL. Hawthorne's *Custom House*, Said's *Orientalism* and Kogawa's *Obasan*: an intertextual reading of an historical fiction. DalR (67:2/3) 1987, 286–96.

**6985.** SAGE, HOWARD. Translating Hawthorne into Chinese: an interview with a translator and teacher of Hawthorne's works (Chen Guan Shang). NHR (15:1) 11–14.

**6986.** SAGHER, SAAD KASSIM. Nathaniel Hawthorne's *The Scarlet Letter*: Hester Prynne as a social rebel. Journal of Education and Science (Univ. of Mosul, Iraq) (7) (Humanities and education) 41–60.

**6987.** SCHARNHORST, GARY. Hawthorne and *The Poetical Works of Edmund Spenser*: a lost review. See **3404.**

**6988.** —— Nathaniel Hawthorne: an annotated bibliography of comment and criticism before 1900. Metuchen, NJ; London: Scarecrow Press, 1988. pp. xii, 404. (Scarecrow author bibliographies, 82.)

**6989.** SCHNEIDER, LON FREDERICK. Transference in four Hawthorne romances. Unpub. doct. diss., Univ. of Iowa, 1988. [Abstr. in DA (49) 3363–4A.] (*The Scarlet Letter, The House of the Seven Gables, The Blithedale Romance, The Marble Faun.*)

**6990.** SMITH, ALLAN LLOYD. Salvos against Hawthorne and the canon. JAStud (23:1) 95–9 (review-article).

**6991.** SWANN, CHARLES. Hawthorne's *The Marble Faun* and Michelangelo's bust of Brutus. NQ (36:2) 185–6.

**6992.** TSOUTSOU, THOMAIS J. The status of the artist in Hawthorne's novels. Unpub. doct. diss., Wayne State Univ., 1988. [Abstr. in DA (50) 445–6A.]

**6993.** WAGENKNECHT, EDWARD. Nathaniel Hawthorne: the man, his tales and romances. New York: Ungar. pp. xii, 264. Rev. by Margaret B. Moore in AL (61:4) 691–2.

**6994.** WEBER, ALFRED. The outlines of *The Story Teller*, the major work of Hawthorne's early years. NHR (15:1) 14–19.

**6995.** WELTZIEN, ALAN O. The picture of history in *The Maypole of Merry Mount*. AQ (45:1) 29–48.

**6996.** WESTBROOK, ELLEN E. Probable improbabilities: verisimilar romance in Hawthorne's *The Birth-mark*. ATQ (3:2) 203–17.

**6997.** WIENK, MARILYN DOWD. Hawthorne's heroines and the feminine ideal: the four major romances in the context of nineteenth-century women's novels. See **5936.**

**6998.** WOHLPART, A. JAMES. The status of the artist in Hawthorne's *The Artist of the Beautiful*. ATQ (3:3) 245–56.

### William Hazlitt

**6999.** GARNETT, MARK A. Hazlitt against Burke: radical versus conservative? See **5120.**

**7000.** JONES, STANLEY. Three additions to the canon of Hazlitt's political writings. RES (38:151) 1987, 355–63.
**7001.** RUDDICK, BILL. Recollecting Coleridge: the internalization of radical energies in Hazlitt's political prose. *See* **6522.**

### Lafcadio Hearn
**7002.** HAYLEY, BARBARA. Lafcadio Hearn, W. B. Yeats and Japan. *In* (pp. 43–60) **37.**

### James Hogg
**7003.** GROVES, DAVID. James Hogg and David Moir. NQ (36:2) 168.
**7004.** —— James Hogg: an early essay. NQ (36:2) 167–8. (*On the Diseases of Sheep.*)
**7005.** —— A pastoral on women by the Ettrick Shepherd. NQ (36:2) 178–81. (*Cuddy Clew: a Pastoral*, published in the Royal Lady's Magazine and Archives of the Court of St James (2) July 1831.)
**7006.** —— (ed.). Tales of love and mystery. (Bibl. 1986, 8536.) Rev. by Fiona Robertson in RES (38:149) 1987, 87–8.
**7007.** HUGHES, GILLIAN. Reading and inspiration: some sources for *The Surpassing Adventures of Allan Gordon*. SLJ (16:1) 21–34.
**7008.** —— (ed.). Papers given at the second James Hogg Society Conference (Edinburgh 1985). Aberdeen: Assn for Scottish Literary Studies; James Hogg Soc., 1988. pp. xi, 148. (Occasional papers, 8.)
**7009.** MACK, DOUGLAS S. Hogg's prose: an annotated listing. Stirling: James Hogg Soc., 1985. leaves 216–63. (Spiral bound.)
**7010.** MACQUEEN, JOHN. The Enlightenment and Scottish literature: vol. 2, The rise of the historical novel. *See* **6449.**
**7011.** PETRIE, ELAINE. James Hogg's *The Private Memoirs and Confessions of a Justified Sinner*. Aberdeen: Assn for Scottish Literary Studies, 1988. pp. 56. (Scotnotes, 4.)
**7012.** —— (ed.). Scottish pastorals: poems, songs, etc., mostly written in the dialect of the south. London: Stirling UP, 1988. pp. xxii, 64.

### Marietta Holley
**7013.** ROSS, CHERI L. Nineteenth-century American feminist humor: Marietta Holley's Samantha novels. JMMLA (22:2) 12–25.

### William Hone
**7014.** WOOD, M. Popular satire in early nineteenth-century radicalism, with special reference to Hone and Cruikshank. *See* **102.**

### Gerard Manley Hopkins
**7015.** BRITTAIN, CLARK MACKLYN. *Logos*, creation, and epiphany in the poetics of Gerard Manley Hopkins. Unpub. doct. diss., Univ. of Virginia, 1988. [Abstr. in DA (49) 3759–60A.]
**7016.** BUMP, JEROME. Hopkins, feminism, and creativity: an overview. TSLL (31:1) 1–30.
**7017.** CAMAIORA, LUISA CONTI. Gray – Keats – Hopkins: poetry and the poetic presence. *See* **5291.**
**7018.** COTTER, JAMES FINN. Hopkins the mythmaker. America (161) 106–8.
**7019.** ELLSBERG, MARGARET R. Created to praise: the language of

Gerard Manley Hopkins. New York; Oxford: OUP, 1987. pp. 145. Rev. by Karen Batley in UES (27:1) 40–1.

**7020.** FEENEY, JOSEPH J. 'Earth is the fairer': the centennial of Gerard Manley Hopkins. America (161) 102–5.

**7021.** GILES, RICHARD F. (ed.). Hopkins among the poets: studies in modern responses to Gerard Manley Hopkins. Hamilton, Ont.: International Hopkins Assn, 1985. pp. viii, 128. (International Hopkins Assn monographs, 3.) Rev. by R. K. R. Thornton in RES (38:150) 1987, 269–70; by Norman White in NQ (36:1) 118–19.

**7022.** KING, SHELLEY MARILYN. 'But meaning motion': movement and change in the poetry of G. M. Hopkins. Unpub. doct. diss., Univ. of Toronto, 1988. [Abstr. in DA (49) 2668A.]

**7023.** LEIMBERG, INGE. Die Andromeda der Zeit: Inkarnation und dichterische Verwirklichung bei Gerard Manley Hopkins. Ang (107: 3/4) 344–79.

**7024.** NIXON, JUDE V. The kindly light: a reappraisal of the influence of Newman on Hopkins. TSLL (31:1) 105–42.

**7025.** ONG, WALTER J. Hopkins, the self, and God. (Bibl. 1988, 5271.) Rev. by Bernard Bergonzi in MLR (84:4) 953–4; by Martha Westwater in DalR (67:1) 1987, 148–51; by R. K. R. Thornton in RES (39:155) 1988, 459–60.

**7026.** PHILLIPS, CATHERINE (ed.). Gerard Manley Hopkins. (Bibl. 1987, 7826.) Rev. by R. K. R. Thornton in RES (39:155) 1988, 460.

**7027.** ROBERTS, GERALD (ed.). Gerard Manley Hopkins: the critical heritage. (Bibl. 1987, 7827.) Rev. by Norman White in NQ (36:1) 118–19; by R. K. R. Thornton in RES (39:155) 1988, 460.

**7028.** SHAW, W. DAVID. Incomprehensible certainties and interesting uncertainties: Hopkins and Tennyson. TSLL (31:1) 66–84.

**7029.** SULLOWAY, ALISON G. Gerard Manley Hopkins and 'women and men' as 'partners in the mystery of redemption'. TSLL (31:1) 31–51.

**7030.** YAMAMURA, TAKEO. Dryden kara Hopkins e: 17 seiki to 20 seiki no soukan kankei. *See* **4464.**

### Pauline Elizabeth Hopkins

**7031.** YARBOROUGH, RICHARD (introd.). Contending forces: a romance illustrative of negro life North and South. New York; Oxford: OUP, 1988. pp. xlviii, 402. (Schomburg library of nineteenth-century Black women writers.)

### Julia Ward Howe

**7032.** SCHRIBER, MARY SUZANNE. Julia Ward Howe and the travel book. NEQ (62:2) 264–79.

### W. D. Howells

**7033.** BASSETT, JOHN E. 'A heart of ideality in my realism': Howells's early criticism. PLL (25:1) 67–82.

**7034.** MERRILL, GINETTE DE B.; ARMS, GEORGE (eds). If not literature: letters of Elinor Mead Howells. (Bibl. 1988, 5281.) Rev. by Henry Claridge in JAStud (23:3) 511–12; by Kenneth E. Eble in RMRLL (43:1/2) 109–10; by John W. Crowley in ALR (22:1) 90–1.

**7035.** MURPHY, BRENDA.   Howells and the popular story paradigm: reading *Silas Lapham*'s proairetic code. ALR (21:2) 21–33.
**7036.** NETTELS, ELSA.   Language, race, and social class in Howells's America. (Bibl. 1988, 5283.) Rev. by Henry Claridge in JAStud (23:3) 511–12.

### Henry Noel Humphreys
**7037.** LEATHLEAN, HOWARD.   Henry Noel Humphreys and the getting-up of books in the mid-nineteenth century. *See* **92.**

### Richard Holt Hutton
**7038.** WOODFIELD, MALCOLM.   R. H. Hutton: critic and theologian: the writings of R. H. Hutton on Newman, Arnold, Tennyson, Wordsworth, and George Eliot. (Bibl. 1987, 7853.) Rev. by Sheridan Gilley in MLR (84:4) 947–8; by Geoffrey Rowell in NQ (35:1) 1988, 112–13.

### Washington Irving
**7039.** MAYFIELD, ARCH RAGAN.   An examination of selected elements of style in Washington Irving's *A Tour on the Prairies*, *Astoria*, and *The Adventures of Captain Bonneville*. Unpub. doct. diss., Texas Tech Univ., 1988. [Abstr. in DA (49) 2221A.]
**7040.** RUBIN-DORSKY, JEFFREY.   Adrift in the Old World: the psychological pilgrimage of Washington Irving. Chicago; London: Chicago UP, 1988. pp. xix, 303. Rev. by William L. Hedges in AL (61:1) 106–8; by Richard D. Rust in EAL (24:2) 155–7.

### Helen Hunt Jackson
**7041.** WHITAKER, ROSEMARY.   Helen Hunt Jackson. (Bibl. 1988, 5300.) Rev. by Richard W. Etulain in OreHQ (90:2) 206–8.

### Henry James
**7042.** ADEGAWA, YUKO.   Henry James kenkyu. (A study of Henry James.) Tokyo: Kirihara. pp. xii, 242.
**7043.** ÁLVAREZ, MARÍA ANTONIA.   Relación Henry–William James y repercusiones en la obra del novelista. RAEI (2) 7–19.
**7044.** ANDERSON, HILTON.   *Daisy Miller* and *The Hotel Child*: a Jamesian influence on F. Scott Fitzgerald. SAF (17:2) 213–18.
**7045.** ANESKO, MICHAEL.   'Friction with the market': Henry James and the profession of authorship. (Bibl. 1988, 5302.) Rev. by C. B. Cox in SewR (96:3) 1988, 505–6; by Susan M. Griffin in MP (86:3) 321–3; by Nicola Bradbury in RES (39:156) 582–3.
**7046.** AUCHARD, JOHN.   Silence in Henry James: the heritage of symbolism and decadence. (Bibl. 1988, 5304.) Rev. by C. B. Cox in SewR (96:3) 1988, 503–5.
**7047.** BAK, YONG-SU.   Henry James eui *The Ambassadors* eui gibeob. (The technique of Henry James's *The Ambassadors*.) JELLC (30) 47–73.
**7048.** BAUER, DALE M.   Feminist dialogics: a theory of failed community. *See* **6469.**
**7049.** BELL, IAN F. A. (ed.).   Henry James: fiction as history. (Bibl. 1988, 5308.) Rev. by David Kirby in DalR (66:3) 1986, 380–2.
**7050.** BELLRINGER, ALAN W.   Henry James. Basingstoke: Macmillan, 1988. pp. viii, 155. (Macmillan modern novelists.)

**7051.** BENDER, TODD K.    A concordance to Henry James's *The Awkward Age*. New York; London: Garland. pp. xi, 693. (Garland reference library of the humanities, 869.)

**7052.** BISHOP, GEORGE.    When the master relents: the neglected short fictions of Henry James. Ann Arbor, MI: UMI Research Press, 1988. pp. 114. (Studies in modern literature, 80.) (Cf. bibl. 1986, 8628.)

**7053.** BOREN, LYNDA S.    Undoing the 'Mona Lisa': Henry James's quarrel with da Vinci and Pater. Mosaic (20:3) 1987, 95–111.

**7054.** BROWN, CHRIS.    Wagner and *The Spoils of Poynton*. CLQ (25:4) 227–36.

**7055.** CAPUTO, PETER.    Selfishness and generosity, isolation and kinship: Melville, James and Flannery O'Connor. Unpub. doct. diss., Columbia Univ., 1988. [Abstr. in DA (49) 3025A.]

**7056.** CHOI, KYUNG-DO.    *Poynton eui yaktalmul*-soyu eui munjae. (The problem of possession in *The Spoils of Poynton*.) YYY (5) 21–35.

**7057.** CUPP, JEFFERY EARNEST.    'Money from elsewhere': donorship and the romance form in the novels of Henry James. Unpub. doct. diss., Univ. of Illinois at Urbana-Champaign, 1988. [Abstr. in DA (49) 2657A.]

**7058.** DAVIES, D. J.    A comparative study of London and Paris in the works of Henry James and Émile Zola. Unpub. doct. diss., CNAA, 1987. [Abstr. in IT (39:2) 482.]

**7059.** EDEL, LEON (ed.).    Henry James: selected letters. (Bibl. 1988, 5320.) Rev. by Bernard Richards in NQ (36:4) 532–5.

**7060.** —— POWERS, LYALL H. (eds).    The complete notebooks of Henry James. (Bibl. 1988, 5321, where second scholar's initial omitted.) Rev. by Richard S. Lyons in SewR (96:3) 1988, 492–7; by Bernard Richards in RES (39:156) 1988, 578–82.

**7061.** —— TINTNER, ADELINE R. (eds).    The library of Henry James. *See* **218.**

**7062.** EVERETT, BARBARA.    Henry James's children. *In* (pp. 317–35) **14.**

**7063.** FEIDELSON, CHARLES.    Henry James, history, and 'story'. *In* (pp. 104–21) **45.**

**7064.** FELMAN, SHOSHANA.    Writing and madness: literature/philosophy/psychoanalysis. Trans. by MARTHA NOEL EVANS and BRIAN MASSUMI. Ithaca, NY; London: Cornell UP, 1985. pp. 255. Rev. by Gillian C. Gill in JA (45:3) 1987, 314–16.

**7065.** FLEMING, BRUCE E.    Floundering about in silence: what the governess couldn't say. SSF (26:2) 135–44.

**7066.** GAGE, RICHARD P.    Order and design: Henry James' titled story sequences. New York; Berne; Frankfurt: Lang, 1988. pp. ii, 315. (American univ. studies, 24: American literature, 1.) (Cf. bibl. 1987, 7891.) Rev. by Barbara J. Eckstein in AL (61:4) 693–4.

**7067.** GARD, ROGER (ed.).    The critical muse: selected literary criticism. (Bibl. 1987, 7892.) Rev. by Pamela Rhodes in DUJ (81:1) 1988, 169–70; by Ronald Mason in NQ (36:4) 535–6.

**7068.** GERVAIS, DAVID.    Deciphering America: *The American Scene*. CamQ (18:4) 349–62.

**7069.** GOETZ, WILLIAM R.    Henry James and the darkest abyss of romance. (Bibl. 1988, 5328.) Rev. by C. B. Cox in SewR (96:3) 1988, 500–2.

**7070.** GOSCILO, MARGARET.    The dual outsider in Henry James's *The Princess Casamassima. In* (pp. 205–18) **26.**

**7071.** GREENWALD, ELISSA.    Realism and the romance: Nathaniel Hawthorne, Henry James, and American fiction. *See* **5826.**

**7072.** GULOTTA, DONNA SHEINBERG.    Fairy tales and Arthurian legends in the novels of Henry James: the emergence of self. *See* **1708.**

**7073.** GURNEY, STEPHEN.    The critical voice of Henry James. ModAge (32:4) 1988, 351–9.

**7074.** HABEGGER, ALFRED.    Henry James and the 'woman business'. Cambridge; New York: CUP. pp. ix, 288. (Cambridge studies in American literature and culture.) Rev. by Wayne C. Booth in NYTB, 24 Sept., 54.

**7075.** —— Henry James's *Bostonians* and the fiction of democratic vulgarity. *In* (pp. 102–21) **1.**

**7076.** HAGBERG, GARRY.    Wittgenstein, Henry James, and epistemological fiction. PhilL (13:1) 75–95.

**7077.** HOFFMANN, CHARLES; HOFFMANN, TESS.    Henry James and the Civil War. NEQ (62:4) 529–52.

**7078.** HORNE, PHILIP.    Writing and rewriting in Henry James. JAStud (23:3) 358–74.

**7079.** AL-ISSA, A.    Polyphony and the anxiety of influence in the fiction of Henry James. Unpub. doct. diss., Univ. of Warwick. [Abstr. in IT (39:4) 1636.]

**7080.** IVY, BENJAMIN.    Portrait of an author. Opera News (53:5) 1988, 20, 22.

**7081.** JOBE, STEVEN HOWARD.    From Stoicism to histrionism: Henry James's pursuit of a dynamic Stoicism. Unpub. doct. diss., Univ. of North Carolina at Chapel Hill, 1988. [Abstr. in DA (50) 684A.]

**7082.** KAHANE, CLAIRE.    Hysteria, feminism, and the case of *The Bostonians. In* (pp. 280–97) **29.**

**7083.** KIBERD, DECLAN.    Isabel Archer: the New Woman as American. *In* (pp. 85–103) **45.**

**7084.** KROOK, DOROTHEA.    *The Aspern Papers*: a counter-introduction. *In* (pp. 223–34) **23.**

**7085.** LINDBERG-SEYERSTED, BRITA.    Ford Madox Ford and his relationship to Stephen Crane and Henry James. *See* **6560.**

**7086.** LONGO, MARIE L.    A study of Henry James's fictional presentation of girls. Unpub. doct. diss., St John's Univ., 1988. [Abstr. in DA (49) 2669A.]

**7087.** LOTT, EDITH ELLEN.    Visual art in the short fiction of Henry James. Unpub. doct. diss., Univ. of South Carolina, 1988. [Abstr. in DA (50) 444A.]

**7088.** LYONS, RICHARD S. The social vision of *The Spoils of Poynton*. AL (61:1) 59–77.

**7089.** MACKENZIE, MANFRED. The way home. Span (28) 63–84.

**7090.** MACNAUGHTON, WILLIAM R. Henry James: the later novels. Boston, MA: G. K. Hall, 1987. pp. v, 154. (Twayne's US authors, 521.) Rev. by Sarah B. Daugherty in ALR (21:3) 82–3.

**7091.** MARTIN, W. R.; OBER, WARREN V. Captain Diamond and Old Hickory: realities and ambivalence in Henry James's *The Ghostly Rental*. SSF (26:1) 1–10.

**7092.** MICHAUX, ARMAND. The innocent and the puritan: Henry James' *Roderick Hudson*. In (pp. 43–54) **2.**

**7093.** MILLIMAN, CRAIG ARTHUR. Lessons of the masters: social tension as a creative necessity in the fiction of Hawthorne, James, and Joyce. See **6974.**

**7094.** MIZRUCHI, SUSAN L. The power of historical knowledge: narrating the past in Hawthorne, James, and Dreiser. See **6975.**

**7095.** MONTEIRO, GEORGE. Henry James and the Secretary of State: a new letter. ALR (22:1) 80–1.

**7096.** PEARSON, JOHN H. Frames of reference: the Prefaces of Henry James. Unpub. doct. diss., Boston Univ. [Abstr. in DA (50) 686A.]

**7097.** PENRICE, AMY WISSINGER. Theodor Fontane and Henry James: configurations of control. Unpub. doct. diss., Harvard Univ., 1988. [Abstr. in DA (49) 3021A.]

**7098.** RASMUSSEN, BARBARA. Re-producing 'James': Marxism, phallocentrism and *Washington Square*. JAStud (23:1) 63–7.

**7099.** RIGHTER, WILLIAM. Golden rules and golden bowls. PhilL (13:2) 262–82.

**7100.** ROWE, JOHN CARLOS. The theoretical dimensions of Henry James. (Bibl. 1988, 5362.) Rev. by C. B. Cox in SewR (96:3) 1988, 497–500.

**7101.** SABIN, MARGERY. The dialect of the tribe: speech and community in modern fiction. See **1418.**

**7102.** SELETRINA, T. L. Dzheĭms i problemy angliĭskogo romana 1880–1890. (James and the problems of the English novel, 1880–1890.) Sverdlovsk, USSR: Izdatel'stvo Ural'skogo universiteta. pp. 125.

**7103.** STEELE, H. MEILI. Realism and the drama of reference: strategies of representation in Balzac, Flaubert, and James. University Park: Pennsylvania State UP, 1988. pp. 162. Rev. by Fred G. See in AL (61:2) 298–9; by Walter G. Putnam, III, in RMRLL (43:4) 261–2.

**7104.** STEMPEL, DANIEL. Biography as dramatic monologue: Henry James, W. W. Story, and the alternate vision. NEQ (62:2) 224–47.

**7105.** STOWE, WILLIAM W. Balzac, James, and the realistic novel. (Bibl. 1988, 5373.) Rev. by C. B. Cox in SewR (96:3) 1988, 502–3.

**7106.** SUTCLIFFE, JAMES HELME. The Argento papers. Opera News (53:5) 1988, 14–18. (Argento's opera based on *The Aspern Papers*.)

**7107.** TINGLE, NICHOLAS. Realism, Naturalism, and Formalism: James and *The Princess Casamassima*. ALR (21:2) 54–66.

**7108.** TINTNER, ADELINE R. The book world of Henry James:

appropriating the classics. (Bibl. 1988, 5378.) Rev. by Robert L. Gale in ALR (21:3) 83–5; by Francis Golffing in PR (56:3) 518–20.

**7109.**  ——James's jury duty and *The Given Case*. CVE (29) 67–72.

**7110.**  TREBISZ, MAŁGORZATA.  The necklace motif in *La Parure, Paste* and *A String of Beads*. *In* (pp. 95–104) **3.**

**7111.**  VAN LEER, DAVID.  The beast of the closet: homosociality and the pathology of manhood. CI (15:3) 587–605. (*The Beast in the Jungle*.)

**7112.**  VEZA, LAURETTE.  Henry James: le champ du regard. Paris: Table Ronde. pp. 348.

**7113.**  WALKER, NANCY.  'Wider than the sky': public presence and private self in Dickinson, James, and Woolf. *In* (pp. 272–303) **51.**

**7114.**  WALKER, PIERRE A.  The Princess Casamassima's 'sudden incarnation' and Octave Feuillet. TSLL (31:2) 257–72.

**7115.**  WARDLEY, LYNN.  Woman's voice, democracy's body, and *The Bostonians*. ELH (56:3) 639–65.

**7116.**  WHITSITT, SAMUEL PORTER.  Putting 'it' in other words: readings of Eco, Deely, Melville and James. Unpub. doct. diss., State Univ. of New York at Buffalo, 1988. [Abstr. in DA (49) 3727A.]

**7117.**  YOUNG, ARLENE.  Hypothetical discourse as *ficelle* in *The Golden Bowl*. AL (61:3) 382–97.

**7118.**  ZACHARIAS, GREG WILLIAM.  Power relations in Henry James's novels: a study of language, characterization and morality. Unpub. doct. diss., New York Univ., 1988. [Abstr. in DA (49) 2663A.]

### William James

**7119.**  ÁLVAREZ, MARÍA ANTONIA.  Relación Henry–William James y repercusiones en la obra del novelista. *See* **7043.**

**7120.**  MYERS, GERALD E.  William James: his life and thought. (Bibl. 1988, 5391.) Rev. by Lawrence Willson in SewR (96:3) 1988, 482–5.

### Anna Jameson

**7121.**  FRIEWALD, BINA.  'Femininely speaking': Anna Jameson's *Winter Studies and Summer Rambles in Canada*. *In* (pp. 61–73) **40.**

### Richard Jefferies

**7122.**  BRATTIN, JOEL J.  From drama into fiction: *The Lamplighter* and *The Lamplighter's Story*. *See* **6597.**

**7123.**  HUNT, PETER (ed.).  Bevis. Oxford: OUP. pp. xxviii, 432. (World's classics.)

### Jerome K. Jerome

**7124.**  CARPENTER, HUMPHREY (introd.).  Three men in a boat: (to say nothing of the dog). Gloucester: Sutton. pp. 248.

**7125.**  LAMB, HUGH (sel. and introd.).  Stories in the dark: tales of terror by Jerome K. Jerome, Robert Barr and Barry Pain. *See* **6252.**

### Sarah Orne Jewett

**7126.**  FRYER, JUDITH.  What goes on in the ladies' room? Sarah Orne Jewett, Annie Fields, and their community of women. *See* **6824.**

**7127.**  MIHĂILĂ, RODICA (introd.).  La ţărm de ape. (Stories and tales.) Bucharest: Sport-Turism. pp. 223.

**7128.**  SHERMAN, SARAH WAY.  Sarah Orne Jewett: an American

Persephone. Hanover, NH; London: New England UP for Univ. of New Hampshire. pp. xiii, 333.

**7129.** STODDART, SCOTT FREDERICK. Selected letters of Sarah Orne Jewett: a critical edition with commentary. Unpub. doct. diss., Univ. of Illinois at Urbana-Champaign, 1988. [Abstr. in DA (49) 2661A.]

**7130.** SUBBARAMAN, SIVAGAMI. Rites of passage: narratorial plurality as structure in Jewett's *The Country of the Pointed Firs*. CR (33:1) 60–74.

### Geraldine Jewsbury

**7131.** LEHMBECK, B. S. Studies in Geraldine Jewsbury's fiction, with particular attention to the woman question. Unpub. M.Litt. diss., Univ. of Edinburgh, 1988. [Abstr. in IT (38:4) 1459–60.]

### Lionel Johnson

**7132.** PITTOCK, MURRAY (ed.). Selected letters. Edinburgh: Tragara, 1988. pp. 39. (Limited ed. of 150 copies.)

### John Keats

**7133.** ASKE, MARTIN. Keats and Hellenism: an essay. (Bibl. 1988, 5402.) Rev. by Richard Jenkyns in RES (39:149) 1987, 94–5.

**7134.** BAKER, JEFFREY. John Keats and symbolism. New York: St Martin's Press, 1986. (Bibl. 1986, 8798.) Rev. by Vincent Newey in RES (38:151) 1987, 399–400.

**7135.** BARNARD, JOHN. John Keats. (Bibl. 1988, 5404.) Rev. by Ronald Tetreault in DalR (67:2/3) 1987, 371–4.

**7136.** BENNETT, ANDREW J. Enticing conclusion: John Keats's *Ode on a Grecian Urn*. Word & Image (5:4) 301–14.

**7137.** CAMAIORA, LUISA CONTI. Gray – Keats – Hopkins: poetry and the poetic presence. *See* **5291.**

**7138.** COOKSON, LINDA; LOUGHREY, BRYAN (eds). Critical essays on Keats: poems and letters. Harlow: Longman, 1988. pp. 143. (Longman literature guides.)

**7139.** DEVINE, KATHLEEN. Rosenberg, Keats, and two Belles Dames Sans Merci. EA (42:2) 188–90.

**7140.** FRY, AUGUST J. A note on *convention* and *innovation*: the *Odes* of John Keats. *In* (pp. 225–34) **16.**

**7141.** FUJIDA, SHINJI. Keats no 'Ode' no sekai. (The world of Keats's odes.) Tokyo: Nan'un-do. pp. 198.

**7142.** GARDNER, JOSEPH H. 'To cease upon the midnight': Keats and Gibbon. *See* **5266.**

**7143.** HAMEED, SALIH MAHDI. Some stylistic features in *To Autumn*. *See* **1406.**

**7144.** HAMILTON, PAUL. Keats and critique. *In* (pp. 108–42) **53.**

**7145.** KERRIGAN, JOHN. Keats and *Lucrece*. *See* **3890.**

**7146.** LAMONT, CLAIRE. Meg the gypsy in Scott and Keats. Eng (36) 1987, 137–45.

**7147.** LE BON-DODAT, ANNE-MARIE. Urgence d'écriture dans la poétique de Keats. Repérages (12) 13–25.

**7148.** LEOFF, EVE. Keats's *Alexandre Fragment* and *La Belle Dame Sans Merci*. ELN (26:3) 46–9.

**7149.** LEVINSON, MARJORIE. Keats's life of allegory: the origins of a style. (Bibl. 1988, 5414.) Rev. by Barbara Hardy in Eng (38) 168–83; by Miriam Allott in NQ (36:3) 405–7.

**7150.** MARQUESS, WILLIAM HENRY.   Lives of the poet: the first century of Keats biography. (Bibl. 1987, 8006.) Rev. by A. F. T. Lurcock in RES (38:152) 1987, 571–2.

**7151.** MORPURGO, J. E.   The poet and Barabbas: Keats, his publishers and editors. In (pp. 112–23) **37.**

**7152.** NEWEY, VINCENT.   'Alternate uproar and sad peace': Keats, politics, and the idea of revolution. YES (19) 265–89.

**7153.** PITE, R. R. G.   Dante's influence on Coleridge and Keats: 'the circle of our vision'. See **6520.**

**7154.** PLASA, C. A.   The economy of revision: Keats, Browning and T. S. Eliot. See **6386.**

**7155.** REED, THOMAS A.   Keats and the gregarious advance of intellect in Hyperion. ELH (55:1) 1988, 195–232.

**7156.** SÁNCHEZ CALVO, ARSENIO.   La naturaleza en Alastor, Childe Harold y Endymion. See **6420.**

**7157.** TAKAHASHI, YUUSHIRO.   John Keats: souzouryoku no hikari to yami. (John Keats: the light and darkness of imagination.) Tokyo: Nan'un-do. pp. 356.

**7158.** WALDOFF, LEON.   Keats and the silent work of imagination. (Bibl. 1988, 5423.) Rev. by Dinah Birch in RES (38:149) 1987, 95–6.

**7159.** WOLFSON, SUSAN J.   The questioning presence: Wordsworth, Keats, and the interrogative mode in Romantic poetry. (Bibl. 1988, 5426.) Rev. by J. R. Watson in RES (39:155) 1988, 453–4.

**7160.** YAMAUCHI, SHOICHI.   The labyrinthian path – Keats's melancholy and his 1820 volume. SEL (English number) 3–20.

### Fanny Kemble

**7161.** LARSON, CYNTHIA MARIE.   A story without an end: Fanny Kemble's Georgia Journal and other autobiographical writings. Unpub. doct. diss., Univ. of Iowa, 1988. [Abstr. in DA (49) 2281A.]

### Adam Kidd

**7162.** BENTLEY, D. M. R. (ed.).   The Huron chief. London, Ont.: Canadian Poetry Press, 1987. pp. xliii, 132. Rev. by David Latham in CanL (122/23) 142–3.

### Francis Kilvert

**7163.** MABER, RICHARD; TREGONING, ANGELA (eds).   Kilvert's Cornish diary: Journal no. 4, 1870, from July 19th to August 6th. Penzance: Hodge. pp. 137. Rev. by Anthony Powell in TLS, 30 June, 716.

### Alice King

**7164.** LAWRENCE, BERTA.   Mary Lamb and Alice King. CLB (65) 33–5.

### Grace King

**7165.** TAYLOR, HELEN.   Gender, race, and region in the writings of Grace King, Ruth McEnery Stuart, and Kate Chopin. See **6474.**

### A. W. Kinglake

**7166.** AL-TAHA, M.   The Orient and three Victorian travellers: Kinglake, Burton and Palgrave. See **6394.**

### Mary Kingsley
**7167.** DOBRZYCKA, IRENA. Mary Kingsley – a Victorian lady in the African bush. KN (35:4) 1988, 431–44.

### The Lambs
**7168.** MISENHEIMER, CAROLYN. The pleasures of early enlightenment: the Lambs' *Tales from Shakespeare*. CLB (67) 69–82.

### Charles Lamb
**7169.** BATE, JONATHAN (ed.). *Elia* and *The Last Essays of Elia*. (Bibl. 1988, 5435.) Rev. by Pierre Coustillas in EA (42:4) 479.
**7170.** NABHOLTZ, JOHN R. Joseph Munden, *Elia* and Charles Lamb in performance. CLB (66) 37–41.
**7171.** RUSSELL, GILLIAN. Lamb's *Specimens of English Dramatic Poets*: the publishing context and the principles of selection. *See* **461.**

### Mary Lamb
**7172.** LAWRENCE, BERTA. Mary Lamb and Alice King. *See* **7164.**
**7173.** WOOF, PAMELA. Dorothy Wordsworth and Mary Lamb, writers. CLB (66) 41–53; (67) 82–93.

### Archibald Lampman
**7174.** ARCHER, ANNE. The story of an affinity: D. G. Jones, Archibald Lampman, and *Kate These Flowers*. CanL (122/23) 42–54.
**7175.** BENTLEY, D. M. R. (ed.). The story of an affinity. London, Ont.: Canadian Poetry Press, 1986. pp. xxxi, 85. Rev. by Len Early in CanL (122/23) 150–2.
**7176.** EARLY, L. R. Archibald Lampman. Boston, MA; London: G. K. Hall, 1986. pp. 175. (Twayne's world authors, 770.) Rev. by John Ower in CanL (115) 1987, 167–9.
**7177.** OWER, JOHN. The story of an affinity: Lampman's *The Frogs* and Tennyson's *The Lotos-Eaters*. CanL (115) 1987, 285–9.

### Andrew Lang
**7178.** DEMOOR, MARYSA. Andrew Lang's letters to Edmund Gosse: the record of a fruitful collaboration as poets, critics, and biographers. RES (38:152) 1987, 492–509.

### Sidney Lanier
**7179.** BARRUCAND, MICHEL. Sidney Lanier: les hymnes aux marais. Caliban (26) 65–80.

### Edward Lear
**7180.** EDE, LISA S. Edward Lear's limericks and their illustrations. *In* (pp. 103–16) **28.**
**7181.** —— An introduction to the nonsense literature of Edward Lear and Lewis Carroll. *In* (pp. 47–60) **28.**
**7182.** NOAKES, VIVIEN (ed.). Selected letters. (Bibl. 1988, 5446.) Rev. by Mitzi Andersen in UES (27:2) 36–7; by MC in Junior Bookshelf (52:5) 1988, 224–5.
**7183.** PITMAN, RUTH (ed.). Edward Lear's Tennyson. (Bibl. 1988, 5447.) Rev. by Vivien Noakes in TRB (5:2) 1988, 69–72.
**7184.** SEWELL, ELIZABETH. Is Flannery O'Connor a nonsense writer? *In* (pp. 183–213) **28.**
**7185.** —— Nonsense verse and the child. *In* (pp. 135–48) **28.**

**7186.** TIGGES, WIM.  An anatomy of literary nonsense. *See* **6466.**

**7187.** —— The limerick: the sonnet of nonsense? *In* (pp. 117–33) **28.**

**7188.** VAN LEEUWEN, HENDRIK.  The liaison of visual and written nonsense. *In* (pp. 61–95) **28.**

### 'Vernon Lee' (Violet Paget)

**7189.** GARDNER, BURDETT.  The lesbian imagination (Victorian style): a psychological and critical study of 'Vernon Lee'. New York; London: Garland, 1987. pp. xxvii, 592. (Harvard dissertations in American and English literature.)

### Sheridan Le Fanu

**7190.** COUGHLAN, PATRICIA.  Doubles, shadows, sedan-chairs and the past: the 'ghost stories' of J. S. Le Fanu. *In* (pp. 17–39) **17.**

**7191.** MILBANK, A.  Daughters of the house: modes of the gothic in the fiction of Wilkie Collins, Charles Dickens and Sheridan Le Fanu. *See* **6542.**

**7192.** MILBANK, ALISON.  Doubting Castle: the gothic mode of questioning. *In* (pp. 104–19) **18.**

### Mark Lemon

**7193.** FISHER, LEONA W.  Mark Lemon's farces on the 'woman question'. SELit (28:4) 1988, 649–70. (*The House of Ladies, The Petticoat Parliament.*)

### G. H. Lewes

**7194.** BARRAT, ALAIN.  George Henry Lewes vulgarisateur scientifique dans *Seaside Studies*. CVE (29) 41–54.

### Elizabeth Lynn Linton

**7195.** OSTERHOLM, KATHRYN KRESS.  Eliza Lynn Linton's female characters and the double bind of the feminine novelist. Unpub. doct. diss., Indiana Univ. of Pennsylvania. [Abstr. in DA (50) 1314A.]

### Henry Wadsworth Longfellow

**7196.** MARTENS, KLAUS.  It was the mockingbird not the nightingale: how an American bird homes in on the German tradition. *In* (pp. 198–208) **4.**

### Franklin Lushington

**7197.** KENNEDY, JUDITH.  Tennyson, the Lushingtons, and Franklin's poem in Fichte. TRB (5:3) 109–20.

### Thomas Babington, Lord Macaulay

**7198.** PHILLIPS, MARK.  Macaulay, Scott, and the literary challenge to historiography. JHI (50:1) 117–33.

### George MacDonald

**7199.** AIURA, R.  Recurring symbols in the fantasies and children's stories of George MacDonald. Unpub. M.Litt. thesis, Univ. of Aberdeen, 1986. [Abstr. in IT (36:1) 20.]

**7200.** CUSICK, E.  George MacDonald and Victorian fantasy. Unpub. doct. diss., Univ. of Oxford, 1988. [Abstr. in IT (39:1) 32.]

**7201.** FILMER, KATH.  La Belle Dame sans merci: cultural criticism and the mythopoeic imagination in George MacDonald's *Lilith*. Mythlore (15:4) 17–20.

**7202.** —— Neither here nor there: the spirit of place in George

MacDonald's *Lilith* and C. S. Lewis's *Till We Have Faces*. Mythlore (16:1) 9–12.

**7203.** Phillips, Michael R. George MacDonald: Scotland's beloved storyteller. Minneapolis, MN: Bethany House, 1987. pp. 390. Rev. by Lesley Smith in SLJ (supp. 30) 24–5.

**7204.** Raeper, William. George MacDonald. Tring; Batavia, IL: Lion, 1987. pp. 432.

**7205.** Reed-Nancarrow, Paula Elizabeth. Remythologizing the Bible: fantasy and the revelatory hermeneutic of George MacDonald. Unpub. doct. diss., Univ. of Minnesota, 1988. [Abstr. in DA (49) 1811a.]

**7206.** Robb, David S. George MacDonald. (Bibl. 1988, 5464.) Rev. by David Groves in NQ (36:2) 254–5; by Lesley Smith in SLJ (supp. 30) 25–8; by Isobel Murray in DUJ (81:1) 1988, 165–6.

**7207.** Triggs, Kathy. The stars and the stillness: a portrait of George MacDonald. (Bibl. 1986, 8888, where title incomplete.) Rev. by Lesley Smith in SLJ (supp. 30) 22–3.

### William McGonagall

**7208.** MacDonald, Robert H. The patriotic muse of William McGonagall: imperialism and the great Scots joke. DalR (67:4) 1987, 480–94.

### W. H. Mallock

**7209.** Kiff, A. Argument and the novel: the dialectical fiction of W. H. Mallock. Unpub. doct. diss., Univ. of Oxford, 1988. [Abstr. in IT (39:2) 487.]

**7210.** al-Sagoubi, S. S. The works of W. H. Mallock in the context of his life and times. Unpub. M.Phil. diss., Univ. of Hull, 1988. [Abstr. in IT (39:3) 1109.]

### James Clarence Mangan

**7211.** Andrews, Jean. James Clarence Mangan and Romantic stereotypes: 'old and hoary at thirty-nine'. IUR (19:2) 240–63.

### Brander Matthews

**7212.** Oliver, Lawrence J. Theodore Roosevelt, Brander Matthews, and the campaign for literary Americanism. See **5695**.

### Herman Melville

**7213.** Bacigalupo, Massimo (ed. and trans.). Herman Melville, gente di mare: *Benito Cereno, Billy Budd, Daniel Orme*. Milan: Mondadori, 1988. pp. 293.

**7214.** Bakker, J. Melville and the West, or, *Israel Potter* reconsidered. DQR (19:1) 18–36.

**7215.** Bryant, John (ed.). A companion to Melville studies. (Bibl. 1986, 8904.) Rev. by Diedrich Knickerbocker in AL (61:2) 283–5.

**7216.** Caputo, Peter. Selfishness and generosity, isolation and kinship: Melville, James and Flannery O'Connor. See **7055**.

**7217.** Clark, James Milton. Melville's use of the confidence man. Unpub. doct. diss., Univ. of California, Riverside, 1988. [Abstr. in DA (49) 1800a.]

**7218.** Dooley, Reinhold James. Herman Melville's short fiction:

ideology and the American confidence game. Unpub. doct. diss., Univ. of Tennessee, 1988. [Abstr. in DA (50) 138A.]

**7219.** DUBAN, JAMES. Chipping with a chisel: the ideology of Melville's narrators. TSLL (31:3) 341–85.

**7220.** DURER, CHRISTOPHER S. *Moby-Dick*'s Ishmael, Burke, and Schopenhauer. MidQ (30:2) 161–78.

**7221.** —— Tommo as an impassioned tourist: a re-reading of Melville's *Typee*. Explorations (12:1/2) 1988/89, 9–24.

**7222.** GARRISON, JOSEPH M., JR. *Billy Budd*: a reconsideration. BSUF (27:1) 1986, 30–41.

**7223.** GOLDMAN, STAN. The small voice of silence: Melville's narrative voices in *Clarel*. TSLL (31:3) 451–73.

**7224.** GRABHER, GUDRUN M. Adding to the myths of *Moby-Dick*: the question of being as shared by existential and oriental philosophy. AAA (14:2) 67–78.

**7225.** GREY, ROBIN SANDRA. The complicity of imagination: seventeenth-century English prose and the ideology of assimilation in Emerson, Thoreau, and Melville. *See* **4249.**

**7226.** HILTNER, JUDITH R. From Pisgah to Egypt: narrative continuities in Melville's *Israel Potter* and *The Two Temples*. JNT (19:3) 300–11.

**7227.** INGERSOLL, EARL. The failure of bloodbrotherhood in Melville's *Moby-Dick* and Lawrence's *Women in Love*. MidQ (30:4) 458–77.

**7228.** KATZ, LESLIE. Flesh of his flesh: amputation in *Moby-Dick* and S. W. Mitchell's medical papers. Genders (4) 1–10.

**7229.** KIMBALL, ARTHUR SAMUEL. Amimesis and the signature: grammatological openings in *The Scarlet Letter* and *Moby-Dick*. *See* **6963.**

**7230.** LEE, SANG-WHA. *Billy Budd* eui jujaejeok baljeon. (Thematic development in *Billy Budd*: the conflict between good and evil and transcendental hope.) JELL (35) 217–34.

**7231.** LEHMAN, ALBERTO; BOGLIOLO, GIULIA BRUNO (eds). Herman Melville: profile di donne. Montebelluna: Amadeus, 1986. pp. 93.

**7232.** LINK, FRANZ. Dickens's Moddle and Melville's Bartleby 'prefer not to'. *See* **6631.**

**7233.** LJUNGQUIST, KENT. 'Meteor of the war': Melville, Thoreau, and Whitman respond to John Brown. AL (61:4) 674–80.

**7234.** McELROY, JOHN HARMON. The uncompromising truth of *Billy Budd*: its miraculous climax. ChrisL (38:3) 47–62.

**7235.** MARTIN, ROBERT K. Hero, captain, and stranger: male friendship, social critique, and literary form in the sea novels of Herman Melville. (Bibl. 1987, 8126.) Rev. by Michael Lynch in MP (86:3) 319–21.

**7236.** MARTIN, TERRY JON. Hawthorne, Poe, Melville, and the rhetoric of deception. *See* **6970.**

**7237.** MATCHIE, THOMAS. *Love Medicine*: a female *Moby-Dick*. MidQ (30:4) 478–91.

**7238.** PATTON, DORIS MILLS. The physeter and the great white whale: the influence of Rabelais on *Moby-Dick*. Unpub. doct. diss., Univ. of Tennessee, 1988. [Abstr. in DA (50) 686A.]

**7239.** PAYNE, DAVID HENRY. Language and myth in Herman Melville's *Moby-Dick* and *Pierre*. Unpub. doct. diss., Univ. of Georgia, 1988. [Abstr. in DA (49) 2660–1A.]

**7240.** PERSON, LELAND S., JR. Aesthetic headaches: women and a masculine poetics in Poe, Melville, and Hawthorne. *See* **6981.**

**7241.** PISANO, FRANK. Melville's 'great haven': a look at Fort Tompkins. SAF (17:1) 111–13.

**7242.** REAGAN, DANIEL. Melville's *Israel Potter* and the nature of biography. ATQ (3:3) 257–76.

**7243.** SANDBERG, ROBERT A. 'The adjustment of screens': putative narrators, authors, and editors in Melville's unfinished 'Burgundy Club' book. *See* **388.**

**7244.** SANDBERG, ROBERT ALLEN. Melville's unfinished 'Burgundy Club' book: a reading edition edited from the manuscripts with introduction and notes. *See* **389.**

**7245.** SEALTS, MERTON M., JR. Melville's reading. (Bibl. 1969, 7423.) Columbia: South Carolina UP, 1988. pp. xviii, 296. (Second ed.: first ed. 1966.) Rev. by Linck C. Johnson in AL (61:2) 285–6.

**7246.** SHETLEY, VERNON. Melville's *After the Pleasure Party*: Venus and virgin. PLL (25:4) 425–42.

**7247.** SHORT, BRYAN C. 'The author at the time': Tommo and Melville's self-discovery in *Typee*. TSLL (31:3) 386–405.

**7248.** STEEDS, W. Herman Melville's *Clarel*: the supreme poem of the faith–doubt crisis: an examination of *Clarel* with specific reference to English and American poets of the nineteenth-century crisis of faith. Unpub. doct. diss., Univ. of Essex, 1988. [Abstr. in IT (39:3) 1118.]

**7249.** STEWART, MARGARET E. The 'romance' *vs* the 'narrative of facts': representational mode and political ambivalence in Melville's *White-Jacket*. ATQ (3:2) 189–202.

**7250.** STRANDBERG, VICTOR. The Frost–Melville connection. *In* (pp. 17–25) **2.**

**7251.** SWEET, TIMOTHY ROBERT. Traces of war: poetry, photography, and the question of representation in the American Civil War. Unpub. doct. diss., Univ. of Minnesota, 1988. [Abstr. in DA (49) 2222–3A.]

**7252.** TANNER, TONY (introd.); DUGDALE, JOHN (notes). The confidence-man: his masquerade. Oxford: OUP. pp. xlvi, 361. (World's classics.)

**7253.** WEINER, SUSAN. 'Law in art': Melville's major fiction and nineteenth-century American law. Unpub. doct. diss., Northwestern Univ. [Abstr. in DA (50) 949A.]

**7254.** WENKE, JOHN. Melville's *Mardi*: narrative self-fashioning and the play of possibility. TSLL (31:3) 406–25.

**7255.** WHITE, BARBARA ANNE. Undercurrent strategies: the encyclopedic narratives of Sterne, Melville, Poe and Rainer. *See* **5520.**

**7256.** WHITSITT, SAMUEL PORTER. Putting 'it' in other words: readings of Eco, Deely, Melville and James. *See* **7116.**

**7257.** YOUNG, PHILIP.   Melville in the Berkshire bishopric: *The Lightning-Rod Man*. CLit (16:3) 201–10.

**7258.** ZIMMERMAN, BRETT.   The Uranic muse: astronomy, Melville, and his contemporaries. Unpub. doct. diss., York Univ. (Ont.), 1988. [Abstr. in DA (49) 3727A.]

### George Meredith

**7259.** BARRETT, ELIZABETH MARY.   Competence, control, and critical practice in three Victorian novels. *See* **6591.**

**7260.** CRAIG, RANDALL.   Promising marriage: *The Egoist*, Don Juan, and the problem of language. ELH (56:4) 897–921.

**7261.** STONE, DONALD D.   Meredith and Bakhtin: polyphony and *Bildung*. SELit (28:4) 1988, 693–712.

**7262.** STONE, JAMES S.   George Meredith's politics: as seen in his life, friendships, and works. Port Credit, Ont.: Meany, 1986. pp. viii, 200. Rev. by Sven-Johan Spånberg in RES (39:154) 1988, 315–16.

### John Stuart Mill

**7263.** SCHARFF, ROBERT C.   Mill's misreading of Comte on 'interior observation'. JHP (27:4) 559–72.

**7264.** SMART, P. T.   Mill and Marx: human nature, the individual and freedom. Unpub. doct. diss., Univ. of Keele. [Abstr. in IT (38:4) 1444–5.]

**7265.** TULLOCH, GAIL.   Mill and sexual equality. Hemel Hempstead: Harvester Wheatsheaf. pp. xviii, 212.

**7266.** WELCH, KATHLEEN E.   Logical writing in the education of John Stuart Mill: the *Autobiography* and the privileging of reason. BIS (16) 1988, 153–67.

### Mary Russell Mitford

**7267.** PIGROME, STELLA.   Mary Russell Mitford. CLB (66) 53–62.

### David Macbeth Moir

**7268.** GROVES, DAVID.   James Hogg and David Moir. *See* **7003.**

### Susanna Moodie

**7269.** MURRAY, HEATHER.   Women in the wilderness. *In* (pp. 74–83) **40.**

**7270.** PETERMAN, MICHAEL.   In search of Agnes Strickland's sisters. CanL (121) 115–24.

### Clement Clarke Moore

**7271.** HOWARTH, WILLIAM.   Visions of sugarplums. BkW, 3 Dec., 1, 19. (*'Twas the Night Before Christmas*.)

### Tom Moore

**7272.** SULTANA, FEHMIDA.   Romantic Orientalism and Islam: Southey, Shelley, Moore, and Byron. *See* **6428.**

### William Morris

**7273.** BLANCHON, MARIE-THÉRÈSE.   William Morris, gothique et socialisme. CVE (28) 1988, 53–63.

**7274.** HODGSON, AMANDA.   The romances of William Morris. New York: CUP, 1987. pp. xii, 219. (Bibl. 1987, 8186, where pagination incorrect.) Rev. by Peter Faulkner in MLR (84:2) 448–9.

**7275.** JULIAN, LINDA ANNE.   William Morris: the Icelandic influence on his writing. Unpub. doct. diss., Boston Univ., [Abstr. in DA (49) 1809A.]

**7276.** KELVIN, NORMAN. Patterns in time: the decorative and the narrative in the work of William Morris. *In* (pp. 140–68) **44.**

**7277.** —— (ed.). The collected letters of William Morris: vol. 2, 1881–1884 & 1885–1888. (Bibl. 1988, 5526.) Rev. by William E. Fredeman in MP (87:2) 200–5.

**7278.** MILBRANDT, ROGER DOUGLAS. Three late Victorian models of artistic production: a study of Arnold, Pater and Morris. *See* **6106.**

**7279.** RICHARDSON, L. A. William Morris and women: experience and representation. Unpub. doct. diss., Univ. of Oxford. [Abstr. in IT (39:3) 1113.]

**7280.** SILVANI, GIOVANNA. Woman in Utopia from More to Huxley. *See* **3286.**

**7281.** SMITH, L. The enigma of visibility: theories of visual perception in the early poetry of William Morris and in the work of Ruskin and the pre-Raphaelites. *See* **5997.**

**7282.** TOMPKINS, J. M. S. William Morris: an approach to the poetry. (Bibl. 1988, 5530.) Rev. by Brian Maidment in TRB (5:3) 148–9.

### Mary N. Murfree ('Charles Egbert Craddock')

**7283.** TAYLOR, ALICE FAY. Mary Noailles Murfree: Southern woman writer. Unpub. doct. diss., Emory Univ., 1988. [Abstr. in DA (49) 3066A.]

### John Henry Newman

**7284.** KENWAY, I. M. Rationality, judgment and certainty: a study of the philosophical significance of John Henry Newman's account of imagination and reason in religious faith. Unpub. doct. diss., Univ. of Bristol, 1986. [Abstr. in IT (36:3) 884–5.]

**7285.** KER, IAN. John Henry Newman: a biography. Oxford: Clarendon Press, 1988. pp. xiii, 762. Rev. by Rosemary Ashton in LRB (11:4) 13–14; by Richard Shannon in TLS, 10 Mar., 242.

**7286.** KULISHECK, PATRICIA JO. John Henry Newman at Alton. NQ (36:2) 188–90.

**7287.** McGRATH, F. J. Newman on revelation and its existence outside Christianity. Unpub. doct. diss., Univ. of Oxford, 1988. [Abstr. in IT (39:1) 6.]

**7288.** NIXON, JUDE V. The kindly light: a reappraisal of the influence of Newman on Hopkins. *See* **7024.**

**7289.** NOONKESTER, MYRON C. An unpublished letter of J. H. Newman. NQ (36:2) 188.

**7290.** SCHENKER, MARK JOHN. Historical transcendentalism in the works of Carlyle, Newman, and Browning. *See* **6387.**

**7291.** THOMAS, S. C. Newman and heresy: the Anglican writings. Unpub. doct. diss., Univ. of Durham, 1988. [Abstr. in IT (38:4) 1441.]

### Solomon Northrup

**7292.** WATERS, CARVER WENDELL. Voice in the slave narratives of Olaudah Equiano, Frederick Douglass, and Solomon Northrup. *See* **5222.**

## Mrs Oliphant

**7293.** CLARKE, JOHN STOCK. The 'rival novelist' – Hardy and Mrs Oliphant. *See* **6878.**

**7294.** FITZGERALD, PENELOPE (introd.). Phoebe, junior. London: Virago Press. pp. xvi, 341. (Virago modern classics, 310.) (Chronicles of Carlingford.)

**7295.** WILLIAMS, MERRYN. Margaret Oliphant, novelist. Cencrastus (34) 20–2.

## Frederick Law Olmsted (1822–1903)

**7296.** SCHEPER, GEORGE L. The reformist vision of Olmsted and the poetics of park design. NEQ (62:3) 369–402.

## Barry Pain

**7297.** LAMB, HUGH (sel. and introd.). Stories in the dark: tales of terror by Jerome K. Jerome, Robert Barr and Barry Pain. *See* **6252.**

## Francis Turner Palgrave

**7298.** TILLOTSON, KATHLEEN. Palgrave's *Golden Treasury* and Tennyson: another source. *See* **2110.**

## William Gifford Palgrave

**7299.** AL-TAHA, M. The Orient and three Victorian travellers: Kinglake, Burton and Palgrave. *See* **6394.**

## Gilbert Parker

**7300.** RIPLEY, JOHN (ed.). Gilbert Parker and Herbert Beerbohm Tree stage *The Seats of the Mighty* in Washington (1896) and London (1897): the promptbooks for the production at Her Majesty's Theatre, London, 28 April 1897. Toronto: Simon & Pierre, 1986. pp. 141. Rev. by Moira Day in CanL (121) 146–7.

## Walter Pater

**7301.** BAROLSKY, PAUL. Walter Pater's *Renaissance*. (Bibl. 1988, 5539.) Rev. by Leonée Ormond in Word & Image (5:2) 219–21.

**7302.** CONNOR, STEVEN. Conclusion: myth and meta-myth in Max Müller and Walter Pater. *In* (pp. 199–222) **59.**

**7303.** ISER, WOLFGANG. Walter Pater: the aesthetic moment. Trans. by DAVID HENRY WILSON. (Bibl. 1988, 5543.) Rev. by Clive Scott in CompCrit (10) 1988, 275–7.

**7304.** JARRATT, SUSAN C. Walter Pater and the sophistication of rhetoric. CE (51:1) 73–87.

**7305.** MCGRATH, F. C. The sensible spirit: Walter Pater and the Modernist paradigm. (Bibl. 1988, 5544.) Rev. by Steven Connor in MLR (84:3) 699–700; by Dietrich Schwanitz in Ang (107:1/2) 247–51.

**7306.** MILBRANDT, ROGER DOUGLAS. Three late Victorian models of artistic production: a study of Arnold, Pater and Morris. *See* **6106.**

## Coventry Patmore

**7307.** DANCHIN, PIERRE. Coventry Patmore and Francis Thompson: the story of a brief friendship (1894–1896). *In* (pp. 27–37) **42.**

## James Ohio Pattie

**7308.** BATMAN, RICHARD. James Pattie's West: the drama and the reality. Norman: Oklahoma UP, 1986. pp. 284. Rev. by Paul Witkowsky in WAL (22:1) 1987, 93–4.

### Thomas Love Peacock

**7309.** BROOKS, HAROLD. 'A song from Mr Cypress'. *See* **6401.**

**7310.** McKAY, MARGARET. Thomas Love Peacock in the diaries of Sir Henry Cole. NQ (36:2) 176–8.

### Wendell Phillips

**7311.** BARTLETT, IRVING H. (ed.). The philosopher and the activist: new letters from Emerson to Wendell Phillips. *See* **6799.**

### Edgar Allan Poe

**7312.** BACHINGER, KATRINA. Gender positions: the intertextuality of gender difference in Margaret Atwood, Katherine Mansfield, Joyce Carol Oates, Edgar Allan Poe, Sir Philip Sidney and others. *See* **3306.**

**7313.** —— The multi-man genre and Poe's Byrons. *See* **6397.**

**7314.** BAUER, STEFAN. Das wahrscheinliche Unwahrscheinliche. Realitätsansprüche in der Kriminalliteratur. *See* **5784.**

**7315.** BEAVER, HAROLD. Doodling America: Poe's *MS. Found in a Bottle*. *In* (pp. 15–27) **13.**

**7316.** BLOOM, CLIVE. Reading Poe, reading Freud: the romantic imagination in crisis. (Bibl. 1988, 5559.) Rev. by Peter Brooks in TLS, 13 Jan., 40.

**7317.** BRODY, SELMA B. Poe's use of Brewster's *Letters on Natural Magic*. ELN (27:1) 50–4.

**7318.** CARLSON, ERIC W. (ed.). Critical essays on Edgar Allan Poe. Boston, MA: G. K. Hall, 1987. pp. 223. (Critical essays on American literature.) Rev. by Henri Justin in EA (42:3) 360–1.

**7319.** GRUESSER, JOHN C. *Ligeia* and Orientalism. SSF (26:2) 145–50.

**7320.** HUTTAR, CHARLES A. Poe's angels. *In* (pp. 82–4) **45.**

**7321.** IRWIN, JOHN T. Handedness and the self: Poe's chess player. AQ (45:1) 1–28.

**7322.** KENNEDY, J. GERALD. Poe, death, and the life of writing. (Bibl. 1988, 5567, where title incomplete.) Rev. by Liliane Weissberg in AL (61:2) 292–4; by Christine Gerrard in RES (39:156) 1988, 598–9.

**7323.** KESTING, MARIANNE. Chiffren der Imagination: phantastische Tiere bei Edgar Allan Poe. PoetA (21:3/4) 329–52.

**7324.** LEE, A. ROBERT (ed.). Edgar Allan Poe: the design of order. (Bibl. 1988, 5569.) Rev. by Christine Gerrard in RES (39:156) 1988, 599–600.

**7325.** LINK, FRANZ. Poe's *Tamerlane*, Shakespeare, Keats und Emily Dickinson. LJGG (29) 1988, 323–5.

**7326.** MARTIN, TERRY JON. Hawthorne, Poe, Melville, and the rhetoric of deception. *See* **6970.**

**7327.** MICHAEL, JOHN. Narration and reflection: the search for grounds in Poe's *The Power of Words* and *The Domain of Arnheim*. AQ (45:3) 1–22.

**7328.** MONTES PAZO, FERNANDO. El narcisismo esquizofrénico de Poe. Atlantis (11:1/2) 151–7.

**7329.** NANKOV, NIKITA. Părvi kritičeski otzivi za Edgar Po v Bălgaria. (The first critical essays in Bulgaria on Edgar Poe.) Ezik i literatura (44:1) 91–100.

**7330.** PAPAZU, MÓNICA.   The search for life and truth in Edgar Allan Poe's tales. Atlantis (11:1/2) 125–36.

**7331.** PERSON, LELAND S., JR.   Aesthetic headaches: women and a masculine poetics in Poe, Melville, and Hawthorne. *See* **6981.**

**7332.** ROSENHEIM, SHAWN.   'The king of "secret readers"': Edgar Poe, cryptography, and the origins of the detective story. ELH (56:2) 375–400.

**7333.** SEAMAN, ROBERT E.   Lacan, Poe, and the descent of the self. TSLL (31:2) 196–214.

**7334.** SZÁSZ, JÁNOS (postscr.).   A Kút és az inga. (The pit and the pendulum.) Bucharest: Kriterion. pp. 311.

**7335.** THOMAS, DWIGHT; JACKSON, DAVID K.   The Poe log: a documentary life of Edgar Allan Poe, 1809–1849. Boston: G. K. Hall, 1987. pp. xlix, 919. (American authors' logs.) Rev. by David Ketterer in JAStud (23:1) 130–1; by Benjamin Franklin Fisher, IV, in AL (60:1) 1988, 115–17; by F. R. Shivers, Jr, in MHM (83) 1988, 274–7.

**7336.** TORRY, ROBERT LYNN.   Keeping watch: vigilance and desire in Poe's fiction. Unpub. doct. diss., State Univ. of New York at Buffalo, 1988. [Abstr. in DA (49) 3726–7A.]

**7337.** TSUJIMOTO, ICHIRO.   Poe no tanpenron kenkyu. (A study of Poe's theory of short stories.) Tokyo: Kazama. pp. ii, 430.

**7338.** VOLOSHIN, BEVERLY.   Transcendence downward: an essay on *Usher* and *Ligeia.* MLS (18:3) 1988, 18–29.

**7339.** WALKER, I. M. (ed.).   Edgar Allan Poe: the critical heritage. (Bibl. 1987, 8264.) Rev. by Christine Gerrard in RES (39:156) 1988, 598.

**7340.** WARE, TRACY.   A note on Poe and Carlyle's *German Romance.* *See* **6454.**

**7341.** —— The two stories of *William Wilson.* SSF (26:1) 43–8.

**7342.** WHITE, BARBARA ANNE.   Undercurrent strategies: the encyclopedic narratives of Sterne, Melville, Poe and Rainer. *See* **5520.**

**7343.** WILLIAMS, MICHAEL J. S.   A world of words: language and displacement in the fiction of Edgar Allan Poe. (Bibl. 1988, 5581.) Rev. by Kenneth Watson in SoQ (27:2) 99–101.

**7344.** ZAPF, HUBERT.   Entropic imagination in Poe's *The Masque of the Red Death.* CLit (16:3) 211–18.

### Thomas Pringle

**7345.** PEREIRA, E.   Thomas Pringle: a bicentenary appraisal. Lantern (38:4) 25–40.

### Howard Pyle

**7346.** AGOSTA, LUCIEN L.   Howard Pyle. Boston, MA: G. K. Hall, 1987. pp. 162. (Twayne's US authors, 514.)

### Charles Reade

**7347.** HAMMET, MICHAEL (ed.).   Plays by Charles Reade. (Bibl. 1986, 9096.) Rev. by Georges Bas in EA (42:4) 487; by Michael R. Booth in YES (19) 344–5.

### Anne Thackeray Ritchie

**7348.** MCCAIL, RONALD.   A family matter: *Night and Day* and *Old Kensington.* RES (38:149) 1987, 23–39.

## Sir Charles G. D. Roberts

**7349.** ADAMS, JOHN COLDWELL. Sir Charles God Damn: the life of Sir Charles G. D. Roberts. (Bibl. 1986, 9101.) Rev. by Laurie Ricou in CanL (121) 143–4.

**7350.** CLEVER, GLENN (ed.). The Charles G. D. Roberts symposium. (Bibl. 1985, 7830.) Rev. by I. S. MacLaren in DalR (67:1) 1987, 109–15.

**7351.** WARE, TRACY. Charles G. D. Roberts's introduction to *Walden*. DalR (67:1) 1987, 99–108.

## Christina Rossetti

**7352.** CASTLE, TONY (ed.). The prayers of Christina Rossetti. London: Marshall Pickering. pp. 32.

**7353.** HARRISON, ANTONY H. Christina Rossetti in context. (Bibl. 1988, 5584, where scholar's forename misspelt.) Rev. by Patrice Caldwell in RMRLL (43:1/2) 101–2.

**7354.** SCHOFIELD, LINDA KATHRYN. Christina Rossetti's poetic identity: a study of secular and religious modes. Unpub. doct. diss., Univ. of Toronto. [Abstr. in DA (50) 1669A.]

**7355.** SMULDERS, SHARON G. M. Christina Rossetti: response and responsibility. Unpub. doct. diss., Univ. of Sussex, 1987. [Abstr. in DA (49) 3736–7A.]

**7356.** TAKACS, K. LINNEA. Amatory strains: erotic love in the poetry of Emily Dickinson and Christina Rossetti. *See* **6707.**

## Dante Gabriel Rossetti

**7357.** ANDERSON, AMANDA S. D. G. Rossetti's *Jenny*: agency, inter-subjectivity, and the prostitute. Genders (4) 103–21.

**7358.** DEMOOR, MARYSA. The whisper of John Donne in Dante Gabriel Rossetti's *The Stream's Secret*. *See* **4396.**

**7359.** RICHARDSON, JAMES. Vanishing lives: style and self in Tennyson, D. G. Rossetti, Swinburne and Yeats. Charlottesville: Virginia UP. pp. x, 240.

**7360.** SLAYTON, WILLIAM TAFT, JR. Dante Gabriel Rossetti's narratives. Unpub. doct. diss., Duke Univ., 1987. [Abstr. in DA (49) 2235A.]

## Josiah Royce

**7361.** HINE, ROBERT. The American West as metaphysics: a perspective on Josiah Royce. PacHR (58:3) 267–91.

**7362.** MICHAELS, WALTER BENN. Frank Norris, Josiah Royce and the ontology of corporations. *In* (pp. 122–51) **1.**

## John Ruskin

**7363.** ALI, K. I. The reception of the third volume of Ruskin's *Modern Painters*. Explorations (12:1/2) 1988/89, 47–64.

**7364.** BIRCH, DINAH. Ruskin's myths. (Bibl. 1988, 5596.) Rev. by E. D. Mackerness in NQ (36:4) 530–1.

**7365.** —— 'The sun is god': Ruskin's solar mythology. *In* (pp. 109–23) **59.**

**7366.** BRADLEY, JOHN LEWIS; OUSBY, IAN (eds). The correspondence of John Ruskin and Charles Eliot Norton. New York: CUP, 1987. (Bibl. 1987, 8293.) Rev. by Malcolm Hardman in MLR (84:2) 446–7; by J. B. Bullen in RES (39:156) 1988, 574–6.

**7367.** ———— 'My first real tutor': John Ruskin and Charles Eliot Norton. NEQ (62:4) 572–86.

**7368.** DEARDEN, JAMES. John Ruskin's *Poems*, 1850. BC (38:1) 114–16.

**7369.** FONTANEY, PIERRE. Ordre et désordre selon Ruskin: le grotesque. CVE (28) 1988, 7–16.

**7370.** MILLER, J. HILLIS. Prosopopoeia and *Praeterita*. *In* (pp. 125–39) **44**.

**7371.** READ, RICHARD. 'A name that makes it looked after': Turner, Ruskin and the visual–verbal sublime. Word & Image (5:4) 315–29.

**7372.** SMITH, L. The enigma of visibility: theories of visual perception in the early poetry of William Morris and in the work of Ruskin and the pre-Raphaelites. *See* **5997**.

**7373.** WALSH, SUSAN ANN. Ruskin's 'many-towered city': fragmentation and unity in the later works. Unpub. doct. diss., Duke Univ., 1988. [Abstr. in DA (49) 2235–6A.]

**7374.** WIHL, GARY. Ruskin and the rhetoric of infallibility. (Bibl. 1987, 8308.) Rev. by Phillip Mallett in YES (19) 345–6.

### Olive Schreiner

**7375.** CLAYTON, CHERRY. Olive Schreiner and Katherine Mansfield: artistic transformations of the outcast figure by two colonial writers. ESA (32:2) 109–19.

**7376.** GORDON, MARCIA MACKE. Absence and presence in *Wuthering Heights* and *The Story of an African Farm*: charting the feminine in language. *See* **6330**.

**7377.** HOLLOWAY, MYLES. Thematic and structural organization in Olive Schreiner's *The Story of an African Farm*. EngA (16:2) 77–89.

**7378.** MARTIN, C. E. Outspoken dreams: selfhood, sex and spirituality in the writings of Olive Schreiner. Unpub. M.Litt. thesis, Univ. of Durham, 1987. [Abstr. in IT (36:4) 1393.]

**7379.** VISEL, ROBIN ELLEN. White Eve in the 'petrified garden': the colonial African heroine in the writing of Olive Schreiner, Isak Dinesen, Doris Lessing and Nadine Gordimer. Unpub. doct. diss., Univ. of British Columbia, 1988. [Abstr. in DA (49) 3721A.]

### Sir Walter Scott

**7380.** BROWN, IAIN GORDON (ed.). Scott's interleaved Waverley novels (the 'Magnum Opus': National Library of Scotland MSS 23001–41): an introduction and commentary. (Bibl. 1987, 139.) Rev. by David Hewitt in AUR (53) 48–51.

**7381.** CAMPBELL, JAMES (introd.). Guy Mannering; or, The astrologer: a novel. London: Soho, 1987. pp. x, 447.

**7382.** GILBERT, G. L. Criticism of the Waverley novels over the period 1932–1982. Unpub. doct. diss., Univ. of Oxford. [Abstr. in IT (39:4) 1638.]

**7383.** GROVES, DAVID. De Quincey and Scott. *See* **6583**.

**7384.** KERR, JAMES. Fiction against history: Scott as storyteller. Cambridge: CUP. pp. ix, 142.

**7385.** LAMONT, CLAIRE. Meg the gipsy in Scott and Keats. *See* **7146**.

**7386.** MacQueen, John. The Enlightenment and Scottish literature: vol. 2, The rise of the historical novel. *See* **6449.**

**7387.** Mitchell, Jerome. Scott, Chaucer, and medieval romance: a study in Sir Walter Scott's indebtedness to the literature of the Middle Ages. *See* **2856.**

**7388.** —— Scott and Malory. *In* (pp. 211–26) **38.**

**7389.** Nayak, J. K. Scott in our time: aspects of Waverley criticism, 1932–82. Unpub. M.Litt. diss., Univ of Oxford, 1988. [Abstr. in IT (39:2) 487.]

**7390.** Orr, Marilyn. Voices and text: Scott the storyteller, Scott the novelist. SLJ (16:2) 41–59.

**7391.** Pavel, Dan Sergiu. Natura ironiei la Walter Scott și Mihail Sadoveanu (The nature of irony in Walter Scott and Mihail Sadoveanu.) Steaua (40:3) 44–5.

**7392.** Phillips, Mark. Macaulay, Scott, and the literary challenge to historiography. *See* **7198.**

**7393.** Rigney, Ann. Adapting history to the novel. NC (8) 127–43.

**7394.** Robertson, F.. The function of gothic elements in relation to Walter Scott's narrative technique. Unpub. doct. diss., Univ. of Oxford, 1988. [Abstr. in IT (39:2) 487.]

**7395.** Robertson, J. F. The construction and expression of Scottish patriotism in the works of Walter Scott. Unpub. doct. diss., Univ. of Edinburgh. [Abstr. in IT (39:4) 1631.]

**7396.** Ruddick, Bill. Scott on the drama: a series of ascriptions. ScottN (14) 2–6.

**7397.** Schöwerling, Rainer. Sir Walter Scott and the tradition of the historical novel before 1814 – with a checklist. *In* (pp. 227–62) **38.**

**7398.** Sultana, Donald. The journey of Sir Walter Scott to Malta. (Bibl. 1988, 5629.) Rev. by J. H. Alexander in YES (19) 331–2.

**7399.** Tait, Margaret. The Mysore War novels. ScottN (15) 7–9.

**7400.** —— *Young Lochinvar.* ScottN (14) 13.

**7401.** Walker, Alistair D. The tentative Romantic: an aspect of *The Heart of Midlothian.* EngS (69:2) 1988, 146–57.

**7402.** Wallace, Tara Ghoshal. Walter Scott and feminine discourse: the case of *St Ronan's Well.* JNT (19:2) 233–47.

### 'Charles Sealsfield' (Karl Postl)

**7403.** Schnitzler, Günter. Erfahrung und Bild: die dichterische Wirklichkeit des Charles Sealsfield (Karl Postl). (Bibl. 1988, 5636.) Rev. by Walter Grünzweig in AAA (14:2) 198–9.

### Canon Sheehan (Patrick Augustine Sheehan)

**7404.** Brown, Terence. Canon Sheehan and the Catholic intellectual. *In* (pp. 7–17) **37.**

### Mary Shelley

**7405.** Alexander, Meena. Women in Romanticism: Mary Wollstonecraft, Dorothy Wordsworth and Mary Shelley. *See* **5581.**

**7406.** Bennett, Betty T. (ed.). The letters of Mary Wollstonecraft Shelley: vol. 3, 'What years I have spent!'. (Bibl. 1988, 5638.) Rev. by David Womersley in NQ (36:4) 523–4.

**7407.** CLEMIT, P.   The intellectual novel in the Romantic period: William Godwin and his school. *See* **5271.**

**7408.** COOK, A. E. M.   Mary Shelley's exploration of creativity and the responsibilities of the poet. Unpub. M.Phil. diss., Univ. of Leeds. [Abstr. in IT (39:3) 1110.]

**7409.** COUCHMAN, B. J.   Cassandra (un)bound: an examination of the fiction of Mary Shelley. Unpub. M.Phil. diss., Univ. of York. [Abstr. in IT (38:4) 1458–9.]

**7410.** FELDMAN, PAULA R.; SCOTT-KILVERT, DIANA (eds).   The journals of Mary Shelley, 1814–1844. (Bibl. 1988, 5641.) Rev. by Angela Leighton in RES (39:156) 1988, 566–7.

**7411.** KLEIN, ROXANNE VERONICA.   Reading and writing the place of difference: Mary Wollstonecraft, Mary Shelley and women's discourse in late eighteenth- and early nineteenth-century Britain. *See* **5585.**

**7412.** LECERCLE, JEAN-JACQUES.   Frankenstein: mythe et philosophie. Paris: Presses Universitaires de France, 1988. pp. 125.

**7413.** MELLOR, ANNE K.   Mary Shelley: her life, her fiction, her monsters. (Bibl. 1988, 5645.) Rev. by Ann Owens Weekes in RMRLL (43:1/2) 107–9; by Lucy Newlyn in TLS, 17 Feb., 171.

**7414.** MICHIE, ELSIE B.   Production replaces creation: market forces and *Frankenstein* as critique of Romanticism. NCC (12:1) 1988, 27–33.

**7415.** MISHRA, V. C.   The gothic sublime: theory, practice and interpretation. *See* **4942.**

**7416.** O'ROURKE, JAMES.   'Nothing more unnatural': Mary Shelley's revision of Rousseau. ELH (56:3) 543–69.

**7417.** PING, TANG SOO.   *Frankenstein, Paradise Lost*, and 'the majesty of goodness'. *See* **4731.**

**7418.** POWER, HENRIETTE LAZARIDIS.   The text as trap: the problem of difference in Mary Shelley's *Frankenstein*. NCC (12:1) 1988, 85–103.

**7419.** ST CLAIR, WILLIAM.   The Godwins and the Shelleys: the biography of a family. *See* **5278.**

**7420.** SOFOULIS (SOFIA), ZOË.   Through the *lumen: Frankenstein* and the optics of re-origination. Unpub. doct. diss., Univ. of California, Santa Cruz, 1988. [Abstr. in DA (49) 3755A.]

**7421.** SUNSTEIN, EMILY W.   Mary Shelley: romance and reality. Boston, MA: Little, Brown. pp. xi, 478. Rev. by Nancy W. Ellenberger in BkW, 19 Feb., 6; by Carolyn Heilbrun in NYTB, 12 Feb., 14.

**7422.** VEEDER, WILLIAM.   Mary Shelley and Frankenstein: the fate of androgyny. (Bibl. 1986, 9201.) Rev. by Anne F. Janowitz in MLR (84:4) 938–9; by Janice Witherspoon Neuleib in ChrisL (39:1) 98–9; by Molly Smith in SoHR (22:1) 1988, 78–9; by Angela Leighton in KSR (2) 1987, 150–4; by Chris Baldick in TLS, 1 May 1987, 471; by David Ketterer in SFS (14:2) 1987, 267–70.

### Percy Bysshe Shelley

**7423.** ADAMSON, C. A.   Materials towards an edition of MS Shelley Adds.e.8. *See* **279.**

**7424.** BAKER, JOHN JAY.   Myth, subjectivity, and the problem of historical time in Shelley's *Lines Written among the Euganean Hills*. ELH (56:1) 149–72.

**7425.** BROOKS, HAROLD F.   Shaw and Shelley. NQ (36:2) 196.

**7426.** BUTLER, MARILYN.   Romantic manichaeism: Shelley's *On the Devil, and Devils* and Byron's mythological dramas. *In* (pp. 13–37) **59.**

**7427.** CLARK, TIMOTHY.   Embodying revolution: the figure of the poet in Shelley. Oxford: Clarendon Press. pp. x, 300. (Oxford English monographs.)

**7428.** D'IAKONOVA, N. IA.   Poeticheskie avtoportrety Shelli. (A poetic self-portrait of Shelley.) NDFN (1989:1) 19–23.

**7429.** DOD, ELMAR.   Die Vernünftigkeit der Imagination in Aufklärung und Romantik: eine komparatistische Studie zu Schillers und Shelleys ästhetischen Theorien in ihrem europäischen Kontext. (Bibl. 1988, 5653.) Rev. by Ralf Simon in arcadia (24:1) 95–8.

**7430.** DUERKSEN, ROLAND A.   Shelley's poetry of involvement. Basingstoke: Macmillan, 1988. pp. ix, 140. (Macmillan studies in Romanticism.)

**7431.** ENGELBERG, KARSTEN KLEJS.   The making of the Shelley myth: an annotated bibliography of criticism of Percy Bysshe Shelley, 1822–1860. (Bibl. 1988, 5655.) Rev. by Elizabeth James in BC (38:1) 124.

**7432.** HAINES, S.   A critical study of the poetry and prose of Percy Bysshe Shelley illustrating the limiting effect of his ideas on his imagination. Unpub. doct. diss., Univ. of Oxford. [Abstr. in IT (39:3) 1111.]

**7433.** HOGLE, JERROLD E.   Shelley's process: radical transference and the development of his major works. New York; Oxford: OUP, 1988. pp. xvi, 416.

**7434.** JONES, LILLA MARIA CRISAFULLI.   Shelley's Utopia from *Queen Mab* to *Prometheus Unbound*: a journey towards silence. *In* (pp. 103–22) CARMELINA IMBROSCIO (ed.), Requiem pour l'utopie? Tendances autodestructives du paradigme utopique. Introd. by RAYMOND TROUSSON. Pisa: Goliardica, 1986. pp. 222. (Histoire et critiques des idées, 6.) Rev. by Abigail E. Lee in MLR (84:4) 902–4.

**7435.** JONES, STEVEN EDWARD.   Satire in Shelley's poetry. Unpub. doct. diss., Columbia Univ., 1988. [Abstr. in DA (49) 3034A.]

**7436.** KEACH, WILLIAM.   Shelley's style. (Bibl. 1987, 8374.) Rev. by Robert C. Casto in RES (38:149) 1987, 93–4.

**7437.** KUCICH, GREG.   The Spenserian psychodrama of *Prometheus Unbound*. *See* **3387.**

**7438.** LEIGHTON, ANGELA.   Shelley and the sublime: an interpretation of the major poems. (Bibl. 1988, 5662.) Rev. by V. A. De Luca in UTQ (56:4) 1987, 582–3.

**7439.** MAXWELL, CATHERINE.   Shelley's *Medusa*: the sixth stanza. NQ (36:2) 173–4.

**7440.** MURPHY, JOHN FRANCIS.   'Woven hymns' of lyric and narrative: plotting nature in Coleridge and Shelley. *See* **6516.**

**7441.** NABLOW, RALPH A.    Shelley, *Ozymandias*, and Volney's *Les Ruines*. NQ (36:2) 172–3.

**7442.** O'NEILL, MICHAEL.    The human mind's imaginings: conflict and achievement in Shelley's poetry. Oxford: Clarendon Press; New York: OUP. pp. xii, 216.

**7443.** —— A more hazardous exercise: Shelley's revolutionary imaginings. YES (19) 256–64.

**7444.** PERUGI, MAURIZIO.    Pascoli, Shelley, and Isabella Anderton, 'Gentle Rotskettow'. MLR (84:1) 51–65.

**7445.** PIRIE, DAVID B.    Shelley. Milton Keynes: Open UP, 1988. pp. 121. (Open guides to literature.)

**7446.** ST CLAIR, WILLIAM.    The Godwins and the Shelleys: the biography of a family. *See* **5278.**

**7447.** SÁNCHEZ CALVO, ARSENIO.    La naturaleza en *Alastor, Childe Harold*, y *Endymion*. *See* **6420.**

**7448.** SHELLEY, BRYAN.    The interpreting angel in *The Triumph of Life*. RES (39:155) 1988, 386–99.

**7449.** SIMPSON, M.    Closet reading and political writing in the dramas of Byron and Shelley. *See* **6423.**

**7450.** SPENCE, GORDON.    Ahasuerus on the one: Shelley, Plato, and Parmenides. AUMLA (72) 261–74.

**7451.** SULTANA, FEHMIDA.    Romantic Orientalism and Islam: Southey, Shelley, Moore, and Byron. *See* **6428.**

**7452.** TOKOO, TATSUO (ed.).    Percy Bysshe Shelley: vol. 8, Bodleian MS Shelley d.3: a facsimile edition with full transcription and textual notes. *See* **183.**

**7453.** WHEELER, KATHLEEN M.    Kant and Romanticism. *See* **5738.**

**7454.** YOST, GEORGE.    Pieracci and Shelley: an Italian 'Ur-*Cenci*'. Potomac, MD: Scripta Humanistica, 1986. pp. x, 141. (Scripta humanistica, 19.) Rev. by Jeremy Tambling in MLR (84:4) 937–8.

### W. W. Skeat

**7455.** SHERBO, ARTHUR.    Walter William Skeat (1835–1912) in the *Cambridge Review*. YLS (3) 109–30.

### Felicia Skene

**7456.** FRYCKSTEDT, MONICA CORREA.    *Hidden Depths*: a new perspective on Victorian fiction. EngS (70:2) 107–14.

### Sydney Smith

**7457.** ARNOLD, DENIS V.    Sydney Smith. N.P.: D. Arnold, 1988. pp. 16.

### Robert Southey

**7458.** BECKWITH, R. T. (ed.).    Poems, hymns, and prose writings by Henry Kirke White (1785–1806) of Nottingham and Cambridge; with the account of his life by Robert Southey. (Bibl. 1985, 8016.) Rev. by Anne Elliott in RES (38:149) 1987, 92–3.

**7459.** BUTLER, MARILYN.    Repossessing the past: the case for an open literary history. *In* (pp. 64–84) **53.**

**7460.** PAULIN, TOM.    English political writers on Ireland: Robert Southey to Douglas Hurd. *In* (pp. 132–45) **17.**

**7461.** RAIMOND, JEAN. Southey's early writings and the Revolution. YES (19) 181–96.

**7462.** SULTANA, FEHMIDA. Romantic Orientalism and Islam: Southey, Shelley, Moore, and Byron. *See* **6428.**

### Catherine Helen Spence

**7463.** ALBINSKI, NAN BOWMAN. *Handfasted*: an Australian feminist's American utopia. JPC (23:2) 15–31.

**7464.** THOMSON, HELEN (ed.). Catherine Helen Spence. St Lucia; London: Queensland UP. pp. xxxvi, 578. (Portable Australian authors.)

### Sir Leslie Stephen

**7465.** ANNAN, NOEL. Leslie Stephen: the godless Victorian. Chicago: Chicago UP, 1986. (Bibl. 1985, 8019.) Rev. by Panthea Reid Broughton in Review (9) 1987, 265–75.

### Robert Louis Stevenson

**7466.** BALDERSTON, DANIEL. The mark of the knife: scars as signs in Borges. MLR (83:1) 1988, 67–75.

**7467.** GELDER, KENNETH (ed.). The Scottish stories and essays. Edinburgh: Edinburgh UP. pp. 311.

**7468.** VEEDER, WILLIAM; HIRSCH, GORDON (eds). *Dr Jekyll and Mr Hyde* after one hundred years. Chicago; London: Chicago UP, 1988. pp. xx, 312.

### Charles Warren Stoddard

**7469.** AUSTEN, ROGER (introd.). For the pleasure of his company. San Francisco, CA: Gay Sunshine Press, 1987. pp. 188. Rev. by Thomas Yingling in ALR (21:3) 91–3.

### Elizabeth Drew Barstow Stoddard

**7470.** CROCE, ANN JEROME. Phantoms from an ancient loom: Elizabeth Barstow Stoddard and the American novel, 1860–1900. Unpub. doct. diss., Brown Univ., 1988. [Abstr. in DA (49) 2701A.]

### Bram Stoker

**7471.** JANN, ROSEMARY. Saved by science? The mixed messages of Stoker's *Dracula*. TSLL (31:2) 273–87.

**7472.** LEATHERDALE, CLIVE. Dracula, the novel and the legend: a study of Bram Stoker's gothic masterpiece. (Bibl. 1985, 8033.) Rev. by Jacques Finné in EA (42:4) 483–5.

**7473.** —— (ed.). The origins of Dracula: the background to Bram Stoker's gothic masterpiece. (Bibl. 1987, 8413.) Rev. by Jacques Finné in EA (42:4) 485–6.

**7474.** NOLDEN, THOMAS. Der Décadent und sein Arzt. Bemerkungen zur europäischen Literatur der Jahrhundertwende. arcadia (24:2) 157–88.

**7475.** POZZUOLI, ALAIN. Bram Stoker, princes des ténèbres. Paris: Librairie Séguier. pp. 173.

**7476.** STOTT, R. The kiss of death: a demystification of the late-nineteenth-century 'femme fatale' in the selected works of Bram Stoker, Rider Haggard, Joseph Conrad and Thomas Hardy. *See* **6868.**

### Elizabeth Stone

**7477.** WHEELER, MICHAEL. Two tales of Manchester life. *See* **6850.**

### Harriet Beecher Stowe
**7478.** BERGHORN, DONNA E. 'The mother's struggle': Harriet Beecher Stowe and the American antislavery debate. Unpub. doct. diss., Rensselaer Polytechnic Inst., 1988. [Abstr. in DA (49) 3199A.]

**7479.** BOYDSTON, JEANNE; KELLEY, MARY; MARGOLIS, ANNE. The limits of sisterhood: the Beecher sisters on women's rights and woman's sphere. Chapel Hill; London: North Carolina UP, 1988. pp. xxiv, 369. (Gender and American culture.) Rev. by Amy Dru Stanley in CWH (35:4) 349–50.

**7480.** HOVET, THEODORE R. The master narrative: Harriet Beecher Stowe's subversive story of master and slave in *Uncle Tom's Cabin* and *Dred*. Lanham, MD; London: UP of America. pp. x, 111. Rev. by Elizabeth Ammons in SAF (17:2) 254–5.

**7481.** ROMERO, LORA PATRICIA. The government of the body: health reform and the American antebellum novel. *See* **6551.**

**7482.** SARSON, STEVEN. Harriet Beecher Stowe and American slavery. NC (7) 33–45.

### Ruth McEnery Stuart
**7483.** TAYLOR, HELEN. Gender, race, and region in the writings of Grace King, Ruth McEnery Stuart, and Kate Chopin. *See* **6474.**

### Algernon Charles Swinburne
**7484.** HARRISON, ANTONY H. Swinburne's medievalism: a study in Victorian love poetry. Baton Rouge; London: Louisiana State UP, 1988. pp. xi, 205. Rev. by Rikky Rooksby in NQ (36:2) 253–4.

**7485.** LAVABRE, SIMONE. Swinburne et la beauté. *In* (pp. 125–30) **10.**

**7486.** MONNEYRON, FRÉDÉRIC. L'androgyne dans *Lesbia Brandon* de Swinburne. CVE (29) 55–65.

**7487.** MORGAN, THAÏS E. The sun of faith, the shadow of doubt: language and knowledge in Swinburne's myth of Apollo. *In* (pp. 125–58) **59.**

**7488.** RICHARDSON, JAMES. Vanishing lives: style and self in Tennyson, D. G. Rossetti, Swinburne and Yeats. *See* **7359.**

### Arthur Symons
**7489.** BECKSON, KARL. Arthur Symons: a life. (Bibl. 1988, 5696.) Rev. by Francis Austin in EngS (70:1) 95–6; by John Stokes in MLR (84:2) 450–1; by Jacqueline Genet in EA (42:2) 223–4.

**7490.** —— MUNRO, JOHN M. (eds). Arthur Symons: selected letters, 1880–1935. Basingstoke: Macmillan; Iowa City: Iowa UP. pp. xx, 289. Rev. by John Stokes in TLS, 16 June, 668; by Michael Dirda in BkW, 18 June, 3, 10.

**7491.** RIX, WALTER. James Joyce's *The Dead*: the symbolist inspiration and its narrative reflection. *In* (pp. 146–65) **17.**

### Bayard Taylor
**7492.** GRANQVIST, RAOUL. Us and them: distancing practices of the colonialist travelogue. *In* (pp. 69–86) **34.**

### Alfred, Lord Tennyson
**7493.** ARMSTRONG, ISOBEL. Tennyson's *The Lady of Shalott*: Victorian mythography and the politics of narcissism. *In* (pp. 49–107) **59.**

**7494.** BARCUS, JAMES E.   The successful failure of ordering structures in Tennyson's *Idylls of the King. In* (pp. 131–44) **18.**

**7495.** BEASLEY, VIOLET E.   A centred, glory-circled memory: memory in Tennyson's early poems. TRB (5:2) 121–9.

**7496.** BELCHER, MARGARET.   A forgotten poem by Tennyson? TRB (5:2) 1988, 64–7. (Final version of bibl. 1986, 9303.)

**7497.** BOYD, DAVID L.   Tennyson's Camelot revisited: an Augustinian approach to the *Idylls. In* (pp. 163–74) **8.**

**7498.** CAMPBELL, M.   Summary of Tennyson's *Will*. Unpub. doct. diss., Univ. of Cambridge. [Abstr. in IT (39:2) 486.]

**7499.** DILLON, STEVEN C.   Tragic idyll: studies in the poetics of Virgil, Milton, and Tennyson. *See* **4681.**

**7500.** DINGLEY, R. J.   Tennyson, Woolner, and Sir Henry Parkes. TRB (5:2) 1988, 55–9.

**7501.** HARRIS, DANIEL A.   Tennyson and personification: the rhetoric of *Tithonus*. (Bibl. 1988, 5703.) Rev. by Dinah Birch in RES (39:153) 1988, 135–6.

**7502.** HAWES, DONALD.   Thackeray, Tennyson, and Bulwer Lytton. *See* **6392.**

**7503.** HUGHES, LINDA K.   The many-facèd glass: Tennyson's dramatic monologues. (Bibl. 1988, 5706.) Rev. by Arthur Pollard in TRB (5:2) 1988, 76.

**7504.** HUNEYCUTT, KEITH LEE.   Tennyson's *The Princess*: an experiment in narrative structure and genre. Unpub. doct. diss., Univ. of North Carolina at Chapel Hill, 1988. [Abstr. in DA (50) 690A.]

**7505.** JORDAN, ELAINE.   Alfred Tennyson. Cambridge: CUP, 1988. pp. xvi, 191. (British and Irish authors.) Rev. by Rikky Rooksby in Eng (38) 83–7; by Leonée Ormond in TRB (5:3) 147–8.

**7506.** JOSEPH, GERHARD.   Poetic and photographic frames: Tennyson and Julia Margaret Cameron. TRB (5:2) 1988, 43–8.

**7507.** KENNEDY, JUDITH.   Tennyson, the Lushingtons, and Franklin's poem in Fichte. *See* **7197.**

**7508.** KHEIRI, OBEID.   Melancholic thoughts, pathetic fallacy and water images in Tennyson's nature poetry. Explorations (12:1/2) 1988/89, 25–38.

**7509.** LANG, CECIL Y.; SHANNON, EDGAR F., JR (eds).   The letters of Alfred Lord Tennyson: vol. 2, 1851–1870. (Bibl. 1988, 5707.) Rev. by Clyde de L. Ryals in MLR (84:2) 445–6.

**7510.** O'DONNELL, ANGELA G.   Tennyson's *English Idyls*: studies in poetic decorum. SP (85:1) 1988, 125–44.

**7511.** OWER, JOHN.   The story of an affinity: Lampman's *The Frogs* and Tennyson's *The Lotos-Eaters*. *See* **7177.**

**7512.** PEARCE, LYNNE.   Tennyson: a select bibliography for 1988. TRB (5:3) 153–9.

**7513.** PELTASON, TIMOTHY.   Reading *In Memoriam*. (Bibl. 1988, 5708.) Rev. by Marion Shaw in RES (38:151) 1987, 401–2.

**7514.** REGAN, STEPHEN.   Tennyson: a select bibliography for 1987. TRB (5:2) 1988, 78–82.

**7515.** RICHARDSON, JAMES.   Vanishing lives: style and self in Tennyson, D. G. Rossetti, Swinburne and Yeats. *See* **7359.**

**7516.** RICKS, CHRISTOPHER (ed.).   Tennyson: a selected edition. Harlow: Longman. pp. xxxi, 1032. (Longman annotated English poets.) Rev. by Marion Shaw in TRB (5:3) 149–50.

**7517.** —— DAY, AIDAN (eds).   Tennyson: the manuscripts and proofs at the Tennyson Research Centre: Lincoln M1–M37, N12, P7–P38. *See* **163.**

**7318.** —— —— Tennyson: the manuscripts and proofs at the Tennyson Research Centre: Lincoln P85++–P109. *See* **164.**

**7519.** —— —— Tennyson: the manuscripts and proofs at the Tennyson Research Centre: Lincoln P109–P179. *See* **165.**

**7520.** —— —— Tennyson: the manuscripts and proofs at the Tennyson Research Centre: Lincoln P179–P194. *See* **166.**

**7521.** —— —— Tennyson: the manuscripts and proofs at the Tennyson Research Centre: Lincoln P194–P205. *See* **167.**

**7522.** —— —— Tennyson: the manuscripts and proofs at the Tennyson Research Centre: Lincoln P205–P210++. *See* **168.**

**7523.** —— —— Tennyson: the manuscripts and proofs at the Tennyson Research Centre: Lincoln P213–P216. *See* **169.**

**7524.** —— —— Tennyson: the manuscripts and proofs at the Tennyson Research Centre: Lincoln P217 and miscellaneous poems. *See* **170.**

**7525.** —— —— Tennyson; the manuscripts at Trinity College Cambridge: loose papers, *In Memoriam* (notebook 13) and notebooks 14–17. *See* **171.**

**7526.** —— —— Tennyson: the manuscripts at Trinity College Cambridge: notebooks 18–25. *See* **172.**

**7527.** —— —— Tennyson: the manuscripts at Trinity College Cambridge: notebooks 26–29. *See* **173.**

**7528.** —— —— Tennyson: the manuscripts at Trinity College Cambridge: notebooks 30–36. *See* **174.**

**7529.** —— —— Tennyson: the manuscripts from Trinity College Cambridge: notebooks 37–40 and loose papers O.15.42, O.15.42(A), Add. MS a.187(16) and R.7.50. *See* **175.**

**7530.** RYALS, CLYDE DE L.   *Idylls of the King*: 'margins scribbled, crost, and crammed with comment'. TRB (5:3) 101–8.

**7531.** RYAN, ROBERT M.   The genealogy of honest doubt: F. D. Maurice and *In Memoriam*. *In* (pp. 120–30) **18.**

**7532.** SHATTO, SUSAN (ed.).   Tennyson's *Maud*: a definitive edition. (Bibl. 1988, 5715.) Rev. by Alastair W. Thomson in RES (38:152) 1987, 577–8.

**7533.** SHAW, MARION.   Alfred Lord Tennyson. Hemel Hempstead: Harvester Wheatsheaf, 1988. pp. xv, 173. (Feminist readings.) Rev. by Leonée Ormond in TRB (5:3) 146–7.

**7534.** SHAW, W. DAVID.   Incomprehensible certainties and interesting uncertainties: Hopkins and Tennyson. *See* **7028.**

**7535.** SIMPSON, JAMES ROGER.   The Arthurian revival and Tennyson,

1800–1849. Unpub. doct. diss., Univ. of East Anglia, 1987. [Abstr. in DA (49) 3036–7A.]

**7536.** SIMPSON, ROGER. A letter from James Knowles: Tennyson on Frederick Maurice and James Martineau. TRB (5:2) 1988, 60–3.

**7537.** SINFIELD, ALAN. Alfred Tennyson. (Bibl. 1988, 5717.) Rev. by Marion Shaw in RES (38:151) 1987, 402–3; by Michael Ackland in AUMLA (72) 348–50.

**7538.** STURMAN, CHRISTOPHER. Arthur Eden and Harrington Hall. TRB (5:2) 130–43.

**7539.** SYLVIA, RICHARD. 'The genuine poet of our time': Emerson's views on Tennyson. See **6820.**

**7540.** THOMSON, ALASTAIR W. The poetry of Tennyson. New York: Routledge & Kegan Paul, 1986. (Bibl. 1986, 9330.) Rev. by Arthur Pollard in TRB (5:2) 1988, 76–7; by Dinah Birch in RES (39:153) 1988, 135.

**7541.** TILLOTSON, KATHLEEN. Palgrave's *Golden Treasury* and Tennyson: another source. See **2110.**

**7542.** TUCKER, HERBERT F. Tennyson and the doom of Romanticism. (Bibl. 1988, 5718.) Rev. by Dale K. Boyer in RMRLL (43:4) 267–8; by Linda H. Peterson in ELN (27:2) 73–5; by Danny Karlin in LRB (11:16) 19–21; by Lee Erickson in MP (87:2) 195–8.

**7543.** ULLMANN, S. O. A. Arnold on Tennyson. See **6113.**

**7544.** WARNER, JANET. Emily Carr's Tennyson. CanL (113/14) 1987, 114–26.

**7545.** WILSON, WILLIAM A. Victorian philology and the anxiety of language in Tennyson's *In Memoriam*. TSLL (30:1) 1988, 28–48.

### William Makepeace Thackeray

**7546.** ALTICK, RICHARD D. Writing the life of J. J. Ridley. *In* (pp. 26–58) **44.**

**7547.** BARRETT, ELIZABETH MARY. Competence, control, and critical practice in three Victorian novels. See **6591.**

**7548.** GENIEVA, E. ÎU. Uil'îam Meĭkpis Tekkereĭ: tvorchestvo, vospominaniîa, bibliograficheskie razyskaniîa. (William Makepeace Thackeray: works, reminiscences, bibliographical research.) Moscow: Knizhnaîa palata. pp. 487.

**7549.** HARDEN, EDGAR F. Thackeray's *English Humourists* and *Four Georges*. (Bibl. 1987, 8481, where title misspelt.) Rev. by Gerald C. Sorensen in RES (38:150) 1987, 264–5.

**7550.** HAWES, DONALD. Thackeray, Tennyson, and Bulwer Lytton. See **6392.**

**7551.** KENNEDY, VICTOR ROBERT. Thackeray's visual imagination. Unpub. doct. diss., Univ. of Toronto, 1988. [Abstr. in DA (50) 147A.]

**7552.** LAW, JOE K. Thackeray and the uses of opera. RES (39:156) 1988, 502–12.

**7553.** LUND, MICHAEL. Reading Thackeray. Detroit, MI: Wayne State UP. pp. 173. Rev. by S. S. Prawer in TLS, 12 May, 521.

**7554.** PETERS, CATHERINE. Thackeray's universe: shifting worlds of imagination and reality. (Bibl. 1988, 5721.) Rev. by Robert A. Colby in MP (86:4) 441–2; by Karen Scherzinger in UES (27:2) 30–2.

**7555.** RADER, RALPH W. The comparative anatomy of three baggy monsters: *Bleak House, Vanity Fair, Middlemarch. See* **6653.**

**7556.** SORENSEN, GAIL D. Thackeray's *The Rose and the Ring*: a novelist's fairy tale. Mythlore (15:3) 37–8, 43.

**7557.** TOTEV, PLAMEN. Takări i negovata očarovatelna geroinja. (Thackeray and his charming heroine.) RodR (33:2) 48–51.

**7558.** TYSON, NANCY JANE. Thackeray and Bulwer: between the lines in *Barry Lyndon. See* **6393.**

**7559.** VÉGA-RITTER, MAX. Dickens et Thackeray, essai d'analyse psychocritique: dès *Pickwick Papers* à *David Copperfield* et de *Barry Lyndon* à *Henry Esmond. See* **6675.**

### Francis Thompson

**7560.** BOARDMAN, BRIGID M. Between heaven and Charing Cross: the life of Francis Thompson. (Bibl. 1988, 5724.) Rev. by Charmazel Dudt in ChrisL (39:1) 103–4; by Julian North in NQ (36:4) 531–2.

**7561.** DANCHIN, PIERRE. Coventry Patmore and Francis Thompson: the story of a brief friendship (1894–1896.) *In* (pp. 27–37) **42.**

### Henry David Thoreau

**7562.** ADAMS, STEPHEN; ROSS, DONALD, JR. Revising mythologies: the composition of Thoreau's major works. Charlottesville: Virginia UP, 1988. pp. xii, 271. Rev. by Robert Sattelmeyer in AL (61:4) 689–91.

**7563.** BUELL, LAWRENCE. The Thoreauvian pilgrimage: the structure of an American cult. AL (61:2) 175–99.

**7564.** BURBICK, JOAN. Thoreau's alternative history: changing perspectives on nature, culture, and language. (Bibl. 1988, 5727.) Rev. by Amy Schrager Lang in AL (61:2) 291–2.

**7565.** GREY, ROBIN SANDRA. The complicity of imagination: seventeenth-century English prose and the ideology of assimilation in Emerson, Thoreau, and Melville. *See* **4249.**

**7566.** HOAGLAND, EDWARD (introd.). The Maine woods. New York; London: Penguin, 1988. pp. xxxiii, 442. (Penguin nature library.)

**7567.** HOCHFIELD, GEORGE. Revaluation: anti-Thoreau. SewR (96:3) 1988, 433–43.

**7568.** HOVDE, CARL F. *The Maine Woods, Cape Cod* and the shape of Thoreau's career. *In* (pp. 87–98) **34.**

**7569.** HOWELL, A. J. *The Scarlet Letter* and *Walden*: two strategies of liberation. *See* **6956.**

**7570.** ITOH, SHOKO. A study of Cape Cod; from wilderness to wasteland. SEL (65:2) 193–207.

**7571.** KRITZBERG, BARRY. Thoreau, slavery, and resistance to civil government. MassR (30:4) 535–65.

**7572.** LJUNGQUIST, KENT. 'Meteor of the war': Melville, Thoreau, and Whitman respond to John Brown. *See* **7233.**

**7573.** NEUFELDT, LEONARD N. Neopragmatism and convention in textual editing, with examples from the editing of Thoreau's autograph journal. *See* **360.**

**7574.** NIIBO, TETSU. Thoreau sono ikikata. (Thoreau's attitude to life.) Tokyo: Hokuju. pp. 198.

**7575.** OKUDA, JOUICHI. Kesshouka suru Thoreau. (Thoreau and crystalization.) Tokyo: Kirihara. pp. xii, 186.

**7576.** POKROVSKIĬ, N. E. Genri Toro. Perevod s russkogo S. SY-ROVATKIN. (Henry Thoreau. Translated into English from Russian.) Moscow: Progress. pp. 242.

**7577.** SATTELMEYER, ROBERT. Thoreau's reading: a study in intellectual history with bibliographical catalogue. Princeton, NJ; Guildford: Princeton UP, 1988. pp. xv, 333. Rev. by Ron Thomas in AL (61:3) 476–7.

**7578.** —— 'When he became my enemy': Emerson and Thoreau, 1848–49. *See* **6817.**

**7579.** WARE, TRACY. Charles G. D. Roberts's introduction to *Walden*. *See* **7351.**

### Catharine Parr Traill

**7580.** PETERMAN, MICHAEL. In search of Agnes Strickland's sisters. *See* **7270.**

### Edward Tregear

**7581.** HOWE, K. R. (ed.). The verse of Edward Tregear. Palmerston North, NZ: Nagare Press. pp. 140.

### Anthony Trollope

**7582.** BELL, A. CRAIG. A guide to Trollope. Braunton, Devonshire: Merlin. pp. 206.

**7583.** DEAL, NANCY BETH. The lady as criminal: Anthony Trollope's adaptation of the Victorian sensation novel. Unpub. doct. diss., Michigan State Univ., 1988. [Abstr. in DA (49) 2666A.]

**7584.** EPPERLY, ELIZABETH R. Anthony Trollope's notes on the old drama. Victoria, B.C.: Univ. of Victoria, 1988. pp. 143. (English literary studies monographs, 42.)

**7585.** HAMER, MARY. Writing by numbers: Trollope's serial fiction. (Bibl. 1987, 8530.) Rev. by Jonathan Freedman in MLR (84:3) 724–5; by Sheila M. Smith in RES (39:156) 1988, 569–70.

**7586.** HANDLEY, GRAHAM. Anthony Trollope: *Barchester Towers*. Harmondsworth: Penguin, 1987. pp. 122. (Penguin masterstudies.)

**7587.** HERBERT, CHRISTOPHER. Trollope and comic pleasure. (Bibl. 1987, 8531.) Rev. by Jonathan Freedman in MLR (84:3) 725–6; by Sheila M. Smith in RES (39:156) 1988, 569–70.

**7588.** HYNES, JOHN G. *The American Senator*: Anthony Trollope's critical 'Chronicle of a Winter at Dillsborough'. EngS (69:1) 1988, 48–54.

**7589.** KUCICH, JOHN K. Transgression in Trollope: dishonesty and the antibourgeois elite. ELH (56:3) 593–618.

**7590.** LINNÉ, CAROL LEE. Trollope's isolates: the price of connection. Unpub. doct. diss., Univ. of Colorado at Boulder, 1988. [Abstr. in DA (49) 3370A.]

**7591.** SUPER, R. H. The chronicler of Barsetshire: a life of Anthony Trollope. Ann Arbor; London: Michigan UP. pp. xvi, 528. Rev. by

Stefan Collini in TLS, 30 June, 712; by John Sutherland in LRB (11:3) 19–22.

**7592.** TERRY, R. C.   A Trollope chronology. Basingstoke: Macmillan. pp. xxxiii, 167. (Macmillan author chronologies.)

**7593.** THOMPSON, JULIAN (ed.).   Cousin Henry. (Bibl. 1987, 8541.) Rev. by Pierre Coustillas in EA (42:4) 481–2.

**7594.** TRACY, ROBERT (ed.).   The Macdermots of Ballycloran. Oxford: OUP. pp. xxxviii, 694. (World's classics.)

**7595.** WALL, STEPHEN.   Trollope and character. (Bibl. 1988, 5751.) Rev. by John Sutherland in LRB (11:3) 19–22; by Patrick Swinden in NQ (36:4) 527–9.

### Frederick Goddard Tuckerman

**7596.** GROVES, JEFFREY D.   A letter from Frederick Goddard Tuckerman to James T. Fields. *See* **6825.**

### 'Mark Twain' (Samuel L. Clemens)

**7597.** ALTSCHULER, MARK.   Motherless child: Huck Finn and a theory of moral development. ALR (22:1) 31–42.

**7598.** BEAVER, HAROLD.   Huckleberry Finn. (Bibl. 1988, 5753.) Rev. by Louis Budd in MLR (84:4) 964–5; by Christine Gerrard in RES (39:156) 1988, 601.

**7599.** BLAIR, WALTER: FISCHER, VICTOR (eds).   Adventures of Huckleberry Finn. (Bibl. 1988, 5756.) Rev. by Harold Beaver in YES (19) 350–1.

**7600.** BRANCH, EDGAR MARQUESS; FRANK, MICHAEL B.; SANDERSON, KENNETH M. (eds).   Mark Twain's letters: vol. 1, 1853–1866. Berkeley; London: California UP, 1988. pp. xlvi, 616. (Mark Twain papers.) Rev. by Alan Gribben in ALR (22:1) 85–5; by Gerald Weales in Smithsonian (20:1) 170–2; by Jeffrey Steinbrink in AL (61:1) 102–4; by Stephen Fender in LRB (11:2) 22–3.

**7601.** BRIDEN, EARL F.   Twainian epistemology and the satiric design of *Tom Sawyer Abroad.* ALR (22:1) 43–52.

**7602.** BRIDGMAN, RICHARD.   Traveling in Mark Twain. (Bibl. 1988, 5758.) Rev. by John S. Whitley in JAStud (23:3) 496–7.

**7603.** BRITTON, WESLEY.   Mark Twain on tape. Mark Twain Circular (1) Aug. 1987, 1–2.

**7604.** BUDD, LOUIS J.   Mark Twain and the West: a selective bibliography. Mark Twain Circular (1) Nov. 1987, 2–4.

**7605.** —— Who's been demeaning whom? *See* **6432.**

**7606.** —— (ed.).   New essays on *Adventures of Huckleberry Finn.* (Bibl. 1988, 5759.) Rev. by Robert Bellflower in RES (39:154) 1988, 333–4; by Harold Beaver in YES (19) 354–5; by James H. Justus in AL (59:1) 1987, 129–32.

**7607.** —— CADY, EDWIN H. (eds).   On Mark Twain: the best from *American Literature.* (Bibl. 1988, 5760.) Rev. by Andrew Hook in NQ (36:2) 271–2; by John S. Whitley in JAStud (23:1) 137–8.

**7608.** BULGER, THOMAS.   Mark Twain's ambivalent utopianism. SAF (17:2) 235–42.

**7609.** CUMMINGS, SHERWOOD.   Mark Twain and science: adventures of a mind. Baton Rouge; London: Louisiana State UP, 1988. pp. xiii, 217. Rev. by Susan K. Harris in AL (61:3) 480–1; by Paul C. Wermuth in NEQ (62:4) 625–6.

**7610.** EVANS, CHARLENE TAYLOR. In defense of *Huckleberry Finn*: anti-racism motifs in *Huckleberry Finn* and a review of racial criticism in Twain's work. Unpub. doct. diss., Rice Univ., 1988. [Abstr. in DA (49) 3025–6A.]

**7611.** GALLIGAN, EDWARD L. Rereading Mark Twain. SewR (96:2) 1988, 265–70 (review-article).

**7612.** GUNN, DREWEY WAYNE. The monomythic structure of *Roughing It*. AL (61:4) 563–85.

**7613.** HOAG, GERALD. The delicate art of geography: the whereabouts of the Phelps plantation in *Huckleberry Finn*. ELN (26:4) 63–6.

**7614.** HOFFMAN, ANDREW JAY. Twain's heroes, Twain's worlds: Mark Twain's *Adventures of Huckleberry Finn*, *A Connecticut Yankee in King Arthur's Court*, and *Pudd'nhead Wilson*. Philadelphia: Pennsylvania UP, 1988. pp. xvii, 210. Rev. by Paul Baender in AL (61:4) 701–2.

**7615.** KAPLAN, JUSTIN. Mr Clemens at home. Art & Antiques (New York) (6:4) 62–7. (Twain's 19-room mansion in Hartford, CT.)

**7616.** KŘEHLÍKOVÁ, EVA. Interpretace povídek Marka Twaina v českých překladech 19. století. (Mark Twain's short stories as interpreted in Czech translations of the nineteenth century.) *In* (pp. 26) **6.**

**7617.** LAWSON, LEWIS. A Connecticut gnostic in King Arthur's court. *In* (pp. 67–76) **2.**

**7618.** LEONARD, JAMES S. More about the Hollywood letters. Mark Twain Circular (1) May 1987, 1.

**7619.** MATHEWSON, STEPHEN. Thomas Hart Benton's centennial, with attention to the Missouri regionalist's illustrations of Mark Twain's books. *See* **96.**

**7620.** MICHAELS, WALTER BENN. An American tragedy, or the promise of American life. *See* **6259.**

**7621.** MICHELSON, BRUCE. Ever such a good time: the structure of Mark Twain's *Roughing It*. *In* (pp. 27–41) **2.**

**7622.** NAGAWARA, MAKOTO. *A True Story* and its manuscript: Mark Twain's image of the American Black. *See* **356.**

**7623.** PECK, RICHARD E. The campaign that . . . succeeded. ALR (21:3) 3–12.

**7624.** ROBINSON, FORREST G. In bad faith: the dynamics of deception in Mark Twain's America. (Bibl. 1987, 8582.) Rev. by James Hurt in MLR (84:3) 730–1; by John S. Whitley in JAStud (23:3) 496–7.

**7625.** SCHARNHORST, GARY. Mark Twain and the Millerites: notes on Millenarianism and *A Connecticut Yankee*. ATQ (3:3) 297–304.

**7626.** SCHIRER, THOMAS E. Mark Twain's theatrical dealings with three English dramatists: Charles Reade, Tom Taylor and Henry J. Byron. *See* **5773.**

**7627.** SCHROETER, JAMES. *Huckleberry Finn*: form and language. *In* (pp. 55–65) **2.**

**7628.** SEWELL, DAVID R. Hank Morgan and the colonization of utopia. ATQ (3:1) 27–44.

**7629.** —— Mark Twain's languages: dialogue and linguistic variety. *See* **1419.**

**7630.** SHILLINGSBURG, MIRIAM JONES. At home abroad: Mark Twain in Australasia. Jackson; London: Mississippi UP, 1988. pp. xiii, 241.

**7631.** SKANDERA, LAURA. Letters from Hollywood. Mark Twain Circular (1) Feb. 1987, 1–3.

**7632.** SUMIDA, STEPHEN H. Re-evaluating Mark Twain's novel of Hawaii. AL (61:4) 586–609.

**7633.** Entry cancelled.

**7634.** SUNDQUIST, ERIC J. Mark Twain and Homer Plessy. Representations (24) 1988, 102–28.

**7635.** TENNEY, THOMAS A. About Mark Twain (an annotated bibliography). Mark Twain Circular (1) Feb. 1987, 5–6; (1) Apr. 1987, 3–4; (1) May 1987, 3–4; (1) June 1987, 5–6; (1) July 1987, 3–4; (1) Aug. 1987, 3–4; (1) Sept. 1987, 3–4; (1) Oct. 1987, 3–4; (1) Nov. 1987, 5–6; (1) Dec. 1987, 5–6, (2) Jan./Feb. 1988, 7–10; (2) Mar./Apr. 1988, 7–10; (2) May/June 1988, 5–8; (2) July/Aug. 1988, 5–8; (2) Sept./Oct. 1988, 5–8; (2) Nov./Dec. 1988, 5–6.

**7636.** TUCKEY, JOHN. Mark Twain's last years. Mark Twain Circular (1) Dec. 1987, 1–3.

**7637.** TURNER, BARNARD EDWARD. Networks of discourse, networks of power: the Foucauldian thesis of 'carceral society' and its application to selected narratives of Balzac, Doyle and Twain. *See* **6743.**

**7638.** WESTENDORP, TJEBBE A. 'He backed me into a corner and blockaded me with a chair': strategies of Mark Twain's literary campaigns. *In* (pp. 49–63) **13.**

**7639.** WILLIAMS, DAVID R. Experience and appearance in America's moral wilderness: Edwards' humiliation, Franklin's rationalization, and Huck Finn's damnation. *See* **5218.**

### Mrs Humphry Ward (Mary Augusta Arnold)

**7640.** ASHTON, ROSEMARY. Doubting clerics: from James Anthony Froude to *Robert Elsmere* via George Eliot. *In* (pp. 69–87) **18.**

**7641.** COLLISTER, PETER. 'A fresh and supplementary language': some quotations in *Robert Elsmere*. DUJ (81:2) 253–64.

### Susan Warner

**7642.** SCHNOG, NANCY. Inside the sentimental: the psychological work of *The Wide Wide World*. Genders (4) 11–25.

### Jane West

**7643.** PEDLEY, COLIN. 'The inward dispositions of the heart': Jane Austen and Jane West. *See* **6228.**

### William Whewell

**7644.** PREYER, ROBERT O. The language of discovery: William Whewell and George Eliot. *See* **6782.**

### Walt Whitman

**7645.** BAUERLEIN, MARK WEIGHTMAN. The signs of feeling: a study of

Whitman's poetics and poetry. Unpub. doct. diss., Univ. of California, Los Angeles, 1988. [Abstr. in DA (49) 2656A.]

**7646.** CADY, EDWIN H.; BUDD, LOUIS J. (eds). On Whitman: the best from American literature. Durham, NC; London: Duke UP, 1987. pp. 295. Rev. by Kristiaan Versluys in JAStud (23:1) 107–8.

**7647.** CLARKE, GRAHAM. 'To emanate a look': Whitman, photography and the spectacle of self. *In* (pp. 78–101) **1.**

**7648.** DeLANCEY, MARK. Texts, interpretations, and Whitman's *Song of Myself.* AL (61:3) 359–81.

**7649.** ERKKILA, BETSY. Whitman the political poet. New York; Oxford: OUP. pp. vi, 360. Rev. by Herbert J. Levine in AL (61:4) 696–7.

**7650.** HUTCHINSON, GEORGE B. Whitman and the Black poet: Kelly Miller's speech to the Walt Whitman Fellowship. AL (61:1) 46–58.

**7651.** KILLINGSWORTH, M. JIMMIE. Whitman's poetry of the body: sexuality, politics and the text. Chapel Hill; London: North Carolina UP. pp. xix, 195.

**7652.** LARSON, KERRY C. Whitman's drama of consensus. Chicago; London: Chicago UP, 1988. pp. xxiv, 269.

**7653.** LEONARD, GEORGE J. Emerson, Whitman, and conceptual art. *See* **6812.**

**7654.** LINK, FRANZ. Walt Whitman und Wilhelm Raabes Schulmeister Eyring 'singen sich selbst'. LJGG (30) 324–5. (Parody.)

**7655.** LJUNGQUIST, KENT. 'Meteor of the war': Melville, Thoreau, and Whitman respond to John Brown. *See* **7233.**

**7656.** MOON, MICHAEL. Disseminating Whitman. SAQ (88:1) 247–65.

**7657.** MOON, MICHAEL DAVID. Whitman in revision: the politics of corporeality and textuality in the first four editions of *Leaves of Grass.* Unpub. doct. diss., Johns Hopkins Univ., 1988. [Abstr. in DA (50) 140A.]

**7658.** NOLAN, JAMES F. Chants democratic: the Native American poetics of Walt Whitman and Pablo Neruda. Unpub. doct. diss., Univ. of California, Santa Cruz, 1988. [Abstr. in DA (50) 1300A.]

**7659.** PERELMAN-HALL, DAVID K. Wolfe and Whitman. TWR (13:1) 15–25.

**7660.** SANCHEZ-EPPLER, KAREN. To stand between: a political perspective on Whitman's poetics of merger and embodiment. ELH (56:4) 923–49.

**7661.** SMITH, MARC DOUGLAS. Self, center, silence: a study of *Song of Myself.* Unpub. doct. diss., State Univ. of New York at Buffalo. [Abstr. in DA (50) 948–9A.]

**7662.** SWEET, TIMOTHY ROBERT. Traces of war: poetry, photography, and the question of representation in the American Civil War. *See* **7252.**

**7663.** TANENBAUM, MILES. Walt Whitman and American art. Unpub. doct. diss., Univ. of Tennessee, 1988. [Abstr. in DA (50) 687A.]

**7664.** TAPSCOTT, STEPHEN. American beauty: William Carlos

Williams and the modernist Whitman. (Bibl. 1986, 9517.) Rev. by
George S. Lensing in SewR (96:1) 1988, 119–20.

**7665.** THOMAS, DAVID LEE.  Loss, mourning and the vatic dispersal of
self in the long poems of Whitman, Eliot, Pound, Berryman and Lowell.
Unpub. doct. diss., Univ. of California, Riverside, 1988. [Abstr. in DA
(49) 3028A.]

**7666.** THOMAS, M. WYNN.  The lunar light of Whitman's poetry.
(Bibl. 1988, 5794.) Rev. by R. W. Butterfield in JAStud (23:1) 157–8; by
David Kuebrich in MP (86:4) 445–8; by Robert Rehder in RES (39:156)
1988, 570–2.

**7667.** WARTOFSKY, STEVEN ANDREW.  The crisis of the whole:
national and personal identity in Walt Whitman's poetry, 1855–1865.
Unpub. doct. diss., Univ. of California, Berkeley, 1988. [Abstr. in DA
(49) 3364–5A.]

### Oscar Wilde

**7668.** ANDERSEN, M. C.  Document of division: Oscar Wilde's *De
Profundis*. UES (27:2) 1–11.

**7669.** COHEN, ED.  Talk on the Wilde side: towards a genealogy of the
discourse on male homosexuality. Unpub. doct. diss., Stanford Univ.,
1988. [Abstr. in DA (49) 3730A.]

**7670.** COHEN, WILLIAM A.  Willie and Wilde: reading *The Portrait of
Mr W. H.*  SAQ (88:1) 219–45.

**7671.** CULLER, JONATHAN.  Wilde's criticism: theory and practice.
*In* (pp. 402–6) **45.**

**7672.** EDWARDS, OWEN DUDLEY (ed.).  The fireworks of Oscar Wilde.
London: Barrie & Jenkins. pp. 282.

**7673.** ELLMANN, RICHARD.  Oscar Wilde. (Bibl. 1988, 5804.) Rev. by
Michael Patrick Gillespie in StudN (20:3) 1988, 343–5; by M. Diane
Denny in TJ (41:2) 264–5; by Isobel Murray in DUJ (81:1) 1988, 141–3.

**7674.** GATTON, JOHN SPALDING.  'Informal wind-like music': two
unpublished letters from Oscar Wilde. ELN (27:1) 48–9.

**7675.** KELLY, G. P.  The 'Christian aesthetic' of Oscar Wilde.
Unpub. doct. diss., Univ. of Oxford, 1988. [Abstr. in IT (39:2) 486–7.]

**7676.** KOHL, NORBERT.  Oscar Wilde: the works of a conformist rebel.
Trans. by DAVID HENRY WILSON. Cambridge: CUP. pp. x, 439.
(European studies in English literature.)

**7677.** KORITZ, AMY E.  Gendering bodies, performing art: theatrical
dancing and the performance aesthetics of Wilde, Shaw and Yeats.
Unpub. doct. diss., Univ. of North Carolina at Chapel Hill, 1988.
[Abstr. in DA (50) 691A.]

**7678.** MANGANIELLO, DOMINIC.  The consolation of art: Oscar Wilde
and Dante. *In* (pp. 394–401) **45.**

**7679.** MURRAY, ISOBEL (ed.).  The writings of Oscar Wilde. Oxford:
OUP. pp. xxiv, 636. (Oxford authors.)

**7680.** NELSON, WALTER.  Oscar Wilde and the dramatic critics: a
study in Victorian theatre. *See* **5768.**

**7681.** PESTKA, DARIUSZ.  A typology of Oscar Wilde's comic devices.
SAP (22) 175–92.

**7682.** POZNAR, WALTER. Life and play in Wilde's *The Importance of Being Earnest*. MidQ (30:4) 515–28.

**7683.** PRICE, JODY LAUREN. 'A map with utopia': Oscar Wilde's vision for social change. Unpub. doct. diss., Univ. of Rhode Island, 1988. [Abstr. in DA (49) 3372A.]

**7684.** SMITH, PHILIP E., II; HELFAND, MICHAEL S. (eds). Oscar Wilde's Oxford notebooks: a portrait of mind in the making. New York; Oxford: OUP. pp. xviii, 256. Rev. by John Stokes in TLS, 16 June, 668.

**7685.** STREITFELD, DAVID. In the margin. BkW, 19 Nov., 15. (Speculation on the cause of Wilde's death.)

**7686.** WHITAKER, THOMAS R. Playing in earnest. *In* (pp. 407–23) **45.**

**7687.** WILLOUGHBY, GUY. Oscar Wilde and poststructuralism. PhilL (13:2) 316–24.

### Espy Williams

**7688.** WATSON, CHARLES S. The first modern dramatist of the South. SoQ (27:2) 77–91.

### Harriette Wilson

**7688a.** GATES, HENRY LOUIS, JR (introd.). Our nig, or Sketches from the life of a free Black in a two-story white house, North: showing that slavery's shadows fall even there. New York: Random House, 1983; London: Allison & Busby, 1984. pp. lix, 140, xxxiii. (Facsim. of first ed. pub. 1859.)

### Constance Fenimore Woolson

**7689.** MYERS, JOAN (ed.). Women artists, women exiles: *Miss Grief* and other stories. New Brunswick, NJ; London: Rutgers UP, 1988. pp. xlviii, 292. (American women writers.)

### Dorothy Wordsworth

**7690.** ALEXANDER, MEENA. Women in Romanticism: Mary Wollstonecraft, Dorothy Wordsworth and Mary Shelley. *See* **5581.**

**7691.** FAY, ELIZABETH ANNE. Realignments: the poetry of the Wordsworths. Unpub. doct. diss., State Univ. of New York at Stony Brook, 1988. [Abstr. in DA (49) 3031–2A.]

**7692.** McGAVRAN, JAMES HOLT, JR. Dorothy Wordsworth's journals: putting herself down. *In* (pp. 230–53) **51.**

**7693.** WOOF, PAMELA. Dorothy Wordsworth and Mary Lamb, writers. *See* **7173.**

### William Wordsworth

**7694.** ALEXANDER, J. H. Reading Wordsworth. (Bibl. 1988, 5821.) Rev. by E. D. Mackerness in NQ (36:2) 247–8.

**7695.** BAKER, HAROLD DEAN. The pleasure of landscape: insistent description in nineteenth-century prose. *See* **6004.**

**7696.** BAKER, JEFFREY. Casualties of the Revolution: Wordsworth and his 'solitary' self. YES (19) 94–111.

**7697.** BIALOSTOSKY, DON. Wordsworth, Allan Bloom, and liberal education. CR (33:4) 419–40.

**7698.** BIALOSTOSKY, DON H. Making tales: the poetics of Wordsworth's narrative experiments. (Bibl. 1987, 8688.) Rev. by June Sturrock in YES (19) 337–8.

**7699.** BRUNS, GERALD L.    Wordsworth at the limits of Romantic hermeneutics. CR (33:4) 393–418.

**7700.** BUTTERWORTH, DANIEL SCOTT.    The narrator of Wordsworth's *The Excursion*. Unpub. doct. diss., Univ. of North Carolina at Chapel Hill, 1988. [Abstr. in DA (49) 2665A.]

**7701.** CARUTH, CATHY LYNNE.    Empirical truths and critical fictions: Locke, Wordsworth, Kant, Freud. *See* **4604.**

**7702.** CHEW, SHIRLEY.    Wordsworth's *Prelude*: a prospect in the mind. *In* (pp. 133–46) **19.**

**7703.** COLEMAN, DEIRDRE.    Re-living Jacobinism: Wordsworth and the Convention of Cintra. YES (19) 144–61.

**7704.** COMENSOLI, VIVIANA.    The literary analogues of Wordsworth's *Goody Blake and Harry Gill*. ELN (26:4) 50–7.

**7705.** CONNORS, S. G.    Living within the light of high endeavours: Wordsworth's poetry of 1800–1805 and the influence of John Milton. *See* **4673.**

**7706.** CROSSAN, GREG.    Irresolution and dependence: the defeat of Wordsworthian ideals in Coleridge's *The Picture* and Browning's *The Last Ride Together*. *See* **6367.**

**7707.** DAVIES, HUGH SYKES.    Wordsworth and the worth of words. Ed. by JOHN KERRIGAN and JONATHAN WORDSWORTH. (Bibl. 1988, 5830.) Rev. by Nicholas Roe in RES (39:154) 1988, 305–6; by J. R. Watson in DUJ (81:1) 162–3.

**7708.** DAWOOD, FATIMA S.    Wordsworth and the theory of imagination. Al-Mustansiriya Literary Review (Al-Mustansiriya Univ., Baghdad) (12) 1985, 121–50.

**7709.** DELLI CARPINI, JOHN JOSEPH.    A formal, historical, and theological study of William Wordsworth's *Ecclesiastical Sonnets*. Unpub. doct. diss., Temple Univ. [Abstr. in DA (50) 1663A.]

**7710.** DILLON, WINT TRACY.    'The splendour of that indefinite abstraction': Wordsworth's language of the imagination. Unpub. doct. diss., Univ. of California, Riverside, 1988. [Abstr. in DA (49) 2226A.]

**7711.** DUGAS, KRISTINE (ed.).    The white doe of Rylstone; or, The fate of the Nortons. Ithaca, NY; London: Cornell UP, 1988. pp. xii, 389. (Cornell Wordsworth.) Rev. by Grevel Lindop in TLS, 5 May, 476.

**7712.** EILENBERG, SUSAN.    Mortal pages: Wordsworth and the reform of copyright. *See* **428.**

**7713.** ELLIS, DAVID.    Realism in Wordsworth's *Michael*. Eng (36) 1987, 38–49.

**7714.** ELLISON, JULIE.    'Nice arts' and 'potent energy': the gendered economy of Wordsworth's fancy. CR (33:4) 441–67.

**7715.** FAY, ELIZABETH ANNE.    Realignments: the poetry of the Wordsworths. *See* **7691.**

**7716.** FEATHER, JOHN.    Publishers and politicians: the remaking of the law of copyright in Britain 1775–1842: 1, Legal deposit and the battle of library tax; 2, The right of authors. *See* **430.**

**7717.** FERREIRA-ROSS, JEANETTE.    Two holistic thinkers: Jan Smuts and William Wordsworth. UES (27:1) 21–7.

**7718.** FRIEDMAN, GERALDINE. History in the background of Wordsworth's *Blind Beggar*. ELH (56:1) 125–48.

**7719.** GARDINER, ALAN. The poetry of William Wordsworth. Harmondsworth: Penguin, 1987. pp. 121. (Penguin masterstudies.)

**7720.** GILL, STEPHEN. William Wordsworth: a life. Oxford: Clarendon Press; New York: OUP. pp. xix, 525. Rev. by Philippa Tristram in LRB (11:8) 17–18; by Norman Fruman in TLS, 5 May, 475–6; by Elizabeth Ward in BkW, 28 May, 1–2; by William Scammell in Listener (121) (misnumbered 122) 16 Mar., 33; by Michael Baron in Eng (38) 255–61.

**7721.** GOODSON, A. C. Elemental Wordsworth: an introduction. CR (33:4) 302–21.

**7722.** GRAVIL, RICHARD. 'Some other being': Wordsworth in *The Prelude*. YES (19) 127–45.

**7723.** GRIFFIN, ROBERT J. Wordsworth's Pope: the language of his former heart. See **5411.**

**7724.** HAIGWOOD, LAURA E. Oedipal revolution in the *Lyrical Ballads*. CR (33:4) 468–89.

**7725.** HALL, SPENCER; RAMSEY, JONATHAN (eds). Approaches to teaching Wordsworth's poetry. (Bibl. 1987, 8702.) Rev. by Matthew C. Brennan in IE (12:2) 1988, 29–30; by June Sturrock in YES (19) 337–8.

**7726.** HAMILTON, PAUL. Wordsworth. (Bibl. 1986, 9602.) Rev. by W. J. B. Owen in RES (39:153) 1988, 123–4.

**7727.** HARDING, ANTHONY JOHN. Did Lucy have to die? Woman as sign in Wordsworth's *Three Years She Grew*. NCC (12:1) 1988, 51–9.

**7728.** HARRISON, GARY. Wordsworth's leech gatherer: liminal power and the 'spirit of independence'. ELH (56:2) 327–50.

**7729.** HARTMAN, GEOFFREY H. The unremarkable Wordsworth. (Bibl. 1988, 5839.) Rev. by J. D. Gutteridge in NQ (36:1) 117; by Peter Swaab in LRB (11:8) 18–19.

**7730.** HARVEY, A. D. Henry Cotes: an early Wordsworthian. *See* **6554.**

**7731.** HEFFERNAN, JAMES A. W. Wordsworth, Constable, and the poetics of chiaroscuro. Word & Image (5:3) 260–77.

**7732.** HOBSBAUM, PHILIP (ed.). William Wordsworth: selected poetry and prose. London: Routledge. pp. xiv, 246. (Routledge English texts.)

**7733.** HOTCHKISS, WILHELMINA LOUISE. Wordsworth, Constable, and the claim of personal geography. Unpub. doct. diss., Univ. of California, Los Angeles, 1988. [Abstr. in DA (49) 3369A.]

**7734.** HUGO, FRANÇOIS JEAN. The struggle to unify: Wordsworth's imagination of the wholeness of being. Unpub. doct. diss., Univ. of Natal (Pietermaritzburg), 1988.

**7735.** JACOBUS, MARY. Romanticism, writing, and sexual difference: essays on *The Prelude*. Oxford: Clarendon Press; New York: OUP. pp. x, 312.

**7736.** JOHNSTON, KENNETH R. Wordsworth and *The Recluse*. (Bibl. 1986, 9606.) Rev. by V. A. De Luca in UTQ (56:4) 1987, 583–5.

**7737.** JONES, MARK CONRAD. Lucy and her readers: a history of the criticism of Wordsworth's Lucy poems. Unpub. doct. diss., Columbia Univ., 1988. [Abstr. in DA (49) 3033–4A.]

**7738.** JORDAN, JOHN E. (ed.).    Peter Bell. Ithaca, NY: Cornell UP. pp. xii, 631. (Cornell Wordsworth.) Rev. by Grevel Lindop in TLS, 5 May, 476.

**7739.** KABITOGLOU, E. DOUKA.    The phenomenology of ascent and descent in Plato and Wordsworth. NC (8) 144–63.

**7740.** KAMRA, SUKESHI.    William Wordsworth's revolutionary view of history: a study of the narratives in the *Lyrical Ballads* (1798 & 1800). Unpub. doct. diss., Simon Fraser Univ. [Abstr. in DA (50) 1665–6A.]

**7741.** KELLEY, THERESA M.    Wordsworth's revisionary aesthetics. (Bibl. 1988, 5846.) Rev. by J. D. Gutteridge in NQ (36:1) 116–17.

**7742.** KISHEL, JOSEPH F. (ed.).    *The Tuft of Primroses* with other late poems for *The Recluse*. (Bibl. 1986, 9613.) Rev. by Christopher Salvesen in RES (38:151) 1987, 397–8; by Grevel Lindop in TLS, 5 May, 476.

**7743.** LAWRENCE, BERTA.    A tragedy remembered. CLB (67) 99–103.

**7744.** LEVINSON, MARJORIE.    Back to the future: Wordsworth's new historicism. SAQ (88:3) 633–59.

**7745.** —— Wordsworth's great period poems: four essays. (Bibl. 1988, 5850.) Rev. by W. J. B. Owen in RES (39:153) 1988, 124–7; by June Sturrock in YES (19) 337–8.

**7746.** MALIK, G. R.    The cultural foundations of Wordsworth's literary criticism. CLB (67) 94–9.

**7747.** MASUGI, SADA.    Wordsworth no shiron. (Wordsworth's theory of poetics.) Tokyo: Senjo. pp. 194.

**7748.** MATTHIAS, DAVID THOMAS.    The concept of sympathy in the early poetry of Samuel Taylor Coleridge and William Wordsworth. *See* **6515.**

**7749.** MORRIS, DAVID B.    Wordsworth and the heartbeat of America: a postmodern fable. CR (33:4) 491–58.

**7750.** O'DONNELL, BRENNAN.    Numerous verse: a guide to the stanzas and metrical structures of Wordsworth's poetry. SP (86:4) 1–136.

**7751.** OH, MOON-KIL.    Nangmanjeok sangsangryeok yeongu: Blake wa Wordsworth bikyo. *See* **5094.**

**7752.** OWEN, W. J. B. (ed.).    The fourteen-book *Prelude*. (Bibl. 1988, 9631.) Rev. by Christopher Salvesen in RES (38:149) 1987, 88–9; by Grevel Lindop in TLS, 5 May, 476.

**7753.** PINCH, ADELA.    Female chatter: meter, masochism, and the *Lyrical Ballads*. ELH (55:4) 1988, 835–52.

**7754.** PINION, F. B.    A Wordsworth chronology. (Bibl. 1988, 5858.) Rev. by L. A. Rabinowitz in UES (27:2) 29–30.

**7755.** PISON, THOMAS ALBERT.    The language of revision: Wordsworth's *Prelude*. Unpub. doct. diss., State Univ. of New York at Buffalo. [Abstr. in DA (50) 1314A.]

**7756.** RICHARDSON, ALAN.    The politics of childhood: Wordsworth, Blake, and catechistic method. *See* **5101.**

**7757.** ROE, NICHOLAS.    *Wordsworth at the Flax-Dam*: an early poem by Seamus Heaney. *In* (pp. 166–70) **17.**

**7758.** —— Wordsworth, Milton, and the politics of poetic influence. *See* **4735.**

**7759.** Rowlett, John Louis.    The generic Wordsworth. Unpub. doct. diss., Univ. of Virginia, 1987. [Abstr. in DA (49) 3735A.]

**7760.** Ruoff, Gene W.    Wordsworth and Coleridge: the making of the major lyrics, 1802–1804. *See* **6523.**

**7761.** Rylestone, Anne Linda.    William Wordsworth's *Ecclesiastical Sonnets* in series: 'recalling the wandering soul to sympathy'. Unpub. doct. diss., Univ. of Massachusetts, 1988. [Abstr. in DA (49) 2235A.]

**7762.** el-Sayid, A. A.    The influence of William Wordsworth on the Dīwān group. Unpub. M.Phil. diss., Univ. of Exeter. [Abstr. in IT (39:4) 1624.]

**7763.** Shin, Kyung-Won.    The English origins of Wordsworth's organicism. Unpub. doct. diss., Univ. of Minnesota, 1988. [Abstr. in DA (49) 1812A.]

**7764.** Shin, Kyung-Won.    Search for personal identity in Locke and Wordsworth. *See* **4611.**

**7765.** Simpson, David.    Figuring class, sex, and gender: what is the subject of Wordsworth's *Gipsies?* SAQ (88:3) 541–67.

**7766.** —— Wordsworth's historical imagination: the poetry of displacement. (Bibl. 1988, 5867.) Rev. by Peter Swaab in LRB (11:8) 18–19; by J. D. Gutteridge in NQ (36:1) 117–18.

**7767.** Sitterson, Joseph C., Jr.    Oedipus in the stolen boat: psychoanalysis and subjectivity in *The Prelude.* SP (86:1) 96–115.

**7768.** Thomas, W. K.; Ober, Warren U.    A mind for ever voyaging: Wordsworth at work portraying Newton and science. Edmonton: Alberta UP. pp. xii, 328.

**7769.** Walker, Eric C.    *Biographia Literaria* and Wordsworth's revisons. *See* **6533.**

**7770.** Wanko, Cheryl.    Leechcraft: Wordsworth's *Resolution and Independence.* ELN (26:4) 58–62.

**7771.** Williams, John.    Wordsworth: Romantic poetry and revolution politics. Manchester: Manchester UP. pp. viii, 203. Rev. by John Bayley in LRB (11:23) 12–14.

**7772.** Wilson, Fred.    Wordsworth and the culture of science. CR (33:4) 322–92.

**7773.** Woodring, Carl.    Shaping life in *The Prelude. In* (pp. 9–25) **44.**

**7774.** Wu, Duncan.    Wordsworth's reading of Bowles. *See* **6272.**

# TWENTIETH CENTURY

## GENERAL

### General Literary Studies

**7775.** ADELAIDE, DEBRA. Australian women writers: a bibliographic guide. *See* **5595.**

**7776.** ALEXANDER, MEENA. Outcaste power: ritual displacement and virile maternity in Indian women writers. *See* **5596.**

**7777.** ALLEN, MICHAEL; WILCOX, ANGELA (eds). Critical approaches to Anglo-Irish literature. *See* **17.**

**7778.** ALTER, ROBERT. The pleasures of reading in an ideological age. *See* **5598.**

**7779.** AMUTA, CHIDI. The theory of African literature: implications for practical criticism. London; Atlantic Highlands, NJ: Zed Books; Inst. for African Alternatives. pp. ix, 206. (Zed cultural studies.)

**7780.** ANON. Aotearoa: an anthology of New Zealand writing. Auckland: Heinemann, 1988. pp. 71.

**7781.** —— (ed.). Les lieux de passage. *See* **35.**

**7782.** ANTOR, HEINZ. The Bloomsbury group: its philosophy, aesthetics, and literary achievement. (Bibl. 1986, 9655.) Rev. by Willi Erzgräber in LJGG (29) 1988, 357–60.

**7783.** APPLEYARD, BRYAN. The pleasures of peace: art and imagination in post-war Britain. London; Boston, MA: Faber & Faber. pp. xv, 367. Rev. by Robert Hewison in Listener (121) 22 June, 5.

**7784.** ARKIN, MARIAN; SHOLLAR, BARBARA (eds). Longman anthology of world literature by women, 1875–1975. *See* **5603.**

**7785.** ARONOWICZ, ANNETTE. Freedom from ideology: secrecy in modern expression. *See* **5604.**

**7786.** ASHCROFT, BILL; GRIFFITHS, GARETH; TIFFIN, HELEN. The Empire writes back: theory and practice in post-colonial literatures. London: Routledge. pp. viii, 246. (New accents.)

**7787.** BACHINGER, KATRINA. 'Sex and power' in der zeitgenössischen nordamerikanischen Frauenliteratur. *In* (pp. 4–18) CHRISTA GÜRTLER and BRIGETTE MAZOHL-WALLNIG (eds), Frauenbilder, Frauenrollen, Frauenforschung. Vienna: Geyer, 1987. pp. 189. (Pubs of the Historical Inst. of the Univ. of Salzburg, 17.)

**7788.** BAKER, CANDIDA (ed.). Yacker 3: Australian writers talk about their work. Sydney: Picador. pp. 333. (Interviews with Glenda Adams, Peter Corris, Robert Drewe, Kate Grenville, Gwen Harwood, A. D. Hope, Christopher Koch, Frank Moorhouse, Louis Nowra, Peter Porter, Randolph Stow, John Tranter.)

**7789.** BANTA, MARTHA. Imaging American women: idea and ideals in cultural history. *See* **5607.**

**7790.** BARNES, JOHN. Home thoughts from abroad: the sense of place in Australian writing. *In* (pp. 52–65) **5.**

**7791.** Baštín, Štefan. Ideové a estetické paralely medzi satirou a čiernym humorom. (Aesthetic boundaries between satire and black humour.) *In* (pp. 16–17) **6.**

**7792.** Bergonzi, Bernard. The myth of Modernism and twentieth-century literature. (Bibl. 1988, 5889.) Rev. by Robert Crawford in RES (38:151) 1987, 417–18.

**7793.** Bertens, Hans, *et al.* (eds). Post war literatures in English: a lexicon of contemporary authors. Alphen aan den Rijn, The Netherlands: Samson; Groningen: Wolters-Noordhoff. Various pagings. (Individual bibliographies of Walter Abish, Allen Ginsberg, Adrienne Kennedy, Geoffrey Hill, Walker Percy.) (Additions to bibl. 1988, 5891.)

**7794.** Binding, Paul. Separate country: a literary journey through the American South. (Bibl. 1981, 2561.) Jackson; London: Mississippi UP, 1988. pp. xi, 195. (Second ed.: first ed. 1979.)

**7795.** Birbalsingh, Frank. Passion and exile: essays on Caribbean literature. London: Hansib, 1988. pp. 186.

**7796.** Blair, Rebecca. The other woman: women authors and cultural stereotypes in American literature. *See* **5611.**

**7797.** Blamires, Harry. Twentieth-century English literature. (Bibl. 1986, 9676.) Rev. by Alan Robinson in MLR (84:3) 726–7.

**7798.** Bongie, Christopher Laurence. Rewriting colonialism: allegories of the 'New Imperialism', 1876–1914. *See* **5613.**

**7799.** Braybrooke, Neville (ed.). Seeds in the wind: juvenilia from W. B. Yeats to Ted Hughes. London: Hutchinson. pp. 208. Rev. by P. N. Furbank in TLS, 17 Nov., 1261.

**7800.** Bredahl, A. Carl, Jr. New ground: Western American narrative and the literary canon. Chapel Hill; London: North Carolina UP. pp. xi, 195.

**7801.** Broich, Ulrich. Apokalypse und Entropie als konkurrierende Konzepte zur Beschreibung des Weltendes in der englischsprachigen Literatur der Gegenwart. LJGG (29) 1988, 291–305.

**7802.** Bromwich, David. A choice of inheritance: self and community from Edmund Burke to Robert Frost. *See* **4833.**

**7803.** Brown, Dennis. The Modernist self in twentieth-century English literature: a study of self-fragmentation. Basingstoke: Macmillan. pp. x, 206.

**7804.** Butler, Christopher. The concept of Modernism. *In* (pp. 49–59) **45.**

**7805.** Butter, P. H. ed.). The truth of imagination: some uncollected reviews and essays. By Edwin Muir. (Bibl. 1988, 5908.) Rev. by Heather Hewitt in SLJ (supp. 31) 26–8.

**7806.** Carpenter, Humphrey. Geniuses together: American writers in Paris in the 1920s. (Bibl. 1988, 5913.) Rev. by Gerald Kennedy in AL (61:1) 114–15; by Herbert Lottman in PR (56:3) 504–7.

**7807.** Charters, Ann. Beats & company: portrait of a literary generation. (Bibl. 1988, 5917.) Rev. by Tim Poland in SoCR (20:1) 1987, 82–3.

**7808.** CHINWEIZU (sel. and introd.).   Voices from twentieth-century Africa: griots and towncriers. London: Faber & Faber, 1988. pp. xl, 424.

**7809.** CHINWEIZU, ONWUCHEKWA JEMIE; MADUBUIKE, IHECHUKWU. Toward the decolonization of African literature: vol. 1, African fiction and poetry and their critics. (Bibl. 1986, 9688.) Rev. by A. Ebeogu in Lore and Language (8:1) 103–5.

**7810.** CHRISTIE, NORTON BRADLEY.   Another war and postmodern memory: remembering Vietnam. Unpub. doct. diss., Duke Univ., 1988. [Abstr. in DA (49) 2218A.]

**7811.** CLIFFORD, JAMES.   The predicament of culture: twentieth-century ethnography, literature, and art. (Bibl. 1988, 5920.) Rev. by Kathleen McGill in JAF (102:406) 485–7.

**7812.** COBB, JAMES C.   The South's South: the enigma of creativity in the Mississippi delta. See **5627.**

**7813.** COLLINS, AILEEN (ed.).   In defence of art: critical essays and reviews. By LOUIS DUDEK. Kingston, Ont.: Quarry Press, 1988. pp. 302. Rev. by Jon Kertzer in CanL (122/23) 172–3.

**7814.** CONKLIN, PAUL K.   The Southern Agrarians. Knoxville: Tennessee UP, 1988. pp. xi, 196. Rev. by Thomas A. Underwood in AL (61:1) 115–17.

**7815.** CONNOR, STEVEN.   Postmodernism and literature. In (pp. 103–31) STEVEN CONNOR, Postmodernist culture: an introduction to theories of the contemporary. Oxford: Blackwell. pp. x, 274.

**7816.** CUNNINGHAM, VALENTINE.   British writers of the thirties. (Bibl. 1988, 5928.) Rev. by Frank McCombie in NQ (36:2) 259–61.

**7817.** DABYDEEN, DAVID; WILSON-TAGOE, NANA.   A reader's guide to West Indian and Black British literature. London: Hansib in assn with the Univ. of Warwick Centre for Caribbean Studies and Dept of Continuing Education. (Bibl. 1986, 9700.)

**7818.** DAHL, ANTHONY GEORGE.   Literature of the Bahamas: the march towards national identity. See **4840.**

**7819.** DAHMS, MOSHIE; NEW, W. H.   Annual bibliography of Commonwealth literature: Canada, 1986–1988. JCL (22:2) 1987, 30–60; (23:2) 1988, 36–74; (24:2) 36–72.

**7820.** DAVEY, FRANK.   Reading Canadian literature. Winnipeg, Man.: Turnstone Press, 1988. pp. 275. Rev. by Stephen Scobie in MalaR (86) 130.

**7821.** DEBUSSCHER, GILBERT; MAUFORT, MARC (eds).   American literature in Belgium. See **2.**

**7822.** DERINGER, LUDWIG.   The Pacific Northwest in American and Canadian literature since 1776: the present state of scholarship. See **4843.**

**7823.** DICK, SUSAN, et al. (eds).   Omnium gatherum: essays for Richard Ellmann. See **45.**

**7824.** DOWLING, DAVID.   Annual bibliography of Commonwealth literature 1987: New Zealand (with the South Pacific Islands). JCL (23:2) 1988, 100–26.

**7825.** DRIVER, DOROTHY.   Annual bibliography of Commonwealth literature: Appendix 2; South Africa, 1986–1988. JCL (22:2) 1987, 124–39; (23:2) 1988, 170–98; (24:2) 133–69.

**7826.** DUBERMAN, MARTIN; VICINUS, MARTHA; CHAUNCEY, GEORGE, JR (eds).   Hidden from history: reclaiming the gay and lesbian past. New York: New American Library; London: Penguin. pp. xi, 579.

**7827.** ELLMANN, RICHARD.   A long the riverrun: selected essays. *See* **5644.**

**7828.** ELSE, ANNE; ROBERTS, HEATHER (eds).   A woman's life: writings by women about female experience in New Zealand. Auckland: Penguin. pp. 267. Rev. by Maud Cahill in NZList, 16 Sept., 66.

**7829.** ENSSLEN, KLAUS.   Einführung in die schwarzamerikanische Literatur. *See* **4849.**

**7830.** EPSTEIN, JOSEPH.   Partial payments: essays on writers and their lives. *See* **5646.**

**7831.** FIELD, G. N.   English left-wing writers and politics in the 1930s. Unpub. doct. diss., Univ. of London, 1986. [Abstr. in IT (36:1) 22.]

**7832.** FOGEL, STANLEY.   The postmodern university: essays on the deconstruction of the humanities. Toronto: ECW Press, 1988. pp. 150. Rev. by Michael H. Keefer in CanL (120) 225–6.

**7833.** FOKKEMA, DOUWE.   Preliminary remarks. *In* (pp. 1–8) **7.**

**7834.** FOSTER, THOMAS C.   Form and society in modern literature. DeKalb: Northern Illinois UP, 1988. pp. xi, 203. Rev. by Susan V. Donaldson in AL (61:2) 316–17.

**7835.** FULTON, ROBIN.   The way the words are taken: selected essays. Edinburgh: Macdonald. pp. 191. (Lines review editions.)

**7836.** GADD, BERNARD (ed.).   Other voices: new writers and writing in New Zealand. Auckland: Brick Row/Hallard Press. pp. 160.

**7837.** —— (sel.).   Pacific voices: an anthology of Maori and Pacific writing. Auckland: Macmillan. pp. viii, 109.

**7838.** GARDNER, RALPH D.   Writers talk to Ralph D. Gardner. Introd. by ROD MCKUEN. Metuchen, NJ; London: Scarecrow Press. pp. xiv, 339.

**7839.** GEDDES, GARY (ed.).   Vancouver: soul of a city. Vancouver: Douglas & McIntyre, 1986. pp. 328. Rev. by Margaret Doyle in CanL (115) 1987, 188–90.

**7840.** GELFANT, BLANCHE H.   Women writing in America: voices in collage. (Bibl. 1987, 8814.) Rev. by Michael Peterman in CanL (115) 1987, 145–6.

**7841.** GEORGINIS, E. G.   Variations of experience: expatriate British writers in the Middle East during the Second World War. Unpub. doct. diss., Univ. of Loughborough. [Abstr. in IT (39:1) 34–5.]

**7842.** GERRARD, NICCI.   Into the mainstream: how feminism has changed women's writing. London: Pandora. pp. ix, 178.

**7843.** GERSTER, R.   Big-noting: the heroic theme in Australian war writing. (Bibl. 1987, 8815.) Rev. by John Rickard in AUMLA (72) 365–7.

**7844.** GILKIN, RONDA. Black American women in literature: a bibliography, 1976 through 1987. Jefferson, NC; London: McFarland. pp. xii, 251.

**7845.** GOETSCH, PAUL. Funktionen der Sprachkritik und -skepsis in der modernen englischen Literatur. LJGG (26) 1985, 227–51.

**7846.** GOLDEN, TAYLOR J., *et al.* (eds). A literary history of the American West. See **5649.**

**7847.** GOONETILLEKE, D. C. R. A. Annual bibliography of Commonwealth literature: Sri Lanka, 1986–88. JCL (22:2) 1987, 91–7; (23:2) 1988, 127–34; (24:2) 117–25.

**7848.** GRAY, NANCY. Slaying the phantom: voices of experience in experimental writing by women. Unpub. doct. diss., Univ. of Washington, 1988. [Abstr. in DA (50) 146A.]

**7849.** GRENVILLE, KATE. From *The Getting of Wisdom* to *Illywhacker*: the library and our literary heritage. See **228.**

**7850.** GUGELBERGER, GEORG M. (ed.). Marxism and African literature. (Bibl. 1987, 8821.) Rev. by Myles Holloway in UES (27:1) 65–6.

**7851.** HAARHOF, DORIAN. Fighting and writing: the origins of indigenous Namibian literature. Current Writing (1) 89–101.

**7852.** HAMILTON, PETER TALBOT. The role of futurism, Dada and Surrealism in the construction of British modernism, 1910–1940. Unpub. doct. diss., Univ. of Oxford, 1987. [Abstr. in DA (50) 680A.]

**7853.** HARLOW, BARBARA. Resistance literature. (Bibl. 1988, 5960.) Rev. by John Walker in QQ (95:4) 1988, 923–5.

**7854.** HARPER, GEORGE MILLS. 'Necessary murder': the Auden circle and the Spanish Civil War. *In* (pp. 67–80) **46.**

**7855.** HARRIS, WILSON. Oedipus and the middle passage. Landfall (43:2) 198–208.

**7856.** HASHIGUCHI, MINORU. Bloomsbury group. Tokyo: Chuokoron. pp. vi, 192. (In Japanese.)

**7857.** HASHMI, ALAMGIR. Annual bibliography of Commonwealth literature: Appendix 1: Pakistan, 1986–88. JCL (22:2) 1987, 112–23; (23:2) 1988, 162–9; (24:2) 126–32.

**7858.** —— The Commonwealth, comparative literature and the world. (Bibl. 1988, 5961.) Rev. by Gary Boire in Span (29) 105–8; by Christopher Smith in NC (7) 182–3.

**7859.** —— Pakistani literature in English 1987–88: a further assessment. Pakistan Times (Islamabad and Lahore) 30 May, C, D.

**7860.** —— (ed.). The worlds of Muslim imagination. (Bibl. 1988, 5963.) Rev. by Annemarie Schimmel in Orientalistische Literaturzeitung (Berlin) (84:2) 196.

**7861.** HERNTON, CALVIN C. The sexual mountain and Black women writers. New York: Doubleday, 1987. pp. 174.

**7862.** HETHERINGTON, CAROL; PETERSSON, IRMTRAUD. Annual bibliography of studies in Australian literature: 1988. See **4853.**

**7863.** HILLIS, DORIS. Voices & visions: interviews with Saskatchewan writers. Moose Jaw, Sask.: Coteau, 1985. pp. iii, 228. Rev. by Patricia Köster in CanL (113/14) 1987, 239–41.

**7864.** HUNTER, JEFFERSON. Image and word: the interaction of twentieth-century photographs and texts. Cambridge, MA; London: Harvard UP, 1987. pp. xi, 233.

**7865.** HYLAND, PETER (ed.). Discharging the canon: cross-cultural readings in literature. *See* **19.**

**7866.** IKIN, VAN; WALKER, BRENDA. Annual bibliography of Commonwealth literature 1986: Australia (with Papua New Guinea). JCL (22:2) 1987, 5–29.

**7867.** —— DOLIN, KIERAN. Annual bibliography of Commonwealth literature 1987: Australia (with Papua New Guinea). JCL (23:2) 1988, 8–35.

**7868.** —— McCOOEY, DAVID. Annual bibliography of Commonwealth literature 1988: Australia (with Papua New Guinea). JCL (24:2) 1–35.

**7869.** ILLMAN, KARL-JOHN. Vad är modern judisk litteratur? (What is modern Jewish literature?) Horisont (36:4) 6–14 (review-article).

**7870.** JACOBS, J. U. The Blues: an Afro-American matrix for Black South African writing. EngA (16:2) 3–17.

**7871.** JACOBSON, DAN. Adult pleasures: essays on writers and readers. (Bibl. 1988, 5975.) Rev. by Stephen Wall in LRB (11:6) 24–6.

**7872.** JAMESON, FREDRIC. Nationalism, colonialism and literature: modernism and imperialism. *See* **4856.**

**7873.** JAMKHANDI, SUDHAKAR R. Australian literary publications in the C. Hartley Grattan Collection. *See* **236.**

**7874.** JOHNSON, BRUCE. A Modernist noesis. *In* (pp. 60–70) **45.**

**7875.** JONES, LAWRENCE. Versions of the dream: literature and the search for identity. *See* **5660.**

**7876.** KAPLAN, AMY. The burden of history. *See* **5662.**

**7877.** KAWAHARADA, DENNIS. The rhetoric of identity in Japanese American writings, 1948–1988. Unpub. doct. diss., Univ. of Washington, 1988. [Abstr. in DA (49) 2659A.]

**7878.** KEARNEY, RICHARD. Transitions: narratives in modern Irish culture. (Bibl. 1988, 5977.) Rev. by Brian Cosgrove in IUR (19:1) 161–4.

**7879.** KEARNS, GODFREY A. United States of America. *In* (pp. 10–43) SPENCER PEARCE and DON PIPER (eds), Literature of Europe and America in the 1960s. Manchester: Manchester UP; New York: St Martin's Press. pp. 286.

**7880.** KEDGLEY, SUE. Our own country: leading New Zealand women writers talk about their writing and their lives. Auckland: Penguin. pp. 192. Rev. by Fiona Farrell Poole in NZList, 27 May, 48.

**7881.** KENNER, HUGH. A sinking island: the modern English writers. (Bibl. 1988, 5979.) Rev. by Cairns Craig in Cencrastus (33) 40–1.

**7882.** KIM, SEONG-KON. Postmodernism gwa post-realism. (Post-modernism *vs* post-realism.) AmeSt (12) 21–43.

**7883.** KROETSCH, ROBERT; NISCHIK, REINGARD M. (eds). Gaining ground: European critics on Canadian literature. (Bibl. 1987, 8851.)

Rev. by Kathy Mezei in YES (19) 359–61; by Stanley S. Atherton in
CanL (115) 1987, 184–6; by John Ferns in RES (38:152) 1987, 584.

**7884.** LEAVIS, LAWRENCE ROBIN. Creative values and contemporary
literature. *See* **5669.**

**7885.** LEVERENZ, DAVID. Manhood and the American renaissance.
*See* **5670.**

**7886.** LIM, SHIRLEY GEOK-LIN. Finding a native voice – Singapore
literature in English. JCL (24:1) 30–48. (Includes select bibliography of
Singaporean literature.)

**7887.** McARTHUR, KATHLEEN MAUREEN. The heroic spirit in the
literature of the Great War. Unpub. doct. diss., Univ. of Cape Town.

**7888.** McCAFFERY, STEVE. North of intention: critical writings,
1973–1986. London, Ont.: Nightwood; New York: Roof, 1986. pp. 239.
Rev. by Karl Jirgens in CanL (121) 144–5.

**7889.** McCASKILL, BARBARA ANN. To rise above race: Black women
writers and their readers, 1859–1939. *See* **5678.**

**7890.** McCORMICK, PETER J. Fictions, philosophies, and the problems of poetics. Ithaca, NY: Cornell UP, 1988. pp. 351. Rev. by Edward
Sankowski in JAE (23:3) 111–13.

**7891.** McDOWELL, DEBORAH E.; RAMPERSAD, ARNOLD (eds). Slavery
and the literary imagination. *See* **5679.**

**7892.** McKERNAN, SUSAN. A question of commitment: Australian
literature in the twenty years after the war. Sydney: Allen & Unwin.
pp. vi, 249.

**7893.** McLAUCHLAN, GORDON (comp.). A history of New Zealand
humour. Auckland: Penguin. pp. 231. Rev. by Craig Harrison in
NZList, 29 Apr., 33.

**7894.** MALABA, M. Z.; STYLE, O-LAN. Annual bibliography of
Commonwealth literature 1987: Africa, Southern; Botswana, Lesotho,
Swaziland, Zimbabwe. JCL (23:2) 1988, 144–61.

**7895.** MANIAM, K. S.; ENG, OOI BOO. Annual bibliography of
Commonwealth literature 1986: Malaysia and Singapore. JCL (22:2)
1987, 83–9.

**7896.** MAPLES, DONNA ELAINE. Building a literary heritage: a study
of three generations of pioneer women, 1880–1930. *See* **5682.**

**7897.** MAUGHAN-BROWN, DAVID. The anthology as reliquary? *Ten
Years of 'Staffrider'* and *The 'Drum' Decade*. *See* **579.**

**7898.** MAYERS, OZZIE J. The power of the pin: sewing as an act of
rootedness in American literature. *See* **5686.**

**7899.** MAYNARD, JOHN ARTHUR. Venice West: the Beat Generation
in Southern California. Unpub. doct. diss., Univ. of Southern
California, 1988. [Abstr. in DA (49) 2281–2A.]

**7900.** MELDRUM, BARBARA HOWARD. Under the sun: myth and
realism in Western American literature. *See* **5688.**

**7901.** METCALF, JOHN (ed.). The bumper book. *See* **12.**

**7902.** MILES, PETER; SMITH, MALCOLM. Cinema, literature and
society: elite and mass culture in inter-war Britain. (Bibl. 1987, 8874.)
Rev. by Richard Maltby in NQ (36:1) 129–30.

**7903.** MILLER, VASSAR (ed.). Despite this flesh: the disabled in stories and poems. Austin: Texas UP, 1985. pp. xviii, 146. Rev. by Peter Bricklebank in DalR (66:3) 1986, 388–91.

**7904.** MOFOKENG, BOITUMELO. Where are the women? *Ten Years of 'Staffrider'. See* **582.**

**7905.** MONTEITH, MOIRA (ed.). Women's writing: a challenge to theory. (Bibl. 1986, 9817.) Rev. by Maria Del Sapio in MLR (84:4) 960.

**7906.** MYERS, THOMAS. Walking point: American narratives of Vietnam. New York; Oxford: OUP, 1988. pp. x, 250. Rev. by M. Gilbert Porter in AL (61:2) 327–8.

**7907.** MZAMANE, MBULELO VIZIKHUNGO. An unhistorical will into past times. Current Writing (1) 36–40.

**7908.** NARAYAN, SHYAMALA A. Annual bibliography of Commonwealth literature: India, 1986–1988. JCL (22:2) 1987, 61–82; (23:2) 1988, 75–99; (24:2) 73–93.

**7909.** NDEBELE, NJABULO S. The ethics of intellectual combat. *See* **583.**

**7910.** NDEGWA, R. N. Annual bibliography of Commonwealth literature: Africa, East and Central, 1986–1987. JCL (22:2) 1987, 1–4; (23:2) 1988, 1–7.

**7911.** NEUMAN, SHIRLEY. Importing difference. *In* (pp. 392–405) **40.**

**7912.** —— KAMBOURELI, SMARO (eds). A mazing space: writing Canadian women writing. *See* **40.**

**7913.** NGUGI WA THIONG'O. Decolonising the mind: the politics of language in African literature. (Bibl. 1988, 6012.) Rev. by Z. B. Molefe in Classic (4:1) 44.

**7914.** NORWOOD, VERA; MONK, JANICE (eds). The desert is no lady: southwestern landscapes in women's writing and art. (Bibl. 1988, 6015.) Rev. by Willard Gingerich in RMRLL (43:1/2) 112–13.

**7915.** OLIVER, LAWRENCE J. Theodore Roosevelt, Brander Matthews, and the campaign for literary Americanism. *See* **5695.**

**7916.** PEPRNÍK, JAROSLAV. Češi v současné britské a americké literatuře. (The Czechs in contemporary British and American literature.) *In* (p. 33) **6.**

**7917.** PRIEBE, RICHARD K. (ed.). Ghanaian literatures. New York; London: Greenwood Press, 1988. pp. x, 300. (Contributions in Afro-American and African studies, 120.)

**7918.** QUARTERMAINE, PETER (ed.). Diversity itself: essays in Australian arts and culture. *See* **20.**

**7919.** RAFF, MELVIN HUNT. This above all: the challenge of identity in modern literature. Unpub. doct. diss., Univ. of Maryland College Park, 1988. [Abstr. in DA (49) 2215A.]

**7920.** RAHMAN, TARIQ. Race relations in Pakistani literature in English. CRNLE Reviews Journal (Flinders Univ. of South Australia, Bedford Park) (1/2) 1988, 140–5.

**7921.** RAMRAJ, VICTOR J. Annual bibliography of Commonwealth literature: the West Indies, 1986–1987. JCL (22:2) 1987, 98–111; (23:2) 1988, 135–43.

**7922.** RICARD, SERGE (ed.).    Les États-Unis: images du travail et des loisirs. *See* **25.**

**7923.** RICHARD, CLAUDE.    Lettres américaines. Aix-en-Provence: Alinéa, 1987. pp. 187. Rev. by Joan Templeton in EA (42:3) 358–60.

**7924.** RICHARDS, SHAUN.    The changing landscape of fact: English as 'necessary sin' in contemporary Irish literature. NC (7) 88–98.

**7925.** RIEDEL, WOLFGANG.    National metaphor in Anglo-Irish literature. *In* (pp. 434–5) **4.** (Abstract.)

**7926.** RITCHIE, HARRY.    Success stories: literature and the media in England, 1950–1959. London; Boston, MA: Faber & Faber, 1988. pp. x, 257. Rev. by James Campbell in TLS, 19 Feb. 1988, 184; by Joseph Coates in BW, 15 May 1988, 7; by Philip Oakes in Listener (119) 17 Mar. 1988, 24.

**7927.** RIVE, RICHARD.    Writing or fighting: the dilemma of the Black South African writer. Staffrider (8:1) 48–54.

**7928.** RUTHERFORD, ANDREW.    The literature of war: five studies in heroic virtue. (Bibl. 1980, 10275.) Basingstoke: Macmillan. pp. 196. (Second ed.: first ed. 1978.) (Kipling, T. E. Lawrence, Le Carré, Evelyn Waugh, *et al.*)

**7929.** RYAN, PAMELA DALE.    What do women want: a psycho-literary investigation into the quest for fulfilment in recent writing by women (1965–1985). Unpub. doct. diss., Univ. of South Africa.

**7930.** SEE, CAROLYN.    Why Australian writers keep their heads down. NYTB, 14 May, 1.

**7931.** SHAVA, PINIEL VIRIRI.    A people's voice: Black South African writing in the twentieth century. London: Zed Books; Athens: Ohio UP. pp. 179. (Zed cultural studies.) Rev. by Michael M. Green in Current Writing (1) 103–5.

**7932.** SHAW, GEORGE P.    Bicentennial writing: revealing the ash in the Australian soil. *In* (pp. 1–15) GEORGE SHAW (ed.), 1988 and all that: new views of Australia's past. Brisbane: Queensland UP, 1988. pp. 140.

**7933.** SHERBO, ARTHUR.    Matters English in *The Critic* (1881–1906). *See* **589.**

**7934.** SHIN, JEONG-HYUN.    Modernism gwa euimi changjo. (Modernism: a creation of meaning.) AmeSt (12) 45–78.

**7935.** SHLOSS, CAROL.    In visible light: photography and the American writer 1840–1940. *See* **5716.**

**7936.** SHOEMAKER, ADAM.    Black words, white page: Aboriginal literature 1929–1988. Brisbane: Queensland UP. pp. viii, 314. (UQP studies in Australian literature.)

**7937.** SIMMS, NORMAN.    Who's writing and why they are writers: a survey of selected authors in the new and emerging literatures of the smaller South Pacific islands and Southeast Asia. Hamilton, NZ: Simms. pp. 151.

**7938.** SINCLAIR, ANDREW (ed.).    The war decade: an anthology of the 1940s. London: Hamilton. pp. xx, 332. Rev. by Humphrey Carpenter in TLS, 10 Nov., 1231.

**7939.** SPENDER, DALE (ed.).    The Penguin anthology of Australian women's writing. Harmondsworth; Melbourne: Penguin, 1988. pp. xxxiii, 891. Rev. by Hilaire Lindsay in Span (29) 108–10.

**7940.** STANZEL, FRANZ K.; ZACHARASIEWICZ, WALDEMAR (eds). Encounters and explorations: Canadian writers and European critics. (Bibl. 1987, 20.) Rev. by Stephen Slemon in CanL (116) 1988, 124–5.

**7941.** STEAD, C. K.    The follies of our age: the new Victorians. Metro (Auckland) Feb., 118–24.

**7942.** STEINER, DOROTHEA.    Definition und Selbstdefinition der Frau in der amerikanischen Lyrik. *In* (pp. 33–49) CHRISTA GÜRTLER and BRIGETTE MAZOHL-WALLNIG (eds), Frauenbilder, Frauenrollen, Frauenforschung. Vienna: Geyer, 1987. pp. 189. (Pubs of the Historical Inst. of the Univ. of Salzburg, 17.)

**7943.** STEMME, FRED.    Left Bank cafés. LGJ (8:2) 1988/89, 13–15.

**7944.** STŘÍBRNÝ, ZDENĚK.    Zpráva o chystaném slovníku spisovatelů píšících anglicky. (A report on a dictionary of authors writing in English.) *In* (p. 42) **6.**

**7945.** SUTHERLAND, FRASER.    Frisking Laura Secord. *In* (pp. 14–25) **12.**

**7946.** —— In defence of Laura Secord. *In* (pp. 6–13) **12.** (Repr.: first pub. 1971.)

**7947.** SVARNY, ERIK.    'The men of 1914': T. S. Eliot and early Modernism. Milton Keynes: Open UP. pp. 268. Rev. by Hugh Haughton in TLS, 17 Mar., 286.

**7948.** SWIFT, PATRICK; WRIGHT, DAVID (eds).    An anthology from *x*: a quarterly review of literature and the arts, 1959–1962. *See* **594.**

**7949.** SWINDEN, PATRICK.    Britain. *In* (pp. 252–86) SPENCER PEARCE and DON PIPER (eds), Literature of Europe and America in the 1960s. Manchester: Manchester UP; New York: St Martin's Press. pp. 286.

**7950.** SYMONS, JULIAN.    Makers of the new: the revolution in literature, 1912–1939. (Bibl. 1988, 6040.) Rev. by Hugh Haughton in TLS, 17 Mar., 286.

**7951.** VEIT-WILD, FLORA.    Creating a new society: women's writing in Zimbabwe. JCL (22:1) 1987, 171–8.

**7952.** WALKER, NANCY A.    A very serious thing: women's humor and American culture. *See* **5729.**

**7953.** WALSH, JEFFREY; AULICH, JAMES (eds).    Vietnam images: war and representation. London: Macmillan. pp. xv, 224.

**7954.** WALTON, DAVID.    An English department's guide to multi-cultural literature. Derby: Derbyshire County Council, 1988.

**7955.** WARD, WILLIAM S.    A literary history of Kentucky. *See* **4896.**

**7956.** WASHINGTON, MARY HELEN.    Invented lives: narratives of Black women, 1860–1960. *See* **5733.**

**7957.** WEISSINGER, THOMAS.    Current bibliography. *See* **4897.** (Afro-American writers.)

**7958.** WEST, JAMES L. W., III.    American authors and the literary marketplace since 1900. *See* **467.**

**7959.** WHITE, LANDEG; COUZENS, TIM (eds).   Literature and society in South Africa: papers from a conference at the University of York, September 1981. (Bibl. 1987, 41.) Rev. by A. Ebeogu in Lore and Language (8:1) 142–3.

**7960.** WIESELTIER, LEON.   American letters: a rude vigour . . . . TLS, 15 Sept., 1002, 1012.

**7961.** WILLIAMS, MARK.   Annual bibliography of Commonwealth literature 1988: New Zealand (with the South Pacific Islands). JCL (24:2) 94–116.

**7962.** —— Looking sideways: English studies, tradition, and cross-cultural comparisons. Span (28) 22–39.

**7963.** WINCHELL, JAMES ARTHUR.   Murdered sleep: crime and aesthetics in France and England, 1850–1910. *See* **5740.**

**7964.** WOODCOCK, GEORGE.   Northern Spring: the flowering of Canadian literature. Vancouver; Toronto: Douglas & McIntyre, 1987. pp. 318. Rev. by Clifford G. Holland in QQ (95:3) 1988, 734–5.

**7965.** YALOM, MARILYN.   Maternity, mortality, and the literature of madness. University Park; London: Pennsylvania State UP, 1985. pp. viii, 133. Rev. by Nina Auerbach in MLR (84:2) 419–20; by Heather Murray in CanL (119) 1988, 145–6.

## Drama, the Theatre, Cinema, and Radio and Television Drama.

For works on modern productions of Shakespeare, see under 'Sixteenth Century: William Shakespeare: Productions'.

**7966.** ALBERSMEIER, FRANZ-JOSEF; ROLOFF, VOLKER (eds).   Literaturverfilmungen. Frankfurt: Suhrkamp. pp. 568.

**7967.** ALLAIN, MATHÉ.   They don't even talk like us: Cajun violence in film and fiction. JPC (23:1) 65–75.

**7968.** ALLEN, ROBERT C. (ed.).   Channels of discourse: television and contemporary criticism. Chapel Hill: North Carolina UP, 1987. (Bibl. 1987, 8945.)

**7969.** ALTMAN, RICK.   Dickens, Griffith, and film theory to-day. *See* **6588.**

**7970.** ANDREW, GEOFF.   The film handbook. Harlow: Longman. pp. 362.

**7971.** ASPINALL, SUE; MURPHY, ROBERT (eds).   Gainsborough melodrama. London: British Film Inst., 1983. pp. 93. (BFI dossiers, 18.)

**7972.** AUSLANDER, PHILIP.   Going with the flow: performance art and mass culture. TDR (33:2) 119–36.

**7973.** AUSTER, ALBERT; QUART, LEONARD.   How the war was remembered: Hollywood and Vietnam. New York; London: Praeger, 1988. pp. xv, 171.

**7974.** AUSTIN, GAYLE.   Feminist theory and postwar American drama. Unpub. doct. diss., City Univ. of New York, 1988. [Abstr. in DA (49) 2023A.]

**7975.** BANK, ROSEMARIE.   Frontier melodrama. *See* **4902.**

**7976.** BANNING, YVONNE. Ghosts with ears: the WESSA in contemporary drama. English Academy Review (6) 19–27. (White English-speaking South Africans in drama.)

**7977.** ——Junction Avenue Theatre Company: *Sophiatown.* SATJ (3:1) 95–102.

**7978.** BARKER, C. J. The culture industry in contemporary Britain: the possibility of political drama in television. Unpub. doct. diss., Univ. of Leeds, 1986. [Abstr. in IT (36:3) 900.]

**7979.** BARNES, JOHN. Pioneers of British film: the beginnings of the cinema in England 1894–1901: vol. 3, 1898: the rise of photoplay. *See* **5747.**

**7980.** BEATY, FREDERICK L. Evelyn Waugh and Lance Sieveking: new light on Waugh's relations with the BBC. PLL (25:2) 186–200.

**7981.** BERGER, ROGER A. 'Ask what you can do for your country': the film version of H. G. Wells's *The Time Machine* and the Cold War. LitFQ (17:3) 177–87.

**7982.** BISHOP, CYNTHIA ANN. The deconstructed actor: towards a postmodern acting theory. Unpub. doct. diss., Univ. of Colorado at Boulder, 1988. [Abstr. in DA (49) 3205A.]

**7983.** BOBO, JACQUELINE. Articulation and hegemony: Black women's response to the film *The Color Purple.* Unpub. doct. diss., Univ. of Oregon. [Abstr. in DA (50) 1481–2A.]

**7984.** BOURGET, EITHNE; BOURGET, JEAN-LOUP. Lubitsch, ou, la satire romanesque. Paris: Stock, 1987. pp. 226. Rev. by Mark Lefanu in EA (42:2) 237–8.

**7985.** BOURGET, JEAN-LOUP. Hollywood, années 30: du Krach à Pearl Harbour. Paris: Hatier, 1986. pp. 160. Rev. by Mark Lefanu in EA (42:2) 237–8.

**7986.** BRAYNE, A. The changing depiction of homosexual people in twentieth-century British drama. Unpub. doct. diss., Univ. of Warwick, 1988. [Abstr. in IT (39:4) 1613.]

**7987.** BROICH, ULRICH. Symposium: das europäische Geschichtsdrama nach 1945. Einleitung. LJGG (28) 1987, 153–65.

**7988.** BROWN-GUILLORY, ELIZABETH. Their place on the stage: Black women playwrights in America. Introd. by MARGARET WALKER ALEXANDER; postscr. by GLORIA T. HULL. New York; London: Greenwood Press, 1988. pp. xiv, 163. (Contributions in Afro-American and African studies, 117.)

**7989.** BUSCOMBE, EDWARD (ed.). The BFI companion to the Western. Introd. by RICHARD SCHICKEL. London: Deutsch, 1988. pp. 432.

**7990.** BYERS, THOMAS R. Kissing Becky: masculine fears and misogynist moments in science fiction films. AQ (45:3) 77–95.

**7991.** CARDULLO, BERT. Four notes on classic films. EA (42:4) 434–40. (*Stagecoach, The Cameraman, Psycho, In Which We Serve.*)

**7992.** CARNEGIE, DAVID. Webster's *The Duchess of Malfi* on TV. *See* **4810.**

**7993.** CARPENTER, CHARLES A. Modern drama scholarship and criticism, 1966–1980: an international bibliography. Buffalo, NY;

Toronto UP, 1986. (Bibl. 1986, 9924.) Rev. by Katharine Worth in MLR (84:3) 706–7.

**7994.** CASTAN, CON. Greek/Australian plays. Australasian Drama Studies (12/13) 1988, 17–33.

**7995.** CAVE, RICHARD ALLEN. New British drama in performance on the London stage: 1970–1985. New York: St Martin's Press, 1988. (Bibl. 1987, 8968.) Rev. by Greg Giesekam in TJ (41:3) 413–15.

**7996.** CHAM, MBYE; ANDRADE-WATKINS, CLAIRE (eds). Blackframes: critical perspectives on Black independent cinema: celebration of Black Cinema Inc. Cambridge, MA; London: MIT Press, 1988. pp. 85.

**7997.** CHAMBERS, COLIN. The story of Unity Theatre. London: Lawrence & Wishart. pp. 446, (plates) 16. Rev. by Benedict Nightingale in TLS, 3 Nov., 1214.

**7998.** CHINOY, HELEN KRICH; JENKINS, LINDA WALSH (eds). Women in American theatre. See **5748.**

**7999.** CLANCY, THOMAS M. The Tiresian influence in Hemingway, hard-boiled fiction, and film noir. Unpub. doct. diss., Oklahoma State Univ., 1988. [Abstr. in DA (49) 3025A.]

**8000.** CLARKE, IAN. Edwardian drama: a critical study. London: Faber & Faber. pp. 125.

**8001.** COLVIN, ANNE HUTTA. The celluloid Crusoe: a study of cinematic Robinsonades. See **5185.**

**8002.** COOK, JUDITH. Directors' theatre: sixteen leading directors on the state of theatre in Britain today. London: Hodder & Stoughton. pp. 157. (Interviews.)

**8003.** CORNISH, ROGER; KETELS, VIOLET (introds). The plays of the seventies. London; New York: Methuen, 1986. pp. xxxi, 623. (Landmarks of modern British drama, 2.)

**8004.** —————— The plays of the sixties. London; New York: Methuen, 1985. pp. xxxvi, 732. (Landmarks of modern British drama, 1.)

**8005.** COSGROVE, JAMES DANIEL. The rebel in modern drama. Unpub. doct. diss., St John's Univ., 1988. [Abstr. in DA (49) 2864A.]

**8006.** COWELL, JOHN. No profit but the name: the Longfords and the Gate Theatre. Dublin: O'Brien, 1988. pp. 224.

**8007.** COWIE, PETER. Coppola. London: Deutsch. pp. ix, 270.

**8008.** CRAVEN, IAN. 'Achieving' culture in the Australian cinema. *In* (pp. 121–41) **20.**

**8009.** CUNNINGHAM, FRANK R. The insistence of memory: the opening sequences of Lumet's *Pawnbroker*. LitFQ (17:1) 39–43.

**8010.** DALRYMPLE, L. Explorations in drama, theatre and education: a critique of theatre studies in South Africa. Unpub. doct. diss., Univ. of Natal, 1988.

**8011.** DE LAURETIS, TERESA. Technologies of gender: essays on theory, film and fiction. Basingstoke: Macmillan. (Language, discourse, society.) (Bibl. 1988, 6091.)

**8012.** DELLAR, PAMELA (ed.). Plays without theatres: recollections of The Compass Players Travelling Theatre, 1944–1952. Introd. by NEIL SISSONS. Beverley: Highgate. pp. 174.

**8013.** DEMASTES, WILLIAM W. Beyond naturalism: a new realism in American theatre. New York; London: Greenwood Press, 1988. pp. viii, 174. (Contributions in drama and theatre studies, 27.) (Cf. bibl. 1987, 8978.) Rev. by Teresa Pyzik in AL (61:3) 502–4.

**8014.** DE NAVACELLE, THIERRY. Woody Allen on location. London: Sidgwick & Jackson, 1987. pp. 464.

**8015.** DERRY, CHARLES. The suspense thriller: films in the shadow of Alfred Hitchcock. Jefferson, NC; London: McFarland, 1988. pp. vii, 351.

**8016.** DESILET, GREGORY. Nietzsche contra Burke: the melodɪama in dramatism. QJS (75:1) 65–83.

**8017.** DESSEN, ALAN C. Modern productions and the Elizabethan scholar. *See* **3058.**

**8018.** DIAMOND, ELIN. Mimesis, mimicry, and the 'true-real'. ModDr (32:1) 58–72.

**8019.** DICKASON, CHRISTIE. Experience and experiment: new theatre workshops 1979–1982. London: Gulbenkian Foundation, 1987. pp. 72.

**8020.** DIELTJENS, LOUIS. The Abbey Theatre as a cultural formation. *In* (pp. 47–65) **32.**

**8021.** DOLAN, JILL. Breaking the code: musings on lesbian sexuality and the performer. ModDr (32:1) 146–58.

**8022.** —— The feminist spectator as critic. Ann Arbor, MI: UMI Research Press. pp. xii, 150. (Theatre and dramatic studies, 52.) Rev. by Helene Keyssar in TJ (41:3) 431–3.

**8023.** DONALD, JAMES (ed.). Fantasy and the cinema. London: British Film Inst. pp. 298.

**8024.** DOOLEY, D. J. *A Handful of Dust* on film: the missing implications. EWN (23:2) 1–4.

**8025.** DURGNAT, RAYMOND; SIMMON, SCOTT. King Vidor, American. Berkeley; London: California UP, 1988. pp. xiii, 382.

**8026.** DUTTON, RICHARD. Modern tragicomedy and the British tradition. (Bibl. 1988, 6098.) Rev. by Peter Hollindale in RES (39:153) 1988, 144–5; by Gerald Mast in MP (86:3) 331–5; by John Stokes in YES (19) 350.

**8027.** EDGERTON, GARY. A visit to the imaginary landscape of Harrison, Texas: sketching the film career of Horton Foote. LitFQ (17:1) 1–12.

**8028.** ENGELL, JOHN. *The Treasure of the Sierra Madre*: B. Traven, John Huston and ideology in film adaptation. LitFQ (17:4) 245–52.

**8029.** ENKEMANN, JÜRGEN. Nichtliterarische Theaterformen: zu ihrem Vordringen in Großbritannien seit den 60er Jahren. *In* (pp. 57–71) **4.**

**8030.** ETHERTON, MICHAEL. Contemporary Irish dramatists. Basingstoke: Macmillan. pp. xvi, 253. (Macmillan modern dramatists.)

**8031.** FAN, ADA MEI. In and out of bounds: marriage, adultery, and women in the plays of Henry Arthur Jones, Arthur Wing Pinero, Harley Granville-Barker, John Galsworthy, and W. Somerset Maugham. *See* **5752.**

**8032.** FENN, JEFFREY WILLIAM.   Culture under stress: American drama and the Vietnam War. Unpub. doct. diss., Univ. of British Columbia, 1988. [Abstr. in DA (49) 3552–3A.]

**8033.** FÉRAL, JOSETTE.   Performance and media: the use of image. Trans. by RON BIRMINGHAM. CanL (118) 1988, 83–95.

**8034.** FILEWOD, ALAN.   Collective encounters: documentary theatre in English Canada. Toronto; London: Toronto UP, 1987. pp. xi, 214. Rev. by Richard Paul Knowles in CanL (122/23) 206–7.

**8035.** FINK, HOWARD; JACKSON, JOHN (eds).   All the bright company: radio drama produced by Andrew Allan. Kingston, Ont.: Quarry Press; Toronto: CBC, 1987. pp. xvi, 336. Rev. by Jill Tomasson Goodwin in CanL (120) 213–15.

**8036.** FISCHER, LUCY.   Shot/countershot: film tradition and women's cinema. Basingstoke: Macmillan. pp. xii, 348.

**8037.** FRICKE, JOHN; SCARFONE, JAY; STILLMAN, WILLIAM.   *The Wizard of Oz*: the official 50th anniversary pictorial history. Introd. by JACK HALEY, JR. London: Hodder & Stoughton. pp. x, 245.

**8038.** GALESTIN, PAUL.   The Marx Brothers: verbal and visual nonsense in their films. *In* (pp. 149–60) **28.**

**8039.** GAREBIAN, KEITH.   Seasons of discontent. *In* (pp. 140–53) **12.**

**8040.** GEIS, DEBORAH R.   Mythmaking and storytelling: the mono-logue in contemporary American drama. Unpub. doct. diss., Univ. of Michigan, 1988. [Abstr. in DA (49) 2025A.]

**8041.** GOSCILO, MARGARET.   Ivory–Merchant's *Maurice*: the hero in absentia. LitFQ (17:2) 99–107.

**8042.** GOSHER, SYDNEY PAUL.   A historical and critical survey of the South African one-act play written in English. *See* **5755.**

**8043.** GREYVENSTEIN, W. R.   Children's theatre in South Africa. Lantern (38:2) 17–24.

**8044.** —— The history and development of children's theatre in English in South Africa. *See* **5757.**

**8045.** GREYVENSTEIN, WALTER.   Let us entertain you! Children's theatre and popular entertainment. *See* **5758.**

**8046.** GROOME, MARGARET ESTELLE.   Canada's Stratford Festival, 1953–1967: hegemony, commodity, institution. Unpub. doct. diss., McGill Univ., 1988. [Abstr. in DA (50) 1486A.]

**8047.** GUSTAFSON, ANTOINETTE MCCLOSKEY.   The image of the West in American popular performance. *See* **5760.**

**8048.** HANSEN, MIRIAM.   The hieroglyph and the whore: D. W. Griffith's *Intolerance*. SAQ (88:2) 361–92.

**8049.** HARBEN, NILOUFER.   Twentieth-century English history plays: from Shaw to Bond. (Bibl. 1988, 6116.) Rev. by Ronald W. Strang in NQ (36:4) 548–9.

**8050.** HARRIS, CLARISSA MYRICK.   Mirror of the movement: the history of the Free Southern Theater as a microcosm of the Civil Rights and Black Power movements. Unpub. doct. diss., Emory Univ., 1988. [Abstr. in DA (49) 3065A.]

**8051.** HARRISON, S. R. American society, cinema and television. Unpub. doct. diss., Univ. of Manchester, 1985. [Abstr. in IT (36:2) 464.]

**8052.** HART, LYNDA. Introduction: performing feminism. *In* (pp. 1–21) **39.**

**8053.** ——— (ed.). Making a spectacle: feminist essays on contemporary women's theatre. *See* **39.**

**8054.** HAUPTFLEISCH, TEMPLE. Citytalk, theatretalk: dialect, dialogue and multilingual theatre in South Africa. *See* **1528.**

**8055.** HEILPERN, JOHN. Conference of the birds: the story of Peter Brook in Africa. (Bibl. 1978, 8850.) London: Methuen. pp. 327. (Revised ed.: first ed. 1977.)

**8056.** HELLE, ANITA PLATH. Re-presenting women writers onstage: a retrospective to the present. *In* (pp. 195–208) **39.**

**8057.** HERMAN, WILLIAM. Understanding contemporary American drama. Columbia: South Carolina UP, 1987. pp. 271. Rev. by Lynda Hart in ModDr (32:2) 324–7.

**8058.** HILL, ANTHONY DUANE. J. A. Jackson's page in *Billboard*: a voice for Black performance during the Harlem renaissance between 1920–25. *See* **573.**

**8059.** HILL, W. J. Class, sexuality and the British cinema, 1956–63. Unpub. doct. diss., Univ. of York, 1986. [Abstr. in IT (36:2) 464.]

**8060.** HOLLADAY, WILLIAM E.; WATT, STEPHEN. Viewing *The Elephant Man*. PMLA (104:5) 868–81.

**8061.** HOPCRAFT, ARTHUR. The spirit of revolution. *See* **6620.**

**8062.** HUGGETT, RICHARD. Binkie Beaumont: *eminence grise* of the West End theatre, 1933–1973. London; Toronto: Hodder & Stoughton. pp. 575.

**8063.** HUMPHRIES, REYNOLD. Fritz Lang: genre and representation in his American films. Baltimore, MD; London: Johns Hopkins UP. pp. xviii, 207.

**8064.** HUSSAIN, SHAISTA. Violence in some twentieth-century plays. Journal of Research (Univ. of the Punjab, Lahore) (15) 1980, 37–60.

**8065.** HUTCHISON, BETH. Gertrude Stein's film scenarios. LitFQ (17:1) 35–8.

**8066.** JAMESON, FREDRIC. Nostalgia for the present. SAQ (88:2) 517–37. (*Time Out of Joint*.)

**8067.** JOHNSON, EDWARD HOTSPUR. *Wuthering Heights*: Bombay style. *See* **6334.**

**8068.** JOHNSON, MARY CHARLOTTE. A critical study of the poetic voice in the narratives of selected documentary films of the 1930s. Unpub. doct. diss., Ohio State Univ. [Abstr. in DA (50) 813A.] (*Night Mail, Power and the Land, Spanish Earth*.)

**8069.** KENNEDY, DOUGLAS. Wars of the words. Listener (121) 8 June, 29–30. (Screenwriting.)

**8070.** KING, ROBERT L. Recent drama. MassR (30:1) 122–36.

8071. KISELINČEVA, KSENIJA. Monologăt v săvremennata ameri-kanska drama. (The monologue in contemporary American drama.) Literaturna misăl (33:2) 79–87.

8072. KOLKER, ROBERT PHILLIP. A cinema of loneliness: Penn, Kubrick, Scorsese, Spielberg, Altman. (Bibl. 1980, 10521.) New York; Oxford: OUP, 1988. pp. xv, 442. (Second ed.: first ed. 1980.)

8073. LARABEE, ANN E. First-wave feminist theatre, 1890–1930. See 5763.

8074. LASKY, ROBERTA LYNNE. The New Playwrights Theatre, 1927–1929. Unpub. doct. diss., Univ. of California, Davis, 1988. [Abstr. in DA (50) 22–3A.]

8075. LAWRENCE, HAPPY JAMES. The state-wide tours of the Florida Federal Theatre Project, October, 1937–June, 1939: a description and evaluation of two seasons on the road for the 'People's Popular Theatre'. Unpub. doct. diss., Florida State Univ., 1988. [Abstr. in DA (49) 3553A.]

8076. LE BLOND, MAX. Drama in Singapore: towards an English language theatre. In (pp. 112–25) 19. (Revised version of conference paper, Singapore, 8–16 April 1981.)

8077. LENNON, PETER. A tale of two dummies. See 6630.

8078. LEO, JOHN R. The familialism of 'man' in American television melodrama. SAQ (88:1) 31–51.

8079. LEONARD, WILLIAM TORBERT. Once was enough. See 5765.

8080. LITTLETON, C. SCOTT. Some implications of the mythology in Star Trek. KF (4:1) 33–42.

8081. LOMONACO, MARTHA SCHMOYER. Broadway in the Poconos: the Tamiment Playhouse, 1921–1960. Unpub. doct. diss., New York Univ., 1988. [Abstr. in DA (50) 23A.]

8082. LOUW, P. ERIC. State-subsidised theatre following the September 1984 Vaal uprising. SATJ (3:2) 101–15.

8083. LURBE, PIERRE. Violence et sacrifice dans Peter Grimes de Benjamin Britten. In (pp. 121–38) 60.

8084. MCCALLUM, JOHN. Studying Australian drama. Australasian Drama Studies (12/13) 1988, 147–66.

8085. MCDERMOTT, KATE (ed.). Places, please! The first anthology of lesbian plays. Iowa City, IA: Aunt Lute Book Co., 1985. pp. xx, 209. Rev. by Jill Dolan in TJ (39:1) 1987, 120–2.

8086. MACDONALD, SCOTT. A critical cinema: interviews with independent filmmakers. Berkeley; London: California UP, 1988. pp. x, 410.

8087. MCGANN, G. K. 'The keys to dreamland': Marxism, aesthetics and film. Unpub. doct. diss., Univ. of Cambridge, 1986. [Abstr. in IT (36:2) 464.]

8088. MACKLIN, JENNY. Film techniques in A Room with a View. Crux (23:4) 8–19.

8089. MAEL, PHYLLIS. Trifles: the path to sisterhood. LitFQ (17:4) 281–4.

**8090.** MAXFIELD, JAMES F. *La Belle Dame sans merci* and the neurotic knight: characterization in *The Maltese Falcon*. LitFQ (17:4) 253–60.

**8091.** MURPHY, ROBERT. Realism and tinsel: cinema and society in Britain, 1939–1948. London: Routledge. pp. xv, 278. (Cinema and society.)

**8092.** MYUNG, INN SEO. A dramatic and theatrical criticism of John Mason Brown. Unpub. doct. diss., Univ. of Michigan, 1988. [Abstr. in DA (49) 2027A.]

**8093.** NAPOLEON, DAVIDA S. The Chelsea Theater Center: a history. Unpub. doct. diss., New York Univ., 1988. [Abstr. in DA (50) 23A.]

**8094.** NAREMORE, JAMES. Acting in the cinema. Berkeley; London: California UP, 1988. pp. ix, 307.

**8095.** NICHOLS, BILL. Form wars: the political unconscious of Formalist theory. SAQ (88:2) 487–515.

**8096.** O'CONNOR, ALAN (ed.). Raymond Williams on television: selected writings. New York; London: Routledge. pp. xvii, 223.

**8097.** O'CONNOR, MARION. William Poel and the Elizabethan Stage Society. *See* **5769.**

**8098.** O'ROURKE, JOYCE WILLIAMS. New female playwrights in the American theatre, 1973–83: a critical analysis of thought in selected plays. Unpub. doct. diss., Louisiana State Univ. and Agricultural and Mechanical College, 1988. [Abstr. in DA (49) 2027–8A.]

**8099.** OSMENT, PHILIP (ed.). Gay Sweatshop: four plays and a company. London: Methuen. pp. lxviii, 148. (Philip Osment, *This Island's Mine*; Noel Greig, *The Dear Love of Comrades*; Andy Kirby, *Compromised Immunity*; Jackie Kay, *Twice Over*.)

**8100.** PALMER, RICHARD H. The critics' canon: standards of theatrical reviewing in America. New York; London: Greenwood Press, 1988. pp. xii, 183. (Contributions in drama and theatre studies, 26.)

**8101.** PATTERSON, TOM; GOULD, ALLAN. First stage: the making of the Stratford festival. Toronto: McLelland & Stewart, 1987. pp. 224. Rev. by Anthony Dawson in CanL (116) 1988, 202–3.

**8102.** PAYNE, DAVID. *The Wizard of Oz*: therapeutic rhetoric in a contemporary media ritual. *See* **1782.**

**8103.** PETER, JOHN. Vladimir's carrot: modern drama and the modern imagination. Chicago: Chicago UP, 1987. (Bibl. 1987, 9064.) Rev. by James Fisher in ModDr (32:2) 318–19.

**8104.** PETTIGREW, JOHN; PORTMAN, JAMIE. Stratford: the first thirty years: vol. 1, 1953–1967; vol. 2, 1968–1982. Introd. by ROBERTSON DAVIES. Basingstoke; Toronto: Macmillan, 1985. pp. xx, 198; 314. Rev. by Anthony Dawson in CanL (116) 1988, 200–2.

**8105.** PHILLIPS, GENE D. Fiction, film, and Faulkner: the art of adaptation. Knoxville: Tennessee UP, 1988. pp. xvii, 217. Rev. by Dana Polan in AL (61:2) 314–16.

**8106.** PIAZZA, ROBERTA. A conversational analysis of theatrical discourse: repair procedures as the expression of dramatic interaction. *See* **1360.**

**8107.** PINKNEY, D. S.   The professional repertory theatre in Yorkshire, 1945–1955. Unpub. doct. diss., Univ. of Leeds, 1986. [Abstr. in IT (36:3) 901.]

**8108.** PLATZ, NORBERT H.   Die Orchestrierung des menschlichen Stimmpotentials: zur Klangästhetik des modernen englischen und amerikanischen Dramas. *In* (pp. 72–90) **4.**

**8109.** PRESSLER, TERRA DAUGIRDA.   Transformative comedy: an emerging genre. Unpub. doct. diss., Univ. of Oregon, 1988. [Abstr. in DA (49) 3553A.]

**8110.** PROEHL, GEOFFREY SCOTT.   Coming home again: American family drama and the figure of the prodigal. *See* **5770.**

**8111.** QUIGLEY, AUSTIN E.   The modern age and other worlds. London: Methuen, 1985. (Bibl. 1987, 9071.) Rev. by Michael Göring in MLR (84:2) 429.

**8112.** QUINCE, W. ROHAN.   'To thine own self be true . . .': adapting E. M. Forster's *Maurice* to the screen. LitFQ (17:2) 108–12.

**8113.** REES, CHARLES A.   Lady Bright and her children: contemporary American gay drama. Unpub. doct. diss., Univ. of Tennessee, 1988. [Abstr. in DA (50) 687A.]

**8114.** REISSIG, ERICH.   Sterne televised. *See* **5515.**

**8115.** REITZ, BERNHARD.   The *telos* of the loss: thematic and structural implications of the concept of identity in British drama since 1956. YREAL (6) 299–342.

**8116.** RENOV, MICHAEL.   Hollywood's wartime woman: representation and ideology. Ann Arbor, MI; London: UMI Research Press, 1988. pp. viii, 275. (Studies in cinema, 42.)

**8117.** RICHARDSON, BRIAN ERLING.   Unlikely stories: causality and interpretation in modern narrative. Unpub. doct. diss., Univ. of Washington, 1988. [Abstr. in DA (49) 3720A.]

**8118.** ROCKETT, WILL H.   Devouring the whirlwind: terror and transcendence in the cinema of cruelty. New York; London: Greenwood Press, 1988. pp. xvii, 204. (Contributions to the study of popular culture, 21.)

**8119.** ROGIN, MICHAEL.   The great mother domesticated: sexual difference and sexual indifference in D. W. Griffith's *Intolerance*. CI (15:3) 510–55.

**8120.** ROONEY, PHILLIP J.   The quest elements in the films of John Boorman. Unpub. doct. diss., Univ. of Nebraska–Lincoln. [Abstr. in DA (50) 1314–15A.]

**8121.** ROOSE-EVANS, JAMES.   Experimental theatre: from Stanislavsky to Peter Brook. (Bibl. 1985, 8833.) London: Routledge. pp. ix, 225. (Fourth ed.: first ed. 1973.)

**8122.** ROSTECK, THOMAS.   Irony, argument, and reportage in television documentary: *See It Now* versus Senator McCarthy. *See* **1319.**

**8123.** ROTHMAN, WILLIAM.   The 'I' of the camera: essays on film criticism, history and aesthetics. Cambridge: CUP, 1988. pp. xix, 210. (Cambridge studies in film.)

**8124.** RUSHING, JANICE HOCKER. Evolution of the new frontier in *Alien* and *Aliens*: patriarchal co-optation of the feminine archetype. QJS (75:1) 1–24.

**8125.** SAMUEL, RAPHAEL. Dickens on stage and screen. *See* **6657.**

**8126.** SANDERS, LESLIE CATHERINE. The development of Black theater in America: from shadows to selves. Baton Rouge; London: Louisiana State UP, 1988. pp. ix, 252. Rev. by Preston M. Yancy in AL (61:1) 134–5; by Eugene Kraft in BALF (23:1) 175–8; by Tim Youngs in ModDr (32:3) 458–9.

**8127.** SANDERSON, JIM. American romanticism in John Ford's *The Grapes of Wrath*: horizontalness, darkness, Christ, and F.D.R. LitFQ (17:4) 231–44.

**8128.** SAURAN, DAVID. In their own words: contemporary American playwrights. New York: Theatre Communications Group, 1988. pp. 320. Rev. by Philip C. Kolin in ModDr (32:2) 327–9.

**8129.** SCHIELE, J. M. Post war theatre in Camden: a study of three theatre enterprises (the Bedford Theatre, the Open Space Theatre, the Round House) between 1949 and 1983. Unpub. doct. diss., CNAA, 1987. [Abstr. in IT (39:2) 478; in DA (50) 1140A.]

**8130.** SCHROEDER, PATRICIA R. The presence of the past in modern American drama. Madison, NJ: Fairleigh Dickinson UP. pp. 148. Rev. by Martha Gilman Bower in AL (61:4) 718–19.

**8131.** SCHWARTZ, PAT. The best of company: the story of Johannesburg's Market Theatre. Johannesburg: Donker, 1988. pp. 280.

**8132.** SCOTT, MICHAEL. Shakespeare and the modern dramatist. *See* **3644.**

**8133.** SCRUGGS, CHARLES. Ethical freedom and visual space: filming *The French Lieutenant's Woman*. Mosaic (20:2) 1987, 13–28.

**8134.** SHOUT, JOHN D. Joyce at twenty-five, Huston at eighty-one: *The Dead*. LitFQ (17:2) 91–4.

**8135.** SILVER, ALAIN, *et al.* (eds). An encyclopedic reference guide to film noir. (Bibl. 1980, 10637.) London: Bloomsbury. pp. 410. (Second ed.: first ed. 1980.)

**8136.** SINCLAIR, MARIANNE. Hollywood Lolita: the nymphet syndrome in the movies. London: Plexus, 1988. pp. 160.

**8137.** SINYARD, NEIL. Dickensian visions in modern British film. *See* **6662.**

**8138.** SMITH, LESLIE. Modern British farce: a selective study of British farce from Pinero to the present day. *See* **5775.**

**8139.** STEPHENS, JUDITH L. Gender ideology and dramatic convention in progressive era plays, 1890–1920. *See* **5776.**

**8140.** STEVENSON, T. M. Modes of Realism: mining drama for the British stage 1900 to the present day. Unpub. M.Phil. diss., Univ. of Nottingham, 1988. [Abstr. in IT (38:4) 1451.]

**8141.** STRASBERG, LEE. A dream of passion: the development of the Method. Edited by EVANGELINE MORPHOS. Boston, MA: Little, Brown, 1987; London: Bloomsbury, 1988; Methuen. pp. xvii, 201.

**8142.** TANITCH, ROBERT.   Guinness. London: Harrap. pp. 168. (Alec Guinness.)

**8143.** TERRIS, OLWEN (ed.).   Twentieth-century dramatists: a list of audio-visual materials available in the UK. London: British Universities Film and Video Council, 1987. pp. vi, 33.

**8144.** THOMPSON, DAVID; CHRISTIE, IAN (eds).   Scorsese on Scorsese. London: Faber & Faber. pp. xxviii, 178.

**8145.** THOMSEN, CHRISTIAN W.; SCHNEIDER, IRMELA (eds).   Grundzüge der Geschichte des europäischen Hörspiels. Darmstadt: Wissenschaftliche Buchgesellschaft, 1985. pp. vi, 233. Rev. by Horst Priessnitz in Ang (107:3/4) 544–9.

**8146.** TICHY, CHARLES ALLEN.   The first seventy years of legitimate theatre in Omaha, Nebraska. Unpub. doct. diss., New York Univ., 1988. [Abstr. in DA (50) 24A.]

**8147.** TOMASELLI, KEYAN.   The cinema of apartheid: race and class in South African film. Sandton: Radix; London: Routledge; New York: Lakeview Press. pp. 299.

**8148.** TURIM, MAUREEN.   Flashbacks in film: memory and history. New York; London: Routledge. pp. ix, 278.

**8149.** TURNER, GRAEME.   Film and fiction: dealing with Australian narrative. In (pp. 109–20) **20.**

**8150.** VANDEN HEUVEL, MICHAEL JOHN.   Performing drama/dramatizing performance: the interface between experimental theatre and postmodern drama, 1960–present. Unpub. doct. diss., Univ. of Wisconsin–Madison, 1988. [Abstr. in DA (49) 3372A.]

**8151.** VAN ZYL, JOHN.   Film adaptation as an interpretation of a play: the case of *Look Back in Anger*. SATJ (3:2) 4–18.

**8152.** VEST, JAMES M.   Reflections of Ophelia (and of Hamlet) in Alfred Hitchcock's *Vertigo. See* **3670.**

**8153.** WARD, KATHRYN ANN.   Clients, colleagues, and consorts: roles of women in American hardboiled detective fiction and film. Unpub. doct. diss., Ohio State Univ., 1988. [Abstr. in DA (49) 2223A.]

**8154.** WEEKS, STEPHEN HYER.   Alternative histories: British historical drama from the Left since 1956. Unpub. doct. diss., Stanford Univ., 1988. [Abstr. in DA (49) 2456A.]

**8155.** WELLWARTH, GEORGE.   Mindlessness in modern drama. SATJ (3:1) 3–17.

**8156.** WESELIŃSKI, ANDRZEJ.   F. Scott Fitzgerald: the novelist looks at Hollywood. KN (36:2) 89–103.

**8157.** WHITEHEAD, KATE.   The Third Programme: a literary history. Oxford: Clarendon Press. pp. 260. (Oxford English monographs.)

**8158.** WHYNOT, CHRIS.   Canadian film: in search of a future. QQ (95:2) 1988, 403–13.

**8159.** WILKERSON, MARGARET B.   Music as metaphor: new plays of Black women. In (pp. 61–75) **39.**

**8160.** WYVER, JOHN.   The moving image: an international history of film, television and video. Oxford: Blackwell. pp. 321.

**8161.** YULE, ANDREW. Enigma: David Puttnam, the story so far . . . . Edinburgh: Mainstream, 1988. pp. 480.

## Fiction

**8162.** ACHEBE, CHINUA. Hopes and impediments: selected essays 1967–87. (Bibl. 1988, 6204.) Rev. by Craig Raine in LRB (11:12) 16–18.

**8163.** AHEARN, EDWARD J. Marx and modern fiction. *See* **5779.**

**8164.** ALBERS, CHRISTINA EDNA. The guardian male figure in selected novels of Hawthorne, James, Howells, Wharton, Cather, and Hemingway. *See* **5780.**

**8165.** ALLAIN, MATHÉ. They don't even talk like us: Cajun violence in film and fiction. *See* **7967.**

**8166.** ANON. The novel in Britain since 1970: a selected bibliography. London: British Council. pp. 68.

**8167.** —— (ed.). Dykeversions: lesbian short fiction. London; Toronto: Women's Press, 1986. pp. 186. Rev. by Roberts Buchanan in CanL (121) 184–6. (Anthology of Canadian lesbian fiction.)

**8168.** —— The self in contemporary American short fiction: who are we? Twenty-one writers of short fiction respond. Mānoa (Honolulu, HI) (1:1/2) 64–80.

**8169.** ARBERY, GLENN CANNON. Victims of likeness: quadroons and octoroons in Southern fiction. *See* **5781.**

**8170.** ASGILL, EDMONDSON OMOTAYO. The endangered species: the African character in American fiction. Unpub. doct. diss., Univ. of South Florida, 1988. [Abstr. in DA (50) 138A.]

**8171.** ASH, SUSAN. Having it both ways: reading related short fiction by post-colonial women writers. Span (28) 40–55.

**8172.** ATWOOD, MARGARET; WEAVER, ROBERT (sels). The Oxford book of Canadian short stories in English. *See* **5783.**

**8173.** BACHINGER, KATRINA. Gender positions: the intertextuality of gender difference in Margaret Atwood, Katherine Mansfield, Joyce Carol Oates, Edgar Allan Poe, Sir Philip Sidney and others. *See* **3306.**

**8174.** BAETENS, JAN. The intermediate domain, or the photographic novel and the problems of value. CI (15:2) 280–91.

**8175.** BAIL, MURRAY (ed.). The Faber book of contemporary Australian short stories. London: Faber & Faber, 1988. pp. 413. Rev. by John Bayley in LRB (10:4) 9.

**8176.** BAKER, CANDIDA (ed.). Yacker: Australian writers talk about their work. Sydney: Pan, 1986. pp. 315.

**8177.** BARMOR, YITZHAK. The father figure in Jewish-American literature. Unpub. doct. diss., Kent State Univ., 1988. [Abstr. in DA (49) 3024A.] (Henry Roth, Bernard Malamud, Saul Bellow, Edward Lewis Wallant, Herbert Gold, Philip Roth.)

**8178.** BARNES, PAULA CASSANDRA. Tradition and innovation: Toni Morrison and the flight motif in Afro-American literature. Unpub. doct. diss., Univ. of Michigan, 1988. [Abstr. in DA (49) 3721A.]

**8179.** BARTLETT, MARY DOUGHERTY (ed.). The new Native American novel: works in progress. Albuquerque: New Mexico UP, 1986. pp. viii, 132. Rev. by Leo E. Oliva in AIQ (11:4) 1987, 354–5.

**8180.** BARTTER, MARTHA A. The way to ground zero: the atomic bomb in American science fiction. New York; London: Greenwood Press, 1988. pp. xii, 278. (Contributions to the study of science fiction and fantasy, 33.)

**8181.** BAUER, STEFAN. Das wahrscheinliche Unwahrscheinliche. Realitätsansprüche in der Kriminalliteratur. See **5784.**

**8182.** BELL, BERNARD W. The Afro-American novel and its tradition. Amherst: Massachusetts UP, 1987; London: Massachusetts UP. pp. 421. Rev. by Mary Ellison in JAStud (23:3) 493–4.

**8183.** BERGER, ALBERT I. Towards a science of the nuclear mind: science-fiction origins of dianetics. SFS (16:2) 123–44.

**8184.** BERTENS, HANS. The attack on epistemology in recent American fiction. In (pp. 249–59) **47.**

**8185.** BIALOSTOSKY, DON H. Dialogics, narratology, and the virtual space of discourse. JNT (19:1) 167–73.

**8186.** BIRD, DELYS. Writing women/reading women: the double-voiced discourse of Australian women's fiction. In (pp. 91–107) **20.**

**8187.** BOBYLEVA, N. E. Angliiskiĭ politicheskiĭ detektiv 70–80-kh godov o vtoroĭ mirovoĭ voĭne. (The English political detective novel of the 70s and 80s about the Second World War.) VKU (23) 111–14.

**8188.** BOLGER, DERMOT (ed.). The Dolmen book of Irish Christmas stories. Portlaoise: Dolmen, 1986. pp. 164.

**8189.** BOSSERT, REX THOMAS. Oneiric architecture: a study in the ideology of modern utopian fiction. See **5792.**

**8190.** BRACCO, R. M. British middlebrow writers and the First World War, 1919–1939. Unpub. doct. diss., Univ. of Cambridge. [Abstr. in IT (39:2) 488.]

**8191.** BRANS, JO. Listen to the voices: conversations with contemporary writers. Dallas, TX: Southern Methodist UP. pp. 260. Rev. by Richard B. Sale in TBR (9:2) 26–7.

**8192.** BRIANS, PAUL. Nuclear holocausts: atomic war in fiction, 1895–1984. Kent, OH: Kent State UP, 1987. pp. 398. Rev. by Alexander H. McIntire, Jr, in SFS (16:1) 110–13; by James Kirkup in NC (8) 190–2.

**8193.** BROMLEY, ROGER. Lost narratives: popular fictions, politics and recent history. London: Routledge, 1988. pp. xv, 230. (Popular fiction.)

**8194.** BUITENHUIS, PETER. The Great War of words: British, American, and Canadian propaganda and fiction, 1914–1933. Vancouver: British Columbia UP, 1987. pp. xviii, 199. Rev. by J. H. Stape in EA (42:4) 487–8; by John Ferns in CanL (120) 173–5.

**8195.** —— The Great War of words: literature as propaganda, 1914–18 and after. London: Batsford, 1987. pp. xviii, 199. Rev. by Dominic Hibberd in TLS, 28 July, 816.

**8196.** BURNARD, BONNIE (ed.).    The old dance: love stories of one kind or another. Moose Jaw, Sask.: Coteau; Thundercreek, 1986. pp. 350. Rev. by Myra Junyk in QQ (95:2) 1988, 450–2.

**8197.** CAMPBELL, ELAINE.    The dichotomized heroine in West Indian fiction. JCL (22:1) 1987, 137–43.

**8198.** CARBY, HAZEL V.    Reconstructing womanhood: the emergence of the Afro-American woman novelist. (Bibl. 1988, 6224.) Rev. by Elizabeth A. Schultz in AmerS (29:2) 1988, 96.

**8199.** CARMIGNANI, PAUL.    Sud historique, Sud mythique, Sud diégétique. *See* **5797.**

**8200.** CAWS, MARY ANN.    Reading frames in modern fiction. (Bibl. 1988, 6225.) Rev. by Alan Kennedy in UTQ (56:3) 1987, 443–6.

**8201.** CAWTHRA, GILLIAN.    Cultural climate and linguistic style: change in English fictional prose from the late Victorian to the early modern period. *See* **5798.**

**8202.** CHAMBERS, ROSS.    Narrative and other triangles. JNT (19:1) 31–48.

**8203.** CHÉNETIER, MARC.    Au-delà du soupçon: la nouvelle fiction américaine de 1960 à nos jours. Paris: Seuil. pp. 453. (Le Don des langues.)

**8204.** —— De drôles de genres, remarques sur l'hybridation générique dans la fiction américaine contemporaine. *In* JEAN BESSIÈRE (ed.), Hybrides romanesques: fiction (1960–1985.) Paris: Presses Universitaires de France, 1988. pp. 143. (Publications du Centre d'Études du Roman et du Romanesque, Université de Picardie.)

**8205.** CHERRY, KELLY.    When all is said and done, how literary theory *really* affects contemporary fiction. NLH (21:1) 21–33.

**8206.** CHESTER, LAURA (ed.).    Deep down: the new sensual writing by women. Boston, MA; London; New York: Faber & Faber, 1988. pp. xii, 330. Rev. in OhioanaQ (32:3) 171.

**8207.** CHRISTIANSON, SCOTT R.    Tough talk and wisecracks: language as power in American detective fiction. JPC (23:2) 151–62.

**8208.** CHRISTIE, CLIVE J.    The quiet American and the ugly American: Western literary perspective on Indo-China in a decade of transition, 1950–1960. Canterbury: Centre of South-East Asian Studies. pp. ii, 70. (Occasional papers, 10.)

**8209.** CLANCY, THOMAS M.    The Tiresian influence in Hemingway, hard-boiled fiction, and film noir. *See* **7999.**

**8210.** CLARY, FRANÇOISE.    L'espoir de vivre: violence et sexualité dans le roman afro-américain, de Chester Himes à Hal Bennett. Berne: Lang, 1988. pp. 374.

**8211.** CLINES, RAYMOND H.    A descriptive analysis of dialogue and inner speech in selected works of fiction. *See* **5800.**

**8212.** CLUTE, JOHN; PRINGLE, DAVID; OUNSLEY, SIMON (eds).    Interzone: the third anthology. New York; London: Simon & Schuster, 1988. pp. viii, 184.

**8213.** COBB, GERALD THOMAS.    Fictive bodies: representation of the human form in twentieth-century American novels. Unpub. doct. diss., Univ. of Washington, 1988. [Abstr. in DA (49) 2656–7A.]

**8214.** COHN, DORRIT.    Fictional versus historical lives: borderlines and borderline cases. JNT (19:1) 3–24.

**8215.** COHN, JAN.    Romance and the erotics of property: mass-market fiction for women. Durham, NC: Duke UP, 1988. pp. 181. Rev. by Sharon Felton in AL (61:1) 148–9.

**8216.** CONTENTO, WILLIAM.    Index to science fiction anthologies and collections, 1977–1983. Boston, MA: G. K. Hall, 1984. pp. 503. (A reference publication in science fiction.) Rev. by Gary K. Wolfe in SFS (14:2) 1987, 252–60.

**8217.** COOK, MICHAEL L.; MILLER, STEPHEN T.    Mystery, detective and espionage fiction: a checklist of fiction in U.S. pulp magazines, 1915–1974. *See* **560.**

**8218.** COUSSY, DENISE.    Le roman nigérian anglophone. Paris: Silex, 1988. pp. 527.

**8219.** COWART, DAVID.    History and the contemporary novel. Carbondale: Southern Illinois UP. pp. xii, 246. Rev. by Robert F. Kiernan in AL (61:4) 713–14.

**8220.** CRAIG, TERRENCE.    Racial attitudes in English-Canadian fiction, 1905–1980. (Bibl. 1987, 9183.) Rev. by K. P. Stich in CanL (120) 168–70.

**8221.** CROOKS, ROBERT C.    The eternal moment: paralysis and stasis in modern British fiction. Unpub. doct. diss., Tufts Univ. [Abstr. in DA (50) 1662A.]

**8222.** CUNLIFFE, MARCUS. America's imaginary wars. *In* (pp. 251–60) **2.**

**8223.** CYGAN, JAN (ed.).    Anglica Wratislaviensia, 14. *See* **3.**

**8224.** DAVIS, SUSAN: HALEY, RUSSELL (eds).    The Penguin book of contemporary New Zealand short stories. Auckland; Harmondsworth: Penguin. pp. 389. Rev. by Andrew Mason in NZList, 18 Dec., 101–3.

**8225.** DEMBO, L. S.    The monological Jew: a literary study. Madison: Wisconsin UP, 1988. pp. xi, 196. Rev. by Sanford E. Marovitz in AL (61:3) 504–5.

**8226.** D'HAEN, THEO.    Genre convention in postmodern fiction. *In* (pp. 405–20) **16.**

**8227.** —— Postmodernism in American fiction and art. *In* (pp. 211–31) **7.**

**8228.** DIPPLE, ELIZABETH.    The unresolvable plot: reading contemporary fiction. (Bibl. 1988, 6239.) Rev. by Daphna Erdinast-Vulcan in NQ (36:4) 553–4.

**8229.** DOWLING, DAVID.    Fictions of nuclear disaster. Iowa City: Iowa UP, 1987. (Bibl. 1987, 9195.) Rev. by Alexander H. McIntire, Jr, in SFS (16:1) 110–13.

**8230.** DRABBLE, MARGARET.    Mimesis: the representation of reality in the post-war British novel. Mosaic (20:1) 1987, 1–14.

**8231.** DRYDEN, EDGAR A.    The form of American romance. *See* **5812.**

**8232.** DRYDEN, PHYLIS CAMPBELL.   Dismemberment motifs in American literature: the incomplete and homeless body as metaphor. *See* **5813.**

**8233.** DUFFY, DENNIS.   Sounding the iceberg: an essay on Canadian historical novels. *See* **5814.**

**8234.** EBY, CLARE VIRGINIA.   Representative men: businessmen in American fiction, 1875–1914. *See* **5815.**

**8235.** EDWARDS, LEE R.   Schizophrenic narrative. JNT (19:1) 25–30.

**8236.** ELAM, DIANE MICHELLE.   Realizing romance: genre, reference, and the novel. *See* **5816.**

**8237.** ELDRED, JANET M.   Gender and creativity: female artist sub-plots from Hawthorne to Fowles. *See* **5817.**

**8238.** FARIS, WENDY B.   Labyrinths of language: symbolic landscape and narrative design in modern fiction. Baltimore, MD; London: Johns Hopkins UP, 1988. pp. viii, 242.

**8239.** FICKEN, CARL.   God's story and modern literature: reading fiction in community. Philadelphia, PA: Fortress Press, 1985. pp. xi, 173. Rev. by George W. Van Devender in ChrisL (36:2) 1987, 42–3.

**8240.** FLETCHER, M. D.   Contemporary political satire: narrative strategies in the post-modern context. Lanham, MD; London: UP of America, 1987. pp. xv, 185.

**8241.** FOKKEMA, DOUWE.   American postmodernism in Germany: a review of reception. CompCrit (10) 1988, 313–26.

**8242.** —— The semantic and syntactic organization of Postmodernist texts. *In* (pp. 81–98) **7.**

**8243.** —— BERTENS, HANS (eds).   Approaching Postmodernism: papers presented at a workshop on Postmodernism, 21–23 September 1984, University of Utrecht. *See* **7.**

**8244.** FORKNER, BEN (ed.).   A new book of Dubliners: short stories of modern Dublin. London: Methuen, 1988. pp. xxxiii, 254.

**8245.** FREIERT, WILLIAM K.   Classical myth in contemporary American fiction. CML (10:1) 47–61.

**8246.** FRIEDMAN, SUSAN STANFORD.   The return of the repressed in women's narrative. JNT (19:1) 141–56.

**8247.** FRITH, G.   The intimacy which is knowledge: female friendship in the novels of women writers. *See* **5821.**

**8248.** FRY, AUGUST J.   The return of Joseph Jefferson Jackson, a study in American myth. *In* (pp. 89–102) **13.**

**8249.** FUENTES, CARLOS.   New novel, new world. MLR (84:4) xxxi–xlii. (Presidential Address, Modern Humanities Research Association, 1989.)

**8250.** GADPAILLE, MICHELLE.   The Canadian short story. Toronto; Oxford: OUP, 1988. pp. viii, 126. (Perspectives on Canadian culture.)

**8251.** GAUGHRAN, RICHARD EDWARD.   Baseball literature's complex pastoralism. Unpub. doct. diss., Lehigh Univ. [Abstr. in DA (50) 1657A.]

**8252.** GELDER, KENNETH; SALZMAN, PAUL.   The new diversity: Australian fiction 1970–88. Melbourne: McPhee Gribble. pp. 296.

**8253.** GIFFORD, ALAN DOUGLAS.    Vietnam War fiction: the narrative quest. Unpub. doct. diss., Univ. of Massachusetts. [Abstr. in DA (50) 1305A.]

**8254.** GILBERT, PAM.    Coming out from under: contemporary Australian women writers. London: Pandora, 1988. pp. 224. (Australian literary heritage.)

**8255.** GODARD, BARBARA.    Voicing difference: the literary production of native women. *In* (pp. 87–107) **40.**

**8256.** GORAK, JAN.    God the artist: American novelists in a postrealist age. (Bibl. 1988, 6258.) Rev. by David Seed in MLR (84:3) 731–2; by Jerome Klinkowitz in AL (59:4) 1987, 688–90.

**8257.** GOTTLIEB, STEPHEN A.    Woman as an alien species in recent fiction. CEACrit (51:2/3) 66–74.

**8258.** GRANT, COLIN.    The fact of fiction. DalR (67:1) 1987, 5–21.

**8259.** GREENFIELD, GEORGE.    Scribblers for bread: aspects of the English novel since 1945. *See* **478.**

**8260.** GRIEM, EBERHARD.    Medieval elements and their functions in some contemporary English novels. *In* (pp. 305–18) **38.**

**8261.** GRIXTI, JOSEPH.    Terrors of uncertainty: the cultural contexts of horror fiction. *See* **5827.**

**8262.** GUNN, DANIEL.    Psychoanalysis and fiction: an exploration of literary and psychoanalytic borders. Cambridge: CUP. pp. xi, 251. Rev. by Peter Brooks in TLS, 13 Jan., 40.

**8263.** HALL, JAMES.    The other crime wave. Bulletin (Sydney) 13 June, 52–9. (Popularity of crime among Australian writers, publishers and readers.)

**8264.** HALPERN, DANIEL (comp.).    The Penguin book of international short stories 1945–85. London: Penguin. pp. xvi, 1061.

**8265.** HAMILTON, CYNTHIA S.    Western and hard-boiled detective fiction in America: from high noon to midnight. (Bibl. 1988, 6266.) Rev. by Christine Bold in JAStud (23:1) 109–11.

**8266.** HARPER, PHILLIP BRIAN.    The recentered subject: marginality in the development of postmodern culture. Unpub. doct. diss., Cornell Univ., 1988. [Abstr. in DA (49) 3026A.]

**8267.** HARRIS, NORMAN.    Connecting times: the sixties in Afro-American fiction. (Bibl. 1988, 6267.) Rev. by Joyce H. Scott in SAF (17:1) 117–20.

**8268.** HASHMI, ALAMGIR.    The postcolonial Pakistani novel. Weekend Post (Lahore and Peshawar) 22 Dec., 3.

**8269.** HAYBALL, C. N. M.    Some aspects of the treatment of India in modern English fiction. Unpub. doct. diss., Univ. of Loughborough, 1987. [Abstr. in IT (39:1) 35.]

**8270.** HAYMAN, DAVID.    Re-forming the narrative: toward a mechanics of modernist fiction. (Bibl. 1987, 9228.) Rev. by Leigh Hafrey in TLS, 13 Jan., 41.

**8271.** HELLER, ARNO.    Gewaltphantasien: ein Phänomen des amerikanischen Gegenwartsromans. Pannonia (Eisenstadt, Austria) (17) 33–4.

**8272.** HENDRICKSON, RUTH ANN. Narrative strategies of erotic fictional autobiography. *See* **5834.**

**8273.** HEWITT, DOUGLAS. English fiction of the early modern period, 1890–1940. *See* **5836.**

**8274.** HITCHENS, CHRISTOPHER. Politics in the novel. BkW, 4 June, 12.

**8275.** HITT, JACK. Forum: in pursuit of pure horror. Harper's (279) Oct., 45–53.

**8276.** HOFFMANN, GERHARD. The absurd and its forms of reduction in Postmodern American fiction. *In* (pp. 185–210) **7.**

**8277.** HÖLBLING, WALTER. Vorstellungen von Krieg und Frieden in der jüngeren amerikanischen Romanliteratur. DIALOG: Beiträge zur Friedensforschung (Stadtschlaining, Austria) (16:3) 61–90.

**8278.** HOLLINGER, VERONICA. The vampire and the alien: variations on the outsider. *See* **5838.**

**8279.** HOLTON, SYLVIA WALLACE. Down home and uptown: the representation of Black speech in American fiction. *See* **1407.**

**8280.** HOWELLS, CORAL ANN. Private and fictional words: Canadian women novelists of the 1970s and 1980s. (Bibl. 1988, 6277.) Rev. by Carla Visser in CanL (122/23) 255–6; by Janice Kulyk Keefer in DalR (67:1) 1987, 141–3; by Peter Quartermaine in NQ (36:2) 277–8.

**8281.** HOYSER, CATHERINE ELIZABETH. Literary viragos: late Victorian and Edwardian female Bildungsromane. *See* **5840.**

**8282.** HUGHES, H. M. Changes in historical romance, 1890s to the 1980s: the development of the genre from Stanley Weyman to Georgette Heyer and her successors. *See* **5841.**

**8283.** HURLEY, KELLY. The novel of the gothic body: deviance, abjection, and late-Victorian popular fiction. *See* **5842.**

**8284.** HUTCHEON, LINDA. A poetics of postmodernism: history, theory, fiction. (Bibl. 1988, 6280.) Rev. by Peter Kitson in NQ (36:4) 555.

**8285.** —— 'Shape shifters': Canadian women novelists and the challenge to tradition. *In* (pp. 219–27) **40.**

**8286.** IRELAND, KEVIN (ed.). The New Zealand collection: a celebration of the New Zealand novel. Auckland: Random House. pp. 223. Rev. by Andrew Mason in NZList, 25 Dec., 138–41.

**8287.** IRVINE, LORNA. Sub/version. Toronto: ECW Press, 1986. pp. 200. Rev. by Stephen Scobie in QQ (95:1) 1988, 191.

**8288.** ISAACS, NEIL D. Fiction night at the comedy club. NER (11:3) 305–19.

**8289.** IWAMOTO, IWAO. Henyou suru 'American fiction'. (The changing face of American fiction.) Tokyo: Nan'un-do. pp. 284.

**8290.** JAŘAB, JOSEF. Americká povídka posledního desetiletí. (The American short story in the last decade.) SvL (34:1) 2–8.

**8291.** —— The recent yet remote war: Vietnam in American literature. Germanica Olomucensia (7) 75–84.

**8292.**  JARRETT, JAMES MICHAEL.   Drifting on a read: jazz as a model for literary and theoretical writing. Unpub. doct. diss., Univ. of Florida, 1988. [Abstr. in DA (49) 3724A.]

**8293.**  JOHANNESSON, HANS-ERIK.   Amerikansk prosa: linjer i USAs och Kanadas litteratur efter 1968 samt kommenterad boklista. (American prose: trends in the literature of the U.S.A. and Canada after 1968, with an annotated list of books.) Lund: Bibliotekstjänst. pp. 136. (Btj, 165.)

**8294.**  JOHNSON, CHARLES.   Being and race: Black writing since 1970. Bloomington: Indiana UP; London: Serpent's Tail, 1988. pp. x, 132. Rev. by Tom LeClair in AL (61:1) 135.

**8295.**  JONES, DOROTHY.   Olivia and Chloe: fictions of female friendship. ALS (14:1) 3–14.

**8296.**  JORDIS, CHRISTINE.   De petits enfers variés: romancières anglaises contemporaines. Paris: Seuil. pp. 256. (Le Don des langues.)

**8297.**  KAPLAN, AMY.   The social construction of American Realism. *See* **5851.**

**8298.**  KARL, FREDERICK R.   American fictions 1940–1980: a comprehensive history and critical evaluation. (Bibl. 1986, 10275.) Rev. by Jerry A. Varsava in RES (38:149) 1987, 110–11.

**8299.**  KAYES, JAMIE BARLOWE.   Reading against the grain: the powers and limits of feminist criticism of American narratives. JNT (19:1) 130–40.

**8300.**  KEATING, H. R. F.   Crime and mystery: the 100 best books. *See* **5853.**

**8301.**  KEATING, PETER.   The haunted study: a social history of the English novel, 1875–1914. *See* **5854.**

**8302.**  KEITEL, EVELYNE.   Reading psychosis: readers, texts and psychoanalysis. Trans. by ANTHEA BALL. Oxford; New York: Blackwell. pp. 160.

**8303.**  KEITH, W. J.   The quest for the (instant) Canadian classic. *In* (pp. 155–65) **12.**

**8304.**  KELLEY, KAROL L.   Models for the multitudes: social values in the American popular novel, 1850–1920. *See* **5858.**

**8305.**  KENNEDY, ALAN.   Thinking the thinking of criticism. *See* **5860.**

**8306.**  KICH, MARTIN.   Everyone goes around acting crazy: a study of recent American hard-core Naturalists. Unpub. doct. diss., Lehigh Univ. [Abstr. in DA (50) 443A.]

**8307.**  KIRPAL, VINEY.   What is the modern Third World novel? JCL (23:1) 1988, 142–56.

**8308.**  KOHLI, DEVINDRA.   Indian English: a *khichri* of words. *See* **1532.**

**8309.**  KOZA, KIMBERLEY ANN.   Women as images of history: contemporary anglophone fiction by minority and post-colonial women writers. Unpub. doct. diss., Indiana Univ., 1988. [Abstr. in DA (50) 953A.]

**8310.**  KREYLING, MICHAEL.   Figures of the hero in Southern narrative. *See* **5862.**

**8311.**  KUROWSKA, ELŻBIETA.  The modern English novel in Polish and English literary criticism in the 1930s. *In* (pp. 136–52) **36.**

**8312.**  LANSFORD, INGRID GIMM.  The rise and fall of the artist aristocrat in the American novel. Unpub. doct. diss., Univ. of Texas at Austin, 1988. [Abstr. in DA (50) 444A.]

**8313.**  LEADBETTER, J. A.  From revolt to redemption: contemporary women writers and fantasy. Unpub. M.Litt. diss., Univ. of Newcastle upon Tyne. [Abstr. in IT (38:4) 1463.]

**8314.**  LEAVIS, L. R.  Creative values and the contemporary novel. EngS (70:4) 328–47.

**8315.**  LECLAIR, TOM.  The art of excess: mastery in contemporary American fiction. Urbana: Illinois UP. pp. 245. Rev. in BkW, 10 Sept., 16; by Claude Clayton Smith in OhioanaQ (32:4) 198–200.

**8316.**  LEE, HERMIONE (introd.).  The secret self: short stories by women. (Bibl. 1985, 9058.) Rev. by Judy Simons in RES (38:150) 1987, 293–4.

**8317.**  LEFANU, SARAH.  In the chinks of the world machine: feminism and science fiction. (Bibl. 1988, 6301.) Rev. by Veronica Hollinger in SFS (16:2) 223–7.

**8318.**  LE GUIN, URSULA K.  The language of the night: essays on fantasy and science fiction. Introd. by SUSAN WOOD. (Bibl. 1982, 9709.) London: Women's Press. pp. 210. (Revised ed.; first ed. 1979.)

**8319.**  LEHMAN, DAVID.  The perfect murder: a study in detection. New York: Free Press. pp. 242. Rev. by T. J. Binyon in BkW, 19 Nov., 11.

**8320.**  LEHNERT-RODIEK, GERTRUD.  Zeitreisen: Untersuchungen zu einem Motiv der erzählenden Literatur des neunzehnten und zwanzigsten Jahrhunderts. *See* **5866.**

**8321.**  LEMMENS, CHERYL ANN.  Dark recesses of the soul: victimization in selected British fiction from *Clarissa* to *The Collector. See* **4938.**

**8322.**  LEONARDI, SUSAN J.  Dangerous by degrees: women at Oxford and the Somerville College novelists. New Brunswick, NJ: Rutgers UP. pp. x, 254. Rev. by Linda Simon in TLS, 1 Sept., 954.

**8323.**  LEVINE, PAUL.  The new realism in American literature. *In* (pp. 175–83) **2.**

**8324.**  LIPSKI, KAROL PAWEL.  Latent mythical patterns in twentieth-century fiction: reversal of the photographic image. Unpub. doct. diss., Brandeis Univ., 1988. [Abstr. in DA (49) 2649A.]

**8325.**  LORENZ, PAUL HOWARD.  Paths to metamorphosis: the quest for whole sight in contemporary British fiction. Unpub. doct. diss., Univ. of Houston, 1988. [Abstr. in DA (50) 450A.]

**8326.**  LYNN, DAVID H.  The hero's tale: narrators in the early modern novel. Basingstoke: Macmillan. pp. 123.

**8327.**  LYONS, P. J.  Literary and theological responses to the Holocaust. Unpub. doct. diss., Univ. of Bristol. [Abstr. in IT (38:3) 1007.]

**8328.**  MCCORMACK, THOMAS.  The fiction editor, the novel, and the novelist. *See* **482.**

**8329.** McCormick, Marjorie Jean.   Mothers in the English novel: from stereotype to archetype. *See* **4941.**

**8330.** Entry cancelled.

**8331.** Mc Elroy, Bernard.   Fiction of the modern grotesque. Basingstoke: Macmillan. pp. xii, 207.

**8332.** McHale, Brian.   Change of dominant from Modernist to Postmodernist writing. *In* (pp. 53–79) **7.**

**8333.** MacLeod, Jack.   The importance of not being earnest: some mutterings on Canadian humour. *In* (pp. 79–88) **12.**

**8334.** MacLulich, T. D.   Between Europe and America: the Canadian tradition in fiction. Toronto: ECW Press, 1988. pp. 255. Rev. by Axel Knoenagel in CanL (120) 227–30.

**8335.** McNaughton, Trudie (ed.).   In deadly earnest: a collection of fiction by New Zealand women 1870s–1980s. *See* **5874.**

**8336.** McVicker, Jeanette Elaine Wewe.   The 'end' of Modernism and postmodern thinking. Unpub. doct. diss., State Univ. of New York at Binghamton, 1988. [Abstr. in DA (49) 2653A.]

**8337.** Maddock-Cowart, Donna Samal.   The word, the flesh, and the devil: the professor in sixteen post-1950 academic novels. Unpub. doct. diss., Univ. of Georgia. [Abstr. in DA (50) 1658A.]

**8338.** Manhire, Bill (ed.).   Six by six: short stories by New Zealand's best writers. Wellington: Victoria UP. pp. 360.

**8339.** Marigny, Jean.   Difficultés de traduction dans les littératures de l'irréel. *In* (pp. 51–65) **22.**

**8340.** Mills, John.   Notes of a natural son. *In* (pp. 28–38) **12.**

**8341.** Mishra, V. C.   The gothic sublime: theory, practice and interpretation. *See* **4942.**

**8342.** Moore, Patricia Ann.   Female emancipation at the turn of the century. *See* **5880.**

**8343.** Mugambi, Helen Nabasuta.   The wounded psyche and beyond: conformity and marginality in selected African and Afro-American novels. Unpub. doct. diss., Indiana Univ., 1988. [Abstr. in DA (50) 944A.] (*The Joys of Motherhood, Efuru, Ripples in the Pool, Quicksand, Their Eyes Were Watching God, Sula.*)

**8344.** Müllenbrock, Heinz Joachim.   Die Entstehung der Anti-utopie im spätviktorianischen England und ihre genetischen Voraussetzungen. *See* **5885.**

**8345.** Murphy, Patrick D.   The verse novel: a modern American poetic genre. CE (51:1) 57–72.

**8346.** Murray, Heather.   Women in the wilderness. *In* (pp. 74–83) **40.**

**8347.** Nadel, Ira B.   Narrative and the popularity of biography. Mosaic (20:4) 1987, 131–41.

**8348.** Nash, Cristopher.   World-games: the tradition of anti-Realist revolt. London: Methuen, 1987. pp. xi, 400.

**8349.** Navajas, Gonzalo.   Mimesis y cultura en la ficción: teoría de la novela. London: Tamesis, 1985. pp. 214. (Colección Tamesis, ser. A: monografías, 115.) Rev. by B. J. McGuirk in MLR (84:2) 414–16.

**8350.** NAYLOR, GLORIA. Love and sex in the Afro-American novel. YR (78:1) 1988, 19–31.

**8351.** NEW, W. H. Canadian short fiction: from myth to modern. *See* **5889.**

**8352.** NILE, RICHARD. The rise of the Australian novel. *See* **5890.**

**8353.** OKONKWO, NELSON CHIDI. The colonial experience and the Third World novel: an exo-cultural study of the novel in Africa, the West Indies and Polynesia. Unpub. doct. diss., Univ. of Auckland, 1988.

**8354.** OLSEN, LANCE. Ellipse of uncertainty: an introduction to postmodern fantasy. (Bibl. 1987, 9307.) Rev. by David W. Madden in StudN (20:3) 1988, 354–6.

**8355.** ORR, JOHN. The making of the twentieth-century novel: Lawrence, Joyce, Faulkner, and beyond. New York: St Martin's Press; Basingstoke: Macmillan, 1987. pp. x, 220. Rev. by Rosemarie A. Battaglia in StudN (20:2) 1988, 230–4.

**8356.** PALENSKÁ, VĚRA. Karibská poválečná románová tvorba. (Postwar fiction in the Caribbean.) *In* (p. 31) **6.**

**8357.** PALMER, PAULINA. Contemporary women's fiction: narrative practice and feminist theory. New York; London: Harvester Wheatsheaf. pp. xii, 192.

**8358.** PATTERSON, ALISTAIR (sel.). Short stories from New Zealand. Petone, NZ: Highgate; Price Milburn, 1988. pp. 176. Rev. by Andrew Mason in NZList, 19 Nov. 1988, 80.

**8359.** PAWLING, CHRISTOPHER (ed.). Popular fiction and social change. (Bibl. 1988, 6329.) Rev. by Margaret Jensen in CanL (115) 1987, 176–7.

**8360.** PERRIN, NOEL. Science fiction: imaginary worlds and real-life questions. NYTB, 9 Apr., 37.

**8361.** PEZE, ESTHER. Situational nonsense in postmodern American fiction. *In* (pp. 215–27) **28.**

**8362.** PLATT, CHARLES. Who writes science fiction? Manchester: Savoy in assn with New English Library, 1980. pp. 313.

**8363.** PLIMPTON, GEORGE (ed.). Women writers at work. New York: Viking. pp. 387. Rev. in BkW, 9 July, 12.

**8364.** PORTER, GERALD (ed.). 'News that stays news': the enactment of present and future in American literature. *See* **43.**

**8365.** PORUSH, DAVID. The soft machine: cybernetic fiction. (Bibl. 1987, 9321.) Rev. by J. R. Wytenbroek in CanL (116) 1988, 141–2.

**8366.** POWELL, B. L. The house beautiful and its mapping of domestic and colonial space: a study of the domestic novel at the turn of the century. *See* **5898.**

**8367.** PROCHÁZKA, MARTIN. Traumata vědomá a kosmické mýty; utopický román a současna britská literatura. (Traumas and cosmic myths: the utopian novel and contemporary British literature.) LitM (18:4) 112–16.

**8368.** RAVENSCROFT, ARTHUR. South African novelists as prophets. *In* (pp. 124–39) **37.**

**8369.** REITENBACH, GAIL GLORIA. Death and the observer: American international novels, 1960–1987. Unpub. doct. diss., Boston College, 1987. [Abstr. in DA (49) 3363A.]

**8370.** RICHARDSON, BRIAN ERLING. Unlikely stories: causality and interpretation in modern narrative. *See* **8117**.

**8371.** RICHTER, DAVID. Murder in jest: serial killing in the post-modern detective story. JNT (19:1) 106–15.

**8372.** ROBERTS, HEATHER. Where did she come from? New Zealand women novelists 1862–1987. *See* **5901**.

**8373.** RUBIN, DAVID. After the Raj: British novels of India since 1947. (Bibl. 1987, 9339.) Rev. by Sara Suleri in MLR (84:3) 728–9.

**8374.** SALE, RICHARD B. Ten interviews: voices of novelists clear and entertaining. TBR (9:2) 26–7 (review-article).

**8375.** SCHAFFELD, NORBERT. Die Darstellung des nationalsozialistischen Deutschland im englischen Roman. Frankfurt; New York; Berne; Paris: Lang, 1987. pp. 393. (European University studies, 14: Anglo-Saxon language and literature, 172.) Rev. by E. A. McCobb in NC (8) 188–90.

**8376.** SCHENK, SUSAN JEAN. 'Burning dinner is not incompetence but war': marriage and madness in contemporary domestic fiction. Unpub. doct. diss., Univ. of Western Ontario. [Abstr. in DA (50) 1315A.]

**8377.** SCHRIBER, MARY SUZANNE. Gender and the writer's imagination from Cooper to Wharton. *See* **5908**.

**8378.** SCHWARZ, DANIEL. Character and characterization: an inquiry. JNT (19:1) 85–105.

**8379.** SCHWARZ, DANIEL R. The transformation of the English novel, 1890–1930. *See* **5909**.

**8380.** SENN, WERNER. Setting up an Australian literature course: some conceptual and practical reflections. *In* (pp. 63–75) **20**.

**8381.** SINGH, G. (ed.). Collected essays by Q. D. LEAVIS: vol. 3, The novel of religious controversy. *See* **5914**.

**8382.** SLEMON, STEPHEN. Post-colonial allegory and the transformation of history. JCL (23:1) 1988, 157–68.

**8383.** SLUSSER, GEORGE E.; RABKIN, ERIC S. (eds). Intersections: fantasy and science fiction. Carbondale: Southern Illinois UP, 1987. pp. x, 252. (Alternatives.) Rev. by Carl D. Malmgren in SFS (16:3) 384–7.

**8384.** SMITH, A. M. 'The transfiguration of the commonplace': a study of the modern Scottish novel. Unpub. M.Litt. thesis, Univ. of Aberdeen, 1984. [Abstr. in IT (36:3) 914.]

**8385.** SMITH, KATHY ANNE. Writing the borderline: journalism's literary contract. Unpub. doct. diss., Univ. of Massachusetts, 1988. [Abstr. in DA (49) 3726A.]

**8386.** SMITH, LARRY; SMITH, LAURA (eds). Best Ohio fiction. Huron, OH: Bottom Dog Press, 1987. pp. 153. Rev. by Edward Lense in OhioanaQ (31:2) 1988, 69–70.

**8387.** SOLOMON, ERIC; ARKIN, STEPHEN (eds). The critic agonistes: psychology, myth and the art of fiction. Essays by DANIEL WEISS. (Bibl. 1987, 9361.) Rev. by Mark Sokolyansky in MLR (84:3) 688–9.

**8388.** SPANGLER, GEORGE M. The idea of degeneration in American fiction 1880–1940. *See* **5918.**

**8389.** SPRENGNETHER, MADELON. (M)other Eve: some revisions of the Fall in fiction by contemporary women writers. *In* (pp. 298–322) **29.**

**8390.** STAFFORD, DAVID. The silent game: the real world of imaginary spies. Harmondsworth: Viking, 1988. pp. viii, 255.

**8391.** STEAD, C. K. Answering to the language: essays on modern writers. Auckland: Auckland UP. pp. 300.

**8392.** STEIG, MICHAEL. Stories of reading: subjectivity and literary understanding. *See* **5920.**

**8393.** STENSON, FRED (ed.). Alberta bound: thirty stories by Alberta writers. Edmonton, Alta: NeWest Press, 1986. pp. viii, 337.

**8394.** STERLING, BRUCE (ed.). Mirrorshades: the cyberpunk anthology. London: Paladin, 1988. pp. xiv, 239.

**8395.** STEVENS, PETER. The fictional look-out, mainly Canadian. QQ (95:3) 1988, 568–79.

**8396.** STEWART, MATTHEW C. Making sense of chaos: prose writing, fictional kind and the reality of Vietnam. Unpub. doct. diss., Emory Univ., 1988. [Abstr. in DA (50) 141A.]

**8397.** STONEHILL, BRIAN. The self-conscious novel: artifice in fiction from Joyce to Pynchon. Philadelphia: Pennsylvania UP, 1988. pp. x, 221.

**8398.** STOWE, WILLIAM W. Critical investigations: convention and ideology in detective fiction. TSLL (31:4) 570–91.

**8399.** STRATFORD, PHILIP. All the polarities: comparative studies in contemporary Canadian novels in French and English. Toronto: ECW Press, 1986. pp. 109. Rev. by Patricia Merivale in CanL (113/14) 1987, 207–12.

**8400.** SULEIMAN, SUSAN RUBIN. Naming and difference: reflections on 'Modernism *versus* Postmodernism' in literature. *In* (pp. 255–70) **7.**

**8401.** SULLIVAN, C. W. Welsh Celtic myth in modern fantasy. *See* **1732.**

**8402.** TANRISAL, MELDAN. New journalism and the nonfiction novel: creating art through facts. Unpub. doct. diss., Hacettepe Universitesi, Turkey, 1988. [Abstr. in DA (50) 1659A.]

**8403.** TAYLOR, D. J. A vain conceit: British fiction in the 1980s. London: Bloomsbury. pp. 135. Rev. by Jan Dalley in TLS, 29 Sept., 1052; by D. A. N. Jones in Listener (122) 5 Oct., 32.

**8404.** THELWELL, MICHAEL. Duties, pleasures, and conflicts: essays in struggle. Introd. by JAMES BALDWIN. Amherst: Massachusetts UP, 1987. pp. xxii, 258.

**8405.** THOMAS, H. NIGEL. From folklore to fiction: a study of folk heroes and rituals in the Black American novel. *See* **1659.**

**8406.** THOMAS, SUE. Indexes to fiction in *Chambers's Journal of Popular Literature, Science and Art*, later *Chambers's Journal*, 3rd to 6th series of *Chambers's Edinburgh Journal*, 1854–1910. *See* **596.**

**8407.** TIFFIN, HELEN. Post-colonialism, post-modernism and the rehabilitation of post-colonial history. JCL (23:1) 1988, 169–81.

**8408.** TODD, RICHARD. The presence of Postmodernism in British fiction: aspects of style and selfhood. *In* (pp. 99–117) **7.**

**8409.** TREVOR, WILLIAM (ed.). The Oxford book of Irish short stories. New York; Oxford: OUP. pp. 569. Rev. by Jack Fuller in BW, 10 Sept., 3–4.

**8410.** VARNADO, S. L. Haunted presence: the numinous in gothic fiction. *See* **4961.**

**8411.** VIRGILI, ELIZABETH SAY. Narrative as expression of women's theological voice. *See* **5931.**

**8412.** WAAGE, FREDERICK O. The environment in American popular fiction of the 1970s. BSUF (26:3) 1985, 52–66.

**8413.** WALD, PRISCILLA BETH. Writing America: the rhetoric of self-authorization in early modern American literature. *See* **5933.**

**8414.** WALSH, JEFFREY; AULICH, JAMES (eds). Vietnam images: war and representation. *See* **7953.**

**8415.** WANAMBISI, MONICA NALYAKA. Eight major exemplars of the twentieth-century American novel, 1900–1959. Unpub. doct. diss., Atlanta Univ., 1987. [Abstr. in DA (49) 2662A.] (Dreiser, Fitzgerald, Hemingway, Faulkner, Salinger, Ellison, Baldwin, Marshall.)

**8416.** WATSON, BRUCE. The night *The Forsyte Saga* struck back. Smithsonian (20:3) 184.

**8417.** WEISS, ALLAN. Professing support: in defence of academia's role in Canadian literature. *In* (pp. 130–9) **12.**

**8418.** WEISS, WOLFGANG. Der anglo-amerikanische Universitäts-roman: eine historische Skizze. *See* **5934.**

**8419.** WHITE, JEAN M. Puzzles and problems. BkW, 16 Apr., 8. (Detective fiction.)

**8420.** WIEGENSTEIN, STEVEN CHRISTOPHER. The contemporary academic novel: a study in genre. Unpub. doct. diss., Univ. of Missouri–Columbia, 1987. [Abstr. in DA (49) 1791A.]

**8421.** WILLIAMS, MERRYN. Six women novelists. *See* **5937.**

**8422.** WILLIS, SUSAN. Specifying: Black women writing the American experience. (Bibl. 1988, 6381.) Rev. by Hazel V. Carby in BALF (23:2) 381–7.

**8423.** WIX, CLARA. East European characters in English-Canadian short stories of the post-war era. CanL (120) 245–50.

**8424.** WOLFE, TOM. Stalking the billion-footed beast: a literary manifesto for the new social novel. Harper's (279) Nov., 45–56.

**8425.** WOLPERT, ILANA PAULA. Crossing the gender line: female novelists and their male voices. *See* **5941.**

**8426.** WRIGHT, ROBERT GLENN. The social Christian novel. Introd. by ROBERT H. WALKER and DEWEY D. WALLACE, JR. *See* **5942.**

**8427.** YANARELLA, ERNEST J.; SIGELMAN, LEE (eds). Political mythology and popular fiction. (Bibl. 1988, 6384.) Rev. by Jan Cohn in AL (61:1) 150–1.

**8428.** YOKE, CARL B. (ed.). Phoenix from the ashes: the literature of the remade world. (Bibl. 1987, 9399.) Rev. by W. Warren Wagar in SFS (16:1) 109–10.

**8429.** YOUNG, MICHAEL ANDREW. The structure and ideology of romance fiction. *See* **5943.**

**8430.** ZAKI, HODA M. Phoenix renewed: the survival and mutation of utopian thought in North American science fiction, 1965–1982. Mercer Island, WA: Starmont House, 1988. pp. 151. Rev. by Tom Moylan in SFS (16:2) 228–31.

**8431.** ZGORZELSKI, ANDRZEJ (ed.). Studies in fantastic fiction. *See* **57.**

### Literature for Children

**8432.** BRIGGS, JULIA. Women writers and writing for children: from Sarah Fielding to E. Nesbit. *In* (pp. 221–50) **14.**

**8433.** CONNOLLY, JOSEPH. Children's modern first editions: their value to collectors. *See* **212.**

**8434.** DENNY, M. Maria Merryweather to Tyke Tyler: the role of the positive heroine in children's fiction 1948–1985. Unpub. M.Phil. diss., Univ. of Loughborough, 1988. [Abstr. in IT (38:4) 1461.]

**8435.** DROTNER, KIRSTEN. English children and their magazines, 1751–1945. *See* **565.**

**8436.** ESTES, GLENN E. (ed.). American writers for children since 1960: poets, illustrators and nonfiction authors. Detroit, MI: Gale Research, 1987. pp. xiii, 430. (Dictionary of literary biography, 61.) Rev. by MC in Junior Bookshelf (52:4) 1988, 177.

**8437.** GOSE, ELLIOTT. Mere creatures: a study of modern fantasy tales for children. Toronto; London: Toronto UP, 1988. pp. x, 202.

**8438.** GREYVENSTEIN, W. R. The history and development of children's theatre in English in South Africa. *See* **5757.**

**8439.** HANSEN, I. V. In context: some recent Australian writing for adolescents. CLEd (20:3) 151–63.

**8440.** HARRISON, BARBARA. Moral intensity and heroic possibility in the postwar children's novel. Unpub. doct. diss., Tufts Univ., 1988. [Abstr. in DA (49) 3360A.]

**8441.** HEBLEY, DIANE. Nightingales and tuis: a survey of New Zealand children's literature in the 1980s. Landfall (43:3) 340–52.

**8442.** LIVINGSTON, MYRA COHN. The child as poet: myth or reality? Boston, MA: Horn Book, 1984. Rev. by Nancy Huse in CLEd (20:2) 121–8.

**8443.** LUKENBILL, W. BERNARD. Children's books and differing views of evolution – past and present. CLEd (19:3) 1988, 156–64.

**8444.** MONROE, SUZANNE STOLZ. Images of Native American female protagonists in children's literature, 1928–1988. Unpub. doct. diss., Univ. of Arizona, 1988. [Abstr. in DA (50) 89A.]

**8445.** NOEL, ROBERTA CHRISTINE. The borrowed cup of courage: a descriptive comparison of archetypes presented by male and female authors in fantasy for adolescents. Unpub. doct. diss., Gonzaga Univ., 1987. [Abstr. in DA (49) 2206A.]

**8446.** PINSENT, PAT. Paradise restored: the significance of coincidence in some children's books. CLEd (20:2) 103–10.

**8447.** REID, C. S. National identity in Scottish and Swiss children's and young people's books: a comparative study. See **5948.**

**8448.** SHAVIT, ZOHAR. Poetics of children's literature. (Bibl. 1986, 10471.) Rev. by Susan Drain in DalR (66:3) 1986, 386–8; by Nancy Huse in CLEd (20:2) 121–8.

**8449.** SHERCLIFF, W. H. Morality to adventure: Manchester Polytechnic's collection of children's books 1840–1939. See **265.**

**8450.** SHIPPEY, T. A. Breton *lais* and modern fantasies. *In* (pp. 69–91) **58.**

**8451.** SMEDMAN, M. SARAH. Not always gladly does she teach, nor gladly learn: teachers in *Kunstlerinromane* for young readers. See **5950.**

**8452.** TROUSDALE, ANN. Who's afraid of the big, bad wolf? CLEd (20:2) 69–79.

**8453.** WEEDMAN, JUDITH ELVIRA. Communication patterns among cultural gatekeepers: a sociometric analysis of interactions among editors, reviewers, and critics of children's literature. Unpub. doct. diss., Univ. of Michigan. [Abstr. in DA (50) 1467A.]

**8454.** WOLF, VIRGINIA L. The gay family in literature for young people. CLEd (20:1) 51–8.

### Poetry

**8455.** ABSE, DANNIE (sel.). The Hutchinson book of post-war British poets. London: Hutchinson. pp. xvii, 275.

**8456.** AHRENDS, GÜNTER; SEEBER, HANS ULRICH (eds). Englische und amerikanische Naturdichtung im 20. Jahrhundert. (Bibl. 1985, 9227.) Rev. by Götz Schmitz in Ang (107:3/4) 530–4.

**8457.** ALTMAN, MERYL BETH. Interlocutions: men, women, and modernisms in American poetry. Unpub. doct. diss., Columbia Univ., 1988. [Abstr. in DA (50) 137A.]

**8458.** AMATESHE, A. D. An anthology of East African poetry. Harlow: Longman, 1988. pp. vii, 136.

**8459.** ANDERSON, DAVID. Women poets and the Midwestern literary traditions. SSMLN (19:1) 25–8.

**8460.** ARMANTROUT, RAE. Not 'literary practitioners of deconstruction'. RCEI (18) 143–6.

**8461.** BEACH, CHRISTOPHER JOHN. ABC of influence: Ezra Pound and the remaking of the American poetic tradition. Unpub. doct. diss., Harvard Univ., 1988. [Abstr. in DA (49) 2217A.]

**8462.** BEDIENT, CALVIN. The wild braid of creation. SewR (96:1) 1988, 137–49.

**8463.** BELL, VEREEN; LERNER, LAURENCE (eds). On modern poetry: essays presented to Donald Davie. See **46.**

**8464.** BERGONZI, BERNARD. Poetry of the Desert War: British poets in Egypt 1940–45. *In* (pp. 15–35) **46.**

**8465.** BIRCH, DAVID. Cunning beneath the verbs: demythologising Singapore English poetry. *In* (pp. 147–90) **19.**

**8466.** BOASE-BEIER, JEAN. Poetic compounds: the principles of poetic language in modern English poetry. *See* **1386.**

**8467.** BOHN, WILLARD. The aesthetics of visual poetry 1914–1928. Cambridge; London; New York: CUP, 1986. pp. x, 228. Rev. by Alan Robinson in MLR (84:2) 454–5.

**8468.** BOURKE, LAWRENCE. 'Avoiding myth and message': contemporary Australian poetry. Poetry Australia (Berrima, N.S.W.) (118) 29–40.

**8469.** BOYM, SVETLANA. Life and death in quotation marks: cultural myth of the modern poet. Unpub. doct. diss., Harvard Univ., 1988. [Abstr. in DA (50) 436A.]

**8470.** BRESLIN, PAUL. The psycho-political muse: American poetry since the fifties. (Bibl. 1987, 9436.) Rev. by Alan Golding in AL (61:1) 143–6; by Mark Halliday in ELN (27:2) 77–81.

**8471.** BRITO, MANUEL. A bibliographical guide to selected 'language poets'; 1, Primary sources (1971–1988). RCEI (18) 187–202.

**8472.** BRITZOLAKIS, CHRISTINA. Imagining the populace: the 'mass' motif in the poetry of high Modernism. ESA (32:2) 95–108.

**8473.** BUTLER, GUY; OPLAND, JEFF (eds). The magic tree: South African stories in verse. Cape Town: Maskew Miller Longman. pp. 243.

**8474.** CASEY, MARIAN (ed.). New beginnings: a reflective anthology of New Zealand verse. Whakatane: NZ Arts Press. pp. 199.

**8475.** CHAPMAN, MICHAEL. The voice of poetry: 10, British poetry – the past fifty years; 11, The Americans. Crux (23:3) 36–46; (23:4) 42–52.

**8476.** CHESS, RICHARD S. Still a small voice: toward an American-Jewish poetry. Unpub. doct. diss., Univ. of Florida, 1988. [Abstr. in DA (50) 946A.]

**8477.** CONTE, JOSEPH MARK. Serial and *a-priori* form in postmodern poetry. Unpub. doct. diss., Stanford Univ., 1988. [Abstr. in DA (49) 2657A.]

**8478.** COOK, ALBERT. Figural choice in poetry and art. (Bibl. 1986, 10499.) Rev. by John E. Stoll in SewR (96:1) 1988, xi–xiii.

**8479.** COOLEY, DENNIS. The vernacular muse: the eye and ear in contemporary literature. Winnipeg, Man.: Turnstone Press, 1987. pp. 311. Rev. by Marcia Macauley in CanL (120) 162–5; by Bert Almon in WAL (23:3) 1988, 243–4.

**8480.** CROZIER, ANDREW; LONGVILLE, TIM (eds). A various art. Manchester: Carcanet Press, 1987. pp. 377.

**8481.** DAMON, MARIA. The poetics of marginality: 'minority discourse' in American Modernist poetry. Unpub. doct. diss., Stanford Univ., 1988. [Abstr. in DA (49) 3722A.]

**8482.** DAVIE, DONALD. Under *Briggflatts*: a history of poetry in Great Britain 1960–1988. Manchester: Carcanet Press. pp. 261. Rev. by Terry Eagleton in TLS, 24 Nov., 1291; by Peter Forbes in Listener (122) 2 Nov., 34.

**8483.** DREXEL, JOHN.   Threaders of double-stranded words: news from the North of Ireland. NER (12:2) 179–92.

**8484.** DYCK, EDWARD FRANK.   Topos and the rhetoric of prairie poetry. Unpub. doct. diss., Univ. of Manitoba, 1988. [Abstr. in DA (49) 2664A.]

**8485.** EASTERBROOK, NEIL GEORGE.   The critical poem: philosophy and modern American poetry. Unpub. doct. diss., State Univ. of New York at Buffalo, 1988. [Abstr. in DA (49) 3723A.]

**8486.** EDMOND, MURRAY; PAUL, MARY (eds).   The new poets: initiatives in New Zealand poetry. Wellington: Allen & Unwin; Port Nicholson Press, 1987. pp. xiv, 132. Rev. by Iain Sharp in NZList, 19 Dec. 1987, 79–81.

**8487.** ENGLER, BERND.   Die amerikanische Ode: Gattungsgeschichtliche Untersuchungen. *See* **4972.**

**8488.** EVANS, MIRIAMA; McQUEEN, HARVEY; WEDDE, IAN (eds).   The Penguin book of contemporary New Zealand poetry. Auckland: Penguin. pp. 536. Rev. by Elizabeth Caffin and Timoti Karetu in NZList, 20 Nov., 111–12.

**8489.** FAWCETT, BRIAN.   Some proposals for the reification of poetry in Canada. *In* (pp. 92–103) **12.**

**8490.** FINKELSTEIN, NORMAN.   The utopian moment in contemporary American poetry. Lewisburg, PA: Bucknell UP, 1988. pp. 135. Rev. by David Porter in AL (61:1) 146–8.

**8491.** FOSTER, JEANNE.   A music of grace: exploring the sacred in contemporary American poetry. Unpub. doct. diss., Graduate Theological Union, 1988. [Abstr. in DA (49) 1801A.]

**8492.** FOWLER, ALASTAIR.   Writing criticism and making poems. NLH (21:1) 1–16.

**8493.** FRIEBERT, STUART; YOUNG, DAVID (eds).   The Longman anthology of contemporary American poetry. New York; London: Longman. pp. xxiv, 629. (Second ed.: first ed. 1983.)

**8494.** GARRATT, ROBERT F.   Modern Irish poetry: tradition and continuity from Yeats to Heaney. (Bibl. 1988, 6414.) Rev. by Bernard O'Donoghue in RES (39:154) 1988, 320–1; by John Cronin in MLR (84:4) 956–7.

**8495.** GELPI, ALBERT.   A coherent splendor: the American poetic renaissance, 1910–1950. (Bibl. 1988, 6416.) Rev. by Suzanne Matson in NEQ (62:3) 473–6; by Alain Suberchicot in EA (42:3) 362–4; by Kathryn Lindberg in JAStud (23:1) 173–5; by Ian F. A. Bell in NQ (36:2) 270–1.

**8496.** GIFFORD, HENRY.   Poetry in a divided world. New York: CUP, 1986. (Bibl. 1986, 2925, where misplaced.) Rev. by Donald Davie in MLR (84:3) 695–6.

**8497.** GOETSCH, PAUL.   Das Kirchenmotiv in der modernen englischen Lyrik. LJGG (30) 281–300.

**8498.** GOODBY, J.   Inner emigrés: a study of seven Irish poets (1955–85). Unpub. doct. diss., Univ. of Leeds, 1986. [Abstr. in IT

(36:4) 1395–6.] (Thomas Kinsella, John Montague, Seamus Heaney, Michael Hartnett, Derek Mahon, Tom Paulin, Paul Muldoon.)

**8499.** GRAY, STEPHEN (ed.). The Penguin book of South African verse. *See* **5965.**

**8500.** HAGENBÜCHLE, ROLAND. Sprachskepsis und Sprachkritik: zum Erkenntnismodus dichterischer Sprache. *See* **5967.**

**8501.** HALL, DONALD. Death to the death of poetry: a response to the elegists. Harper's (279) Sept., 72–6.

**8502.** HARDING, GUNNAR. Amerikansk språkpoesi. (American language-poetry.) Artes (15:4) 5–6, 125–9.

**8503.** HARDWICK, A. Voices from the garden: aspects of women's poetry 1910–1939. Unpub. doct. diss., Univ. of Loughborough, 1988. [Abstr. in IT (39:2) 489.]

**8504.** HARESNAPE, GEOFFREY. Belief in the song: Jack Cope and South African poetry in English. Contrast (17:3) 44–52.

**8505.** HARRIS, CLAIRE. Poets in limbo. *In* (pp. 115–25) **40.**

**8506.** HASSAN, SALEM KADHEM. Time, tense and structure in contemporary English poetry: Larkin and the Movement. Unpub. doct. diss., Univ. of Glasgow, 1985. [Abstr. in DA (50) 952–3A.]

**8507.** HAUSMAN, MARGARET JANE. Syntactic disordering in modern poetry: index, icon, symbol. *See* **5968.**

**8508.** HEALY, MAURA (ed.). Fire the sun: an anthology of poems. Harlow: Longman. pp. xviii, 196. (Modern women writers.)

**8509.** HEANEY, SEAMUS. The government of the tongue: the 1986 T. S. Eliot Memorial Lectures, and other critical writings. New York: Farrar, Straus & Giroux, 1988. (Bibl. 1988, 6418.) Rev. by Lucy McDiarmid in NYTB, 5 Mar., 25; by Helen Vendler in NY, 13 Mar., 102–7; by Peter Sacks in Upstream (7:4) 61–6; by Gerald Dawe in Honest Ulsterman (86) 43–8.

**8510.** HEINEMANN, MARGOT. English poetry and the war in Spain: some records of a generation. *In* (pp. 46–64) STEPHEN M. HART (ed.), '¡No pasarán!': art, literature and the Spanish Civil War. London: Tamesis, 1988. pp. 122. (Colección Tamesis, ser. A: monografías, 136.)

**8511.** HEINZELMAN, KURT. The year in poetry, 1988. MassR (30:1) 137–76.

**8512.** HUDSON, EDWARD (sel.). Poetry in the First World War. Hove: Wayland, 1988. pp. 128.

**8513.** JAŘAB, JOSEF. Beatnik jako moderní klasik. (The beatnik as a modern classic.) SvL (34:1) 241–4.

**8514.** JONES, ELDRED DUROSIMI (ed.); PALMER, EUSTACE (assoc. ed.); JONES, MARJORIE (asst ed.). Oral and written poetry in African literature today: a review. London: Currey, 1988. pp. vi, 162.

**8515.** KART, LARRY. Candor in verse: re-examining the fate of the confessional poet. BW, 5 Mar., 3.

**8516.** KATROVAS, RICHARD. History and the transpersonal talent, or 'I'm just tired of reading guys'. NER (11:3) 340–50.

**8517.** KELLER, LYNN. Re-making it new: contemporary American poetry and the Modernist tradition. (Bibl. 1987, 9466.) Rev. by David

Porter in AL (61:1) 146–8; by Ian F. A. Bell in NQ (36:2) 270–1; by Suzanne Matson in NEQ (62:3) 473–6.

**8518.** KENNELLY, BRENDAN.   Poetry and violence. *In* (pp. 5–28) **32.**

**8519.** KHAN, NOSHEEN.   Women's poetry of the First World War. Brighton; New York: Harvester Press. pp. ix, 226. (Cf. bibl. 1987, 9469.) Rev. by Terry Castle in TLS, 2 June, 607–8.

**8520.** LANE, PATRICK.   The unyielding phrase. CanL (122/23) 57–64.

**8521.** LAVERY, JOHN.   The sense of place in modern Ulster poetry. Unpub. doct. diss., Univ. of Toronto. [Abstr. in DA (50) 449–50A.]

**8522.** McCLATCHY, J. D.   White paper: on contemporary American poetry. New York: Columbia UP. pp. x, 351. Rev. by Mark Ford in TLS, 15 Sept., 1001; by Harold Beaver in NYTB, 9 July, 33.

**8523.** McGOVERN, ROBERT.   The personal poet and our cultural identity. SSMLN (19:3) 12–23.

**8524.** MAZZARO, JEROME.   Varieties of poetic experience. SewR (96:1) 1988, 149–58.

**8525.** MESSERLI, DOUGLAS (ed.).   'Language' poetries: an anthology. New York: New Directions, 1987. pp. 184. Rev. by Jerome J. McGann in LRB (9:18) 1987, 6–8.

**8526.** MEYER, BRUCE MILLER.   Sergeant of *Outposts*: one editor's role in post-war British poetry, 1944–1987. *See* **580.**

**8527.** MOLE, JOHN.   Passing judgements: poetry in the eighties. Bristol: Bristol Classical Press. pp. iv, 188. Rev. by Terry Eagleton in TLS, 24 Nov., 1292.

**8528.** MOLLISON, ELIZABETH; MEIJER, HENK ROMIJN (comps). Spiegel van de Engelse poëzie uit de gehele wereld: deel twee, Dichters van de twintigste eeuw. (A mirror on English poetry from the whole world: part 2, Poets of the twentieth century.) Amsterdam: Meulenhoff. pp. xiv, 383.

**8529.** MORAMARCO, FRED.   Speculations: contemporary poetry and painting. Mosaic (20:3) 1987, 23–36.

**8530.** MURPHY, PATRICK D.   The verse novel: a modern American poetic genre. *See* **8345.**

**8531.** NIELSEN, ALDON LYNN.   Reading race: white American poets and the racial discourse in the twentieth century. Athens; London: Georgia UP, 1988. pp. xii, 178.

**8532.** NIVEN, ALASTAIR (ed.).   Under another sky: an anthology of Commonwealth Poetry Prize winners. Introd. by JAMES PORTER. Manchester: Carcanet Press, 1987. pp. 103.

**8533.** NORTON, JOHN DOUGLAS.   Narcissus *sous rature*: the effacement of the self in contemporary American poetry. Unpub. doct. diss., Univ. of California, Berkeley, 1988. [Abstr. in DA (50) 444A.]

**8534.** O'DRISCOLL, DENNIS.   Eastern ripples. CamQ (18:2) 190–7. (Contemporary British and East European poetry.)

**8535.** OSTRIKER, ALICIA SUSKIN.   Stealing the language: the emergence of women's poetry in America. (Bibl. 1987, 9500.) Rev. by Judith McCombs in CanL (120) 202–3.

**8536.** PARTHASARATHY, R.   The exile as writer: on being an Indian writer in English. *See* **5988.**

**8537.** PERKINS, DAVID. A history of modern poetry: Modernism and after. (Bibl. 1988, 6448.) Rev. by Monroe K. Spears in SewR (96:1) 1988, 95–101.

**8538.** PERLOFF, MARJORIE. The dance of the intellect: studies in the poetry of the Pound tradition. (Bibl. 1988, 6449.) Rev. by Martin Schiralli in JAE (23:3) 123–4; by Reginald Berry in CanL (118) 1988, 147–8; by Anthony Woodward in RES (38:151) 1987, 411–12.

**8539.** —— New poetry: transatlantic disagreements. TLS, 20 Jan., 60, 69.

**8540.** PERLOFF, MARJORIE G. Artifice once more: 'post-structuralist' poetries in the age of Donahue. RCEI (18) 151–67.

**8541.** PETTINGELL, PHOEBE. Poetic personas. NewL (72:18) 15–16.

**8542.** PLIMPTON, GEORGE (ed.). Poets at work. New York: Viking. pp. 512. Rev. in BkW, 9 July, 12.

**8543.** PRIESSNITZ, HORST. The 'vossification' of Ludwig Leichhardt: Leichhardt's career in 19th and 20th century Australian poems. In (pp. 102–14) **5.**

**8544.** REED, JEREMY. Madness: the price of poetry. See **5992.**

**8545.** REED, SABRINA LEE. The place of American poets in the development of Irving Layton, Louis Dudek and Raymond Souster. Unpub. doct. diss., Univ. of Toronto, 1988. [Abstr. in DA (49) 2654A.]

**8546.** REID, CHRISTOPHER (ed.). The Poetry Book Society anthology, 1989–1990. London: Hutchinson. pp. ix, 99.

**8547.** REILLY, CATHERINE W. English poetry of the Second World War: a biobibliography. (Bibl. 1988, 6454.) Rev. by John Gillard Watson in NQ (36:1) 130–2.

**8548.** RIACH, ALAN. Stranger eyes: Charles Olson, 'Pacific Man' and some aspects of New Zealand poetry. Landfall (43:1) 57–73.

**8549.** RICHMAN, ROBERT (ed.). The direction of poetry: an anthology of rhymed and metered verse written in the English language since 1975. New York: Houghton Mifflin. pp. 168. Rev. by Robert Adler in Commentary (87:4) 70–2.

**8550.** ROBINSON, ALAN. Instabilities in contemporary British poetry. (Bibl. 1988, 6456.) Rev. by Terry Eagleton in TLS, 24 Nov., 1291; by Alan Golding in NQ (36:4) 549–51.

**8551.** —— Poetry, painting and ideas, 1885–1914. (Bibl. 1988, 6457.) Rev. by Thomas Gibbons in RES (38:150) 1987, 273–5.

**8552.** RODEFER, STEPHEN. Prologue to language doubling. RCEI (18) 75–6.

**8553.** RUGOFF, KATHY. To purge Auschwitz: the poets' view. PCL (14) 1988, 3–11.

**8554.** SAFARIK, ALLAN (ed.). Vancouver poetry. Vancouver: Polestar Press, 1986. pp. 197. Rev. by Margaret Doyle in CanL (115) 1987, 188–90.

**8555.** SCHMIDT, MICHAEL. Reading modern poetry. London: Routledge. pp. 128. Rev. by Terry Eagleton in TLS, 24 Nov., 1291.

**8556.** SELWYN, VICTOR (gen. ed.). More poems of the Second World War: the Oasis selection. Ed. by ERIK DE MAUNY, IAN FLETCHER, and

ROBIN IVY. London: Dent in assn with Salamander Oasis Trust. pp. xix, 383. (Everyman classics.)

**8557.** SENN, WERNER. Speaking the silence: contemporary poems on paintings. Word & Image (5:2) 181–97.

**8558.** SIMMONS, THOMAS SCOTT. Erotic reckonings: mastery and apprenticeship in the work of poets and lovers. Unpub. doct. diss., Univ. of California, Berkeley, 1988. [Abstr. in DA (49) 3364A.]

**8559.** SMITH, KENNETH R. Praise of the past: the myth of eternal return in women writers. PW (24:4) 50–8.

**8560.** SOLWAY, DAVID. The end of poetry. CanL (115) 1987, 127–34.

**8561.** STEAD, C. K. Answering to the language: essays on modern writers. *See* **8391.**

**8562.** STEINER, DOROTHEA. Definition und Selbstdefinition der Frau in der amerikanischen Lyrik. *See* **7942.**

**8563.** STEINMAN, LISA M. Made in America: science, technology, and American Modernist poets. (Bibl. 1988, 6467.) Rev. by Julian D. Gill in JAStud (23:1) 121–2; by Christopher Brookeman in NQ (36:1) 134–5.

**8564.** STOREY, MARK (ed.). Poetry and Ireland since 1800: a source book. *See* **5998.**

**8565.** TAYLOR, MARTIN (comp.). Lads: love poetry of the trenches. London: Constable. pp. 251.

**8566.** THESEN, SHARON. Poetry and the dilemma of expression. *In* (pp. 380–4) **40.**

**8567.** TOMLINSON, CHARLES. Some presences on the scene: a vista of postwar poetry. *In* (pp. 215–32) **46.**

**8568.** TULIP, JAMES. Poetry since 1965. ALS (13:4) 1988, 475–92.

**8569.** VENDLER, HELEN. The music of what happens: poems, poets, critics. (Bibl. 1988, 6469.) Rev. by Ross Labrie in CanL (122/23) 143–5.

**8570.** —— (ed.). The Harvard book of contemporary American poetry. (Bibl. 1987, 9537.) Rev. by James Gardner in Commentary (81:1) 1986, 50–5.

**8571.** VON HALLBERG, ROBERT. American poetry and culture, 1945–1980. (Bibl. 1987, 9539.) Rev. by Neil Corcoran in MLR (84:1) 149–50.

**8572.** WAH, FRED. Which at first seems to be a going back for origins: notes on a reading of some American women writers. *In* (pp. 374–9) **40.**

**8573.** WALKER, JEFFREY. Bardic ethos and the American epic: Whitman, Pound, Crane, Williams, Olson. *See* **6000.**

**8574.** AL-WASITI, SALMAN. English poetry of the First World War: initial response. Al-Mustansiriya Literary Review (Al-Mustansiriya Univ., Baghdad) (11) 1985, 97–119.

**8575.** WATSON, STEPHEN. Philip Larkin and the situation of poetry. Contrast (17:3) 12–31.

**8576.** WATTEN, BARRETT. 'Language' in poetry. RCEI (18) 45–51.

**8577.** WEBSTER, MICHAEL PAUL. The semiotics of aurally and visually elastic poetries: 1910–1940. Unpub. doct. diss., Indiana Univ., 1988. [Abstr. in DA (50) 134A.]

**8578.** WESLING, DONALD. Late capitalist lyric: politics in American poetry (and poetics) since 1945. RCEI (18) 179–85.

**8579.** WEVERS, LYDIA (sel.). Yellow pencils: contemporary poetry by New Zealand women. Auckland; Oxford: OUP, 1988. pp. xxvi, 221. Rev. by Mary Paul in NZList, 11 Feb., 56.

**8580.** WOODS, GREGORY. Articulate flesh: male homo-eroticism and modern poetry. (Bibl. 1987, 9548.) Rev. by Alan Golding in AL (61:1) 143–6; by C. M. Jackson-Houlston in NQ (36:2) 284–5.

**8581.** WOOLMER, J. HOWARD. The Poetry Bookshop, 1912–1935: a bibliography. Introd. by PENELOPE FITZGERALD. See **471**.

**8582.** YORK, R. A. The poem as utterance. (Bibl. 1986, 7438, where misplaced.) Rev. by Reginald Berry in CanL (118) 1988, 149–50; by Eva Fox Gal in NQ (35:2) 1988, 272.

### Prose

**8583.** DURCZAK, JERZY. Contemporary American literary nonfiction. Lublin, Poland: Uniwersytet Marii Curie-Skłodowskiej, 1988. pp. 165. (Wydział Humanistyczny.)

**8584.** HILL, GEOFFREY. Of diligence and jeopardy. See **3159**.

**8585.** KAZIN, ALFRED. A writer's America: landscape in literature. (Bibl. 1988, 6477.) Rev. by Bryan Wolf in TLS, 16 June, 672; by Stephen Fender in LRB (11:2) 22–3; by William P. Kelly in JAH (76:3) 898–9.

**8586.** PACK, ROBERT; PARINI, JAY (eds). The Bread Loaf anthology of contemporary American essays. Hanover, NH; London: New England UP for Bread Loaf Writers' Conference, Middlebury College. pp. viii, 379.

**8587.** SMITH, KATHY ANNE. Writing the borderline: journalism's literary contract. See **8385**.

**8588.** STANLEY, MARNI L. Travelers' tales: showing and telling, slamming and questing. In (pp. 51–60) **40**.

**8589.** STEWART, MATTHEW C. Making sense of chaos: prose writing, fictional kind and the reality of Vietnam. See **8396**.

**8590.** TANRISAL, MELDAN. New journalism and the nonfiction novel: creating art through facts. See **8402**.

### Biography and Autobiography

**8591.** BUSS, HELEN M. Canadian women's autobiography: some critical directions. In (pp. 154–64) **40**.

**8592.** COLMER, JOHN A. Australian autobiography: a personal quest. Melbourne; Oxford: OUP. pp. 174.

**8593.** DODD, PHILIP. History or fiction: balancing contemporary autobiography's claims. Mosaic (20:4) 1987, 61–9.

**8594.** DOVEY, TERESA. A question of power: Susan Gardner's biography versus Bessie Head's autobiography. EngA (16:1) 29–38.

**8595.** DUDLEY, DAVID LEWIS. 'The trouble I've seen': visions and revisions of bondage, flight, and freedom in Black American auto-biography. See **6020**.

**8596.** FOX-GENOVESE, ELIZABETH. My statue, my self: auto-biographical writings of Afro-American women. In (pp. 63–89) **51**.

**8597.** FRIEDMAN, SUSAN STANFORD.    Women's autobiographical selves: theory and practice. *In* (pp. 34–62) **51.**

**8598.** GILLESPIE, DENNIS PATRICK.    Augustine and America: five contemporary autobiographical works. Unpub. doct. diss., Loyola Univ. of Chicago, 1988. [Abstr. in DA (49) 1801–2A.] (John Ashbery, *Three Poems*; James Merrill, *The Book of Ephraim*; Robert Lowell, *Day by Day*; Lyn Hejinian, *My Life*; Frank Bidart, *Confessional.*)

**8599.** HOBERMAN, RUTH.    Modernizing lives: experiments in English biography, 1918–1939. Carbondale: Southern Illinois UP, 1987. pp. 240. Rev. by Daniel J. Cahill in BMMLA (22:2) 26–9.

**8600.** KENNEALLY, MICHAEL.    The autobiographical imagination and Irish literary autobiographies. *In* (pp. 111–31) **17.**

**8601.** MARCUS, JANE.    Invincible mediocrity: the private selves of public women. *In* (pp. 114–46) **51.**

**8602.** MARGOLIES, EDWARD.    American biography: Anderson, Dreiser, Toomer. EngS (70:4) 372–6 (review-article).

**8603.** MASON, MICHAEL A.    Canadian servicemen's memoirs of the Second World War. Mosaic (20:4) 1987, 11–22.

**8604.** MURRAY, DAVID.    From speech to text: the making of American Indian autobiographies. *In* (pp. 29–43) **1.**

**8605.** NADEL, IRA B.    Narrative and the popularity of biography. *See* **8347.**

**8606.** NOVARR, DAVID.    The lines of life: theories of biography, 1880–1970. *See* **6026.**

**8607.** ORMSBY, FRANK (ed.).    Northern windows: an anthology of Ulster autobiography. Belfast: Blackstaff Press, 1987. pp. ix, 265. Rev. by Adolphe Haberer in EA (42:3) 357–8.

**8608.** PERREAULT, JEANNE MARTHA.    Writing the self: feminist autobiography in the United States. Unpub. doct. diss., Univ. of Alberta, 1988. [Abstr. in DA (49) 3027A.]

**8609.** ROBE, MARGARET ANN.    Conceiving a self in autobiography by women. Unpub. doct. diss., Univ. of California, Los Angeles, 1988. [Abstr. in DA (49) 3720A.]

**8610.** SCHEER-SCHÄZLER, BRIGITTE.    From paracriticism to para-biography? Ihab Hassan's autobiography *Out of Egypt*: scenes and arguments of an autobiography. *In* (pp. 239–50) **2.**

**8611.** SHEAR, KEITH.    Depictions of childhood in South African autobiography, with particular reference to the 1920s. EngA (16:1) 39–69.

### Related Studies

**8612.** BARTLETT, THOMAS, *et al.*    Irish studies: an introduction. Dublin: Gill & Macmillan, 1988. pp. 240.

**8613.** BARZUN, JACQUES.    The culture we deserve. Middletown, CT: Wesleyan UP. pp. 185. Rev. by Michael Dirda in BkW, 16 July, 5.

**8614.** BASSNETT, SUSAN.    Poetry, translation and the process of discovery. *In* (pp. 145–53) **4.**

**8615.** BROOKEMAN, CHRISTOPHER. American culture and society since the 1930s. London: Macmillan, 1984. (Bibl. 1986, 10645.) Rev. by Bruce Michelson in YES (19) 358–9.

**8616.** BURGIN, VICTOR. The end of art theory: criticism and post-modernity. Basingstoke: Macmillan, 1986. pp. x, 221. (Communications and culture.) Rev. by Alan Robinson in MLR (84:2) 416–17.

**8617.** CAIRNS, DAVID; RICHARDS, SHAUN. Writing Ireland: colonialism, nationalism and culture. Manchester: Manchester UP, 1988. pp. 178. Rev. by Eibhear Walshe in IUR (19:1) 186–7.

**8618.** CASE, SUE-ELLEN. Toward a butch-femme aesthetic. *In* (pp. 282–99) **39.** (Revised version of Discourse (Univ. of Wisconsin–Milwaukee) (11:1).)

**8619.** CHEFDOR, MONIQUE; QUINONES, RICARDO; WACHTEL, ALBERT (eds). Modernism: challenges and perspectives. Urbana; Chicago: Illinois UP, 1986. pp. xi, 347. Rev. by Steven Connor in MLR (84:3) 700–1.

**8620.** FEKETE, JOHN (ed.). Life after postmodernism: essays on value and culture. (Bibl. 1988, 6510.) Rev. by Michael H. Keefer in CanL (120) 226–7.

**8621.** FISKE, JOHN. Understanding popular culture. London; Boston, MA: Unwin Hyman. pp. xi, 206. Rev. by David Papineau in TLS, 8 Dec., 1364.

**8622.** FOKKEMA, DOUWE. What is Modernism? *In* (pp. 1–47) DOUWE FOKKEMA and ELRUD IBSCH, Modernist conjectures: a mainstream in European literature 1910–1940. London: Hurst, 1987. pp. xii, 330. Rev. by Naomi Segal in NC (8) 178–80.

**8623.** FOSTER, R. F. Varieties of Irishness. *See* **6037.**

**8624.** GEYER-RYAN, HELGA; LETHEN, HELMUT. The rhetoric of forgetting: Brecht and the historical avant-garde. *In* (pp. 305–48) **16.**

**8625.** GONZÁLEZ, YOLANDA BROYLES. Toward a re-vision of Chicano theatre history: the women of El Teatro Campesino. *In* (pp. 209–38) **39.**

**8626.** GRANT, DON. Australian studies and Australian identity. *In* (pp. 77–90) **20.**

**8627.** GUNEW, SNEJA. Constructing Australian subjects: critics, writers, multicultural writers. *In* (pp. 51–62) **20.**

**8628.** GUNN, GILES. The culture of criticism and the criticism of culture. (Bibl. 1988, 6512.) Rev. by Mireya Folch-Serra in QQ (95:3) 1988, 619–22.

**8629.** HARVEY, DAVID. The condition of postmodernity: an enquiry into the origins of cultural change. Oxford: Blackwell. pp. ix, 378.

**8630.** HOLBROOK, DAVID. Truth, campaigns and freedom. *In* (pp. 197–216) **13.**

**8631.** HUFFSTETLER, EDWARD WRIGHT. The voice from the burning bush: spiritual faith and the religion of American primitivism. *See* **6046.**

**8632.** HUYSSEN, ANDREAS. After the great divide: modernism, mass culture, postmodernism. Bloomington: Indiana UP; Basingstoke: Macmillan, 1986. pp. vii, 244. (Language, discourse, society.) Rev. by Mireya Folch-Serra in QQ (95:3) 1988, 633–6.

**8633.** INGLIS, FRED.    Popular culture and the meaning of feeling. *In* (pp. 145–60) **13.**

**8634.** JONES, D. G.    Text and context: some reflections on translation with examples from Quebec poetry. CanL (117) 1988, 6–10.

**8635.** LAUGHLIN, JAMES.    Richard Ellmann's Michaux: a publisher's recollections. *In* (pp. 23–8) **45.**

**8636.** LEMAHIEU, D. L.    A culture for democracy: mass communication and the cultivated mind in Britain between the wars. Oxford: Clarendon Press. pp. 396. Rev. by Paul Smith in TLS, 20 Jan., 68.

**8637.** LEVINE, LAWRENCE W.    Highbrow/lowbrow: the emergence of cultural hierarchy in America. *See* **6052.**

**8638.** MCPHERSON, I. N.    Wittgenstein's transformation: developing linguistic responsibility. Unpub. doct. diss., Univ. of St Andrews. [Abstr. in IT (39:1) 11.]

**8639.** MALMGREEN, GAIL (ed.).    Religion in the lives of English women, 1760–1930. *See* **5017.**

**8640.** MARCHAND, PHILIP.    Marshall McLuhan: the medium and the messenger. New York: Ticknor & Fields. pp. xiii, 320. Rev. by G. W. in CanL (122/23) 301.

**8641.** MARSHALL, JOYCE.    The writer as translator: a personal view. CanL (117) 1988, 25–9.

**8642.** MEZEI, KATHY.    Speaking white: literary translation as a vehicle of assimilation in Quebec. CanL (117) 1988, 11–23.

**8643.** NAVE, YUDITH (FISCHER).    Biblical motifs representing the 'lyrical self' in the works of: Sholem Aleichem, Natan Alterman, Lea Goldberg, Ariella Deem, Shulamit Hareven. Unpub. doct. diss., Brandeis Univ., 1987. [Abstr. in DA (49) 1800A.]

**8644.** O'CONNOR, JOHN J.    Violets in a crucible: the translating, editing, and reviewing of Canadian books. CanL (117) 1988, 114–25.

**8645.** PFANNER, HELMUT F. (ed.).    Kulturelle Wechselbeziehungen im Exil: exile across cultures. Bonn: Bouvier, 1986. pp. 394. (Studien zur Literatur der Moderne, 14.) Rev. by J. M. Ritchie in MLR (83:4) 1988, 1051.

**8646.** REYER, WILLIAM ROBERT.    Biblical figures in selected short fiction of Isaac Bashevis Singer. Unpub. doct. diss., Bowling Green State Univ., 1988. [Abstr. in DA (49) 2661A.]

**8647.** ROOT, ROBERT L., JR.    The rhetorics of popular culture: advertising, advocacy, and entertainment. New York: Greenwood Press, 1987. pp. xiv, 175. (Contributions to the study of popular culture, 16.)

**8648.** ROSE, DAN.    Patterns of American culture: ethnography and estrangement. Philadelphia: Pennsylvania UP. pp. 123. Rev. by J. J. Patton in Lore and Language (8:2) 126–7.

**8649.** ROSS, ANDREW.    No respect: intellectuals and popular culture. London; New York: Routledge. pp. xi, 269. Rev. by David Paineau in TLS, 8 Dec., 1364.

**8650.** —— (ed.). Universal abandon? The politics of post-modernism. Edinburgh: Edinburgh UP; Minneapolis: Minnesota UP, 1988. pp. xviii, 300. (Cultural politics.)

**8651.** SHERMAN, JOSEPH. A way of dying: problems of Jewish identity and Jewish survival in the novels of Isaac Bashevis Singer. Unpub. doct. diss., Univ. of the Witwatersrand, 1988.

**8652.** SIMON, SHERRY. The true Quebec as revealed to English Canada: translated novels, 1864–1950. *See* **6065.**

**8653.** SINCLAIR, ANDREW. War like a wasp: the lost decade of the 'forties. London: Hamilton. pp. 321. Rev. by Humphrey Carpenter in TLS, 10 Nov., 1231.

**8654.** STEVENS, JOHN D. Media and morality in the twenties. HT (39) Nov., 25–9.

**8655.** TERNAVASIO, PAOLA. Eugenio Montale e la cultura Anglo-Americana: la traduzione come sintesi di esperienze interpretative. Unpub. doct. diss., Univ. of Connecticut, 1988. [Abstr. in DA (49) 3717A.]

**8656.** VAN SCHENDEL, MICHEL. Traduire l'autre, presque le même: réflexions d'un auteur à propos d'une traduction. CanL (117) 1988, 58–60.

**8657.** WINTEROWD, W. ROSS. The culture and politics of literacy. New York; Oxford: OUP. pp. xiv, 226. Rev. in BkW, 6 Aug., 13.

**8658.** WITEK, JOSEPH PATRICK. 'Stranger and more thrilling than fiction': comic books as history. Unpub. doct. diss., Vanderbilt Univ., 1988. [Abstr. in DA (50) 688A.]

## Literary Theory

This section is intended to contain studies **about** the literary theory, literary historiography, literary criticism, etc., produced *in* the twentieth century. For modern works **of** literary history and criticism dealing generally with this period, see under 'Twentieth Century: General Literary Studies'.

**8659.** AGEE, ANNE SCRIVENER. The concept of audience as a tool for composing and interpreting texts. Unpub. doct. diss., Catholic Univ. of America. [Abstr. in DA (50) 1307–8A.]

**8660.** AGOSTINI, RENÉ. Théâtre et narratologie: perspectives d'une esthétique du récit dramatique. *See* **1950.**

**8661.** AIKEN, SUSAN HARDY, *et al.* (eds). Changing our minds: feminist transformations of knowledge. Albany: New York State UP, 1988. pp. xxiv, 171. Rev. by Sharon Groves in AQ (45:3) 97–109.

**8662.** ALTIERI, CHARLES. When the self became the subject: a review essay on Paul Smith. SoHR (23:3) 255–63 (review-article).

**8663.** AMUTA, CHIDI. The theory of African literature: implications for practical criticism. *See* **7779.**

**8664.** ANDERSON, MARY JANELLE. Toward a Christian approach to literature: the critical theories of C. S. Lewis as a model for Christian literary criticism. Unpub. doct. diss., Univ. of South Florida, 1988. [Abstr. in DA (50) 131A.]

**8665.** APPIAH, KWAME ANTHONY.    The conservation of 'race'. BALF (23:1) 37–60. (Racism in contemporary Afro-American literary criticism.)

**8666.** ARAC, JONATHAN (ed.).    Postmodernism and politics. Manchester: Manchester UP; Minneapolis: Minnesota UP, 1986. pp. xliii, 171. (Theory and history of literature, 28.) Rev. by Steven Connor in MLR (84:4) 907–8; by John McGowan in Criticism (29:2) 1987, 257–60; by Philip Auslander in TJ (39:2) 1987, 257–8.

**8667.** —— GODZICH, WLAD; MARTIN, WALLACE (eds).    The Yale critics: deconstruction in America. (Bibl. 1986, 10713.) Rev. by Julian Patrick in UTQ (56:2) 1986/87, 358–9.

**8668.** ATKINS, G. DOUGLAS: MORROW, LAURA (eds).    Contemporary literary theory. Basingstoke: Macmillan. pp. xiv, 249.

**8669.** AUSTIN, GAYLE.    Feminist theory and postwar American drama. See **7974.**

**8670.** BABCOCK, BARBARA A.    'The arts and all things common': Victor Turner's literary anthropology. CompCrit (9) 1987, 39–46.

**8671.** BAL, MIEKE.    Narratology: introduction to the theory of narrative. Trans. by CHRISTINE VAN BOHEEMEN of *De theorie van Vertellen en Verhalen: Inleidung in de Narratologie.* (Bibl. 1986, 10719.) Rev. by Peter Stoicheff in UTQ (56:2) 1986/87, 375–6.

**8672.** BAUMLIN, JAMES S.; BAUMLIN, TITA FRENCH.    Psyche/logos: mapping the terrains of mind and rhetoric. See **1302.**

**8673.** BEACH, CHRISTOPHER.    Ezra Pound and Harold Bloom: influences, canons, traditions, and the making of modern poetry. ELH (56:2) 463–83.

**8674.** BENJAMIN, ANDREW (ed.).    The problems of modernity: Adorno and Benjamin. London: Routledge. pp. xi, 220. (Warwick studies in philosophy and literature.)

**8675.** BENNETT, DONNA.    Naming the way home. *In* (pp. 228–45) **40.**

**8676.** BERGER, HARRY, JR.    Bodies and texts. Representations (17) 1987, 144–66.

**8677.** BERTENS, HANS.    The Postmodern *Weltanschauung* and its relation with Modernism: an introductory survey. *In* (pp. 9–51) **7.**

**8678.** BLACK, PAMELA ANN.    The presence of the unknowable: the question of the universal in Romantic poetics and deconstructive theory. See **5953.**

**8679.** BODE, CHRISTOPH.    How far can you go? Zum Stand der literaturwissenschaftlichen Debatte in Großbritannien. Ang (107:3/4) 380–414.

**8680.** —— Literary value and evaluation: the case for relational concepts. *In* (pp. 309–24) **5.**

**8680a.** BOERCKEL, SUSAN DENISE.    Kenneth Burke's rhetoric of the 1920s, 1930s, and 1940s. Unpub. doct. diss., State Univ. of New York at Stony Brook, 1988. [Abstr. in DA (50) 1649–50A.]

**8681.** BOGDAN, DEANNE.    From stubborn structure to double mirror: the evolution of Northrop Frye's theory of poetic creation and response. JAE (23:2) 33–43.

**8682.** BOKLUND-LAGOPOULOU, KARIN. Materialism and semiotics in contemporary critical theory. Aristotle Univ. of Thessaloniki Yearbook of English Studies (1) 277–96.

**8683.** BORINSKY, ALICIA. No body there: on the politics of interlocution. *In* (pp. 245–56) **61.**

**8684.** BOWKER, VERONICA. Textuality and worldliness: crossing the boundaries: a postmodernist reading of Achebe, Conrad and Lessing. JLS (5:1) 55–67.

**8685.** BRENKMAN, JOHN. Culture and domination. Ithaca, NY; London: Cornell UP, 1987. pp. xi, 239.

**8686.** BRETZIUS, STEPHEN MERRILL. Criticism in style: theory as aesthetic form. Unpub. doct. diss., Harvard Univ., 1988. [Abstr. in DA (50) 436A.]

**8687.** BROICH, ULRICH; PFISTER, MANFRED; SCHULTE-MIDDELICH, BERND (eds). Intertextualität: Formen, Funktionen, anglistische Fallstudien. (Bibl. 1987, 9656.) Rev. by Herbert Grabes in Ang (107:1/2) 275–8.

**8688.** BROWNE, P. L. Lukács's aesthetics and ontology, 1908–23. Unpub. doct. diss., Univ. of Sussex. [Abstr. in IT (39:3) 1084.]

**8689.** BRUNS, GERALD L. Between philosophy and literature: theory, practice, and significance in literary study. Ren (41:4) 233–51.

**8690.** BUCK, C. Reading the feminine self: H.D./Freud/psychoanalysis. Unpub. doct. diss., Univ. of Kent, 1987. [Abstr. in IT (39:4) 1636.]

**8691.** BUTLER, CHRISTOPHER. Interpretation, deconstruction, and ideology: an introduction to some current issues in literary theory. (Bibl. 1986, 10743.) Rev. by Julian Patrick in UTQ (56:2) 1986/87, 359–62.

**8692.** BUTLER, MARILYN. Repossessing the past: the case for an open literary history. *In* (pp. 64–84) **53.**

**8693.** CAIN, WILLIAM E. F. O. Matthiessen and the politics of criticism. Madison; London: Wisconsin UP, 1988. pp. xiv, 238. (Wisconsin project on American writers.) Rev. by Nina Baym in NEQ (62:3) 466–8; by Tim Poland in AL (61:4) 714–16.

**8694.** CALINESCU, MATEI. Postmodernism and some paradoxes of periodization. *In* (pp. 239–54) **7.**

**8695.** CAPUTO, JOHN D. Radical hermeneutics: repetition, deconstruction, and the hermeneutic project. (Bibl. 1988, 6554.) Rev. by Vincent B. Leitch in PhilL (13:1) 151–62.

**8696.** CATANO, JAMES V. Language, history, style: Leo Spitzer and the critical tradition. London: Routledge, 1988. pp. 205.

**8697.** CHAPMAN, MICHAEL. The critic in a state of emergency: towards a theory of reconstruction. Theoria (74) 13–29.

**8698.** CHERRY, KELLY. When all is said and done, how literary theory *really* affects contemporary fiction. *See* **8205.**

**8699.** COBLEY, EVELYN. Mikhail Bakhtin's place in genre theory. Genre (21:3) 1988, 321–38.

**8700.** —— Towards history as discontinuity: the Russian Formalists and Foucault. Mosaic (20:2) 1987, 41–56.

**8701.** COHEN, RALPH; PECK, JEFFREY M. (eds). New Literary History international bibliography of literary theory and criticism. Baltimore, MD; London: Johns Hopkins UP, 1988. pp. xix, 188. (Bibliography for 1984/85.)

**8702.** CONNERTY, J. P. Narrative as an object and a method in philosophy and the human sciences. Unpub. doct. diss., Univ. of Oxford, 1988. [Abstr. in IT (39:3) 1084.]

**8703.** CONNOR, STEVEN. Postmodernism and literature. See **7815.**

**8704.** —— Postmodernities. In (pp. 27–64) STEVEN CONNOR, Postmodernist culture: an introduction to theories of the contemporary. Oxford: Blackwell. pp. x, 274.

**8705.** CRITCHLEY, S. J. The chiasmus: Levinas, Derrida, and the ethics of deconstructive reading. Unpub. doct. diss., Univ. of Essex, 1988. [Abstr. in IT (38:4) 1444.]

**8706.** CULLER, JONATHAN. Framing the sign: criticism and its institutions. Norman; London: Oklahoma UP, 1988. (Oklahoma project for discourse and theory, 3.) (Bibl. 1988, 6562.)

**8707.** —— On deconstruction: theory and criticism after structuralism. (Bibl. 1986, 10755.) Rev. by Stephen Heath in CompCrit (9) 1987, 281–326; by Julian Patrick in UTQ (56:2) 1986/87, 343–52.

**8708.** —— Wilde's criticism: theory and practice. In (pp. 402–6) **45.**

**8709.** DE MAN, PAUL. The resistance to theory. (Bibl. 1988, 6571.) Rev. by Catherine Belsey in MLR (84:3) 683–5; by Frank McCombie in NQ (36:2) 280–2.

**8710.** DENHAM, ROBERT D. Northrop Frye: an annotated bibliography of primary and secondary sources. (Bibl. 1988, 6572.) Rev. by Graham Forst in CanL (122/23) 189–90; by James M. Mellard in AEB (ns 2:3) 1988, 113–21.

**8711.** DÍAZ FERNÁNDEZ, JOSÉ RAMÓN. F. R. Leavis: bibliografía de sus escritos críticos. RAEI (2) 175–202.

**8712.** DICK, SUSAN, et al. Richard Ellmann: the critic as artist. In (pp. xiii–xviii) **45.**

**8713.** DILLON, BRIAN DANIEL. Inevitable fictions: biographically-based discourse in literary criticism. Unpub. doct. diss., Washington State Univ., 1988. [Abstr. in DA (49) 3354A.]

**8714.** DOLAN, JILL. The feminist spectator as critic. See **8022.**

**8715.** DOLAN, JILL S. The feminist spectator as critic: performance criticism and representation. Unpub. doct. diss., New York Univ., 1988. [Abstr. in DA (49) 2864A.]

**8716.** DOLEŽEL, LUBOMÍR. Mimesis and contemporary criticism. CompCrit (11) 253–61 (review-article).

**8717.** DRUCE, ROBERT (ed.). A centre of excellence: essays presented to Seymour Betsky. See **13.**

**8718.** DURRANT, M. J. The ethical function of literature in the criticism of Northrop Frye. Unpub. doct. diss., Univ. of Otago.

**8719.** DUYFHUIZEN, BERNARD. Textual harassment of Marvell's Coy Mistress: the institutionalization of masculine criticism. See **4630.**

**8720.** DUYTSCHAEVER, JORIS.    Faulkner's *Light in August* and the vicissitudes of narcissism: the case of Gail Hightower. *In* (pp. 99–115) **2.**

**8721.** EAGLETON, TERRY.    The emptying of a former self. TLS, 26 May, 573–4 (review-article).

**8722.** —— Literary theory: an introduction. (Bibl. 1986, 3025.) Rev. by Julian Patrick in UTQ (56:2) 1986/87, 352–6; by Stephen Heath in CompCrit (9) 1987, 281–326.

**8723.** EASTHOPE, ANTONY.    British post-structuralism since 1968. London: Routledge, 1988. pp. xiv, 255. Rev. by Maud Ellmann in TLS, 17 Feb., 172.

**8724.** EBERT, TERESA LYNN.    Patriarchy, ideology, subjectivity: towards a theory of feminist critical cultural studies. Unpub. doct. diss., Univ. of Minnesota, 1988. [Abstr. in DA (50) 138–9A.]

**8725.** EDELMAN, LEE.    The plague of discourse: politics, literary theory, and AIDS. SAQ (88:1) 301–17.

**8726.** ELLIS, JOHN.    Against deconstruction. Princeton, NJ; Guildford: Princeton UP. pp. x, 168. Rev. by Frank Kermode in LRB (11:20) 21–3.

**8727.** ESONWANNE, UZOMA MARTIN.    Difference, interpretation and referentiality. Unpub. doct. diss., Univ. of New Brunswick, 1988. [Abstr. in DA (49) 2227A.]

**8728.** EWBANK, INGA-STINA.    Victorian novels and feminist criticism. *In* (pp. 47–66) **47.**

**8729.** FELDSTEIN, RICHARD; ROOF, JUDITH (eds).    Feminism and psychoanalysis. *See* **29.**

**8730.** FELMAN, SHOSHANA.    Writing and madness: literature/philosophy/psychoanalysis. Trans. by MARTHA NOEL EVANS and BRIAN MASSUMI. *See* **7064.**

**8731.** FELPERIN, HOWARD.    Beyond deconstruction: the uses and abuses of literary theory. (Bibl. 1988, 6587.) Rev. by Thomas Docherty in RES (38:149) 1987, 122–3; by Mireya Folch-Serra in QQ (95:3) 1988, 622–5.

**8732.** FISH, STANLEY.    Doing what comes naturally: change, rhetoric and the practice of theory in literary and legal studies. Oxford: Clarendon Press. pp. x, 613. Rev. by John Ellis in LRB (11:14) 20–2.

**8733.** FITE, DAVID.    Harold Bloom: the rhetoric of romantic vision. (Bibl. 1986, 7518, where misplaced.) Rev. by V. A. De Luca in UTQ (56:4) 1987, 579–82.

**8734.** FOGEL, STANLEY.    The postmodern university: essays on the deconstruction of the humanities. *See* **7832.**

**8735.** FOKKEMA, DOUWE.    American postmodernism in Germany: a review of reception. *See* **8241.**

**8736.** —— The concept of convention in literary theory and empirical research. *In* (pp. 1–16) **16.**

**8737.** —— BERTENS, HANS (eds).    Approaching Postmodernism: papers presented at a workshop on Postmodernism, 21–23 September 1984, University of Utrecht. *See* **7.**

**8738.** FOLCH-SERRA, MIREYA.    A postmodern conversation. QQ (95:3) 1988, 568–79 (review-article).

**8739.** FOSTER, JOHN WILSON.    The critical condition of Ulster. *In* (pp. 86–102) **17.**

**8740.** FOWLER, ALASTAIR.    Writing criticism and making poems. *See* **8492.**

**8741.** FREUND, ELIZABETH.    The return of the reader: reader-response criticism. London: Methuen, 1987. pp. xii 184. (New accents.) Rev. by Sue Vice in NQ (36:1) 136.

**8742.** FUSS, DIANA JEAN.    Essential theories/theory's essentialism: feminism, poststructuralism, and contemporary literary criticism. Unpub. doct. diss., Brown Univ., 1988. [Abstr. in DA (49) 2205A.]

**8743.** GADET, FRANÇOISE.    Saussure and contemporary culture. Trans. by GREGORY ELLIOTT. London: Century Hutchinson. pp. 169. Rev. by Michael Sprinker in TLS, 18 Aug., 898.

**8744.** GANE, MIKE (ed.).    Ideological representation and power in social relations: literary and social theory. London: Routledge. pp. 224. (Economy and society.)

**8745.** GASCHÉ, RODOLPHE.    The tain of the mirror: Derrida and the philosophy of reflection. (Bibl. 1988, 6595.) Rev. by Glenn Erickson in SoCR (21:2) 75–9.

**8746.** GERRY, THOMAS M. F.    The literary crisis: the nuclear crisis. DalR (67:2/3) 1987, 297–305.

**8747.** GLABERSON, ERIC.    The literary criticism of the New York intellectuals. AmerS (29:1) 1988, 71–85.

**8748.** GOLDEN, KENNETH L.    Crisis in criticism: textual literalism versus the art of criticism. MidQ (30:2) 151–60.

**8749.** GROENING, LAURA.    Modernizing academia: an American and a Canadian vision. *See* **6071.**

**8750.** GROVES, SHARON.    A question of change. AQ (45:3) 97–109 (review-article).

**8751.** GUAGLIARDO, HUEY S.    Cleanth Brooks: critic in a nutshell? BSUF (26:3) 1985, 67–74.

**8751a.** GUILLÉN, CLAUDIO.    Entre lo uno y lo diverso: introducción a la literatura comparada. Barcelona: Crítica, 1985. Rev. by Arthur Terry in CompCrit (10) 1988, 327–32.

**8752.** GUNN, DANIEL.    Psychoanalysis and fiction: an exploration of literary and psychoanalytic borders. *See* **8262.**

**8753.** HALLIBURTON, DAVID.    Reconstructing theory. CompCrit (11) 71–95.

**8754.** HARLAND, RICHARD.    Superstructuralism: the philosophy of structuralism and post-structuralism. (Bibl. 1988, 6610.) Rev. by David Dowling in CanL (119) 1988, 119.

**8755.** HARRIS, ROBIN.    English studies at Toronto: a history. *See* **6073.**

**8755a.** HARRIS, WENDELL V.    The critics who made us: Kenneth Burke. SewR (96:3) 1988, 452–63.

**8756.** HASSAN, IHAB.    The critical scene: issues in postmodern American criticism. *In* (pp. 5–15) **2.**

**8757.** —— The postmodern turn: essays in postmodern theory and culture. (Bibl. 1987, 9729.) Rev. by Mireya Folch-Serra in QQ (95:3) 1988, 627–30.

**8758.** HEATH, STEPHEN. Literary theory, etc. CompCrit (9) 1987, 281–326 (review-article).

**8759.** HIGDON, DAVID LEON. The relevance of Northrop Frye's *Specific Continuous Forms*. RMRLL (43:4) 223–34.

**8760.** HILLGÄRTNER, RÜDIGER. Das Versprechen des Übersetzers. Dekonstruktion des Subjekts und Benjamin-Lektüre bei Paul de Man. GRM (39) 440–56.

**8761.** HIRSCH, DAVID H. Paul de Man and the politics of deconstruction. SewR (96:2) 1988, 330–8.

**8762.** HOGARTY, KENNETH WILLIAM. Heroes need apply: a critical study of appropriating action in classrooms informed by reader-response theory. Unpub. doct. diss., Univ. of San Francisco, 1988. [Abstr. in DA (49) 2955A.]

**8763.** HOOKER, DEBORAH A. Coming to Cressida through Irigaray. *See* **4037.**

**8764.** HUISMAN, LEO. Twentieth-century British literature: a survey of some recent literary history and criticism. DQR (19:1) 51–73.

**8765.** HUMM, MAGGIE. Feminist criticism: women as contemporary critics. (Bibl. 1986, 10822, where title incomplete.) Rev. by Maria Del Sapio in MLR (84:4) 959–60.

**8766.** HUMPHREYS, ARTHUR. The livingness of literature. *In* (pp. 173–7) **13.**

**8767.** HUNTER, DIANNE (ed.). Seduction & theory: readings of gender, representation, and rhetoric. Urbana; Chicago: Illinois UP. pp. vi, 250.

**8768.** HUTCHEON, LINDA. A theory of parody: the teachings of twentieth-century art forms. (Bibl. 1986, 10824.) Rev. by Lorna Irvine in CanL (115) 1987, 264–5.

**8769.** IRZIK, SIBEL KUVENT. Deconstruction and the politics of criticism. Unpub. doct. diss., Indiana Univ., 1988. [Abstr. in DA (49) 3356A.]

**8770.** JANCOVICH, M. Social and cultural thought in the formation of the New Criticism: the social origins of the American literary criticism. Unpub. doct. diss., Univ. of Kent, 1988. [Abstr. in IT (39:2) 489.]

**8771.** JANG, GYUNG-RYUL. Bipyeong eui gaekgwansung gwa gachi pandan eui munjae: Murray Krieger eui kyoungwu. (Murray Krieger and the problem of value-judgement.) AmeSt (12) 93–111.

**8772.** —— The limits of essentialist critical thinking: a metacritical study of the New Criticism and its theoretical alternatives. Unpub. doct. diss., Univ. of Texas at Austin, 1988. [Abstr. in DA (50) 140A.]

**8773.** JARDINE, ALICE; SMITH, PAUL (eds). Men in feminism. New York; London: Methuen, 1987. pp. viii, 288. Rev. by Naomi Segal in MLR (84:3) 685–6.

**8774.** JARRETT, JAMES MICHAEL. Drifting on a read: jazz as a model for literary and theoretical writing. *See* **8292.**

**8775.** JASEN, PATRICIA. Arnoldian Humanism, English studies, and the Canadian university. *See* **6074.**

**8776.** JAY, GREGORY S.; MILLER, DAVID L. (eds). After strange texts: the role of theory in the study of literature. (Bibl. 1987, 4.) Rev. by Philip Le Brun in RES (38:151) 1987, 427–8.

**8777.** JAY, PAUL. Modernism, postmodernism, and critical style: the case of Burke and Derrida. Genre (21:3) 1988, 339–58.

**8778.** JOHNSON, C. System and writing in the philosophy of Jacques Derrida. Unpub. doct. diss., Univ. of Cambridge. [Abstr. in IT (39:3) 1086.]

**8779.** KAMUF, PEGGY. Floating authorship. *In* (pp. 177–200) PEGGY KAMUF, Signature pieces: on the institution of authorship. Ithaca, NY; London: Cornell UP, 1988. pp. x, 237.

**8780.** —— Pieces of resistance. *In* (pp. 201–27) PEGGY KAMUF, Signature pieces: on the institution of authorship. Ithaca, NY; London: Cornell UP, 1988. pp. x, 237.

**8781.** KAUFFMAN, LINDA (ed.). Gender and theory: dialogues on feminist criticism. Oxford; New York: Blackwell. pp. x, 258.

**8782.** KAYES, JAMIE BARLOWE. Reading against the grain: the powers and limits of feminist criticism of American narratives. *See* **8299.**

**8783.** KAYES, JAMIE R. BARLOWE. The criticism of American literature: the powers and limits of an institutional practice. Unpub. doct. diss., Ohio State Univ., 1988. [Abstr. in DA (49) 2659–60A.]

**8784.** KEITEL, EVELYNE. Reading psychosis: readers, texts and psychoanalysis. Trans. by ANTHEA BALL. *See* **8302.**

**8785.** KENT, THOMAS. Beyond system: the rhetoric of paralogy. *See* **1311.**

**8786.** KERMODE, FRANK. Northrop Frye and the Bible. *In* (pp. 71–81) **45.**

**8787.** KERRIGAN, WILLIAM. Terminating Lacan. SAQ (88:4) 993–1008.

**8788.** KIM, JONGSOON. A study of Fredric Jameson's *The Political Unconscious: Narrative as a Socially Symbolic Act*. JELL (35) 29–39.

**8788a.** KINCH, M. B.; BAKER, WILLIAM; KIMBER, JOHN. F. R. and Q. D. Leavis: an annotated bibliography. New York; London: Garland. pp. xxiii, 531. (Garland bibliographies of modern critics and critical schools, 12.) (Garland reference library of the humanities, 521.)

**8789.** KLUMPP, JAMES F.; HOLLIHAN, THOMAS A. Rhetorical criticism as moral action. *See* **1312.**

**8790.** KNIGHTS, L. C. Cambridge criticism: what was it? *In* (pp. 161–71) **13.** (Talk given at reunion of contributors to *Pelican Guide* and *New Pelican Guide to English Literature*, Cambridge, Sept. 1983.)

**8791.** —— Postscript. *In* (pp. 193–5) **13.**

**8792.** KRONENFELD, JUDY. Post-Saussurean semantics, Reformation religious controversy, and contemporary critical disagreement. *See* **4504.**

**8793.** KRUPNICK, MARK. Lionel Trilling and the politics of style. *In* (pp. 152–70) **1.**

**8794.** KUROWSKA, ELŻBIETA.   The Modern English novel in Polish and English literary criticism in the 1930s. *In* (pp. 136–52) **36.**

**8795.** LANNIN, THOMAS FORREST, JR.   Contemporary critical theory and the literary revisionism of W. B. Yeats' later poetry. Unpub. doct. diss., Univ. of California, Riverside, 1988. [Abstr. in DA (49) 2230–1A.]

**8796.** LEITCH, VINCENT B.   American literary criticism: from the thirties to the eighties. (Bibl. 1988, 6640.) Rev. by Jeffrey A. Steele in AL (61:3) 507–8; by William E. Cain in CE (51:3) 320–4.

**8797.** —— Deconstructive criticism: an advanced introduction. (Bibl. 1987, 9767.) Rev. by Julian Patrick in UTQ (56:2) 1986/87, 357–8.

**8798.** LERNER, LAURENCE.   The author: coroner's report. SoHR (23:3) 201–14.

**8799.** —— On ambiguity, Modernism, and sacred texts. *In* (pp. 133–44) **46.**

**8800.** LETHEN, HELMUT.   Modernism cut in half: the exclusion of the avant-garde and the debate on Postmodernism. *In* (pp. 233–8) **7.**

**8801.** LEVINSON, MARJORIE.   Introduction. *In* (pp. 1–17) **53.**

**8802.** —— The new historicism: back to the future. *In* (pp. 18–63) **53.**

**8803.** LIU, ALAN.   The power of Formalism: the New Historicism. ELH (56:4) 721–71.

**8804.** LODGE, DAVID (ed.).   Modern criticism and theory: a reader. (Bibl. 1988, 6650.) Rev. by Maud Ellmann in TLS, 17 Feb., 172.

**8805.** LORIMER LUNDBERG, PATRICIA.   Gendered reading communities: the feminization of reader response criticism and a dialogics of reading. *See* **6302.**

**8806.** McCAFFERY, STEVE.   North of intention: critical writings, 1973–1986. *See* **7888.**

**8807.** MacCANNELL, JULIET FLOWER.   Figuring Lacan: criticism and the cultural unconscious. (Bibl. 1987, 9771.) Rev. by Elizabeth Wright in RES (38:152) 1987, 590–1.

**8808.** McCORMICK, THOMAS W.   Theories of reading in dialogue: an interdisciplinary study. Lanham, MD; London: UP of America, 1988. pp. x, 399.

**8809.** MACEY, DAVID.   Lacan in contexts. London: Verso. pp. xi, 322. Rev. by John Forrester in TLS, 14 Apr., 392.

**8810.** McGANN, G. K.   'The keys to dreamland': Marxism, aesthetics and film. *See* **8087.**

**8811.** McMAHON, ROBERT.   Kenneth Burke's divine comedy: the literary form of *The Rhetoric of Religion.* PMLA (104:1) 53–63.

**8812.** MARTIN, GRAHAM.   Cambridge criticism & 'history'. *In* (pp. 179–82) **13.**

**8813.** MASON, ELLSWORTH.   Ellmann's road to Xanadu. *In* (pp. 4–12) **45.**

**8814.** MASSEY, M. KATHLEEN.   Post-structuralism, the new rhetoric, and composition: the watershed moment. Unpub. doct. diss., Univ. of Southern California. [Abstr. in DA (50) 1313A.]

**8815.** MELLARD, JAMES M.   Monument or scholarly tool? Denham's Northrop Frye: a review essay. AEB (ns 2:3) 1988, 113–21.

**8816.** MELVILLE, STEPHEN W.    Philosophy beside itself: on deconstruction and Modernism. (Bibl. 1988, 6658.) Rev. by Steven Connor in MLR (84:4) 905–7.

**8817.** MITCHELL, W. J. T. (ed.).    Against theory: literary studies and the new pragmatism. (Bibl. 1988, 6662.) Rev. by Philip Le Brun in RES (38:151) 1987, 426–7.

**8818.** MORRIS, ROBERT.    Words and images in modernism and postmodernism. CI (15:2) 337–47.

**8819.** MULLINS, PHIL.    Recovering the veridical: implications of Michael Polanyi's thought for literary studies. MidQ (31:1) 29–44.

**8820.** NATOLI, JOSEPH (ed.).    Literary theory's future(s). Urbana; Chicago: Illinois UP. pp. vi, 337.

**8821.** NAVAJAS, GONZALO.    Mimesis y cultura en la ficción: teoría de la novela. *See* **8349.**

**8822.** NEEL, JASPER.    Plato, Derrida, and writing. Carbondale: Southern Illinois UP, 1988. pp. 252. Rev. by Miriam Dow in CE (51:8) 878–81.

**8823.** NEUMAN, SHIRLEY.    Importing difference. *In* (pp. 392–405) **40.**

**8824.** NEWTON, JUDITH; ROSENFELT, DEBORAH (eds).    Feminist criticism and social change: sex, class and race in literature and culture. (Bibl. 1987, 9792.) Rev. by Judy Simons in RES (39:153) 1988, 156–7.

**8825.** NEWTON, K. M.    Poststructuralism and the question of interpretation. Eng (38) 117–40.

**8826.** —— (ed.).    Twentieth-century literary theory: a reader. Basingstoke: Macmillan, 1988. pp. 282. Rev. by Peter Kitson in NQ (36:4) 554–5.

**8827.** NIALL, LUCY.    The death of literature. Antithesis (Melbourne) (2:2) 1988/89, 71–84.

**8828.** NICHOLS, BILL.    Form wars: the political unconscious of Formalist theory. *See* **8095.**

**8829.** NIRANJANA, TEJASWINI.    Bringing the text to legibility: translation, post-structuralism, and the colonial context. *See* **1628.**

**8830.** NORRIS, CHRISTOPHER.    The contest of faculties: philosophy and theory after deconstruction. (Bibl. 1986, 10880.) Rev. by Ian Maclean in RES (38:150) 1987, 289–90.

**8831.** —— Deconstruction: theory and practice. (Bibl. 1983, 9985.) Rev. by Mireya Folch-Serra in QQ (95:3) 1988, 630–3.

**8832.** —— Paul de Man: deconstruction and the critique of aesthetic ideology. (Bibl. 1988, 6676.) Rev. by Terry Eagleton in TLS, 26 May, 573–4.

**8833.** O'CONNOR, ALAN.    Raymond Williams: writing, culture, politics. Oxford: Blackwell. pp. 180. Rev. by Chris Baldick in TLS, 3 Nov., 1205.

**8834.** OLSEN, STEIN HAUGOM.    The end of literary theory. (Bibl. 1988, 6682.) Rev. by Adolphe Haberer in EA (42:4) 450–1.

**8835.** ORLANDINI, ROBERTA.    The Italian reception of modern American criticism. Unpub. doct. diss., Drew Univ., 1988. [Abstr. in DA (50) 133A.]

**8836.** PALMER, PAULINA. Contemporary women's fiction: narrative practice and feminist theory. See **8357**.

**8837.** PARK, CHAN-BU. Transferential structure of reading: an essay on psychoanalysis and literary criticism. JELL (35) 41–56.

**8838.** PARRINDER, PATRICK. The failure of theory: essays on criticism and contemporary fiction. (Bibl. 1988, 6685.) Rev. by Rikky Rooksby in NQ (36:2) 282–3; by Raman Selden in YES (19) 363–5.

**8839.** PATRICK, JULIAN. Deconstruction and ideology in current literary theory. UTQ (56:2) 1986/87, 338–64 (review-article).

**8840.** PETTERSSON, TORSTEN. Literary interpretation: current models and a new departure. Åbo: Åbo Academy Press, 1988. pp. 132. Rev. by Peter Kitson in NQ (36:4) 555–6.

**8841.** POTTER, A. M. Religion and the literary critic. Literator (10:1) 66–76. (*As I Lay Dying*.)

**8842.** PRINCE, GERALD. A dictionary of narratology. See **1143**.

**8843.** PRINTZ-PÅHLSON, GÖRAN. Interview with Raymond Williams (1967). CompCrit (11) 3–27. (Trans. of article in Ord och bild (1967:4).)

**8844.** RADNER, HILARY ANN. Shopping around: locating feminine enunciation through textual practice. Unpub. doct. diss., Univ. of Texas at Austin, 1988. [Abstr. in DA (49) 3530A.]

**8845.** RAJCHMAN, JOHN. Crisis. Representations (28) 90–8.

**8846.** RICE, PHILIP: WAUGH, PATRICIA (eds). Modern literary theory: a reader. London: Arnold. pp. x, 286.

**8847.** RIFFATERRE, MICHAEL. Text production. Trans. by THÉRÈSE LYONS. New York: Columbia UP, 1983. pp. 341. Rev. by Julian Patrick in UTQ (56:2) 1986/87, 340–3.

**8848.** ROBSON, W. W. Values and knowledge. In (pp. 185–8) **13**.

**8849.** ROXMAN, SUSANNA. England kan lära oss. (England can teach us.) In (pp. 31–4) BENGT-OLOV LINDER (ed.), Kritik av kritik. (Criticism scrutinized.) Stockholm: Carlsson. pp. 99.

**8850.** RULEWICZ, WANDA. Intertextuality in deconstructive criticism. KN (36:2) 377–87.

**8851.** SAID, EDWARD W. Representing the colonized: anthropology's interlocutors. CI (15:2) 205–25.

**8852.** SAKELLARIDOU, ELIZABETH. The dead ends of the feminist discourse. Aristotle Univ. of Thessaloniki Yearbook of English Studies (1) 437–51.

**8853.** SALINGAR, LEO. Life and thought. In (pp. 189–91) **13**.

**8854.** SARUP, MADAN. An introductory guide to post-structuralism and post-modernism. New York; London: Harvester Wheatsheaf, 1988. pp. viii, 171.

**8855.** SCHAUM, MELITA. 'Ariel, save us': big stick polemics in Frank Lentricchia's *Ariel and the Police*. Genders (4) 122–9.

**8856.** SCHENDLER, SYLVAN. 'Heroic work, heroic being': avoid the valedictory. In (pp. 1–3) **45**.

**8857.** SCHOLES, ROBERT.    Textual power: literary theory and the teaching of English. (Bibl. 1988, 6711.) Rev. by Thomas Docherty in RES (38:149) 1987, 123.

**8858.** SEAMAN, ROBERT E.    Lacan, Poe, and the descent of the self. *See* **7333.**

**8859.** SEAMON, ROGER.    Poetics against itself: on the self-destruction of modern scientific criticism. PMLA (104:3) 294–305.

**8860.** SEEBER, HANS ULRICH.    Auf dem Weg zum Vortex: Zentral-bewegung, Ästhetik des Sublimen und das Wasser der Moderne in englischen London-Texten des 19. Jahrhunderts. *See* **1913.**

**8861.** SELDEN, RAMAN.    Practising theory and reading literature: an introduction. New York; London: Harvester Wheatsheaf. pp. xii, 206. (Pub. in US as *Practicing Theory and Reading Literature: an Introduction* (Lexington: Kentucky UP. (Literary theory: practice and pedagogy.).)

**8862.** SELLARS, R.    Bloom, Freud, and Milton: misprision, psycho-analysis, and the question of the text. *See* **4740.**

**8863.** SHARRATT, BERNARD.    Communications and image studies: notes after Raymond Williams. CompCrit (11) 29–50.

**8864.** SHASHIDHAR, R.    From literary criticism to Marxism – an analysis of the holistic writings of Raymond Williams. Unpub. doct. diss., Univ. of Manchester. [Abstr. in IT (39:4) 1635.]

**8865.** SHEREEN, FAIZA WAHBY.    An introduction to the assumptions, methods, and practices of the Chicago school of criticism. Unpub. doct. diss., Univ. of Cincinnati, 1988. [Abstr. in DA (49) 3361A.]

**8866.** SHERIFF, JOHN K.    The fate of meaning: Charles Peirce, structuralism and literature. *See* **1248.**

**8867.** SMITH, BARBARA HERRNSTEIN.    Contingencies of value: alterna-tive perspectives for critical theory. (Bibl. 1988, 6724.) Rev. by Anthony Savile in NYTB, 4 June, 35.

**8868.** SMITH, PAUL.    Discerning the subject. Minneapolis: Minnesota UP, 1988. pp. xxxv, 185. Rev. by Charles Altieri in SoHR (23:3) 255–63.

**8869.** SÖRENSEN, DOLF.    Theory formation and the study of literature. Amsterdam: Rodopi, 1987. pp. xii, 370. Rev. by Roger Fowler in MLR (84:4) 899.

**8870.** SOUTHWELL, SAMUEL B.    Kenneth Burke and Martin Heideg-ger: with a note against deconstructionism. Gainesville: Florida UP, 1987. pp. ix, 156. Rev. by Clarence Walhout in ChrisL (38:3) 89.

**8871.** SPRINKER, MICHAEL.    The current conjuncture in theory. CE (51:8) 825–31.

**8872.** STONE, DONALD D.    Meredith and Bakhtin: polyphony and *Bildung. See* **7261.**

**8873.** SULEIMAN, SUSAN RUBIN.    Naming and difference: reflections on 'Modernism *versus* Postmodernism' in literature. *In* (pp. 255–70) **7.**

**8874.** TERRY, ARTHUR.    'Between the one and the many': Claudio Guillén on comparative literature. CompCrit (10) 1988, 327–32 (review-article).

**8875.** THOMPSON, DENYS. The Leavises: recollections and impressions. (Bibl. 1987, 11514.) Rev. by G. Singh in ModAge (32:2) 1988, 179–82.

**8876.** TIFFIN, HELEN. Post-colonialism, post-modernism and the rehabilitation of post-colonial history. *See* **8407.**

**8877.** TOSTEVIN, LOLA LEMIRE. Breaking the hold on the story: the feminine economy of language. *In* (pp. 385–91) **40.**

**8878.** VALDÉS, MARIO J. Phenomenological hermeneutics and the study of literature. Toronto; London: Toronto UP, 1987. pp. x, 142. (Univ. of Toronto romance, 56.) Rev. by David Dowling in CanL (117) 1988, 149–51.

**8879.** VAN ALPHEN, ERNST. Naar een theorie van het postmodernisme, over de postmodernisme discussie. (Towards a theory of postmodernism, concerning the postmodernism discussion.) ForumL (30:1) 21–37.

**8880.** VAN DEN HEUVEL, PIERRE. À la recherche du sujet perdu. Neophilologus (73:2) 189–206.

**8881.** VAN MEURS, JOS; KIDD, JOHN. Jungian literary criticism 1920–1980: an annotated, critical bibliography of works in English (with a selection of titles after 1980). Metuchen, NJ; London: Scarecrow Press, 1988. pp. 353.

**8882.** VAUGHAN-LEE, L. C. Imaginal response: an adaptation of Jung's 'active imagination' into a mode of responding to archetypal images in Shakespeare's *Hamlet. See* **3848.**

**8883.** VEESER, H. ARAM (ed.). The new historicism. London; New York: Routledge. pp. xvi, 317. Rev. by Frank Kermode in LRB (11:20) 21–3.

**8884.** WARNER, MARTIN. On not deconstructing the difference between literature and philosophy. PhilL (13:1) 16–27.

**8885.** WASHINGTON, PETER. Fraud: literary theory and the end of English. London: Fontana. pp. 188.

**8886.** WATERS, LINDSAY; GODZICH, WLAD (eds). Reading de Man reading. Minneapolis: Minnesota UP. pp. 312. Rev. by Terry Eagleton in TLS, 26 May, 573–4.

**8887.** WELLEK, RENÉ. A history of modern criticism, 1750–1950: vol. 5, English criticism, 1900–1950; vol. 6, American criticism, 1900–1950. (Bibl. 1988, 6752.) Rev. by Inge Jonsson in Samlaren (110) 170–2.

**8888.** WHITSITT, SAMUEL PORTER. Putting 'it' in other words: readings of Eco, Deely, Melville and James. *See* **7116.**

**8889.** WILLETT, CYNTHIA J. Tropes of orientation: between dialectic and deconstruction. Unpub. doct. diss., Pennsylvania State Univ., 1988. [Abstr. in DA (49) 2689A.]

**8890.** WILLOUGHBY, GUY. Oscar Wilde and poststructuralism. *See* **7687.**

**8891.** WILSON, ELIZABETH ANNE. Criticism, Inc.: a reconsideration of New Criticism and the profession, 1930–1955. Unpub. doct. diss., Univ. of Pennsylvania, 1988. [Abstr. in DA (50) 142A.]

**8892.** WINKGENS, MEINHARD.   Die kulturkritische Verankerung der Literaturkritik bei F. R. Leavis. Paderborn: Schoningh, 1988. pp. 464.

**8893.** WOLF, WERNER.   Literaturtheorie in der Literatur. David Lodges *Small World* als kritische Auseinandersetzung mit dem Dekonstruktivismus. AAA (14:1) 19–38.

**8894.** YE, HUANIAN.   Literary criticism and culture: comparison of American and Chinese scholarly criticism of American literature. Unpub. doct. diss., New York Univ. [Abstr. in DA (50) 1300A.]

## AUTHORS

### Edward Abbey

**8895.** REA, PAUL W.   Abbey's country. Journal of the Southwest (31:2) 264–70.

### Walter Abish

**8896.** SEMRAU, JANUSZ.   Magritte, Godard, and Walter Abish's architectonic fiction. SAP (22) 141–52.

### Peter Abrahams

**8897.** WADE, JEAN-PHILIPPE.   Peter Abrahams's *The Path of Thunder*: the crisis of the liberal subject. EngA (16:2) 61–75.

### Chinua Achebe

**8898.** BOWKER, VERONICA.   Textuality and worldliness: crossing the boundaries: a postmodernist reading of Achebe, Conrad and Lessing. *See* **8684.**

**8899.** ELIAS, KHALIQUZZAMAN M.   The legacies of Prospero: a critique of the colonial and the neo-colonial experiences in selected writings of Richard Wright, Chinua Achebe, and George Lamming. Unpub. doct. diss., Howard Univ. [Abstr. in DA (50) 1651A.]

**8900.** MADUKA, CHIDI T.   African religious beliefs in literary imagination: *ogbanje* and *abiku* in Chinua Achebe, J. P. Clark and Wole Soyinka. JCL (22:1) 1987, 17–30.

**8901.** OKINMAH, UMELO R.   Post-colonial tensions in a cross-cultural milieu: a comparative study of the writings of Witi Ihimaera and Chinua Achebe. Unpub. doct. diss., Univ. of Otago.

### J. R. Ackerley

**8902.** PARKER, PETER.   Ackerley: a life of J. R. Ackerley. London: Constable. pp. xii, 465. Rev. by Humphrey Carpenter in TLS, 15 Sept., 993–4; by John Bayley in LRB (11:18) 3, 5–6; by John Lahr in Listener (122) 21 Sept., 29–30.

**8903.** —— Cousins once removed. HT (39) Sept., 7–8.

**8904.** —— Literary lionheart. Listener (122) 7 Sept., 14–15.

### Peter Ackroyd

**8905.** GELLERSTEDT, MATS.   En playboy i modernismens spegelsal: om Peter Ackroyd och frågan om äkthet i konsten. (A playboy in modernism's hall of mirrors: on Peter Ackroyd and the question of truth in the arts.) Allt om böcker (1989:4) 24–8.

### Milton Acorn

**8906.** DEAHL, JAMES (ed.).   *I Shout Love* and other poems. Toronto: Aya Press, 1987. pp. 96. Rev. by Richard Lemm in DalR (67:1) 1987, 116–23.

**8907.** Purdy, Al (sel.). Dig up my heart: selected poems 1952–83. Toronto: McLelland & Stewart, 1983. pp. 221. Rev. by Richard Lemm in DalR (67:1) 1987, 120–2.

### Alice Adams

**8908.** Upton, Lee. Charming the past: Alice Adams' revisionary nostalgia. SSF (26:1) 33–41.

### Richard Adams

**8909.** Kokot, Joanna. Perspektywy metaliterackie w *Watership Down* Richarda Adamsa. (Metaliterary perspectives in Richard Adams's *Watership Down*.) KN (36:2) 361–75.

**8910.** Schmoll, Edward A. Homeric reminiscence in *Watership Down*. CML (10:1) 21–6.

### Fleur Adcock

**8911.** Duțescu, Dan. Trei p̦oeți englezi contemporani – Fleur Adcock, Alan Brownjohn, Jon Silkin. (Three English contemporary poets–Fleur Adcock, Alan Brownjohn, Jon Silkin.) Bucharest: Univers. pp. 143. Rev. in RomLit, 23 May, 20.

**8912.** Gunn, Kirsty. Fleur Adcock: New Zealand's expatriate poet. More (Auckland) July, 132–4.

### Ama Ata Aidoo

**8913.** Odamtten, Vincent Okpoti. The developing art of Ama Ata Aidoo. Unpub. doct. diss., State Univ. of New York at Stony Brook, 1988. [Abstr. in DA (50) 1303A.]

### Conrad Aiken

**8914.** Butscher, Edward. Conrad Aiken: poet of White Horse Vale. (Bibl. 1988, 6773.) Rev. by Ted R. Spivey in AL (61:3) 485–7.

**8915.** Marten, Harry. The art of knowing: the poetry and prose of Conrad Aiken. Columbia: Missouri UP, 1988. pp. xiii, 191. Rev. by Ted R. Spivey in AL (61:2) 309–10.

**8916.** Swan, Jesse G. At the edge of sound and silence: Conrad Aiken's *Senlin: A Biography* and *Silent Snow, Secret Snow*. SoLJ (22:1) 41–9.

### Edward Albee

**8917.** Byun, Chang-Ku. Edward Albee eui heuigok gwa eoneo. (Dramatic language in Edward Albee's plays.) AmeSt (12) 79–92.

**8918.** Doty, Kathleen. Dialogue, deixis and narration in a dramatic adaptation. *See* **1395.**

**8919.** Fischer-Seidel, Therese. Mythenparodie im modernen englischen und amerikanischen Drama. Tradition und Kommunikation bei Tennessee Williams, Edward Albee, Samuel Beckett und Harold Pinter. (Bibl. 1986, 11011.) Rev. by Hubert Zapf in AAA (13:1) 1988, 81–4.

**8920.** Kolin, Philip C. (ed.). Conversations with Edward Albee. (Bibl. 1988, 6779.) Rev. by Thomas P. Adler in ModDr (32:2) 321–4.

**8921.** —— Davis, J. Madison (eds). Critical essays on Edward Albee. (Bibl. 1988, 6780.) Rev. by Gerald Mast in MP (86:3) 331–5.

**8922.** Mayberry, Bob. Theatre of discord: dissonance in Beckett, Albee, and Pinter. London; Toronto: Assoc. UPs; Rutherford, NJ: Fairleigh Dickinson UP. pp. 90.

**8923.** NILSEN, HELGE NORMANN.   Responsibility, adulthood and the void: a comment on Edward Albee's *A Delicate Balance*. Neophilologus (73:1) 150–7.

**8924.** ROUDANÉ, MATTHEW C.   Understanding Edward Albee. (Bibl. 1988, 6781.) Rev. by Lynda Hart in ModDr (32:2) 324–7.

### Nelson Algren

**8925.** DREW, BETTINA.   Nelson Algren: a life on the wild side. New York: Putnam. pp. 416. Rev. by James Atlas in NYTB, 26 Nov., 18; by Bruce Cook in BkW, 19 Nov., 1–2; by James R. Giles in BW, 15 Oct., 3.

**8926.** PERLONGO, BOB.   Interview with Nelson Algren. AQ (45:1) 101–6.

### Hervey Allen

**8927.** KNEE, STUART.   Hervey Allen (1889–1949): a literary historian in America. Lewiston, NY: Mellen Press, 1988. pp. xiii, 496. Rev. by Randy K. Cross in AL (61:2) 303–5.

### Margery Allingham

**8928.** MORPURGO, J. E. (ed.).   The return of Mr Campion: uncollected stories. London: Hodder & Stoughton. pp. xix, 165.

**8929.** SYMONS, JULIAN.   Snobbery with violence. Listener (121) 26 Jan., 12–13.

### Kingsley Amis

**8930.** EASTMAN, JOHN K.   Dissimilar discourses: the realism of conversation in Amis's *Lucky Jim*. RAEI (2) 43–51.

**8931.** McDERMOTT, JOHN.   Kingsley Amis: an English moralist. Basingstoke: Macmillan. pp. x, 270.

**8932.** RASKIN, MARINA.   The emergence of fantasmagoric realism in contemporary Russian, Hebrew, and British literatures: Vasily Aksenov, Amos Oz, and Kingsley Amis. Unpub. doct. diss., Purdue Univ., 1988. [Abstr. in DA (50) 681A.]

**8933.** SKINNER, JOHN.   Novelist as mimic: a sociolinguistic study of Kingsley Amis. Lore and Language (8:1) 3–17.

### A. R. Ammons

**8934.** LINK, FRANZ.   'Racket's inner silence'. Zur Lyrik A. R. Ammons'. LJGG (28) 1987, 133–51.

### Mulk Raj Anand

**8935.** PONTES, HILDA.   A select checklist of critical responses to Mulk Raj Anand's *Untouchable*. JCL (23:1) 1988, 189–97.

### Rudolfo Anaya

**8936.** DASENBROCK, REED WAY.   Forms of biculturalism in Southwestern literature: the work of Rudulfo Anaya and Leslie Marmon Silko. Genre (21:3) 1988, 307–19.

### Maxwell Anderson

**8937.** ADAM, JULIE.   Versions of heroism in modern American drama: selected plays by Miller, Williams, Anderson and O'Neill. Unpub. doct. diss., Univ. of Toronto, 1988. [Abstr. in DA (49) 2655A.]

### Patrick Anderson

**8938.** CAMPBELL, PATRICK.   Attic shapes and empty attics: Patrick Anderson – a memoir. CanL (121) 86–99.

### Sherwood Anderson
**8939.** BIDNEY, MARTIN. Anderson and the androgyne: 'something more than man or woman'. SSF (25:3) 1988, 261–74.

**8940.** BRUYÈRE, CLAIRE. Sherwood Anderson: l'impuissance créatrice. Paris: Klincksieck, 1985. pp. 370. (Études anglo-américaines, 8.) Rev. by Joan Templeton in EA (42:2) 234–6.

**8941.** IAKIMENKO, N. L. *Uaĭnsburg, Ogaĭo* Sh. Andersona v kontekste dukhovnykh iskaniĭ amerikanskoĭ literatury 10–20-kh godov XX veka. (*Winesburg, Ohio* by Sherwood Anderson in the context of the spiritual quest in American literature, 1910–1920.) NDFN (1989:2) 32–8.

**8942.** LEE, HAIYOUNG. Sherwood Anderson's *Winesburg, Ohio*: alienation *vs* imagination. JELL (35) 103–13.

**8943.** RIDEOUT, WALTER B. Sherwood Anderson and the industrial age in Clyde, Ohio. NwOQ (61:2/4) 64–72.

**8944.** TOBIN, MARY-ELISABETH FOWKES. The composition of Sherwood Anderson's short story *Not Sixteen*. SB (42) 293–300.

**8945.** TOWNSEND, KIM. Sherwood Anderson: a biography. (Bibl. 1987, 9918, where subtitle omitted.) Rev. by Walter B. Rideout in SewR (96:3) 1988, liii–lv; by Edward Margolies in EngS (70:4) 372–3; by David Anderson in SSMLN (18:2) 1988, 23–8; by David D. Anderson in NwOQ (61:2/4) 95–8.

**8946.** WILLIAMS, KENNY J. A storyteller and a city: Sherwood Anderson's Chicago. (Bibl. 1988, 6808.) Rev. by Hilbert H. Campbell in AL (61:2) 302–3; by L. Moody Simms, Jr, in IHJ (83:3) 207.

### Maya Angelou
**8947.** ELLIOT, JEFFREY M. (ed.). Conversations with Maya Angelou. London: Virago Press. pp. xvi, 246.

### Ayi Kwei Armah
**8948.** WRIGHT, DEREK. Ayi Kwei Armah's Africa: the sources of his fiction. London: Zell. pp. ix, 334. (New perspectives on African literature, 1.)

**8949.** —— Orality in the African historical novel: Yambo Ouologuem's *Bound to Violence* and Ayi Kwei Armah's *Two Thousand Seasons*. JCL (23:1) 1988, 91–101.

### Harriette Arnow
**8950.** MILLER, DANNY L. Harriette Simpson and Harold Arnow in Cincinnati: 1934–1939. Queen City Heritage (47:2) 41–8.

### John Ashbery
**8951.** DIEPEVEEN, LEONARD. The problem of Ashbery's reputation. DalR (67:2/3) 1987, 345–54.

**8952.** PAPAGEORGIOU, VASILIS. Jag kan tygla mitt undermedvetna: John Ashbery samtalar med Vasilis Papageorgiou. (I can restrain my subconscious: John Ashbery talks to Vasilis Papageorgiou.) Artes (15:4) 45–53.

**8953.** RAWSON, CLAUDE. Bards, boardrooms, and blackboards: John Ashbery, Wallace Stevens, and the academicization of poetry. *In* (pp. 181–91) **46.**

### Sylvia Ashton-Warner (Sylvia Henderson)

**8954.** HOOD, LYNLEY.    Sylvia! The biography of Sylvia Ashton-Warner. (Bibl. 1988, 6821.) Rev. by Susan Ash in Landfall (43:1) 114–16.

### Isaac Asimov

**8955.** COWAN, S. A.    Five-finger exercise: Asimov's clues to the plot-solution of *Catch that Rabbit*. SFS (16:1) 90–3.

### Margaret Atwood

**8956.** ATWOOD, MARGARET.    Biographobia: some personal reflections on the act of biography. *In* (pp. 1–8) **44.**

**8957.** BERGMANN, HARRIET F.    'Teaching them to read': a fishing expedition in *The Handmaid's Tale*. CE (51:8) 847–54.

**8958.** CENTING, RICHARD (comp.).    Ohio magazines. See **559.**

**8959.** HENGEN, SHANNON EILEEN.    Margaret Atwood's power. Unpub. doct. diss., Univ. of Iowa, 1988. [Abstr. in DA (49) 2224–5A.]

**8960.** KALER, ANNE K.    'A sister, dipped in blood': satiric inversion of the formation techniques of women religious in Margaret Atwood's *The Handmaid's Tale*. ChrisL (38:2) 43–62.

**8961.** KAUFFMAN, LINDA.    Special delivery: twenty-first-century epistolarity in *The Handmaid's Tale*. *In* (pp. 221–44) **61.**

**8962.** KETTERER, DAVID.    Margaret Atwood's *The Handmaid's Tale*: a contextual dystopia. SFS (16:2) 209–17.

**8963.** McCOMBS, JUDITH.    *Up in the Air so Blue*: vampires and victims, great mother myth and gothic allegory in Margaret Atwood's first, unpublished novel. CR (33:3) 251–7.

**8964.** NAULTY, PATRICIA MARY.    'I never talk of hunger': self-starvation as women's language of protest in novels by Barbara Pym, Margaret Atwood, and Anne Tyler. Unpub. doct. diss., Ohio State Univ., 1988. [Abstr. in DA (50) 140–1A.] (Barbara Pym, *Quartet in Autumn*; Margaret Atwood, *The Edible Woman*; Anne Tyler, *Dinner at the Homesick Restaurant*.)

**8965.** NICHOLSON, MERVYN.    Food and power: Homer, Carroll, Atwood and others. See **6462.**

**8966.** RIGNEY, BARBARA HILL.    Margaret Atwood. (Bibl. 1987, 9942.) Rev. by Glenn Deer in CanL (120) 151–2.

**8967.** YALOM, MARILYN.    Maternity, mortality, and the literature of madness. See **7965.**

### Alvin Aubert

**8968.** WARD, JERRY W., JR.    Alvin Aubert: the levee, the blues, the mighty Mississippi. BALF (23:3) 415–40. (Interview.)

**8969.** —— Alvin Aubert: a primary bibliography. BALF (23:3) 445–9.

### Louis Auchincloss

**8970.** PIKET, VINCENT.    Louis Auchincloss: the growth of a novelist. Nijmegen, The Netherlands: European UP. pp. 350.

### W. H. Auden

**8971.** COWAN, LAURA JEAN.    'An altering speech': syntax in the early poetry of W. H. Auden. See **1392.**

**8972.** HARPER, GEORGE MILLS.    'Necessary murder': the Auden circle and the Spanish Civil War. *In* (pp. 67–80) **46.**

**8973.** JOHNSON, MARY CHARLOTTE.    A critical study of the poetic voice in the narratives of selected documentary films of the 1930s. *See* **8068.**

**8974.** LAHEY, PHILIP.    *The Prolific and the Devourer* (1939): W. H. Auden's 'pensées'. EA (43:3) 270–81.

**8975.** MASLEN, ELIZABETH.    'The menacing shapes of our fever': looking back at Auden's *Spain. In* (pp. 65–82) STEPHEN M. HART (ed.), '¡No pasarán!': art, literature and the Spanish Civil War. London: Tamesis, 1988. pp. 122. (Colección Tamesis, ser. A: monografías, 136.)

**8976.** MENDELSON, EDWARD (ed.).    Plays and other dramatic writings by W. H. Auden, 1928–1938. London: Faber & Faber. pp. xxxiii, 680. Rev. by Michael Wood in TLS, 4 Aug., 849.

**8977.** MINOGUE, VALERIE.    Sarraute, Auden, and the Great Tall Tailor. MLR (84:2) 331–6.

**8978.** ROBB, M. P.    The sacramental vision: belief and art in the poetry of David Jones, Charles Williams and W. H. Auden. Unpub. doct. diss., Univ. of Manchester. [Abstr. in IT (39:4) 1634–5.]

**8979.** SERVOTTE, HERMAN.    Auden and Kierkegaard. *In* (pp. 275–82) **42.**

**8980.** SMITH, STAN.    A Helensburgh source for Auden's Airman. NQ (36:2) 206–7.

**8981.** —— Two unknown holograph poems by W. H. Auden and C. Day Lewis. NQ (36:2) 205–6.

**8982.** —— W. H. Auden. (Bibl. 1988, 6841.) Rev. by Michael Ackland in AUMLA (72) 344–8.

**8983.** STEWART, JAMES C. Q.    An Auden repudiation. NQ (36:2) 204.

**8984.** —— Auden's *The Double Man.* NQ (36:2) 204–5.

### Mary Austin

**8985.** PRYSE, MARJORIE (ed.).    Stories from the country of *Lost Borders.* (Bibl. 1988, 6847.) Rev. by Susan K. Harris in ALR (21:3) 87–8.

**8986.** STINEMAN, ESTHER LANIGAN.    Mary Austin: song of a maverick. New Haven, CT; London: Yale UP. pp. ix, 269. Rev. in BkW, 12 Nov., 17.

### Alan Ayckbourn ('Roland Allen')

**8987.** DUKORE, BERNARD F.    Alan Ayckbourn's Liza Doolittle. ModDr (32:3) 425–39.

**8988.** GORE-LANGTON, ROBERT.    Darkness on the edge of town. Listener (121) 13 Apr., 29–30.

**8989.** GOULD, GERARD (ed.).    Sisterly feelings. Harlow: Longman. pp. xxviii, 191. (Longman study texts.)

**8990.** PAGE, MALCOLM (comp.).    File on Ayckbourn. London: Methuen. pp. 95. (Writer-files.)

### Beryl Bainbridge

**8991.** STAMIROWSKA, KRYSTYNA.    The bustle and the crudity of life: the novels of Beryl Bainbridge. KN (35:4) 1988, 445–56.

### James Baldwin

**8992.** BELL, BERNARD W.    The Afro-American novel and its tradition. *See* **8182.**

**8993.** CUNNINGHAM, JAMES.    Baldwinian aesthetics in Sterling
Plumpp's Mojo poems. BALF (23:3) 505–18.
**8994.** PORTER, HORACE.    Stealing the fire: the art and protest of James
Baldwin. Middletown, CT: Wesleyan UP, 1988. pp. 220. Rev. by
Maurice J. Bennett in BkW, 12 Feb., 10.
**8995.** THUM, D. MAUREEN.    Rufus' journey to suicide in James
Baldwin's *Another Country*. MichA (20:2) 1988, 211–20.
**8996.** TROUPE, QUINCY (ed.).    James Baldwin: the legacy. New York;
London: Simon & Schuster. pp. 267. Rev. by Charles R. Larson in
BkW, 16 Apr., 1, 6.
**8997.** WEATHERBY, W. J.    James Baldwin: artist on fire. New York:
Fine. pp. 412. Rev. by Charles R. Larson in BkW, 16 Apr., 1, 6.

### J. G. Ballard
**8998.** BENISON, J.    Postmodernity and science fiction: an approach to
the social relevance of J. G. Ballard's fiction. Unpub. doct. diss., Univ.
of Essex. [Abstr. in IT (39:3) 1114.]

### Toni Cade Bambara
**8999.** CARBY, HAZEL V.    Reinventing history/imagining the future.
BALF (23:2) 381–7 (review-article).

### John Banville
**9000.** LERNOUT, GEERT.    Banville and being: *The Newton Letter* and
history. *In* (pp. 67–77) **32.**

### Amiri Baraka (LeRoi Jones)
**9001.** DUVAL, ELAINE ISOLYN.    Theatre and the double: revolutionary
consciousness in Baraka and Artaud. Unpub. doct. diss., Univ. of
Tennessee, 1988. [Abstr. in DA (50) 305A.]
**9002.** KENNEDY, WILLIAM.    Two writers' beginnings. BkW, 19 Nov., 5.
**9003.** SUNG, BYEONG-HWI.    LeRoi Jones eui *Dutchman* sogo. (A study
of LeRoi Jones's *Dutchman*.) YYY (5) 37–47.

### Howard Barker
**9004.** IMRAN, M. Y.    A study of the plays of Howard Barker, with
special reference to the artist figures. Unpub. doct. diss., Univ. of Kent.
[Abstr. in IT (39:4) 1633.]
**9005.** RABEY, DAVID IAN.    Howard Barker: politics and desire: an
expository study of his drama and poetry, 1969–87. Basingstoke:
Macmillan. pp. ix, 298.

### Djuna Barnes
**9006.** CLARK, SUSAN F.    Misalliance: Djuna Barnes and the American
theatre. Unpub. doct. diss., Tufts Univ. [Abstr. in DA (50) 1486A.]

### Peter Barnes
**9007.** RAMANATHAN, GEETHA RAMANATHAN.    Gender and madness in
five modern plays. Unpub. doct. diss., Univ. of Illinois at Urbana-
Champaign, 1988. [Abstr. in DA (49) 2455–6A.] (*The Ruling Class*.)

### J. M. Barrie
**9008.** BALSARI-SHAH, SHEFALI (ed.).    The admirable Crichton.
London: Sangam. pp. xvii, 71.
**9009.** CAREY, REBECCA A.    J. M. Barrie and the Du Mauriers.
*See* **6747.**

**9010.** MURRAY, THOMAS J.     J. M. Barrie and the search for self. Unpub. doct. diss., Harvard Univ., 1988. [Abstr. in DA (50) 450–1A.]

### John Barth

**9011.** CHRZANOWSKA-KARPIŃSKA, EWA.     The aesthetics of parody in postmodernist fiction: John Barth's *Giles Goat-Boy. In* (pp. 115–30) **3.**

**9012.** —— John Barth's *Lost in the Fun-House* as a comic metafiction. *In* (pp. 209–27) **36.**

**9013.** COOKE, STEWART JON.     Received melodies: the new, old novel. Unpub. doct. diss., McGill Univ., 1988. [Abstr. in DA (50) 131–2A.] (John Barth, *The Sot-Weed Factor*, and *Letters*; T. Coraghessan Boyle, *Water Music*; John Fowles, *The French Lieutenant's Woman*; Erica Jong, *Fanny*.)

**9014.** COSENZA, JOSEPH A.     The structure of John Barth's *Anonymiad.* NCL (19:3) 6.

**9015.** HOFFMANN, GERHARD.     The absurd and its forms of reduction in Postmodern American fiction. *In* (pp. 185–210) **7.**

**9016.** MARGOLIES, EDWARD.     John Barth and the barbarities of history. *In* (pp. 205–11) **2.**

**9017.** RAPER, JULIUS ROWAN.     John Barth's *Chimera*: men and women under the myth. SoLJ (22:1) 17–31.

**9018.** SAFER, ELAINE B.     The contemporary American comic epic: the novels of Barth, Pynchon, Gaddis, and Kesey. Detroit, MI: Wayne State UP, 1988. pp. 216. Rev. by Vernon Hyles in AL (61:3) 497–8; by Stanley Trachtenberg in SAF (17:2) 251–2.

### Donald Barthelme

**9019.** BERMAN, JAYE ELLYN.     Parody as cultural criticism in the Postmodern American novel: Donald Barthelme, Gilbert Sorrentino, and Thomas Pynchon. Unpub. doct. diss., Univ. of Wisconsin–Milwaukee, 1988. [Abstr. in DA (49) 2217A.]

**9020.** MALTBY, P. L.     Dissident postmodernists: Barthelme, Coover, Pynchon. Unpub. doct. diss., Univ. of Sussex. [Abstr. in IT (39:4) 1637.]

**9021.** STREITFELD, DAVID.     Remembering Barthelme. BkW, 17 Dec., 15.

### Blanche Edith Baughan

**9022.** ALCOCK, PETER.     A catch and a cantata in the wilderness: two unabashed exhibits from Miss Baughan. JCL (24:1) 103–13.

### Frank Baum

**9023.** FRICKE, JOHN; SCARFONE, JAY; STILLMAN, WILLIAM.     *The Wizard of Oz*: the official 50th anniversary pictorial history. Introd. by JACK HALEY, JR. *See* **8037.**

**9024.** HUDLIN, EDWARD W.     The mythology of 'Oz': an interpretation. PLL (25:4) 443–62.

**9025.** PAYNE, DAVID.     *The Wizard of Oz*: therapeutic rhetoric in a contemporary media ritual. *See* **1782.**

### James K. Baxter

**9026.** WEIR, JOHN.     James K. Baxter: a voice for the living. New Zealandia (Auckland) (4) 19–22.

**Barbara Baynton**

**9027.** SHERIDAN, SUSAN. Gender and genre in Barbara Baynton's *Human Toll*. ALS (14:1) 66–77.

**9028.** WALKER, SHIRLEY. Barbara Baynton's *Human Toll*: a modernist text? Southerly (49:2) 131–48.

**Peter S. Beagle**

**9029.** PENNINGTON, JOHN. Innocence and experience and the imagination in the world of Peter Beagle. Mythlore (15:4) 10–16.

**Ann Beattie**

**9030.** DEZURE, DEBORAH. Images of shifting in Beattie's *Shifting*. SSF (26:1) 11–15.

**Samuel Beckett**

**9031.** ACHESON, JAMES; ARTHUR, KATERYNA (eds). Beckett's later fiction and drama: texts for company. (Bibl. 1988, 6898.) Rev. by David Bradby in MLR (84:1) 188.

**9032.** ALBRIGHT, DANIEL. Beckett's recent activities: the liveliness of dead imagination. *In* (pp. 374–83) **45.**

**9033.** AXELROD, MARK RICHARD. *Scapigliatura*; or, The politics of style in Balzac's *Le Père Goriot*, Beckett's *Watt* and Cortázar's *Rayuela*. Unpub. doct. diss., Univ. of Minnesota, 1988. [Abstr. in DA (50) 435–6A.]

**9034.** BRATER, ENOCH. Beyond minimalism: Beckett's late style in the theater. Oxford; New York: OUP, 1987. pp. x, 209. Rev. by Lois Oppenheim in TJ (41:1) 119–20.

**9035.** —— (ed.). Beckett at 80/Beckett in context. (Bibl. 1986, 11163, where '(ed.)' omitted.) Rev. by James Hansford in RES (39:153) 1988, 145–6.

**9036.** BRIENZA, SUSAN D. Samuel Beckett's new worlds: style in metafiction. Norman: Oklahoma UP, 1987. pp. xviii, 290. Rev. by Michael Patrick Gillespie in StudN (20:1) 1988, 100–1.

**9037.** BRYDEN, MARY. Coils of the cobra: the predatory woman of Shaw and Beckett. NC (7) 160–71.

**9038.** BUTLER, LANCE ST JOHN. Samuel Beckett and the meaning of being: a study in ontological parable. (Bibl. 1986, 11165.) Rev. by Peter Müller in Archiv (225:2) 1988, 411–15.

**9039.** CALDER, JOHN (ed.). As no other dare fail: for Samuel Beckett on his 80th birthday by his friends and admirers. (Bibl. 1986, 11166.) Rev. by John Pilling in MLR (84:4) 957–9.

**9040.** CAREY, PHYLLIS. Beckett's Pim and Joyce's Shem. JJQ (26:3) 435–9.

**9041.** CATANZARO, MARY F. The voice of absent love in *Krapp's Last Tape* and *Company*. ModDr (32:3) 401–12.

**9042.** COHEN, DAVID. Conclusion of the foregoing: James Joyce, Samuel Beckett and Flann O'Brien. Unpub. doct. diss., State Univ. of New York at Buffalo, 1988. [Abstr. in DA (49) 2665A.]

**9043.** COHN, RUBY (ed.). Samuel Beckett: *Waiting for Godot*: a casebook. (Bibl. 1987, 10028, where title and scholar's description incorrect.) Rev. by John Pilling in NQ (36:1) 127–8.

**9044.** COMO, ROBERT M. O'Neill, Beckett, and Dürrenmatt: the shared genre. EOR (13:2) 63–72.

**9045.** DAVIES, PAUL. The ideal real: imagination and knowledge in the prose of Samuel Beckett. Unpub. doct. diss., Univ. of Reading, 1988. [Abstr. in DA (49) 3731A.]

**9046.** DAVIS, ROBIN J.; BUTLER, LANCE ST J. (eds). 'Make sense who may': essays on Samuel Beckett's later works. Gerrards Cross: Smythe. pp. 175. (Irish literary studies, 30.) Rev. by Patrick Parrinder in LRB (11:21) 26–7.

**9047.** DOHERTY, FRANCIS. Beckett and the life sentence. JSSE (13) 25–32.

**9048.** ELLIS, REUBEN J. 'Matrix of surds': Heisenberg's algebra in Beckett's *Murphy*. PLL (25:1) 120–3.

**9049.** ENGELBERTS, MATTHIJS. Stiltes rond Godot: het Nederlands debat over de vrouwlijke rolebezetting van *Wachten op Godot*. (Silences around Godot: the Dutch debate about women acting in *Waiting for Godot*.) ForumL (30:3) 174–9.

**9050.** FISCHER-SEIDEL, THERESE. Die unausweichliche Modalität des Sichtbaren: Wahrnehmung und Kategorien des Dramas im Theater Becketts. *In* (pp. 106–23) **4.**

**9051.** FRIEDMAN, ALAN WARREN; ROSSMAN, CHARLES; SHERZER, DINA (eds). Beckett translating/Translating Beckett. (Bibl. 1988, 6902.) Rev. by Rosemary Pountney in NQ (36:2) 265–6.

**9052.** FUß, ALBERT. Das dichterische Wort als Weg zum Nichts oder zur Fülle: Samuel Beckett und Paul Claudel. LJGG (26) 1985, 253–69.

**9053.** GONTARSKI, S. E. The intent of *undoing* in Samuel Beckett's dramatic texts. (Bibl. 1986, 11179.) Rev. by Robert N. Scanlan in TJ (39:2) 1987, 255–6; by Marilyn Roberts in RMRLL (40:1/2) 1987, 101–2.

**9054.** HOLLAND, PETER. Space: the final frontier. *In* (pp. 45–62) **50.**

**9055.** HUBER, WERNER. Transformations of Beckett: the case of Athol Fugard. Literator (10:3) 48–54.

**9056.** JOH, CHO-HEE. Beckett's capacity for differentiation: some observations on reading his works. JELL (35) 759–73.

**9057.** JOHNSON, TONI O'BRIEN. An ante-text for Samuel Beckett's *Happy Days*. IUR (19:2) 302–9.

**9058.** KARÁTSON, ANDRÉ. Le nirvana comme supplice de tantale: note sur Beckett et Schopenhauer. *In* (pp. 217–23) ANNE HENRY (ed.), Schopenhauer et la création littéraire en Europe. Paris: Méridiens Klincksieck. pp. 230.

**9059.** KIM, JIN-A. An extended notion of recognition: a study of *Hamlet, The Three Sisters*, and *Footfalls*. *See* **3835.**

**9060.** MCBRIDE, WILLIAM THOMAS. In the name of beauty: the terrible alphabet of Samuel Beckett. Unpub. doct. diss., State Univ. of New York at Buffalo. [Abstr. in DA (50) 1667A.]

**9061.** MCMILLAN, DOUGALD. The fatal circle: composition and direction of *Come and Go. In* (pp. 384–93) **45.**

**9062.** —— FEHSENFELD, MARTHA. Beckett in the theatre: the author as practical playwright and director: vol. I, From *Waiting for Godot* to *Krapp's Last Tape*. (Bibl. 1988, 6908.) Rev. by W. B. Worthen in TJ (41:4) 561–2.

**9063.** McMULLAN, AUDREY ELIZABETH. Between spaces: the dynamic principle in Samuel Beckett's later drama. Unpub. doct. diss., Univ. of Reading, 1988. [Abstr. in DA (50) 962A.]

**9064.** MARVEL, LAURA MELISSA. Tragedies of identity in the works of Shakespeare and Beckett. *See* **3598.**

**9065.** MAYBERRY, BOB. Theatre of discord: dissonance in Beckett, Albee, and Pinter. *See* **8922.**

**9066.** MENZIE, A. E. Puns and wordplay on the themes of sex and food in Samuel Beckett's *How It Is*. Unpub. doct. diss., Univ. of Liverpool, 1986. [Abstr. in IT (36:4) 1401.]

**9067.** MERCIER, VIVIAN. *All That Fall*: Samuel Beckett and the Bible. *In* (pp. 360–73) **45.**

**9068.** MURRAY, FRANK J., JR. Speaking the unspeakable: theatrical language in the plays of Samuel Beckett and Sam Shepard. Unpub. doct. diss., Stanford Univ., 1988. [Abstr. in DA (49) 2454–5A.]

**9069.** O'BRIEN, EOIN. The Beckett country: Samuel Beckett's Ireland. Foreword by JAMES KNOWLSON. (Bibl. 1987, 10048.) Rev. by J. C. C. Mays in RES (39:154) 1988, 324–5.

**9070.** PIETTE, A. C. Rhyme and memory in the prose of Proust, Joyce and Beckett. Unpub. doct. diss., Univ. of Cambridge, 1988. [Abstr. in IT (39:2) 483.]

**9071.** RAGHAVAN, HEMA V. Samuel Beckett: rebels and exiles in his plays. Liverpool: Lucas, 1988. pp. 149.

**9072.** RUSTAM, ANEED THANWAN. Man's suffering in Beckett's *Waiting for Godot* and *Endgame*. Al-Mustansiriya Literary Review (Al-Mustansiriya Univ., Baghdad) (11) 1985, 121–34.

**9073.** SABIN, MARGERY. The dialect of the tribe: speech and community in modern fiction. *See* **1418.**

**9074.** SIMON, ALFRED. Beckett. Paris: Belfond. pp. 296.

**9075.** SWANDER, HOMER. Shakespeare and Beckett: what the words know. *In* (pp. 60–78) **55.**

**9076.** THOMAS, RONALD R. The novel and the afterlife: the end of the line in Bunyan and Beckett. *See* **4340.**

**9077.** VERDICCHIO, MASSIMO. Exagmination round the fictification of Vico and Joyce. JJQ (26:4) 531–9.

**9078.** WALTON, S. JEAN. Expression as extortion: saying the self in the works of Samuel Beckett. Unpub. doct. diss., State Univ. of New York at Buffalo. [Abstr. in DA (50) 945A.]

**9079.** WEITZ, SHOSHANA. Mr Godot will not come today. *In* (pp. 186–98) **50.**

### Thomas Beer

**9080.** ANDERSON, DAVID. Thomas Beer. SSMLN (19:2) 2–10.

### Sir Max Beerbohm

**9081.** DANSON, LAWRENCE. Max Beerbohm and the act of writing. Oxford: Clarendon Press. pp. xii, 264.

**9082.** HART-DAVIS, RUPERT (ed.). Letters of Max Beerbohm, 1892–1956. New York: Norton. (Bibl. 1988, 6923.) Rev. by Michael Dirda in BkW, 18 June, 3, 10.

**9083.** RIEWALD, J. G. Sir Max Beerbohm: a bibliographical checklist 1950–1985. *In* (pp. 192–222) **23.**

### Saul Bellow

**9084.** BAKKER, J. Saul Bellow: a writer's despair. *In* (pp. 177–90) **23.**

**9085.** CHAVKIN, ALLAN; CHAVKIN, NANCY FEYL. Bellow's dire prophecy. CR (33:2) 93–107.

**9086.** CLAYTON, JOHN J. Saul Bellow's *Seize the Day*: a study in midlife transition. *In* (pp. 135–47) **2.**

**9087.** FUCHS, DANIEL. Saul Bellow: vision and revision. (Bibl. 1984, 10129.) Rev. by Eugene Hollahan in StudN (20:1) 1988, 104–7.

### Stephen Vincent Benét

**9088.** JOHNSON, MARY CHARLOTTE. A critical study of the poetic voice in the narratives of selected documentary films of the 1930s. *See* **8068.**

### E. F. Benson

**9089.** BURTON, PETER (introd.). David Blaize. London: Hogarth Press. pp. 316.

**9090.** LEONARDI, SUSAN J. Recipes for reading: summer pasta, lobster à la Riseholme, and key lime pie. PMLA (104:3) 340–7.

### John Berger

**9091.** CARLBERG, ANDERS J. Det var en gång ett Europa: om ett tema hos John Berger och V. S. Naipaul. (There was a Europe once: on a theme in John Berger and V. S. Naipaul.) Allt om böcker (1989:2) 62–6.

### Thomas Berger

**9092.** LANDON, BROOKS. The measure of *Little Big Man*. SAF (17:2) 131–42.

### Robert Berold

**9093.** GARDNER, SUSAN. Four South African poets: interviews with Robert Berold, Jeremy Cronin, Douglas Reid Skinner and Stephen Watson. (Bibl. 1986, 11248.) Rev. by David Levey in UES (27:1) 61–2.

### Francis Berry

**9094.** KNIGHT, G. WILSON. My life's work, with a discussion of Francis Berry's poetry. *In* (pp. 71–80) **37.**

### Wendell Berry

**9095.** TRIGGS, JEFFREY ALAN. Farm as form: Wendell Berry's *Sabbaths*. SDR (27:4) 76–87.

### John Berryman

**9096.** BAWER. BRUCE. The middle generation: the lives and poetry of Delmore Schwartz, Randall Jarrell, John Berryman, and Robert Lowell. (Bibl. 1987, 10090.) Rev. by Monroe K. Spears in SewR (96:1) 1988, 101–3.

**9097.** HALLIDAY, E. M.   John Berryman and the thirties: a memoir. (Bibl. 1988, 6942, where subtitle omitted.) Rev. by Kathe Davis in AL (61:1) 141–3.

**9098.** KELLY, RICHARD J. (ed.).   We dream of honour: John Berryman's letters to his mother. (Bibl. 1988, 6943.) Rev. by Kathe Davis in AL (61:1) 141–3.

**9099.** MATTERSON, STEPHEN.   Berryman and Lowell: the art of losing. Totowa, NJ: Barnes & Noble, 1988. (Bibl. 1987, 10094.) Rev. by Michael Hofmann in TLS, 26 May, 578; by William V. Davis in AL (61:4) 723–4.

**9100.** THOMAS, DAVID LEE.   Loss, mourning and the vatic dispersal of self in the long poems of Whitman, Eliot, Pound, Berryman and Lowell. *See* **7665.**

## Earle Birney

**9101.** ADAM, IAN.   Marginality and the tradition: Earle Birney and Wilson Harris. JCL (24:1) 88–102.

**9102.** McDONALD, LARRY.   The politics of influence: Birney, Scott, Livesay and the influence of politics. DalR (67:4) 1987, 425–35.

## Elizabeth Bishop

**9103.** BRIEFS-ELGIN, REGINA.   To keep it forever: deanimating metaphor in the poetry of Elizabeth Bishop. Unpub. doct. diss., Univ. of Virginia, 1988. [Abstr. in DA (50) 689A.]

**9104.** HARRISON, VICTORIA GAIL.   Rebel in 'shades and shadows': the poetics and politics of Elizabeth Bishop. Unpub. doct. diss., Rutgers Univ., 1988. [Abstr. in DA (49) 3027A.]

**9105.** PAGE, BARBARA.   Nature, history, and art in Elizabeth Bishop's *Brazil, January 1, 1502.* PCL (14) 1988, 39–46.

**9106.** PARKER, ROBERT DALE.   The unbeliever: the poetry of Elizabeth Bishop. Urbana: Illinois UP, 1988. pp. xi, 169. Rev. by Lisa Steinman in AL (61:2) 319–21; by Bonnie Costello in NEQ (62:2) 312–14; by Brett Candlish Millier in TLS, 12 May, 516.

**9107.** TRAVISANO, THOMAS J.   Elizabeth Bishop: her artistic development. (Bibl. 1988, 6952.) Rev. by Bonnie Costello in NEQ (62:2) 310–12; by Brett Candlish Millier in TLS, 12 May, 516.

## John Peale Bishop

**9108.** FOSSUM, KRISTIN.   Distinguished friendship: selected letters of John Peale Bishop. Unpub. doct. diss., Princeton Univ. [Abstr. in DA (50) 1656A.]

## Stephen Black

**9109.** GRAY, STEPHEN.   Stephen Black, man of letters. Contrast (17:4) 73–80.

## Algernon Blackwood

**9110.** DALBY, RICHARD (ed.).   Dracula's brood: neglected vampire classics by Sir Arthur Conan Doyle, Algernon Blackwood, M. R. James and others. *See* **6729.**

## James Blish

**9111.** KETTERER, DAVID.   Imprisoned in a tesseract: the life and work of James Blish. Kent, OH: Kent State UP, 1987. pp. xvi, 410. Rev. by

Desmond Tarrant in SFS (16:2) 390–3; by Roz Kaveney in SFS (16:3) 393–7.

## Judy Blume

**9112.** EALES, DEREK. Enid Blyton, Judy Blume, and cultural impossibilities. CLEd (20:2) 81–9.

## Enid Blyton

**9113.** EALES, DEREK. Enid Blyton, Judy Blume, and cultural impossibilities. *See* **9112.**

## Louise Bogan

**9114.** BRIDGFORD, KIM SUZANNE. Discoveries of the not-known: Louise Bogan, Murel Rukeyser, Sylvia Plath, May Swenson, and Adrienne Rich. Unpub. doct. diss., Univ. of Illinois at Urbana-Champaign, 1988. [Abstr. in DA (50) 558A.]

## Robert Bolt

**9115.** DE ITUARTE, MAITE. *A Man for All Seasons*: a bold and beautiful verbal architecture. LDeus (19:45) 165–72.

## Edward Bond

**9116.** AHRENDS, GÜNTER. Vom Text des Autors zum Text der Aufführung: Andrea Breths Interpretation von Edward Bonds *Summer*. *In* (pp. 124–39) **4.**

**9117.** HIRST, DAVID L. Edward Bond. (Bibl. 1987, 10116.) Rev. by Michael Göring in MLR (84:2) 428.

**9118.** VON LEDEBUR, RUTH. The adaptation and reception in Germany of Edward Bond's *Saved*. *In* (pp. 199–213) **50.**

## Roo Borson

**9119.** HARASYM, SARAH. Ringing rounds on the proper name. *In* (pp. 324–33) **40.**

## Herman Charles Bosman

**9120.** GRAY, STEPHEN. Herman Charles Bosman's use of short fictional forms. EngA (16:1) 1–8.

## Elizabeth Bowen

**9121.** LASSNER, PHYLLIS. Reimagining the acts of war: language and history in Elizabeth Bowen's *The Heat of the Day* and Rose Macaulay's *The World My Wilderness*. PCL (14) 1988, 30–8.

## George Bowering

**9122.** KAMBOURELI, SMARO. Stealing the text: George Bowering's *Kerrisdale Elegies* and Dennis Cooley's *Bloody Jack*. CanL (115) 1987, 9–23.

## Jane Bowles

**9123.** BRIATTE, ROBERT. Paul Bowles: 2117, Tanger Socco. Paris: Plon. pp. 338. (Collection biographique.) (Includes bibliography of the work of Jane and Paul Bowles.)

## Paul Bowles

**9124.** BRIATTE, ROBERT. Paul Bowles: 2117, Tanger Socco. *See* **9123.**

**9125.** CAMPBELL, N. H. The unfinished scream: the disintegration of the self and society in the works of Paul Bowles. Unpub. doct. diss., Univ. of Wales, 1988. [Abstr. in IT (39:3) 1116–17.]

**9126.** SAWYER-LAUÇANNO, CHRISTOPHER. An invisible spectator: a biography of Paul Bowles. London: Bloomsbury; New York: Weidenfeld & Nicolson. pp. 501. Rev. by John Ryle in TLS, 15 Sept., 995–6; by Dennis Drubelle in BkW, 11 June, 3–4; by Anatole Broyard in NYTB, 6 Aug., 3; by John Clute in Listener (122) 24 Aug., 28.

### John Boyd

**9127.** PILKINGTON, ULICK LIONEL. Representations of the Northern Ireland crisis in contemporary drama: 1968–80. Unpub. doct. diss., Univ. of Toronto. [Abstr. in DA (50) 24A.] (John Boyd, *The Flats*; Brian Friel, *Translations* and *The Freedom of the City*; Bill Morrison, *Flying Blind*; Graham Reid, *The Death of Humpty Dumpty*.)

### Martin Boyd

**9128.** CROCKER, WALTER. Martin Boyd. Overland (114) 9–15.

### T. Coraghessan Boyle

**9129.** COOKE, STEWART JON. Received melodies: the new, old novel. *See* **9013.**

### Leigh Brackett

**9130.** CARR, JOHN LEONARD. Leigh Brackett: American science fiction writer – her life and work. Unpub. doct. diss., Ohio State Univ., 1988. [Abstr. in DA (49) 2218A.]

### Malcolm Bradbury

**9131.** ELPHICK, LINDA LOIS. 'A world without real deliverances': liberal humanism in the novels of Malcolm Bradbury. Unpub. doct. diss., Ball State Univ., 1988. [Abstr. in DA (49) 2227A.]

**9132.** McLEOD, MARION. The television man. NZList, 14 Oct., 42–6.

**9133.** TODD, RICHARD. Convention and innovation in British fiction 1981–1984: the contemporaneity of magic realism. *In* (pp. 361–88) **16.**

### Ray Bradbury

**9134.** SZCZERBICKA, ANNA. The child motif in the short stories of R. Bradbury. *In* (pp. 31–74) **57.**

### Scott Bradfield

**9135.** STREITFELD, DAVID. One writer's beginnings. BkW, 23 July, 15.

### Edward Kamau Brathwaite

**9136.** BRATHWAITE, DORIS MONICA. A descriptive and chronological bibliography (1950–1982) of the work of Edward Kamau Brathwaite. London: New Beacon Books, 1988. pp. ix, 97.

### Richard Brautigan

**9137.** BOYER, JAY. Richard Brautigan. (Bibl. 1988, 6985.) Rev. by Richard W. Etulain in OreHQ (90:2) 206–8.

**9138.** ELÍASSON, GYRÐIR. Richard Brautigan. TMM (50:4) 496–8.

**9139.** STREITFELD, DAVID. Hippie poet laureate. BkW, 9 Apr., 15.

### Christopher Brennan

**9140.** CROFT, JULIAN. The federal and national impulse in Australian literature, 1890–1958. Townsville, Qld: Foundation for Australian Literary Studies. pp. 60.

**9141.** MACAINSH, NOEL. Steps into the forest: Christopher Brennan's fatal attraction. AUMLA (72) 229–51.

### Howard Brenton

**9142.** BOON, RICHARD. Writers with dirty hands: Howard Brenton's *A Sky Blue Life: Scenes After Maxim Gorki*. ModDr (32:2) 183–91.

**9143.** CAULFIELD, CARL. 'What the bomb does to our minds': Sewell's *Welcome the Bright World* and Brenton's *The Genius*. Australasian Drama Studies (14) 19–32.

### Simon Brett

**9144.** MASLON, LAURENCE. Author, author! AD (22:4) 340–51.

### Ann Bridge

**9145.** KELLAWAY, KATE (introd.). Peking picnic. London: Virago Press. pp. 328. (Virago modern classics, 330.)

### 'James Bridie' (Osborne Henry Mavor)

**9146.** MAVOR, RONALD. Dr Mavor and Mr Bridie: memoirs of James Bridie. Edinburgh: Canongate; National Library of Scotland, 1988. pp. 150. Rev. by David Hutchison in SLJ (supp. 31) 29–30.

### Katharine Briggs

**9147.** DAVIDSON, H. R. ELLIS. Katharine Briggs; story-teller. *See* **1652.**

### Robert Bringhurst

**9148.** WHATLEY, JOHN. Readings of nothing: Robert Bringhurst's *Hachadura*. CanL (122/23) 108–22.

### Harold Brodkey

**9149.** IANNONE, CAROL. The Brodkey question. Commentary (87:4) 58–61.

### Louis Bromfield

**9150.** LITTLE, CHARLES E. (ed.). Louis Bromfield at Malabar: writings on farming and country life. Baltimore, MD; London: Johns Hopkins UP, 1988. pp. xx, 239. Rev. by Don E. Weaver in OhioanaQ (32:2) 94–5.

### Rupert Brooke

**9151.** VICHY, THÉRÈSE. Rupert Brooke. Europe (721) 147–54.

### Christine Brooke-Rose

**9152.** BROOKE-ROSE, CHRISTINE. Ill wit and good humour: women's comedy and the canon. CompCrit (10) 1988, 121–38.

### James Ambrose Brown

**9153.** HAARHOFF, DORIAN. Bondels and bombs: the Bondelswarts Rebellion in historical fiction. ESA (32:1) 25–39. (James Ambrose Brown, *The Return*; Thomas Pynchon, *V*.)

### Rita Mae Brown

**9154.** LEVINE, DANIEL B. Uses of Classical mythology in Rita Mae Brown's *Southern Discomfort*. CML (10:1) 63–70.

### Sterling A. Brown

**9155.** CALLAHAN, JOHN F. Sterling Brown ain't dead nothing . . . . He ain't even passed. BALF (23:1) 91–4.

**9156.** TIDWELL, JOHN EDGAR. Sterling A. Brown remembered. BALF (23:1) 109–11.

**9157.** WILLIAMS, SHERLEY ANNE. Remembering Prof. Sterling A. Brown, 1901–1989. BALF (23:1) 106–8.

**9158.** WRIGHT, JOHN S.   The new negro poet and the nachal man: Sterling Brown's folk odyssey. BALF (23:1) 95–105.

### Alan Brownjohn

**9159.** CHIFU, GABRIEL.   Interview. Ramuri, May, 5.

**9160.** DUȚESCU, DAN.   Trei p̦oeți englezi contemporani – Fleur Adcock, Alan Brownjohn, Jon Silkin. *See* **8911.**

**9161.** NISTOR, EUGENIU.   Interview. Orizont, 15 Sept., 8.

### John Brunner

**9162.** WĄGROCKA, JADWIGA.   *The Whole Man*: autothematic use of fairy tale. *In* (pp. 91–100) **57.**

### Ernest Buckler

**9163.** MATHESON, SUE.   Creation, incest, and individuation: the ritual underpinnings of *The Mountain and the Valley*. DalR (67:4) 1987, 402–10.

**9164.** MATHEWS, LAWRENCE.   Hacking at the parsnips: *The Mountain and the Valley* and the critics. *In* (pp. 188–201) **12.**

### Vincent Buckley

**9165.** CRABBE, CHRIS WALLACE.   Vincent Buckley and the poetry of presence. JPC (23:2) 81–91.

**9166.** O'SULLIVAN, VINCENT.   Singing mastery: the poetics of Vincent Buckley. Westerly (34:2) 50–7.

### Frederick Buechner

**9167.** ANDERSON, CHRIS.   The very style of faith: Frederick Buechner as homilist and essayist. ChrisL (38:2) 7–21.

### Charles Bukowski

**9168.** HARRISON, RUSSELL.   The blue suit: an episode from Charles Bukowski's *Factotum*. Germanica Olomucensia (7) 85–93.

**9169.** SMITH, J. P.   The poetry of Charles Bukowski. Unpub. doct. diss., Univ. of Hull. [Abstr. in IT (39:4) 1637.]

### Michael Bullock

**9170.** STEWART, JACK F.   Image and mood: recent poems by Michael Bullock. CanL (115) 1987, 107–21.

### Anthony Burgess

**9171.** BURGESS, ANTHONY.   Little Wilson and big God: being the first part of the confessions of Anthony Burgess. Toronto: Stoddart, 1987. (Bibl. 1988, 7008.) Rev. by Paul Boytinck in QQ (95:2) 1988, 448–50.

**9172.** CASSOLA, ARNOLD.   *MF*: a glossary of Anthony Burgess's Castitan language. ELN (26:4) 72–9.

**9173.** NICHOL, DONALD W.   'Flagrant' versus 'fragrant' in Beaumont, Pope, Pound, and Burgess. *See* **1048.**

### Kenneth Burke

**9174.** BOERCKEL, SUSAN DENISE.   Kenneth Burke's rhetoric of the 1920's, 1930's, and 1940's. *See* **8680a.**

**9175.** DESILET, GREGORY.   Nietzsche contra Burke: the melodrama in dramatism. *See* **8016.**

**9176.** HARRIS, WENDELL V.   The critics who made us: Kenneth Burke. *See* **8755a.**

**9177.** HENDERSON, GREIG E.   Kenneth Burke: literature and language as symbolic action. Athens; London: Georgia UP, 1988. pp. 216.

**9178.** JAY, PAUL (ed.). The selected correspondence of Kenneth Burke and Malcolm Cowley, 1915–1981. New York: Viking, 1988. pp. xi, 448. Rev. by Tim Poland in AL (61:3) 505–7; by Harrison E. Salisbury in BW, 1 Jan., 3; by Monroe K. Spears in BkW, 1 Jan., 3.

**9179.** McMAHON, ROBERT. Kenneth Burke's divine comedy: the literary form of *The Rhetoric of Religion*. *See* **8811**.

**9180.** SOUTHWELL, SAMUEL B. Kenneth Burke and Martin Heidegger: with a note against deconstructionism. *See* **8870**.

### Sam Burnside

**9181.** SMYTH, DAMIAN. Defining the inheritance: Sam Burnside interviewed. Linen Hall Review (6:3) 5–9.

### William Burroughs

**9182.** LYDENBERG, ROBIN. Word cultures: radical theory and practice in William S. Burroughs' fiction. (Bibl. 1988, 7013.) Rev. by David Glover in JAStud (23:1) 172–3.

**9183.** MORGAN, TED. Literary outlaw: the life and times of William S. Burroughs. (Bibl. 1988, 7014.) Rev. by Leigh Kirkland Pietschner in AL (61:4) 710–11.

**9184.** PRIGENT, CHRISTIAN. La langue et ses monstres. Montpellier: Cadex. pp. 208. (L'Ostiaque.)

### Octavia Butler

**9185.** BARR, MARLEEN S.; SALVAGGIO, RUTH; LAW, RICHARD. Suzy McKee Charnas/Octavia Butler/Joan D. Vinge. Mercer Island, WA: Starmont House, 1986. pp. 171. (Starmont reader's guide.) Rev. by Kathleen L. Spencer in SFS (14:3) 1987, 407–10.

### Mary Butts

**9186.** BAGG, CAMILLA (introd.); WAGSTAFF, BARBARA (postscr.). The crystal cabinet: my childhood at Salterns. Manchester: Carcanet Press, 1988. pp. 280.

### A. S. Byatt

**9187.** CREIGHTON, JOANNE V. Sisterly symbiosis: Margaret Drabble's *The Waterfall* and A. S. Byatt's *The Game*. Mosaic (20:1) 1987, 15–29.

### James Branch Cabell

**9188.** RIEMER, JAMES D. From satire to subversion: the fantasies of James Branch Cabell. New York; London: Greenwood Press. pp. xxii, 106. (Contributions to the study of science fiction and fantasy, 38.)

### Abraham Cahan

**9189.** RISCHIN, MOSES (ed.). Grandma never lived in America: the New Journalism of Abraham Cahan. Bloomington: Indiana UP, 1985. pp. xliv, 538. Rev. by Albert Waldinger in ALR (21:3) 74–5.

### Hall Caine

**9190.** SHIMMIN, N. L. The making of a Manx literature: regional identity in the writings of Hall Caine and T. E. Brown. *See* **6347**.

### Hortense Calisher

**9191.** SNODGRASS, KATHLEEN. Coming down from the heights: three novels of Hortense Calisher. TSLL (31:4) 554–69.

### Roy Campbell

**9192.** LE BON, PIERRE.   Uys Krige et Roy Campbell: première rencontre de deux poètes sud-africains. Repérages (11) 29–45.

### Truman Capote

**9193.** CLARKE, GERALD.   Capote: a biography. (Bibl. 1988, 7031.) Rev. by Adam Begley in LRB (11:1) 23.

**9194.** FOX, JOSEPH (ed.).   *Answered Prayers*: the unfinished novel. New York: Random House; London: Hamilton, 1986. pp. 180. Rev. by R. Z. Sheppard in Time, 7 Sept. 1987, 65.

**9195.** GOING, WILLIAM T.   Truman Capote: Harper Lee's fictional portrait of the artist as an Alabama child. AlaR (42:2) 136–49.

**9196.** STEFANOV, HRISTO (introd.).   Sbădnati molitvi. (Answered prayers.) Varna, Bulgaria: Bakalov. pp. 179.

### Bliss Carman

**9197.** MILLER, MURIEL.   Bliss Carman: quest & revolt. St John's Nfld: Jesperson Press, 1985. pp. xv, 304. Rev. by Ronald Hatch in CanL (115) 1987, 224–5.

**9198.** SOUSTER, RAYMOND; LOCHHEAD, DOUGLAS (eds).   Windflower: poems of Bliss Carman. Ottawa: Tecumseh Press, 1985. pp. xvi, 251. Rev. by Ronald Hatch in CanL (115) 1987, 224–5.

### Emily Carr

**9199.** BLANCHARD, PAULA.   The life of Emily Carr. Vancouver: Douglas & McIntyre; Seattle: Washington UP, 1987. pp. 331. Rev. by Emily-Jane Orford in CanL (120) 233–4.

**9200.** GOWERS, RUTH.   Emily Carr. Leamington Spa: Berg, 1987. pp. 126. (Berg women's series.) Rev. by Glenn Deer in CanL (120) 150–1; by Dorothy Farr in QQ (95:4) 1988, 894–5.

**9201.** WARNER, JANET.   Emily Carr's Tennyson. *See* **7544.**

### Catherine Carswell

**9202.** CARSWELL, IANTHE (introd.).   The camomile: an invention. London: Virago Press, 1987. pp. xv, 305. (Virago modern classics; 261.)

### Angela Carter

**9203.** TODD, RICHARD.   Convention and innovation in British fiction 1981–1984: the contemporaneity of magic realism. *In* (pp. 361–88) **16.**

### Raymond Carver

**9204.** McINERNEY, JAY.   Raymond Carver: a still small voice. NYTB, 6 Aug., 1.

**9205.** VERLEY, CLAUDINE.   Narration and interiority in Raymond Carver's *Where I'm Calling From*. JSSE (13) 91–102.

**9206.** WOLFF, TOBIAS.   Raymond Carver had his cake and ate it too. Esquire (112:3) 240–2, 244, 247–8.

### Joyce Cary

**9207.** BISHOP, ALAN.   Gentleman rider: a biography of Joyce Cary. (Bibl. 1988, 7045, where title incorrect.) Rev. by Martin Fagg in Listener (121) 5 Jan., 24–5; by D. A. N. Jones in TLS, 21 July, 805.

**9208.** BRADBURY, MALCOLM.   Persons of letters. *In* (pp. 5–14) **42.**

## Willa Cather

**9209.** AMBROSE, JAMIE. Willa Cather: writing at the frontier. Oxford: Berg, 1988. pp. xv, 173. (Berg women's series.)

**9210.** ARNOLD, MARILYN. Willa Cather: a reference guide. Boston, MA: G. K. Hall, 1986. pp. xxii, 415. (A reference guide to literature.) Rev. by Mildred R. Bennett in WAL (22:2) 1987, 182.

**9211.** —— Willa Cather's artistic 'radicalism'. CEACrit (51:4) 2–10.

**9212.** BOHLKE, L. BRENT (ed.). Willa Cather in person: interviews, speeches, and letters. (Bibl. 1988, 7054.) Rev. by Barbara Barr in StudN (20:3) 1988, 340–1; by Patrick Reilly in NQ (36:1) 133–4; by Christine Bold in JAStud (23:1) 163–4.

**9213.** BROWN, MARY RUTH (COX). A pilgrim's progress toward faith: Willa Cather's quest for the 'thing not named'. Unpub. doct. diss., Oklahoma State Univ., 1988. [Abstr. in DA (49) 3025A.]

**9214.** COLLINS, JEANNE COOKE. 'A green thought in a green shade': the garden motif in Willa Cather's fiction. Unpub. doct. diss., Univ. of Northern Colorado, 1988. [Abstr. in DA (49) 2218A.]

**9215.** FRYER, JUDITH. Felicitous space: the imaginative structures of Edith Wharton and Willa Cather. Chapel Hill: North Carolina UP, 1986. pp. xvii, 403. Rev. by Ellen Powers Stengel in AL (61:1) 117–18; by Alice Hall Petry in AmerS (29:2) 1988, 97; by Barbara Barr in StudN (20:3) 1988, 342–3.

**9216.** HARRIS, RICHARD C. First loves: Willa Cather's Niel Herbert and Ivan Turgenev's Vladimir Petrovich. SAF (17:1) 81–91.

**9217.** LEE, HERMIONE. Willa Cather: a life saved up. London: Virago Press. pp. vii, 409. Rev. by Christine Bold in TLS, 17 Nov., 1259–60; by Janet Todd in LRB (11:24) 18–19; by Paul Binding in Listener (122) 19 Oct., 24–5.

**9218.** —— (ed.). The short stories of Willa Cather. London: Virago Press. pp. xviii, 490.

**9219.** NELSON, ROBERT J. Willa Cather and France: in search of the lost language. Urbana: Illinois UP, 1988. pp. xii, 173. Rev. by Ann Romines in AL (61:1) 119–20.

**9220.** O'BRIEN, SHARON. Willa Cather: the emerging voice. (Bibl. 1988, 7062.) Rev. by Judy Simons in RES (39:156) 1988, 587–8.

**9221.** PASTOURMATZI, DOMNA A. Shaking the pillars of patriarchy: a gender analysis of Willa Cather's Nebraska and Colorado novels. Unpub. doct. diss., Bowling Green State Univ., 1988. [Abstr. in DA (50) 686A.]

**9222.** RYDER, MARY R. 'All wheat and no chaff': Frank Norris' *Blix* and Willa Cather's literary vision. ALR (22:1) 17–30.

**9223.** SEDGWICK, EVE KOSOFSKY. Across gender, across sexuality: Willa Cather and others. SAQ (88:1) 53–72.

**9224.** SHAW, PATRICK W. Women and the father: psychosexual ambiguity in *Death Comes for the Archbishop*. AI (46:1) 61–76.

**9225.** SLOTE, BERNICE. Willa Cather: a pictorial memoir. (Bibl. 1987, 10235.) Rev. by Barbara W. Rippey in JWest (28:1) 123.

**9226.** Stevens, Diane Prenatt.    Willa Cather and the art of civilization. Unpub. doct. diss., Indiana Univ., 1988. [Abstr. in DA (49) 2661A.]

**9227.** Urgo, Joseph R.    How context determines fact: historicism in Willa Cather's *A Lost Lady*. SAF (17:2) 183–92.

**9228.** Vrydaghs, Carol Marlene.    Willa Cather's odyssey of the soul: sex, spirit, and society in her vision. Unpub. doct. diss., Indiana Univ., 1988. [Abstr. in DA (49) 2662A.]

**9229.** Woodress, James.    Willa Cather: a literary life. (Bibl. 1988, 7069.) Rev. by Mona Pers in SN (61:1) 120–1.

## William Caunitz

**9230.** Tsunoda, Waka.    On the beat with William Caunitz. AD (22:2) 136–41.

## Raymond Chandler

**9231.** Smith, Johanna M.    Raymond Chandler and the business of literature. TSLL (31:4) 592–610.

**9232.** Ward, Kathryn Ann.    Clients, colleagues, and consorts: roles of women in American hardboiled detective fiction and film. See **8153.**

## Sid Chaplin

**9233.** Pickering, Michael; Robins, Kevin.    Between determinism and disruption: the working-class novels of Sid Chaplin. CE (51:4) 357–76.

## Suzy McKee Charnas

**9234.** Barr, Marleen S.; Salvaggio, Ruth; Law, Richard.    Suzy McKee Charnas/Octavia Butler/Joan D. Vinge. See **9185.**

## Nirad C. Chaudhuri

**9235.** Mishra, Sudesh.    The two Chaudhuris: historical witness and pseudo-historian. JCL (23:1) 1988, 7–15.

## John Cheever

**9236.** Cheever, Benjamin (ed.).    The letters of John Cheever. London: Cape. (Bibl. 1988, 7080.) Rev. in BkW, 27 Aug., 12; by Jackson J. Benson in AL (61:3) 468; by Nigel Andrew in Listener (122) 12 Oct., 32; by James Campbell in TLS, 15 Sept., 996; by John Lanchester in LRB (11:20) 29–30.

**9237.** Donaldson, Scott.    John Cheever: a biography. (Bibl. 1988, 7082.) Rev. by Jackson J. Benson in AL (61:3) 466–7; by Roderick T. Leupp in ChrisL (38:3) 78–9; by John W. Crowley in NEQ (62:2) 297–301.

**9238.** Thomas, Jim.    A changing American family: Cheever, Gardner, Irving, Updike. Unpub. doct. diss., Univ. of Missouri–Columbia, 1988. [Abstr. in DA (50) 949A.]

**9239.** Woodward, Lynne.    Isolation and integration: John Cheever's *The Country Husband*. BSUF (27:1) 1986, 5–11.

## Kelly Cherry

**9240.** Cherry, Kelly.    When all is said and done, how literary theory *really* affects contemporary fiction. See **8205.**

## G. K. Chesterton

**9241.** Coren, Michael.    Gilbert: the man who was G. K. Chesterton. London: Cape. pp. 270.

**9242.** LAUER, QUENTIN.    G. K. Chesterton: philosopher without portfolio. New York: Fordham UP, 1988. pp. 191.

**9243.** SMITH, MARIE (ed.).    Thirteen detectives: classic mystery stories by the creator of Father Brown. London: Xanadu, 1987. pp. 256.

### Agatha Christie ('Mary Westmacott')

**9244.** ANON. (ed.).    Agatha Christie. Paris: Gallimard, 1988. pp. 125. (Cahiers Renaud-Barrault, 115.)

**9245.** COMBES, ANNIE.    Agatha Christie: l'écriture du crime. Paris: Impressions nouvelles. pp. 298.

**9246.** PARDUE, MARY JANE.    The mystery of mass appeal: critical clues to the success of Agatha Christie. Unpub. doct. diss., Middle Tennessee State Univ., 1988. [Abstr. in DA (49) 2653A.]

### Caryl Churchill

**9247.** COUSIN, GERALDINE.    Churchill the playwright. London: Methuen. pp. 135.

**9248.** DIAMOND, ELIN.    (In)visible bodies in Churchill's theater. In (pp. 259–81) **39.** (Repr. from TJ (40:2) 1988, 189–205.)

**9249.** FITZSIMMONS, LINDA (comp.).    File on Churchill. London: Methuen. pp. 95. (Writer-files.)

**9250.** HERRMAN, ANNE.    Travesty and transgression: transvestism in Shakespeare, Brecht and Churchill. See **3559.**

**9251.** KRITZER, AMELIA HOWE.    Open-ended inquiries: the plays of Caryl Churchill. Unpub. doct. diss., Univ. of Wisconsin–Madison, 1988. [Abstr. in DA (49) 3553A.]

**9252.** REINELT, JANELLE.    Feminist theory and the problem of performance. ModDr (32:1) 48–57.

### Sir Winston Churchill

**9253.** CANNADINE, DAVID (ed.).    Blood, toil, tears and sweat: Winston Churchill's famous speeches. London: Cassell. pp. xi, 355.

### Tom Clancy

**9254.** SHAPIRO, WALTER.    Of arms and the man: Tom Clancy, the military minstrel, longs to live the life he writes about. Time, 21 Aug., 66–8.

### Brian Clark

**9255.** GLAAP, ALBERT-REINER.    *Whose Life is it Anyway?* in London and on Broadway: a contrastive analysis of the British and American versions of Brian Clark's play. In (pp. 214–23) **50.**

### John Pepper Clark

**9256.** MADUKA, CHIDI T.    African religious beliefs in literary imagination: *ogbanje* and *abiku* in Chinua Achebe, J. P. Clark and Wole Soyinka. See **8900.**

### Arthur C. Clarke

**9257.** CLARKE, ARTHUR C.    Astounding days: a science fictional autobiography. London: Gollancz. pp. 224.

### Austin Clarke

**9258.** HARMON, MAURICE.    Austin Clarke: a critical introduction. Dublin: Wolfhound Press. pp. 208.

**Jack Clemo**

**9259.** LANE, S. J. Jack Clemo: cartographer of grace. Unpub. doct. diss., Univ. of Newcastle upon Tyne. [Abstr. in IT (39:4) 1633.]

**George Clutesi**

**9260.** BRINGHURST, ROBERT. Nootka rag: funeral music for George Clutesi. CanL (118) 1988, 190–3.

**John Coates**

**9260a.** TERRY, JUDITH. 'Knit your own stuff'; or, Finishing off Jane Austen. See **6241.**

**J. M. Coetzee**

**9261.** ATTWELL, DAVID. The political unconsciousness in *Foe*. JLS (5:2) 255–6.

**9262.** BJÖRKSTÉN, INGMAR. J. M. Coetzee och den sydafrikanska konsekvensen. (J. M. Coetzee and South-African consequence.) Allt om böcker (1989:5) 40–2.

**9263.** CARUSI, ANNAMARIA. *Foe*: the narrative and power. JLS (5:2) 134–44.

**9264.** DE JONG, MARIANNE. Foe and Friday: blueprints for the 'differand'. JLS (5:2) 215–18.

**9265.** —— Introduction. JLS (5:2) 106–18. (Introduction to a special issue on Coetzee's *Foe*.)

**9266.** DOVEY, THERESA. The intersection of postmodern, post-colonial and feminist discourse in J. M. Coetzee's *Foe*. JLS (5:2) 119–33.

**9267.** GLENN-LAUGA, CATHERINE. The 'hearerly' text: seashells on the seashore. See **5191.**

**9268.** GRÄBE, INA. Postmodernist narrative strategies in *Foe*. JLS (5:2) 145–82.

**9269.** HEWSON, KELLY LEIGH. Writers and responsibility: George Orwell, Nadine Gordimer, John Coetzee and Salman Rushdie. Unpub. doct. diss., Univ. of Alberta, 1988. [Abstr. in DA (49) 3033A.]

**9270.** McDERMOTT, LYDIA EVE. Narrative duality and the novels of J. M. Coetzee: a semiotic study. Unpub. doct. diss., Univ. of Pretoria.

**9271.** MAES-JELINEK, HENA. Ambivalent Clio: J. M. Coetzee's *In the Heart of the Country* and Wilson Harris's *Carnival*. JCL (22:1) 1987, 87–98.

**9272.** MARAIS, M. J. The deployment of metafiction in an aesthetic of engagement in J. M. Coetzee's *Foe*. JLS (5:2) 183–93.

**9273.** MARAIS, MICHAEL. Interpretative authoritarianism: reading/ colonizing Coetzee's *Foe*. EngA (16:1) 9–16.

**9274.** VAN LIEROP, KARIN. J. M. Coetzees Zuidafrikaanse robinso-nade. (J. M. Coetzee's South African Robinsonade.) De Gids (151:2) 154–60.

**9275.** VAUGHAN, MICHAEL. Marxism and J. M. Coetzee's writing. JLS (5:2) 218–23.

**9276.** WAGNER, KATHRIN M. *Dichter* and *Dichtung*: Susan Barton and the 'truth' of autobiography. ESA (32:1) 1–11. (*Foe*.)

## Wanda Coleman

**9277.** MAGISTRALE, TONY.   Doing battle with the wolf: a critical introduction to Wanda Coleman's poetry. BALF (23:3) 539–54.

## Pádraic Colum

**9278.** STERNLICHT, SANFORD.   Padraic Colum: poet of the 1960s. CLQ (25:4) 253–7.

## Ivy Compton-Burnett

**9279.** LERAY, JOSETTE.   Lieux et langages du pouvoir dans les romans d'Ivy Compton-Burnett. *In* (pp. 163–76) **14.**

**9280.** SPURLING, HILARY.   Ivy: the life of I. Compton-Burnett. (Bibl. 1986, 11468.) Rev. by William H. Pritchard in HR (38:2) 1985, 259–64.

## Cyril Connolly

**9281.** KERTZER, J. M.   Cyril Connolly's *The Unquiet Grave*: the pilot and the noonday devil. Mosaic (20:4) 1987, 23–36.

**9282.** SHELDEN, MICHAEL.   Friends of promise: Cyril Connolly and the world of *Horizon*. *See* **587.**

## Joseph Conrad

**9283.** BATCHELOR, JOHN.   Lord Jim. London; Boston, MA: Unwin Hyman, 1988. pp. xiv, 241. (Unwin critical library.) Rev. by Allan Hunter in NQ (36:2) 257–8.

**9284.** BENASSI, MARÍA CLAUDIA.   Conquering history: Conrad's *Nostromo* and García Márquez' *One Hundred Years of Solitude* as counter-historical novels. Unpub. doct. diss., Brown Univ., 1988. [Abstr. in DA (49) 2209A.]

**9285.** BIGNAMI, MARIALUISA.   Joseph Conrad, the Malay archipelego, and the decadent hero. RES (38:150) 1987, 199–210.

**9286.** BOWKER, VERONICA.   Textuality and worldliness: crossing the boundaries: a postmodernist reading of Achebe, Conrad and Lessing. *See* **8684.**

**9287.** BRADBURY, MALCOLM.   The modern world: ten great writers. London: Secker & Warburg, 1988. pp. xix, 294. Rev. by Gerald Gillespie in NC (8) 180–2. (English writers discussed: Conrad, T. S. Eliot, Joyce and Virginia Woolf.)

**9288.** BRODSKY, G. W. S.   Victory in defeat: Joseph Conrad and the idea of honour. Unpub. doct. diss., Univ. of York. [Abstr. in IT (38:4) 1458.]

**9289.** CAMPBELL, G.   Kipling and Conrad: precursors of modernity. Unpub. M.Phil. diss., Univ. of Liverpool. [Abstr. in IT (39:3) 1110.]

**9290.** CARACCIOLO, P. L.; HAMPSON, R. G.   'Money turned to leaves': Conrad, Collins, Dickens, and the barber's fourth brother. NQ (36:2) 193–6.

**9291.** CHON, SOO-YOUNG.   Conrad's *Victory*: an elusive allegory. JELL (35) 83–101.

**9292.** DILWORTH, THOMAS.   Listeners and lies in *Heart of Darkness*. RES (38:152) 1987, 510–22.

**9293.** ENGLISH, JAMES F.   Comic transactions: humor as communication in four modern novels. Unpub. doct. diss., Stanford Univ., 1988.

[Abstr. in DA (49) 2652A.] (*The Secret Agent, The Golden Notebook, Miss Lonelyhearts, Pale Fire.*)

**9294.** FLOOD, TRACY SEELEY.   Gnostic romance: Dickens, Conrad and the advent of Modernism. *See* **6613.**

**9295.** FOGEL, AARON.   Coercion to speak: Conrad's poetics of dialogue. (Bibl. 1986, 11489.) Rev. by John Batchelor in RES (39:156) 1988, 585–7.

**9296.** GALEA, ILEANA.   Romanul istoric al lui J. Conrad. (Conrad's historical novels.) Steaua (40:6) 52.

**9297.** GOETSCH, PAUL.   Fictive oral storytelling in *Lord Jim. In* (pp. 179–95) **5.**

**9298.** GoGWILT, CHRISTOPHER LLOYD.   Joseph Conrad and the invention of the West. Unpub. doct. diss., Princeton Univ., 1988. [Abstr. in DA (49) 3719A.]

**9299.** GRANQVIST, RAOUL.   Us and them: distancing practices of the colonial travelogue. *In* (pp. 69–86) **34.**

**9300.** HEWITT, DOUGLAS.   *Heart of Darkness* and some 'old and unpleasant reports'. RES (38:151) 1987, 374–6.

**9301.** HIGDON, DAVID LEON.   Conrad, *Under Western Eyes*, and the mysteries of revision. *See* **322.**

**9302.** HOLM, BIRGITTA.   Hjärta av mörker: om Orfeus, Eurydike och Joseph Conrads roman. (Heart of darkness: on Orpheus, Eurydice and Joseph Conrad's novel.) BLM (58:5) 281–92.

**9303.** HONG, SUNG-JOO.   The reversal of the role between men and things in *The Secret Agent.* INH (17) 79–90.

**9304.** JAUDEL, PHILIPPE.   Traduire Conrad. *In* (pp. 37–49) **22.**

**9305.** KARL, FREDERICK R.; DAVIES, LAURENCE (eds).   Collected letters of Joseph Conrad: vol. 2, 1898–1902. (Bibl. 1988, 7123.) Rev. by John Batchelor in RES (39:156) 1988, 583–5.

**9306.** KIM, SOO-JONG.   Joseph Conrad soseol eui ingan siljon munjae. (The problem of human existence as considered in the novels of Joseph Conrad.) Unpub. doct. diss., Chungnam National Univ., Daejeon, Korea.

**9307.** KIMBROUGH, ROBERT (ed.).   *Heart of Darkness*: an authoritative texts, backgrounds and sources, criticism. (Bibl. 1988, 7125.) Rev. by Douglas Hewitt in NQ (36:2) 274–5.

**9308.** KOPPER, EDWARD A., JR.   Conrad in Michael Crichton's *Sphere.* NCL (19:4) 11–12.

**9309.** KU, MI-HYANG.   Joseph Conrad soseol eui goripsung. (Alienation in Joseph Conrad's novels.) YYY (5) 49–67.

**9310.** LORIMER LUNDBERG, PATRICIA.   Gendered reading communities: the feminization of reader response criticism and a dialogics of reading. *See* **6302.**

**9311.** LOWE, THERESA CECILIA.   Concepts of the self and isolation in Conrad's Malaysian novels. Unpub. doct. diss., Univ. of South Florida, 1988. [Abstr. in DA (49) 3034A.]

**9312.** MANDEL, MIRIAM B.   Significant patterns of colour and animal imagery in Conrad's *Heart of Darkness.* Neophilologus (73:2) 305–19.

**9313.** MIHĂIEŞ, MIRCEA.     Ultimul Conrad. (The latest Conrad.) RomLit, 6 Apr., 20 (review-article).

**9314.** MONK, LELAND R.     Standard deviations: chance and the modern novel. *See* **6778.**

**9315.** NAYDER, LILLIAN ROSE.     Fictional economies: a study of Dickens and Conrad. *See* **6647.**

**9316.** NIEKER, MARK.     Apprehensive moments: Conrad, Chaucer, and the *Sefer Yetsira*. *See* **2859.**

**9317.** PACCAUD, JOSIANE.     Hypertextuality in Joseph Conrad's *Under Western Eyes*. CVE (29) 73–82.

**9318.** RAY, MARTIN (ed.).     Chance: a tale in two parts. Oxford; New York: OUP, 1988. pp. xxxvi, 476. (World's classics.) Rev. by Sylvère Monod in EA (42:2) 224–5.

**9319.** RESSLER, S.     Joseph Conrad: consciousness and integrity. New York: New York UP, 1988. pp. ix, 167. Rev. by Allan Hunter in NQ (36:4) 538–9.

**9320.** RUPPEL, RICHARD JEFFREY.     Kipling, Conrad, and the popular exotic short fiction of the 1890's. *See* **5905.**

**9321.** STAPE, J. H.     Conrad to T. F. Unwin and Neil Monro: two unpublished letters. NQ (36:2) 192–3.

**9322.** STOTT, R.     The kiss of death: a demystification of the late-nineteenth-century 'femme fatale' in the selected works of Bram Stoker, Rider Haggard, Joseph Conrad and Thomas Hardy. *See* **6865.**

**9323.** SULLIVAN, ERNEST W., II; MURRAH, DAVID J.     The Donne Dalhousie discovery: proceedings of a symposium on the acquisition and study of the John Donne and Joseph Conrad collections at Texas Tech University. *See* **267.**

**9324.** TALIB, I. BIN S.     Towards an understanding of coherence, with the example of Conrad's *Nostromo*. Unpub. doct. diss., Univ. of East Anglia, 1986. [Abstr. in IT (36:4) 1397.]

**9325.** VERLEUN, JAN.     Conrad's modernity and humanity. *In* (pp. 131–40) **23.**

**9326.** VERLEUN-VAN DE VRIESENAERDE, JETTY.     Conrad criticism 1965–1985: *The Nigger of the 'Narcissus'*; Conrad criticism 1965–1985: *Heart of Darkness*. Niebert, The Netherlands: Phoenix Press, 1988. 2 vols. pp. xi, 117; ix, 188.

**9327.** VLAD, ALEXANDRU (introd.).     Duelistii. (The duelists.) Bucharest: Editura militara. pp. 272.

**9328.** WHITELEY, PATRICK J.     Knowledge and experimental realism in Conrad, Lawrence and Woolf. Baton Rouge; London: Louisiana State UP, 1987. pp. 235. Rev. by Emile Delavenay in EA (42:1) 107–8.

**9329.** YONG, MARGARET.     Explorations in the heart of darkness: turning landscape into art in *Slipstream* and *The Year of Living Dangerously*. *In* (pp. 10–37) **19.**

### Dennis Cooley

**9330.** KAMBOURELI, SMARO.     Stealing the text: George Bowering's *Kerrisdale Elegies* and Denis Cooley's *Bloody Jack*. *See* **9122.**

## Robert Coover
**9331.** CAMPBELL, GREGOR DUNCAN. Historical consciousness in the fiction of William Gaddis, Thomas Pynchon, and Robert Coover: a reading of *The Recognitions*, *Gravity's Rainbow*, and *The Public Burning*. Unpub. doct. diss., Univ. of Toronto. [Abstr. in DA (50) 1661A.]

**9332.** MALTBY, P. L. Dissident postmodernists: Barthelme, Coover, Pynchon. See **9020**.

**9333.** STENGEL, WAYNE B. Robert Coover's 'writing degree zero': *The Magic Poker*. AQ (45:2) 101–10.

## 'Jack Cope' (Robert Knox Cope)
**9334.** HARESNAPE, GEOFFREY. Belief in the song: Jack Cope and South African poetry in English. See **8504**.

## John William Corrington
**9335.** MILLS, WILLIAM. Risking the bait: John William Corrington, 1932–1988. SoR (25:3) 586–94.

## Peter Cowan
**9336.** BENNETT, BRUCE. Of books and covers: Peter Cowan. See **71**.

## Sir Noel Coward
**9337.** GREY, FRANCIS. Noel Coward. New York: St Martin's Press, 1987. pp. viii, 216. Rev. by Robert F. Gross in TJ (41:2) 263.

## Malcolm Cowley
**9338.** DOLAN, MARC. 'True stories' of 'the Lost Generation': an exploration of narrative truth in memoirs of Hemingway, Cowley, and Fitzgerald. Unpub. doct. diss., Harvard Univ., 1988. [Abstr. in DA (50) 471A.]

**9339.** DORMAN, ROBIN. 90 candles for Malcolm Cowley. LGJ (8:2) 1988/89, 2–8.

**9340.** JAY, PAUL (ed.). The selected correspondence of Kenneth Burke and Malcolm Cowley, 1915–1981. See **9178**.

**9341.** KEMPF, JAMES M. *Exile's Return*: a final farewell to Cowley. LGJ (8:2) 1988/89, 12, 15.

**9342.** McCALL, JOHN. Lost Generation chronicler: Malcolm Cowley. LGJ (8:2) 1988/89, 9–11.

## James Gould Cozzens
**9343.** BRUCCOLI, MATTHEW J. James Gould Cozzens: a life apart. (Bibl. 1985, 10289.) Rev. by Francis X. Duggon in ModAge (32:2) 1988, 184–6.

## Hart Crane
**9344.** BERTHOFF, WARNER. Hart Crane: a re-introduction. Minneapolis: Minnesota UP. pp. xi, 138. Rev. by Leonora Woodman in AL (61:4) 719–20.

**9345.** GAUTHIER, DOMINIQUE. Du labyrinthe au temple: le pont comme seuil mythique dans *The Bridge* de Hart Crane. *In* (pp. 135–44) **35**.

**9346.** GILES, PAUL. Hart Crane: the contexts of *The Bridge*. (Bibl. 1988, 7149.) Rev. by Marjorie Perloff in MLR (84:4) 965–7.

**9347.** GUNNER, RAPHAEL ISAAC.　Originality, representation, and irony in Hart Crane's poetics and *The Bridge*. Unpub. doct. diss., Harvard Univ. [Abstr. in DA (50) 1305A.]

**9348.** YINGLING, THOMAS E.　'New thresholds, new anatomies': Hart Crane and the homosexual text. Unpub. doct. diss., Univ. of Pennsylvania, 1988. [Abstr. in DA (49) 3365A.]

**9349.** Entry cancelled.

### Adelaide Crapsey

**9350.** ALKALAY-GUT, KAREN.　Alone in the dawn: the life of Adelaide Crapsey. Athens; London: Georgia UP, 1988. pp. x, 364.

### Michael Crichton

**9351.** KOPPER, EDWARD A., JR.　Conrad in Michael Crichton's *Sphere*. *See* **9308.**

### e. e. cummings

**9352.** GRABHER, GUDRUN M.　E. E. Cummings: the ontologica dangling of his poetry. Interspace (Berlin) (4) 43–62.

**9353.** VERSLUYS, KRISTIAAN.　'the season 'tis, my lively lambs': E. E. Cummings' quarrel with the language of politics. *In* (pp. 77–88) **2.**

### Allen Curnow

**9354.** JAMES, TREVOR.　'Errors and omissions excepted': Allen Curnow's philosophical scepticism. JCL (22:1) 1987, 55–72.

**9355.** RIACH, ALAN.　Stranger eyes; Charles Olson, 'Pacific Man' and some aspects of New Zealand poetry. *See* **8548.**

**9356.** SIMPSON, PETER (ed.).　Look back harder: critical writings, 1935–1984. (Bibl. 1988, 7160.) Rev. by Peter Quartermaine in NQ (36:2) 278–9.

### Blanche d'Alpuget

**9357.** LITTLE, GRAHAM. Blanche D'Alpuget. *In* (pp. 157–69) GRAHAM LITTLE, Speaking for myself. Melbourne: McPhee Gribble. pp. 269. (Interview.)

### Sarah Daniels

**9358.** DAVIS, TRACY C.　*Extremities* and *Masterpieces*: a feminist paradigm of art and politics. ModDr (32:1) 89–103.

### Eleanor Dark

**9359.** O'REILLY, HELEN.　The timeless Eleanor Dark. Outrider (Indooroopilly, Qld) (6:1) 42–7.

### Donald Davie

**9360.** HEANEY, SEAMUS.　*Or, Solitude*: a reading. *In* (pp. 81–7) **46.**

**9361.** JARMAN, MARK.　A shared humanity: *In the Stopping Train* and *The Whitsun Weddings*. *In* (pp. 89–101) **46.**

**9362.** VENDLER, HELEN.　Donald Davie: self-portraits in verse. *In* (pp. 233–53) **46.**

### Idris Davies

**9363.** BEDNAR, Y. N.　Idris Davies – a study of a South Wales valley poet. Unpub. M.Litt. diss., Univ. of Oxford, 1988. [Abstr. in IT (39:2) 490.]

### John Davies

**9364.** POOLE, RICHARD.　Two kinds of poetic thought: Robert Minhinnick and John Davies. AWR (88) 1988, 67–77.

### Robertson Davies
**9365.** HULSE, MICHAEL. Robertson Davies in conversation with Michael Hulse. JCL (22:1) 1987, 119–35.

**9366.** KÖSTER, PATRICIA. 'A rum start': the redoubled baptisms of Francis Chegwidden Cornish. CanL (116) 1988, 248–53.

**9367.** PETERMAN, MICHAEL. Robertson Davies. Boston, MA; London: G. K. Hall; Toronto: ECW Press, 1986. pp. 178. (Twayne's world authors, 780.) Rev. by Shirley Buswell in CanL (116) 1988, 149–51; by Patricia Monk in DalR (66:3) 1986, 366–7.

**9368.** SNIDER, NORMAN. Robertson Davies: the view from High Table. *In* (pp. 69–72) **12.**

### W. H. Davies
**9369.** BARKER, JONATHAN (ed.). Selected poems. (Bibl. 1986, 11622.) Rev. by W. S. Milne in Agenda (24:1) 1986, 50–3.

### William Arthur Deacon
**9370.** LENNOX, JOHN; LACOMBE, MICHÈLE (eds). Dear Bill: the correspondence of William Arthur Deacon. Toronto; London: Toronto UP, 1988. pp. xxxii, 368.

### Walter de la Mare
**9371.** BAYLEY, JOHN. The child in Walter de la Mare. *In* (pp. 337–49) **14.**

**9372.** BENTINCK, A. Tolkien and de la Mare: the fantastic secondary worlds of *The Hobbit* and *The Three Mulla-Mulgars*. Mythlore (15:3) 39–43.

**9373.** REID-WALSH, JACQUELINE JANE AYER. The burning-glass: a developmental study of Walter de la Mare's poetry. Unpub. doct. diss., McGill Univ. [Abstr. in DA (50) 956A.]

### Mazo de la Roche
**9374.** GIVNER, JOAN. Mazo de la Roche: the hidden life. Oxford; Toronto: OUP. pp. x, 273. Rev. by Alexandra Pringle in TLS, 10 Nov., 1230.

### Don DeLillo
**9375.** HIGGINBOTHAM, J. K. The 'queer' in Don DeLillo's *End Zone*. NCL (19:1) 5–7.

**9376.** LECLAIR, TOM. In the loop: Don DeLillo and the system novel. Urbana: Illinois UP, 1987. pp. xiii, 244. Rev. by Wayne B. Stengel in AL (61:1) 132–3.

**9377.** WILLSON, ROBERT F., JR. DeLillo's *Libra*: fiction and pseudo-history? NCL (19:4) 8–9.

### Anita Desai
**9378.** SHAMSIE, MUNEEZA. A coat of many colours. Dawn Magazine (Karachi) 21 Apr., 1, 4.

**9379.** SIDHWA, BAPSI. Seamier side of Indian life. Dawn Magazine (Karachi) 13 Jan., 1, 8.

### Peter De Vries
**9380.** WOOD, RALPH C. The comedy of redemption: Christian faith in four American novelists. Notre Dame, IN: Notre Dame UP, 1988.

pp. xi, 310.(Peter De Vries, Flannery O'Connor, Walker Percy, John Updike.) Rev. by Elizabeth Brown-Guillory in AL (61:4) 711–12.

### John Dewey
**9381.** BOISVERT, RAYMOND D.    Dewey's metaphysics. New York: Fordham UP, 1988. pp. xii, 227.

### Philip K. Dick ('Richard Phillips')
**9382.** BARLOW, AARON JOHN.    Reality, religion, and politics in Philip K. Dick's fiction. Unpub. doct. diss., Univ. of Iowa, 1988. [Abstr. in DA (49) 2216A.]

**9383.** JAMESON, FREDRIC.    Nostalgia for the present. *See* **8066.**

**9384.** MACKEY, DOUGLAS.    Philip K. Dick. Boston, MA: G. K. Hall, 1988. pp. 157. (Twayne's US authors, 533.) Rev. by Peter Fitting in SFS (16:2) 233–6.

**9385.** PEACOCK, J. W.    The unreconstructed man: the fiction of Philip K. Dick. Unpub. doct. diss., Univ. of Liverpool, 1988. [Abstr. in IT (39:3) 1118.]

**9386.** RICKMAN, GREGG.    To the high castle: Philip K. Dick, a life 1928–1962. Long Beach, CA: Fragments West/Valentine Press. pp. 451. Rev. by Peter Nicholls in BkW, 31 Dec., 5.

**9387.** SUTIN, LAWRENCE.    Divine invasions: a life of Philip K. Dick. New York: Harmony. pp. 352. Rev. by Peter Nicholls in BkW, 31 Dec., 5.

### James Dickey
**9388.** BLAIR, JAMES.    The question of race in James Dickey's *Cherrylog Road*. NCL (19:1) 2.

**9389.** TSCHACHLER, HEINZ.    '*Un principe d'insuffisance*': Dickey's dialogue with Bataille. Mosaic (20:3) 1987, 81–93.

### Joan Didion
**9390.** FELTON, SHARON.    Joan Didion: a writer of scope and substance. HC (26:10) 1–10.

**9391.** JULIER, LAURA STEPHANIE.    We tell ourselves stories in order to live: patriarchal fictions and the narrative essays of Joan Didion. Unpub. doct. diss., Univ. of Iowa, 1988. [Abstr. in DA (49) 3363A.]

**9392.** MOSLEY, MERRITT.    Joan Didion's symbolic landscapes. SoCR (21:2) 55–64.

### Annie Dillard
**9393.** DILLARD, ANNIE.    An American childhood. London: Picador. pp. 255.

### 'Isak Dinesen' (Karen Blixen)
**9394.** VISEL, ROBIN ELLEN.    White Eve in the 'petrified garden': the colonial African heroine in the writing of Olive Schreiner, Isak Dinesen, Doris Lessing and Nadine Gordimer. *See* **7379.**

### E. L. Doctorow
**9395.** ANCONA, FRANK.    The tripartite maternal identity in E. L. Doctorow's *Loon Lake*. NCL (19:5) 7–8.

**9396.** BEVILACQUA, WINIFRED FARRANT.    The revision of the Western in E. L. Doctorow's *Welcome to Hard Times*. AL (61:1) 78–95.

**9397.** BUSBY, MARK. E. L. Doctorow's *Ragtime* and the dialectics of change. BSUF (26:3) 1985, 39–44.

**9398.** EIDSVIK, CHARLES. Playful perceptions: E. L. Doctorow's use of media structures and conventions in *Ragtime*. LJGG (30) 301–9.

**9399.** GELLERSTEDT, MATS. Det var en gång i Amerika . . .: gangster-epokens USA: E. L. Doctorows roman *Billy Bathgate*. (Once upon a time in America . . .: the gangster era in the USA: E. L. Doctorow's novel *Billy Bathgate*.) Allt om böcker (1989:5) 70–5.

**9400.** POSPÍŠIL, TOMÁŠ. Ctyři romány E. L. Doctorowa ve světle jeho autoiských zájmů. (Four novels by E. L. Doctorow in the light of his interests.) *In* (pp. 35–6) **6.**

### Hilda Doolittle ('H.D.')

**9401.** AUGUSTINE, JANE. *The Mystery*: H.D.'s unpublished Moravian novel edited and annotated: towards a study in the sources of a poet's religious thinking. Unpub. doct. diss., City Univ. of New York, 1988. [Abstr. in DA (49) 2216A.]

**9402.** BUCK, C. Reading the feminine self: H.D./Freud/psycho-analysis. *See* **8690.**

**9403.** CHISHOLM, D. L. H.D.'s Freudian poetics: psychoanalysis in translation. Unpub. doct. diss., Univ. of Oxford, 1988. [Abstr. in IT (39:1) 34.]

**9404.** COHEN, PAUL. Contraries and language in *Helen in Egypt*. CEACrit (51:2/3) 75–85.

**9405.** FREEMAN, CLARA JEAN. Magdalene before and after: H.D.'s poetic sequences. Unpub. doct. diss., New York Univ., 1988. [Abstr. in DA (49) 2652A.]

**9406.** GUNN, THOM. Three hard women: HD, Marianne Moore, Mina Loy. *In* (pp. 37–52) **46.**

**9407.** SCHAUM, MELITA. Lyric resistance: views of the political in the poetics of Wallace Stevens and H.D. WSJ (13:2) 191–205.

### John Dos Passos

**9408.** CARR, VIRGINIA SPENCER. Dos Passos: a life. (Bibl. 1985, 10418.) Rev. by Francis Russell in ModAge (32:2) 1988, 182–4.

**9409.** GUTMAN, HUCK. Alienation and form in Dos Passos's *U.S.A.* trilogy. PCL (14) 1988, 22–9.

**9410.** MAINE, BARRY (ed.). Dos Passos: the critical heritage. (Bibl. 1988, 7215.) Rev. by Simon Stevens in CamQ (18:2) 223–6.

**9411.** MÉRAL, JEAN. La représentation romanesque de New York dans *Manhattan Transfer*. Littératures (21) 107–15.

**9412.** MONTANELLI, INDRO. Dos Passos. Trans. by MARK T. BASSETT. LGJ (8:2) 1988/89, 16–18.

### Margaret Drabble

**9413.** CREIGHTON, JOANNE V. Sisterly symbiosis: Margaret Drabble's *The Waterfall* and A. S. Byatt's *The Game*. *See* **9187.**

**9414.** GOSS, MARJORIE. Murder and martyrdom in Margaret Drabble's *The Radiant Way*. NCL (19:3) 2.

**9415.** SKOLLER, ELEANOR HONIG. The in-between of writing: experi-ence and experiment in the work of Margaret Drabble, Marguerite

Duras, and Hannah Arendt. Unpub. doct. diss., Univ. of Wisconsin–Milwaukee, 1988. [Abstr. in DA (49) 3736A.]

### Theodore Dreiser

**9416.** EL-BAAJ, H. Thomas Hardy and Theodore Dreiser: a comparative study. *See* **6870.**

**9417.** BARRINEAU, NANCY WARNER. Journalism in the 1890s: the origins of Theodore Dreiser's fiction. Unpub. doct. diss., Univ. of Georgia, 1988. [Abstr. in DA (49) 2656A.]

**9418.** BENDJEDDOU, MOHAMED YAZID. Two literary responses to American society in the early modern era: a comparison of selected novels by Theodore Dreiser and Upton Sinclair in relation to their portrayal of the immigrant, the city, the business tycoon, women, and the problem of labour, 1900–1929. Unpub. doct. diss., Univ. of Warwick, 1985. [Abstr. in DA (50) 1655–6A.]

**9419.** DAVIS, JOSEPH K. Dreiser and the time of Realism. SewR (96:3) 1988, 507–10 (review-article).

**9420.** HAYES, KEVIN J. Textual anomalies in the 1900 Doubleday, Page *Sister Carrie*. *See* **320.**

**9421.** LINGEMAN, RICHARD. Theodore Dreiser: at the gates of the city 1871–1907. (Bibl. 1988, 7228.) Rev. by Edward Margolies in EngS (70:4) 373–5; by Joseph K. Davis in SewR (96:3) 1988, 507–8.

**9422.** MIZRUCHI, SUSAN L. The power of historical knowledge: narrating the past in Hawthorne, James, and Dreiser. *See* **6975.**

**9423.** NOSTWICH, T. D. (ed.). Theodore Dreiser's *Heard in the Corridors*: articles and related writings. Ames: Iowa State UP, 1988. pp. xxiv, 155. Rev. by Richard W. Dowell in ALR (21:3) 93–4; by John C. Hirsh in JAStud (23:1) 182–4.

**9424.** ORLOV, PAUL A. Theodore Dreiser's *Ev'ry Month*, I, 1, found at last: revealing more roots of a writer's thought. ALR (22:1) 69–79.

**9425.** RIGGIO, THOMAS P. (ed.). Dreiser–Mencken letters: the correspondence of Theodore Dreiser and H. L. Mencken, 1907–1945. (Bibl. 1988, 7229.) Rev. by Joseph Griffin in DalR (67:2/3) 1987, 374–5; by Yoshinobu Hakutani in SAF (17:2) 249–51.

**9426.** WEST, JAMES L. W., III. A *Sister Carrie* portfolio. (Bibl. 1987, 10466.) Rev. by Joseph K. Davis in SewR (96:3) 1988, 509–10.

### Robert Drewe

**9427.** EDELSON, PHYLLIS FAHRIE. The role of history in three contemporary Australian novels. JPC (23:2) 63–71. (Robert Drewe, *The Savage Crows*; Tom Winton, *Shallows*; Nigel Krauth, *Matilda, My Darling*.)

### W. E. B. DuBois

**9428.** APTHEKER, HERBERT (ed.). Newspaper columns by W. E. B. DuBois. White Plains, NY: Kraus-Thomson, 1986. 2 vols. pp. xxv, 1150. Rev. by John M. Reilly in Criticism (29:2) 1987, 250–3.

### Louis Dudek

**9428a.** REED, SABRINA LEE. The place of American poets in the development of Irving Layton, Louis Dudek and Raymond Souster. *See* **8545.**

## Daphne Du Maurier
**9429.** CODACCIONI, MARIE-JOSÉ.    L'étrangère dans le temps. *In* (pp. 237–45) **26.** (*Split Second.*)
## John Gregory Dunne
**9430.** WINCHELL, MARK ROYDEN.    John Gregory Dunne. Boise, ID: Boise State UP, 1986. pp. 53. (Western writers.) Rev. by David Fine in SoCR (22:1) 139–40.
## Lawrence Durrell
**9431.** BOONE, JOSEPH A.    Mappings of male desire in Durrell's *Alexandria Quartet.* SAQ (88:1) 73–106.
**9432.** FERTILE, CANDACE EVELYN.    Love and narrative in the novels of Lawrence Durrell. Unpub. doct. diss., Univ. of Alberta, 1988. [Abstr. in DA (49) 3032A.]
**9433.** HALL, T.    Lawrence Durrell's *The Alexandria Quartet*: conflicting metaphysics and the escape from Alexandria. Unpub. doct. diss., Univ. of Oxford, 1988. [Abstr. in IT (39:3) 1115.]
**9434.** VON RICHTHOFEN, P. M.    The *Booster/Delta* nexus: Henry Miller and his friends in the literary world of Paris and London on the eve of the Second World War. *See* **598.**
## William Eastlake
**9435.** DOS DANTOS, ELOINA PRATI.    William Eastlake's undiscovered country: a portrait of the artist. Unpub. doct. diss., State Univ. of New York at Buffalo, 1988. [Abstr. in DA (49) 3722–3A.]
## Richard Eberhart
**9436.** GUTIERREZ, DONALD.    Light in Richard Eberhart's verse. BSUF (27:1) 1986, 59–71.
## Lauris Edmond
**9437.** EDMOND, LAURIS.    True fiction. NZList, 13 May, 26–7.
**9438.** ROSIER, PAT.    *Hot October*: an interview with writer Lauris Edmond. Broadsheet (170) 37–9.
## Loren Eiseley
**9439.** FRANKE, ROBERT G.    Loren Eiseley and the Transcendentalist tradition. Mosaic (20:3) 1987, 15–22.
## Stevan Eldred-Grigg
**9440.** MCLEOD, MARION.    The history man. NZList, 7 Oct., 42–6.
## T. S. Eliot
**9441.** ACKERLEY, C. J.    *The Waste Land*'s sylvan scene. NQ (36:2) 203.
**9442.** ACKROYD, PETER.    T. S. Eliot: a life. (Bibl. 1988, 7301.) Rev. by Gregory Wolfe in ModAge (32:2) 1988, 172–5.
**9443.** ADLER, ROBERT.    What was T. S. Eliot? Commentary (87:3) 31–7.
**9444.** ANDTBACKA, RALF.    Om mötet mellan metafysik och sexualitet i T. S. Eliots diktning. (On the encounter of metaphysics and sexuality in T. S. Eliot's poetry.) Horisont (36:6) 63–71.
**9445.** ANSARI, A. A.    Time and history in *Little Gidding*. ACM (2:1) 112–25.
**9446.** ARROWSMITH, WILLIAM.    Grave prattle: Eliot's *Le Directeur*. YR (78:2) 166–95.

**9447.** ASHER, KENNETH.    T. S. Eliot and ideology. ELH (55:4) 1988, 895–915.

**9448.** BAKER, WILLIAM.    Some T. S. Eliot inscribed copies – an addendum. BC (38:2) 253–7.

**9449.** BEDIENT, CALVIN.    He do the police in different voices: *The Waste Land* and its protagonist. (Bibl. 1988, 7305.) Rev. by Mary O'Connor in QQ (95:4) 1988, 927–9; by William Harmon in SewR (96:1) 1988, 112.

**9450.** BEEHLER, MICHAEL.    T. S. Eliot, Wallace Stevens, and the discourses of difference. (Bibl. 1988, 7306.) Rev. by William Harmon in SewR (96:1) 1988, 109–10.

**9451.** BELL, VEREEN.    Grace dissolved in place: a reading of *Ash Wednesday*. *In* (pp. 1–14) **46.**

**9452.** BOITANI, PIERO.    Some dead master: Brunetto, Dante and Eliot. *In* (pp. 277–93) **38.**

**9453.** BRADBURY, MALCOLM.    The modern world: ten great writers. *See* **9287.**

**9454.** BROOKS, CLEATH.    *The Waste Land*: a prophetic document. YR (78:2) 318–32.

**9455.** CARPENTER, HUMPHREY.    Poor Tom: Mary Trevelyan's view of T. S. Eliot. Eng (38) 37–52.

**9456.** CARPENTIER, MARTHA CELESTE.    Mother, maid, and witch: Hellenic female archetypes in modern British literature. Unpub. doct. diss., Fordham Univ., 1988. [Abstr. in DA (49) 1807A.]

**9457.** CHANDRAN, K. NARAYANA.    'Shantih' in *The Waste Land*. AL (61:4) 681–3.

**9458.** CHOE, YOUNG-SUNG.    T. S. Eliot si eui du jujae: sowoe wa guwon. (Two themes in T. S. Eliot's poetry: alienation and salvation.) JELL (35) 385–405.

**9459.** COOKSON, LINDA; LOUGHREY, BRYAN (eds).    Critical essays on *The Waste Land*: T. S. Eliot. Harlow: Longman, 1988. pp. 155. (Longman literature guides.)

**9460.** CRANE, DAVID.    On Eliot's *Four Quartets*. Durham: New Century Press, 1985. pp. 150. Rev. by Sylvie Bruce in DUJ (81:1) 1988, 171–2.

**9461.** CRAWFORD, ROBERT.    The savage and the city in the work of T. S. Eliot. (Bibl. 1988, 7318.) Rev. by Frank McCombie in NQ (36:2) 263–4; by Ronald Bush in MP (87:1) 104–6.

**9462.** DALE, ALZINA STONE.    T. S. Eliot: the philosopher poet. Wheaton, Il.: Shaw, 1988. pp. 209. Rev. by Peter Milward in ChrisL (38:3) 83–4.

**9463.** DONOGHUE, DENIS.    The idea of a Christian society. YR (78:2) 218–34.

**9464.** DOUGLASS, PAUL.    Bergson, Eliot, and American literature. (Bibl. 1988, 7321.) Rev. by William Harmon in SewR (96:1) 1988, 108–9; by Peter Lamarque in YES (19) 355–7; by Claus Daufenbach in arcadia (24:3) 327–9; by Alan Robinson in RES (39:155) 1988, 463–4.

**9465.** ELIOT, VALERIE (ed.).    The letters of T. S. Eliot: vol. 1, 1898–1922. (Bibl. 1988, 7324.) Rev. by Martin Scofield in Eng (38) 267–72; by Robert Spoo in AL (61:3) 463–5; by Sanford Schwartz in NEQ (62:3) 445–7; by James Longenback in HLQ (52:3) 421–32; by Dominic Manganiello in ChrisL (39:1) 104–5; by Neville Braybrooke in UES (27:2) 36–8.

**9466.** FADDUL, ATIF YUSUF.    A comparative study of the poetics of T. S. Eliot and Adunis. Unpub. doct. diss., Univ. of Pennsylvania, 1988. [Abstr. in DA (50) 132A.]

**9467.** FOKKEMA, DOUWE.    Thomas Stearns Eliot. *In* (pp. 75–101) DOUWE FOKKEMA and ELRUD IBSCH, Modernist conjectures: a mainstream in European literature 1910–1940. London: Hurst, 1987. pp. xii, 330. Rev. by Naomi Segal in NC (8) 178–80.

**9468.** FROULA, CHRISTINE.    Eliot's Grail quest; or, The lover, the police, and *The Waste Land*. YR (78:2) 235–53.

**9469.** GORDON, LYNDALL.    Eliot's new life. (Bibl. 1988, 7329.) Rev. by Sanford Schwartz in NEQ (62:3) 447–9; by Stephen Watson in Upstream (7:2) 59–61.

**9470.** GRABES, HERBERT.    Deliberate intertextuality: the function of quotation and allusion in the early poetry of T. S. Eliot. *In* (pp. 139–52) **42.**

**9471.** HARMON, WILLIAM.    A dry season. SewR (96:1) 1988, 105–12 (review-article).

**9472.** HECHT, ANTHONY.    The first eighteen lines of *The Waste Land*. YR (78:2) 202–9.

**9473.** HELMLING, STEVEN.    The success and failure of T. S. Eliot. SewR (96:1) 1988, 55–76.

**9474.** —— T. S. Eliot and Ralph Ellison: insiders, outsiders, and cultural authority. SoR (25:4) 841–58.

**9475.** HINCHLIFFE, ARNOLD P. (ed.).    T. S. Eliot: plays: a casebook. (Bibl. 1987, 10519.) Rev. by Georges Bas in EA (42:2) 228–9.

**9476.** HONG, KEE-JONG.    T. S. Eliot wa hyungisang si eui buwhal. (T. S. Eliot and the rebirth of metaphysical poems.) UJH (34) 143–62.

**9477.** HOUGHTON, R. L.    Eliot's first quartet. CamQ (18:3) 239–70.

**9478.** —— *The Waste Land* revisited. CamQ (18:1) 34–62.

**9479.** JACOBSON, DAN.    Of time and poetry. *See* **6900.**

**9480.** KADOKURA, YASUO.    T. S. Eliot to Irving Babbitt. (T. S. Eliot and Irving Babbitt.) Tokyo: Apollon. pp. 266.

**9481.** KEARNS, CLEO MCNELLY.    T. S. Eliot and Indic traditions: a study in poetry and belief. (Bibl. 1988, 7339.) Rev. by William Harmon in SewR (96:1) 1988, 110–11.

**9482.** KERMODE, FRANK.    The last classic. YR (78:2) 147–65.

**9483.** LITZ, A. WALTON.    The allusive poet: Eliot and his sources. YR (78:2) 254–64.

**9484.** —— Strange meetings: Eliot, Pound, and Laforgue. *In* (pp. 146–52) **45.**

**9485.** LONGENBACH, JAMES. Modernist poetics of history: Pound, Eliot, and the sense of the past. Princeton, NJ: Princeton UP, 1987. pp. xviii, 279. Rev. by Lawrence S. Rainey in MP (87:1) 106–11.

**9486.** McDIARMID, LUCY. Eliot: the dead, the living, and the end of poetry. YR (78:2) 265–78.

**9487.** MAGOON, JOSEPH. Bibliography of writings about T.S. Eliot for the years 1970 to 1987. Bournemouth: Magoon. pp. xi, 95 (in various pagings).

**9488.** MANGANIELLO, DOMINIC. T. S. Eliot and Dante. Basingstoke: Macmillan. pp. x, 212.

**9489.** MASON, H. A. The Lithuanian whore in *The Waste Land*. CamQ (18:1) 63–72.

**9490.** MENAGHAN, JOHN MICHAEL. Text as stage: Donne, Browning, Eliot and the idea of the 'dramatic'. *See* **4412.**

**9491.** MENAND, LOUIS. Discovering Modernism: T. S. Eliot and his context. (Bibl. 1988, 7350.) Rev by William Harmon in SewR (96:1) 1988, 109; by Ruth Pulik in UES (27:2) 38–9.

**9492.** MERRILL, JAMES. *The Love Song of J. Alfred Prufrock*. YR (78:2) 209–10.

**9493.** MORRISON, JAMES EMERSON. The last testament and the Modernist imagination. Unpub. doct. diss., State Univ. of New York at Buffalo, 1988. [Abstr. in DA (49) 3733A.]

**9494.** MURATA, SHUNICHI. T. S. Eliot no fuukei ni tsuite. (T. S. Eliot's landscape.) SEL (66:1) 17–32.

**9495.** OLNEY, JAMES. T. S. Eliot and the interpretation of experience: a slightly polemical inquiry. SoR (25:2) 503–13.

**9496.** —— (ed.). T. S. Eliot: essays from the *Southern Review*. Oxford: Clarendon Press, 1988. pp. xiv, 351.

**9497.** OZICK, CYNTHIA. A critic at large: T. S. Eliot at 101. NY, 20 Nov., 119–54.

**9498.** PARK, TAE-RYONG. T. S. Eliot munhak eui heuiseng gwa guwon eui sasang yeongu. (A study of the theme of salvation through sacrifice in T. S. Eliot's literature.) Unpub. doct. diss., Dongguk Univ., Seoul.

**9499.** PATRIDES, C. A. T. S. Eliot: alliances of levity and seriousness. SewR (96:1) 1988, 77–94.

**9500.** PLASA, C. A. The economy of revision: Keats, Browning and T. S. Eliot. *See* **6386.**

**9501.** RAINEY, LAWRENCE S. The price of Modernism: reconsidering the publication of *The Waste Land*. *See* **458.**

**9502.** REEVES, GARETH. T. S. Eliot: a Virgilian poet. Basingstoke: Macmillan. pp. vii, 181.

**9503.** —— T. S. Eliot's Virgilian hauntings: *La Figlia che Piange* and the *Aeneid*. NC (7) 113–24.

**9504.** RICKS, CHRISTOPHER. T. S. Eliot and prejudice. (Bibl. 1988, 7361.) Rev. by Hugh Haughton in TLS, 17 Mar., 285–6.

**9505.** SCHMIDT, GERD. Sweeneys düstere Begleiter. LJGG (30) 195–209.

**9506.** SCHNACKENBERG, GJERTRUD.  *Marina.* YR (78:2) 210–15.

**9507.** SCHWARTZ, SANFORD.  The matrix of Modernism: Pound, Eliot, and early twentieth-century thought. (Bibl. 1988, 7365.) Rev. by Robert Crawford in RES (38:151) 1987, 418–19.

**9508.** SCHWEIK, ROBERT C.  T. S. Eliot's *Four Quartets* and the uses of 'referred forms'. Cithara (28:2) 43–64.

**9509.** SCOFIELD, MARTIN.  T. S. Eliot: the poems. (Bibl. 1988, 7366.) Rev. by Frank McCombie in NQ (36:4) 541–4; by Julian D. Gill in JAStud (23:1) 166–7.

**9510.** SHUSTERMAN, RICHARD.  Aesthetic education or aesthetic ideology: T. S. Eliot on art's moral critique. PhilL (13:1) 96–114.

**9511.** —— T. S. Eliot and the philosophy of criticism. (Bibl. 1988, 7369.) Rev. by John Xiros Cooper in AL (61:1) 137–8; by Ronald Bush in ELN (27:1) 74–7.

**9512.** SKAFF, WILLIAM.  The philosophy of T. S. Eliot: from skepticism to a surrealist poetic, 1909–1927. (Bibl. 1988, 7374.) Rev. by William Harmon in SewR (96:1) 1988, 105–8; by Peter Lamarque in YES (19) 355–7.

**9513.** SÖDERLIND, JOHANNES.  Immediate phrase repetition in language and in music. *In* (pp. 345–54) **24.**

**9514.** SULTAN, STANLEY.  Eliot, Joyce and company. (Bibl. 1988, 7375.) Rev. by Jean-Michel Rabaté in EA (42:3) 351–2; by Deirdre Byrne in UES (27:1) 41–2; by Hugh Haughton in TLS, 17 Mar., 286; by Joseph Buttigieg in JJQ (26:2) 287–91.

**9515.** SVARNY, ERIK.  'The men of 1914': T. S. Eliot and early Modernism. *See* **7947.**

**9516.** THOMAS, DAVID LEE.  Loss, mourning and the vatic dispersal of self in the long poems of Whitman, Eliot, Pound, Berryman and Lowell. *See* **7665.**

**9517.** TOMLIN, E. W. F.  T. S. Eliot: a friendship. London: Routledge, 1988. pp. vii, 241. Rev. by Robert Crawford in NQ (36:4) 541.

**9518.** WAJIMA, SHIRO.  T. S. Eliot no shi to shinjitsu. (Truth and the poetry of T. S. Eliot.) Tokyo: Takashima. pp. viii, 264, 12.

**9519.** WESTENDORP, TJEBBE.  How pleasant to meet Mr Eliot! An account of a forgotten interview. *In* (pp. 173–6) **23.**

**9520.** WHITEHEAD, JOHN.  T. S. Eliot and Edgar Wallace. NQ (36:2) 203–4.

**9521.** WILBER, RICHARD.  *Ash Wednesday.* YR (78:2) 215–17.

**9522.** WINTLE, SARAH.  Wagner and *The Waste Land* — again. Eng (38:162) 227–50.

### Stanley Elkin

**9523.** PENZENSTADLER, JOAN ELIZABETH.  Mythological mapping in recent American fiction. Unpub. doct. diss., Texas A&M Univ., 1988. [Abstr. in DA (50) 686–7A.]

### Ralph Ellison

**9524.** BELL, BERNARD W.  The Afro-American novel: and its tradition. *See* **8182.**

**9525.** BENTSON, KIMBERLY (ed.).    Speaking for you: the vision of Ralph Ellison. Washington, DC: Howard UP, 1988. pp. 438. Rev. by Maurice J. Bennett in BkW, 12 Feb., 10.

**9526.** HARPER, PHILLIP BRIAN.    'To become one and yet many': psychic fragmentation and aesthetic synthesis in Ralph Ellison's *Invisible Man*. BALF (23:4) 681–700.

**9527.** HELMLING, STEVEN.    T. S. Eliot and Ralph Ellison: insiders, outsiders, and cultural authority. *See* **9474.**

**9528.** LYONS, ELEANOR.    Ellison and the twentieth-century American scholar. *See* **6813.**

**9529.** MARX, STEVEN.    Beyond hibernation: Ralph Ellison's 1982 version of *Invisible Man*. BALF (23:4) 701–21.

**9530.** NADEL, ALAN.    Invisible criticism: Ralph Ellison and the American canon. (Bibl. 1988, 7384.) Rev. by Rita R. Dandridge in AL (61:1) 128–30; by Elizabeth A. Schultz in AmerS (29:2) 1988, 96.

**9531.** O'MEALLY, ROBERT (ed.).    New essays on *Invisible Man*. (Bibl. 1988, 7385.) Rev. by Ralph Willett in NQ (36:4) 560–1.

**9532.** SMITH, ANGELEAN VANDORA.    Patterns of authenticity: a search for self in American novels. Unpub. doct. diss., Emory Univ. [Abstr. in DA (50) 948A.] (*Invisible Man, One Flew Over the Cuckoo's Nest, The Bluest Eye, The Bell Jar, The Catcher in the Rye.*)

**9533.** STROUT, CUSHING.    Going into Ellison territory. BALF (23:4) 808–14.

## Buchi Emecheta

**9534.** EMENYONU, ERNEST N.    Technique and language in Buchi Emecheta's *The Bride Price, The Slave Girl* and *The Joys of Motherhood*. JCL (23:1) 1988, 130–41.

**9535.** KATRAK, KETU H.    Womanhood/motherhood: variations on a theme in selected novels of Buchi Emecheta. JCL (22:1) 1987, 159–70.

## Nora Ephron

**9536.** LEONARDI, SUSAN J.    Recipes for reading: summer pasta, lobster à la Riseholme, and key lime pie. *See* **9090.**

## Louise Erdrich

**9537.** MATCHIE, THOMAS.    *Love Medicine*: a female *Moby-Dick*. *See* **7237.**

## St John Ervine

**9538.** CRONIN, JOHN (ed.).    Selected plays of St John Ervine. Gerrards Cross: Smythe, 1988. pp. 387. Rev. by John Boyd in Fortnight (272) 21.

## Louis Esson

**9539.** BLAIR, RON.    Yeats lights the candles. Westerly (34:2) 41–9.

**9540.** McCALLUM, JOHN.    Irish memories and Australian hopes: William Butler Yeats and Louis Esson. Westerly (34:2) 33–40.

## Caradoc Evans

**9541.** HARRIS, L. J.    The early career of Caradoc Evans. Unpub. doct. diss., Univ. of Wales, 1986. [Abstr. in IT (39:1) 35.]

## William Everson ('Brother Antonius')

**9542.** BARTLETT, LEE.    William Everson: the life of Brother Antonius. New York: New Directions, 1988. pp. 288. Rev. by Ann Charters in AL (61:2) 322–3.

## Nuruddin Farah

**9543.** BARDOLPH, JACQUELINE. Time and history in Nuruddin Farah's *Close Sesame*. JCL (24:1) 193–206.

**9544.** SPARROW, FIONA. Telling the story yet again: oral traditions in Nuruddin Farah's fiction. JCL (24:1) 164–72.

**9545.** TURFAN, BARBARA. Opposing dictatorship: a comment on Nuruddin Farah's *Variations on the Theme of an African Dictatorship*. JCL (24:1) 173–84.

**9546.** WRIGHT, DEREK. Unwritable realities: the orality of power in Nuruddin Farah's *Sweet and Sour Milk*. JCL (24:1) 185–92.

## J. G. Farrell

**9547.** FERNS, CHRIS. 'First as tragedy, then as farce': J. G. Farrell's retelling of history. DalR (67:2/3) 1987, 275–85.

**9548.** HARTVEIT, LARS. The 'jolting passage over switched points of history' and the experience of disclocation in J. G. Farrell's *The Singapore Grip*. EngS (70:6) 566–80.

## James T. Farrell

**9549.** MURPHY, JACQUELINE L. The silence of history: the later works of James T. Farrell in cultural context. Unpub. doct. diss., Temple Univ. [Abstr. in DA (50) 1659A.]

## William Faulkner

**9550.** ANDERSON, CARL L. Faulkner's *Was*: 'a deadlier purpose than simple pleasure'. AL (61:3) 414–28.

**9551.** BARKER, STEPHEN. From old gold to I.O.U.s: Ike McCaslin's debased genealogical coin. FJ (3:1) 1987, 2–25.

**9552.** BASSETT, JOHN E. Faulkner in the eighties: crosscurrents in criticism. CLit (16:1) 1–27.

**9553.** BOWMAN, MICHAEL STUART. The Yoknapatawpha theatre: performance, popular culture, and authority in the Faulknerian novel. Unpub. doct. diss., Northwestern Univ. [Abstr. in DA (50) 945–6A.]

**9554.** BROOKS, CLEANTH. On the prejudices, predilections, and firm beliefs of William Faulkner. (Bibl. 1988, 7398.) Rev. by Ian Jackson in NQ (36:2) 272–3; by David Rogers in JAStud (23:1) 140–2.

**9555.** BROWN, CALVIN S. No Faulkner moratorium needed. SewR (96:2) 271–9 (review-article).

**9556.** CHAPPELL, CHARLES M. Faulkner's arch-villain: Eupheus ('Doc') Hines. CLit (16:1) 66–74.

**9557.** CLARKE, DEBORAH. Gender, race, and language in *Light in August*. AL (61:3) 398–413.

**9558.** COHEN, PHILIP. A previously unpublished Faulkner letter. CLit (16:1) 103–5.

**9559.** CONNOR, W. M. Vardaman Bundren, the child in William Faulkner's *As I Lay Dying*. Unpub. M.Litt. thesis, Trinity Coll. Dublin, 1985–86. [Abstr. in IT (36:3) 915.]

**9560.** CRANE, JOHN KENNY. The Yoknapatawpha chronicle of Gavin Stephens. Cranbury, NJ: Susquehanna UP; London: Assoc. UP's, 1988. pp. 308. Rev. by Bruce Kawin in AL (61:2) 313–14; by David Rogers in JAStud (23:3) 501.

**9561.** Desmond, John F.  The scriptural tradition and Faulkner's gnostic style. SoR (25:3) 563–8.

**9562.** Dowling, David.  William Faulkner. Basingstoke: Macmillan. pp. xi, 183. (Macmillan modern novelists.)

**9563.** Duvall, John N.  Paternity in *Pylon*: 'some little sign'? FJ (3:1) 1987, 39–51.

**9564.** —— Silencing women in *The Fire and the Hearth* and *Tomorrow*. CLit (16:1) 75–82.

**9565.** Duytschaever, Joris.  Faulkner's *Light in August* and the vicissitudes of narcissism: the case of Gail Hightower. *In* (pp. 99–115) **2.**

**9566.** Engler, Bernd.  Kontingenz und Kohärenz. Zur Problematik fiktionaler Sinnkonstitution in William Faulkners *Absalom, Absalom!*. LJGG (29) 1988, 159–87.

**9567.** Ford, Daniel G.  New directions in Faulkner studies. SoLJ (22:1) 128–34.

**9568.** Fowler, Doreen; Abadie, Ann J. (eds).  Faulkner and humor: Faulkner and Yoknapatawpha, 1984. (Bibl. 1986, 11876.) Rev. by Calvin S. Brown in SewR (96:2) 1988, 273–5.

**9569.** Garfield, Deborah.  To love as 'fiery ancients' would: eros, narrative and Rosa Coldfield in *Absalom, Absalom!*. SoLJ (22:1) 61–79.

**9570.** Garner, Linda Mebane.  Twentieth-century marble goddesses: Victorian and modernist portrayals of the antebellum Southern lady in Stark Young's *So Red the Rose*, William Faulkner's *The Unvanquished* and *Absalom, Absalom!*, and Margaret Walker's *Jubilee*. Unpub. doct. diss., Univ. of Missouri–Columbia, 1987. [Abstr. in DA (49) 1801A.]

**9571.** Gauch, Patricia Lee.  Faulkner and beyond: a biography of Joan Williams. Unpub. doct. diss., Drew Univ., 1988. [Abstr. in DA (49) 1801A.]

**9572.** Gresset, Michel.  A Faulkner chronology. (Bibl. 1986, 11879.) Rev. by Calvin S. Brown in SewR (96:2) 1988, 272–3.

**9573.** —— Faulkner's fiction, 1919–1936. Durham, NC; London: Duke UP. pp. 305. Rev. by David Rogers in JAStud (23:3) 500–1.

**9574.** —— Ohashi, Kenzaburo (eds).  Faulkner: after the Nobel Prize. (Bibl. 1987, 10614.) Rev. by Martin Kreiswirth in AL (61:1) 125–6; by David Rogers in JAStud (23:3) 502.

**9575.** Grimwood, Michael.  Heart in conflict: Faulkner's struggles with vocation. (Bibl. 1988, 7411.) Rev. by Peter Verney in DalR (67:2/3) 1987, 375–7; by Leonard Butts in StudN (20:4) 1988, 430–1.

**9576.** Harrison, Robert L.  Aviation lore in Faulkner. (Bibl. 1987, 10619.) Rev. by Robert Dale Parker in MLR (84:1) 149.

**9577.** Hasegawa, Yoshio.  William Faulkner no bungaku. (The literature of William Faulkner.) Tokyo: Kirihara. pp. vi, 270.

**9578.** Herring, Gina.  Mental retardation and William Faulkner's ironic vision. Unpub. doct. diss., Auburn Univ., 1988. [Abstr. in DA (50) 2658A.]

**9579.** Ho, WEN-CHING.   Miscegenation in William Faulkner: a synecdoche for slavery/caste system. Unpub. doct. diss., Univ. of Michigan. [Abstr. in DA (49) 1658A.]

**9580.** HOFFMAN, DANIEL.   Faulkner's country matters: folklore and fable in Yoknapatawpha. Baton Rouge: Louisiana State UP. pp. xviii, 181. Rev. by Sanford Pinsker in GaR (43:4) 798–800.

**9581.** HÖNNIGHAUSEN, LOTHAR.   William Faulkner: the art of stylization in his early graphic and literary work. pp. xiv, 215. (Bibl. 1987, 10620, where pagination incorrect.) Rev. by Milton A. Cohen in AL (61:3) 496–7.

**9582.** —— (ed.).   Faulkner's discourse: an international symposium. Tübingen: Niemeyer. pp. xix, 292.

**9583.** JOHNSON, KAREN RAMSAY.   Gender, sexuality, and the artist in Faulkner's novels. AL (61:1) 1–15.

**9584.** JUERGENSEN, JAMES E., SR.   Nihilism and religion in Faulkner's prose. Unpub. doct. diss., Kent State Univ., 1988. [Abstr. in DA (50) 1658A.]

**9585.** KARL, FREDERICK R.   William Faulkner: American writer: a biography. London: Faber & Faber; New York: Weidenfeld & Nicolson. pp. xvi, 1131. Rev. by Sanford Pinsker in GaR (43:4) 796–8; by Judith L. Sensibar in BW, 21 May, 6; by John W. Aldridge in NYTB, 14 May, 3; by Paul Binding in Listener (122) 31 Aug., 24–5.

**9586.** KINNEY, ARTHUR F.   The family-centred nature of Faulkner's world. CLit (16:1) 83–102.

**9587.** KOYAMA, TOSHIO.   William Faulkner no tanpen shōsetsu no sekai. (The world of William Faulkner's short stories.) Tokyo: Yamaguchi. pp. iv, 432.

**9588.** LALONDE, CHRIS.   Story, myth, rite of passage, and *Mosquitoes*. FJ (3:1) 1987, 26–38.

**9589.** MACHINEK, ANNA.   William Faulkner and the gothic tradition. KN (36:2) 105–14.

**9590.** McMASTER, MARIAN BABIRECKI.   Jorge Luis Borges, traductor de William Faulkner. Unpub. doct. diss., Middlebury College, 1988. [Abstr. in DA (50) 942A.]

**9591.** MICHEL, PIERRE.   Quentin Compson and the narrative perspective in Faulkner's *Absalom, Absalom!*. In (pp. 193–202) **42**.

**9592.** —— Shreve McCannon: the outside voice in *Absalom, Absalom!*. In (pp. 117–26) **2**.

**9593.** MILLGATE, MICHAEL (ed.).   New essays on *Light in August*. (Bibl. 1987, 10650.) Rev. by David Rogers in JAStud (23:3) 502–3.

**9594.** MINTER, DAVID (ed.).   *The Sound and the Fury*: an authoritative text, backgrounds and contexts, criticism. New York; London: Norton, 1987. pp. xiii, 417. (Norton critical editions.) Rev. by David Rogers in JAStud (23:3) 502; by Douglas Hewitt in NQ (36:2) 273–4.

**9595.** MORELAND, RICHARD C.   Antisemitism, humor and rage in Faulkner's *The Hamlet*. FJ (3:1) 1987, 52–70.

**9596.** MORTIMER, GAIL L.   Faulkner's rhetoric of loss: a study in perception and meaning. (Bibl. 1987, 10652.) Rev. by Robert Dale Parker in MLR (84:1) 148.

**9597.** O'DONNELL, PATRICK.   *Sub rosa*: voice, body, and history in *Absalom, Absalom!*. CLit (16:1) 28–47.

**9598.** ORR, JOHN.   The making of the twentieth-century novel: Lawrence, Joyce, Faulkner, and beyond. *See* **8355.**

**9599.** PARKER, ROBERT DALE.   Faulkner and the novelistic imagination. (Bibl. 1988, 7429.) Rev. by Calvin S. Brown in SewR (96:2) 1988, 277–9.

**9600.** PETTEY, HOMER B.   Reading and raping in *Sanctuary*. FJ (3:1) 1987, 71–84.

**9601.** PETTEY, HOMER BOYD.   Faulkner and fetishism. Unpub. doct. diss., Univ. of Arizona. [Abstr. in DA (50) 1306A.]

**9602.** PHILLIPS, GENE D.   Fiction, films, and Faulkner: the art of adaptation. *See* **8105.**

**9603.** PHILLIPS, LOUIS.   Answering Faulkner. America (160) 452–3.

**9604.** PINSKER, SANFORD.   Faulkner criticism's inexhaustible voice. GaR (43:4) 795–803 (review-article).

**9605.** POTTER, A. M.   Religion and the literary critic. *See* **8841.**

**9606.** RABBETTS, JOHN.   From Hardy to Faulkner: Wessex to Yoknapatawpha. *See* **6922.**

**9607.** ROSS, STEPHEN M.   Fiction's inexhaustible voice: speech and writing in Faulkner. Athens; London: Georgia UP. pp. xviii, 286. Rev. by Sanford Pinsker in GaR (43:4) 800–2.

**9608.** ROUBEROL, JEAN.   De Falkner à Faulkner: *La rose blanche de Memphis*. *See* **6821.**

**9609.** RUZICKA, WILLIAM T.   Faulkner's fictive architecture: the meaning of place in the Yoknapatawpha novels. Ann Arbor, MI; London: UMI Research Press, 1987. pp. viii, 157. (Studies in modern literature, 67.)

**9610.** SAPORTA, MARC.   Les erres du faucon: une psychobiographie de William Faulkner. Paris: Seghers. pp. 411. (Collection biographie.)

**9611.** SHERRY, CHARLES.   Being otherwise: nature, history, and tragedy in *Absalom, Absalom!*. AQ (45:3) 47–76.

**9612.** SKEI, HANS HANSSEN.   William Faulkner: the novelist as short story writer: a study of William Faulkner's short fiction. pp. 332. (Bibl. 1987, 10677, where pagination incorrect and second subtitle omitted.) Rev. by Calvin S. Brown in SewR (96:2) 275–6; by Richard H. King in RES (38:151) 1987, 412–13.

**9613.** SLAUGHTER, CAROLYN NORMAN.   *As I Lay Dying*: demise of vision. AL (61:1) 16–30.

**9614.** SNEAD, JAMES A.   Figures of division: William Faulkner's major novels. (Bibl. 1988, 7441.) Rev. by Robinson Blann in StudN (20:4) 1988, 440–3.

**9615.** TEBBETTS, TERRELL L.   Shadows of Jung: a psychological approach to *Light in August*. SoLJ (22:1) 80–95.

**9616.** VOLPE, EDMOND L. *Dry September*: metaphor for despair. CLit (16:1) 60–5.

**9617.** WADLINGTON, WARWICK. Reading Faulknerian tragedy. (Bibl. 1987, 10683.) Rev. by O. B. Emerson in AL (61:1) 124–5.

**9618.** ZEITLIN, MICHAEL. Faulkner and *Ulysses*: a psychoanalytic inquiry. Unpub. doct. diss., Univ. of Toronto, 1988. [Abstr. in DA (50) 137A.]

**9619.** ZENDER, KARL F. Character and symbol in *Barn Burning*. CLit (16:1) 48–59.

**9620.** —— The crossing of the ways: William Faulkner, the South, and the modern world. New Brunswick, NJ: Rutgers UP. pp. xiv, 206. Rev. by Carolyn Norman in AL (61:4) 708–9; by Sanford Pinsker in GaR (43:4) 802–3.

### Brian Fawcett

**9621.** FAWCETT, BRIAN. Some proposals for the reification of poetry in Canada. *In* (pp. 92–103) **12.**

### Raymond Federman

**9622.** KUTNIK, JERZY. The novel as performance: the fiction of Ronald Sukenick and Raymond Federman. Carbondale: Southern Illinois UP, 1986. pp. xxviii, 275. (Crosscurrents: modern critiques, ser. 3: 7.) Rev. by Christoph Bode in GRM (39) 365–7.

**9623.** —— The reader's plight in Raymond Federman's fiction. *In* (pp. 223–34) **36.**

**9624.** RALIAN, ANTOANETA (introd.). Indoita vibraţie; Zîmbete în Washington Square. (The two-fold vibration; Smiles on Washington Square.) Bucharest: Univers. pp. 324. Rev. by Radu Surdelescu in RomLit, 7 Sept., 20.

**9625.** SURDELESCU, RADU. Scenariul ipotezelor şi ipotezele scenariu-lui. (The scenario of conjecture and hypothetical scenarios.) RomLit, 7 Sept., 20 (review-article). (*The Two-fold Vibration, Smiles on Washington Square.*)

### Harvey Fergusson

**9626.** GISH, ROBERT F. Frontier's end: the life and literature of Harvey Fergusson. Lincoln: Nebraska UP, 1988. pp. xv, 363. Rev. by Louis Owens in AL (61:4) 712–13; by Peter Wild in Journal of the Southwest (31:3) 433–5.

### Lawrence Ferlinghetti

**9627.** BUSH, GLEN. Revolutionary visions: Blake, Ginsberg and Ferlinghetti. *See* **5061.**

### Lloyd Fernando

**9628.** KOH TAI ANN. The Empire's orphans: stayers and quitters in *A Bend in the River* and *Scorpion Orchid*. *In* (pp. 38–53) **19.**

### Timothy Findley

**9629.** SHIELDS, E. F. 'The perfect voice': Mauberley as narrator in Timothy Findley's *Famous Last Words*. CanL (119) 1988, 84–98.

**9630.** SPARLING, DON. Timothy Findley's fictions. *In* (p. 41) **6.**

### F. Scott Fitzgerald

**9631.** ANDERSON, HILTON. *Daisy Miller* and *The Hotel Child*: a Jamesian influence on F. Scott Fitzgerald. *See* **7044.**

**9632.** —— Weight and balance in *The Great Gatsby*. ELN (27:1) 58–60.
**9633.** BERMAN, RONALD. 'Oh, science and art, and all that': reflections on *The Great Gatsby*. JAE (23:3) 85–95.
**9634.** BRUCCOLI, MATTHEW J. (ed.). New essays on *The Great Gatsby*. (Bibl. 1988, 7458.) Rev. by Robert Bellflower in RES (39:154) 1988, 333–4; by Harold Beaver in YES (19) 354–5; by James H. Justus in AL (59:1) 1987, 129–32.
**9635.** CROFT, JULIAN. The federal and national impulse in Australian literature, 1890–1958. *See* **9140.**
**9636.** DAVISON, RICHARD ALLAN. *Of Mice and Men* and *McTeague*: Steinbeck, Fitzgerald, and Frank Norris. SAF (17:2) 219–26.
**9637.** DOLAN, MARC. 'True stories' of 'the Lost Generation': an exploration of narrative truth in memoirs of Hemingway, Cowley, and Fitzgerald. *See* **9338.**
**9638.** DONALDSON, SCOTT. Fool for love: a biography of F. Scott Fitzgerald. New York: Delta. pp. xi, 262. Rev. in BkW, 17 Sept., 17.
**9639.** FRYER, SARAH BEEBE. Fitzgerald's New Women: harbingers of change. Ann Arbor, MI; London: UMI Research Press, 1988. pp. 119. (Studies in modern literature, 86.) Rev. by Robert Wexelblatt in AL (61:2) 305–6; by Linda Miller in SAF (17:2) 253–4.
**9640.** —— Fitzgerald's New Women: harbingers of change. Unpub. doct. diss., Michigan State Univ., 1988. [Abstr. in DA (49) 2658A.]
**9641.** MAGISTRALE, TONY; DICKERSON, MARY JANE. The language of time in *The Great Gatsby*. CLit (16:2) 117–28.
**9642.** SMITH, FELIPE. The dark side of paradise: race and ethnicity in the novels of F. Scott Fitzgerald. Unpub. doct. diss., Louisiana State Univ. and Agricultural and Mechanical College, 1988. [Abstr. in DA (50) 1307A.]
**9643.** TOWN, CAREN J. 'Uncommunicable forever': Nick's dilemma in *The Great Gatsby*. TSLL (31:4) 497–513.
**9644.** WESELIŃSKI, ANDRZEJ. F. Scott Fitzgerald: the novelist looks at Hollywood. *See* **8156.**
**9645.** WESTON, ELIZABETH ANNE. The international theme in F. Scott Fitzgerald's literature. Unpub. doct. diss., New York Univ., 1988. [Abstr. in DA (49) 2662–3A.]

### John Gould Fletcher

**9646.** CARPENTER, LUCAS; RUDOLPH, LEIGHTON (eds). Selected poems. Fayetteville: Arkansas UP. pp. xi, 340. Rev. by Dick Davis in TLS, 5 May, 478.

### Horton Foote

**9647.** EDGERTON, GARY. A visit to the imaginary landscape of Harrison, Texas: sketching the film career of Horton Foote. *See* **8027.**

### Shelby Foote

**9648.** CARTER, WILLIAM (ed.). Conversations with Shelby Foote. Jackson; London: Mississippi UP. pp. xviii, 276. (Literary conversations.)

### Hulbert Footner

**9649.** LYBECK, ALVIN. Call of the wild. AD (22:4) 406–19.

## 'Ford Madox Ford' (Ford Madox Hueffer)
**9650.** DOOLEY, MICHAEL.   Readers and writers. Ford's narrative technique in stories from the past: *Zeppelin Nights*. JSSE (13) 39–55.
**9651.** LINDBERG-SEYERSTED, BRITA.   Ford Madox Ford and his relationship to Stephen Crane and Henry James. *See* **6560**.
**9652.** RITTENBERG, DAVID JONATHAN.   Ford Madox Ford: culture and society in Edwardian England. Unpub. doct. diss., Columbia Univ., 1988. [Abstr. in DA (49) 3035A.]
**9653.** SKINNER, JOHN.   Ford Madox Ford's *The Good Soldier*: a narratological *cas limite*. JNT (19:3) 287–999.
## 'Leslie Ford' ('David Frome', 'Brenda Conrad', Zenith Jones Brown)
**9654.** CLEARY, MARYELL.   Money makes the world go around. AD (22:2) 158–65.
## R. A. D. Ford
**9655.** MUNTON, ANN.   R. A. D. Ford, poet and diplomat: a poetry of tact. CanL (120) 133–42.
## Maria Irene Fornes
**9656.** AUSTIN, GAYLE.   The madwoman in the spotlight: plays of Maria Irene Fornes. *In* (pp. 76–85) **39**.
## E. M. Forster
**9657.** ABE, SACHIKO.   E. M. Forster kenkyu. (A study of E. M. Forster.) Tokyo: New Current International. pp. x, 274.
**9658.** BEYER, KATHLEEN COLLINS.   Mutability as theme: *Marianne Thornton, Goldsworthy Lowes Dickinson*, and *The Hill of Devi*. CEACrit (51:4) 64–74.
**9659.** DOVER, R. J.   E. M. Forster and the English liberal tradition. Unpub. doct. diss., Univ. of Sussex, 1988. [Abstr. in IT (38:4) 1461–2.]
**9660.** FORD, ELIZABETH ANNE.   Nursery tea: child characters in the novels of Virginia Woolf and E. M. Forster. Unpub. doct. diss., Kent State Univ. [Abstr. in DA (50) 1663–4A.]
**9661.** GOSCILO, MARGARET.   Ivory–Merchant's *Maurice*: the hero in absentia. *See* **8041**.
**9662.** HERZ, JUDITH SCHERER.   The short narratives of E. M. Forster. New York: St Martin's Press, 1988. (Bibl. 1988, 7487.) Rev. by Claude J. Summers in MP (87:2) 205–9.
**9663.** KIM, YONG-CHOL.   Humanism and E. M. Forster's criticism of fiction. JELL (35) 695–715.
**9664.** KIRKPATRICK, B. J.   A bibliography of E. M. Forster. (Bibl. 1986, 12019.) Rev. by Tony Brown in RES (38:151) 1987, 408–9.
**9665.** LAGO, MARY.   Calendar of the letters of E. M. Forster. (Bibl. 1985, 10848.) Rev. by John Batchelor in RES (38:149) 1987, 103–5.
**9666.** —— FURBANK, P. N. (eds).   Selected letters of E. M. Forster: vol. 2, 1921–1970. (Bibl. 1988, 10746.) Rev. by John Batchelor in RES (38:149) 1987, 102–5.
**9667.** LUBICZ-PYRZOWSKA, BARBARA.   Perspectives of semiotization in E. M. Forster's short stories in the light of genological and supragenological categories. *In* (pp. 7–18) **57**.

**9668.** LUBICZ-PYRZOWSKA, BARBARA. Perspektywy semiotyzacji opowiadań E. M. Forstera w świetle kategorii gatunkowych i pondagatunkowych. *In* (pp. 178–93) **36.**

**9669.** McGUINESS, ILONA MARIA KUEHNHACKL. Only connections: rhetoric as collaborative impulse in E. M. Forster's non-fiction. Unpub. doct. diss., Univ. of Iowa, 1988. [Abstr. in DA (49) 2232A.]

**9670.** MACKLIN, JENNY. Film techniques in *A Room with a View*. *See* **8088.**

**9671.** MEMON, MOHAMMAD ALIM. E. M. Forster's *A Passage to India*: a revaluation. ARIEL (Jamshoro, Pakistan) (13) 1987/88, 55–72.

**9672.** POOLE, ROBERT. Bloomsbury and bicycles. ELH (56:4) 951–66.

**9673.** QUINCE, W. ROHAN. 'To thine own self be true . . .': adapting E. M. Forster's *Maurice* to the screen. *See* **8112.**

**9674.** VARTY, ANNE. E. M. Forster, Arnold Böcklin, and Pan. RES (39:156) 1988, 513–18.

**9675.** WOODS, E. A darkness visible: Gissing, Masterman and the metaphors of class 1880–1914. *See* **6860.**

### John Fowles

**9676.** COOKE, STEWART JON. Received melodies: the new, old novel. *See* **9013.**

**9677.** KERSNOWSKI, FRANK. John Fowles and *The Ebony Tower*. JSSE (13) 57–65.

**9678.** McSWEENEY, KERRY. Four contemporary novelists. (Bibl. 1986, 12039.) Rev. by Paul Tiessen in CanL (115) 1987, 157–9.

**9679.** MICHEL-MICHOT, PAULETTE. Fowles's 'Poor Koko': a metaphor of the quest. *In* (pp. 203–11) **42.**

**9680.** OLIVA CRUZ, JUAN IGNACIO. Parodia y pastiche en la obra de John Fowles. RCEI (18) 221–9.

**9681.** SCRUGGS, CHARLES. Ethical freedom and visual space: filming *The French Lieutenant's Woman*. *See* **8133.**

**9682.** TARBOX, KATHERINE. The art of John Fowles. Athens; London: Georgia UP, 1988. pp. x, 210.

**9683.** WILSON, JOAN MARGARET. Time as the organizing principle in the romances of John Fowles. Unpub. doct. diss., Southern Illinois Univ. at Carbondale, 1988. [Abstr. in DA (50) 1671A.]

### Janet Frame

**9684.** MacLENNAN, CAROL. Dichotomous values in the novels of Janet Frame. JCL (22:1) 1987, 179–89.

### 'Miles Franklin' (Stella Maria Sarah Miles Franklin, 'Brent of Bin Bin', 'Mrs Ogniblat l'Artsau')

**9685.** JONES, NANCY LEE. Reality and the shadow: the adventure of identity in twentieth-century Australian women's fiction. Unpub. doct. diss., Tufts Univ. [Abstr. in DA (50) 1665A.]

**9686.** ROE, JILL. 'Tremenjus good for what ails us': the correspondence of Miles Franklin and C. Hartley Grattan. LCUT (42/43) 1988, 77–101.

**9687.** RUTHERFORD, ANNA.    Miles Franklin: the outside track. *In* (pp. 239–56) **42.**

### Michael Frayn

**9688.** ANTIP, FELICIA.    Inocenții bine intenționați: despre romanele *Spre Sfîrșitul Dimineții* și *Vise Dulci* ale lui Michael Frayn. (Well-intentioned innocents: on the novels *Towards the End of the Morning* and *Sweet Dreams* by Michael Frayn.) RomLit, 5 Jan., 22.

### Anne French

**9689.** WEVERS, LYDIA.    'A partial version of the facts': a conversation between Anne French and Lydia Wevers. Landfall (43:3) 310–27.

### Brian Friel

**9690.** FITZGIBBON, GERALD.    Garnering the facts: unreliable narrators in some plays of Brian Friel. *In* (pp. 53–62) **17.**

**9691.** PILKINGTON, ULICK LIONEL.    Representations of the Northern Ireland crisis in contemporary drama: 1968–80. *See* **9127.**

**9692.** VERSTRAETE, GINETTE.    Brian Friel's drama and the limits of language. *In* (pp. 85–96) **32.**

### Robert Frost

**9693.** BÄCKMAN, SVEN.    Diktarmöte i krigets skugga. (A meeting of poets in the shadow of war.) Lundaforskare föreläser 1988, 36–41.

**9694.** BURNSHAW, STANLEY.    Robert Frost himself. (Bibl. 1987, 10790.) Rev. by Robert Zaller in Agenda (26:3) 65–8.

**9695.** CLARK, JOHN R.    Left on the right track with Robert Frost. NCL (19:1) 10–12.

**9696.** COULTHARD, A. R.    Three wrong turns on Frost's *The Road Not Taken*. NCL (19:3) 11–12.

**9697.** FAGGEN, ROBERT.    Robert Frost and the challenge of Darwin. Unpub. doct. diss., Harvard Univ., 1988. [Abstr. in DA (49) 3026A.]

**9698.** FLEISSNER, ROBERT F.    Robert Frost stonewalls it again: the newly discovered variant lines. *See* **314.**

**9699.** FRATTALI, STEVEN VINCENT.    Across the field: nature and selfhood in the poetry of Robert Frost. Unpub. doct. diss., State Univ. of New York at Binghamton, 1988. [Abstr. in DA (50) 1305A.]

**9700.** HOGGARD, JAMES.    Correcting an error: *The Road Not Taken*. NCL (19:1) 7–8.

**9701.** HOLLAND, NORMAN N.    The brain of Robert Frost: a cognitive approach to literature. New York; London: Routledge, 1988. pp. viii, 200. Rev. by Richard Wakefield in AL (61:3) 488–90.

**9702.** INGEBRETSEN, EDWARD J.    Love's sentence: domesticity as religious discourse in Robert Frost's poetry. ChrisL (39:1) 51–62.

**9703.** KATZ, SANDRA L.    Elinor Frost: a poet's wife. Westfield, MA: Westfield State Coll., Inst. for Massachusetts Studies, 1988. pp. xiv, 193. Rev. by Edward J. Ingebretsen in AL (61:4) 704–7.

**9704.** MONTEIRO, GEORGE.    Robert Frost and the New England Renaissance. Lexington: Kentucky UP, 1988. pp. xii, 176. Rev. by Edward J. Ingebretsen in AL (61:4) 704–7.

**9705.** PERKINS, DAVID.    Robert Frost and romantic irony. SoCR (22:1) 33–7.

**9706.** SCRIMGEOUR, J. D. Another path: an alternative reading of *A Road Not Taken*. NCL (19:1) 8–10.

**9707.** STANLEY-SMITH, J. R. Language, vision and reality: a study of the poetry of Edward Thomas, Robert Frost and Wallace Stevens. Unpub. doct. diss., Univ. of Wales, 1987. [Abstr. in IT (39:1) 29.]

**9708.** STRANDBERG, VICTOR. The Frost–Melville connection. *In* (pp. 17–25) **2.**

**9709.** WALSH, JOHN EVANGELIST. Into my own: the English years of Robert Frost, 1912–1915. (Bibl. 1988, 7545.) Rev. by Edward J. Ingebretsen in AL (61:4) 704–7.

### Athol Fugard

**9710.** ANGOVE, COLEEN. Afrikaner sterotypes and mavericks in selected Fugard plays. SATJ (3:1) 55–68.

**9711.** COLLERAN, JEANNE MARIE. The dissenting writer in South Africa: a rhetorical analysis of the drama of Athol Fugard and the short fiction of Nadine Gordimer. Unpub. doct. diss., Ohio State Univ., 1988. [Abstr. in DA (49) 2655A.]

**9712.** HUBER, WERNER. Transformations of Beckett: the case of Athol Fugard. *See* **9055.**

**9713.** MACKAY, E. A. Antigone and Orestes in the works of Athol Fugard. Theoria (74) 31–42.

### Robin Fulton

**9714.** GUSTAVSSON, BO. Robin Fulton och det visionära seendet. (Robin Fulton and visionary sight.) Horisont (36:6) 74–5.

### Joseph Furphy ('Tom Collins')

**9715.** CROFT, JULIAN. The federal and national impulse in Australian literature 1890–1958. *See* **9140.**

**9716.** ZELLER, ROBERT. 'I hope here be truths': R. G. Howarth as editor of Joseph Furphy. *See* **278.**

### William Gaddis

**9717.** CAMPBELL, GREGOR DUNCAN. Historical consciousness in the fiction of William Gaddis, Thomas Pynchon, and Robert Coover: a reading of *The Recognitions, Gravity's Rainbow,* and *The Public Burning. See* **9331.**

**9718.** JOHNSTON, JOHN. Double-voicing, intertextuality and the pro-liferation of simulacra in William Gaddis's *The Recognitions.* Genre (22:1) 41–67.

**9719.** MOORE, STEVEN DANA. William Gaddis and the alchemy of art: the intellectual traditions behind his novels. Unpub. doct. diss., Rutgers Univ., 1988. [Abstr. in DA (49) 3363A.]

**9720.** PETILLON, PIERRE-YVES. William Gaddis et le babil des ténèbres. Critique (502) 133–53 (review-article).

**9721.** SAFER, ELAINE B. The contemporary American comic epic: the novels of Barth, Pynchon, Gaddis, and Kesey. *See* **9018.**

### Ernest J. Gaines

**9722.** ANTHONY, BOOKER T. The individual and tradition in the fiction of Ernest J. Gaines. Unpub. doct. diss., Ohio State Univ., 1988. [Abstr. in DA (49) 2655–6A.]

**9723.** Griffin, Joseph.    Ernest J. Gaines's good news: sacrifice and redemption in *Of Love and Dust.* MLS (18:3) 1988, 75–85.

### Mavis Gallant

**9724.** Irvine, Lorna.    Starting from the beginning every time. *In* (pp. 246–55) **40.**

**9725.** Rooke, Constance.    Fear of the open heart. *In* (pp. 256–69) **40.**

**9726.** Schaub, Danielle.    Narrative strategies in *Overhead in a Balloon.* JSSE (12) 53–62.

**9727.** Sturgess, Charlotte.    Narrative strategies in *Overhead in a Balloon.* JSSE (12) 45–52.

### John Galsworthy

**9728.** Innes, Christopher.    Granville Barker and Galsworthy: questions of censorship. ModDr (32:3) 331–44.

**9729.** Strahan, Linda Lee.    Comedy and desire: revision in Galsworthy's *The Forsyte Saga.* Unpub. doct. diss., Univ. of California, Riverside, 1988. [Abstr. in DA (49) 1812A.]

**9730.** Watson, Bruce.    The night *The Forsyte Saga* struck back. *See* **8416.**

### John Gardner

**9731.** Berman, Steven David.    The reconstruction of character and culture in the fiction of John Gardner. Unpub. doct. diss., Univ. of Missouri–Columbia, 1988. [Abstr. in DA (49) 3361–2A.]

**9732.** Butts, Leonard.    The novels of John Gardner: making life art as a moral process. Baton Rouge; London: Louisiana State UP, 1988. pp. xxii, 143. Rev. by Susan Strehle in AL (61:1) 130–1.

**9733.** Thomas, Jim.    A changing American family: Cheever, Gardner, Irving, Updike. *See* **9238.**

### Silvana Gardner

**9734.** Hatzimanolis, Efi.    *Big Words, Little Words (Naturally)*: an unnatural reading. Span (29) 21–30.

### Hamlin Garland

**9735.** Rocha, Mark William.    The feminization of failure in American historiography: the case of the invisible drama in the life of Hamlin Garland (1860–1940). Unpub. doct. diss., Univ. of Southern California, 1988. [Abstr. in DA (49) 1804A.]

**9736.** —— Hamlin Garland's temperance play. ALR (21:3) 67–71.

### Alan Garner

**9737.** Elliott, Ralph W. V.    Literary dialect in Chaucer, Hardy, and Alan Garner. *See* **2827.**

### David Gascoyne

**9738.** Benford, Colin T.    David Gascoyne: a bibliography of his works (1929–1985). Ryde: Heritage, 1986. pp. xvi, 148.

### William Gass

**9739.** Eckford-Prossor, Melanie Charlotte.    Ambivalence sustained: William Gass, language theory and the problem of romantic integration in the twentieth century. Unpub. doct. diss., Univ. of California, Los Angeles, 1988. [Abstr. in DA (49) 2220A.]

## Pam Gems

**9740.** CARLSON, SUSAN. Revisionary endings: Pam Gems's *Aunt Mary* and *Camille*. *In* (pp. 103–17) **39.**

## 'Lewis Grassic Gibbon' (James Leslie Mitchell)

**9741.** ANON. An early poem by J. Leslie Mitchell (Lewis Grassic Gibbon). AUR (53:1) 37–40. (*To Marguerite ('Peggy')*.)

## Robert Gibbs

**9742.** DORSCHT, SUSAN RUDY. A space to play in; or, Telling the (w)hole story: the recent poetry of Robert Gibbs. CanL (116) 1988, 87–93.

## Barbara Giles

**9743.** STONE, MICHAEL. Interview with Barbara Giles. *See* **2063.**

## Charlotte Perkins Gilman (Mrs Stetson)

**9744.** FELDSTEIN, RICHARD. Reader, text, and ambiguous referentiality in *The Yellow Wallpaper*. *In* (pp. 269–79) **29.**

**9745.** GOLDEN, CATHERINE. The writing of *The Yellow Wallpaper*: a double palimpsest. SAF (17:2) 193–201.

**9746.** JOHNSON, BARBARA. Is female to male as ground is to figure? *In* (pp. 255–68) **29.**

**9747.** KING, JEANNETTE; MORRIS, PAM. On not reading between the lines: models of reading in *The Yellow Wallpaper*. SSF (26:1) 23–32.

**9748.** SMITH, MARSHA A. The disoriented male narrator and social conversion: Charlotte Perkins Gilman's feminist Utopia vision. ATQ (3:1) 123–33.

## Allen Ginsberg

**9749.** BUSH, GLEN. Revolutionary visions: Blake, Ginsberg and Ferlinghetti. *See* **5061.**

**9750.** JAŘAB, JOSEF. Allen Ginsberg po letech. (Allen Ginsberg several years later.) *In* (pp. 22–3) **6.**

**9751.** —— Beatnik jako moderní klasik. *See* **8513.**

**9752.** KERBLAT-HOUGHTON, JEANNE. 'Work and leisure': to revise or not: Ginsberg his method, or, 'First thought, best thought'. *In* (pp. 181–92) **25.**

**9753.** MILES, BARRY. Ginsberg: a biography. New York: Simon & Schuster. pp. 588. Rev. by Paul Berman in NYTB, 1 Oct., 3; by Amiri Baraka in BkW, 24 Dec., 9; by Barry Silesky in BW, 3 Sept., 4.

**9754.** PETTINGELL, PHOEBE. Poetic personas. *See* **8541.**

## Ellen Glasgow

**9755.** GOODMAN, SUSAN. Competing visions of Freud in the memoirs of Ellen Glasgow and Edith Wharton. CLQ (25:4) 218–26.

**9756.** MATTHEWS, PAMELA RAE. 'Two women blended': Ellen Glasgow and her fictions. Unpub. doct. diss., Duke Univ., 1988. [Abstr. in DA (50) 947–8A.]

**9757.** RAPER, JULIUS ROWAN (ed.). Ellen Glasgow's reasonable doubts: a collection of her writings. Baton Rouge: Louisiana State UP, 1988. pp. xix, 262. (Southern literary studies.) Rev. by Pamela R. Matthews in AL (61:2) 301–2.

## Susan Glaspell

**9758.** MAEL, PHYLLIS. *Trifles*: the path to sisterhood. *See* **8089.**

## William Golding

**9759.** DELBAERE-GARANT, JEANNE. The artist as clown of God: Golding's *The Paper Man*. *In* (pp. 39–49) **42.**

**9760.** JACQUIN, BERNARD. Enfermement et rites de passage dans la fiction de William Golding. *In* (pp. 93–100) **35.**

**9761.** KAMM, JÜRGEN. Narrative cross-references as a structural device in William Golding's *Free Fall*. Ang (107:1/2) 89–92.

**9762.** KRAHÉ, PETER. William Golding als 'moving target'. Von den Schwierigkeiten des Umgangs mit einem zietgenössischen Autor. LJGG (26) 1985, 307–27.

**9763.** MATHIS, GILLES. En tête à texte avec l'étrange: la métamorphose de Jack dans *Lord of the Flies*. *In* (pp. 247–78) **26.**

**9764.** MITTOO, RAKESH C. Myth, ritual, and the numinous in the novels of William Golding. Unpub. doct. diss., Univ. of Manitoba, 1988. [Abstr. in DA (49) 3371A.]

**9765.** RUSTAM, ANEED T. Fable and Golding's *The Inheritors*. Journal of Education and Science (Univ. of Mosul, Iraq) (8) (Humanities and education) 41–57.

**9766.** STAPE, J. H. James Hanley, William Golding, Muriel Spark: additional primary works. AEB (ns 2:3) 1988, 110–12.

**9767.** SUGIMURA, YASUNORI. Hallucination and plotmaking principle in *Pincher Martin* by William Golding. SEL (English number) 21–36.

## Nadine Gordimer

**9768.** CLINGMAN, STEPHEN (ed.). The essential gesture: writing, politics and places. Cape Town: Philip, 1988. (Bibl. 1988, 7585.) Rev. by Menán du Plessis in Contrast (17:3) 74–8; by Mike Marais in Upstream (7:2) 63–4.

**9769.** COLLERAN, JEANNE MARIE. The dissenting writer in South Africa: a rhetorical analysis of the drama of Athol Fugard and the short fiction of Nadine Gordimer. *See* **9711.**

**9770.** FONTENOT, DEBORAH YVONNE B. A vision of anarchy: correlate structures of exile and madness in selected works of Doris Lessing and her South African contemporaries. Unpub. doct. diss., Univ. of Illinois at Urbana-Champaign, 1988. [Abstr. in DA (50) 449A.]

**9771.** GORDIMER, NADINE. Censorship and the artist. *See* **1846.**

**9772.** HEWSON, KELLY LEIGH. Writers and responsibility: George Orwell, Nadine Gordimer, John Coetzee and Salman Rushdie. *See* **9269.**

**9773.** MACLENNAN, DON. The vacuum pump: the fiction of Nadine Gordimer. Upstream (7:1) 30–3.

**9774.** O'CONNELL, JOANNA. Prospero's daughters: language and allegiance in the novels of Rosario Castellanos and Nadine Gordimer. Unpub. doct. diss., Univ. of California, Berkeley, 1988. [Abstr. in DA (50) 944A.]

**9775.** RASEBOTSA, NOBANTU NKWANE LORATO. The language of possibilities: domination and demythicization in Gordimer's art.

Unpub. doct. diss., State Univ. of New York at Stony Brook, 1988. [Abstr. in DA (50) 1303–4A.]

**9776.** VISEL, ROBIN ELLEN. White Eve in the 'petrified garden': the colonial African heroine in the writing of Olive Schreiner, Isak Dinesen, Doris Lessing and Nadine Gordimer. *See* **7379.**

### Caroline Gordon

**9777.** MAKOWSKY, VERONICA A. Caroline Gordon: a biography. Oxford; New York: OUP. pp. x, 260. Rev. by Ann Hulbert in TLS, 17 Nov., 1260.

**9778.** WALDRON, ANN. Close connections: Caroline Gordon and the Southern renaissance. (Bibl. 1987, 10879.) Rev. by Donald R. Noble in SoQ (27:2) 95–7.

**9779.** WEAKS, MARY LOUISE. A 'little postage stamp of native soil' in the upper South: the poetry and fiction of Caroline Gordon, Allen Tate, and Robert Penn Warren. Unpub. doct. diss., Univ. of Missouri–Columbia, 1988. [Abstr. in DA (50) 446A.]

### Edward Gorey

**9780.** TIGGES, WIM. An anatomy of literary nonsense. *See* **6466.**

**9781.** —— The limerick: the sonnet of nonsense? *In* (pp. 117–33) **28.**

**9782.** VAN LEEUWEN, HENDRIK. The liaison of visual and written nonsense. *In* (pp. 61–95) **28.**

### Sir Edmund Gosse

**9783.** DEMOOR, MARYSA. Andrew Lang's letters to Edmund Gosse: the record of a fruitful collaboration as poets, critics, and biographers. *See* **7178.**

**9784.** HARPER, MARCIA MITCHELL. The literary influence of Sir Edmund Gosse upon the Victorian age. *See* **5653.**

### Michael Gow

**9785.** AKERHOLT, MAY-BRIT. Interview with Michael Gow. Australasian Drama Studies (12/13) 1988, 73–84.

### Sue Grafton

**9786.** TAYLOR, BRUCE. G is for (Sue) Grafton. AD (22:1) 4–13. (Interview).

### W. S. Graham

**9787.** LOPEZ, TONY. The poetry of W. S. Graham. Edinburgh: Edinburgh UP. pp. vi, 170.

### Kenneth Grahame

**9788.** DEFOREST, MARY. *The Wind in the Willows*: a tale for two readers. CML (10:1) 81–7.

**9789.** PHILIP, NEIL. *The Wind in the Willows*: the vitality of a classic. *In* (pp. 299–316) **14.**

### Harley Granville-Barker

**9790.** INNES, CHRISTOPHER. Granville Barker and Galsworthy: questions of censorship. *See* **9728.**

**9791.** KENNEDY, DENNIS (ed.). Plays by Harley Granville-Barker. (Bibl. 1987, 10905.) Rev. by Georges Bas in EA (42:4) 487; by Peter Mudford in NQ (36:2) 255–6.

## Robert Graves

**9792.** BRYANT, HALLMAN BELL.    Robert Graves: an annotated bibliography. (Bibl. 1988, 7593.) Rev. by Kieran Quinlan in SoCR (22:1) 144–5.

**9793.** CARTER, D. N. G.    Robert Graves: the lasting poetic achievement. Totowa, NJ: Barnes & Noble, 1988; Basingstoke: Macmillan. pp. x, 285. (Macmillan studies in twentieth-century literature.)

**9794.** GRAVES, RICHARD PERCEVAL.    Robert Graves: the assault heroic, 1895–1926. (Bibl. 1988, 7594.) Rev. by P. E. Mitchell in DalR (67:1) 1987, 151–2.

**9795.** MITCHELL, P. E.    Robert Graves's *Goodbye to All That*. DalR (66:3) 1986, 341–53.

**9796.** QUINN, P. J. M.    Robert Graves and Siegfried Sassoon: from early poetry to autobiography. Unpub. doct. diss., Univ. of Warwick, 1988. [Abstr. in IT (39:4) 1634.]

**9797.** SMEDS, JOHN.    Robert Graves och den poetiska inspirationen. (Robert Graves and poetic inspiration.) Horisont (36:6) 56–62.

**9798.** WILLIAMS, WILLIAM PROCTOR (ed.).    A bibliography of the writings of Robert Graves. By FRED. H. HIGGINSON. (Bibl. 1988, 7595.) Rev. by Stephen Hills in BC (38:1) 119–22.

## Alasdair Gray

**9799.** CHARLTON, BRUCE.    An Alasdair Gray source book. Durham: Charlton, 1988. pp. 116.

## John Gray

**9800.** BESSAI, DIANE.    Discovering the popular audience. CanL (118) 1988, 7–28.

## Simon Gray

**9801.** MILLS, JOHN A.    'Old Mr Prickle-pin': Simon Gray's *Butley*. AI (45:4) 1988, 411–29.

## Spalding Gray

**9802.** DEMASTES, WILLIAM W.    Spalding Gray's *Swimming to Cambodia* and the evolution of an ironic presence. TJ (41:1) 75–94.

## 'Henry Green' (Henry Vincent Yorke)

**9803.** SALMON, A.    The novels of Henry Green: 'a life continuing beyond the book'. Unpub. doct. diss., Univ. of Liverpool, 1988. [Abstr. in IT (39:3) 1115–16.]

## Graham Greene

**9804.** COUTO, MARIA.    Graham Greene: on the frontier: politics and religion in the novels. (Bibl. 1988, 7603.) Rev. by Andrew Gibson in Eng (38:162) 273–7; by Judie Newman in DUJ (81:1) 1988, 173–4.

**9805.** ERDINAST-VULCAN, DAPHNA.    Graham Greene's childless fathers. Basingstoke: Macmillan, 1988. pp. ix, 115. (Macmillan studies in twentieth-century literature.) Rev. by Andrew Gibson in Eng (38:162) 273–7.

**9806.** GREENE, GRAHAM; LOW, DAVID.    Dear David, Dear Graham: a bibliophilic correspondence. Oxford: Alembic Press; Amate Press. pp. 91. (Limited ed. of 250 copies.)

**9807.** GROSSMAN, EWA.    Another trip into Greeneland – some reflections on Graham Greene's novel *Monsignor Quixote*. *In* (pp. 105–14) **3**.

**9808.** HAWTREE, CHRISTOPHER (ed.).    Yours etc.: letters to the press 1945–89. Harmondsworth: Reinhardt in assn with Viking. pp. xx, 268. Rev. by Julian Symons in TLS, 10 Nov., 1231; by Ian Thomson in Listener (122) 2 Nov., 33.

**9809.** LARSON, MICHAEL.    Laughing till the tears come: Greene's failed comedian. Ren (41:3) 177–87.

**9810.** ROBB, PAUL H.    Graham Greene's use of evil in selected novels. Unpub. doct. diss., Ball State Univ., 1988. [Abstr. in DA (49) 2672A.] (*This Gun for Hire, The Confidential Agent, The Ministry of Fear, Brighton Rock*.)

**9811.** SHERRY, NORMAN.    The life of Graham Greene: vol. 1, 1904–1939. New York: Viking; London: Cape. pp. xxi, 783. Rev. by R. Z. Sheppard in Time, 12 June, 69; by John Bayley in LRB (11:11) 3, 5; by Philip French in Listener (121) 27 Apr., 25–6; by Jonathan Yardley in BkW, 25 June, 3; by Peter Conn in BW, 18 June, 1, 9; by Robert Coles in NYTB, 18 June, 1; by Michael Dirda in Smithsonian (20:7) 225–6.

**9812.** SMITH, GRAHAME.    The achievement of Graham Greene. (Bibl. 1987, 10927.) Rev. by Nicola Bradbury in RES (38:150) 1987, 275–6.

**9813.** THOMAS, BRIAN.    An underground fate: the idiom of romance in the later novels of Graham Greene. Athens; London: Georgia UP, 1988. pp. xix, 232. (Cf. bibl. 1988, 7611.) Rev. by Daphna Erdinast-Vulcan in NQ (36:4) 548.

### Augusta, Lady Gregory

**9814.** HIGDON, DAVID LEON.    A George Russell letter to Lady Augusta Gregory. IUR (19:2) 209–12.

**9815.** KELLY, JOAN TANTUM.    Four Irish writers: 1800–1932: nationalism and gender in a changing Ireland. *See* **6750**.

**9816.** LEERSSEN, JOEP.    Táin after táin: the mythical past and the Anglo-Irish. *In* (pp. 29–46) **32**.

### Frederick Philip Grove

**9817.** HJARTARSON, PAUL (ed.).    A stranger to my time: essays by and about Frederick Philip Grove. Edmonton, Alta: NeWest Press, 1986. pp. xii, 356. Rev. by Ed Jewinski in CanL (120) 159–61; by Mary Rubio in QQ (95:4) 1988, 934–7.

**9818.** STICH, K. P.    Grove's 'Stella'. CanL (113/14) 1987, 258–62.

### Neil M. Gunn

**9819.** BURNS, JOHN.    A celebration of the light: Zen in the novels of Neil Gunn. Edinburgh: Canongate, 1988. pp. xii, 188. Rev. by Margery McCulloch in SLJ (supp. 30) 11–13.

### Thom Gunn

**9820.** GUNN, THOM.    Three hard women: HD, Marianne Moore, Mina Loy. *In* (pp. 37–52) **46**.

### Ivor Gurney

**9821.** ACTON, CAROL GILLIAN.    Paradox in parenthesis: a comparative study of the war poetry of Wilfred Owen, Charles Sorley, Isaac

Rosenberg, Ivor Gurney, and David Jones. Unpub. doct. diss., Queen's Univ. at Kingston (Ont.). [Abstr. in DA (49) 3359A.]

**9822.** BANERJEE, JACQUELINE.    Ivor Gurney's 'dark march' – is it really over? EngS (70:2) 115–31.

### Mafika Gwala
**9823.** NGWENYA, THENGAMEHLO.    Mafika Gwala: towards a national culture. Staffrider (8:1) 68–74.

### Alex Haley
**9824.** HÜLLEN, WERNER.    On the translation of English compound verbs into German: an investigation based on Alex Haley's *Roots/Wurzeln. In* (pp. 238–57) **4.**

### Donald Hall
**9825.** RECTOR, LIAM (ed.).    The day I was older: on the poetry of Donald Hall. Santa Cruz, CA: Story Line Press. pp. 288. Rev. in BkW, 24 Sept., 12.

### Radclyffe Hall
**9826.** ORMROD, RICHARD.    Gabriel D'Annunzio and Radclyffe Hall. MLR (84:4) 842–5.

**9827.** O'ROURKE, REBECCA.    Reflecting on *The Well of Loneliness.* London: Routledge. pp. x, 146. (Heroines.)

### Michael Hamburger
**9828.** HAMBURGER, MICHAEL.    Testimonies: selected shorter prose, 1950–1987. Manchester: Carcanet Press. pp. 348.

### Dashiell Hammett
**9829.** DOOGAN, G. MICHAEL.    Dash-ing through the snow. AD (22:1) 82–91.

**9830.** MAXFIELD, JAMES F.    *La Belle Dame sans merci* and the neurotic knight: characterization in *The Maltese Falcon. See* **8090.**

**9831.** MURRAY, WALTER.    The riddle of the key. AD (22:3) 290–3.

**9832.** WARD, KATHRYN ANN.    Clients, colleagues, and consorts: roles of women in American hardboiled detective fiction and film. *See* **8153.**

### James Hanley
**9833.** STAPE, J. H.    James Hanley, William Golding, Muriel Spark: additional primary works. *See* **9766.**

### Lorraine Hansberry
**9834.** CARTER, STEVEN R.    Lorraine Hansberry's *Toussaint.* BALF (23:1) 139–48.

**9835.** HUMPHRIES, EUGENIA.    Lorraine Hansberry: the visionary American playwright. Unpub. doct. diss., State Univ. of New York at Stony Brook, 1988. [Abstr. in DA (50) 1305A.]

### David Hare
**9836.** DONESKY, FINLAY JAMES.    Historical perspective in David Hare's drama. Unpub. doct. diss., Univ. of Michigan, 1988. [Abstr. in DA (49) 1798A.]

**9837.** OLIVA, JUDY LEE.    Theatricalizing politics: David Hare and a tradition of British political drama. *See* **1970.**

### Wilson Harris
**9838.** ADAM, IAN.    Marginality and the tradition: Earle Birney and Wilson Harris. *See* **9101.**

**9839.** MAES-JELINEK, HENA. Ambivalent Clio: J. M. Coetzee's *In the Heart of the Country* and Wilson Harris's *Carnival*. *See* **9271**.

### Gerald Haslam

**9840.** LOCKLIN, GERALD. Gerald Haslam. (Bibl. 1988, 7653.) Rev. by Richard W. Etulain in OreHQ (90:2) 206–8.

### Robert Hass

**9841.** GUSTAVSSON, BO. The discursive muse: Robert Hass's *Songs to Survive the Summer*. SN (61:2) 193–201.

### Epeli Hau'ofa

**9842.** SUBRAMANI. Interview with Epeli Hau'ofa. Landfall (43:1) 35–51.

### Stratis Haviaras

**9843.** KALOGERAS, GEORGE D. Magic realism and the carnivalesque in a Greek-American spiritual journey. Aristotle Univ. of Thessaloniki Yearbook of English Studies (1) 353–64.

### Bessie Head

**9844.** CHETIN, SARA. Myth, exile, and the female condition: Bessie Head's *The Collector of Treasures*. JCL (24:1) 114–37.

**9845.** DOVEY, TERESA. A question of power: Susan Gardner's biography versus Bessie Head's autobiography. *See* **8594**.

**9846.** EILERSEN, GILLIAN STEAD (introd.). Tales of tenderness and power. Johannesburg: Donker. pp. 144.

**9847.** FONTENOT, DEBORAH YVONNE B. A vision of anarchy: correlate structures of exile and madness in selected works of Doris Lessing and her South African contemporaries. *See* **9770**.

**9848.** IBRAHIM, HUMA. Bessie Head: a third-world woman writer in exile. Unpub. doct. diss., Indiana Univ., 1988. [Abstr. in DA (49) 2655A.]

**9849.** MacKENZIE, CRAIG. Bessie Head: an introduction. Grahamstown: National English Literary Museum. pp. 52. (NELM introduction ser., 1.)

**9850.** MACKENZIE, CRAIG. From oral tradition to literary form: the short stories of Bessie Head. *In* (pp. 256–68) EDGARD SIENAERT and NIGEL BELL (eds), Catching winged words: oral tradition and education. Durban: Natal Univ. Oral Documentation and Research Centre, 1988. pp. vii, 282.

**9851.** —— Short fiction in the making: the case of Bessie Head. EngA (16:1) 17–28.

### Seamus Heaney

**9852.** ADAIR, TOM. Calling the tune: Seamus Heaney interviewed. Linen Hall Review (6:2) 5–8.

**9853.** ALLISON, JONATHAN. Community and individualism in the poetry of W. B. Yeats and Seamus Heaney. Unpub. doct. diss., Univ. of Michigan, 1988. [Abstr. in DA (49) 2225A.]

**9854.** ANDREWS, ELMER. The poetry of Seamus Heaney: all the realms of whisper. New York: St Martin's Press; Basingstoke: Macmillan, 1988. pp. 219. Rev. by Stephen Smith in FQ (ns 3:2) 57–8; by Dillon Johnston in TLS, 8 Sept., 983.

**9855.** BROWN, DUNCAN. Seamus Heaney's 'book of changes': *The Haw Lantern*. Theoria (74) 79–96.

**9856.** CORCORAN, NEIL. Seamus Heaney. (Bibl. 1987, 10977.) Rev. by R. J. C. Watt in RES (39:156) 1988, 592–3.

**9857.** HART, HENRY. Crossing divisions and differences: Seamus Heaney's prose poems. SoR (25:4) 803–21.

**9858.** HEANEY, SEAMUS. *Or, Solitude*: a reading. *In* (pp. 81–7) **46.**

**9859.** HOGAN, KATHERINE M. The political poetry of Seamus Heaney: an explication of poetic strategies. Unpub. doct. diss., New York Univ. [Abstr. in DA (50) 1312A.]

**9860.** HUGHES, GEORGE. Myth and poetics in the work of Seamus Heaney. PoetT (29/30) 126–42.

**9861.** McLOUGHLIN, D. J. Tradition and nationality in the work of three Irish poets: W. B. Yeats, Patrick Kavanagh and Seamus Heaney. Unpub. M.Phil. diss., Univ. of Manchester, 1987. [Abstr. in IT (39:3) 1115.]

**9862.** McLOUGHLIN, DEBORAH. 'An ear to the line': modes of receptivity in Seamus Heaney's *Glanmore Sonnets*. PLL (25:2) 201–15.

**9863.** ROE, NICHOLAS. *Wordsworth at the Flax-Dam*: an early poem by Seamus Heaney. *In* (pp. 166–70) **17.**

**9864.** SCHMIDT, MICHAEL. Samtal mellan fyra poeter. (A conversation with four poets.) Lyrikvännen (1989:2/3) 121–31.

**9865.** SCRUTON, JAMES ALBERT. A vocable ground: the poetry of Seamus Heaney. Unpub. doct. diss., Univ. of Tennessee, 1988. [Abstr. in DA (49) 3361A.]

**9866.** SINNER, A. T. Y. Protective colouring: the political commitment in the poetry of Seamus Heaney. Unpub. doct. diss., Univ. of Hull, 1988. [Abstr. in IT (38:4) 1463.]

### John Hearne

**9867.** SAMAD, DAIZAL RAFEEK LIQUAT. Characters in crisis: the novels of John Hearne. Unpub. doct. diss., Univ. of New Brunswick. [Abstr. in DA (50) 683A.]

### Robert A. Heinlein

**9868.** MALCOLM, DAVID. Two *Theys*: a comparison of the fantastic in two texts. *In* (pp. 19–30) **57.**

**9869.** SLUSSER, GEORGE E. Structures of apprehension: Lem, Heinlein, and the Strugatskys. SFS (16:1) 1–37.

**9870.** STOVER, LEON. Robert A. Heinlein. (Bibl. 1988, 7676.) Rev. by Roger Asselineau in EA (42:2) 238–9.

### Joseph Heller

**9871.** BAŠTÍN, ŠTEFAN. The comic vision of life in the fiction of Joseph Heller. *In* (pp. 89–103) **62.**

**9872.** MERRILL, ROBERT. Joseph Heller. Boston, MA: G. K. Hall, 1987. pp. xiv, 153. (Twayne's US authors, 512.) Rev. by Louise K. Barnett in MLR (84:3) 732–3.

**9873.** PROTSENKO, I. B. Kompozitsionno-stilisticheskie osobennosti p'esy Dzhozefa Khellera *N'iu Kheĭven my bombili. See* **1416.**

**9874.** SEED, DAVID. The fiction of Joseph Heller: against the grain. New York: St Martin's Press; Basingstoke: Macmillan. pp. viii, 224. Rev. in BkW 17 Sept., 17.

**9875.** TOMAN, MARSHALL B. Nonsense and sensibility: negation in the novels of Joseph Heller. Unpub. doct. diss., Boston College, 1988. [Abstr. in DA (50) 141–2A.]

### Lillian Hellman

**9876.** FEIBLEMAN, PETER. Lilly: reminiscences of Lillian Hellman. London: Chatto & Windus. (Bibl. 1988, 7683.) Rev. by Patrick Taylor-Martin in Listener (121) 2 Mar., 33; by Donna Rifkind in TLS, 17 Mar., 275.

**9877.** NEWMAN, ROBERT P. The Cold War romance of Lillian Hellman and John Melby. Chapel Hill; London: North Carolina UP. pp. xiv, 375.

**9878.** PATRAKA, VIVIAN M. Lillian Hellman's *Watch on the Rhine*: realism, gender, and historical crisis. ModDr (32:1) 128–45.

**9879.** RECKNAGEL, MARSHA LEE. Lillian Hellman's memoirs: 'writing is oneself'. Unpub. doct. diss., Rice Univ., 1988. [Abstr. in DA (49) 3028A.]

**9880.** ROLLYSON, CARL. Lillian Hellman: her legend and her legacy. (Bibl. 1988, 7684.) Rev. by Thomas P. Adler in ModDr (32:3) 454–6.

### Ernest Hemingway

**9881.** BAKKER, J. Ernest Hemingway in Holland, 1925–1981: a comparative analysis of the contemporary Dutch and American critical reception of his work. (Bibl. 1987, 11010.) Rev. by Harold Beaver in MLR (84:4) 969–70.

**9882.** BENSON, JACKSON J. Ernest Hemingway: the life as fiction and the fiction as life. AL (61:3) 345–58.

**9883.** BUDICK, E. MILLER. *The Sun Also Rises*: Hemingway and the art of repetition. UTQ (56:2) 1986/87, 319–37.

**9884.** COX, JAMES M. Getting the best of Ernest. SewR (96:3) 1988, 511–15 (review-article).

**9885.** DAVIS, JUDY W. Three novels mentioned in *A Farewell to Arms*. NCL (19:4) 4–5.

**9886.** DOLAN, MARC. 'True stories' of 'the Lost Generation': an exploration of narrative truth in memoirs of Hemingway, Cowley, and Fitzgerald. *See* **9338.**

**9887.** FITCH, NOEL RILEY. Hemingway in Paris: Parisian walks for the literary traveller. Wellingborough: Equation. pp. 195.

**9888.** FLEMING, ROBERT E. American nightmare: Hemingway and the West. MidQ (30:3) 361–71.

**9889.** —— The endings of Hemingway's *Garden of Eden*. AL (61:2) 261–70.

**9890.** FUENTES, NORBERTO; HERRERA SOTOO; LONGO, ROBERTO. Ernest Hemingway rediscovered. Trans. by MARIANNE SINCLAIR. London: Plexus; New York: Scribner's, 1988. pp. 192. (Trans. of bibl. 1987, 11023.)

**9891.** GRIFFIN, PETER. Along with youth: Hemingway, the early years. (Bibl. 1987, 11027.) Rev. by Ellen Pifer in YES (19) 351–3; by Julian P. Smith in JAStud (23:1) 112–13; by David Seed in RES (38:151) 1987, 414.

**9892.** HAN, JIN-SUK. *The Killers* eui eoneohakjeok haesuk. (A linguistic interpretation of *The Killers.*) Unpub. doct. diss., Chungnam National Univ., Daejeon, Korea.

**9893.** HILY MANE, GENEVIÈVE. *The Garden of Eden*, du manuscrit au roman publié: le vrai paradis perdu de Hemingway. EA (42:3) 282–303.

**9894.** HOWARD, SUSAN F. A study of Jungian archetypes in three Hemingway novels. Unpub. doct. diss., Michigan State Univ., 1988. [Abstr. in DA (49) 2659A.] (*The Sun Also Rises, For Whom the Bell Tolls, The Old Man and the Sea.*)

**9895.** JOHNSON, MARY CHARLOTTE. A critical study of the poetic voice in the narratives of selected documentary films of the 1930s. *See* **8068.**

**9896.** JOHNSON, PAUL. Hemingway: portrait of the artist as intellectual. Commentary (87:2) 49–59.

**9897.** KIM, YOO-JO. Ernest Hemingway mikonggae danpyeon wisang: tonggwa jaeeui eui gwanjeom eseo. (The theme of initiation in Ernest Hemingway's unpublished short stories.) JELL (35) 463–83.

**9898.** LAMB, ROBERT PAUL. Hemingway and the short story: a study in craft. Unpub. doct. diss., Harvard Univ., 1988. [Abstr. in DA (50) 444A.]

**9899.** LaPRADE, DOUGLAS EDWARD. The censorship of Hemingway in Spain. Unpub. doct. diss., Univ. of Illinois at Urbana-Champaign, 1988. [Abstr. in DA (49) 2660A.]

**9900.** LARSEN, KEVIN S. Rounds with Mr Cervantes: Don Quijote and *For Whom the Bell Tolls*. OL (43:2) 1988, 108–28.

**9901.** LYNN, KENNETH S. Hemingway. (Bibl. 1988, 7706.) Rev. by Thomas K. Meier in ELN (26:3) 92–4; by James M. Cox in SewR (96:3) 1988, 511–15.

**9902.** McDOWELL, NICHOLAS. Hemingway. Hove: Wayland, 1988. pp. 112. (Life and works.)

**9903.** McKELLY, JAMES C. From whom the bull flows: Hemingway in parody. AL (61:4) 547–62.

**9904.** MEYERS, JEFFREY. Hemingway: a biography. (Bibl. 1987, 11042.) Rev. by Felicity Horne in UES (27:1) 48–9.

**9905.** MORELAND, KIM. Plumbing the iceberg: a review essay on recent Hemingway biographies. SoHR (23:2) 145–64.

**9906.** NAGEL, JAMES (ed.). Ernest Hemingway: the writer in context. (Bibl. 1987, 11043.) Rev. by Ellen Pifer in YES (19) 351–3.

**9907.** ORLOVA, R. Russkaia sud'ba Khemingveia. (The Russian fate of Hemingway.) VLit (1989:6) 77–107.

**9908.** PEDOTO, CONSTANCE ANNE. *Il Gioco del Nulla*: Ernest Hemingway and Italo Calvino's construction of 'nothingness'. Unpub. doct. diss., Univ. of South Florida, 1988. [Abstr. in DA (50) 133A.]

**9909.** RENZA, LOUIS A. The importance of being Ernest. SAQ (88:3) 661–89.

**9910.** REYNOLDS, MICHAEL. Hemingway: the Paris years. New York; Oxford: Blackwell. pp. xvii, 402. Rev. by Michael Shnayerson in BkW, 24 Dec., 1–2.

**9911.** —— The young Hemingway. (Bibl. 1987, 11049.) Rev. by David Seed in RES (38:151) 1987, 414–15; by Ellen Pifer in YES (19) 351–3.

**9912.** SEED, DAVID. The ravages of time in Hemingway's *A Farewell to Arms*. DUJ (81:2) 265–9.

**9913.** SONNE, HARLY; GRAMBYE, CHRISTIAN. Narrativité et représentation psychologique. Neophilologus (73:2) 162–82.

**9914.** STRONG, PAUL. Gathering the pieces and filling in the gaps: Hemingway's *Fathers and Sons*. SSF (26:1) 49–58.

**9915.** STRYCHACZ, THOMAS. Dramatizations of manhood in Hemingway's *In Our Time* and *The Sun Also Rises*. AL (61:2) 245–60.

**9916.** VAN DEN HEUVEL, PIERRE. À la recherche du suject perdu. *See* **8880.**

**9917.** VAN GUNTEN, MARK CHARLES. The manly art: Ernest Hemingway and the scene of writing. Unpub. doct. diss., Univ. of South Carolina. [Abstr. in DA (50) 1659A.]

**9918.** VILLARD, HENRY SERRANO; NAGEL, JAMES. Hemingway in love and war: the lost diary of Agnes von Kurowsky, her letters, and correspondence of Ernest Hemingway. Boston, MA: Northeastern UP. pp. 303. Rev. by Justin Kaplan in NYTB, 22 Oct., 7; by Michael Shnayerson in BkW, 24 Dec., 1–2.

**9919.** WAGNER-MARTIN, LINDA (ed.). New essays on *The Sun Also Rises*. (Bibl. 1987, 11060, where '(ed.)' omitted.) Rev. by Julian P. Smith in JAStud (23:1) 112–13.

### Beth Henley

**9920.** GUERRA, JONNIE. Beth Henley: female quest and the family-play tradition. *In* (pp. 118–30) **39.**

### Mark Henshaw

**9921.** ARTHUR, KATERYNA OLIJNYK. Interview with Mark Henshaw. Span (28) 1–10.

### Xavier Herbert

**9922.** ROSS, ROBERT L. Xavier Herbert's *Poor Fellow My Country*: in search of an American audience. JPC (23:2) 55–62.

### Michael Herr

**9923.** FURNISS, DAVID WEST. Making sense of the war: Vietnam and American prose. Unpub. doct. diss., Univ. of Minnesota, 1988. [Abstr. in DA (49) 1860A.]

### John Hewitt

**9924.** BROWN, TERENCE. The poet's shadow. Fortnight (275: supp.) vii.

**9925.** BURNSIDE, SAM. Preparing lonely defences. Fortnight (275: supp.) iii–iv.

**9926.** CRAIG, PATRICIA.    Finding hope in the weavers. Fortnight (275: supp.) vi.

**9927.** SMYTH, DAMIAN.    Speaking a common tongue. Fortnight (275: supp.) ii–iii.

**9928.** WATTS, GERALDINE.    Utility clashes with emotion. Fortnight (275: supp.) v.

### Paul Hiebert

**9929.** NICOL, ERIC.    Paul Hiebert (1892–1987). CanL (117) 1988, 175. (Obituary.)

### Aidan Higgins

**9930.** CALLAHAN, DENIS JOSEPH F.    James Joyce and the novels of Aidan Higgins, Jennifer Johnston, John McGahern and Brian Moore. Unpub. doct. diss., Univ. of Notre Dame, 1988. [Abstr. in DA (49) 3360A.]

### George V. Higgins

**9931.** FORD, ERWIN H., II.    Expiation ritual in the crime novels of George V. Higgins. Unpub. doct. diss., State Univ. of New York at Buffalo, 1988. [Abstr. in DA (49) 3723–4A.]

### Geoffrey Hill

**9932.** BARFOOT, C. C.    Reading the word in Geoffrey Hill. *In* (pp. 65–88) **13.**

**9933.** BARNDEN, SASKIA (GAIL).    Voice in contemporary British poetry, with special attention to Philip Larkin, Ted Hughes and Geoffrey Hill. Unpub. doct. diss., Indiana Univ., 1988. [Abstr. in DA (49) 2664A]

**9934.** GARDNER, PHILIP.    'Make me an Offa': Geoffrey Hill and *Mercian Hymns*. DalR (67:2/3) 1987, 202–16.

**9935.** GLYNN, STEPHEN T.    'Biting nothings to the bone': the exemplary failure of Geoffrey Hill. Eng (36) 1987, 235–64.

**9936.** HORNER, AVRIL.    Geoffrey Hill, Dietrich Bonhoeffer, and *Christmas Trees*. NQ (36:2) 209–10.

**9937.** WALTHEER, ELIZABETH.    Geoffrey Hill's critical nostalgia. *In* (pp. 165–71) **23.**

### Tony Hillerman

**9938.** GAUGENMAIER, JUDITH TABOR.    The mysteries of Tony Hillerman. AWest (26:6) 46–7, 56–8.

### Jack Hodgins

**9939.** SLEMON, STEPHEN.    Magic realism as post-colonial discourse. CanL (116) 1988, 9–24. (*The Invention of the World, What the Crow Said.*)

### David Hogan

**9940.** ROHMAN, GERD.    David Hogan's Irish civil war story *The Leaping Trout*. JSSE (12) 79–85.

### Desmond Hogan

**9941.** D'HAEN, THEO.    Desmond Hogan and Ireland's postmodern past. *In* (pp. 79–84) **32.**

### Margaret Hollingsworth

**9942.** PARKER, DOROTHY.    Alienation and identity: the plays of Margaret Hollingsworth. CanL (118) 1988, 97–113.

### Timothy Holme
**9943.** BARNARD, ROBERT.    The Neapolitan knight. AD (22:3) 266–70.

### Hugh Hood
**9944.** HOOD, HUGH.    The elephant in the next room: anatomy of a long work. CanL (116) 1988, 97–108.

### A. D. Hope
**9945.** DARLING, ROBERT JAMES.    The poetry of A. D. Hope. Unpub. doct. diss., Univ. of Rhode Island, 1988. [Abstr. in DA (49) 3360A.]

### Christopher Hope
**9946.** JOFFE, PHIL.    An interview with Christopher Hope. EngA (16:2) 91–105.

### A. E. Housman
**9947.** BROWNE, PIERS.    An elegy in Arcady: an artist's view of Housman's poetry. Southampton: Ashford. pp. xii, 164.

### Velina Houston
**9948.** ARNOLD, STEPHANIE.    Dissolving the half shadows: Japanese American women playwrights. *In* (pp. 181–94) **39.**

### Richard Howard
**9949.** STANTON, JOSEPH CHARLES.    A Langerian analysis of Richard Howard's iconic poems and their referents. Unpub. doct. diss., New York Univ. [Abstr. in DA (50) 1239A.]

### Tina Howe
**9950.** BACKES, NANCY.    Body art: hunger and satiation in the plays of Tina Howe. *In* (pp. 41–60) **39.**

### L. Ron Hubbard
**9951.** BERGER, ALBERT I.    Towards a science of the nuclear mind: science-fiction origins of dianetics. *See* **8183.**

### W. H. Hudson
**9952.** GRIGNANI, MARIA A. (ed.).    La vita della foresta di W. H. Hudson nella traduzione di Eugenio Montale. Turin: Einaudi, 1987. pp. 342. Rev. by Diego Zancani in MLR (84:2) 492–3.

### Langston Hughes
**9953.** RAMPERSAD, ARNOLD.    The life of Langston Hughes: vol. 1, 1902–1941: I, too, sing America. (Bibl. 1988, 7771.) Rev. by Holly Eley in TLS, 16 June, 671–2.
**9954.** —— The life of Langston Hughes: vol. 2, 1941–1967: I dream a world. (Bibl. 1988, 7772.) Rev. in BkW, 3 Sept., 12; by Holly Eley in TLS, 16 June, 671–2.
**9955.** TRACY, STEVEN C.    Langston Hughes and the blues. Urbana: Illinois UP, 1988. pp. xiii, 251. Rev. by John McCluskey, Jr, in AL (61:3) 487–8.

### Ted Hughes
**9956.** BARNDEN, SASKIA (GAIL).    Voice in contemporary British poetry, with special attention to Philip Larkin, Ted Hughes and Geoffrey Hill. *See* **9933.**
**9957.** Cox, C. B.    British poetry since 1945: Philip Larkin and Ted Hughes. YYY (5) 1–13.

**9958.** DIENHART, JOHN M.    Form and function in Ted Hughes's poem *The Jaguar*. EngS (70:3) 248–52.

**9959.** WALDER, DENNIS.    Ted Hughes. (Bibl. 1987, 11118.) Rev. by Adolphe Haberer in EA (42:3) 356–7.

### Keri Hulme

**9960.** CHARMAN, JANET. Keri Hulme. Broadsheet (173) 14–16. (Interview.)

### William Humphrey

**9961.** WINCHELL, MARK ROYDEN.    Beyond regionalism: the growth of William Humphrey. SewR (96:2) 1988, 287–92.

### Sam Hunt

**9962.** O'HARE, NOEL.    Lonesome cowboy. NZList, 27 May, 27–8.

### Violet Hunt

**9963.** WIESENFARTH, JOSEPH.    Violet Hunt rewrites Jane Austen: *Pride and Prejudice* (1813) and *Their Lives* (1916). *See* **6245.**

### Douglas Hurd

**9964.** PAULIN, TOM.    English political writers on Ireland: Robert Southey to Douglas Hurd. *In* (pp. 132–45) **17.**

### Zora Neale Hurston

**9965.** AALTONEN, SIRKKU.    'De muleuh de world': patterns of dominance in Zora Neale Hurston's *Their Eyes Were Watching God*. *In* (pp. 22–30) **43.**

**9966.** BLOOM, HAROLD (ed.).    Zora Neale Hurston's *Their Eyes Were Watching God*. New York: Chelsea House, 1987. pp. 130. (Modern critical interpretations.) Rev. by Eva Boesenberg in BALF (23:4) 799–807.

**9967.** CARBY, HAZEL V.    Reinventing history/imagining the future. *See* **8999.**

**9968.** FISHER-PETERS, PEARLIE MAE.    'Don' say mo' wid yo' mouf dan yo' back kin stan''': the assertive woman in Zora Neale Hurston's fiction, folklore and drama. Unpub. doct. diss., State Univ. of New York at Buffalo, 1988. [Abstr. in DA (50) 139A.]

**9969.** FOX-GENOVESE, ELIZABETH.    My statue, my self: autobiographical writings of Afro-American women. *In* (pp. 63–89) **51.**

**9970.** JARRETT, MARY.    The idea of audience in the short stories of Zora Neale Hurston and Alice Walker. JSSE (12) 33–44.

**9971.** KRASNER, JAMES.    The life of women: Zora Neale Hurston and female autobiography. BALF (23:1) 113–26.

**9972.** PLANT, DEBORAH G.    Zora Neale Hurston's *Dust Tracks on a Road*: Black autobiography in a different voice. Unpub. doct. diss., Univ. of Nebraska–Lincoln, 1988. [Abstr. in DA (49) 3725A.]

**9973.** WALL, CHERYL A.    *Mules and Men*: Zora Neale Hurston's strategies of narration and visions of female empowerment. BALF (23:4) 661–80.

**9974.** WALLINGER-NOWAK, HANNA.    Traditionsbildung in der schwarzamerikanischen Frauenliteratur: Zora Neale Hurston und Alice Walker. *In* (pp. 19–32) CHRISTA GÜRTLER and BRIGETTE MAZOHL-WALLNIG (eds), Frauenbilder, Frauenrollen, Frauenforschung. Vienna:

Geyer, 1987. pp. 189. (Pubs of the Historical Inst. of the Univ. of Salzburg, 17.)

## Aldous Huxley

**9975.** DEERY, J. Doors of perception: science, literature, and mysticism in the works of Aldous Huxley. Unpub. doct. diss., Univ. of Oxford. [Abstr. in IT (39:3) 1115.]

**9976.** DOMMERGUES, ANDRÉ. Aldous Huxley: pouvoir et société. *In* (pp. 123–35) **14.**

**9977.** HERBRÜGGEN, HUBERTUS SCHULTE. Formen und Entwicklungslinien der Utopie bei Aldous Huxley. LJGG (27) 1986, 285–96.

**9978.** PARSONS, DAVID. Dartington: a principle source of inspiration behind Aldous Huxley's *Island*. JGE (39:1) 1987, 10–25.

**9979.** PIEPER, ANNEMARIE. Der philosophische Begriff der Utopie und die klassischen Utopisten. *See* **3285.**

**9980.** REESE, STEVEN CASE. Modernism and the march of science: four novelists. Unpub. doct. diss., Univ. of Delaware, 1988. [Abstr. in DA (49) 2234A.]

**9981.** SILVANI, GIOVANNA. Woman in Utopia from More to Huxley. *See* **3286.**

## 'Robin Hyde' (Iris Guiver Wilkinson)

**9982.** ASH, SUSAN (introd.). Wednesday's children. Auckland: New Women's Press. pp. 296.

## Witi Ihimaera

**9983.** OJINMAH, UMELO R. Post-colonial tensions in a cross-cultural milieu: a comparative study of the writings of Witi Ihimaera and Chinua Achebe. *See* **8901.**

## Momoko Iko

**9984.** ARNOLD, STEPHANIE. Dissolving the half shadows: Japanese American women playwrights. *In* (pp. 181–94) **39.**

## William Inge

**9985.** BAILEY, JEFFREY. William Inge: an appreciation in retrospect. KQ (18:4) 1986, 139–47.

**9986.** KNUDSEN, JAMES. Last words: the novels of William Inge. KQ (18:4) 1986, 121–9.

**9987.** LANGE, JANE W. 'Forces get loose': social prophecy in William Inge's *Picnic*. KQ (18:4) 1986, 57–70.

**9988.** MCILRATH, PATRICIA. William Inge, great voice of the heart of America. KQ (18:4) 1986, 45–53.

**9989.** VOIS, RALPH F. William Inge and the savior/specter of celebrity. KQ (18:4) 1986, 25–40.

**9990.** WENTWORTH, MICHAEL. The convergence of fairy tale and myth in William Inge's *Picnic*. KQ (18:4) 1986, 75–85.

## David Ireland

**9991.** JONES, DOROTHY. Serious laughter: on defining Australian humour. JCL (23:1) 1988, 76–90.

**9992.** STEIN, THOMAS MICHAEL. 'You have work to do, my reader': David Ireland's *A Woman of the Future* as modernist fictional autobiography. *In* (pp. 146–55) **5.**

## John Irving

**9993.** THOMAS, JIM. A changing American family: Cheever, Gardner, Irving, Updike. *See* **9238.**

## Christopher Isherwood

**9994.** MENDELSON, EDWARD (ed.). Plays and other dramatic writings by W. H. Auden, 1928–1938. *See* **8976.**

**9995.** SCHWERDT, LISA M. Isherwood's fiction: the self and technique. Basingstoke: Macmillan. pp. ix, 214. (Macmillan studies in twentieth-century literature.)

**9996.** STĂNESCU, ALEXANDRA. Reţea de producţie. (Production network.) RomLit, 1 June, 20 (review-article). (*Mr Norris Changes Trains*; *Goodbye to Berlin*.)

## W. W. Jacobs

**9997.** LAMERTON, CHRIS. W. W. Jacobs: a bibliography. Margate: Greystone, 1988. pp. 172.

## C. L. R. James

**9998.** BUHLE, PAUL. C. L. R. James: the artist as revolutionary. New York; London: Verso. pp. 197. Rev. by Edward W. Said in BkW, 5 Mar., 5.

## M. R. James

**9999.** DALBY, RICHARD (ed.). Dracula's brood: neglected vampire classics by Sir Arthur Conan Doyle, Algernon Blackwood, M. R. James and others. *See* **6729.**

## Randall Jarrell

**10000.** BRYANT, J. A., JR. Understanding Randall Jarrell. Columbia: South Carolina UP, 1986. pp. 194. Rev. by Monroe K. Spears in SewR (96:1) 1988, 103.

**10001.** HAGENBÜCHLE, HELEN. Laurels for a bat: aesthetic theories in Randall Jarrell's *The Bat-Poet*. LJGG (28) 1987, 115–31.

**10002.** ROSS, ROBERT. Christina Stead's encounter with 'the true reader': the origin and outgrowth of Randall Jarrell's introduction to *The Man Who Loved Children*. LCUT (42/43) 1988, 161–79.

## Robinson Jeffers

**10003.** BOSWELL, JEANETTA. Robinson Jeffers and the critics, 1912–1983: a bibliography of secondary sources with selective annotations. Metuchen, NJ; London: Scarecrow Press, 1986. pp. ix, 170. (Scarecrow author bibliographies, 77.) Rev. by Robert J. Brophy in WAL (23:4) 367–70.

**10004.** EVERSON, WILLIAM. The excesses of God: Robinson Jeffers as a religious figure. Introd. by ALBERT GELPI. Stanford, CA: Stanford UP, 1988. pp. xv, 190. Rev. by Robert Kern in AL (61:2) 323–5; by Linda Wagner-Martin in CR (33:2) 187–8.

**10005.** FALCK, COLIN (ed.). Selected poems: the centenary edition. (Bibl. 1987, 11160.) Rev. by Robert Zaller in Agenda (26:3) 1988, 54–5.

**10006.** HASS, ROBERT. Rock and hawk: a selection of shorter poems by Robinson Jeffers. (Bibl. 1988, 7810.) Rev. by Robert Zaller in Agenda (26:3) 1988, 55–6.

**10007.** HUNT, TIM. A voice in nature: Jeffers' *Tamar and Other Poems*. AL (61:2) 230–44.
**10008.** —— (ed.). The collected poetry of Robinson Jeffers: vol. 1, 1920–1928. Stanford, CA: Stanford UP, 1988. pp. 521. Rev. by Linda Wagner-Martin in CR (33:2) 187–8.
**10009.** JOHNSTON, ALLAN JAMES. Reinventing the metaphors: toward an ecological aesthetics in the writings of Robinson Jeffers, Kenneth Rexroth, and Gary Snyder. Unpub. doct. diss., Univ. of California, Davis, 1988. [Abstr. in DA (50) 684–5A.]
**10010.** SHARON, CAROL BOOTH. The tension of the mind: Robinson Jeffers' rhetoric of violence. Unpub. doct. diss., Univ. of California, Berkeley, 1988. [Abstr. in DA (49) 3364A.]
**10011.** VARDANIS, ALEX A. The temptations of despaire: Jeffers and *The Faerie Queene*. See **3419**.
**10012.** ZALLER, ROBERT. The cliffs of solitude: a reading of Robinson Jeffers. (Bibl. 1987, 11168.) Rev. by W. S. Milne in Agenda (26:3) 57–61.

### Ruth Prawer Jhabvala

**10013.** SUCHER, LAURIE. The fiction of Ruth Prawer Jhabvala: the politics of passion. London: Macmillan. pp. x, 251.
**10014.** WILLIAMS, HAYDN. Mad seekers, doomed lovers and cemeteries in India: or, R. P. Jhabvala's *Heat and Dust* and *A New Dominion*. New Literature Review (15) 1988, 11–20.

### James Weldon Johnson

**10015.** HARMON, JUDITH EILENE BROWN. James Weldon Johnson, a new Negro: a study of his early life and literary career, 1871–1916. Unpub. doct. diss., Emory Univ., 1988. [Abstr. in DA (49) 3065A.]

### Denis Johnston

**10016.** RONSLEY, JOSEPH. The difficult debut of Denis Johnston's *Old Lady. In* (pp. 175–90) **45**.

### Jennifer Johnston

**10017.** CALLAHAN, DENIS JOSEPH F. James Joyce and the novels of Aidan Higgins, Jennifer Johnston, John McGahern and Brian Moore. *See* **9930**.

### Mary Johnston

**10018.** MIXON, WAYNE. What's in a name? Mary Johnston's *Audrey*. SoLJ (22:1) 96–106.

### D. G. Jones

**10019.** ARCHER, ANNE. The story of an affinity: D. G. Jones, Archibald Lampman, and *Kate These Flowers. See* **7174**.

### David Jones

**10020.** ACTON, CAROL GILLIAN. Paradox in parenthesis: a comparative study of the war poetry of Wilfred Owen, Charles Sorley, Isaac Rosenberg, Ivor Gurney, and David Jones. *See* **9821**.
**10021.** AUSTIN, D. L. Literature as history: misreading David Jones's *In Parenthesis*. DalR (67:2/3) 1987, 217–27.
**10022.** DILWORTH, THOMAS. The shape of meaning in the poetry of David Jones. Toronto; London: Toronto UP, 1988. pp. xii, 434.

**10023.** PAGNOULLE, CHRISTINE.   David Jones: a commentary on some poetic fragments. (Bibl. 1988, 7827.) Rev. by Alain Cazade in EA (42:4) 492–3; by Bart Eeckhout in EngS (70:2) 169–70.

**10024.** —— Dramatic irony in David Jones's poem *The Tribune's Visitation. In* (pp. 229–37) **42.**

**10025.** ROBB, M. P.   The sacramental vision: belief and art in the poetry of David Jones, Charles Williams and W. H. Auden. *See* **8978.**

### James Jones

**10026.** HENDRICK, GEORGE (ed.).   To reach eternity: the letters of James Jones. New York: Random House. pp. 379. Rev. by Kenneth S. Lynn in BkW, 18 June, 1–2; by Benjamin DeMott in NYTB, 30 July, 10; by J. Michael Lennon in BW, 14 May, 1, 4.

### Madison Jones

**10027.** WALSH, WILLIAM.   An interview with Madison Jones. SoHR (23:1) 39–51.

### Erica Jong

**10028.** COOKE, STEWART JON.   Received melodies: the new, old novel. *See* **9013.**

### Gabriel Josipovici

**10029.** JOSIPOVICI, GABRIEL.   Writing, reading, and the study of literature. *See* **1863.**

### Elsa Joubert

**10030.** CARLEAN, KEVIN.   The narrative functions of Elsa Joubert's *Poppie Nongena.* EngA (16:2) 49–59.

### James Joyce

**10031.** ARMSTRONG, ALISON.   Transition years: James Joyce and Modernist art. *In* (pp. 351–9) **45.**

**10032.** ATTRIDGE, DEREK.   Finnegans awake: the dream of interpretation. JJQ (27:1) 11–29.

**10033.** —— FERRER, DANIEL (comps).   Post-structuralist Joyce: essays from the French. (Bibl. 1986, 12611.) Rev. by R. A. Cave in RES (39:154) 1988, 322.

**10034.** BECKMAN, RICHARD.   'Them boys is so contrairy', *FW* 620.12. JJQ (26:4) 515–29.

**10035.** BEGUM, KHANI.   James Joyce and Simone de Beauvoir: the myth of woman re-visioned. Unpub. doct. diss., Southern Illinois Univ. at Carbondale, 1988. [Abstr. in DA (50) 1660A.]

**10036.** BEJA, MORRIS, *et al.* (eds).   James Joyce: the centennial symposium: papers presented at the eighth international James Joyce symposium, Dublin, Ireland, 1982. Urbana: Illinois UP, 1986. pp. xv, 234. Rev. by Vincent J. Cheng in MP (86:3) 328–31; by J. C. C. Mays in RES (39:156) 1988, 588–9.

**10037.** —— BENSTOCK, SHARI (eds).   Coping with Joyce: essays from the Copenhagen symposium. Columbus: Ohio State UP. pp. xviii, 280. Rev. by John S. Phillipson in OhioanaQ (32:4) 220.

**10038.** BENZENHÖFER, UDO.   Joyce and embryology: Giulio Valenti's *Lezioni Elementari di Embriologia* as a source for 'Oxen of the Sun'. JJQ (26:4) 608–11.

**10039.** BISHOP, JOHN. Joyce's book of the dark: *Finnegans Wake*. (Bibl. 1988, 7837.) Rev. by Michael Patrick Gillespie in PLL (24:4) 1988, 450–3; by J. C. C. Mays in RES (39:156) 1988, 590–1.

**10040.** BLONDEL, JACQUES. Pathos in *The Dead* (James Joyce, 1904). Repérages (12) 1–5.

**10041.** BOGUMIL, MARY LOUISE. Joyce's use of synaesthesia: the intra- and the inter-episodic recurrence of sensory impressions in *Ulysses*. Unpub. doct. diss., Univ. of South Florida, 1988. [Abstr. in DA (49) 3031A.]

**10042.** BOWEN, ZACK; CARENS, JAMES F. (eds). A companion to Joyce studies. (Bibl. 1985, 11449.) Rev. by Willi Erzgräber in LJGG (27) 1986, 360–4.

**10043.** BRADBURY, MALCOLM. The modern world: ten great writers. *See* **9287.**

**10044.** BRIVIC, SHELDON. Joyce the creator. (Bibl. 1987, 11212.) Rev. by R. A. Cave in RES (39:154) 1988, 321–2.

**10045.** BUCKWALD, CRAIG MARTIN. Transforming vision: the authority of romantic nature in the fiction of James Joyce. Unpub. doct. diss., Univ. of California, Berkeley, 1988. [Abstr. in DA (50) 951A.]

**10046.** CAESAR, TERRY P. Joycing parody. JJQ (26:2) 227–37.

**10047.** CALLAHAN, DENIS JOSEPH F. James Joyce and the novels of Aidan Higgins, Jennifer Johnston, John McGahern and Brian Moore. *See* **9930.**

**10048.** CAREY, PHYLLIS. Beckett's Pim and Joyce's Shem. *See* **9040.**

**10049.** CARPENTIER, MARTHA CELESTE. Mother, maid, and witch: Hellenic female archetypes in modern British literature. *See* **9456.**

**10050.** CASTLE, GREGORY. The book of youth: reading Joyce's Bildungsroman. Genre (22:1) 21–40.

**10051.** CHILDRESS, LYNN D. Les Phéniciens et l'Odyssée: a source for 'Lestrygonians'. JJQ (26:2) 259–69.

**10052.** CHIN, SHEON-JOO. The death of Rudy: James Joyce's use of the doctrine of prenatal influence in *Ulysses*. JELL (35) 115–30.

**10053.** CLARK, JOHN M. Writing *Jerusalem* backwards: William Blake in *Exiles*. *See* **5065.**

**10054.** COHEN, DAVID. Conclusion of the foregoing: James Joyce, Samuel Beckett, and Flann O'Brien. *See* **9042.**

**10055.** COHN, ALAN M. Current JJ checklist (47–49). JJQ (26:2) 271–7; (26:3) 425–34; (26:4) 573–81.

**10056.** COWART, DAVID. From Nuns' Island to Monkstown: celibacy, concupiscence, and sterility in *The Dead*. JJQ (26:4) 499–504.

**10057.** CRONIN, RICHARD. Gabriel Conroy's Three Graces. NQ (36:2) 200.

**10058.** CULLETON, CLAIRE A. Joycean synchronicity in Wolfe's *Look Homeward, Angel*. TWR (13:2) 49–52.

**10059.** CUMPIANO, MARION W. The impact of James Joyce on William Carlos Williams: an uneasy ambivalence. WCWR (15:1) 48–58.

**10060.**  DALESKI, H. M.   Joyce's 'Circe': a tale of dragons. *In* (pp. 151–63) **23.**

**10061.**  DAWSON, HUGH J.   Thomas MacGreevy and Joyce. JJQ (25:3) 1988, 305–21.

**10062.**  DEVLIN, KIMBERLY J.   'See ourselves as other see us': Joyce's look at the eye of the other. PMLA (104:5) 882–93.

**10063.**  DIGGORY, TERENCE.   Yeats's stream of consciousness. *In* (pp. 253–66) **45.**

**10064.**  DOMENICHELLI, MARIO.   Paradoxes: Joyce's opus in-interruptum. JJQ (27:1) 111–19.

**10065.**  DORSEY, PETER.   From *Hero* to *Portrait*: the de-Christification of Stephen Dedalus. JJQ (26:4) 505–13.

**10066.**  DU SAUTOY, PETER.   Editing *Ulysses*: a personal account. *See* **306.**

**10067.**  EAGLETON, TERRY.   Joyce and mythology. *In* (pp. 310–19) **45.**

**10068.**  EASTMAN, JACQUELINE F.   The language of flowers: a new source for 'Lotus Eaters'. JJQ (26:3) 379–96.

**10069.**  ECKLEY, GRACE.   Children's lore in *Finnegans Wake*. *See* **1788.**

**10070.**  ELBARBARY, SAMIR.   The image of the goat in *Portrait of the Artist as a Young Man*. CLit (16:3) 261–73.

**10071.**  ELLMANN, RICHARD.   James Joyce. (Bibl. 1985, 11470.) Rev. by Deirdre Byrne in UES (27:1) 41.

**10072.**  —— Joyce as letter writer. *In* (pp. 304–9) **45.** (Text of radio broadcast, 28 April 1984.)

**10073.**  FERNANDES DE TOLENTINO, MAGDA VELLOSO.   Family bonds and bondage within the family: a study of family ties in Clarice Lispector and James Joyce. MLS (18:2) 1988, 73–7.

**10074.**  FESHBACH, SIDNEY.   Marcel Duchamp; or, Being taken for a ride: Duchamp was a Cubist, a Mechanomorphist, a Dadaist, a Surrealist, a Conceptualist, a Modernist, a Post-Modernist – and none of the above. JJQ (26:4) 541–60.

**10075.**  FOKKEMA, DOUWE.   James Joyce. *In* (pp. 48–74) DOUWE FOKKEMA and ELRUD IBSCH, Modernist conjectures: a mainstream in European literature 1910–1940. London: Hurst, 1987. pp. xii, 330. Rev. by Naomi Segal in NC (8) 178–80.

**10076.**  FÜGER, WILHELM.   Crosslocution in *Dubliners*. JJQ (27:1) 87–99.

**10077.**  GARDT, ANDREAS.   James Joyce auf deutsch: Möglichkeiten der literarischen Übersetzung. Frankfurt; Berne; New York; Paris: Lang. pp. 297. (Apekte der englischen Geistes- und Kulturgeschichte, 18.)

**10078.**  GORDON, LINDA ADRIAN.   Parallax as a model of perspective in *Ulysses* and *À la Recherche du temps perdu*. Unpub. doct. diss., Univ. of Colorado at Boulder, 1988. [Abstr. in DA (49) 2210A.]

**10079.**  HAYMAN, DAVID.   *Ulysses* and Motherwell: illustrating an affinity. *See* **88.**

**10080.**  HERR, CHERYL.   Joyce's anatomy of culture. (Bibl. 1988, 7861.) Rev. by J. C. C. Mays in RES (39:156) 1988, 590.

**10081.** HIGGINS, MICHAEL.   A note on 'time or setdown' in *Ulysses*. *See* **1074.**

**10082.** HYLES, VERNON.   Ben, Rudy, and the fantastic: Wolfe's journey to Nighttown. TWR (13:2) 44–8.

**10083.** JOLAS, EUGÈNE.   James Joyce. Paris: Plon. pp. 200.

**10084.** KAIN, RICHARD M.   The case of the lost cyclist; or, What happened to Harry Thrift (*U*10.1259). *See* **336.**

**10085.** KEANE, PATRICK J.   Terrible beauty: Yeats, Joyce, Ireland, and the myth of the devouring female. St Louis: Missouri UP, 1988. pp. xvii, 146.

**10086.** KERSHNER, R. B.   Joyce, Bakhtin, and popular literature: chronicles of disorder. Chapel Hill; London: North Carolina UP. pp. xi, 338. Rev. by Cheryl Herr in JJQ (27:1) 146–52.

**10087.** KERSHNER, R. B., JR.   Joyce and Dujardin's *L'Initiation au péché et à l'amour*: an unacknowledged debt? JJQ (26:2) 213–25.

**10088.** KIMBALL, JEAN.   From Eve to Helen: stages of the *anima*-figure in Joyce's *Ulysses*. Mosaic (20:2) 1987, 29–40.

**10089.** KLEIN, SCOTT W.   Odysseus as 'new womanly man'. JJQ (26:4) 617–19.

**10090.** KWON, OH-KUNG.   James Joyce eui *Ulysses* yeongu: dawonronjeok jeupgeun. (A study of James Joyce's *Ulysses*: a pluralistic approach.) Unpub. doct. diss., Chung Ang Univ., Seoul.

**10091.** LELAND, BLAKE THOMAS.   Heroic economies: Ezra Pound, James Joyce and Modernist epic between the wars. Unpub. doct. diss., Cornell Univ., 1988. [Abstr. in DA (50) 685A.]

**10092.** LIND, L. R.   The uses of Homer. CML (10:1) 7–20.

**10093.** LOSEY, JAY B.   Dream-epiphanies in *Finnegans Wake*. JJQ (26:4) 611–17.

**10094.** McARTHUR, MURRAY.   Stolen writings: Blake's *Milton*, Joyce's *Ulysses*, and the nature of influence. *See* **5087.**

**10095.** McCORMACK, W. J.   *Finnegans Wake* in Irish literary history. *In* (pp. 111–35) **32.**

**10096.** McDONALD, CHRISTIE.   'Oranges – apples – sugarsticks' Joycean associations: an interview with Richard Ellmann. *In* (pp. 37–41) **45.**

**10097.** MC ELROY, BERNARD.   Fiction of the modern grotesque. *See* **8331.**

**10098.** MARTÍ-OLIVELLA, JAUME.   Estructuras Joyceanas en la narrativa catalana y latinoamericana contemporanea. Unpub. doct. diss., Univ. of Illinois at Urbana-Champaign, 1988. [Abstr. in DA (49) 2650A.]

**10099.** MELCHIORI, GIORGIO.   Mr Bloom in Venice. JJQ (27:1) 121–4.

**10100.** —— The Rev. John Flynn and Buck Mulligan. JJQ (27:1) 124–6.

**10101.** MIHĂIEŞ, MIRCEA.   Cealaltă rătăcire a lui Ulise. (*Ulysses*'s other wanderings.) Orizont, 28 July, 16 (review-article).

**10102.** MILLIMAN, CRAIG ARTHUR. Lessons of the masters: social tension as a creative necessity in the fiction of Hawthorne, James, and Joyce. *See* **6974.**

**10103.** MIRZA, SHIKOH MOHSIN. Narration and theme in James Joyce's *Two Gallants*. ACM (2:1) 101–11.

**10104.** MIYATA, KYOUKO. Joyce no toshi: Trieste to Zurich. (Joyce's cities: Trieste and Zurich.) Tokyo: Ozawa. pp. x, 268.

**10105.** MONK, LELAND R. Standard deviations: chance and the modern novel. *See* **6778.**

**10106.** NADEL, IRA B. 'Finn Redux': a new source for the title of *Finnegans Wake*. JJQ (26:2) 279–84.

**10107.** ——Joyce and the Jews: culture and texts. Basingstoke: Macmillan; Iowa City: Iowa UP. pp. xii, 290. Rev. by Dominic Manganiello in JJQ (27:1) 152–5.

**10108.** OLOFSSON, TOMMY. 'Away! Away!': om James Joyce i lands-flykt och dramat *Exiles*. ('Away! Away!': on James Joyce in exile and his play *Exiles*.) Allt om böcker (1989:4) 10–15.

**10109.** ORR, JOHN. The making of the twentieth-century novel: Lawrence, Joyce, Faulkner, and beyond. *See* **8355.**

**10110.** O'SHEA, MICHAEL J. James Joyce and heraldry. (Bibl. 1987, 11289.) Rev. by Patrick Parrinder in MLR (84:1) 142–3.

**10111.** PEARCE, SANDRA MANOOGIAN. A reading of the comic elements in James Joyce's *Exiles*: the Bergsonian clown in the Dionysian vineyard. Unpub. doct. diss., Oklahoma State Univ., 1988. [Abstr. in DA (49) 3035A.]

**10112.** PESCH, JOSEF W. Dot dropping(s) . . . a 'pre-text'? *See* **367.**

**10113.** PETERSON, RICHARD F.; COHN, ALAN M.; EPSTEIN, EDMUND L. (eds). Work in progress: Joyce centenary essays. (Bibl. 1984, 11618.) Rev. by Patrick Parrinder in MLR (84:1) 143.

**10114.** PIETTE, A. C. Rhyme and memory in the prose of Proust, Joyce and Beckett. *See* **9070.**

**10115.** PLATT, L. H. The buckeen and the dogsbody: aspects of history and culture in 'Telemachus'. JJQ (27:1) 77–86.

**10116.** POPLAWSKI, GARY J. Stasis and paralysis: Stephen Dedalus and Gabriel Conroy. BSUF (27:3) 1986, 43–54.

**10117.** PUGLIATTI, PAOLA. Who's afraid of the 1984 *Ulysses*? JJQ (27:1) 41–53.

**10118.** PURDY, STROTHER B. Vico's *verum-factum* and the status of the object in *Finnegans Wake*. JJQ (26:3) 367–78.

**10119.** RABATÉ, JEAN-MICHEL. Bruno *no*, Bruno *si*: note on a contradiction in Joyce. JJQ (27:1) 31–9.

**10120.** RADER, RALPH W. Why Stephen's hand hurts: Joyce as Narcissus in *Ulysses*. JJQ (26:3) 440–5.

**10121.** REESE, STEVEN CASE. Modernism and the march of science: four novelists. *See* **9980.**

**10122.** REIZBAUM, MARILYN. Zurich James Joyce Foundation. *See* **259.**

**10123.** Reynolds, Mary T. Mr Leopold Bloom and the lost Vermeer. *In* (pp. 320–32) **45.**

**10124.** Rix, Walter. James Joyce's *The Dead*: the symbolist inspiration and its narrative reflection. *In* (pp. 146–65) **17.**

**10125.** Robertson, William K. A portrait of James Joyce's biographer. *In* (pp. 42–8) **45.** (Interview with Richard Ellmann.)

**10126.** Roughley, Alan Robert. *Finnegans Wake* as a deconstructive text. Unpub. doct. diss., Univ. of British Columbia, 1987. [Abstr. in DA (49) 2234A.]

**10127.** Ryu, Ju-Hyun. Jakga wa kyoungheom: *Ulysses* eui Scylla and Charybdis. (The author and his experiences: Scylla and Charybdis in *Ulysses*.) JELL (35) 445–62.

**10128.** Sabin, Margery. The dialect of the tribe: speech and community in modern fiction. See **1418.**

**10129.** Sagher, Saad Kassim. Alienation in James Joyce's *Dubliners*. Journal of Education and Science (Univ. of Mosul, Iraq) (5) (Humanities and education) 1987, 19–51.

**10130.** Sandulescu, C. George. The language of the devil: texture and archetype in *Finnegans Wake*. (Bibl. 1987, 11311.) Rev. by Geert Lernout in IUR (19:2) 397–400.

**10131.** Sayers, William. A schoolmaster's June day walk round the city: Joyce and Strindberg's Albert Blom. SN (61:2) 183–92.

**10132.** Schiralli, Martin. Art and the Joycean artist. JAE (23:4) 37–50.

**10133.** Schlossman, Beryl. Joyce's Catholic comedy of language. (Bibl. 1987, 11313.) Rev. by Patrick Parrinder in MLR (84:1) 144–5.

**10134.** Schneider, Ulrich. James Joyce, *Dubliners*. (Bibl. 1986, 12723.) Rev. by Willi Erzgräber in LJGG (26) 1985, 422–5.

**10135.** Schork, R. J. Plautus and Martial in Joyce. NQ (36:2) 198–200.

**10136.** Senn, Fritz. Bucolic strands in 'Aeolus'. JJQ (27:1) 129–32.

**10137.** —— Cold comfort. JJQ (27:1) 126–8.

**10138.** —— *Habent sua fata*. JJQ (27:1) 132–4.

**10139.** —— Micro-Cycloptics. JJQ (27:1) 134–6.

**10140.** —— 'There's a medium in all things': Joycean readings. *In* (pp. 333–50) **45.**

**10141.** Shaffer, Brian W. Kindred by choice: Joyce's *Exiles* and Goethe's *Elective Affinities*. JJQ (26:2) 199–212.

**10142.** Shout, John D. Joyce at twenty-five, Huston at eighty-one: *The Dead*. See **8134.**

**10143.** Sims, Peter. A pocket guide to *Ulysses*. JJQ (26:2) 239–58.

**10144.** Sisson, Annette. Constructing the human conscience in Joyce's *Dubliners*. MidQ (30:4) 492–514.

**10145.** Smidt, Kristian. 'I'm not half Norawain for nothing': Joyce and Norway. JJQ (26:3) 333–50.

**10146.** Smith, Craig Stanley. The web of Nausicaa: a study of Joyce's *Ulysses*. Unpub. doct. diss., Southern Illinois Univ. at Carbondale, 1988. [Abstr. in DA (49) 3372A.]

**10147.**  Spoo, Robert.    Jules Laforgue and the nightmare of Stephen Dedalus. JJQ (26:3) 445–9.

**10148.**  —— Rival confessors in *Chamber Music*: meaning and narrative in Joyce's lyric mode. JJQ (26:4) 483–98.

**10149.**  —— Teleology, monocausality, and marriage in *Ulysses*. ELH (56:2) 439–62.

**10150.**  —— 'Usurper': a word on the last word in 'Telemachus'. JJQ (26:3) 450–1.

**10151.**  Staley, Thomas F.    An annotated critical bibliography of James Joyce. New York; London: Harvester Wheatsheaf. pp. viii, 182. (Harvester Wheatsheaf annotated critical bibliographies.)

**10152.**  Steinberg, Erwin R.    Reading Leopold Bloom/1904 in 1989. JJQ (26:3) 397–416.

**10153.**  Steppe, Wolfhard.    Reply to Paola Pugliatti's 'Who's Afraid of the 1984 *Ulysses*?'. JJQ (27:1) 55–68.

**10154.**  Swartzlander, Susan.    'Yclept from Clio's clippings': James Joyce's use of history. Unpub. doct. diss., Pennsylvania State Univ., 1988. [Abstr. in DA (50) 451A.]

**10155.**  Torchiana, Donald T.    Backgrounds for Joyce's *Dubliners*. (Bibl. 1986, 12738.) Rev. by Patrick Parrinder in MLR (84:1) 142; by Klaus P. Müller in Ang (107:1/2) 263–6; by R. A. Cave in RES (39:154) 1988, 322–3.

**10156.**  Trela, Julia.    Joyce a zen. (Joyce and Zen.) Twórczość (45:11) 70–84.

**10157.**  Tristram, Hildegarde L. C.    Why James Joyce also lost his 'brain of forgetting': patterns of memory and media in Irish writing. *In* (pp. 220–33) **5.**

**10158.**  Tweedie, Gordon.    'Common sense': James to Joyce and the pragmatic L. Bloom. JJQ (26:3) 351–66.

**10159.**  Unal-Hodson, H. C.    A stylistic evaluation of point of view in James Joyce's *The Boarding House*. See **1427.**

**10160.**  van Boheemen, Christine (ed.).    Joyce, modernity and its mediation. Amsterdam: Rodopi. pp. 228. (European Joyce studies, 1.)

**10161.**  van Caspel, Paul.    Bloomers on the Liffey: eisegetical readings of Joyce's *Ulysses*. (Bibl. 1987, 11337.) Rev. by Patrick Parrinder in MLR (84:1) 142.

**10162.**  van Caspel, Paul P. J.    Blake and Joyce: strange syzygy. *In* (pp. 101–17) **23.**

**10163.**  Verdicchio, Massimo.    Exagmination round the fictification of Vico and Joyce. See **9077.**

**10164.**  Versteegen, Heinrich.    James Joyces *Ulysses* in vier deutschen Übersetzungen: samt einem Ausblick auf die niederländische Übersetzung. Frankfurt; Berne; New York; Paris: Lang, 1988. pp. 349. (Studien zur englischen und amerikanischen Literatur, 12.)

**10165.**  Wales, Kathleen.    The 'Oxen of the Sun' in *Ulysses*: Joyce and Anglo-Saxon. JJQ (26:3) 319–32.

**10166.**  Wasserman, Julian N.    James Joyce and the left hand of God: Hinduism in *Ulysses*. BSUF (27:3) 1986, 55–70.

**10167.** YEE, CORDELL D. K.  Between word and world: language and representation in Joyce. Unpub. doct. diss., Univ. of Wisconsin–Madison. [Abstr. in DA (50) 452A.]

**10168.** ZACCHI, ROMANA.  Quoting words and worlds: discourse strategies in *Ulysses*. JJQ (27:1) 101–9.

**10169.** ZEITLIN, MICHAEL.  Faulkner and *Ulysses*: a psychoanalytic inquiry. *See* **9618.**

### George S. Kaufman

**10170.** MASON, JEFFREY D.  Wisecracks: the farces of George S. Kaufman. Ann Arbor, MI; London: UMI Research Press, 1988. pp. xi, 134. (Theater and dramatic studies, 53.) Rev. by Don B. Wilmeth in TJ (41:4) 565–6.

### Patrick Kavanagh (1905–1967)

**10171.** HUGHES, EAMONN.  The political unconscious in the auto-biographical writings of Patrick Kavanagh.  *In* (pp. 103–10) **17.**

**10172.** KAVANAGH, PETER.  Sacred keeper: a biography of Patrick Kavanagh. (Bibl. 1981, 11768.) Newbridge, Co. Kildare: Goldsmith Press, 1986. pp. 404.( Second ed.: first ed. 1979.)

**10173.** MCLOUGHLIN, D. J.  Tradition and nationality in the work of three Irish poets: W. B. Yeats, Patrick Kavanagh and Seamus Heaney. *See* **9861.**

### John B. Keane

**10174.** KEALY, MARIE HUBERT.  Spirit of place: a context for social criticism in John B. Keane's *The Field* and *Big Maggie*. IUR (19:2) 287–301.

### Molly Keane ('M. J. Farrell')

**10175.** PETRE, DIANA (introd.).  Young entry. London: Virago Press. pp. 320. (Virago modern classics, 324.)

### Weldon Kees

**10176.** ABBOTT, CRAIG S.  The guidebook source for Weldon Kees' *Travels in North America*. NCL (19:3) 8.

### Adrienne Kennedy

**10177.** FORTE, JEANIE.  Realism, narrative, and the feminist play-wright – a problem of reception. ModDr (32:1) 115–27.

### William Kennedy

**10178.** KENNEDY, WILLIAM.  Two writers' beginnings. *See* **9002.**

**10179.** REILLY, EDWARD C.  John the Brawn McGree in *Quinn's Book*: a probable source. NCL (19:3) 4–5.

### Jack Kerouac

**10180.** BIRKERTS, SVEN.  On the road to nowhere: Kerouac re-read and regretted. Harper's (279) July, 74–6.

**10181.** MALMGREN, CARL D.  *On the Road* reconsidered: Kerouac and the modernist tradition. BSUF (30:1) 59–67.

**10182.** PENZENSTADLER, JOAN ELIZABETH.  Mythical mapping in recent American fiction. *See* **9523.**

**10183.** ROUS, JEAN-MARIE.  Jack Kerouac, le clochard céleste. Paris: Renaudot. pp. 251.

## Ken Kesey

**10184.** FICK, THOMAS H.   The hipster, the hero, and the psychic frontier in *One Flew Over the Cuckoo's Nest*. RMRLL (43:1/2) 19–34.

**10185.** SAFER, ELAINE B.   The contemporary American comic epic: the novels of Barth, Pynchon, Gaddis, and Kesey. *See* **9018.**

**10186.** SMITH, ANGELEAN VANDORA.   Patterns of authenticity: a search for self in American novels. *See* **9532.**

## Wendy Kesselman

**10187.** HART, LYNDA.   'They don't even look like maids any more': Wendy Kesselman's *My Sister in This House*. In (pp. 131–46) **39.**

**10188.** SCHROEDER, PATRICIA R.   Locked behind the proscenium: feminist strategies in *Getting Out* and *My Sister in This House*. ModDr (32:1) 104–14.

## Francis King

**10189.** TRENDAFILOV, VLADIMIR (introd.).   Čovekăt sam e brodnik. (One is a wanderer.) Sofia: Narodna kultura. pp. 280.

## Stephen King

**10190.** MAGISTRALE, TONY.   Hawthorne's woods revisited: Stephen King's *Pet Sematary*. *See* **6969.**

**10191.** UNDERWOOD, TIM; MILLER, CHUCK (eds).   Bare bones: conversations on terror with Stephen King. London: New English Library. pp. 217.

## Galway Kinnell

**10192.** TUTEN, NANCY LEWIS.   In the Romantic tradition: the poetry of Galway Kinnell. Unpub. doct. diss., Univ. of South Carolina, 1988. [Abstr. in DA (49) 3028A.]

**10193.** ZIMMERMAN, LEE.   Intricate and simple things: the poetry of Galway Kinnell. Urbana: Illinois UP, 1987. pp. xiv, 246. (Cf. bibl. 1985, 11618.) Rev. by Allen Dunn in AL (61:3) 494–6.

## Thomas Kinsella

**10194.** LEERSSEN, JOEP.   Táin after táin: the mythical past and the Anglo-Irish. In (pp. 29–46) **32.**

## W. P. Kinsella

**10195.** FRY, AUGUST J.   The return of Joseph Jefferson Jackson, a study in American myth. In (pp. 89–102) **13.**

## Rudyard Kipling

**10196.** CAMPBELL, G.   Kipling and Conrad: precursors of modernity. *See* **9289.**

**10197.** CORNELL, LOUIS L. (ed.).   *The Man who Would be King* and other stories. (Bibl. 1987, 11378.) Rev. by Zohreh T. Sullivan in MLR (84:4) 951–3.

**10198.** HELDMAN, JAMES.   Kipling, *Jane's Marriage*, and *The Janeites*. *See* **6174.**

**10199.** KEMP, SANDRA.   Kipling's hidden narratives. Oxford: Blackwell, 1988. pp. x, 132. Rev. by Brian Gasser in NQ (36:4) 537–8.

**10200.** —— (ed.).   Selected stories. (Bibl. 1987, 11384.) Rev. by Zohreh T. Sullivan in MLR (84:4) 951–3.

**10201.**	MALCOLM, DAVID.	Two *Theys*: a comparison of the fantastic in two texts. *In* (pp. 19–30) **57.**

**10202.**	MOORE-GILBERT, B. J.	Kipling and 'orientalism'. (Bibl. 1987, 11387.) Rev. by Alan Sandison in DUJ (81:1) 1988, 167–8; by Zohreh T. Sullivan in MLR (84:1) 140–1.

**10203.**	PETZOLD, DIETER.	The female of the species. Frauenfiguren in Kiplings Werk. AAA (14:1) 3–18.

**10204.**	PINNEY, THOMAS (ed.).	The day's work. (Bibl. 1987, 11391.) Rev. by Zohreh T. Sullivan in MLR (84:4) 951–3.

**10205.**	ROBSON, W. W. (ed.).	The jungle book. New York: OUP, 1987. (Bibl. 1987, 11396.) Rev. by Zoreh T. Sullivan in MLR (84:4) 951–3.

**10206.**	RUPPEL, RICHARD JEFFREY.	Kipling, Conrad, and the popular exotic short fiction of the 1890's. *See* **5905.**

**10207.**	RUTHERFORD, ANDREW (ed.).	Plain tales from the hills. (Bibl. 1987, 11400.) Rev. by Zohreh T. Sullivan in MLR (84:4) 951–3.

**10208.**	SEYMOUR-SMITH, MARTIN.	Rudyard Kipling. London: Mac-Donald. pp. 373. Rev. by Harry Ricketts in LRB (11:6) 13–14.

### A. M. Klein

**10209.**	CAPLAN, USHER; STEINBERG, M. W. (eds).	Literary essays and reviews. (Bibl. 1987, 11408.) Rev. by Laura Groening in CanL (119) 1988, 131–3.

**10210.**	FINKELSTEIN, MARK.	The style of A. M. Klein. Unpub. doct. diss., Univ. of Toronto, 1988. [Abstr. in DA (50) 145A.]

**10211.**	STEINBERG, M. W. (ed.).	Short stories. (Bibl. 1984, 11730.) Rev. by D. O. Spettique in DalR (66:3) 1986, 368–71.

### C. J. Koch

**10212.**	MAES-JELINEK, HENA.	A web of horizons: 'Otherland' in Christopher Koch's *The Doubleman*. *In* (pp. 161–73) **42.**

**10213.**	YONG, MARGARET.	Explorations in the heart of darkness: turning landscape into art in *Slipstream* and *The Year of Living Dangerously*. *In* (pp. 10–37) **19.**

### Arthur Koestler

**10214.**	DAY, FRANK.	Arthur Koestler: a guide to research. New York: Garland, 1987. pp. xxi, 248. (Garland reference library of the humanities, 612.) Rev. by Paul G. Reeve in SoCR (22:1) 140–1.

### Joy Kogawa

**10215.**	MAGNUSSON, A. LYNNE.	Language and longing in Joy Kogawa's *Obasan*. CanL (116) 1988, 58–66.

**10216.**	MERIVALE, P.	Framed voices: the polyphonic elegies of Hébert and Kogawa. CanL (116) 1988, 68–82.

**10217.**	ROSE, MARILYN RUSSELL.	Hawthorne's *Custom House*, Said's *Orientalism* and Kogawa's *Obasan*: an intertextual reading of an historical fiction. *See* **6984.**

**10218.**	ST ANDREWS, B. A.	New voices in the Canadian choir: Kogawa and Mukherjee. SDR (27:4) 17–39.

### Arthur Kopit

**10219.**	CAMERON-WEBB, GAVIN.	*End of the World* and *Hamlet*. *See* **3698.**

## Bernard Kops

**10220.** MANOR, E.   The Anglo-Jewish predicament in the plays of Bernard Kops, Arnold Wesker, Harold Pinter, and Peter Shaffer. Unpub. M.Litt. thesis, Univ. of Cambridge, 1986. [Abstr. in IT (36:2) 473–4.]

## Jerzy Kosinski

**10221.** GLADSKY, THOMAS S.   Jerzy Kosinski: the Polish Cooper. NCL (19:2) 11–12.

**10222.** GORDON, ANDREW.   Jerzy Kosinski's *Being There* and the 'oral triad'. NCL (19:2) 3–5.

**10223.** GRIGSBY, JOHN L.   Jerzy Kosinski's *Cockpit*: a twentieth-century *Gulliver's Travels*? See **5528.**

**10224.** HIRSCHBERG, STUART.   A note on an episode in Jerzy Kosinski's *The Hermit of 69th Street*. NCL (19:2) 5–6.

**10225.** LILLY, PAUL R., JR.   Words in search of victims: the achievement of Jerzy Kosinski. Kent, OH; London: Kent State UP, 1988. pp. x, 199.

**10226.** MURRAY, RAYMOND B.   'That certain Krylovian touch': an insight into Jerzy Kosinski's *Being There*. NCL (19:2) 6–8.

**10227.** ZIEGLER, ROBERT.   Electing the video self: a note on *Being There*. NCL (19:2) 2–3.

## Nigel Krauth

**10228.** EDELSON, PHYLLIS FAHRIE.   The role of history in three contemporary Australian novels. See **9427.**

## Henry Kreisel

**10229.** NEUMAN, SHIRLEY (ed.).   Another country: writings by and about Henry Kreisel. Edmonton, Alta: NeWest Press, 1985. pp. 362. (NeWest literary documents, 7.) Rev. by F. W. Watt in CanL (115) 1987, 202–3.

## Uys Krige

**10230.** LE BON, PIERRE.   Uys Krige et Roy Campbell: première rencontre de deux poètes sud-africains. See **9192.**

## Seymour Krim

**10231.** NICOSIA, GERALD.   Seymour Krim: making every word count. BkW, 29 Oct., 1, 10.

## Robert Kroetsch

**10232.** DORSCHT, SUSAN RUDY.   How *The Studhorse Man* makes love: a post-feminist analysis. CanL (119) 1988, 25–31.

**10233.** LECKER, ROBERT.   Robert Kroetsch.   (Bibl. 1986, 12835.) Rev. by Anne Hicks in CanL (118) 1988, 141–3.

**10234.** RUDY DORSCHT, SUSAN ARLENE.   Telling the difference: rereading 'woman', with Robert Kroetsch's writing. Unpub. doct. diss., York Univ. (Ont.), 1988. [Abstr. in DA (49) 3728A.]

**10235.** SLEMON, STEPHEN.   Magic realism as post-colonial discourse. See **9939.**

**10236.** TENER, J., *et al.* (eds).   The Robert Kroetsch papers: first accession. See **270.**

**10237.** TURNER, M. E. Canadian literature and Robert Kroetsch: a case of canonization. DalR (67:1) 1987, 56–72.

**10238.** TURNER, MARGARET E. Endings be damned: Robert Kroetsch's *Gone Indian*. CanL (119) 1988, 57–71.

### Maxine Kumin

**10239.** VOSSEKUIL, CHERYL LYNN. Making the connection: a thematic analysis of Maxine Kumin's poetry. Unpub. doct. diss., Michigan State Univ., 1988. [Abstr. in DA (49) 3028–9A.]

### Oliver La Farge

**10240.** CAFFEY, DAVID L. (ed.). Yellow sun, bright sky: the Indian country stories of Oliver La Farge. Albuquerque: New Mexico UP, 1988. pp. 212. Rev. by Robert F. Gish in Journal of the Southwest (31:3) 435–7.

### Alex La Guma

**10241.** CHANDRAMOHAN, B. The writings of Alex La Guma: a study in transethnicity. Unpub. doct. diss., Univ. of Sheffield, 1988. [Abstr. in IT (38:4) 1461.]

### Betty Lambert

**10242.** VAN HERK, ARITHA. Double crossings: booking the lover. *In* (pp. 276–86) **40.**

### George Lamming

**10243.** BIRBALSINGH, FRANK. George Lamming in conversation with Frank Birbalsingh. JCL (23:1) 1988, 182–8.

**10244.** ELIAS, KHALIQUZZAMAN M. The legacies of Prospero: a critique of the colonial and the neo-colonial experiences in selected writings of Richard Wright, Chinua Achebe, and George Lamming. *See* **8899.**

**10245.** MCDONALD, AVIS G. 'Within the orbit of power': reading allegory in George Lamming's *Natives of My Person*. JCL (22:1) 1987, 73–86.

### Patrick Lane

**10246.** LANE, PATRICK. The unyielding phrase. *See* **8520.**

### Rose Wilder Lane

**10247.** ANDERSON, WILLIAM T. (ed.). A *Little House* sampler. Lincoln: Nebraska UP. pp. 243. Rev. by Gillian Avery in TLS, 7 Apr., 377.

### Eve Langley

**10248.** JONES, NANCY LEE. Reality and the shadow: the adventure of identity in twentieth-century Australian women's fiction. *See* **9685.**

### Philip Larkin

**10249.** BARNDEN, SASKIA (GAIL). Voice in contemporary British poetry, with special attention to Philip Larkin, Ted Hughes and Geoffrey Hill. *See* **9933.**

**10250.** COOKSON, LINDA; LOUGHREY, BRYAN (eds). Critical essays on Philip Larkin: the poems. Harlow: Longman. pp. 135. (Longman literature guides.)

**10251.** COX, C. B. British poetry since 1945: Philip Larkin and Ted Hughes. *See* **9957.**

**10252.** DAY, ROGER.    Larkin. (Bibl. 1987, 11426.) Rev. by Adolphe Haberer in EA (42:3) 355–6.

**10253.** HARTLEY, JEAN.    Philip Larkin, the Marvell Press and me. *See* **435.**

**10254.** HASSAN, SALEM KADHEM.    Time, tense and structure in contemporary English poetry: Larkin and the Movement. *See* **8506.**

**10255.** JARMAN, MARK.    A shared humanity: *In the Stopping Train* and *The Whitsun Weddings. In* (pp. 89–101) **46.**

**10256.** LI, VICTOR.    Reverence or resistance? Reading Larkin's poetry. DalR (67:2/3) 1987, 355–64 (review-article).

**10257.** LONGINO, VICTORIA.    'Smaller and clearer as the years go by': women and girls in the works of Philip Larkin. Unpub. doct. diss., Univ. of Cincinnati. [Abstr. in DA (50) 1312–13A.]

**10258.** ROWE, M. W.    The transcendental Larkin. Eng (38) 143–52.

**10259.** SALWAK, DALE (ed.).    Philip Larkin: the man and his work. Basingstoke: Macmillan. pp. xviii, 184.

**10260.** SHARROCK, ROGER.    Private faces in public places: the poetry of Larkin and Lowell. Eng (36) 1987, 113–32.

**10261.** SMITH, PETER MACDONALD.    The postmodernist Larkin. Eng (38) 153–61.

**10262.** SPURR, BARRY.    Alienation and affirmation in the poetry of Philip Larkin. Sydney Studies in English (14) 1988/89, 52–71.

**10263.** THWAITE, ANTHONY (ed.).    Collected poems. New York: Farrar, Straus & Giroux; London: Marvell Press; Faber & Faber. pp. xxvii, 330. Rev. by Paul Gray in Time, 8 May, 97; by Patrick Williams in Honest Ulsterman (88) 41–7; by Blake Morrison in TLS, 14 Oct. 1988, 1151–2; by Peter Forbes in Listener (120) 13 Oct. 1988, 33; by Ian Hamilton in LRB (10:18) 1988, 3, 5.

**10264.** WATSON, STEPHEN.    Philip Larkin and the situation of poetry. *See* **8575.**

**10265.** WHALEN, TERRY.    Philip Larkin and English poetry. Vancouver: British Columbia UP, 1986. (Bibl. 1987, 11431.) Rev. by Victor Li in DalR (67:2/3) 1987, 356–64; by A. T. Tolley in QQ (95:4) 1988, 931–3.

### Margaret Laurence

**10266.** ROOKE, CONSTANCE.    Fear of the open heart. *In* (pp. 256–69) **40.**

**10267.** SCOTT, JAMIE S.    Self-writing, self-transcendence, commemoration: Margaret Laurence's *A Bird in the House.* JSSE (12) 87–105.

**10268.** SPARROW, FIONA MARY.    'The spirit in the ascent': the African writings of Margaret Laurence. Unpub. doct. diss., Univ. of Toronto. [Abstr. in DA (50) 1660A.]

### D. H. Lawrence

**10269.** ASAI, M.    Fullness of being: a study of D. H. Lawrence. Unpub. doct. diss., Univ. of Manchester, 1988. [Abstr. in IT (39:2) 488.]

**10270.** BALBERT, PETER.    D. H. Lawrence and the phallic imagination: essays on sexual identity and feminist misreading. Basingstoke: Macmillan. pp. xi, 190. Rev. by David Trotter in LRB (11:17) 16–17.

**10271.** —— Marcus, Phillip L. (eds). D. H. Lawrence: a centenary consideration. Ithaca, NY; London: Cornell UP, 1985. pp. 261. Rev. by Michael Bell in MLR (84:1) 146–7.

**10272.** Betsky-Zweig, Sarah. Lawrence and Cézanne. *In* (pp. 103–26) **13.** (Conference paper, Leiden, Sept. 1983.)

**10273.** Black, Michael. D. H. Lawrence: the early fiction: a commentary. (Bibl. 1988, 7970.) Rev. by Karen McLeod Hewitt in RES (38:151) 1987, 409; by Jeff Wallace in Eng (36:154) 1987, 77–84.

**10274.** Britton, Derek. Lady Chatterley: the making of the novel. (Bibl. 1988, 7972.) Rev. by Roy Booth in Eng (38) 87–92; by John Worthen in NQ (36:4) 544.

**10275.** Burgess, Anthony. Flame into being: the life and work of D. H. Lawrence. (Bibl. 1987, 11447.) Rev. by Michael Bell in MLR (84:1) 147.

**10276.** Chong, Nam-Young. D. H. Lawrence eui munhak yesulron. (D. H. Lawrence's theory of literature.) EngSt (13) 46–57.

**10277.** Chua Chen Lok. The European participant and the third-world revolution: André Malraux's *Les Conquérants* and D. H. Lawrence's *The Plumed Serpent. In* (pp. 101–11) **19.**

**10278.** Clark, L. D. (ed.). The plumed serpent (Quetzalcoatl). Cambridge: CUP, 1987. pp. xlviii, 571. (Cambridge edition of the letters and works of D. H. Lawrence.) Rev. by Émile Delavenay in EA (42:1) 112–13.

**10279.** —— The plumed serpent. Introd. by Melvyn Bragg. London: Grafton. pp. viii, 423. (Cambridge edition of the works of D. H. Lawrence.)

**10280.** Dallaportas, Joyce. D. H. Lawrence and Henry Moore: the positive and negative manifestations of the archetypal feminine. Unpub. doct. diss., Syracuse Univ., 1988. [Abstr. in DA (50) 4A.]

**10281.** D'Andrea, Ben. The modern apocalyptic imagination of D. H. Lawrence. Unpub. doct. diss., Univ. of Toronto. [Abstr. in DA (50) 1654A.]

**10282.** Ellis, David; Mills, Howard. D. H. Lawrence's non-fiction: art, thought and genre. Cambridge: CUP, 1988. pp. vi, 193.

**10283.** Farmer, David; Vasey, Lindeth; Worthen, John (eds). Women in love. (Bibl. 1988, 7979.) Rev. by Peter Preston in NQ (36:2) 262–3.

**10284.** Fjågesund, P. Apocalyptic and millennial ideas in D. H. Lawrence: a contextual exploration. Unpub. doct. diss., Univ. of Oxford, 1988. [Abstr. in IT (39:2) 488.]

**10285.** Floc'h, Sylvain. Arches et arcanes: la mystique de l'échange chez D. H. Lawrence. *In* (pp. 129–34) **35.**

**10286.** Freije, George F. Equine names in *The Rocking-Horse Winner.* CEACrit (51:4) 75–84.

**10287.** Gates, Susan Fielding. George Eliot and D. H. Lawrence: a study in influence. *See* **6765.**

**10288.** GORHAM, R. ELAINE.   Mythic reconstruction: the new beginning of D. H. Lawrence's late work. Unpub. doct. diss., Univ. of Michigan, 1988. [Abstr. in DA (49) 2229A.]

**10289.** GRMELOVÁ, ANNA.   Tématické a strukturální diversifikace povídek D. H. Lawrence pod vlivem 1. světové války. (Thematic and structural diversification of D. H. Lawrence's stories as influenced by World War I.) *In* (p. 20) **6.**

**10290.** HARVEY, GEOFFREY.   Sons and lovers. (Bibl. 1987, 11461.) Rev. by Margaret Storch in MLR (84:4) 955; by Gail Cunningham in RES (39:156) 1988, 591–2.

**10291.** HYDE, VIRGINIA.   *Aaron's Rod*: D. H. Lawrence's revisionist typology. Mosaic (20:2) 1987, 111–26.

**10292.** IIDA, TAKERO; IIDA, MASAMI (eds).   D. H. Lawrence: shouden to shi no kanshou. (D. H. Lawrence: a short biography and an interpretation of his poems.) Tokyo: Yamaguchi. pp. vi, 192.

**10293.** INGERSOLL, EARL.   The failure of bloodbrotherhood in Melville's *Moby-Dick* and Lawrence's *Women in Love. See* **7227.**

**10294.** INGERSOLL, EARL G.   The progress towards marriage in D. H. Lawrence's *Mr Noon*. DQR (19:4) 294–306.

**10295.** JANSOHN, CHRISTA.   Lawrence's 'book of French verse'. NQ (36:2) 201–2.

**10296.** KALNINS, MARA (ed.).   Aaron's rod. (Bibl. 1988, 7988.) Rev. by Émile Delavenay in EA (42:1) 111–12.

**10297.** KATZ-ROY, GINETTE; LIBRACH, MIRIAM (eds).   D. H. Lawrence. Paris: L'Herne, 1988. pp. 397.

**10298.** KINKEAD-WEEKES, MARK (ed.).   The rainbow. Cambridge: CUP. pp. lxxvi, 672. (Cambridge edition of the letters and works of D. H. Lawrence.) Rev. by David Trotter in LRB (11:17) 16–17.

**10299.** LAVRIN, NORA.   D. H. Lawrence: Nottingham connections. Nottingham: Astra Press, 1986. pp. viii, 187. Rev. by Margaret Storch in MLR (84:4) 955–6.

**10300.** LEE, SEOG-JANG.   D. H. Lawrence eui soseol gibeob: *The Rainbow* reul jungsim euro. (D. H. Lawrence's narrative technique in *The Rainbow*.) Unpub. doct. diss., Dongguk Univ., Seoul.

**10301.** LINDSKOLD, JANE MAUREEN.   The Persephone myth in D. H. Lawrence. Unpub. doct. diss., Fordham Univ. [Abstr. in DA (49) 3733A.]

**10302.** MACLEOD, SHEILA.   Lawrence's men and women. (Bibl. 1987, 11477.) Rev. by Karen McLeod Hewitt in RES (38:149) 1987, 106; by Michael Bell in MLR (84:1) 147.

**10303.** MAHON, ELLEN MACLEOD.   Behind the dancing: D. H. Lawrence's *Apocalypse* and *Last Poems*. Unpub. doct. diss., Fordham Univ., 1988. [Abstr. in DA (49) 2669–70A.]

**10304.** MASSON, M. J.   The influence of Congregationalism on the first four novels of D. H. Lawrence. Unpub. doct. diss., Univ. of Durham, 1988. [Abstr. in IT (39:3) 1115; in DA (50) 1313A.]

**10305.** MAY, KEITH M.   Nietzsche and modern literature: themes in Yeats, Rilke, Mann and Lawrence. Basingstoke: Macmillan, 1988. pp. ix, 175.

**10306.** MEHL, DIETER.   D. H. Lawrence und sein 'neuer' Roman *Mr Noon.* PoetA (21:1/2) 164–78.

**10307.** MEMON, MUHAMMAD ALIM.   D. H. Lawrence's vision of man: a study of flesh and spirit. Sind Quarterly (Karachi) (17:2) 53–70.

**10308.** MILIARAS, BARBARA A.   Pillar of flame: the mythological foundations of D. H. Lawrence's sexual philosophy. New York; Berne; Frankfurt: Lang, 1987. pp. xi, 301. (American univ. studies, 4: English language and literature, 33.) Rev. by Émile Delavenay in EA (42:1) 109–10.

**10309.** MILTON, COLIN.   Lawrence and Nietzsche: a study in influence. Aberdeen: Aberdeen UP, 1987. pp. xi, 244. Rev. by Eleanor H. Green in AUR (53:1) 44; by Émile Delavenay in EA (42:1) 108–9.

**10310.** NEWMARCH, DAVID.   Literary and kindred evenings in D. H. Lawrence's Eastwood: the Eastwood Congregational Literary Society 1899–1909. ESA (32:2) 121–33.

**10311.** NIXON, CORNELIA.   Lawrence's leadership politics and the turn against women. Berkeley; Los Angeles; London: California UP, 1986. pp. xii, 239. Rev. by Margaret Storch in MLR (84:4) 954–5; by Karen McLeod Hewitt in RES (39:153) 1988, 143–4.

**10312.** ORR, JOHN.   The making of the twentieth-century novel: Lawrence, Joyce, Faulkner, and beyond. *See* **8355.**

**10313.** POLE, S.   'The utmost response': a comparison of the writing and thought of Antonin Artaud and D. H. Lawrence. Unpub. doct. diss., Univ. of Reading. [Abstr. in IT (39:2) 483.]

**10314.** PRESTON, PETER; HOARE, PETER (eds).   D. H. Lawrence in the modern world. London: Macmillan. pp. xvi, 221. Rev. by David Trotter in LRB (11:17) 16–17.

**10315.** RADI, A.   The man–woman relationship: conflicts and dualities. (*Sons and Lovers, The Rainbow, Women in Love.*) Unpub. M.Litt. thesis, Univ. of Strathclyde, 1984. [Abstr. in IT (36:3) 914.]

**10316.** REESE, STEVEN CASE.   Modernism and the march of science: four novelists. *See* **9980.**

**10317.** REEVES, MARJORIE; GOULD, WARWICK.   Joachim of Fiore and the myth of the eternal evangel in the nineteenth century. *See* **6109.**

**10318.** RICHARDS, BERNARD.   A botanical mistake in Lawrence's *The White Peacock.* NQ (36:2) 202.

**10319.** SABIN, MARGERY.   The dialect of the tribe: speech and community in modern fiction. *See* **1418.**

**10320.** SALGĀDO, GĀMINI; DAS, G. K. (eds).   The spirit of D. H. Lawrence: centenary studies. Introd. by RAYMOND WILLIAMS. Basingstoke: Macmillan, 1988. pp. xx, 335.

**10321.** SCHECKNER, PETER.   Class, politics, and the individual: a study of the major works of D. H. Lawrence. Rutherford, NJ: Fairleigh Dickinson UP, 1985. pp. 176. Rev. by Jennings Blackman in MidQ (30:3) 387–8.

**10322.** SCHNEIDER, DANIEL J.   D. H. Lawrence's physical religion: the debt to Tylor, Frobenius, and Nuttall. *In* (pp. 161–6) **45.**

**10323.** SNYDER, PHILLIP ASA.   Constructional codes in the *Künstler-roman: Sons and Lovers* and *Look Homeward, Angel* as exemplars. Unpub. doct. diss., Univ. of North Carolina at Chapel Hill, 1988. [Abstr. in DA (50) 683A.]

**10324.** SQUIRES, MICHAEL; JACKSON, DENNIS (eds).   D. H. Lawrence's *Lady*: a new look at *Lady Chatterley's Lover.* (Bibl. 1986, 12951.) Rev. by Michael Bell in MLR (84:1) 146.

**10325.** VASEY, LINDETH (ed.).   Mr Noon. (Bibl. 1986, 12963.) Rev. by Karen Scherzinger in UES (25:1) 1987, 51–2.

**10326.** VERHOEVEN, WILHELMUS MARIA.   D. H. Lawrence's duality concept: its development in the novels of the early and major phase. (Bibl. 1987, 11500.) Rev. by M. J. Klay in EngS (70:2) 189–90.

**10327.** VITOUX, PIERRE.   Le fleuve souterrain dans *Women in Love.* EA (42:1) 13–26.

**10328.** WHITELEY, PATRICK J.   Knowledge and experimental realism in Conrad, Lawrence and Woolf. *See* **9328.**

**10329.** WILLIAMS, L. R.   Misogynistic knowledge and the 'cocksure' woman: Freud, Nietzsche, and feminism in the interpretation of D. H. Lawrence. Unpub. doct. diss., Univ. of Sussex, 1988. [Abstr. in IT (38:4) 1463–4.]

**10330.** WINKGENS, MEINHARD.   Zivilisationskritik und Lebens-affirmation bei D. H. Lawrence. Der paradigmatische Bildungsweg von Ursula Brangwen. LJGG (27) 1986, 123–40.

**10331.** WUSSOW, H.   The nightmare of history: the Great War and the work of Virginia Woolf and D. H. Lawrence. Unpub. doct. diss., Univ. of Oxford, 1988. [Abstr. in IT (39:2) 489.]

**10332.** YAMAGUCHI, TETSUO.   D. H. Lawrence ni okeru haha. (The mother in D. H. Lawrence's work.) Tokyo: Yumi Press. pp. viii, 174.

### T. E. Lawrence

**10333.** ANON.   T. E. Lawrence: the legend and the man: an exhibition held in the Bodleian Library, 12 September to 26 November 1988, to mark the centenary of the birth of Thomas Edward Lawrence, 'Lawrence of Arabia'. Oxford: Bodleian Library, 1988. pp. 112.

**10334.** BROWN, MALCOLM (ed.).   T. E. Lawrence: the selected letters. New York: Norton. pp. 568. Rev. by Paul Gray in Time, 15 May, 80–1; by Stephen E. Tabachnick in NYTB, 16 July, 19; by Warren O. Ault in BkW, 21 May, 5; by Jeffrey Meyers in BW, 7 May, 6.

**10335.** MEYERS, JEFFREY.   The wounded spirit: T. E. Lawrence's *Seven Pillars of Wisdom.* New York: St Martin's Press; Basingstoke: Macmillan. pp. 239. (Second ed.: first ed. 1973.) Rev. in BkW, 10 Dec., 17.

**10336.** PFAFF, WILLIAM.   A critic at large: the fallen hero. NY, 1 May, 105–15.

**10337.** WILSON, JEREMY.   Lawrence of Arabia: the authorised bio-graphy of T. E. Lawrence. London: Heinemann. pp. xi, 1188. Rev. by Robert Irwin in Listener (122) 21 Dec., 62–3.

### Henry Lawson
**10338.** JONES, DOROTHY.   Serious laughter: on defining Australian humour. *See* **9991.**

**10339.** TURNER, GRAEME.   Film and fiction: dealing with Australian narrative. *In* (pp. 109–20) **20.**

### John Howard Lawson
**10340.** BLOCH, BEVERLE ROCHELLE.   John Howard Lawson's *Processional*: Modernism in American theatre in the twenties. Unpub. doct. diss., Univ. of Denver, 1988. [Abstr. in DA (49) 2863–4A.]

### Irving Layton
**10341.** CAMERON, ELSPETH.   Irving Layton: a portrait. Toronto: Stoddart, 1985. pp. 518. Rev. by Ben Jones in CanL (115) 1987, 160–2; by Patricia Keeney Smith in UTQ (56:3) 1987, 467–8.

**10342.** LAYTON, IRVING; O'ROURKE, DAVID.   Waiting for the Messiah. Toronto: McLelland & Stewart, 1985. pp. 264. Rev. by Patricia Keeney Smith in UTQ (56:3) 1987, 468–70.

**10343.** REED, SABRINA LEE.   The place of American poets in the development of Irving Layton, Louis Dudek and Raymond Souster. *See* **8545.**

### Stephen Leacock
**10344.** CHOPRA, VISHNU R.   From manuscript to print: Stephen Leacock's *The Transit of Venus*. *See* **127.**

**10345.** STAINES, DAVID (ed.).   Stephen Leacock: a reappraisal. Ottawa: Ottawa UP, 1986. pp. 170. (Reappraisals: Canadian writers, 12.) Rev. by Gerald Noonan in CanL (122/23) 234–6.

### David Leavitt
**10346.** KLARER, MARIO.   Homoerotische Trigonometrie. Zu David Leavitts *Territory* (Revieransprüche). Forum Homosexualität und Literatur (Siegen, Germany) (7) 51–69.

### 'John le Carré' (David John Cornwell)
**10347.** MARTIN, B. K.   Le Carré's *The Spy Who Came in from the Cold*: a structuralist reading. Sydney Studies in English (14) 1988/89, 72–88.

### Harper Lee
**10348.** CHAPPELL, CHARLES M.   The unity of *To Kill a Mockingbird*. AlaR (42:1) 32–48.

**10349.** GOING, WILLIAM T.   Truman Capote: Harper Lee's fictional portrait of the artist as an Alabama child. *See* **9195.**

### Ursula K. Le Guin
**10350.** BARROW, CRAIG; BARROW, DIANA.   *The Left Hand of Darkness*: feminism for men. Mosaic (20:1) 1987, 83–96.

**10351.** BLOOM, HAROLD (ed.).   Ursula K. Le Guin. New York: Chelsea House, 1986. pp. x, 274. (Modern critical views.) Rev. by Elizabeth Cummins in SFS (15:1) 99–101.

**10352.** BUCKNALL, BARBARA J.   Rilke and Le Guin. Mythlore (16:2) 62–5.

**10353.** CZEŻYK, MARIOLA.   Extratextual perspectives of two trilogies. *In* (pp. 75–89) **57.**

**10354.** Franko, Carol.   Self-conscious narration as the complex representation of hope in Le Guin's *Always Coming Home*. Mythlore (15:3) 57–60.

**10355.** Heldrech, Lillian M.   To defend or to correct: patterns of culture in *Always Coming Home*. Mythlore (16:1) 58–62, 66.

**10356.** Lebioda, Tadeusz Tomasz.   Obcy wśród hermafrodytów. (A stranger among hermaphrodites.) Míesíęczník líterackí (24:11/12) 131–2.

### Elmore Leonard

**10357.** Sandels, Robert.   Common criminals and ordinary heroes. AD (22:1) 14–20.

### Doris Lessing ('Jane Somers')

**10358.** Bowker, Veronica.   Textuality and worldliness: crossing the boundaries: a postmodernist reading of Achebe, Conrad and Lessing. *See* **8684.**

**10359.** Cook, S.   A personal polyphony: narrative voice in Doris Lessing's novels of the 1970s. Unpub. M.Phil. diss., Univ. of York. [Abstr. in IT (39:1) 34.]

**10360.** Dvorak, Angeline Godwin.   Surrogate motherhood and the quest for self in selected novels of Doris Lessing. Unpub. doct. diss., Florida State Univ. [Abstr. in DA (50) 1663a.]

**10361.** English, James F.   Comic transactions: humor as communication in four modern novels. *See* **9293.**

**10362.** Fahim, S. S.   Doris Lessing: the theme of equilibrium and the form of the novel. Unpub. doct. diss., Univ. of Exeter. [Abstr. in IT (38:4) 1462.]

**10363.** Fontenot, Deborah Yvonne B.   A vision of anarchy: correlate structures of exile and madness in selected works of Doris Lessing and her South African contemporaries. *See* **9770.**

**10364.** Magie, Lynne Adele.   The daemon Eros: gothic elements in the novels of Emily and Charlotte Brontë, Doris Lessing, and Iris Murdoch. *See* **6304.**

**10365.** Mihăieş, Mircea (introd.).   Povestiri africane. (Collected African stories.) Bucharest: Univers. pp. 636.

**10366.** Pilet, Françoise.   Une lecture de *Through the Tunnel* de Doris Lessing. *In* (pp. 101–8) **35.**

**10367.** Visel, Robin Ellen.   White Eve in the 'petrified garden': the colonial African heroine in the writing of Olive Schreiner, Isak Dinesen, Doris Lessing and Nadine Gordimer. *See* **7379.**

**10368.** Whittaker, Ruth.   Doris Lessing. Basingstoke: Macmillan, 1988. pp. viii, 144. (Modern novelists.)

### Denise Levertov

**10369.** Georgoudaki, Catherine.   The human body as poetic tool and subject matter in Denise Levertov's poems. AAA (14:1) 57–72.

**10370.** Sakelliou-Schultz, Liana.   Denise Levertov: an annotated primary and secondary bibliography. New York; London: Garland, 1988. pp. xviii, 321. (Garland reference library of the humanities, 856.)

## Norman Levine
**10371.** GREENSTEIN, MICHAEL.  Between Ottawa and St Ives: Norman Levine's tight-rope walkers. JCL (23:1) 1988, 61–75.

## Alun Lewis
**10372.** LEWIS, GWENO (ed.).  Alun Lewis: letters to my wife. Bridgend: Seren. pp. 425. Rev. by William Scammell in Listener (122) 17 Aug., 28.

## C. Day Lewis ('Nicholas Blake')
**10373.** SMITH, STAN.  Text of unpublished holograph verses by C. Day Lewis. NQ (36:2) 207–8.

**10374.** —— Two unknown holograph poems by W. H. Auden and C. Day Lewis. *See* **8981.**

## C. S. Lewis
**10375.** ANDERSON, MARY JANELLE.  Toward a Christian approach to literature: the critical theories of C. S. Lewis as a model for Christian literary criticism. *See* **8664.**

**10376.** CARTER, MARGARET.  Perpetual winter in C. S. Lewis and Patricia McKillip. Mythlore (16:1) 35–6, 57.

**10377.** FILMER, KATH.  Neither here nor there: the spirit of place in George MacDonald's *Lilith* and C. S. Lewis's *Till We Have Faces.* *See* **7202.**

**10378.** GRESHAM, DOUGLAS H.  Lenten lands: my childhood with Joy Davidman and C. S. Lewis. New York: Macmillan; London: Collins, 1988. pp. x, 225.

**10379.** HOOPER, WALTER (ed.).  Letters of C. S. Lewis, edited with a memoir by W. H. LEWIS. (Bibl. 1967, 9065.) London: Fount, 1988. pp. 528. (Revised ed.: first ed. 1966.)

**10380.** JONES, CARLA FAUST.  The Literary Detective computer analysis of stylistic differences between *The Dark Tower* and C. S. Lewis' Deep Space trilogy. *See* **528.**

**10381.** KENNEDY, EUGENE.  Luminous spirit: the life and work of writer–theologian C. S. Lewis. BW, 1 Jan., 4.

**10381a.** LINDSKOOG, KATHRYN.  The C. S. Lewis hoax. Portland, OR: Multnomah Press, 1988. pp. 175. Rev. by Claude Rawson in TLS, 11 Aug., 864.

**10382.** —— Golden chains of coincidence: a C. S. Lewis puzzle solved and mystery to ponder. Mythlore (15:4) 21–5.

**10383.** LONEY, DOUGLAS.  Humpty Dumpty in the heavens: perspective in *Out of the Silent Planet.* Mythlore (16:2) 14–20.

**10384.** MANLOVE, C. N.  C. S. Lewis: his literary achievement. (Bibl. 1987, 11564.) Rev. by Peter J. Schakel in ChrisL (38:2) 82–3.

**10385.** MOYNIHAN, MARTIN (ed. and trans.).  C. S. Lewis–Don Giovanni Calabria: letters. London: Collins; Ann Arbor, MI: Servant. pp. 125. Rev. by Claude Rawson in TLS, 11 Aug., 864.

**10386.** RAWSON, CLAUDE.  The schoolboy Johnson. TLS, 11 Aug., 863–4 (review-article).

**10387.** SAYER, GEORGE.  Jack: C. S. Lewis and his times. Basingstoke: Macmillan. (Bibl. 1988, 8054.) Rev. by Claude Rawson in TLS,

11 Aug., 863–4; by John Bayley in LRB (11:1) 26–7; by David Hein in AEH (58:4) 551–3; by Dabney Hart in ChrisL (38:3) 70–2.

**10388.** WILSON, A. N.   C. S. Lewis, sins and all. NYTB, 24 Dec., 1.

### Sinclair Lewis

**10389.** McKENNA, BRUCE A.   Sinclair Lewis, a professional writer. Unpub. doct. diss., Brandeis Univ., 1988. [Abstr. in DA (49) 1803A.]

**10390.** PARRY, SALLY E.   The changing fictional faces of Sinclair Lewis' wives. SAF (17:1) 65–79.

**10391.** PORTER, M. GILBERT.   From Babbitt to Rabbit: the American materialist in search of a soul. In (pp. 185–96) **2.**

### Wyndham Lewis

**10392.** AYERS, D. S.   Wyndham Lewis and the self. Unpub. doct. diss., Univ. of Southampton. [Abstr. in IT (39:4) 1636.]

**10393.** DE VOOGD, P. J.   Literature of displacement: René Harding rejects George Eliot. In (pp. 349–59) **16.**

**10394.** O'KEEFFE, P.   Wyndham Lewis's *Tarr*: an edition of the novel, based on the 1918 American version. See **362.**

**10395.** SYMONS, JULIAN (ed.).   The essential Wyndham Lewis: an introduction to his work. London: Deutsch. pp. ix, 380. Rev. by John Bayley in LRB (11:12) 19–20.

### Shirley Lim

**10396.** LIM, SHIRLEY.   The dispossessing eye: reading Wordsworth on the equatorial line. In (pp. 126–32) **19.**

### Anne Morrow Lindbergh

**10397.** WURZ, TRUDE.   Anne Morrow Lindbergh: the literary reputation: a primary and annotated secondary bibliography. New York; London: Garland, 1988. pp. xxv, 92. (Garland reference library of the humanities, 556.)

### Jack Lindsay

**10398.** SMITH, BERNARD (ed.).   Culture and history: essays presented to Jack Lindsay. (Bibl. 1988, 8069.) Rev. by Stephen Ingle in NQ (36:2) 266–8.

### Joan Lindsay

**10399.** BARRETT, DONALD.   Some correspondence with Joan Lindsay. ALS (14:1) 104–7

### Gordon Lish

**10400.** GRUNWALD, LISA.   Captain Fiction rides again. Esquire (111:3) 160–2. (Interview.)

### Penelope Lively

**10401.** YVARD, PIERRE.   *Pack of Cards*, a theme and a technique. JSSE (13) 103–11.

### Dorothy Livesay

**10402.** DORNEY, LINDSAY; NOONAN, GERALD; TIESSEN, PAUL (eds).   A public and private voice: essays on the life and work of Dorothy Livesay. Waterloo, Ont.: Waterloo UP, 1986. pp. 139. Rev. by Sandra Hutchison in CanL (116) 1988, 208–9.

**10403.** McDONALD, LARRY.   The politics of influence: Birney, Scott, Livesay and the influence of politics. See **9102.**

## Ross Lockridge, Jr
**10404.** PENZENSTADLER, JOAN ELIZABETH.   Mythical mapping in recent American fiction. *See* **9523.**
## David Lodge
**10405.** GIBERT MACEDA, MARÍA TERESA.   *Small World* ... y baldío. (*Small World* ... and an empty one.) RAEI (2) 83–90.
**10406.** WOLF, WERNER.   Literaturtheorie in der Literatur. David Lodges *Small World* als kritische Auseinandersetzung mit dem Dekonstruktivismus. *See* **8893.**
## Jack London
**10407.** CREWS, BRIAN.   Fate, naturalism and the individual in Jack London's fiction. RCEI (18) 205–20.
**10408.** GATTI, SUSAN IRVIN.   Jack London on the job: a writer's representation of work. Unpub. doct. diss., Univ. of Pittsburgh. [Abstr. in DA (50) 1656–7A.]
**10409.** LABOR, EARLE; LEITZ, ROBERT C., III.   Jack London on Alexander Berkman: an unpublished introduction. AL (61:3) 447–56.
**10410.** ————SHEPARD, I. MILO (eds).   The letters of Jack London. (Bibl. 1988, 8075.) Rev. by Charles N. Watson, Jr, in AL (61:4) 684–6; by Peter Kemp in TLS, 9 June, 627–8; by John Sutherland in LRB (11:14) 17–19.
**10411.** McINTYRE, JOHN C.   Horacio Quiroga and Jack London compared: *A la deriva*, *El hombre muerto*, and *To Build a Fire*. NC (7) 143–59.
**10412.** PORTER, GERALD.   The art of the impossible: two early American utopias. *In* (pp. 42–54) **43.**
**10413.** SINCLAIR, ANDREW (introd. and postscr.).   *The Sea-Wolf* and other stories. Harmondsworth: Penguin. pp. 319. (Twentieth-century classics.)
**10414.** ———— Tales of the Pacific. Harmondsworth: Penguin. pp. 232. (Twentieth-century classics.)
**10415.** STASZ, CLARICE.   American dreamers: Charmian and Jack London. (Bibl. 1988, 8080.) Rev. by Charles N. Watson, Jr., in AL (61:4) 684–6.
**10416.** STEFANOV, HRISTO (postscr.).   Martin Ídan. (Martin Eden.) Varna, Bulgaria: Bakalov, 1988. pp. 435.
## Michael Longley
**10417.** GAUTHIER, DOMINIQUE.   Fragments de beauté chez deux poètes d'Irlande du Nord: Derek Mahon et Michael Longley. *In* (pp. 109–24) **10.**
## Anna M. Louw
**10418.** SMITH, MARIETJIE.   Anna M. Louw – 'n skryfster wat kan lag. (An authoress who can laugh.) Lantern (38:2) 11–14.
## H. P. Lovecraft
**10419.** LÉVY, MAURICE.   Etranges étrangers: ou, le fantastique selon Lovecraft. *In* (pp. 219–36) **26.**
## Amy Lowell
**10420.** AMBROSE, JAMES.   Amy Lowell and the music of her poetry. NEQ (62:1) 45–62.

**Robert Lowell**

**10421.** AXELROD, STEVEN GOULD; DEESE, HELEN (eds). Robert Lowell: essays on the poetry. (Bibl. 1988, 8085.) Rev. by Monroe K. Spears in SewR (96:1) 1988, 103–4.

**10422.** DORESKI, WILLIAM. Dante and the Roman poets in Robert Lowell's *History*. MLS (18:2) 1988, 47–59.

**10423.** HOBSBAUM, PHILIP. A reader's guide to Robert Lowell. (Bibl. 1988, 8087.) Rev. by Michael Hofmann in TLS, 26 May, 578.

**10424.** MEYERS, JEFFREY. Manic power: Robert Lowell and his circle. (Bibl. 1988, 8088.) Rev. by Michael Hofmann in TLS, 26 May, 578.

**10425.** SHARROCK, ROGER. Private faces in public places: the poetry of Larkin and Lowell. See **10260.**

**10426.** THOMAS, DAVID LEE. Loss, mourning and the vatic dispersal of self in the long poems of Whitman, Eliot, Pound, Berryman and Lowell. See **7665.**

**10427.** WALLINGFORD, KATHARINE. Robert Lowell's language of the self. Chapel Hill; London: North Carolina UP, 1988. pp. xi, 179. Rev. by Ronald A. Sharp in AL (61:4) 724–5; by Michael Hofmann in TLS, 26 May, 578.

**10428.** WITEK, THERESE DAMM. The *Life Studies* manuscripts: Robert Lowell and the revisable self. See **410.**

**Malcolm Lowry**

**10429.** BINNS, RONALD. Malcolm Lowry. (Bibl. 1987, 11633.) Rev. by Paul Tiessen in CanL (115) 1987, 157–9.

**10430.** HOVEN, HERIBERT. Malcolm Lowry: mit Seblstzeugnissen und Bilddokumenten. Reinbek: Rowohlt, 1988. pp. 155. (Rowohlts Monographien, 414.) Rev. by Stefan Haag in CanL (122/23) 168–9.

**10431.** SALLOUM, SHERYL. Malcolm Lowry: Vancouver days. (Bibl. 1987, 11640.) Rev. by Charles Lillard in CanL (118) 1988, 155.

**10432.** SCHERF, KATHLEEN. Three new poems by Malcolm Lowry. See **177.**

**10433.** SCHERF, KATHLEEN DOROTHY. The collected poetry of Malcolm Lowry: a critical edition with a commentary. See **392.**

**10434.** WILLIAMS, MARK. Muscular aesthete: Malcolm Lowry and 1930s English literary culture. JCL (24:1) 65–87.

**Mina Loy**

**10435.** GUNN, THOM. Three hard women: HD, Marianne Moore, Mina Loy. In (pp. 37–52) **46.**

**Alison Lurie**

**10436.** STARK, JOHN. Alison Lurie's career. HC (26:2) 1–7.

**Andrew Lytle**

**10437.** YOUNG, THOMAS DANIEL; SARCONE, ELIZABETH (eds). The Lytle–Tate letters: the correspondence of Andrew Lytle and Allen Tate. (Bibl. 1988, 8100.) Rev. by Robert C. Peterson in SoQ (27:2) 93–5.

**Rose Macaulay**

**10438.** LASSNER, PHYLLIS. Reimagining the acts of war: language and history in Elizabeth Bowen's *The Heat of the Day* and Rose Macaulay's *The World My Wilderness*. See **9121.**

### James McAuley
**10439.** McCredden, Lyn.   Any  hope  of  self-construction?  SoRA
(22:1) 61–74.   **George MacBeth**
**10440.** Ieronim, Ioana.   George Macbeth. RomLit 2 Mar., 20.
### Norman MacCaig
**10441.** Ross, Raymond.   Norman MacCaig: the history man. Cencrastus (33) 10–14.   **Mary McCarthy**
**10442.** Gelderman, Carol.   Mary McCarthy: a life. London: Sidgwick & Jackson. (Bibl. 1988, 8101.) Rev. by Frances Spalding in
Listener (121) 6 Apr., 31; by Anne Chisholm in TLS, 16 June, 672; by
John Lanchester in LRB (11:20) 29–30.
**10443.** McCarthy, Mary.   How I grew. London: Weidenfeld &
Nicolson, 1987. pp. 278.   **Jill McCorkle**
**10444.** Kane, Patricia.   When women tell stories: Jill McCorkle's
*Tending to Virginia*. NCL (19:3) 7.
### Carson McCullers
**10445.** Doty, Kathleen.   Dialogue, deixis and narrative in a
dramatic adaptation. See **1395.**
### Colleen McCullough
**10446.** Kaplan, Cora.   *The Thorn Birds*: fiction, fantasy, femininity.
*In* (pp. 142–66) Victor Burgin, James Donald, and Cora Kaplan
(eds), Formations of fantasy. London; New York: Methuen, 1986. pp. x,
221. Rev. by Maria Del Sapio in YES (19) 362–3.
### 'Hugh MacDiarmid' (C. M. Grieve)
**10447.** Bold, Alan.   MacDiarmid: Christopher Murray Grieve: a
critical biography. (Bibl. 1988, 8108.) Rev. by Raymond Ross in
Cencrastus (32) 29; by Patrick Crotty in SLJ (supp. 30) 16–19.
**10448.** Buthlay, Kenneth (ed.).   A drunk man looks at the thistle.
(Bibl. 1988, 8110.) Rev. by Patrick Crotty in SLJ (supp. 31) 23–6.
**10449.** Kerrigan, Catherine.   The nightmare of history: Hugh
MacDiarmid and the problem of the past. DalR (67:2/3) 1987, 306–13.
**10450.** —— (ed.).   The Hugh MacDiarmid–George Ogilvie letters.
(Bibl. 1988, 8114.) Rev. in Edinburgh Review (83) 139–40.
**10451.** McCarey, Peter.   Hugh MacDiarmid and the Russians.
(Bibl. 1988, 8115.) Rev. by Avril Pyman in MLR (84:4) 1053–4.
**10452.** Stephens, Charles.   The poet and revolution: MacDiarmid
and Blok. Cencrastus (32) 26–8.
**10453.** Watson, Roderick.   MacDiarmid. (Bibl. 1986, 13135.) Rev.
by Bruce Charlton in DUJ (81:1) 1988, 172–3.
### Roger McDonald
**10454.** Yong, Margaret.   Explorations in the heart of darkness:
turning landscape into art in *Slipstream* and *The Year of Living Dangerously*.
*In* (pp. 10–37) **19.**
### 'Ross MacDonald' (Kenneth Millar)
**10455.** Ward, Kathryn Ann.   Clients, colleagues, and consorts:
roles of women in American hardboiled detective fiction and film.
*See* **8153.**

## Ian McEwan
**10456.** DUPERRAY, MAX. L'étranger dans le contexte post-moderniste: *The Comfort of Strangers* d'Ian McEwan. *In* (pp. 291–306) **26.**

## John McGahern
**10457.** CALLAHAN, DENIS JOSEPH F. James Joyce and the novels of Aidan Higgins, Jennifer Johnston, John McGahern and Brian Moore. *See* **9930.**

**10458.** QUINN, ANTOINETTE. Varieties of disenchantment: narrative techniques in John McGahern's short stories. JSSE (13) 77–89.

## John McGrath
**10459.** DORNAN, READE WHITING. Committed theatre in post-war Britain: the approaches of Arnold Wesker and John McGrath. Unpub. doct. diss., Michigan State Univ., 1988. [Abstr. in DA (49) 3031A.]

## Thomas MacGreevy
**10460.** DAWSON, HUGH J. Thomas MacGreevy and Joyce. *See* **10061.**

## Thomas McGuane
**10461.** WIELAND, DENNIS PAUL. The transformation of the Cooper *mythos* in the writings of Thomas McGuane. *See* **6553.**

## Medbh McGuckian
**10462.** MELANDER, INGRID. The use of traditional symbol in three poems by Medbh McGuckian. MS (83:4) 298–303.

**10463.** WILLS, C. Language, history and sex in the poetry of Paul Muldoon and Medbh McGuckian. Unpub. doct. diss., Univ. of Oxford. [Abstr. in IT (39:3) 1116.]

## Arthur Machen
**10464.** DOBSON, ROGER; BRANGHAM, GODREY; GILBERT, R. A. (eds). Selected letters: the private writings of the master of the macabre. Wellingborough: Aquarian, 1988. pp. 256. Rev. by Timothy d'Arch Smith in TLS, 10 Mar., 253.

**10465.** PALMER, CHRISTOPHER (ed.). The collected Arthur Machen. London: Duckworth, 1988. pp. 376. Rev. by Timothy d'Arch Smith in TLS, 10 Mar., 253.

## Sir Compton Mackenzie
**10466.** THOMAS, DAVID; THOMAS, JOYCE. Compton Mackenzie: a bibliography. (Bibl. 1986, 13161.) Rev. by John Gillard Watson in NQ (36:1) 125–7.

## Patricia McKillip
**10467.** CARTER, MARGARET. Perpetual winter in C. S. Lewis and Patricia McKillip. *See* **10376.**

## Michael McLaverty
**10468.** KING, SOPHIA HILLAN. Conscience and the novelist: Michael McLaverty's journals and critical writings of the forties. Studies (78:309) 58–71.

## Archibald MacLeish
**10469.** BARBER, DAVID. In search of an 'image of mankind': the public poetry and prose of Archibald MacLeish. AmerS (29:2) 1988, 31–56.

**10470.** JONES, VICTOR H. MacLeish: on the poet. BSUF (27:1) 1986, 20–9.

**10471.** LANE, LAURIAT, JR. The publication history of MacLeish's longer poems. AL (61:2) 273–8.

**10472.** MACLEISH, ARCHIBALD. Reflections. Amherst; Massachusetts UP, 1986. pp. xiii, 291.

### Alistair MacLeod

**10473.** DAVIDSON, ARNOLD E. As birds bring forth the story: the elusive art of Alistair MacLeod. CanL (119) 1988, 32–42.

**10474.** —— Blindness and second sight in Alistair MacLeod's *Vision*. JSSE (12) 21–31.

### Bryan MacMahon

**10475.** MALLOY, KRISTIN. The short stories of Bryan MacMahon: theme and craft. Unpub. doct. diss., Univ. of Minnesota, 1988. [Abstr. in DA (49) 2231–2A.]

### 'Brinsley MacNamara' (John Weldon)

**10476.** GONZALEZ, ALEXANDER G. The novels of Brinsley Mac-Namara's later period. IUR (19:2) 272–86.

### Louis MacNeice

**10477.** GARDINER, MARGARET. A scatter of memories. London: Free Association, 1988. pp. 280. Rev. by Samuel Hynes in LRB (11:5) 6–7.

**10478.** HEUSER, ALAN (ed.). Selected literary criticism of Louis MacNeice. (Bibl. 1987, 11695.) Rev. by Jacqueline Banerjee in EngS (69:2) 1988, 280–2; by C. A. Buckley in NQ (35:3) 1988, 397–8.

**10479.** KIRKHAM, MICHAEL. Louis MacNeice's poetry of ambivalence. UTQ (56:4) 1987, 540–56.

**10480.** LONGLEY, EDNA. Louis MacNeice: a study. (Bibl. 1988, 8133.) Rev. by Samuel Hynes in LRB (11:5) 6–7; by Peter McDonald in TLS, 6 Jan., 16; by Sean O'Brien in Honest Ulsterman (87) 53–61.

**10481.** LONGLEY, MICHAEL (ed.). Selected poems. (Bibl. 1988, 8134.) Rev. by Peter McDonald in TLS, 6 Jan., 16.

### D'Arcy McNickle

**10482.** HANS, BIRGIT. Surrounded: the fiction of D'Arcy McNickle. Unpub. doct. diss., Univ. of Arizona, 1988. [Abstr. in DA (49) 2220A.]

**10483.** PARKER, DOROTHY RAGON. Choosing an Indian identity: a biography of D'Arcy McNickle. Unpub. doct. diss., Univ. of New Mexico, 1988. [Abstr. in DA (49) 2368A.]

### Derek Mahon

**10484.** DUYTSCHAEVER, JORIS. History in the poetry of Derek Mahon. *In* (pp. 97–110) **32.**

**10485.** GAUTHIER, DOMINIQUE. Fragments de beauté chez deux poètes d'Irlande du Nord: Derek Mahon et Michael Longley. *In* (pp. 109–24) **10.**

### Margaret Mahy

**10486.** GILDERDALE, BETTY. Introducing Margaret Mahy. Auckland: Viking Kestrel, 1987. pp. 90.

### Norman Mailer

**10487.** FICK, THOMAS H. The hipster, the hero, and the psychic frontier in *One Flew Over the Cuckoo's Nest*. *See* **10184.**

**10488.** KUBERSKI, PHILIP. The metaphysics of postmodern death: Mailer's *Ancient Evenings* and Merrill's *The Changing Light at Sandover.* ELH (56:1) 229–54.

**10489.** STANÍK, IVAN. Norman Mailer as a radical and observer. *In* (pp. 125–37) **62.**

**10490.** TABBI, JOSEPH PAUL. The psychology of machines: technology and personal identity in the work of Norman Mailer and Thomas Pynchon. Unpub. doct. diss., Univ. of Toronto. [Abstr. in DA (50) 1670A.]

**10491.** VĂLČEV, TODOR (introd.). Armiite na noštta. (The armies of the night.) Sofia: Narodna kultura. pp. 312.

**10492.** WENKE, JOSEPH. Mailer's America. (Bibl. 1988, 8141.) Rev. by Barbara Lounsberry in AmerS (29:2) 1988, 98.

### Bernard Malamud

**10493.** ADLER, BRIAN UNGAR. Liberty and the strongest bonds: fathers and sons in selected short works of Bernard Malamud. Unpub. doct. diss., Univ. of Tennessee, 1988. [Abstr. in DA (50) 684A.]

**10494.** CHOI, JAE-SUCK. Bernard Malamud eui *God's Grace*: jagi jungsimjeok sago eui gamok. (Bernard Malamud's *God's Grace*: the prison of egoism.) JELL (33) 1987, 691–708.

**10495.** LEE, CREMILDA TOLEDO. Freedom and responsibility in Bernard Malamud's *The Fixer.* CAE (22) 447–52.

**10496.** SALZBURG, JOEL (ed.). Critical essays on Bernard Malamud. Boston, MA: G. K. Hall, 1987. pp. viii, 229. (Critical essays on American literature.) Rev. by Daniel Walden in SAF (17:1) 120–1.

**10497.** VALEVA, ALEKSANDRA (introd.). Govoreštijat kon. (The short stories.) Sofia: Profizdat, 1988. pp. 151.

### David Malouf

**10498.** HESELTINE, HARRY. *An Imaginary Life*: the dimensions of self. ALS (14:1) 26–40.

**10499.** MANSFIELD, NICK. Body talk: the prose of David Malouf. Southerly (49:2) 230–8.

**10500.** NEILSEN, PHILIP. Breaking the myth: David Malouf's *Fly Away Peter.* Outrider (Indooroopilly, Qld) (6:1) 75–88.

**10501.** NETTELBECK, AMANDA. The pattern of history: discursive conflicts in David Malouf's *Child's Play.* Span (29) 31–44.

### David Mamet

**10502.** KOLIN, PHILIP C. David Mamet's *Writing in Restaurants*: a bibliography. AEB (ns 2:4) 1988, 160–7.

**10503.** RYAN, STEVEN DANIEL. David Mamet: dramatic craftsman. Unpub. doct. diss., Fordham Univ., 1988. [Abstr. in DA (49) 1800A.]

### Eli Mandel

**10504.** STUBBS, ANDREW. The politics of art: Eli Mandel's 'Journals'. CanL (122/23) 10–25.

### Frederick Manfred ('Feike Feikema VII')

**10505.** ANDERSON, DAVID. Frederick Manfred's mid-America. SSMLN (19:3) 24–33.

**10506.** WHIPP, LES. Frederick Manfred's *The Wind Blows Free*: autobiographical mythology. SDR (27:2) 100–28.

**10507.** WHIPP, LESLIE. Frederick Manfred's *The Golden Bowl* – the novel and novelist emerging. SDR (27:3) 54–73.

### F. E. Maning

**10508.** FITZGERALD, JOAN. Images of the self: two early New Zealand autobiographies by John Logan Campbell and Frederick Edward Maning. *See* **6439.**

### Chris Mann

**10509.** MANN, CHRIS ZITHULELE. A poem called *Farmyard in the City* with a few observations on prosody and quantum mechanics. *See* **2095.**

### Frederic Manning

**10510.** HOWARD, MICHAEL (introd.). The middle parts of fortune: Somme and Ancre, 1916. London: Buchan & Enright, 1986. pp. vii, 246. (Echoes of war.)

**10511.** MARWIL, JONATHAN L. Frederic Manning: an unfinished life. Durham, NC: Duke UP, 1988. pp. xx, 380. Rev. by Douglas Hewitt in NQ (36:2) 261–2.

### 'Katherine Mansfield'
### (Kathleen Mansfield Beauchamp, 'Julian Mark')

**10512.** ALPERS, ANTONY (ed.). The stories of Katherine Mansfield. (Bibl. 1985, 12046.) Rev. by David Bradshaw in MLR (82:1) 1987, 193–4.

**10513.** ANON. Katherine Mansfield manuscripts in the Alexander Turnbull Library. *See* **121.**

**10514.** CALDER, ALEX. My Katherine Mansfield. Landfall (43:4) 483–99.

**10515.** CLAYTON, CHERRY. Olive Schreiner and Katherine Mansfield: artistic transformations of the outcast figure by two colonial writers. *See* **7375.**

**10516.** DALE, JUDITH. Performing Katherine Mansfield. Landfall (43:4) 503–11.

**10517.** HANKIN, CHERRY A. (ed.). Letters between Katherine Mansfield and John Middleton Murry. London: Virago Press, 1988. pp. 425. Rev. by Dennis McEldowney in Landfall (43:4) 512–16; by Gillian Boddy in NZList, 6 May, 54–5, 59.

**10518.** HARDY, LINDA. The ghost of Katherine Mansfield. Landfall (43:4) 416–32.

**10519.** HARLOW, MICHAEL. The Katherine Mansfield centennial. English in Aotearoa (7) 2–3.

**10520.** McNEISH, JAMES. Katherine Mansfield's ambitious legacy. BkW, 1 Jan., 15.

**10521.** MIKAMI, KAZUKO. Rakuen no motomete: Katherine Mansfield no kenkyu. (In search of paradise: a study of Katherine Mansfield.) Tokyo: Kobundo. pp. 222.

**10522.** MIZUTA, KEIKO. Katherine Mansfield and the prose poem. RES (39:153) 1988, 75–83.

**10523.** MORAN, PATRICIA LOUISE. (S)mothering and the production(s) of the female artist: Katherine Mansfield and Virginia Woolf. Unpub. doct. diss., Univ. of California, Berkeley, 1988. [Abstr. in DA (50) 956A.]

**10524.** ORR, BRIDGET. Reading with the taint of the pioneer: Katherine Mansfield and settler criticism. Landfall (43:4) 447–61.

**10525.** O'SULLIVAN, VINCENT (ed.). Poems of Katherine Mansfield. (Bibl. 1988, 8181.) Rev. by Elizabeth Caffin in NZList, 6 May, 54.

**10526.** —— SCOTT, MARGARET (eds). The collected letters of Katherine Mansfied: vol. 1, 1903–1917. (Bibl. 1988, 8182.) Rev. by Valerie Shaw in THES (750) 1987, 24; by Samuel Hynes in SewR (94:4) 1986, 639–44; by David Bradshaw in MLR (82:1) 1987, 192–3; by Rosemary Dinnage in TLS, 13 Feb. 1987, 156; by Karina Williamson in NQ (36:1) 121–2.

**10527.** —— —— The collected letters of Katherine Mansfield: vol. 2, 1918–1919. (Bibl. 1988, 8183.) Rev. by Elizabeth Caffin in NZList, 26 Sept. 1987, 58; by Valerie Shaw in THES (750) 1987, 24; by Rosemary Dinnage in TLS, 13 Feb. 1987, 156; by Karina Williamson in NQ (36:1) 121–2.

**10528.** ROBINSON, ROGER. Mansfield celebrated. Landfall (43:3) 332–40.

**10529.** XU, ZHIMO. Mansfield. Trans. by SHIFEN GONG. TLR (22:2) 85–97.

### Jack Mapanje

**10530.** CHIMOMBO, STEVE. The chameleon in lore, life and literature – the poetry of Jack Mapanje. JCL (23:1) 1988, 102–15.

**10531.** GIBBS, JAMES. 'Whiskers, Alberto' and the 'township lambs' – towards an interpretation of Jack Mapanje's poem *We Wondered About the Mellow Peaches*. JCL (22:1) 1987, 31–46.

### 'William March' (William Edward March Campbell)

**10532.** CANFIELD-REISMAN, ROSEMARY M. (introd.). Trial balance: the collected short stories. Tuscaloosa; London: Alabama UP, 1987. pp. xxiii, 506.

### Archie Markham

**10533.** FITZPATRICK, JANICE. Engaging in a small act of exploration. Fortnight (275) 26. (Interview.)

### Daphne Marlatt

**10534.** RICOU, LAURIE. Phyllis Webb, Daphne Marlatt and simultitude: journal entries from a capitalist bourgeois patriarchal Anglo-Saxon mainstream critic. *In* (pp. 205–15) **40.**

### Owen Marshall

**10535.** CORBETT, FRANK. Owen Marshall: Timaru's writer in residence. North and South (Auckland) Sept., 84–91.

**10536.** O'SULLIVAN, VINCENT. The naming of parts: Owen Marshall and the short story. Sport (3) 67–74.

### Paule Marshall

**10537.** CARBY, HAZEL V. Reinventing history/imagining the future. *See* **8999.**

**10538.** CHRISTOL, HÉLÈNE. 'The Black woman's burden': Black women and work in *The Street* (Ann Petry) and *Brown Girls, Brownstones* (Paule Marshall). *In* (pp. 145–58) **25.**

**10539.** SHATTUCK, SANDRA DICKINSON. Personal and political histories: the hard work of remembering in Paule Marshall's *The Chosen Place, The Timeless People* and Christa Wolf's *Kindheitsmuster.* Unpub. doct. diss., Univ. of Texas at Austin, 1988. [Abstr. in DA (49) 1794A.]

### John Masefield

**10540.** FAROOQUI, KHALIDA SALEEM. A textual analysis of John Masefield's poem *A Consecration.* ARIEL (Jamshoro, Pakistan) (13) 1987/88, 41–8.

### C. F. G. Masterman

**10541.** WOODS, E. A darkness visible: Gissing, Masterman and the metaphors of class 1880–1914. *See* **6860.**

### William Mastrosimone

**10542.** DAVIS, TRACY C. *Extremities* and *Masterpieces*: a feminist paradigm of art and politics. *See* **9358.**

### Greg Matthews

**10543.** KRATZ, HENRY. Raunch. *See* **1003.**

### W. Somerset Maugham

**10544.** BARKER, DEBRA KAY STONER. Ironic designs in the exotic short fiction of W. Somerset Maugham. Unpub. doct. diss., Ball State Univ. [Abstr. in DA (50) 1308–9A.]

**10545.** CALDER, ROBERT. Willie: the life of W. Somerset Maugham. London: Heinemann. pp. xviii, 429. Rev. by Peter Parker in Listener (121) 30 Mar., 27.

**10546.** LE BON-DODAT, ANNE-MARIE. W. Somerset Maugham, poète malgré lui? Repérages (11) 21–7.

**10547.** TREBISZ, MAŁGORZATA. The necklace motif in *La Parure, Paste* and *A String of Beads. In* (pp. 95–104) **3.**

**10548.** WHITEHEAD, JOHN. Maugham: a reappraisal. London: Vision Press; Totowa, NJ: Barnes & Noble, 1987. (Critical studies.) Rev. by Peter Miles in NQ (36:1) 124–5.

### William Mayne

**10549.** LURIE, ALISON. William Mayne. *In* (pp. 369–79) **14.**

### Zakes Mda

**10550.** GORAN, JAN. Nothing to root for: Zakes Mda and South African resistance theatre. TJ (41:4) 478–91.

**10551.** HOLLOWAY, MYLES. Discordant voices of a lived reality: Zakes Mda's *The Hill.* SATJ (3:2) 33–50.

**10552.** — Social commentary and artistic mediation in Zakes Mda's early plays. English Academy Review (6) 28–41.

### Ved Mehta

**10553.** MEHTA, VED. The stolen light. London: Collins. pp. 462. (Continents of exile.) Rev. by John Grigg in Listener (121) 22 June, 28.

### H. L. Mencken

**10554.** FECHER, CHARLES A. (ed.). The diary of H. L. Mencken. New York: Knopf. pp. 476. Rev. by Jonathan Yardley in BkW, 10 Dec., 3; by

Robert Ward in NYTB, 24 Dec., 3; by Harry S. Ashmore in BW, 17 Dec., 1, 4.

## James Merrill

**10555.** KUBERSKI, PHILIP.   The metaphysics of postmodern death: Mailer's *Ancient Evenings* and Merrill's *The Changing Light at Sandover*. *See* **10488.**

**10556.** YENSER, STEPHEN.   The consuming myth: the work of James Merrill. (Bibl. 1987, 11781.) Rev. by Tim Armstrong in JAStud (23:1) 148–9.

## Thomas Merton

**10557.** CARR, ANNE E.   A search for wisdom and spirit: Thomas Merton's theology of the self. Notre Dame, IN: Notre Dame UP, 1988. pp. xii, 171. Rev. by M. Basil Pennington in Cithara (28:2) 71–2.

## W. S. Merwin

**10558.** DAVIS, WILLIAM V.   Influence without anxiety: Dylan Thomas and W. S. Merwin. NCL (19:5) 6–7.

**10559.** FINLEY, ROBERT STUART MARTIN.   Difficult language in the poetry of W. S. Merwin. Unpub. doct. diss., Univ. of Toronto. [Abstr. in DA (50) 1663A.]

**10560.** WILSON, REED DANIEL.   Words on a journey: vision and religion in the poetry of W. S. Merwin. Unpub. doct. diss., Univ. of California, Los Angeles, 1988. [Abstr. in DA (49) 3727A.]

## John Metcalf

**10561.** SOLECKI, SAM.   Some kicks against the prick: John Metcalf in his essays. *In* (pp. 207–23) **12.**

## Charlotte Mew

**10562.** HARDWICK, A.   Voices from the garden: aspects of women's poetry 1910–1939. *See* **8503.**

## Nicholas Meyer

**10563.** GORDON, STUART; BOLCHAZY, LADISLAUS J.   Detecting the real Sherlock Holmes: a stylometric comparison of Doyle and Meyer. *See* **6732.**

## Oscar Micheaux

**10564.** HEBERT, JANIS.   Oscar Micheaux: a Black pioneer. SDR (27:1) 62–70.

**10565.** YOUNG, JOSEPH A.   Black novelist as white racist: the myth of Black inferiority in the novels of Oscar Micheaux. New York; London: Greenwood Press. pp. xii, 178. (Contributions in Afro-American and African studies, 123.)

## Edna St Vincent Millay

**10566.** CHEVALIER, JEAN-LOUIS.   Sur la beauté: étude d'un sonnet de St Vincent Millay. *In* (pp. 37–50) **10.**

## Arthur Miller

**10567.** ADAM, JULIE.   Versions of heroism in modern American drama: selected plays by Miller, Williams, Anderson and O'Neill. *See* **8937.**

**10568.** BIGSBY, CHRISTOPHER (postscr.).   The golden years; The man who had all the luck. London: Methuen. pp. 235.

**10569.** DUKORE, BERNARD F.  *Death of a Salesman* and *The Crucible*: text and performance. Basingstoke: Macmillan. pp. 108. (Text and performance.)

**10570.** PORTER, M. GILBERT.  From Babbitt to Rabbit: the American materialist in search of a soul. *In* (pp. 185–96) **2.**

**10571.** ROUDANÉ, MATTHEW C. (ed.).  Conversations with Arthur Miller. Jackson; London: Mississippi UP, 1987. pp. xvii, 394. (Literary conversations.) Rev. by Thomas P. Adler in ModDr (32:2) 322–3; by John H. Lutterbie in TJ (41:4) 567–8.

**10572.** SCHLUETER, JUNE; FLANAGAN, JAMES K.  Arthur Miller. New York: Ungar, 1987. pp. xix, 143. Rev. by John H. Lutterbie in TJ (41:4) 568–9; by Thomas P. Adler in ModDr (32:2) 323–4.

**10573.** SPAULDING, PETER.  *Death of a Salesman* by Arthur Miller. Basingstoke: Macmillan, 1987. pp. vii, 85. (Macmillan master guides.)

### Henry Miller

**10574.** VON RICHTOFEN, P. M.  The *Booster/Delta* nexus: Henry Miller and his friends in the literary world of Paris and London on the eve of the Second World War. *See* **598.**

### Kelly Miller

**10575.** HUTCHINSON, GEORGE B.  Whitman and the Black poet: Kelly Miller's speech to the Walt Whitman Fellowship. *See* **7650.**

### Iris Milutinovic

**10576.** McLAREN, JOHN.  Iris Milutinovic – between two worlds. *See* **249.**

### Robert Minhinnick

**10577.** POOLE, RICHARD.  Two kinds of poetic thought: Robert Minhinnick and John Davies. *See* **9364.**

### Margaret Mitchell

**10578.** HAAG, JOHN.  *Gone with the Wind* in Germany. GaHQ (73:2) 278–304.

**10579.** PETRY, ALICE HALL.  Miss O'Connor and Mrs Mitchell: the example of *Everything That Rises*. SoQ (27:4) 5–15.

### W. O. Mitchell

**10580.** MITCHELL, BARBARA.  The long and short of it: two versions of *Who Has Seen the Wind*. *See* **354.**

### Timothy Mo

**10581.** ROTHFORK, JOHN.  Confucianism in Timothy Mo's *Sour Sweet*. JCL (24:1) 49–64.

### Bloke Modisane (William Modisane)

**10582.** NGWENYA, THENGANI H.  The ontological status of self in autobiography: the case of Bloke Modisane's *Blame Me on History*. Current Writing (1) 67–76.

### N. Scott Momaday

**10583.** HANSON, ELIZABETH I.  N. Scott Momaday: evocations of disruption and defeat. *In* (pp. 197–204) **2.**

### John Montague

**10584.** BROWN, TERENCE.  *The Dead Kingdom*: a reading. IUR (19:1) 103–9.

**10585.**  DENMAN, PETER.  'The executioner's boots': the fiction of John Montague. IUR (19:1) 129–38.

**10586.**  GARRATT, ROBERT F.  John Montague and the poetry of history. IUR (19:1) 91–102.

**10587.**  GRENNAN, EAMON.  'Of so, and so, and so': re-reading some details in Montague. IUR (19:1) 110–28.

**10588.**  JOHNSTON, DILLON.  Eros in Eire: Montague's romantic poetry. IUR (19:1) 44–57.

**10589.**  MONTAGUE, JOHN.  'The figure in the cave': a chapter of autobiography. IUR (19:1) 73–88.

**10590.**  O'DRISCOLL, DENNIS.  An interview with John Montague. IUR (19:1) 58–72.

**10591.**  QUINN, ANTOINETTE.  *The Well-Beloved*: Montague and the Muse. IUR (19:1) 27–43.

**10592.**  REDSHAW, THOMAS DILLON.  Books by John Montague: a descriptive checklist, 1958–1988. IUR (19:1) 139–58.

**10593.**  SEALY, DOUGLAS.  *The Sound of a Wound*: an introduction to the poetry of John Montague from 1958 to 1988. IUR (19:1) 8–26.

### L. M. Montgomery

**10594.**  GATES, CHARLENE E.  Image, imagination, and initiation: teaching as a rite of passage in the novels of L. M. Montgomery and Laura Ingalls Wilder. CLEd (20:3) 165–73.

**10595.**  RUSSELL, RUTH WEBER; RUSSELL, D. W.; WILMSHURST, REA.  Lucy Maud Montgomery: a preliminary bibliography. Waterloo, Ont.: Waterloo Univ. Library, 1986. pp. xxiii, 175. Rev. by Karen Smith in DalR (67:1) 1987, 143–5.

### Brian Moore

**10596.**  CALLAHAN, DENIS JOSEPH F.  James Joyce and the novels of Aidan Higgins, Jennifer Johnston, John McGahern and Brian Moore. *See* **9930.**

**10597.**  AL-JABBARI, E. H.  A study of women in the novels of Brian Moore. Unpub. doct. diss., Univ. of Dundee, 1988. [Abstr. in IT (39:1) 33–4.]

**10598.**  O'DONOGHUE, J.  Religion and belief in the novels of Brian Moore. Unpub. M.Litt. diss., Trinity Coll. Dublin, 1988. [Abstr. in IT (39:4) 1634.]

### George Moore

**10599.**  BEASLEY, MURRAY JOHN.  Alcoves in Cythera: George Moore's appeal to eighteenth-century antiquity. Unpub. doct. diss., Univ. of Auckland.

**10600.**  BRIDGWATER, PATRICK.  George Moore and German pessimism. London: Grant & Cutler, 1988. pp. 81.

**10601.**  EAKIN, DAVID B.; GERBER, HELMUT E. (eds).  In minor keys: the uncollected short stories of George Moore. (Bibl. 1986, 13295.) Rev. by Hilary Pyle in RES (38:149) 1987, 100–1.

**10602.**  GERBER, HELMUT E.; BRACK, O. M., JR (eds).  George Moore on Parnassus: letters (1900–1933) to secretaries, publishers, printers, agents, literati, friends, and acquaintances. Newark: Delaware UP; London: Assoc. UPs. pp. 896. Rev. by John Kelly in TLS, 28 Apr., 451.

**10603.** MARTIN, AUGUSTINE. Julia Cahill, Father McTurnan, and the geography of nowhere. *In* (pp. 98–111) **37.**

### Marianne Moore

**10604.** DAVIS, ELIZABETH H. Utility and contrast: stylistic revision in Marianne Moore's *The Paper Nautilus*. NCL (19:5) 10–11.

**10605.** DAVIS, ELIZABETH HAWK. The rhetorical poetics of Marianne Moore: a structuralist and semiotic analysis of style. Unpub. doct. diss., East Texas State Univ. [Abstr. in DA (50) 1304A.]

**10606.** ERICKSON, DARLENE ELLEN. Illusion is more precise than precision: the poetry of Marianne Moore. Unpub. doct. diss., Miami Univ. [Abstr. in DA (50) 1656A.]

**10607.** GUNN, THOM. Three hard women: HD, Marianne Moore, Mina Loy. *In* (pp. 37–52) **46.**

**10608.** HEUVING, JEANNE DIANE. Marianne Moore and gender construction. Unpub. doct. diss., Univ. of Washington, 1988. [Abstr. in DA (49) 2652A.]

**10609.** HOLLEY, MARGARET. The poetry of Marianne Moore: a study in voice and value. New York: CUP, 1987. (Bibl. 1987, 11828.) Rev. by Helen Deese in AL (61:1) 140–1; by Michael L. Johnson in AmerS (29:2) 1988, 97.

**10610.** MONROE, MELISSA. The expressive function of nominal structure in Marianne Moore and Wallace Stevens. Unpub. doct. diss., Stanford Univ. [Abstr. in DA (50) 1313A.]

**10611.** WILLIS, PATRICIA C. American modern: Scofield Thayer, Marianne Moore, and *The Dial. See* **601.**

**10612.** —— (ed.). The complete prose of Marianne Moore. (Bibl. 1987, 11840.) Rev. by Jonathan Barker in Agenda (26:3) 63–4.

### Thomas Sturge Moore

**10613.** TILBY, MICHAEL. An early English admirer of Paul Valéry: Thomas Sturge Moore. MLR (84:3) 565–88.

### Robert Morgan

**10614.** LIOTTA, P. H. Pieces of the Morgenland: the recent achievements in Robert Morgan's poetry. SoLJ (22:1) 32–40.

### Bill Morrison

**10615.** PILKINGTON, ULICK LIONEL. Representations of the Northern Ireland crisis in contemporary drama: 1968–80. *See* **9127.**

### Toni Morrison

**10616.** BARNES, PAULA CASSANDRA. Tradition and innovation: Toni Morrison and the flight motif in Afro-American literature. *See* **8178.**

**10617.** CARBY, HAZEL V. Reinventing history/imagining the future. *See* **8999.**

**10618.** DEO, VEENA S. The creative Black woman in Toni Morrison's novels. Unpub. doct. diss., Univ. of Kentucky. [Abstr. in DA (50) 946A.]

**10619.** DURÁN GIMÉNEZ-RICO, ISABEL. La tradición afroamericana en *Beloved* de Toni Morrison. RAEI (2) 31–41.

**10620.** FLICK, THOMAS H.   Toni Morrison's 'allegories of the cave': movies, consumption, and Platonic realism in *The Bluest Eye*. JMMLA (22:1) 10–22.

**10621.** HORVITZ, DEBORAH.   Nameless ghosts: possession and dispossession in *Beloved*. SAF (17:2) 157–67.

**10622.** KANKAANRANTA, ANNE.   A different quest of roots as shown in Toni Morrison's novel *Song of Solomon*. In (pp. 31–41) **43.**

**10623.** McLEOD, MARION.   Out of slavery. NZList, 20 May, 59–60.

**10624.** MIHĂILĂ, RODICA.   In căutarea integrității eului: Toni Morrison. (In search of the integrity of the ego: Toni Morrison.) RomLit, 2 Mar., 21.

**10625.** MONTGOMERY, MAXINE LAVON.   A pilgrimage to the origins: the apocalypse as structure and theme in Toni Morrison's *Sula*. BALF (23:1) 127–37.

**10626.** OPYR, LINDA ELENA.   The Black woman in the novels of Alice Walker and Toni Morrison. Unpub. doct. diss., St John's Univ., 1988. [Abstr. in DA (49) 3027A.]

**10627.** SMITH, ANGELEAN VANDORA.   Patterns of authenticity: a search for self in American novels. *See* **9532.**

### John Mortimer

**10628.** MENGEL, EWALD.   Strategies of dealing with 'alterity' in John Mortimer's *The Captain of Köpernick*. In (pp. 222–37) **4.**

**10629.** TUCKER, MARTIN.   All quiet on the English front: silence as escapism. Confrontation (39/40) 1988/89, 256–9.

### Willard Motley

**10630.** NELLES, WILLIAM.   From 'Tourist Town' to *Let Noon Be Fair*: the posthumous revision of Motley's last novel. *See* **357.**

### Es'kia Mphahlele

**10631.** FONTENOT, DEBORAH YVONNE B.   A vision of anarchy: correlate structures of exile and madness in selected works of Doris Lessing and her South African contemporaries. *See* **9770.**

**10632.** SEMPLE, HILARY.   'Brother-mortals': Robert Burns and Es'kia Mphahlele. *See* **5147.**

### Edwin Muir

**10633.** AITCHISON, JAMES.   The golden harvester: the vision of Edwin Muir. Aberdeen: Aberdeen UP, 1988. pp. vii, 215. Rev. by Margery McCulloch in Cencrastus (33) 29; by Heather Hewitt in SLJ (supp. 30) 13–15.

**10634.** BROWN, GEORGE MACKAY (sel. and introd.).   Edwin Muir: selected prose. (Bibl. 1987, 11872.) Rev. by Susan Manning in CamQ (18:4) 401–12.

**10635.** MANNING, SUSAN.   Edwin Muir and the modern. CamQ (18:4) 401–12 (review-article).

### Bharati Mukherjee

**10636.** ST ANDREWS, B. A.   New voices in the Canadian choir: Kogawa and Mukherjee. *See* **10218.**

**10637.** STREITFELD, DAVID.   A colonial legacy. BkW, 12 Nov., 19.

## Paul Muldoon
**10638.** WILLS, C. Language, history and sex in the poetry of Paul Muldoon and Medbh McGuckian. *See* **10463.**

## Alice Munro
**10639.** HOY, HELEN. 'Rose and Janet': Alice Munro's metafiction. *See* **330.**

**10640.** KAMBOURELI, SMARO. The body as audience and performance in the writing of Alice Munro. *In* (pp. 31–8) **40.**

**10641.** MILLER, JUDITH (ed.). The art of Alice Munro: saying the unsayable: papers from the Waterloo conference. Waterloo, Ont.: Waterloo UP, 1984. pp. vi, 135. Rev. by Patricia Köstler in CanL (117) 1988, 166–7.

**10642.** MOORE, J.; TENER, J.; STEELE, A. (eds). The Alice Munro papers: first accession. *See* **252.**

**10643.** ROOKE, CONSTANCE. Fear of the open heart. *In* (pp. 256–69) **40.**

## Neil Munro
**10644.** STAPE, J. H. Conrad to T. F. Unwin and Neil Munro: two unpublished letters. *See* **9321.**

## Iris Murdoch
**10645.** CONRADI, PETER J. Iris Murdoch: the saint and the artist. Basingstoke: Macmillan. pp. xvi, 328. (Second ed.: first ed. 1986.)

**10646.** CORIN, FERNAND. Rites of passage in Iris Murdoch's *The Good Apprentice*. *In* (pp. 15–25) **42.**

**10647.** ČUROVA, MARGARITA. Iris Murdoch's ethical and aesthetic views. GSUFNF (79:1) 151–87.

**10648.** GRIFFIN, G. The influence of the writings of Simone Weil on the fiction of Iris Murdoch. Unpub. doct. diss., Univ. of Leicester. [Abstr. in IT (39:2) 483.]

**10649.** MAGIE, LYNNE ADELE. The daemon Eros: gothic elements in the novels of Emily and Charlotte Brontë, Doris Lessing, and Iris Murdoch. *See* **6304.**

**10650.** JEDRZEJKIEWICZ, MARIA. Problemy recepcji powieści Iris Murdoch (na przykładzie lektury *The Sea, the Sea*. (The problem of the reception of Iris Murdoch's novels (exemplified by *The Sea, the Sea*).) *In* (pp. 153–77) **36.**

**10651.** O'CONNOR, PATRICIA J. Iris Murdoch: philosophical novelist. NC (8) 164–76.

## Thomas Murphy (1935– )
**10652.** MURRAY, CHRISTOPHER (introd.). After tragedy: three Irish plays. London: Methuen, 1988. pp. ix, 115. Rev. by Ulf Dantanus in IUR (19:1) 180–2.

## Les Murray
**10653.** MURRAY, LES. Poems and the mystery of embodiment. *See* **2097.**

**10654.** ROSS, BRUCE CLUNIES. Les Murray's vernacular republic. *In* (pp. 21–37) **20.**

**10655.** SCHMIDT, MICHAEL. Samtal mellan fyra poeter. *See* **9864.**

**10656.** SINGH, KIRPAL.   Landscape as revelation: the case of Les Murry. Span (28) 90–6.

**10657.** SYKES, NICK.   Les Murray. Studio (Albury, N.S.W.) (33) 1988/89, 13–20. (Interview.)

### John Middleton Murry

**10658.** HANKIN, CHERRY A. (ed.).   Letters between Katherine Mansfield and John Middleton Murry. *See* **10517.**

### Meja Mwangi

**10659.** JOHANSSON, LARS.   Images and counter-images in Meja Mwangi's novel *The Cockroach Dance. In* (pp. 25–37) RAOUL GRANQVIST (ed.), Distorted perspectives: five papers on the image of Africa. Umeå: Umeå Univ., 1987. pp. 110. (Umeå papers in English, 9.)

### Vladimir Nabokov

**10660.** ENGELKING, LESZEK.   Vladimir Nabokov. Warsaw: Czytelnik. pp. 146. (Klasycy Literatury 20 wieku.)

**10661.** ENGLISH, JAMES F.   Comic transactions: humor as communication in four modern novels. *See* **9293.**

**10662.** FISHWICK, I. R.   'Conventions are conventions . . .': some thoughts about the techniques of direction and misdirection – with particular reference to genre features – in the novels of Vladimir Nabokov, and an assessment of their intentions and effects. Unpub. doct. diss., Univ. of Durham, 1988. [Abstr. in IT (38:4) 1464.] (Restricted access.)

**10663.** HAMEL, BERNARD.   Poétique du nom: sur l'introït de *Lolita.* Repérages (12) 7–12.

**10664.** JACKSON, PAUL R.   *Pale Fire*'s Simplon Pass. NCL (19:1) 2–4.

**10665.** MORRISON, JAMES EMERSON.   The last testament and the Modernist imagination. *See* **9493.**

**10666.** MROZ, EDITH MARIA FAY.   Vladimir Nabokov and romantic irony. Unpub. doct. diss., Univ. of Delaware, 1988. [Abstr. in DA (49) 3734A.]

**10667.** PARKER, MARY ELIZABETH.   Nabokov: the artist against caprice. Unpub. doct. diss., Univ. of North Carolina at Greensboro, 1987. [Abstr. in DA (49) 1804A.]

**10668.** SCHUMAN, SAMUEL.   Nabokov and Shakespeare's trees. *See* **3643.**

**10669.** STREITFELD, DAVID.   Nabokov's *Laura.* BkW, 19 Nov., 15. (The fate of the manuscript of the unfinished novel *The Original of Laura.*)

**10670.** WOOD, MICHAEL.   Lolita in wonderland. CompCrit (10) 1988, 159–69.

### V. S. Naipaul

**10671.** CARLBERG, ANDERS J.   Det var en gång ett Europa: om ett tema hos John Berger och V. S. Naipaul. *See* **9091.**

**10672.** DUYCK, RUDY.   V. S. Naipaul and John Donne: the morning after. *See* **4399.**

**10673.** KOH TAI ANN.   The Empire's orphans: stayers and quitters in *A Bend in the River* and *Scorpion Orchid. In* (pp. 38–53) **19.**

**10674.** Langran, P. R. K. Narayan and V. S. Naipaul: a comparative study of some Hindu aspects of their work. Unpub. doct. diss., Univ. of Leeds, 1988. [Abstr. in IT (38:4) 1463.]

**10675.** Mair, Christian. Naipaul's *Miguel Street* and Selvon's *Lonely Londoners* — two approaches to the use of Caribbean creole in fiction. *See* **1551.**

**10676.** Mann, Harveen Sachdeva. Among the mimic men: the fictional works of V. S. Naipaul. Unpub. doct. diss., Purdue Univ., 1986. [Abstr. in DA (49) 3720A.]

**10677.** Riley, Geoffrey. Echoes of Wells in Naipaul's *A House for Mr Biswas*. NQ (36:2) 208–9.

**10678.** Shelnutt, Eve. Estimating V. S. Naipaul: an oblique approach. Genre (22:1) 69–84.

**10679.** Singh, Vidya Devi. V. S. Naipaul: an exile at home. Unpub. doct. diss., Southern Illinois Univ. at Carbondale, 1988. [Abstr. in DA (49) 3361A.]

**10680.** Stewart, Frank E. L. Naipaul's vision of the land in his later works. SEL (65:2) 175–92.

**10681.** ten Kortenaar, Neil. History in the fiction of V. S. Naipaul. Unpub. doct. diss., Univ. of Toronto, 1988. [Abstr. in DA (50) 147A.]

**10682.** Theime, John. The web of tradition: uses of allusion in V. S. Naipaul's fiction. London: Hansib, 1987. pp. 224.

### R. K. Narayan

**10683.** Langran, P. R. K. Narayan and V. S. Naipaul: a comparative study of some Hindu aspects of their work. *See* **10674.**

### Peter Neagoe

**10684.** Le Goff, Denise-Claude. Peter Neagoe: l'homme et l'œuvre. New York; Berne; Frankfurt; Paris: Lang, 1988. pp. 413. (American univ. studies, 19: 219; General literature, 16.)

### Howard Nemerov

**10685.** Vendler, Helen. Books: the man in the street, the man in the air, the man in the heavens. NY, 18 Sept., 133–9.

### E. Nesbit

**10686.** Robson, W. W. E. Nesbit and *The Book of Dragons*. *In* (pp. 251–70) **14.**

**10687.** Streatfeild, Noel (introd.). Long ago when I was young. London: Beehive, 1987. pp. 127, (plates) 6. Rev. by MC in Junior Bookshelf (51:4) 1987, 157.

### John Newlove

**10688.** Dyck, E. F. Place in the poetry of John Newlove. CanL (122/23) 69–91.

### bp Nichol

**10689.** Bowering, George. bp Nichol: 1944–1988. CanL (122/23) 294–7.

### Lorine Niedecker

**10690.** Kilroy, James. Four late poems of Lorine Niedecker. *In* (pp. 119–32) **46.**

## Anaïs Nin
**10691.** RICHARD-ALLERDYCE, DIANE.   The feminine creativity of Anaïs Nin: a Lacanian view. Unpub. doct. diss., Univ. of Florida, 1988. [Abstr. in DA (50) 441A.]

**10692.** ROBE, MARGARET ANN.   Conceiving a self in autobiography by women. *See* **8609.**

**10693.** VON RICHTOFEN, P. M.   The *Booster/Delta* nexus: Henry Miller and his friends in the literary world of Paris and London on the eve of the Second World War. *See* **598.**

## Marsha Norman
**10694.** DOLAN, JILL.   Bending gender to fit the canon: the politics of production. *In* (pp. 318–44) **39.**

**10695.** DOLAN, JILL S.   The feminist spectator as critic: performance criticism and representation, *See* **8715.**

**10696.** FORTE, JEANIE.   Realism, narrative, and the feminist playwright – a problem of reception. *See* **10177.**

**10697.** SCHROEDER, PATRICIA R.   Locked behind the proscenium: feminist strategies in *Getting Out* and *My Sister in This House*. *See* **10188.**

**10698.** SPENCER, JENNY S.   Marsha Norman's 'she-tragedies'. *In* (pp. 147–65) **39.**

## Frank Norris
**10699.** BEVILACQUA, WINIFRED FARRANT.   From the ideal to its reverse: key sociocultural concepts in *McTeague*. CR (33:1) 75–88.

**10700.** CARON, JAMES E.   Grotesque naturalism: the significance of the comic in *McTeague*. TSLL (31:2) 288–317.

**10701.** DAVISON, RICHARD ALLAN.   *Of Mice and Men* and *McTeague*: Steinbeck, Fitzgerald, and Frank Norris. *See* **9636.**

**10702.** HOCHMAN, BARBARA.   The art of Frank Norris, storyteller. Columbia: Missouri UP, 1988. pp. viii, 149. Rev. by Jesse S. Crisler in AL (61:3) 481–3.

**10703.** MCELRATH, JOSEPH R., JR; CRISLER, JESSE S.   The bowdlerization of *McTeague*. *See* **448.**

**10704.** MICHAELS, WALTER BENN.   Frank Norris, Josiah Royce and the ontology of corporations. *In* (pp. 122–51) **1.**

**10705.** RYDER, MARY R.   'All wheat and no chaff': Frank Norris' *Blix* and Willa Cather's literary vision. *See* **9222.**

## Robert Norwood
**10706.** KIZUK, ALEX.   Religion, place, & self in early twentieth-century Canada: Robert Norwood's poetry. CanL (115) 1987, 66–77.

## Joyce Carol Oates
**10707.** COLAKIS, MARIANTHE.   The House of Atreus myth in the seventies and eighties: David Rabe's *The Orphan* and Joyce Carol Oates's *Angel of Light*. CML (9:2) 125–30.

**10708.** STRANDBERG, VICTOR.   Sex, violence, and philosophy in *You Must Remember This*. SAF (17:1) 3–17.

**10709.** WESLEY, MARILYN CLARKE.   Transgression and refusal: the dynamic of power in the domestic fiction of Joyce Carol Oates. Unpub. doct. diss., Syracuse Univ., 1988. [Abstr. in DA (49) 3365A.]

## Flann O'Brien (Brian O'Nolan, 'Myles na gCopaleen')

**10710.** ADRIAN, JACK. A Sexton Blake mystery. TLS, 10 Nov., 1239. (Letter to the editor.)

**10711.** COHEN, DAVID. Conclusion of the foregoing: James Joyce, Samuel Beckett and Flann O'Brien. See **9042**.

**10712.** CRONIN, ANTHONY. No laughing matter: the life and times of Flann O'Brien. London: Grafton. pp. xii, 260. Rev. by William Scammell in Listener (122) 26 Oct., 34; by Denis Donoghue in TLS, 27 Oct., 1171.

**10713.** LANTERS, JOSÉ. 'Still life' versus real life: the English writings of Brian O'Nolan. *In* (pp. 161–81) **28**.

**10714.** SHEA, THOMAS F. The craft of seeming pedestrian: Flann O'Brien's *The Hard Life*. CLQ (25:4) 258–67.

**10715.** TIGGES, WIM. An anatomy of literary nonsense. See **6466**.

### Kate O'Brien

**10716.** MADDEN, DEIRDRE (postscr.). The ante-room. London: Virago Press. pp. 306. (Virago modern classics, 325.)

### Tim O'Brien

**10717.** FURNISS, DAVID WEST. Making sense of the war: Vietnam and American prose. See **9923**.

### Sean O'Casey

**10718.** AYLING, RONALD. The 'politics' of childhood auto-biographies: O'Casey and Soyinka. Mosaic (20:4) 1987, 37–48.

**10719.** JONES, NESTA. O'Casey and expressionism. Cambridge: Chadwyck-Healey; Consortium for Drama and Media in Higher Education, 1988. pp. 102. (Theatre in focus.)

**10720.** KISELINČEVA, KSENIJA. Judžin O'Nijl i Šon O'Kejsi – žreci na teatralnata magija. (Eugene O'Neill and Sean O'Casey, priests of the magic of theatre.) T (42:4) 53–6.

**10721.** O'CASEY, EILEEN. Cheerio, Titan: the friendship between George Bernard Shaw and Eileen and Sean O'Casey. New York: Scribner's. pp. 141. Rev. in BkW, 26 Nov., 13; by Joseph Coates in BW, 10 Dec., 7.

**10722.** O'CONNOR, GARRY. Sean O'Casey: a life. (Bibl. 1988, 8390.) Rev. by John Countryman in TJ (41:4) 560–1.

### Flannery O'Connor

**10723.** ANDREAS, JAMES. 'If it's a symbol, the hell with it': the medieval gothic style of Flannery O'Connor in *Everything That Rises Must Converge*. ChrisL (38:2) 23–41.

**10724.** BAUMGAERTNER, JILL P. Flannery O'Connor: a proper scaring. (Bibl. 1988, 8393.) Rev. by Kathleen Feeley in ChrisL (38:2) 78–9.

**10725.** BEHRENDT, STEPHEN C. Knowledge and innocence in Flannery O'Connor's *The River*. SAF (17:2) 143–55.

**10726.** BROWN, HUGH R. Savannah landmark: Flannery O'Connor's childhood home. FOB (18) 43–5.

**10727.** BURKLE, HOWARD R. The child in Flannery O'Connor. FOB (18) 59–69.

**10728.** CAPUTO, PETER.   Selfishness and generosity, isolation and kinship: Melville, James and Flannery O'Connor. *See* **7055.**

**10729.** CASH, JEAN W.   O'Connor on *The Violent Bear it Away*: an unpublished letter. ELN (26:4) 71.

**10730.** DESMOND, JOHN F.   Risen sons: Flannery O'Connor's vision of history. (Bibl. 1988, 8396.) Rev. by Michael Kowalewski in SoQ (27:4) 112–14; by Patrick W. Carey in CathW (232) 183–4.

**10731.** DONAHOO, ROBERT EARL.   Comic forms and social meanings in the fiction of Flannery O'Connor. Unpub. doct. diss., Duke Univ., 1988. [Abstr. in DA (49) 2219A.]

**10732.** EMERICK, RONALD.   Hawthorne and O'Connor: a literary kinship. *See* **6950.**

**10733.** GIANNONE, RICHARD.   Flannery O'Connor and the mystery of love. Urbana; Chicago: Illinois UP. pp. xi, 269. Rev. by Ralph C. Wood in FOB (18) 99–102.

**10734.** HIGDON, DAVID LEON.   Flannery O'Connor's sentence titles. SAF (17:2) 227–34.

**10735.** HOPKINS, MARY FRANCES.   The rhetoric of heteroglossia in Flannery O'Connor's *Wise Blood*. *See* **1408.**

**10736.** KESSLER, EDWARD.   Flannery O'Connor and the language of apocalypse. (Bibl. 1987, 12044.) Rev. by Ted R. Spivey in ChrisL (38:4) 90–2.

**10737.** KIRKLAND, WILLIAM M.   Baron von Hügel and Flannery O'Connor. FOB (18) 28–42.

**10738.** LUDWIG, DALE LESLIE.   Controlled distance: internal character presentation in Flannery O'Connor's short stories. Unpub. doct. diss., Univ. of Illinois at Urbana-Champaign, 1988. [Abstr. in DA (50) 302A.]

**10739.** MELLARD, JAMES M.   Flannery O'Connor's Others: Freud, Lacan, and the unconscious. AL (61:4) 625–43.

**10740.** PAULSON, SUZANNE MORROW.   Flannery O'Connor: a study of the short fiction. (Bibl. 1988, 8404.) Rev. by Paul W. Nisley in ChrisL (39:1) 107–8; by Ted R. Spivey in ChrisL (38:4) 90–2.

**10741.** PETRY, ALICE HALL.   Miss O'Connor and Mrs Mitchell: the example of *Everything That Rises*. *See* **10579.**

**10742.** POWERS, DOUGLAS.   Ruller McFarney's cutting loose. FOB (18) 70–8.

**10743.** SATTERFIELD, BEN.   *Wise Blood*, artistic anemia, and the hemorrhaging of O'Connor criticism. SAF (17:1) 33–50.

**10744.** SEWELL, ELIZABETH.   Is Flannery O'Connor a nonsense writer? *In* (pp. 183–213) **28.**

**10745.** SEXTON, MARK S.   Flannery O'Connor's presentation of vernacular religion in *The River*. FOB (18) 1–12.

**10746.** SHACKELFORD, D. DEAN.   The Black outsider in O'Connor's fiction. FOB (18) 79–90.

**10747.** SMITH, MARCUS A. J.   Another desert: Hazel Motes's missing years. FOB (18) 55–8.

**10748.** STEPHENS, C. RALPH (ed.).    The correspondence of Flannery O'Connor and the Brainard Cheneys. pp. xviii, 220. (Bibl. 1986, 13578, where pagination incorrect.) Rev. by Lawrence Willson in SewR (96:2) 1988, 283–6.

**10749.** WOOD, RALPH C.    The comedy of redemption: Christian faith in four American novelists. *See* **9380.**

**10750.** —— The long-run efficacy of love: four books on Flannery O'Connor. FOB (18) 99–105 (review-article).

### Sean O'Faolain

**10751.** BONACCORSO, RICHARD.    Sean O'Faolain's Irish vision. (Bibl. 1987, 12066.) Rev. by C. A. Buckley in NQ (36:1) 128–9.

### Tillie Olsen

**10752.** FAULKNER, MARA.    Blight, fruit, and possibility in the writing of Tillie Olsen. Unpub. doct. diss., Univ. of Minnesota, 1988. [Abstr. in DA (49) 3723A.]

### Charles Olson

**10753.** PRUS, RANDY THOMAS.    Olson's dance: the poetics of place in American poetry. Unpub. doct. diss., State Univ. of New York at Buffalo. [Abstr. in DA (50) 1306A.]

**10754.** RIACH, ALAN.    Stranger eyes: Charles Olson, 'Pacific Man' and some aspects of New Zealand poetry. *See* **8548.**

**10755.** STEIN, CHARLES.    The secret of the black chrysanthemum: the poetic cosmology of Charles Olson and his use of the writings of C. G. Jung. Barrytown, NY: Station Hill Press, 1987. pp. xxvii, 224. (Clinamen studies.) Rev. by Lisa M. Steinman in AL (61:2) 319–21.

**10756.** STOICHEFF, PETER.    Poem's poetics or poet's death: what ends *The Cantos*, *Maximus*, and *Paterson*? Genre (22:2) 175–93.

### Michael Ondaatje

**10757.** BUTTERFIELD, MARTHA.    The one lighted room: *In the Skin of a Lion*. CanL (119) 1988, 162–7.

**10758.** JONES, MANINA.    *The Collected Works of Billy the Kid*: scripting the docudrama. CanL (122/23) 26–38.

**10759.** SOLECKI, SAM (ed.).    Spider blues: essays on Michael Ondaatje. (Bibl. 1986, 13601.) Rev. by Susan Gingell in CanL (113/14) 1987, 214–17.

### Eugene O'Neill

**10760.** ADAM, JULIE.    Version of heroism in modern American drama: selected plays by Miller, Williams, Anderson and O'Neill. *See* **8937.**

**10761.** ANTUSH, JOHN V.    Eugene O'Neill: modern and postmodern. EOR (13:1) 14–26.

**10762.** BERLIN, NORMAND.    O'Neill's Shakespeare. *See* **3815.**

**10763.** —— (ed.).    Eugene O'Neill, three plays: *Mourning Becomes Electra*, *The Iceman Cometh*, *Long Day's Journey into Night*: a casebook. Basingstoke: Macmillan. pp. 189. (Casebook.)

**10764.** BOGARD, TRAVIS (ed.).    Complete plays. (Bibl. 1988, 8423.) Rev. by Gerald Weales in Smithsonian (20:5) 130–3.

**10765.** —— The unknown O'Neill: unpublished or unfamiliar writings of Eugene O'Neill. New Haven, CT; London: Yale UP, 1988.

pp. ix, 434. Rev. by Jean Chothia in JAStud (23:2) 313; by Jonathan Veitch in NEQ (62:4) 603–4.

**10766.** —— BRYER, JACKSON R. (eds). Selected letters of Eugene O'Neill. (Bibl. 1988, 8424.) Rev. by Stephen A. Black in AL (61:2) 310–12; by Jonathan Veitch in NEQ (26:4) 604–6.

**10767.** BOWER, MARTHA GILMAN (ed.). More stately mansions. Oxford; New York: OUP, 1988. pp. viii, 313. (Unexpurgated ed.)

**10768.** CARPENTER, FREDERIC I. Eugene O'Neill and the Orient: a forward glance. EOR (13:1) 27–8.

**10769.** CHOTHIA, JEAN. Questions of significance: some recent work in O'Neill studies. JAStud (23:2) 311–14 (review-article).

**10770.** COMO, ROBERT M. O'Neill, Beckett, and Dürrenmatt: the shared genre. *See* **9044.**

**10771.** COOPERMAN, ROBERT. *Marco Millions*: O'Neill's other comedy. EOR (13:2) 37–44.

**10772.** CUNNINGHAM, FRANK R. 'Authentic tidings of invisible things': beyond James Robinson's *Eugene O'Neill and Oriental Thought*. FOR (13:1) 29–39.

**10773.** DLOYD, VIRGINIA. Eugene O'Neill: the unfinished plays. New York: Ungar, 1988. pp. 213. Rev. by Jean Chothia in JAStud (23:2) 311–14.

**10774.** —— (ed.). Eugene O'Neill at work: newly released ideas for plays. (Bibl. 1984, 12455.) Rev. by Jean Chothia in JAStud (23:2) 313–14.

**10775.** HAHN, MIN. Eugene O'Neill geuk eui kyeoljungronjeok yoin. (Determinism in O'Neill.) Unpub. doct. diss., Busan National Univ. (Korea).

**10776.** HALFMANN, ULRICH (ed.). Eugene O'Neill: comments on the drama and the theater: a source book. Tübingen: Narr, 1987. pp. xxv, 255. (Studies & texts in English, 7.) Rev. by Jean Chothia in JAStud (23:2) 312–13.

**10777.** HALL, ANN CHRISTINE. 'A kind of Alaska': the representation of women in the plays of Eugene O'Neill, Harold Pinter, and Sam Shepard. Unpub. doct. diss., Ohio State Univ., 1988. [Abstr. in DA (49) 2214A.]

**10778.** HAMMERMAN, HARLEY J. On collecting O'Neill. *See* **229.**

**10779.** HINDEN, MICHAEL. Missing lines in *Long Day's Journey into Night*. *See* **323.**

**10780.** KISELINČEVA, KSENIJA. Judžin O'Nijl i Šon O'Kejsi — žreci na teatralnata magija. *See* **10720.**

**10781.** KOBERNICK, MARK. Semiotics of the drama and the style of Eugene O'Neill. *See* **1409.**

**10782.** KOLIN, PHILIP C. Parallels between *Desire Under the Elms* and *Sweet Bird of Youth*. EOR (13:2) 23–35.

**10783.** LAHR, JOHN (introd.). The collected plays of Eugene O'Neill. (Bibl. 1988, 8438.) Rev. by L. H. Hugo in UES (27:1) 47–8.

**10784.** LARSON, KELLI A. O'Neill's tragic quest for belonging: psychological determinism in the S.S. *Glencairn* plays. EOR (13:2) 12–22.

**10785.** LINDMAN-STRAFFORD, KERSTIN. Modern som martyr. (The mother as martyr.) Finsk tidskrift (Helsinki) (1989:7) 414–23.

**10786.** MAUFORT, MARC. Eugene O'Neill and the shadow of Edmond Dantès: the pursuit of dramatic unity in *Where the Cross is Made* (1918) and *Gold* (1920). *In* (pp. 89–97) **2.**

**10787.** MOORTON, RICHARD F., JR. The author as Oedipus in *Mourning Becomes Electra* and *Long Day's Journey into Night*. PLL (25:3) 304–25.

**10788.** ONUNWA, PASCHAL U. Eugene O'Neill: the evolution of racial justice and brotherhood in five plays. Unpub. doct. diss., Fordham Univ., 1988. [Abstr. in DA (49) 1803–4A.] (*Thirst, The Dreamy Kid, The Emperor Jones, All God's Chillun Got Wings, The Iceman Cometh.*)

**10789.** PORTER, LAURIN. The banished prince: time, memory, and ritual in the late plays of Eugene O'Neill. Ann Arbor, MI: UMI Research Press, 1988. pp. 134. (Theater and dramatic studies, 54.) Rev. by James A. Robinson in AL (61:4) 716–17.

**10790.** PRASAD, HARI MOHAN. The dramatic art of Eugene O'Neill. New Delhi: Associated Publishing House, 1987. pp. x, 113. Rev. by Ronald H. Wainscott in TJ (41:1) 121.

**10791.** ROBINSON, JAMES A. O'Neill's Indian *Elms*. EOR (13:1) 40–6.

**10792.** SHAUGHNESSY, EDWARD L. Eugene O'Neill in Ireland: the critical reception. Westport, CT: Greenwood Press, 1988. pp. xv, 221. (Contributions in drama and theatre studies, 25.) Rev. by Judith E. Barlow in AL (61:3) 501–2.

**10793.** SPÅNBERG, SVEN-JOHAN. *A Moon for the Misbegotten* as elegy: an intertextual reading. SN (61:1) 23–36.

**10794.** STANICH, LINDA K. *The Iceman Cometh* as ethnographic text. EOR (13:2) 55–62.

**10795.** STROUPE, JOHN H. Critical approaches to O'Neill. New York: AMS Press, 1988. pp. x, 219. (AMS studies in modern literature, 17.) Rev. by Ronald H. Wainscott in TJ (41:1) 120–1.

**10796.** VENA, GARY. *The Iceman Cometh*: reconstructing the première. Ann Arbor: Michigan UP, 1988. pp. 251. Rev. by Jean Chothia in JAStud (23:2) 311–12.

**10797.** VORHEES, DUANE LEROY. Hitler, Jung: O'Neill. EngSt (13) 58–71.

**10798.** WAINSCOTT, RONALD H. Staging O'Neill: the experimental years, 1920–1934. New Haven, CT; London: Yale UP, 1988. pp. xviii, 337. Rev. by Jonathan Veitch in NEQ (62:4) 603.

**10799.** WERNER, BETTE CHARLENE. Eugene O'Neill's Paradise lost: the theme of the islands in *Mourning Becomes Electra*. BSUF (27:1) 1986, 46–52.

## George Oppen

**10800.** YOUNG, DENNIS PATRICK. The possibilities of being: the poetry of George Oppen. Unpub. doct. diss., Univ. of Iowa, 1988. [Abstr. in DA (49) 3365–6A.]

## Simon Ortiz

**10801.** MANLEY, KATHLEEN; REA, PAUL W.    An interview with Simon Ortiz. Journal of the Southwest (31:3) 362–77.

## Joe Orton

**10802.** HARVEY, S. M.    The plays of Joe Orton: an analysis of his dialogue as dramatic technique. Unpub. M.Phil. diss., Univ. of Surrey, 1987. [Abstr. in IT (39:1) 35.]

**10803.** SHEPHERD, SIMON.    Because we're queers: the life and crimes of Kenneth Halliwell and Joe Orton. London: GMP. pp. 173.

**10804.** WHITAKER, THOMAS R.    Playing in earnest. *In* (pp. 407–23) **45.**

## 'George Orwell' (Eric Blair)

**10805.** BOLTON, W. F.    The language of 1984: Orwell's English and ours. (Bibl. 1987, 12133.) Rev. by B. D. H. Miller in RES (38:149) 62–3.

**10806.** BOUCHARD, GUY; ROCQUE, ANDRÉ; RUELLAND, JACQUES.    Orwell et *1984*: trois approches. Paris: Bellarmin, 1988. pp. 273.

**10807.** CASEMENT, WILLIAM.    *Nineteen Eighty-Four* and philosophical realism. MidQ (30:2) 215–28.

**10808.** FÜGER, WILHELM.    Intertextualia Orwelliana: Untersuchungen zur Theorie und Praxis der Markierung von Intertextualität. PoetA (21:1/2) 197–200.

**10809.** HEWSON, KELLY LEIGH.    Writers and responsibility: George Orwell, Nadine Gordimer, John Coetzee and Salman Rushdie. *See* **9269.**

**10810.** LASKOWSKI, WILLIAM EDWARD, JR.    George Orwell and the Tory–Radical tradition. Unpub. doct. diss., Univ. of Illinois at Chicago, 1988. [Abstr. in DA (49) 2231A.]

**10811.** MULVIHILL, ROBERT (ed.).    Reflections on America, 1984: an Orwell symposium. Athens; London: Georgia UP, 1986. pp. x, 221.

**10812.** RODDEN, JOHN.    George Orwell and British Catholicism. Ren (41:3) 143–68.

**10813.** —— Orwell as Quixote: analogy, anecdote, and repute. CLit (16:2) 129–47.

**10814.** —— The politics of literary reputation: George Woodcock and the anarchists' Orwell. QQ (95:2) 1988, 330–49.

**10815.** —— The politics of literary reputation: the making and claiming of 'St George' Orwell. Oxford; New York: OUP. pp. xiii, 478. Rev. by Julian Symons in NYTB, 4 June, 25; by the same in LRB (11:21) 20–1.

**10816.** —— Soviet literary policy, 1945–1989: the case of George Orwell. ModAge (32:2) 1988, 131–9.

**10817.** RODDEN, JOHN GALLAGHER.    The politics of literary reputation: the 'making' and 'claiming' of 'St George' Orwell. Unpub. doct. diss., Univ. of Virginia, 1987. [Abstr. in DA (49) 3372A.]

**10818.** SILVANI, GIOVANNA.    Women in Utopia from More to Huxley. *See* **3286.**

**10819.** ZVEREV, A.    Bez Starshego Brata . . .: o slozhnom cheloveke i neprostom avtore – Dzh. Oruelle. (Without Big Brother . . .: a complicated man and equally complex author – George Orwell.) Novoe vremîa (Moscow) (1989:37) 38–40.

**10820.** —— O starshem brate i chreve kite: shtrikhi k portretu Dzh. Oruèlla. (Big Brother and the belly of the whale: a portrait of George Orwell.) Literaturnoe obozrenie (Moscow) (1989:9) 56–61.

### John Osborne

**10821.** EGAN, ROBERT G.    *Anger* and the actor: another look back. ModDr (32:3) 413–24.

**10822.** GOMEZ, CHRISTINE.    Profaning the sacred: the juxtaposition of incest and marriage in Ford, Ibsen and Osborne. *See* **4487.**

**10823.** VAN ZYL, JOHN.    Film adaptation as an interpretation of a play: the case of *Look Back in Anger*. *See* **8151.**

### Wilfred Owen

**10824.** ACTON, CAROL GILLIAN.    Paradox in parenthesis: a comparative study of the war poetry of Wilfred Owen, Charles Sorley, Isaac Rosenberg, Ivor Gurney, and David Jones. *See* **9821.**

**10825.** HIBBERD, DOMINIC.    A donation to the Wilfred Owen Collection at Oxford. *See* **231.**

**10826.** NORGATE, PAUL.    Shell-shock and poetry: Wilfred Owen at Craiglockhart Hospital. Eng (36) 1987, 1–35.

### Sara Paretsky

**10827.** SANDELS, ROBERT.    It was a man's world. AD (22:4) 388–96.

### Dorothy Parker

**10828.** KINNEY, ARTHUR F.    Dorothy Parker's letters to Alexander Woollcott. MassR (30:3) 487–515.

### Stewart Parker

**10829.** COLLINS, GAIL.    Partisan position on pizzas. Fortnight (278: supp.) vi.

**10830.** COOPER, ROBERT.    Riveting exchanges. Fortnight (278: supp.) v. (Parker's early radio plays.)

**10831.** DAVEY, SHAUN.    Well-crafted cigarette packets. Fortnight (278: supp.) iii–iv.

**10832.** GINGOLD, ALFRED.    Valuing the individual moment. Fortnight (278: supp.) i–ii.

**10833.** KENT, NICHOLAS.    A wonderfully brave ending. Fortnight (278: supp.) x–xi.

**10834.** PARKER, LYNNE.    Wrestling with flesh and blood. Fortnight (278: supp.) vii.

**10835.** SMYTH, DAMIAN.    Descent, dissent, 'tradition'. Fortnight (278: supp.) ix–x.

### R. Parthasarathy

**10836.** PARTHASARATHY, R.    The exile as writer: on being an Indian writer in English. *See* **5988.**

### Alan Paton

**10837.** HOOPER, MYRTLE.    Paton and the silence of Stephanie. ESA (32:1) 53–62.

**10838.** RUTHERFORD, ANNA.    Stone people in a stone country: Alan Paton's *Too Late the Phalarope*. *In* (pp. 140–52) **37.**

**10839.** STUART, RONALD KEITH.  Incarnational hermeneutics in the writings of Alan Paton. Unpub. doct. diss., Southern Baptist Theological Seminary, 1988. [Abstr. in DA (49) 2698A.]

### Orlando Patterson

**10840.** McDONALD, AVIS G.  Writing down Babylon: movement and stasis in Orlando Patterson's *The Children of Sisyphus.* Span (29) 62–76.

### Walker Percy

**10841.** ALLEN, WILLIAM RODNEY.  Walker Percy: a Southern wayfarer. Jackson: Mississippi UP, 1986. pp. xx, 160. Rev. by James H. Justus in AL (61:1) 127–8.

**10842.** BIZET, JEAN-MICHEL.  Re-ligion, ré-ticence et ex-sistence dans *The Moviegoer* de Walker Percy. EA (42:4) 424–33.

**10843.** BUGGE, JOHN.  Arthurian myth devalued in Walker Percy's *Lancelot. In* (pp. 175–87) **8.**

**10844.** DERWIN, SUSAN.  Orality, aggression, and epistemology in Walker Percy's *The Second Coming.* AQ (45:2) 63–99.

**10845.** —— The renunciation of mimesis: theory and practice of the novel. *See* **2008.**

**10846.** GANČEVA, VERA.  Ricari na pečalnata duša. (Knights of sadness.) *In* (pp. 5–31) UOKĂR PĂRSI, Kinomanat. (The moviegoer.) Sofia: Narodna kultura. pp. 232.

**10847.** HARDY, JOHN EDWARD.  The fiction of Walker Percy. Urbana: Illinois UP, 1987. pp. ix, 317. Rev. by Zoltán Abádi-Nagy in AL (61:3) 500–1; by John F. Desmond in ChrisL (38:2) 75–6.

**10848.** HUGHES, ROBERT.  Walker Percy's comedy and *The Thanatos Syndrome.* SoLJ (22:1) 3–16.

**10849.** OLEKSY, ELŻBIETA.  Theistic existentialism in American letters – Hawthorne and Percy. *See* **6979.**

**10850.** WOOD, RALPH C.  The comedy of redemption: Christian faith in four American novelists. *See* **9380.**

### S. J. Perelman

**10851.** GALE, S. H.  S. J. Perelman: a critical study. Westport, CT; London: Greenwood Press, 1987. (Contributions in popular culture, 15.) Rev. in AmerS (29:1) 1988, 90.

### Ann Petry

**10852.** CHRISTOL, HÉLÈNE.  'The Black woman's burden': Black women and work in *The Street* (Ann Petry) and *Brown Girls, Brownstones* (Paule Marshall). *In* (pp. 145–58) **25.**

### Robert Phelps

**10853.** STREITFELD, DAVID.  A literary life. BkW, 26 Nov., 15.

### Marjorie Pickthall

**10854.** RELKE, DIANA M. A.  Demeter's daughter: Marjorie Pickthall and the quest for poetic identity. CanL (115) 1987, 28–43.

**10855.** WILLIAMSON, JANICE.  Framed by history: Marjorie Pickthall's devices and desire. *In* (pp. 167–78) **40.**

## Harold Pinter

**10856.** CHOI, JEONG-MEE. Harold Pinter's portrayal of women's hollow marriages: passionate attempts at escape from the shackles of reality. YYY (5) 69–114.

**10857.** DICKEY, JOHANNA SUSAN. Strategies of menace in the plays of John Whiting, Harold Pinter and Sam Shepard. Unpub. doct. diss., Stanford Univ., 1988. [Abstr. in DA (49) 3552A.]

**10858.** GALE, STEVEN H. (ed.). Harold Pinter: critical approaches. Rutherford, NJ: Fairleigh Dickinson UP; London; Toronto: Assoc. UPs, 1986. pp. 232. Rev. by Susan Hollis Merritt in ModDr (32:3) 459–61.

**10859.** HALL, ANN CHRISTINE. 'A kind of Alaska': the representation of women in the plays of Eugene O'Neill, Harold Pinter, and Sam Shepard. *See* **10777.**

**10860.** MANOR, E. The Anglo-Jewish predicament in the plays of Bernard Kops, Arnold Wesker, Harold Pinter, and Peter Shaffer. *See* **10220.**

**10861.** MAYBERRY, BOB. Theatre of discord: dissonance in Beckett, Albee, and Pinter. *See* **8922.**

**10862.** POTTER, A. 'What do you think of these Buddhas?': the function of the Buddha in Harold Pinter's *The Caretaker.* SATJ (3:2) 19–32.

**10863.** SAKELLARIDOU, ELIZABETH. How absurd? Some reflections on Pinter's position in the contemporary theatre. Aristotle Univ. of Thessaloniki Yearbook of English Studies (1) 423–33.

**10864.** —— Pinter's female portraits: a study of female characters in the plays of Harold Pinter. Totowa, NJ: Barnes & Noble, 1988. (Bibl. 1988, 8510.) Rev. by Peter Mudford in NQ (36:2) 265; by Susan Hollis Merritt in ModDr (32:1) 171–3.

**10865.** SALEM, DANIEL. L'étranger dans *A Slight Ache* de Pinter. *In* (pp. 279–90) **26.**

**10866.** SCOTT, MICHAEL (ed.). *The Birthday Party, The Caretaker, The Homecoming*: a casebook. (Bibl. 1988, 8511.) Rev. by Susan Hollis Merritt in ModDr (32:3) 461–2.

## Sylvia Plath

**10867.** ANNAS, PAMELA J. A disturbance in mirrors: the poetry of Sylvia Plath. (Bibl. 1988, 8517.) Rev. by Susan Lurie in AL (61:3) 492–4.

**10868.** BRIDGFORD, KIM SUZANNE. Discoveries of the not-known: Louise Bogan, Muriel Rukeyser, Sylvia Plath, May Swenson, and Adrienne Rich. *See* **9114.**

**10869.** HARGROVE, NANCY D. Christian imagery in the poetry of Sylvia Plath. MidQ (31:1) 9–28.

**10870.** PETTINGELL, PHOEBE. Poetic personas. *See* **8541.**

**10871.** SMITH, ANGELEAN VANDORA. Patterns of authenticity: a search for self in American novels. *See* **9532.**

**10872.** STEVENSON, ANNE. Bitter fame: a life of Sylvia Plath. London: Viking; Boston, MA: Houghton Mifflin. pp. xvi, 413. Rev. by William

Scammell in Listener (122) 9 Nov., 31; by Anthony Thwaite in LRB (11:20) 28–9; by Diane Middlebrook in TLS, 27 Oct., 1179; by David Roberts in BW, 13 Aug., 3; by Elizabeth Ward in BkW, 20 Aug., 5.

**10873.** —— 'The dark forces of lust': Plath at Cambridge. NYTB, 13 Aug., 1.

**10874.** STREITFELD, DAVID. Lives of the poets. BkW, 30 July, 15.

**10875.** TALBOT, MARY PATRICIA. The poetry of Sylvia Plath: a critical revision. Unpub. doct. diss., Brown Univ., 1988. [Abstr. in DA (49) 2223A.]

**10876.** WAGNER-MARTIN, LINDA. Sylvia Plath: a biography. (Bibl. 1988, 8526.) Rev. by Jill Farringdon in PW (25:1) 27–30.

**10877.** YALOM, MARILYN. Maternity, mortality, and the literature of madness. See **7965.**

### William Plomer

**10878.** ALEXANDER, PETER F. The archetypal anti-apartheid novel: the writing of *Turbott Wolfe.* DUJ (81:2) 281–7.

**10879.** —— William Plomer: a biography. Oxford: OUP. pp. xvii, 397. (Oxford lives.) Rev. by Peter Parker in Listener (121) 9 Mar., 34; by John Bayley in LRB (11:5) 3, 5.

**10880.** SNELL, JOYCE. William Plomer. Lantern (38:2) 3–8.

### Sterling Plumpp

**10881.** CUNNINGHAM, JAMES. Baldwinian aesthetics in Sterling Plumpp's *Mojo* poems. See **8993.**

### William Poel

**10882.** O'CONNOR, MARION. William Poel and the Elizabethan Stage Society. See **5769.**

### Sharon Pollock

**10883.** BESSAI, DIANE. Sharon Pollock's women: a study in dramatic process. In (pp. 126–36) **40.**

**10884.** KNOWLES, RICHARD PAUL. Replaying history: Canadian historiographic metadrama. DalR (67:2/3) 1987, 228–43.

### Bernard Pomerance

**10885.** HOLLADAY, WILLIAM E.; WATT, STEPHEN. Viewing *The Elephant Man. See* **8060.**

### Katherine Anne Porter

**10886.** BREEDLOVE, LAURA D. Diary of a craftsman: the fiction and nonfiction of Katherine Anne Porter. Unpub. doct. diss., Univ. of Georgia, 1988. [Abstr. in DA (50) 684A.]

**10887.** CHEATHAM, GEORGE. Death and repetition in Porter's Miranda stories. AL (61:4) 610–24.

### Chaim Potok

**10888.** ABRAMSON, EDWARD A. Chaim Potok. Boston, MA: G. K. Hall, 1986. pp. 159. (Twayne's US authors, 503.)

### Beatrix Potter

**10889.** CARPENTER, HUMPHREY. Excessively impertinent bunnies: the subversive element in Beatrix Potter. In (pp. 271–98) **14.**

**10890.** LINDER, LESLIE (ed.). The journal of Beatrix Potter, 1881–1897. Introd. by JUDY TAYLOR. London: Warne. pp. xxviii, 468. (Revised ed.) Rev. by Eva Tucker in Listener (122) 14 Dec., 31.

## Ezra Pound

**10891.** AHEARN, BARRY (ed.). Pound/Zukofsky: selected letters of Ezra Pound and Louis Zukofsky. (Bibl. 1987, 12234.) Rev. by Kenneth Cox in Agenda (26:1) 1988, 60–8.

**10892.** ANTONSSON, GÖRGEN; HENDERSON, ARCHIE. Ezra Pound och nobelpriset. (Ezra Pound and the Nobel Prize.) Lyrikvännen (1989:4) 198–206.

**10893.** BEACH, CHRISTOPHER. Ezra Pound and Harold Bloom: influences, canons, traditions, and the making of modern poetry. See **8673.**

**10894.** BEACH, CHRISTOPHER JOHN. ABC of influence: Ezra Pound and the remaking of the American poetic tradition. See **8461.**

**10895.** BELL, T. A. The hero *polumetis*: a new interpretation of *The Cantos* of Ezra Pound. Unpub. doct. diss., Univ. of Oxford, 1988. [Abstr. in IT (39:1) 36.]

**10896.** BISHOP, PHILIP E. 'And will the world take up its course again?': paranoia and experience in the *Pisan Cantos*. TSLL (31:4) 536–53.

**10897.** BORNSTEIN, GEORGE. Poetic remaking: the art of Browning, Yeats and Pound. See **6365.**

**10898.** —— (ed.). Ezra Pound among the poets. (Bibl. 1987, 12241.) Rev. by Anthony Woodward in RES (38:152) 1987, 581–2.

**10899.** BURNS, PHILIP J. 'Dear Uncle George': Ezra Pound's letters to Congressman Tinkham of Massachusetts. Unpub. doct. diss., Univ. of Rhode Island, 1988. [Abstr. in DA (49) 3362A.]

**10900.** CANTRELL, CAROL H. 'Sufficient ground to stand on': Pound, Williams, and American history. *In* (pp. 153–60) **45.**

**10901.** CARPENTER, HUMPHREY. A serious character: the life of Ezra Pound. (Bibl. 1988, 8537.) Rev. by William H. Gass in TLS, 13 Jan., 27–8; by John Whalen-Bridge in AL (61:3) 484–5; by G. Singh in ACM (2:1) 126–35.

**10902.** COOK, ALBERT. Projections of measure: the continued synergies of Pound and Williams. AQ (45:2) 35–61.

**10903.** COOKSON, WILLIAM. A guide to the *Cantos* of Ezra Pound. (Bibl. 1988, 8542.) Rev. by Anthony Woodward in RES (38:151) 1987, 412.

**10904.** DIGGORY, TERENCE. Yeats's stream of consciousness. *In* (pp. 253–66) **45.**

**10905.** FOGELMAN, BRUCE. Shapes of power: the development of Ezra Pound's poetic sequences. Ann Arbor, MI: UMI Research Press, 1988. pp. xii, 223. (Studies in modern literature, 95.) (Cf. bibl. 1988, 8548.) Rev. by Cordell D. K. Yee in AL (61:2) 306–7.

**10906.** FRIBERG, GÖSTA. 'Sextus Pound': om Pound, personan & Propertius. ('Sextus Pound': on Pound, the persona and Propertius.) Lyrikvännen (1989:4) 182–5.

**10907.** HAMILTON, ROBERT SCOTT. Ezra Pound and the Symbolist inheritance. Unpub. doct. diss., Univ. of California, Berkeley, 1988. [Abstr. in DA (50) 146–7A.]

**10908.** HOOGESTRAAT, JANE. 'Akin to nothing but language': Pound, Laforgue, and logopoeia. ELH (55:1) 1988, 259–85.

**10909.** HOOLEY, DANIEL M. The classics in paraphrase: Ezra Pound and modern translators of Latin poetry. Selinsgrove, PA: Susquehanna UP; London; Toronto: Assoc. UPs, 1988. pp. 146. (Cf. bibl. 1986, 10668.) Rev. by Richard G. Landini and William J. O'Neal in CML (9:2) 153–7.

**10910.** KRONICK, JOSEPH. Reading Pound against Pound. SoR (25:4) 859–76.

**10911.** LAUGHLIN, JAMES. Pound as wuz: recollections and interpretations. (Pub. in USA as *Pound as Wuz: Essays and Lectures on Ezra Pound.*) London: Owen. (Bibl. 1988, 8553.)

**10912.** LELAND, BLAKE THOMAS. Heroic economies: Ezra Pound, James Joyce and Modernist epic between the wars. See **10091.**

**10913.** LITZ, A. WALTON. Strange meetings: Eliot, Pound, and Laforgue. *In* (pp. 146–52) **45.**

**10914.** LONGENBACH, JAMES. Modernist poetics of history: Pound, Eliot, and the sense of the past. See **9485.**

**10915.** —— Stone Cottage: Pound, Yeats, and Modernism. (Bibl. 1988, 8556.) Rev. by Hugh Haughton in TLS, 17 Mar., 286; by Nicholas Grene in NQ (36:4) 546.

**10916.** McGANN, JEROME. The third world of criticism. *In* (pp. 85–107) **53.**

**10917.** NICHOL, DONALD W. 'Flagrant' versus 'fragrant' in Beaumont, Pope, Pound, and Burgess. See **1048.**

**10918.** OLSON, PETER DAVID. Seizing *Hagoromo*: Ezra Pound's imaged drama and *The Cantos.* Unpub. doct. diss., Univ. of Michigan, 1988. [Abstr. in DA (49) 2211–12A.]

**10919.** OZTURK, T. A. Ezra Pound and visual art. Unpub. doct. diss., Univ. of Oxford, 1987. [Abstr. in IT (39:2) 490.]

**10920.** PERLOFF, MARJORIE. Ezra Pound and *The Prose Tradition in Verse. In* (pp. 162–93) MARJORIE PERLOFF, The futurist moment: avant-garde, avant-guerre, and the language of rupture. Chicago; London: Chicago UP, 1986. pp. xxiii, 288. Rev. by Timothy Matterer in JEGP (87:1) 1988, 153–5; by Gregory L. Ulmer in Criticism (30:2) 1988, 263–5; by Jacob Korg in PLL (24:2) 1988, 212–18; by Steven Connor in MLR (84:4) 904–5.

**10921.** PRATT, WILLIAM. Pound and Yeats: the poetics of friendship. *In* (pp. 159–80) **46.**

**10922.** RAE, PATRICIA. From mystical gaze to pragmatic game: representations of truth in vorticist art. ELH (56:3) 689–720.

**10923.** SMITH, MARCEL; ULMER, WILLIAM A. (eds). Ezra Pound: the legacy of Kulchur. Tuscaloosa; London: Alabama UP, 1988. pp. vi, 179. Rev. by Martin Schiralli in JAE (23:3) 124.

**10924.** SOMMARDAL, GÖRAN. Folklorism och modernism. (Folklorism and Modernism.) Lyrikvännen (1989:4) 172–8. (Pound's interpretations of Chinese poetry.)

**10925.** STOICHEFF, PETER.   Poem's poetics or poet's death: what ends *The Cantos, Maximus,* and *Paterson? See* **10756.**
**10926.** TERRELL, CARROLL F.   A companion to the *Cantos* of Ezra Pound: vol. 2 (Cantos 74–117). 1984. (Bibl. 1986, 13913, where date of publication incorrect.) Rev. by Peter Makin in MLR (83:2) 1988, 435–6.
**10927.** THOMAS, DAVID LEE.   Loss, mourning and the vatic dispersal of self in the long poems of Whitman, Eliot, Pound, Berryman, and Lowell. *See* **7665.**
**10928.** VAUGHAN, T. S.   A discussion of Ezra Pound's early work. Unpub. M.Litt. thesis, Univ. of Edinburgh, 1986. [Abstr. in IT (36:4) 1399.]
**10929.** VON HALLBERG, ROBERT.   Ezra Pound in Paris. *In* (pp. 53–65) **46.**
**10930.** WARD, J.   Myth, history and the early poetics of Ezra Pound, 1904–1930 (up to a draft of xxx Cantos). Unpub. doct. diss., Univ. of Leeds, 1988. [Abstr. in IT (39:3) 1118.]
**10931.** WILSON, JAMES ALAN.   Ritual and reception: Ezra Pound's translations of troubadour and Chinese lyrics. Unpub. doct. diss., Univ. of California, Berkeley, 1987. [Abstr. in DA (49) 1795A.]

### Anthony Powell

**10932.** FROST, LAURIE ANNE ADAMS.   Reminiscent scrutinies: individual memory and social life in Anthony Powell's *A Dance to the Music of Time.* Unpub. doct. diss., Rice Univ., 1988. [Abstr. in DA (49) 3032A.]

### The Powys Brothers

**10933.** STINTON, JUDITH.   Chaldon Herring: the Powys Circle in a Dorset village. Woodbridge: Boydell Press, 1988. pp. 184.

### Llewelyn Powys

**10934.** FOSS, P. J.   Epicurean–mystic: a study of Llewelyn Powys, the man and his work. Unpub. doct. diss., Univ. of Wales, 1988. [Abstr. in IT (39:3) 1115.]

### E. J. Pratt

**10935.** PITT, DAVID G.   E. J. Pratt: the master years: 1927–1964. Toronto; London: Toronto UP, 1987. pp. xviii, 555.
**10936.** TSCHACHLER, HEINZ.   The cost of a story: ideology and ambivalence in the verse narratives of E.J. Pratt. CanL (122/23) 93–106.

### John Clark Pratt

**10937.** CRUZ, JUAN J.   Gone to pieces everyone: an interiew with John Clark Pratt. RCEI (18) 251–6.

### J. B. Priestley

**10938.** BRADBURY, MALCOLM.   Persons of letters. *In* (pp. 5–14) **42.**
**10939.** BROME, VINCENT.   J. B. Priestley. (Bibl. 1988, 8574.) Rev. by John Bayley in LRB (11:1) 26–7.
**10940.** DAKHNO, M. P.   Rol' stilisticheskikh priemov formirovanii kontŝeptual'noĭ informatŝii dramaturgicheskogo teksta: na materiale p'es Dzh. B. Pristli. *See* **1394.**

## J. H. Prynne

**10941.** HARDY, STEPHEN. The poetry of J. H. Prynne: a suitable case for further critical treatment? Germanica Olomucensia (7) 95–102.

## Al Purdy

**10942.** BROWN, RUSSELL (ed.). The collected poems of Al Purdy. Toronto: McClelland & Stewart, 1986. pp. xviii, 396. Rev. by Don Gutteridge in CanL (116) 1988, 159–61.

## James Purdy

**10943.** MILLER, PAUL W. James Purdy's fiction as shaped by the American Midwest: the Chicago novels. In (pp. 149–61) **2.**

## Rodney Pybus

**10944.** SUBERCHICOT, ALAIN. La beauté dans l'œuvre poétique de Rodney Pybus. In (pp. 169–84) **10.**

## Barbara Pym

**10945.** COTSELL, MICHAEL. Barbara Pym. Basingstoke: Macmillan. pp. ix, 153. (Macmillan modern novelists.) Rev. by Margaret Bradham in TLS, 8 Sept., 967.

**10946.** GRONER, MARLENE SAN MIGUEL. The novels of Barbara Pym. Unpub. doct. diss., St John's Univ., 1988. [Abstr. in DA (49) 3033A.]

**10947.** LIDDELL, ROBERT. A mind at ease: Barabara Pym and her novels. London: Owen. pp. 143. Rev. by Margaret Bradham in TLS, 8 Sept., 967.

**10948.** NAULTY, PATRICIA MARY. 'I never talk of hunger': self-starvation as women's language of protest in novels by Barbara Pym, Margaret Atwood, and Anne Tyler. See **8964.**

## Thomas Pynchon

**10949.** BERMAN, JAYE ELLYN. Parody as cultural criticism in the postmodern American novel: Donald Barthelme, Gilbert Sorrentino, and Thomas Pynchon. See **9019.**

**10950.** BERSANI, LEO. Pynchon, paranoia, and literature. Representations (25) 99–118.

**10951.** BRETT, LAUREL KAYE. Toto, I have a feeling we're not in Kansas anymore: discussions of Pynchon's novels. Unpub. doct. diss., State Univ. of New York at Stony Brook, 1987. [Abstr. in DA (49) 3024A.]

**10952.** CAMPBELL, GREGOR DUNCAN. Historical consciousness in the fiction of William Gaddis, Thomas Pynchon, and Robert Coover: a reading of *The Recognitions*, *Gravity's Rainbow*, and *The Public Burning*. See **9331.**

**10953.** CARTER, J. C. Pynchon's transmarginal leaps. Unpub. M.Litt. diss., Univ. of Edinburgh. [Abstr. in IT (39:4) 1636.]

**10954.** COWLEY, JULIAN. The eternal centre/the final zero: the fiction of Thomas Pynchon. DQR (19:1) 1–17.

**10955.** EDMUNDSON, MARK. Prophet of a new postmodernism: the greater challenge of Salman Rushdie. Harper's (279) Dec., 62–71 (review-article).

**10956.** Farrell, John Charles. Thomas Pynchon and the post-modern language. Unpub. doct. diss., Harvard Univ., 1988. [Abstr. in DA (49) 3026A.]

**10957.** Fludernik, Monika. *Hänsel und Gretel*, and Dante: the coordinates of hope in Pynchon's *Gravity's Rainbow*. AAA (14:1) 39–56.

**10958.** Fry, August J. The clouding of the wine: reading Thomas Pynchon's *The Crying of Lot 49*. In (pp. 143–9) **23.**

**10959.** Haarhoff, Dorian. Bondels and bombs: the Bondelswarts Rebellion in historical fiction. See **9153.**

**10960.** James, A. Pynchon, the postmodern and the postwar: a reading of *Gravity's Rainbow*. Unpub. doct. diss., Univ. of Sussex. [Abstr. in IT (39:4) 1636–7.]

**10961.** Keesey, Douglas. Rereading Thomas Pynchon. Unpub. doct. diss., Princeton Univ., 1988. [Abstr. in DA (49) 3027A.]

**10962.** Kim, Sang-Koo. Soseol eui haesukhakjeok jeopgeun: *Gravity's Rainbow* eui kyoungwu. (A hermeneutical approach to *Gravity's Rainbow*.) JELL (35) 485–509.

**10963.** Kozlowski, Lisa M. The truth behind the catenary in Pynchon's *V*: a dream that will help you not at all. NCL (19:4) 2–4.

**10964.** McCarron, William E. The figurative made literal in *Gravity's Rainbow*. NCL (19:5) 2–3.

**10965.** —— Pynchon and Zener cards. NCL (19:3) 9–11.

**10966.** Mc Elroy, Bernard. Fiction of the modern grotesque. See **8331.**

**10967.** Maltby, P. L. Dissident postmodernists: Barthelme, Coover, Pynchon. See **9020.**

**10968.** Mead, Clifford. Thomas Pynchon: a bibliography of primary and secondary materials. Elmwood Park, IL: Dalkey Archive. pp. viii, 175. Rev. in BkW, 13 Aug., 13.

**10969.** Measom, J. N. Black and white and the abolition of the spectrum: an approach to the writings of Thomas Pynchon. Unpub. M.Phil. diss., Univ. of Manchester, 1988. [Abstr. in IT (39:2) 490.]

**10970.** Miyamoto, Yoichiro. *Gravity's Rainbow* and the question of postmodernism. SEL (65:2) 209–22.

**10971.** Moore, Thomas. The style of connectedness: *Gravity's Rainbow* and Thomas Pynchon. (Bibl. 1988, 8598.) Rev. by J. Madison Davis in StudN (20:4) 1988, 436–7.

**10972.** Redfield, Marc W. Pynchon's postmodern sublime. PMLA (104:2) 152–62.

**10973.** Safer, Elaine B. The contemporary American comic epic: the novels of Barth, Pynchon, Gaddis, and Kesey. See **9018.**

**10974.** Seed, David. The fictional labyrinths of Thomas Pynchon. Iowa City: Iowa UP, 1988. (Bibl. 1988, 8602.) Rev. by James M. Mellard in AL (61:1) 131–2.

**10975.** Tabbi, Joseph Paul. The psychology of machines: technology and personal identity in the work of Norman Mailer and Thomas Pynchon. See **10490.**

**10976.** TAYLOR, JANE H. M.   The *Danse macabre*: reflections on black humour. CompCrit (10) 1988, 139–57.

**10977.** THIELEMANS, JOHAN.   MBA-Kayere and the routes of power: Pynchon's *Gravity's Rainbow* read from Enzian's point of view. *In* (pp. 213–25) **2.**

**10978.** WARD, DEAN ALAN.   The fictive 'experiments' of George Eliot and Thomas Pynchon: science, literary models, and human experience. *See* **6795.**

**10979.** WEISENBURGER, STEVEN.   A *Gravity's Rainbow* companion: sources and contexts for Pynchon's novel. Athens; London: Georgia UP, 1988. pp. 345.

### David Rabe

**10980.** COLAKIS, MARIANTHE.   The House of Atreus myth in the seventies and eighties: David Rabe's *The Orphan* and Joyce Carol Oates's *Angel of Light*. *See* **10707.**

**10981.** KOLIN, PHILIP C.   David Rabe: a stage history and a primary and secondary bibliography. (Bibl. 1988, 8604. Rev. by Mark Charney in SoCR (21:2) 86–7; by Jennifer Lynn McMillion in TJ (41:3) 433–4; by Laura Morrow in ModDr (32:3) 456–8.

### Kathleen Raine

**10982.** EL-SHAER, M. S.   Mysticism in the poetry of Kathleen Raine. Unpub. doct. diss., Univ. of Durham, 1987. [Abstr. in IT (38:4) 1462.]

### Ayn Rand

**10983.** BAKER, JAMES T.   Ayn Rand. Boston, MA: G. K. Hall, 1987. pp. 168. (Twayne's US authors, 501.) Rev. by John Braeman in AmerS (29:2) 1988, 97–8.

**10984.** BRANDEN, NATHANIEL.   Judgment day: my years with Ayn Rand. Boston, MA: Houghton Mifflin. pp. 436. Rev. by Charles Paul Freund in BkW, 10 Sept., 10.

### Arthur Ransome

**10985.** BROGAN, HUGH (ed.).   *Coots in the North* and other stories. London: Cape, 1988. pp. 114. Rev. by T. J. Binyon in TLS, 6 Jan., 22.

**10986.** SMITH, J. B.   'The old eel that come up through Breydon Water': Arthur Ransome's work as a key to folklife and folk speech. *See* **1483.**

### Terence Rattigan

**10987.** YOUNG, B. A.   The Rattigan version: Sir Terence Rattigan and the theatre of character. New York: Atheneum, 1988. (Bibl. 1986, 13983.) Rev. by Robert F. Gross in TJ (41:2) 263–4.

### James Reaney

**10988.** KNOWLES, RICHARD PAUL.   Replaying history: Canadian historiographic metadrama. *See* **10884.**

### Ishmael Reed

**10989.** DE FILIPPO, BERNARD JOHN.   HooDoo, voodoo, and conjure: the novels of Ishmael Reed. Unpub. doct. diss., Carnegie–Mellon Univ., 1987. [Abstr. in DA (49) 3025A.]

### Graham Reid

**10990.** PILKINGTON, ULICK LIONEL.   Representations of the Northern Ireland crisis in contemporary drama: 1968–80. *See* **9127.**

### Ruth Rendell ('Barbara Vine')

**10991.** CLARK, SUSAN L. A fearful symmetry. AD (22:3) 228–35.

### Kenneth Rexroth

**10992.** BARTLETT, LEE. The community of love: reading Kenneth Rexroth's long poems. CR (33:1) 13–31.

**10993.** HAMALIAN, LEO. Scanning the self: the influence of Emerson on Kenneth Rexroth. See **6809.**

**10994.** JOHNSTON, ALLAN JAMES. Reinventing the metaphors: toward an ecological aesthetics in the writings of Robinson Jeffers, Kenneth Rexroth and Gary Snyder. See **10009.**

**10995.** TRITICA, JOHN MICHAEL. Kenneth Rexroth and the poetics of commitment and mysticism. Unpub. doct. diss., Univ. of New Mexico, 1988. [Abstr. in DA (49) 3727A.]

### Jean Rhys

**10996.** CURTIS, JAN. Jean Rhys's *Voyage in the Dark*: a re-assessment. JCL (22:1) 1987, 144–58.

**10997.** DELOURME, CHANTAL. La mémoire fécondée: réflexions sur l'intertextualité: *Jane Eyre, Wide Sargasso Sea.* See **6290.**

**10998.** HARRISON, NANCY R. Jean Rhys and the novel as women's text. Chapel Hill; London: North Carolina UP. pp. xvi, 289. Rev. by Sue Roe in TLS, 2 June, 608.

**10999.** KAVANAGH, DESMOND. Jean Rhys and God. DUJ (81:2) 275–80.

**11000.** O'CONNOR, TERESA F. Jean Rhys: the West Indian fictions. New York: New York UP, 1986. pp. x, 247. Rev. by Coral Ann Howells in RES (39:155) 1988, 464–6.

### Adrienne Rich

**11001.** BRIDGFORD, KIM SUZANNE. Discoveries of the not-known: Louise Bogan, Muriel Rukeyser, Sylvia Plath, May Swenson, and Adrienne Rich. See **9114.**

**11002.** HERZOG, ANNE. Adrienne Rich and the discourse of decolonization. CR (33:3) 258–77.

**11003.** RATCLIFFE, KRISTA L. Words of one's own: toward a rhetoric of feminism in selected essays of Virginia Woolf and Adrienne Rich. Unpub. doct. diss., Ohio State Univ., 1988. [Abstr. in DA (49) 2653–4A.]

**11004.** WERNER, CRAIG. Adrienne Rich: the poet and her critics. Chicago: American Library Assn, 1988. pp. ix, 199. Rev. by Gertrude Reif Hughes in AL (61:2) 321–2.

**11005.** WILSON, SUSAN RUTH. Adrienne Rich: the conscious rhetorician. Unpub. doct. diss., Northwestern Univ., 1988. [Abstr. in DA (49) 2223–4A.]

### 'Frank Richards' (Charles Harold St John Hamilton)

**11006.** CADOGAN, MARY. Frank Richards: the chap behind the chums. (Bibl. 1988, 8638.) Rev. by Patricia Craig in LRB (11:11) 26–7.

### Henry Handel Richardson
### (Ethel Florence Lindesay Robertson)

**11007.** MACKENZIE, MANFRED. The way home. See **7089.**

**11008.** PLATZ, NORBERT H.   Influence or choice? Henry Handel Richardson's *Maurice Guest* and its relation to German culture. *In* (pp. 115–25) **5.**

### Jack Richardson

**11009.** CALLENS, JOHAN.   Initiation in Jack Richardson's *In the Final Year of Grace*. *In* (pp. 163–74) **2.**

### Mordecai Richler

**11010.** DARLING, MICHAEL (ed.).   Perspectives on Mordecai Richler. Toronto: ECW Press, 1986. pp. 183. Rev. by I. S. Maclaren in CanL (120) 196–8.

### Edgell Rickword

**11011.** HOBDAY, CHARLES.   Edgell Rickword: a poet at war. Manchester: Carcanet Press. pp. 337. Rev. by John Lucas in TLS, 3 Nov., 1204; by C. H. Sisson in LRB (11:21) 21.

### Lynn Riggs

**11012.** BRAUNLICH, PHYLLIS COLE.   Haunted by home: the life and letters of Lynn Riggs. Norman; London: Oklahoma UP, 1988. pp. xvi, 233.

### Sharon Riis

**11013.** PERREAULT, JEANNE.   Narrative strategies and feminist fundamentals in *The True Story of Ida Johnson*. *In* (pp. 270–5) **40.**

### Mary Roberts Rinehart

**11014.** DANCE, JAMES C.   Spinsters in jeopardy. AD (22:1) 28–37.

### Richard Rive

**11015.** DE VRIES, ABRAHAM H.   An interview with Richard Rive. Current Writing (1) 45–55.

**11016.** GRAY, STEPHEN.   Richard Moore Rive (1932–1989). Current Writing (1) 1.

**11017.** HARESNAPE, GEOFFREY.   Memorial for Richard Rive. Contrast (17:3) 6–8.

**11018.** HOLTZHAUSEN, EVELYN JOHN.   An interview with Richard Rive. Upstream (7:3) 4–6.

**11019.** RABIE, JAN.   Richard Rive ons mis jou. (Richard Rive, we miss you.) Contrast (17:3) 9–11.

**11020.** RAJU, JAYARANI; DUBBELD, CATHERINE.   Richard Rive: a select bibliography. Current Writing (1) 56–65.

### Eric Roach

**11021.** BREINER, LAURENCE A.   History, nature, and people in the poetry of Eric Roach. JCL (23:1) 1988, 43–60.

### Elizabeth Madox Roberts

**11022.** BENIGNI, HELEN.   Portraits from the Bluegrass: the main characters in the short fiction of Elizabeth Madox Roberts. Unpub. doct. diss., Indiana Univ. of Pennsylvania. [Abstr. in DA (50) 1656A.]

### Edwin Arlington Robinson

**11023.** BOSWELL, JEANETTA.   Edwin Arlington Robinson and the critics: a bibliography of secondary sources with selective annotations. Metuchen, NJ; London: Scarecrow Press, 1988. pp. vii, 285. (Scarecrow author bibliographies, 80.)

**Marilynne Robinson**

**11024.** RAVITS, MARTHA.   Extending the American range: Marilynne Robinson's *Housekeeping*. AL (61:4) 644–66.

**Stephen Rodefer**

**11025.** RODEFER, STEPHEN.   A note on realism. RCEI (18) 77.

**Theodore Roethke**

**11026.** NORDSTRÖM, LARS.   Theodore Roethke, William Stafford, and Gary Snyder: the ecological metaphor as transformed regionalism. Uppsala: Acta Universitatis Upsaliensis; Stockholm: Almqvist & Wiksell. pp. 197. (Studia anglistica upsaliensia, 67.) (Doct. diss., Uppsala Univ.)

**11027.** YVARD, PIERRE.   Theodore Roethke, *In a Dark Time*, explication et traduction. Repérages (11) 73–80.

**Isaac Rosenberg**

**11028.** ACTON, CAROL GILLIAN.   Paradox in parenthesis: a comparative study of the war poetry of Wilfred Owen, Charles Sorley, Isaac Rosenberg, Ivor Gurney, and David Jones. *See* **9821.**

**11029.** DEVINE, KATHLEEN.   Rosenberg, Keats, and two Belles Dames Sans Merci. *See* **7139.**

**Sinclair Ross**

**11030.** MATHESON, T. J.   'But do your thing': conformity, self-reliance, and Sinclair Ross's *As For Me and My House*. DalR (66:4) 1986, 497–512.

**11031.** ROSS, MORTON L.   The canonization of *As for Me and My House*: a case study. *In* (pp. 170–85) **12.**

**Philip Roth**

**11032.** MILBAUER, ASHER Z.; WATSON, DONALD G. (eds).   Reading Philip Roth. New York: St Martin's Press; Basingstoke: Macmillan, 1988. pp. xiv, 205. Rev. by James H. Justus in SAF (17:1) 115–16.

**11033.** ROTH, PHILIP.   The facts: a novelist's autobiography. (Bibl. 1988, 8647.) Rev. in BkW, 8 Oct., 12; by Stephen Fender in Listener (121) 23 Feb., 32; by Bryan Cheyette in TLS, 17 Feb., 159.

**11034.** STOUT, JANIS P.   The misogyny of Philip Roth's *The Great American Novel*. BSUF (27:1) 1986, 72–5.

**11035.** STREITFELD, DAVID.   Grapes of Roth. BkW, 27 Aug., 15.

**11036.** TRACHTENBERG, STANLEY.   In the egosphere: Philip Roth's anti-Bildungsroman. PLL (25:3) 326–41. (*The Ghost Writer*.)

**Jerome Rothenberg**

**11037.** POLKINHORN, HARRY.   Jerome Rothenberg: a descriptive bibliography. Jefferson, NC; London: McFarland, 1988. pp. xii, 178. (American contemporary poetry bibliographies, 3.)

**Muriel Rukeyser**

**11038.** BRIDGFORD, KIM SUZANNE.   Discoveries of the not-known: Louise Bogan, Muriel Rukeyser, Sylvia Plath, May Swenson, and Adrienne Rich. *See* **9114.**

**Salman Rushdie**

**11039.** APPIGNANESI, LISA; MAITLAND, SARA (eds).   The Rushdie file. London: Fourth Estate in assn with ICA. pp. x, 258. Rev. by Bob

Woffinden in Listener (122) 10 Aug., 27; by Christopher Hitchens in LRB (11:20) 11–15.

**11040.** BRENNAN, TIMOTHY. Salman Rushdie and the Third World: myths of the nation. London: Macmillan. pp. xv, 203. Rev. by Christopher Hitchens in LRB (11:20) 11–15.

**11041.** EDMUNDSON, MARK. Prophet of a new postmodernism: the greater challenge of Salman Rushdie. *See* **10955.**

**11042.** HEWSON, KELLY. Opening up the universe a little more: Salman Rushdie and the migrant as story-teller. Span (29) 82–93.

**11043.** HEWSON, KELLY LEIGH. Writers and responsibility: George Orwell, Nadine Gordimer, John Coetzee and Salman Rushdie. *See* **9269.**

**11044.** KANAGANAYAKAM, C. Myth and fabulosity in *Midnight's Children*. DalR (67:1) 1987, 86–98.

**11045.** MICHELL, JOHN. Rushdie's insult. London: Michell. pp. 8. (Radical traditionalist papers, 7; Blasphemy, 2.)

**11046.** MORRISON, BLAKE. In the matter of Rushdie. BkW, 6 Aug., 15.

**11047.** PASHA-ZADE, A.; ALIEV, S. Sataninskaia kniga: o romane S. Rushdi *Sataninskie stikhi.* (The satanic book: on Salman Rushdie's *Satanic Verses.*) Aziia Afrika segodnia (Moscow) (1989:7) 12–15.

**11048.** TELLEKAMP, D. W. S. Salman Rushdie's *History in My Vision.* Rotterdam: Slootweg & Tromp Meesters. pp. 43.

**11049.** TODD, RICHARD. Convention and innovation in British fiction 1981–1984: the contemporaneity of magic realism. *In* (pp. 361–88) **16.**

**11050.** WELDON, FAY. Sacred cows. London: Chatto & Windus. pp. 43. (Chatto CounterBlasts, 4.) Rev. by Christopher Hitchens in LRB (11:20) 11–15. (The *Satanic Verses* affair.)

### George William Russell ('Æ')

**11051.** HIGDON, DAVID LEON. A George Russell letter to Lady Augusta Gregory. *See* **9814.**

### George Ryga

**11052.** BOIRE, GARY. George Ryga: a tribute. CanL (118) 1988, 189–90.

**11053.** —— Wheels on fire: the train of thought in George Ryga's *The Ecstasy of Rita Joe.* CanL (113/14) 1987, 62–74.

**11054.** GRACE, SHERRILL. The expressionist legacy in the Canadian theatre: George Ryga and Robert Gurik. CanL (118) 1988, 47–58.

### Edward Sackville-West

**11055.** DE-LA-NOY, MICHAEL. Eddy: the life of Edward Sackville-West. (Bibl. 1988, 8657.) Rev. by John Bayley in LRB (11:1) 26–7.

### V. Sackville-West

**11056.** LEASKA, MITCHELL A.; PHILLIPS, JOHN (eds). Violet to Vita: the letters of Violet Trefusis to Vita Sackville-West, 1910–21. London: Methuen. pp. xii, 303. Rev. by Claire Harman in TLS, 29 Sept., 1053; by Ann Geneva in Listener (122) 21 Sept., 34.

**11057.** NICOLSON, NIGEL (introd.). *The Land*; and *The Garden.* Exeter: Webb & Bower in assn with Joseph. pp. 190.

**11058.** RAITT, S. The texture of a friendship: V. Sackville-West and Virginia Woolf. Unpub. doct. diss., Univ. of Cambridge. [Abstr. in IT (38:3) 1013.]

### J. D. Salinger

**11059.** COTTER, JAMES FINN. A source for Seymour's suicide: Rilke's *Voices* and Salinger's *Nine Stories*. PLL (25:1) 83–98.

**11060.** HAMILTON, IAN. In search of J. D. Salinger. (Bibl. 1988, 8661.) Rev. by Jackson J. Benson in AL (61:3) 465–8; by Stephen Turner in Landfall (43:1) 124–6; by Clarence Petersen in BW, 27 Aug., 4; in BkW, 27 Aug., 12.

**11061.** SMITH, ANGELEAN VANDORA. Patterns of authenticity: a search for self in American novels. *See* **9532.**

### James Salter

**11062.** STREITFELD, DAVID. Salter's sport. BkW, 23 Apr., 15.

### Rick Salutin

**11063.** KNOWLES, RICHARD PAUL. Replaying history: Canadian historiographic metadrama. *See* **10884.**

### Laura Goodman Salverson

**11064.** GUNNARS, KRISTJANA. Laura Goodman Salverson's confessions of a divided self. *In* (pp. 148–53) **40.**

### Carl Sandburg

**11065.** CALLAHAN, NORTH. Carl Sandburg: his life and works. (Bibl. 1988, 8667.) Rev. by Robert W. Johannsen in IHJ (82:1) 56–7; by Richard Gray in NQ (36:2) 276–7; by Mark E. Neely, Jr, in AHR (94:5) 1496.

### Pamela Sargent

**11066.** MORRISSEY, THOMAS J. Pamela Sargent's science fiction for young adults: celebrations of change. SFS (16:2) 184–90.

### Siegfried Sassoon

**11067.** QUINN, P. J. M. Robert Graves and Siegfried Sassoon: from early poetry to autobiography. *See* **9796.**

### Dorothy L. Sayers

**11068.** HAHN, STEPHEN. Theodicy in Dorothy Sayers' *Murder Must Advertise*. Ren (41:3) 169–76.

**11069.** PATTERSON, NANCY-LOU. A comedy of masks: Lord Peter as Harlequin in *Murder Must Advertise*. Mythlore (15:3) 22–8.

**11070.** —— A ring of good bells: providence and judgement in Dorothy L. Sayers' *The Nine Tailors*. Mythlore (16:1) 50–2.

### Jack Schaefer

**11071.** ROBINSON, FORREST G. Heroism, home, and the telling of *Shane*. AQ (45:1) 72–100.

### Joan Schenkar

**11072.** PATRAKA, VIVIAN M. Mass culture and metaphors of menace in Joan Schenkar's plays. *In* (pp. 25–40) **39.**

**11073.** WILSON, ANN. History and hysteria: writing the body in *Portrait of Dora* and *Signs of Life*. ModDr (32:1) 73–88.

### Stephen Scobie

**11074.** FEE, MARGERY. Stephen Scobie: biographical. CanL (115) 1987, 81–102.

### Duncan Campbell Scott

**11075.** SOUSTER, RAYMOND; LOCHHEAD, DOUGLAS (eds). Powassan's drum: poems of Duncan Campbell Scott. Ottawa: Tecumseh Press, 1985. pp. xii, 200. Rev. by Ronald Hatch in CanL (115) 1987, 223–4.

### F. R. Scott

**11076.** DJWA, SANDRA. The politics of the imagination: a life of F. R. Scott. Toronto: McClelland & Stewart, 1987. pp. 528. Rev. by Al Purdy in CanL (121) 126–31.

**11077.** MCDONALD, LARRY. The politics of influence: Birney, Scott, Livesay and the influence of politics. *See* **9102.**

**11078.** PURDY, AL. Purdy's Scott: a memoir in response to Sandra Djwa's *The Politics of the Imagination: a Life of F. R. Scott.* CanL (121) 126–31 (review-article).

### Paul Scott

**11079.** SRIVASTAVA, ARUNA. The pageant of empire: Paul Scott's The Raj Quartet and related versions of imperialism in the Anglo-Indian novel. Unpub. doct. diss., McMaster Univ. [Abstr. in DA (50) 1315A.]

### Samuel Selvon

**11080.** MAIR, CHRISTIAN. Naipaul's *Miguel Street* and Selvon's *Lonely Londoners* – two approaches to the use of Caribbean creole in fiction. *See* **1551.**

### Richard Selzer

**11081.** WHITTIER, GAYLE. Richard Selzer's evolving paradigms of creativity. CR (33:3) 278–301.

### Mongane Wally Serote

**11082.** GAGIANO, ANNIE. Serote's novel and Visser's criticism. English Academy Review (6) 84–91. (*To Every Birth its Blood.*)

### Mary Lee Settle

**11083.** GARRETT, GEORGE. Understanding Mary Lee Settle. Columbia: South Carolina UP, 1988. pp. 187. Rev. by Jane Gentry Vance in SoLJ (22:1) 135–8.

**11084.** ROSENBERG, BRIAN. The price of freedom: an interview with Mary Lee Settle. SoR (25:2) 351–65.

### Stephen Sewell

**11085.** CAULFIELD, CARL. 'What the bomb does to our minds': Sewell's *Welcome the Bright World* and Brenton's *The Genius. See* **9143.**

**11086.** HUNTER, MARY ANN. Casebook: Stephen Sewell's *Miranda.* Australasian Drama Studies (14) 47–63.

**11087.** —— Stephen Sewell talks to Mary Ann Hunter. Australasian Drama Studies (14) 33–45.

### Anne Sexton

**11088.** GEORGOUDAKI, CATHERINE. Kitchen imagery in Anne Sexton's poetry. Aristotle Univ. of Thessaloniki Yearbook of English Studies (1) 323–49.

### Maurice Shadbolt

**11089.** MANN, PHILLIP. The first production of *Once on Chunuk Bair.* Illusions (11) 14–18.

### Peter Shaffer

**11090.** MANOR, E. The Anglo-Jewish predicament in the plays of Bernard Kops, Arnold Wesker, Harold Pinter, and Peter Shaffer. *See* **10220.**

**11091.** PLUNKA, GENE A. Roles, rites, and rituals: Peter Shaffer's *The Royal Hunt of the Sun.* BSUF (27:3) 1986, 71–9.

### Ntozake Shange

**11092.** DeSHAZER, MARY K. Rejecting necrophilia: Ntozake Shange and the warrior re-visioned. *In* (pp. 86–100) **39.**

**11093.** SPLAWN, P. JANE. Rites of passage in the writings of Ntozake Shange: the poetry, drama, and novels. Unpub. doct. diss., Univ. of Wisconsin–Madison, 1988. [Abstr. in DA (50) 687A.]

### Thomas Shapcott

**11094.** WILLIAMS, BARBARA. Interview with Thomas Shapcott. Westerly (34:1) 43–52.

### George Bernard Shaw

**11095.** BERDAN, MARSHALL S. Watson and Shaw: subtle echoes in the canon. *See* **6726.**

**11096.** BROOKS, HAROLD F. Shaw and Shelley. *See* **7425.**

**11097.** BRYDEN, MARY. Coils of the cobra: the predatory woman of Shaw and Beckett. *See* **9037.**

**11098.** CHAMEEV, A. A. Zhanrovoe svoeobrazie dramaturgii Shou 1920-kh godov. (The originality of genre in Shaw's plays of the 1920s.) NDFN (1989:2) 25–32.

**11099.** DECKER, DAVID JOHN. The temptation of Saint George: a critical study of the 1880's novels of Bernard Shaw. Unpub. doct. diss., Univ. of Washington, 1988. [Abstr. in DA (50) 689–90A.]

**11100.** DUKORE, BERNARD F. Alan Ayckbourn's Liza Doolittle. *See* **8987.**

**11101.** GAINOR, J. ELLEN. Shaw's daughters: discourses of gender and female identity in the work of George Bernard Shaw. Unpub. doct. diss., Princeton Univ. [Abstr. in DA (49) 3732A.]

**11102.** HARLESS, WINSTON NEELY. Characterization in selected one-act plays of George Bernard Shaw: a display of enthymematic argument. Unpub. doct. diss., Ohio State Univ., 1988. [Abstr. in DA (49) 2864A.] (*O'Flaherty, V. C., The Shewing-Up of Blanco Posnet, Augustus Does His Bit, The Six of Calais, The Man of Destiny, Overruled.*)

**11103.** HENDERSON, HEATHER DONIELSON. 'All life transfigured': structural and thematic disillusionment in Shaw's *Heartbreak House.* Unpub. doct. diss., Yale Univ., 1988. [Abstr. in DA (50) 1311A.]

**11104.** HILTON, JULIAN. The Galatea principle: learning machines. *See* **4058.**

**11105.** HOLROYD, MICHAEL. Bernard Shaw: vol.1, 1856–1898: The search for love. (Bibl. 1988, 8706.) Rev. by Bernard Crick in HT (39) Jan., 49; by John Updike in NY, 2 Jan., 62–5; by Gale K. Larson in TJ (41:3) 426–9; by Damon Galgut in Upstream (7:3) 68–70; by Christopher Murray in IUR (19:1) 165–7.

**11106.** —— Bernard Shaw: vol. 2, 1898–1918: The pursuit of power. London: Chatto & Windus; New York: Random House. pp. ix, 422. Rev. by Nicholas Rudall in BW, 10 Sept., 6; by Peter Kemp in Listener (122) 14 Sept., 24–5; by John Sutherland in TLS, 8 Sept., 965–6; by Frank Kermode in LRB (11:19) 14; by Michael Dirda in BkW, 24 Sept., 3, 7; by Margot Peters in NYTB, 17 Sept., 9.

**11107.** INNES, CHRISTOPHER. Granville Barker and Galsworthy: questions of censorship. *See* **9728.**

**11108.** JOYCE, STEVEN JAMES. Transformations and text: the rehearsal copies of George Bernard Shaw's *Buoyant Billions* in critical perspective. *See* **334.**

**11109.** KORITZ, AMY E. Gendering bodies, performing art: theatrical dancing and the performance aesthetics of Wilde, Shaw and Yeats. *See* **7677.**

**11110.** LAURENCE, DAN H. (ed.). Bernard Shaw: collected letters: vol. 4, 1926–1950. (Bibl. 1988, 8708.) Rev. by John Updike in NY, 2 Jan., 65–8.

**11111.** LEE, HAENG-SOO. George Bernard Shaw heuigok eui isang segae. (The ideal world in the drama of George Bernard Shaw.) Unpub. doct. diss., Chungnam National Univ., Daejeon (Korea). pp. 109.

**11112.** MORGAN, MARGERY (comp.). File on Shaw. London: Methuen. pp. 124. (Writer-files.)

**11113.** O'CASEY, EILEEN. Cheerio, Titan: the friendship between George Bernard Shaw and Eileen and Sean O'Casey. *See* **10721.**

**11114.** PARSONS, MELINDA BOYD. The 'unmechanicalness' of photography: Bernard Shaw's activist photographic philosophy. CLQ (25:2) 64–73.

**11115.** REDMOND, JAMES. 'If the salt have lost his savour': some 'useful' plays in and out of context on the London stage. *In* (pp. 63–88) **50.**

**11116.** REYNOLDS, JEAN. Immodest proposals: the performer in Shaw's prose. Unpub. doct. diss., Univ. of South Florida, 1988. [Abstr. in DA (49) 1811A.]

**11117.** SUMMERS, ELLEN. Shaw and Henderson: autobiographer versus biographer. SB (42) 284–93.

**11118.** VON ALBRECHT, MICHAEL. Fate or hate? A textual problem in Shaw's *Major Barbara. See* **404.**

**11119.** WHITAKER, THOMAS R. Playing in earnest. *In* (pp. 407–23) **45.**

**11120.** WISENTHAL, J. L. Shaw's sense of history. (Bibl. 1988, 8715.) Rev. by Nicholas Grene in NQ (36:2) 256–7.

### Irwin Shaw

**11121.** SALTER, JAMES. Winter of the lion. Esquire (112:1) 69–76.

**11122.** SHNAYERSON, MICHAEL. Irwin Shaw: a biography. New York: Putnam. pp. 447. Rev. by Richard Schickel in Time, 14 Aug., 68; by Jonathan Yardley in BkW, 6 Aug., 3.

### Sam Shepard

**11123.** CHO, EUN-YOUNG. *Operation Sidewinder*: apocalypse, hyeokmyoung geurigo pokryeok eui wonmugok. (*Operation Sidewinder*: a vicious circle of apocalypse, revolution and violence.) JELL (35) 286–312.

**11124.** DICKEY, JOHANNA SUSAN. Strategies of menace in the plays of John Whiting, Harold Pinter and Sam Shepard. *See* **10857.**

**11125.** DUGDALE, JOHN (comp.). File on Shepard. London: Methuen. pp. 69. (Writer-files.)

**11126.** GILMEN, R. Nevedomaîa zemlîa Sèma Sheparda. (The mysterious land of Sam Shepard.) Te (1989:9) 58–62.

**11127.** HALL, ANN CHRISTINE. 'A kind of Alaska': the representation of women in the plays of Eugene O'Neill, Harold Pinter, and Sam Shepard. *See* **10777.**

**11128.** MURRAY, FRANK J., JR. Speaking the unspeakable: theatrical language in the plays of Samuel Beckett and Sam Shepard. *See* **9068.**

**11129.** RAMSEY, ALLEN. The boundaries of illusion in *Fool for Love.* NCL (19:4) 9–11.

**11130.** SESSUMS, KEVIN. En hästdrömmares geografi: Sam Shepard samtalar med Kevin Sessums. (A horse-dreamer's geography: Sam Shepard talks to Kevin Sessums.) Artes (15:4) 93–106.

### R. C. Sherriff

**11131.** BRACCO, R. M. British middlebrow writers and the First World War, 1919–1939. *See* **8190.**

### George Shiels

**11132.** MACDONALD, J. W. The realism of George Shiels. Unpub. doct. diss., Univ. of Exeter. [Abstr. in IT (39:4) 1633–4.]

### Ann Allen Shockley

**11133.** BOGUS, SDIANE ADAMS. Theme and portraiture in the fiction of Ann Allen Shockley. Unpub. doct. diss., Miami Univ., 1988. [Abstr. in DA (49) 1800A.]

### Sandra Shotlander

**11134.** CURB, ROSEMARY. Mirrors moving beyond frames: Sandra Shotlander's *Framework* and *Blind Salome. In* (pp. 300–17) **39.**

### Jon Silkin

**11135.** DUŢESCU, DAN. Trei p̌oeţi englezi contemporani – Fleur Adcock, Alan Brownjohn, Jon Silkin. *See* **8911.**

### Leslie Marmon Silko

**11136.** DASENBROCK, REED WAY. Forms of biculturalism in Southwestern literature: the work of Rudolfo Anaya and Leslie Marmon Silko. *See* **8936.**

**11137.** EKRA, SOUMALEY MARIE-OLGA. Native American religion in the work of Leslie Marmon Silko. Unpub. doct. diss., Indiana Univ., 1988. [Abstr. in DA (50) 946–7A.]

**11138.** MANLEY, KATHLEEN. Leslie Marmon Silko's use of color in *Ceremony.* SF (46:2) 133–46.

**11139.** WRIGHT, ANNE (ed.). The delicacy and strength of lace: letters between Leslie Marmon Silko and James Wright. (Bibl. 1987, 12496.) Rev. by Renée Staton in OhioanaQ (32:4) 217–19.

### Alan Sillitoe
**11140.** PRICE, TIM. The politics of culture: *Saturday Night and Sunday Morning*. Unpub. doct. diss., Univ. of Nottingham, 1987. [Abstr. in DA (49) 643A.]

### Clifford D. Simak
**11141.** SLAVČEV, SVETOSLAV (introd.). Otnovo i otnovo. (Time and again.) Varna, Bulgaria: Bakalov, 1988. pp. 288.

### Paul Simon
**11142.** GARCÍA MARTOS, SOFÍA. La voz interior: una nueva definición de la canción protesta en la obra de Paul Simon. Atlantis (11:1/2) 79–87.

### 'Jo Sinclair' (Ruth Seid)
**11143.** MASLEKOFF, BARBARA. Jo Sinclair and Ohioana. OhioanaQ (32:2) 64.

### Upton Sinclair
**11144.** BARRETT, JAMES R. Work and community in the jungle: Chicago's packinghouse workers, 1894–1922. Urbana; Chicago: Illinois UP, 1987. pp. xvi, 290. (The working class in American history.) Rev. by Alun Munslow in JAStud (23:1) 102–3.

**11145.** BENDJEDDOU, MOHAMED YAZID. Two literary responses to American society in the early modern era: a comparison of selected novels by Theodore Dreiser and Upton Sinclair in relation to their portrayal of the immigrant, the city, the business tycoon, women, and the problem of labour, 1900–1929. *See* **9418.**

**11146.** DE GRUSON, GENE (ed.). The lost first edition of Upton Sinclair's *The Jungle*. *See* **301.**

**11147.** SIMON, LINDA. Socialism at home: the case of Upton Sinclair. NJH (107:1/2) 48–57.

### C. H. Sisson
**11148.** SISSON, C. H. On the look-out: a partial autobiography. Manchester: Carcanet Press. pp. 234. Rev. by Alan Ross in TLS, 6 Oct., 1091.

### The Sitwells
**11149.** RITCHIE, NEIL. Collecting Sitwelliana. *See* **261.**

### Sacheverell Sitwell
**11150.** RITCHIE, NEIL. Sacheverell Sitwell: an annotated and descriptive bibliography 1916–1986. Florence: Giardo Press. pp. 391. (Limited edition of 425 copies, signed by the author.) Rev. by Anthony Hobson in TLS, 21 Apr., 437.

### Robin Skelton
**11151.** SKELTON, ROBIN. The memoirs of a literary blockhead. Basingstoke; Toronto: Macmillan, 1988. pp. x, 326. Rev. by George Woodcock in CanL (122/23) 275–6: by Peter J. Clark in MalaR (83) 1988, 197.

### Elizabeth Smart
**11152.** VAN WART, ALICE (ed.). In the meantime. Ottawa: Deneau, 1984. pp. vii, 159. Rev. by Lola Lemire Tostevin in CanL (122/23) 169–70.

**11153.** —— Necessary secrets: the journals of Elizabeth Smart. Ottawa: Deneau, 1986. pp. x, 305. Rev. by Patricia Morley in CanL (116) 1988, 225–7.

### A. J. M. Smith

**11154.** COMPTON, HAZEL ANNE. A. J. M. Smith: Canadian metaphysical. Unpub. doct. diss., Univ. of New Brunswick, 1988. [Abstr. in DA (49) 2663–4A.]

### Clark Ashton Smith

**11155.** BEHRENDS, STEVE; SIDNEY-FRYER, DONALD; HOFFMAN, RAH (eds). Strange shadows: the uncollected fiction and essays of Clark Ashton Smith. Introd. by ROBERT BLOCH. New York; London: Greenwood Press. pp. xiv, 281. (Contributions to the study of science fiction and fantasy, 36.)

### Iain Crichton Smith

**11156.** GOW, C. A. Iain Crichton Smith: a poetry of opposition. Unpub. doct. diss., Univ. of Dundee. [Abstr. in IT (39:2) 488–9.]

**11157.** GOW, CAROL. Bourgeois land: another country. Cencrastus (35) 3–5.

### Lee Smith

**11158.** HILL, DOROTHY COMBS. The female imagination in an age of transition: the fiction of Lee Smith. Unpub. doct. diss., Univ. of North Carolina at Chapel Hill, 1988. [Abstr. in DA (49) 3724A.]

### Stevie Smith

**11159.** BARBERA, JACK; MCBRIEN, WILLIAM. Stevie: a biography of Stevie Smith. (Bibl. 1987, 12507.) Rev. by Paul Breslin in MP (87:2) 209–12.

### Sydney Goodsir Smith

**11160.** NAIRN, THOM. A route maist devious: Sydney Goodsir Smith and Edinburgh. Cencrastus (33) 6–9.

### Vivian Smith

**11161.** GAFFNEY, CARMEL. The poetry of Vivian Smith. Quadrant (34:7) 61–5.

### Kendrick Smithyman

**11162.** CARTWRIGHT, GARTH. Interview: poet Kendrick Smithyman. Metro (Auckland), Sept., 134–9.

### C. P. Snow

**11163.** GRYTA, CAROLINE NOBILE. Selected letters of C. P. Snow: a critical edition. Unpub. doct. diss., Pennsylvania State Univ., 1988. [Abstr. in DA (49) 2667A.]

### Gary Snyder

**11164.** JOHNSTON, ALLAN JAMES. Reinventing the metaphors: toward an ecological aesthetics in the writings of Robinson Jeffers, Kenneth Rexroth, and Gary Snyder. *See* **10009.**

**11165.** NORDSTRÖM, LARS. Theodore Roethke, William Stafford, and Gary Snyder: the ecological metaphor as transformed regionalism. *See* **11026.**

### 'Somerville and Ross' (Edith Somerville and Violet Martin)

**11166.** BEARDS, VIRGINIA (ed.). The real Charlotte. New Brunswick, NJ: Rutgers UP, 1986. pp. xxii, 298. Rev. by George O'Brien in MLR (84:2) 457.

**11167.** COWART, CLAIRE DENELLE. Webs of heredity: a study of the Anglo-Irish in the novels and stories of Somerville and Ross. Unpub. doct. diss., State Univ. of New York at Stony Brook, 1988. [Abstr. in DA (50) 1662A.]

**11168.** KELLEGHER, J. M. A view from the Big House at sunset: the fictional Ireland of E. Somerville and Martin Ross. Unpub. doct. diss., Univ. of Bradford, 1982. [Abstr. in IT (38:4) 1459.]

**11169.** KELLY, JOAN TANTUM. Four Irish writers: 1800–1932: nationalism and gender in a changing Ireland. *See* **6750.**

**11170.** LEWIS, GIFFORD (ed.). The selected letters of Somerville and Ross. Introd. by MOLLY KEANE. London: Faber & Faber. pp. xxxiii, 308. Rev. by Roy Foster in TLS, 27 Oct., 1191; by Maeve Binchy in Listener (122) 3 Aug., 27.

### Susan Sontag

**11171.** BRANHAM, ROBERT J. Speaking itself: Susan Sontag's Town Hall address. Q JS (75:3) 259–76.

**11172.** JONSSON, STEFAN. Man måste försvara allvaret: ett samtal med Susan Sontag. (Seriousness has to be defended: a conversation with Susan Sontag.) BLM (58:2) 84–93.

### Charles Hamilton Sorley

**11173.** ACTON, CAROL GILLIAN. Paradox in parenthesis: a comparative study of the war poetry of Wilfred Owen, Charles Sorley, Isaac Rosenberg, Ivor Gurney, and David Jones. *See* **9821.**

### Gilbert Sorrentino

**11174.** BERMAN, JAYE ELLYN. Parody as cultural criticism in the postmodern American novel: Donald Barthelme, Gilbert Sorrentino, and Thomas Pynchon. *See* **9019.**

### Raymond Souster

**11175.** REED, SABRINA LEE. The place of American poets in the development of Irving Layton, Louis Dudek and Raymond Souster. *See* **8545.**

### Wole Soyinka

**11176.** AMUTA, CHIDI. From myth to ideology: the socio-political content of Soyinka's war writings. JCL (23:1) 1988, 116–29.

**11177.** AYLING, RONALD. The 'politics' of childhood auto-biographies: O'Casey and Soyinka. *See* **10718.**

**11178.** COUSSY, DENISE. Le roman nigérian anglophone. *See* **8218.**

**11179.** GILBERTOVÁ, IVA. Wole Soyinka – dvě rané hry. (Wole Soyinka: two early plays.) *In* (pp. 18–19) **6.**

**11180.** KLÍMA, VLADIMÍR. The African Nobel Prize winner. PP (32:3) 117–26.

**11181.** MADUKA, CHIDI T. African religious beliefs in literary imagination: *ogbanje* and *abiku* in Chinua Achebe, J. P. Clark and Wole Soyinka. *See* **8900.**

### Muriel Spark

**11182.** CALDER, ANGUS. Miss Jean Brodie and the Kaledonian Klan. Cencrastus (33) 20–1.

**11183.** DEVOIZE, JEANNE; VALETTE, PAMELA. An interview with Muriel Spark. JSSE (13) 11–22.

**11184.** RAMADOSS, HARIPRIYA. Beyond surface reality: the aesthetic theme in Muriel Spark's fiction. Unpub. doct. diss., Purdue Univ., 1988. [Abstr. in DA (50) 693A.]

**11185.** STAPE, J. H. James Hanley, William Golding, Muriel Spark: additional primary works. *See* **9766.**

**11186.** TUCKER, MARTIN. All quiet on the English front: silence as escapism. *See* **10629.**

### Jean Stafford

**11187.** ROBERTS, DAVID. Jean Stafford: a biography. (Bibl. 1988, 8800.) Rev. by Joseph J. Firebaugh in AL (61:2) 312–13; by Adam Begley in LRB (11:1) 23.

**11188.** RYAN, MAUREEN. Innocence and estrangement in the fiction of Jean Stafford. (Bibl. 1988, 8801.) Rev. by William Leary in SewR (96:3) 1988, lv–lvii.

### William Stafford

**11189.** ANDREWS, TOM. Glimpses into something ever larger. Field (41) 38–40.

**11190.** ATWOOD, MARGARET. *Waking at 3 a.m.* Field (41) 29–33.

**11191.** HOLDEN, JONATHAN. *With Kit, Age 7, at the Beach.* Field (41) 25–8.

**11192.** NORDSTRÖM, LARS. Theodore Roethke, William Stafford, and Gary Snyder: the ecological metaphor as transformed regionalism. *See* **11026.**

**11193.** PASTAN, LINDA. *Ask Me.* Field (41) 34–6.

**11194.** SIMIC, CHARLES. *At the Bomb Testing Site.* Field (41) 8–10.

**11195.** TAYLOR, HENRY. Millions of intricate moves. Field (41) 12–24.

**11196.** TURNER, ALBERTA. *Things I Learned Last Week.* Field (41) 41–3.

**11197.** YOUNG, DAVID. Shivers of summer wind. Field (41) 45–52.

### Frank Stanford

**11198.** LAUNIUS, CARL JUDSON. It was a flood: the life and poetry of Frank Stanford. Unpub. doct. diss., Univ. of California, Davis, 1988. [Abstr. in DA (50) 685A.]

### Barrie Stavis

**11199.** STŘÍBRNÝ, ZDENĚK. Americký dramatik Barrie Stavis. (The American dramatist Barrie Stavis.) Světové divadlo (Prague) (15) 194–200.

### C. K. Stead

**11200.** STEAD, C. K. Stendhal's mirror and Yeats's looking-glass: a reconsideration of *The Tower. In* (pp. 193–211) **46.**

### Christina Stead

**11201.** JONES, NANCY LEE. Reality and the shadow: the adventure of identity in twentieth-century Australian women's fiction. *See* **9685.**

**11202.** ROSS, ROBERT. Christina Stead's encounter with 'the true reader': the origin and outgrowth of Randall Jarrell's introduction to *The Man Who Loved Children. See* **10002.**

**11203.** Seet, K. K.    The shackled soul: the theme of entrapment in the fiction of Christina Stead. Unpub. doct. diss., Univ. of Exeter. [Abstr. in IT (39:3) 1116.]

**11204.** Segerberg, Anita.    A fiction of sisters: Christina Stead's *Letty Fox* and *For Love Alone*. ALS (14:1) 15–25.

### Wallace Stegner

**11205.** Swingrover, Elizabeth Anne.    'The way things are': the later novels of Wallace Stegner. Unpub. doct. diss., Univ. of Nevada, Reno, 1988. [Abstr. in DA (50) 445A.]

### Gertrude Stein

**11206.** Berry, Ellen E.    On reading Gertrude Stein. Genders (5) 1–20.

**11207.** Duberman, Martin; Vicinus, Martha; Chauncey, George, Jr (eds).    Hidden from history: reclaiming the gay and lesbian past. *See* **7826.**

**11208.** Hutchison, Beth.    Gertrude Stein's film scenarios. *See* **8065.**

**11209.** Winston, Elizabeth.    Making history in *The Mother of Us All*. Mosaic (20:4) 1987, 117–29.

### John Steinbeck

**11210.** Benson, Jackson J.    Looking for Steinbeck's ghost. Norman; London: Oklahoma UP, 1988. pp. viii, 231. Rev. by Nancy E. Zane in AL (61:4) 707–8.

**11211.** —— Steinbeck – a defense of biographical criticism. CLit (16:2) 109–16.

**11212.** Davison, Richard Allan.    *Of Mice and Men* and *McTeague*: Steinbeck, Fitzgerald, and Frank Norris. *See* **9636.**

**11213.** E Jeon, Jo-Young.    John Steinbeck eui *In Dubious Battle* gwa John Milton eui Paradise Lost eui sinwha wa yeongwanhayeo. *See* **4683.**

**11214.** Fensch, Thomas (ed.).    Conversations with John Steinbeck. Jackson; London: Mississippi UP, 1988. pp. xxi, 116. (Literary conversations.)

**11215.** Mulcahy, Judith M.    John Steinbeck's non-fiction. Unpub. doct. diss., Univ. of Delaware, 1988. [Abstr. in DA (49) 2221A.]

**11216.** Nakayama, Kiyoichi.    Steinbeck no bungaku kenkyu: California jidai. (A study of Steinbeck's California period.) Osaka: Kansai UP. pp. viii, 414, xxx.

**11217.** Sanderson, Jim.    American romanticism in John Ford's *The Grapes of Wrath*: horizontalness, darkness, Christ, and F.D.R. *See* **8127.**

**11218.** Timmerman, John H.    The squatter's circle in *The Grapes of Wrath*. SAF (17:2) 203–11.

### A. M. Stephen

**11219.** Kizuk, A. R.    The vernacular in early twentieth-century Canadian poetry: Arthur Stringer and A. M. Stephen. DalR (66:4) 1986, 483–96.

### Wallace Stevens

**11220.** Arbuthnot, Nancy Prothro.    Wallace Stevens and I in Montana. SDR (27:2) 36–42.

**11221.** BATES, MILTON J. *Sur plusieurs beaux sujets*: Wallace Stevens' commonplace book: a facsimile and transcription. Stanford, CA: Stanford UP; San Marino, CA: Huntington Library. pp. 117.

**11222.** —— Wallace Stevens: a mythology of self. (Bibl. 1987, 12595.) Rev. by James Applewhite in SewR (96:1) 1988, 123–5.

**11223.** BEVIS, WILLIAM W. Mind of winter: Wallace Stevens, meditation and literature. Pittsburgh, PA: Pittsburgh UP, 1988. pp. xi, 343. (Critical essays in modern literature.)

**11224.** BRAZEAU, PETER. Parts of a world: Wallace Stevens remembered, an oral biography. (Bibl. 1985, 13105.) Rev. by Eugene Paul Nassar in ModAge (32:2) 1988, 166–9.

**11225.** BROGAN, JACQUELINE VAUGHT. Stevens and simile: a theory of language. (Bibl. 1988, 8828.) Rev. by Margaret Dickie in YES (19) 365–6; by Peter McDonald in RES (39:155) 1988, 461–3.

**11226.** —— Stevens in history and not in history: the poet and the Second World War. WSJ (13:2) 168–90.

**11227.** BURNSHAW, STANLEY. Reflections on Wallace Stevens. WSJ (13:2) 122–6.

**11228.** CARROLL, JOSEPH. Wallace Stevens' supreme fiction: a new romanticism. (Bibl. 1988, 8831.) Rev. by Julian D. Gill in JAStud (23:1) 166–7.

**11229.** COOK, ELEANOR. Poetry, word-play and word-war in Wallace Stevens. (Bibl. 1988, 8832.) Rev. by Glen MacLeod in AL (61:3) 490–1.

**11230.** COZENS, I. J. 'Forging' as 'fake/make' in Wallace Stevens' *The Doctor of Geneva*. Unpub. doct. diss., Univ. of Keele, 1988. [Abstr. in IT (38:4) 1464.]

**11231.** DICICCO, LORRAINE CHRISTINE. Wallace Stevens and the long poem: constructing a new stage. Unpub. doct. diss., Univ. of Western Ontario. [Abstr. in DA (50) 1304A.]

**11232.** DOGGETT, FRANK; EMERSON, DOROTHY. A primer of possibility for *The Auroras of Autumn*. WSJ (13:1) 53–66.

**11233.** DONOGHUE, DENIS. Notes on a late poem by Stevens. *In* (pp. 167–74) **45.** (*Of Mere Being*.)

**11234.** DOUGHERTY, JAY. *Sunday Morning* and *Sunday Morning*. ELN (27:1) 61–8.

**11235.** FORD, BRIAN WILLIAMS. The incipient cosmos: the problem of religion in the poetry of Wallace Stevens. Unpub. doct. diss., Tufts Univ., 1988. [Abstr. in DA (49) 2658A.]

**11236.** FRIEND, ROBERT. Poverty and plenitude: the struggle for belief in the poetry of Wallace Stevens. Neophilologus (73:4) 620–32.

**11237.** GELPI, ALBERT (ed.). Wallace Stevens: the poetics of Modernism. (Bibl. 1987, 12611.) Rev. by Reginald Berry in CanL (118) 1988, 148; by Peter McDonald in RES (38:151) 1987, 406–8.

**11238.** KANG, DU-HYOUNG. Stasis versus continuity: Mallarmé and Wallace Stevens. WSJ (13:1) 38–52.

**11239.** KWAN-TERRY, JOHN. Of pines, beards and several Chinamen: one way of looking at Wallace Stevens. *In* (pp. 54–72) **19.**

**11240.**  LEE, CHONG-HO.   Tal jungsimwha doen segae eseoeui 'iss-eum' eui sihak: Wallace Stevens si eui kyungwoo. (Wallace Stevens' poetics of being in the de-centered world.) EngSt (13) 72–92.

**11241.**  LENSING, GEORGE S.   Wallace Stevens: a poet's growth. (Bibl. 1988, 8839.) Rev. by Peter McDonald in RES (39:155) 1988, 461–3.

**11242.**  LEONARD, J. S.; WHARTON, C. E.   The fluent mundo: Wallace Stevens and the structure of reality. (Bibl. 1988, 8841.) Rev. by Jacqueline Vaught Brogan in AL (61:2) 317–19.

**11243.**  LONGENBACH, JAMES.   The 'fellowship of men that perish': Wallace Stevens and the First World War. WSJ (13:2) 85–108.

**11244.**  MALIK, FARIDA.   Imagination and reality in Wallace Stevens's poetry. Explorations (12:1/2) 1988/89, 77–85.

**11245.**  MONROE, MELISSA.   The expressive function of nominal structure in Marianne Moore and Wallace Stevens. See **10610.**

**11246.**  MONROE, ROBERT EMMETT.   Figuration and society in *Owl's Cover*. WSJ (13:2) 127–49.

**11247.**  PATKE, RAJEEV S.   The long poems of Wallace Stevens: an interpretative study. (Bibl. 1987, 12629, where title incorrect.) Rev. by Robert Belflower in RES (38:149) 1987, 102–3.

**11248.**  PRASAD, VEENA RANI.   Wallace Stevens: the symbolic dimensions of his poetry. Liverpool: Lucas; New Delhi: Arnold-Heinemann, 1987. pp. xiii, 208.

**11249.**  QUINN, BERNETTA.   Wallace Stevens: 'the peace of the last intelligence'. Ren (41:4) 191–204.

**11250.**  QUIRK, TOM.   Realism, the 'real', and the poet of reality: some reflections on American Realists and the poetry of Wallace Stevens. ALR (21:2) 34–53.

**11251.**  RAWSON, CLAUDE.   Bards, boardrooms, and blackboards: John Ashbery, Wallace Stevens, and the academicization of poetry. *In* (pp. 181–91) **46.**

**11252.**  REHDER, ROBERT.   *Description Without Place*: the language of poetry and the language of philosophy. YREAL (6) 39–66.

**11253.**  RICHARDSON, JOAN.   Wallace Stevens: the early years, 1879–1923. (Bibl. 1988, 8849.) Rev. by James Applewhite in SewR (96:1) 1988, 121–3.

**11254.**  —— Wallace Stevens: the later years, 1923–1955. New York: Morrow, 1988. pp. 462. Rev. by Jacqueline Vaught Brogan in AL (61:3) 491–2; by Milton J. Bates in NYTB, 5 Feb., 27; by Joseph Parisi in BW, 6 Nov. 1988, 6.

**11255.**  SCHAUM, MELITA.   Lyric resistance: views of the political in the poetics of Wallace Stevens and H.D. See **9407.**

**11256.**  SHERBURN-ZIMMER, PETER NEILS.   Poetry: open to interpretation. A postmodern *essai* of Wallace Stevens. Unpub. doct. diss., State Univ. of New York at Binghamton, 1988. [Abstr. in DA (49) 2221–2A.]

**11257.**  STANLEY-SMITH, J. R.   Language, vision and reality: a study of the poetry of Edward Thomas, Robert Frost and Wallace Stevens. See **9707.**

**11258.** STEGMAN, MICHAEL O. Variations on a theme in *Peter Quince at the Clavier*. WSJ (13:1) 3–14.

**11259.** TERES, HARVEY. Notes toward the supreme Soviet: Stevens and doctrinaire Marxism. WSJ (13:2) 150–67.

**11260.** WALKER, DAVID. The transparent lyric: reading and meaning in the poetry of Stevens and Williams. (Bibl. 1987, 12637.) Rev. by James Applewhite in SewR (96:1) 1988, 126–7.

**11261.** WEINFIELD, HENRY. Wallace Stevens' *Esthétique du mal* and the evils of aestheticism. WSJ (13:1) 27–39.

### Robert Stone

**11262.** FURNISS, DAVID WEST. Making sense of the war: Vietnam and American prose. *See* **9923.**

### Phil Stong

**11263.** McCOWN, ROBERT A. Phil Stong's *State Fair*. BkIA (50) 35–9.

### Tom Stoppard

**11264.** BILLINGTON, MICHAEL. Stoppard: the playwright. (Bibl. 1987, 12643. Rev. by J. Janisch in UES (27:2) 41–2.

**11265.** CASEY, ROGER N. Stoppard's clean well-lighted place. NCL (19:5) 3–4.

**11266.** KELLY, KATHERINE E. Tom Stoppard radioactive: a sounding of the radio plays. ModDr (32:3) 440–52.

**11267.** PATSALIDES, SAVVAS. The players vis-à-vis the play's design: *Rosencrantz and Guildenstern Are Dead*. Aristotle Univ. of Thessaloniki Yearbook of English Studies (1) 403–20.

**11268.** SAMMELLS, NEIL. Tom Stoppard: the artist as critic. New York: St Martin's Press, 1988. (Bibl. 1988, 8858.) Rev. by Johanna S. Dickey in TJ (41:2) 266–7.

**11269.** TAN, P. K. W. A stylistics of drama, with particular reference to Stoppard's *Travesties* and parody. *See* **1425.**

**11270.** WARD, DANA DERRICK. Dramas of defamiliarization and distantiation: a comparative study of the selected works of Eugene Ionesco, Tom Stoppard, and Antonio Buero Vallejo. Unpub. doct. diss., Univ. of Arkansas, 1987. [Abstr. in DA (49) 1795A.] (*Jumpers, Every Good Boy Deserves Favour.*)

**11271.** WHITAKER, THOMAS R. Playing in earnest. *In* (pp. 407–23) **45.**

**11272.** YUN, MIDUCK. Stoppard eui *Rosencrantz and Guildenstern Are Dead* eseo play world eui euimi wa the player eui yeokwhal. (The significance of the play world and the role of the player in Stoppard's *Rosencrantz and Guildenstern Are Dead*.) JELL (35) 259–85.

### Randolph Stow

**11273.** WILLBANKS, RAY. Keys to *The Suburbs of Hell*: a study of Randolph Stow's novel. JCL (22:1) 1987, 47–54.

### Lytton Strachey

**11274.** FERNS, JOHN. Lytton Strachey. Boston, MA: G. K. Hall, 1988. pp. x, 133. (Twayne's English authors, 462.) Rev. by Gabriel Merle in EA (42:3) 304–7.

**11275.** ROSENBAUM, S. P. Lytton Strachey and the prose of Empire. *In* (pp. 122–33) **45.**

## T. S. Stribling

**11276.** PIACENTINO, EDWARD J.    T. S. Stribling: pioneer realist in modern Southern literature. Lanham, MD; London: UP of America, 1988. pp. xvi, 174. Rev. by Fred Hobson in AL (61:1) 121–2.

## Arthur Stringer

**11277.** KIZUK, A. R.    The vernacular in early twentieth-century Canadian poetry: Arthur Stringer and A. M. Stephen. *See* **11219.**

## 'Patience Strong' (Winifred May)

**11278.** JOHNSON, TONI O'BRIEN.    An ante-text for Samuel Beckett's *Happy Days. See* **9057.**

## Jan Struther

**11279.** GROVE, VALERIE (introd.).    Mrs Miniver. London: Virago Press. pp. xxi, 145. (Virago modern classics, 329.)

## William Styron

**11280.** COLOGNE-BROOKES, B.    From harmony to history: the shifting patterns of discourse in the novels of William Styron. Unpub. doct. diss., Univ. of Nottingham. [Abstr. in IT (39:3) 1117.]

**11281.** SIRLIN, RHODA A.    William Styron's *Sophie's Choice*: a wisdom that is woe, a woe that is madness. Unpub. doct. diss., City Univ. of New York, 1988. [Abstr. in DA (50) 1306–7A.]

## Ronald Sukenick

**11282.** KUTNIK, JERZY.    The novel as performance: the fiction of Ronald Sukenick and Raymond Federman. *See* **9622.**

## Montague Summers

**11283.** FRANK, FREDERICK S.    Montague Summers: a bibliographical portrait. *See* **64.**

## May Swenson

**11284.** BRIDGFORD, KIM SUZANNE.    Discoveries of the not-known: Louise Bogan, Muriel Rukeyser, Sylvia Plath, May Swenson, and Adrienne Rich. *See* **9114.**

## Graham Swift

**11285.** SÖDERQVIST, JAN.    Att acceptera tillvarons gåtfullhet: Jan Söderqvist intervjuar Graham Swift. (To accept the mystery of existence: Jan Söderqvist talks to Graham Swift.) Allt om böcker (1989:4) 32–6.

## Julian Symons

**11286.** ÁLVAREZ-BUYLIA BUSTILLO, VIRGINIA.    Entrevista a Julian Symons. Atlantis (11:1/2) 157–66.

## J. M. Synge

**11287.** CHAUDHURI, UNA.    The dramaturgy of the other: diegetic patterns in Synge's *The Playboy of the Western World*. ModDr (32:3) 374–86.

**11288.** FLEISCHMANN, RUTH.    Fathers vanquished and victorious: a historical reading of Synge's *Playboy. In* (pp. 63–74) **17.**

**11289.** HULL, KEITH N.    Natural supernaturalism in *Riders to the Sea*. CLQ (25:4) 245–52.

**11290.** TAWFEEK, S. B.; AZIZ, SHATHA A.    Variations on old themes in J. M. Synge's *The Playboy of the Western World*. Journal of Education and Science (Univ. of Mosul, Iraq) (7) (Humanities and education) 25–40.

**Netta Syrett**

**11291.** MILLS, DAVID. Netta Syrett and *The Old Miracle Plays of England. See* **2567.**

**Thurairajah Tambimuttu**

**11292.** WILLIAMS, JANE (ed.). Tambimuttu: bridge between two worlds. *See* **600.**

**Allen Tate**

**11293.** ARBEIT, MARCEL. Allen Tate – prozaik. (Allen Tate the prose writer.) *In* (pp. 16) **6.**

**11294.** BANDY, W. T. Allen Tate's juvenilia. SoR (25:1) 86–94.

**11295.** WEAKS, MARY LOUISE. A 'little postage stamp of native soil' in the upper South: the poetry and fiction of Caroline Gordon, Allen Tate, and Robert Penn Warren. *See* **9779.**

**Peter Taylor**

**11296.** KUEHL, LINDA KANDEL. Voices and victims: a study of Peter Taylor's *In the Miro District and Other Stories.* Unpub. doct. diss., Lehigh Univ., 1988. [Abstr. in DA (49) 1799A.]

**Megan Terry**

**11297.** BRESLAUER, JAN; KEYSSAR, HELENE. Making magic public: Megan Terry's traveling family circus. *In* (pp. 169–80) **39.**

**11298.** LARSON, JAMES WALLACE. Public dreams: a critical investigation of the plays of Megan Terry, 1955–1986. Unpub. doct. diss., Univ. of Kansas, 1988. [Abstr. in DA (49) 3207A.]

**Can Themba**

**11299.** CHAPMAN, MICHAEL. Can Themba, storyteller and journalist of the 1950s: the text in context. EngA (16:2) 19–29.

**Stefan Themerson**

**11300.** BOELENS, TYSGER. The bad manners of nonsense: an inquiry into the nonsensical orthodoxy of Stefan Themerson's *The Adventures of Peddy Bottom. In* (pp. 229–44) **28.**

**11301.** STACHNIAK, EWA MARIA. The positive philosophy of exile in contemporary literature: Stefan Themerson and his fiction. Unpub. doct. diss., McGill Univ., 1988. [Abstr. in DA (50) 137A.]

**11302.** THEMERSON, STEFAN. On nonsense and on logic-fiction. *In* (pp. 3–16) **28.**

**Alexander Theroux**

**11303.** KOHL, STEPHAN. The Renaissance lover, the medieval sinner, and timelessness: Alexander Theroux's *Darconville's Cat. In* (pp. 295–304) **38.**

**Paul Theroux**

**11304.** BERTENS, HANS. The convention of the new beginning in Theroux's *The Mosquito Coast. In* (pp. 389–403) **16.**

**11305.** GLASER, ELTON. The self-reflexive traveler: Paul Theroux on the art of travel and travel writing. CR (33:3) 193–206.

**Sharon Thesen**

**11306.** THESEN, SHARON. Poetry and the dilemma of expression. *In* (pp. 380–4) **40.**

## D. M. Thomas

**11307.** DUPERRAY, MAX.    Enchaînements et déchaînements: la violence et la répétition dans *The White Hotel* (1981) de D. M. Thomas. *In* (pp. 159–74) **60.**

**11308.** ELLERY, CHRIS.    Oracle and womb: delphic myth in D. M. Thomas's *The White Hotel*. NCL (19:4) 3–4.

**11309.** TODD, RICHARD.    Convention and innovation in British fiction 1981–1984: the contemporaneity of magic realism. *In* (pp. 361–88) **16.**

## Dylan Thomas

**11310.** DAVIES, WALFORD; MAUD, RALPH (eds).    Collected poems, 1934–53. (Bibl. 1988, 8889.) Rev. by John Ackerman in PW (24:4) 66–7.

**11311.** DAVIS, WILLIAM V.    Influence without anxiety: Dylan Thomas and W. S. Merwin. *See* **10558.**

**11312.** FERRIS, PAUL (ed.).    The collected letters of Dylan Thomas. (Bibl. 1987, 12708.) Rev. by Nicolas Jacobs in RES (38:151) 1987, 416–17.

**11313.** GREENWAY, WILLIAM.    Dylan Thomas and 'the flesh's vision'. CLit (16:3) 274–80.

**11314.** LE BON, PIERRE.    Approche thématique, symbolique et rythmique du poème *After the Funeral* de Dylan Thomas. Repérages (12) 26–35.

**11315.** MAUD, RALPH (ed.).    The notebook poems 1930–34. London: Dent, 1988. pp. xvi, 288.

**11316.** SCHOPF, ALFRED.    *Especially When the October Wind* von Dylan Thomas. Ein poetologisches Gedicht? LJGG (28) 1987, 99–113.

**11317.** VOLSIK, PAUL.    Neo-Romanticism and the poetry of Dylan Thomas. EA (42:1) 39–54.

## Edward Thomas

**11318.** BÄCKMAN, SVEN.    Diktarmöte i krigets skugga. *See* **9693.**

**11319.** KIRKHAM, MICHAEL.    The imagination of Edward Thomas. (Bibl. 1988, 8896.) Rev. by Peter McDonald in RES (39:154) 1988, 316–17; by Murray G. H. Pittock in YES (19) 347–8; by Adolphe Haberer in EA (42:2) 228.

**11320.** SMITH, STAN.    Edward Thomas. (Bibl. 1988, 8898.) Rev. by Murray G. H. Pittock in YES (19) 347.

**11321.** STANLEY-SMITH, J. R.    Language, vision and reality: a study of the poetry of Edward Thomas, Robert Frost and Wallace Stevens. *See* **9707.**

**11322.** THOMAS, R. GEORGE.    Edward Thomas: a portrait. (Bibl. 1988, 8899.) Rev. by Peter McDonald in RES (38:149) 1987, 101–2; by Murray G. H. Pittock in YES (19) 348.

## 'Maria Thomas' (Roberta Worrick)

**11323.** WEST, PAUL.    Maria Thomas, 1941–1989. BkW, 10 Dec., 18–19.

## R. S. Thomas

**11324.** THOMAS, R. S.    Neb. (No one.)    Caernarvon: Gwasg Gwynedd, 1985. pp. 131. (Autobiography: in Welsh.) Rev. by Idris Jones in AWR (86) 1987, 134–6.

## Judith Thompson

**11325.** TOLES, GEORGE. 'Cause you're the only one I want': the anatomy of love in the plays of Judith Thompson. CanL (118) 1988, 116–35.

## David Thomson

**11326.** DELANEY, JAMES G. David Thomson. *See* **1694.**

## James Thurber

**11327.** LONG, ROBERT EMMET. James Thurber. New York: Ungar, 1988. pp. xv, 236. (Literature and life.) Rev. by Michael J. Rosen in OhioanaQ (32:2) 84–5.

**11328.** ROSEN, MICHAEL J. (ed.). Collecting himself: James Thurber on writing and writers, humor and himself. New York: Harper & Row; London: Hamilton. pp. xx, 263. Rev. by Edward Sorel in NYTB, 5 Nov., 36.

## Alice B. Toklas

**11329.** DUBERMAN, MARTIN; VICINUS, MARTHA; CHAUNCEY, GEORGE, JR (eds). Hidden from history: reclaiming the gay and lesbian past. *See* **7826.**

**11330.** FRIEDRICH, OTTO. The grave of Alice B. Toklas and other reports from the past. New York: Holt. pp. 384. Rev. by Judith Chettle in BkW, 13 Aug., 6.

## J. R. R. Tolkien

**11331.** ABBOTT, JOE. Tolkien's monsters: concept and function in *The Lord of the Rings*: 1, The Balrog of Khazad-dum. Mythlore (16:1) 19–26, 33.

**11332.** ANDERSON, DOUGLAS A. (ed.). The annotated *Hobbit*. London: Unwin Hyman. pp. x, 335.

**11333.** APENKO, E. M. *Sil'marillion* Dzhona Tolkina: k voprosu ob odnom zhranrovom èksperimente. (J. R. R. Tolkien's *Silmarillion*: an experiment in genre.) VLU (1989:1) 41–6. (English summary.)

**11334.** BEACH, SARAH. 'A myth for Angle-land': J. R. R. Tolkien and creative mythology. Mythlore (15:4) 31–6.

**11335.** BENTINCK, A. Tolkien and de la Mare: the fantastic secondary worlds of *The Hobbit* and *The Three Mulla-Mulgars*. *See* **9372.**

**11336.** BROGAN, HUGH. Tolkien's Great War. *In* (pp. 351–67) **14.**

**11337.** BURNS, MARJORIE J. J. R. R. Tolkien and the journey north. Mythlore (15:4) 5–9.

**11338.** CHRISTENSEN, BONNIEJEAN. Tolkien's creative technique: *Beowulf* and *The Hobbit*. *See* **2339.**

**11339.** CZEŻYK, MARIOLA. Extratextual perspectives of two trilogies. *In* (pp. 75–89) **57.**

**11340.** HYDE, PAUL NOLAN. Mythos: the daughter of mountains, the mother of pearls. Mythlore (16:1) 27–33.

**11341.** O'BRIEN, DONALD. On the origin of the name 'Hobbit'. *See* **1186.**

**11342.** RIDDEN, GEOFFREY. J. R. R. Tolkien: *The Lord of the Rings*: notes. Beirut: York Press; Harlow: Longman, 1984. pp. 80. (York notes, 230.) Rev. by Hanna Stenström in Arda (4) 1984, 124–5.

**11343.** Shorto, Russell.   J. R. R. Tolkien: man of fantasy. New York: Kipling Press, 1988. pp. 48.

**11344.** Startzman, L. Eugene.   Goldberry and Galadriel: the quality of joy. Mythlore (16:2) 5–13.

**11345.** Stratyner, Leslie.   'Ðe us ðas beagas geaf' ('He who gave us these rings'): Sauron and the perversion of Anglo-Saxon ethos. Mythlore (16:1) 5–8.

**11346.** Syme, Margaret Ruth.   Tolkien as gospel writer. Unpub. doct. diss., McGill Univ. [Abstr. in DA (50) 973A.]

**11347.** Tolkien, Christopher (ed.).   The return of the shadow: the history of *The Lord of the Rings*, part 1. Boston, MA: Houghton Mifflin; London: Unwin, 1988. pp. xii, 497. (History of Middle-Earth, 6.) Rev. by Wayne G. Hammond in Mythlore (15:4) 49–50.

**11348.** —— The treason of Isengard: the history of *The Lord of the Rings*, part 2. Boston, MA: Houghton Mifflin; London: Unwin Hyman. pp. 504. (History of Middle-Earth, 7.)

**11349.** Treloar, John L.   The Middle-Earth epic and the seven capital vices. Mythlore (16:1) 37–41.

### Charles Tomlinson

**11350.** Bachem, Walter.   Self and other in Charles Tomlinson's poetry of perception. Aristotle Univ. of Thessaloniki Yearbook of English Studies (1) 255–73.

**11351.** Chevalier, Jean-Louis.   *The Door* et quelques autres portes: à propos d'un poème de Charles Tomlinson. *In* (pp. 119–28) **35.**

**11352.** Ponsford, Michael.   'To wish back Eden': the community theme in Charles Tomlinson's verse. MidQ (30:3) 346–60.

**11353.** Tomlinson, Charles.   Some presences on the scene: a vista of postwar poetry. *In* (pp. 215–32) **46.**

### Jean Toomer

**11354.** Kerman, Cynthia Earl; Eldridge, Richard.   The lives of Jean Toomer: a hunger for wholeness. London: Louisiana State UP, 1987. (Bibl. 1987, 12801.) Rev. by Edward Margolies in EngS (70:4) 375–6.

**11355.** Rice, H. William.   Two work songs in *Cane*. See **1755.**

**11356.** Turner, Darwin T. (ed.).   *Cane*: an authoritative text, backgrounds, criticism. New York; London: Norton, 1988. pp. ix, 246. (Norton critical editions.) Rev. by James Booth in NQ (36:4) 561–2.

### Philip Toynbee

**11357.** Bullimore, John (ed.).   The end of a journey: an autobiographical journal 1979–81. London: Bloomsbury, 1988. pp. ix, 422.

### John Tranter

**11358.** Lilley, Kate.   Tranter's plots. ALS (14:1) 41–50.

### 'B. Traven'

**11359.** Engell, John.   *The Treasure of the Sierra Madre*: B. Traven, John Huston and ideology in film adaptation. See **8028.**

### Violet Trefusis

**11360.** Leaska, Mitchell A.; Phillips, John (eds).   Violet to Vita: the letters of Violet Trefusis to Vita Sackville-West, 1910–21. See **11056.**

### 'Robert Tressell' (Robert Noonan)

**11361.**  ALFRED, DAVID (ed.).   The Robert Tressell lectures, 1981–88. Rochester: WEA, 1988. pp. xvi, 115.

### William Trevor

**11362.**  MacKenna, M. D.   William Trevor: the moral landscape. Unpub. doct. diss., National Univ. of Ireland, Dublin, 1987. [Abstr. in IT (39:4) 1634.]

### Lionel Trilling

**11363.**  HAGOPIAN, JOHN V.   A reader's moral dissent from Lionel Trilling's *Of This Time, Of That Place*. *In* (pp. 227–38) **2.**

**11364.**  KRUPNICK, MARK.   Lionel Trilling and the politics of style. *In* (pp. 152–70) **1.**

### John Tripp

**11365.**  JENKINS, NIGEL.   John Tripp. Cardiff: Wales UP. pp. 117. (Writers of Wales.)

### Amos Tutuola

**11366.**  BELVAUDE, CATHERINE E.   Amos Tutuola et l'univers du conte africain. Paris: L'Harmattan. pp. 204.

### Anne Tyler

**11367.**  FREIERT, WILLIAM K.   Anne Tyler's accidental Ulysses. CML (10:1) 71–9. (*The Accidental Tourist*.)

**11368.**  GAITENS, JUDI.   The web of connection: a study of family patterns in the fiction of Anne Tyler. Unpub. doct. diss., Kent State Univ., 1988. [Abstr. in DA (49) 3026A.]

**11369.**  LINTON, KARIN.   The temporal horizon: a study of the theme of time in Anne Tyler's major novels. Uppsala: Acta Universitatis Upsaliensis: Stockholm: Almqvist & Wiksell. pp. 145. (Studia anglistica upsaliensia, 68.) (Doct. diss., Uppsala Univ.)

**11370.**  NAULTY, PATRICIA MARY.   'I never talk of hunger': self-starvation as women's language of protest in novels by Barbara Pym, Margaret Atwood, and Anne Tyler. *See* **8964.**

### John Updike

**11371.**  LASSETER, VICTOR K.   *Rabbit Is Rich* as a naturalistic novel. AL (61:3) 429–45.

**11372.**  LEMEUNIER, BARBARA SMITH.   'The same thing as being dead': images of work and leisure in John Updike's three Rabbit novels. *In* (pp. 159–80) **25.**

**11373.**  NEWMAN, JUDIE.   John Updike. New York: St Martin's Press, 1988. (Bibl. 1988, 8941.) Rev. by W. R. MacNaughton in SAF (17:1) 124–5; by Robert M. Luscher in AL (61:2) 325–7; by Eugene Hollahan in StudN (20:1) 1988, 104–7.

**11374.**  PLATH, JAMES WALTER.   The painterly aspects of John Updike's fiction. Unpub. doct. diss., Univ. of Wisconsin–Milwaukee, 1988. [Abstr. in DA (49) 2221A.]

**11375.**  PORTER, M. GILBERT.   From Babbitt to Rabbit: the American materialist in search of a soul. *In* (pp. 185–96) **2.**

**11376.**  RISTOFF, DILVO I.   Updike's America: the presence of contemporary American history in John Updike's Rabbit novels. Unpub.

doct. diss., Univ. of Southern California, 1987. [Abstr. in DA (49) 1804A.]

**11377.** THOMAS, JIM.   A changing American family: Cheever, Gardner, Irving, Updike. *See* **9238.**

**11378.** UPDIKE, JOHN.   Self-consciousness: memoirs. New York: Knopf; London: Deutsch. pp. x, 245. Rev. by Paul Gray in Time, 13 Mar., 77; by Philip Oakes in Listener (121) 11 May, 26.

**11379.** WOOD, RALPH C.   The comedy of redemption: Christian faith in four American novelists. *See* **9380.**

### Thorstein Veblen

**11380.** ERWIN, ROBERT.   The man who discovered America. YR (78:1) 1988, 46–61.

### Joan D. Vinge

**11381.** BARR, MARLEEN S.; SALVAGGIO, RUTH; LAW, RICHARD.   Suzy McKee Charnas/Octavia Butler/Joan D. Vinge. *See* **9185.**

### Kurt Vonnegut, Jr

**11382.** GREER, CREED.   Kurt Vonnegut and the character of words. JNT (19:3) 312–30.

**11383.** MUSTAZZA, LEONARD.   The machine within: mechanization, human discontent, and the genre of Vonnegut's *Player Piano*. PLL (25:1) 99–113.

**11384.** NANDYAL, RAMAKRISHNA.   Thematic unity in the early Vonnegut fiction: *Player Piano* (1952) to *Slapstick* (1976). Unpub. doct. diss., Oklahoma State Univ., 1988. [Abstr. in DA (49) 3027A.]

**11385.** PEZE, ESTHER.   Situational nonsense in postmodern American fiction. *In* (pp. 215–27) **28.**

**11386.** SNIDER, MERLIN.   Morals and irreligion: Kurt Vonnegut as social ethicist. Unpub. doct. diss., Univ. of Southern California, 1988. [Abstr. in DA (49) 2255A.]

### Derek Walcott

**11387.** ESPINOSA, MÓNICA JEANNE.   A terrible beauty is born: problems of identity in two Caribbean poets. Unpub. doct. diss., Univ. of California, San Diego, 1987. [Abstr. in DA (49) 3020A.]

**11388.** SCHMIDT, MICHAEL.   Samtal mellan fyra poeter. *See* **9864.**

### Alice Walker

**11389.** BOBO, JACQUELINE.   Articulation and hegemony: Black women's response to the film *The Color Purple*. *See* **7983.**

**11390.** CARBY, HAZEL V.   Reinventing history/imagining the future. *See* **8999.**

**11391.** JARRETT, MARY.   The idea of audience in the short stories of Zora Neale Hurston and Alice Walker. *See* **9970.**

**11392.** OPYR, LINDA ELENA.   The Black woman in the novels of Alice Walker and Toni Morrison. *See* **10626.**

**11393.** STREITFELD, DAVID.   Deep purple. BkW, 12 Feb., 15.

**11394.** WALLINGER-NOWAK, HANNA.   Traditionsbildung in der schwarzamerikanischen Frauenliteratur: Zora Neale Hurston und Alice Walker. *See* **9974.**

**11395.** WEISENBURGER, STEVEN C.    Errant narrative and *The Color Purple.* JNT (19:3) 257–75.

**11396.** WILLIAMS, CAROLYN.    'Trying to do without God': the revision of epistolary address in *The Color Purple. In* (pp. 273–85) **61.**

### Margaret Walker

**11397.** GARNER, LINDA MEBANE.    Twentieth-century marble goddesses: Victorian and modernist portrayals of the antebellum Southern lady in Stark Young's *So Red the Rose,* William Faulkner's *The Unvanquished* and *Absalom, Absalom!,* and Margaret Walker's *Jubilee. See* **9570.**

### Edgar Wallace

**11398.** WHITEHEAD, JOHN.    T. S. Eliot and Edgar Wallace. *See* **9520.**

### Edward Lewis Wallant

**11399.** CUNNINGHAM, FRANK R.    The insistence of memory: the opening sequences of Lumet's *Pawnbroker. See* **8009.**

### Michelene Wandor

**11400.** REINELT, JANELLE.    Michelene Wandor: artist and ideologue. *In* (pp. 239–55) **39.**

### Sylvia Townsend Warner

**11401.** ACKLAND, VALENTINE.    For Sylvia: an honest account. Introd. by BEA HOWE. London: Chatto & Windus, 1985. pp. 135. Rev. by P. N. Furbank in TLS, 28 July, 815–16; by Susannah Clapp in LRB (11:20) 31–2.

**11402.** FURBANK, P. N.    A dangerous relevance.    TLS, 28 July, 815–16 (review-article).

**11403.** HARDWICK, A.    Voices from the garden: aspects of women's poetry 1910–1939. *See* **8503.**

**11404.** HARMAN, CLAIRE.    Sylvia Townsend Warner: a biography. London: Chatto & Windus. pp. 358. Rev. by P. N. Furbank in TLS, 28 July, 815–16; by Susannah Clapp in LRB (11:20) 31–2; by Christopher Potter in Listener (122) 27 July, 27.

### Robert Penn Warren

**11405.** BEDIENT, CALVIN.    In the heart's last kingdom: Robert Penn Warren's major poetry. (Bibl. 1986, 14472.) Rev. by Richard Gray in YES (19) 357–8.

**11406.** BURT, JOHN.    Robert Penn Warren and American idealism. New Haven, CT; London: Yale UP, 1988. pp. xi, 238. Rev. by John Rabbetts in JAStud (23:1) 186–7.

**11407.** DJANKOV, KRĂSTAN (introd.).    Nošten ezdač. (Night rider.) Sofia: Profizdat, 1988. pp. 408.

**11408.** SCOTT, NATHAN A., JR.    Warren's career in poetry: taking counsel of the heart alone. CR (33:2) 141–86.

**11409.** WALKER, MARSHALL.    Robert Penn Warren, Audubon and imagination. SAP (22) 153–62.

**11410.** WEAKS, MARY LOUISE.    A 'little postage stamp of native soil' in the upper South: the poetry and fiction of Caroline Gordon, Allen Tate, and Robert Penn Warren. *See* **9779.**

**11411.**  WILHELM, ALBERT E.    The gate as metaphor in Robert Penn Warren's short fiction. BSUF (30:1) 52–8.

### Booker T. Washington
**11412.**  SMOCK, RAYMOND W. (ed.).    Booker T. Washington in perspective: essays of LOUIS R. HARLAN. Jackson; London: Mississippi UP, 1988. pp. xii, 210.

### Judah Waten
**11413.**  CARTER, DAVID.    Biography, politics, a novel: reading Judah Waten. SoRA (22:1) 35–52.

### Frank Waters
**11414.**  MALPEZZI, FRANCES M.    Meru, the voice of the mountain. SDR (27:2) 27–35.

### Sheila Watson
**11415.**  BOWERING, ANGELA.    Figures cut in sacred ground: illuminati in *The Double Hook*. Edmonton, Alta: NeWest Press, 1988. pp. 160. Rev. by Jon Kertzer in CanL (122/23) 173; by Linda Lamont-Stewart in CanL (122/23) 174–5; by Stephen Scobie in MalaR (85) 1988, 141.

**11416.**  BOWERING, GEORGE (ed.).    Sheila Watson and *The Double Hook*. Ottawa: Golden Dog Press, 1985. pp. iv, 199. (Critical views on Canadian writers.) Rev. by Michael Peterman in CanL (115) 1987, 144–5.

**11417.**  DAVIDSON, ARNOLD E.    *The Double Hook*'s double hooks. CanL (116) 1988, 29–41.

### Evelyn Waugh
**11418.**  BEATY, FREDERICK L.    Evelyn Waugh and Lance Sieveking: new light on Waugh's relations with the BBC. *See* **7980.**

**11419.**  CARPENTER, HUMPHREY.    The Brideshead generation: Evelyn Waugh and his friends. London: Weidenfeld & Nicolson. pp. ix, 523. Rev. by Peter Kemp in TLS, 8 Sept., 967; by Peter Parker in Listener (122) 14 Sept., 28; by John Bayley in LRB (11:18) 3, 5–6.

**11420.**  CELAÁ, ISABEL.    Evelyn Waugh en *Brideshead Revisited*. LDeus (19:45) 173–7.

**11421.**  DAVIS, ROBERT MURRAY.    Chronology in *Brideshead Revisited*. EWN (23:2) 4–6.

**11422.**  DOOLEY, D. J.    *A Handful of Dust* on film: the missing implications. *See* **8024.**

**11423.**  GREENE, DONALD.    The fountain in *Brideshead Revisited*. EWN (23:2) 4.

**11424.**  —— More on Charles Ryder's conversion. EWN (23:3) 1–3.

**11425.**  —— Notes on Waugh and the military. EWN (23:1) 1–3.

**11426.**  McCANN, WESLEY.    Speedy recovery. Listener (122) 10 Aug., 23.

**11427.**  McCARTNEY, GEORGE.    Confused roaring: Evelyn Waugh and the Modernist tradition. (Bibl. 1988, 8992.) Rev. by Alain Blayac in EA (42:4) 489–90.

**11428.**  MAHON, JOHN W.    Charles Ryder's Catholicism. EWN (23:1) 5–7.

**11429.** Morris, Mary Josephine Ann. Evelyn Waugh: the novel and its relation to other media. Unpub. doct. diss., Univ. of Toronto, 1988. [Abstr. in DA (50) 149A.]

**11430.** Morriss, Margaret; Dooley, D. J. Evelyn Waugh: a reference guide. (Bibl. 1984, 13385, where first scholar's surname misspelled.) Rev. by Robert Murray Davis in PLL (22:1) 1986, 218–20.

**11431.** Osborne, John W. A reply to Donald Greene about Charles Ryder's conversion. EWN (23:1) 3–5. (*Refers to* bibl. 1988, 8989.)

**11432.** —— Sebastian Flyte as a homosexual. EWN (23:3) 7–8.

**11433.** —— Waugh and the Spanish Civil War in *Brideshead Revisited*. EWN (23:2) 6.

**11434.** Stannard, Martin (ed.). Evelyn Waugh: the critical heritage. (Bibl. 1986, 14498.) Rev. by Robert Murray Davis in PLL (22:1) 217.

**11435.** Wilson, John H. A sense of importance. EWN (23:3) 3–6.

**11436.** Wilson, John Howard, Jr. Art imitating life: the writings of Evelyn Waugh. Unpub. doct. diss., Univ. of Michigan, 1988. [Abstr. in DA (49) 3737A.]

**11437.** Wise, Brian. Additional Waugh bibliography, 3. EWN (23:1) 8.

**11438.** Wolk, Gerhard. Evelyn Waugh: a supplementary checklist of criticism. EWN (23:2) 6–7.

### Mary Webb

**11439.** Edgerton, Becky Richards. Bright glass: the fictional world of Mary Webb. Unpub. doct. diss., Univ. of Northern Colorado, 1988. [Abstr. in DA (49) 2226A.]

### Phyllis Webb

**11440.** Butling, Pauline. Paradox and play in the poetry of Phyllis Webb. *In* (pp. 191–204) **40.**

**11441.** Glickman, Susan. 'Proceeding before the amorous invisible': Phyllis Webb and the *ghazal*. CanL (115) 1987, 48–61.

**11442.** Ricou, Laurie. Phyllis Webb, Daphne Marlatt and simultitude: journal entries from a capitalist bourgeois patriarchal Anglo-Saxon mainstream critic. *In* (pp. 205–15) **40.**

### Fay Weldon

**11443.** Kossick, Shirley. The fiction of Fay Weldon: a critical survey. UES (27:1) 28–34.

### H. G. Wells

**11444.** Aldiss, Brian (introd.). The world set free. London: Hogarth Press, 1988. pp. 191.

**11445.** Batchelor, John. H. G. Wells. (Bibl. 1986, 14510.) Rev. by Douglas Hewitt in RES (38:150) 1987, 272–3.

**11446.** Berger, Roger A. 'Ask what you can do for your country': the film version of H. G. Wells's *The Time Machine* and the Cold War. *See* **7981.**

**11447.** Draper, Michael. H. G. Wells. (Bibl. 1987, 12903.) Rev. by David Y. Hughes in SFS (16:1) 103–8; by Patrick Parrinder in NQ (36:3) 411–12.

**11448.** EGE, S. E.   A comparative study of the works of Edward Bellamy and H. G. Wells with special reference to their utopian fiction (1888–1945). *See* **6256.**

**11449.** HUGHES, DAVID Y.   God, the devil, and H. G. Wells. SFS (16:1) 103–8 (review-article).

**11450.** RILEY, GEOFFREY.   Echoes of Wells in Naipaul's *A House for Mr Biswas*. *See* **10677.**

### Robert Wells

**11451.** EDGECOMBE, RODNEY.   'Incidentals of remoteness': Robert Wells and the idea of pastoral. ESA (32:1) 13–24.

### Eudora Welty

**11452.** ARNOLD, MARILYN.   'The magical percussion': Eudora Welty's human recital on art and time. SoHR (23:2) 101–18.

**11453.** BERLANT, LAUREN.   Re-writing the Medusa: Welty's *Petrified Man*. SSF (26:1) 59–70.

**11454.** COLE, HUNTER; SRINIVASAN, SEETHA.   Eudora Welty, inquiring photographer. NYTB, 22 Oct., 1.

**11455.** HARRISON, MARTHA SUZAN.   A sweet devouring: Eudora Welty's reading and writing of Virginia Woolf. Unpub. doct. diss., Univ. of North Carolina at Chapel Hill, 1988. [Abstr. in DA (49) 2658A.]

**11456.** MARRS, SUZANNE.   The Welty collection: a guide to the Eudora Welty manuscripts and documents at the Mississippi Department of Archives and History. *See* **250.**

**11457.** MATTHAEUS, DOROTHEA CHRISTIANE.   Eudora Welty and the humor of the Old Southwest. Unpub. doct. diss., State Univ. of New York at Stony Brook, 1988. [Abstr. in DA (50) 1306A.]

**11458.** SIMPSON, BEVERLY HURLEY.   Discovering the heart's truth: female initiation in the novels of Eudora Welty. Unpub. doct. diss., Ball State Univ., 1988. [Abstr. in DA (49) 3726A.]

**11459.** THEODOSIADOU, GEORGIA A.   The use of myth in five of Eudora Welty's novels. Unpub. doct. diss., Arizona State Univ., 1988. [Abstr. in DA (49) 2662A.] (*The Golden Apples, The Robber Bridegroom, Delta Wedding, Losing Battles, The Ponder Heart.*)

### Arnold Wesker

**11460.** DORNAN, READE WHITING.   Committed theatre in post-war Britain: the approaches of Arnold Wesker and John McGrath. *See* **10459.**

**11461.** HANSEN, NIELS BUGGE.   The metamorphosis of Shylock. *See* **3925.**

**11462.** LINDEMANN, KLAUS; LINDEMANN, VALESKA.   Arnold Wesker. (Bibl. 1985, 13436.) Rev. by Michael Göring in MLR (84:2) 428–9.

**11463.** MANOR, E.   The Anglo-Jewish predicament in the plays of Bernard Kops, Arnold Wesker, Harold Pinter, and Peter Shaffer. *See* **10220.**

### Mary Wesley

**11464.** ROBERTS, NIGEL.   Hail Mary.   Listener (121) 11 May, 6–7.

### 'Nathanael West' (Nathan Wallenstein Weinstein)

**11465.**  ENGLISH, JAMES F.   Comic transactions: humor as communication in four modern novels. *See* **9293.**

**11466.**  MERRILL, CATHERINE OSBORNE.   Nathanael West and the tradition of the grotesque. Unpub. doct. diss., Univ. of South Florida. [Abstr. in DA (50) 1306A.]

**11467.**  WEXELBLATT, ROBERT.   *Miss Lonelyhearts* and the rhetoric of disintegration. CLit (16:3) 219–31.

### 'Rebecca West' (Mrs H. M. Andrews)

**11468.**  URIE, DALE MARIE.   Rebecca West: a worthy legacy. Unpub. doct. diss., Univ. of North Texas. [Abstr. in DA (50) 1778A.]

### George Whalley

**11469.**  JOHNSTON, GEORGE (ed.).   The collected poems of George Whalley. Kingston, Ont.: Quarry Press, 1986. pp. 128. Rev. by David Lewis in QQ (95:3) 1988, 731–2.

### Edith Wharton

**11470.**  BAUER, DALE M.   Feminist dialogics: a theory of failed community. *See* **6469.**

**11471.**  —— *Twilight Sleep*: Edith Wharton's brave new politics. AQ (45:1) 49–51.

**11472.**  BLOOM, HAROLD (ed.).   Edith Wharton. New York: Chelsea House, 1986. pp. viii, 176. (Modern critical views.) Rev. by Patricia Lee Yongue in ALR (21:1) 1988, 82–3.

**11473.**  FRACASSO, EVELYN ESPOSITO.   Prisoners of consciousness: theme and technique in the tales of Edith Wharton. Unpub. doct. diss., Fordham Univ., 1988. [Abstr. in DA (49) 1801A.]

**11474.**  FRYER, JUDITH.   Felicitous space: the imaginative structures of Edith Wharton and Willa Cather. *See* **9215.**

**11475.**  GOODMAN, SUSAN.   Competing visions of Freud in the memoirs of Ellen Glasgow and Edith Wharton. *See* **9755.**

**11476.**  GOODMAN, SUSAN L.   Friends and rivals, Edith Wharton's women. Unpub. doct. diss., Univ. of New Hampshire, 1988. [Abstr. in DA (50) 1664A.]

**11477.**  HAYS, PETER L.   Signs in *Summer*: words and metaphors. PLL (25:1) 114–19.

**11478.**  HERMAN, BARBARA ALLRAN.   The marriage question: a study of selected novels by Edith Wharton. Unpub. doct. diss., Univ. of North Carolina at Chapel Hill, 1987. [Abstr. in DA (49) 2220–1A.]

**11479.**  KIM, WOOK-DONG.   Theme and symbol in Wharton's *Ethan Frome*. JELL (35) 677–94.

**11480.**  LEWIS, R. W. B.; LEWIS, NANCY (eds).   The letters of Edith Wharton. (Bibl. 1988, 9040.) Rev. by Carol J. Singley in AL (61:3) 461–3; by Ruth Bernard Yeazell in LRB (11:2) 11–12; by Elizabeth Ammons in NEQ (62:3) 441–2; by Tony Tanner in Listener (121) 5 Jan., 26–7.

**11481.**  PIERCE, ROSEMARY ERICKSON.   Clare Van Degen in *The Custom of the Country*. SAF (17:1) 107–10.

**11482.**  SEELBINDER, EMILY.   Writing like a man: gender and readers in *Adam Bede* and *The House of Mirth. See* **6787.**

**11483.**  STENGEL, ELLEN POWERS.   The terror of the usual: the supernatural short stories of Edith Wharton. Unpub. doct. diss., Duke Univ., 1987. [Abstr. in DA (49) 2222A.]

### E. B. White

**11484.**  RUSSELL, ISABEL.   Katharine and E. B. White: an affectionate memoir. New York; London: Norton, 1988. pp. 269.

### Kenneth White

**11485.**  McMANUS, TONY.   Entering the White world. Cencrastus (35) 32–5.

### Patrick White

**11486.**  AKERHOLT, MAY-BRIT.   Patrick White. Amsterdam: Rodopi, 1988. pp. iv, 206. (Australian playwrights, 2.)

**11487.**  ARENS, WERNER.   Destruction and regeneration as Blakean contraries in Patrick White's *Riders in the Chariot. In* (pp. 126–45) **5.**

**11488.**  BRUGMAN, ALBERT PETER.   Torture in the country of the mind: a study of suffering and self in the novels of Patrick White. Unpub. doct. diss., Univ. of the Orange Free State.

**11489.**  DAWSON, S.   'A variation of the rainbow': an examination of pastoral in Patrick White's prose fiction. Unpub. doct. diss., Univ. of Leeds. [Abstr. in IT (39:3) 1114.]

**11490.**  JOHNSON, MANLY.   Patrick White: 'failure' as ontology. JPC (23:2) 73–80.

**11491.**  LAIGLE, GENEVIÈVE.   Le sens du mystère dans l'œuvre romanesque de Patrick White. Paris: Didier; Atelier national de reproduction des thèses. 2 vols. pp. 983.

### T. H. White

**11492.**  CHAPMAN, S. E.   A study of the genre of T. H. White's Arthurian books. Unpub. doct. diss., Univ. of Wales, 1988. [Abstr. in IT (39:1) 34.]

### John Whiting

**11493.**  DICKEY, JOHANNA SUSAN.   Strategies of menace in the plays of John Whiting, Harold Pinter and Sam Shepard. *See* **10857.**

### Rudy Wiebe

**11494.**  BOWEN, DEBORAH.   Squaring the circle: the problem of translation in *The Temptations of Big Bear.* CanL (117) 1988, 62–70.

### Richard Wilbur

**11495.**  COULTHARD, A. R.   Poetic justice in Wilbur's *A Game of Catch.* NCL (19:5) 5.

**11496.**  PAYNE, MARJORY SCHEIDT.   'Giver of due regard': the religious vision of Richard Wilbur. Unpub. doct. diss., Univ. of Rochester, 1988. [Abstr. in DA (50) 136–7A.]

**11497.**  SCOTT, NATHAN, JR.   The poetry of Richard Wilbur — 'the splendor of mere being'. ChrisL (39:1) 7–33.

### Laura Ingalls Wilder

**11498.**  ANDERSON, WILLIAM T. (ed.).   A *Little House* sampler. *See* **10247.**

**11499.** GATES, CHARLENE E. Image, imagination, and initiation: teaching as a rite of passage in the novels of L. M. Montgomery and Laura Ingalls Wilder. *See* **10595.**

## Michael Wilding

**11500.** VAUTHIER, SIMONE. Lost and found: the narrative and the descriptive modes in Michael Wilding's *What It Was Like, Sometimes.* JSSE (12) 63–75.

## Anne Wilkinson

**11501.** BARBOUR, DOUGLAS. Day thoughts on Anne Wilkinson's poetry. *In* (pp. 179–90) **40.**

## Charles Williams

**11502.** ANDERSON, ANGELEE SAIFER. The nature of the city: visions of the kingdom and its saints in Charles Williams' *All Hallows' Eve.* Mythlore (15:3) 16–21.

**11503.** ENRIGHT, NANCY. Charles Williams and his theology of romantic love: a Dantean interpretation of the Christian doctrines of the Incarnation and the Trinity. Mythlore (16:2) 22–5.

**11504.** McKINLEY, MARLENE MARIE. 'To live from a new root': the uneasy consolation of *All Hallows' Eve.* Mythlore (16:1) 13–17.

**11505.** ROBB, M. P. The sacramental vision: belief and art in the poetry of David Jones, Charles Williams and W. H. Auden. *See* **8978.**

**11506.** TILLEY, ELIZABETH SUSAN. 'Vitalizing abstractions': the fiction of Charles Williams. Unpub. doct. diss., Univ. of Toronto, 1988. [Abstr. in DA (50) 150A.]

## Joan Williams

**11507.** GAUCH, PATRICIA LEE. Faulkner and beyond: a biography of Joan Williams. *See* **9571.**

## Miller Williams

**11508.** TURCO, LEWIS. Miller Williams. HC (26:4) 1–9.

## Raymond Williams

**11509.** O'CONNOR, ALAN. Raymond Williams: writing, culture, politics. *See* **8833.**

**11510.** —— (ed.). Raymond Williams on television: selected writings. *See* **8096.**

**11511.** SHARRATT, BERNARD. Communications and image studies: notes after Raymond Williams. *See* **8863.**

**11512.** WILLIAMS, RAYMOND. What I came to say. Introd. by FRANCIS MULHERN. *See* **1939.**

## Sherley Anne Williams

**11513.** HENDERSON, MAE G. (W)riting *The Work* and working the rites. BALF (23:4) 631–60.

## Tennessee Williams

**11514.** ADAM, JULIE. Versions of heroism in modern American drama: selected plays by Miller, Williams, Anderson and O'Neill. *See* **8937.**

**11515.** CLUM, JOHN M. 'Something cloudy, something clear': homo-phobic discourse in Tennessee Williams. SAQ (88:1) 161–79.

**11516.** DEBUSSCHER, GILBERT.   Tennessee Williams's Black Nativity: an unpublished libretto. *In* (pp. 127–33) **2.**

**11517.** JINDRA, MIROSLAV.   K jednomu nevýročí aneb jak Tennessee Williams o tři roky omládl. (On a non-anniversary, or, How Tennessee Williams became younger.) LitM (18:3) 141–2.

**11518.** JOHNSON, CARLA JEAN.   A tiger by the tail: the five finished versions of Tennessee Williams' *Twenty-Seven Wagons Full of Cotton*. Unpub. doct. diss., Univ. of Notre Dame, 1988. [Abstr. in DA (49) 1802A.]

**11519.** KOLIN, PHILIP C.   Parallels between *Desire Under the Elms* and *Sweet Bird of Youth*. *See* **10782.**

**11520.** —— 'Red-hot!' in *A Streetcar Named Desire*. NCL (19:4) 6–8.

**11521.** LEE, HAIYOUNG.   Humanism in Tennessee Williams' major plays. Unpub. doct. diss., Sogang Univ., Seoul.

**11522.** PETTINELLI, FRANCES.   Tennessee Williams: a study of the dramaturgical evolution of three later plays, 1969–78. Unpub. doct. diss., City Univ. of New York, 1988. [Abstr. in DA (49) 2028A.] (*The Two-Character Play, Small Craft Warnings, Vieux Carré*.)

## William Carlos Williams

**11523.** CANTRELL, CAROL H.   'Sufficient ground to stand on': Pound, Williams, and American history. *In* (pp. 153–60) **45.**

**11524.** CHAPPELL, CHARLES.   Botched romantic strategy in Williams' *Portrait of a Lady*. WCWR (15:1) 41–7.

**11525.** CIRASA, ROBERT JOHN.   Lyrically-based coherence in the structure of William Carlos Williams's volumes of collected poetry. Unpub. doct. diss., New York Univ., 1988. [Abstr. in DA (49) 3722A.]

**11526.** CONRAD, BRYCE.   The deceptive ground of history: the sources of William Carlos Williams' *In the American Grain*. WCWR (15:1) 22–40.

**11527.** CONRAD, BRYCE D.   The sources of America: a study of *In the American Grain*. Unpub. doct. diss., Univ. of Iowa, 1988. [Abstr. in DA (49) 2218–19A.]

**11528.** COOK, ALBERT.   Projections of measure: the continued synergies of Pound and Williams. *See* **10902.**

**11529.** CORONITI, JOSEPH A., JR.   Scoring the 'absolute rhythm' of William Carlos Williams: Steve Reich's *The Desert Music*. WCWR (15:2) 36–48.

**11530.** CRAWFORD, THOMAS HUGH.   The rhetoric of medical authority: the early writing of William Carlos Williams. Unpub. doct. diss., Duke Univ., 1988. [Abstr. in DA (49) 2657A.]

**11531.** CUMPIANO, MARION W.   The impact of James Joyce on William Carlos Williams: an uneasy ambivalence. *See* **10059.**

**11532.** DONLEY, CAROL.   William Carlos Williams and *Ol' Bunk's Band*. WCWR (15:2) 9–16.

**11533.** DRISCOLL, KERRY.   William Carlos Williams and the maternal muse. Ann Arbor, MI: UMI Research Press, 1987. pp. xv, 196. (Studies in modern literature, 72.) Rev. by T. Hugh Crawford in AL (61:4) 720–3.

**11534.** DUFFEY, BERNARD.   A poetry of presence: the writing of William Carlos Williams. (Bibl. 1988, 9094.) Rev. by George S. Lensing in SewR (96:1) 115–17.

**11535.** FIGGIS, S. E.   Toward spring and all: the gestation of William Carlos Williams' poetic. Unpub. doct. diss., Univ. of Hull, 1988. [Abstr. in IT (39:3) 1117.]

**11536.** FRAIL, DAVID.   Citizen Williams: thirty new items from the Rutherford newspaper. WCWR (15:1) 4–21.

**11537.** KALLET, MARILYN.   Honest simplicity in William Carlos Williams' *Asphodel, That Greeny Flower*. (Bibl. 1987, 13027.) Rev. by George S. Lensing in SewR (96:1) 118–19.

**11538.** KNAPP, JAMES F.   Not wholeness but multiplicity: the primitivism of William Carlos Williams. Mosaic (20:1) 1987, 71–81.

**11539.** KNIGHT, CHRISTOPHER J.   William Carlos Williams, Paul Cézanne and the 'technique of originality'. Mosaic (20:2) 1987, 83–96.

**11540.** LAWSON, A. J.   The poetry of William Carlos Williams. Unpub. doct. diss., Univ. of Oxford. [Abstr. in IT (39:3) 1117.]

**11541.** LENSING, GEORGE S.   Williams after the first quarter-century. SewR (96:1) 1988, 113–20 (review-article).

**11542.** LIM, YONG-MOOK.   W. C. Williams eui Americanism gwa hoewhajeok baekyung. (William Carlos Williams' Americanism against the background of the visual arts.) JELLC (30) 103–28.

**11543.** LITZ, A. WALTON; MACGOWAN, CHRISTOPHER (introds).   A new Williams poem: *Peter Kipp to the High School*. WCWR (15:1) 1–3.

**11544.** MAHFOUD, H.   William Carlos Williams: towards a democratic art. Unpub. doct. diss., Univ. of Essex. [Abstr. in IT (39:2) 489–90.]

**11545.** MONTEIRO, GEORGE.   A note on William Carlos Williams' *Comedy Entombed: 1930*. WCWR (15:2) 49–50.

**11546.** NIELSEN, ALDON L.   Whose blues? WCWR (15:2) 1–8.

**11547.** SCHMIDT, PETER.   William Carlos Williams, the arts, and literary tradition. Baton Rouge; London: Louisiana State UP, 1988. pp. xiii, 268. Rev. by T. Hugh Crawford in AL (61:4) 720–3; by Jacqueline Doyle in RMRLL (43:1/2) 126–7.

**11548.** STOICHEFF, PETER.   Poem's poetics or poet's death: what ends *The Cantos*, *Maximus*, and *Paterson*? *See* **10756.**

**11549.** TRACY, STEVEN C.   William Carlos Williams and *Blues: A Magazine of New Rhythms*. WCWR (15:2) 17–29.

### Henry Williamson

**11550.** BLENCH, J. W.   Henry Williamson and the romantic appeal of Fascism: part II. DUJ (81:2) 289–305.

**11551.** GREGORY, JOHN (introd.).   From a country hilltop. [London]: Henry Williamson Soc., 1988. pp. 130. Rev. by J. W. Blench in DUJ (81:2) 330–1.

**11552.** WILLIAMSON, RICHARD (introd.).   Days of wonder. (Bibl. 1987, 13052.) Rev. by J. W. Blench in DUJ (81:2) 329–30.

## A. N. Wilson
**11553.** ANTIP, FELICIA. Formarea unui tînăr de viitor: A. N. Wilson. (The development of a most promising young man: A. N. Wilson.) RomLit, 20 Apr., 22.

**11554.** STEUHL, WOLFGANG. Die roman-gewordene Heilsbotschaft des Erzählers A. N. Wilson. GRM (39) 73–89.
## Angus Wilson
**11555.** STAPE, J. H.; THOMAS, ANNE N. Angus Wilson: a bibliography, 1947–1987. New York: Mansell, 1988. (Bibl. 1988, 9114.) Rev. by L. Wood in Library (11:2) 174–5; by B. C. Bloomfield in BC (38:3) 416–17.

**11556.** TOBOUL, DENISE. Violence et irrationalité dans l'œuvre romanesque d'Angus Wilson. In (pp. 139–58) **60.**
## Edmund Wilson
**11557.** JOHNSTON, PAUL KEITH. The confidence of Edmund Wilson. Unpub. doct. diss., Univ. of Michigan, 1988. [Abstr. in DA (49) 3719–20A.]

**11558.** WILSON, ROSALIND BAKER. Near the magician: a memoir of my father, Edmund Wilson. New York: Weidenfeld & Nicolson. pp. 257. Rev. by Monroe Engel in BkW, 19 Nov., 4–5; by Pearl K. Bell in NYTB, 10 Dec., 26.
## Ethel Wilson
**11559.** STOUCK, DAVID (ed.). Ethel Wilson: stories, essays, letters. Vancouver: British Columbia UP. Rev. by Margaret Doyle in CanL (121) 141–3.
## Lanford Wilson
**11560.** BUSBY, MARK. Lanford Wilson. (Bibl. 1988, 9119.) Rev. by Richard W. Etulain in OreHQ (90:2) 206–8.

**11561.** WILLIAMS, PHILIP MIDDLETON. 'A comfortable house': the collaboration of Lanford Wilson and Marshall W. Mason on *Fifth of July*, *Talley's Folly*, and *Talley & Son*. Unpub. doct. diss., Univ. of Colorado at Boulder, 1988. [Abstr. in DA (50) 1487A.]
## Yvor Winters
**11562.** COMITO, TERRY. In defense of Winters: the poetry and prose of Yvor Winters. (Bibl. 1988, 9121.) Rev. by Francis Murphy in SewR (96:3) 1988, lvii–lix.
## Tom Winton
**11563.** EDELSON, PHYLLIS FAHRIE. The role of history in three contemporary Australian novels. See **9427.**
## Adele Wiseman
**11564.** WISEMAN, ADELE. *Memoirs of a Book Molesting Childhood* and other essays. See **1940.**
## P. G. Wodehouse
**11565.** RAFFERTY, TERRENCE. Satisfaction. NY, 22 May, 94–100.

**11566.** TROUPP, HENRY. P. G. Wodehouse och jag. (P. G. Wodehouse and I.) Nya Argus (Helsinki) (82:5/6) 95–9.
## Thomas Wolfe (1900–1938)
**11567.** BORNEMANN, ALFRED H. Thomas Wolfe's economics. TWR (13:1) 26–8.

**11568.** BOYER, JAMES D. Allegory as subterfuge in Wolfe's *Fame and the Poet*. TWR (13:1) 11–14.

**11569.** CULLETON, CLAIRE A. Joycean synchronicity in Wolfe's *Look Homeward, Angel*. See **10058.**

**11570.** DEDMOND, FRANCIS B. Shaping Frings's *Look Homeward, Angel*: the 'jelly roll' scene. TWR (13:1) 29–32.

**11571.** DOLL, MARY ASWELL; STITES, CLARA (eds). In the shadow of the giant: Thomas Wolfe: correspondence of Edward C. Aswell and Elizabeth Nowell, 1949–1958. Athens: Ohio UP, 1988. pp. xx, 256. Rev. by John S. Phillipson in OhioanaQ (32:3) 156; by John Halberstadt in NYTB, 30 July, 14.

**11572.** DONALD, DAVID HERBERT. Look homeward: a life of Thomas Wolfe. (Bibl. 1988, 9128.) Rev. by John Howland, Jr, in SewR (96:2) 1988, 280–2.

**11573.** HOWLAND, JOHN, JR. Descending into the maelstrom. SewR (96:2) 1988, 280–3 (review-article).

**11574.** HUNTLEY, REID. Wolfe's obsession with time: a philosophical problem. TWR (13:1) 33–45.

**11575.** HYLES, VERNON. Ben, Rudy, and the fantastic: Wolfe's journey to Nighttown. See **10082.**

**11576.** IDOL, JOHN L., JR. A Thomas Wolfe companion. (Bibl. 1987, 13082.) Rev. by Ruel Foster in SoCR (22:1) 147–9.

**11577.** JOHNSTON, CAROL. Thomas Wolfe: a descriptive bibliography. Pittsburgh, PA: Pittsburgh UP, 1987. pp. xix, 295. (Pittsburgh series in bibliography.) Rev. by Ruel Foster in SoCR (22:1) 147–9.

**11578.** —— Thomas Wolfe's first triumph: *An Angel on the Porch*. TWR (13:2) 53–62.

**11579.** PEDOTO, CONSTANCE. A deconstructive approach to Thomas Wolfe's *Look Homeward, Angel*. TWR (13:2) 23–30.

**11580.** PERELMAN-HALL, DAVID K. Wolfe and Whitman. See **7659.**

**11581.** ROBERTS, TERRY. Narrative distance in *Look Homeward, Angel*. TWR (13:2) 13–19.

**11582.** SNYDER, PHILLIP ASA. Constructional codes in the *Künstlerroman*: *Sons and Lovers* and *Look Homeward, Angel* as exemplars. See **10323.**

**11583.** STUTMAN, SUZANNE. 'Esther' Bernstein and 'Eugene' Wolfe: fact versus fiction. TWR (13:1) 1–10.

**11584.** UNDERWOOD, THOMAS A. Autobiography and ideology in the South: Thomas Wolfe and the Vanderbilt Agrarians. AL (61:1) 31–45.

**11585.** VAUGHAN, ROBERT. *Look Homeward, Angel*'s Helen: portrait of conflict. TWR (13:2) 34–9.

**11586.** WALSER, RICHARD. Concerning the form of *Look Homeward, Angel*. TWR (13:2) 2–9.

**11587.** WILSON, FRANK C. In search of the tubercle bacillus: the death of Thomas Wolfe. Mosaic (20:3) 1987, 57–63.

## Tom Wolfe (1931– )

**11588.** WOLFE, TOM. Stalking the billion-footed beast: a literary manifesto for the new social novel. See **8424.**

### Tobias Wolff

**11589.** AUGUSTSSON, LARS ÅKE.   Under realismens skitiga yta: om
Tobias Wolffs prosa. (Under the dirty surface of realism: on Tobias
Wolff's prose.) BLM (58:3) 177–82.

### Leonard Woolf

**11590.** SPOTTS, FREDERIC.   Letters of Leonard Woolf. San Diego, CA:
Harcourt Brace Jovanovich; London: Weidenfeld & Nicolson. pp. xxxvi,
616. Rev. by Leon Edel in NYTB, 29 Oct., 7.

### Virginia Woolf

**11591.** ALLEN, ANNETTE C.   A phenomenological exploration of time,
self, and narrative in the major novels of Virginia Woolf. Unpub. doct.
diss., Univ. of Texas at Dallas, 1988. [Abstr. in DA (49) 1806A.]

**11592.**   Entry cancelled.

**11593.** BENSTOCK, SHARI.   Authorizing the autobiographical. *In* (pp.
10–33) **51.**

**11594.** BISHOP, EDWARD.   A Virginia Woolf chronology. Basingstoke:
Macmillan. pp. xvii, 268. (Macmillan author chronologies.)

**11595.** BOWLBY, RACHEL.   Virginia Woolf: feminist destinations.
(Bibl. 1988, 9143.) Rev. by Rikky Rooksby in NQ (36:4) 540–1.

**11596.** BRADBURY, MALCOLM.   The modern world: ten great writers.
*See* **9287.**

**11597.** BULLOCK, LINDA CAROL.   *The Waves*: Virginia Woolf's mirror
of consciousness. Unpub. doct. diss., Univ. of Tennessee. [Abstr. in DA
(50) 1661A.]

**11598.** CAUGHIE, PAMELA LOUISE.   Virginia Woolf and the postmodern tradition: literature in quest and question of itself. Unpub. doct.
diss., Univ. of Virginia, 1988. [Abstr. in DA (49) 3729–30A.]

**11599.** CHAMBERLAIN, DANIEL FRANK.   Figures and facets of narrative perspective in fiction. *See* **2002.**

**11600.** COOLEY, ELIZABETH WILLIAMS.   'One must stop to find a
word': language and communication in the novels of Virginia Woolf.
Unpub. doct. diss., Univ. of North Carolina at Chapel Hill, 1988.
[Abstr. in DA (49) 3730A.]

**11601.** DAVIES, STEVIE.   Virginia Woolf: *To the Lighthouse*. Harmondsworth: Penguin. pp. 142. (Penguin critical studies.)

**11602.** DESALVO, LOUISE.   Virginia Woolf: the impact of childhood
sexual abuse on her life and work. London: Women's Press;
Boston, MA: Beacon Press. pp. xxiii, 372. Rev. by Andrew Motion in
TLS, 10 Nov., 1230; by Julia Epstein in BkW, 14 May, 4–5; by Kennedy
Fraser in NY, 6 Nov., 154–63.

**11603.** DICK, SUSAN.   'The writing "I" has vanished': Virginia
Woolf's last short fictions. *In* (pp. 134–45) **45.**

**11604.** —— (ed.).   The complete shorter fiction of Virginia Woolf.
(Bibl. 1985, 13614.) London: Hogarth Press. pp. 346. (Revised and
expanded ed.: first ed. 1985.)

**11605.** FOKKEMA, DOUWE.   Virginia Woolf. *In* (pp. 102–22) DOUWE
FOKKEMA and ELRUD IBSCH, Modernist conjectures: a mainstream in

European literature 1910–1940. London: Hurst, 1987. pp. xii, 330. Rev. by Naomi Segal in NC (8) 178–80.

**11606.** FORD, ELIZABETH ANNE. Nursery tea: child characters in the novels of Virginia Woolf and E. M. Forster. *See* **9660.**

**11607.** GALEF, DAVID. Mrs Woolf and Mr Browne. *See* **4329.**

**11608.** GILLESPIE, DIANE FILBY. The sisters' arts: the writing and painting of Virginia Woolf and Vanessa Bell. (Bibl. 1988, 9156.) Rev. by Peter Collier in Word & Image (5:4) 393–4.

**11609.** GUTH, DEBORAH. 'What a lark! What a plunge!': fiction as self-evasion in *Mrs Dalloway.* MLR (84:1) 18–25.

**11610.** HARRISON, MARTHA SUZAN. A sweet devouring: Eudora Welty's reading and writing of Virginia Woolf. *See* **11455.**

**11611.** HENKE, SUZETTE A. Virginia Woolf's *The Waves*: a phenomenological reading. Neophilologus (73:3) 461–72.

**11612.** HUSSEY, MARK. The singing of the real world: the philosophy of Virginia Woolf's fiction. (Bibl. 1988, 9160.) Rev. by Harvena Richter in StudN (20:4) 1988, 417–18.

**11613.** JOHNSON, BRUCE. A Modernist noesis. *In* (pp. 60–70) **45.**

**11614.** JOSEPH, GERHARD. Poetic and photographic frames: Tennyson and Julia Margaret Cameron. *See* **7506.**

**11615.** KAMUF, PEGGY. Penelope at work. *In* (pp. 144–73) PEGGY KAMUF, Signature pieces: on the institution of authorship. Ithaca, NY; London: Cornell UP, 1988. pp. x, 237.

**11616.** LUCEY, JOHN MICHAEL. Culture inclined to ideology: problems of style and grammar in André Gide and Virginia Woolf. Unpub. doct. diss., Princeton Univ. [Abstr. in DA (50) 438A.]

**11617.** McCAIL, RONALD. A family matter: *Night and Day* and *Old Kensington. See* **7348.**

**11618.** McMANUS, DIANE PATRICIA. Resurrecting Shakespeare's sister: the evolution of Virginia Woolf's narrative voice from the Common Reader to Anon. Unpub. doct. diss., Temple Univ. [Abstr. in DA (50) 1667A.]

**11619.** McNEILLIE, ANDREW (ed.). The essays of Virginia Woolf: vol. 1, 1904–1912; vol. 2, 1912–1918. (Bibl. 1988, 9168, 9169.) Rev. in PR (56:3) 489–94; by M. A. Curr in UES (27:1) 45–7.

**11620.** —— The essays of Virginia Woolf: vol. 3, 1919–1924. London: Hogarth Press, 1988. pp. xxx, 551.

**11621.** MARCUS, JANE. Invincible mediocrity: the private selves of public women. *In* (pp. 114–46) **51.**

**11622.** —— Virginia Woolf and the languages of patriarchy. Bloomington: Indiana UP, 1987. pp. xviii, 219. Rev. by Harvena Richter in StudN (20:4) 1988, 418–20.

**11623.** —— (ed.). New feminist essays on Virginia Woolf. (Bibl. 1982, 14103.) Rev. by Herbert Marder in MLR (83:3) 1988, 706–7.

**11624.** —— Virginia Woolf and Bloomsbury: a centenary celebration. Bloomington: Indiana UP, 1987. (Bibl. 1987, 13124.) Rev. by Harvena Richter in StudN (20:4) 1988, 420.

**11625.** MARTIN, BILL. *To the Lighthouse* and the feminist path to postmodernity. PhilL (13:2) 307–15.

**11626.** MORAN, PATRICIA LOUISE. (S)mothering and the production(s) of the female artist: Katherine Mansfield and Virginia Woolf. *See* **10523.**

**11627.** MOSES, JOHN WILLIAM. 'Soliloquies in solitude': Virginia Woolf and the Romantic imagination. Unpub. doct. diss., Miami Univ. [Abstr. in DA (50) 1668A.]

**11628.** NEDELČEVA, MARIANA. Tazi treska, životat . . . (Life, this fever. . .) *In* (pp. 5–10) Misis Dalauej. (Mrs Dalloway.) Sofia: Narodna kultura. pp. 192.

**11629.** PARK, HEE-JIN. Euisik eui heureum soseol eui wichi wa munjaejeom: 'makgan' *Between the Acts* reul jungsim euro. (A study of *Between the Acts* as stream of consciousness.) EngSt (13) 29–45.

**11630.** PAUL, JANIS M. The Victorian heritage of Virginia Woolf: the external world in her novels. Norman, OK: Pilgrim, 1987. pp. ix, 217. Rev. by Harvena Richter in StudN (20:4) 1988, 421.

**11631.** POOLE, ROBERT. Bloomsbury and bicycles. *See* **9672.**

**11632.** RAITT, S. The texture of a friendship: V. Sackville-West and Virginia Woolf. *See* **11058.**

**11633.** RATCLIFFE, KRISTA L. Words of one's own: toward a rhetoric of feminism in selected essays of Virginia Woolf and Adrienne Rich. *See* **11003.**

**11634.** REESE, STEVEN CASE. Modernism and the march of science: four novelists. *See* **9980.**

**11635.** ROBE, MARGARET ANN. Conceiving a self in autobiography by women. *See* **8609.**

**11636.** ROE, S. M. Virginia Woolf, writing and gender. Unpub. doct. diss., Univ. of Kent, 1988. [Abstr. in IT (39:1) 35–6.]

**11636a.** ROSENMAN, ELLEN BAYUK. The invisible presence: Virginia Woolf and the mother–daughter relationship. Baton Rouge: Louisiana State UP, 1986. pp. xiv, 181. Rev. by Thomas C. Caramagno in MP (86:3) 326–8.

**11637.** ROY, GERALDINE RACHEL GROSS. A pattern of timeless moments: metaphor and temporal order in Proust's *À la Recherche du temps perdu* and selected novels by Virginia Woolf. Unpub. doct. diss., Univ. of Toronto. [Abstr. in DA (50) 1652A.]

**11638.** RUOTOLO, LUCIO P. The interrupted moment: a view of Virginia Woolf's novels. (Bibl. 1987, 13135.) Rev. by Harvena Richter in StudN (20:4) 1988, 421–2.

**11639.** RYBÁROVÁ, VIERA. Rozprávačská situácia v románe Virginie Woolfovej *K majáku*. (The narrator's position in Virginia Woolf's novel *To the Lighthouse*.) *In* (pp. 40–1) **6.**

**11640.** SWEENEY, SHARON HOHNER. Using Gérard Genette's narrative theory to study Virginia Woolf's narrative strategies. Unpub. doct. diss., Drew Univ. [Abstr. in DA (50) 1670A.]

**11641.** TRANSUE, PAMELA J.   Virginia Woolf and the politics of style. Albany: New York State UP, 1986. pp. viii, 222. Rev. by Nicola Bradbury in RES (39:154) 1988, 317–18.

**11642.** WALKER, NANCY.   'Wider than the sky': public presence and private self in Dickinson, James, and Woolf. *In* (pp. 272–303) **51.**

**11643.** WARNER, ERIC.   Virginia Woolf, *The Waves.* (Bibl. 1987, 13151.) Rev. by Gail Cunningham in RES (39:156) 1988, 592.

**11644.** WHEARE, JANE.   Virginia Woolf: dramatic novelist. Basingstoke: Macmillan. pp. x, 238.

**11645.** WHITELEY, PATRICK J.   Knowledge and experimental realism in Conrad, Lawrence and Woolf. *See* **9328.**

**11646.** WOODS, MICHAEL J.   'But we have other lives, I think, I hope': the quest for transcendence in selected novels of Virginia Woolf. Unpub. doct. diss., Univ. of Rhode Island, 1988. [Abstr. in DA (50) 452A.] (*The Voyage Out, Mrs Dalloway, To the Lighthouse, Between the Acts.*)

**11647.** WUSSOW, H.   The nightmare of history: the Great War and the work of Virginia Woolf and D. H. Lawrence. *See* **10331.**

**11648.** ZWERDLING, ALEX.   Virginia Woolf and the real world. (Bibl. 1988, 9185.) Rev. by Thomas C. Caramagno in MP (86:3) 324–6; by Karen L. Levenback in ModAge (32:2) 1988, 169–72.

### Alexander Woollcott

**11649.** KINNEY, ARTHUR F.   Dorothy Parker's letters to Alexander Woollcott. *See* **10828.**

### Cornell Woolrich

**11650.** SERED, JEAN.   The dark side. AD (22:2) 116–34, 240–58.

### James Wright

**11651.** MORRIS, JOHN GRAVES, JR, III.   The book as twenty-fifth poem: the craftsmanship of James Wright. Unpub. doct. diss., Arizona State Univ. [Abstr. in DA (50) 1659A.]

**11652.** STEIN, KEVIN.   The poetry of a grown man: constancy and transition in the works of James Wright. Athens: Ohio UP. pp. xviii, 222. Rev. by David Galef in AL (61:4) 725–6; by Edward Lense in OhioanaQ (32:3) 145–6.

**11653.** TERMAN, PHILIP S.   James Wright's poetry of intimacy. Unpub. doct. diss., Ohio State Univ., 1988. [Abstr. in DA (49) 2662A.]

### Richard Wright

**11654.** ELIAS, KHALIQUZZAMAN M.   The legacies of Prospero: a critique of the colonial and the neo-colonial experiences in selected writings of Richard Wright, Chinua Achebe, and George Lamming. *See* **8899.**

**11655.** KINNAMON, KENETH, *et al.*   A Richard Wright bibliography: fifty years of criticism and commentary, 1933–1982. (Bibl. 1988, 9198.) Rev. by Yoshinobu Hakutani in SAF (17:1) 116–17.

**11656.** WALKER, MARGARET.   Richard Wright, daemonic genius: a portrait of the man, a critical look at his work. New York: Warner. pp. xix, 428. Rev. by Waldo E. Martin, Jr, in BkW, 16 Apr., 6.

**11657.** WATKINS, PATRICIA D.    The paradoxical structure of Richard Wright's *The Man Who Lived Underground*. BALF (23:4) 767–83.

### Stephen Wright

**11658.** MARÍN, PILAR.    Entropy in *Meditations in Green*. Atlantis (11:1/2) 137–47.

### Hisaye Yamamoto

**11659.** YOGI, STAN.    Legacies revealed: uncovering buried plots in the stories of Hisaye Yamamoto. SAF (17:2) 169–81.

### Wakako Yamauchi

**11660.** ARNOLD, STEPHANIE.    Dissolving the half shadows: Japanese American women playwrights. *In* (pp. 181–94) **39.**

### Dornford Yates

**11661.** ADRIAN, JACK (ed.).    The best of Berry: selected stories of Dornford Yates. London: Dent. pp. xix, 281. (Classic thrillers.)

### W. B. Yeats

**11662.** ALLISON, JONATHAN.    Community and individualism in the poetry of W. B. Yeats and Seamus Heaney. *See* **9853.**

**11663.** BELSEY, CATHERINE.    Mobilizing Byzantium. *In* (pp. 1–16) **17.**

**11664.** BLAIR, RON.    Yeats lights the candles. *See* **9539.**

**11665.** BORNSTEIN, GEORGE.    Poetic remaking: the art of Browning, Yeats, and Pound. *See* **6365.**

**11666.** BREEN, MARGARET SOENSER.    The feminine position of auditor in Yeats's *Purgatory*. CLQ (25:1) 42–54.

**11667.** CHADWICK, JOSEPH.    Violence in Yeats's later politics and poetry. ELH (55:4) 1988, 869–93.

**11668.** CHAPMAN, WAYNE KENNETH.    Yeats and the English literary Renaissance: adaptation and development in the craft of poetry. Unpub. doct. diss., Washington State Univ., 1988. [Abstr. in DA (50) 448A.]

**11669.** CHIBA, YOKO.    W. B. Yeats and *Noh*: from *Japonisme* to Zen. Unpub. doct. diss., Univ. of Toronto. [Abstr. in DA (50) 1486A.]

**11670.** CULLINGFORD, ELIZABETH BUTLER.    Labour and memory in the love poetry of W. B. Yeats. *In* (pp. 204–19) **45.**

**11671.** DAICHES, DAVID.    W. B. Yeats: tones of voice. *In* (pp. 18–25) **37.**

**11672.** DEANE, SEAMUS.    National character and national audience: races, crowds and readers. *In* (pp. 40–52) **17.**

**11673.** DESAI, R. W.    In search of Horatio's identity (via Yeats). *In* (pp. 191–203) **45.**

**11674.** DIGGORY, TERENCE.    Yeats's stream of consciousness. *In* (pp. 253–66) **45.**

**11675.** DONOGHUE, DENIS.    Blind bitter land. Listener (121) 12 Jan., 6–7.

**11676.** FLANNERY, JAMES.    Yeats: the masker and the masks. *In* (pp. 267–79) **45.**

**11677.** FOGARTY, MARGARET E.    'It is myself that I remake': the shaping self of W. B. Yeats's *Autobiographies*. *In* (pp. 75–85) **17.**

**11678.** GENET, JACQUELINE.    Yeats's *Deirdre* as a chess-game and a poet's game. *In* (pp. 123–38) **42.**

**11679.** GURNEY, STEPHEN. Images of Yeats. ModAge (32:1) 1988, 81–7 (review-article).

**11680.** HAYLEY, BARBARA. Lafcadio Hearn, W. B. Yeats and Japan. *In* (pp. 43–60) **37.**

**11681.** HEANEY, SEAMUS. Yeats' nobility. FQ (ns 3:2) 11–14; Fortnight (271: supp.) ii–iii.

**11682.** JEFFARES, A. NORMAN. W. B. Yeats: a new biography. London: Century Hutchinson, 1988; New York: Farrar Straus Giroux. pp. x, 374. Rev. by Bernard O'Donoghue in TLS, 10 Mar., 252; by Joseph Coates in BkW, 19 Nov., 5.

**11683.** —— (ed.). Yeats the European. Gerrards Cross: Smythe. pp. xv, 340. (Princess Grace Irish library, 3.)

**11684.** JORDAN, CARMEL. A terrible beauty: the Easter rebellion and Yeats's 'great tapestry'. Lewisburg, PA: Bucknell UP; London; Toronto: Assoc. UPs, 1987. pp. 132.

**11685.** KEANE, PATRICK J. Terrible beauty: Yeats, Joyce, Ireland, and the myth of the devouring female. *See* **10085.**

**11686.** —— Yeats's interactions with tradition. Columbia: Missouri UP, 1987. pp. xx, 332. Rev. by Rikky Rooksby in NQ (36:2) 258–9.

**11687.** KELLY, JOHN (ed.); DOMVILLE, ERIC (assoc. ed.). The collected letters of W. B. Yeats: vol. 1, 1865–1895. (Bibl. 1988, 9222.) Rev. by Alan Robinson in RES (38:150) 1987, 271–2; by Stephen Gurney in ModAge (32:1) 1988, 81–7.

**11688.** KINAHAN, FRANK. Yeats, folklore and occultism: contexts of the early work and thought. London; Boston, MA: Unwin Hyman, 1988. pp. xxiii, 255. Rev. by Rikky Rooksby in NQ (36:4) 544–5.

**11689.** KINANE, VINCENT. Some aspects of the Cuala Press. *See* **440.**

**11690.** KORITZ, AMY. Women dancing: the structure of gender in Yeats's early plays for dancers. ModDr (32:3) 387–400.

**11691.** KORITZ, AMY E. Gendering bodies, performing art: theatrical dancing and the performance aesthetics of Wilde, Shaw and Yeats. *See* **7677.**

**11692.** KUCH, PETER. 'What can I but enumerate old themes?' *In* (pp. 234–52) **45.**

**11693.** LANNIN, THOMAS FORREST, JR. Contemporary critical theory and the literary revisionism of W. B. Yeats' later poetry. *See* **8795.**

**11694.** LOIZEAUX, ELIZABETH BERGMANN. Yeats and the visual arts. New Brunswick, NJ: Rutgers UP, 1986. pp. xviii, 238. Rev. by Stephen Gurney in ModAge (32:1) 1988, 81–7.

**11695.** LONGLEY, EDNA. W. B. and cultural politics today. Fortnight (271: supp.) iii–v.

**11696.** MCCALLUM, JOHN. Irish memories and Australian hopes: William Butler Yeats and Louis Esson. *See* **9540.**

**11697.** MACINTYRE, ALASDAIR. Poetry as political philosophy: notes on Burke and Yeats. *In* (pp. 145–57) **46.**

**11698.** MCLOUGHLIN, D. J. Tradition and nationality in the work of three Irish poets: W. B. Yeats, Patrick Kavanagh and Seamus Heaney. *See* **9861.**

**11699.** MAHONY, ROBERT.   Yeats and the Irish language revival: an unpublished lecture. IUR (19:2) 220–6.

**11700.** MANICOM, DAVID ALTON.   Romantic nationalism and the unease of history: the depiction of political violence in Yeats's poetry. Unpub. doct. diss., McGill Univ. [Abstr. in DA (50) 955A.]

**11701.** MAY, KEITH M.   Nietzsche and modern literature: themes in Yeats, Rilke, Mann and Lawrence. *See* **10305.**

**11702.** MORIARTY, MARY; SWEENEY, CATHERINE.   W. B. Yeats. Dublin: O'Brien, 1988. pp. 58.

**11703.** OPPEL, FRANCES NESBITT.   Mask and tragedy: Yeats and Nietzsche, 1902–10. (Bibl. 1988, 9233.) Rev. by L. Santoro in IUR (19:1) 188–90.

**11704.** PASCHEN, E.   Yeats's revisions of his female personae poems. Unpub. doct. diss., Univ. of Oxford, 1988. [Abstr. in IT (39:2) 489.]

**11705.** PITTOCK, MURRAY G. H.   Yeats, Plotinus, and *Among Schoolchildren.* IUR (19:2) 213–19.

**11706.** PRATT, WILLIAM.   Pound and Yeats: the poetics of friendship. *In* (pp. 159–80) **46.**

**11707.** RAINE, KATHLEEN (introd.).   Fairy and folk tales of Ireland. Ed. by W. B. Yeats. *See* **1728.**

**11708.** RAMAZANI, R. JAHAN.   Yeats: tragic joy and the sublime. PMLA (104:2) 163–77.

**11709.** REEVES, MARJORIE; GOULD, WARWICK.   Joachim of Fiore and the myth of the eternal evangel in the nineteenth century. *See* **6109.**

**11710.** RHEE, YOUNG-SUCK.   Invention rules: a look into the creative process of Yeats's *Sailing to Byzantium.* INH (17) 55–77.

**11711.** RICHARDSON, JAMES.   Vanishing lives: style and self in Tennyson, D. G. Rossetti, Swinburne and Yeats. *See* **7359.**

**11712.** RICHMAN, ROBERT.   Reclaiming Yeats. Commentary (88:6) 57–9.

**11713.** ROESSEL, DAVID.   The historical context of Yeats's Byzantium. PCL (14) 1988, 55–63.

**11714.** RUDE, DONALD W.; NEEPER, L. LAYNE.   Some new light on W. B. Yeats' *Eight Poems.* AEB (ns 3:1) 11–15.

**11715.** SADDLEMYER, ANN.   The theatrical voice: *The Words upon the Window-Pane. In* (pp. 153–73) **37.**

**11716.** —— 'Yours affly, Dobbs': George Yeats to her husband, winter 1931–32. *In* (pp. 280–303) **45.**

**11717.** STALLWORTHY, JON.   W. B. Yeats and that high horse. *In* (pp. 220–33) **45.**

**11718.** STANFORD, MICHAEL KENT.   W. B. Yeats and the modern political poem. Unpub. doct. diss., Univ. of Virginia, 1988. [Abstr. in DA (50) 1315–16A.]

**11719.** STEAD, C. K.   Stendhal's mirror and Yeats's looking-glass: a reconsideration of *The Tower. In* (pp. 193–211) **46.**

**11720.** SUGIYAMA, SUMIKO.   The dream of Eros: Yeats's *His Dream.* IUR (19:2) 227–39.

**11721.** TRISTRAM, HILDEGARDE L. C. Why James Joyce also lost his 'brain of forgetting': patterns of memory and media in Irish writing. *In* (pp. 220–33) **5.**

### Anzia Yezierska

**11722.** HENRIKSEN, LOUISE LEVITAS; BOYDSTON, JO ANN. Anzia Yezierska: a writer's life. (Bibl. 1988, 9245.) Rev. by Eric J. Sundquist in AL (61:1) 120–1.

### Stark Young

**11723.** GARNER, LINDA MEBANE. Twentieth-century marble goddesses: Victorian and modernist portrayals of the antebellum Southern lady in Stark Young's *So Red the Rose*, William Faulkner's *The Unvanquished* and *Absalom, Absalom!*, and Margaret Walker's *Jubilee*. *See* **9570.**

### Robert Zend

**11724.** GRACE, SHERRILL. In the name-of-the-father: Robert Zend's *Oāb* (or the up(Z)ènding of trïdution). CanL (120) 91–7.

### Louis Zukofsky

**11725.** HOOLEY, DANIEL M. The classics in paraphrase: Ezra Pound and modern translators of Latin poetry. *See* **10909.**

**11726.** STANLEY, SANDRA L. Among American friends: Louis Zukofsky and the making of a modern American poetics. Unpub. doct. diss., Univ. of Southern California, 1988. [Abstr. in DA (50) 137A.]

# INDEXES

## INDEX OF AUTHORS AND SUBJECTS

This index consists mainly of authors' names, titles and subjects which appear as headings in the main body of the work, with some explanatory additions, cross-references, etc. For a breakdown, by genre, of the various periods within the 'English Literature' section, see the Table of Contents.

# INDEX OF SCHOLARS

including compilers, critics, editors and translators.
Reviewers are included only when the item has been counted as a review-article.

Eland-Jankowska, Ewa, 3712
Elbarbary, Samir, 10070
Elbaz, Robert, 2126
Elbert, Sarah, 6085–6
Elderhorst, Constance, 4400
Eldred, Janet M., 5817
Eldredge, L. M., 1077
Eldridge, Richard, 11354
Elert, Claes-Christian, 1164
— Kerstin, 1164
Eliade, Mircea, 3172
Elian, Abbas Abdelrahman, 6887
Elias, Khaliquzzaman M., 8899
Elíasson, Gyrðir, 9138
Eliot, Simon, 429
— Valerie, 9465
El Itreby, Elizabeth J., 2554
Elledge, W. Paul, 6408
Ellery, Chris, 11308
Elliot, Jeffrey M., 8947
Elliott, Emory, 1836
— Gregory, 8743
— R. W. V., 2419
— Ralph, 2890
— Ralph W. V., 2293, 2827
Ellis, A. C. O., 219
— Bill, 1699
— David, 3529, 7713, 10282
— Frank H., 567
— H. F., 6148
— John, 8726
— Michael Edmond, 777
— Reuben J., 9048
— Roger, 2613, 2891
Ellison, Julie, 7714
Ellmann, Richard, 5644, 7673, 10071–2
Ellrodt, Robert, 1837, 4326
Ellsberg, Margaret R., 7019
Elphick, Linda Lois, 9131
Else, Anne, 7828
Elshershabi, Muhammad Attia Hasan, 1432
Elsness, Johan, 895
Emeljanow, Victor, 5751
Emenyonu, Ernest N., 9534
Emerson, Dorothy, 11232
Emerick, Ronald, 6950
Emery, Ted A., 5234
Empson, William, 3256, 3530
Enemark, Richard D., 6609
Eng, Ooi Boo, 7895
Engehausen, Frank, 3922
Engelberg, Karsten Klejs, 7431
Engelberts, Matthijs, 9049
Engelking, Leszek, 10660
Engell, James, 4298, 5333
— John, 5565, 8028
Engle, Lars, 2892–3, 4003

Engler, Balz, 1078
— Bernd, 4972, 9566
English, James F., 9293
Enkemann, Jürgen, 8029
Enright, D. J., 1838–9
— Nancy, 11503
Ensslen, Klaus, 4849
Entzminger, Robert L., 4684
Epp, Garrett Peter Jantz, 2555
Epperly, Elizabeth R., 7584
Epstein, Edmund L., 10113
— Joseph, 5646
— Julia, 5162
— William H., 2127
Erdinast-Vulcan, Daphna, 9805
Erdmann, Peter, 1340
Erickson, Darlene Ellen, 10606
— Peter, 3531
Eriksen, Roy T., 3225, 3257
Erkkila, Betsy, 7649
Erler, Mary, 2614
Ernst, Charles Albert Scheuringer, 4248
Erwin, Robert, 11380
Erzgräber, Willi, 2226, 2615, 2723
Esolen, Anthony M., 3361
— Anthony Michael, 3362
Esonwanne, Uzoma Martin, 8727
Espinosa, Mónica Jeanne, 11387
Espy, Willard R., 1305
Esser, Jürgen, 744, 1263
Essick, Robert N., 5070
Esslin, Martin, 1958
Estes, Glenn E., 8436
Etchells, Ruth, 4499, 4685, 6369
Etherton, Michael, 8030
Evans, Arthur B., 2009
— Charlene Taylor, 7610
— D. Simon, 2420
— Deanna Delmar, 2685
— Faith, 3756
— G. Blakemore, 4352
— G. R., 676
— George Ewart, 1654
— Gwladys, 1700
— Malcolm, 3532
— Martha Noel, 7064
— Mary, 6149
— Maurice, 3447
— Miriama, 8488
— Robert C., 4324
Everett, Barbara, 2075, 3448, 7062
— Glenn Sawyer, 5964
Evers, M., 418

Everson, William, 10004
Ewald, Helen Rothschild, 1433
Ewbank, Inga-Stina, 3231, 3689, 6293
Exell, A. W., 1679

Faas, Ekbert, 3533
Fabb, Nigel, 1397
Faber, David, 745
Facinelli, Diane A., 2421
Faddul, Atif Yusuf, 9466
Faggen, Robert, 9697
Fahim, S. S., 10362
Fairbanks, Carol, 2010
Fairer, David, 5408
Fajardo-Acosta, Fidel, 2342
Falck, Colin, 10005
Falih, Haleem H., 747
Faller, Lincoln B., 4253
Faltz, Leonard, 1210
Fan, Ada Mei, 5752
Fanto, James Anthony, 2176
Farag, S. M., 1341
Fareh, Shehdeh Ismail, 1434
Faris, Wendy B., 8238
Farmer, David, 10283
Farnie, D. A., 220
Farooqui, Khalida Saleem, 10540
Farrell, James M., 5039
— John Charles, 10956
— John P., 6326
— Kirby, 3534
— Thomas J., 2894–5
Farringdon, Jill, 2076
Faulkner, Mara, 10752
— Peter, 6270
— Thomas C., 4342, 5173
Fausbøll, Else, 2316
Favre, Albert, 4327
Favret, Mary A., 4989
Fawcett, Brian, 8489
— Mary Laughlin, 3952
— Nancy Ruth, 5444
Fay, Elizabeth Anne, 7691
Feather, John, 430
Featheringill, Ron Charles, 4687
Fecher, Charles A., 10554
Federico, Annette Rose, 6858
Fee, Margery, 11074
Feeney, Joseph J., 7020
Fees, C., 1764
Fehsenfeld, Martha, 9062
Feibleman, Peter, 9876
Feidelson, Charles, 7063
Fein, Susanna, 2422
— Susanna Greer, 136
Feinberg, Anat, 3061

McKernan, Susan, 7892
Mackey, Douglas, 9384
McKillop, I. D., 6053
Mackin, James Andrew, Jr,
  1316
McKinley, M., 4650
— Marlene Marie, 11504
McKinnell, John, 2303, 3090
Mackinnon, A. H., 4869
— Lachlan, 3589
McKitterick, David, 247–8
Macklem, Michael, 483
Macklin, Jenny, 8088
McKusick, James C., 709
McLaren, John, 249
McLauchlan, Gordon, 7893
McLaughlin, Peter, 4268
MacLean, Patrick, 3838
— Sally-Beth, 3091
McLeish, Kenneth, 2028
MacLennan, Carol, 9684
Maclennan, Don, 9773
Macleod, Iseabail, 1135, 1149,
  1472
MacLeod, Jack, 8333
McLeod, Marion, 9132, 9440,
  10623
MacLeod, Sheila, 10302
McLoughlin, D. L., 9861
— Deborah, 9862
— J. P., 2644a
MacLulich, T. D., 8334
McMahon, Robert, 8811
— Sean, 2094
McManus, Diane Patricia,
  11618
— Eva Beasley, 3802
— Tony, 11485
McMaster, Juliet, 6209–11
— Marian Babirecki, 9590
McMillan, Dougald, 346, 9062
McMillin, Scott, 3092
McMullan, Audrey Elizabeth,
  9063
McMullen, Lorraine, 6716
McNaughton, Trudie, 5874
Macnaughton, William R.,
  7090
McNeely, Trevor, 3956
McNees, Eleanor, 6906
McNeil, David, 5540
MacNeil, Joe Neil, 1675
McNeillie, Andrew, 11619–20
McNeish, James, 10520
McNulty, Elaine Marie, 925
McPherson, David, 3093
— I. N., 8638
Macpherson, Pat, 6303
McQuain, Jeff, 651
MacQueen, Angus, 2741

McQueen, Harvey, 8488
MacQueen, John, 6449
McSparran, Frances, 2470
McSweeney, Kerry, 6777, 9678
McVicker, Jeanette Elaine
  Wewe, 8336
McWhir, Anne, 4461
McWilliams, Debra, 6738
— John, 6968
Madden, Deirdre, 10716
Maddock-Cowart, Donna
  Samal, 8337
Madigan, Mary Kathleen, 5454
Madubuike, Ihechukwu, 7809
Maduka, Chidi T., 8900
Maekawa, Tetsuro, 6907
Mael, Phyllis, 8089
Maertz, Gregory George, 5681
Maes-Jelinek, Hena, 42, 9271,
  10212
Magie, Lynne Adele, 6304
Maginn, Diane, 6739
Magister, Karl-Heinz, 3590
Magistrale, Tony, 6969, 9277,
  9641
Magnet, Myron, 6634
Magnusson, A. Lynne, 10215
— Ulf, 534
Magoon, Joseph, 6908, 9487
Maguire, Nancy Klein, 3094
Mahfoud, H., 11544
Mahon, Ellen Macleod, 10303
— John W., 3591, 11428
Mahoney, Dhira B., 2777
Mahony, Robert, 11699
Mahood, M. M., 3457, 3592
Maidment, Brian, 5979
Maik, Linda L., 1749
Maine, Barry, 9410
Mair, Christian, 1551
Maitland, Sara, 11039
Makowsky, Veronica A., 9777
Makurenkova, S. A., 4409
Malaba, M. Z., 7894
Malcolm, David, 9868
Maley, William, 3393
Malik, Farida, 11244
— G. R., 7746
Malless, Stan, 651
Mallett, Phillip, 6382, 6909
Mallette, Richard, 3394–5
Malloy, Kristin, 10475
Malmgreen, Gail, 5017
Malmgren, Carl D., 10181
Malotki, Ekkehart, 1718
Malpezzi, Frances M., 11414
Maltby, P. L., 9020
Maltz, Harold P., 6635
Manabe, Kazumi, 968
Mancoff, Debra N., 6055

Mandel, Miriam B., 9312
Maner, Martin, 5351
Manes, Joan, 1587
Manganaro, Elise Salem, 3321
Manganiello, Dominic, 7678,
  9488
Manhire, Bill, 8338
Maniam, K. S., 7895
Manicom, David Alton, 11700
Manley, Kathleen, 10801,
  11138
— Kathleen E. B., 1744
— Lawrence, 3185
Manlove, C. N., 10384
— Colin, 2188
Mann, Chris Zithulele, 2095
— Harveen Sachdeva, 10676
— Jill, 2812, 2950–1
— Maureen Ruth Forbes, 6305
— Phillip, 11089
Manning, Gillian, 4547
— John, 95, 1023–4
— Susan, 1474, 10635
Manor, E., 10220
Manser, Martin H., 1136
Mansfield, Nick, 10499
— R. G., 3095
Manvell, Roger, 5314–15
Maples, Donna Elaine, 5682
Mara, Gerald, 4540
Maragou, Helena, 4321
Marais, M. J., 9272
— Michael, 9273
Marc'hadour, Germain, 3283
Marchand, Philip, 8640
Marcus, Jane, 6025, 11622–4
— Leah S., 347, 3594, 3810,
  4103
— Phillip L., 10271
Marder, Louis, 535, 3096–7,
  3973
Marenbon, John, 2304
Margolies, Edward, 8602, 9016
Margolis, Anne, 7479
Marigny, Jean, 1624
Marín, Pilar, 11658
Marius, Richard, 3284
Markley, Robert, 4283, 5463
Marks, Sylvia Kasey, 5449
Markus, Manfred, 38, 731, 736
Marotti, Arthur F., 4410
Marowitz, Charles, 3597
Marquess, William Henry,
  7150
Marquis, Greg, 1750
Marr, David, 5683
Marrs, Suzanne, 250
Marsden, Hilda, 6278
— Peter H., 629
Marsh, Derick, 3957

Plunka, Gene A., 11091
Podgorskiĭ, A. V., 4766
Pöhl, Esther, 1110
Poirier, Richard, 1903
Pokrovskiĭ, N. E., 7576
Poláčková, Milena, 932, 1009
Pole, S., 10313
Polkinhorn, Harry, 11037
Pollak, Ellen, 5420
— Vivian R., 6701–2
Pollard, Arthur, 5172, 6847
Pollner, Clausdirk, 624
Pollock, Beth Ruby, 6982
Polomski, Andrzej, 744
Pomorska, Krystyna, 1415
Ponsford, Michael, 11352
Pontes, Hilda, 8935
Poole, Adrian, 3625
— Richard, 9364
— Robert, 9672
Poovey, Mary, 6061, 6229, 6311
Popham, Shelby Anne, 3108
Popkin, Richard H., 4286
— Susan M., 4109
Poplawski, Gary J., 10116
Popowich, F. P., 818
Porter, Gerald, 43, 1754, 6260
— Horace, 8994
— James, 8532
— Joseph A., 3270, 3995
— Laurin, 10789
— M. Gilbert, 10391
— Roy, 4287, 4885, 5267
Portier, François, 5464
Portman, Jamie, 8104
Porush, David, 8365
Posner, Richard A., 1904
Pospíšil, Tomáš, 9400
Posthumus, J., 1633
Potter, A., 10862
— A. M., 8841
— Lois, 3109
— Nick, 3564
Pottle, Frederick A., 5111a
Pounds, Norman J. G., 1787
Poussa, Patricia, 1053
Powell, B. L., 5898
— David, 256, 5388, 6484
— John Weldon, 1238
— Susan, 2499
Power, Henriette Lazaridis, 7418
Powers, Douglas, 10742
— Kathleen Emily, 3627
— Lyall H., 7060
Poyas, Frank B., 257
Poyet, Albert, 4456
Poynton, Cate, 1173
Poznar, Walter, 7682
Pozzuoli, Alain, 7475

Pradeilles, Anne, 541
Prado, C. G., 2035
Prager, Carolyn, 4474
Prasad, Hari Mohan, 10790
— Veena Rani, 11248
Pratt, T. K., 1142
— William, 10921
Prebensen, Henrik, 542
Preisler, Bent, 1580
Prescott, Anne Lake, 3324, 3399–400
— Robert Allen, 5989
Pressler, Terra Daugirda, 8109
Preston, C. E., 3325
— Peter, 10314
Preyer, Robert O., 6782
Price, Jocelyn, 2659
— Jody Lauren, 7683
— Tim, 11140
Prickett, Stephen, 710, 4879, 5899
Priebe, Richard K., 7917
Priessnitz, Horst, 5990
Priest, Dale G., 3798
Prigent, Christian, 9184
Primatarova-Miltscheva, Antoinette, 1280
Prince, Gerald, 1143
Pringle, David, 8212
Printz-Påhlson, Göran, 8843
Prior, R. J., 4415
— Roger, 3996
Probyn, Clive T., 4947, 5545
Procházka, Martin, 1634, 8367
Procter, Johanna, 4585
Proehl, Geoffrey Scott, 5770
Progovac, Ljiljana, 631
Prostko, Jack, 5465
Protšenko, I. B., 1416
Prunet, Jean-François, 769
Prus, Randy Thomas, 10753
Pruss, Ingrid, 4511
— Ingrid R., 4512
Pryor, Felix, 2114
Pryse, Marjorie, 8985
Psaki, Francies Regina, 2500
Puci, Ján, 1446
Pugliatti, Paola, 10117
Punter, David, 1905
Purdon, L. O., 2865
Purdy, Al, 8907, 11078
— Richard Little, 6920–1
— Strother B., 10118
Putnam, Hilary, 1239
Pütz, Manfred, 1061
Pyle, Forest Barnett, III, 5700
Pylkkö, Pauli Olavi, 632

Qi-Bo, Zhu, 543
Quart, Leonard, 7973
Quartermaine, Peter, 20
Questier, M. C., 3189
Quick, Anne, 2849
Quigley, Austin E., 8111
— Daniel James, 4586
Quilligan, Maureen, 54, 3326
Quince, W. Rohan, 8112
Quinn, Antoinette, 10458, 10591
— Bernetta, 11249
— P. J. M., 9796
Quinones, Ricardo, 8619
Quint, David, 3016
Quintero, Ruben David, 5421
Quirk, Randolph, 1281
— Thomas, 4257
— Tom, 11250

Rabaiotti, Renato, 5049
Rabaté, Jean-Michel, 10119
Rabb, J. Douglas, 6450
— Melinda Alliker, 4948
Rabbetts, John, 6922
Rabey, David Ian, 9005
Rabie, Jan, 11019
Rabkin, Eric S., 8383
— Gerald, 3628
Race, William H., 5991
Rackin, Phyllis, 3629
Radcliffe, David Hill, 4110, 4371
Radel, Nicholas F., 4310
Rader, Ralph W., 6653, 10120
Radford, Andrew, 819
Radi, A., 10315
Radner, Hilary Ann, 8844
— Joan N., 1727
Radzinowicz, Mary Ann, 4416
Rae, Patrick, 10922
Raeper, William, 7204
Raff, Melvin Hunt, 7919
Rafferty, Terrence, 11565
Rafroidi, Patrick, 5546
Raghavan, Hema V., 9071
Rahman, Tariq, 7920
Railey, Kevin, 6348–9
Raimond, Jean, 7461
Raina, Badri, 6654
Raine, Kathleen, 1728, 5099
Rainer, Maria Eva, 972
Rainey, Lawrence S., 458
Raitt, S., 11058
Raizis, Marios Byron, 6418
Rajan, Balachandra, 2193
Rajchman, John, 8845
Raju, Jayarani, 11020
Ralian, Antoaneta, 9624

Ramadoss, Haripriya, 11184
Ramanathan, Geetha
  Ramanathan, 9007
Ramat, Paolo, 633
Ramazani, R. Jahan, 11708
Rampersad, Arnold, 2135,
  5679, 9953–4
Ramraj, Victor J., 7921
Ramsey, Allen, 11129
— Jonathan, 7725
— M. K., 5100
— Roy Vance, 368
Ranald, Margaret Loftus, 3630
Randall, Dale B. J., 4614, 4647,
  4817
Ranger, Paul, 5470
Ransom, Daniel, 2501
Raper, Julius Rowan, 9017,
  9757
Rapple, Brendan A., 6108
Rasebotsa, Nobantu Nkwane
  Lorato, 9775
Rashkow, Ilona Nemesnyik,
  3161
Raskin, Marina, 8932
Rasmussen, Barbara, 7098
— Carl J., 207
— Eric, 3631
Raspa, Anthony, 82
Rastelli, Lucy Gordon, 258
Rastetter, S. J., 2978
Ratcliffe, Krista L., 11003
Rathbone, N., 3751
Rauff, James Vernon, 544
Ravenscroft, Arthur, 8368
Ravits, Martha, 11024
Rawlinson, David H., 5356
Rawson, Claude, 4881, 5390,
  8953, 10386
Ray, Joan Klingel, 4513
— Martin, 9318
— Martin S., 6886
— Robert H., 3884
Rayan, Krishna, 5701
Raylor, Timothy, 369
Rayment, N., 2115
Raymo, Robert R., 2440
Razzak, Fakhir Abdul, 5023
Rea, Paul W., 8895, 10801
Read, Richard, 7371
Reagan, Daniel, 7242
Real, Hermann J., 5548
Reaver, J. Russell, 1729
Rebeck, Theresa, 5771
Rebelo, Ethelwyn, 6340
Reboul, Anne, 1282
Recknagel, Marsha Lee, 9879
Rector, Liam, 9825
Redekop, Ernst, 6550
Redfield, Marc W., 10972

Redford, Bruce, 4990
Redmond, Christopher, 6741
— James, 1973–4, 5371
— Kate Karlson, 6742
— Luanne Bethke, 6230
Redshaw, Thomas Dillon,
  10592
Reed, Arden, 5702
— Jeremy, 5992
— John O., 711
— John R., 5900
— Melissa Ann, 3997
— Sabrina Lee, 8545
— Thomas A., 7155
Reed-Nancarrow, Paula
  Elizabeth, 7205
Rees, Charles A., 8113
— Joan, 3853
Rees-Mogg, Emma, 5589
Reese, Steven Case, 9980
Reeve, Jan, 1581
Reeves, Florence, 6488
— Gareth, 9502–3
— Marjorie, 6109
Regan, Stephen, 7514
— Tom, 2092, 6064
— Vincent David, 1101
Regnier-Bohler, Danielle, 2502
Rehder, Robert, 11252
Reichl, Karl, 2260, 2953
Reid, C. S., 5948
— Christopher, 1448, 8546
Reid-Walsh, Jacqueline Jane
  Ayer, 9373
Reilly, Catherine, 8547
— Edward C., 10179
— Patrick, 5548
Reiman, Donald H., 5703
Reimer, Stephen R., 2694
Reinelt, Janelle, 9252, 11400
Reinert, Thomas, 5357
Reinhard, Kenneth, 3844
Reinsma, Luke M., 2318
Reissig, Erich, 5515
Reitenbach, Gail Gloria, 8369
Reitz, Bernhard, 8115
Reizbaum, Marilyn, 259
Relke, Diana M. A., 10854
Relph, J. T., 1730
Remley, Paul G., 2503
Renoir, Alain, 2261
Renov, Michael, 8116
Renza, Louis A., 9909
Ressler, S., 9319
Revard, Carter, 1038
— Stella P., 4372
Reyer, William Robert, 8646
Reyes, Marie, 1417
Reynolds, David S., 5704
— Jean, 11116

— Larry J., 5705
— M. L., 370
— Mary T., 10123
— Michael, 9910–11
— Susan, 2309
Rhee, Young-Suck, 11710
Riach, Alan, 8548
— D. W., 3245
— W. A. D., 1482
Riaz, Sahibzada M., 3960
Ricard, Serge, 25
Ricci, Digby, 3752
Rice, H. William, 1755
— Philip, 8846
— Sally Ann, 820
Richard, Claude, 7923
— Jean-Pierre, 6419
Richard-Allerdyce, Diane,
  10691
Richards, Bernard, 1361, 4417,
  10318
— Donna Jean, 1498
— Mary P., 162
— Shaun, 7924, 8617
Richardson, Alan, 5101
— Brian Erling, 8117
— J. A., 5549
— James, 7359
— Joan, 11253–4
— John, 2263
— L. A., 7279
— Malcolm, 2504
— P., 5260
Richer, Jean, 3632
Richetti, John, 5199
— John J., 5200
Richman, Gerald, 2924
— Robert, 8549, 11712
Richmond, Hugh M., 3018,
  3753–4
Richter, David, 8371
— David H., 4949
Rickman, Gregg, 9386
Ricks, Christopher, 163–75,
  5993, 7516, 9504
— David, 3961
Ricou, Laurie, 10534
Ridden, Geoffrey, 11342
Riddy, Felicity, 2379, 2781
Rideout, Walter B., 8943
Rider, Jeff, 2505, 2765
Ridgway, Jim, 2036
Riedel, Wolfgang, 5707
Riehle, Wolfgang, 3803
Riely, John, 5516
Riemer, James D., 9188
Riewald, J. G., 9083
Riffaterre, Michael, 8847
Rigaud, N. J., 26, 4187, 4475
— Nadia, 60

Rigg, A. G., 1191
Riggio, Milla Cozart, 2570
— Thomas P., 9425
Riggs, David, 4588
Righter, William, 7099
Rigney, Ann, 7393
— Barbara Hill, 8966
Rigter, Bob, 934
Riley, David W., 260
— Geoffrey, 10677
Rimmer, E. M., 2506
Ringler, William A., Jr, 2507, 3211
Ripley, John, 7300
Rischin, Moses, 9189
Rissanen, Matti, 545
Ristoff, Dilvo I., 11376
Ritchie, Harry, 7926
— Neil, 261, 11150
Ritt, Nikolaus, 736
Rittenberg, David Jonathan, 9652
Rive, Richard, 7927
Rivers, Isabel, 459
Rix, Walter, 7491
Roark, Christopher, 3782
Robb, David S., 7206
— M. P., 8978
— Paul H., 9810
Robbins, Bruce, 2038
— Helen Walker, 6312
— Stephen Lee, 4289
Robe, Margaret Ann, 8609
Roberts, David, 4188, 11187
— Gerald, 7027
— Heather, 5901, 7828
— Jane, 385, 1064, 2264
— John R., 4377, 4514
— Lorraine, 4378
— Marie, 2101
— Nigel, 11464
— P. M., 634
— Terry, 11581
Robertson, F., 7394
— J. F., 7395
— Karen, 4624
— William K., 10125
Robin, Maurice, 15
Robins, Kevin, 9233
Robinson, Alan, 8550-1
— Eric, 6440, 6483-4
— Forrest G., 7624, 11071
— Fred C., 2217
— Ian, 3983
— J. W., 3110
— James A., 10791
— Michèle, 2925
— Roger, 10528
Robson, John M., 1174
— W. W., 8848, 10205, 10686

Rocha, Mark William, 9735-6
Roche, Thomas P., Jr, 3401
Rockett, Will H., 8118
Rocque, André, 10806
Rodden, John, 10812-16
— John Gallagher, 10817
Rodefer, Stephen, 8552
Roe, Jill, 9686
— Nicholas, 4735, 6501, 6521, 7757
— Richard Paul, 4017
— S. M., 11636
Roemer, Kenneth M., 6261
Roessel, David, 11713
Rogal, Samuel J., 4770
Rogers, Pat, 1908, 4882-3, 5424
— William E., 2926
Rogin, Michael, 8119
Rohman, Gerd, 9940
Rohmer, Rolf, 3633
Rokošná, Daniela, 546
Rollinson, Philip, 3402
Rollyson, Carl, 9880
Roloff, Volker, 7966
Romaine, Suzanne, 1552, 1582
Romero, Lora Patricia, 6551
Rommetveit, Ragnar, 1240
Rompkey, Ronald, 5319
Ronan, Clifford J., 4589
Ronsley, Joseph, 10016
Roof, Judith, 29
Rooke, Constance, 9725
Rooks, John, 3403
Room, Adrian, 1144-5
Rooney, Anne, 2866
— Phillip J., 8120
Roose-Evans, James, 8121
Roosen, William, 5201
Root, Robert L., Jr, 8647
Roper, Alan, 4457-8
Rose, Dan, 8648
— Jane Atteridge, 6573
— Marilyn Russell, 6984
— Mary Beth, 2508, 3111-12
— Phyllis, 6028
Rose-Innes, Henrietta, 2102
Rosen, Alan, 4736
— Alan Charles, 3885
— Michael J., 11328
Rosenbaum, S. P., 11275
Rosenberg, Brian, 11084
— Brian C., 6655
— John D., 6451, 6569
— Marvin, 1241, 3755
— Neil V., 1756
Rosenfelt, Deborah, 8824
Rosengarten, Herbert, 6313, 6316
Rosenheim, Shawn, 7332
Rosenman, Ellen B., 6785

— Ellen Bayuk, 11636a
Rosenthal, M. L., 2103
Rosenwald, Lawrence, 6816
Rosier, Pat, 9438
Ross, Alexander M., 5902
— Andrew, 8649-50
— Angus, 5551
— Anne, 1783
— Bruce Clunies, 10654
— Cheri L., 7013
— Donald, Jr, 7563
— Háj, 1267
— Harry J., 4111
— Ian Campbell, 5517
— Malcolm, 1909
— Morton L., 11031
— Raymond, 10441
— Robert, 10002
— Robert L., 9922
— Stephen M., 9607
— Trevor Thornton, 1910
Rossenbeck, Klaus, 1103
Rosser, Marion Dortch, 386
Rosslyn, Felicity, 2194, 3962, 5423
Rossman, Charles, 9051
Rosteck, Thomas, 1319
Rosten, Leo, 1499
Roston, Murray, 2510
Rothfield, Lawrence I., Jr, 5903
Rothfork, John, 10581
Rothman, William, 8123
Rouberol, Jean, 6821
Roudané, Matthew C., 8924, 10571
Roughley, Alan Robert, 10126
Rous, Jean-Marie, 10183
Rouse, R. H., 217
Rousseau, G. S., 4885, 5424
Roussel, Roy, 4112
Rovine, Harvey, 3635
Rowe, Anne E., 5709
— Donald W., 2867
— Elizabeth Ashman, 2266
— George E., 4590
— J. G., 2661
— Jeremy, 5471
— John Carlos, 7100
— Karen E., 4790
— M. W., 10258
Rowland, Beryl, 2809
— William Gordon, Jr, 5710
Rowlett, John Louis, 7759
Rowse, A. L., 3636-7
Roxman, Susanna, 8849
Roy, G. Ross, 460, 5146
— Geraldine Rachel Gross, 11637
— Parama, 5904
Royot, Daniel, 6940